W9-BNO-553

Peru

Sara Benson

Paul Hellander, Rafael Wlodarski

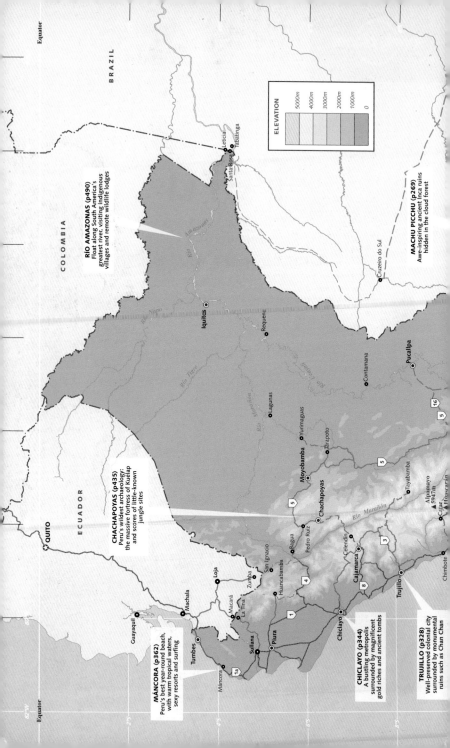

Equator

BRAZIL

ELEVATION

| 5000m |
| 4000m |
| 3000m |
| 2000m |
| 1000m |
| 0 |

COLOMBIA

RIO AMAZONAS (p490)
Float along South America's
greatest river, visiting indigenous
villages and remote wildlife lodges

Leticia
Tabatinga
Santa Rosa

MACHU PICCHU (p269)
Awe-inspiring ancient Inca ruins
hidden in the cloud forest

Cruzeiro do Sul

Iquitos

Requena

Pucallpa

Contamana

Río Tigre

Río Ucayali

Río Marañón

Lagunas

Yurimaguas

Moyobamba

Tarapoto

CHACHAPOYAS (p435)
Peru's wildest archaeology:
the massive fortress of Kuelap
and scores of little-known
jungle sites

QUITO

ECUADOR

Chachapoyas

Tayabamba

Alpamayo
5947m

Huascarán
César

Bagua
Pedro Ruíz

Celendín

Río Marañón

San Ignacio

Huancabamba

Zumba

Loja

Macará

La Tina

Cajamarca

Chimbote

Trujillo

TRUJILLO (p328)
Well-preserved colonial city
surrounded by monumental
ruins such as Chan Chan

CHICLAYO (p344)
A bustling metropolis
surrounded by magnificent
gold riches and ancient tombs

Machala

Guayaquil

Tumbes

Máncora

Sullana

Piura

Chiclayo

MÁNCORA (p362)
Peru's best year-round beach,
with warm tropical waters,
sexy resorts and surfing

Equator

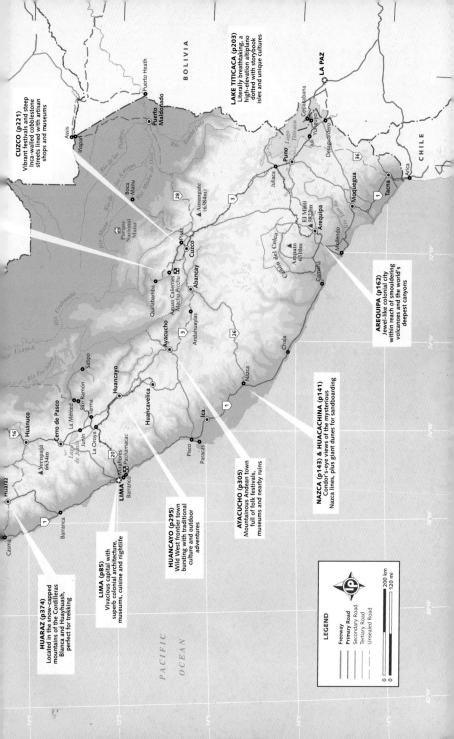

CUZCO (p221)
Vibrant festivals and steep Inca-walled cobblestone streets lined with artisan shops and museums

LAKE TITICACA (p203)
Literally breathtaking, a high-elevation altiplano dotted with storybook isles and unique cultures

AREQUIPA (p162)
Jewel-like colonial city within reach of smouldering volcanoes and the world's deepest canyons

NAZCA (p143) & HUACACHINA (p141)
Condor's-eye views of the mysterious Nazca lines, plus giant dunes for sandboarding

AYACUCHO (p305)
Mountainous Andean town full of folk festivals, museums and nearby ruins

HUANCAYO (p295)
Wild West frontier town bursting with traditional culture and outdoor adventures

LIMA (p85)
Vivacious capital with superb colonial architecture, museums, cuisine and nightlife

HUARAZ (p374)
Located in the snow-capped mountains of the Cordilleras Blanca and Huayhuash, perfect for trekking

BOLIVIA

CHILE

PACIFIC OCEAN

LEGEND
Freeway
Primary Road
Secondary Road
Tertiary Road
Unsealed Road

0 ———— 200 km
0 ———— 120 mi

Destination Peru

Peru is an epic fantasyland. Imagine scenery on the scale of an Indiana Jones or Lara Croft flick, with forgotten temples entangled in jungle vines, cobwebbed imperial tombs baking in the desert sun and ancient bejeweled treasures beyond reckoning. Wild rivers that rage, pumas that prowl in the night and hallucinogenic shaman rituals that are centuries old – and it's not just a movie here, it's real life.

After all, this is the South American country that chewed up and spat out empire after empire – even Inca warriors and Spanish conquistadors didn't stand a lasting chance. No one could completely conquer this jaw-dropping terrain, from glaciated Andean peaks where condors soar, down to the vast coastal deserts and the hot, steamy rainforests of the Amazon Basin.

Almost like a continent in miniature, Peru will astound you with its diversity, from its countless indigenous peoples, languages and traditions to its rainbow variety of wildlife. Whether it's your first trip to South America or your fiftieth, Peru is the perfect launchpad. Travel however and wherever the spirit moves you – a luxury lodge in the Amazon, cheap ceviche (raw seafood marinated in lime juice) at a beachfront café or a panoramic train ride through the Andes – because it's all surprisingly affordable.

Wanna take it easy? Follow the Gringo Trail that connects the country's highlights, winding up to the mountaintop Inca citadel of Machu Picchu. Or step off the beaten path and groove to Afro-Peruvian beats during Carnaval, float in a slow boat down the Amazon and chase that perfect wave along a paradisiacal Pacific coastline.

In short, if you crave adventure, jump on the next plane to Peru.

RICHARD I'ANS

Fiesta Time

RICHARD I'ANSON

Dig out your glad rags for Inti Raymi (p239), Peru's biggest festival

GRANT DIXON

Join the weird and wonderful dances for Virgen del Carmen in Paucartambo (p283)

OTHER HIGHLIGHTS

- Experience the music and mayhem of Cajamarca's Carnaval (p426) celebrations – just mind the water!
- Make a midnight trek up Ausangate at Q'oyoriti (p284)
- Piety and partying – no wonder the Semana Santa celebrations in Ayacucho (p309) are considered the country's finest

Pipe in the new year at Año Nuevo (p504)

ERIC L WHEATER

Ancient Treasures

COREY WISE

Tomb raiders: inspect the grisly remains at Sipán (p350)

Admire the craftsmanship on display at Saqsaywamán (p254)

RYAN FOX

OTHER HIGHLIGHTS

- Create your own theories about the origins of the mysterious Nazca Lines (p144)
- Pretend you're Indiana Jones at the untouristed ruins of Kuélap (p440)

Opposite:
Exhaust your stock of superlatives at Machu Picchu (p269)

WES WALKER

Marvel at the friezes at mammoth Chan Chan (p336)

JANE SWEE

People of Peru

Make friends in the Amazon Basin (p450)

Knit one, purl one: gain first-hand experience of Peruvian craftwork (p49)

OTHER HIGHLIGHTS

- Develop a taste for the finer things in life in the company of fashionable *arequipeños* (inhabitants of Arequipa; p162)
- Party with the Peruvian jet set at Máncora (p362)

A *cuzqueño* (inhabitant of Cuzco) baby hitches a ride, Cuzco (p221)

Devour the secrets of Peruvian cooking (p77)

A wealth of experience: learn from the people of Ica (p137)

Shoot the breeze in Lima (p85)

Alpacas are a girl's best friend: meet the locals at Saqsaywamán (p254)

Natural Wonders

JASON EDWARDS

Who's watching who? Eyeball owl monkeys in the Amazon Basin (p450)

Look but don't touch: admire the cacti on the Cordillera Huayhuash Circuit (p392)

PAUL KENNEDY

OTHER HIGHLIGHTS

- Plumb the depths of Cañón del Cotahuasi (p186), the world's deepest canyon
- Let your imagination take flight while watching the majestic Andean condors at Cruz del Condor (p184)

Catch your breath at the 5100m-high Cerani pass on the trek from Cabanconde to Andagua (p185)

GRANT D

JEFF CANTARUTTI

Take away golden memories of the flora at Machu Picchu (p269)

LEANNE WALKER

Leapfrog over lily pads near Iquitos (p490)

ERIC L WHEATER

An islander paddles across the placid waters of Lake Titicaca (p203)

Gold, lemon, burnt orange – count the colors as the sun rises over Reserva Nacional Tambopata (p462)

ALFREDO MAIQUEZ

Adrenaline Highs

Bag another peak (or five) in the Cordillera Blanca (p387)

GRANT D

Condor's-eye view: a paraglider escapes from the hustle and bustle of Miraflores (p105)

PAUL KENNEDY

Surfin' safari: catch a ride on the 3m pipeline at Cabo Blanco (p361)

OTHER HIGHLIGHTS

- Discover sand *everywhere* after sandboarding the giant dunes at Huacachina (p141)
- Receive a round of applause from fellow trekkers after scaling 4198m-high Warmiwañusca (Dead Woman's Pass) on the Inca Trail (p276)
- Travel from the Andes to the Amazon in 10 heart-pounding days on the Río Tambopata (p236)

Contents

Regional Map Contents

The Authors

SARA BENSON
Coordinating Author, South Coast, Arequipa & Canyon Country, Lake Titicaca, Cuzco & the Sacred Valley

After graduating with a liberal arts degree from university in Chicago, Sara jumped on a plane headed to California with just one suitcase and $100 in her pocket. More than a decade later, she still calls the San Francisco Bay Area home – when she's not off traipsing around Asia, Oceania and the Americas. Already the author of more than 20 travel and nonfiction books, she also has written for newspapers and magazines from coast to coast, including the *Los Angeles Times*, *Miami Herald* and *National Geographic Adventure*. She recently contributed to Lonely Planet's *South America on a Shoestring*.

Sara also wrote the Destination Peru, Getting Started, Itineraries, Snapshot, History, Environment, Peru Outdoors, Directory, Transportation and Glossary chapters.

My Favorite Trip

Dozens of detours off the Gringo Trail led me into the heart of rural Peru. I climbed through the ghoulish catacombs at Hacienda San José and watched Carnaval dancers groove to Afro-Peruvian beats in Chincha (p130), rafted the Río Cañete and cycled between vineyards outside Lunahuaná (p129), hiked through coastal sand dunes at the lagoon sanctuary near Mejía (p152) and trekked by Yanque and Cabanaconde in Cañón del Colca (p181). I hopped between traditional villages on the shores of Lake Titicaca (p215) and crossed the Bolivian border to visit Isla del Sol (p218), then explored remote ruins in the Sacred Valley (p255) and, finally, tackled spectacular alternatives to the Inca Trail (p277).

PAUL HELLANDER
Lima, Central Highlands, Amazon Basin

Paul has been trekking around the world for as long as he can remember. He has contributed to over 30 Lonely Planet guides and visited some 50 countries. South America was a long time coming, but the wait was worth it. Updating this edition of *Peru* was Paul's second visit for Lonely Planet to this archetypally Andean nation, and it was by far the most rewarding. Paul is a linguist by profession, a photographer by design and an author with a passion. When not sampling ceviche (raw seafood marinated in lime juice) in Miraflores, sipping *mate de coca* (coca-leaf tea) in the Andes or meandering along Amazonian rivers, Paul lives in Adelaide, South Australia, where he is always planning even more trips.

LONELY PLANET AUTHORS

Why is our travel information the best in the world? It's simple: our authors are independent, dedicated travellers. They don't research using just the internet or phone, and they don't take freebies in exchange for positive coverage. They travel widely, to all the popular spots and off the beaten track. They personally visit thousands of hotels, restaurants, cafés, bars, galleries, palaces, museums and more – and they take pride in getting all the details right, and telling it how it is. For more, see the authors section on www.lonelyplanet.com.

RAFAEL WLODARSKI

North Coast, Huaraz & the Cordilleras, Northern Highlands

After completing degrees in marketing and psychology in Melbourne, Rafael vowed never to use either of them and set off on a six-month round-the-world trip. Seven years and three passports later, he is yet to come home. Rafael spent most of his twenties traveling overland through the Middle East, the Indian subcontinent and North and South America. In 2000 he spent over a year traipsing around South America and is one of the few gringos around who has managed to develop a fondness for fried guinea pig. He currently calls foggy San Francisco home.

CONTRIBUTING AUTHORS

Dr David Goldberg completed his training in internal medicine and infectious diseases at Columbia-Presbyterian Medical Center in New York City, where he has also served as voluntary faculty. At present, he is an infectious diseases specialist in Scarsdale, NY, and the editor-in-chief of the website MDTravel-Health.com. He wrote the Health chapter.

Carolina A Miranda has been making ceviche since she was old enough to chop onions and is a long-time devotee of poet Cesar Vallejo. These interests prepared her to write the Food & Drink and Culture chapters for this book. In addition, she has traveled extensively throughout Peru, including long stints in Lima, Cuzco, the Urubamba valley and Chiclayo, her father's birthplace on the northern coast.

Hugh Thomson is the author of *The White Rock: An Exploration of the Inca Heartland* and *A Sacred Landscape: The Search for Ancient Peru*. He led several research expeditions to the area around Cuzco and made the first reports of some previously unknown Inca sites. Hugh wrote the Inca World chapter.

Getting Started

Peru has it all. Mystical archaeological sites, amazing Amazonian rainforest, the world's highest tropical mountains and an endless desert coastline will keep you traveling for months. Diverse and welcoming peoples, even more varied wildlife and some of the continent's gutsiest food all await adventurers. Best of all, transportation is efficient and relatively inexpensive, and accommodations are available to suit every budget, from cheapie backpackers hostels to beautifully converted colonial mansions.

This chapter will help you know when to go to Peru, what to pack, how much you'll spend while you're there and which places you won't want to miss visiting.

WHEN TO GO

Peru's climate has two main seasons – wet and dry – though the weather varies greatly depending on the geographical region. Temperature is mostly influenced by elevation: the higher you climb, the cooler it becomes.

A Peruvian weather site, in Spanish, is www.senamhi.gob.pe.

The peak tourist season is from June to August, which coincides with the cooler dry season in the Andean highlands and summer vacation in North America and Europe. This is the best (and busiest) time to go trekking on the Inca Trail to Machu Picchu, or climbing, hiking and mountain biking elsewhere.

People can and do visit the highlands year-round, though the wettest months of December to March make it a wet and muddy proposition. Many of the major fiestas (see p504), such as La Virgen de la Candelaria, Carnaval and Semana Santa, occur in the wettest months and continue undiminished even during heavy rainstorms.

On the arid coast, Peruvians visit the beaches during the most hot and humid time of the year, from late December through March. In central and southern Peru, the coast is cloaked in *garúa* (coastal fog) for the rest of the

---

DON'T LEAVE HOME WITHOUT...

- A passport valid for six months beyond your trip and, if necessary, a visa (p513).
- All recommended immunizations (p529) – make sure any prior vaccinations are up-to-date before setting off.
- A copy of your travel insurance policy details (p506).
- An ATM or traveler's-check card with a four-digit PIN (p507).
- Reservations for trekking the Inca Trail (p274) – or better yet, plan to take an alternative route (p277).
- A lightweight, wind-resistant and rainproof jacket – it'll shield you from the sun, and keep you dry when it rains.
- Earplugs – long-distance buses and many hotels enjoy ear-splitting entertainment at all hours.
- A Swiss Army–style penknife – do remember to place it in your checked luggage when flying or it'll be confiscated.
- Duct tape – make a mini-roll around a pencil, then use it to repair backpacks, seal shut leaky bottles etc.
- A roll of toilet-paper – essential as public toilets (p511) and most restaurants don't supply it.

year. Although the southern beaches are deserted then, the coastal cities can be visited at any time. In the north, the coast usually sees more sun, so beach lovers can hang out there year-round.

In the eastern rainforest, of course, it rains. The wettest months are December through May, but even then it rarely rains for more than a few hours at a time, so there's still plenty of sunshine to enjoy. Follow the locals' example: briefly take cover during the heaviest downpours. It's not a big deal.

See Climate Charts (p499) for more information.

COSTS & MONEY

Shoestring travelers watching their céntimos – by sleeping in dormitory rooms, traveling on economy buses, eating set menus – can easily get by on US$20 to US$25 a day, and even less if frugality is one of their strong points. Visitors who prefer private hot showers, à la carte meals in moderately priced restaurants, comfortable buses and occasional flights will find that US$35 to US$75 a day should meet their needs. Staying at luxury hotels and dining at top-end restaurants can cost up to several hundred dollars a day, especially if you're doing your trip by organized tour (see p520) or visiting only the most expensive cities of Cuzco and Lima.

You can stretch your budget by traveling with a partner as double rooms are usually less expensive than two singles (see p496). Hone your bargaining skills – taxi cabs don't have meters, and drivers routinely overcharge gringos. Hotels often give discounts if you simply ask for their 'best price,' or if you inquire about promotional, student or business rates. Many restaurants offer filling three-course set lunches for around S/5 (about US$1.50), while eating à la carte will triple your bill. Pay with cash rather than credit cards, in order to avoid hefty surcharges. Peruvian ATMs dispense both local currency (nuevos soles) and US dollars. Above all, keep your money safely stashed – an economical trip can get expensive fast if you are pickpocketed! For tips on avoiding theft, see p501.

Adventurers on a tight budget will be dismayed at the high costs of hiking the famed Inca Trail to Machu Picchu. Unguided trips are now illegal (and this is strictly enforced) and the cheapest four-day trips start around US$300 per person, not including equipment rental, tips for the guides and porters, or any incidental expenses, such as bottled water. A day trip to Machu Picchu via train and bus isn't cheap either (see p253 and p274).

For exchange rates, see the inside front cover of this book. For more advice on ATMs, currency exchange, traveler's checks, taxes and tipping, see p507.

HOW MUCH?

Local phone call US$0.15

Short taxi ride (not in Lima) US$1

Internet café per hour US$0.60

Two-star hotel room with bathroom and TV US$20

Flight between most cities US$95

See also the Lonely Planet Index, inside front cover.

TRAVEL LITERATURE

Inca Land: Explorations in the Highlands of Peru, by Hiram Bingham, is the classic traveler's tale. The book was first published in 1922, just over a decade after the American author 're-discovered' the ancient Inca citadel of Machu Picchu.

Eight Feet in the Andes: Travels with a Donkey from Ecuador to Cuzco, by Dervla Murphy, is an insightful, witty travelogue of this peripatetic travel writer's 1300-mile journey with her daughter through remote regions, ending at Machu Picchu.

The White Rock: An Exploration of the Inca Heartland, by Hugh Thomson, describes a filmmaker's search for hidden archaeological sites throughout the Peruvian Andes and Bolivia. It includes a lot of background on earlier travelers and explorers.

The Peru Reader: History, Culture, Politics, edited by Orin Starn, Carlos Ivan Degregori and Robin Kirk, is a literary and journalistic look at

TOP TENS

Festivals & Events

From colorful religious processions to Inca festivals in the Andean highlands, Peru's fiestas go off year-round. The following are just a few of our favorites.

- Virgen de la Candelaria (p504) – highland folk music and dance celebrations on February 2
- Carnaval (p504) – water fights and highland fiestas before the start of Lent
- Semana Santa (p504) – spectacular pageantry during Holy Week
- Q'oyoriti (p284) – Andean mountain worship and spiritual pilgrimages in May/June
- Inti Raymi (p239) – ancient Inca festival of the sun held on June 24
- Fiestas Patrias (p504) – Peru's festive National Independence Days on July 28–29
- Feast of Santa Rosa de Lima (p504) – honoring the patron saint of the Americas on August 30
- El Señor de los Milagros (p107) – on October 18, with religious processions bedecked in purple, plus bullfights
- Día de los Muertos (p505) – food, drink and flowers taken to family graves on November 2
- Puno Week (p196) – starting on November 5, among the Americas' best folkloric celebrations

Outdoor Adventures

From Andean highlands to Amazon rainforests to arid coastal deserts, Peru is an all-seasons playground. See p60 for an insider's guide to outdoor adventures. For Peru's top national parks, wildlife reserves and natural areas, turn to p56.

- Trekking to Machu Picchu (p274) – deservedly world-famous trails to ancient Inca ruins
- Trekking the Ausangate Circuit (p283) – six days of high-altitude trekking alongside alpacas
- Mountaineering around Huaraz (p377) – experts can scale Peru's highest peak, Huascarán (6768m)

everything from the conquest of the Incas to cocaine production, guerrilla warfare and gay activism.

At Play in the Fields of the Lord, by Peter Matthiessen, is a classic, superb and believable novel about the conflicts between the forces of 'development' and indigenous peoples in the Amazon jungle.

Trail of Feathers: In Search of the Birdmen of Peru, by Tahir Shah, is an amusing tall tale about what lies behind the 'birdmen' legends of the Peruvian desert, eventually leading the author to a tribe of cannibals in the Amazon.

Cut Stones and Crossroads: A Journey in the Two Worlds of Peru, by Ronald Wright, is a comprehensive journey through some of Peru's ancient cities and archaeological sites, and it comes with helpful guides to Quechua terminology and traditional Andean music.

INTERNET RESOURCES

For many more websites targeted to specific topics, such as volunteering in Peru or gay and lesbian travel, thumb through the Directory at the back of this book, starting on p496.

Andean Travel Web (www.andeantravelweb.com/peru) Independent travel directory with loads of links to hotels, tour companies, volunteer programs etc.

Latin America Network Information Center (www.lanic.utexas.edu) The University of Texas provides hundreds of informative links on all subjects.

- Trekking in the Cordilleras Blanca and Huayhuash (p385) – prime tramping past scores of glaciated peaks
- River running (white-water rafting) on the Río Tambopata (p236) and the rivers around Arequipa (p171) – multiday Andes-to-Amazon descents or through deep canyons
- Mountain biking around Arequipa (p172) and the Cordillera Blanca (p378) – easy trails and demanding single-track await
- Trekking in the Cañóns del Colca and Cotahuasi (p181 and p186) – get down into the world's deepest canyons
- Reaching remote archaeological sites from Chachapoyas (p438) – hire a guide, machete and pack mule to thrash through cloud forest
- Sandboarding at Huacachina (p142) – slide down humungous dunes at a desert oasis
- Surfing on the north coast (p340) – adventurers don't stop at 10!

Weird, Wacky & Wonderful
When it's time to fly your freak flag, here's a bizarre checklist of Peru's oddest experiences.

- Nazca Lines (p145) – one of the world's great archaeological mysteries
- Museo Santury (p166) – home to the frozen Inca maiden Juanita
- Islas Flotantes (p203) – artificial islands made entirely of reeds
- Visiting a shaman in Huancabamba (p360) – all-night ceremonies with hallucinogenic plants
- Feasting on roast *cuy* (guinea pigs; p432) – they're not just pets anymore
- Museo Nacional Sicán (p352) – the life and death of the paranoid Lord of Sicán
- Paragliding off Lima's beachfront cliffs (p105) – urban adventure taken to extremes
- Fiesta de los Gatos (p417) – dine on felines in Huari
- Riding high-altitude rails to Huancayo (p301) – via the world's second-highest train station
- Golfing in the Amazon (p486) – nine holes of expat-inspired madness in Iquitos

Living in Peru (www.livinginperu.com) This English-speaking expats' guide is an excellent source of local (albeit Lima-centric) news, plus an events calendar.
Peru Links (www.perulinks.com) Thousands of links on a range of topics; many are in Spanish, some in English. Editor's picks and top 10 sites are always good.
PromPerú (www.peru.info) The official government tourism agency, with a good overview of Peru in Spanish, English, French, German, Italian and Portuguese.

Itineraries
CLASSIC ROUTES

THE GRINGO TRAIL
Two Weeks / Lima to Cuzco

Leaving **Lima** (p85), journey south to **Pisco** and **Paracas** (p131), where there are tours to the wildlife-rich **Islas Ballestas** (p132). Then it's on to **Ica** (p137), Peru's wine and pisco (grape brandy) capital, and the palm-fringed oasis of **Huacachina** (p141), famous for sandboarding. Next is **Nazca** (p142) for a flight over the mysterious Nazca Lines.

Turn inland for the 'white city' of **Arequipa** (p162), with its colonial architecture and stylish nightlife. While there, go trekking in **Cañón del Colca** (p181) or **Cañón del Cotahuasi** (p186), the world's deepest, or climb **El Misti** (p170), a breathless 5822m high. Then it's upwards to **Puno** (p193), Peru's port on **Lake Titicaca** (p203), the world's highest navigable lake, where you can visit traditional islands and the *chullpas* (funerary towers) at **Sillustani** (p202) or **Cutimbo** (p202).

Wind through the Andes to **Cuzco** (p221), South America's oldest continuously inhabited city. Browse colorful markets and explore archaeological sites in the **Sacred Valley** (p255), then trek along the **Inca Trail** (p274) to **Machu Picchu** (p269) – or better yet, take a more adventurous **alternative route** (p277).

This loop starting from Lima, zooming through the coastal desert, up to Lake Titicaca and ending at Machu Picchu, is one of the most popular routes on the continent. You could do much of this route in two weeks, but a meandering month is ideal.

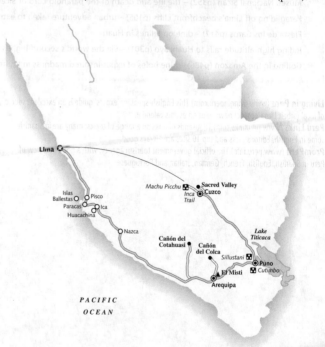

Lima

Machu Picchu · Sacred Valley
Inca · Cuzco
Trail

Islas
Ballestas · Pisco
Paracas · Ica
Huacachina

Nazca

Lake
Titicaca

Cañón del
Cotahuasi · Cañón
del Colca · Sillustani · Puno
Cutimbo

El Misti

Arequipa

*PACIFIC
OCEAN*

ONLY THE BEST OF PERU   Four Weeks / Lima to Máncora

Overcome your jet lag in **Lima** (p85), Peru's historic capital, then zoom south through the coastal desert for a flyover of the **Nazca Lines** (p145) before arriving in stylish, cosmopolitan **Arequipa** (p162), with its mysterious monasteries, deep canyons and smoking volcanoes. Fly high into the Andes to reach colonial **Cuzco** (p221) for a few days of acclimatization before boarding the train to **Machu Picchu** (p269), the most visited archaeological site in South America.

From Cuzco, fly to **Puerto Maldonado** (p452) to stay at a wildlife lodge along one of the mighty rivers in the Amazon Basin. Alternatively, take an overland tour from Cuzco to the **Manu area** (p465), where a Unesco-listed haven of biodiversity protects the priceless rainforest. Another option for exploring the Amazonian *selva* (jungle) is to first fly back to Lima, then onward to **Iquitos** (p483).

Back in Lima, take a bus northward to the adventurers' base camp of **Huaraz** (p374), where a short trek will take you to the precipitous peaks and languid lakes of the **Cordillera Blanca** (p385). Rumble back down to the coast at **Chimbote** (p326), then dash north to historic **Trujillo** (p328), surrounded by a cornucopia of archaeological sites, including the ruins of the largest pre-Columbian city in the Americas, **Chan Chan** (p336), and the fascinating **Huacas del Sol y de la Luna** (p339). Finish up with a sunny seaside break at the bustling beach resort and surf town of **Máncora** (p362).

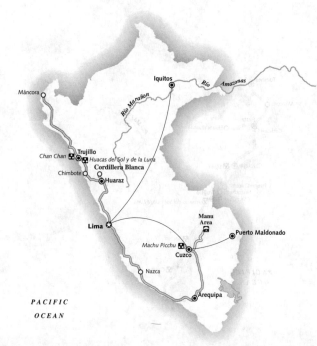

Are you the kind of person who has to do it all? This whirlwind tour hits Peru's must-see attractions. Be sure to give yourself a full month if you want to brag that you've really seen it all.

ROADS LESS TRAVELED

NORTH COASTIN'   Three Weeks / Lima to Tumbes

The first stop north of **Lima** (p85) could be **Caral** (p324), where the oldest known civilization in South America arose. Further north is the gruesome site of **Sechín** (p325), although many travelers prefer to continue to **Trujillo** (p328). Nearby attractions include the well-preserved Moche pyramids of **Huacas del Sol y de la Luna** (p339), and the ruins of the once mighty **Chan Chan** (p336).

Off the sleepy beaches at **Huanchaco** (p340), modern surfers paddle out to the breakers alongside local fishers in traditional *totora* canoes. En route to Chiclayo is **Puerto Chicama** (p343), which boasts one of the world's longest left-hand breaks, attracting international surfers. Then it's **Chiclayo** (p344), with several nearby towns that contain world-class museums showcasing riches from the important archaeological site of **Sipán** (p350).

Piura (p353) is a hub for visiting the witch doctors of **Huancabamba** (p359), hidden away in the Andes, or the craft markets and *picanterías* (local restaurants) of dusty **Catacaos** (p357). Peru's best beaches lie along the Pacific shoreline heading further north, and resorts such as **Máncora** (p362) offer lots of places to munch on great seafood and dance the balmy nights away.

The journey ends at **Tumbes** (p367), a gateway to Ecuador. It's the jumping-off point for visiting Peru's only mangrove swamps (watch out for those crocodiles!) and vast tracts of protected forests.

Straight as an arrow, the Panamericana Norte passes archaeological sites, great beaches, colonial cities and museums with fascinating artifacts. Hemingway liked it – you will too. Unless you're in a hurry to reach Ecuador, you'll want to spend a minimum of two weeks on your journey.

BACK DOOR INTO THE AMAZON   Two Weeks / Chiclayo to Iquitos

Leaving fascinating **Chiclayo** (p344), with its ancient ruins and witches' market, take a bus over the Andean continental divide to **Chachapoyas** (p435), a base for visiting the isolated, untouristed fortress of **Kuélap** (p440), dating from AD 1000, and many other remote, barely known archaeological sites. Chachapoyas can easily be reached in 10 hours from Chiclayo, traveling along the quicker paved road via the highland jungle town of **Jaén** (p434), a remote border crossing to Ecuador.

Hardier travelers will take the wild, unpaved, longer route to first visit **Cajamarca** (p421), a lovely highland provincial town where the Inca Atahualpa was imprisoned by Spanish conquistadors. Outside of the wet season, continue on the slow, spectacular route to friendly **Celendín** (p433) and **Leimebamba** (p442), surrounded by many archaeological sites, on a scenic but kidney-busting drive to Chachapoyas (p434).

From Chachapoyas, take the scenic but unpaved road to **Pedro Ruíz** (p443), where transportation is readily available to **Tarapoto** (p444). Break your journey here to hike to high jungle waterfalls. The last road section to **Yurimaguas** (p480) is a seven-hour unpaved gut-wrencher. Cargo boats leave here most days on the two-day trip to **Iquitos** (p483) via the village of **Lagunas** (p482), a good entry point to the **Reserva Nacional Pacaya-Samiria** (p482). Hammock or cabin space is readily available. Don't expect much comfort, but the trip will be an absolutely unforgettable experience of how people live on the world's greatest river. At Iquitos, you can arrange boat trips that go deep into the Amazon Basin or Brazil.

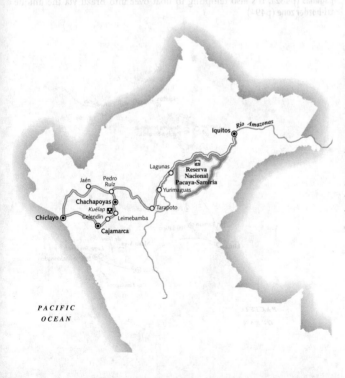

This route crosses the northern highlands by road and ends at Amazonian Iquitos, the largest city in the world that cannot be reached by road. Hurrying locals get from Chiclayo to Iquitos in less than a week; curious travelers might take a month or more.

JUNGLE BOOGIE   Four Weeks / Cuzco to Iquitos

Although it's Brazil that springs to mind when you think of the Amazon, Peru shouldn't be far behind. Over half of the country is made up of jungle, which dramatically drops away from the eastern slopes of the Andes and deep into the Amazon Basin.

The most popular excursion starts from **Cuzco** (p221 and p282) and heads to the **Manu area** (p465), itself the size of a small country and full of jungle lodges and wildlife-watching opportunities. Or you can fly from Cuzco to **Puerto Maldonado** (p452), and rent a thatch-roofed bungalow with a view either along the **Río Madre de Dios** (p458), the gateway to lovely **Lago Sandoval** (p460), or along the **Río Tambopata** (p462), where a national reserve protects one of the country's largest clay licks.

During the dry season, it's possible for hard-core types to travel overland back to Cuzco. But most travelers elect to fly back to Lima, then onward to **Pucallpa** (p474), near the lake **Yarinacocha** (p478). The lake is ringed by tribal villages, including those of the matriarchal Shipibo people, renowned for their pottery. A more challenging bus journey reaches Pucallpa from Lima via the boomtown of **Satipo** (p472), at the heart of Peru's coffee-growing region, and **Puerto Bermúdez** (p473), the stronghold of Peru's largest indigenous Amazonian tribe, the Asháninka.

Pucallpa is the start of a classic slow riverboat journey north along the **Río Ucayali** (p477) to **Iquitos** (p483). This northern jungle capital has a floating market and a bustling port where you can catch a more comfortable cruise into Peru's largest national park, **Reserva Nacional Pacaya-Samiria** (p482), via **Lagunas** (p482). It's also tempting to float over into Brazil via the unique **tri-border zone** (p494).

Expect to fly a lot (if your time is limited) or spend weeks on epic river and road journeys through the unforgettable Amazon Basin, populated by spectacular wildlife and tribal peoples. Bring bucketloads of patience and self-reliance – a lot of luck never hurts either.

TAILORED TRIPS

ANCIENT TREASURES

Peru's main attractions are its Inca ruins, especially **Machu Picchu** (p269) and the bounty of the **Sacred Valley** (p255). But there is a wealth of sites from other cultures to see, too.

Trujillo is an excellent base for seeing **Chan Chan** (p336), as well as ongoing excavations of the Moche pyramids of **Huacas del Sol y de la Luna** (p339). If you have time in Huaraz, the 3000-year-old ruins of the **Chavín de Huántar** (p414) are worth a trip. Or keep going north to **Chiclayo** (p344), another treasure-house of ancient sites. Nearby, gold and other riches from the excavated site of **Sipán** (p350) are found in the museum at **Lambayeque** (p351). Chiclayo is also the springboard for side trips into the northern highlands, where more archaeological sites await hidden in the cloud forest outside **Chachapoyas** (p438), like **Kuélap** (p440), a monolithic monument that gives Machu Picchu a run for its money.

The wonderfully woven artifacts of the Paracas are best seen in museums – Lima's **Museo de la Nación** (p99) and **Museo Rafael Larco Herrera** (p100) in particular – while the **Nazca Lines** (p145) can only be appreciated properly from the air. The funerary towers of the Colla, Lupaca and Inca cultures at **Sillustani** (p202) and **Cutimbo** (p202), near Lake Titicaca, are worth seeing while in Puno.

ADRENALINE HIGHS

Forget the crowds in Patagonia and go to Peru instead. Extreme-sports fanatics, expedition experts and daydreaming adventurers can all get their kicks right here.

Surf's up at some of the top spots on the Americas' Pacific coast. Drag your board up the coast in search of that elusive perfect swell at **Huanchaco** (p340), **Puerto Chicama** (p343), **Pacasmayo** (p343) or around **Máncora** (p362). Or head in the opposite direction to Lima's **southern beaches** (p125), **Cerro Azul** (p129) and all the way south to **Boca del Río** (p157), near the Chilean border. Don't forget sandboarding on Peru's coastal dunes at **Huacachina** (p142) and **Cerro Blanco** (p146).

Try mountain biking the rugged trails around **Huaraz** (p378) to the sight of the highest glimmering, ice-capped peaks on the continent. Hundreds of rock-climbing routes are being bolted every year in the **Cordillera Blanca** region (p377), while challenging treks await in the **Cordilleras Blanca and Huayhuash** (p385) and around **Cuzco** (p235).

Civilized **Arequipa** (p169) is a launching pad for rugged climbs of nearby volcanoes, such as **El Misti** (p170) and in the remote **El Valle de los Volcanes** (p186). Then head to the world's deepest canyons, the **Cañón del Colca** (p181) and **Cañón del Cotahuasi** (p186), for trekking between rural villages and wild river running (white-water rafting).

Snapshot

It's a nation on the brink.

Although known to the outside world for its ancient ruins, Peru is modernizing at a breakneck pace. Where once there were only chicken buses, now comfortable *bus-camas* (bed buses) ply newly paved highways. The construction of an ambitious interoceanic highway and the opening of the new Integration Bridge between Peru and Brazil signals a cross-border trade and travel boom ahead.

In fact, average Peruvians today are economically far better off than they were even just five years ago. Nevertheless, everyday life still consists mostly of chronic poverty and unemployment that's so out of control it can't be reliably measured.

It's hardly surprising, then, that labor strikes for higher wages and political protests happen quite often: farmers march against the US-backed eradication of traditional coca crops, villagers fight environmental pollution by international mining corporations, doctors boycott US trade pacts that would drive up the price of drugs desperately needed to treat HIV/AIDS – the controversies never stop. This unrest can be tiresome for travelers, who may find their trip suddenly delayed. It's not really a big deal to Peruvians, though, who are used to accepting such disturbances as facts of life.

As it tries to exorcise the demons from its political past, Peru is haunted by all-too-familiar ghosts. In 2005, disgraced ex-president Alberto Fujimori returned from exile in Japan and announced that he planned to run for the presidency again, only to be arrested in Chile on an extradition warrant to face charges of corruption and human rights abuses. Peruvians look back with mixed feelings to the days of Fujimori's strongman style of rule (see p37), and his cult of personality lingers on.

In the 2006 presidential elections, Fujimori was constitutionally banned from appearing on the ballot, so it narrowed to a face-off between the popular nationalist Ollanta Humala, an ex-army officer under Fujimori, and left-leaning Alan García, another ex-president who put Peru on the path to financial ruin during the late 1980s. In the end, Peruvians decided that the devil you know is better than the one you don't, and voted silver-tongued García back into office. Outgoing president Alejandro Toledo may have been the first indigenous president of an Andean nation, but after failing to deliver new jobs and an administration plagued by corruption scandals, Toledo's popularity ratings dropped below 10%, the lowest of any South American president.

Armed attacks along the famous Inca Trail and on trekking routes in the mountains around Huaraz, muggings on overnight buses, terrorist threats against train routes and express kidnappings from taxis don't happen often, but they do happen. Meanwhile, the feared Sendero Luminoso (Shining Path) guerrillas may be making a comeback, thanks to profits from cocaine trafficking with drug cartels in neighboring Colombia (see p501). Such unfortunate events are just as worrying to Peruvians – whose economic success and development depend heavily on tourist dollars – as they are to foreign visitors.

Yet Peru overall is a safer, easier and more insanely popular place to travel than ever before. Thankfully, responsible tourism is finally on the agenda, from Inca Trail porter welfare to sustainable ecotourism in the Amazon to protecting loved-to-death sites such as Machu Picchu and the Nazca Lines. Every year archaeologists are finding more amazing sites hidden in the

FAST FACTS

Population: 27.2 million

Median age: 25 years

Peruvians who live in poverty: 54%

Gross Domestic Product (GDP): US$72 billion

Estimated hectares of coca production: 38,000

Number of taxis in Lima: one in every seven cars

Rate of inflation: 1.6%

Navigable tributaries in the Amazon Basin: 8600km

Average daily visitors to Machu Picchu: 1000

Native varieties of Peruvian potatoes: almost 4000

cloud forests, desert and jungle, including those built by some of the oldest cultures in the Americas. Peruvians also are reclaiming more of their heritage, with racism against indigenous peoples now recognized as unjust and a debate underway to have Inca artifacts repatriated from Yale University in the USA.

When it comes to Peru, there's always news. Come see its evolution for yourself.

History

For many travelers, the first word that comes to mind when thinking of Peruvian history is 'Inca.' Indeed the Inca civilization, the best-known and most-studied of South America's pre-Columbian cultures, is the one you're most likely to encounter on the road. Yet the mighty Incas are merely the tip of the archaeological iceberg. Peru had a bounty of pre-Columbian cultures, some preceding the Incas by millennia.

Peru is unequaled in South America for its archaeological wealth, and many archaeologists find Peru's ancient sites and cultures as endlessly fascinating as those of Mexico, Egypt or the Mediterranean. Learning about and visiting these centuries-old ruins is the highlight of many travelers' journeys as well, and even those travelers with limited interest in archaeology will find seeing some of the main sites rewarding.

What we know of Peru's pre-Columbian civilizations has been gleaned almost entirely from archaeological excavation. With no written records available, archaeologists have had to derive historical information from the realistic and expressive decoration found on ancient ceramics, textiles and other artifacts. These relics are worth examining wherever they are on display in Peru's many archaeological museums.

It's illegal to buy pre-Columbian antiques and take them out of the country.

PRECERAMIC PERIOD

Humans are relatively recent arrivals in the New World, probably spreading throughout the Americas after migrating across the Bering Strait about 20,000 years ago. Peru's first inhabitants were nomadic hunters and gatherers who roamed the country in loose-knit bands, living in caves and hunting fearsome (and now extinct) animals such as giant sloths, saber-toothed tigers and mastodons. Hunting scenes were recorded in cave paintings made by Peru's early inhabitants at Lauricocha near Huánuco and Toquepala near Tacna.

Domestication of the llama, alpaca and guinea pig began by about 4000 BC, though some sources claim that it may have begun as early as 7000 BC. Around the same time, people began planting seeds and learning how to improve crops by simple horticultural methods such as weeding.

TOP 10 ARCHAEOLOGICAL MUSEUMS

Museo de la Nación (p99) Lima
Museo Rafael Larco Herrera (p100) Lima
Qorikancha (p233), Cuzco
Museo de Sitio Manuel Chávez Ballón (p266) Aguas Calientes
Museo de Arte Precolombino (p232) Cuzco
Museo Santury (p166) Arequipa
Museo Tumbas Reales de Sipán (p351) North coast
Museo Nacional Sicán (p352) North coast
Museo Inka (p232) Cuzco
Museo Regional de Ica (p139) Ica

TIMELINE	12,000 BC	4000 BC
	Peru's oldest known archaeological site, the Pikimachay caves near Ayacucho, are used by hunters and gatherers	Settlement of Peru's coastal oases; farming, fishing and construction of burial pyramids

The coastal strip of Peru was wetter than today's desert, and a number of small settlements were established, thus changing the way of life of people living there from nomadic hunters and gatherers to settled agriculturists and fisherfolk. The inhabitants fished with nets or bone hooks, sometimes using rafts, and collected food such as shellfish, sea urchins, seabird eggs and even sea lions. Various forms of the Andean staple, the potato, began to be grown as a crop around 3000 BC, along with beans, quinoa, cotton, squashes and corn. Cotton was used to make clothing, mainly by using simple twining techniques and, later, by weaving.

Manioc (also called cassava) and sweet potatoes appeared on the coast early on, indicating trade links with the Amazon basin. Trade occurring between the Andean and Amazon regions was evidenced also by the use of the coca leaf for ritual purposes and the introduction of exotic rainforest bird feathers. Ceramics and metalwork were still unknown during this period in either area, although jewelry made of bone and shell has been found.

The coastal people lived in simple one-room dwellings, lined with stone or made from branches and reeds. These early Peruvians also built many structures for ceremonial or ritual purposes. Some of the oldest – raised temple platforms facing the ocean and containing human burials – date from the third millennium BC, indicating a prosperity based on the rich marine life of the coast. Some of these platforms were decorated with painted mud friezes. The more complex coastal ruins of Caral (p324) are unique: dating from as early as 3000 BC, they are evidence of the oldest civilization in South America, contemporaneous with more-famous ancient civilizations in Egypt, India and China. More recently the ruins of the oldest astronomical observatory in the Western Hemisphere were discovered on the coast just north of Lima.

Discover Peru's most recent archaeological finds at www .archaeologynews.org.

Roughly contemporary with coastal settlements of the later Preceramic Period, the enigmatic site of the Temple of Kotosh (p315) near Huánuco is one of the earliest ruins in highland Peru. Little is known about the people who lived there, but their buildings rated among the most developed for that period, and pottery fragments found here predate those found in other parts of Peru by several hundred years.

INITIAL PERIOD

This period, so named for the initiation of ceramics production, extended from approximately 2000 to 1000 BC. What is known about it today has been gleaned from remains found in the Virú valley and Guañape area, just south of Trujillo on Peru's north coast. More recently, large ceremonial temples from this period have been discovered in the Rímac valley above Lima and other coastal sites. Funerary offerings were made at many of them. During this time, ceramics developed from basic undecorated pots to sculpted, incised and simply colored pots of high quality. Weaving, fishing and horticulture also improved, the latter particularly through the development of irrigation. Toward the end of this time, agricultural terraces were first constructed in the highlands.

EARLY HORIZON

Lasting roughly from 1000 to 300 BC, this period has also been called the Chavín Horizon, after the site of Chavín de Huántar (p414), east of Huaraz.

1000–300 BC	300 BC–AD 800
Period of the Chavín Horizon; several cultures share developments in weaving, pottery, sculpture, agriculture, religion and architecture	The Paracas create the finest textiles; the Moche build huge adobe platform mounds; the Nazca construct the Nazca Lines

It's termed a 'horizon' because artistic and religious phenomena appeared, perhaps independently, within several cultures in different places at about the same time, indicating some kind of interchange of ideas and increasing cultural complexity. This horizon extended throughout much of the highlands and the coast.

The salient feature of the Chavín influence is the repeated representation of a stylized feline (jaguar or puma) face with prominently religious overtones, perhaps symbolizing spiritual transformations experienced under the influence of hallucinogenic plants. Other animal faces, some mythical, and human faces are also found. Most importantly, this period represents the greatest early development in weaving, pottery, agriculture, religion and architecture – in a word, culture. For more about the Chavín culture, see p415.

During this time, methods of working with gold, silver and copper also developed on the north coast.

Get a sneak cyber-peek
at the rainbow variety
of Peru's archaeological
sites at www.naya.org
.ar/peru/index.html.

EARLY INTERMEDIATE PERIOD

Around 300 BC, the Chavín culture inexplicably lost its unifying influence. Over the next thousand or so years, several cultures became locally important, of which the best known is the unusually named Paracas Necropolis (named after the burial site discovered south of Lima), which produced cotton and wool textiles considered to be the finest pre-Columbian textiles of the Americas – with up to 398 threads per linear inch! See p135 for more about the Paracas culture.

From about AD 100 to 700 pottery, metalwork and weaving reached a pinnacle of technological development in several regions. Two distinct cultures are particularly noted for their exceptional pottery: the Moche from the Trujillo area produced pottery from press molds, and the Nazca from the south coast introduced polychrome techniques. Both of these cultures recorded their life in intricate detail on their ceramics, leaving archaeologists with plentiful clues about this period.

These cultures also left behind impressive sites that are worth visiting today. The Moche built massive platform mounds (popularly called 'pyramids') such as the Huacas del Sol y de la Luna (Temples of the Sun and Moon; p339), which are located near Trujillo. Sipán (p350), another Moche site situated near Chiclayo, contains a series of tombs that have been under excavation since 1987 and may be the most important archaeological discovery in South America since Machu Picchu. The Temple of the Moon is currently under excavation, and amazing friezes have been uncovered. Most recently, the elaborately tattooed mummy of a female Moche leader was discovered in 2006 at another coastal site. See p336 for more about the Moche culture.

The Nazca made enigmatic giant designs in the desert, known as the Nazca Lines (p145). At the turn of the 20th century, it was Peruvian archaeologist Max Uhle who first realized that the drifting desert sands hid remnants of a culture distinct from other coastal peoples. Soon *huaqueros* (grave robbers) came to plunder many of the most fascinating sites and sold their finds to individuals and museums. But you can view Nazca mummies at the Chauchilla Cemetery (p146), and also visit the pyramids of Cahuachi (p146), which are still undergoing excavations.

600–1100	900–1470
The expansionist, militaristic Wari culture emerges and spreads throughout the central Andes	The Chimu build Chan Chan, the largest pre-Columbian city in the Americas; fierce Chachapoyas warriors construct Kuélap

MIDDLE HORIZON

Most of the latter half of the 6th century was marked by a catastrophic drought along the coast, contributing to the otherwise mysterious demise of the Moche.

From AD 600 to about 1100, the Wari (or Huari) emerged as the first expansionist peoples known in the Andes. Unlike the earlier Chavín, expansion was not limited to the diffusion of artistic and religious influence. Based in the Ayacucho region of the central highlands, the Wari were vigorous military conquerors who built and maintained important outposts throughout much of Peru. The sprawling ruins of their ancient capital can still be visited outside Ayacucho (p313).

The Wari attempted to subdue the cultures they conquered by emphasizing their own values and suppressing local oral traditions and regional self-expression. Thus from about AD 700 to 1100, Wari influence is noted in the art, technology and architecture of most areas in Peru. More significantly, from an archaeologist's point of view, any local oral traditions that may have existed were discouraged by these conquerors and slowly forgotten. With no written language to study either, archaeologists must rely entirely on the examination of excavated artifacts to gain an idea of what life during this period was like.

The Wari too, in their turn, were replaced by other cultures.

LATE INTERMEDIATE PERIOD

Because of their cultural dominance and oppressive rule, it is not surprising that the Wari were generally not welcomed by other cultures, despite the improvements they made in urban development and organization. By about AD 1000, their governance had been replaced by individual groups in local areas. These separate regional states thrived for the next 400 years. The best-known is the Chimu kingdom in the Trujillo area. Its capital was Chan Chan (p336), famed as the largest adobe city in the world.

Several other cultures existed around roughly the same time as the Chimu. The cloud-forest-dwelling Chachapoyas warrior culture erected Kuélap (p440), one of the most intriguing and significant of the highland ruins, and reasonably accessible to travelers. Back on the coast, the Sicán (see also p336) were descendants of the Moche culture. They were also excellent metalsmiths who actively traded with other tribes in the regions of present-day Ecuador, Chile and Colombia. Also contemporary with the Chimu were the Chancay people just north of Lima. The best collection of Chancay artifacts is at the Fundacion Museo Amano in Lima (p102). Further south were the Ica and Chincha cultures, whose artifacts can be seen in the Museo Regional de Ica (p139). At this time there were also several small altiplano (Andean plateau) kingdoms situated near Lake Titicaca that frequently warred with one another. They left impressive *chullpas* (funerary towers) dotting the bleak landscape – the best remaining examples are at Sillustani (p202) and Cutimbo (p202). Last but not least, the formation of chiefdoms and social development in the Amazon jungle had already begun by the end of this period.

Prior to the Incas, there were scores of different cultures and civilizations dating back at least to 2500 BC – and *The Ancient Kingdoms of Peru*, by Nigel Davies, covers almost all of them.

INCA EMPIRE

For all its glory, the Inca empire really only existed for barely a century. The reign of the first eight *incas* (kings) spanned the period from the 12th

1100–1200	1438–1470
Emergence of the Inca tribe in the valley around Cuzco, founded by Manco Capac	Inca Pachacutec defeats the Chanka and embarks upon aggressive empire building; Machu Picchu and Qorikancha constructed

century to the early 15th century. But prior to 1438, the Incas, a small tribe who believed themselves to have descended from the ancestral sun god Inti, ruled over only the valley of Cuzco.

It was the ninth *inca*, Pachacutec, that gave the empire its first bloody taste of conquest. A growing thirst for expansion had led the neighboring highland tribe, the Chankas, to Cuzco's doorstep around 1438, and Viracocha Inca fled in the belief that his small empire was lost. However, his son Pachacutec rallied the Inca army and, in a desperate battle, he famously routed the Chanka. This marked the beginning of a remarkably rapid military expansion.

Buoyed by his victory in Cuzco, Pachacutec promptly bagged much of the central Andes over the next 25 years. The Inca empire, known as Tahuantinsuyo (Land of Four Quarters), conquered most of the cultures in the area stretching from southern Colombia to central Chile, including also the Andean regions of Bolivia and northern Argentina. It was also during this time that scores of fabulous mountaintop citadels were built, including famous Machu Picchu (p269).

Like the Wari before them, the Incas imposed their way of life on the peoples they conquered. Thus when the Spanish arrived, most of the Andean area had been politically unified by Inca rule. This unification did not extend to many of the everyday facets of life for the conquered, and many of them felt some resentment toward the Inca leaders. This was a significant factor in the success of the Spaniards during their invasion of the New World. See p67 for more information on the Incas.

SPANISH INVASION

When Europeans 'discovered' the New World, epidemics, including smallpox, swept down from Central America and the Caribbean. In 1527, the 11th *inca* Huayna Capac died of such an epidemic. Before expiring, he divided his empire between his two sons, Atahualpa, possibly born of a *quiteña* (inhabitant of Quito) mother, who took the north, and the pure-blooded native *cuzqueño* (inhabitant of Cuzco) Huascar, who took Cuzco and the south. Civil war promptly ensued, and the slow downfall of the Inca empire began.

After Columbus' first landfall, the Spanish rapidly invaded and conquered the Caribbean islands and the Aztec and Mayan cultures of Mexico and Central America. By the 1520s, the conquistadors were ready to turn their attentions to the South American continent. In 1522 Pascual de Andagoya sailed as far as the Río San Juan in Ecuador. Two years later, Francisco Pizarro headed south but was unable to reach even the San Juan. In November 1526, Pizarro again headed south, this time with more success. By 1528 he had discovered the rich coastal settlements of the Inca empire.

After returning to Spain to court money and men for the impending conquest, he returned. Pizarro's third expedition left Panama late in 1530. He landed on the Ecuadorian coast and began to march overland toward Peru. In September 1532, Pizarro founded the first Spanish town in Peru, naming it San Miguel de Piura. He then marched inland into the heart of the Inca empire. Pizarro succeeded in reaching Cajamarca in 1532, by which time Atahualpa had defeated his half-brother Huascar.

This meeting between Incas and Spaniards was to radically change the course of South American history. Atahualpa was ambushed by a few dozen armed conquistadors, who succeeded in capturing him, killing thousands

The Incas in Cuzco ate fresh seafood that was delivered by runners from the coast near Quito in less than six days – quite a feat!

1532–33	1780
Spanish conquistadors arrive at Cajamarca, capturing, and later executing, Atahualpa, putting an end to the Inca empire	Inca Túpac Amaru II leads a bloody, but unsuccessful rebellion against the Spanish colonialists

THE SPANISH INQUISITION, AMERICAN-STYLE

In 1569, King Phillip II of Spain decreed that Lima, the capital of the colonial viceroyalty of Peru, would become the largest tribunal of the Spanish Inquisition in the Americas, to which prisoners from as far away as Panama and Cuba were sent. Although gruesome images spring to mind almost immediately when you hear the words 'Spanish Inquisition,' the scope of the dreaded process here in the colonies was less far-reaching than in the mother country. Torture was usually only applied after a prisoner had been given several opportunities to confess to heresy, and only Spanish colonists or *mestizos* (people of mixed indigenous and Spanish descent) were ever brought before the tribunal. Of those 2000 or so prisoners detained in Lima during the 150 years of the Inquisition in the Americas, just over 40 were executed. Indigenous peoples were given a free pass, as they were not considered fully converted to Christianity. Today you can inspect the torture chambers and courtroom used at Lima's **Museo de la Inquisición** (p97).

of unarmed indigenous tribespeople. In an attempt to regain his freedom, the Inca offered a ransom of gold and silver from Cuzco, including that stripped from the walls of Qorikancha, the most glorious temple in the Inca empire.

But after holding Atahualpa prisoner for a number of months and teasing the Incas with ransom requests, Pizarro murdered the Inca leader anyway, and quickly marched on Cuzco. Mounted on horseback, protected by armor and swinging steel swords, the Spanish cavalry was virtually unstoppable. Despite sporadic rebellions, the Inca empire was forced to retreat into the mountains and jungle, and never recovered its glorious prestige or extent.

European diseases traveled faster than the Spanish conquistadors: the 11th Inca, Huayna Capac, died of smallpox eight years before Pizarro founded Lima.

COLONIAL PERU

The Inca capital of Cuzco was of little use to the Spaniards, who were a seafaring people and needed a coastal capital to maintain communication with Spain. Accordingly, Pizarro founded Lima as the 'City of Kings' on the Feast of Epiphany, January 6, 1535, and this became the capital of the viceroyalty of Peru, as the colony was named.

The next three decades were a period of great turmoil, with the Incas fighting against their conquerors, and the conquistadors fighting among themselves for control of the rich colony. The conquistador Diego de Almagro was assassinated in 1538 and Francisco Pizarro suffered the same fate three years later at the hands of Almagro's avenging son. Meanwhile, Manco Inca tried to regain control of the highlands and was almost successful in 1536, but he was forced to retreat to Vilcabamba in the jungle, where he was killed in 1544. Succeeding Incas were less defiant until 1572 when the last ruling Inca, Túpac Amaru, organized a rebellion in which he was defeated and eventually beheaded by the Spaniards in front of the cathedral in Cuzco's main plaza.

Horrible Histories: The Angry Aztecs and the Incredible Incas by Terry Deary is a great book for kids, with some meaty history mixed in with the juicy bits.

Things were relatively peaceful, however, during the next 200 years. Lima became the main political, social and commercial center of the Andean nations. Cuzco became a backwater, its main mark on the colonial period being the development of the Cuzco school of art, the *escuela cuzqueña*, which blended Spanish and indigenous influences. Cuzco school canvases can be admired now in Lima's museums and in the many colonial churches that were built in the highlands during the 17th and 18th centuries.

1824	1879–83
The battles of Junín and Ayacucho lead to the birth of Peru as an independent state	Peru wars with Chile over the nitrate-rich northern Atacama Desert and loses a large area of southern coastal land

The rulers of the colony were the Spanish-born viceroys appointed by the Spanish crown. Immigrants from Spain held the most prestigious positions, while Spaniards born in the colony were generally less important. This is how the Spanish crown was able to control its colonies. *Mestizos* were placed still further down the social scale. Lowest of all were the indigenous peoples, who were exploited and treated as *peones* (expendable laborers,) under the *encomienda* system. This feudal system granted Spanish colonists land titles that included as property all of the indigenous people living within that area.

This finally boiled over into the 1780 indigenous uprising, led by Túpac Amaru II. Educated by Jesuits, this *cuzqueño* of royal Inca descent served his Spanish colonial masters at first while working to improve conditions for indigenous workers, especially in Peru's mines. As his politics grew more radical, Túpac Amaru II adopted his great-grandfather's Incan name and staged an all-out rebellion. When that struggle was quashed by the Spanish, the indigenous leaders were cruelly executed in Cuzco. Túpac Amaru II himself was drawn and quartered in Cuzco's main plaza, the same place that his great-grandfather had been executed. No one knows whether any of the Inca royal line survived past this date.

> Tupac Amur Shakur, the US rap star who was slain in Las Vegas in 1996, was named after 18th-century Inca revolutionary Túpac Amaru II.

INDEPENDENCE

By the early 19th century, the inhabitants of Spain's Latin American colonies were dissatisfied with their lack of freedom and high taxation; South America was ripe for revolt and independence. In Peru's case, what paved the way toward independence was the discovery and exploitation of a variety of rich mineral deposits, beginning with the seemingly inauspicious guano (seabird droppings) used for fertilizer.

The winds of change arrived in Peru from two directions. José de San Martín liberated Argentina and Chile, and in 1821 he entered Lima and formally proclaimed independence. Meanwhile, Simón Bolívar had freed Venezuela, Colombia and Ecuador.

In 1822 San Martín and Bolívar met privately in Guayaquil, Ecuador. What transpired during that heart-to-heart conversation is still a mystery, but afterward San Martín left Latin America altogether to live in France, while Bolívar continued with the liberation of Peru.

The most decisive battles for Peruvian independence were fought at Junín on August 6, 1824 and Ayacucho on December 9. But it wasn't until 1826 that the Spanish finally surrendered.

DISORDER AT THE BORDERS

Unfortunately, independence didn't spell the end of warfare for Peru. A brief war broke out with Spain in 1866, which Peru won, and was followed shortly by a longer war with Chile (1879–83), which Peru lost. The latter was over the nitrate-rich areas of the northern Atacama Desert and resulted in Chile annexing a large portion of coastal southern Peru. The area around Tacna wasn't returned until 1929.

Peru went to war with Ecuador over a border dispute in 1941. A treaty drawn up in Rio de Janeiro in 1942 gave Peru jurisdiction over the northern sections of the departments of Amazonas and Loreto, but Ecuador disputed this border, and deadly skirmishes occurred between the two countries every few years. Finally, in 1998, the border issue was resolved, with Peru granting

1911	1964
US historian Hiram Bingham arrives at the ruins of Machu Picchu	The world's worst soccer disaster occurred in Lima when over 300 fans were killed in a riot following a disputed referee call

Ecuador access to the Amazon and leaving a tiny area in Ecuador's control. Essentially, the 1942 border remains almost intact and the two countries are now at peace, although much unexploded ordinance (UXO) is waiting to be cleaned up.

DICTATORSHIPS & REVOLUTIONARIES

For much of the 20th century, especially during the 1960s and '70s, the governing of Peru was marked by a series of military dictatorships and coups.

Civilian rule returned in 1980 with President Fernando Belaúnde Terry, who had been ousted by a military coup in 1968. His earlier administration had been mired in disputes with a US-owned oil company when the military stepped in and took control of some of Peru's most lucrative oil fields. After being exiled to Argentina for more than a decade, Belaúnde was allowed by the military to come back to Peru and run for office again. Although Belaúnde was admired for his staunch commitment to the democratic process, his second presidential term was marred by radical inflation, domestic terrorism and human-rights violations by the Peruvian armed forces.

The Maoist group Sendero Luminoso (Shining Path) waged a terrorist campaign against the central government from 1980 until the early 1990s, and the struggle led to between 40,000 and 60,000 deaths and 'disappearances.' The guerrilla group was linked to drug cartels and active mainly in Peru's central highlands, but the effects of its activities were often felt in Lima. A smaller, unrelated guerrilla group, the Marxist-Leninist Movimiento Revolucionario Túpac Amaru (MRTA) also waged a war against the government, but this conflict was largely localized within the department of San Martín.

In 1985 Peru's presidential elections were won by Alan García Pérez. Alan García, as he's better known, was Peru's youngest president ever and delighted the passionately proud populace with his weekly *balconazos,* oratory-filled appearances on the balcony of the Presidential Palace. He further pleased Peruvians by cutting taxes and freezing prices. For a while he was Peru's shining star, but the economy could not support García's largesse, and the currency was massively devalued.

The last years of the García presidency were grim – no more *balconazos,* hyperinflation (at one point, it reached 10,000%!), Sendero Luminoso guerrillas heightening their activities, and a national state of emergency with a 1am to 5am curfew in Lima. Demonstrations and protests were an almost daily occurrence. By the end of García's five-year term, the country was in economic and political chaos. García went into exile after being accused of embezzling millions of dollars, and thereafter lived in luxurious apartments in Columbia, France and Germany. Amazingly, after the statute of limitations had run out, he returned to Peru to run for president again – twice!

The Monkey's Paw by Robin Kirk covers Peru during the violent 1980s – it's an excellent, if chaotic examination of how individuals manage to survive terror.

FUJIMORI MANIA

The socioeconomic situation improved after the 1990 elections when Alberto Fujimori, a Japanese-Peruvian, defeated the novelist Mario Vargas Llosa (see p45), a right-winger who advocated pro-business, free-market 'shock treatment' for Peru's ailing economy. Fujimori capitalized on fears that such treatment would mean more poverty and increased unemployment, and he was seen as an alternative to the established parties and policies.

1970	1985
A 7.7 magnitude earthquake kills 70,000 people in northern Peru, destroying 90% of Huaraz and burying the town of Yungay	Alan García Pérez is elected president; his five-year term is marked by hyperinflation and the resurgence of the Sendero Luminoso

Fujimori's austere program of economic reform resulted in unprecedented rises in the cost of food and other essentials, but it also allowed a liberal reformation of import/export, tax and foreign-investment regulations, leading to international financial support. He favored gradual reforms, deregulation of state monopolies and a new currency pegged to the US dollar. When the nuevo sol became Peru's new currency in 1991, it had an incredible equivalent worth of one billion old soles.

In April 1992 Fujimori suspended the constitution and dissolved congress in an *autogolpe* (coup from within). This perceived dictatorial, antidemocratic move led to a suspension of foreign aid, as well as outcry within Peruvian governmental circles. Nevertheless, Fujimori had the backing of the majority of the population and proceeded to catalyze the greatest economic and social improvements Peru had seen in decades.

Check out the scandalous 'Vladivideos' that brought down the Fujimori government in 2001 at www.agenciaperu.com /archivo/vladivideos /vladivideos.htm.

Fortunately for Fujimori, the major leaders of both the Sendero Luminoso and the MRTA were captured in 1992, which helped keep his popular support intact following the *autogolpe*. In 1993 a new constitution was approved that changed the law stipulating a president could not run for two successive terms, conveniently allowing Fujimori to run for re-election. Other changes included the approval of a new, 120-member unicameral congress (previously bicameral) and the institution of the death penalty for terrorists. Meanwhile, inflation dropped to under 20% and the Peruvian currency stabilized.

In 1995 Fujimori ran for a second term, easily beating opponent Javier Pérez de Cuellar, a former UN secretary general. A notable incident during Fujimori's second term was the seizure of the Japanese ambassador's residence during an official reception in December 1996 by 14 members of the MRTA. Hundreds of prominent people were taken hostage. The guerrillas demanded, among other things, the release of MRTA members currently in prison, a rollback of the government's free-market reforms and improvement in the cruel and inhuman treatment of prisoners, which is still common in Peruvian jails. Most of the hostages were soon released, although 72 men were held until 22 April 1997 when Peruvian commandos stormed the embassy, killing the captors and releasing all of the hostages except one who died along with two soldiers. This action came under criticism as it was claimed that some of the MRTA members were repeatedly shot, despite attempts to surrender.

In 2000 Fujimori again ran for office, claiming that a third term was possible because his first term predated the 1993 constitutional change. He received 49.9% of the vote, just short of the 50% needed to win outright. His main challenger was Alejandro Toledo, a leftist of indigenous Andean highlands descent and a shoeshine-boy-turned-economist who had little political experience. Toledo received 40.2% of the vote but claimed that the elections had been fraudulent, with some departments casting more votes than there were voters.

A run-off was scheduled for May 2000. Toledo refused to run, citing electoral fraud. The Organization of American States (OAS) sent a team of investigators, and the international community threatened sanctions against Peru unless the run-off was postponed, irregularities were corrected and the election was held in a democratic manner. Fujimori did not allow the run-off to be postponed and, despite having no opponent, allowed the apparently flawed electoral process to vote him in. The pressure from the

1990	1996
Alberto Fujimori is elected president; his semi-dictatorial style of rule leads to unprecedented improvements in the economy	Túpac Amaru guerrillas enter the Japanese ambassador's residence in Lima and hold hostages for four months

VLADIVISION

In September 2000, a video was released showing Vladimiro Montesinos, President Alberto Fujimori's hawkish head of intelligence, bribing a Peruvian congressman, and Fujimori's 10-year presidency spiraled out of control. In November, Fujimori ordered the military to arrest Montesinos, but the spymaster had already fled the country. Within days approximately 2700 so-called 'Vladivideos' were discovered, implicating key figures in money laundering and government corruption. After several months of flight through Latin America, Montesinos was captured in Venezuela in June 2001 and extradited. Ironically, he is now jailed in the same Peruvian maximum-security prison that he himself designed to hold terrorist leaders.

OAS diminished as world leaders realized that they had nothing to gain and much to lose by imposing economic sanctions on the country.

Meanwhile, Fujimori claimed he knew nothing about the money laundering and corruption scandals that his intelligence chief Vladimiro Montesinos had been involved in and he continued his presidential duties, including a state trip to Asia. While there, the Peruvian Congress declared him to be morally unfit to govern, and on November 20, 2000 Fujimori sent in his resignation while visiting Japan.

Normally one of two vice-presidents would have taken on the presidency, but both resigned following Fujimori's disgraceful exit. Instead, the opposition head of congress, Valentin Paniagua, was sworn in as interim president on November 22. Despite calls to return and face the charges made against him, Fujimori claimed his ancestral Japanese citizenship and stayed on in self-imposed exile in Japan.

TWENTY-FIRST CENTURY

When new presidential elections were held in April 2001, Peruvians seemed to have completely forgotten the grim 1980s and almost voted the silver-tongued orator Alan García back into office. The former president was beaten, but only by a slim margin, by Alejandro Toledo.

Cocaine: White Gold Rush in Peru, by Edmundo Morales, a Peruvian-born drug researcher, provides an insider's look at the nuts and bolts of the underground economy of coca production.

During the campaign, Toledo had made much of his indigenous heritage in a country where most of the populations is of indigenous or mixed heritage. Symbolically, he staged some of his inauguration ceremonies at the mountaintop Inca citadel of Machu Picchu. As priests offered coca leaves and *chicha* (fermented corn beer) to the heavens, more pragmatic pundits below wondered if Toledo could live up to the grandiose promises he made during his campaign.

Toledo took over a country struggling to come to terms with its past. His inexperience eventually led to an administration plagued by corruption scandals and a complete failure to deliver new jobs. By 2003, although the currency remained strongly pegged to the US dollar, Peruvians were again facing increased unemployment, stagnant wages and a higher cost of living. Toledo's popularity was at an all-time low (below 10%, the lowest of any South American president). For the first time in almost a decade, the country was again plagued by strikes and demonstrations.

That same year, Peru's Truth and Reconciliation Commission (CVR) presented its findings on human rights abuses and violence during the 1980s and '90s, a first step toward justice for victims. Meanwhile, an inter-

2000	2001
Fujimori, disgraced by the corrupt actions of his head of intelligence, Vladimir Montesinos, resigns and escapes into exile in Japan	Alejandro Toledo becomes the first president of indigenous descent of any Andean country

national warrant for the arrest of Fujimori was filed with Interpol, stepping up the country's efforts to extradite the former leader from Japan. The arrest warrant, issued by a supreme court judge and based on Fujimori's alleged involvement in massacres undertaken by the paramilitary death squad Grupo Colina, did not convince Japanese authorities to return the exiled Fujimori for trial.

State of Fear: The Truth About Terrorism (2005) directed by Pamela Yates is a hard-hitting documentary that examines the Sendero Luminoso's devastating effects on everyday life in Peru and the erosion of democracy under Alberto Fujimori.

In 2005, Fujimori voluntarily returned from exile in Japan and announced that he planned to run for the presidency again, only to be arrested in Chile on an extradition warrant to face long-standing charges of corruption and human rights abuses. Although he was barred from placing his name on the presidential ballot, his daughter Keiko ran a successful campaign of her own and became one of Lima's congressional representatives. It proved in part how much of a hold Fujimori still had on the Peruvian populace.

With Fujimori out of the way, the 2006 presidential elections eventually narrowed to a face-off between the populist nationalist Ollanta Humala, an indigenous Andean ex–army officer who had served under Fujimori, and ex-president Alan García, who had put Peru on the path to financial ruin during the 1980s. Early polls showed the right-wing National Unity candidate Lourdes Flores pulling ahead, but her early momentum faded.

Voters apparently decided that the devil you know is better than the one that you don't, and elected the more conservative candidate García. This was quite a blow to Venezuelan President Hugo Chávez, who many Peruvians perceived had meddled in their elections by stridently voicing his support of Humala, whose political positions against foreign investment and in favor of a strong central government and income redistribution fit perfectly with Chávez' dream of South American socialist solidarity. The diplomatic flare-up between Peru and Venezuela only intensified after the elections, when Chávez called Peru the lapdog of the USA and initially refused ties with the new García administration.

Meanwhile, foreign investors breathed a sigh of relief at the presidential election results, predicting business as usual in Peru, and the nuevo sol currency remains stable – for now.

2002

Before a state visit by US President George W Bush, a car bomb explodes outside the US Embassy in Lima

2005

Construction of the Interoceanic Hwy, which will open trading routes between Peru and Brazil, starts in the Amazon Basin

The Culture

THE NATIONAL PSYCHE

During the 1990s, a drive through Lima would have taken you past a most unusual public works project: an endless series of cylindrical concrete pillars topped by a mangled web of reinforced steel. These monuments were a tribute to a long-running government enterprise: corruption. Intended as supports for an elevated trans-Lima railway, construction on the project stalled in 1992 when President Alan García found himself on the wrong end of a coup and decamped to France, allegedly taking the bulk of the railway's funds with him.

The reaction? Most Peruvians shrugged. And a group of enterprising *limeños* (inhabitants of Lima) got to work decorating the dreary structures with pastoral murals and other works of art. No anecdote better defines the national character: Peruvians may be cynical about their leaders, but it doesn't suppress an inherent optimism, a trait that compels them to make the most of a bad situation – or art of a government boondoggle.

Peru's spirit, however, has been sorely tested, particularly in the central Andes. The area surrounding the department of Ayacucho was the site of a vicious guerilla war in the 1980s that left hundreds of thousands of civilians trapped in a spin-cycle of violence between the Sendero Luminoso (Shining Path) guerrillas and the heavy-handed Peruvian military. During this time, almost 63,000 people died or disappeared. Peasant indigenous populations bore the brunt of the suffering. For this reason, communities in the central highlands can be rather cool (though always cordial) to outsiders.

In recent years, issues of race and class have bubbled to the surface. Long dominated by a fair-skinned oligarchy in Lima, Peruvian society has begun to slowly embrace its indigenous roots. In 2001, Alejandro Toledo became the first indigenous Peruvian to be elected to the presidency. Regardless, racism persists, especially among the urban elite, most of whom live by the maxim that whiter is somehow better. More significant are the economic issues. There is an extraordinary disparity between the wealthy few and the struggling masses, with more than half the nation living under the poverty line. The country's stagnant economy in recent years has not ameliorated this problem and the vast majority of Peruvians are consumed with making it to the next paycheck. In other parts of society, highly traditional notions of gender roles – men at work, women at home – remain firmly in place. Aside from a burgeoning new generation of professional women in the big cities, Peru remains quite comfortable with old world machismo. Attitudes towards homosexuality remain equally conservative.

Even as the last few decades have brought an onslaught of social and political turmoil, people have managed to maintain a zeal for all things worth living for. A room full of Peruvians is a snap and crackle of discussion and debate, of melancholic reminiscing and boisterous laughter. There is a fervor for robust cuisine, soulful music and the thrill of a neck-and-neck soccer match. At any time, a small gathering can turn into an impromptu party. This is a country that takes family and friendship seriously, treating its guests with warmth and consideration. It is a culture, ultimately, that faces its setbacks with stoicism and plenty of dark humor – but also lots of hope.

Julio Ramón Ribeyro's *Chronicle of San Gabriel* is the poignant coming-of-age tale of a young man from Lima named Lucho who goes to live with his frayed, extended family at a highland ranch.

LIFESTYLE

With a geography that encompasses everything from windswept altiplano (Andean plateau) to lowland jungle, Peru is relentlessly touted as a land of contrasts. This metaphor couldn't be more appropriate in describing its society: a mixture of rich and poor, indigenous and white, young and old. Nowhere is this more obvious than in Lima, where shiny office towers abut shantytowns and ragged children beg among crowds of well-dressed business people.

As in much of Latin America, the global economic boom of the late 1990s has benefited only a chosen few. The richest 10th of the country receives 37% of the income, while the bottom 10th makes do with less than 1%. The poverty is grinding: according to a 2003 estimate, 54% of the population lives below the poverty line, surviving on less than US$58 per month. One in four children under the age of five is malnourished and almost a quarter of the population does not have electricity. Naturally, it is the rural, indigenous people who make up an overwhelming majority of the country's poor and represent an outsized share of the extreme poverty cases. In rural areas, the poor survive largely from subsistence agriculture, living in traditional adobe or corrugated tin houses that frequently lack electricity and indoor plumbing.

In cities, the lower and middle classes live in concrete, apartment-style housing or small stand-alone homes. Much of the housing is architecturally nondescript. Units have a shared living area, a kitchen and one or more bedrooms, the latter of which are generally shared by more than one generation; the average Peruvian home offers little individual space. More affluent urban homes consist of stand-alone houses, many built in a modernist or Spanish style and bordered by gardens and high walls.

The national life expectancy has reached an all-time high of 70 years – a vast improvement from 1960, when it stood at a meager 48. (As a comparison: life expectancy in the United States is 77 years.) However, the numbers aren't as good for the rural poor. A lack of good sanitation and access to reliable medical care keeps life expectancy in the Andes to an estimated average of 55 years. Though the big cities feature all the amenities of modern life – from internet cafés to cell phones – access to technology remains a luxury. Peru has only 64 telephone main lines per 1000 people, compared to 700 in the US and 221 in neighboring Chile.

Family remains the nucleus of social and cultural life in Peru and groups of the same clan will often live near each other. Couples have an average of 2.5 children, though rural families tend to be bigger and poor extended families are more likely to live together. For those who reside in urban centers, modernization continues to impact traditional family ways. Society is becoming more geographically mobile. The villager born in Alca might one day find himself working in Arequipa. But most likely, he will go to Lima, which continues to serve as the center of industry, business and government life in Peru.

SOCIAL GRACES

Peruvians are polite, indeed, rather formal, in their interactions. Even a brief interchange, such as giving a taxi driver your destination, is preceded by a *buenos días* (good morning). A hearty handshake is normally given at the beginning and end of even the briefest meeting. Among friends, an *abrazo* (back-slapping hug) is in order. Women will often greet each other with a kiss, as will men and women – except in business settings, where a handshake is appropriate. Indigenous people don't kiss and their handshakes, when offered, tend to have a light touch. A gentle nod of the head in combination with a greeting is the preferred way of saying hello. If invited to visit a Peruvian home, it is considered good manners to take a gift such as flowers or candy.

Let Julia Meyerson take you on a tour of daily life in the Andes in her engagingly written memoir *Tambo: Life in an Andean Village.*

Death in the Andes by Mario Vargas Llosa is a solemn, fictional examination of the violence that gripped the country in the 1980s. Be forewarned: this isn't a beach read, but its characterization of Peruvian society is, as always, revealing.

As in the rest of Latin America, the concept of time is extraordinarily elastic; the concept of 'on time' is almost non-existent. Moreover, the locals are used to less personal space than some Western travelers may be accustomed to: expect seating in public areas, such as buses and trains, to be thisclose.

POPULATION

Peru is essentially a bicultural society, comprised of two roughly same-sized parts: those who are indigenous and those who are not. It's a division that breaks out roughly along class lines. The more affluent urban class is made up largely of whites and fair-skinned *mestizos* (people of mixed indigenous and Spanish descent) – the latter of whom refer to themselves as *criollos* (natives of Peru). Within this segment, a wealthy upper class has historically taken the top roles in politics and business, while the middle class has filled lower level white-collar positions, such as clerks, teachers and entrepreneurs.

The other half of the country is made up primarily of indigenous *campesinos* (peasants). About 45% of Peru's population is pure *indígena* (people of indigenous descent) – making it one of three countries in Latin America to have such high indigenous representation. (Note: in Spanish, *indígenas* is the appropriate term; *indios* is insulting.) Most *indígenas* are Quechua-speaking and live in the highlands, while a smaller percentage speak Aymara and inhabit the Lake Titicaca region. In the Amazon, which contains about 6% of the country's total population, various indigenous ethnicities speak a plethora of other languages.

Afro-Peruvians, Asians and other immigrant groups are also represented – primarily along the coast – but cumulatively make up only 3% of the population. Among the elite, retrograde ideas about race persist. Nonwhite people are sometimes discriminated against, especially in upmarket bars, nightclubs and discos in Lima; less so elsewhere.

More than a quarter of all Peruvians – mostly *indígenas* – live in a rural setting, surviving from subsistence farming or working as laborers. This statistic represents a significant change from Peru's agrarian past. In the early 1960s, more than half the population lived in the countryside. It was the turmoil of the 1980s that helped fuel an exodus from the highland. Hundreds of thousands of people moved to cities, taxing overburdened municipal infrastructures, particularly in Lima. Issues of effective sanitation and electrification remain significant challenges for informal squatter settlements known as *pueblos jovenes* (young towns). Life doesn't necessarily get better for people who move to the cities. The national unemployment rate is almost 8% and underemployment is rampant; more than half of Peruvians are underemployed.

MEDIA

The situation for the working press has improved greatly since the 1980s when civil strife resulted in the deaths of both foreign and domestic journalists. But Alberto Fujimori's regime still casts a shadow on the industry. His administration was renowned for spying on opposition journalists and bribing broadcasters for favorable coverage (see When Life Imitates Soap Operas, p44). Alejandro Toledo's administration saw some improvements, but he was not without his clumsy – largely legislative – attempts at controlling what was reported.

The situation has remained most difficult for journalists who work in the provinces. In 2003, the most recent year for which there are statistics, at least 15 reporters nationwide were physically attacked for their work, according to Reporters Without Borders, an international organization that supports press freedom.

The Motorcycle Diaries, a film about Argentine revolutionary Che Guevara's travels through South America, makes pit stops in Cuzco and Machu Picchu.

For the kids: pick up The Way of the Condor by Nathan Kravetz, which tells the story of a young boy who must leave the Andes to go work in Lima. (Good for ages 9–12.)

WHEN LIFE IMITATES SOAP OPERAS

Blonde, tanned and rail-thin, Laura Bozzo is the kind of feisty heroine that could only exist on a *telenovela*, the Spanish-language serials that are wildly popular in Latin America. She is over-the-top flamboyant in her wardrobe (curve-hugging outfits and sky-high heels) and her love-life (younger or mercurial powerful men). It'd be 100% soap-opera fare if it weren't all real. Bozzo is the fifty-something host of a TV talk show called *Laura en América*, a program devoted to put-upon wives, philandering men, incest victims and transvestites. As part of the proceedings, there is usually at least one fist fight. The show is no *Masterpiece Theatre* – not that it matters. In 2001, *Laura* was picked up for international syndication. Her worldwide audience couldn't get enough of her. Neither could the Peruvian attorney general, who accused her of receiving US$3 million in bribes from Alberto Fujimori's administration in exchange for bashing his opponents on air. (She was the first to report that then-presidential candidate Alejandro Toledo had a daughter out of wedlock.)

The case has all the trappings of a TV melodrama: Bozzo was put under house arrest for three years, during which she lived in her production studio in Lima with her much-younger boyfriend and continued to broadcast. In 2005, she testified in court that she was hopelessly enamored of Vladimiro Montesinos, Fujimori's corrupt former spymaster. Bozzo has firmly (and repeatedly) declared her innocence, saying that she never received so much as a nuevo sol for expressing her views. In July 2006, Bozzo was convicted of all charges and given a suspended prison sentence of four years, during which she cannot leave the country without a judge's permission. She has filed an appeal. This modern-day morality play has riveted Peruvians and it seems that Bozzo's every utterance is duly noted in the papers. After all, who needs a *telenovela* when real life is this entertaining?

RELIGION

Though there is widespread freedom of religion, Peru remains largely Roman Catholic. About 80% of the population identifies as such (though only 15% of them attend services on a weekly basis). The Church enjoys a cozy relationship with the state: they have a largely tax-exempt status and Catholicism is the official religion of the military. Moreover, bishops and other clergy get monthly government stipends, reportedly as much as US$3000 a month. This has generated outcries from some evangelical groups, most of whom do not receive this generous treatment. Even so, evangelicals and other Protestants are a growing force, representing up to 12% of the nation's population. The Peruvian Church is also growing increasingly divided along political lines, in which a conservative hierarchy is pitted against a more freethinking clergy.

It was a Peruvian priest, Gustavo Gutiérrez, who, in 1971, first articulated the principles of liberation theology – the theory that links Christian thought to social justice. He now teaches at Notre Dame University in the United States.

Indigenous people have largely adapted Catholic deities to their own beliefs. Viracocha (the creator) is symbolized by the Christian God, while Pachamama (the earth mother) is represented by the Virgin Mary. Indigenous festivities that are purportedly Catholic have many layers of meaning. In Puno, for example, the locals host a festival in honor of La Virgen de la Candelaria every February 2 (Candlemas). The virgin, however, is closely identified with Pachamama, as well as natural elements such as lightning. Moreover, she is often referred to as Mamacha Candelaria and is upheld as a symbol of fertility. The feast can last up to two weeks, during which time local dancers – dressed in colorful outfits and large animal masks – take to the streets in her honor.

WOMEN IN PERU

Women can vote and own property, but the situation remains challenging in a country where the unwritten laws of machismo are widely accepted. For starters, the female illiteracy rate of 15% is almost three times that of men and maternal mortality rates are among the highest in Latin America. Also an issue is the high adolescent birth rate: in 1999, 13% of women between the ages of 15 and 19 were mothers or pregnant for the first time. Access to health care is limited and gynecological cancer is the leading cause of death among women of childbearing age. In the mid '90s, under Fujimori, a number of civil organizations alleged that the government forcibly sterilized tens of thousands of women in poor, rural areas. As a result, a law was passed in 1999 requiring informed consent for any sterilization procedure. Lately, the situation for women has improved: a number of laws barring domestic violence and sexual assault have been passed in the last decade, and in 1999, women were allowed to pursue the same rank and careers as men in the Merchant Marine Academy – once a bastion of male power. Other visible gains have come in politics. In 2006, right-of-center candidate Lourdes Flores ran for the presidency, losing a chance at the final run-off by only 1% of the vote.

ARTS
Literature
Mario Vargas Llosa (1936–) is Peru's most famous writer, hailed alongside Latin American literary luminaries such as Gabriel García Márquez, Julio Cortázar and Carlos Fuentes. His novels evoke James Joyce in their complexity, meandering through time and shifting perspectives, keeping the reader alert through the turn of each page. Beyond his artistry, Vargas Llosa is a keen social observer, casting a spotlight on the naked corruption of the ruling class and the peculiarities of Peruvian society. (This instinct is what led him to make his failed bid for the presidency in 1989.) Luckily for English-language readers, his more than two dozen novels are available in translation. The best place to start is *La ciudad y los perros* (The Time of the Hero) which is based on his experience at a Peruvian military academy. (The soldiers at his old academy responded to this novel by burning it.) Other stand-outs include *La fiesta del chivo* (The Feast of the Goat), which takes place in the Dominican Republic, and *Historia de Mayta* (The Real Life of Alejandro Mayta) a bleak, multi-faceted look at the life of a fictional revolutionary.

A detailed biography of Mario Vargas Llosa, along with a bibliography of his works is available at www.kirjasto.sci .fi/vargas.htm.

Alfredo Bryce Echenique (1939–) is another incisive Peruvian observer. His most well-known book, *Un mundo para Julius* (A World for Julius), published in 1972, tracks a bourgeois child's relationship to a distant mother and his loyalty to the servants with whom he spends much of his time. In 2002, Echenique won the Planeta literary award, Spain's most lucrative literary prize, for *El huerto de mi amada* (My Beloved's Garden), which recounts an affair between a 30-year-old woman and a teenage boy in 1950s Lima. Demonstrating that Peruvian penchant for dark humor is Julio Ramón Ribeyro (1929–94). Though never a best-selling author, Ribeyro is critically acclaimed for his short stories and essays that focus on the vagaries of lower middle class life. His work is available in English in *Marginal Voices: Selected Stories*.

Read Daniel Alarcón's melancholic tale of a family touched by death in the story *City of Clowns*, featured on the *New Yorker's* website at www.newyorker.com /fiction/content/?030616 fi_fiction2.

Two Peruvian writers are noted for their portrayals of indigenous reality. José María Arguedas (1911–69), who was born in the Andes, introduced a Quechua syntax to Spanish fiction in novels such as *Los ríos profundos* (Deep Rivers) and *Yawar fiesta*, among others. Ciro Alegría (1909–67) covered the repression of Andean communities in *El mundo es ancho y ajeno* (Broad and Alien is the World).

One rising literary star is the Peruvian-American author Daniel Alarcón (1977–), whose short stories have been featured in the *New Yorker* magazine. His work is now available in the collection War by Candlelight. For a worthwhile compilation of women writers, pick up *Fire From the Andes: Short*

A PERUVIAN PRIMER: A FEW DELIGHTS FOR THE EYES & EARS

The Dancer Upstairs Based on the real-life search for the elusive leader of Sendero Luminoso (Shining Path), this gripping novel by British author Nicholas Shakespeare is a fascinating examination of an upstanding government investigator trying to maneuver between violent terrorists and corrupt government officials. In 2002, the book was made into a movie of the same name starring Spanish actor Javier Bardem.

The War of the End of the World Considered Mario Vargas Llosa's reigning literary masterpiece, this historical novel, published in 1981, examines the disaffected sides of a bloody uprising in Brazil in rich, psychological detail.

Afro-Peruvian Classics – The Soul of Black Peru This 15-track compilation featuring various artists is a fantastic primer to a genre that is just coming into its own.

Three must-have albums for the CD library The best of Peruvian *criollo* music can be had in three CDs: *Susana Baca* by Susana Baca, *Eva! Leyenda Peruana* by Eva Ayllón and *La flor de la canela* by the celebrated Chabuca Granda. All that's missing is the pisco sour (grape brandy cocktail).

La muralla verde This 1970 film, whose title translates into *The Green Wall*, can be difficult to find on video (it is not yet out on DVD), but is well worth it if you do. Directed by Armando Robles Godoy, it tells the story of a disaffected government clerk who moves to the jungle after growing increasingly disenchanted with life in Lima.

Fiction by Women From Bolivia, Ecuador and Peru, which includes stories by Peruvian authors such as Catalina Lohmann and Pilar Dughi.

Go to www.poets.org for an extensive biography and bibliography of Peru's greatest poet, César Vallejo.

If Vargas Llosa is Peru's greatest novelist, then César Vallejo (1892–1938) is its greatest poet. Though he published only three slim books – *Los heraldos negros* (The Black Heralds), *Trilce* and *Poemas humanos* (Human Poems) – he has long been regarded as one of the most important and innovative Spanish-language poets of the 20th century. Vallejo frequently touched on existential themes and was known for pushing the language to its limits, inventing words when real ones no longer served him.

Cinema & Television

The state of Peruvian cinema and TV is anemic. Cinema, especially, has suffered since 1992 when Fujimori overturned a law that helped promote and display domestic films. Almost 15 years later, the government institute devoted to film production, CONACINE, remains toothless and underfunded. Despite that, a few filmmakers, such as Francisco Lombardi, still manage to produce feature-length movies. Lombardi, who has been working since the '70s, is best known for producing a film version of Vargas Llosa's *The Time of the Hero* in 1985 and *Tinta roja* (Red Ink) in 2000, a feature based on Chilean author Alberto Fuguet's novel of the same name.

German director Werner Herzog's film *Fitzcarraldo,* about a man who builds an opera house in the Amazon, was shot in various locations in Peru, including Lima and Iquitos.

The bulk of the programming on Peruvian TV consists largely of imported *telenovelas* (Spanish-language soaps) and locally made low-budget talk and news shows. The TV news industry is just beginning to regain its credibility after it was revealed in 2001 that executives from the four principal networks took money from Fujimori spymaster/briber-in-chief Vladimiro Montesinos in exchange for positive coverage (see When Life Imitates Soap Operas, p44). Many of the deals were captured on film and showed Montesinos giving network heads cash pay-offs that amounted to hundreds of thousands of dollars. The 'Vladivideos,' as they were called, riveted the country when they began surfacing at the beginning of Toledo's presidency.

Music

Like its food, traditional Peruvian music is a fusion of ingredients, an intercontinental mix of instruments and styles. Pre-Columbian cultures contributed omnipresent bamboo flutes, the Spaniards brought stringed instruments like guitars and violins and the Africans gave it a backbone of fluid percussive rhythm. And though music is a highly regional affair – African-influenced *landós* are predominant on the coast, indigenous *huaynos* in the Andes and *criollo* waltzes in the Spanish urban centers – Peruvian music is united by a festiveness that is imbued with a soulful sense of melancholy.

In the Andes, *huayno* is perhaps the purest expression of pre-Columbian music. It is heavy on bamboo wind instruments such as *quenas* (bamboo flutes of varying lengths) and *zampoñas* (a set of panpipes with two rows of bamboo canes). *Zampoñas* range from tiny, high-pitched *chulis* to meter-long, bass *toyos*. Also seen are *ocarinas*, small, oval clay instruments with up to 12 holes. Drums are typically made from hollowed tree trunks covered with a stretched goatskin. A more Hispanicized version of *huayno*, typically referred to as *música folklórica*, includes the use of string instruments, the most typical being the *charango*, a tiny 10-stringed mandolin with a box made of armadillo shell. More recent additions to these instruments include harps and a variety of brass instruments which can generally be seen in the cacophonous strolling bands that parade through small mountain towns on fiesta days.

Andean music's biggest moment of international fame came in 1970 when US duo Simon & Garfunkel produced a pop version of the traditional *huayno El Cóndor Pasa*. Since then, the musical genre seems to have become a favorite of 'lite' music enthusiasts, who have put forth dozens of bland albums with names like *Hooked on Pan Flute* in which American pop standards are replayed on Andean instruments. (Poison for the ears as far as this reviewer is concerned.) For a worthwhile – and far more authentic – round-up of good *música folklórica*, pick up *Andean Legacy* by Narada, a label specializing in global sounds.

In the past three decades, the *huayno* has mixed with other musical styles such as rock and Colombian *cumbia* to produce an exclusively local genre known as *chicha* – and it is what you will most likely hear if holed up in some high-altitude bar. It is the music of the indigenous working class, combining less-than-subtle beats with lyrics about demanding respect and saving up for a home of one's own. Famous *chicha* performers include Belem and Los Shapis.

On the coast, the more danceable *música criolla* (*criollo* music) has its roots in both Spain and Africa. The main instrumentation consists of guitars and a *cajón*, a wooden box on which the player sits and drums out a rhythm with his hands. Its origins has been attributed to slaves who allegedly used empty vegetable crates as percussion instruments. The most famous of *criollo* styles is the *vals peruano* (Peruvian waltz), a 3/4-time waltz that in no way resembles anything coming out of Vienna. It is fast-moving, rhythmic and full of complex Spanish-guitar melodies – perfect for dancing. The most legendary *música criolla* singer and composer of the 20th century is Chabuca Granda (1920–1983). Her smooth, breathy vocals and expressive lyrics, full of longing and nostalgia, turned the art form into a global phenomenon; Brazilian master Caetano Veloso honored Granda's song *Fina estampa* in his 1996 album of the same name.

Also sharing African-Spanish roots is *landó*, which lies on the bluesier end of the *criolla* scale. These include elements of call-and-response backed up by guitar and several layers of percussion. The lyrics focus on slavery, violence and other social issues. Stand-out performers in the genre are contemporary singers Susana Baca and Eva Ayllón, both of whom have toured internationally. But the best way to enjoy *música criolla* is to feel the energy it exudes when performed live. The best places for this are at one of the many *peñas* (bars or clubs featuring live folkloric music) in Lima (p119) or by traveling to Chincha on the southern coast for *Verano Negro*, an Afro-Peruvian cultural festival that takes place every February.

Perú Negro, a band that has been together for more than 35 years, has long captured the spirited beauty of Afro-Peruvian music. Two albums worth a listen are *Sangre de un Don* and *Jolgorio*.

Peruvian singer Tania Libertad has achieved an international following with melancholy interpretations of Latin American standards. Her album *Negro Color* – which includes a duet with Brazilian crooner Chico Buarque – captures her voice at its operatic finest.

Interested in high camp? Check out *The Ultimate Yma Sumac Collection* by the popular 1950s lounge singer. Sumac claimed to be a descendant of Atahualpa and was renowned for her exotic floor shows and startling four-octave voice range.

Modern popular music includes the usual selection of rock, pop, blues, reggae, hip-hop and punk – most of which is imported. The home-grown Peruvian rock scene is limited, but, as a genre, it is making a small comeback after being outcast as 'alienating and Yankee' by the military in the '60s and '70s. In the '80s a small underground music scene emerged, led by bands such as Leusemia, Narcosis and Autopsia. Other newer groups have met with more mainstream success. The band Libido, for example, has produced consistently solid rock albums since 1998 and has achieved a significant level of worldwide acclaim. The foursome has sold millions of albums and has received two Video Music Awards from MTV Latin America. Other popular acts include Uchpa (who sing in Quechua), Anna Carina and Los Fuckin' Sombreros.

Delve into rock *en español* with two of Libido's top albums – *Pop*Porn* and *Hembra*. Their songs are straightforward, guitar-driven rock; think the Strokes with a Peruvian flourish.

Architecture

From Inca monumentalism to Spanish baroque to boxy modernist, an extraordinarily varied assortment of architectural styles can be found in Peru. Naturally, the most famous example of pre-Colombian architecture is the impressive mountaintop retreat built by the Incas at Machu Picchu, a site that dates back to 1440. Composed of roughly 140 constructions connected by more than 100 flights of stone steps, Machu Picchu epitomizes the grand scale of Inca architecture. The engineering is equally impressive: dry-stone walls are polished and put into place without mortar. Other period structures can be found throughout Cuzco, as well as Pisac and Saqsaywamán.

Also a significant pre-Colombian site is the city of Chan Chan, north of Trujillo, erected by the Chimu civilization some time between AD 850 and 1470. If Inca architecture appears to reach for the clouds, Chimu structures do quite the opposite. Built entirely out of adobe brick, Chan Chan's temples and houses are flat, blending seamlessly into the broad desert horizon. It's the type of design that would have made Frank Lloyd Wright proud.

Art of the Andes: From Chavín to Inca by Rebecca Stone-Miller is a comprehensive introduction to Andean art and architecture, with more than 180 images to accompany and explain the text.

Juxtaposed against the austerity of indigenous architecture are the hundreds of ornate Spanish churches and colonial houses that serve as the center of so many cities and towns. The 16th century saw a veritable building boom of structures built in what is referred to as 'Andean baroque' – baroque with indigenous flourishes. Prime examples are Iglesia de la Compañía de Jesús (p231) in Cuzco and the fabulously ornate Jesuit church in Andahuaylillas (p279), referred to locally as the 'Sistine Chapel of Latin America' for its elaborate décor. For a less flamboyant colonial architecture, the city of Arequipa is unbeatable. Its buildings, made largely from a white volcanic rock called *sillar* are beautifully constructed and maintained. Particularly worthwhile is the block-sized Santa Catalina Convent – even if you think you've already been at every church worth seeing in Peru.

The contemporary architecture, particularly in Lima, leans toward modernism. Unfortunately, the local interpretation of it has been less than inspiring. Lima is a vast suburban sprawl of grey, boxy blandness. However, some newer structures, such as the glassy, new Marriott Hotel in Miraflores and the curvy Torre Siglo XXI in San Isidro are fine examples of a more fluid and compelling Peruvian modernism.

Painting & Sculpture

The country's most famous artistic movement took place during the 17th and 18th century when the artists of the Cuzco School produced thousands of paintings and sculptures – the vast majority of which remain entirely unattributed. The paintings, produced by *mestizo* artists, were influenced by Spanish, Netherlandish and Late Gothic art and consist of finely detailed portraits of holy figures embroidered with gold paint. (Reproductions of these canvases are sold just about everywhere.)

In the early 20th century, an indigenous movement led by painter José Sabogal (1888–1956) achieved national prominence. Like his contemporaries in Mexico (Diego Rivera and Rufino Tamayo), Sabogal was interested in integrating pre-Columbian design with Peruvian fine art. He painted Indian women and incorporated images from pottery and textiles into his work. As director of the National School of Arts in Lima, he influenced a whole generation of painters, including Julia Codesido (1892–1979) and Mario Urteaga (1875–1957). By the 1960s, abstract art had taken hold, led by artists such as Fernando de Szyszlo (1925–), who still managed to keep Peruvian themes, such as pre-Columbian myth an integral part of his work. Other well-known contemporary artists include sculptor/painter Victor Delfín (1927–) and painter Alberto Quintanilla (1934–). Two contemporary photographers worth viewing are Natalia Iguíñiz (1973–), whose stark portraits illustrate issues of race and class, and Andrea Miranda (1978–) who specializes in arresting, oversized images of urban landscapes.

Crafts

Peru has long had a bounty of finely produced crafts and folk art. Intricately woven textiles have an extensive history among both Andean and coastal indigenous cultures. Rugs, ponchos, belts and wall-hangings are decorated with elaborate anthropomorphic designs, images of local flora and other graphic elements. On the coast, it is the region of Paracas that is most famous for its weaving. The Paracas Textile, which dates back to 300 BC, is the most renowned example of this fine tradition (and, unfortunately for anyone in Peru, it resides at the Brooklyn Museum in New York City).

Pottery represents one of Peru's more well-developed crafts. The most stunning designs are those made in the tradition of the Moche people of the northern coast, who thrived in the six centuries beginning in AD 100. Vases and other vessels are made to depict humans in a realist style. The most famous of these – the *huacos eróticos* – depict a variety of sexual acts.

Other popular items include hand-tooled leather, filigree jewelry in gold and silver, woven baskets and religious icons. Textiles, pottery and other items can easily be found in Lima (p120), as well as in other major Peruvian cities such as Cuzco (p250) and Arequipa (p179).

Dance

The national dance is the *marinera*, which has its roots in Peruvian colonial history. Performed to *música criolla*, the dance is a flirtation between a man and woman who circle each other in a rhythmic courtship. The man uses a straw hat to make way for a woman while she coyly hides her face behind a white handkerchief. Other dances include the *zamacueca* (which is closely related to the *marinera*) and the *vals peruano* the latter of which is danced by a couple. *Zapateo* (literally, foot-stomping) is a popular black Peruvian dance.

SPORTS

Fútbol (soccer) is the most sanctified spectator sport, followed with a fervor that borders on religious piety. The soccer season is from late March to November and though there are many teams, their abilities are not exceptional. Peru hasn't qualified to play in the World Cup since 1982, but they have taken home two Copa América trophies (a competition among South American nations). The best teams are from Lima, and the traditional *clásico* is the match between Alianza Lima and the Universitario de Deportes (La U).

Art history buffs will appreciate *The Stone and the Thread* by César Patternosto, the first comprehensive, scholarly analysis to examine the complex abstract art forms inherent in pre-Columbian Andean crafts.

For a visual overview of some of the most stunning works of pre-Columbian ceramic portraiture, pick up *Moche Portraits from Ancient Peru* by Christopher Donnan.

Lima's Museo Rafael Larco Herrera features an extensive photo gallery of pre-Hispanic pottery, jewelry and textiles on its website, http://museo larco.perucultural.org.pe.

Everything you ever
needed to know about
every regional Peruvian
soccer team large and
small is available at
www.peru.com/futbol
(in Spanish).

Bullfighting is also well attended, particularly in Lima, where it is most popular. The traditional season runs from October to early December and Lima's Plaza de Acho attracts internationally famous matadors. Outside of Lima, small bullfights occur at fiestas, but are rarely of a high standard. Travelers should be aware that the bulls are killed in Peruvian fights; if you want to witness this popular national sport, you'll need to be prepared for a gory (and often confronting) spectacle.

Other sports, though not necessarily popular in Peru, have been well-represented by some athletes. In 1988, for example, the Peruvian women's volleyball team won the silver medal at the Seoul Olympics. In tennis, the now-retired Jaime Yzaga reached 18 in career rankings in the world. And more recently, in 2004, surfer Sofia Mulanovich became the first South American to win the world title.

Environment

THE LAND

At 1,285,220 sq km, Peru is the third-largest country in South America, about five times larger than the UK and over five times smaller than Australia. It lies in the tropics south of the equator and is divided into three strikingly different geographical regions: the Pacific coastal strip, the Andes mountains and the Amazonian lowlands.

The narrow coastal strip below 1000m in elevation is mainly desert, merging at its southern end into Chile's Atacama Desert, one of the driest places on earth. The coast includes Lima, the capital, and several major cities – oases watered by dozens of rivers that cascade from the Andes. These oases have been developed as agricultural centers where the creation of irrigation channels over the centuries has utilized the fertile soil deposited as silt by the rivers. It's a strange sight to see green fields morph into sandy or rocky desert at the point where irrigation ends. The country's best road, the Carretera Panamericana (Pan-American Hwy), slices through coastal Peru from border to border.

The Andes, the world's second-greatest mountain chain, rise rapidly from the coast to reach spectacular heights of over 6000m just 100km inland. Peru's highest peak, Huascarán (6768m), is the world's highest tropical summit and the sixth highest peak in the Americas. Tropical they may be, but the Andes have year-round glaciers above 5000m. Between 3000m and 4000m lie the agricultural Andean highlands supporting half of Peru's population. The rugged landscape brims with jagged ranges separated by deep, vertiginous canyons, rewarding travelers with spectacular scenery.

The eastern Andean slopes receive much more rainfall than the dry western slopes and are clothed in lush cloud forests as they drop into the fabled rainforests of the Amazon basin. Only two other countries in the world (Brazil and the Democratic Republic of Congo) have more tropical rainforest than Peru. In the low-lying Amazon basin, the undulating land rarely rises more than 500m above sea level and varied tributary systems all feed into the mighty Río Amazonas. Weather conditions are hot and humid year-round, with the most precipitation falling between December and May. Roads into and within the Peruvian Amazon region are few, and travelers typically venture forth on river voyages – or fly.

The Andes don't stop at the Pacific coast; 100km offshore there is a trench that's as deep as the Andes are high.

The Living Edens: Manu, Peru's Hidden Rain Forest, produced and written by Kim McQuarrie, is a public TV program about a journey deep into the Peruvian Amazon; check out the free website at www.pbs.org/edens /manu.

WILDLIFE

With its great variety of ecosystems, resulting from multifarious variations in climate, elevation and soils in the tropics, Peru boasts a menagerie of wildlife that is almost unequalled anywhere else in the world. The only downside is

THE DEEPEST CANYON

Not far outside of Arequipa in southern Peru, the Cañón del Colca (p181), 3191m deep, has in the past been claimed to be the deepest canyon on earth. However, that tag is currently considered to belong to Cañón del Cotahuasi (p186), beyond Nevado Coropuna to the west, with its floor 3345m below adjacent snowy peaks. Both are more than twice as deep as Colorado's Grand Canyon (which has a depth of about 1500m). Elsewhere in the world, Nepal's Kali Gandaki valley floor lies some 6000m below the neighboring 8000m-plus summits of Dhaulagiri and Annapurna, but this is apparently considered a gorge rather than a more extensive canyon. It seems a bit arbitrary, but regardless of the ultimate outcome of these debates, all are impressive sights.

that seeing all these animals takes time and effort. Many of them live in the rainforest, where you can be a scant 20m away from a jaguar and never know it is there. In the highlands, flocks of vicuñas (threatened wild relatives of alpacas) vanish over the horizon as soon as they catch sight of an intruder. When you do go wildlife watching, start with a heavy dose of patience, be prepared for dawn wake-up calls (when the animals are most active), travel in slow and quiet groups, carry binoculars and hire a local guide. Then you're ready for memorable sightings of Peru's profusion of tropical wildlife.

Rainforest Publications (www.rainforestpublica tions.com) sells pocket-sized, laminated, color foldout guides for quickly identifying common forest birds, mammals, raptors, marine mammals, reef fish and birds in Peru.

Animals

Wildlife enthusiasts come to see Peru to see a rainbow variety of bird species, as well as pink freshwater dolphins, condors, jaguars and spectacled bears, to name just a few engrossing species. With coastal, mountain and rainforest habitats, Peru is one of only a dozen or so countries in the world considered to be 'megadiverse.' There is so much to spot, you'd better bring binoculars.

Bird and marine life is abundant along the coast, with colonies of sea lions, Humboldt penguins, Chilean flamingos, Peruvian pelicans, Inca terns and the brown booby endemic to the region. Remarkable highland birds include the majestic Andean condor, puna ibis and a variety of hummingbirds. The highlands are also home to camelids such as llamas, alpacas, guanacos and vicuñas, while cloud forests are the haunts of jaguars, tapirs and the endangered spectacled bear.

The best field guide for Peru's highlands is *Birds of the High Andes* by Jon Fjeldsa and Niels Krabbe. It's heavy and expensive but excellent.

Swoop down toward the Amazon and with luck you'll spot all the iconic tropical birds – parrots, macaws, toucans and many more. The Amazon is home to over a dozen species of monkeys, plus river dolphins, frogs, reptiles, fish and insects galore. Snakes? Don't panic. Many species live here, but they're mostly shy of humans.

BIRDS

Peru has over 1800 bird species – more than what is found on the continents of North America and Europe taken together. No wonder ornithologists flock to Peru. From the tiniest hummingbirds (see Frequent Flyers, below) to the majestic Andean condor, the variety is colorful and seemingly endless: new

---

FREQUENT FLYERS

For many visitors to Peru, the diminutive hummingbirds are the most delightful birds to observe. Over 100 species have been recorded in Peru, and their exquisite beauty is matched by their extravagant names, such as 'green-tailed goldenthroat,' 'spangled coquette,' 'fawn-breasted brilliant' and 'amethyst-throated sunangel.'

Hummingbirds are capable of beating their wings in a figure-eight pattern up to almost 80 times a second, thus producing the typical hum for which they are named. This exceptionally rapid wing-beat enables them to hover in place when feeding on nectar, or even to fly backward. These tiny birds must feed frequently to gain the energy needed to keep them flying.

Species such as the redheaded Andean hillstar, living in the *puna* (high Andean grasslands of the altiplano), have evolved an amazing strategy to survive a cold night. They go into a state of torpor, which is like a nightly hibernation, by lowering their body temperature by up to 30°C, thus drastically slowing their metabolism.

One of the most unusual and exotic species of hummingbird is the marvelous spatuletail, found only in a remote valley of northern Peru. Full-grown adult males have the feathery spatules for which the species is named. These showy spatules are used during mating displays to attract females. Now endangered by the loss of its forest habitat due to logging and wildfires, this species is rarely seen.

species are discovered every year. The best thing about watching birds here is that you can do it anywhere. Even in the center of Lima you'll see rufous-collared sparrows and Pacific doves, neither of which are found on other continents. If you journey down the south coast to Pucusana (p128) or the Islas Ballestas (p132), you'll spot thousands of cormorants and boobies, and a few flamingos and penguins thrown in for good measure. And of course, how can you visit the coast and not see gulls galore?

A more incisive question is: how can you also see gulls galore without visiting the coast? Head into the highlands to see the Andean gull, commonly sighted around lakes and along rivers as high as about 4500m. Just don't mistakenly call it a seagull! Other highland birds include: several species of ibis, with their distinctively down-curved bills; the strangely named cinclodes (a type of ovenbird), found only in Andean countries; torrent ducks with a taste for highland whitewater; and a gaggle of Andean geese, Andean flickers, Andean siskins and Andean swallows – you get the picture.

Most famous of all is the Andean condor. Weighing up to 10kg and with a 3m wingspan, this monarch of the air once ranged over the entire Andean mountain chain from Venezuela down to Tierra del Fuego at the tip of the continent. Considered the largest flying bird in the world, the Andean condor was put on the endangered species list in the 1970s, due mostly to loss of its natural habitat and to environmental pollution. But it was also hunted to the brink of extinction because its body parts were believed to cure a variety of physical ailments, even to increase male virility or ward off nightmares. These condors usually nest in inaccessible mountain cliffs that prevent predators from snatching their young. Their main food source is carrion and they're most easily spotted riding thermal air currents above their wide-open hunting grounds, such as the canyons around Arequipa (see p184).

Swoop down towards the Amazon and you'll sight the iconic tropical birds – parrots, macaws, toucans and more. But it's hard to see them for all the trees. The best idea is to take a quiet river trip. This way you can see Amazonian umbrella birds and toucans gliding across the river, and parrots perched in the riverside trees. Many lodges know a local salt lick where, soon after dawn, flocks of macaws and parakeets come to feed on the mineral-laden clay.

MAMMALS

The Amazon is also home to many exciting mammals. Almost two dozen species of monkeys are found here, many of which are commonly seen, as are sloths and bats. With a guide, you may also see piglike peccaries, anteaters, ambling armadillos, curious coatis (ring-tailed members of the raccoon family) and perhaps giant river otters, capybara, river dolphins, tapirs or one of a half dozen elusive cat species, including jaguars.

The cloud forests rimming the Amazon are home to the endangered spectacled bear, South America's only bear. Named for the distinctive individualistic markings on its face and chest, the spectacled bear has adapted to range from the high-canopy rainforests of the Amazon all the way up to the high-elevation Andes mountains. Spectacled bears do not hibernate, though they may hole up in a den during particularly nasty weather.

Andean mammals include the domesticated llamas and alpacas, and their wild relatives, the vicuñas and guanacos. You can see llamas, alpacas and vicuñas at the Reserva Nacional Salinas y Aguada Blanca (p181) outside Arequipa. Far inland from Nazca, the Reserva Nacional Pampas Galeras (p146) is a vicuña sanctuary with a biannual round-up and ceremonial shearing in late May or early June. On highland talus slopes, watch out for the viscacha, which looks like a cross between a rabbit and giant squirrel (and maybe a

During the mid-19th century, mineral-rich *guano* (seabird droppings) accounted for as much as 80 percent of Peru's national revenue.

A Parrot Without a Name: The Search for the Last Unknown Birds on Earth, by Don Stap, is the true story of a modern expedition into the remotest reaches of the Peruvian Amazon.

Perú: The Travellers' Wildlife Guide, by David L Pearson and Les Beletsky, handily focuses on the country's most important and frequently seen birds, mammals, amphibians, reptiles and ecosystem habitats.

guinea pig, too). Foxes, deer and domesticated guinea pigs are also highland dwellers, as is the puma (cougar or mountain lion).

On the coast, huge numbers of sea lions and seals are easily seen on the Islas Ballestas (p132). Dolphins are commonly seen offshore, but whales very rarely. In the coastal desert strip, there are few unique species of land animals. One is the Sechura fox, the smallest of the South American foxes, which has a black-tipped tail and pale agouti fur.

Sloths slowly descend from their trees about once a week to urinate and defecate on the ground. Scientists don't know why.

REPTILES, AMPHIBIANS, FISH & INSECTS
Other creatures, especially found in the Amazon, include frogs, reptiles, fish and insects galore. The electric blue morpho butterfly is unmistakable as it flaps along jungle rivers; it feeds not on nectar, but on rotting fruit or tree sap that has fermented. Tiny but brightly colored poison-dart frogs, once used by indigenous peoples to poison the points of their blow-pipe darts, can be found with a careful search. Avoid the green anaconda, an aquatic boa snake that can measure over 10m in length. After ambushing its prey by the water's edge, the green anaconda kills it by constricting its body around it and drowning it in the river. Caimans, tapirs, deer, turtles and peccaries are all tasty meals for this killer snake, though human victims are almost unheard of.

Plants
At high elevations in the Andes mountains, especially in the Cordilleras Blanca and Huayhuash around Huaraz, there is a cornucopia of distinctive alpine flora and fauna. Plants encountered in this region include native lupins, spiky tussocks of ichu grass, striking quenua trees with their distinctive curly red paperbark and bromeliads. Many alpine wildflowers bloom during the trekking season, roughly between May and September.

Neotropical Rainforest Mammals, by Louise Emmons and Francois Feer, is an illustrated full-color field guide to over 300 species of rainforest animals, including handy distribution and range maps. A companion CD-ROM of vocalizations is also available.

In Peru's highlands, you'll find the distinctive *puna*, which is made up of shrublands and grasslands that act as a natural 'sponge' to the Andes. These areas have a fairly limited flora of hard grasses, cushion plants, small herbaceous plants, shrubs and dwarf trees. Many plants in this environment have developed small, thick leaves that are less susceptible to frost, and curved leaves to reflect extreme radiation. In the north of the country there is some *páramo*, which has a harsher climate, is less grassy and has an odd mixture of landscapes, including peat bogs, glacier-formed valleys, alpine lakes, wet grasslands and patches of shrubland and forest.

As the eastern Andean slopes descend into the western Amazon uplands, the scenery becomes more rugged and remote. Here are the little-known tropical cloud forests, so named because they trap (and help create) clouds that drench the forest in a fine mist, allowing some delicate forms of plant life to survive. Cloud forest trees are adapted to steep slopes, rocky soils and a rugged climate. They are characterized by low, gnarled growth, dense small-leafed canopies and moss-covered branches supporting a host of plants such as orchids, ferns and bromeliads. These aerial plants, which gather

GIANTS OF THE MOUNTAINS
One member of the bromeliad family, *Puya raimondii*, is the world's tallest flowering plant. These showy, 10m-plus tall members of the pineapple family can take up to a century or more to mature and in full bloom flaunt up to 8000 white flowers each! After blooming only once in its lifetime, the plant dies. Some of the most famous stands of *Puya raimondii* in Peru are found in the Andes mountains outside of Huaraz, specifically near Catac (p413) and Punta Winchus (p403), both of which can easily be visited on organized day tours from Huaraz (see p378).

LEAF-CUTTER ANTS

One of hundreds of ant species in the Amazon's rainforests, leaf-cutter ants live in colonies numbering in the hundreds of thousands. Their homes are huge nests dug deep into the ground. Foraging ants search the vegetation for particular types of leaves, cut out small sections and, holding the leaf segments above their heads like a small umbrella, bring them back to the nest. Travelers frequently come across a long line of them in the jungle, scurrying along carrying leaf sections back to the nest, or returning for another load. Amazingly, they consume over 10% of all available leaves in the world's neotropical zones each year.

Workers within the nest sort out the leaves that will easily decompose into a type of compost; unsuitable material is ejected from the nest. The composted leaves form a mulch, on which a fungus grows. The ants tend these fungal gardens, for they provide the colony's main diet. The bodies of the queen ants genetically secrete an antibiotic strain of bacteria to combat any alien fungi that might try to invade their gardens.

Army ants and other species prey upon this ready and constant supply of foragers. To combat this, leaf-cutter ants are morphologically separated by size and jaw structure into different castes. Some specialize in tending the fungal gardens, others have vibrating jaws designed for cutting leaf segments, and yet others are soldier ants (armed with huge mandibles) which accompany the foragers to protect them from attackers. Close observation reveals yet another caste – a microscopic ant that rides along on the leaf segments without disturbing the foragers. The riders' function is unclear, but biologists suggest that they act as protection against parasitizing wasps that try to lay eggs on the foragers while they are carrying leaves.

their moisture and some nutrients without ground roots, are collectively termed epiphytes. The dense vegetation at all levels of the cloud forest gives it a mysterious and delicate, fairytale appearance. It is also important as a source of freshwater and for controlling erosion.

Below the cloud forest is the Amazon rainforest, with its untold wealth of flora and fauna. A short walk into this tropical forest will reveal that it is vastly different from the temperate forests that many North Americans and Europeans are used to. Tropical forests have great variety. If you stand in one spot and look around, you see scores of different species of trees, but you often have to walk several hundred meters to find another example of any particular species.

One thing that often astounds visitors is the sheer immensity of some trees. A good example is the ceiba tree (also called the kapok or cotton silk tree), which has huge flattened supports, or buttresses, around its base and may easily reach three meters across. The smooth gray trunk often grows straight up for 50m before the branches are reached. These spread out into a huge crown with a slightly flattened appearance. The shape is distinctive, and the tree is often the last to be logged in a ranching area. When you see a huge, buttressed, and flattened looking tree in a pasture in the Amazon lowlands, it very often is a ceiba.

Some rainforest trees are supported by strange roots that look like props or stilts. These trees are most frequently found where periodic floods occur – the stilt roots are thought to play a role in keeping the tree upright during the inundation. Rainforest palms are among the trees that have these kinds of roots.

In areas that have been cleared (often naturally, by a flash flood or when a gap is created by an ancient forest giant falling during a storm) various fast-growing pioneer species appear. These may grow several meters a year in areas where abundant sunlight is suddenly available. Some of the most common and easily recognized of these are in the nettle family of the genus *Cecropia*, often found on riverbanks. Their gray trunks are often circled by

Tropical Nature, by Adrian Forsyth and Ken Miyata, satisfyingly subtitled 'Life and Death in the Rain Forests of Central and South America', is an eminently readable and often humorous book that introduces rainforests.

A Neotropical Companion, by John Kricher, provides an introduction to the wildlife and ecosystems of the New World tropics, including coastal and highland regions. It's dry but aimed at lay readers.

ridges at intervals of a few centimeters, but they are otherwise fairly smooth, and their branches form a canopy at the top of the trunk. The leaves are very large, palmate (like a human hand) and lobed, with the underside a much lighter green than the top – particularly noticeable when winds make the leaves display alternately light and dark green shades in a chaotic manner.

In stark contrast, the coastal desert is generally barren of vegetation, apart from around water sources, which may spring into palm-fringed lagoons. Otherwise, the only forests you'll occasionally glimpse will be those made up either of cacti or, if you happen to be visiting the ecological reserves around Tumbes (p372) on Peru's north coast, mangroves.

NATIONAL PARKS

Peru's vast wealth of wildlife is protected by a system of national parks and reserves with 60 areas covering almost 15% of the country. The newest is the Sierra del Divisor Reserve Zone, which encompasses 4 million acres of rainforest near the Brazilian border. All of these protected areas are administered by the **Instituto Nacional de Recursos Nacionales** (Inrena; www.inrena.gob.pe), a division of the Ministry of Agriculture. Protected areas unfortunately lack the fundamental infrastructure needed to conserve them and are subject to illegal hunting, fishing, logging and mining. The government simply doesn't have the money to hire enough rangers and buy necessary equipment to patrol the parks. Often, what you'll find is only a scanty information center with some outdated maps and one lone ranger at the road's end. Nevertheless, the parks do receive some measure of protection, and various international agencies contribute money and resources to help with conservation and local education projects.

ENVIRONMENTAL ISSUES

Andean Botanical Information System (www.sacha.org) is a veritable online encyclopedia of flowering plants in Peru's coastal areas and the Andes.

Major economic activities, which include farming, grazing, mining, drilling and logging, cause serious environmental problems in Peru.

Deforestation of the highlands for firewood, of the rainforests for valuable hardwoods, and of both to clear land for agricultural use has led to severe erosion, causing soil to deteriorate and get blown off the mountains or washed away down the rivers. Deforestation of the rainforest has caught international attention among the environmentally aware (though fixing it remains problematic). But in the highlands, where many people live, deforestation and overgrazing are also severe problems. The soil needs its protective cover of Andean woodlands and *puna* grasslands. With the

---

TOP 10 WILDLIFE-WATCHING SPOTS

Parque Nacional Manu (p467) Remote jungle; your best chance to see jaguars, tapirs and monkeys

Islas Ballestas (p132) and **Reserva Nacional de Paracas** (p133) Coastal reserve with penguins, flamingos and sea lions

Parque Nacional Huascarán (p387) Andean condors, giant Puya raimondii plants, vicuñas and viscachas in the Cordillera Blanca

Iquitos (p483) Canopy walkways, jungle lodges and river cruises

Puerto Maldonado (p452) Capybara sightings while cruising to a lowland macaw lick

Cañón del Colca (p181) The easiest place to spot Andean condors

Santuario Nacional Lagunas de Mejía (p152) Desert oasis of coastal lagoons with abundant native and migratory birds

Reserva Nacional Pacaya-Samiria (p482) Little-known rainforest reserve explored by dugout canoe

Tumbes (p371) Huge swathes of mangrove forests with crocodiles, birds, jaguars, anteaters and parrots

Machu Picchu (p269) Rainbow of rare and endemic birds – over 400 species!

ongoing removal of its protective cover, the soil's quality, never good to begin with, is rapidly deteriorating.

This erosion has led to decreased water quality, particularly in the Amazon basin, where silt-laden water is unable to support microorganisms at the base of the food chain. Other water-related problems include pollution from mining in the highlands and from industrial waste and sewage along the coast. Because of sewage contamination, many beaches around Lima and other coastal cities have been declared unfit for swimming. Coastal pollution, combined with overfishing, is a serious threat to Peru's rich marine resources, as is the El Niño effect (p500).

In the early 1990s, Peru took steps to formulate a national environmental and natural resource code, but the government lacked the funding to enforce it. Then in 1995, Peru's congress created a National Environmental Council (CONAM) to further refine and carry out national environmental policy. Unfortunately, law enforcement remains weak today. There just isn't enough money in this economically hard-hit nation to protect all of its amazing natural resources.

Mongo Bay (www .mongobay.com) is an excellent resource for news, education and conservation issues related to rainforests.

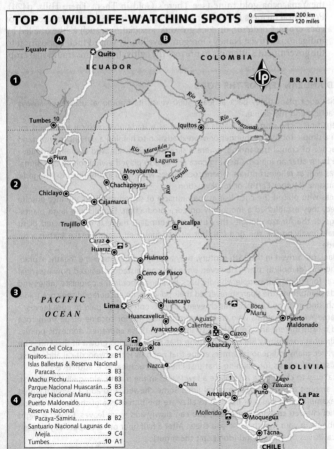

TOP 10 WILDLIFE-WATCHING SPOTS

0 — 200 km
0 — 120 miles

Breakfast of Biodiversity: The Truth about Rain Forest Destruction, by John Vandermeer, is a balanced account of the causes of rainforest destruction worldwide, including in the Peruvian Amazon.

The Nature Conservancy (www.nature.org /wherewework/south america/peru) and WWF (www.wwf.biz/about _wwf/where_we_work /latin_america_and _caribbean/where/peru /index.cfm) keep an eye on Peru's environmental and conservation hot buttons.

But there's good news. The Peruvian government and various private interests within the tourism industry have recently begun to cooperate in order to save some of Peru's premier natural attractions. Responsible tourism is finally on the national agenda, especially in the Amazon basin.

In September 2005, Peru became one of 17 Latin American countries along with Spain to sign the Amazon River Declaration, which calls for environmental safeguards to ensure biodiversity and also sustainable tourism strategies to fight rural poverty and spur regional development. Of course, development has its drawbacks, too. Critics predict that the opening of the Integration Bridge between Peru and Brazil and the construction of a new interoceanic highway linking the Atlantic and the Pacific along a transcontinental trading route will increase illegal logging and poaching and accelerate the acculturation of indigenous tribal communities into the modern mainstream.

In the central and northern Andean highlands, rural *campesinos* (peasants) have protested with partial success against the long-term environmental damage being caused by foreign-owned mining companies, including at the Yanacocha gold mine (see There's Gold in Them There Hills, p424). Poor rural farmers have also risen up against the US-backed eradication of coca crops. *Cocaleros*, or coca growers' associations, such as the one led by indigenous activist Nancy Obregón, have loudly voiced their opposition to the government's attempts to prevent the cultivation of this traditional crop.

COCA: SACRED ANDEAN LEAF OF THE GODS

Cultivation of the coca plant dates back at least 5000 years. Its traditional uses have always included the practical and the divine.

During ancient times, chewing coca leaves was used as a traditional medical treatment for everything from a simple toothache, hunger or overexhaustion to helping a patient to withstand the surgical practice of cranial trepanning, where a slice of skull is removed (usually to relieve pressure on the brain after an injury). Chewing coca leaves also played a vital role in communal and family life, as well as religious rituals, where coca leaves were used as offerings to the gods, including Pachamama (Mother Earth), or for divination.

It was the Incas who placed the coca leaf at the pinnacle of sacred ritual. As the Inca empire rapidly expanded, they established a monopoly on coca production. Establishing large plantations at the edge of the Amazon jungle, they used the abundant harvests of the sacred plant not only in rituals involving the sun god Inti, but also to fuel their armies, make friends with allies and to trade.

When the Spaniards arrived in the 15th century, they attempted to outlaw the 'heathen' practice of cultivating this 'diabolical' plant. However, once the conquistadors realized how essential chewing coca was for indigenous people who did back-breaking labor in the colonists' mines and on their hacienda plantations, the Spanish reversed their policies and encouraged the coca trade. Even the Spanish king and the Catholic church eventually accepted taxes paid in coca leaves.

Today, the same Western nations who create the most demand for cocaine made from coca crops cultivated mostly in Peru and Columbia also interfere in these countries' domestic politics and disrupt traditional community life by demanding that all coca crops grown in the Andes be eradicated. However, many indigenous farmers argue that not only is this hypocritical and unjust, there is also no scientific basis for claiming that just chewing coca leaves is addictive.

The traditional way to chew coca is to place a few leaves in the mouth, along with a catalyst, such as a small amount of wood ash or mineral lime. Some chewers also add a sweet flavored substance (for example, cane sugar or licorice) to alleviate the bitter taste of the leaves. As you build up a wad of chewed coca in your cheek, you can slowly add more leaves. Expect a slight tingling or numbness in your mouth while you chew. After a half hour or so, respectfully deposit the chewed coca leaves on the ground (don't spit them out).

Of course, Peru and Columbia are still the world's top cocaine-producing countries, but not all harvests are bought by drug cartels. Alternative political voices, such as Bolivian President Evo Morales, suggest that the answer to the coca-growing problem is not criminalization, but regulations and industrialization of the coca industry to produce alternative health products for legal export instead. For more on narcotrafficking in Peru, see p319.

Elsewhere in the southern Andean highlands, Peru has started to act on a $130 million master plan submitted to Unesco to preserve Machu Picchu, which has become a victim of its own success and now rates among the world's top 100 most endangered monuments. Experts say unrestricted tourism and landslides have damaged the ancient citadel and the nearby Inca trail that leads to it. Proposals include a daily limit of 2,500 tourists, a number that critics say is too high (and too close to the actual figure). Unesco has often threatened to list it as an 'at-risk' World Heritage Site if the Peruvian government does not move more quickly and strongly to protect it.

Peru is looking toward future options for tourism development. Spas are being developed around the country's many hot springs. 'Mystic tourism' is another trend, with visits to jungle and highland shamans at the top of many travelers' lists of adventures. Meanwhile, the government is heavily promoting tourism in northern Peru to steer more visitors away from the country's well-trammeled Gringo Trail in southern Peru. To this end, there's talk of building a highway between Cajamarca and Chachapoyas, with the eventual goal of more easily linking the archaeological treasures of the north coast with the Cajamarca countryside and the fortress of Kuélap, as well as the rainforests of the northern Amazon.

Sponsored by the US public TV program *Frontline*, the online travel journal at www .pbs.org/frontline world/fellows/peru0803 disturbingly documents a corporate search for natural gas reservoirs hidden beneath Peru's Amazon jungle.

Planeta Peru (www .planeta.com/peru.html) offers ecotourism links along with plenty of environmental news and recommended reading.

Peru Outdoors

The land of the Incas is a modern mecca for outdoor adventurers. Whether you want to scale Andean peaks or smoking volcanoes, go rafting in the world's deepest canyon or sandboarding down humongous desert dunes by the sparkling waters of the Pacific, Peru will give you a head rush. It's a wonderland for adrenaline junkies of all types.

Most activities are available year-round, but of course certain times of year are better than others, depending on what you want to do. Peak season for most outdoor activities is during the dry winter season (roughly from late May until early September). Trekking in the highlands is a muddy proposition during the wet season, especially from December to March, when the heaviest rains fall. However, those warmer summer months are the best for swimming and surfing along the Pacific coast.

The fledgling status of many outdoor activities in Peru is both an advantage and a drawback. While it may sound like paradise to have a surf break, single-track trail or rapids run all to yourself, it's not always so. Equipment rental can be expensive, at least by local standards, and sometimes difficult to find. For highly specialized activities, such as mountaineering, bring your own high-quality gear from home. Peru is probably not the place to try out riskier sports for the first time either – absolute beginners shouldn't expect to get their feet wet, for example, on a river running (white-water rafting) trip here.

Activity guides in Peru are largely unregulated, untrained and inexperienced, which can lead to injury or even death for their paying clients. In addition, some outdoor outfitters and tour operators may have little concern for safeguarding the environment or working cooperatively with local communities. Always avoid the cheapest, cut-rate travel agencies – it's far better to spend a bit more cash on a well-trained guide and a trip organized by a reputable agency, if only to assure your greater safety, not to mention enjoyment. For professionally organized activity tours from Australia, New Zealand, North America and Europe, see p520.

TREKKING & HIKING

Pack your hiking boots – the variety of trails in Peru is staggering. Trekking is most rewarding during the May to September dry season in the Andes. It

---

RESPONSIBLE TREKKING

The Andean mountains are part of a sensitive ecological environment, so it's important to be conscious of the impact of mass tourism.

With the amount of traffic some treks see, litter can be a huge problem. Marking your path with a trail of trash is just plain thoughtless, rude and illegal. Locals may be among the worst offenders, but 'When in Rome…' is not an excuse – if you carry it in, you can carry it out. If you can pick up and carry out some extra garbage, all the better.

Avoid disturbing flora or fauna when trekking, and do not cut down trees or live branches for fires or other use (open fires are illegal).

Don't give children money, sweets or gifts – it encourages persistent begging, which has become a major problem on busy routes. If you wish to help the communities you are visiting, consider donating directly to local schools, NGOs and other volunteer organizations. See also p513.

Remember that often the gear you are carrying is extremely expensive for a local: be sensitive and do not flaunt your relative wealth. Stow everything inside your tent overnight.

is certainly possible to trek during the wet season; just be prepared for daily downpours, cloudy viewing conditions and soggy, damp tents! Hikers will find many easily accessible trails around Peru's archaeological ruins, which are also the final destinations for more challenging trekking routes.

The main trekking centers are Cuzco in the Andes of southern Peru and Huaraz inland from the north coast. Both towns have countless outfitters who will provide rental equipment and guides – and even *arrieros* (mule drivers) and pack animals. Most trekking gear can be hired, but your own broken-in boots will save you from horrific blisters inflicted by poorly fitting rental boots. If you prefer to trek ultralight, you might want to bring all of your own gear, especially a sleeping bag, as old-generation rental items tend to be heavy.

Whether or not you'll need a guide depends on where you'll be trekking. Certain areas of Peru require a trekking guide, such as along the Inca Trail or for entry to Machu Picchu. In more dangerous and remote places, such as the Cordillera Huayhuash, having a guide may help deter potential attackers. But scores of other trekking routes are wonderfully DIY. Whenever you do go without a guide, at least talk to a reliable outdoor outfitter about weather and trail conditions and safety before heading out. Topographic maps for major trekking routes are usually sold in the nearest major gateway town, such as Cuzco, Huaraz or Arequipa. For more obscure routes, buy topo maps from the Instituto Geográfico Nacional (IGN) in Lima (p507).

The Cordillera Blanca (p387) can't be beat for peaks, while the nearby Cordillera Huayhuash (p391) is similarly stunning. The classic and favorite trekking route is the four-day Llanganuco to Santa Cruz trek (p387), climbing the 4760m Punta Union pass surrounded by ice-clad peaks. Longer treks include the northern route around Alpamayo (p391), which needs at least a week. Shorter overnight trips in the Cordillera Blanca go to mountain base camps, alpine lakes and even along an old Inca route. The more demanding 10-day Cordillera Huayhuash circuit (p392), which is not as busy, shares impressive scenery and high-elevation passes that guarantee you bragging rights afterward.

But if you've heard of *any* trek in Peru, it'll be the world-famous Inca Trail to Machu Picchu (p274). Of course, everyone else knows about it, too, so we highly recommend that you think about taking an alternative route to Machu Picchu (see p277). The spectacular six-day trek around awesome Ausangate (6384m; p283) will take you over 5000m passes, through huge herds of alpacas, and past tiny hamlets unchanged in centuries. The Inca site Choquequirau (p285) near Cuzco and ancient ruins hidden in cloud forests outside Chachapoyas (p438) in Peru's northern highlands are two of the more remote trekking possibilities.

Alternatively, you can get down into the world's deepest canyons – the world-famous Cañón del Colca (p181) and Cañón del Cotahuasi (p186). Though the elevations in the canyon country outside Arequipa are less breathtaking than around Huaraz or Cuzco, the scenery will knock you off your feet. During the wet season, when some Andean trekking routes may be impassable, everything in the Cañón del Colca is invitingly lush and green. It's also the best place in Peru for DIY trekking between rural villages. The more remote and rugged Cañón del Cotahuasi is best visited with an experienced local guide and only during the dry season.

Wherever you choose to hike or trek in Peru, be prepared for altitude sickness (p534). Give yourself enough time – which means at least a few days – to acclimatize to higher elevations in nearby cities (eg Cuzco, Huaraz, Arequipa, Puno) before tackling any trails. You'll enjoy the trek more if you're not laboring for every breath and step along the way. The biggest mistake

The Inka Porter Project website (www.peruweb .org/porters) has excellent advice and guidelines for trekking responsibly and ensuring the ethical treatment of porters and *arrieros* (mule drivers).

Lonely Planet's *Trekking in the Central Andes* has excellent DIY information on dozens of popular and little-known trails in Peru.

Peruvian Andean Adventures (www.cain gram.info/Peru_climbs .htm) has scores of photos of trekking and climbing around Peru, along with helpful links to more practical information.

you can make is to fly directly from the coast to Cuzco, then expect to start the Inca Trail the very next day – it'll make you (and your entire trekking group and tour guides) miserable.

MOUNTAIN, ROCK & ICE CLIMBING

Spin the globe and you'll see that Peru has the highest tropical mountains in the world. Don't miss them. High-elevation climbing is best done during the dry season, with mid-June to mid-July considered the best time. Acclimatization to altitude is essential (see p534 for details).

LIGHT AT THE END OF THE INCA TRAIL   Sara Benson

Sometimes everything just goes awry.

When you're on the road, you have to go with the flow. And when you're a travel writer, you're on the road almost all the time. So, I've learned to grab onto every opportunity that passes my way. That's how I ended up starting on the Inca Trail at an altitude of more than 3000m just 48 hours after flying into Cuzco from sea level on the California coast.

Not exactly the brightest idea, I know. But isn't that how it always is when you're backpacking? Travel plans are hatched at the last minute ('Hey, wanna go to Peru next week?'), which in this case meant that there was only one spot left on the Inca Trail trek, and hey, when was I ever coming back to South America?

Altitude sickness be damned; I started trekking. I had extreme confidence in the mantra 'mind over matter.' Besides, I'd already been on more challenging trails in the Himalayas. I was an experienced hiker. I knew wilderness first aid. And I had top-flight outdoor gear. This was going to be a breeze.

Wrong. Our bus from Cuzco had to ford a stream just to get to the trailhead and bounced precariously from side to side. I stepped off the bus unsteadily and felt a cold dampness running down my back. The water-bladder insert in my backpack had sprung a leak. Not an auspicious start, but I was undaunted.

By the time we made camp the first night, my head was spinning from the altitude and I was breathless – not in awe at the magnificent scenery, but from lack of oxygen. As we settled in for the night, my tentmate burst out with, 'Look at my scar!' He'd just had open-heart surgery. I immediately nicknamed our tent 'The Nursing Home.' As thirty-somethings, we were among the oldest people on our trek. And after one day on the Inca Trail, I felt more like a senior citizen.

At dawn the next morning it started to rain. And then it rained some more, all day, So much for Andean vistas. It was all I could do to see the stones in front of me, which were obscured by mist and low-hanging clouds. Meanwhile, the trail led relentlessly upward. I reached 'Dead Woman's Pass' at almost 4200m. Believe me, no place I'd ever been seemed so appropriately named. I was lagging so far behind my fellow trekkers at this point, they actually broke out into applause as I struggled up the final stretch.

Then something quixotic happened: I found my second wind. I almost skipped down the stones into the next valley. It didn't stop raining for the next two days, but I no longer minded the weather. Raindrops quivering on orchids just made them more beautiful to me. Coming upon Inca ruins shrouded in fog suddenly made me feel like Indiana Jones. The trail was still very hard work, but it now felt more like an epic pilgrimage.

When I passed through the Intipunku (Sun Gate) at some ungodly hour of the final morning, I saw nothing. All of the promised grand views of the mountaintop citadel, Machu Picchu, were obscured. I suddenly got choked up. All this trekking for nothing? I thought. But as we ambled downward toward the ancient ruins, the mist started to lift. By the time we entered the sacred site, dazzling sunlight reflected off the zigzag stone fortifications, a monument to a lost time and empire. It was everything I'd dared to dream it would be.

In the end, there are some wonders of the world that you have to earn the right to appreciate. For me, all the trials and tribulations of the Inca Trail only made the journey's end more unforgettable.

For beginners looking to bag their first serious peaks, Peru may not be the best place to start. Many so-called guides are inexperienced and don't even know the basics of first aid, let alone wilderness search and rescue. Even experienced mountaineers may want to hire a local guide who knows exactly what has been happening recently in the mountains. Check out all guides' credentials carefully and try to get personal references before hiring anyone.

The Cordillera Blanca, with dozens of peaks exceeding 5000m, is arguably the most inspiring climbing area in South America. The Andean base camp town of Huaraz (see p377) has tour agencies, outdoor outfitters, local guides, information and climbing equipment for hire, although it's best to bring your own gear for more serious ascents. Ishinca (5530m) and Pisco (5752m) are snow peaks considered easy enough for relatively inexperienced climbers. These mountains are also good warm-up climbs for experienced climbers who are acclimatizing for bigger adventures such as Huascarán (6768m), the highest peak in Peru and a fairly challenging climb for experts only. In between are many difficult peaks, including the knife-edged Alpamayo (5947m), considered by many to be the most beautiful mountain in Peru, and dozens of possible new routes for highly experienced climbers. South of the Cordillera Blanca, the Cordillera Huayhuash offers many other possibilities, including Yerupajá (6634m), Peru's second-highest peak.

Rock and ice climbing are taking off in a big way around Huaraz (see p377), where a few travel agencies and outdoor outfitters have indoor climbing walls, rent out technical equipment and organize group climbing trips.

In the south of Peru, there is no shortage of highs. Before attempting any high-altitude expedition in this region, however, you should first spend some time in Cuzco or Puno to acclimatize. Arequipa (p170) is surrounded by snowy volcanic peaks, some of which are scaleable even by beginners, as long as you've got plenty of determination and some wilderness experience. Many outdoor outfitters and travel agencies in Arequipa are less than reliable, so check all rental equipment carefully before setting out and only hire really qualified guides. The most popular climb around Arequipa is El Misti (5822m), which, despite its height, is basically a very long, tough walk. Chachani (6075m) is one of the easiest 6000m peaks in the world, though you'll need crampons, an ice axe and a good guide. There are many other tempting peaks towering above the Cañón del Colca (p181) outside Arequipa, too.

RIVER RUNNING

Also known as white-water rafting, river running is a popular activity year-round. Adventurers are discovering the unspoiled rivers plunging from the Andes into the lush canyons of the upper Amazon. Commercial rafting trips and kayaking are both possible; trips can range from a few hours to more than two weeks.

Cuzco (p235) is undoubtedly the main town in which to find the greatest variety of river possibilities. The choices range from a few hours of mild rapids on the Urubamba to several days on the Apurímac (technically the source of the Amazon and with some world-class rafting between May and November). A river-running trip on the Tambopata, available from June through October, tumbles down the eastern slopes of the Andes, culminating in a couple of days of floating in unspoiled rainforest. Rafting down the Río Urubamba in the Sacred Valley is popular. It's not very wild and offers some spectacular scenery and a chance to visit some of the best Inca ruins near Cuzco.

Classic Climbs of the Cordillera Blanca, by Brad Johnson, is a well-reviewed mountaineering guide for first-timers and experts alike, with good maps and photographs.

National Geographic (www.national geographic.com/andes/) covered a 1995 climbing expedition to recover the mummified body of the Inca ice maiden Juanita, now on display in Arequipa's Museo Santury (p166).

Outside Arequipa, Nevado Ampato (6288m) was a sacred mountain to the Incas, who climbed it to offer human sacrifices as gifts to the gods.

Other rafting centers include Arequipa (p171). There the Río Chili is the most frequently run local river, with a half-day beginners' trip leaving daily between March and November. Further afield from Arequipa, the expert-level Río Majes passes class II and III rapids. Over on the south coast, Lunahuaná (p129) is a prime spot for both beginners and experts. Between December and April, the rapids of the Río Cañete can reach class IV.

On the more difficult Apurímac and Tambopata rivers, paying customers and guides have died in accidents in recent years. These and other rivers are remote, and rescues can take days. It is therefore worth investing in a well-run expedition with a reputable company and avoiding the cut-price trips. To guarantee an expertly professional trip, consider booking a specialty tour from abroad (see p520).

A good operator will have insurance, provide you with a Boleta de Venta (a legal document indicating the operator is registered), have highly experienced guides with certified first-aid training who carry a properly stocked medical kit, and provide top-notch equipment including self-bailing rafts, US Coast Guard–approved life jackets, first-class helmets and spare paddles. Many good companies raft rivers accompanied by a kayaker who is experienced in river rescue.

As with the cheaper trekking outfitters, some river-running companies in Peru are not environmentally sensitive, resulting in dirty camping beaches. The only way to protect yourself *and* the river is to ask the tough questions and inspect equipment.

SURFING

Surfing has a big fan base in Peru. It's enjoyed mainly by local young people with money to burn and also a handful of international surfers who come here searching for that perfect break. The surfing is good, it's uncrowded and there are plenty of places to explore. Just ask around, or surf the Web for sites such as www.peruazul.com, www.vivamancora.com and www .wannasurf.com.

The water is cold from April to mid-December (as low as 15°C, or 60°F), when locals wear wetsuits to surf. Indeed, many surfers wear wetsuits year-round, even though you can get away with not using them in the January to March period, when the water is a little warmer (around 20°C, or 68°F, in the Lima area). The far north coast (north of Talara) stays above 21°C (70°F) most of the year. The surfing is quite challenging, and available facilities and equipment are limited and expensive. You'll find a few surf shops and hostels that offer advice, rental boards and surfing day-trips and tours only at the most popular beaches along the north coast. Otherwise, if you're serious about surfing Peru's Pacific coast, bring your own board from home – it may be awkward to travel with, but you'll become instant friends with local surfers just by walking down the street.

In Lima (p105) surfers can be found on the crowded Miraflores, Barranco and Costa Verde beaches. Slightly south in Chorrillos, La Herradura, with an outstanding left point-break, gets crowded when there is a strong swell. In-the-know surfers prefer the smaller crowds further south at Punta Hermosa (p125). Near here is Punta Rocas (p125), where international and national championships are held annually. Isla San Gallán, off the Península de Paracas, is accessible only by boat (ask local fishers or at hotels) and provides an epic right point-break for world-class surfers.

There are some radical waves along Peru's north coast (see p343), most of which have reliable swell from April through October. Máncora (p362) and Huanchaco (p340) have good lefts, but the left at Cabo Blanco (p362) can be tricky when conditions are intimidating. The most famous wave is at

Puerto Chicama (p343), where rides of over 2km in length are possible on a wave considered to be the world's longest. Los Organos, south of Máncora, has tubular rights and lefts – they're for experienced surfers only, though. Pacasmayo (p343), just to the north of Máncora, and Pimintel (p349) and Santa Rosa (p350), nearby Chiclayo, are also good.

SANDBOARDING

For something completely different, go sandboarding down the humongous desert dunes at Huacachina (p142) and near Nazca (p146) along Peru's south coast. Though it's softer, warmer and safer than snowboarding or surfing, don't be lulled into a false sense of security – several people have seriously injured themselves after losing control of their sandboards. Some hotels and travel agencies offer tours in *areneros* (dune buggies), where you are hauled up to the top of the dunes, then picked up at the bottom, but the drivers are notoriously reckless, so watch out. Cerro Blanco outside Nazca is the highest known sand dune in the world at 2078m – a pretty radical challenge for experienced boarders.

Sandboard (www.sandboard.com) is a free online magazine for aspiring dune riders.

MOUNTAIN BIKING & CYCLING

In Peru mountain biking is still a fledgling sport. That said, both easy and demanding single-track trails await mountain bikers outside of Huaraz (p378) and Arequipa (p172). If you're experienced, there are awesome mountain-biking possibilities around the Sacred Valley and downhill trips to the Amazon jungle, all accessible from Cuzco (p236). Easier cycling routes include the wine country around Lunahuaná (p129) and in the Cañón del Colca, starting from Chivay (p182).

Be aware that, with the exceptions of Huaraz, Cuzco and Arequipa, rental mountain bikes in Peru tend to be pretty basic, so if you are planning on some serious biking, it's best to bring your own. Airlines' bicycle-carrying policies vary, so shop around. Some airlines will fly your bike as checked baggage (either for free or for a hefty surcharge) if it's boxed. However, boxing the bike gives baggage handlers little clue to the contents, and it may be roughly handled. If it's OK with the airline, try wrapping it in heavy-duty plastic; this way baggage handlers can see the contents.

Even with your own bike, it's still worth hiring a guide or getting local information about the best biking routes. Most of them aren't very well known. Always wear a helmet and make yourself as visible as possible. You'll also need a repair kit and extra parts (and familiarity with how to use them), some good directions (maps can be dangerously unreliable, especially when it comes to unpaved roads) and enough food and water to get you to the next town.

SWIMMING

Swimming is popular along the Peruvian coast from January to March, when the Pacific Ocean waters are warmest, although the beaches may often be contaminated near the major coastal cities and there are many dangerous currents. Only north of Talara does the water stay warm year-round. It sure ain't Ibiza or Brazil, but the biggest beach scenes in Peru are just south of Lima (p125) and along the north coast, especially at laid-back Huanchaco (p340), around Chiclayo (p349) and the perennially busy, jet-set resorts of Máncora (p362).

Playas Peru (www.playasperu.com) is a hip, in-the-know guide to Peruvian beaches from Tumbes all the way to Tacna, listing hot surf spots and cool nightlife.

SCUBA DIVING

Scuba diving in Peru is limited. The water is cold except from mid-December to March. During these months the water is cloudiest because of run-off from

WATCHING WILDLIFE IN PERU

Sea lions, seabirds, vicuñas (threatened wild relatives of alpacas), condors, scarlet macaws, hummingbirds, sloths, leaf-cutter ants, monkeys, caimans, toucans, iguanas, parrots, freshwater dolphins – the list of wildlife in this 'megadiverse' country seems endless, and there are many opportunities to see these animals. A lot of travelers come specifically to spend their days watching wildlife. Many adventure travel companies and tour agencies can arrange guided natural-history tours from abroad or after you've arrived in Peru.

Peru's national parks, reserves and wildlife sanctuaries (see p56) are all good places for observation, but private areas such as Amazon jungle lodges around Iquitos and Puerto Maldonando can also yield a good number of birds, insects, reptiles and even monkeys. Early morning and late afternoon are the best times to watch for wildlife activity anywhere; the hot middle part of the day is when many animals rest – out of sight. A lightweight pair of binoculars will improve wildlife observation tremendously; it's better to purchase them at home before your trip.

Have realistic expectations. The coastal desert has limited wildlife – go to the Península de Paracas and Islas Ballestas (p132) or Santuario Nacional Lagunas de Mejía (p152) for the best experience. The canyon country surrounding Arequipa (p181) can be a good place to spot Andean condors and camelids, including wild vicuñas. The rugged highlands have Andean wildlife, but much of it has been hunted out, so try to visit more remote trekking areas.

The Amazonian rainforest is a fantastic environment with plenty of wildlife, but animals are hard to see because the vegetation is so thick. You could be 15m from a jaguar and not even know it is there. Don't expect to see jaguars, ocelots, tapirs, and many other mammals, which are shy, well camouflaged and rare. Concentrate on wildlife that is easier to observe and enjoy them – many of the animals described in the Environment chapter (p51) can be seen fairly easily if you take time to visit different parts of the country. Walk slowly and quietly; listen as well as look; and be patient.

mountain rivers, as it's the wet season. A couple of dive shops in Lima (p105) offer PADI certification classes, rent scuba equipment and offer diving trips along the coast. The best diving areas are the warm waters near the Ecuador border and the clear waters around the Península de Paracas.

HORSEBACK RIDING

Horse rentals can be arranged in many tourist destinations, but the rental stock is not always treated well, so stop to think before you saddle up. For a real splurge, take a ride on a graceful Peruvian Paso horse, allegedly possessing the world's smoothest gait. They are descendants of horses with royal Spanish and Moorish lineage ridden by Spanish conquistadors. Today the most impressive *caballos de paso* (horseback dressage displays) are held in Trujillo (p329). Several stables in Peru advertise half-day or longer rides, especially in the Sacred Valley outside Cuzco at Urubamba (p259).

Bird-watching alert: Peru has the most breeding avian species of any country in the world.

PARAGLIDING

Paragliding is an up-and-coming sport in Peru, especially from the coastal clifftops of suburban Miraflores in Lima (p105) and at various points along the south coast, including Pisco and Paracas, Ica and even possibly over the Nazca Lines. Because there are so few paragliding operators so far in Peru, you'll have to ask around or search online. It's best to either be experienced or take tandem flights.

The Inca World Hugh Thomson

The civilizations of ancient Peru were some of the oldest on earth, yet also the most isolated. Until the relatively late arrival of the Spanish in 1532, the Incas and the many cultures that preceded them had a quite unique way of life – one that excluded writing, the wheel and many other necessities of the so-called Old World, but managed to build magnificent monuments and a stable society in a terrifyingly unstable landscape.

HISTORY
The Incas & their Predecessors

The Incas were relative newcomers themselves when the Spanish arrived. The Inca empire had only begun expanding after AD 1400, so had been around for a mere century before being so brutally cut short by the Spanish. The Incas were only the last in a whole series of cultures predating the Spanish conquest, but it has taken a while for the world to appreciate the achievements of these earlier Peruvian civilizations, not least because the Incas liked to pretend that it was all their own work.

There is some evidence that the Incas substantially retold the history of preceding civilizations to downplay their achievements, and in some cases to ignore those achievements completely. In *Crónica del Perú*, one of the best of the early Spanish chroniclers, Pedro de Cieza de León, quoted his Inca sources as saying that before them there were only 'naked savages' and that 'these natives were stupid and brutish beyond belief. They say they were like animals, and that many ate human flesh, and others took their daughters and mothers to wife and committed other even graver sins.'

This manipulative distortion of history was so successful – the same myth was repeated by other chroniclers like Garcilaso de la Vega in the early 17th century – that the truth has only emerged comparatively recently. Far from imposing order on an unruly bunch of savages, the Incas were merely the latest dominant tribe (and a short-lived one at that) in a series of Andean civilizations that had flourished over the preceding 4000 years, including the Moche in the north of Peru, the Wari of the central states and the Tiahuanaco culture near Lake Titicaca.

It was a German archaeologist, Max Uhle, who first began to reveal how literally deep the roots of Andean culture were. In dig after dig in southern and central Peru in the early 20th century, he showed conclusively that the Inca had been preceded by earlier cultures, and that some of these cultures had built up similar empires. In the north, the doyen of Peruvian archaeologists, Julio C Tello, started in 1919 to excavate the extraordinary Chavín de Huántar, with its jungle iconography of snakes and jaguars dating from as early as 1200 BC – over two millennia before the arriviste Incas.

So where did the Incas come from? The prosaic response is that up until around AD 1400, they were just one of a number of competing tribes in the area around Cuzco, before they built up their enormous empire under a series of dynamic and capable emperors. The Incas evolved their own religious explanation (p73).

Birth of the Inca Empire

Many chroniclers of the Inca empire attribute its phenomenal growth to the achievements of one man: the emperor Pachacutec, who according to these accounts, deserves to be as well known as Alexander the Great or Napoleon.

Hugh Thomson is the author of *The White Rock: An Exploration of the Inca Heartland* and *Sacred Landscape: The Search for Ancient Peru*. He led several research expeditions to the area around Cuzco and made the first reports of some previously unknown Inca sites.

María Rostworowski de Diez Canseco's *History of the Inca Realm* is a brilliant and accessible book that gives a Peruvian perspective on the Incas. Her website at http://incas.perucultural.org.pe/ is also excellent.

Pachacutec (originally known as Inca Yupanqui), was a younger son of the emperor Viracocha. During Viracocha's reign, the Incas had been no more than one of the many small tribes dotted around this area. Then, some time around 1438, the Chanka, a rival tribe to the north of Cuzco, attacked the Incas with such ferocity that Viracocha and his designated heir, Inca Urcon, fled the capital. Only a small band of captains, led by Inca Yupanqui, remained to provide a last-ditch defense.

Although facing seemingly hopeless odds, they managed to defeat the enemy with the help, so it was said, of the very stones of Cuzco, which rose up from the ground to fight alongside them. Not only were the Chanka sent packing, but Inca Yupanqui (who now adopted the soubriquet Pachacutec, 'Transformer of the Earth,' and took the throne from his disgraced father and brother) embarked on an ambitious program of conquest that initiated the imperial phase of Inca culture. Within a generation the Incas had grown from an anonymous small tribe of the Cuzco valley to become the dominant force of the Andes.

Pachacutec's achievements seem almost to defy geographical comprehension. During his reign from around 1438 to 1471, he led the first wave of conquests over to Bolivia and Lake Titicaca. His son Túpac Yupanqui, working under his direction, followed with further expansion north to Ecuador, until the whole chain of the Andes from Colombia to Chile was under Inca control, a distance of some 3000 miles and an area the size of continental Europe.

Nor was Pachacutec's achievement purely military. After his victory over the Chanka, he gathered the stones that were supposed to have helped him in his fight and set them up as *huacas* (sacred temples) in places where they could be worshipped in gratitude for the assistance they had given. He inculcated the Incas with the idea that they were a people of power, of destiny, and created an elaborate hierarchy devolving from his own position as the *sapa inca,* the emperor. The nobility became a separate tier in this hierarchy and were allowed to wear earplugs as a distinguishing feature. Tribes living close to Cuzco were accommodated by being made honorary Incas.

Pachacutec also ensured that impressive stone monuments were erected to this idea of an imperial destiny. Inca leaders had always been expected to build; one of the slurs perpetuated about the disgraced Inca Urcon, the brother that Pachacutec had usurped, was that he was too weak to leave a building to his name. But Pachacutec, a true emperor, took this principle to new, grandiose extremes. He ordered the construction of Saqsaywamán (p254), of the temple-fortress at Ollantaytambo (p262) and, possibly, of Machu Picchu (p269). He also built great roads across the continent.

According to later Inca accounts, Pachacutec was said to have laid down all the basic framework for the institutions of state over his reign of approximately thirty years – institutions that his successors were ritualistically to preserve in his name. For the first time, the peoples of the coast and the mountains were given a unified administration that allowed peaceful trading and cooperation, with Quechua as the lingua franca. Where there had previously been darkness, so this story went, the Inca empire brought order.

However, this account of Pachacutec needs to be treated with some care. It is a seductive idea – an empire carved out by the sheer willpower of one individual, who single-handedly turned the tide of a nation's destiny – and as such was appealing to Spanish chroniclers reared on just such chivalric exploits themselves. Pachacutec was undoubtedly a dynamic and capable leader. But what has come down to us is very much the 'official version' of the history, carefully propagated by Pachacutec and his descendants. As a usurping family, they had an interest in denigrating the achievements of their predecessors, who consequently may have received short shrift.

William Prescott's *History of the Conquest of Peru* is still a terrific read, despite being written in 1847 by a Boston lawyer who had never been to Peru.

The Land of Four Quarters

While Pachacutec initially concentrated on the southern Andes and Bolivia, his son Túpac Yupanqui began the expansion into the northern ranges and Ecuador that was to have such a profound consequence for the Inca empire of Tahuantinsuyo (Land of Four Quarters).

It seems that the Incas had a prolonged love affair with the warm climate of Ecuador; fertile land, the trade in exotic desirables such as sea shells and the attractions of the local girls combined to make it irresistible to the aesthetes from the highlands. Successive emperors spent more and more time campaigning there. The rhythm of such campaigns allowed plenty of time to enjoy the place: the normal, very civilized practice of pre-Columbian peoples was for fighting to pause during harvesttime to allow both sides to gather in crops (when the Spanish arrived, they disconcerted the locals by ignoring this convention). Cieza de León also reports that the Incas often found it too hot to fight in the summer anyway.

During these long campaigns, Túpac Yupanqui founded the city of Tumipampa (modern day Cuenca, in Ecuador), where his son Huayna, the future emperor, was born. When Huayna Capac succeeded to the throne, Ecuador clearly appealed more to him than the harsher climate of the Inca heartland. He chose to stay for many years in his birthplace, and was said to have preferred it to Cuzco as a capital.

John Hemming's *The Conquest of the Incas* is a magisterial read.

By Inca standards Huayna seems to have been a bit of a bon vivant: he was said to be able to drink three times as much as any of his subjects. When asked how it was that he never became intoxicated, he replied that 'he drank for the poor, of whom he supported many.'

Yet the Inca push into Ecuador can with hindsight be seen as an expansion too far. In just three generations, the Inca empire had grown from an enclave around Cuzco to one that stretched several thousand miles along the Andes. In the process it had become fatally distended.

Guns & Germs

There has long been a debate, both among chroniclers of the time and modern scholars, as to whether Huayna Capac may have fathered Atahualpa by an Ecuadorian princess, which would have made his son illegitimate by the Inca rules of succession. Whatever the truth, the mere attribution shows the extent to which Atahualpa has always been inextricably associated with the north. The endless campaigns that Huayna waged in Ecuador left a permanent standing army in the North, an exception to the normal Inca convention that armies were temporary and centered on Cuzco.

In around 1527 came disaster: a fatal epidemic killed as much as half the population of 25 million, including the emperor Huayna Capac.

The cracks in the new Inca empire quickly started to show. The empire was split between Atahualpa and Huayna Capac's other son, Huascar, and the resulting civil war was devastating. It was the turning point in Inca fortunes, much more so than the Spanish conquest of 1532, which simply exploited the wreckage it caused. The two sides were evenly matched: Huascar had all the resources of the Cuzco state behind him, while Atahualpa was the more experienced soldier, with a strong Ecuadorian power base and a ruthless streak. Indeed, far from being passive and noble as he is sometimes portrayed, Atahualpa was one of the most brutal of all Inca emperors – and this was a category in which he had stiff competition. Atahualpa eventually defeated Huascar, but not before the country had been laid to waste.

By 1532, the Spanish could simply walk in and take the empire. The conquistadors, as so often, were incredibly lucky; after landing on the coast at Tumbes, they traveled south down the Royal Road towards the Inca capital, moving through a civilization that had been fatally weakened by first disease and then internal divisions. They also had superior weapons and the psychological advantage of horses, which were unknown to the locals.

It was not long before Francisco Pizarro and his men kidnapped Atahualpa in the main square at Cajamarca (p421); after extorting a huge ransom of gold and silver from the Incas, they executed him and marched on Cuzco to claim the empire for themselves.

Although the conquistadors scorned the Incas for lacking a writing system, Francisco Pizarro was himself illiterate.

Inca Resistance

It would be a great mistake to think that the Incas simply surrendered to the Spanish, despite the initial success of the conquistadors.

After Atahualpa's death, the Spanish decided to install a puppet emperor on the throne, a half-brother of Atahualpa and Huascar called Manco, but this proved to be a costly error. After a few years of obedience, Manco revolted, calling troops up from all over Tahuantinsuyo for one last stand.

Many of Pizarro's comrades had gone to Chile on an expedition, while others were in the newly founded city of Lima. The remaining Spanish were taken by surprise and trapped in the streets of the town, while the Incas gathered outside the walls and in the great fortress above at Saqsaywamán. Pedro de Cieza de León described the conquistadors' dismay at suddenly seeing the strength of Manco's forces camped around Cuzco: 'So numerous were the troops who came here that they covered the fields, and by day it looked as if a black cloth had been spread over the ground for half a league.'

The Incas came remarkably close to finishing the Spanish off, setting fire to the roofs of Cuzco and keeping up a punishing siege. There were fewer than two hundred of the conquistadors and, of these, as Pedro candidly admits, only the cavalrymen really mattered, as the Spanish on foot were no match for the agile *indígenas* (people of indigenous descent).

It was the European horses which were the Spaniards' only hope if they were to hold over 100,000 Inca soldiers at bay. On open ground, an armored Spanish horseman with steel weapons against an indigenous infantryman was

---

CLOTHES MAKETH THE MAN

Pedro Pizarro was a young cousin of Franciso Pizarro's, and he spent a considerable amount of time in Atahualpa's company, which he later recorded in his memoirs.

It seems that even after his capture, the Inca tried to keep up the pretense that he could still preside over the affairs of his empire, as if being held by the Spanish were merely a temporary inconvenience. Like Pedro, Atahualpa was still virtually a teenager, but he had the fully developed appetite for power of a natural autocrat, and even in captivity enjoyed all the trappings of a rock star of the most demanding sort (think a 16th-century Jim Morrison).

As an emperor he had been supremely arrogant, and even in defeat, Atahualpa had plenty of attitude. One day Pedro was sitting with him when Atahualpa dropped a bit of food on his clothing. The Inca immediately got up and changed, coming back in a much finer dark brown *manta* (cloak). When Pedro felt the cloth, and realized that even by Quechuan high standards it was an exceptionally rich cloak, he asked Atahualpa what it was made from. 'The finest hair of vampire bats,' replied the Inca haughtily. Pedro asked how it had been possible to catch enough bats to make an entire cloak. 'Those dogs of Tumbez and Puerto Viejo [Inca settlements in the North], what else have they to do there but to capture such animals so as to make clothes for me?'

Pedro became fascinated by Atahualpa's wardrobe. He discovered that all his clothes were only worn once, after which they were guarded in special chests by his retainers – to prevent others from ever touching them – and burnt at an annual ceremony. Appalled by this profligacy, the young Pizarro noted that this applied even to those garments that the Inca had handled but then rejected, indeed 'to everything which he had ever touched.'

like a tank against an archer. But in the cramped streets of Cuzco, the horses were no longer so agile or effective. The *indígenas* built palisades to contain them, and used slings to hurl burning cloth at the buildings the Spanish were sheltering in. The defenders realized they were in an impossible position.

They mounted a despairing charge and rode up to take Saqsaywamán itself, before Manco could assemble more troops for the siege. However much one might dislike the motives or morals of the conquistadors, this was a bold and brave move given how few of them there were and the overwhelming superiority of the Incas.

The Incas under Manco were forced to retreat. He led his men into the wild Vilcabamba area to the west of Cuzco, from where he and his successors managed to hold out against the Spanish for another remarkable forty years, waging intermittent guerrilla attacks. It is in this area that some of the most deliberately inaccessible Inca ruins can still be found.

Manco used the emotive power of the mummies (below) during his exile, carrying the surviving bodies of previous Inca emperors with him into the Vilcabamba. Even though the mummies were captured by the Spanish and brought back to Cuzco, they passed back into indigenous hands and continued to be used by the underground resistance movement for the next twenty years.

In some ways, Manco Inca is the forgotten hero of Inca history. His predecessor Atahualpa is remembered as the emperor whom Pizarro and his men first seized and ransomed for rooms full of gold and silver before executing, while the name of Túpac Amaru, the very last king, lives on for its symbolic value and has been sporadically revived as the focus for later resistance groups. But Manco was a more admirable character than either of them. At the time of the rebellion, he had survived both a brutal civil war and the Spanish conquest, which along with the epidemic had managed to lay to waste one of the world's great empires in less than 10 years. The world he had known had crumbled around him. Out of the ashes, and with some consummate political maneuvering, he somehow managed to rally a rebellion which, if not ultimately successful, at least gave heart to his people.

For a vivid eyewitness account of the Spanish conquest, try Titu Cusi's *An Inca Account of the Conquest of Peru*. As a young boy, Titu Cusi watched his father Manco Inca being hacked to death, and he later went on to lead the Incas in exile in the mountains.

INCA EXPANSIONISM

The astonishing expansion of the Incas across a few generations before the arrival of the Spanish can only partly be explained by dynamic leadership. Other factors contributed to their success: their facility for trade, their opportunism and an occasionally overlooked factor – the curious Inca laws of dynastic inheritance.

The Inca Mummies

When each Inca emperor died, his *panaca* (estate) continued to maintain his household as if he were still alive – he remained 'resident' in his old palace as a mummy, and was brought out on feast days or for the coronation of his successors; each of those successors, therefore, would have to build themselves a new palace. When a new emperor was crowned, the mummies of the whole previous dynasty were carried in procession alongside him (along with their fingernail and hair trimmings, which had been scrupulously preserved while they were alive). The sense of a 'living' dynastic succession must have been overwhelming.

At the time of the Spanish conquest there were twelve such *panacas* in existence. Each mummy would have its own litter, bearers and attendants from that *panaca*, and a pavilion would be erected for them on the main square where the coronation took place. In a ceremony that extended the traditional consumption of vast quantities of alcohol by the emperor's new subjects, the incoming *sapa inca* would also exchange toasts with each of his dead ancestors, with the mummy's attendants drinking on behalf of the corpse.

It's clear that the 'mummy lobby' had grown very powerful towards the end of the Inca empire and precipitated a bitter divide in Cuzco. The problem was that the mummies' attendants had free license to 'interpret' what the needs of the mummy might be: if he was said to need more provisions, *chicha* (fermented corn beer) and concubines to keep him happy, then these had to be provided. One suspects that the cry 'He needs more alcohol and women – *now!*' must often have reverberated around the main square of Cuzco. Huascar Inca, who had a reforming agenda during his brief tenure as emperor, tried to limit the abuses that had grown up.

It must have been particularly galling for each new emperor that the mummy of his predecessor got to keep all his land, wealth and particularly palaces, so that the incoming emperor would have to build a new one. The main square of Cuzco when the conquistadors arrived was witness to this: each side was lined with the palaces of past emperors, still inhabited by their mummies. Indeed there had been no space left for Huascar on the square itself and he had been forced, to his fury, to build a new palace on the hill above (he caused outrage at one point by threatening to confiscate one of the palaces of his dead forebears instead).

Huascar met a bad end – quietly killed in the mountains on his way to meet the Spanish, when he was supposedly being protected by an escort provided by his half-brother Atahualpa. The story has a another twist: Huascar himself belonged to the *panaca* of the dead emperor Túpac Yupanqui and so to attack him further, Atahualpa arranged for Túpac Yupanqui's mummy to be burnt – an act which must have seemed deeply sacrilegious to the Inca population.

But as well as being a colorful and striking part of the Inca world view, the mummies' influence had one important implication: the fact that the mummy of a departed Inca and his *panaca* continued to own his palaces and land even after his death was a powerful incentive for every new emperor to go out and conquer new lands.

Geography & Trade

The whole dynamic of Inca expansion was also determined by the unique geography of Peru. The great desert kingdoms of earlier millennia, such as the Paracas, the Nazca and the Moche, had arisen as a result of the riches of the sea. However, the climatic conditions that gave rise to the rich seas – colder surface waters and an upwelling from the ocean deep – also created very little rainfall, which was why the desert coast was one of the most barren on earth.

For other foodstuffs, the coastal peoples were forced to turn to the valleys and the mountains, and the mountain peoples in their turn looked to the jungles for tropical fruits and coca. These trade exchanges and the obvious advantages of an integrated market created various successive dominant cultures and, finally, Tahuantinsuyo, which contained all three of the productive zones: jungle, mountains and coast.

Tahuantinsuyo was in some ways more like a huge trading association than a formal empire. This also explained why not all Inca conquests were military: Tahuantinsuyo was more like an aggressive modern corporation that offered an overwhelmingly compelling reason to each client tribe why it had to join – consumer benefits.

The Inca technique with a potential client tribe was first to send in spies. Then, after carefully weighing up the local situation, the Incas would let the

The one territory the Incas had little success in conquering was the Amazon rainforest to their east. Their name for the disorientating network of rivers and tributaries that twisted into their empire was Amaru-Mayu, 'Great Serpent-Mother of Men.'

old chiefs know that they could still keep their positions if they joined the empire. Judicious bribery with concubines and textiles – cloth had enormous value in the Andes – further lubricated the transition.

Above all, the Incas made it clear that they would win whatever happened. Cieza de León reported one Inca emperor as saying to a prospective new tribe, 'These lands will soon be ours, like those we already possess.' This proved effective diplomacy and many tribes gave in without a fight.

The Incas were adept at incorporating such new tribes into the empire. Pachacutec had instigated a typically efficient method for achieving this. Local populations had always carried out *mita* (works of communal labor), such as the building and maintenance of the terraces and irrigation canals that kept so much of the country under cultivation.

Now large numbers of people were taken from their homelands to serve as tribute labor elsewhere, in a new system called *mitamayo*. The workers themselves were known as *mitimaes*. To take their place in their own community would come other workers from other tribes, so the *mitimaes* feared the locals, and the locals feared the *mitimaes*. It was a system of divide and rule that appealed to the Incas, and one that they were often brutal in enforcing, sending large communities into internal exile, just as Stalin was to do in Russia.

Cieza de León got lost once leaving the Inca town of Vilcas. He found that three roads seemed to point to precisely the same destination. One had been built by the emperor Pachacutec with *mita* labor, another by his son Túpac Yupanqui, and the road actually in use had been built by Huayna Capac, who clearly believed in the dangers of idle hands. It was only after several frustrating false starts that Cieza managed to get on the right one.

It's estimated that by running in relays, the Inca messengers could cover 150 miles in a day.

For the tribes who had been conquered by the Incas, the roads must have been a continual sign of the Imperial presence. As subjects, they had to contribute to the upkeep of those roads as part of the *mita* system of communal labor, even if they themselves were not always allowed to use them; these were not highways in the European sense, democratically open to all – only those on state business were allowed to use the most important roads.

The roads were even more important in a society without writing; most communication would have been done by the famous state couriers, the *chasqui*, who would run between staging posts to carry messages.

INCA RELIGION

Inca religion was a relatively loose-knit, pragmatic one – not for them any Aztec-style slaughtering of thousands of human victims.

Creation Myth

One myth gives Inca's place of origin as the Isla del Sol (Island of the Sun) on distant Lake Titicaca. The myth claimed that the original Incas, Manco Capac and his sister Mama Huaca (or Mama Ocllo), had emerged from this island, which was revered as the birthplace of the sun. It was also an island that the earlier Tiahuanaco civilization had strong connections with.

By claiming that they too had come from the Isla del Sol, the Incas were not simply making a claim for a mystical origin themselves – they also were harnessing the cultural power of an earlier mighty civilization, from whose great ruins, the Incas implied, they somehow drew some of their own strength.

The Incas & Stone

One of the first things even the most casual visitor to Peru notices is the Inca facility with stone. And if they don't, a guide will soon point it out, from the seeming ease with which great stones are slotted together at Saqsaywamán or along the streets around Cuzco's main square to the monumental buildings at Machu Picchu or in the Sacred Valley.

For the Incas, stone was far more than just a building material; they worshipped some of the region's naturally occurring boulders, such as Q'enqo, making them into *huacas* with elaborate carvings. Stone was something that reminded them of their mountain heritage.

In one creation myth, Viracocha, the Inca creator god, formed the first man out of stone. Later, when the greatest of all Inca emperors, Pachacutec, successfully defeated the rival Chanka tribe at the beginning of his imperial Inca dynasty, he was said to have summoned the very stones around Cuzco to rise up and fight with him in a desperate defense of the capital against the invaders.

While in most traditions, stone implies a notion of permanence, this is not necessarily true in the Andes. In an area of incipient volcanic activity and landslides, with recurring and violent El Niño activity over the millennia, the landscape has always been changing, and for the Incas, stone was a volatile, organic medium. This sense of stone as a life force is crucial to understanding the Inca architectural and sculptural aesthetic.

The primacy given to monumental stonework by the Incas and the earlier Andean civilizations is also remarkable. Whereas in most early civilizations, including those further north in Central America, such building only occurred after an earlier stage of experimentation with ceramics and smaller-scale fabrication, in the Andes monumental architecture predates even the earliest known pottery. Indeed, it could be argued that the Incas worked stone with more facility than they did clay, as their pottery is functional rather than memorable.

The great architectural achievement of the Incas was their ability to shape a building in the wildest and most inaccessible environment, as anyone who has seen Machu Picchu or the other Inca sites will testify.

In working stone with such facility, the Incas again claimed descent – and legitimacy – from the great Tiahuanaco civilization, whose ruined city with its monoliths was still admired across the Andes. Pachacutec

While the Incas had no writing, they did keep records on knotted cords called *quipus*. These have yet to be fully deciphered, but the hope is that they may prove to be more than just numerical accounts.

RECIPROCITY

When the Inca emperor Atahualpa first met the Spanish conquistadors, he offered them a drink from a *qeros* (drinking flask), in the traditional ceremony of reciprocal toasting that had always been practiced in the Andes. The Spanish refused, showing him a Bible instead – which Atahualpa, insulted by their refusal to drink with him, spurned. Nor had the Spanish arrived with the traditional gifts, so the Inca emperor sent them an insulting present of ducks gutted and filled with straw. This, went the inference, was what he could do to the conquistadors whenever he wanted. The Spanish, in their turn, were outraged at Atahualpa's insult to the Bible.

A more telling instance of mutual misunderstanding could not be imagined, for in the Andean world, nothing was more important than the idea of reciprocity. Returning the favor done to you was what bound people together.

We are familiar with this from Japanese and to a lesser extent Western customs ('we must invite them to our wedding as they invited us to theirs'), but in the Andes reciprocity was such a dominating cultural influence that it became even more important than military considerations. Some of the large regional centers, like Huánuco Pampa, were built not to impose military order on the local population – the European model – but to host festivals of reciprocity with the local tribes. Toasts would be drunk in matching *qeros*, and allegiances would be confirmed. It is clear that the Incas adopted this pattern from their predecessors, such as the Wari and the Nazca, who likewise built such ritual centers.

TOP FIVE INCA SITES

Ollantaytambo (p262) This is really two sites: the imposing set of terraces that rise up to the magnificent remains of a sun temple, from which Manco Inca routed the Spanish, and the town below, which preserves the street plan and waterways of an Inca settlement better than anywhere else in Peru.

Pisac (p256) Although surprisingly little is known about this site, its position overlooking the Sacred Valley perfectly demonstrates the Incas' ability to build 'organically' out of a mountain setting.

Machu Picchu (p269) No amount of visits can exhaust the infinite variety of the richest of all Inca sites. Ruth Wright's excellent *The Machu Picchu Guidebook: A Self-Guided Tour* is essential reading.

Choquequirau (p285) Positioned over a deep river canyon and probably used as a 'country estate' by Inca emperors, this site's Inca architecture shows both playfulness and grandeur. The walk up to Choquequirau from Río Apurímac is not for the fainthearted.

Raqchi (p279) In some ways the birthplace of the classic Inca architectural style, this site should on no account be missed when traveling between Cuzco and Bolivia. The use of adobe together with stone in the construction of its monumental walls is particularly striking.

---

even brought Colla stonemasons all the way from Lake Titicaca to try to replicate the look of Tiahuanaco at some of the great sites he built, such as Ollantaytambo.

A Sacred Landscape

Central to the Inca religion was the notion of *ceques*, lines that radiated out from their capital Cuzco and divided their kingdom into a 'sacred landscape'; *huacas* were placed at points along these lines, and there was an intricate system of sightlines to sacred mountains.

The very occasional human sacrifice would be made, say at the coronation of an Inca emperor, but this was an exception rather than a rule. In this situation, children called *capacochas* were sacrificed either by burial or on mountain tops (as the famous 'ice mummies' found by Johan Reinhard near Arequipa were; see p168 for more details). Before being sacrificed, these children would walk along the *ceques* that ran from Cuzco back to their home territories.

Inca Worship

Inti, the sun god, was an important deity who was intricately allied with the figure of the emperor. The festival of Inti Raymi, which marked the June Solstice, an important agricultural time, was celebrated throughout the empire. Central to the main ceremony in Cuzco was the imperial *punchao* (sun shield), an enormous image made from beaten gold, which was meant to contain the dried hearts of previous rulers.

Also important were the rise and fall of the Pleiades (the Seven Sisters), and the worship of the moon, which was conducted by priestesses; so mysterious were the rites of these female celebrants at places such as the Isla de la Luna (Island of the Moon) that even the Inca emperor was said by one commentator to be unsure of what they were.

Corn, the basic foodstuff of the empire, was also grown for ritual occasions in places including the Isla del Sol and the Sacred Valley. The *chicha* drink made from it was consumed in such quantities at these festivities that it is said there are more words for the different stages of intoxication in the Quechua language than in any other.

A common pan-Andean practice was binding the skulls of children, particularly those born to the nobility and priesthood. This created deformations such as elongated or flattened foreheads, which were considered attractive and prestigious.

THE INCA INHERITANCE

Certain aspects of the Inca worldview – the belief in cooperative labor by communities, the superb agriculture and husbandry of shared resources,

The celebrated photographer Martín Chambi was one of the first *indigenas* (indigenous people) to photograph his people from their own perspective. See his images of Cuzco at www .martinchambi.com.

and a spirituality rooted in stone and corn and the mountains – still run deep within the Quechua people, despite the intervening 300 years of Spanish rule. In the political arena, the *indigenismo* (indigenous) movement of the 20th century and various political initiatives have again sought to place the Inca empire and its beliefs at the heart of Peru's sense of national identity.

But we still know far less about the Incas and their predecessors than we do of other ancient civilizations, partly because they left no written records but also because we have come to a true study of their culture surprisingly late. Above all, it would be a mistake to underestimate the difference in outlook of the Incas and their Andean forbears to the modern world. When offered a cup by the Incas, as the conquistadors were by Atahualpa, we should choose to drink deeply from it if we want to understand them.

Food & Drink

Decades before the word 'fusion' was appropriated by food writers and celebrity chefs, the concept was being quietly and deliciously implemented in daily Peruvian cooking. Nutty Andean stews mingled with Asian stir-fry techniques. Spanish rice dishes absorbed flavors from the Amazon. And Peru's 3000km coastline provided a bounty of sublime seafood concoctions.

It is only in the past decade that the world has discovered this rich culinary tradition. High-end restaurants in international capitals now serve Peruvian staples such as ceviche (raw seafood marinated in lime juice) and pisco sour (grape brandy cocktail). Peruvian chefs have responded by launching *novoandina* (Peruvian nouvelle cuisine), taking traditional dishes to new gastronomic heights. The short of it is that you will never go hungry in Peru: from trendy boîtes in Miraflores to humble eateries in Moyobambo, this is a country devoted to the art of keeping the human palate entertained.

Peruvian chef Gastón Acurio has led a culinary trend called *novoandina*, which updates indigenous dishes with sophisticated cooking techniques. He runs the eateries Astrid y Gastón, Tanta and La Mar in Lima.

STAPLES & SPECIALTIES

Peruvians typically begin their day with bread and coffee or tea, although American-style egg breakfasts are available in most restaurants. Lunch is the main meal of the day and generally includes three courses: an appetizer, main and dessert. This is usually followed by coffee or *té de manzanilla* (chamomile tea). Dinner tends to be smaller – often consisting of just one dish and a light dessert.

Peruvian cuisine begins and ends with the humble potato. The tuber is from Peru – and it is here that hundreds of regional varieties are transformed into a mind-boggling number of dishes. Standouts include cold salad dishes such as *ocopa* (potatoes with a spicy peanut sauce), *papa a la huancaína* (potato bathed in a creamy cheese sauce) and *causa* (smashed potato salad served with salsa or seafood). Also popular is *papa rellena*, a mashed potato filled with well-seasoned ground beef and then deep-fried. Potatoes are also found in the chowdery soups known as *chupe* and in *lomo saltado*, the simple beef stir-fries that headline practically every Peruvian menu.

LIMA'S TOP FIVE EATING SPOTS *Sara Benson & Paul Hellander*

Astrid y Gastón (Map p102; ☎ 01-242 5387; Cantuarias 175, Miraflores) Renowned for its A-list *novoandina* cuisine prepared by celebrity chef Gastón Acurio, this is the place for gourmet *tiraditos* (a Japanese-influenced version of ceviche, served in thin slices and without onions) and crisp roasted duck.

Las Brujas de Cachiche (Map p102; ☎ 01-444 5310; Bolognesi 460, Miraflores) For hearty, down-home Peruvian cooking, you can't go wrong with Las Brujas, where you can dig in to deliciously prepared *lomo saltado* (strips of beef stir-fried with onions, tomatoes, potatoes and chili) and an array of seafood specialties.

El Señorío de Sulco (Map p102; ☎ 01-441 0389; Malecón Cisneros 1470, Miraflores) Critically acclaimed for 20 years, El Señorío is run by Isabel Alvarez, a noted local food writer. The sublime *criollo* dishes (spicy Peruvian fare with Spanish and African influences) are what keep the crowds coming back. The artisanal ice cream doesn't hurt either.

La Rosa Nautica (Map p102; ☎ 01-445 0149; Circuito de Playas, Miraflores) Seafood-aholics eat here! Situated at the end of Playa Costa Verde, on the historic pier, this restaurant offers half a dozen original ceviches along with a handful of specially prepared *tiraditos*.

Bircher Benner (Map pp88-9; ☎ 01-463 0276; San Felipe 720, Jesús María) For the vegetarian who has endured weeks in the hinterlands eating nothing but *tacu tacu* (pan-fried rice and beans), a stop at this innovative eatery is practically required. On the menu: imaginative veggie dishes such as mushroom ceviche.

While the potato is the backbone of Peruvian cuisine, ceviche is the star. An allegedly aphrodisiacal concoction of fish, shrimp or other seafood marinated in lime juice, onions and chili peppers, it is typically served with wedges of boiled corn and sweet potato. *Tiradito* is a Japanese-influenced version, with thinly sliced fish and no onions. (These dishes are glorious, but they can be devastating on the stomach if not fresh. It is not recommended to eat ceviche from street stands.)

Seafood is a major facet of Peruvian cuisine. Fish is prepared dozens of ways: *al ajo* (bathed in garlic), *frito* (fried in batter) or *a la chorrillana* (cooked in white wine, tomatoes, garlic and onions). Similarly, crab, mussels, clams and scallops appear regularly in soups, stews and Spanish omelets. *Choros a la chalaca* (mussels in fresh corn salsa) and *conchitas a la parmesana* (scallops in cheese) are coastal favorites. Many dishes – from steak to chicken – are served *a lo macho* (in seafood sauce).

Soups are extraordinarily popular, especially in the chilly highlands, where these tend to be a generous, gut-filling experience. *Chupe de camarones* (shrimp chowder) is a spicy favorite, along with *sopa a la criolla* (a milder, creamy noodle soup with beef and vegetables).

Among the more common mains are *lomo saltado,* along with *ají de gallina* (shredded chicken in a spicy walnut sauce) and *picante de pollo* (spicy chicken stew in turmeric and cilantro). The Latin American staple of *arroz con pollo* (chicken with rice) is found in several guises, some with tomato as a base, others with cilantro. *Aguaditos* are soupy risottos made with chicken, seafood or beef.

Desserts tend to be diabetes-inducing concoctions. *Suspiro limeño* is the most famous: *manjar blanco* (caramel pudding) topped with sweet meringue. Also favored are *alfajores* (cookie sandwiches with caramel) and 'king kong' (giant cookie sandwiches). *Crema volteada* (flan) is also very popular. For something fruitier, try *mazamorra morada,* a purple-corn pudding with fresh fruit.

DRINKS

All of the main soft drink brands are available here, though the locals have a passion for the bubble-gum-flavored Inca Kola, the nuclear-yellow national favorite. Fresh fruit juices are also available, as are traditional drinks such as *chicha morada,* a sweet, noncarbonated beverage made from purple corn. *Agua con/sin gas* (carbonated/noncarbonated water) is available in restaurants, corner shops and supermarkets. Don't drink unpurified tap water – it will make you sick.

Though Peru exports coffee to the world, the locals drink it instant. Most restaurants provide hot water and a jar of Nescafé. Others serve a liquid concentrate diluted with hot milk or water. (It looks like soy sauce, so check before pouring it into your milk – or over your rice.) In more cosmopolitan cities, cafés serving espresso have popped up as well. Tea and *mates* (herbal teas) are widely available. The latter includes *manzanilla* (chamomile), *menta* (mint) and *mate de coca,* a coca-leaf tea. (It won't get you high, but it does help with high-altitude acclimatization.)

Local beers are good and generally inexpensive. The best-known brands are Pilsen Callao, Brahma, Cristal and Cusqueña, all of which are light lagers. Arequipeña and Trujillana are regional brews served in and around those cities. Some brands, such as Pilsen, offer *cerveza negra* (dark beer) as well.

In the Andes, homemade *chicha* (corn beer) is very popular. The brewing process, which has remained unchanged since pre-Columbian times, is begun by chewing and spitting corn into a vat. This is then sealed and stored for several weeks to allow for fermentation. *Chicha,* which tastes bitter, is

---

Today's potatoes can be traced back to a single progenitor from Peru. The tuber has been cultivated in the Andes for at least 7000 years.

The origin of the word 'ceviche' is unclear. Some say it's derived from the Spanish word for pickle, escabeche, or the Quechua word for the dish, siwichi.

The Exotic Kitchens of Peru by noted food writer Copeland Marks is not only a great cookbook – from hors d'oeuvres to dessert – but an excellent guide to understanding the origins and history of Peru's complex cooking.

POUR ON THE PISCO *Carolina A Miranda*

It is the national beverage: pisco, the omnipresent grape brandy served at events from the insignificant to the momentous. Production dates back to the early days of the Spanish colony in Ica, where it was distilled on private haciendas and then sold to sailors making their way through the port of Pisco. By the mid-20th century, it was a staple in every Peruvian bar.

In recent years, it's become a continuing source of friction with Chile, Peru's neighbor to the south. It turns out that pisco has long been manufactured there and the Chileans consider it *their* national drink as well. Combine this with the fact that the two countries are still sore over a war they fought in the 1880s and you get a lot of squabbling over who has the right to call their brandy 'pisco.' Peru has history on its side. The first known reference to pisco was in the will of an Ica landowner in 1631. But it is Chile who has the stronger marketing muscle: it sells more than six times as much internationally than Peru.

For me (I am of both Peruvian and Chilean origin), it doesn't matter where the heck pisco comes from – as long as it keeps on coming. The liquor has an uncomplicated, light, woody taste. When made into a sour, it is smoother and more refreshing than any margarita.

My father, who is from Chiclayo, has – thankfully – agreed to share the family recipe:

Felipe's Pisco Sour

1 part freshly squeezed lime juice
3 parts pisco
ice
sugar to taste
1 teaspoon egg white (for frothiness)
Angostura bitters

Combine the lime juice and pisco in a blender. Add sugar to taste. (I use less than one part.) Add plenty of ice and blend. Spoon in egg white and blend again. Serve immediately in highball or rocks glasses. Add a drop of bitters to the top for decoration. *¡Salud!*

low in alcoholic content and is found almost exclusively at small markets and private homes. A red flag posted near the door indicates that *chicha* is available. Pack the Pepto-Bismol for this one.

Local wines aren't anything exceptional, but they have become better over the years. The best local labels are Tacama, Ocucaje and Vista Alegre from the Ica Valley. Also very popular is pisco (see above).

CELEBRATIONS

Every Peruvian town has some celebratory day in which everyone pours into the streets to drink, dance and eat – and then drink some more. These events are usually centered on religious holidays, such as Carnaval (Shrove Tuesday), or civil ones, such as Fiestas Patrias (National Independence Days). For these occasions, entire marketplaces spring up in town squares selling *chicharrones* (pork cracklings), *lechón* (suckling pig) and plenty of beer. During the month of October, bakeries are stocked with *turrón de Doña Pepa,* a honey-laced cake eaten in honor of El Señor de los Milagros (the Christ of Miracles).

In the Andes, festivals are infused with indigenous foodstuffs such as *chicha* and roasted *cuy* (guinea pig). For special occasions and weddings, families will gather to make *pachamanca:* a mix of marinated meats, vegetables, cheese, chilies and fragrant herbs that are buried in the ground and baked on hot rocks. This pre-Columbian tradition has its roots in nature worship: by using the earth – or Pachamama – to cook, it is being honored as well.

For hip entertaining, pick up *Latin Chic* by Isabel González and Carolina Buia. The recipes are from all over the Americas, but Peruvian flourishes abound: from a spicy ceviche to a sticky-sweet *alfajor* cookie with caramel.

WHERE TO EAT & DRINK

For the most part, restaurants in Peru are a community affair, and local places will cater to a combination of families, tourists, teenagers and packs of chatty businessmen. *Almuerzo* (lunch), served at around 1pm, is the main meal of the day. This is when many eateries serve a *menú*, the set meal of the day, consisting of an *entrada* (appetizer), *segundo* (main course) and *postre* (dessert). This is generally good value. (Note: if you request the *menú*, you'll get the special. If you want the menu, ask for *la carta*.) In tiny towns, the *menú* may be all that is available.

Peru is also home to an endless number of Chinese eateries known as *chifas*, which generally serve food of Cantonese origin. At lunch, they offer a variety of *menús* for all tastes and budgets. Appetizers consist of *wantan frito* (fried wontons) or *enrollado con verduras* (spring rolls), followed by a main course of stir-fried chicken, beef or seafood with rice or noodles.

Outside of the tourist areas, an early *desayuno* (breakfast) can be problematic since most restaurants don't open until at least 8am. If you need to eat early, high-end hotel restaurants often have more flexible hours.

Cena (dinner) is eaten late, and restaurants, which may be dead at 7:30pm, come alive at 9pm. In tiny, remote towns, however, everything may be closed by 9pm.

Quick Eats

Peruvians love to eat on the street and the most popular items are *anticuchos* (shish kebabs), ceviche and *choclo con queso* (boiled corn with cheese). Also popular – and quite delicious – are *picarones* (fritters). Street stands can be extraordinarily cheap and efficient; they can also be spectacularly unhygienic. Approach with caution.

A safer bet would be the many *pollerías* (restaurant specializing in roast chicken) that can be found in just about every town. These are quick, cheap and tasty, too. Bakeries are also an excellent way to eat well and maintain a tight budget. Most sell empanadas (meat or cheese turnovers), cakes and bread – and some sell coffee as well.

VEGETARIANS & VEGANS

In a country where most people survive on potatoes, there can be a general befuddlement over why anyone would choose to be vegetarian. This attitude is changing, however, and many large cities and tourist-heavy towns have restaurants that are strictly veggie. Among other things, these places serve popular national dishes, such as *lomo saltado*, using soy substitutes. Vegetarian restaurants are found primarily in Lima and cities such as Cuzco and Arequipa.

It is possible, however, to eat veggie at the average restaurant. Many of the potato salads, such as *papas a la huancaína*, *ocopa* and *causa* are made without meat, as is *palta a la jardinera*, an avocado stuffed with vegetable salad. *Sopa de verduras* (vegetable soup), *tortilla* (Spanish omelet) and *tacu tacu* (beans and rice mixed together) are other options. If there isn't anything veggie on the menu, just ask. Most restaurants will make accommodations. Be sure to ask specifically for *un plato vegetariano* (a vegetarian dish). The term *sin carne* (without meat) refers only to red meat or pork and you could end up with chicken or seafood instead. *Chifas* are always a good bet since they generally always feature a meat-free *menú*.

Vegans will have a harder time. An overwhelming number of dishes in Peru are cooked with eggs, cheese or milk – or a combination of all three. Self-catering is perhaps the best option; markets have wide selections of grains, legumes, fruits and vegetables.

Inka Kola, the neon-yellow soft drink, outsells global behemoths Coke and Pepsi in Peru.

In 2003 President Alejandro Toledo designated the first Saturday of every February 'Pisco Sour Day' as a way to promote the Peruvian liquor.

The dessert *turrón de Doña Pepa* was first made by a slave woman, in 1800, to honor the Christ of Miracles after she regained the use of her paralyzed arms.

TRAVEL YOUR TASTEBUDS

In the Andes, nutty, spicy stews are de rigueur but it is the roasted *cuy* (guinea pig) that grabs every traveler's attention (see A Brief History of the Guinea Pig, p432). On the Pacific coast, where seafood reigns supreme, ceviche attracts the most inspection. (Though most people assume it's raw fish – it isn't. The fish is 'cooked' by the lime juice through a process of oxidation.) The Amazon region adds tropical dashes to the national menu. You might sink your teeth into grilled piranhas and monkey soup. But keep an eye peeled for *juanes*, banana-leaf tamales made of rice, chicken and garlic.

EATING WITH KIDS

If you're traveling with the tots, you'll find that 'kids' meals' (small portions at small prices) are not normally offered in restaurants. However, Peruvian establishments are quite family-friendly. Most restaurants have simple grilled foods, such as *bistec* (steak) and *pollo a la plancha* (chicken). Other basic items include cheese and ham sandwiches, pasta and hamburgers. Among Peruvian kids, the perennial dinnertime favorite is *arroz con huevo frito* (rice with a fried egg).

If traveling with an infant, stock up on formula and baby food before heading into rural areas. Avocados are safe and nutritious, and can be served to children as young as six months old. Bananas are found just about everywhere and make a great snack, mashed or whole. Young children should avoid water and ice as they are more susceptible to stomach illnesses.

For other tips on traveling with tykes, see p499.

The most sumptuous recipes and photographs of Peruvian cooking are available in Tony Custer's and Miguel Etchepare's hardback tome *The Art of Peruvian Cuisine*. Log on to their website www .artperucuisine.com for a preview.

HABITS & CUSTOMS

Meals in Peru are a conversational, leisurely affair. Other than in the bustling business-district restaurants in downtown Lima, don't expect anyone to be in much of a hurry – including your server.

When sitting down, it is polite to say *buenos días* or *buenas tardes* to the server. And when dining with locals, wish them *buen provecho* (bon appétit) before eating. Tips of 10% or more are customary at finer restaurants, but not expected at casual dining establishments such as *pollerías*. More upscale places will also include the *propina* (tip) in the bill – along with an 18% tax.

Do note that if you invite the locals out to eat, the expectation is that you will pay. Likewise, if you are invited to someone's home, it is considered good manners to bring a gift. Flowers, dessert or pisco are customary items.

Alpaca meat tastes like beef but has only half the fat.

EAT YOUR WORDS

The following is a list of foods, drinks and other useful culinary words and phrases, with their English translations and pronunciations. These should provide a good start to your comprehension of Peruvian menus. For further pronunciation guidelines, see the Language chapter (p537).

Useful Phrases

I'd like ...
    Quisiera ...   kee·*sye*·ra ...

I'd like the set lunch, please.
    Quisiera el menú por favor.   kee·*sye*·ra el me·*noo* por fa·*vor*

I'm a vegetarian.
    Soy vegetariano/a. (m/f)   soy ve·he·ta·*rya*·no/a

The menu/bill, please.
    La carta/cuenta, por favor.   la *kar*·ta/*kwen*·ta por fa·*vor*

Is service included in the bill?

¿El servicio está incluido en la cuenta?   el ser·*vee*·syo es·*ta* een·*klwee*·do en la *kwen*·ta

Thank you, that was delicious.

Muchas gracias, estaba buenísimo.   moo·chas *gra*·syas es·*ta*·ba bwe·*nee*·see·mo

breakfast
desayuno   de·sa·*yoo*·no

lunch
almuerzo   al·*mwer*·so

dinner
cena   *se*·na

(cheap) restaurant
restaurante (barato)   re·stow·*ran*·te (ba·*ra*·to)

set meal
(el) menú   el me·*noo*

Food Glossary

agua con/sin gas	*a*·gwa kon/seen gas	water (carbonated/noncarbonated)
agua mineral	*a*·gwa mee·ne·*ral*	water (mineral)
agua potable	*a*·gwa po·*ta*·ble	water (drinking)
aguardiente	a·gwar·*dyen*·te	cane alcohol
ají de gallina	a·*hee* de ga·*lee*·na	a spicy stew of shredded chicken with walnuts served over potatoes and rice
ají	a·*hee*	chili condiments
alfajor	al·*fa*·khor	a cookie sandwich of thick, sweet caramel
almejas	al·*me*·khas	clams
anticucho	an·tee·*koo*·cho	shish kebab
arroz	a·*ros*	rice
atún	ah·*toon*	tuna fish; generally canned
azúcar	a·*soo*·kar	sugar
bistec	bee·*stek*	steak
cabro, cabrito	ka·bro, ka·*bree*·to	goat
calamares	ka·la·*ma*·res	squid
caldo	*kal*·do	broth
camarones	ka·ma·*ro*·nes	shrimp
camote	ka·*mo*·te	sweet potato
cancha	*kan*·cha	roasted, dried corn kernels eaten like nuts
cangrejo	kan·*gre*·kho	crab
carne	*kar*·ne	meat
carne de res	*kar*·ne de res	beef
cau cau	kow kow	a tripe stew served with beans and potatoes over rice
causa	*kaw*·sa	a cold, smashed potato salad topped with some salsa or seafood
cecina	se·*see*·na	jungle dish of dehydrated pork
cerdo, chancho	ser·do, chan·cho	pork
cerveza	ser·*ve*·sa	beer
ceviche	se·*vee*·che	raw seafood marinated in lime juice
charqui	char·kee	beef jerky; biltong
chaufa, chaulafan	chow·fa, chow·la·*fan*	fried rice (Chinese style)
chicha	*chee*·cha	fermented corn beer
chicha morada	*chee*·cha mo·*ra*·da	a sweet, non-alcoholic purple corn drink

chicharrones	chee·cha·*ro*·nes	pork cracklings
chirimoya	chee·ree·mo·ya	a white-fleshed highland fruit served on its own or in orange juice
choclo	cho·klo	corn on the cob
choclo con queso	cho·klo kon *ke*·so	boiled corn with cheese
choros	cho·ros	mussels
choros a la chalaca	cho·ros a la cha·*la*·ka	steamed, fresh mussels served in a tomato and corn salsa
chupe	*choo*·pe	a hearty chowder-style soup generally made with seafood
conchitas	kon·*chee*·tas	scallops
cordero	kor·*de*·ro	mutton
cuy	kwee	guinea pig
empanadas	em·pa·*na*·das	meat and/or cheese turnovers
ensalada	en·sa·*la*·da	salad
estofado	es·to·*fa*·do	stew
farína	fa·*ree*·na	muesli-like yucca concoction eaten fried or in lemonade
frijoles	free·*ho*·les	beans
frutas	*froo*·tas	fruit
galleta de soda	ga·*ye*·ta de *so*·da	soda cracker
gallina	ga·*lee*·na	chicken
helado	e·*la*·do	ice cream
huacatay	wa·*ka*·tay	a mintlike herb frequently used in sauces
huevos	*we*·vos	eggs
huevos fritos/revueltos	*we*·vos free·tos/re·*vwel*·tos	fried/scrambled eggs
jamón	kha·*mon*	ham
juane	*khwa*·ne	jungle dish of steamed rice with fish or chicken, wrapped in a banana leaf
jugo	*hoo*·go	juice
langosta	lan·*gos*·ta	lobster
leche	*le*·che	milk
lechón	le·*chon*	suckling pig
licór	lee·*kor*	liquor
locro	*lo*·kro	meat and vegetable stew
lomo	*lo*·mo	beef
lomo saltado	*lo*·mo sal·*ta*·do	strips of beef stir-fried with onions, tomatoes, potatoes and chili
manjar blanco	man·khar *blan*·ko	caramel
mantequilla	man·te·*kee*·ya	butter
manzana	mahn·*sah*·nah	apple
maracuyá	ma·ra·koo·*ya*	passion fruit
mariscos	ma·*rees*·kos	seafood
mate	ma·*teh*	herbal tea
mazamorra morada	ma·sa·*mo*·rra mo·*ra*·da	a sweet, purple corn pudding served for dessert
mora	*mo*·ra	blackberry
naranja	na·*ran*·kha	orange
ocopa	o·*ko*·pa	potatoes served with a spicy, creamy peanut sauce
pachamanca	pa·cha·*man*·ka	meat, potatoes and vegetables cooked in an earthen 'oven' of hot rocks
palta	*pal*·ta	avocado
pan	pan	bread

papa a la huancaína	*pa·pa a la hwan·kay·na*	boiled potato topped with a creamy cheese sauce
papa rellena	*pa·pa re·ye·na*	a deep-fried, mashed potato filled with ground beef
papas fritas	*pa·pas free·tas*	french fries
parrillada	*pa·ree·ya·da*	grilled meats
pastel	*pas·tel*	cake
pescado	*pes·ka·do*	fish
pescado a la chorrillana	*pes·ka·do a la cho·ree·ya·na*	a fish filet served with a sauté of onions, garlic and tomatoes
picante de pollo	*pee·kan·te de po·yo*	spicy chicken stew made with turmeric and cilantro
picarones	*pee·ka·ro·nes*	a sweet fritter often served with molasses syrup
piña	*pee·nya*	pineapple
plátano	*pla·ta·no*	plantain
pollo	*po·lyo*	chicken
postre	*pos·tre*	dessert
queso	*ke·so*	cheese
quinua	*kee·noo·a*	a highly nutritious, protein-rich grain of the high Andes
rocoto	*ro·ko·to*	a spicy hot pepper resembling a red bell pepper
rocoto relleno	*ro·ko·to re·ye·no*	a *rocoto* stuffed with rice and meat
sandía	*san·dee·a*	watermelon
seco de cabrito	*se·ko de ka·bree·to*	roasted kid goat
solterito arequipeño	*sol·te·ree·to a·re·kee·pe·nyo*	a fava bean salad typical of Arequipa
sopa, chupe	*so·pa, choo·pe*	soup
sopa a la criolla	*so·pa a la kree·ol·la*	a mildly spiced, creamy noodle soup with beef and peppers
sudado	*soo·da·do*	fish (or seafood) soup or stew
suprema de pollo	*soo·pre·ma de po·yo*	breaded chicken fillet
suspiro limeño	*soos·pee·ro lee·me·nyo*	a caramel meringue dessert
tacu tacu	*ta·koo ta·koo*	pan-fried rice and beans served with steak, seafood or fried eggs
tallarines	*ta·ya·ree·nes*	noodles
tamal	*ta·mal*	corn dough stuffed with meat, beans or chilies
toronja	*to·ron·kha*	grapefruit
torta	*tor·ta*	cake
tortilla	*tor·tee·ya*	Spanish omelet
trucha	*troo·cha*	trout
verduras	*ver·doo·ras*	vegetables
vino	*vee·no*	wine

Lima

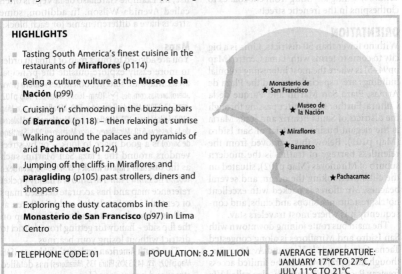

It's wacky, it's wonderful – yet it sometimes feels like the Wild West. Just over eight million inhabitants crowd into Peru's capital, giving it an edge that few other cities in South America have. The second-largest desert city in the world, Lima has shantytowns that look like something from the developing world, yet the malls and business districts of its coastal suburbs are Europe away from home.

Few travelers linger long in this bustling, fast-moving modern metropolis, yet Lima has a lot on offer. Peru's capital city is an ever-evolving conurbation imbued with fascinating contrasts and nuances that can transport you in no time from the waning splendor of colonial architecture to pre-Inca pyramids to ultramodern shopping malls. In the midst of these, you'll find many of the country's best museums, historic churches and stately mansions.

And as if sightseeing was not enough, Lima justifiably boasts some of the finest dining opportunities on the continent – from fresh seafood in suave seaside restaurants to hole-in-the-wall eateries where lunch costs under a dollar. You want sports? Try paragliding off the cliffs of Miraflores, surfing off the cliff-backed beaches of Barranco and Costa Verde, or practicing your cycling, tennis or even cricket. Nightlife? The bars and clubs of Miraflores and Barranco provide entertainment to a city that never sleeps.

Lima will appeal to you in different ways. It may take a while, but your investment in exploring one of South America's happening cities will pay off.

HIGHLIGHTS

- Tasting South America's finest cuisine in the restaurants of **Miraflores** (p114)
- Being a culture vulture at the **Museo de la Nación** (p99)
- Cruising 'n' schmoozing in the buzzing bars of **Barranco** (p118) – then relaxing at sunrise
- Walking around the palaces and pyramids of arid **Pachacamac** (p124)
- Jumping off the cliffs in Miraflores and **paragliding** (p105) past strollers, diners and shoppers
- Exploring the dusty catacombs in the **Monasterio de San Francisco** (p97) in Lima Centro

Monasterio de
★ San Francisco

Museo de
★ la Nación

★ Miraflores

★ Barranco

★ Pachacamac

| ■ TELEPHONE CODE: 01 | ■ POPULATION: 8.2 MILLION | ■ AVERAGE TEMPERATURE: JANUARY 17°C TO 27°C, JULY 11°C TO 21°C |

HISTORY

Lima was dubbed the City of Kings when it was founded by Francisco Pizarro in 1535 on the Catholic feast day of Epiphany, or the Day of the Kings. A university opened in 1551, and Lima became the Americas' seat of the Spanish Inquisition in 1569. The city grew quickly and was the continent's richest and most important town during early colonial times, though this all changed in 1746, when a disastrous earthquake wiped out most of the city. However, rebuilding was rapid, and most of the old colonial buildings still to be seen here date from after the earthquake. Following the wars of independence from Spain in the 1820s, other cities were crowned as capitals of the newly independent states, and Lima's importance as a colonial center faded.

For almost 400 years, Lima was a relatively small city. However, a population explosion began in the 1920s with an influx of rural poor from throughout Peru, especially the highlands. The urban population of 173,000 in 1919 more than tripled in the next 20 years, and since 1940 there has been a further 13-fold increase. The vast numbers of migrants spawned the *pueblos jovenes* (young towns) that surround the capital, many of which still lack electricity, water and adequate sanitation. Jobs are scarce, though entrepreneurial energy is strong; many work as *ambulantes* (street vendors) selling anything from chocolates to clothespins in the frenetic streets.

ORIENTATION

With no fewer than 50 districts, Lima is a big city to come to terms with. Lima Centro (Map pp94–5) is where the most interesting colonial buildings are, especially around the Plaza de Armas, Plaza San Martín and Parque de la Cultura. Further south, after passing through the districts of Santa Beatriz and Jesús María is the elegant business district of San Isidro (Map p101). Below this, removed from the relentless barrage of traffic, is the modern suburb of Miraflores (Map p102), situated on the cliffs overlooking the ocean, and several beaches. Miraflores is packed with excellent hotels, restaurants, shops and clubs, and consequently it is where most travelers stay.

The main bus route joining downtown with San Isidro and Miraflores is along congested Tacna, Garcilaso de la Vega and Av Arequipa, though taxis prefer to take the limited access freeway Paseo de la República, also called Vía Expresa, which is sunken below ground level and is nicknamed *el zanjón* (the ditch).

Further south of Miraflores is the small cliff-top community of Barranco (Map p104). An artists and poets' colony with up-and-coming accommodations and the liveliest nightlife in town, Barranco also boasts attractive 19th-and early-20th-century architecture around El Puente de los Suspiros (Bridge of Sighs).

Many of Lima's excellent museums are scattered through other suburbs, including Pueblo Libre (Map pp88–9) to the west of San Isidro, and San Borja and Monterrico (Map pp88–9) to the east of the city centre.

The international and domestic airport is in Callao (Map pp88–9) – about 12km west of downtown or 16km northwest of Miraflores – but there is no expressway connecting the airport with the rest of the city. Callao also features Lima's port, naval base and an old colonial fort.

Street Names

The Spanish built downtown Lima in the colonial style, with streets in a checkerboard pattern surrounding the central Plaza de Armas. Though street numbers are easy to follow, jumping to the next 100 for each *cuadra* (block; ie '*cuadra* 5' will be numbered from 500 to 599), street names can be confusing for visitors. Both old and new names are in use; for example Garcilaso de la Vega is often called Avenida Wilson. In addition, some streets have a different name for each block.

Maps

You are advised to buy a map of Lima in order to more easily explore outside the principal areas. Maps are sold in bookstores – **Ibero** (www.iberolibrerias.com.pe; 🕙 10am-10pm; Benavides **Map p102**; ☎ 242 2798; Alfredo Benavides 500, Miraflores; Larco **Map p102**; Av José Larco 199, Miraflores; LarcoMar **Map p102**; Malecon de la Reserva 610, Miraflores; Surco Monterrey 170, Santiago de Surco) is a good place to look – or by street vendors around the Plaza San Martín, such as the **Caseta el Viajero Kiosk** (☎ 423 5436; Jirón Belén 1002). The *Lima Plan Turistico* is a handy pocket reference map and has accurate detailed maps of central Lima, San Isidro and Miraflores, as well as a broader metropolitan Lima map on the flip side – handy for getting from district to district without losing your bearings.

The **South American Explorers' clubhouse** (SAE; Map p102; ☎ 445 3306; Piura 135, Miraflores) has detailed street and bus maps of Lima.

INFORMATION
Bookstores
Crisol (Map p102; ☎ 221 1010; Av Santa Cruz 816, Miraflores; ⊗ 10am-11pm daily) A big and showy bookstore, with some novels and travel guides in English and French.
El Virrey (Map pp94-5; ☎ 440 0607; Dasso 141, Lima Centro; ⊗ 10am-6:30pm Mon-Sat) This place has a limited selection of glossy travel books.
Ibero (www.iberolibrerias.com.pe; ⊗ 10am-10pm); Benavides (Map p102; ☎ 242 2798; Alfredo Benavides 500, Miraflores); Surco (Monterrey 170, Santiago de Surco); Larco (Map p102; Av José Larco 199, Miraflores); LarcoMar (Map p102; Malecon de la Reserva 610, Miraflores) A modern bookstore chain with a modest but catholic selection of English-language classic texts and modern novels plus a decent range of Lonely Planet titles.
South American Explorers' clubhouse (Map p102; ☎ 445 3306; Piura 135, Miraflores) SAE members can access Lima's best selection of English-language guidebooks; there's also a members-only book exchange.
Zeta (Map p102; ☎ 446 5139; booksell@zetabook.com .pe; ⊗ 10am-8pm Mon-Sat); Espinar (Av Espinar 219, Miraflores); LarcoMar (Malecon de la Reserva 610, Miraflores) A small but helpful shop, this has a varied foreign-language selection plus a few Lonely Planet titles.

Cultural Centers
All of the following present a variety of plays, film screenings, art shows and more at irregular intervals. Check the newspapers or the *Peru Guide* for details.
Alianza Francesa (Map p102; ☎ 241 7014; Av Arequipa 4598, Miraflores) Has French-language cultural events.
Goethe Institut (☎ 433 3180; Jirón Nazca 722, Jesús María) For German speakers.
Instituto Cultural Peruano-Norteamericano (http://icpnacultural.perucultural.org.pe in Spanish); Lima Centro (Map pp94-5; ☎ 428 3530; Cuzco 446); Miraflores (Map p102; ☎ 241 1940; Av Arequipa 4798) Offers US newspapers, a library and Spanish courses, plus visiting art displays.
Peruvian-British Cultural Association (www.britan ico.edu.pe); Miraflores (Map p102; ☎ 447 1135; Jirón Bellavista 531); San Isidro (Map p101; ☎ 221 7550; Av Arequipa 3495) British newspapers and English-language books are available in the library here.

Emergency
Policía de Turismo (Poltur; Map pp94-5; ☎ 424 2053; Pasaje Tambo de Belén 106, Pachitea, Lima Centro; ⊗ 24hr) Poltur gives advice and assistance on anything from robberies to rabies. English-speaking police are usually available, and will provide reports to make insurance claims or get a traveler's-check refund. It's southwest of Plaza San Martín.

Policía head office (Map pp88-9; ☎ 460 0921; Moore 268, Magdalena del Mar; ⊗ 24 hr)

Immigration
For general information about visas and stay extensions, see p513. See p503 for a list of embassies in Lima.

Go first thing in the morning to the **oficina de migraciónes** (immigration office; Map pp94-5; ☎ 330 4144; España 734, Breña; ⊗ 8am-1pm Mon-Fri) if you want to get your tourist-card extension (US$20) on the same day. The specially stamped paperwork can be bought beforehand at the neighboring Banco de la Nación (US$7). You will also need your passport and the immigration slip you received upon entry into Peru (it's more time consuming and expensive if you've lost it). You may be asked to show a ticket out of the country, or prove that you have sufficient funds – the more affluent you look, the less hassle you'll have.

Internet Access
Many hotels have internet access. The following places have fast public access for about US$0.60 an hour.
Dragon Fans Internet (Map p102; ☎ 446 6814; Pasaje Tarata 230, Miraflores; ⊗ 24 hr)
Internet Mundonet (Map pp94-5; Ancash, Lima Centro)
Telefónica-Perú (Map p102; Alfredo Benavides cuadra 4, Miraflores; ⊗ 24 hr)

Laundry
Many hotels can have your laundry done for you – the more expensive the hotel, the more expensive the laundry. Many *lavanderías* (laundries) only do dry cleaning, and those that wash and dry may charge per item rather than by weight. Most have overnight laundry; some will have it ready the same day if it's left first thing in the morning.
KTO (Map pp94-5; ☎ 332 9035; España 481, Lima Centro; per kg US$1.40; ⊗ 7am-8pm Mon-Sat)
Lavandaria 40 Minutos (Map p102; ☎ 446 5928; Av Espinar 154, Miraflores; loads up to 4kg US$4.20; ⊗ 8am-8pm Mon-Sat, 9am-1pm Sun)
Lavandería Neptuno (Map p104; ☎ 477 4472; Av Grau 912, Barranco; per kg US$2)
Press To (Map pp94-5; ☎ 426 2660; Cuzco, Lima Centro; per item US$1.40-3; ⊗ 9am-10pm Mon-Sat, 9am-9pm Sun) In the Metro supermarket.
Servirap (Map p102; ☎ 241 0759; cnr Schell & Grimaldo del Solar, Miraflores; per kg US$2.30; ⊗ 8am-10pm Mon-Sat, 9am-6pm Sun) Also has self-service.

LIMA

METROPOLITAN LIMA

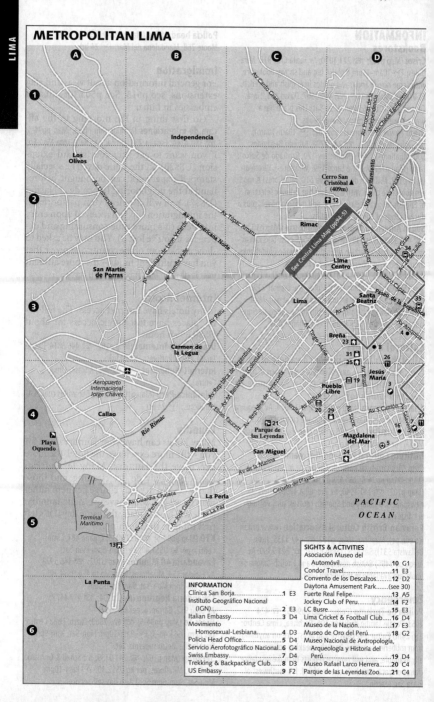

Independencia

Los Olivos

Cerro San Cristóbal ▲ (409m)

🏛 12

Av Panamericana Norte

Av Túpac Amaru

Rímac

See Central Lima Map (pp94-5)

San Martín de Porras

Lima Centro

Santa Beatriz

Lima

🏛 34

Breña

23 🏛

35

Carmen de la Legua

31 🏛
25 🏛

26

8

Aeropuerto Internacional Jorge Chávez

Callao

🏛 19

Jesús María

3

Río Rímac

21 🏛
Parque de las Leyendas

Pueblo Libre

20
29

Av S Carrión

16

27

Magdalena del Mar

5

Playa Oquendo

Bellavista

San Miguel

24

Av de la Marina

PACIFIC OCEAN

Terminal Marítimo

13 🏛

La Perla

Av La Paz

Circuito de Playas

La Punta

SIGHTS & ACTIVITIES
Asociación Museo del Automóvil	10 G1
Condor Travel	11 E3
Convento de los Descalzos	12 D2
Daytona Amusement Park	(see 30)
Fuerte Real Felipe	13 A5
Jockey Club of Peru	14 F2
LC Busre	15 E3
Lima Cricket & Football Club	16 D4
Museo de la Nación	17 E3
Museo de Oro del Perú	18 G2
Museo Nacional de Antropología, Arqueología y Historia del Perú	19 D4
Museo Rafael Larco Herrera	20 C4
Parque de las Leyendas Zoo	21 C4

INFORMATION
Clínica San Borja	1 E3
Instituto Geográfico Nacional (IGN)	2 E3
Italian Embassy	3 D4
Movimiento Homosexual-Lesbiana	4 D3
Policia Head Office	5 D4
Servicio Aerofotográfico Nacional	6 G4
Swiss Embassy	7 D4
Trekking & Backpacking Club	8 D3
US Embassy	9 F2

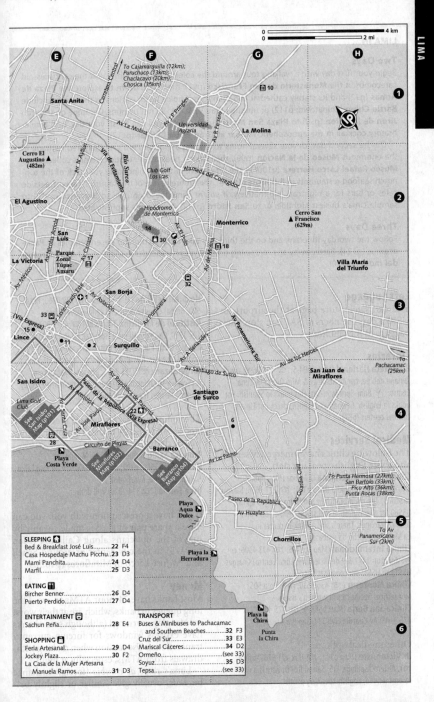

SLEEPING
Bed & Breakfast José Luis	22 F4
Casa Hospedaje Machu Picchu	23 D3
Mami Panchita	24 D4
Marfil	25 D3

EATING
| Bircher Benner | 26 D4 |
| Puerto Perdido | 27 D4 |

ENTERTAINMENT
| Sachun Peña | 28 E4 |

SHOPPING
Feria Artesanal	29 D4
Jockey Plaza	30 F2
La Casa de la Mujer Artesana	
Manuela Ramos	31 D3

TRANSPORT
Buses & Minibuses to Pachacamac	
and Southern Beaches	32 F3
Cruz del Sur	33 E3
Mariscal Cáceres	34 D2
Ormeño	(see 33)
Soyuz	35 D3
Tepsa	(see 33)

LIMA IN...

Two Days

Begin your first day with a walking tour around the colonial heart of Lima. Visit the centuries-old catacombs at the **Monasterio de San Francisco** (p97), then head down to explore the **Plaza de Armas** (p92) and its stately cathedral and mansions. Choice lunch options in the center include **Barrio Chino** (Chinatown; p112) or unique **L'Eau Vive** (p113), run by nuns. Continue on through **Jirón de la Union** (p98) to **Plaza San Martín** (p98), where you can finish your day with a celebratory cocktail in the atmospheric old bar at **Gran Hotel Bolívar** (p117).

On the second day, devote several hours to getting a grip on Peru's multilayered heritage in the enormous **Museo de la Nación** (p99), then take a peek at the erotic ceramics collection at **Museo Rafael Larco Herrera** (p100) in the afternoon. In the evening, take your pick of the top-notch seafood restaurants in **Miraflores** (p114), then retire to one of the suburb's many streetside cafés or bars for a nightcap. Alternatively, if you're game, head on over to **Barranco** (p118) to sample Lima's busiest nightlife, or to **San Isidro** (p117) for its most sophisticated.

Three Days

Follow the two-day itinerary, and on the third day take a trip to the arid desert temples at **Pachacamac** (p124). Barter away any remaining time buying handicrafts in Miraflores' huge **Mercado del Indios** (p120).

Left Luggage

You can safely store bags at the airport for US$6 a day. Members of SAE can store their baggage at the clubhouse.

Libraries

Biblioteca Nacional (Map pp94-5; ☎ 428 7690; www .binape.gob.pe; cnr Av Abancay & Miró Quesada, Lima Centro; ☺ 8am-8pm Mon-Sat) Has books in Spanish. For books in English, German and French, check out Lima's cultural centers (p87).

Medical Services

The following clinics have emergency service and some English-speaking staff.

Clínica Anglo-Americana La Molina (Map pp88-9; ☎ 436 9933); San Isidro (Map p101; ☎ 221 3656; Salazar cuadra 3) The main branch in San Isidro charges up to US$60 for a consultation and stocks yellow-fever and tetanus vaccines. There's also a walk-in center in La Molina, near the US embassy.

Clínica Internacional (Map pp94-5; ☎ 433 4306; cnr Washington 1471 & 9 de Diciembre, Lima Centro) Charges US$17 to US$35 for consultations.

Clínica Montesur (☎ 436 3630; Av El Polo 505, Monterrico) Specializes in women's issues.

Clínica San Borja (Map pp88-9; ☎ 475 4000, 475 3141; Av Guardia Civil 337, San Borja)

Other medical options:

Dr Victor Aste (Map p101; ☎ /fax 421 9169; office 101, Antero Aspillaga 415, San Isidro) Dr Aste is a well-recommended, English-speaking dentist.

Hospital del Niño (Map pp94-5; ☎ 330 0066; Brasil 600, Breña) Gives tetanus and yellow-fever jabs.

Instituto de Medicina Tropical (☎ 482 3903, 482 3910; Cayetano Heredia Hospital, Honorio Delgado, San Martín de Porres) The institute is good for treating tropical diseases. It is also one of the cheapest places.

Jorge Bazan (☎ 9735 2668; jrbazanj@yahoo.com) An English-speaking backpacker medic recommended by readers; he sees travelers at their hotel.

The following pharmacies are modern, well stocked and open 24 hours. They often deliver free of charge.

America Salud (Armendariz 215, Miraflores)

Botica Fasa (Map p102; ☎ 619 0000; cnr Av José Larco & Ricardo Palma, Miraflores)

Inka Farma (☎ 314 2020) Will deliver.

If you have a prescription with you, you can have a spare pair of glasses made cheaply by one of the opticians along Cailloma (Map pp94–5) in the city center or around Schell and Av José Larco in Miraflores (p102).

Money

Most banks have 24-hour ATMs to avoid the long queues in banks, which are at their worst on Monday mornings (although some banks have express windows for foreign-currency transactions). Use caution when making withdrawals from ATMs, especially at night.

Lima's *casas de cambio* (foreign-exchange bureaus) usually give similar or slightly better rates than banks for cash (although not traveler's checks); they are also quicker and open longer. There are several *casas de cambio* downtown on Ocoña and Camaná (Map pp94–5), as well as along Av José Larco in Miraflores (Map p102). Street moneychangers hang around the *casas de cambio*. Those around Parque Kennedy in Miraflores have uniforms and badges, and are generally the safest option outside of business hours.

The following are some of the most useful options:

American Express (Amex; Map p102; ☎ 221 8204; amexcard@travex.com.pe; Santa Cruz 621, Miraflores; ⏰ 9am-5:30pm Mon-Fri, 9am-1pm Sat) Amex will replace stolen or lost Amex traveler's checks, but will not cash its own checks. Somebody is usually there after hours to take telephone reports about lost checks. Most of the banks will cash Amex checks; you get the best rates if you cash them in for nuevos soles.

Banco Continental Lima Centro (Map pp94–5; Cuzco 286); Miraflores (Map p102; cnr Av José Larco & Tarata; ⏰ 9am-6pm Mon-Fri, 9:30am-12:30pm Sat) A representative of Visa; its ATMs also take Cirrus, Plus and MasterCard.

BCP (⏰ 9am-6pm Mon-Fri, 9:30am-12:30pm Sat); Lima Centro (Map pp94–5; Lampa 499); José Gonzales (Map p102; cnr Av José Larco & José Gonzales, Miraflores); José Pardo (Map p102; Av José Pardo 491, Miraflores); Schell (Map p102; cnr Av José Larco & Schell, Miraflores) All these branches have 24-hour Visa and Plus ATMs, and make cash advances on Visa. The bank also changes Amex, Citicorp and Visa traveler's checks.

Banco Santander Central Hispano (BSCH; Agusto Tamayo 120, San Isidro; ⏰ 9am-6pm Mon-Fri) It has Visa and Plus ATMs and changes Visa and Citicorp traveler's checks.

Banco Wiese (Map p102; Av José Larco 1123, Miraflores; ⏰ 9:15am-6pm Mon-Fri, 9:30am-12:30pm Sat) This bank is a MasterCard representative and changes Amex and Citicorp traveler's checks.

Interbank (⏰ 9am-6pm Mon-Fri); Lima Centro (Map pp94–5; Jirón de la Unión 600); Larco (Map p102; Av José Larco 690, Miraflores) Interbank has ATMs with Cirrus, Plus, Visa and MasterCard.

LAC Dólar (⏰ 9:30am-6:30pm Mon-Sat, 9am-2pm Sun); Lima Centro (Map pp94–5; ☎ 428 8127; fax 427 3906; Camaná 779); Miraflores (Map p102; ☎ 242 4069; Av de la Paz 211) LAC Dólar is safe, reliable, and changes cash and traveler's checks at reasonable rates. It will also deliver the money for free if you phone and give the numbers of your traveler's checks.

Moneygram (Map p102; ☎ 0800 15821, 241 2222; moneyexpress@terra.com.pe; Alfredo Benavides 735, Miraflores; ⏰ 10am-6:30pm Mon-Sat)

Photography

Slide- and print-film developing tends to be mediocre in Lima.

Taller de Fotografía Profesional (Map p102; ☎ 241-1015; Alfredo Benavides 1171, Miraflores) The best photo shop in the city, with top-quality processing, camera repairs and sales.

Post

Members of the **SAE** (Map p102; ☎ 445 3306; Piura 135, Miraflores) can have mail held at the clubhouse.

Main post office (Map pp94–5; ☎ 427 9370; Pasaje Piura, Lima Centro; ⏰ 8:15am-8:15pm Mon-Fri, 9am-1:30pm Sat, 8am-4pm Sun) It's inside the city block on the northwest corner of the Plaza de Armas. Mail sent to you at Lista de Correos (Poste Restante), Correos Central, Lima, can be collected here, though it is not 100% reliable. Bring some identification.

Miraflores post office (Map p102; ☎ 445 0697; Av Petit Thouars 5201; ⏰ 8:15am-8:15pm Mon-Fri, 9am-1:30pm Sat, 8am-4pm Sun) Located east of Av Arequipa.

Faster, more expensive postal services:

DHL (Map p101; ☎ 422 5232, 517 2500; Los Castaños 225, San Isidro)

Federal Express (FedEx; ☎ 242 2280; Pasaje Olaya 260, Santiago de Surco)

Telephone & Fax

Telefónica-Perú has pay phones on almost every street corner in Lima (many accept only telephone cards). Call ☎ 103 (no charge) for directory inquiries within Lima and ☎ 109 for assistance with provincial numbers. Some offices of **Telefónica-Perú** (Lima Centro Map pp94–5; Bolivia 347; Miraflores Map p102; Alfredo Benavides cuadra 4; ⏰ 24 hr; Tarata Map p102; Pasaje Tarata 280) also have fax services.

Tourist Information

iPerú (iperulima@promperu.gob.pe); Aeropuerto Internacional Jorge Chávez (Map pp88-9; ☎ 574 8000; iperulimaapto@promperu.gob.pe; Main Hall; ⏰ 24hr); Miraflores (Map p102; ☎ 445 9400; Module 14, Plaza Gourmet, LarcoMar, Malecon de la Reserva 610; ⏰ noon-8pm); San Isidro (Map p101; ☎ 421 1627; Jorge Basadre 610; ⏰ 8:30am-6:30pm Mon-Fri) The San Isidro office combines the services of the tourist protection agency Indecopi and the information office iPerú, dispensing maps and useful advice, as well as dealing with tourist complaints. The Miraflores office is tiny but it's useful on weekends.

Tourist office (Map pp94–5; ☎ 427 6080 ex 222-83; Pasaje de los Escribanos 145, Lima Centro; ⏰ 9am-6pm

Mon-Fri, 11am-3pm Sat & Sun) Has limited information that is not always up to date.

Trekking & Backpacking Club (Map pp88-9; ☎ 423 2515; tebac@yahoo.com; Huascar 1152, Jesús María) Provides information in Spanish for independent trekkers and has maps, brochures, equipment rental and guides.

Travel Agencies

For details of companies in Lima offering local tours, including visits to archaeological sites such as Pachacamac, as well as tours around Peru, see p106. For travel agencies to organize your travel arrangements try the following:

Fertur Peru (Map pp94-5; ☎ 427 1958; fertur@terra .com.pe; Jirón Junín 211, Lima Centro; ☺ 9am-7pm Mon-Sat) Fertur is a small agency recommended for countrywide information and good prices on national and international flights. It has discounts for students and SAE members.

Infotur (Map pp94-5; ☎ 431 0117; Jirón Belén 1066, Lima Centro; ☺ 9:30am-6pm Mon-Fri, 10am-2pm Sat) Infotur has reliable information about transportation, hotels and sightseeing.

Intej (Map p104; ☎ 247 3230; intej@intej.org; San Martín 240, Barranco) The official International Student Identity Card (ISIC) office; Intej organizes student air fares and changes flight details.

Lima Tours (Map pp94-5; ☎ 424 5110; www.lima tours.com.pe; Jirón Belén 1040, Lima Centro; ☺ 8:30am-5:30pm Mon-Fri, 9am-1pm Sat) Perhaps the best-known agency in Lima.

Pro Peru Travel (Map pp94-5; ☎ 433 4170; www .properutravel.com; República de Chile 225, Santa Beatriz) This professional outfit is handy for people staying in Santa Beatriz. It will have tickets delivered to your hotel.

Victor Travel Services (Map pp94-5; ☎ 431 4195; victortravel@terra.com.pe; Jirón de la Unión 1068, Lima Centro) Helpful for local information.

DANGERS & ANNOYANCES

With large numbers of poor and unemployed people, it is inevitable that Lima suffers from opportunistic crime. While you are unlikely to physically hurt, travelers do regularly have their belongings stolen and muggings can happen. Re-read p500 before arriving in Lima. The basic precaution is to look as little like an affluent traveler as possible. That means not wearing expensive watches or jewelry, using a small pocket-sized camera and taking it out only when you use it. Carry your money as loose pocket change and take only as much as you need for your outing. Move around confidently and don't use a map unless seated at a café or restaurant: it's a dead giveaway.

Central Lima and the area around the bus terminals have many pickpockets, but even ritzy Miraflores has its opportunist thieves. Take extra care on the beaches with your belongings and look out for gangs of youths playing soccer – they've been known to mug hapless lone travelers. Use taxis to get around at night and generally adapt a streetwise attitude to keep yourself out of potential strife.

SIGHTS

Lima has enough museums, churches and colonial houses to keep a sightseer happy for weeks. The museums are among the best in the country. The many churches, monasteries and convents are a welcome break from the city's noisy traffic and incessant crowds, though they are often closed for restoration, services or because the caretaker fancies an extended lunch. Several of the main parks and plazas of central Lima are within easy walking distance of each other. There are several pre-Inca ruins within the city, oddly juxtaposed with the modern urban landscape; the main ones are in San Isidro and Miraflores.

Central Lima
PLAZA DE ARMAS

Also called Plaza Mayor, the 140-sq-meter Plaza de Armas (Map pp94–5) was once the heart of Lima. Though not one original building remains, the impressive bronze fountain in the center is its oldest feature, erected in 1650, and its oldest building is the cathedral, which was reconstructed after the 1746 earthquake.

The exquisitely balconied Palacio Arzobispal (Archbishop's Palace) to the left of the cathedral is a relatively modern building, dating to 1924. On the northeast side, the **Palacio de Gobierno** was built in 1937 and is the residence of Peru's president. A handsomely uniformed presidential guard is on duty here all day; the ceremonial changing of the guard takes place at noon. It's a struggle to get into the palace, which is by free guided tour only (Spanish and English) and has to be organized 48 hours in advance at the nearby **Office of Public Relations** (Map pp94-5; ☎ 311 3908; Jirón de la Unión, Plaza Pizarro 201; admission free). Ask a guard to point you in the right direction.

On the corner of the plaza, opposite the cathedral, there is an impressive statue of Francisco Pizarro on horseback – though, just for the record, he was actually a mediocre horseman. The statue once sat in the center of the plaza, but the clergy apparently took a dim view of the horse's rear end facing the cathedral, so the statue was moved to its present position, with its backside safely averted. There is an identical statue in Pizarro's hometown of Trujillo, Spain.

La Catedral de Lima

The original cathedral (1555) on the southeast side of the Plaza de Armas, was deemed too small for its congregation within a single decade, and work on its successor began in 1564, which was still unfinished when it was consecrated in 1625. It was badly damaged in the 1687 earthquake and almost totally destroyed by another earthquake in 1746. The **reconstruction** (Map pp94-5; ☎ 427 9647; adult/child US$1.40/1; ⊙ 9am-4:30pm Mon-Fri, 10am-4:30pm Sat) is based on the early plans.

The interior is stark but impressive, with a beautifully carved **choir** and a **religious museum** in the rear. Look for the coffin and remains of Francisco Pizarro in the mosaic-covered chapel just to the right of the main door. A debate over the authenticity of the remains raged during the 1980s and early 1990s, especially after several bodies and a mysterious

SOUTH AMERICAN EXPLORERS (SAE)

For many long-term travelers, journalists, scientists and expat residents, this club has become almost legendary. Since it was founded by Don Montague and Linda Rojas in 1977, SAE has been involved in activities ranging from the first cleanup of the Inca Trail to medicine drives for local nonprofit organizations. However, it functions primarily as an information center for travelers, adventurers and scientific expeditions, providing excellent advice about Latin American travel, especially in Peru, Ecuador and Bolivia and Argentina.

The club has an extensive library of books, maps and trip reports of other travelers, indexed by region and date. Various useful books and maps are sold, and there are trail maps for the Inca Trail, Mt Ausangate area, Cordillera Blanca and Cordillera Huayhuash, as well as general maps of South America. You can also get useful current information on travel conditions, currency regulations, weather and so on.

The club is a member-supported, nonprofit organization. Annual membership costs US$50 per person (US$80 for a couple), which covers four issues of their quarterly *South American Explorer* magazine. (Members outside the USA have to add US$10 for postage. Membership dues and donations to the club are tax-deductible in the USA.) Special discounts are available for ISIC holders and volunteers.

Members receive full use of the clubhouse and its facilities, including introductions to other travelers and notification of expedition opportunities; long- or short-term luggage storage; poste restante or forwarding of mail addressed to you at the club; a book exchange; buying and selling of used equipment; and discounts on the books, maps and gear sold at the clubhouse. It's also a relaxing place to do research or just chat with the friendly staff and make use of the free internet for members. Another big advantage for members is that they receive scores of significant discounts (ranging from 5% to 30% off) throughout Peru; pick up the list of participants from the club. Weekly events are organized, and anyone is welcome to attend; the events include salsa classes, presentations, and social and cultural events. Nonmembers are also welcome to browse for information, and the staff are happy to answer quick questions, but at the end of the day, staff are volunteers and members' needs come first.

If you're in Lima, simply go to the **SAE clubhouse** (Map p102; ☎ 445 3306; Piura 135, Miraflores; ⊙ 9:30am-5pm Mon-Fri, 9:30am-8pm Wed, 9:30am-1pm Sat), just off Av Arequipa, and sign up.

There are also clubhouses in **Cuzco** (☎ 084-245 484; No 4, Choquechaca 188; ⊙ 9:30am-5pm Mon-Fri, 9:30am-1pm Sat), **Quito** (☎ /fax 02-222 5228; Jorge Washington 311 y Leonidas Plaza, Mariscal Sucre; ⊙ 9:30am-5pm Mon-Wed & Fri, 9:30am-8pm Thu, 9:30am-1pm Sat) in Ecuador and **Buenos Aires** (☎ 011-4861 7571; Jeronimo Salguero 553; ⊙ 10am-6pm Mon-Thu, 1-5pm Fri & Sat) in Argentina.

The club's US office in **New York** (☎ 607-277 0488; 126 Indian Creek Rd, Ithaca) publishes the magazine; send them US$6 for a sample copy of the *South American Explorer* and check the **website** (www.saexplorers.org) for further information. Nonmember subscriptions are US$22 for one year and US$35 for two.

LIMA

CENTRAL LIMA

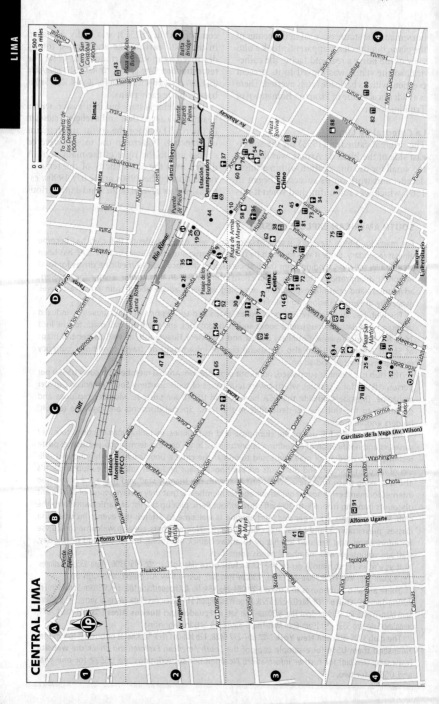

disembodied head were unearthed in the crypt in the late 1970s. After a battery of tests and speculation, the authorities concluded that the body previously on display was an unknown church official and that a brutally stabbed and headless body from the crypt was indeed Pizarro's, and was reunited with the head and transferred to the chapel.

Tours in English and several other languages are available for a tip. Only flashless photography is allowed.

AROUND THE PLAZA DE ARMAS
Iglesia de la Merced
The **Iglesia de la Merced** (Map pp94-5; ☎ 427 8199; cnr Jirón de la Unión & Miró Quesada; admission free; ☻ 8am-noon & 4-8pm) has a multilayered history. It was

built on the site of the first Mass celebrated in Lima (which was held in 1534), but the original church was soon replaced by a larger version. This in turn, was torn down, rebuilt in 1628, promptly flattened by the 1687 earthquake, then once again rebuilt. Work started on a new façade after more damage in the 1746 earthquake, and in 1773 the church was gutted by a fire that destroyed all paintings and vestments in the sacristy. Most of today's church dates from the 18th century.

Museo Banco Central de Reserva del Perú
This **museum** (Map pp94-5; ☎ 613 2000; http://museo bcr.perucultural.org.pe; Banco Central de Reserva, cnr Lampa & Ucayali; admission free; ☻ 10am-4:30pm Mon-Fri, 10am-1pm

Sat & Sun) specializes in pre-Columbian archaeology, especially from the Vicus culture, and
houses 19th- and 20th-century Peruvian art
and an exhibit of Peruvian monies. Strolling in
and out of the bank's old high-security vault
also has a certain appeal.

You need to show a passport or national
ID card to get in.

Museo Postal y Filatelico
Stamp buffs will want to visit the **Postal & Phila-
telic Museum** (Map pp94-5; Pasaje Piura; admission free;
⏱ 8:30am-6:30pm Mon-Sat, 9am-12:30pm Sun), appropriately housed in Lima Centro's main post
office just off the Plaza de Armas. You can
examine, buy and trade Peruvian stamps.

Museo de la Inquisición
This **building** (Map pp94-5; ☎ 311 7777 ext 2910; www
.congreso.gob.pe/museo.htm; Jirón Junín 548; admission
free; ⏱ 9am-5pm daily) was used by the Spanish Inquisition from 1570 to 1820 (see p35)
and subsequently became the senate building. Visitors can explore the basement where
prisoners were tortured, and there's a ghoulish waxwork exhibit of life-size unfortunates
being stretched on the rack or having their
feet roasted. The university library upstairs
has a remarkable wooden ceiling.

Entry is only by half-hourly guided tours,
which are conducted in Spanish, English,
Italian, French and Portuguese.

Parque de la Muralla
At the northern end of city center are the
remains of the *muralla* (city walls) that once
protected the original inner-city precinct. Now
protected in the aptly named **Parque de la Muralla** (Map pp94-5; ☎ 433 1546; parquedelamuralla@yahoo
.com; Amazonas, cuadra 1; admission US$0.30, free Wed;
⏱ 9:30am-9:30pm), the original walls have been
excavated to reveal a fairly extensive set of
remains. Of interest are the objects that were
discovered during the excavations. These are
now housed inside a well-presented on-site
museum where a developmental history of
the city of Lima is expounded via a series of
graphic boards and display cabinets containing all kinds of curious objects that range from
plates to plumbing. The on-site restaurant
makes the visit all the more worthwhile.

Monasterio de San Francisco
This Franciscan **monastery and church** (Map
pp94-5; cnr Lampa & Ancash; adult/student US$1.40/0.75;

⏱ 9:45am-6pm) is famous for its catacombs
and its remarkable library, where you can
see thousands of antique texts, some dating
as far back as the conquistadors. It also has a
very fine museum of religious art.

The underground catacombs are the
site of an estimated 70,000 burials and the
faint-hearted may find the bone-filled crypts
unnerving – if only for the conservationists' bizarre decision to rearrange the skulls
and femurs into striking rings of concentric
circles.

The building, which is one of the best preserved of Lima's early colonial churches, was
finished before the earthquake of 1687 and
withstood both this and the quake of 1746
better than many others. However, the 1970
earthquake caused considerable damage.
Much of the church has been well restored in
its original baroque style with Moorish influences. Admission to the monastery includes
a 45-minute guided tour. Spanish-speaking
tours leave regularly, and there are hourly
tours led by English-speaking guides.

Other Colonial Churches
Santuario de Santa Rosa de Lima (Map pp94-5; ☎ 425
1279; Tacna; admission free; ⏱ 9am-1pm & 3-6pm) honors
the first saint of the Americas in her hometown of Lima. The church and its garden have
been built at roughly the site of her birth, and
you can find a modest adobe sanctuary in the
gardens, built in the early 17th century for her
prayers and meditation.

Iglesia de Santo Domingo (Map pp94-5; ☎ 427
6793; cnr Camaná & Conde de Superunda; admission US$1;
⏱ 9am-12:30pm & 3-6pm Mon-Sat, 9am-1pm Sun) is one
of Lima's most historic churches, built on land
granted by Francisco Pizarro to the Dominican Friar Vicente Valverde, who accompanied
Pizarro throughout the conquest and was
instrumental in persuading him to execute
the captured and ransomed Inca Atahualpa.
Construction began in 1540, though much of
the interior was modernized late in the 18th
century. The church contains the tombs of
Saint Rose and Saint Martín de Porres (one of
the few black saints), plus an alabaster statue
of Saint Rose presented to the church by Pope
Clement in 1669. There is also fine tile work
showing the life of Saint Dominic.

Iglesia de San Pedro (Map pp94-5; ☎ 428 3010; cnr
Azangaro & Ucayali; admission free; ⏱ 10am-noon & 5-6pm
Mon-Fri) is a small baroque church considered to
be one of the finest examples of early colonial

architecture in Lima. It was consecrated by the Jesuits in 1638 and has changed little since. The interior is sumptuously decorated with gilded altars, Moorish-influenced carvings and an abundance of beautiful glazed tilework.

Iglesia de San Agustín (Map pp94–5; ☎ 427 7548; cnr Ica & Camaná; admission free) has been significantly altered over the years, though the *churrigueresque* (an elaborate and intricately decorated Spanish style) façade dates from the early 1700s. The church has limited opening times, but the drab interior is inferior to the elaborate exterior in any case.

Colonial Mansions

Built in 1735, the famous **Palacio Torre Tagle** (Map pp94–5; ☎ 427 3860; Ucayali 363) is the best surviving colonial mansion in Lima, with striking carved wooden balconies that demonstrate a Moorish influence. It now contains the offices of the Foreign Ministry, so entry on weekdays is prohibited or restricted to the patio. On some Saturdays, a tip to the caretaker may allow you access to the fine rooms and balconies upstairs. More extensive preorganized visits need to be arranged with the **oficina cultural** (☎ 311 2400).

Casa Aliaga (Map pp94–5; ☎ 619 6900; Jirón de la Unión 224) is another of Lima's most historic houses, furnished completely in the colonial style. It stands on land given in 1535 to Jerónimo de Aliaga, one of Pizarro's faithful 13 followers, and has been occupied by the Aliaga family ever since. The Aliaga's house can be visited only by appointment or through local tour agencies.

The easiest mansion to visit is **Casa Pilatos** (Map pp94–5; ☎ 427 7212; Ancash 390; admission free; ☽ 2-6pm Mon-Fri, 9am-5pm Sat & Sun), which houses the National Culture Institute; simply knock on the door and a guard will usually let you in for a look around. **Casa de la Riva** (Map pp94–5; Ica 426; admission US$1; ☽ 10am-1pm & 2-4pm Mon-Fri) is run by the Entre Nous Society. It's a handsome mansion with an elegant porch and windows built in the 18th century. Outside you can see beautiful carved wooden balconies, while inside the rooms remain little changed since the colonial era. **Casa de Riva-Aguero** (Map pp94–5; ☎ 427 9275; Camaná 459; ☽ 10am-1pm & 2-8pm Mon-Fri, 9am-1pm Sat & Sun) houses a small folk-art collection. The rest of the house is shown only by appointment. **Casa de Oquendo** (Casa Osambela; Map pp94–5; ☎ 427 7987; Superunda 298; ☽ 9:30am-4pm Mon-Fri) is a 19th-century house with a look-

out tower from where you can see the port in Callao.

Jirón de la Unión

As you walk down the five pedestrianized blocks of the jirón (Map pp94–5) from the Plaza de Armas to Plaza San Martín, you'll pass a multitude of fashion and sporting stores, cinemas and fast-food joints. The jirón is always very crowded with shoppers, sightseers, street performers and, of course, the inevitable pickpockets, so keep an eye on your valuables.

PLAZA SAN MARTÍN

The early-20th-century Plaza San Martín (Map pp94–5) has French-influenced architecture and a bronze equestrian statue of liberator General San Martín erected in 1921. But get closer and you'll also discover the overlooked statue of Madre Patria, the symbolic mother of Peru. Commissioned in Spain under instruction to give the good lady a crown of flames, nobody thought to iron out the double meaning of the word flame in Spanish (*llama*), and the hapless craftsmen duly placed a delightful little llama on her head.

The **Gran Hotel Bolívar** (p117) presides over the square and it's well worth a stop in its stately bar for a sip or two of its famous pisco sour (grape brandy cocktail).

PARQUE DE LA CULTURA

Originally known as Parque de la Exposition, this newly revamped park (Map pp94–5) has Japanese gardens and a small amphitheater for outdoor performances. It's a welcome relief from the crowds and traffic of Lima's boisterous center. Two of Lima's major art museums are in the park.

From Miraflores, catch a *combi* (minibus) marked 'Todo Arequipa' from Av Arequipa to 9 de Diciembre (US$0.30, 10 to 15 minutes).

Museo de Arte de Lima

The **Lima Art Museum** (Map pp94–5; ☎ 423 6332; www.museodearte.org; Paseo de Colón 125; adult/student US$1/0.70; ☽ 10am-5pm) is housed in a very handsome building. It exhibits far more than art, and its collection ranges from colonial furniture to pre-Columbian artifacts, as well as canvases spanning 400 years of Peruvian art. Photography is not allowed. Temporary shows cost extra. There is a café and the cinema Filmoteca (p120).

Museo de Arte Italiano

Located just north of the Museo de Arte, the **Italian Art Museum** (Map pp94-5; ☎ 423 9932; Paseo de la República 250; adult/student/child US$1/0.60/0.30; ☼ 10am-5pm Mon-Fri) is housed in a fairy-tale neoclassical building, and exhibits paintings, sculptures and prints mainly from the early 20th century. Italian and other European art is represented, and don't miss the detailed mosaic murals on the outside walls.

OTHER SIGHTS
Museo de la Cultura Peruana

The **Museum of Peruvian Culture** (Map pp94-5; ☎ 423 5892; museodelacultura.perucultural.org.pe; Alfonso Ugarte 650; adult/student US$1/0.60; ☼ 10am-5pm Tue-Fri, 10am-2pm Sat) specializes in items closely allied to popular art and handicrafts. Exhibits include ceramics, carved gourds, traditional folk art and costumes from various periods and places. It also runs classes for Peruvian instruments and dances.

Las Nazarenas

The most passionate of Lima's traditional religious feasts centers on the 18th-century **Iglesia de las Nazarenas** (Map pp94-5; ☎ 423 5718; cnr Huancavelica & Tacna; admission free; ☼ 7am-noon & 5-8:30pm Mon-Sat, 6:30am-1pm & 5-8:30pm Sun). A shanty town inhabited by liberated black slaves once sprawled on this site, and it was here that an ex-slave painted an image of the Crucifixion of Christ on a wall that miraculously survived when the area was leveled by the 1655 earthquake. The church of the Nazarene was later built around this wall, and on October 18 of each year a copy of the mural, known as the Lord of the Miracles, is carried from church to church in a thousands-strong procession that lasts two to three days.

Rímac
MUSEO TAURINO

Located just north of the Río Rímac, the **Bullfight Museum** (Map pp94-5; ☎ 481 1467; museotaurino@hotmail.com; Hualgayoc 332; admission US$1.50; ☼ 8am-4:30pm Mon-Fri) is at the Plaza de Acho, Lima's bullring. It boasts all manner of matadors' relics, including a holed and blood-stained costume worn by a Spanish matador who was famously gored and killed in the Lima bullring years ago – score one for the bulls! There are also paintings and drawings of bullfighting scenes by various artists, notably Picasso. The Spanish-speaking staff may

give you a free tour, but if you're opposed to bullfighting you may wish to give the museum a miss altogether.

CERRO SAN CRISTÓBAL

This 409m-high hill (Map pp88–9) to the northeast of Lima Centro has a **mirador** (lookout) at its crown, with views of Lima stretching off into the *garúa* (coastal fog). A huge **cross**, built in 1928 and illuminated at night, is a Lima landmark and is the object of a pilgrimage every May 1. There is also a small **museum** (Map pp88-9; admission US$0.30; ☼ 8am-6pm Tue-Thu, 8am-10pm Fri & Sat). The route up to the *mirador* is through a poor area, so take a taxi (US$5 to US$6 round-trip) or wait for the erratic tourist bus (US$1.40, 15 minutes) that passes through the Plaza de Armas. It is more frequent at weekends.

CONVENTO DE LOS DESCALZOS

At the end of Alameda de los Descalzos, an attractive if somewhat forgotten avenue, is this typical meditation **convent and museum** (Map pp88-9; ☎ 481 0441; Alameda de los Descalzos; adult/child US$1.40/0.60; ☼ 10am-1pm & 3-6pm Tue-Sat, 11:30am-6pm Sun), run by the Descalzos ('the Barefooted,' a reference to the Franciscan friars). Visitors can see old wine-making equipment in the 17th-century kitchen, a refectory, an infirmary and the typical cells of the Descalzos. There are also some 300 colonial paintings here of the Quito and Cuzco schools. The convent is in a poor area of Lima, so take a taxi and ask the driver to wait.

Spanish-speaking guides with a little English will show you around. A tour lasts about 45 minutes, and a small tip is appreciated.

East Lima
MUSEO DE LA NACIÓN

This dominating concrete block houses the best **museum** (Map pp88-9; ☎ 476 9878; www.inc .gob.pe; Javier Prado Este 2466, San Borja; adult/student US$2/1, special shows US$3.30; ☼ 9am-6pm Tue-Sun) in the country to get your head around Peru's myriad prehistoric civilizations. It has excellent models of Peru's well-known ruins and three levels of extensive exhibits about Peru's heritage, all at a much more affordable price than at the private collections. Everything from Chavín stone carvings to Nazca ceramics and Paracas weavings is represented, and there are also exhibits from the now defunct Museo de Ciencias de la Salud describing medical practices in pre-Columbian and colonial times. Besides the permanent collections, there are often special shows, lectures and other events.

French and English guided tours are available (about US$3 per group). A taxi from Miraflores will cost about US$1.50.

MUSEO DE ORO DEL PERÚ

This now notorious **private museum** (Map pp88-9; ☎ 345 1292; www.museooroperu.com.pe; Alonso de Molina 1100, Monterrico; adult/child US$9/4.50; ☢ 11:30am-7pm) was at the top of Lima's 'must-see' list until 2001, when it was rocked by a scandal that claimed between 10% and an incredible 98% of the museum's collection were fakes. The museum was reopened with an assurance that all pieces now on display in its huge basement are bona fide, but the confusion is yet to be completely cleared up. The thousands of remaining gold pieces range from ponchos embroidered with hundreds of solid-gold plates to huge earrings that make your ears ache just looking at them.

The **Arms Museum**, housed in the top half of the building, is reputedly the largest in the world and even those with no interest in guns can't fail to be fascinated by the mammoth collection of ancient and bizarre firearms. Look for the 2m-long blunderbuss with a 5cm bore and a flaring, trumpetlike muzzle. Though it looks more suitable for hunting elephants, this 19th-century gun was supposedly a mere duck-hunting rifle.

Photography is prohibited. A taxi from Miraflores costs US$2 to US$2.50.

ASOCIACIÓN MUSEO DEL AUTOMÓVIL

The **Automobile Museum** (Map pp88-9; ☎ 368 0373; www.museodelautomovilnicolini.com; cnr La Molina & Totoritas, La Molina; adult/student US$6/3; ☢ 9am-9pm daily) has an impressive array of 64 classic cars (mostly imported), which were manufactured between 1901 and 1973. The cars were collected and restored by millionaire Jorge Nicolini. The collection includes a Cadillac Fleetwood that was used by no fewer than four Peruvian presidents. English-speaking guides are available.

San Isidro & Around

MUSEO RAFAEL LARCO HERRERA

An 18th-century viceroy mansion built on the site of a pre-Columbian pyramid houses this highly recommended private **museum**

(Map pp88-9; ☎ 461 1312; museolarco.perucultural .org.pe; Bolívar 1515, Pueblo Libre; adult/student US$8/4; ☢ 9am-6pm daily) has one of the largest ceramics collections to be found anywhere. It is said to include over 50,000 pots, many of which were collected in the 1920s by a former vice president of Peru. The first rooms resemble a storeroom, stacked right to the ceilings with an overwhelming jumble of ceramics. Further into the museum, the best pieces are displayed in the uncluttered manner they deserve. They include a selection of gold and silver pieces, feathered textiles and an astonishing Paracas weaving that contains 398 threads to the linear inch – a world record. But for all this, many tourists are lured here simply by the famous collection of pre-Columbian erotic pots that illustrate, with remarkable explicitness, the sexual practices of ancient Peruvian men, women, skeletons and animals in all combinations of the above.

Photography is not allowed. Catch a bus from Av Arequipa in Miraflores marked 'Todo Bolívar' to Bolívar's 15th block. A taxi costs about US$1.40. A painted blue line should link this building to the Museo Nacional de Antropología, Arqueología y Historía del Perú, located a 10- to 15-minute walk away.

MUSEO NACIONAL DE ANTROPOLOGÍA, ARQUEOLOGÍA Y HISTORÍA DEL PERÚ

The **National Museum of Anthropology, Archaeology & History of Peru** (Map pp88-9; ☎ 463 5070; http:// museonacional.perucultural.org.pe; Plaza Bolívar, cnr San Martín & Vivanco, Pueblo Libre; adult/student US$3.20/1; ☢ 9am-5pm Tue-Sat, 9am-4pm Sun) traces the history of Peru from the Preceramic Period to independence. Some exhibits have been moved to the Museo de la Nación, but a worthwhile collection remains, including scale models of the big archaeological sites, as well as some of the original stelae and obelisks from Chavín. The building was once the home of revolutionary heroes San Martín (from 1821 to 1822) and Bolívar (from 1823 to 1826) and the museum contains late-colonial and early-republican paintings, furnishings and independence artifacts.

From Miraflores, take a 'Todo Brasil' *combi* from Av Arequipa (just north from Óvalo) to *cuadra* 22 on the corner of Vivanco, then walk seven blocks up that street. A blue line connects this museum with Museo Rafael Larco Herrera.

MUSEO DE HISTORIA NATURAL UNMSM

One block west of *cuadra* 12 of Av Arequipa, the **Natural History Museum** (Map p101; ☎ 471 0117; http://museohn.unmsm.edu.pe; Arenales 1256, Jesús Maria; adult/student US$1.20/0.60; ☺ 9am-3pm Mon-Fri, 9am-5pm Sat, 9am-1pm Sun) has a modest taxidermy collection that's useful for familiarizing yourself with the fauna of Peru.

HUACA HUALLAMARCA

Also known as Pan de Azúcar (Sugar Loaf), this **huaca** (Map p101; ☎ 222 4124; Nicolás de Rivera 201, San Isidro; adult/student/child US$1.70/1/0.30; ☺ 9am-5pm Tue-Sun) is a highly restored Maranga adobe pyramid dating from AD 200 to 500. Walking up to the ceremonial platform provides a novel perspective on contemporary San Isidro.

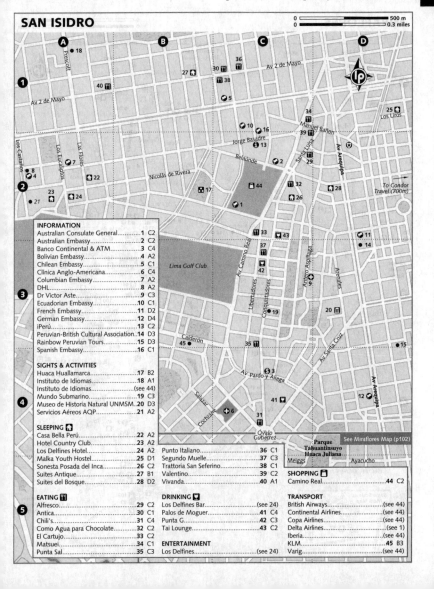

SAN ISIDRO

0 ————— 500 m
0 ————— 0.3 miles

INFORMATION	
Australian Consulate General	**1** C2
Australian Embassy	**2** C2
Banco Continental & ATM	**3** C4
Bolivian Embassy	**4** A2
Chilean Embassy	**5** C1
Clínica Anglo-Americana	**6** C4
Columbian Embassy	**7** A2
DHL	**8** A2
Dr Victor Aste	**9** C3
Ecuadorian Embassy	**10** C1
French Embassy	**11** D2
German Embassy	**12** D4
iPerú	**13** C2
Peruvian-British Cultural Association	**14** D3
Rainbow Peruvian Tours	**15** D3
Spanish Embassy	**16** C1

SIGHTS & ACTIVITIES	
Huaca Huallamarca	**17** B2
Instituto de Idiomas	**18** A1
Instituto de Idiomas	(see 44)
Mundo Submarino	**19** C3
Museo de Historia Natural UNMSM	**20** D3
Servicios Aéreos AQP	**21** A2

SLEEPING 🛏	
Casa Bella Perú	**22** A2
Hotel Country Club	**23** A2
Los Delfines Hotel	**24** A2
Malka Youth Hostel	**25** D1
Sonesta Posada del Inca	**26** C2
Suites Antique	**27** B1
Suites del Bosque	**28** D2

EATING 🍽	
Alfresco	**29** C2
Antica	**30** C1
Chili's	**31** C4
Como Agua para Chocolate	**32** C2
El Cartujo	**33** C2
Matsuei	**34** C1
Punta Sal	**35** C3

Punto Italiano	**36** C1
Segundo Muelle	**37** C3
Trattoria San Seferino	**38** C1
Valentino	**39** C2
Vivanda	**40** A1

DRINKING 🍷	
Los Delfines Bar	(see 24)
Palos de Moguer	**41** C4
Punta G	**42** C3
Tai Lounge	**43** C2

ENTERTAINMENT	
Los Delfines	(see 24)

SHOPPING 🛍	
Camino Real	**44** C2

TRANSPORT	
British Airways	(see 44)
Continental Airlines	(see 44)
Copa Airlines	(see 44)
Delta Airlines	(see 1)
Iberia	(see 44)
KLM	**45** B3
Varig	(see 44)

See Miraflores Map (p102)

To Condor Travel (700m)

Miraflores

FUNDACION MUSEO AMANO

This **museum** (Map p102; ☎ 441 2909; museoam ano@hotmail.com; Retiro 160; admission free; ✆ 3-5pm) has a fine private ceramics collection following the development of pottery through Peru's various pre-Columbian cultures, including the Chimú and Nazca cultures. It specializes in the little-known Chancay culture, from which it has a remarkable collection of textiles. The one-hour tours are available for small groups only (no individuals or large groups) at 3pm, 4pm and 5pm on weekdays; make an appointment in advance. It's best if you understand Spanish or have someone to interpret.

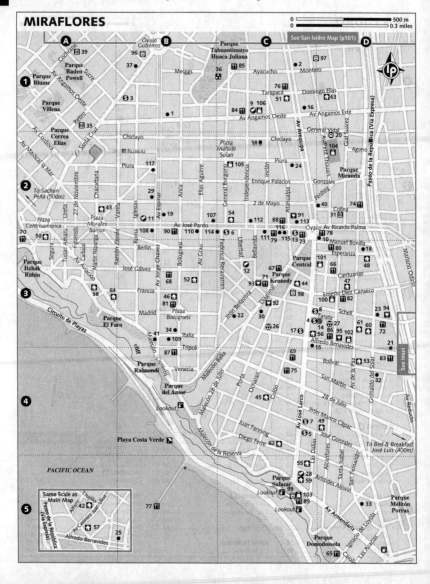

MUSEO ENRICO POLI BIANCHI

This **museum** (Map p102; ☎ 422 2437; Cochrane 400; admission US$10; ☒ 4-6pm Tue-Fri, appointments only) has a collection of gold textiles, colonial silver and paintings that was featured in *National Geographic*. Prearranged tours by the owner are given in Spanish only.

CASA DE RICARDO PALMA

This **house** (Map p102; ☎ 445 5836; Gral Suarez 189; adult/student US$1/0.25; ☒ 9:15am- 12:45pm & 2:30-5pm Mon-Fri) was the home of the Peruvian author of that name from 1913 until his death in 1919.

HUACA PUCLLANA

Easily accessible, this **huaca** (Map p102; ☎ 445 8695; cnr Borgoña & Tarapaca, Miraflores; admission free; ☒ 9am-5pm Wed-Mon) is an adobe pyramidal structure that dates back to AD 400 and was

remodeled over three centuries. Though vigorous excavations continue, the site is open to regular guided tours (in Spanish) and there's a tiny museum with finds and a reconstructed burial.

Barranco

MUSEO DE ARTE VIRREYNAL PEDRO DE OSMA

This private **art museum** (Map p104; ☎ 467 0141; museo@fundacionosma.org; Av San Pedro de Osma 421; admission US$3; ☒ 10am-1:30pm & 2:30-6pm Tue-Sun) has an exquisite collection of colonial art and furniture, as well as metalwork and sculpture from all over Peru. It is housed in one of Barranco's older mansions. Take a *combi* or *colectivo* (shared transportation) from Tacna/Garcilaso de la Vega in central Lima or Diagonal in Miraflores.

LIMA

MUSEO DE LA ELECTRICIDAD

The **Museum of Electricity** (Map p104; ☎ 477 6577; Av San Pedro de Osma 105; admission free; ☒ 9am-1pm & 2-5pm Mon-Sun) has a small exhibit on electricity in Lima, including the electric tramway system that used to link Barranco with Miraflores and Lima. Outside, a restored electric tram runs along rails for a few blocks of Av San Pedro de Osma on weekends (US$0.60).

West Lima
PARQUE DE LAS LEYENDAS ZOO

This **zoo** (Map pp88-9; ☎ 464 4282; Av la Marina, cuadra 24, San Miguel; adult/child under 11 US$2.50/1.20; ☒ 9am-5:30pm), between Lima Centro and Callao, is divided into three areas representing the three major geographical divisions of Peru:

the coast, the sierra (the Andes) and the Amazon Basin. Up to 210 native Peruvian animals make up the majority of the exhibits, though there are also typical international zoo animals. You might finally get to see those animals and birds you only heard in the jungle! The conditions are OK, and the zoo is well maintained and popular.

Irregular buses and *colectivos* (US$0.30 to US$0.60, 25 to 35 minutes) go past the park; catch them from Av Abancay and Garcilaso de la Vega in central Lima. A taxi from Miraflores will cost about US$2 to US$2.50.

FUERTE REAL FELIPE

This historic **fort** (Map pp88-9; ☎ 429 0532; Plaza Independencia, Callao; foreigner/Peruvian/student US$2/1.20/0.60;

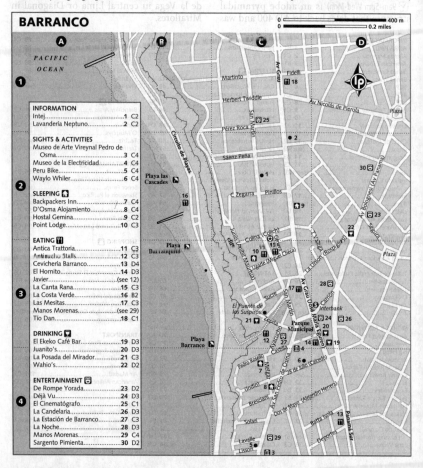

BARRANCO

0 ——— 400 m
0 ——— 0.2 miles

INFORMATION
Intej..1 C2
Lavandería Neptuno.....................2 C2

SIGHTS & ACTIVITIES
Museo de Arte Vireynal Pedro de
Osma..3 C4
Museo de la Electricidad...............4 C4
Peru Bike...................................5 C4
Waylo Whiler..............................6 C4

SLEEPING
Backpackers Inn...........................7 C4
D'Osma Alojamiento.....................8 C4
Hostal Gemina.............................9 C2
Point Lodge...............................10 C3

EATING
Antica Trattoria..........................11 C3
Antinucho 9talls..........................12 C3
Cevichería Barranco....................13 D4
El Hornito.................................14 D3
Javier...................................(see 12)
La Canta Rana............................15 C3
La Costa Verde...........................16 B2
Las Mesitas...............................17 C3
Manos Morenas......................(see 29)
Tío Dan...................................18 C1

DRINKING
El Ekeko Café Bar.......................19 D3
Juanito's..................................20 D3
La Posada del Mirador..................21 C3
Wahio's...................................22 D2

ENTERTAINMENT
De Rompe Yorada........................23 D2
Déjà Vu...................................24 D3
El Cinematógrafo.........................25 C1
La Candelaria.............................26 D3
La Estación de Barranco.................27 C3
La Noche..................................28 D3
Manos Morenas...........................29 C4
Sargento Pimienta........................30 D2

(☉ 9am-2pm) was built in 1747 to guard the coast against pirates, and is where the Spanish royalists made their last stand during the battles of independence in the 1820s. It still houses a small military contingent, complete with an assault course and the soldiers' *fútbol* (soccer) pitch. Visits are by guided tours in Spanish only. Note that the nearby dock area is a rough neighborhood.

ACTIVITIES
Cycling
Popular excursions from Lima include the 31km ride to Pachacamac, where there are several good local circuits open between April and December. Experts can also inquire about the circuit from Olleros to San Bartolo south of Lima. For general information in Spanish on cycling, try **Federación Deportiva Peruana de Ciclismo** (☎ 929 8137; fedepeci@hotmail .com; San Luis 1308).

Dozens of bike shops are listed in Lima's yellow pages under 'Bicicletas.' Check out the following places:
Explore Bicycle Rentals (Map p102; ☎ 241 7494; iexplore@terra.com; Bolognesi 381, Miraflores; ☉ 8am-5pm Mon-Fri) This shop (no sign) rents out mountain bikes with helmet and lock, charging US$3 per hour, US$5 per day and US$45 per week.
Peru Bike (Map p104; ☎ 467 0757; Av San Pedro de Osma 560, Barranco; ☉ 9am-1pm & 4-8pm Mon-Sat) Peru Bike is a recommended shop that also does repairs.
Willy Pro (☎ 346 0468; Javier Prado Este 3339, San Borja; ☉ 8am-8pm Mon-Sat)

Paragliding
For paragliding off the clifftops of Lima or around the south of Peru, including Lunahuaná, Ica and Paracas, contact **Peru Fly** (Map p102; ☎ /fax 444 5004; www.perufly.com; Jorge Chavez 666, Miraflores). Tandem flights take off from the clifftop Parque Raimondi close to the company's office in Miraflores and cost US$25. Alternatively, intensive six-day courses are offered (US$450). Be sure to wave at the bemused coffee drinkers in the cliffside LarcoMar shopping mall as you glide past.

Swimming & Surfing
Despite plenty of newspaper warnings of pollution and health hazards, *limeños* hit the beaches in their droves during the summer months of January, February and March. If you decide to join them, be aware of local thieves and don't leave anything unattended

for a second. **Playa Costa Verde** in Miraflores (also called Waikiki) is a favorite of local surfers and has good breaks year-round. Barranco's beaches have waves that are better for long boards. There are seven other beaches in Miraflores and four more in Barranco. Serious surfers can also try **Playa la Herradura** in Chorrillos, which has waves up to 5m high. For information on cleaner beaches and good surfing close to the south of Lima, see p125.

The following stores sell surfing equipment and provide information:
Big Head (Map p102; ☎ 818 4156; LarcoMar, Malecon de la Reserva 610, Miraflores)
Focus (☎ 475 8459; Leonardo da Vinci 208, San Borja)
Waylo Whiler (Map p104; ☎ 247 6343; 28 de Julio 287, Barranco)

Scuba Diving
There's reasonable deep-sea diving off Peru's southern coast. Contact **Peru Divers** (☎ 251 6231; perudivers@bellnet.com.pe; Huaylas 205, Chorrillos), an excellent dive shop owned by Luis Rodriguez, a PADI-certified instructor who sells gear, provides diving information, and arranges certification and diving trips. Also good is **Mundo Submarino** (Map p101; ☎ 441 7604; Conquistadores 791, San Isidro; ☉ 9:30am-1:30pm & 4-8pm Mon-Sat), which has equipment and organizes classes. It is run by Alejandro Pez, who speaks English, German, French, Italian and Portuguese.

Other Activities
You can go tenpin bowling at **Cosmic Bowling** (Map p102; ☎ 445 7776; LarcoMar, Malecon de la Reserva 610, Miraflores; per hr US$12; ☉ 10am-midnight) in the LarcoMar shopping mall. At night, the lanes are illuminated by 'cosmic' lighting. There's also tenpin bowling (US$7 per hour, including a drink) and pool (US$1.50 per hour) at the more run-down **Brunswick Bowl** (Map p102; ☎ 801 5786; Malecón Balta 135, Miraflores; 9am-3pm Mon-Sat).

Daytona Amusement Park (Map pp88-9; ☎ 435 6130; Av El Derby, Monterrico; admission US$7), though lacking major-league thrills, has laser quest, go-cart racing and minicars, and you can even go paint-balling.

Lima has several tennis and golf clubs, and the first-class hotels and tour agencies can help organize games, but it's extremely pricey for nonmembers. **Lima Cricket & Football Club** (Map pp88-9; ☎ 264 0027; Justo Vigil 200, Magdalena del Mar) is popular with expats and allows English-speaking visitors with passports to participate for free in their activities.

Sailors can contact the **Yacht Club Peruano** (☎ 429 0775; yatchclubperuano@infonegocio.net.pe; Bolognesi 761, La Punta, Callao).

People wishing to visit English-speaking foreign prisoners, who are mainly in jail on drug charges, can ask the **SAE** (Map p102; ☎ 445 3306; Piura 135, Miraflores) for a list of prisoners, prison addresses and visiting hours.

COURSES
Language
Though Lima has plenty of language schools, most cater to Peruvians learning English and tend to be far more expensive than in other parts of Peru. You can try the following places:

El Sol (Map p102; ☎ 242 7763; lsol1@terra.com.pe, Grimaldo del Solar 469, Miraflores) El Sol charges US$11/14 per hour for group/individual classes.

Inlingua (Map p102; ☎ 422 0915; www.inlingua.com; Av Santa Cruz 888, Miraflores) Individual classes are US$25 per hour.

Instituto Cultural Peruano-Norteamericano (Map p102; ☎ 241 1940; Av Arequipa 4798, Miraflores) It's US$95 per month for five two-hour group classes per week.

Instituto de Idiomas Universidad Católica (Map p101; ☎ 442 8761; Camino Real 1037, San Isidro); Universidad del Pacífico (Map p101; ☎ 421 2969; Prescott 333, San Isidro) The Universidad Católica branch of this language school charges US$140 per month for five two-hour group classes per week, while at Universidad del Pacífico it costs US$250 for three months with three 90-minute group classes per week.

You can also try a private teacher for between US$4 and US$8 per hour:
Alex Boris (☎ 423 0697, 9989 2771)
Carol Zuniga (☎ 495 2581)
Lourdes Galvaz (☎ 435 3910) Also teaches Quechua.
Luis Alberto Rivas Valcarcel (☎ 444 3652, 9962 9930)
Sonia (☎ 251 3191 before 10am)

Music & Dance
In Lima, other classes are usually conducted over several months in Spanish, but you may be able to organize flexible schedules if you contact the organizers directly.

Biblioteca Nacional (Map pp94-5; ☎ 428 7690; cafaebnp@binape.gob.pe; cnr Av Abancay & Miró Quesada, Lima Centro) This library sometimes has weekend courses in Quechua and the *zampoña* (Andean panpipes).

Museo de Arte de Lima (Map pp94-5; ☎ 423 4732; areaeducativa@terra.com.pe; Paseo de Colón 125, Lima Centro) Offers four- to eight-month courses in traditional

and modern Peruvian dances including Latin dances, Andean folk dances and the Afro-Latino *danzas negras*, as well as in typical Andean instruments such as the *zampoña*.

Museo de la Cultura Peruana (Map pp94-5; ☎ 423 5892; Alfonso Ugarte 650, Lima Centro) Runs limited classes for Peruvian instruments and typical dances from US$10 per class.

TOURS & GUIDES
For guided tours of Lima and nearby archaeological sites such as Pachacamac, as well as trips around Peru, try the following companies. In addition to these, many travel agencies (see p92), including Fertur Peru, Infotur and Lima Tours, also organize tours. Tours for elsewhere in Peru, though, will be cheaper if organized in the nearest major town to the area you want to visit.

Aero Condor Perú (Map p102; ☎ 441 1354, 442 5215; www.aerocondor.com.pe; Av José Pardo, Miraflores) Has flights over the Nazca Lines for around US$300. It's much cheaper, though, to take a bus to Nazca and fly from there.

Aventours (Map p102; ☎ 444 9060; www.aventours.com; Av Arequipa 4799, Miraflores) Aventours offers private overland tours or guided trips using public transport, and also arranges guided treks.

Condor Travel (Map pp88-9; ☎ 615 3000; www.condortravel.com.pe; Blondet 249, San Isidro) Recommended for top-end touring.

Ecoaventura Vida (☎ /fax 461 2555; www.ecoaventuravida.com) It runs alternative circuits to areas on the coast, such as the Ancon Islands and up to Paramonga.

Explorandes (Map p102; ☎ 445 8683; www.explorandes.com; San Fernando 320, Miraflores) Explorandes specializes in trekking and adventure sports.

Lima Vision (Map p102; ☎ 447 0482; www.limavision.com; Chiclayo 444, Miraflores) Lima Vision has daily four-hour city tours for US$20 and one-day tours for US$70.

Peru Expeditions (Map p102; ☎ 447 2057; www.peru-expeditions.com; office 504, Av Arequipa 5241, Miraflores; ⏱ 10am-5:30pm Mon-Fri, 9am-noon Sat) It has trips in 4WDs around Lima and beyond, and can also arrange trekking, biking and rafting around Peru.

Servicios Aéreos AQP (Map p101; ☎ 222 3312; www.saaqp.com.pe; Los Castaños 347, San Isidro) This company offers top-end tours throughout Peru.

The following guides are officially registered with **Agotour** (☎ 571 1305), the Peruvian guide organization. The telephone numbers are for Peruvian daytime use only.

Gladis Araujo (☎ 463 3642, 9966 4780) Gladis speaks English.

Maria Kralewska de Canchaya (☎ 470 9888, 461 4061; canchaya@terra.com.pe) Speaks Polish.

Monica Velásquez (☎ 9943 0796; vc_monica@ hotmail.com) Speaks English; airport pickups offered if you sign for a tour.

Nila Soto (☎ 452 5483, 9965 0951) Speaks English and Italian.

Silvia Rodrich (☎ 446 0391, 446 8185) Speaks English.

Tino Guzman (☎ /fax 429 5779, 9909 5805) Speaks English; member of SAE.

Toshie Matsumura De Irikura (☎ 476 5101) Speaks Japanese.

FESTIVALS & EVENTS

See p504 for major festivals and special events, and p505 for national holidays. For other events, see local newspapers and the useful *Peru Guide*. Holidays specific to Lima:

Festival of Lima Celebrates the anniversary of Lima's founding on January 18.

Feast of Santa Rosa de Lima Held on August 30, this feast has processions in honor of Saint Rose, the patron saint of Lima and the Americas.

El Señor de los Milagros (Lord of the Miracles) Huge religious processions on October 18 celebrate the Lord of the Miracles, with smaller processions occurring on Sundays in October.

SLEEPING

Apart from the tourist mecca of Cuzco, hotels are more expensive here than in any other Peruvian city. The cheapest are generally in central Lima, though it's not as salubrious here as in the more upmarket neighborhoods of Miraflores, Barranco and San Isidro. Wherever you stay, always ask about discounts if you're planning to spend more than a few days in Lima as most places offer good weekly rates. Off season is generally from December to March.

It's also worth contacting hotels in advance to find out if they will pick you up from the airport; even budget hostels often arrange for secure taxis for a few dollars less than the official airport taxi service.

Be aware that hostels in Lima face a lot of expensive red tape to put up a sign on the front of their establishment, so many of the following budget options have no sign and can look for all the world like ordinary houses from the outside.

Central Lima
BUDGET

Hostal España (Map pp94-5; ☎ 428 5546; hotel _espana@hotmail.com; Azangaro 105; dm/d US$3.50/10; 🖳) The long-running Hostal España is in a rambling old mansion full of classical busts, birds and paintings. It's an established backpackers' scene with basic but not unlovely accommodations. Service can be pretty surly at times and you can expect some noise from fellow travelers. There are limited hot showers in the early morning or late evening, as well as internet access, laundry services and a rooftop café surrounded by a veritable jungle of trailing plants. Nevertheless, it's the best spot in central Lima to meet other travelers.

Hostal San Francisco (Map pp94-5; ☎ 426 2735; hostal_san _francisco@terramail.com.pe; Azangaro 127; dm US$5-6; 🖳) This is a clean and modern escape from the travelers' scene next door and, though it has less character, is friendly and has good soft beds.

Hostal Belén (Map pp94-5; ☎ 427 8995; arco bel@terra.com.pe; Jirón Belén 1049; s/d/tr with shared bathroom US$6/12/18, s/d US$9/12) Housed in a characterful, lofty-ceilinged colonial building, Belén has quite basic but good rooms and very hot water, though the popular bar downstairs gets rowdy at weekends.

Familia Rodríguez (Map pp94-5; ☎ 423 6465; jjr -art@mail.cosapidata.com.pe; No 3, 2nd fl, Nicolás de Piérola 730; dm incl breakfast US$6) This is an informal and very friendly family home in a central position. Recommended.

Pensión Ibarra (Map pp94-5; ☎ /fax 427 8603; pension_ibarra@ekno.com; 14th & 15th fl, Tacna 359; s/d with shared bathroom US$7/10) Situated high above the city in an apartment block, this homely place is run by the helpful Ibarra sisters, who make a real effort to keep it safe, comfortable and clean. Rooms are simple and there is a kitchen. It's good for long-term stays.

Hostal Iquique (Map pp94-5; ☎ 433 4724; hiqui que@terra.com.pe; Iquique 758; s/d with shared bathroom US$7/10, s/d US$10/16) This recommended spot is clean, safe and has warm showers at any time. There is a rooftop terrace, decorative tiling and most rooms have national TV. Kitchen facilities are available – the amiable owner, Fernando, is an excellent cook, and if you're lucky he might help you with a good meal.

Hostal de las Artes (Map pp94-5; ☎ 433 0031; artes@terra.com.pe; Chota 1469; s US$8, d US$14-17) This gay-friendly Dutch-Peruvian-owned hostel has well-maintained rooms that have bathrooms with hot water. It is located on a quiet street in an atmospheric, high-ceilinged *casa antigua* (old house) with colorful tiling and a glass ceiling.

Hostal Roma (Map pp94-5; ☎ 427 7576; resroma@terra .com.pe; Ica 326; s/d with shared bathroom US$13/20, s/d US$25/36; 💻) This friendly old hostel is clean, central and a little camp with quirky, varied rooms – some are windowless so look at a few. There is a good choice of breakfasts. Off-season discounts are as much as US$5.

Others to try:

Hotel Europa (Map pp94-5; ☎ 427 3351; Ancash 376; s/d US$5/7) Worn budget alternative with flimsy and dark rooms but friendly service.

Hostal Wiracocha (Map pp94-5; ☎ 427 1178; fax 427 4406; Jirón Junín 284; s/d with shared bathroom US$6/7, s/d US$10/12) Superb location but has some damp rooms. The private showers are hot.

MIDRANGE

Hotel Internacional (Map pp94-5; ☎ 433 5517; fax 330 4754; 28 de Julio 763; s/d incl breakfast US$20/26) It's a good value but nondescript choice. Rooms are tidy and comfortable, and windows have double glazing.

Posada del Parque (Map pp94-5; ☎ 433 2412, 9945 4260; posada@incacountry.com; Parque Hernán Velarde 60; s/d/tr US$27/33/48) Surrounded by an elegant wrought-iron fence, this graceful, butter yellow colonial house sits on a tranquil, tree-lined cul-de-sac just south of Lima Centro and is ideally situated for both central Lima and Miraflores. Run by the friendly, helpful English-speaking Leo and Mónica, the guesthouse boasts spotless rooms with antique-looking furniture and eclectic artwork. All rooms have cable TV and airport pickups are available.

Kamana Hotel (Map pp94-5; ☎ 426 7204; res ervas@hotelkamana.com; Camaná 547; s/d/tr incl breakfast US$28/35/45) Popular with overseas tour groups, this secure, smart and relatively modern hotel has clean, comfortable rooms. English and French are spoken. For the location, it's exceptional value, especially during the off-season, when discounts are available.

Hostal Bonbini (Map pp94-5; ☎ 427 6477; hostal bonbini@hotmail.com; Cailloma 209; s/d US$30/40) This central hotel is a comfy, well-manicured spot with spick-and-span bathrooms and cable TV. It's a refreshingly good find in an area short on quality midrange options.

Hotel Continental (Map pp94-5; ☎ 427 5890; contihot@terra.com.pe; Puno 196; s/d/tr incl breakfast US$36/45/55) The Continental is a large but faded hotel with spacious rooms decorated by somebody with a penchant for the color beige. The 7th floor and up have newer rooms with cable TV.

Hotel Maury (Map pp94-5; ☎ 428 8188; hotmaury@ amauta.rcp.net.pe; Ucayali 201; s/d/ste incl breakfast US$48/59/108) Newly renovated and looking very well for it, this option borders on the top-end and has been given the thumbs-up by readers. The smart rooms boast all the mod cons.

Clifford Hotel (Map pp94-5; ☎ 433 4249; www .theclifffordhotel.com.pe; Parque Hernán Velarde 27; s/d/tr US$50/55/70) Located on the same cul-de-sac as Posada del Parque is this rather smart newcomer to the hotel scene. Comprising 21 rooms in a former private mansion, all rooms are large and airy with fans, cable TV and a phone. The breezy marbled and chandeliered entry is most welcoming. There's a bar and restaurant, and a pleasant garden to relax in.

TOP END

Central Lima has seen its business slipping away in recent years and top end establishments have been suffering. In response to their plight, many offer periodic promotional rates to woo customers back, so contact them in advance for the latest discounts.

Gran Hotel Bolívar (Map pp94-5; ☎ 619 7171; www .granhotelbolivarperu.com; Jirón de la Unión 958; s/d US$70/80) Nostalgia strikes at this venerable 1920s hotel on Plaza San Martín. Sadly, the hotel has had chronic plumbing problems and its rooms, though retaining a rare finesse, are increasingly musty from disuse. Yet for anyone chasing the retro atmosphere of this era, it's a rare treat. Posted rates are usually ignored in favor of promotional discount rates of US$50/60 for singles/doubles.

Lima Sheraton (Map pp94-5; ☎ 315 5000; www .sheraton.com.pe; Paseo de la República 170; d US$90-230) Over 400 spacious rooms and suites are contained in this vertigo-inducing tower that overlooks the venerable Palacio de Justicia. Abstract designs and muted desert tones unify the public and private spaces, with convenient amenities geared for business travelers. There's a Visa ATM, and a casino to spend your freshly withdrawn cash in. Promotional discount prices bring the rates down a fair slice. Rooms on special can be had for as low as US$49; check the website for details or just turn up.

West Lima

Casa Hospedaje Machu Picchu (Map pp88-9; ☎ 424 3479; vanessa_new@hotmail.com; Juan Pablo Ferandini 1015, Breña; dm US$3.50) A family homestay a block off the 10th *cuadra* of Brasil, this place is highly recommended by readers. It is very friendly, secure, has kitchen privileges and a lounge with cable TV. Some English is spoken.

Mami Panchita (Map pp88-9; ☎ 263 7203; www .mamipanchita.com; Avenida Federico Gallesi 198, San Miguel; d US$20/30; 🖳) An amiable Dutch-Peruvian guesthouse in the municipality of San Miguel, Mami Panchita is a secret gem. Its golden reputation relies on word of mouth and repeat visitors, as well as convenient proximity to the airport. A safe, familial atmosphere and a relaxing, flower-bedecked environment are its big draws.

San Isidro

Accommodation in San Isidro is most definitely pitched at the middle to upper income brackets, with scant budget or backpacker options. San Isidro is a little quieter than lively Miraflores, but is a solid locale for people looking for midrange-priced accommodation for a longer period of time or a quiet, secure place to stay.

Malka Youth Hostel (Map p101; ☎ 442 0162; www .youthhostelperu.com; Los Lirios 165; dm student/nonstudent US$6/7; 🖳) Near Parque Americas, this neat little hostel has clean, quiet rooms that sleep three to eight people, plus a couple of private rooms. There are kitchen and laundry facilities, and a TV room with a DVD player and a good selection of titles; in addition there is a games room, luggage storage, 24-hour hot water and even a small climbing wall in its neat, relaxing garden.

Casa Bella Perú (Map p101; ☎ 441 0643; www.casa bellaperu.net; Las Flores 459; s/d/tr US$30/35/42; 🖳) If you are looking for a quiet, well-priced place in a pleasant part of town, this is it. Formerly a private house, this expansive property now boasts eight very comfortable rooms. There's a kitchen, a relaxing common area, a big garden and a US$5 laundry service. Airport pickups are available upon request.

Suites Antique (Map p101; ☎ 222 1094; www.suites antique.com; Av 2 de Mayo 954; s/d/ste US$85/85/100; 🞲 🖳) Comfortable, spacious and convenient are the three words that best describe this suite complex located close to a brace of decent restaurants. The rooms are generally large, airy and tastefully decorated. There is also a cozy in-house café-restaurant.

Suites del Bosque (Map p101; ☎ 221 1108; www .suitesdelbosque.com; Paz Soldán 165; executive ste s/d US$140/150, master ste US$200; 🞲 🖳) Unapolo-

getically upmarket, suites here come in two flavors: executive and master. They are very swish and comfortable, and boast all the latest gadgets. The in-house Los Cristales restaurant does a sumptuous daily buffet lunch.

Hotel Country Club (Map p101; ☎ 611 9000; www .hotelcountry.com; Los Eucaliptos 590; s/d US$175/250; 🞲 🖳) Built in 1927, this hotel is housed in one of Lima's finest buildings, which has been superbly renovated with a glorious lobby covered by a stained-glass dome. The hotel manages to meld slick modern class with a carefully nurtured colonial charm. The rooms range from the simply luxurious master to the decadently opulent presidential suite.

Sonesta Posada del Inca (Map p101; ☎ 712 6000; www.sonesta.com/peru_lima; Pancho Fiero 194; s/d US$205/235; 🞲 🖳 🞲) Yet another upper-range accommodation choice. This rather expansive complex right in the centre of San Isidro is downright comfortable. The large, airy rooms have all the facilities: minibar, marble bathrooms, data ports for laptops, air-con and suchlike. Disabled visitors are also catered for upon request.

Los Delfines Hotel (Map p101; ☎ 215 7000; www .losdelfineshotel.com; Los Eucaliptos 555; s/d incl breakfast US$220/250; 🞲 🖳) This hotel is famous as much for its long-term guests Yaku and Wayra – dolphins kept in a cramped pool alongside the hotel's lobby bar – as it is for its luxurious rooms and casino. The dolphins perform at regular intervals, including an evening show at 8:30pm Tuesday to Sunday.

Miraflores
BUDGET

Casa del Mochilero (Map p102; ☎ 444 9089; pil aryv@hotmail.com; 2nd fl, Chacaltana 130A; r with shared bathroom per person US$4) This youthful homestay is a popular enough lodging and has a rather laidback casual atmosphere. The place has simple rooms, shared hot showers and kitchen usage. There's a DVD setup in the small downstairs casual lounge.

Friend's House (Map p102; ☎ 446 6248; friendsho use_peru@yahoo.com.mx; Jirón Manco Cápac 368; dm/d US$6/14) This backpacker-friendly hostel has a highly sociable atmosphere – perhaps inescapable given the cramped nature of the dorms. Kitchen privileges are available, as well as a small lounge with cable TV and bicycle rental.

Hitchhikers (Map p102; ☎ 242 3008; www.hhikers peru.com; Bolognesi 400; dm/s/d US$8/16/18) One of the newer additions to the ever expanding (and occasionally contracting) backpacker scene in Miraflores, Hitchhikers has got a good balance of features: security, comfort, cleanliness and sleeper-friendliness. The bare courtyard could do with some greenery, but the rooms and standard packie comforts are all present. A good choice.

Bed & Breakfast José Luis (Map pp88–9; ☎ 444 1015; hsjluis@terra.com.pe; Paula de Ugarriza 727; r per person incl breakfast US$10) On a quiet residential street off 28 de Julio east of Paseo de la República, this huge rabbit warren of a place is popular with guests appreciative of the friendly English-speaking host and the characterful old building. All but three of the basic rooms have bathrooms. Reservations only.

Inkawasi (Map p102; ☎ 241 8218; backpackerinkawasi@hotmail.com; Av de la Aviación 210; dm US$10, d US$25-30, all incl breakfast) This small budget place is modern, well furnished and close to clifftop parks. There's a small interior garden for relaxing. The owner speaks fluent English.

Flying Dog Backpackers (Map p102; ☎ 445 6745; www.flyingdogperu.com; Ernesto Diez Canseco 117; dm/d incl breakfast US$10/25; ☒) In the pulsing heart of Miraflores, the Flying Dog is run by laid-back, youthful staff who speak fluent English. There's a common kitchen, cable TV and a billiards lounge. Cheap rates include the works: local phone calls, luggage storage and unlimited filtered water. They also have two other accommodation properties; see website for details.

Albergue Turístico Juvenil Internacional (Map p102; ☎ 446 5488; www.limahostell.com.pe; Av Casimiro Juan Ulloa 328; dm/d US$11/28) Tucked away on a residential street, this renovated hostel is an excellent choice for its spotless dorms, though the private rooms aren't such a bargain. The hostel also offers a large lounge, good kitchen facilities, plentiful travel information and a spacious garden with an outdoor pool.

Pensión Yolanda (Map p102; ☎ 445 7565; pension yolanda@hotmail.com; Domingo Elías 230; s/d with shared bathroom US$12/24, d US$30) Rooms here are plain and a shade overpriced, but the hostel provides very helpful tourist information and the friendly manager speaks fluent English, French and German.

MIDRANGE

Olimpus Hostel (Map p102; ☎ 242 6077; olimpusperu@terra.com.pe; Diego Ferre 365; dm/s/d incl breakfast US$15/38 /56) This is another friendly hostel with well-decorated, spotless rooms, welcoming communal areas and a gregarious owner. The rates are flexible.

Residencial Alfa (Map p102; ☎ 241 1446; residencial_alfa@yahoo.com; Av de la Aviación 565; s/d incl breakfast US$25/35 ☒) Close to the green and relaxing clifftop park on the north side of Miraflores you'll find this discerning option in a quiet neighborhood. There's no sign – just look for the international flags on the gate. Rooms are airy, tidy and very well appointed. Internet access is free and airport pickups can be arranged.

Hostal Señorial (Map p102; ☎ 445 7306; www.senorial.net; José Gonzalez 567; s/d incl breakfast US$35/45; ☒) Some rooms are better than others at this popular hostel, which has a tranquil internal lawn and a novel visitors' book scrawled on the walls. The good-sized rooms include cable TV, plus there's a solarium.

Hostal el Patio (Map p102; ☎ 444 2107, www.hostalelpatio.net; Ernesto Diez Canseco 341A; d/ste incl breakfast US$45/65; ☒) This little gem of a guesthouse has a cheery English-speaking owner. The quaint inn has a sunny courtyard with a fountain and trailing plants, and several terraces upon which to chill. Rooms are very comfortable and the suites have kitchens and minifridges. Filtered water is supplied to all rooms.

Hotel Alemán (Map p102; ☎ 445 6999; www.hotelalema.com.pe; Av Arequipa 4704; s/d incl breakfast $42/55) The clean and secure Hotel Alemán has exceptionally spacious rooms with colonial furnishings, private bathrooms, cable TV, telephones, large desks and minifridges. It gives discounts for long stays.

Hotel San Antonio Abad (Map p102; ☎ 447 6766; www.hotelsanantonioabad.com; Ramón Ribeyro 301; s/d incl breakfast US$45/55) This is a popular and pleasant hotel set back from the road. It has grassy gardens and comfy rooms with cable TV and phone, and offers free airport pickup with advance notice.

Hostal Torreblanca (Map p102; ☎ 447 3363; www.torreblancaperu.com; Av José Pardo 1453; s/d US$45/55) Though the narrow corridors look pretty haphazard as you stand waiting in the cramped lobby, the varied rooms are actually in very good nick. A few on the top floor have wood-beamed ceilings, red tiling and fireplaces. The amenities are above average.

Hotel Larcomar View (Map p102; ☎ 445 7321; Las Dalias 276; s/d US$45/55) This vaguely Swiss, odd-looking hotel has a cozy atmosphere and comfortable rooms with TV; four of the rooms have balconies overlooking a nice little garden. You may get a 20% discount if you show this book.

Hostal Esperanza (Map p102; ☎ 444 2411; htl esperanza@terra.com.pe; Esperanza 350; s/d US$45/60) This place is an externally ugly high-rise that is safe and clean within. It's main advantage is its very central location.

La Castellana (Map p102; ☎ 444 4662; www.hotel -lacastellana.com; Grimaldo del Solar 222; s/d incl breakfast US$50/60) Housed in a colonial-style villa, alluring La Castellana offers pleasant, if slightly dark, rooms with cable TV, direct-dial phones and dual-voltage outlets. There's a grassy interior garden and a terrace for partaking of your continental breakfast.

Hotel El Doral (Map p102; ☎ 242 7799; www.eldoral .com.pe; Av José Pardo 486; s/d US$54/61 incl breakfast; 🖳 🖳) Rooms in this high-rise hotel have cable TV, minibars and small sitting rooms plus that all-important double-glazing fronting onto one of Miraflores' busiest streets. There's a very small open-air swimming pool and bar on a high terrace.

La Paz Apart Hotel (Map p102; ☎ 242 9350; www .lapazaparthotel.com; Av de la Paz 679; s/d incl breakfast US$70/75; 🖃 🖳) This modern high-rise still looks brand spanking new. All of the sparklingly clean suites have kitchenettes, separate bedrooms, direct-dial telephones and dual-voltage outlets. The most spacious suites sleep up to five people. Wi-fi internet is available on the 3rd and 6th floors.

Hotel Ariosto (Map p102; ☎ 444 1414; www.hotelari osto.com.pe; Av de la Paz 769; s/d/tr incl breakfast US$75/75/90; 🖃 🖳) This time-warped hotel, which attracts a fair quota of jazz musicians and writers, attempts – and partially pulls off – a woody, country charm. It has a 24-hour restaurant service and a sauna, and rates include free airport pickup. Discounted rates are frequently arranged for long stays or in the off-season.

TOP END

Miraflores has numerous top-class establishments, and only a selection of the most noteworthy is given here. All of the following have a restaurant, and phones and cable TV in the rooms.

Hotel Antigua Miraflores (Map p102; ☎ 241 6116; www.peru-hotels-inns.com; Av Grau 350; s $64-74, d US$74-89, ste US$89-104; 🖃 🖳) In a converted early-20th-century mansion, the Hotel Antigua Miraflores is situated in a quiet spot. Its elegant lounges are decorated with colonial and mod-

ern Peruvian art. The rooms, while sporting all the expected modern facilities, also have intriguing antique flourishes. Rooms vary in size and style; the suites are most sumptuous, with Jacuzzi, kitchen and air-con.

JW Marriott Hotel Lima (Map p102; ☎ 217 7000; www.marriotthotels.com/limdt; Malecón de la Reserva 615; s/d/ste US$155/175/375; 🅿 🖃 🖳 🖳) The luxurious, space-age, five-star Marriott is perhaps the flashiest of them all, with a superb seafront location by the LarcoMar shopping center. The sparkling rooms seem to have every amenity going, including temperature regulation and no fewer than three phones in each room, and there are glass-fronted restaurants and bars, a large casino, plus an open-air tennis court and pool.

Hotel las Américas (Map p102; ☎ 444 7272; www .hoteleslasamericas.com; Alfredo Benavides 415; r US$180-330; 🖃 🖳 🖳) This standard five-star hotel has all the luxury and services you would expect for the price tag.

Miraflores Park Hotel (Map p102; ☎ 242 3000; www.mira-park.com; Malecón de la Reserva 1035; s/d/ste US$295/295/340; 🅿 🖃 🖳 🖳) Surely the best of Lima's smaller luxury hotels, the Miraflores Park Hotel has glorious ocean views and all the frills expected of a five-star hotel, including a gym, a sauna, a squash court and a small outdoor pool overlooking the ocean. Some rooms have glass walls with stunning views. Want to indulge? For US$40 let the bath butler run an aphrodisiac-salt-infused, flower-petal-strewn, candle-lit bath for you and a guest.

Barranco

Once a holiday resort for upper-crust *limeños*, Barranco's budget scene is now blossoming, with several top-notch new hostels to rival anything in Miraflores.

Point Lodge (Map p104; ☎ 247 7997; www.the pointhostels.com; Junín 300; dm US$7-9, d US$18; 🖳) This whitewashed villa is a popular, long-running hostel with fairly comfortable dorms as well as the toys that backpackers crave: cable TV and a DVD collection, free internet access, pool and table-tennis tables, hammocks, a shared kitchen and a popular in-house bar. The staff are only too willing to act as guides on the Friday evening pub trawl.

D'Osma Alojamiento (Map p104; ☎ 251 4178; deosma@ec-red.com; Av San Pedro de Osma 240; s/d incl breakfast US$10/20) Far less of a backpacker scene, this family home has a quiet environment good for long-term stays. There are only a few rooms so book ahead. Some English and German is spoken. There is no obvious sign; look for the big wooden gate and ring the bell.

Backpackers Inn (Map p104; ☎ 247 1326; www .barrancobackpackers.com; Mariscal Castilla 260; dm/d incl breakfast US$12/28) In a renovated mansion with ocean views, this friendly hostel is popular with surfers. It has light-filled dorms with big windows and attached bathrooms with 24-hour hot water. Rates include free internet access. There's a common kitchen and TV lounge, too.

Hostal Gemina (Map p104; ☎ 477 0712; hostal gemina@yahoo.com; Av Grau 620; s/d/tr incl breakfast US$29/42/55) A smart, modern hotel on Barranco's main street, Gemina has been recommended for endless hot water and friendly service. Rates are flexible. There's an on-site cafeteria.

EATING

Lima is arguably the gastronomic capital of the continent, boasting high-quality restaurants in every price range. Seafood is a local specialty, but you'll find restaurants specializing in all types of national and international fare. Don't leave without trying the distinctive sweets *mazamorra morada* (a purple corn pudding), or *suspiro limeño* (a caramel meringue dessert). *Limeños* are primarily beer drinkers, though wine is beginning to be preferred by young professionals. Starting a meal with a pisco sour is very common.

Unless otherwise indicated, restaurants are open for lunch and dinner daily.

Central Lima
BUDGET
Menús (set meals) that cost about US$1.50 to US$2 can be found in many of the cheaper restaurants.

Azato (Map pp94-5; ☎ 423 0278; Arica 298; menús US$1.50-2) It's a recommended spot for fast *criollo* food (spicy fare with Spanish and African influences). It's a fast-food-style joint and is easy to spot with its prominent sign on Arica.

Villa Natura (Map pp94-5; ☎ 426 3944; Ucayali 326; 3-course menús US$1.50-2; ☾ closed Sun) This is one of a proliferation of no-frills, vegetarian pit stops in central Lima. There's no obvious sign; just locate the street number and put your head inside the door.

Panko's (Map pp94-5; ☎ 424 9079; Garcilaso de la Vega 1296; items US$2-4) Panko's is a busy central Lima bakery offering a mouthwatering array of sweets, pastries and drinks, as well as pies and hamburgers.

Pachamanca (Map pp94-5; ☎ 428 7920; Ancash 400; mains US$2-5) This spot, with a have-a-go-at-anything menu and a location near the backpackers' hotels, is popular with gringos and locals alike.

La Merced (Map pp94-5; ☎ 427 7933; Miró Quesada 158; mains US$2-6) This restaurant, usually bustling with businesspeople doing lunch, has a bland exterior that gives no clue to its spacious interior and intricately carved wooden ceiling. At busy times you may have to wait for a table.

El Cordano (Map pp94-5; ☎ 427 0181; Ancash 202; snacks US$2-4, mains US$4-7) Though looking a shade run-down these days, El Cordano is a long standing downtown bar-cum-restaurant with 1920s décor. It serves typical Peruvian snacks – the country ham rolls are popular – and a top selection of Peruvian beers, wines and excellent pisco sours.

La Casera (Map pp94-5; ☎ 427 2380; Huancavelica 244; menús US$2.50; ☾ closed Sun) Little more than a relaxed fast-food joint, this simple and brusque place serves typical Peruvian food at economical prices.

Queirolo (Map pp94-5; ☎ 425 0421; Camaná 900; mains US$3-5; ☾ closed dinner Sun) An atmospheric old restaurant popular for its set lunches and its role as a drinking-and-gathering spot for *limeños*. You can't mistake it – its walls are filled with wine and spirit bottles.

Rovegno (Map pp94-5; ☎ 424 8465; Arenales, 456; mains US$3-7) A cross between a delicatessen and a snack bar, this Italian-style *pastelería-bodega* (pastry-shop-cum-wine-shop) is very handy for travelers staying in nearby Santa Beatriz. Dishes run the gamut of stock Peruvian staples, from *lomo saltado* (strips of beef stir-fried with onions, tomatoes, potatoes and chili) to fish and vegetarian options.

Self-Catering
In central Lima, the best supermarket is **Metro** (Map pp94-5; Cuzco; ☾ 8am-10pm daily).

MIDRANGE
If you can, don't miss a trip to Lima's Barrio Chino (Chinatown), southeast of the Plaza de Armas. Lima houses about 200,000 first-generation Chinese immigrants and its Chi-

nese quarter is blessed with numerous authentic restaurants in a lively pedestrian mall lined with paving slabs inscribed with news of weddings, births and other happy events.

El Estadio Futbol Club (Map pp94-5; ☎ 428 8866; Nicolás de Piérola 926; mains US$4-9; ☺ noon-midnight Mon-Wed, noon-2am Thu-Sat) On Plaza San Martín, this *fútbol*-themed bar serves hearty food, with over 22 choices on the menu. Chicken and fish dishes predominate. Sit at indoor or outdoor tables, a few of which are already occupied by waxwork soccer stars such as Maradona and Pelé.

Manhattan Restaurant (Map pp94-5; ☎ 428 2117; Miró Quesada 253; mains US$4-10; ☺ 8am-7pm Mon-Fri) This sophisticated, mellow hideaway has good *menús*, as well as a happy hour from 5pm to closing time at 7pm. The tasty *sopa a la criolla* (mildly spiced, creamy noodle soup with beef and peppers) and the *escalope pollo con verdana* (chicken escalopes) make for a filling meal.

Cevichería la Choza Nautica (Map pp94-5; ☎ 261 5537; Breña 204; mains US$6-10; ☺ lunch & dinner) *La choza* means 'the shack,' a conscious play of words with the upscale La Rosa Nautica restaurant in Miraflores. And this popular little *cevichería* (restaurant serving raw seafood marinated in lime juice) doesn't miss the opportunity to play on the aphrodisiac qualities of seafood either – just look for their 'ceviche erotica' *menú*.

Wa Lok (Map pp94-5; ☎ 447 1329; Paruro 864; mains US$5-12; ☺ closed dinner Sun) This is one of the better *chifas* (Chinese restaurants) in Chinatown, though it is better if you ask for the English-language version of the menu. The portions are enormous so don't overorder.

Salon Capon (Map pp94-5; ☎ 426 9286; Paruro 819; mains US$6-10; ☺ closes 8pm Sun) Similar to Wa Lok, though somewhat smaller, Salon Capon has particularly good dim sum.

San Remo Restaurant (Map pp94-5; ☎ 427 9102; Pasaje de los Escribanos; 2-course menús US$7) Half a block from the Plaza de Armas, Pasaje de los Escribanos has several upscale cafés, including this welcoming outdoor spot.

La Muralla (Map pp94-5; ☎ 426 6113; Parque de la Muralla, Amazonas cuadra 1; buffet US$8; ☺ 9am-9pm) Handily located in the Parque de la Muralla archaeological complex (p97), La Muralla is a smart and newish dining venue. Its daily buffet is its main attraction and has a wide array of carefully prepared Peruvian dishes. You can also get a late breakfast here too.

TOP END
L'Eau Vive (Map pp94-5; ☎ 427 5612; Ucayali 370; lunch US$10, dinner US$25; ☺ 12:30-3pm & 7:30-9:30pm Mon-Sat) This unique restaurant has *menús* prepared and served by a French order of nuns; it features dishes from all over the world, as well as some exotic cocktails. The restaurant is in a quiet, colonial-style house and is a welcome relief from the Lima madhouse, though it can be a bit hard to find. Ring the doorbell to gain access. The nuns are supposed to sing 'Ave Maria' at 9pm.

West Lima
Bircher Benner (Map pp88-9; ☎ 463 0276; www.bircher benner.com; San Felipe 720, Jesús María; mains US$3-7; ☺ closed Sun) Established in 1972 to provide a healthy alternative to Lima's meat- and fish-heavy food, this vegetarian restaurant and shop produces many imaginative creations. Mushroom ceviche is one – an enticing mix of mushroom, onions, coriander, tomato and ricotta. You'll need a cab to get here.

San Isidro
In San Isidro there is a noticeable absence of cheap hole-in-the-wall eateries such as you will find in central Lima or even in Miraflores. This is the enclave of fine dining places and haute cuisine – even the streets are noticeably more refined. The two main dining strips are Av 2 de Mayo and Conquistadores, the latter of which also hosts most of the nightspots. Italian-style restaurants predominate, though there are some fine ceviche places and at least a couple of Mexican restaurants.

For self-catering, **Vivanda** (Map p101; Av 2 de Mayo; ☺ 8am-10:30pm) is one of the best supermarket options in Lima.

MIDRANGE
Como Agua para Chocolate (Map p101; ☎ 222 0297; Pancho Fierro 108; mains US$4-9) Taking its cue from the movie *Like Water for Chocolate*, this Mexican has made its home in San Isidro. Chocolate only appears in its desserts, while the food runs the gamut of standard Mexican staples. The lunchtime *menús* (US$6) are a good option and offer imaginative choices. Excellent wine list.

Puerto Perdido (Map pp88-9; ☎ 264 3435; Pezet 1455; mains US$5-7; ☺ lunch only) Two blocks southwest of Lima Golf Club, this seafood restaurant serves excellent ceviche and is popular with a young crowd.

Chili's (Map p101; ☎ 222 8917; Óvalo Gutierrez; mains US$5-8; ☻ noon-1am) 'Like no other place' goes the slogan at this Tex-Mex grill and bar. It's hip and happy, the food sparkles and you'll have a spicy time. Ribs, fajitas, quesadillas and shrimp dishes are all on offer. Enjoy them with a classic margarita.

Antica (Map p101; ☎ 222 9488; Av 2 de Mayo 732; mains US$5-9; ☻ noon-midnight) With rustic knick-knack-covered walls, candle-bedecked tables and solid wooden benches, this place has wood-fired-oven-cooked pizza and calzone that taste just that little bit more authentic. Order the very reasonable house wine to wash it all down.

El Cartujo (Map p101; ☎ 221 4962; Libertadores 108; mains US$6-8; ☻ 8-1pm) Have a refreshing pisco sour at the long wooden cocktail bar then select a table for gastronomic treats that range from Argentinean beef to ceviche to lobster to pasta. This is a very atmospheric place for lunch.

TOP END

Punta Sal (Map p101; ☎ 441 7431; Conquistadores 958; mains US$9-15) Another great seafood restaurant, Punta Sal is one of the best places for traditional ceviche. Try the assassin ceviche with black scallops and sea urchins if you dare. Very reasonably priced for a classy restaurant.

Punto Italiano (Map p101; ☎ 221 3167; Av 2 de Mayo 647; mains US$10-16 ☻ lunch & dinner) Italian cuisine with a Sardinian twist is dished up at this popular and homey trattoria-style venue. Handmade ravioli is filling and full of taste while the *carne tagliata* (veal with tagliatelle) with Sardinian cheese is divine. Don't forget the top Punto Italian pizza.

Alfresco (Map p101; ☎ 422 8915; www.alfrescoperu .com; Santa Luisa 295; mains US$10-18) Part of a well-known and well-appreciated restaurant chain, this quality eatery is presided over by chef Alfredo Aramburú Picasso. With a name like that you'd expect his food to be artwork – and it is. The fish creations are quite stunning; try the charcoal fillet of sea bream.

Valentino (Map p101; ☎ 441 6174; Manuel Bañon 215; mains US$10-20) Mediterranean in outlook, discreet and classy in delivery, Valentino serves up gastronomic treats with a seductive touch. Tuna tartare, glazed duck breast and gnocchi in lobster sauce are among the tempting options on offer.

Trattoria San Seferino (Map p101; ☎ 422 8242; Av 2 de Mayo 793; mains US$11-19) Yet another Italian eating place, this time a trattoria specializing in hearty country fare. *Bife de chorizo* – similar to a New York strip steak, but bigger – is popular, as is the unusual dishes of potted duck and green risotto with homemade pesto.

Matsuei (Map p101; ☎ 422 4323; Manuel Bañon 260; mains US$12-17; ☻ lunch & dinner) Japanese cuisine can be enjoyed at it best at this classy restaurant-cum-sushi-bar. The sashimi and *maki* rolls beg for consumption, yet you won't go wrong with the delicate texture of the tempura and yakitori dishes.

Miraflores

BUDGET

Restaurants are more expensive in Miraflores, but if you keep your eyes peeled there's still a few hole-in-the-wall cafés selling cheap *menús*; check out the places on Berlin between Av Grau and Diagonal. US-style fast-food joints cluster around Óvalo Gutierrez, in the northwest of Miraflores. Vegetarian options

---

THE AUTHOR'S CHOICE

Segundo Muelle (Map p101; ☎ 421 1206; www.segundomuelle.com; Conquistadores 490; mains US$6-8; ☻ noon-5pm) You know your lunch is going to be a pleasurable one when you see the crowded tables and animated faces of discerning diners at this *cevichería* (restaurant serving raw seafood marinated in lime juice). Ceviche is a lunchtime dish in Peru and it is eaten with full seriousness. It helps when a local is your host and can guide you through the maze of visually stunning dishes (the picture menu helps!). Secundo Muelle is one of four restaurants bearing the same name, and this one really buzzes when hungry and fussy San Isidrans come for their lunchtime ceviche. The *ceviche de mariscos a los tres ajies* (shellfish in three-chili sauce) is one obvious choice; it won first prize for the best Peruvian ceviche and it's deservedly worthy (see how it is made at their website). The *parrilla marina* (seafood grill) is also a top-notch option, and was the host's choice. Whatever you choose it will be guaranteed to be of high quality. It also helps that the service is quick, professional & diligent. Top marks to this excellent *cevichería*.

are thin on the ground but are reasonably cheap. Miraflores has by far the best pavement cafés in Lima for people-watching.

Café Café (Map p102; drinks US$1.50-6, snacks & sandwiches US$2-4); Mártir Olaya (☎ 445 1165; Mártir Olaya 250); LarcoMar (☎ 445 9499; Malecon de la Reserva 610, Miraflores; ⏰ to 3am Fri & Sat) With two branches in Miraflores, this place advertises 120 different drinks, gourmet coffees, sandwiches and desserts. The LarcoMar branch is the place to see and be seen, with a great location looking directly out to sea and down to the surfers below; it's not for sufferers of vertigo.

Ima Sumac (Map p102; ☎ 446 2713; Colón 241; 3-course menús US$2; ⏰ lunch only) It's a warm and friendly little place with great-value menús. Take-away or delivery (extra US$0.30) is possible if you're in Miraflores.

Quattro D (Map p102; ☎ 447 1523; Av Angamos Oeste 408; items $2.50-5) This place has perhaps the best Italian ice cream in town, boasting 36 different flavors, as well as delicious cakes and good coffee. It even offers up their own take on pizza if coffee and cakes are not sufficient for you.

Santa Isabel (Map p102; Alfredo Benavides 487; mains US$2.50-6; ⏰ 24 hr) Open all night, this café-restaurant has a varied buffet.

Govinda (Map p102; ☎ 444 2871; Schell 634; 3-course menús US$3-4; ⏰ closed dinner Sun) A cheap-and-cheerful café run by the Hare Krishna; there are lots of healthy veggie options for meat avoiders.

Chifa Kun Fa (Map p102; ☎ 447 8634; San Martín 459; mains US$3-6) Good Peruvian-style Chinese food is served here.

Self-Catering

There are many supermarkets loaded with both local and imported food, drink, toiletries and medicines. One of the best is **Vivanda** (Map p102; Benavides Alfredo Benavides 487; ⏰ 24 hr; Pardo Av José Pardo; ⏰ 8am-10:30pm), which rivals any North American mall hangout.

MIDRANGE

The trendiest spot to dine in Miraflores is currently in the LarcoMar shopping mall, with its spectacular location teetering on the brink of the coastal cliffs. The complex is packed with smart cafés and a young crowd partaking of their pricey beverages, and there's even a sushi bar.

Several British-style pubs in Miraflores offer international pub grub (p118).

Pardo's Chicken (Map p102; ☎ 446 4790; Alfredo Benavides 730; mains US$3-9) An ubiquitous chicken-and-fries restaurant that largely manages to escape the atmosphere of a fast-food place. Pardo's also does ribs and *anticuchos* (shish kebabs).

Haiti (Map p102; ☎ 445 0539; Parque Central; mains US$4-8) Located right opposite Parque Central, this is an excellent spot to watch the world go by – its tables spill out onto one of the busiest pedestrian areas in Miraflores. The bow-tied waiters are very suave and a little overformal, but there's not a better place to go for breakfast after a hard night out or for an evening pisco sour to massage your thoughts.

El Parquetito (Map p102; ☎ 444 0490; Lima 373; mains US$4-8) El Parquetito has shady outdoor tables on a pedestrian street and good breakfasts.

Solari (Map p102; ☎ 242 3100; Av José Pardo 216; mains US$4-9) Serving a mix of international dishes in a flashy, modern glass building complete with plants and an artificial waterfall, this restaurant has an atmosphere that only slightly resembles that of an indoor swimming pool.

Glorietta (Map p102; ☎ 445 0498; Diagonal 181; mains US$5-10) Parque Kennedy and Diagonal, nicknamed 'Pizza Street,' have numerous open-fronted Italian joints to choose from, including this reasonable spot.

Sí Señor (Map p102; ☎ 445 3789; Bolognesi 706; mains US$6-10; ⏰ evening only). This lively place serves Tex-Mex food, usually accompanied by Mexican beer and, of course, plenty of tequila.

Vista al Mar (Map p102; ☎ 242 5705; Malecon de la Reserva 610; mains US$6-12) When the smell of garlic hits your nose on a Pacific sea breeze, you know you will dine well. Built into the clifftop and with its balcony dangling out over the sea, Vista al Mar is an elegant, modern restaurant serving a variety of meals and snacks. Fish and ceviche are wise options. It also does a great breakfast buffet at weekends. Watch for the occasional paraglider floating past along the cliffs.

La Tranquera (Map p102; ☎ 447 5111; Av José Pardo 285; mains US$7-16) This 30-year-old favorite is an Argentine-influenced recommendation for meat, meat and more meat. It serves a US$75 *parrillada* (grilled meats) that supposedly serves five, but looks more fit for 10. There's also a special selection of meats, such as *cuy* (guinea pig; US$14), rabbit and game.

La Trattoria (Map p102; ☎ 446 7002; Manuel Bonilla 106; mains US$7-16; ⏰ dinner) Recommended for tasty, homemade pasta that you can watch being made, La Trattoria is a simple, laid-back Italian restaurant with a quiet ambience.

Il Postino (Map p102; ☎ 446 8381; Colina 401; mains US$8-13; ☒ closed dinner Sun) This is one of Miraflores' best Italian restaurants, with an informal Mediterranean atmosphere and a great collection of reasonably priced international wines.

TOP END

La Tiendecita Blanca (Map p102; ☎ 445 9797; Av José Larco 111; mains US$9-16) On the Óvalo by Parque Central, this has been a Miraflores landmark for over half a century. It has a superb, if pricey, Swiss pastry selection.

Cebichería Don Beta (Map p102; ☎ 445 8370; José Gálvez 667; 3-course menús US$10-13) Don't be put off by the tiny exterior of this locally popular seafood restaurant; it opens up into an attractive room with a thatched roof and nautical theme. It tends to be quiet midweek, but picks up on weekends. The seafood is exceptionally fresh and the range of ceviche choices is quite broad.

Las Tejas (Map p102; ☎ 444 4360; Ernesto Diez Canseco 340; mains US$10-15) For a good variety of Peruvian fare featuring shellfish, kebabs and rice-based dishes, try this small snug place, set below road level near Hostal el Patio. It has live *criollo* (coastal) music at 8pm from Thursday to Saturday.

La Hamaca (Map p102; ☎ 242 7978; Av Arequipa 4698; mains US$6-18; ☒ closed dinner Sun) This high-class restaurant takes an intimate atmosphere to another level with tables in private booths, each carefully decorated with antique touches. It serves a limited menu of typical Peruvian food. You'll know you've arrived when you see the outdoor *hamaca* (hammock).

Restaurant Huaca Pucllana (Map p102; ☎ 445 4042; General Borgoño cuadra 8; mains US$8-20) This mellow, sophisticated establishment sits overlooking the pre-Inca pyramidal temple Huaca Pucllana and serves wonderful contemporary Peruvian cuisine plus a smattering of Italian specialties. Check the daily specials board.

Ambrosia (Map p102; ☎ 242 3000; Malecón de la Reserva 1035; mains US$8-20) Based in the Miraflores Park Hotel, this sophisticated, highbrow restaurant gets the culinary thumbs-up for its international gourmet meals.

Las Brujas de Cachiche (Map p102; ☎ 444 5310; alcorta@brujasdecachiche.com.pe; Bolognesi 460; mains US$9-15, 3-course menús US$25) Las Brujas weaves its image around the tale of the village of Ca-

chiche near Ica, where legendary temptresses and sorcerers meddled with the populace. It's one of the best places in town for quality Peruvian food.

Astrid y Gaston (Map p102; ☎ 242 5387; Cantuarias 175; mains US$10-22; ☒ lunch & dinner) This elegant upper-class *limeño* mainstay has Cordon Bleu–trained chefs who create excellent international food. Dishes to watch out for are tuna *tiradito* (Japanese-influenced ceviche, served in thin slices without onion), veal osso buco and Piuran groper. Owner Gastón Acurio is quite a culinary media personality in his own right and has been the capital's flavor of the month, after month, after month.

La Rosa Nautica (Map p102; ☎ 445 0149; Circuito de Playas; mains US$11-25, 3-course menús US$17) This famous restaurant is in a fabulous building at the end of Playa Costa Verde's historic pier. The location and atmosphere are unique: the ocean is floodlit, surfers sometimes skim through the pilings, and you can clearly hear and smell the waves below. Take a taxi to the pier and walk the last 100m. Recommended dishes include the grilled sea bass, and the mouthwatering crayfish, crab and tomato cocktail.

El Señorio de Sulco (Map p102; ☎ 441-0389; Malecón Cisneros 1470; buffet US$25) A well-known restaurant close to the clifftops of Miraflores, El Señorio is known for its excellent *criollo* seafood and meats.

Barranco

BUDGET

Barranco is a very pleasant place to get away and dine. The passageway under El Puente de los Suspiros leads to several *anticucho* stalls and restaurants, though they tend to have pushy touts vying for business. The *anticucho de corazón* (beef-heart *anticucho*) served up here are great right off the grill.

Las Mesitas (Map p104; ☎ 477 4199; Av Grau 341; mains US$3-5) A good but run-of-the-mill choice, Las Mesitas has decent service, light meals and an array of tempting Peruvian desserts.

El Hornito (Map p104; ☎ 477 2465; Av Grau 209; mains US$3-7) As well as excellent pizzas, this very central dining venue offers up a wide range of *parrilladas* and pasta dishes. The vine-covered patio with fairy-light-illuminated trees is pleasant at night.

Javier (Map p104; ☎ 477 5339; Barjada de los Baños 403B; mains US$3.50-6) One of three adjoining restaurants, Javier is recommended for its wide range of offerings, including the ubiquitous *anticuchos*.

MIDRANGE

While there is not a huge range of choices in Barranco, places tend to be atmospheric, cozy and distinguished by good and attentive service.

Cevichería Barranco (Map p104; ☎ 467 4560; Panamá Sur 270; mains US$4-7; ☽ lunch only) This cheap seafood restaurant has a welcoming patio with a thatched roof. Yet again there is no sign; look for the imposing brick wall and wooden gate. It's a 15-minute walk from central Barranco.

Manos Morenas (Map p104; ☎ 467 0421; Av San Pedro de Osma 409; mains US$5-12; ☽ closed dinner Sun) Manos Morenas is an informal *peña* (bar or club featuring live folkloric music) that's highly recommended locally for both its top-notch *criollo* food and its live *criollo* music (after 10pm) Tuesday to Saturday. There's a cover charge of US$10.

Antica Trattoria (Map p104; ☎ 247 3443; San Martín 201; mains US$6-9; ☽ noon-4pm & 7pm-1am) This classy Italian joint with a nouveau-rustic air serves up pizza, but it is better recommended for its pasta concoctions and generic Italian cuisine. Dishes to savor include ravioli stuffed with crab, osso buco with polenta, and filling risottos.

La Canta Rana (Map p104; ☎ 477 8934; Génova 101; mains US$7-10; ☽ lunch only) Literally translated as 'the Singing Frog,' this unpretentious place is a great *cevichería* serving all manner of seafood. Portions tend to be small, but it has great lunchtime and weekend ambience. There's no obvious sign; look for the green walls.

TOP END

La Costa Verde (Map p104; ☎ 477 5228; Playa Barranquito; mains US$10-40) Located directly on the Barranco beachfront, this sophisticated restaurant is recommended for its excellent seafood. It has a Sunday buffet for about US$43 per person including wine. Take a taxi there and away at night from Miraflores (US$1 to US$1.50).

DRINKING

Lima is overflowing with bars of every description – from San Isidro's havens for the modern elite to Barranco's cheap-and-cheerful stomping grounds. Weekends from January to March also see the fresh-from-the-beach summer crowds heading down to Kilometer 97 on the Panamericana for the nightlife.

Unfortunately, several bars and nightclubs discriminate against nonwhites. Be aware, and if you find one, walk on and drink elsewhere. As a quick comparison of prices, drinks in Barranco cost between US$2.50 and US$4, while in San Isidro they can go as high as US$4 to US$6.

Central Lima

The nightlife in central Lima is limited. Most *limeños* on the lookout for a party or even just a night out with friends tend to head to Miraflores or Barranco, where there is an almost unlimited selection of nightspots. Travelers based in central Lima tend to congregate in small gringo restaurants near their accommodation, or occasionally gather at one of the many cafés that border the two main plazas, Plaza de Armas and Plaza San Martín. The two plazas offer a world of people-watching and relaxed schmoozing rather than the frenetic rhythms of the two coastal hot spots.

El Estadio Futbol Club (Map pp94-5; ☎ 428 8866; Nicolás de Piérola 926; ☽ noon-midnight Mon-Wed, noon-2am Thu-Sun) For something a little unusual, dribble your way towards this soccer-themed bar on Plaza San Martín. It is a great illustration of soccer fanaticism Peruvian style, where you can literally rub shoulders with waxwork models of famous soccer players. It's a bit unnerving being welcomed by David Beckham or sitting with Pelé in the corner. Notwithstanding, the beer is good and is served in 1.5L jugs or steinlike pots. Every chair is named after a soccer player and there is as much soccer-related paraphernalia as will fit on the walls.

Gran Hotel Bolívar (Map pp94-5; ☎ 619 7171; Jirón de la Unión 958) If you really fancy a trip back to yesteryear don your glad rags and step into the cavernous interior of Lima's most famous hotel. Oozing dusty, faded charm and elegance, the streetside bar at this grand old hotel serves up an infamously good pisco sour; if you dare, order the *pisco catedral*, a double-sized pisco sour! You may occasionally get a solo piano player tinkling out a few nostalgic classics.

San Isidro

For the most modern bars (with the most elevated prices), head to San Isidro.

Tai Lounge (Map p101; ☎ 422 7351; Conquistadores 325; ☽ Mon-Sat) One of Lima's most exclusive spots, Tai Lounge draws the cream of young *limeños*, who appreciate the plush lounging areas, cool outside patios and suave clientele. It also hosts a good Thai restaurant.

Punta G (Map p101; ☎ 440 5237; Conquistadores 510; ✆ Mon-Sat) Another cosmopolitan bar frequented by the in crowd, the intimate Punta G boasts some terrific cocktails. There's no sign; look for the white doors.

Palos de Moguer (Map p101; ☎ 221 8363; Cavenecia 129; ✆ evenings Mon-Sat) This lively alehouse is a little away from the main drag – about 100m north of Óvalo Gutierrez – but is worth a look-in. The pub features a dozen Peruvian boutique beers brewed by Colon, including a very passable brown ale, and can be ordered in enormous 1.5L glasses. If beer is not your drop, there are 17 variations on the pisco sour to sip from.

Los Delfines Bar (Map p101; Los Delfines Hotel, Los Eucaliptos 555) Punters come to this top hotel's elegant bar to watch the resident dolphins do somersaults as they (the patrons) knock back cocktails and try not to think about the conditions the animals are kept in. The show is at 8:30pm from Tuesday to Sunday.

Miraflores

Miraflores has a scattering of would-be British pubs, which serve as haunts of upper-class *limeños* and expats. That said, there is little British about them other than their superficial décor. There is also a dense collection of small, loud bars to which ordinary *limeños* flock on weekends.

Brenchley Arms (Map p102; ☎ 445 9680; Atahualpa 174; ✆ evenings Mon-Sat) A lookalike British bar serving a limited but honest selection of pub grub (US$3 to US$10) – liver and onions features, though the favorite is the hearty chili. There is a dart board as concession to its British heritage, but only one draft beer – and it's Peruvian. Service is attentive and the atmosphere is laid-back.

Old Pub (Map p102; ☎ 242 8155; San Ramón 295; ✆ evenings) At the far end of a busy restaurant-and-bar alley located just west of Parque Kennedy you'll find what purports to be a British pub. Owned by English-speaking expats, this central pub has darts, cable TV and an international dinner menu specializing in beef. Again, there is no draft British beer in sight.

Treff's (Map p102; ☎ 440 0148; Alfredo Benavides 571) This German-style tavern, tucked away from the street through a winding colonial passageway, is another international favorite. It offers friendly service and a pool table, and is a little quieter than the previously listed drinking holes.

Teatriz (Map p102; ☎ 242 3084; LarcoMar, Malecon de la Reserva 610; admission US$8-10; ✆ Mon-Sat) In LarcoMar, the modern Teatriz draws an older clientele who later spill out into the mall's late-night cafés to cool their aching feet.

O'Murphys (Map p102; Schell 627; ✆ evening Mon-Sat) This Irish pub has – sadly – no Irish beer or much ale choice at all. It's nonetheless popular and less sardine-can-like than many of the hole-in-the-wall bars that abound in central Miraflores.

Media Naranja (Map p102; ☎ 446 6946; Schell 130; ✆ Mon-Sat) You can hardly miss the enormous, brightly colored flags on the awnings of this lively Brazilian-themed bar-cum-café wedged into the southwest side of Parque Kennedy.

Barranco

Barranco's tight-knit bars and clubs are concentrated around Barranco's Parque Municipal, which is thronged with revelers on Friday and Saturday nights.

Juanito's (Map p104; Av Grau 274) One of the oldest haunts in Barranco, this was a leftist *peña* of the 1960s; it retains its traditional décor and is still very popular. You can't miss it, though the sign is nowhere to be seen; just look for the room filled with bottles of wine.

El Ekeko Café Bar (Map p104; ☎ 247 3148; Av Grau 266; ✆ 10am-midnight Mon-Wed, 10am-3am Thu-Sat) A generally more sedate option, with free poetry readings on Monday, this faithful old bar comes alive at weekends when the grandfathers of bohemia play live music (US$5 to US$7 cover), trotting out their lively tango, *música folklórica* and cha-cha-chas. The bar also serves up a range of hors d'oeuvres.

La Posada del Mirador (Map p104; ☎ 477 1120; Ermita 104) A *cevichería* by day and a laid-back drinking hole at night, the clifftop Posada del Mirador has outdoor tables that are great for catching the sunset.

Wahio's (Map p104; ☎ 477 4110; Plaza Espinosa; ✆ Thu-Sat) A lively little bar with its fair share of dreadlocks and a classic soundtrack of reggae, ska and dub.

ENTERTAINMENT

Cinemas, theaters, art galleries and music shows are listed in *El Comercio* daily newspaper, with the most detailed listings found in Monday's 'Luces' section. Another useful source of general information is the *Peru Guide*, a free booklet published monthly that can be found at hotels and tourist spots in Lima. The free *Lima Night* guide is distributed in nightspots throughout Lima, with scores of addresses for everything from *peñas* to pubs.

Live Music

Live Peruvian music and dance is performed from Thursday to Saturday at *peñas*, which also double as bars and serve up typical Peruvian food. The programs usually have free sessions for you to strut your own stuff as well. There are two main types of Peruvian music, *folklórica* and *criollo*; the first is more typical of the Andean highlands, while the second is more coastal and therefore more popular in Lima.

Las Brisas de Titicaca (Map pp94-5; ☎ 332 1901; www .brisasdeltiticaca.com; Wakuski 168, Lima Centro; admission general/front row US$8/12.50; ☉ 7pm-late Wed, 9:30pm-late Thu, 10:30pm-late Fri & Sat) This well-recommended – and spectacular – *folklórica peña*, near Plaza Bolognesi in Lima Centro, is popular with *limeños*.

La Candelaria (Map p104; ☎ 247 1314; www.lacan delariaperu.com; Bolognesi 292, Barranco; admission US$7; ☉ 9:30pm-late Fri & Sat) This is a good *peña* that has lively *criollo* music and dancing, with plenty of audience participation.

Sachun Peña (Map p102; ☎ 441 0123; Av del Ejército 657, Miraflores; admission US$10) This recommended place has a variety of acts that get under way in the late evening.

Other rousing *peñas*:

De Rompe Yorada (Map p104; ☎ 247 3271; cnr Bolognesi & Segura, Barranco; ☉ 9:30pm-late Thu-Sat) Good atmospheric place near La Candelaria.

La Estación de Barranco (Map p104; ☎ 247 0344; Av San Pedro de Osma 112, Barranco; admission US$7-15) A well-known *peña* for *criollo* music.

Manos Morenos ((Map p104; ☎ 467 0421; Av San Pedro de Osma 409; admission $10 ☉ closed dinner Sun) Also popular for *criollo* music, which is played after 10pm Tuesday to Saturday.

Nightclubs

The clubs in Lima get going from 11pm or midnight, and continue going strong till dawn. Many have happy hours during the week, but rarely during the crowded weekends, when cover charges can sometimes be as much as US$10.

With a dozen or so bars and clubs, Barranco is by far the simplest place in Lima to go club-hopping, and the action is so tightly packed that you only need to walk a few steps to find an entirely different vibe. Miraflores also has some busy clubs, centered on Parque Central and the LarcoMar shopping center.

Tequila Rocks (Map p102; Ernesto Diez Canseco 146, Miraflores; admission US$3; ☉ Mon-Sat) This long-established clubbing haunt plays all the crowd-pleasing favorites and has a well-deserved reputation as a travelers' pickup joint.

La Noche (Map p104; ☎ 247 2186; Av Bolognesi 307, Barranco; admission US$3) The party crowd is often to be found at this well-known tri-level bar nestled snugly at the end of a busy parade. La Noche prides itself on playing a wide mix of music, with everything from modern Latin pop to the occasional highland tune.

Señor Frogs (Map p102; LarcoMar, Malecon de la Reserva 610, Miraflores; admission US$8-10; ☉ Mon-Sat) A very flashy, electric club, Señor Frogs attracts a young local crowd.

Sargento Pimienta (Map p104; ☎ 477 0308; Bolognesi 755, Barranco; ☉ Wed-Sat) The name of this huge barnlike place is 'Sergeant Pepper' in Spanish, and true to form it plays a mix of international retro from the 1970s to the 1990s, plus occasional live rock. Alcohol is cheap, and somehow the enormous dance floor becomes miraculously packed by midnight.

Déjà Vu (Map p104; ☎ 247 3742; Av Grau 294-296, Barranco; ☉ 6:30pm-4am) A bohemian club with a dual personality, Déjà Vu's upper tier has thumping international music, while below there are usually performances of live Peruvian music. There are also *peña* performances by the group Oita Norma on occasion.

Cinemas

The latest international films are usually screened with their original soundtrack and Spanish subtitles, except films for children, which are always dubbed. Some cinemas offer half-price entry midweek. Listings are in newspapers' cultural-events sections.

UVK Multicines LarcoMar (Map p102; ☎ 446 7336; LarcoMar, Malecon de la Reserva 610, Miraflores; admission US$4)

Starvision el Pacífico (Map p102; ☎ 445 6990; Av José Pardo 121, Miraflores; admission US$3.50)

Cine Planet Miraflores (Map p102; ☎ 452 7000; Av Santa Cruz 814; admission US$4); Lima Centro (Map pp94-5; ☎ 452 7000; Jirón de la Unión 819; admission US$1.50-2.50)

Smaller and more esoteric options:

Filmoteca (Map pp94-5; ☎ 423 4732; Museo de Arte, Paseo Colón 125, Lima Centro; US$1.50-4.50)

El Cinematógrafo (Map p104; ☎ 477 1961; Pérez Roca 196, Barranco; US$3.50) For arty and alternative movies.

Theater

Pickings are a little thin on this score, but the following are worth noting. **Teatro Segura** (Map pp94-5; ☎ 426 7189; Huancavelica 265, Lima Centro) puts on opera, plays and ballet, while others include **Teatro Canut** (Map p102; ☎ 422 5373; Petit Thouars 4550, Miraflores) and **Teatro Britanico** (Map p102; ☎ 447 9760; Bellavista 527; Miraflores), which sometimes has plays in English.

For big-name music concerts, check the 'Luces' section of *El Comercio* on Mondays.

Casinos

Many top-end hotels have casinos and there are slot-machine halls scattered all around Lima, especially in Miraflores. While you are unlikely to walk away a nuevo sol millionaire, you can bet with small denomination coins and dress standards are pretty slack, though security guards will vet you for 'suitability'.

Some options:

JW Marriott Hotel Lima (Map p102; ☎ 217 7000; www.marriotthotels.com/limdt; Malecón de la Reserva 615)

Lima Sheraton (Map pp94-5; ☎ 315 5000; www .sheraton.com.pe; Paseo de la República 170)

Los Delfines Hotel (Map p101; ☎ 215 7000; www .losdelfineshotel.com; Los Eucaliptos 555)

Sports

Estadio Nacional (Map pp94-5; Lima Centro) *Fútbol* is the national sport, and Peru's Estadio Nacional, off *cuadras* 7 to 9 of the Paseo de la República, is the venue for the most important *fútbol* matches and other events.

Jockey Club of Peru (Map pp88-9; ☎ 435 1035; Hipódromo de Monterrico) Located at the junction of the Panamericana Sur and Javier Prado, the Jockey Club of Peru has horse races at 6pm every Tuesday and Thursday, and at 2pm on weekends. Betting starts at US$1. The members' stand is open to nonmembers for US$3.

SHOPPING

Clothing, jewelry and handicrafts from all over Peru are available in Lima. Shop prices tend to be high, but those with a little less capital can haggle their hearts out at several good craft markets. Shopping hours are usu-

ally 10am to 8pm Monday to Saturday, with variable lunchtime hours. Prices are generally fixed, but it's always worth trying for a discount. US dollars can be used in some of the better stores, and exchange rates are often within 1% of the best rates in town. Traveler's checks and credit cards can also be used, but receive less favorable rates.

Conquistadors (Map p101), a street in San Isidro, has a series of small, select boutiques and is a popular shopping precinct.

Handicrafts

Small art galleries selling wares are dotted around downtown: Try Pasaje de los Escribanos in Lima Centro, Ernesto Diez Canseco in Miraflores, and the area around Barranco's Parque Municipal. Miraflores, in particular, has plenty of good but pricey shops with quality wares.

A small artisans' market, with work ranging from garish painting-by-numbers to some good watercolors, functions informally on Parque Kennedy, in the heart of Miraflores, most days.

Mercado del Indios (Map p102; Av Petit Thouars 5245, Miraflores) This enormous market is the best place to browse through handicrafts from all over Peru. Prices are varied so shop carefully.

Feria Artesanal (Map pp88-9; Av de la Marina, Pueblo Libre) This artisan market is another option for handicrafts.

Centro Comercial El Suche (Map p102; Av de la Paz, Miraflores) This shady colonial passageway houses highly exclusive jewelry and handicrafts stores.

Agua y Tierra (Map p102; ☎ 444 6980; Ernesto Diez Canseco 298; Miraflores) This shop specializes in Amazonian ornaments.

La Casa de la Mujer Artesana Manuela Ramos (Map pp88-9; ☎ 423 8840; Juan Pablo Fernandini 1550, Pueblo Libre; ☯ 9am-5pm Mon-Fri), at *cuadra* 15 of Brasil, is a crafts cooperative with good-quality work from all over Peru. The proceeds support women's programs that are funded by the Movimiento Manuela Ramos.

Alpaca 111 (Map p102; ☎ 241 3484; LarcoMar, Malecon de la Reserva 610, Miraflores) has high-quality alpaca products as does **La Casa de la Alpaca** (Map p102; ☎ 447 6271; Av de la Paz 665, Miraflores).

Local Markets

Mercado Central (Map pp94-5; cnr Ayacucho & Ucayali, Lima Centro) You can buy almost anything at this crowded market, located to the southeast of Av Abancay and close to Barrio Chino.

Flower market (Map pp94-5; Puente Santa Rosa) Located where Tacna crosses the Río Rímac, this morning market is a kaleidoscopic scene of beautiful flowers at bargain prices.

South of Plaza Grau is a black-market area known as Polvos Azules (Map pp88-9); this is the place to find cheap luxuries and consumer goods – even that camera that was stolen from you. The government turns a blind eye to this market, and people from all social strata wander around, but watch your pockets carefully.

Shopping Malls

On Sundays, your best bets are Lima's US-style malls.

Jockey Plaza (Map pp88-9; Javier Prado Este 4200, Monterrico) This huge mall has department stores, a movie theater, food court and a range of specialty stores that will make you forget you're in Peru.

LarcoMar (Map p102; Malecon de la Reserva 610, Miraflores) Hiding below the Parque Salazar in Miraflores, LarcoMar is a smaller mall with a spectacular location built into the cliffs.

Camino Real (Map p101; Camino Real, Belaúnde 147, San Isidro) A large mall in San Isidro with a smaller, less ostentatious collection of shops.

Camping Equipment

For camping gear, try the expensive **Alpamayo** (Map p102; ☎ 445 1671; Av José Larco 345, Miraflores), or **Todo Camping** (Map p102; ☎ 242 1318; Angamos Oeste 350, Miraflores). **Mountain Worker** (Map p102; ☎ 445 2197; General Borgoño 394, Miraflores) has also been recommended. **Tattoo Adventure Gear** (Map p102; LarcoMar, Malecon de la Reserva 610, Miraflores) sells quality trekking gear as well as brand-name backpacks and day packs.

GETTING THERE & AWAY
Air

Lima's **Aeropuerto Internacional Jorge Chávez** (code LIM; Map pp88-9; ☎ 595 0606; www.lap.com.pe; Callao) is divided into two sections. Looking at the building from the parking area, the domestic arrivals and departures section is to the right. To the left is the international section. The usual airport facilities are available at the international airport: local, long-distance and international phone offices; public phones; banks; snack bars; sundry stores and a post office. Internet access is available on the second

floor. A 24-hour left-luggage room charges about US$6 per item per day. For information on international flights, see p516.

Many domestic airlines have sprung up in recent years only to fold or be forced into early retirement. The closure of TANS Peru, the main government-sponsored airline, has reduced competitiveness for now, making the airways a seller's market. Official prices are at an unprecedented high and bargains are hard to come by.

The principle destinations from Lima are Arequipa, Cuzco, Iquitos, Puerto Maldonado, Chiclayo, Trujillo, Juliaca, Pucallpa, Piura, Cajamarca, Ayacucho, Trujillo, Tacna, Tarapoto and Tumbes. Getting flight information, buying tickets and reconfirming flights is best done at the airline offices.

For more general information on air travel in Peru, see p521. For domestic flights, the departure tax is US$6.05.

The following are the Lima offices of current domestic operators:

Aero Condor Perú (Map p102; ☎ 441 1354, 442 5215; www.aerocondor.com.pe; Av José Pardo, Miraflores) Flies to Andahuaylas, Arequipa, Ayacucho, Cajamarca, Cuzco, Chiclayo, Iquitos, Piura, Puerto Maldonado and Tacna. Additionally it offers link services between Ayacucho and Andahuaylas, Arequipa and Tacna, Chiclayo and Piura, and Cuzco and Puerto Maldonado.

LAN (Map p102; ☎ 213 8200; www.lan.com; Av José Pardo 513, Miraflores) LAN goes to Arequipa, Chiclayo, Cuzco, Iquitos, Juliaca, Piura, Puerto Maldonado, Tacna, Tarapoto and Trujillo. Additionally it offers link services between Arequipa and Cuzco, Arequipa and Juliaca, Arequipa and Tacna, Cuzco and Juliaca, Cuzco and Puerto Maldonado, Tarapoto and Iquitos, Chiclayo and Piura, and Trujillo and Chiclayo.

LC Busre (Map pp88-9; ☎ 619 1313; www.lcbusre .com.pe; Los Tulipones 218, Lince) Flies to Cajamarca, Ayacucho, Huánuco and Pucallpa on smaller turbo-prop aircraft.

Star Perú (Map p102; ☎ 705 9000; www.starperu.com; Av José Pardo 269, Miraflores) Flies to Chiclayo, Cuzco, Iquitos, Pucallpa, Tarapoto and Trujillo. Additionally it offers link services between Tarapoto and Iquitos, and Trujillo and Chiclayo.

TACA (Map p102; ☎ 511 8222, 800 18222; www.taca.com; Av Espinar 331) Flies to Cuzco.

Bus

The most important road out of Lima is the Carretera Panamericana (Pan-American Highway), which runs northwest and southeast roughly parallel to the coast. Long-distance buses leave Lima every few minutes; it takes about 24 hours to get to either the Ecuadorian or the Chilean border. Buses also ply the usually rougher roads inland into the Andes and across into the eastern jungles.

There is no central bus terminal; each bus company runs its own offices and terminals. Some major companies have several terminals; always clarify where the bus leaves from when buying tickets. Be aware that Lima's bus terminals tend to be in disadvantaged neighborhoods and are notorious for theft, so if possible buy your tickets in advance, and take a taxi when carrying luggage.

The busiest times of year are Semana Santa (the week before Easter) and the week before and after Fiestas Patrias (July 28 to 29), when thousands of *limeños* make a dash out of the city and fares double. At these times, book well ahead.

There are scores of long-distance bus companies operating from Lima, though not all are recommended. The following are good, convenient companies:

Civa (Map pp94-5; ☎ 332 5236, 332 5264; www.civa .com.pe; cnr 28 de Julio & Paseo de la República 575, Lima Centro) For Cajamarca, Tumbes, Máncora, Chachapoyas, Chiclayo, Piura and Trujillo, plus south coast towns en route to Arequipa and Tacna.

Cruz del Sur (☎ 225 5748; www.cruzdelsur.com.pe); Lima Centro (Map pp94-5; ☎ 431 5125; Quilca 531); La Victoria (Map pp88-9; ☎ 225 6163, 225 5748; Javier Prado Este 1109) This is one of the biggest companies and serves the entire coast plus Arequipa, Cuzco, Huancayo, Huaraz and Puno. The old terminal on Quilca is mostly for its cheaper Ideal services, while the terminal on Javier Prado Este offers the more luxurious Imperiale and 1st-class Cruzero services – about twice the cost of normal services. Buses sometimes stop at both terminals: ask when buying your ticket.

Empresa Atahualpa (Map pp94-5; ☎ 427 7324, 427 7338; Jirón Sandía 266, Lima Centro) For the Cajamarca and Celendín areas.

Empresa Molina (Map pp94-5; ☎ 428 0617; Ayacucho 1141-1145, Lima Centro) Nicolás Arriola (☎ 324 2137, 324 2131; cnr Av Nicolás Arriola & Av San Luis) Has services to Ayacucho and Cuzco via the newly paved road from Pisco.

Flores (Map pp94-5; ☎ 424 3278; cnr Paseo de la República & 28 de Julio, Lima Centro) Flores runs regular buses to Arequipa and all south coast destinations.

Ittsa (Map pp94-5; ☎ 423 5232; Paseo de la República 809, cuadra 6, Lima Centro) Ittsa is a newer company with good services all along the north coast, including Trujillo, Chiclayo and Piura.

Mariscal Cáceres (☎ 427 2844); 28 de Julio (Map pp88-9; ☎ 474 7850; 28 de Julio 2195, Lima Centro); Carlos Zavala Loayza (Map pp94-5; Carlos Zavala Loayza 217, Lima Centro) For the Huancayo area and Jauja.

Movil Tours (Map pp94-5; ☎ 332 0004; Paseo de la República 749, Lima Centro) For Huaraz, Chachapoyas, Tarapoto and Caraz.

Ormeño (☎ 427 5679; www.grupo-ormeno.com); Lima Centro (Map pp94-5; Carlos Zavala Loayza 177); La Victoria (Map pp88-9; ☎ 472 1710; Javier Prado Este 1059) Ormeño is another of the biggest bus companies in Lima, with various subsidiaries at the same address, such as Expreso Ancash (for Huaraz), Expreso Continental (northern Peru), Expreso Chinchano (south coast and Arequipa) and San Cristóbal (Puno and Cuzco). It also offers faster, more comfortable business class and Royal Class services to Arequipa, Chiclayo, Ica, Piura, Trujillo and Tumbes, all of which leave from the international terminal on Javier Prado Este.

Soyuz (Map pp88-9; ☎ 226 1515; cnr Mexico 333 & Paseo de la República, Lima Centro) Runs every 20 minutes along the Pan-American Hwy to Ica.

Tepsa Lima Centro (Map pp94-5; ☎ 427 5642/3; www .tepsa.com.pe; Lampa 1237, Lima Centro); Javier Prado (Map pp88-9; ☎ 470 6666; Javier Prado Oeste 1091) Serves northern destinations and many inland places, including Arequipa, Tacna, Piura, Máncora, Cajamarca, Chiclayo and Trujillo.

Transportes Chanchamayo (Map pp94-5; ☎ 265 6850; Manco Cápac 1052, La Victoria) Runs services to Tarma and La Merced.

destination	cost* (US$)	duration (hr)
Arequipa	15/30	16
Ayacucho	6/15	9
Cajamarca	18/27	13
Chachapoyas	20/27	20-23
Chiclayo	15/27	12
Cuzco	25/48	30
Huancayo	6/14	7
Huaraz	9/17	8
Ica	5/15	4½
Nazca	8/27	6
Pisco	4/12	3
Piura	24/38	14
Puno	11/45	21
Tacna	18/42	18
Trujillo	10/28	9
Tumbes	25/40	18

* prices given are for normal/luxury buses

Transportes León de Huánuco (Map pp94-5; ☎ 424 3893; 28 de Julio 1520, La Victoria) For Pucallpa via Huánuco and Tingo María.

Transportes Rodríguez (Map pp94-5; ☎ 428 0506; turismo_rodriguez@yahoo.com; Roosevelt 350, Lima Centro) For Huaraz and Caraz.

Car

Lima is very congested and parking is difficult, so you're advised to take taxis within the city. However, if you do want to hire a car, the following hire companies all have 24-hour desks at the airport. Prices vary from US$40 per day to US$75 per day inclusive of 300km. Delivery is possible.

Budget (☎ 442 8706; www.budgetperu.com)
Dollar (☎ 444 3050; reservas@dollarperu.com)
Hertz (☎ 447 2129; www.hertz.com.pe)
Mitsui (☎ 349 2000; www.mitsuiautomotriz.com)
National (☎ 575 1111; www.nationalcar.com.pe)

Train

The Ferrocarril Central Andino railway line runs from Estación Desamparado in Lima inland to Huancayo, climbing from sea level to 4829m – the second-highest point for passenger trains in the world – before descending to Huancayo at 3260m. It's an exciting trip, with dozens of tunnels and bridges and interesting views. Though regular passenger service was canceled several years ago, a limited service runs weekly from mid-April to October. The round-trip costs US$55.

It is essential to check well beforehand for current schedules; for up-to-date information and bookings see www.incasdelperu.org/statusofthetrain.htm or phone ☎ 064-22 2395. Alternatively, you could visit the official, though less informative, site at www.ferroviasperu.com.pe.

GETTING AROUND
To/From the Airport

Arrival at the airport can be a little confusing for first-time visitors. After passing through customs, it's only a few meters to taxis and other transportation, so avoid porters in the baggage-claim area unless you want to have your luggage trundled 20m outside the door and dumped into the most expensive taxi available.

Within the airport concourse are official taxi booking desks; outside the airport arrivals area are official and semiofficial taxis, and outside the airport perimeter itself are 'local' taxis. For an official taxi you will pay between US$20 and US$23 to get to central Lima or Miraflores. You will pay between US$10 and US$15 for a taxi outside the arrivals concourse, and you will get a local taxi for under $10. Official taxis have the advantage of being safer and less intimidating than running the gauntlet of taxi drivers outside the arrivals concourse. The official vehicles are in better condition than the sometimes ramshackle state of the local taxis, which are usually tiny Daewoo Ticos that have barely enough room for passengers, let alone any bulky luggage. If you book a hotel in advance, the owners will often offer to arrange a free pickup. A travel desk at the airport can arrange taxis and make hotel reservations, but these tend to be more expensive.

A good alternative to a taxi is to catch the safe and easy Urbanito bus (US$4.50/6 to the center/Miraflores), which will take you to the hotel you want; organize it at the airport if your hotel is a bit out of the way. Urbanito has a desk near the official taxi counter, but someone usually approaches with a sign as travelers come out of customs. There are also a few *colectivo* taxis available that charge about US$5 per person and drop you off at your chosen hotel. These leave from the same place as the regulated taxis.

The cheapest way to get to the airport from the center is by the buses marked 'Faucett/Aeropuerto' that run south along Alfonso Ugarte and cost US$0.30.

Taxis are recommended if you're going to the airport from Miraflores. Getting to the airport by taxi is cheapest if you just flag one down and bargain. For better security, you can call a taxi in advance (see p124) and pay the full US$15 to US$25 fare, which again varies according to your location, the company and the time of day.

Allow over an hour to the airport from either central Lima, San Isidro or Miraflores – the exception is before 6:30am, when traffic is light.

Bus

Taking local minibuses (also called *combis* or *micros*) around Lima is something of an adventure. They're often slow and crowded, but numerous and startlingly cheap (fares are approximately US$0.35 Monday to Saturday and US$0.45 on Sunday). Look for the destination cards placed in the windshield and ignore any signs on the side of the bus. The most useful routes link central Lima with Miraflores along Av Arequipa or Paseo de la República. Minibuses going Garcilaso de la Vega (also called Av Wilson) and Av Arequipa are labeled 'Todo Arequipa' or 'Larco/Schell/ Miraflores' when heading to Miraflores and, likewise, 'Todo Arequipa' and 'Wilson/Tacna' when leaving Miraflores for central Lima. Catch these buses along Av José Larco or Av Arequipa in Miraflores.

From Plaza Grau (Map pp94–5; there's a stop in front of the Museo de Arte Italiano), minibuses travel along the Paseo de la República to Alfredo Benavides in Miraflores, with regular stops along the way.

A slower, full-sized green bus (marked 73A) runs regularly from the center to Barranco via Miraflores, passing along Tacna and Garcilaso de la Vega, down Av Arequipa and Av José Larco in Miraflores, and on to Barranco, where it can drop you along San Martín. Alternatively, for Barranco, catch any bus with the sign 'Chorrillos/Huaylas/Metro' from Diagonal, which runs off Óvalo in Miraflores.

Taxi

Lima's taxis don't have meters, so negotiate a price with the driver before getting in. As a rough guide for taxis flagged down on the streets, a trip from central Lima to Miraflores costs around US$3, and to the Museo de Oro del Peru or airport costs around US$5. The trip from Miraflores to the airport costs US$6 to US$10 (the higher price is for night-time travel). Be aware that foreigners are often charged more, and that you'll have to haggle harder in rush hour. If there are two or more of you be clear on whether the fare is per person or for the car.

The majority of taxis in Lima are unregistered (ie unofficial); indeed, surveys have indicated that no less than one vehicle in seven here is a taxi. It is safer to use registered taxis, which have either a taxi sign or a phone number on the roof and an authorization sticker with the word SETAME on the inner windshield. Registered taxis also usually have a yellow paint job and a license number painted on the sides. Flimsy Daewoo Ticos are the most common taxi.

Taxi companies can be called by phone or you can pick up registered taxis from taxi stands, such as the one outside the Sheraton

in central Lima or outside the LarcoMar shopping mall in Miraflores. Registered taxis cost about 30% to 50% more than regular street taxis. Taxis can be hired; registered taxis charge about US$6 per hour and street taxis charge between US$3.50 and US$6 per hour for trips in and around central Lima and Miraflores. Outside these areas the fee is higher.

The following companies all work 24 hours and accept advance reservations:

Moli Taxi (☎ 479 0030)
Taxi Fono (☎ 226 0866)
Taxi Lima (☎ 271 1763)
Taxi Miraflores (☎ 446 3953)
Taxi Móvil (☎ 422 6890)
Taxi Real (☎ 470 6263)
Taxi Seguro (☎ 241 9292)

Colectivo taxis drive up and down the same streets all day long. The most useful service goes from central Lima to Miraflores along Tacna, Garcilaso de la Vega and Av Arequipa. Another goes from Plaza San Martín to Callao (passing the airport). A third goes along Paseo de la República down to Barranco and Chorrillos. These *colectivos* can be identified by colorful window stickers. When seats are available, the driver may hold his hand out of the window indicating how many seats are left. You can flag them down and get off anywhere on the route. The fare is about US$0.50.

AROUND LIMA

PACHACAMAC
☎ 01

Situated about 31km southeast of the city center, this extensive **archaeological complex** (☎ 430 0168; http://pachacamac.perucultural.org.pe; adult/student/child US$1.70/0.60/0.30; ⏱ 9am-5pm Mon-Fri) made up of palaces and temple-pyramids is the closest major site to Lima. Although Pachacamac was an important Inca site and a major city when the Spanish arrived, it had been a ceremonial center on the central coast about 1000 years before the Inca empire. Begun in AD 200, the site was later expanded by the Wari culture before being conquered and added to by the Incas; each palace and temple thus is the work of a different culture. The name Pachacamac, which can be variously translated as 'He who Animated the

World' or 'He who Created Land and Time,' comes from the Wari god, whose wooden, two-faced image can be seen in the on-site **museum**.

Though most of the buildings are now little more than walls of piled rubble dotted around the desert landscape, the main temples and huge pyramids have been excavated, with their ramps and stepped sides revealed. You can climb the stairs to the top of the impressive **Templo del Sol** (Temple of the Sun), which on clear days offers excellent views of the coast. One Inca complex that has been completely excavated and rebuilt is the **Palacio de las Mamacuña** (House of the Chosen Women), which can only be entered with a guide (US$3.50 to US$4.50 for the whole site). The complex is surrounded by a garden and the roof beams are home to innumerable swallows.

A visitors center, its small museum and a café are by the site entrance, which is on the road to Lurin, not far from the Panamericana. A simple map can be obtained from the office in the visitors center, and a track leads from here into the complex. Those on foot should allow a leisurely two hours. Those with a vehicle can leave their car in a string of parking spots as they go from site to site. Many people cycle to the site, where there are some pleasant tracks to take.

Various tour agencies in Lima (see p106) offer guided tours to Pachacamac that include round-trip transport and a guide. Costs depend on the size of the group and the quality of the guide, but are around US$30 to US$35 per person. Alternatively, catch a minibus signed 'Pachacamac' from the corner of Ayacucho and Grau in central Lima (US$0.60, 45 minutes); minibuses leave every 15 minutes during daylight hours. From Miraflores, catch a taxi to the intersection of Angamos and the Panamericana, also known as the Primavera Bridge (US$1.20), then take the bus signed 'Pachacamac/Lurin' (US$0.30, 25 minutes). For both services, tell the driver to let you off near the *ruinas* (ruins) or you'll end up at Pachacamac village, about 1km beyond the entrance.

To get back to Lima, flag down any bus outside the gate but expect to stand. It's best not to wait until late in the afternoon.

You can hire a taxi from Lima that will wait for you at the ruins for two or three hours. Expect to pay US$5 to US$6 per hour.

SOUTHERN BEACHES
☎ 01

Limeños make a beeline for their southern beaches during the January to March summer. The exodus peaks at weekends, which are occasionally so congested that the highway becomes temporarily one way and incoming traffic is diverted to an older stretch of the Panamericana. The beaches south of Lima include El Silencio, Señoritas, Caballeros, Punta Hermosa, Punta Negra, San Bartolo, Santa María, Naplo and Pucusana. Despite their popularity, don't expect the tropical beach resorts of other South American countries; many have cold water and strong currents, so inquire locally before swimming as drownings occur annually. Some beaches have private clubs used by *limeños*.

Camping is possible outside of the Lima metropolitan area; go with a large group and watch your belongings closely. **Punta Hermosa** and the popular **San Bartolo** have hostels near the beach at budget to midrange rates during the busy summer. One good midrange option sitting above the bay in San Bartolo is **Hostal 110** (☎ 430 7559; Malecón San Martín Norte 110; d Sun-Thu/ Fri & Sat US$25/35; 🅿), run by an Italian pilot.

For surfers, San Bartolo is great for beginners, but the largest wave in Peru is to be found near Punta Hermosa at **Pico Alto** (Panamericana Km 43), though it's not for the inexperienced and requires a long paddle out. **Punta Rocas**, a little further south, is also popular with experienced surfers and hosts international surfing competitions. At Punta Rocas, you can crash at the basic **Hostal Hamacas** (☎ 231 5498, 9985 4766; surfresortperu@terra .com.pe; Panamericana Km 47; dm US$5). Unfortunately, surfboard rental is almost nonexistent along these beaches so you'll have to buy or rent one in Lima, and hire a taxi to transport it (US$10 to US$15 one way).

To get to the southern beaches, take a bus signed 'San Bartolo' from the Panamericana Sur at the Primavera Bridge (taxi from Miraflores US$1.20). You can get off the bus where you want and hike down to the beaches, which are mostly 1km or 2km away from the highway.

CARRETERA CENTRAL
The Carretera Central (Central Hwy) heads directly east from Lima, following the Rímac valley into the foothills of the Andes and on to La Oroya in Peru's central highlands.

Buses to Chosica leave frequently from Lima and can be used to get to Puruchuco (US$0.45, 50 minutes), Cajamarquilla (US$0.45, 1¼ hours), Chaclacayo (US$0.60, 1½ hours) and Chosica (US$0.75, two hours). Many are minibuses signed 'Chosica,' and they can be picked up at Arica at the Plaza Bolognesi. Recognizing the sites from the road can be difficult, so tell your bus driver where you want to be let off.

Puruchuco
☎ 01

The site of **Puruchuco** (☎ 494 2641; admission US$1.70; 🕑 9am-4:30pm Mon-Sat) hit the news in 2002 when a huge stash of about 2000 well-preserved mummy bundles was unearthed from its enormous Inca cemetery. It's one of the biggest finds of its kind, and the multitude of grave goods buried with the bundles has already revealed fresh insights into the Inca civilization. The site has a highly reconstructed Inca chief's house, with one room identified as a guinea-pig ranch. Situated amid the shantytown of Túpac Amaru, Puruchuco is 13km from central Lima. A signpost on the highway marks the turn-off, and from here it is several hundred meters along a road to the right.

Cajamarquilla
☎ 01

The large site of **Cajamarquilla** (admission US$1.40; 🕑 9am-5pm) dates from the Wari culture of AD 700 to 1100 and consists mainly of adobe walls, some sections of which have been restored. A road to the left from Lima at about Km 10 (18km from central Lima) goes to the Cajamarquilla zinc refinery, almost 5km from the highway. The ruins are located about halfway along the refinery road; you take a turn to the right along a short road. There are signs, but ask the locals for the *zona arqueológica* if you have trouble finding them.

Chaclacayo
☎ 01

The village of Chaclacayo, at Km 27, is about 660m above sea level – just high enough to rise above Lima's coastal *garúa*. You can often bask in sunshine here while 8.2 million people in the capital below languish in the gray fog.

Simple cabins are available at midrange 'vacation hotels,' such as **Centro Vacacional Huampani** (☎ 497-1188, in Lima 497-1683; Km 26; s/d with shared bathroom US$14, d US$24), and there are decent dining, swimming pool and horseback-riding facilities. Peruvians usually come to the vacation complexes on day trips.

Chosica
☎ 01

The resort town of Chosica, 860m above sea level and almost 40km along the Carretera Central, was very popular with *limeños* early in the 20th century. Today, its popularity has declined, though escapees from Lima's *garúa* will still find it a convenient spot to take advantage of several variously priced hotels in the sun. From Chosica, a minor road leads to the ruins of **Marcahuasi** (see p289 for more details).

South Coast

Peru's southern coastal desert is refreshed by palm oases and spanned by a ribbon of pavement, the Carretera Panamericana (Pan-American Hwy), which slices all the way through the country from Ecuador to Chile. It's the best overland route to Arequipa, Lake Titicaca and of course, Cuzco. Yes, you guessed it: this is the start of Peru's well-beaten Gringo Trail.

But the south coast holds far more depth and diversity than the kilometer upon kilometer of arid desert and coastline viewed from a bus window. These lowlands gave birth to some extraordinary pre-Columbian civilizations, especially the Nazca – remembered for their cryptic lines etched across 500 sq km of desolate land – and the Paracas Necropolis culture, whose burial sites still lie in the sands. Spanish haciendas became the birthplace of Afro-Peruvian music and dance, whose untamed protest strains live on, especially around Chincha.

That said, it's also the wildness of the territory that brings travelers here today. Pacific beaches issue a siren's call to surfers, while river runners get their feet wet in Lunahuaná. Pisco is famous not only for the national drink, pisco (Peruvian brandy), but also for its marine wildlife and rugged coastline. Ica is surrounded by vineyards and the monstrous sand dunes of Huacachina. Closer to Chile, bird-watchers flock to the coastal lagoons of Mejía.

Peru's south coast is an ideal place to let your wanderlust run wild. Just jump off your bus along the Panamericana wherever some dusty track catches your eye; you'll always find something quirky or interesting at the end of these desert roads.

SOUTH COAST

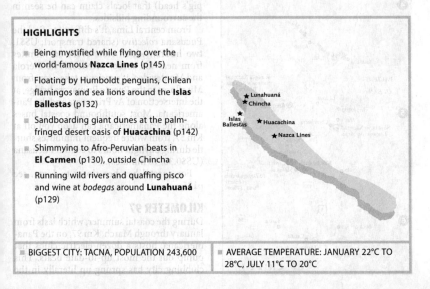

HIGHLIGHTS

- Being mystified while flying over the world-famous **Nazca Lines** (p145)
- Floating by Humboldt penguins, Chilean flamingos and sea lions around the **Islas Ballestas** (p132)
- Sandboarding giant dunes at the palm-fringed desert oasis of **Huacachina** (p142)
- Shimmying to Afro-Peruvian beats in **El Carmen** (p130), outside Chincha
- Running wild rivers and quaffing pisco and wine at *bodegas* around **Lunahuaná** (p129)

- BIGGEST CITY: TACNA, POPULATION 243,600
- AVERAGE TEMPERATURE: JANUARY 22°C TO 28°C, JULY 11°C TO 20°C

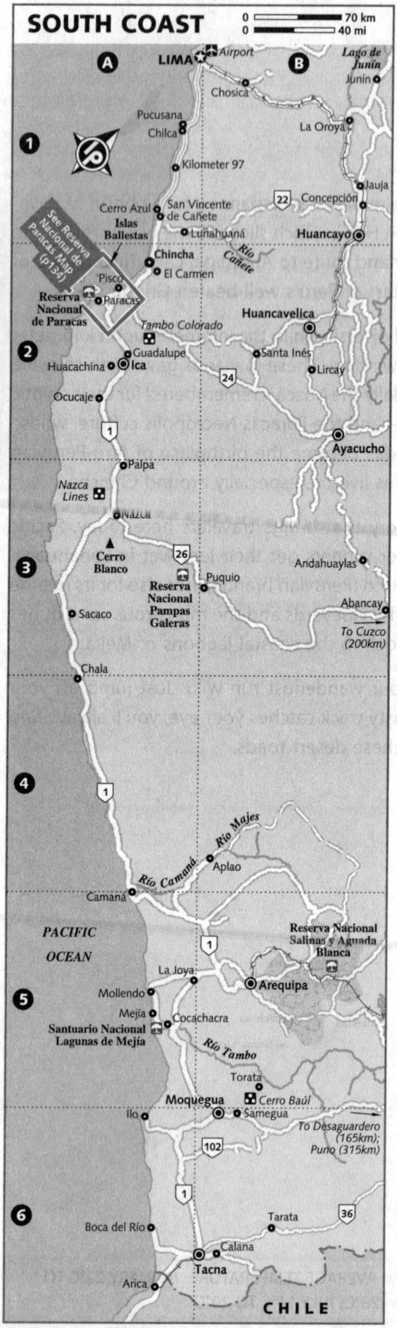

PUCUSANA

☎ 01 / pop 4400

This small fishing village, 65km south of Lima, is a popular locals' beach resort from January to April. The small Pucusana and Las Ninfas beaches are on the town's seafront and at low tide you can wade to La Isla, an offshore island with a strand of sand. The most isolated beach in the area is Naplo, 1km away and reached through a tunnel. If you're interested in fishing or bird-watching, boats can be hired (from US$6) at the marina, which is two blocks from the main plaza.

South of Pucusana, off Km 64 along the Panamericana Sur, is the turnoff to the village of **Chilca**, famed for its muddy and mineral-rich **lagoons** (admission US$0.30; 24hr), one of which is nicknamed La Milagrosa (the Miracle). The bathing pools allegedly have power to heal everything from infertility to acne – and some believers credit this to intervention by aliens in UFOs! A *mototaxi* (three-wheeled motorcycle rickshaw taxi) from the Panamericana to the pools costs about US$1.50 each way.

The best of the simple hotels in Pucusana, **El Mirador de Pucusana** (☎ 430 9228; d US$10-13.50;) has a breathtaking location atop the bayfront with fantastic views. Rooms are basic, but do have hot water. It's a great place to savor the scenery as you sip on a pisco sour in its seafood **restaurant** (mains US$3-5). Try to distinguish the various shapes (including a pig's head) that locals claim can be seen in the surrounding hillsides.

From central Lima, it's difficult to find the Pucusana *colectivo* (shared transport; US$1, two hours), which runs every 30 minutes from near the corner of Nicolás de Piérola and Montevideo. It's easier to take a taxi from Miraflores to the Puente Primavera bridge, at the intersection of Av Primavera and the Panamericana. Most southbound coastal buses along the Panamericana can drop you off at Km 57, from where frequent minibuses shuttle during daylight hours to central Pucusana (US$0.30, 10 minutes).

For coastal beaches closer to Lima, see p125.

KILOMETER 97

During the coastal summer, which lasts from January through March, Km 97, on the Panamericana, hosts a dozen electric clubs that pump out the most up-to-date beats. This clubbing city has sprung up literally in the middle of nowhere, where DJs can happily crank up the volume with a clear conscience. However, it firmly shuts its doors from April until December, when all the hottest action migrates back to the capital city.

Almost any bus along the Panamericana can drop you here upon request. Most *limeños* (inhabitants of Lima) party all night, then catch a bus back next morning, but there are some basic guesthouses on the main boulevard where you can crash for around US$10 per person. Otherwise, you can flag down any southbound bus or hire a taxi to reach the beach at Cerro Azul, which has more appealing lodgings.

CAÑETE
☎ 056 / pop 22,000

The full name of this small market town, about 145km south of Lima, is San Vicente de Cañete. Most Peruvian holidaymakers head north of town to **Cerro Azul**, a beach that's popular with experienced surfers. It's a 15-minute walk west of Km 131 on the Panamericana, about 15km north of town. There's also a small Inca sea fort in the area, known as **Huarco**, but it's in a poor state of repair.

In Cerro Azul, the surfer-friendly **Hostal Cerro Azul** (☎ 271 1302, 9763 1969; Puerto Viejo; www .cerroazulhostal.com; d/tr/q US$39/43/52, ste US$90-104) is less than 100m from the shoreline. **Hostal Las Palmeras** (☎ 284 6005; Puerto Viejo; tw/d/tr/q Sun-Thu US$40/45/55/70, Fri & Sat US$60/65/70/90; 🏊) has a gorgeous location looking onto the beach and the pier. Prices vary according to the season. On the main commercial strip just back from the beach, **Casa Hospedaje Los Delfines** (Comercio 723; r from US$10) is an immaculately kept, family-run guesthouse that's often full. If you're hungry, beachfront shacks and large roadside restaurants right on the Panamericana all serve fresh seafood.

From Lima, buses for Pisco or Ica can drop you at Cañete or maybe even Cerro Azul (US$1.50, 2½ hours). Buses back to Lima are invariably crowded, especially on Sundays from January to April. There are also *combis* (minibuses) between Cañete and Cerro Azul (US$0.30, 30 minutes) or south to Chincha (US$0.60, one hour).

LUNAHUANÁ
☎ 056 / pop 3600 / elev 1700m

Detouring inland from Cañete, a curvy road slopes through the steep-walled Río Cañete

valley and after 38km reaches the pastoral village of Lunahuaná, which offers great opportunities for river running (white-water rafting) and kayaking. Lunahuaná is also the gateway to one of Peru's coastal wine countries, with several *bodegas* (wine shops and cellars) proffering free samples year-round. The best time to show up is during the second week of March for the wine harvest, **Fiesta de la Vendimia**. An adventure sports festival is usually held in late February or early March.

Sights

A rustic *bodega* producing both wines and piscos, venerable **La Reyna de Lunahuaná** (admission & tours free; ☯ 9am-5pm) presides over the main plaza in Catapalla, about 6km east of Lunahuaná; a round-trip taxi ride costs from US$3, including waiting time. Closer to town, **Bodega Los Reyes** (☎ 284 1206; ☯ 9am-4pm) is also generous in its measures, and it retains the traditional method of treading the grapes, which you can see for yourself in February or March.

Nearby archaeological sites in the Cañete valley include **Incawasi**, the rough-walled ruins of the military headquarters of Túpac Yupanqui, located on the western outskirts of Lunahuaná; and the small pre-Inca fort of **Ungara**, situated closer to Imperial. Either site can be visited by taxi, though there's really not much left to see.

Activities

The river-running season runs from December to April, the rainy months in the Andes when the Río Cañete runs high; in February the rapids can reach class IV. River-running championships are often held here in late February. At most times this trip is suitable for beginners, and outfitters in Lima often take groups on weekends from US$25 per person. If you want to organize it in Lunahuaná, **Río Cañete Expediciones** (☎ in Lima 01-284 1271; www.riocanete.com.pe) requires a minimum of four people, and trips that last between 40 minutes and four hours cost US$10.50 to US$36. The tour company is based at **Camping San Jerónimo** (☎ 9635 3921; Km 33 Carretera Cañete-Lunahuaná), which also has a rock-climbing wall.

If you'd like to cycle out to visit some *bodegas*, basic mountain bikes can be rented from many storefronts near the plaza and along Av Grau.

Sleeping & Eating

Hostal Casuarinas (☎ 581 2627; Grau 295; s/d US$6/12) A couple of blocks from the plaza in the direction of the main road, this secure budget hotel has tidy rooms with TVs and hot showers.

Hostal Río Alto (☎ 284 1125; Km 39 Carretera Cañete-Lunahuaná; s/d US$28/40; 🛋) About 1km along the highway east of Lunahuaná, this friendly guesthouse looks down to the river from a shady terrace overrun with plants. Rooms, though plain, are modern and have hot showers.

Hotel Campestre Embassy (☎ 284 1194; Km 39 Carretera Cañete-Lunahuaná; d US$40-70; 🛋) A gathering spot for locals, this upscale hotel farther east of town has a restaurant and a disco. The most expensive rooms have breezy balconies overlooking the river.

There are several private campgrounds spread out along the river outside town.

Camping San Jerónimo (☎ 9635 3921; Km 33 Carretera Cañete-Luanahuaná; campsites per person US$3) This campground borders the river far west of town. Base camp for Río Cañete Expediciones (p129), it has good facilities and a free artificial rock-climbing wall for guests.

Several local seafood restaurants are found around the main plaza and along Av Grau; the local specialty is crawfish.

Getting There & Away

From Cañete, catch a *micro* to Imperial (US$0.20, 10 minutes), from where *micros* also run to Lunahuaná (US$1, 45 minutes). Faster *colectivo* taxis wait for passengers on the main road, just downhill from the plaza in Lunahuaná, and then race back to Imperial (US$1.50, 25 minutes).

CHINCHA

☎ 056 / pop 140,000

The sprawling town of Chincha is the next landmark, some 55km south of Cañete, at Km 202 along the Panamericana. Once a Spanish colonial stronghold, today it's the beating heart of Afro-Peruvian culture, and it makes an interesting stopover to catch a vibrant music-and-dance performance or to tour a ghostly former slave plantation.

Orientation & Information

The main plaza is a long walk inland from the Panamericana, so take a taxi (US$1.50). Banks with international ATMs line Benavides west of the plaza heading toward the market area. Cybercafés are all around the plaza.

Sights

There's not much to see in the city center, but the outlying sites are fascinating.

EL CARMEN DISTRICT

Chincha is famous for the vibrant and wild Afro-Peruvian music heard in the *peñas* (bars and clubs featuring live traditional music) of the El Carmen district, about 15km outside town. The best times to visit are during Verano Negro (late February/early March), Fiestas Patrias (late July) and La Virgen del Carmen de Chincha (December 27). During these times, minibuses run from Chincha to El Carmen all night long, and the *peñas* are full of frenzied *limeños* and locals dancing. One traditional dance not to try at home is 'El Alcatraz,' when a gyrating male dancer with a candle attempts to set on fire a handkerchief attached to the back of his partner's skirt.

HACIENDA SAN JOSÉ

A slightly ramshackle but grand old Spanish colonial hacienda, **Hacienda San José** (☎ 22 1458; www.haciendasanjose.com.pe; tours per person US$3) is packed with 300 years' worth of history, surrounded by lovely orange groves and suffused with the scent of flowers. The hacienda, built in 1688, was a sugar and honey plantation that was worked by black African slaves until a rebellion broke out in 1879, leading to the master being dramatically hacked down by the former slaves. The hacienda also has an atmospheric old chapel and spooky catacombs. Guided tours are available in Spanish.

To visit the hacienda, drive 5km south of Chincha along the Panamericana, then head 9km inland over bumpy country roads. If you don't have your own transport, a taxi costs about US$4 each way, or you can catch one of the minivans that frequently run back and forth between El Carmen and Chincha, but be sure to ask the driver (in Spanish) exactly where to get off, then expect to walk at least 2km.

ARCHAEOLOGICAL SITES

In ancient times, the small Chincha empire long flourished in this region until it was clobbered by the Incas in the late 15th century. The best surviving archaeological sites in the area are **Tambo de Mora**, on the coast about 10km from Chincha, and the temple of

La Centinela northwest of the city, about 8km off the Panamericana. Both can be visited by taxi (about US$10).

Sleeping & Eating

Bare-bones cheap hotels and *chifas* (Chinese restaurants) surround Chincha's main plaza. Most fill up and double or triple their prices during festivals, though you can always avoid this problem by dancing all night and taking an early morning bus back to Lima or further south down the coast.

Hostal La Posada (☎ 26 2042; Santo Domingo 200; s/d US$9/15) Run by a gregarious Italian-Peruvian couple, this simple guesthouse is one of the most secure choices in the city center, just a stone's throw from the main plaza. The rooms are antique-looking, but decently kept. Ask for one facing away from the street.

Casa Hacienda San José (☎ 22 1458, in Lima 01-444 5242; www.haciendasanjose.com.pe; d/ste incl breakfast Sun-Thu US$27/33, Fri & Sat $38/43; ⚡) On the grounds of a historic colonial plantation (opposite), this genteel hotel boasts rooms with real character, but also modern amenities. It also has great Sunday buffet lunches with shows of African-Peruvian and *criollo* dance and music that are open to nonguests (US$20). There are also dance classes.

El Sausal (☎ 26 2451, in Lima 01-222 0155; www.sausal .com.pe; Km 197.5 Carretera Panamericana; d/ste US$49/58, 5-person bungalows US$116; ⚡) A surprisingly plush spot to kick back, right on the Panamericana, this hotel has a spacious country-club feel with a big swimming pool, sun loungers, lush gardens, a billiards room and alas, a karaoke bar.

In El Carmen, a few local families will take in overnight guests and cook meals for under US$10 per person per night – just ask around.

Getting There & Around

There are many companies based on the Panamericana with buses running through Chincha en route between Lima (US$2, 2½ hours) and Ica (US$2, two hours). Most southbound buses can drop you off at the San Clemente turnoff on the Panamericana (US$1), from where you can catch frequent *colectivo* taxis and minivans for the 6km trip into Pisco (US$1). From Chincha, *combis* headed north to Cañete (US$0.60, one hour) and south to Paracas (US$0.60, one hour) leave from near Plazuela Bolognesi.

Minivans to El Carmen (US$0.50, 30 minutes) leave from Chincha's central market area, a few blocks from the main plaza.

The plaza is a short taxi ride (US$1.50) from the Panamericana where the coastal buses stop.

PISCO

☎ 056 / pop 58,000

Sharing its name with the brandy produced from white muscat grapes in this region, Pisco is an important port 235km south of Lima. Generally used as a base to see the abundant wildlife of the Islas Ballestas and Península de Paracas, the area is also of historical and archaeological interest, having hosted one of the most highly developed pre-Inca civilizations – the Paracas culture from 900 BC until AD 200 (p135), after which the nearby town of Paracas is named. Later it acted as a base for Peru's revolutionary fever in the 1800s.

Orientation & Information

Although the Pisco–Paracas area is spread out, it's easy to get around. Most long-distance buses drop passengers off at the San Clemente turnoff on the Panamericana, from where frequent *colectivos* shuttle to central Pisco's Plaza de Armas. Public transport to the beaches and harbor at Paracas, 15km further south along the coast, leaves from Pisco's market area.

There's no tourist office in Pisco, but travel agencies (see p135), the *municipalidad* (town hall) and **police** (☎ 53 5343; San Francisco 139; ☯ 24hr) help when they can. Everything else you'll need is found around the Plaza de Armas,

---

THE FLAMINGO FLAG

Locals like to tell a fanciful yarn of how the Peruvian flag was born on the beaches of the Península de Paracas. The story goes that *libertador* (liberator) José de San Martín landed here in 1820 and, exhausted after a long journey, fell into a deep sleep. When he awoke, he was dazzled by the flamboyance of flamingos flying overhead, their outstretched wings catching the light of the setting sun. It was those flashes of red that allegedly gave him the inspiration for the scarlet outer panels of what is now Peru's national flag.

including cybercafés. **BCP** (Figueroa 162) has a Visa/MasterCard ATM and changes US dollars and travelers' checks. **Interbank** (San Martín 101) has a 24-hour global ATM.

Dangers & Annoyances

Never walk alone at night. Central Pisco is fairly safe, but the market and nearby beaches should be avoided after dark and visited only in a group during the day. Muggings at gunpoint are not unheard of, even on busy pedestrian streets, so always take a taxi after sunset. Women can expect lots of unwanted attention while they walk around here, day or night. Touts for tours and hotels swarm incoming buses, and in the melee your luggage may disappear, so watch out.

Sights & Activities

PLAZA DE ARMAS & AROUND

Since Pisco was once a revolutionary base for liberator José de San Martín, the general's **statue** now peers down on the main plaza. His headquarters, the **Club Social Pisco** (San Martín 132), still stands nearby; it's now open to the public as a Peruvian restaurant.

East of the plaza, the town's **cemetery** has a few hidden secrets. Taxi drivers like to tell the story of 19th-century Englishwoman Sarah Ellen Roberts, a suspected vampire whose body was refused by all graveyards until Pisco was paid handsomely to bury it. Before dying, she boasted that she would rise again after 100 years – though much to everyone's disappointment in 1993, she didn't.

The dusty **Acorema Interpretation Center** (☎ 53 2046; www.acorema.org.pe; San Martín 1471; admission US$1; ☒ hrs vary), housed in a curious old Swiss-style building, has tame exhibits on biodiversity and conservation in Paracas plus a large whale skeleton tucked away to one side. It's in a dangerous part of town near the beach, so take a *mototaxi* (US$1.20).

ISLAS BALLESTAS

Although grandiosely nicknamed the 'poor man's Galapagos,' the Islas Ballestas make for a memorable excursion. The only way to get there is with a boat tour, offered by many travel agencies (p135). None of the small boats have a cabin, so dress to protect against the wind, spray and sun. The sea can get rough, so

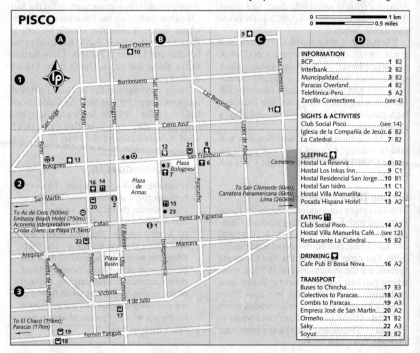

PISCO

0 ———————— 1 km
0 ———————— 0.5 miles

To As de Oros (500m);
Embassy Beach Hotel (750m);
Acorema Interpretation
Center (1km); La Playa (1.5km)

To San Clemente (6km);
Carratera Panamericana (6km);
Lima (260km)

To El Chaco (15km);
Paracas (17km)

sufferers of motion sickness should take medication before boarding. Wear a hat (cheap ones are sold at the harbor), as it's not unusual to receive a direct hit of *guano* (droppings) from the seabirds.

On the outward boat journey, which takes about 1½ hours, you can't miss the famous three-pronged **Candelabra** geoglyph, a giant figure etched into the sandy hills, which is over 150m high and 50m wide. No one knows exactly who made the geoglyph, or when, or what it signifies, but theories abound. Some connect it to the Nazca Lines, while others propound that it served as a navigational guide for ancient sailors and was based on the constellation of the Southern Cross. Some even believe it to have been inspired by a local cactus species with hallucinogenic properties.

An hour is spent cruising around the islands' arches and caves, watching large herds of noisy sea lions sprawl on the rocks. The most common *guano*-producing birds in this area are the guanay cormorant, the Peruvian booby and the Peruvian pelican, seen in colonies several thousand strong. You'll also see pelicans, cormorants, Humboldt penguins and, if your luck is in, dolphins.

Although you can get close enough to the wildlife for a good look, some species, especially the penguins, are more visible with binoculars. On your return trip, ask to see the Chilean flamingos, which are usually found in the southern part of the bay and not on the direct boat route. The flamingos aren't always there, however – the best time is June to August.

Back on shore, a minibus whisks tour groups back to Pisco in time for lunch, or you can continue on a tour of the Reserva Nacional de Paracas. If you decide to grab a bite to eat at the waterfront shacks in Paracas, you can take a *combi* back to Pisco later.

RESERVA NACIONAL DE PARACAS

This vast desert reserve occupies most of the Península de Paracas. For tour operators, see p135. Alternatively, hire a taxi in Pisco for around US$5 per hour, or take a *combi* into the village of Paracas and then walk – make sure to allow lots of time, and bring food and plenty of water.

Near the entrance to Paracas village, past Playa El Chaco, is an **obelisk** commemorating the landing of the liberator General José de San Martín. The *combi* continues further in and, if asked, will drop you in front of Hotel Paracas. Continue on foot either along the tarmac road south of Paracas, or the beach, looking out for seashore life.

About 3km south is a park entry point, where a US$1.50 fee is charged. Another 2km beyond the entrance is the **park visitor center**, which has kid-friendly exhibits on conservation and ecology. Next door is the **Museo JC Tello** (adult/child/student US$2.50/0.30/0.60; ☺ 9am-5pm). Unfortunately, the museum's best pieces were stolen a few years ago, but an interesting collection of weavings, trophy heads and trepanned skulls (showing an ancient medical technique wherein a slice of the skull is removed, relieving pressure on the brain resulting from injuries) remains. Chilean flamingos often hang out in the bay in front of the complex, and there's now a walkway down to a *mirador* (lookout). Try not to step outside the designated route as this can interfere with the flamingos' food supply.

A few hundred meters behind the visitor complex is the 5000-year-old remains of the **Paracas Necropolis**, a late site of the Paracas culture, which predated the Incas by more than a thousand years. A stash of over 400 funerary bundles was found here, each wrapped in many layers of colorful woven shrouds for which the Paracas culture is famous. There's

---

DROPPINGS TO DIE FOR

Layers of sun-baked, nitrogen-rich *guano* (seabird droppings) have been diligently deposited over millennia on the Islas Ballestas and Península de Paracas by large resident bird colonies – in places, the guano is as much as 50m deep. Guano's recognition as a first-class fertilizer dates back to pre-Inca times, but few would have predicted that these filthy riches were to become Peru's principal export during the mid-19th century, being shipped in vast quantities to Europe and America. In fact, the trade was so lucrative that Spain precipitated the so-called Guano War of 1865–66 over possession of the nearby Chincha Islands. Nowadays, over-exploitation and synthetic fertilizers have taken their toll and the birds are largely left to their steady production process in peace, but for licensed extraction every 10 years – and boatloads of day-trippers, of course.

little to see now though. Lima's Museo de la Nación (p99) and Ica's Museo Regional de Ica (p139) exhibit some exquisite textiles and other finds from the site.

Beyond the visitor complex, the tarmac road continues around the peninsula, past a 'graveyard' of old fishing boats to Puerto General San Martín, which has a smelly fishmeal plant and a port on the northern tip of the peninsula. Forget this road and head out on the dirt road that branches off a few hundred meters beyond the museum. After about 6km it reaches the tiny fishing village of **Lagunillas**, where you can usually find someone to cook fresh fish for you; it's sometimes possible to catch a ride back to town, squeezed in alongside the fresh fish catch. From the village, the road continues a few kilometers to a parking area near a **clifftop lookout**, which has grand views of the ocean, with a sea-lion colony on the rocks below and plenty of seabirds gliding by.

Other seashore life around the reserve includes flotillas of jellyfish (swimmers beware!), some of which reach about 70cm in diameter with trailing stinging tentacles up to

1m. They are often washed up on the shore, where they quickly dry to form mandalalike patterns on the sand. Beachcombers can also find sea hares, ghost crabs and seashells along the shoreline, and the Andean condor occasionally descends to the coast in search of rich pickings.

You can ask at the visitor center for designated areas to pitch tents, but never camp alone as violent robberies have been reported. To really explore, the entire peninsula is covered by topographic map 28-K from the Instituto Geográfico Nacional (IGN) in Lima (see p507).

TAMBO COLORADO

This early Inca lowland **outpost** (admission US$2; ☼ dawn-dusk), about 45km northeast of Pisco, was named for the red paint that once completely covered its adobe walls. It's one of the best-preserved sites on the south coast and is thought to have served as an administrative base and control point for passing traffic, mostly conquered peoples. An on-site caretaker will collect the fee and can answer questions in Spanish.

RESERVA NACIONAL DE PARACAS

0 —— 10 km
0 —— 6 miles

INFORMATION
Paracas Explorer......................(see 9)
Park Visitor Center.................**1** B3

SIGHTS & ACTIVITIES
Candelabra............................**2** B2
Fish-Meal Factories.................**3** B2
Flamingos Often Seen Here.....**4** B3
'Graveyard' of Fishing Boats.....**5** B3
Mirador................................**6** B3
Museo JC Tello....................(see 1)
Obelisk................................**7** B3
Paracas Necropolis.................**8** B3
Playa El Chaco.......................**9** D3

SLEEPING
El Amigo..............................(see 9)
Hostal Los Frayles...................(see 9)
Hostal Refugio del Pirata.........(see 9)
Hotel El Mirador....................**10** C2
Hotel Paracas........................**11** B3
Posada del Libertador.............**12** B3

TRANSPORT
Boats to Islas Ballestas............**13** B3

To Lima (250km)

To Tambo Colorado (40km); Ayacucho (310km)

Pisco

San Clemente

Islas Ballestas

Islas Tres Marías

Isla Blanca

San Andrés

Puerto General San Martín

Península de Paracas

Bahía de Paracas

Isla Sangayán

Reserva Nacional de Paracas

Paracas

Carretera Panamericana Sur

Lagunillas

PACIFIC OCEAN

Clifftop Lookout

To Ica (60km)

From Pisco, it takes about an hour to get there by car. Hire a taxi for half a day (US$15) or take a tour from Pisco (US$25, two-person minimum). A *combi* through the village of Humay passes Tambo Colorado 20 minutes beyond the village; it leaves from the Pisco market early in the morning (US$2, three hours). Once there, ask the locals about when to expect a return bus, but you could get really stuck out there, as transport back to Pisco is infrequent and often full.

Tours & Guides

Prices and service for tours of Islas Ballestas and Reserva Nacional de Paracas are usually very similar. The better tours are escorted by a qualified naturalist who at least speaks Spanish and English. Most island boat tours leave daily around 7am and cost around US$10 per person. They either leave from Pisco's Plaza de Armas or will pick you up from your hotel before driving to Paracas to board the boats. The cheapest tours are usually pooled into one vessel. Less-than-interesting afternoon land tours of the Península de Paracas (US$8) briefly stop at the national reserve's visitor center and museum (entry fees not included), breeze by coastal geological formations and spend a long time having lunch in a remote fishing village. Tours of the reserve can be combined with an Islas Ballestas tour to make a full-day excursion (US$16).

THE PARACAS CULTURE

Little is known about the early Paracas culture, Paracas Antiguo, except that it was influenced by the Chavín Horizon, an early artistic and religious historical period (see p31). Most of our knowledge is about the middle and later Paracas cultures, which existed from about 500 BC to 200 AD. This is divided into two periods known as Paracas Cavernas and Paracas Necropolis, named after the main burial sites discovered.

Paracas Cavernas is the middle period (500 BC to 300 BC) and is characterized by communal bottle-shaped tombs dug into the ground at the bottom of a vertical shaft, often to a depth of 6m or more. Several dozen bodies of varying ages and both sexes – possibly family groups – were buried in some of these tombs. They were wrapped in relatively coarse cloth and accompanied by funereal offerings of bone and clay musical instruments, decorated gourds and well-made ceramics.

Paracas Necropolis (300 BC to 200 AD) is the site that yielded the treasure of exquisite textiles for which the Paracas culture is now known. This burial site can still be seen, despite the coverage of drifting sands on the north side of Cerro Colorado, on the isthmus joining the Península de Paracas with the mainland.

The Necropolis consisted of a roughly rectangular walled enclosure in which more than 400 funerary bundles were found. Each contained an older mummified man (who was probably a nobleman or priest) wrapped in many layers of weavings. It is these textiles that are marveled at by visitors now. The textiles consist of a wool or cotton background embroidered with multicolored and exceptionally detailed small figures. These are repeated again and again, until often the entire weaving is covered by a pattern of embroidered designs. Motifs such as fish and seabirds, reflecting the proximity to the ocean, are popular, as are other zoomorphic and geometric designs.

Our knowledge is vague about what happened in the area during the thousand years after the Paracas culture disintegrated. A short distance to the southeast, the Nazca culture became important for several centuries after the disappearance of the Paracas culture. This in turn gave way to Wari influence from the mountains. After the sudden disappearance of the Wari empire, the area became dominated by the Ica culture, which was similar to and perhaps part of the Chincha empire. They in turn were conquered by the Incas.

About this time, a remarkable settlement was built by the expanding Incas, one that is perhaps the best-preserved early Inca site to be found in the desert lowlands today. This is Tambo Colorado, so called for the red-painted walls of some of the buildings. Hallmarks of Inca architecture – such as trapezoid-shaped niches, windows and doorways – are evident, although the buildings were made not from rock, but from adobe bricks. While not as spectacular as the Inca ruins in the Cuzco area, archaeology enthusiasts will find it worth a visit.

Established tour operators:

Paracas Overland (☎ 53 3855; paracasoverland@ hotmail.com; San Francisco 111) Popular with backpackers, this new agency offers tours of the Islas Ballestas and Reserva Nacional de Paracas. It can arrange for a trustworthy taxi driver to take you to Tambo Colorado.

Zarcillo Connections (☎ 53 6543; www.ballestasislands.com; Suite B, Callao 137) Zarcillo has daily tours to the Islas Ballestas and Reserva Nacional de Paracas with guides who speak English and some French and Italian, too. It occasionally takes groups to Tambo Colorado and will arrange customized trips to Nazca. Mountain bikes may be rented at US$10 per day.

Paracas Explorer (☎ 54 5141, 54 5089; www.paracasexplorer.com) In the El Chacho beach district of Paracas, this backpacker travel agency offers the usual island and reserve tours, as well as three-hour dune-buggy and sandboarding trips into the desert (US$15 to US$20 per person).

Guests at the **Hotel Paracas** (☎ 54 5100, in Lima 01-445 9376; www.hotelparacas.com; Av Paracas 173) can arrange reliable, if expensive, Islas Ballestas tours in fast boats. For budget adventure tours, including sandboarding, contact **Hostal San Isidro** (☎ 53 6471; www.sanisidrohostal.com; San Clemente 103). Affiliated with Alegría Tours in Nazca (p147), **Alas Peruanas** (☎ 962 1673; www.alasperuanas.com) offers flights from the Pisco area to the Nazca Lines and back for around US$150 per person (four-passenger minimum).

Sleeping
Many hotels in Pisco and Paracas are noisy at night with street commotion, and in the morning with guests departing for tours.

PISCO
Most travelers stay in central Pisco.

Hostal Los Inkas Inn (☎ 53 6634, 54 5149; www.losinkasinn.com; Barrio Nuevo 14; s/d/tr US$9/13.50/18; 🖵 🖭) This small, family-owned guesthouse has basic but tidy rooms, plus a mini swimming pool, a rooftop terrace with games and free internet access for nuevo sole–pinchers.

Hostal San Isidro (☎ 53 6471; www.sanisidrohostal.com; San Clemente 103; dm US$7, s/d/tr US$10/20/30; 🖭) In a sketchy area near the cemetery, this backpacker inn has a free games room with all the toys (pool, table tennis etc). Modern, decent-value rooms come with fans, cable TV and hot-water showers. There's also a shared kitchen, indoor swimming pool and tiny bar. Some travelers have reported being mugged returning late at night, so take a taxi.

Hostal La Reserva (☎ 53 5643; lareserva_hostal@hotmail.com; San Francisco 327; s/d/tr incl breakfast US$10/20/30) For something way sharper, the whitewashed, oval-shaped La Reserva has sparkling rooms with modish furnishings, fans, cable TV and erratic hot water. Touts hang out here, but the front-desk staff are chilled.

Posada Hispana Hotel (☎ 53 6363; www.posadahispana.com; Bolognesi 236; s/d US$15/30) With legions of fans, this friendly hostel has attractive bamboo and wooden fittings, an espresso café and a terrace for kicking back. Most of the well-worn rooms are musty, however, and only a good deal if you negotiate; some have cable TV. English, French and Italian are spoken.

Hostal Residencial San Jorge (☎ 53 2885; www.hotelsanjorgeresidencial.com; Juán Osores 267-269; r incl breakfast US$16-20) On a quieter residential street, this newly renovated hotel has spotless, spacious rooms with cable TV, plus breezy modern décor with a splash of tropical color and style. A sun-drenched back garden has lounge chairs and tables for picnicking. If it's full, the San Jorge Suite Hostal (Comercio 187) is closer to the plaza.

Hostal Villa Manuelita (☎ 53 5218; hostalvillamanuelita@hotmail.com; San Francisco 227; s/d US$18/28) In an antique colonial building near the Plaza de Armas, this charming small hotel has spacious rooms with hot water and cable TV, an Italianesque café and ornamental gardens out back. Women will feel especially welcome here.

Embassy Beach Hotel (☎ 53 2568; fax 53 2256; San Martín 1119; s/d/tr US$40/60/80; 🖭) About 1km west of town but still distant from the beach, this bland modern hotel has all the expected creature comforts including rooms with cable TV, telephone and minibar, a decent restaurant and a games room.

PARACAS
El Amigo (☎ 54 5042; Av Paracas s/n, Playa El Chaco; s/d US$10/15) El Amigo is Paracas' original budget option for those needing that extra half-hour in bed before tours. It has basic rooms with TV; some rooms have views. It's often cheaper in the off-season.

Posada del Libertador (☎ 967 2163; www.posadadellibertador.com; Av Paracas 25; s/d US$15/30; 🖭) Perfect for families and large groups, this modern condo complex rents well-maintained two-story bungalows, each with four bedrooms, a private bathroom, living room, kitchenette and balcony overlooking the pool. Such luxury!

Hotel El Mirador (☎ 54 5086, in Lima 01-241 6803; www.elmiradorhotel.com; Km 20 Carretera Paracas; s/d/tr $31/41/54, breakfast US$3-4; ☒) Hidden in the sand dunes before the entrance to Paracas, El Mirador is a peaceful, get-away-from-it-all oasis – in fact, it's often empty in low season. And with views like these, it's almost as if you're in the Sahara.

Hotel Paracas (☎ 54 5100, in Lima 01-445 9376; www .hotelparacas.com; Av Paracas 173; r US$79-137, bungalows US$119-260, ste US$126-381; ☒) Bordering the bay, this exclusive resort hotel built in the 1940s has a swish dining room and bar, manicured gardens and a small ancient ceramics museum. Its tasteful rooms boast pleasant porches, too. It's also a good spot to see the amazilia hummingbird. Islas Ballestas and dune-buggy tours can be arranged.

There are several work-in-progress backpacker guesthouses in nearby El Chaco beach district, including generic **Hostal Los Frayles** (☎ 54 5141; Av Paracas s/n; r US$10-20) and cozy **Hostal Refugio del Pirata** (☎ 54 5054; Av Paracas s/n; r US$12-18), where some rooms have ocean views.

Eating & Drinking

Only a few cafés in Pisco open early enough for breakfast before an Islas Ballestas tour, so many hotels include breakfast in their rates. Otherwise, try the **Hostal Villa Manuelita Café** (☎ 53 5218; San Francisco 227). For cheap local *menús* (set meals), there's the historic **Club Social Pisco** (San Martín 132; ☺ lunch & dinner).

In the waterfront El Chaco district of Paracas, there are loads of look-alike beachfront seafood shacks. Unfortunately turtle meat *(motelo)* still winds up on some menus, so please don't encourage the catching of this endangered creature by ordering dishes made with its meat.

As de Oros (☎ 53 2010; San Martín 472; mains US$3-12; ☺ noon-2am) A few blocks west of the Plaza de Armas, this is a good modern restaurant that hosts the only notable disco in town on Friday and Saturday nights. There's also a poolside bar.

Restaurante La Catedral (Plaza de Armas, 108 San Juan de Dios; mains US$4.50-6; ☺ 11am-8pm) As brightly lit as a grade-school cafeteria, this cheerful locals' favorite on the plaza serves up heaped plates of Peruvian seafood, fried bananas, mashed potatoes layered with farm-fresh veggies and much more.

Café Pub El Bossa Nova (San Martín 176; ☺ 5pm-late Mon-Sat) This is an intimate balcony bar from which to peer down on local folks strutting by. Take care negotiating the steep, rickety staircase after a few exquisitely made pisco sours.

Getting There & Around

Pisco is 6km west of the Panamericana, and only buses with Pisco as the final destination actually go to town. If you're not on a direct bus, ask to be left at the San Clemente turnoff on the Panamericana, where fast and frequent *colectivos* wait to shuttle passenger to central Pisco's Plaza de Armas (US$1, 10 minutes). In the reverse direction, *colectivos* for the San Clemente turnoff leave frequently from near Pisco's central market. After dark, avoid the dangerous market area and take a taxi instead (US$1.50).

Soyuz, which has a **ticket office** (☎ 53 5526; Plaza de Armas, Juan de Dios 100) in central Pisco, usually runs the fastest buses along the Panamericana. Near the plaza, **Ormeño** (☎ 53 2764) has six daily buses to Lima (US$5 to US$10, four hours), two of which go direct with the luxurious Royal Class and do not require a change of bus on the highway. It also has two daily buses to Ica (US$3 to US$4.50, 1½ to two hours) and Nazca (US$6 to US$12, four hours), plus two buses a day on the paved road to Arequipa (US$12 to US$18, 12 to 15 hours). It advertises daily buses to Ayacucho, Cuzco, Moquegua, Ilo and Tacna, but most of these do not go directly; you will most likely be put on a Lima-bound bus as far as the Panamericana and have to wait there at a 'terminal' (a shack) for connecting buses.

A short taxi ride around town costs US$1. *Combis* to Paracas leave from near Pisco's central market every half-hour from 6am until 6:30pm daily (US$0.60, 30 minutes). After dark, though, take a taxi to Paracas (US$3). Minibuses to Chincha leave from two blocks south of Plaza Belén (US$0.60, one hour).

ICA

☎ 056 / pop 217,700 / elev 420m

The capital of its department, Ica may have a downtrodden air, but it boasts a thriving wine and pisco industry, with grapes irrigated by the river that shares its name, plus an excellent museum, colonial churches and rowdy annual fiestas. Its slightly elevated position means that it sits above the coastal mist and the climate is dry and sunny.

SOUTH COAST

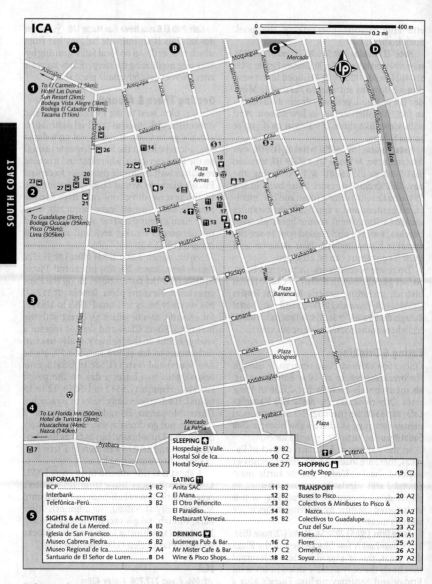

ICA

To El Carmelo (1.5km);
Hotel Las Dunas
Sun Resort (2km);
Bodega Vista Alegre (3km);
Bodega El Catador (10km);
Tacama (11km)

To Guadalupe (3km);
Bodega Ocucaje (35km);
Pisco (75km);
Lima (305km)

To La Florida Inn (500m);
Hotel de Turistas (2km);
Huacachina (4km);
Nazca (140km)

INFORMATION	
BCP	1 B2
Interbank	2 C2
Telefónica-Perú	3 B2

SIGHTS & ACTIVITIES	
Catedral de La Merced	4 B2
Iglesia de San Francisco	5 B2
Museo Cabrera Piedra	6 B2
Museo Regional de Ica	7 A4
Santuario de El Señor de Luren	8 D4

SLEEPING	
Hospedaje El Valle	9 B2
Hostal Sol de Ica	10 C2
Hostal Soyuz	(see 27)

EATING	
Anita SAC	11 B2
El Mana	12 B2
El Otro Peñoncito	13 B2
El Paraidiso	14 B2
Restaurant Venezia	15 B2

DRINKING	
lucienega Pub & Bar	16 C2
Mr Mister Cafe & Bar	17 C2
Wine & Pisco Shops	18 B2

SHOPPING	
Candy Shop	19 C2

TRANSPORT	
Buses to Pisco	20 A2
Colectivos & Minibuses to Pisco & Nazca	21 A2
Colectivos to Guadalupe	22 B2
Cruz del Sur	23 A2
Flores	24 A1
Flores	25 A2
Ormeño	26 A2
Soyuz	27 A2

Information

At the time of research there were rumors of a tourism office opening on the Plaza de Armas, where you'll also find several cybercafés.

BCP (Plaza de Armas) Has a Visa/MasterCard ATM and changes US dollars and travelers' checks.

Hospital (☎ 23 4798, 23 4450; Cutervo 104; 24hr) For emergency services.

Interbank (Grau cuadra 2) Has a 24-hour global ATM; on *cuadra* (block) 2 of Grau.

Police (☎ 23 5421; JJ Elias cuadra 5; 24hr) At the city center's edge.

Serpost (San Martín 156) Southwest of the Plaza de Armas.

Telefónica-Peru (Plaza de Armas, Lima 149) Stays open late for local, long-distance and international calls.

Dangers & Annoyances

Ica has a richly deserved reputation for theft. Stay alert, particularly around the bus terminals and market areas. Sunday is said to be the prime day for petty crimes against tourists, Peruvians and foreigners alike.

Sights & Activities

MUSEO REGIONAL DE ICA

In suburban San Isidro, don't miss this gem of a **museum** (☎ 23 4383; Jirón Ayabaca cuadra 8; adult/child/student US$4/2.50/1; 🕑 8am-7pm Mon-Fri, 9am-6pm Sat & Sun). Despite being robbed in 2004, it still has an impressive collection of artifacts from the Paracas, Nazca and Inca cultures, including superb examples of Paracas weavings, as well as textiles made of feathers. There are beautiful Nazca ceramics, scarily well-preserved mummies of everything from children to a small macaw, trepanned skulls and shrunken trophy heads, enormous wigs and tresses of hair. Out back look for a scale model of the Nazca Lines.

The museum is 1.5km southwest of the city center. Take a taxi from the Plaza de Armas (US$1). You could walk, but it's usually not safe to do so alone, and even larger groups may get hassled.

MUSEO CABRERA PIEDRA

On the Plaza de Armas, this unsigned **museum** (☎ 23 1933; Bolívar 174; adult/student US$3/1.50; 🕑 hrs vary, closed Sun) has an oddball collection of thousands of carved stones and boulders graphically depicting diverse pre-Columbian themes, from astronomy to surgical techniques and sexual practices. The eccentric collector, Dr Cabrera, claimed the stones were ancient, but they're very likely elaborate fakes. If you'd rather not pay, you can sneak a peek at some of the carvings outside the museum entrance.

COLONIAL CHURCHES & MANSIONS

The hulking **Iglesia de San Francisco** (cnr Municipalidad & San Martín) has some fine stained-glass windows. Ica's cathedral, **Iglesia de La Merced** (cnr Bolívar & Libertad), was rebuilt in the late 19th century and contains a finely carved wooden altar. The **Santuario de El Señor de Luren** (Cutervo, btwn Piura & Ayacucho) boasts an image of the patron saint that is venerated by pilgrims during Semana Santa and again in October (p140). The streets surrounding the Plaza de Armas boast a few impressive Spanish colonial mansions, including along the first block of Libertad.

WINERIES

Local wines and piscos can be bought around Ica's Plaza de Armas, but it's more fun to track them down at their source. *Bodegas* (wineries) can be visited year-round, but the best time is during the grape harvest from late February until early April.

Some of Peru's finest wine comes from **Bodega Ocucaje** (☎ 40 8011; www.hotelocucaje.com; Av Principal s/n; admission free, 1hr tour US$3; 🕑 tastings 9am-noon & 2-5pm Mon-Fri, 9am-noon Sat, tours 11am-3pm Mon-Fri), but unfortunately it's fairly isolated, over 30km south of Ica off the Panamericana. Hiring a taxi to reach the winery costs around US$10 each way, or you can join a local tour leaving from Ica (see below).

Another touristy *bodega* less than 10km north of Ica, **Bodega El Catador** (☎ 40 3295; off Km 334 Carretera Panamericana) does wine pressing by foot during February and March, and runs free tours and wine and pisco tastings all year. It also has a restaurant with dancing in the evenings during harvest time. The surrounding neighborhoods can be dicey, so take a taxi each way (US$4.50).

Bodega Vista Alegre (☎ 23 2919; 🕑 8am-noon & 1:45-4:45pm Mon-Fri, 7am-1pm Sat), 3km northeast of Ica in the La Tinguiña district, is the easiest of the large commercial wineries to visit (taxi one way US$1.50). It's best to go in the morning, as the winery occasionally closes in the afternoon. Another place producing the right stuff is **Bodega Tacama** (☎ 22 8395; www.tacama.com; 🕑 9am-4pm), 11km northeast of Ica, which offers interesting tours of its industrial facilities. Again, you'll have to hire a taxi to get here (US$6 each way).

The most convenient of Ica's family-owned artisanal *bodegas* are found in the suburb of **Guadalupe**, less than 3km from Ica on the road to Lima. There are many stalls selling huge bottles of various kinds of pisco, wine, fruit, jams etc. *Micros* bound for Guadalupe (US$0.30, 15 minutes) pass by Iglesia de San Francisco near Ica's Plaza de Armas, or a taxi costs around US$3 each way.

Tours & Guides

Travel agencies around the Plaza de Armas offer city tours and winery excursions. **Aero Condor Perú** (☎ 25 6230; www.aerocondor.com.pe; Hotel Las Dunas, Av La Angostura 400) offers tourist overflights

SOUTH COAST

of the Nazca Lines for about US$150 per person (three-person minimum).

Festivals & Events

Ica has more than its share of fiestas. February inspires the water-throwing antics typical of any Latin American carnival, plus dancers in beautiful costumes. In early to mid-March, it's time for the famous grape-harvest festival, **Fiesta de la Vendimia**, with all manner of processions, beauty contests, cockfights and horse shows, music and dancing, and of course, free-flowing pisco and wine. Most of the events are reserved for evenings and weekends at the festival site of Campo Feriado, on the outskirts of town, but during the week, the tasting and buying of wine and honey throughout the town dominates. The founding of the city by the Spanish conquistadors on 17 June 1563 is celebrated during **Ica Week**, while **Tourist Week** happens during mid-September. In late October, the religious pilgrimage of **El Señor de Luren** culminates in fireworks and a traditional procession of the faithful that keeps going all night.

Sleeping

Beware that hotels fill up and double or triple their prices during the festivals, of which there are many in Ica (above).

BUDGET

Most travelers head for Huacachina (p142), about 4km west of the city. If you get stuck in Ica overnight, dozens of depressing, cheap hotels line the side streets east of the bus terminals and north of the Plaza de Armas, particularly along Tacna.

Hospedaje El Valle (☎ 21 6801; San Martín 151; s/d US$7.50/11) More sprightly than the budget-guesthouse competition, this old-fashioned hostelry run by gracious elderly ladies faces an inner courtyard and has a securely gated entrance. It's a short walk west of the plaza.

La Florida Inn (☎ 23 7313; http://hometown.aol3 .com/lemco3/laflorida.html; Residencial La Florida B-1; dm/s/d with shared bathroom US$8/10/20, s/d US$15/30; ✕ 🖵) Getting rave reviews from Lonely Planet readers, this small, family-owned hotel located not too far from the regional museum has quirkily decorated rooms with TVs. There are solar hot-water showers. Call ahead for reservations and directions.

Hostal Soyuz (☎ 22 4743; Manzanilla 164; s/d/ tr US$13.50/18/21; ✕) Sitting directly over

Soyuz bus terminal, this handy option for late arrivals or early departures has carpeted rooms with air-con and cable TV, but is only for heavy sleepers on account of the rumpus below.

MIDRANGE

Hotel Sol de Ica (☎ 23 6168; www.hotelsoldeica.com; Lima 265; s/d/tr US$32/38/46, ste US$75; 🏊) This dazzlingly white, three-story central hotel gives personalized service. Remarkably small rooms have unusual wood paneling, TVs and phones. There's limited hot water, but the hotel has a sauna and two swimming pools.

El Carmelo (☎ 23 2191; www.elcarmelohotelhacienda .com; Km 301 Carretera Panamericana; s/d/tr/q from US$25/ 35/50/60; 🏊) This romantic roadside hotel on the outskirts of town inhabits a delightful 200-year-old hacienda that has undeniable rustic charm. There's a good restaurant plus a winery on-site. Take a taxi from the city center (US$1).

TOP END

Hotel Hacienda Ocucaje (☎ 83 7049; www.hotelocucaje .com; off Km 334 Carretera Panamericana; d/tr/q Sun-Thu US$64/77/87, Fri & Sat US$77/87/103; 🏊) The Ocucaje winery (p139) has built an upmarket resort hotel with a relaxed ambience and a billiards room, kids' playground, swimming pool, sauna and Jacuzzi. Rooms are modern, but it's the rural getaway you're paying for.

Hotel Las Dunas Sun Resort (☎ 25 6224; www .lasdunashotel.com/hotel; Av La Angostura 40; s/d Sun-Thu US$64/76, Fri & Sat US$77/93, ste US$150, chalet US$300; 🏊) By far the most luxurious hotel in town, the sprawling Las Dunas resort boasts a swimming pool, sauna, tennis courts, mini-golf course, business center, restaurants and bars. Various excursions are offered (for an additional fee), including cycling, horse riding, sandboarding and winery tours. Service can be haphazard, however. The resort is located off Km 300 Carretera Panamericana.

Eating

Two no-frills vegetarian places are **El Mana** (San Martín cuadra 2; menús US$1) and **El Paraidiso** (Loreto 176-178; menús US$1.50; ☽ closed Sat), which serve filling set meals for small change.

Anita SAC (☎ 21 8582; Libertad 133; menús US$3-3.60, mains US$3.25-10; ☽ 10am-10pm) Right smack on the Plaza de Armas, this elegant café dishes up heaped plates of regional Peruvian specialties, plus lip-smacking desserts.

Restaurant Venezia (☎ 23 2241; Lima 230; mains US$3.50-10; ☯ lunch Mon-Sat, dinner daily) Just around the corner from the plaza, the elegant Venezia is a popular family-run Italian restaurant. It's a bit on the expensive side but with an ace wine list.

El Otro Peñoncito (☎ 23 3921; Bolívar 255; mains US$4-10; ☯ lunch & dinner) Ica's most historic and characterful restaurant serves a varied menu of Peruvian and international fare. The formal bartenders here shake a mean pisco sour, too.

Several shops in the streets east of the plaza sell *tejas* (caramel-wrapped candies flavored with fruits, nuts etc).

Drinking

There's not much happening in Ica outside of fiesta times (see opposite), though nearby Huacachina has some friendly watering holes. On Ica's Plaza de Armas, you'll find several wine and pisco tasting rooms to pop into for a quick tipple. South of the plaza along Lima, innovative local bars and clubs advertise live music, DJs and dancing, including Mr Mister Café & Bar and lucienega Pub & Bar. The craziest late-night disco is situated on the north side of the **Hotel de Turistas** (Av de Los Maestros 500), 3km southwest of the plaza; it's a US$1 taxi ride.

Getting There & Away

Ica is a main destination for buses along the Panamericana, so it's easy to get to/from Lima or Nazca. Most of the bus companies are clustered in a high-crime area at the west end of Salaverry, and also Manzanilla west of Lambayeque.

For Lima (US$3.50 to US$13.50, 4½ hours), **Soyuz** (☎ 23 3312) and **Flores** (☎ 21 2266) have departures every 15 minutes, while luxury services go a few times daily with **Cruz del Sur** (☎ 22 3333) and **Ormeño** (☎ 21 5600). Many companies have daytime buses to Nazca (US$2, 2½ hours), while services to Arequipa (US$15 to US$24, 12 hours) are mostly overnight. However, these night buses are notoriously unsafe and recently there have been reports of robberies and hijackings.

To reach Pisco (US$2 to US$4.50, 1½ to two hours), Ormeño is the only major bus company that has direct buses from Ica. Other bus companies drop passengers at the San Clemente turnoff on the Panamericana, about 6km east of Pisco, where a variety of

colectivo taxis and minivans wait to shuttle passengers into town (US$1, 10 minutes). Some faster, but slightly more expensive *colectivos* and minibuses headed for Pisco and Nazca leave when full from near the intersection of Lambayeque and Municipalidad in Ica.

Some small companies may serve destinations around Peru's central highlands, such as Ayacucho and Huancavelica. Check the ever-changing schedules and fares in person at various bus company offices at the west end of Salaverry.

HUACACHINA
☎ 056 / pop 200

Just 5km west of Ica, this tiny oasis surrounded by towering sand dunes nestles next to a picturesque (if smelly) lagoon that features on the back of Peru's S/50 note. Graceful palm trees, exotic flowers and attractive antique buildings testify to the bygone glamour of this resort, which was once a playground for Peruvian elite. These days, it's totally ruled by party-seeking crowds of international backpackers.

Dangers & Annoyances

Though safer than Ica, Huacachina is not a place to be lax about your personal safety or to forget to look after your property. Many guesthouses have well-deserved reputations for ripping off travelers and also harassing young women with sexual advances. Check out all of your options carefully before accepting a room, and never pay for more than a night in advance in case you need to quickly change lodgings.

TOP FIVE CHILL-OUT SPOTS ALONG PERU'S GRINGO TRAIL

Lunahuaná (p129) Floating by rural vineyards on the Río Cañete, plus all the crawfish you can eat

Huacachina (above) Sandboard down gigantic dunes all day long, then party by the oasis till the break of dawn

Cabanaconde (p184) Trek where Andean condors soar into one of the world's deepest canyons

Isla del Sol (p218) Go bravely border-hopping to Bolivia on the shores of aquamarine Lake Titicaca

Sacred Valley (p255) Leave behind the Machu Picchu crowds and explore quaint colonial towns, lively markets and more untrammeled Inca ruins

Activities

The lagoon's murky waters supposedly have curative properties, though hotel swimming pools are far more inviting.

You can rent sandboards for US$1.50 an hour to slide, surf or ski your way down the irresistible dunes, getting sand lodged into bodily nooks and crannies. Though softer, warmer and safer than snowboarding, don't be lulled into a false sense of security – several people have seriously injured themselves losing control of their sandboards. Many hotels offers tours in *areneros* (dune buggies), where you are hauled up to the top of the dunes, sandboard down, then are picked up at the bottom. Drivers are notoriously unsafe, so go at your own risk. The going rate for tours at the time of research was US$12 per person, but ask first if sandboard rental is included and how long the tour lasts.

Sleeping & Eating

Camping is normally possible in the dunes around the lagoon, so ask around and bring at least a sleeping bag for those cold desert nights.

Hostal Salvatierra (☎ 23 2352; Malecón de Huacachina s/n; s/d with shared bathroom US$3/6, s/d US$4.50/7.50; ☒ ☐) The only budget guesthouse actually sitting beside the lagoon, this family-run place is a real bargain. It has a low-key atmosphere, spacious rooms with comfortable beds and a small private pool.

Casa de Arena (☎ 21 5439/5274; casadearena@hotmail .com; Perotti s/n; dm US$3.60, s/d with shared bathroom US$5/7.50, s/d US$7.50/9, ☒ ☐) At this perennially popular place with an outdoor poolside bar perfect for all-night parties, the staff can be notoriously shifty and most women will want to give this place a miss. Private rooms at the back have better views of the oasis.

Hostal Rocha (☎ 22 9987, 22 2256; kikerocha@hotmail .com; Perotti s/n; s/d incl breakfast US$7.50/9; ☒) A more efficiently run backpacker guesthouse closer to the taxi stand, Rocha has the same carefree, anything-goes atmosphere as Casa de Arena and an identical poolside party scene. Rooms can be claustrophobic, but there are hammocks outside to laze around in. Rates include kitchen access.

Hospedaje El Huacanicero (☎ 21 7435; Perotti s/n; www.elhuacachinero.com; r US$7.50; ☒) Easily spotted by their green *areneros* parked out front, this two-story guesthouse is currently a work-in-progress. Rickety rooms with shuttered windows are just a stone's throw from the dunes, though. There's a shared kitchen, garden hammocks and, of course, a poolside bar.

Hostería Suiza (☎ 23 8762; www.hostesuiza.5u.com; Malecón de Huacachina; s/d/tr/q incl continental breakfast US$25/35/50/70; ☒) At the far end of the road beside the oasis, this is a tranquil alternative: no pumping bars here, just an elegant, characterful building and a restful garden. Most extras such as towels are not included, however, and there's not always hot water either. Yet the peace and quiet is priceless. Dutch, French, Italian and English are spoken.

Hotel Mossone (☎ 21 3630; fax 23 6137; s/d/tr/q US$42/60/70/80, ste US$80-103; ☒ ☐) The resort's original grand hotel has simple yet stylish rooms carefully arranged around an almost Mediterranean-style courtyard. All rooms have hot showers and TVs. There's also an upscale restaurant with a convivial waterfront bar. Walk-in guests can score big discounts in the off-season.

Most hotels have a café of sorts and there are a few touristy restaurants near the waterfront. Readers have recommended Restaurant Sol de Ica, which sells homemade chocolates, and the men's social club, Restaurant Mayo.

Getting There & Away

The only way to get to Huacachina from Ica is by taxi or *mototaxi* (US$1.20), or *colectivo* taxi (US$0.60).

PALPA

☎ 056 / pop 14,000 / elev 300m

From Ica, the Panamericana heads southeast through the small oasis of Palpa, famous for its orange groves. Like Nazca, Palpa is surrounded by perplexing **geoglyphs** in the pampa (large, flat area). The best way to see these lines is on a combined overflight from Nazca (p145). Spanish-speaking guides at the **municipalidad** (☎ 40 4488) may be able to take you around local archaeological sites with advance warning.

NAZCA

☎ 056 / pop 53,000 / elev 590m

As the Panamericana rises through coastal mountains and stretches across the arid flats to Nazca, you'd be forgiven for thinking that this desolate pampa holds little of interest. And indeed this sun-bleached expanse was largely ignored by the outside world until 1939, when North American scientist Paul Kosok flew across the desert and noticed a series of extensive lines and figures etched below, which he initially took to be an elaborate pre-Inca irrigation system. In fact, what he had stumbled across was one of ancient Peru's most impressive and enigmatic achievements: the world-famous Nazca Lines. Today the small town of Nazca is continually inundated by travelers who show up to marvel and scratch their heads over the purpose of these mysterious lines, which were declared a Unesco World Heritage Site in 1994.

History

In 1901 the Peruvian archaeologist Max Uhle was the first to realize that the drifting desert sands hid remnants of a Nazca culture distinct from other coastal peoples. Thousands

of ceramics have since been uncovered, mostly by careless *huaqueros* (grave robbers) who plundered burial sites and sold off their finds to individuals and museums. Archaeologists pieced together the story of this unique culture from its highly distinctive ceramics, from the brightly colored and naturalistic early pottery (AD 200 to 500) to the more stylized and sophisticated designs characterizing the late period (AD 500 to 700), and also the simpler designs of the terminal period (AD 700 to 800), influenced by the conquering Wari people. Invaluable tools for unraveling Peru's ancient past, the ceramics depict everything from everyday plants and animals to fetishes and divinities; some even echo the Nazca Lines themselves. Even the most heedless observer

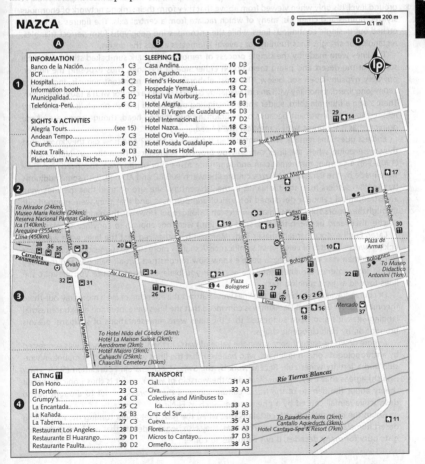

NAZCA

0 _____ 200 m
0 _____ 0.1 mi

INFORMATION	
Banco de la Nación	1 C3
BCP	2 D3
Hospital	3 C2
Information booth	4 C3
Municipalidad	5 D2
Telefónica-Perú	6 C3

SIGHTS & ACTIVITIES	
Alegría Tours	(see 15)
Andean Tempo	7 C3
Church	8 D2
Nazca Trails	9 D3
Planetarium Maria Reiche	(see 21)

SLEEPING	
Casa Andina	10 D3
Don Agucho	11 D4
Friend's House	12 C2
Hospedaje Yemayá	13 C2
Hostal Vía Morburg	14 D1
Hotel Alegría	15 B3
Hotel El Virgen de Guadalupe	16 D3
Hotel Internacional	17 D2
Hotel Nazca	18 C3
Hotel Oro Viejo	19 C2
Hotel Posada Guadalupe	20 B3
Nazca Lines Hotel	21 C3

To Mirador (24km);
Museo Maria Reiche (29km);
Reserva Nacional Pampas Galeras (90km);
Ica (140km);
Arequipa (355km);
Lima (450km)

Carretera Panamericana

Óvalo

Av Los Incas

Carretera Panamericana

San Bastidas

San Martín

Simón Bolívar

Ignacio Morsesky

Fermín del Castillo

Callao

Grau

José Maria Mejia

Juan Matta

Arica

Maria Reiche

Lima

Bolognesi

Plaza de Armas

Bolognesi

To Museo Didáctico Antonini (1km)

Plaza Bolognesi

Mercado

To Hotel Nido del Cóndor (2km);
Hotel La Maison Suisse (2km);
Aerodrome (2km);
Hotel Majoro (3km);
Cahuachi (25km);
Chaucilla Cemetery (30km)

Río Tierras Blancas

To Paredones Ruins (2km);
Cantallo Aqueducts (3km);
Hotel Cantayo Spa & Resort (7km)

EATING	
Don Hono	22 D3
El Portón	23 C3
Grumpy's	24 C3
La Encantada	25 C2
La Kañada	26 B3
La Taberna	27 C3
Restaurant Los Angeles	28 D3
Restaurante El Huarango	29 D1
Restaurante Paulita	30 D2

TRANSPORT	
Cial	31 A3
Civa	32 A3
Colectivos and Minibuses to	
Ica	33 A3
Cruz del Sur	34 B3
Cueva	35 A3
Flores	36 A3
Micros to Cantayo	37 D3
Ormeño	38 A3

SOUTH COAST

will soon learn to recognize the strikingly different Nazca ceramics, some of which can be seen in the local archaeological museum and at the Museo Regional de Ica (p139), though the best collections are stashed away at museums in Lima.

Orientation & Information

All buses arrive and depart near the óvalo (main roundabout) at the west end of town.

From there, it's about a 15-minute walk east to the Plaza de Armas. Cybercafés are on every other street. A few international tourist hotels will exchange US dollars cash or cash travelers' checks, but it's nearly impossible to get euros exchanged here.

BCP (Lima 495) Has a Visa/MasterCard ATM and changes US dollars and travelers' checks.

Casa Andina (Bolognesi 367) Has a global ATM that's often out of service.

ANCIENT MYSTERIES IN THE SAND

Spread across an incredible 500 sq km of arid, rock-strewn plain in the Pampa Colorada (Red Plain), the Nazca Lines remain one of the world's great archaeological mysteries. Consisting of over 800 straight lines, 300 geometric figures (geoglyphs) and, concentrated in a relatively small area, some 70 spectacular animal and plant drawings (biomorphs), the lines are almost imperceptible at ground level. It's only when viewed from above that they form their striking network of enormous stylized figures and channels, many of which radiate from a central axis. The figures are mostly etched out in single continuous lines, while the encompassing geoglyphs form perfect triangles, rectangles or straight lines running for several kilometers across the desert.

The lines were made by the simple process of removing the dark sun-baked stones from the surface of the desert and piling them up on either side of the lines, thus exposing the lighter, powdery gypsum-laden soil below. The most elaborate designs represent animals, including a 180m-long lizard, a monkey with an extravagantly curled tail, and a condor with a 130m wingspan. There's also a hummingbird, spider and an intriguing owl-headed person on a hillside, popularly referred to as an astronaut because of its goldfish-bowl shaped head, though some are of the opinion that it's a priest with a mystical owl's head.

Endless questions remain. Who constructed the lines and why? And how did they know what they were doing when the lines can only be properly appreciated from the air? Maria Reiche (1903–98), a German mathematician and long-time researcher of the lines, theorized that they were made by the Paracas and Nazca cultures between 900 BC and AD 600, with some additions by the Wari settlers from the highlands in the 7th century. She also claimed that the lines were an astronomical calendar developed for agricultural purposes, and that they were mapped out through the use of sophisticated mathematics (and a long rope). However, the handful of alignments Reiche discovered between the sun, stars and lines were not enough to convince scholars.

Later, English documentary-maker Tony Morrison hypothesized that the lines were walkways linking huacas, or sites of ceremonial significance. A slightly more surreal suggestion from explorer Jim Woodman was that the Nazca people knew how to construct hot-air balloons and that they did, in fact, observe the lines from the air. Or, if you believe author George Von Breunig, the lines formed a giant running track.

Of course, it was inevitable that the lines would attract the attention of even more way-out-there theorists. Author Erich von Daniken was convinced that the lines were intended as extraterrestrial landing sites. It's also been suggested that the lines were representations of shamans' dreams brought on by hallucinogenic drugs.

A more down-to-earth theory, given the value of water in the sun-baked desert, was suggested by anthropologist Johann Reinhard, who believed that the lines were involved in mountain worship and a fertility/water cult. Recent work by the Swiss–Liechtenstein Foundation (SLSA; www .slsa.ch) agrees that they were dedicated to the worship of water, and it is thus ironic that their theory about the demise of the Nazca culture suggests that it was due not to drought but to destructive rainfall caused by a phenomenon such as El Niño!

About the only thing that is certain is that when the Nazca set about turning their sprawling desert homeland into an elaborate art canvas, they also began a debate that will keep archaeologists busy for many decades, if not centuries to come.

Hospital (☎ 52 2586; Callao s/n; ☼ 24hr) For emergency services.

Post office (Castillo 379) Two blocks west of the Plaza de Armas.

Telefónica-Perú (Lima 525) Stays open late for local, long-distance and international calls.

Dangers & Annoyances

Travelers arriving by bus will be met by persistent touts trying to sell tours or take arriving passengers to hotels. These touts may use the names of places listed here but are never to be trusted. They'll tell you anything you want to hear to secure a commission. Never hand over any money until you can personally talk to the hotel or tour-company owner and get a confirmed itinerary in writing. It's best to go with a reliable agency for land tours of the surrounding area, as a few violent assaults and robberies of foreign tourists have been reported recently.

Sights
NAZCA LINES

The best-known lines are found in the desert 20km north of Nazca, and by far the best way to appreciate them is to get a bird's-eye view from a *sobrevuelo* (overflight).

Mirador

You'll get only a sketchy idea of the lines at the **observation tower** (admission US$0.30) on the Panamericana 20km north of Nazca, which has an oblique view of three figures: the lizard, tree and hands (or frog, depending on your point of view). It's also a lesson in the damage to which the lines are vulnerable: the Panamericana runs smack through the tail of the lizard, which from nearby seems all but obliterated. Signs warning of landmines are a reminder that walking on the lines is strictly forbidden. It irreparably damages them, and besides, you can't see anything at ground level anyway. To get to the observation tower from Nazca, catch any bus or *colectivo* northbound along the Panamericana (US$0.75, 30 minutes).

Museo Maria Reiche

When Maria Reiche, the German mathematician and long-term researcher of the Nazca Lines, died in 1998, her house, which stands another 5km north along the Panamericana, was made into a small **museum** (Museo de Sitio; admission US$1.50; ☼ 9am-6pm). Though disappointingly scant on information, you can see where she lived, amid the clutter of her tools and obsessive sketches, and pay your respects to her tomb. Though the sun can be punishing, it's possible to walk here from the *mirador* in a sweaty hour or so, or passing *colectivos* can sometimes take you (US$0.30). To return to Nazca, just ask the guard to help you flag down any southbound bus or *colectivo*.

Overflights

Flights over the lines are taken in light aircraft (three to nine seats) in the morning and early afternoon. The optimal time is usually between 7:30am and 10am, when the sun is low, though flights are at the mercy of the weather. Planes won't take off without good visibility, and there's often a low mist over the desert in the morning. Strong winds in the late afternoon also make flying impractical.

Passengers are usually taken on a first-come, first-served basis, with priority given to tour groups or those who have made reservations in Lima. The flight lasts approximately 30 minutes. Because the small aircraft bank left and right, it can be a stomach-churning experience, so motion-sickness sufferers should skip breakfast. Looking at the horizon may help mild nausea.

The standard overflight costs from US$40 per person. Special discount deals are sometimes available, though prices may climb above US$50 in peak season, especially during June and July. In addition, the aerodrome charges a departure tax of US$5. Combination flights that include the Palpa geoglyphs (p142) may be available; these cost about US$80 per person and last roughly one hour. Tour packages include transport to the aerodrome, about 2km outside town. Make reservations as far in advance as possible. It's cheaper to do this in Nazca, but travel agencies in other major cities, such as Lima, Ica and Arequipa, can also arrange this for a small commission.

Companies that fly over the lines have ticket offices near the aerodrome. The biggest is **Aero Condor Perú** (☎ 52 2402; www.aerocondor.com.pe; Hotel Nido del Cóndor), which has offices in Lima and Ica, followed by **Aerolca** (☎ 52 2434; www.areoica .net; Hotel La Maison Suisse), which also has an office in Lima. **Alas Peruanas** (☎ 52 2444; www.alasperuanas .com) is affiliated with Alegrías Tours (p147). Flights can also be booked at travel agencies and many of the hotels in town. Going directly to the aerodrome to arrange a flight is not reliable, but you might save a few dollars.

MUSEO DIDACTICO ANTONINI
On the east side of town, this excellent **ar-chaeological museum** (☎ 52 3444; http://digilander
.libero.it/MDAntonini; Av de la Cultura 600; admission US$3,
cameras US$1.50; ☉ 9am-7pm) boasts an aqueduct
running through the back garden, as well as
interesting reproductions of burial tombs,
a valuable collection of ceramic pan flutes
and a scale model of the lines. You can get
an overview of both the Nazca culture and
a glimpse of most of Nazca's outlying sites
here. Though the exhibit labels are in Spanish, the front desk lends translation booklets
in various languages for you to carry around.
The museum can be hard to find, so take a
taxi (US$1.20).

PLANETARIUM MARIA REICHE
This small **planetarium** (☎ 52 2293; www.concytec
.gob.pe/ipa/inicio_ingles.htm; Nazca Lines Hotel, Bolognesi
s/n; adult/student US$6/3) offers scripted evening
lectures on the Nazca Lines with graphical
displays on a domed projection screen that
last approximately 45 minutes. Call ahead or
check the posted schedules for show times
in Spanish or English (French and Italian by
reservation only).

OUTLYING SIGHTS
All of the sights listed below can be visited
on tours from Nazca (see opposite), although
individual travelers or pairs may have to wait
a day or two before the agency finds enough
people who are also interested in going.

Chauchilla Cemetery
The most popular excursion from Nazca,
this **cemetery** (admission US$1.50), 30km south of
Nazca, will satisfy any urges you have to see
ancient bones, skulls and mummies. Dating
back to the Nazca culture around AD 1000,
the mummies were, until recently, scattered
haphazardly across the desert, left by ransack-
ing tomb-robbers. Now they are seen carefully
rearranged inside a dozen or so tombs, though
cloth fragments and pottery and bone shards
still litter the ground outside the demarcated
trail. Organized tours last three hours and cost
US$5 to US$20 per person.

Pardeones Ruins & Cantallo Aqueducts
The **Pardeones ruins**, 2km southeast of town
via Arica over the river, are not very well
preserved. About 5km further are the underground **Cantallo aqueducts** (admission US$1), which

are still in working order and essential to
irrigate the surrounding fields. The Nazca's
stonework is fine, and it is possible to enter
the aqueducts through the spiraling *ventanas*
(windows), which local people use to clean the
aqueducts each year – it's a wet, weird and
claustrophobic experience. It's possible, but
not necessarily safe, to walk to the aqueducts;
at least, don't carry any valuables. It's better to
catch a minibus leaving from the first block of
Arica (US$0.80, 20 minutes), which passes by
the entrance to the aqueducts, or take a taxi
(around US$9 round-trip with waiting time).
Tours from Nazca that take 2½ hours are
available for around US$5 per person (four-
passenger minimum) and may be combined
with a guided walk through **Buena Fe**, where
some small geoglyphs are found.

Cahuachi
A dirt road travels 25km west from Nazca to
Cahuachi, the most important known Nazca
center, which is still undergoing excavation.
It consists of several pyramids, a graveyard
and an enigmatic site called Estaquería, which
may have been used as a place of mummifica-
tion. Tours from Nazca take three hours, cost
US$8 to US$35 per person, and may include
a side trip to **Pueblo Viejo**, a nearby pre-Nazca
residential settlement.

Reserva Nacional Pampas Galeras
This national reserve is a vicuña (threatened
wild relatives of alpacas) sanctuary high in
the mountains 90km east of Nazca on the
road to Cuzco. It is the best place to see these
shy animals in Peru, though tourist services
are virtually nonexistent. Every other year in
late May or early June is the *chaccu*, when
hundreds of villagers round up the vicuñas for
shearing and three festive days of traditional
ceremonies, with music and dancing, and of
course, drinking. Full-day or overnight tours
from Nazca cost US$30 to US90 per person.

Activities
Need to beat the heat? Go swimming at the
Nazca Lines Hotel (☎ 52 2293; Bolognesi s/n; entry incl
snack & drink US$5).

Off-the-beaten-track expeditions offered by
several outdoor outfitters include a **sandboarding** trip down nearby Cerro Blanco (2078m),
the highest-known sand dune in the world,
and a real challenge for sandboarders fresh
from Huacachina. Half-day **mountain biking**

tours cost about the same (US$35). Ask other travelers to recommend agencies, as some folks have had disappointing and even dangerous experiences with unqualified guides and poor equipment.

Tours & Guides

Most people fly over the lines then leave, but there's much more to see around Nazca. If you take one of the many local tours on offer, they typically include a torturously long stop at a potter's and/or gold-miner's workshop for a demonstration of their techniques (tips for those who show you their trade are expected, too).

Hotels and travel agencies tirelessly promote their own tours. Aggressive touts meeting all arriving buses will try to hard-sell you before you've even picked up your bag.

Some established agencies:

Alegría Tours (☎ /fax 52 2444; www.alegriatoursperu .com; Hotel Alegría, Lima 168) Behemoth agency offers all the usual local tours, plus off-the-beaten-track and sandboarding options. The tours are expensive for one person, so ask to join up with other travelers to receive a group discount. Alegría can arrange guides in Spanish, English, French and German in some cases.

Nasca Trails (☎ 52 2858; nascatrails@terra.com.pe; Bolognesi 550) Recommended by readers, it's run by the friendly Juan Tohalino Vera, an experienced guide who speaks excellent English, as well as German, French and Italian. Not all the agency's tours have such experienced guides, however. They'll pick you up at the bus station if you phone ahead.

For more unusual adventure tours, including desert trekking, **Jorge Echeandia** (☎ 52 1134, 971 4038; jorgenasca17@yahoo.com) is a reliable local guide. The well-educated staff at the Museo Didactico Antonini (opposite) can sometimes be hired on their off-duty time to guide you around local archaeological sites.

Sleeping

Prices drop by up to 50% outside of peak season, which runs from May until August.

BUDGET

Friend's House (☎ 52 3630, 52 2684; elmochilero _1000@hotmail.com; Juan Matt 712; s/d with shared bathroom incl breakfast US$4.50/6; ☐) This fly-by-night backpacker hostel is staffed by young, laid-back local guys. Guests have access to a common kitchen, laundry facilities, TV lounge and a small workout room.

Hostal Posada Guadalupe (☎ 52 2249; San Martín 225; s/d with shared bathroom US$5/7.50) Hidden on a residential block at the far western edge of town, this relaxed family-run guesthouse is a stone's throw from the bus stations. Some of the rooms have private bathrooms, while others are basically just a bed in a box.

Hotel Alegría (☎ 52 2702; www.nazcaperu.com; Lima 168; r with shared bathroom per person US$4.50-7.50) This hotel keeps a dozen basic but clean rooms with shared hot showers for budget travelers.

Hospedaje Yemeyá (☎ 52 3416; Callao 578; r incl breakfast from US$7.50; ☐) An indefatigably hospitable family deftly deals with all of the backpackers that stream through their doorway. They offer a few floors of small but well-cared-for rooms with hot showers and cable TV. There's a sociable terrace and café.

Hostal Vía Morburg (☎ 52 2141; hotelviamorburg@ yahoo.es; José María Mejía 108; s/d US$7.50/10.50; ☒) A noisy, but secure guesthouse, the Vía Morburg has small rooms with cramped showers but plenty of hot water. There's a rooftop café and a miniature swimming pool – more of a bathtub, really. Light sleepers should be forewarned about the crowing roosters next door.

Hotel Nazca (☎ 52 2085; marionasca13@hotmail.com; Lima 438; s with shared bathroom US$3, s/d US$8.50/$12.50) A friendly, older place, it offers basic courtyard rooms, some with communal tepid showers. Ticket touts often hang around here offering cheap tours – don't pay for anything until you have it in writing.

Hotel Internacional (☎ 55 2744; Maria Reiche 112; r/bungalows US$8.50/12.50) Don't let the lackluster entrance fool you: the Internacional may have only standard rooms in the main building, but bigger and better duplex-style bungalows with front porches await out back.

Camping

Hotel Nido del Cóndor (☎ 52 3520; contanas@terra.com .pe; Panamericana Sur Km 447; camping per person US$3) Out by Nazca's aerodrome, this hotel sometimes allows camping on its grassy front lawn.

MIDRANGE

All of the following offer private bathrooms with hot water.

Don Agucho (☎ 52 2048; donagucho@hotmail.com; San Carlos 100; s/d/tr incl breakfast $25/30/40; ☒) The Don Agucho provides chatty service, nice rooms and a great terrace for lounging; the terrace is filled with cacti, wickerwork and

SOUTH COAST

wagon wheels. Breakfasts are filling, though hot water is erratic. It's a short walk over the bridge from town.

Hotel Alegría (☎ 52 2702; www.nazcaperu.com; Lima 168; s/d/tr incl continental breakfast US$18/25/33; 🖥 🖭) This is a classic travelers' haunt with a restaurant, garden, and a busy travel agency. It has narrow, carpeted rooms with TVs and fans. English, French, German, Italian and Hebrew are spoken. Rates include a free half-hour of internet access and a pickup from the bus stations, where you should ignore touts from the Hotel Alegría II – it's *not* recommended.

Hotel Oro Viejo (☎ 52 3332, 52 1112; www.hoteloro viejo.com; Callao 483; s/d US$27/32, ste US$75, all incl breakfast; 🖥) This charming small hotel retains a familial atmosphere and has airy, well-furnished rooms, a welcoming common lounge and an exquisitely tended garden.

Also recommended:

Hotel El Virgen de Guadalupe (☎ 52 1221; hotel-v -guadalupe@speedy.com.pe; Lima 488; r per person incl breakfast US$10-20) A secure, good-value guesthouse near the market.

Hotel Nido del Cóndor (☎ 52 3520; contanas@terra .com.pe; Panamericana Sur Km 447; s/d from US$25/35; 🖭) Modern place opposite the aerodrome with a small swimming pool. It shows free films on the Nazca Lines. English and German are spoken.

TOP END

Catering mostly to tour groups, Nazca's top hotels just aren't that luxurious.

Hotel La Maison Suisse (☎ 52 2434; www.aeroica .net; Km 447 Panamericana; s/d/tr US$50/60/80; 🔀 🖭) This securely gated place, opposite the aerodrome, has a large grassy area with hammocks. The rooms are comfortable enough, with TVs and phones, while suites have air-con, Jacuzzis and minibars. Check online for discount packages, including overflights of the lines.

Casa Andina (☎ 52 3563; www.casa-andina.com; Bolognesi 367; s US$60, d $US70-80, all incl buffet breakfast; 🔀 🖥 🖭) This newly renovated Peruvian chain hotel, poised midway between the bus stations and the Plaza de Armas, offers the best value for money of any of Nazca's up-market hotels. Rooms have eminently stylish, modern furnishings with bold color schemes, air-con and cable TV.

Hotel Majoro (☎ 52 2490; www.hotelmajoro.com; Km 452 Carretera Panamericana Sur, Vista Alegre; s/d/tr/q US$65/80/100/120; 🖭) Housed in a lovely converted hacienda out in the middle of nowhere, this place has simple rooms but tranquil gardens plus a peacock and alpaca. It's 3km out of town beyond the aerodrome (taxi US$1).

Nazca Lines Hotel (☎ 52 2293; fax 52 2112; Bolognesi s/n; s/d/ste $65/85/101; 🔀 🖭) Overrun nightly by huge European and Japanese tour groups, the staff here manage to be exceptionally polite and courteous. The hotel boasts rooms with all mod cons, a tennis court, restaurant and nightly lectures on the lines (see p146).

Hotel Cantayo Spa & Resort (☎ 52 2345; www.ho telcantayo.com; r incl breakfast from US$160; 🔀 🖭) The ultimate escape from grimy central Nazca, the Hotel Cantayo is run by Italians, and overrun with monkeys, a family of peacocks, alpacas and horses for riding. It's just 500m from the Cantallo aqueducts (p146). The rooms are top quality and have various bedroom styles, including four-poster beds and Japanese-style furnishings. The hotel also has a top-notch pool amid extensive gardens.

Eating & Drinking

West of the Plaza de Armas, Bolognesi is stuffed full of foreigner-friendly pizzerias, restaurants and bars, including **Grumpy's** (Bolognesi 182), which gets rave reviews from starving and homesick backpackers.

Restaurant Paulita (Tacna cuadra 2; menús US$1.50-2, mains US$2-4.50; 🕙 11am-9pm) With two tiny open-air tables facing the Plaza de Armas, this locals' fave serves homestyle Peruvian food and a few *criollo* specialties. Don't delay having dinner too late, as it may shut early.

Restaurant Los Angeles (Bolognesi 266; mains US$2-5; 🕙 11:30am-8:30pm) This meticulously run Peruvian and international eatery is known for especially delicious soups and salads. It's owned by a local tour guide who speaks French and English.

La Taberna (☎ 52 1411; Lima 321; menús US$1.50-4.50, mains from US$5; 🕙 lunch & dinner) It's a touristy hole-in-the-wall place: the scribbles covering every inch of wall are a testament to its popularity. Try the spicy fish, challengingly named 'Pescado a lo Macho,' or various vegetarian dishes. There's live music many evenings.

Don Hono (☎ 52 3066; Arica 254; mains US$2-6; 🕙 closed Sun) Just off the Plaza de Armas, this venerable restaurant serves farm-fresh produce and is justifiably proud of its pisco sour. It's a few notches above other touristy eateries around the plaza.

La Kañada (☎ 52 2917; Lima 160; menús US$3, mains around US$5; 🕙 9am-9pm) Handy to the bus stations, this old standby still serves tasty Peruvian food. A decent list of cocktails includes Algarrobina, made with pisco, milk and syrup from the *huarango* (carob) tree. There's occasionally live music in the evening.

Also recommended:

La Encantada (☎ 52 2930; Callao 592; mains US$4.50-10; ☒ lunch & dinner) A stylish seafood restaurant serving excellent ceviche (raw seafood marinated in lime juice); it's next to a disco.

Restaurante El Huarango (☎ 52 1287; Arica 602; mains US$4.50-12; ☒ dinner) A swish two-story restaurant with a rooftop terrace and top-rated *criollo* coastal fare.

Getting There & Around

AIR

People who fly into Nazca normally fly over the Nazca Lines and return the same day. Aero Condor Perú offers overflight tour packages for small groups departing from Ica (p139) and Lima (p106).

BUS & TAXI

Nazca is a major destination for buses on the Panamericana and is easy to get to from Lima, Ica or Arequipa. Bus companies cluster at the west end of Lima, near the *óvalo* (main roundabout). Buses to Arequipa generally originate in Lima, and to get a seat you have to pay the Lima fare. Be aware that hijackings and violent robberies have recently occurred on night buses, especially between Nazca and Arequipa, so take an overnight service only at your own risk.

Almost all services to Lima (US$5 to US$22.50, eight hours), Arequipa (US$7 to US$36, 10 to 12 hours) and for those heading to Chile, Tacna (US$7 to US$30, 13 to 15 hours), leave in the late afternoon or evening. Those bound for Arequipa will often stop en route upon request at Chala (US$3, three hours) and Camaná (US$6, seven hours). **Cruz del Sur** (☎ 52 3713) and **Ormeño** (☎ 52 2058) have a few luxury buses daily to Lima. Intermediate points such as Ica and Pisco are more speedily served by smaller, though less-safe *económico* bus companies, such as Flores.

To go direct to Cuzco (US$15 to US$30, 14 hours), several companies, including Cruz del Sur, take the paved road east via Abancay. This route climbs over 4000m and gets very cold, so wear your warmest clothes and bring your sleeping bag on board if you have one. The alternative is to go via Arequipa, where you can transfer to a more comfortable Cuzco-bound bus along an entirely paved route.

For Ica, fast *colectivo* taxis (US$3.60, two hours) and slower minibuses (US$2.70, 2½ hours) leave when full from near the gas station on the *óvalo*. On the south side of the main roundabout, antiquated *colectivo* taxis wait for enough passengers to make the run down to Chala (US$3.50, 2½ hours).

A taxi from central Nazca to the aerodrome, 2km away, costs about US$1.

SACACO

About 100km south of Nazca toward Chala in the desert is Sacaco, where the sand is made of crushed shells; keep your eyes peeled for fossilized crocodile teeth. There is a small on-site **museum** (admission US$1.50) with a fossilized whale in the middle of nowhere. The 3km road to Sacaco is marked by a sign at Km 539 on the Panamericana. You can hire a taxi from Nazca to Chala with a stop at Sacaco (US$30 to US$35), but the museum's opening hours are erratic and it may be closed when you show up. Alegría Tours (p147) occasionally runs tours from Nazca.

CHALA

☎ 054 / pop 2500

The tiny, ramshackle fishing village of Chala, about 170km from Nazca, presents intrepid travelers with an opportunity to break the journey to Arequipa and visit the archaeological site of **Puerto Inca** (admission free; ☒ 24hr), from whence fresh fish was once sent all the way to Cuzco by runners – no mean effort! The well-marked turnoff is 10km north of town, at Km 603 along the Panamericana, from where a dirt road leads 3km west to the coastal ruins.

Near the ruins, **Hotel Puerto Inca** (☎ 25 8798; www.puertoinka.com.pe; Km 603 Carretera Panamericana; s/d/tr/q US$35/53/73/91; ☒) is a large resort set in a pretty bay. It has a campground that costs US$3 per person, with a shower complex by the sea. It also offers horse riding and body-board, kayak and jet ski rentals.

In humble Chala itself are many more-basic guesthouses. The clean, friendly **Hostal Grau** (☎ 50 1009; Comercio 701; s/d US$3/6) has shared cold showers; ask for a room at the back with sea views. Local restaurants along the highway serve set lunches – trout is the special of the day, every day – from US$1.

Colectivo taxis to Chala (US$3.50, 2½ hours) leave from the *óvalo* in Nazca when full from the early morning until mid-afternoon. Onward buses to Arequipa (US$6, eight hours) via Camaná (US$4.50, 4½ hours) stop in Chala at small ticket offices along the Panamericana, with most buses departing between 6pm and 8pm. At the time of research, Transportes Camino del Inka had the only early bus to Arequipa leaving in the early afternoon, around 1pm. Major bus companies such as Cruz del Sur and Flores also have daily buses to Lima (US$7.50 to US$25, 11 hours) via Nazca (US$3, three hours) that stop in Chala.

CAMANÁ

☎ 054 / pop 12,500

After leaving Chala in the dust, the Panamericana heads south for 220km, clinging tortuously to sand dunes dropping down to the sea, until it reaches positively urban Camaná. This coastal city has long been a summer resort popular with *arequipeños* (inhabitants of Arequipa) who flock to its beaches, about 5km from the center. Sadly, the earthquake of June 2001 sparked a tidal wave that devastated the beachside community and its tourism industry. Nonetheless, Camaná is still a possible place to break the journey to Arequipa. Its town center is largely unaffected, and its beaches are uncrowded.

Orientation & Information

The main plaza is about a 15-minute walk along the road where all the buses stop toward the coast. On the plaza, **BCP** (9 de Noviembre 139) changes US dollars and has a 24-hour Visa/MasterCard ATM.

Sleeping & Eating

To get to the coast, take a *combi* to La Punta beach (US$0.30, 10 minutes), where there are a few sparse restaurants and hotels, some bearing scars from the tsunami. Hotels get busy on summer weekends from January to April, even in the city center.

Hostal Montecarlo (☎ 57 1110; Lima 514; s/d/tr with bathroom US$9/12/14) The main road along which the bus stations are lined up is chock-a-block with cheap, bare-bones hotels. This is one of the flashier ones, with clean rooms, 24-hour hot water, cable TV and phone.

Hotel Sun Valley (☎ 28 3056, 969 4235; eridv@hotmail .com; Km 843, Cerrillos 2; r from US$15; 🏊) Outside town and close to the beach, this squeaky-clean hotel has friendly owners that have put comfy beds in every room. It also has a sunny terrace and a restaurant that comes highly recommended. Infrequent minibuses from

the center go to the beach, but taking a taxi is faster (US$1.50).

Hotel de Turistas (☎ 57 1113; htouristcamana@yahoo .com; Lima 138; s/d/tr US$21/28/39, ste US$58, all incl breakfast; 🏊) Housed in a large elegant building set in spacious gardens, this place is a cut above the competition. It has a restaurant and is just a short walk or taxi ride from the bus stations.

Getting There & Away

Frequent bus services to Arequipa (US$4.50, 3½ hours) are provided by several companies, all of which are found along Lima, including luxurious **Cruz del Sur** (☎ 57 1491; Lima 474), newcomer **Cromotex** (☎ 57 1752; Lima 301) and the always-economical **Flores** (☎ 57 1013; Lima 200). Cruz del Sur and other smaller bus companies also have daily services to Lima (US$12, 12 hours) that stop at most intermediate coastal points, such as Chala (US$4.50, 4½ hours) and Nazca (US$6, seven hours).

MOLLENDO

☎ 054 / pop 29,000

Reached via a desert landscape of delicate pinks, browns and grays, this old-fashioned beach resort is a popular getaway for *arequipeños* during the coastal summer, from January to early April. Beyond the sand dunes the desert becomes very rocky, with brave cacti eking out an existence in the salt-laden soil.

Orientation & Information

Mollendo is a pleasant colonial town, with hilly streets and a long beach. The bus terminal is a quick ride from the town's main plazas, which are just up from the beach. **BCP** (Arequipa 330) has a Visa/MasterCard ATM and changes US dollars. Internet cafés are everywhere; **StarNet** (Arequipa 624; per hr US$0.30; 🕙 8:30am-10pm) has fast connections. **Telefónica-Perú** (Arequipa 675) is north of the central market.

Sights & Activities

When temperatures are searing from January through to at least March, **swimming pools** (entry per adult/child US$1/0.50) open alongside the sea, and beachfront discos stay thumping until the wee hours of the morning. But Mollendo can be like a ghost town throughout the rest of the year. Once a bustling port, most ships now dock in the larger port of Matarani, 15km to the northwest.

Sleeping

Single rooms are difficult to find, especially on weekends in high season. Prices listed may be bargained down midweek and during the off-season.

La Posada Inn (☎ 53 4610; Arequipa 337; s/d with shared bathroom US$5/10, s/d US$7.50/12, all incl breakfast) This is an excellent, well-cared-for option run by a welcoming family and scented with honeysuckle in summer. Rooms in the lower area have hot water, and some have local TV.

Hostal Los Balcones (☎ 53 5087; Dean Valdivia 511; s/d from US$10/20) Just around the corner from all the hubbub, this airy colonial building may have seen better days, but it's a fair deal for rooms with cable TV. Never mind the surly staff.

El Plaza Hostal (☎ 53 2460; plazamollendo@hotmail .com; Arequipa 209; s/d/tr/q US$13.50/18/21/24) This large new hotel has spacious rooms, hot showers and local TV. It's another flower-bedecked spot with smiling employees.

Hostal La Casona (☎ 53 3160; Arequipa 188-192; s/d US$13.50/18) Just as central as El Plaza, La Casona has high-ceilinged, airy rooms with cable TV and hot water. The staff can be stiff necked, but the atmosphere is casual.

Hostal La Villa (☎ 53 5051; fax 53 2700; Mariscal Castilla 366; s/d/tr US$20/25/30, ste from US$33; ☒) Bedraggled and showing its age, this historic high mansion is a chilled place to lie back on a sun lounger with a cold drink and one foot dangling into the plunge pool. It has carpeted rooms with cable TV, plus a garden terrace and restaurant.

Eating

Cevicherías (restaurants serving ceviche) and seafood restaurants abound in town and near the beach. For ice cream and snacks, **Helad-ería Venecia** (Comercio at Blondell; ice cream US$0.70-2; ☯ noon-8pm) has some intriguing local fruit flavors and may tempt you with free samples. **Marco Antonio** (Plaza Bolognesi, Comercio 254; mains US$2-5.50; ☯ 11am-9pm) is a good no-frills Peruvian café with bargain set meals. There are dozens of snack bars near the beach, too.

Getting There & Around

The bus station, Terminal Terrestre, is about 1.5km northwest of the center; there's a US$0.30 departure tax. A couple of small bus companies have frequent departures throughout the day for Arequipa (US$1.50 to US$2.50, 1½ to 2½ hours). **Tepsa** (☎ 53 2872) has one

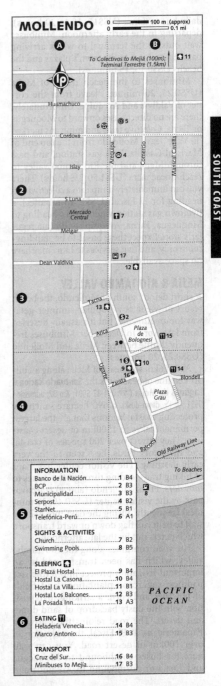

MOLLENDO

0 — 100 m (approx)
0 — 0.1 mi

To Colectivos to Mejiá (100m);
Terminal Terrestre (1.5km)

Huamachuco
Cordova
Islay
S Luna
Mercado Central
Melgar
Dean Valdivia
Tacna
Arica
Plaza de Bolognesi
Ugarte
Zarata
Plaza Grau
Balcony
Old Railway Line

To Beaches

PACIFIC OCEAN

INFORMATION	
Banco de la Nación	1 B4
BCP	2 B3
Municipalidad	3 B3
Serpost	4 B2
StarNet	5 B1
Telefónica-Perú	6 A1

SIGHTS & ACTIVITIES	
Church	7 B2
Swimming Pools	8 B5

SLEEPING ⌂	
El Plaza Hostal	9 B4
Hostal La Casona	10 B4
Hostal La Villa	11 B1
Hostal Los Balcones	12 B3
La Posada Inn	13 A3

EATING ⊓	
Heladería Venecia	14 B4
Marco Antonio	15 B3

TRANSPORT	
Cruz del Sur	16 B4
Minibuses to Mejía	17 B3

daily bus to Lima (US$15, 18 to 20 hours), departing in the early afternoon. Minibuses wait outside the terminal to whisk arriving passengers down to the town's plazas and the beach (US$0.15, 15 minutes).

Minibuses to the beach resort of Mejía (US$0.25, 20 minutes) leave from the corner of Valdivia and Arequipa. Unfortunately, there are no direct buses onward to Moquegua or Tacna. Colectivo taxis and minivans marked 'El Valle' leave Mollendo from the top end of Mariscal Castilla, by a gas station, and pass through Mejía and the Río Tambo valley to reach Cocachacra (US$1.50, 1½ hours). There you can immediately jump into a colectivo taxi heading for El Fiscal (US$1, 15 minutes), a flyblown gas station where buses heading to Moquegua, Tacna, Arequipa and Lima regularly stop. Expect these buses to be standing-room only, and that services to Lima may have no space available.

MEJÍA & RÍO TAMBO VALLEY

A short detour south of Mollendo, the beach resort of Mejía is a popular summer getaway for arequipeños, but it's usually deserted from late April to December. Minibuses frequently shuttle between Mejía and Mollendo (US$0.25, 20 minutes).

About 6km southeast of Mejía along an unbroken line of beaches is the **Santuario Nacional Lagunas de Mejía** (☎ 054-83 5001; Km 32; admission US$1.50; ☉ dawn-dusk), a 690-hectare sanctuary protecting coastal lagoons that are the largest permanent lakes in 1500km of desert coastline. They attract over 200 species of coastal and migratory birds, best seen in the very early morning. The visitor center has maps of hiking trails leading through the dunes to miradors. From Mollendo (above) colectivos pass by the visitor center (US$0.40, 30 minutes) frequently during the daytime. Ask the staff to help you flag down onward transport, which peters out by the late afternoon.

The road continues along the Río Tambo valley, which has been transformed by an important irrigation project into fertile rice paddies, sugarcane plantations and fields of potatoes and corn: a striking juxtaposition with the dusty backdrop of sand dunes and desert. The road rejoins the Carretera Panamericana at El Fiscal, the only stop in over 100km of desert road. You can wait here for buses southbound to Moquegua and Tacna or northbound to Arequipa and

Lima, but expect them to be standing-room only. Long-distance services to Lima may be completely full.

MOQUEGUA

☎ 053 / pop 57,300 / elev 1420m

This parched, dusty inland town survives in the driest part of the Peruvian coastal desert, soon to merge into northern Chile's Atacama Desert – the driest in the world. The Río Moquegua delivers enough moisture to the surrounding rural areas to grow avocados and grapes (the latter often used to make Pisco Biondi, one of the nation's top-shelf brandies), but as you walk away from the river it becomes hard to believe that any agriculture is possible here.

Moquegua means 'quiet place' in Quechua, and the region has long been culturally linked with the Andes. It has peaceful cobblestone streets, a shady central plaza with flower gardens and some unusual buildings that are roofed with a type of wattle-and-daub mixture mixed from sugar-cane thatch and clay. Sadly, many of these structures sustained significant damage during the 2001 earthquake, which hit Moquegua harder than any other settlement in the region.

Orientation & Information

The main plaza is a long walk uphill from where the buses stop. After dark, don't risk being in the dangerous market area and take a taxi instead (US$1.20). Cheap but slow cybercafés are near the Plaza de Armas.

BCP (Moquegua 861) Has a 24-hour Visa/MasterCard ATM.

Regional Tourist Office (☎ 46 2236; Ayacucho 1060; ☉ 7:30am-3:30pm Mon-Fri) Primarily administrative, but the staff are happy to answer questions and provide some brochures.

Serpost (Ayacucho 560; ☉ 8am-noon & 3-6:30pm Mon-Sat) On the Plaza de Armas.

Sights & Activities
PLAZA DE ARMAS & AROUND

The town's small and shady plaza boasts a 19th-century wrought-iron fountain, thought by some to have been designed by Alexandre Gustave Eiffel, and flower gardens that make it a welcome oasis away from the encroaching desert.

The foreign-funded **Museo Contisuyo** (☎ 76 1844; http://bruccowen.com/contisuyo/MuseoE.html; Tacna 294; adult/student US$1/0.30; ☉ 8am-1pm & 12:30-5:30pm) is an excellent little repository of local archaeological artifacts, including photographs of recent excavations, along with exhibitions of new works by local artists. The labels are in Spanish and English.

Opposite the façade of the town's oldest **church**, which mostly collapsed during a massive earthquake in 1868, is an 18th-century Spanish **colonial jail**, with intimidating iron-grilled windows. Next door is the **La Casa Tradicional de Moquegua** (Ayacucho cuadra 5; admission by donation; 8am-noon & 4-7pm Mon-Sat, 8am-noon Sun), which is an interesting living history museum, though it may be shut.

Walk around the town center to see some of the typical sugar-cane thatching, especially along Calle Moquegua, and have a peek inside **Catedral Santa Catalina**, which houses the body of 18th-century St Fortunata, whose hair and nails are said to be still growing.

CERRO BAÚL

A worthwhile excursion outside the city is to the flat-topped and steep-sided hill of **Cerro Baúl**, 18km northeast of Moquegua, once a royal brewery built by the Wari people. As was the case with succeeding Inca traditions,

it was upper-class Wari women who were the skilled brewers here. Archaeologists who are still at work excavating the site believe that it was ceremonially destroyed by fire after one last, drunken *chicha* (fermented corn beer) bash, though why it was abandoned in such a rush remains a mystery so far. The rugged walk to the top of the site, which boasts panoramic views, takes about an hour. From Moquegua, a round-trip taxi costs about US$10, or simply catch a *micro* headed for Torata from central Moquegua and ask to be let off at Cerro Baúl (US$0.60).

Tours & Guides

Architectural walking tours of the town can be arranged at the Museo Contisuyo. **Ledelca Tours** (76 2342; ledelca_tours@hotmail.com; Ayacucho 625) is a travel agency near the plaza that organizes guided trips to *bodegas*, geoglyphs and Cerro Baúl.

Sleeping

There are plenty of dirt-cheap, but not necessarily safe hotels near the bus stations and the market area.

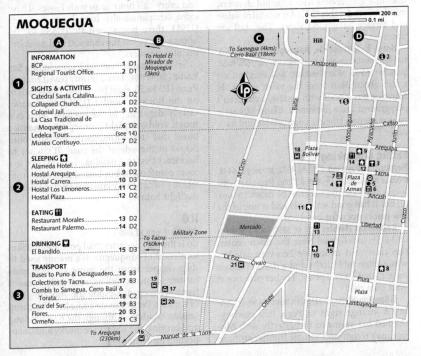

Hostal Carrera (☎ 46 2113; Lima 320; s/d with shared bathroom US$3.60/6, s/d US$4.50/8) Sitting pretty, safe and secure behind its own garden gate, this pastel-colored little hostel has basic rooms and a convivial owner. There may be limited hot water in the communal bathrooms.

Hostal Arequipa (☎ 46 1338; Arequipa 360; s/d/tr US$8.50/12.50/15.50) Located on a busy main street not far from the plaza, the Arequipa has clean and cozy rooms with hot showers and cable TV. Service here is reasonably friendly and helpful.

Hostal Plaza (☎ 46 1612; Ayacucho 675; s/d/tr US$9/11.50/16.50) This is a neat spot by the plaza, opposite the cathedral, with airy, good-value rooms sporting large-screen cable TVs.

Hostal Los Limoneros (☎ 46 1600; Lima 441; s/d US$12/16.50) It's the quiet garden, with its shady patios and delicious smells, that makes this the most attractive and traditional guesthouse in town. Though not as luxurious as some hotels, the restful high-ceilinged rooms have hot water and cable TV.

Alameda Hotel (☎ /fax 46 3971; Junín 322; s/d/tr/q US$20.50/23.50/29/38, ste US$41, all incl breakfast) This bland, out-of-the-way hotel has quality, spic-and-span rooms with sofa, hot showers, minibars and cable TV. An upstairs salon and terrace have good views. The staff are unsmiling.

Hotel El Mirador de Moquegua (☎ 46 1765; mirador@inventur.com.pe; Alto de la Villa s/n; s/d/tr US$26/40/50, bungalow $55-85, all incl breakfast;) Perched on a cliff about 3km from the town center, El Mirador has a pool with a view, a children's playground and a restaurant. Bland '60s-style rooms are nevertheless comfortable and have cable TV.

Eating & Drinking

Restaurant Palermo (☎ 46 4072; Moquegua 644A; 3-course menús US$2; 9am-8:30pm) Popular with locals, the Palermo may not be much to look at, but it has good set meals and is one of the few places open for breakfast.

Restaurant Morales (☎ 46 3084; Lima 398; mains US$2-6; lunch & dinner) Near the town center, this classy but affordable Peruvian café has white-linen tablecloths and a *dueña* (female owner) that's a real pistol. Try her patience at your own risk!

El Bandido (Moquegua 333; pizzas from US$4.50; 5pm-late) A strange sight in Peru, this cowboy-themed bar seems to fit perfectly with Moquegua's rough-and-tumble frontier attitude.

Wood-fired pizzas are made to order, and the beer just keeps flowing.

For open-air terrace restaurants serving typical regional food with live *folklórica* (folkloric) music on weekends, catch a taxi to nearby Samegua (US$1).

Getting There & Away

A new bus terminal being built 2km east of the city may be open by the time you read this. For now, buses leave from several small terminals downhill southwest of the Plaza de Armas. There you'll also find faster, though less safe and more expensive *colectivo* taxis that leave when full for Tacna (US$4.50, 2½ hours) and sometimes Ilo.

Buses to Lima (US$15 to US$21, 16 to 20 hours) leave with **Ormeño** (☎ 46 1149; Av La Paz 524), which has two luxury-class services daily; **Cruz del Sur** (☎ 46 1405), which has three luxury services; and **Flores** (☎ 46 2647), which has two *económico* services. These buses often make intermediate coastal stops, for example at Nazca and Ica. Other buses to Arequipa (US$4.50, four hours) leave three times daily with Cruz del Sur, twice daily with Ormeño and every half hour or so with Flores. These same companies also have buses to Tacna (US$3, three hours) and Ilo (US$2.40, 1½ hours); Flores has the cheapest and most frequent departures.

Several smaller companies, including **San Martín** (☎ 46 3584), take a mostly paved route to Puno (US$6.50, eight hours) via Desaguadero on the Bolivian border (US$5, six hours), usually departing in the evening. This is a rough, cold overnight journey on *económico* buses that stop infrequently for bathroom breaks at the side of the road. It's wiser to backtrack first to Arequipa, then transfer to a more comfortable bus bound for Puno, from where you can easily cross into Bolivia during daylight hours.

ILO
☎ 053 / pop 82,000

Ilo is the ugly departamental port, about 95km southwest of Moquegua. It's mainly used to ship copper from the mine at Toquepala further south, as well as wine and avocados from Moquegua. Despite the shocking lack of scenery, Peruvians do come here for cheap seaside holidays. Although the beach is long and curving, the waters are murky and unappealing for swimming.

Sights

About 15km inland at El Algarrobal is the **Museo Municipal de Sitio** (☎ 83 5000; Centro Mallqui; adult/student US$1/0.30; ☺ 10am-3pm Mon-Sat, 10am-2pm Sun), which hosts a surprisingly noteworthy collection of exhibits on the area's archaeology and agriculture, including ceramics, textiles, a collection of feather-topped hats and a mummified llama. A round-trip by taxi costs around US$10.

Sleeping & Eating

There's no need to stay overnight, but if you get stuck there are plenty of options.

Hotel San Martín (☎ 48 1082; Matará 325; s/d US$7.50/10.50) Near the bus companies, this is a good-value hostel with large decent rooms and private hot showers. The staff are extremely eager to rent you a room.

Hostal Plaza (☎ 48 2146; 2 de Mayo 514; s/d/tr US$9/12/15) Who says there's no truth in advertising? Just off the plaza, this is a well-kept hotel with good, if bland rooms with hot showers and cable TV.

VIP Hotel (☎ 48 1492; www.viphotel.corporacionadc .net; 2 de Mayo 608; s/d US$28.50/37, with air-con US$35/43.50; ⌨) A swish hotel by the plaza, the VIP has a refined restaurant, wi-fi internet access and spacious rooms with all the frills, from minibars to cable TV. The higher the floor, the better the sea views.

Happy Cow (Moquegua 133; menús from US$2; ☺ 11am-10pm) A short walk from the plaza, this cheerful subterranean *parrillada* (grill house) has a sign (in English) that will make you laugh. It serves all sorts of barbecue-style fried meats and yummy snacks. It's opposite a popular pub and disco.

Restaurant El Peñon (☎ 48 2929; 2 de Mayo 100; mains US$2-5; ☺ lunch & dinner) It has a prime shorefront position, looking down on pelicans and across to the port, but you may not be able to enjoy the seafood or panoramic views due to the port's distinctive smell.

Getting There & Away

There is an oddly ship-shaped bus terminal 1km northeast of town, but most companies continue to leave from smaller stations in the town center, a short walk from the plaza and the beach.

Cruz del Sur (☎ 48 2206; cnr Moquegua & Matará) and **Ormeño** (☎ 48 1415; cnr Junín & Matará) each have daily buses to Lima (US$18 to US$42, 16 to 18 hours) as well as Moquegua (US$2.40, 1½

hours), where you can transfer to other buses bound for Arequipa. **Flores** (☎ 48 2512; cnr Ilo & Matará) goes to the same destinations more frequently, with direct services to Tacna (US$3, 3½ hours, every 45 minutes) and Arequipa (US$5.50, five hours, every 2½ hours).

Faster, slightly pricier *colectivo* taxis to Tacna and sometimes Moqegua leave when full from the side streets near the smaller bus stations.

TACNA

☎ 052 / pop 243,600 / elev 460m

At the tail end of the Panamericana, almost 1300km southeast of Lima, the hectic border outpost of Tacna is Peru's southernmost city and the capital of its department. It is situated about 40km from the Chilean border and was occupied by Chile in 1880 after the War of the Pacific, until its people voted to return to Peru in 1929. Incidentally, Tacna has some of Peru's best schools and hospitals; whether this is due to its Chilean ties is a matter of hotly debated opinion. The city also shows off British and French influences in its architecture and train system. Yet it remains staunchly, even defiantly patriotic. You'll never be in doubt as to which side of the border you're actually on.

Information

Internet cafés are everywhere, and most offer inexpensive local, long-distance and international phone calls. Chilean pesos, Peruvian nuevos soles and US dollars can all be easily exchanged in Tacna. There's a global ATM at Terminal Terrestre.

BCP (San Martín 574) Has a Visa/MasterCard ATM, changes travelers' checks and gives cash advances on Visa cards.

Bolivian Consulate (☎ 42 3063; Bolognesi 1721; ☺ 9am-3pm Mon-Fri) Most travelers can enter Bolivia without a visa; there's another Bolivian consulate located in Puno.

Chilean Consulate (☎ 42 3063; www.minrel.cl; Presbitero Andía at Saucini; ☺ 8am-1pm Mon-Fri) Most travelers don't need a Chilean visa and head straight for the border instead.

Hospital (☎ 72 2121, 72 3361; Blondell s/n; ☺ 24hr) For emergency services.

Interbank (San Martín 646) Has a 24-hour global ATM.

Lavandería Latina (Vizcarra 264b; per kg US$1.40; ☺ 8am-9pm Mon-Sat) Laundry service.

Oficina de migraciones (immigration office; ☎ 74 3231; Av Circunvalación s/n, Urb Él Triángulo; ☺ 8am-1pm Mon-Fri)

Police (☎ 71 4141; Calderón de la Barca 353; ☺ 24hr)
Serpost (Bolognesi 361; ☺ 8am-8pm Mon-Sat) South of the Plaza de Armas.
Regional Tourist Office (☎ 22 2784; Blondell 280; ☺ 7:30am-3:15pm Mon-Fri) Only limited advice and brochures.
Zesal Tour Agency (☎ 24 2851; zesaltacna@hotmail .com; 2nd fl, international bus terminal; ☺ 7am-8pm Mon-Sat) Provides free tourist information.

Dangers & Annoyances

Remember that international border traffic attracts thieves and other criminals. Keep a close watch on your belongings at all times, especially at the bus terminals, and don't wander around alone after dark. When in doubt, take a taxi instead of walking.

Sights & Activities

You won't need much more than an afternoon to see everything Tacna has to offer. If you're coming from Chile, you may want to continue on immediately to Arequipa instead.

PLAZA DE ARMAS

Tacna's main plaza, which is studded with palm trees and large pergolas topped by bizarre mushroomlike bushes, is a popular meeting place and has a patriotic flag-raising ceremony every Sunday morning. The plaza, famously pictured on the front of Peru's S/100 note, features a huge arch – a monument to the heroes of the War of the Pacific. It is flanked by larger-than-life bronze statues of Admiral Grau and Colonel Bolognesi. Nearby,

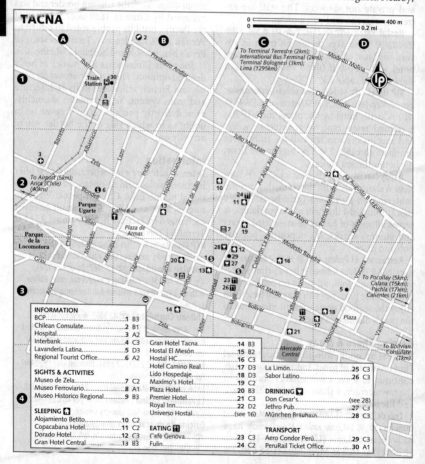

TACNA

0 _____ 400 m
0 _____ 0.2 mi

INFORMATION	
BCP	1 B3
Chilean Consulate	2 B1
Hospital	3 A2
Interbank	4 C3
Lavandería Latina	5 D3
Regional Tourist Office	6 A2

SIGHTS & ACTIVITIES	
Museo de Zela	7 C2
Museo Ferroviario	8 A1
Museo Historico Regional	9 B3

SLEEPING	
Alojamiento Betito	10 C2
Copacabana Hotel	11 C2
Dorado Hotel	12 C2
Gran Hotel Central	13 B3
Gran Hotel Tacna	14 B3
Hostal El Mesón	15 B2
Hostal HC	16 C3
Hotel Camino Real	17 D3
Lido Hospedaje	18 D3
Máximo's Hotel	19 C2
Plaza Hotel	20 B3
Premier Hotel	21 C3
Royal Inn	22 D2
Universo Hostal	(see 16)

EATING	
Cafe Genova	23 C3
Fulin	24 C2
La Limón	25 C3
Sabor Latino	26 C3

DRINKING	
Don Cesar's	(see 28)
Jethro Pub	27 C3
München Brauhaus	28 C3

TRANSPORT	
Aero Condor Perú	29 C3
PeruRail Ticket Office	30 A1

the 6m-high bronze **fountain** was created by the French engineer Alexandre Gustave Eiffel (of eponymous tower fame), who also designed the **cathedral**, noted for its fine stained-glass windows and onyx high altar.

MUSEO FERROVIARIO & EL PARQUE DE LA LOCOMOTORA

This **museum** (☎ 72 4981; admission US$0.30; ☼ 8am-5:30pm), located inside the train station – just ring the bell at the southern gates – gives the impression of stepping back in time. You can wander amid beautiful though poorly maintained 20th-century steam engines and rolling stock, plus atmospheric salons filled with historic paraphernalia, including a curious collection of international postage stamps, all to the tune of the lonely tap-tapping of the station master's ancient typewriter.

About a 15-minute walk south of the train station, a British locomotive built in 1859 and used as a troop train in the War of the Pacific is the centerpiece of **El Parque de la Locomotora**, an otherwise empty roadside park.

OTHER MUSEUMS

The small, musty **Museo de Zela** (Zela 542; admission free; ☼ 8:30am-12:30pm & 3:30-6:30pm Mon-Sat) provides a look at the interior of one of Tacna's oldest colonial buildings, the Casa de Zela. It houses a motley collection of 19th-century paintings of stately folk.

If the tiny **Museo Historico Regional** (Casa de la Cultura; adult/student US$1/0.30; ☼ 8am-1pm & 2-5pm) is closed, ask someone in the library below to open it. The main exhibit deals with the War of the Pacific, and features paintings and maps. There's also a small collection of art and archaeological pieces.

BEACHES

Tacna's main seaside resort is **Boca del Río**, about 50km southwest of the city. Minibuses from Terminal Bolognesi go here along a good road (US$1.50, one hour).

Sleeping

There's no shortage of hotels catering to Tacna's cross-border traffic. That said, almost all are overpriced and fill up very fast, especially on weekends. No matter what time you arrive in Tacna, your first order of business is to find a room, which may take quite a while. And if you don't grab the first decent room you are able to find, they may all be gone just a few minutes later.

BUDGET

Alojamiento Betito (☎ 70 7429; 2 de Mayo 493; s/d with shared bathroom US$4.50/7.50) Offers basic rooms with communal cold-water bathrooms in a quirky, old high-ceilinged building with a likably shambolic feel, plus a bohemian bar downstairs.

Marinas (☎ 44 6014; Av Circunvalación Sur; s/d with shared bathroom US$5/10, s/d US$8/12) Positioned near the bus terminals, Marinas is clean, secure and handy for dropping your stuff off when arriving late at night. Rooms with en-suite bathrooms also have cable TV.

Lido Hospedaje (☎ 57 7001; San Martín 876A; s/d/tr US$7/10/13) An unusually well-run and secure guesthouse that many travelers say is the most welcoming budget option in Tacna. Compact

---

DETOUR: TACNA'S WINE COUNTRY

The countryside around Tacna is known for its vineyards, olive groves and orchards, and the small *bodegas* produce a few thousand liters of *vino de chacra* – a rough but pleasing red table wine.

The suburb of **Pocollay** is just a few kilometers from central Tacna, easily reached by catching a bus or *micro* along Bolognesi (US$0.15, 10 minutes). It's popular with *tacneños* for its traditional rural restaurants, which often have live bands on weekends.

Further northeast of Tacna are the villages of **Calana**, **Pachía** and **Calientes**, which are about 15km, 17km and 21km from Tacna, respectively. Calana and Pachía have many rural restaurants, while Calientes has hot springs.

Past Pachia is where the road forks, heading left toward Calientes or right toward the **Complejo Arqueológico de Miculla**, with drawings spread over 20km of human figures, animals and symbols of a fertility cult estimated to be 1500 years old.

Local buses and minivans go to most of these places from Tacna's Terminal Bolognesi, or you can hire a taxi for the day (around US$30).

and spotlessly clean rooms have hot water and local TV.

Royal Inn (☎ 42 6094; Patricio Melendez 574; s/d US$7.50/10.50) A short walk north of a sketchy market area, this enormous, bare-bones hotel has decently clean rooms with limited hot water. Conveniently, there's a minibar by the front desk.

Hostal HC (☎ 24 2042; Zela 734; s/d US$7.50/10.50) A decently clean, if kinda claustrophobic place with talkative staff who are knowledgeable about local excursions. Basic rooms have cable TV and hot showers.

Universo Hostal (☎ 41 5441; Zela 724; s/d US$7.50/10.50) Just as central as the Hostal HC, this broken-in small hotel next door has smaller rooms with hot shower and cable TV.

MIDRANGE

Many hotels raise their rates just before holidays and on weekends, when international shoppers from Chile hit town. All of the following have rooms with private hot-water bathrooms, cable TV and telephones.

Premier Hotel (☎ 24 6045; www.premierhoteltacna .com; Bolognesi 804; s/d US$15/20) Surprisingly popular with travelers, the tired-looking Premier has comfy rooms with a snack bar below. The busy street outside near the central market area can be noisy, though.

Plaza Hotel (☎ 42 2101; www.plazahoteltacna.com; San Martín 421; s/d/tr US$15/20/27) There's a hospital-like atmosphere to this cool, blocky option by the plaza. Ubiquitous white linoleum lends the corridors a clinical look, which is reflected in the staff's attitude, but rooms are more worn It has a cafeteria and rates may include breakfast.

Copacabana Hotel (☎ 42 1721; hotelcopacabana@ speedy.com.pe; Arias Araguez 370; s/d US$16.50/19.50) The popular, youthful Copacabana has simple, cute rooms with private hot showers, cable TV and good amenities, but some rooms can get very noisy on weekends due to the nearby disco.

Gran Hotel Central (☎ 41 5051; www.hotelcentral tacna.com; San Martín 561; s/d/tr/q incl continental breakfast US$20/28/35/41) The entrance to this once-plush hotel has a loudly buzzing neon sign that heralds slightly seedy, worn-around-the-edges rooms that are nevertheless spacious and have long sofas.

Hostal El Mesón (☎ 41 4070; www.mesonhotel.com; Hipólito Unanue 175; s/d/tr/q from US$22.50/28.50/31/36) El Mesón is a clean, modern and friendly option

close to the plaza. It also has a cafeteria and in-room minibars.

Hotel Camino Real (☎ 42 1891; creal-hotel@star.com .pe; San Martín 855; s/d US$22.50/30, ste US$53.50, all incl breakfast) The flashy-looking Camino Real has comfy rooms with good amenities that include a minibar, but disappointing '70s décor. It also has a startlingly red bar and a cafeteria.

Dorado Hotel (☎ 41 5741, 42 1111; www.doradohotel .com; Arias Araguez 145; s/d/ste from US$27/36/50, all incl breakfast) Undoubtedly Tacna's top hotel, the elegant Dorado has artistically designed modern rooms with heavenly beds a grand lobby bar and public spaces that exude an exclusive ambience.

Maximo's Hotel (☎ 24 2604; www.maximoshotel.com; Arias Araguez 281; s/d US$30/35, ste US$40, all incl breakfast & lunch; ▢) Quirky Maximo's has a lobby that's overladen with plants, balconies and candelabra, all suffused by green-tinted light. There's also a snack bar and good clean rooms with fans. The hotel sauna (entry US$2.40) is open from 2pm to 10pm daily.

Gran Hotel Tacna (☎ 42 4193; Bolognesi 300; s/d/tr/ste incl breakfast US$43/52/63/75; ▨) The blocky Gran Hotel Tacna has a choice of suites and many rooms with a balcony. Rooms are plush, and there are pleasant grounds and a pool, a restaurant with 24-hour room service and a bar with dancing.

Eating

Popular local dishes include *patasca a la tacneña*, a thick, spicy vegetable-and-meat soup, and *picante a la tacneña*, hot peppered tripe (it's better than it sounds). Southeast of the Plaza de Armas is a good hunting ground for inexpensive restaurants. A surprising number of hole-in-the-wall cafés serve fresh fruit and yogurt, as well as other healthy, vegetarian snacks.

Fulin (Arias Araguez 396; menús US$1.50; ☼ lunch Mon-Fri) This is a cheap vegetarian *chifa* in a rickety old building that somehow manages to deny the passing of time. Just look for the sign with Chinese characters outside.

Sabor Latino (☎ 44 6845; Vigil 68; meals US$1.50-6; ☼ 11am-8pm) You'll almost always find every table taken at this bustling café, which has lazy tropical ceiling fans and a spicy Latin soundtrack. It's especially recommended for filling set lunches and dinners, *criollo*-style.

Café Genova (☎ 24 4809; San Martín 649; mains US$4-10; ☼ 11am-2am) Brush shoulders with local socialites at this open-fronted streetside café with good espresso and cocktails, along with a variety of Peruvian and international snacks, desserts and light meals. It's the atmosphere you're paying for, not quality fare, though service is flawless.

La Limón (San Martín 981; mains US$3.50-12; ⊙ lunch & dinner Mon-Sat) With its own private entryway guarded by modelesque staff, this courtyard restaurant is the city's most modish spot to dine. On the innovative menu are traditional Peruvian dishes done with fusion flair, accompanied by a top-notch South American wine list.

In the *campiña* (countryside) outside Tacna (see Detour: Tacna's Wine Country, p157), several rustic restaurants come alive for weekend lunches, offering traditional fare and live music. In the nearby suburb of Pocollay, **La Huerta** (☎ 41 3080; Zela 1327) is a pleasant outdoor place with uproarious birdsong and a terrace with vine-covered trellising; there's often music between noon and 2pm. Further outside the city, Calana and Pachía also have many open-air restaurants.

Drinking

The small pedestrian streets of Libertad and Vigil are ground zero for Tacna's limited nightlife. There you'll find a couple of pubs and clubs, some with live music and dancing on weekends. On the first block of Arias Araguez are more urbane bars. Beer geeks imbibe at the flashy München Brauhaus, while rockers get down 'n' dirty at Jethro Pub. Stop by Don Cesar's for a taste of fine Peruvian pisco.

Getting There & Away
AIR
Tacna's **airport** (code TCQ; ☎ 84 4503) is 5km west of town. At the time of research, **Aero Condor Perú** (☎ 24 8187; Arias Araguez 135) was the only company offering regularly scheduled passenger services, though its dirt-cheap, thrice-weekly flights to Arequipa were often fully booked weeks ahead of time.

BUS
There are a few major bus terminals. Most long-distance departures leave from **Terminal Terrestre** (☎ 72 7007) on Hipólito Unanue, at the northeast edge of town. **Terminal Bolognesi** (☎ 71 1786), a 1km walk uphill and to the right from Terminal Terrestre, is for regional buses and *combis* to the beach at Boca del Río and

other villages outside the city limits but within the department of Tacna.

International
Infrequent buses (US$3) to Arica, Chile, leave between 6am and 10pm from the international terminal across the street from Terminal Terrestre.

Overnight *económico* buses to Puno (US$7.50, 10 hours) via Desaguadero on the Bolivian border (US$6, eight hours) mostly leave from Av Circumvalación, east of the main terminals. There are about a dozen companies with offices lined up next to one another here; all buses leave in the late afternoon or evening. But this is a rough, cold overnight journey with limited bathroom breaks at the side of the road in the middle of the night. It's much better to go to Arequipa first, then transfer – trust us! Exceptions to that rule are the comfortable luxury buses that often go via Desaguadero.

Long-Distance
Buses are frequently stopped and searched by immigration and/or customs officials not far north of Tacna. Have your passport handy, and beware of passengers asking you to hold a package for them while they go to the bathroom or smoke a cigarette.

A US$0.30 terminal-use tax is levied at Terminal Terrestre. For Lima (US$18 to US$43, 18 to 22 hours) there are luxury services run by **Cruz del Sur** (☎ 42 5729), **Ormeño** (☎ 42 3292) and at least a half-dozen smaller, cheaper but less-reliable companies. Most Lima-bound buses leave in the afternoon or evening and will drop you off at other south-coast towns, including Nazca and Ica. Cruz del Sur also has a daily direct overnight bus to Cuzco (US$22.50, 16 hours) via Puno (US$15, 10 hours) and Desaguadero (US$12, eight hours). **Flores** (☎ 42 6691) has hourly *económico* buses to Moquegua (US$3, three hours) and Arequipa (US$6.50, seven hours) from 5:30am until 10pm, plus 10 buses daily to Ilo (US$3, 3½ hours). Many other bus companies serve these destinations, but not as cheaply or frequently.

TAXI
Numerous *colectivo* taxis (US$3.60 to US$4.50, two hours) to Arica, Chile, leave between 6am and 10pm from the international terminal across the street from Terminal Terrestre. On Friday and Saturday, you may also find taxis

> **BORDER CROSSING: CHILE VIA TACNA**
>
> Border-crossing formalities are fairly straightforward, except if you take a public bus, which can't be recommended. While trains (below) are the cheapest way of crossing into Chile, *colectivo* taxis (p159) are the quickest. Taxi drivers usually help you through the border formalities, making them a safer, more convenient option than the ratty local buses. Allow at least two hours for the 65km trip by road between Tacna and Arica.
>
> The Chilean border post is open 8am to midnight from Sunday to Thursday, and 24 hours on Friday and Saturday. Note that Chile is an hour ahead of Peru, or two hours during daylight saving time (DST) from the first Sunday in April until the last Sunday in October. From Arica, you can continue south into Chile by air or bus, or northeast into Bolivia by air or bus. For more information, consult Lonely Planet's *South America on a Shoestring*, *Chile & Easter Island* and *Bolivia*.

willing to go outside these times, but expect to pay over the odds.

Fast, though notoriously unsafe, *colectivo* taxis to Moquegua (US$1.50, 2½ hours) and sometimes Ilo leave when full from Mercado Grau, a short walk uphill from Terminal Terrestre. Be sure to keep your wits about you in the dangerous market area.

TRAIN

Trains between Tacna's **train station** (☎ 42 4981) and Arica, Chile (US$1.50, 1½ hours) are the cheapest and most charming but also the slowest way to cross the border. Your passport is stamped at the station before boarding the train in Tacna. There is no stop at the actual border and you receive your entry stamp

when you arrive in Chile near Arica's Plaza de Armas. Though this historic railway is a must for train buffs, service can be erratic and inconveniently timed. There's usually one train in the early morning before dawn and another in the late afternoon. Always double-check at the station for the latest schedules and book tickets at least a day in advance.

Getting Around

A taxi between the airport and the city center costs about US$1, or you can go from the airport to Arica, with stops at the border, for US$40. Alternatively, walk out of the airport parking area and get the same cross-border service for half-price. A taxi from the center to the bus terminals costs about US$0.75.

Arequipa & Canyon Country

The irresistibly sexy city of Arequipa, known as the White City, is surrounded by some of the wildest terrain in Peru. This is a land of active snowy volcanoes, high-altitude deserts, thermal hot springs, salt lakes and, last but not least, the world's deepest canyons.

Whether your heart desires to go trekking, mountain biking, river running (white-water rafing) or clambering up Andean peaks, Arequipa makes the perfect base camp. No other place in southern Peru delivers the best of both urban and outdoor life – you can slalom down from a sandy volcanic summit and still be back in your colonial mansion guesthouse in time for a dinner of spicy *arequipeño* food and all-night dancing in a sizzling-hot nightclub.

Peru's second-largest city is often dismissed as an overland layover en route from Nazca to Lake Titicaca and Cuzco. True, it's an invaluable intermediate stop for acclimatization to high altitudes. But don't leave before exploring the city itself – at least to wander down the hidden passageways of the Monasterio de Santa Catalina and marvel at the icy Inca mummies in the Museo Santury.

Don't miss exploring the spectacular landscape that surrounds the city either – not least, the famous Cañón del Colca, shadowed by snow-topped volcanoes, and possessing one of the best places to marvel at the flight of the Andean condor. More untrammeled roads, such as those in the Cañón del Cotahuasi, await adventurous souls, passing ancient ruins, waterfalls, hot springs and even dinosaur footprints. What more could you possibly ask for?

AREQUIPA & CANYON COUNTRY

HIGHLIGHTS

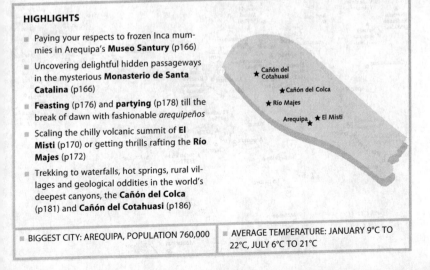

- Paying your respects to frozen Inca mummies in Arequipa's **Museo Santury** (p166)
- Uncovering delightful hidden passageways in the mysterious **Monasterio de Santa Catalina** (p166)
- **Feasting** (p176) and **partying** (p178) till the break of dawn with fashionable *arequipeños*
- Scaling the chilly volcanic summit of **El Misti** (p170) or getting thrills rafting the **Río Majes** (p172)
- Trekking to waterfalls, hot springs, rural villages and geological oddities in the world's deepest canyons, the **Cañón del Colca** (p181) and **Cañón del Cotahuasi** (p186)

★ Cañón del Cotahuasi
★ Cañón del Colca
★ Río Majes
Arequipa ★ ★ El Misti

■ BIGGEST CITY: AREQUIPA, POPULATION 760,000

■ AVERAGE TEMPERATURE: JANUARY 9°C TO 22°C, JULY 6°C TO 21°C

AREQUIPA

☎ 054 / pop 760,000 / elev 2350m

Rocked by volcanic eruptions and earthquakes nearly every century since the Spanish arrived in 1540, Peru's second-largest city doesn't lack for drama. Locals sometimes say 'When the moon separated from the earth, it forgot to take Arequipa,' waxing lyrical about the city's grand colonial buildings, built from an off-white volcanic rock called *sillar* that dazzles in the sun. As a result, Arequipa has been baptized the White City. Its distinctive stonework graces the stately Plaza de Armas, along with countless beautiful colonial churches, monasteries and mansions scattered throughout the city.

What makes Peru's second-biggest city so irresistible is the obvious relish with which its citizens enjoy all the good things in life, especially the region's spicy food, stylish shopping and nightlife. The pulse of city life is upbeat. The streets are full of jostling vendors, bankers, artists, students and nuns – in short, a microcosm of modern Peru.

There's no better place in the south to rejuvenate your weary bones, especially while waiting a few days to acclimatize before scaling the higher elevations of Lake Titicaca and Cuzco.

Arequipeños (inhabitants of Arequipa) themselves are a proud people fond of intellectual debate, especially about their fervent political beliefs, which find voice through regular demonstrations in the Plaza de Armas. In fact, their stubborn intellectual independence from Lima is so strong that at one time they even designed their own passport and flag. The celebration of the city's founding every August 15 passionately puts an exclamation point on that regionalist pride.

HISTORY

Evidence of pre-Inca settlement by indigenous peoples from the Lake Titicaca area leads some scholars to think the Aymara people first named the city (*ari* means 'peak' and *quipa* means 'lying behind' in Aymara; hence, Arequipa is 'the place lying behind the peak' of El Misti). However, another oft-heard legend

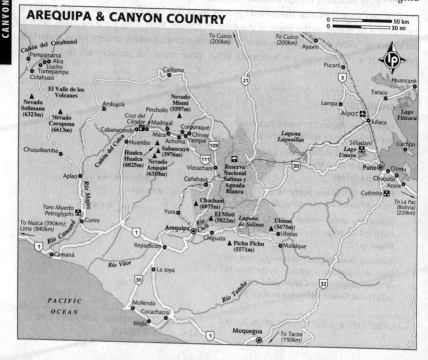

AREQUIPA & CANYON COUNTRY

0   50 km
0   30 mi

To Cuzco (200km)
To Cuzco (200km)

Cañon del Cotahuasi
Pampamarca
Alca
Lluacho
Tomepampa
Cotahuasi

El Valle de los Volcanes

Nevado Solimana (6323m)

Nevado Coropuna (6613m)

Chuquibamba

Aplao

Río Majes

Toro Muerto Petroglyphs

To Nazca (390km); Lima (840km)

Corire

Río Camaná

Camaná

Andagua

Cruz del Cóndor

Cabanaconde

Cañón del Colca

Huambo

Hualca Hualca (6025m)

Pinchollo

Madrigal

Maca

Nevado Mismi (5597m)

Corporaque

Achoma

Chivay

Yanque

Sabancaya (5976m)

Nevado Ampato (6310m)

Vizcachani

Cañahuas

109

111

Caylloma

21

Reserva Nacional Salinas y Aguada Blanca

Chachani (6075m)

Yura

El Misti (5822m)

Río Chili

Arequipa

Chiguata

Repartición

Río Vítor

La Joya

30

Laguna de Salinas

Pichu Pichu (5571m)

Pucará

Lampa

Laguna Lagunillas

Ayavirí

3

Huancané

Taraco

Airport

Lago Titicaca

Juliaca

Sillustani

Lago Umayo

Puno

Chucuito

Acora

Cutimbo

Llachón

Chimu

To La Paz (Bolivia) (220km)

Ubinas (5675m)

Ubinas

Matalque

30

32

1

PACIFIC OCEAN

Mollendo

Cocachacra

Mejía

Río Tambo

Moquegua

To Tacna (150km)

1

says that the fourth Inca, Mayta Capac, was traveling through the valley and became enchanted by it. He ordered his retinue to stop, saying, '*Ari, quipay*,' which translates as 'Yes, stay.' The Spaniards refounded the city on August 15, 1540, and the date is remembered with a week-long fair.

Unfortunately, Arequipa is built in an area highly prone to natural disasters; the city was totally destroyed by earthquakes and volcanic eruptions in 1600 and has since been rocked by major earthquakes in 1687, 1868, 1958, 1960 and, most recently, in 2001. For this reason, many of the city's buildings are built low for stability. However, despite these disasters, many fetching historic structures survive.

ORIENTATION

The city of Arequipa nestles in a fertile valley under the perfect cone-shaped volcano of El Misti (5822m). Rising majestically behind the cathedral, El Misti can be viewed from the plaza and is flanked to the left by the higher and more ragged Chachani (6075m) and to the right by the lower peak of Pichu Pichu (5571m).

The city center is based on a checkerboard pattern around the Plaza de Armas. Because streets change names every few blocks, addresses can be confusing. Generally, streets have different names north, south, east, and west of the Plaza de Armas, then change names again further out from the center.

INFORMATION
Bookstores

Colca Trek (☎ 20 6217, 960 0170; www.colcatrek.com.pe; colcatrek@gmail.com; Jerusalén 401-B) The best place for topographic and DIY trekking maps of the region.
Librería el Lector (☎ 28 8677; San Francisco 221; ☽ 9am-noon & 1-9pm) Book exchange and an excellent selection of new local-interest titles, guidebooks and music CDs.
Zeta (☎ 20 0747; Casona Santa Catalina, Santa Catalina 210; ☽ 10am-6pm) A limited selection of travel literature, coffee-table books and cultural tomes.

Cultural Centers

There are a few cultural centers around town that host art shows, music concerts and film screenings, and have libraries and cafés that welcome travelers.
Alianza Francesa (☎ 21 5579; www.afarequipa.org.pe; Santa Catalina 208)
Centro Cultural Peruano Norteamericano (ICPNA; ☎ 89 1020; Melgar 109)

Emergency

Policía de Turismo (Tourist Police; ☎ 20 1258; Jerusalén 315-317; ☽ 24hr) May be helpful if you need an official theft report for insurance claims.

Immigration

Oficina de migraciónes (immigration office; ☎ 42 1759; Parque 2, cnr Bustamente & Rivero, Urb Quinta Tristán; ☽ 8-11am Mon-Fri) Come here for a visa extension; a taxi from the city center costs around US$1.

AREQUIPA IN...

One Day
Start your day with a quick coffee at one of the balcony restaurants on the **Plaza de Armas** (p167), looking out at the cathedral, then head down to the **Museo Santury** (p166) to shiver at the grisly beauty of the frozen sun-bride Juanita and her fellow ice mummies. Afterwards, walk up Calle Santa Catalina and wander the hushed passageways of the **Monasterio de Santa Catalina** (p166), wondering at its risqué history. After sunset, stroll up to San Francisco to splash out on the city's hottest **restaurants** (p176) and **nightlife** (p178).

Two Days
Follow the one-day itinerary, then in the morning of the second day take a detour to the historic neighborhood of **Yanahuara** (p169), a brisk walk across the Puente Grau. It's worthwhile, if only to snap a photo from the main plaza's *mirador* (lookout). For lunch, sit yourself down at one of the traditional restaurants around the city and discuss the hot topics of Peruvian politics over a similarly spicy *arequipeño* meal. Spend the afternoon **shopping** (p179) for quality antiques and artisan crafts, or stop by one of the city's less visited historical religious complexes, such as the learned **Monasterio de la Recoleta** (p167) or the beautiful **Museo de Arte Virreinal de Santa Teresa** (p168).

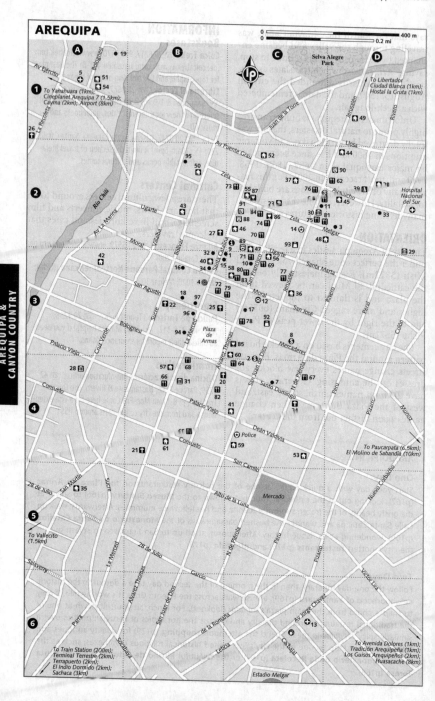

AREQUIPA

AREQUIPA & CANYON COUNTRY

Selva Alegre Park

To Libertador Ciudad Blanca (1km); Hostal la Gruta (1km)

Hospital Nacional del Sur

Plaza de Armas

Police

Mercado

To Paucarpata (6.5km); El Molino de Sabandía (10km)

To Vallecito (1.5km)

To Train Station (200m); Terminal Terrestre (2km); Terrapuerto (2km); El Indio Dormido (2km); Sachaca (3km)

To Avenida Dolores (1km); Tradición Arequipeña (1km); Los Guisos Arequipeños (2km); Huasacache (8km)

Estadio Melgar

AREQUIPA & CANYON COUNTRY

Internet Access

Most internet cafés charge about US$0.50 per hour. Many cybercafés also offer cheap local and international phone calls.

Ciber Market (☎ 28 4306; Santa Catalina 115B; ⏰ 8:30am-11pm) Private booths, fast computers with printers available, plus net-to-phone and digital photo CD-burning services.

Cusco Coffee Company (☎ 28 1152; La Merced 135; ⏰ 9am-7pm) For laptop users, there's a wi-fi hot spot here.

Laundry

Calle Jerusalén has many spots for having your kit washed.

Magic Laundry (Jerusalén 404; per kg US$1.20; ⏰ 9am-1pm & 2:30-7pm Mon-Sat) If you're lucky, clothes can be washed, dried and folded in about three hours.

Left Luggage

Most guesthouses and hotels will store your bags for free for a few days while you explore the surrounding countryside. Always lock your bags securely, keep a list of the contents with you and check over everything carefully when you return.

Medical Services

Clínica Arequipa (☎ 25 3424, 25 3416; Bolognesi at Puente Grau; ⏰ 8am-8pm Mon-Fri, 8am-12:30pm Sat) Arequipa's best and most expensive clinic.

Hogar Clínica San Juan de Dios (☎ 25 1560, 25 2256; Av Ejército 1020, Cayma) In the suburb of Cayma, this is also recommended; call ahead for hours.

Hospital Regional Honorio Delgado Espinoza (☎ 21 9702, 23 3812; Av Daniel Alcides Carrión s/n; ⏰ 24hr) Emergency 24-hour services.

InkaFarma (☎ 20 4685; Santo Domingo 113; ⏱ 24hr) One of Peru's biggest pharmacy chains; it's well-stocked.

Paz Holandesa Policlinic (☎ 20 6720; www.paz holandesa.com; Av Jorge Chavez 527; ⏱ 8am-8pm Mon-Sat) This appointment-only travel clinic provides vaccinations as well. Doctors here speak English and Dutch. Profits go toward providing free medical services for underprivileged Peruvian children.

Money

There are moneychangers and ATMs on streets east of the Plaza de Armas. There are global ATMs inside the Casona Santa Catalina complex, Terminal Terrestre and the airport.

BCP (San Juan de Dios 125) Has a Visa ATM and changes traveler's checks.

Interbank (Mercaderes 217) Has a global ATM and changes traveler's checks.

Post

FedEx (☎ 25 6464; Casona Santa Catalina, Santa Catalina 210; ⏱ 9am-5pm Mon-Sat)

DHL (☎ 22 0045; Santa Catalina 115; ⏱ 8:30am- 7:30pm Mon-Fri, 9am-noon Sat)

Main post office (Moral 118; ⏱ 8am-8pm Mon-Sat, 9am-1pm Sun)

Tourist Information

iPerú airport (☎ 44 4564; 1st fl, Main Hall, Aeropuerto Rodríguez Ballón; ⏱ 6:30am-6pm); city center (☎ 22 1228; Casona Santa Catalina, Santa Catalina 210; ⏱ 9am-7pm) The main office also runs Indecopi, which is the tourist-protection agency and deals with complaints against local firms, including tour operators and travel agencies. Check with them first if you have doubts about a certain company.

DANGERS & ANNOYANCES

Petty theft is often reported in Arequipa, so travelers are urged to hide their valuables. Most crime is opportunistic, so keep your stuff in sight while in restaurants and internet cafés. Also be aware of distraction techniques like spitting or tapping your shoulder. Take great care in Selva Alegre Park, north of the city center, as muggings have been reported there. Only pay for tours in a recognized agency and never trust touts in the street – they bamboozle cash out of a surprisingly high number of travelers.

SIGHTS
Monasterio de Santa Catalina

Even if you've already overdosed on colonial edifices of yesteryear, this **convent** (☎ 22 9798; www.santacatalina.org.pe; Santa Catalina 301; admission US$10.50; ⏱ 9am-5pm, last entry 4pm) shouldn't be missed. Occupying a whole block and guarded by imposing high walls, it is one of the most fascinating colonial religious buildings in Peru. Nor is it just a religious building – this 20,000-sq-meter complex is almost a citadel within the city.

Today, it's a disorientating place that allows you to step back in time to a forgotten world of narrow twisting streets and tiny fruit-filled plazas, hidden staircases, beautiful courtyards and ascetic living quarters. A paradise for photographers, the convent has been wonderfully restored, and the delicate pastel-colored buildings contrast attractively with bright flowers, period furnishings and religious art. Don't miss the tranquil café, which sells freshly baked pastries and espresso drinks.

There are two ways of visiting Santa Catalina. One is to wander around at your own pace, discovering the mazelike architecture, soaking up the meditative atmosphere and getting slightly lost (there's a finely printed miniature map on the back of your ticket if you're up for an orienteering challenge). Alternatively, wonderfully informative guides are available for a tip of US$3 to US$4.50. Among them, they speak Spanish, English, French, German, Italian and Portuguese. The tours last about an hour, after which you're welcome to keep exploring by yourself until the gates close.

Museo Santury

Officially the Museo de la Universidad Católica de Santa María, this **museum** (☎ 20 0345; www.ucsm.edu.pe/santury; La Merced 110; admission US$4.50; ⏱ 9am-6pm Mon-Sat & 9am-3pm Sun) exhibits 'Juanita, the ice princess' – the frozen body of an Inca maiden sacrificed on the summit of Nevado Ampato over 500 years ago (see p168). Multilingual tours (available in Spanish, English, French, German and Italian) consist of a video followed by an examination of various burial artifacts, culminating in a respectful viewing of a frozen mummy preserved in a carefully monitored glass-walled exhibition freezer. Although Juanita is not on display from January to April, another child sacrifice discovered in the mountains around Arequipa is. Only guided visits are permitted (expect to tip the guide), and the whole spectacle is done in a respectful, nonghoulish manner. Allow about an hour for a visit.

MONASTERIO MISTERIOSO

The Monasterio de Santa Catalina was founded in 1580 by a rich widow, Doña María de Guzmán, who was very selective in choosing her nuns. They came from the best Spanish families, who naturally had to pay a substantial dowry.

Traditionally, the second son or daughter of upper-class Spanish families would enter religious service. For women, this meant going to a nunnery to live in chaste poverty. However, in this particularly privileged convent each nun had between one and four servants or slaves (usually black), and the nuns would invite musicians, have parties and generally live it up in the style to which they had always been accustomed.

After about three centuries of these hedonistic goings-on, Pope Pius IX sent Sister Josefa Cadena, a strict Dominican nun, to straighten things out. She arrived like a hurricane in 1871 and set about sending the rich dowries back to Europe and freeing the myriad servants and slaves, some of whom stayed on as nuns. From this point, the vast majority of the 450 people who once lived here never ventured outside the convent's imposing high walls and the convent was shrouded in mystery until it opened to the public in 1970, when the mayor of Arequipa forced the convent to modernize, including opening its doors to tourism.

Today, the three dozen or so remaining nuns continue to live a cloistered life in a far corner of the complex while the rest remains open to the public.

Plaza de Armas

Arequipa's main plaza showcases the city's *sillar* architecture and the cathedral. The colonnaded balconies overlooking the plaza are a great place to relax over a snack or a coffee, though it's the views you're paying for, not the bland, overpriced café fare.

The history of **La Catedral** (☎ 23 2635; admission free; ☉ 7-11:30am & 5-7:30pm Mon-Sat, 7am-1pm & 5-7pm Sun), the cathedral that dominates Arequipa's main plaza, is one filled with doggedness. The original structure, dating from 1656, was gutted by fire in 1844. It was consequently rebuilt, but was then promptly flattened by the earthquake of 1868. Most of what you now see has been rebuilt since then. The earthquake of June 2001 toppled one enormous tower and the other slumped precariously, yet by the end of the following year the cathedral looked as good as new once again.

The cathedral is the only one in Peru that stretches the length of a plaza. The interior is simple and airy, with a luminous quality, and the high vaults are uncluttered. The cathedral also has a distinctly international flair; it is one of less than 100 basilicas in the world that are entitled to display the Vatican flag, which is to the right of the altar. Both the altar and the 12 columns (depicting the 12 apostles) are made of Italian marble: the huge Byzantine-style brass lamp hanging in front of the altar is from Spain; and the pulpit was carved in France. In 1870, Belgium provided the impressive organ, said to be the largest in South America, though damage during shipping condemned the devout to wince at its distorted playing for over a century.

Iglesia de la Compañía

Just off the southeastern corner of the Plaza de Armas, this **Jesuit church** (☎ 21 2141; admission free; ☉ 9am-noon & 3-6pm) is one of the oldest in Arequipa and is noted for its ornate main façade and main altar, which is carved in *churrigueresque* style (an elaborate and intricately decorated Latin American adaptation of Spanish baroque) and completely covered in gold leaf. To the left of the altar is the **San Ignacio chapel** (☉ 9am-12:30pm & 3-6pm Mon-Fri, 11:30am-12:30pm & 3-6pm Sat, 9am-12:30pm & 5-6pm Sun), with a polychrome cupola smothered in junglelike murals of tropical flowers, fruit and birds, among which mingle warriors and angels.

Monasterio de la Recoleta

A short cab ride from the city center in a dicey neighborhood, this musty **monastery** (☎ 27 0966; La Recoleta 117; admission US$1.50; ☉ 9am-noon & 3-5pm Mon-Sat) was constructed on the west side of the Río Chili in 1648 by Franciscan friars, though now it has been completely rebuilt. Scholarship was an integral part of the Franciscans' order, and bibliophiles will delight in their huge library, which contains more than 20,000 dusty books and maps; the oldest volume dates back to 1494. The library opens for supervised 15-minute visits starting at 9:45am, then every hour thereafter. There is a well-known museum of Amazonian exhibits collected by the missionaries, and an extensive collection of preconquest artifacts and religious art of the *escuela cuzqueña* (Cuzco school). Guides who speak Spanish, English, French and Italian are available (small tip expected).

Museo de Arte Virreinal de Santa Teresa

This gorgeous 17th-century Carmelite **convent** (☎ 28 1188; www.museocarmelitas.com; Melgar 303; admission US$3; ❧ 9am-4:30pm Mon-Sat, 9am-12:30pm Sun) was only recently opened to the public as a living museum. The colonial-era buildings are justifiably famed for their decoratively painted walls and restored rooms filled with priceless votive *objets d'art*, murals, precious metalworks, colonial-era paintings and other historical artifacts, all capably explained by student tour guides who speak Spanish, English, French, German and Portuguese (tips appreciated). A charming shop at the front of the complex sells baked goods and rose-scented soap made by the nuns.

Colonial Mansions

Some of Arequipa's stately colonial *sillar* mansions can be visited – a real treat.

Built in 1730, **Casa de Moral** (☎ 21 4907; Moral 318; adult/student US$1.40/1; ❧ 9am-5pm Mon-Sat) is named after the 200-year-old mulberry tree in its central courtyard. Owned by BCP, the house is now one of the most accessible for snooping, and bilingual guides are available. It has a fascinating little map collection charting South American development.

Another mansion that's easy to visit is **Casa Ricketts** (Casa Tristán del Pozo; ☎ 21 5070; San Francisco 108; admission free; ❧ 9:15am-12:45pm & 4:30-6:30pm Mon-Fri, 9:30am-12:45pm Sat). Built in 1738, it has served as a seminary, archbishop's palace, school, home to well-to-do families, and now as a working bank. Look for the puma-headed fountains in the interior courtyard.

Also worth a peek is the **Casona Iriberry** (Casa Arróspide; Santa Catalina 115; admission free; ❧ hrs vary), housing the Universidad Nacional de San Agustín (UNSA) within its 18th-century colonial halls and patios.

The 17th-century **La Mansión del Fundador** (☎ 44 2460; admission US$2.10; ❧ 9am-6pm), once owned by Arequipa's founder Garcí Manuel de Carbajal, has been restored with its original furnishings and paintings, and even has its own chapel. The mansion is in the village of Huasacache, 9km from Arequipa's city center, most easily reached by taxi (round-

HUMAN SACRIFICE IN THE ANDES

In 1992 local climber Miguel Zárate was guiding an expedition on Nevado Ampato (6310m) when he found curious wooden remnants, suggestive of a burial site, exposed near the icy summit. In September 1995 he convinced American mountaineer and archaeologist Johan Reinhard to climb the peak, which following recent eruptions of nearby Sabancaya had been coated by ash, melting the snow below and exposing the site more fully. Upon arrival, they immediately found a statue and other offerings, but the burial site had collapsed and there was no sign of a body. Ingeniously, the team rolled rocks down the mountainside and, by following them, Zárate was able to spot the bundled mummy of an Inca girl, which had tumbled down the same path when the icy tomb had crumbled.

Wrapped in finely woven blankets, the girl had been almost perfectly preserved by the icy temperatures for about 500 years, and it was immediately apparent from the remote location of her tomb and from the care and ceremony surrounding her death (as well as the crushing blow to her right eyebrow) that this 12- to 14-year-old girl had been sacrificed to the gods at the summit. For the Incas, mountains were gods who could kill by volcanic eruption, avalanche or climatic catastrophes. These violent deities could only be appeased by sacrifices from their subjects, and the ultimate sacrifice was that of a human child.

It took the men days to carry the frozen bundle down to the village of Cabanaconde, from where she was carried to a princely bed of frozen foodstuffs in Zárate's own domestic freezer, before being taken to the Universidad Católica in Arequipa to undergo a battery of scientific examinations. Quickly dubbed 'Juanita, the ice princess,' the mummy was given her own museum in 1998 (see p166). In total, almost two dozen similar Inca sacrifices have been discovered atop various Andean mountains since the 1950s.

DETOUR: YANAHUARA & CAYMA

The peaceful neighborhood of Yanahuara makes a diverting excursion from the city center. It's within walking distance: go west on Av Puente Grau over the Puente Grau (Grau Bridge), and continue on Av Ejército for half a dozen blocks. Turn right on Av Lima and walk five blocks to a small plaza, where you'll find the **Iglesia San Juan Batista** (admission free), which dates from 1750. It housed the highly venerated Virgen de Chapi after the 2001 earthquake brought her church tumbling down about her ears. The popular Fiesta de la Virgen de Chapi is held on May 1. At the side of the plaza there's a *mirador* (lookout) with excellent views of Arequipa and El Misti.

Head back along Av Jerusalén, parallel to Av Lima, and just before reaching Av Ejército you'll see the well-known restaurant Sol de Mayo (p177), where you can stop for a tasty lunch of typical *arequipeño* food. The round-trip walk should take around two hours, but there are also *combis* (minibuses) to Yanahuara from along Av Puente Grau (and returning from Yanahuara's plaza to the city) every few minutes to speed you along (US$0.30, 10 minutes).

Beyond Yanahuara is Cayma, another inner suburb of Arequipa's city center, nicknamed El Balcón (the Balcony) for its privileged views. Here you'll also find the eye-catching **Iglesia de San Miguel Arcángel** (admission free), dating from 1730. For a tip, the church warden may take you up the small tower, which has panoramic views. To reach Cayma from Yanahuara, walk along San Vicente and then take Av Leon Velarde, or catch one of the regular *combis* marked 'Cayma' from Av Puente Grau (US$0.30, 15 minutes).

---

trip US$4.50). Local city tours occasionally stop here.

Other Churches

Visiting hours for smaller churches in Arequipa are erratic, but most are open for sincere worshippers from 7am to 9am and 5pm to 8pm. Originally built in the 16th century, **Iglesia de San Francisco** (☎ 22 3048; Zela cuadra 1; admission US$1.50; ☽ church 7am-9am & 5-8pm Mon-Sat & 7am-noon & 5-8pm Sun, convent 9am-12:30pm & 3-5pm daily) has been badly damaged by several earthquakes. It still stands, however, and visitors can see a large crack in the cupola – testimony to the power of the quakes. Other colonial churches around the city center include San Agustín, La Merced and Santo Domingo.

Other Museums

The university-run **Museo de Arqueológico de Universidad Católica de Santa María** (☎ 95 9636; Cruz Verde 303; admission free; ☽ 8:15am-noon & 2-5:30pm Mon-Fri) has interesting little displays on local excavation sites, as well as some artifacts, including surprisingly well-preserved ancient ceramics. The student guides can be less than enthusiastic, though their spiels are well rehearsed (small tips expected).

The small **Museo Regional Histórico Etnológico Municipal** (☎ 20 0096; Jerusalén 402; adult/student US$2.40/1.50; ☽ 9am-3pm Mon-Fri) is housed in a tumbledown colonial building. Paintings, historical documents, maps and other para-

phernalia pertaining to the city's history are displayed here. Most interesting are the satirical caricatures of stately 19th-century Peruvian elite.

El Molina de Sabandía

The rural suburb of Paucarpata, about 8km southeast of the city center, makes a pleasant country escape. *Combis* (minibuses) can be caught along Goyeneche, Independencia and Paucarpata, which is the eastern continuation of Mercaderes (US$0.60, 25 minutes), or you can take a taxi (round-trip US$4). Paucarpata itself features an attractive colonial church on the main plaza and several good *picanterías* (local restaurants).

A 3km walk from the plaza past notable Inca terracing brings you to **El Molino de Sabandía** (adult/child US$1.50/0.60; ☽ 9am-5pm). This mill was built in 1785, fell into disrepair and was restored two centuries later; it now grinds once more for visitors. The neat grounds, shaded with weeping willows and providing great views of El Misti, are a favorite of picnickers. Horseback rides are available outside the restaurant.

ACTIVITIES

Trekking, mountaineering and rafting trips are offered everywhere in central Arequipa. Always check the ID of guides carefully and ask to see the little black book that identifies trained and registered guides. Make sure that the guide you hire has a guiding card and a booklet listing all the places he or she has guided. Because the very best guides are often away on trips, try to make arrangements in advance. Of course, no travel agency or guide can ever be 100% recommended, so check everything exhaustively before shelling out for any trip. The following outdoor outfitters can usually put you in touch with reliable guides:

Colca Trek (☎ 20 6217, 960 0170; www.colcatrek.com .pe; colcatrek@gmail.com; Jerusalén 401-B) Colca Trek is an ecoconscious adventure-tour agency and shop run by the knowledgeable, English-speaking Vlado Soto. In addition to trekking tours, it organizes mountaineering, mountain-biking and river-running trips; it buys, sells and rents many kinds of equipment, including climbing gear and bikes; and it is one of the few shops selling decent topographical maps of the area and a full complement of camp-stove gas canisters. Be careful of copycat travel agencies that illegally use the Colca Trek name and/or web addresses that are similar to the agency's official site .

Carlos Zarate Adventures (☎ 20 2461; www.zara teadventures.com; Santa Catalina 204) This company was founded in 1954 by Carlos Zárate, the great-grandfather of climbing in Arequipa. He is still going strong at over 80 years of age, and his son Carlos Zárate Flores is also an experienced guide. Spanish and a little English, French and German are spoken. The company arranges all manner of treks, and climbs all the local peaks, charging US$50 plus expenses per day for the guide, plus the vehicle rental to get to base camp (US$50 to US$150, depending on the mountain). Pack mules may be hired for an extra fee.

Mountaineering

Superb mountains for climbing surround Arequipa. Adequate acclimatization for this area is essential and it's best to have spent some time in Cuzco or Puno immediately before a high-altitude expedition. Lack of water can also be a problem, as can the icy temperatures, which sometimes drop to -29°C at the highest camps. The best months for mountain climbing are between April and December.

Though many climbs in the area are not technically difficult, they should never be undertaken lightly. Watch for the symptoms of altitude sickness and if in doubt, go back down. You should be well-informed about medical and wilderness-survival issues, as many guides are dangerously untrained and even careless.

Maps of the area can be obtained from **Colca Trek** (☎ 20 6217, 960 0170; www.colcatrek.com.pe; colcatrek@gmail.com; Jerusalén 401-B) in Arequipa or the **Instituto Geográfico Nacional** (IGN; Map pp88-9; ☎ 01-475 9960; ventaign@ignperu.gob.pe; Aramburu 1198, Surquillo; ☾ 9am-4pm Mon-Fri) in Lima. Colca Trek and **Carlos Zarate Adventures** (☎ 20 2461; www .zarateadventures.com; Santa Catalina 204) rent tents, ice axes and crampons, but climbers should bring their own sleeping bags, climbing boots and very warm clothes. The standard rate for hiring a mountain guide is currently at least US$60 per day, plus at least the cost of transport; one guide can take a group of up to three or four climbers for this price.

EL MISTI

Looming 5822m above Arequipa, the city's guardian volcano El Misti is the most popular climb in the area. It is technically one of the easiest ascents of any mountain of this size in the world, but it's hard work nonetheless and you normally need an ice ax and,

---

THE NEXT BIG BANG

El Misti is one of several active volcanoes in the Arequipa region. There were five minor eruptions of El Misti during the 20th century, and deposits from at least 20 eruptions in the last 14,000 years have been noted in the region. A relatively minor eruption during the 15th century caused the Incas and other tribespeople living in the area to flee Arequipa in a panic.

The current interior crater probably formed in an eruption about 2000 years ago. This eruption covered the Arequipa area with a layer of pumice, and pyroclastic material then flowed down the various *quebradas* (steep ravines or gulches) to the outskirts of present-day Arequipa.

The center of Arequipa is only 17km from El Misti's summit, which towers above the city. Planning controls regulating the locations of the city's growth are lacking, and the suburbs extend up along gullies on the slopes of the volcano – channels for lava, ash and mud in the event of an eruption.

Currently El Misti's activity is limited to the fumaroles around the crater rim, but geologists have pointed out the inevitability of another major eruption – sometime!

sometimes, crampons. The mountain is best climbed from July to November, with the later months being the least cold. At the top is a 10m-high iron cross, which was erected in 1901. Below the summit is a sulfurous yellow crater with volcanic fumaroles hissing gas, and there are spectacular views down to the Laguna de Salinas and back to the city.

There are several routes, but none are clearly marked and at least one (notably the Apurímac route) is notorious for robberies, so taking a guide is highly recommended. A two-day trip costs about US$60 to US$80. One popular route starting from Chiguata is an eight-hour hard uphill slog on rough trails to base camp (4500m); from there to the summit and back takes eight hours, while the sliding return from base camp to Chiguata takes three hours or less.

Any way you tackle it, public transport to the mountain base is scarce. You can hire a 4WD vehicle for US$50 to take you up to about 3300m and pick you up on your return. Another route, on the back of the mountain, allows you to get up to 4000m by 4WD, but it costs up to US$150 for the vehicle.

OTHER MOUNTAINS

One of the easiest 6000m peaks in the world is **Chachani** (6075m), which is as close to Arequipa as El Misti. You need crampons, an ice ax and good equipment. There are various routes up the mountain, one of which involves going by 4WD (US$100) to Campamento de Azufrera at 4950m. From there you can reach the summit in about nine hours and return in under four. Alternatively, for a two-day trip, there is a good spot to camp at 5200m. Other routes take three days but are easier to get to by 4WD (US$50).

Sabancaya (5976m) is part of a massif on the south rim of the Cañón del Colca that also includes extinct **Hualca Hualca** (6025m) and **Nevado Ampato** (6310m). Sabancaya is currently the most active of the region's volcanoes and has erupted in recent years. The crater can be approached between eruptions if you have an experienced guide, but neighboring Ampato is a fairly straightforward, if strenuous, three-day ascent, and you get safer views of the active Sabancaya from here.

Other mountains of interest near Arequipa include **Ubinas** (5675m), which is a gentler two-day climb and has a lot of geothermal activity. **Nevado Mismi** (5597m) is a fairly easy three- or four-day climb on the north side of the Cañón del Colca. You can approach it on public transportation and, with a guide, find the lake that is reputedly the source of the Amazon. The highest mountain in southern Peru is the difficult **Nevado Coropuna** (6613m).

Trekking

The spectacular canyons around Arequipa offer many excellent hiking options. Trekking agencies can arrange a whole array of off-the-beaten-track routes to suit your timescale and fitness level. Although you can trek year-round, the best (ie driest) time is from May to November. There is more danger of rockfalls in the canyons during the wet season (between December and April). Easier treks in the Cañón del Colca can be beautifully lush during the wet season, however, while more remote trails, especially those in the Cañón del Cotahuasi, become inaccessible.

Our best advice is that if you're already an experienced trekker and you're trekking in a well-traveled area like the Cañón del Colca, you don't need to go with a guide at all. Hiking from village to village is the simplest DIY trekking option. In the Cañón del Colca, the main roads are scenic routes, though there are dozens of more challenging trails. The roads are a good, easy way to experience village life at a slower pace, although they are dusty and passing traffic can be unnerving.

If you're nervous about hiking solo or want to tackle more untrammeled routes, there are dozens of tour companies based in Arequipa that can arrange guided treks. Be sure you book with a reputable company, never exchange money with touts on the street and always ask to see your guide's guiding card and booklet listing all the places that he or she has experience guiding.

For indispensable topographic maps for trekking, as well as top-notch guided trips (including of the Cañón del Cotahuasi), contact **Colca Trek** (☎ 20 6217, 960 0170; www.colcatrek.com.pe; colcatrek@gmail.com; Jerusalén 401-B).

River Running

Arequipa is one of Peru's premier bases for white-water rafting and kayaking. Many trips are unavailable during the rainy season (between December and March), when water levels can be dangerously high. For more information and advice, surf to www .peruwhitewater.com.

AREQUIPA & CANYON COUNTRY

The **Río Chili**, about 7km from Arequipa, is the most frequently run local river, with a half-day trip suitable for beginners leaving almost daily from April to November (from US$25). Further afield, you can also do relatively easy trips on the **Río Majes**, into which the Río Colca flows. The commonly run stretches pass class II and III rapids.

A more off-the-beaten-track possibility is the remote **Río Cotahuasi**, a relatively new white-water discovery reaching into the deepest sections of the world's deepest known canyon. Expeditions here are infrequent and only for the experienced, usually taking nine days and passing through several class IV and V rapids. The **Río Colca** was first run back in 1981, but this is a dangerous, difficult trip and not to be undertaken lightly. However, a few outfitters will do infrequent and expensive rafting trips, and easier sections can be found upriver from the canyon.

A number of rafting outfitters have been recommended by travelers:

Amazonas Explorer (☎ in Cuzco 084-25 2846, 976 5448, 976 5447; www.amazonas-explorer.com; Collasuyo 910, Urb Marivelle, Cuzco) Located in Cuzco, this company can arrange private trips on the Río Cotahuasi.

Casa de Mauro (Ongoro) In the village of Ongoro, 190km by road west of Arequipa, this is one of the most convenient base camps for rafting the Río Majes. A one-hour class III white-water run in inflatable rafts costs about US$16. Experienced river runners can take a 25km, class IV run lasting three hours for US$29. The lodge, which has camping (US$2 per person) and dorm beds (US$3), and a restaurant famed for its shrimp dinners and pisco (Peruvian grape brandy), can be contacted in advance through Colca Trek (p170). It is cheapest to take a Transportes del Carpio bus from Arequipa's Terminal Terrestre to Aplao (US$3, three hours, hourly) and then a minibus to Ongoro (or a taxi for US$3.50).

Cusipata (☎ 20 3966, 986 0950; www.cusipata.com; Jerusalén 408) Cusipata is currently the best river-running company in Arequipa. It leads recommended white-water and kayaking trips to all the major destinations, including the Ríos Colca and Cotahuasi (US$2000), with the English-speaking Vellutino brothers, Gian Marco and Piero. They also organize introductory kayaking courses.

Majes River Raft Co (☎ 28 0205, 47 1162, 83 2105; www.majesriver.com) Offers daily departures at 9am for easy seven-mile rafting trips (US$16) on the Río Majes. More challenging 20-mile trips that pass through class IV rapids depart at 8am (US$29). Overnight accommodations in rustic bungalows with solar hot-water showers cost US$10 per person; camping (US$2 per person) and meals (US$2 to US$3) are also available. From Arequipa's

Terminal Terrestre, catch a bus with Transportes Carpio to Aplao (US$3, three hours, hourly), then a taxi to the Hotel Majes River (US$3), where the outfit is based.

Mountain Biking

The area around Arequipa has mountain-biking possibilities. Try the following companies for rental and tours:

Colca Trek (☎ 20 6217, 960 0170; www.colcatrek.com .pe; colcatrek@gmail.com; Jerusalén 401-B) Colca Trek organizes downhill volcano mountain-biking trips to Chachani and El Misti, and can also arrange tailor-made tours. If you're an experienced biker with an adventuresome spirit, you can rent high-end mountain bikes, buy topographic maps and get trip-planning advice here.

Naturaleza Activa (☎ 22 2257; www.peruexploration .com; Santa Catalina 211) This company is slowly making a name for itself with adventure tours, especially mountain biking trips. Popular tours include a five- to six-hour bike tour of Chachani and the *salinas* (salt flats or salt lagoons; US$55 per person for a group of four), and a three- to four-hour bike trip down El Misti (US$35). All prices include transportation and bike, helmet, guide and snacks. It's also possible to hire mountain bikes for US$30 day, or US$5 per hour.

Other Activities

A 15-minute walk north of the Puente Grau, **Club Internacional** (☎ 25 3384; Bolognesi s/n; admission Mon-Fri US$3, Sat & Sun US$4.50; ⏰ 6am-midnight Mon-Sat, 7am-5pm Sun) has two swimming pools, a soccer field, tennis courts and a bowling alley by the river. It's popular with local families.

COURSES

For Spanish-language courses, there are literally dozens of schools in Arequipa. Ask around for recent recommendations from other travelers. Also try:

CEICA (☎ 22 1165; www.ceica-peru.com/arequipa.htm; Urb Universitaria G-9) It charges US$120 for 20 hours of private lessons per week and can arrange family homestays for US$70/40 a week including/excluding meals. Call in advance and they'll pick you up from the airport or bus terminal.

CEPESMA (☎ 40 5927; cepesma.idiomas@peru.com; La Marina 141) It charges around US$6 per hour for private classes.

EDEAQ (☎ 22 6784, 962 8217; www.edeaq.com; Casilla 11) This Peruvian- and Swiss-managed school is located close to the Plaza de Armas. It's more expensive, but also more intensive than most, costing from US$435 per week for lessons plus homestay or hotel accommodations with breakfast.

AREQUIPA & CANYON COUNTRY

ICPNA (☎ 89 1020; www.icpna.edu.pe; Melgar 109) It offers private Spanish classes for US$10 per hour.

Juanjo (www.spanishlanguageperu.com; 2nd epata C-4, Urb Magisterial, Yanahuara) Recommended by travelers, it arranges individual, small-group classes from US$6 per hour to US$170 per week. Homestays and volunteer work can also be arranged.

ROCIO (☎ 28 6929; www.spanish-peru.com; Ayacucho 208) Charges US$3.25 per hour for an individual class of 60 minutes. Group lessons cost US$65 per person for 20 classes per week, starting every Monday.

Spanish Café Arequipa (☎ 22 2052; www.spanish cafeperu.com; Santa Catalina 203) A European-Peruvian venture featuring a unique Spanish conversation café with a small classroom at the back. Salsa lessons, social activities and volunteer opportunities are available. Rates vary.

TOURS & GUIDES

The streets of Santa Catalina and Jerusalén harbor dozens of travel agencies offering ho-hum city tours and excursions to the canyon country, most with daily departures. While some agencies are professional, there are also plenty of carpetbaggers muscling in on the action, so shop carefully. Never accept tours from street touts and, where possible, tours should be paid for in cash, as occasional credit-card fraud is reported. Most agencies pool their clients into one bus, even though they charge different rates for the tours. Minibuses are the norm for these trips, and the small vehicles are cramped and overcrowded – tall people should get ready to tuck knees under chins. Guides usually speak some level of English and/or other languages, but some garble a memorized and hard-to-follow script.

The standard two-day tour of the Cañón del Colca (p181) costs US$20 to US$75 per person, depending on the season, group size and the comfort level of the hotel you choose to stay at in Chivay. All tours leave Arequipa between 7am and 9am, passing through the Reserva Nacional Salinas y Aguada Blanca (p181). A stop is usually made at a teahouse and, later, at the highest point to take in the views before descending to Chivay for lunch. Some agencies then take their groups on a short hike, and the hot springs of Chivay are almost always visited before sunset, so bring a swimsuit and towel. There is usually a visit to a lively, if touristy *peña* (bar or club featuring live folkloric music) in the evening. Be aware that the cost of the tour includes lodging with breakfast in Chivay, but other

meals are paid for out of your own pocket, as is the canyon's *boleto turístico* (tourism ticket) and small tips for your guide and driver. On the second morning the group leaves around 6am to reach Cruz del Cóndor by 8:30am for an hour or so of condor-spotting, before returning to Arequipa. A quick stop is made along the way at a colonial church in one of the canyon villages, such as Yanque. Many groups are approached by locals toting captive birds of prey in the hope that tourists will pay a tip to have their picture taken. Please do not encourage the capture of these endangered wild birds.

For agencies offering outdoor activity-based tours, see p170.

FESTIVALS & EVENTS

Semana Santa (Holy Week) *Arequipeños* claim that their Semana Santa celebrations leading up to Easter are similar to the very solemn and traditional Spanish observances from Seville. Maundy Thursday, Good Friday and Holy Saturday processions are particularly colorful and sometimes end with the burning of an effigy of Judas.

Fiesta de la Virgen de Chapi Arequipa also fills up for this festival, celebrated on May 1 in Yanahuara (p169).

August 15 The founding day of the city is celebrated with parades, dancing, beauty pageants, climbing competitions on El Misti and other energetic events over the course of several days. The fireworks show in the Plaza de Armas on the evening of August 14 is definitely worth catching.

SLEEPING

Arequipa has been experiencing a hotel boom for quite some time now, and competition is stiff. It's always worth asking for discounts, especially if you stay put for a few days, though the prices quoted skyrocket around holidays and festivals, and sometimes during the high season (June to August).

Budget

Unless otherwise indicated, all accommodations listed here have some hot water. Many are unmarked or are recognizable by a sign proclaiming 'Rooms for Tourist.'

Home Sweet Home (☎ 40 5982; www.homesweet home-peru.com; Rivero 509A; dm/s/d/tr with shared bathroom US$3/5/10/15, s/d US$7.50/14, all incl breakfast) This genuinely friendly homestay has won over countless backpackers with its huge breakfasts and cute, if a bit musty, rooms. Upstairs there's a TV, and downstairs there's a small common kitchen. It's reliably secure and is family run.

El Indio Dormido (☎ 42 7401; www.elindiodormido
.com; Av Andrés Avelino Cáceres B-9; dm/s/d with shared
bathroom US$4.50/6/9) Conveniently near Termi-
nal Terrestre, this off-the-beaten-path hostel
relies on word of mouth from happy guests.
It has a pretty (but noisy) terrace garden on
top with hammocks to laze in. Call ahead for
directions.

La Reyna (☎ 28 6578; Zela 209; dm/s/d/tr US$4.50/
6/12/18) A rickety old standby, La Reyna has
rooftop balconies with pleasant mountain
and monastery views, as well as reasonably
tidy rooms and kitchen privileges on request.
It's cheek-to-jowl with much of Arequipa's
nightlife, which can be a plus or minus.

Le Foyer (☎ 28 6473; hostallefoyer@yahoo.com; Ugarte
114; s/d with bathroom US$5/9, s/d US$10/13) Though
pervaded with hunger-inducing smells from
the Mexican restaurant below, this place is a
decent-value option if you want to be in the
thick of Arequipa's nocturnal action. Rooms
have TVs.

Los Andes Bed & Breakfast (☎ 033 0015; los
andesaqp@hotmail.com; La Merced 123; s/d with shared bathroom US$5/10, s/d US$10/20) Just a stone's throw
south of the Plaza de Armas, this airy guesthouse has spacious, if spartan, rooms and
sun-drenched common lounges. Justifiably
popular with foreign students and volunteers,
it's especially comfy for extended stays.

La Posada del Cacique (☎ 20 2170; posadadel
cacique@yahoo.es; Av Puente Grau 219; s/d with shared bathroom US$6/12, s/d US$13.50/18) A smiley option near
the Puente Grau bridge, this family-run guesthouse has basic but cavernous high-ceilinged
rooms and a sunny terrace for chilling out.
There's a small common kitchen.

Colonial House Inn II (☎ 28 4249; Rivero 504; s/d with
shared bathroom US$7/13, s/d US$9/15) This good-value
option is owned by the English-speaking boss
of Los Leños pizzeria. Housed in a capacious
colonial building tucked down a side alley, the
rooms combine rustic style with convenience.
There's a huge common kitchen, but no sign
outside.

Point Hostel (☎ 28 6920; www.thepointhostels.com;
Av Lima 515, Vallecito; dm US$7-8, s/d with shared bathroom
from US$10/16, all incl breakfast; 🖳) Located in the
verdant suburb of Vallecito, this rambling
hostel has a slew of the kind of amenities
that backpackers love, including free internet
access, a games room, a library and socializing spaces that make it almost worth the
above-average price. Get here before the
crowds do.

Hostal el Tumi de Oro (☎ 28 1319; San Agustín 311A;
s/d US$9/12) Run by chirpy elderly folks, this
cheerful guesthouse is hidden away on a side
street. It boasts a prettily tiled terrace, plus a
book exchange and games. The private rooms
are spotless, and there are shared kitchen and
laundry facilities. Recommended.

Hostal Núñez (☎ 21 8648; hostal_nunez@terra.com;
Jerusalén 528; s/d US$10/17) On a street full of not-
so-great guesthouses, this secure, friendly
hostel is always stuffed with gringos. There's
laundry service and the colorful rooms sport
frilly décor, a bathroom and TV, though the
singles are a bit of a squeeze.

Hospedaje el Caminante Class (☎ 20 3444; 2nd
fl, Santa Catalina 207A; d with shared/private bathroom
US$10.50/15) Repeatedly recommended by
readers, this overcrowded guesthouse near
the plaza is overpriced. It has decent rooms,
kitchen privileges and all the *mate de coca*
(coca-leaf tea) you can drink. There's a rooftop
terrace with views, too. Be careful when taking
a taxi from the bus terminals and only give the
driver the address, not the name of the hostel,
or you may find yourself taken to a guesthouse
in a dangerous part of town.

Casa de Avila (☎ 21 3177; San Martín 116; r from
US$12.50; 🖳) A breezy walk southwest of the
Plaza de Armas, this family-run guesthouse
does everything it can to entice travelers, including providing hot water showers, a sunny
garden ('for taking a beer'), unlimited coffee,
free internet access and taxi pickups.

Also recommended:

La Posada del Parque (☎ 21 2275; Deán Valdivia
238A; dm/s/d with shared bathroom US$2/4/7, s/d
US$7.50/9) A low-rent budget choice in an odd location
near the market, but with a gracious hostess.

Hospedaje Familiar Thelma (☎ 28 6357;
pensionthelma@hotmail.com; Palacio Viejo 107; s/d with
shared bathroom US$5/10) Recommended by readers, this
quiet homestay's hostess speaks Spanish, French, German
and Italian (no English).

Hostal Solar (☎ 24 1793; www.hostalsolar.com;
Ayacucho 108; s/d incl breakfast US$5/10; 🖳) A tidy,
secure and family-run colonial guesthouse with a library
and sunny terrace.

Hotel Regis (☎ 22 6111; Ugarte 202; s/d with shared
bathroom US$5.50/10.50, d US$16.50) Clean, safe and
chaotically close to the action, this place has a rooftop
mirador.

Colonial House Inn (☎ 22 3533; colonialhouseinn@
hotmail.com; Av Puente Grau 114; s/d incl breakfast
US$7/11.50; 🖳) Peaceful, if slightly run-down, colonial
house with a garden and friendly staff.

Midrange

All hotels listed here have cable TV, unless otherwise stated.

Hostal las Torres de Ugarte (☎ 28 3532; www .hotelista.com; Ugarte 401A; s/d/tr incl breakfast US$20/30/36; 🖳) This is a friendly hostel in a quiet location behind the Monasterio Santa Catalina. It has immaculate rooms with TVs and colorful woolly bedspreads. You'll just have to ignore the cacophonous echoing hallways. Rates drop 25% in the low season.

La Casa de Mi Abuela (☎ 24 1206; www.lacasa demiabuela.com; Jerusalén 606; s/d/tr incl breakfast US$30/33/37.50; 🖳 🕿) This secure hotel, which is often booked out by tour groups, has an extensive garden full of bird song, plus deck chairs, swings, loungers and hammocks for kicking back. There's also a small pool, games area, library and an excellent Peruvian restaurant with live piano music. The rooms are disappointingly substandard, however, with bizarre floor plans and a hodgepodge of differently aged and styled furniture. The front-desk staff can be brusque.

Hostal la Gruta (☎ 22 4631; www.lagrutahotel .com; La Gruta 304, Selva Alegre; s/d/ste incl breakfast from US$35/45/55) Situated over 1km north of the city center, La Gruta (the Grotto) is a beautiful small hotel tucked away on a quiet residential street. Rooms are all tastefully furnished and have large windows or glass walls with views of the garden, as well as a refrigerator and bar; some also have fireplaces. The staff are wonderfully welcoming, too. Rates include airport pickup on request.

THE AUTHOR'S CHOICE

La Casa de Melgar (☎ 22 2459; www.lacasa delmelgar.com; Melgar 108A; s/d from US$20/30) Housed in an 18th-century building made from *sillar* (off-white volcanic rock) blocks, La Casa de Melgar is nonetheless fitted with all the expected creature comforts. The ground-floor rooms of this colonial inn have high-domed ceilings and shared walls (so unfortunately you can't escape the noise from your neighbors' TV), and the whole place has a gothic Catholic air. Rooms have divinely comfy beds, and there's a good café and several small sunny patios and gardens to relax in. In our humble opinion, it's the most romantic secret hideaway within the city limits.

La Hostería (☎ 28 9269; www.lahosteriaqp.com; Bolívar 405; s/d US$45/55, ste from US$65) Worth every dollar is this picturesque colonial hotel with a flower-bedecked courtyard, light and quiet rooms (with minibar), carefully chosen antiques, a sunny terrace and a lounge. Some rooms suffer from street noise, so request one in the back. Apartment-style suites on the upper floors have stellar city views.

Casa Arequipa (☎ 28 4219; www.arequipacasa.com; Av Lima 409, Vallecito; s US$35-55, d US$45-65) Inside a cotton-candy pink colonial mansion in the gardens of suburban Vallecito, this gay-friendly B&B offers over half a dozen guest rooms with fine design touches such as richly painted walls, pedestal sinks, antique handmade furnishings and alpaca-wool blankets. A sociable cocktail bar is in the lobby.

Hotel la Posada del Monasterio (☎ 20 6565; www .posadadelmonasterio.com.pe; Santa Catalina 300; s/d/tr incl breakfast from US$45/57/68; 🕿) On a prime pedestrian corner, this hotel gracefully inhabits an architecturally mix-and-match building combining the best of the Old and New Worlds. Especially popular with European tour groups, the comfortable modern rooms here have all the expected facilities. From the rooftop terrace there are fine views of the Santa Catalina convent across the street.

Also recommended:

Lula's B&B (☎ 27 2517, 934 2660; http://bbaqpe.com; Cerro San Jacinto, Cayma; s/d US$13/19, per week $60/119) A charming apartment-style B&B run by a friendly Spanish teacher in the suburb of Cayma. Big discounts are given for extended stays. Meals (vegetarians OK) and airport and bus terminal pickups also available.

Los Balcones de Santa Catalina (☎ 20 1291; Moral 217; s/d incl breakfast US$18/27) This place was originally a budget hotel; some rooms have wooden floors and a balcony with a back view of the cathedral.

Nueva España Hotel (☎ 25 2941; Antiquilla 106, Yanahuara; s/d/tr incl breakfast US$20/25/35) This distinguished 19th-century colonial house has just over a dozen rooms with solar hot showers. It's in the quaint suburb of Yanahuara; call for free pickups. Spanish, French, German and English are spoken.

Real San Felipe (☎ 28 5010; www.geocities.com/hrs faqp; San Juan de Dios 304; s/d incl breakfast US$20/35) Glass-walled modern rooms have fully stocked minibars, phones and tiny bathtub-shower combos.

La Maison d'Elise (☎ 25 6185, 25 3343; www.aqplink .com/hotel/maison; Av Bolognesi 104; s/d/tr US$54/70/86, ste $78-96; 🕿) An elegant colonial mansion retreat just north of the Puente Grau bridge. Rooms have telephones, fridges and cable TV.

Tierrasur Hotel (☎ 22 7132; www.tierrasur.com; Consuelo 210; s/d incl breakfast US$60/75) Clean, quiet and reminiscent of a good American chain hotel, this place boasts a restaurant, bar, gym and a terrace.

Top End

There's no shortage of full-service hotels in Peru's second-largest city.

La Posada del Puente (☎ 25 3132; www.posada delpuente.com; Bolognesi 101; s/d US$85/97, ste US$149-203; ☐) Dipping down to the river, the extensive gardens of this high-end hotel make for a tranquil setting that's surprisingly removed from the bustling traffic above. The hotel has business-class rooms, wi-fi access and a good restaurant and bar. Staying here gives you free access to the sports facilities and swimming pool at nearby Club Internacional (p172).

Sonesta Posada del Inca (☎ 21 5530; www.sonesta .com; Portal de Flores 116; s/d incl breakfast from US$69/79, ste $105-155; ☒ ☐ ☒) On the Plaza de Armas, this hotel has some rooms at the front with private terraces and a view of the cathedral through the arches. Other guests can compensate by frequenting the rooftop pool and terrace, which also boasts a fine panorama of the plaza, although the café is disappointing.

Libertador Ciudad Blanca (☎ 215110; www.libertador .com.pe; Plaza Bolívar s/n, Selva Alegre; r US$150-210, ste US$170-280; ☒ ☐ ☒) This is the grande dame of Arequipa's hotels, situated 1km north of the center. The stylish building is nicely set in gardens with a pool and playground. It has spacious rooms and opulent public areas with wi-fi access, plus its spa boasts a sauna, Jacuzzi and fitness room. The sedate restaurant serves a fine Sunday brunch. Neighboring Selva Alegre park is beautiful, but don't wander too far from the crowds, and avoid it after dark.

EATING

Trendy upscale restaurants line Calle San Francisco north of the Plaza de Armas, while touristy outdoor cafés huddle together on Pasaje Catedral behind the cathedral.

Budget

Cafe Casa Verde (☎ 22 6376; Jerusalén 406; snacks US$0.60-1.50; ☽ 10am-8pm) This nonprofit court-yard café staffed by underprivileged kids is the perfect morning- or afternoon-break spot. It dishes up yummy German-style pastries, sandwiches, cappuccinos and fresh juices, so why not set up the chessboard and stay a while?

Restaurante Gopal (☎ 21 2193; Melgar 101B; menús US$1-2, mains US$1.50-3; ☽ 9am-9pm) This basic, health-conscious vegetarian café specializes in traditional Peruvian dishes made with imitation meats, so you can enjoy *lomo saltado* (strips of beef stir-fried with onions, tomatoes, potatoes and chili) without guilt.

Sunlight Vegetarian House (Moral 205; menús US$1.50; ☽ lunch) This no-frills Chinese vegetarian café has a faithful local following. You may have to shout your order because the dining room is open to the chaotic street.

Mandala (☎ 28 7086; Jerusalén 207; 3-course menús US$1.50-2; ☽ 9am-9pm) This humble, health-minded café affably cooks up quick, quality vegetarian fare (breakfasts are huge!) in a subterranean space with tables that probably look just like the ones at your grandmother's house.

Lakshmivan (☎ 22 8768; Jerusalén 400; menús US$1.50-3.60; ☽ 11:30am-9:30pm) Set in a colorful old building with a tiny outdoor courtyard, this place has various *menús* (set meals) and an extensive à la carte selection, all with South Asian flair. Service can be slow.

Cusco Coffee Company (☎ 28 1152; La Merced 135; drinks US$1.50-3.60; ☽ 9am-7pm) This Starbucks-style Peruvian coffee shop has the most chatty baristas in town selling sugary baked goods and a full menu of espresso drinks made from beans grown in the Amazon jungle.

Ribs Cafe (☎ 28 8188; Alvarez Thomas 107; mains US$2-3; ☽ noon-8:30pm) This surprising store-front cooks up BBQ ribs in a rainbow variety of sauces, ranging from honey-mustard to chocolate to red wine, as well as empanadas (meat or cheese turnovers) stuffed with everything imaginable and solid American breakfasts.

El Turko I (☎ 20 3862; San Francisco 216; mains US$2.50-6; ☽ 7am-midnight Sun-Wed, 24hr Thu-Sat) Part of an ever expanding Ottoman empire, this funky little joint serves a hungry crowd its late-night kebabs and vegetarian Middle Eastern salads, but is also an excellent java and sweet pastries stop during the day. There's another branch, El Turko III, at the airport.

Fez (☎ 20 5930; San Francisco 229; mains US$2.50-6; ☽ 7am-midnight Sun-Thu, 7am-4am Fri & Sat) Have you been craving authentic falafel ever since you landed in South America? Step right up to the counter here and order yourself a sandwich dripping with juicy goodness – and don't forget the rich coffee either. Garden tables are out the back.

Zig Zag Crêperie (☎ 20 6620; Alianza Francesa, Santa Catalina 208; mains US$2.50-7; ⏱ 8am-midnight) Yet another cozy place to get your caffeine fix, this cultural café has a crackling fireplace, balcony tables, board games and over 100 kinds of sweet and savory crepes filled with anything from Chilean smoked trout to wild Swiss mushrooms to exotic South American fruits.

Inkari Pub Pizzeria (Pasaje Catedral; ⏱ 11am-10pm) This pizzeria has a delicious happy-hour special of a personal pizza and a *copa de vino* (glass of wine) for just US$3.

SELF-CATERING
Pick up groceries at **El Super** (⏱ 9am-2pm & 4-8:30pm Mon-Sat, 9am-2pm Sun); Plaza de Armas (Portal de la Municipalidad 130); Piérola (N de Pierola, cuadra 1).

Midrange
Cafe Restaurant Antojitos de Arequipa (Morán cuadra 1; mains US$3-7.50; ⏱ 24hr) This café-restaurant is a bright beacon in the dead of night. An enormous menu of comfort food and Peruvian favorites, plus espresso machines and locks on the chairs for safeguarding your pack make it ideal for waiting out that tiresome late-night bus departure.

Manolo's (☎ 21 9009; Mercaderes 113; mains US$3-10; ⏱ 10am-10pm) With a decidedly retro atmosphere, this mirror-filled café looks as if it were established in the early days of the Republic. Its endless menu lists coffees, ice creams, desserts, sandwiches and full Peruvian home-style meals.

Nina-Yaku (San Francisco 211; menús US$3, mains US$3.50-7; ⏱ lunch & dinner) This nouveau Peruvian eatery wouldn't look a bit out of place in NYC's Soho or Buenos Aires' Palermo Hollywood. The modern menu includes reinventions of traditional *arequipeño* tastes, with salads, sandwiches and tastebud-tingling desserts, plus coffees and cocktails.

Mixtos (☎ 20 5343; Pasaje Catedral 115; mains US$4-8; ⏱ 11:30am-9:30pm) Tucked away in the alley behind the cathedral on the Plaza de Armas is this popular and quaint restaurant that serves mainly Italian and *criollo* (spicy Peruvian fare with Spanish and African influences) seafood dishes. It has outdoor balconies and tables.

Cevichería Fory Fay (☎ 24 2400; Thomas 221; mains US$4.50-6; ⏱ lunch) Small and to-the-point, it

---

THE SPICE OF LIFE, AREQUIPEÑO STYLE

The best *picanterías* (local restaurants) for traditional regional food are outside Arequipa's city center, and most are open for lunch only. Try tasting the explosively spicy *rocoto relleno* (hot peppers stuffed with meat, rice and vegetables), *ocopa* (potatoes served with a spicy, creamy peanut sauce), *chupe de camarones* (shrimp chowder) or *chancho al horno* (roast suckling pig), and wash it down with *chicha* (fermented corn beer).

Ary Quepay (☎ 20 4583; Jerusalén 502; mains US$4-8; ⏱ lunch & dinner) This place offers traditional plates, including alpaca and *cuy* (guinea pig), in a colonial-style building that extends out to a dimly lit rustic area dripping with plants. There's enthusiastic *música folklórica* most evenings.

Sol de Mayo (☎ 25 4148; Jerusalén 207; mains US$5-8, 4/8-course tasting menús US$40/80; ⏱ lunch only) Serving good Peruvian food in the Yanahuara district, Sol de Mayo has live *música folklórica* every afternoon from 1pm to 2pm. Book a table in advance. You can combine a visit here with a stop-off at the *mirador* (lookout) in Yanahuara (p169).

Tradición Arequipeña (☎ 42 6467; Av Dolores 111; meals US$4-10; ⏱ noon-7pm Sun-Thu, noon-10pm Fri & Sat) This locally famous restaurant has mazelike gardens, fountains and terrace tables. Live music includes *folklórica* and *criollo*. It's 2km southeast of the center; a taxi ride here should cost US$1.20.

Los Guisos Arequipeños (☎ 46 5151; Av Pizarro 111; mains US$5-10; ⏱ noon-6:30pm Mon-Thu, noon-9pm Fri-Sun) This huge, barnlike formal restaurant is in the suburb of Lambramani, 2km southeast of the center. Along with bow-tied waiters, it has bountiful gardens and occasional live music.

La Cantarilla (☎ 25 1515; Tahuaycani 106; mains US$5-10; ⏱ lunch only) You'll be greeted by an ostrich statue at this rustic open-air restaurant in the southwestern suburb of Sachaca. Mostly catering to tour groups, it serves some international fare as well as good-quality Arequipeño food, including freshwater shrimp. Take a taxi (US$1.50).

For dinner shows with live traditional music, see p179.

serves only the best ceviche (raw seafood marinated in lime juice) – and nothing else. Pull up a chair at a rickety table and crack open a beer – limit one per person, though! By the way, here is a phonetic spelling of how Peruvians say '45' in English.

Los Leños (☎ 28 9179; Jerusalén 407; pizzas US$4.50-6; ⏲ 6-10:30pm Mon-Sat) Pizzas for homesick travelers are baked in a wood-burning oven that adds warmth to the laid-back atmosphere. Rock music is the only soundtrack. If you're more impressed by the food than we were, add your personalized scribble to the already-covered-with-graffiti walls.

Paquita Sim (☎ 25 1915, 22 1059; Granada 102, Cayma; mains US$4.50-8; ⏲ noon-3:30pm & 6-10.30pm Tue-Sat, noon-4pm Sun) Worth going out of your way for, this family-run Asian fusion restaurant is a feast for the senses, with Chinese, Japanese and Thai influences on the gourmet menu. It's one block southeast of the intersection of Avs Ejercito and Cayma.

El Turko II (☎ 21 5729; San Francisco 315; mains US$5-12; ⏲ 8am-midnight) Right in the thick of things on San Francisco, the brother of El Turko I is a highly recommended Middle Eastern restaurant. Sizzling platters of kebabs and other carnivorous and vegetarian specialties are served in surroundings worthy of an art gallery. It's romantic and the service is well polished.

Top End

La Viñeda (☎ 20 5053; San Francisco 319; mains US$4.50-12; ⏲ dinner) An intimate spot, this is one of the best places to knock back a steak or platters of traditional Peruvian food, all in an ornate Victorian atmosphere. The wine list features South American varietals.

Sambambaia's (☎ 24 1209; www.sambambaias.com .pe; Luna Pizarro 304, Vallecito; mains US$6-10; ⏲ noon-3pm Mon, Wed, Fri-Sun, noon-11pm Tue & Thu) Located just 2km outside of the city center, this restaurant is an elegant upper-crust alternative with Brazilian specialties, live piano music and a tropical garden setting. Call ahead for reservations.

El Gaucho Parrilladas (☎ 22 0301; Portal de Flores 112; mains US$6-16; ⏲ dinner Mon-Sat) Not one for vegetarians – these guys are experts in steak and steak alone, and they don't skimp on portions. On a lower level off the Plaza de Armas, the restaurant has a snug atmosphere. All the city's movers and shakers dine here, so make reservations in advance.

Zig Zag Restaurant (☎ 20 6020; Zela 212; mains US$7-15; ⏲ 6pm-midnight) The upscale sister of Zig Zag Crêperie, this European restaurant inhabits a two-story colonial house with an iron stairway designed by Gustave Eiffel. The spendy menu features decadent fondues, stone-grilled steaks, other South American game dishes and even Swiss *rösti*.

La Trattoria del Monasterio (☎ 20 4062; Santa Catalina 309; mains US$7.50-13.50; ⏲ lunch from noon daily, dinner from 7pm Mon-Sat) A helping of epicurean delight has finally descended upon the Monasterio Santa Catalina. In a gracious light-filled dining room with colonial walls, the menu of Italian specialties is infused with the flavors of Arequipa, all from the imagination of superstar Peruvian chef Gastón Arcurio. Reservations are essential.

DRINKING

The nocturnal scene in Arequipa is pretty slow midweek but takes off at weekends. It's worth keeping an eye out for the free-drinks fliers distributed around town. For the spiciest nightlife, head for the bars and clubs along San Francisco north of the plaza. Beyond the tourist haunts, the hottest local action is to be had at nightclubs strung along Av Dolores, 2km southeast of the center (a taxi costs around US$1).

Déjà Vu (☎ 28 3428; San Francisco 319B; ⏲ 6pm-2am) With a rooftop terrace overlooking the church of San Francisco, this eternally popular haunt has a long list of crazy cocktails, including some outrageous specialties – try its *diablo rojo* ('red devil;' US$3) – along with decent DJs after dark. This bar is good on weekdays and weekends alike.

Forum Rock Cafe (☎ 20 2697; www.forumrockcafé .com; Casona Forum, San Francisco 317; ⏲ 10pm-4am Tue-Sat) It's a gutsy Latin rock bar with a thing for bamboo and waterfalls. Food is sometimes served but the specialties are bands and booze – burgers are just an afterthought. In the same building, Zero Bar & Pool is a busy nightspot with pool tables and spacious booths.

Istanbul (☎ 20 5930; San Francisco 231A; ⏲ 10am-3am) Owned by the same folks as El Turko, this Middle Eastern-themed bar has stained-glass windows and overstuffed couches on which to sip exotic liquor concoctions, beers or jet-fuel coffee.

Kibosch (Zela 205; ⏲ 9pm-late Thu-Sat) This hectic club has no shortage of bars and dance space, and plays an energetic mix of salsa and rock music.

Dady'o Disco Pub & Karaoke (Portal de Flores 112; ☺ 10pm-3am Thu-Sat) On the Plaza de Armas, raucous Dady'o Disco Pub & Karaoke throws open its doors for go-go dancing, live bands and digital karaoke, plus wickedly cheap beers.

Farren's Irish Pub (Pasaje Catedral; ☺ noon-11pm) Tucked behind the cathedral, this touristy Irish-themed watering hole is the place to go for deliciously cheap happy-hour pints and sports on satellite TV.

ENTERTAINMENT
Live Music
Be aware that some places advertise a nightly *peña*, but there's rarely anything going on except from Thursday to Saturday nights.

Las Quenas (☎ 28 1115; Santa Catalina 302; admission US$3; ☺ closed Sun) An exception to the rule, this traditional *peña* features performances almost nightly starting around 9pm. The music varies, although *música folklórica* predominates. It also serves decent *arequipeño* food starting at 8pm.

Boulevard Café (Santa Catalina 300B; ☺ noon-11pm Thu-Sun) Just a few doors south of Las Quenas, the contemporary Boulevard Café has live local indie music acts with no cover charge from Thursday to Sunday nights.

Café Art Montréal (Ugarte 210; ☺ 6-11pm) This smoky, intimate little bar with live bands playing on a stage at the back would be equally at home as a bohemian students' hangout on Paris' Left Bank.

La Quinta (☎ 20 0964; Jerusalén 522; admission US$1.50; ☺ closed Sun) Another good spot for local food and boisterous live bands on weekends, but it's potluck as to whether you get live music on other nights.

La Troica (☎ 22 5690; Jerusalén 522A; admission US$2) Next door to La Quinta, La Troica also has food and a variety of live music, including Afro-Peruvian and Latin, in addition to more traditional *folklórica* sounds.

Cinema
A handful of cinemas show English-language movies dubbed or with Spanish subtitles. Local newspapers have listings. It's also worth checking at the various cultural centers (p163) for film festivals and other screenings. Déjà Vu (opposite) sometimes shows free DVDs in the afternoons.

Showing blockbuster movies, **Cineplanet Arequipa 7** (☎ 270 1945; www.cineplanet.com.pe; Los Arces s/n at Av del Ejercito) is in a shopping mall just a short taxi ride from the center.

Sports
Conducted *arequipeño* style, the bullfights of the grand *peleas de toros* are less bloodthirsty than most. They involve pitting two bulls against each other for the favors of a fertile female until one realizes he's beaten. The fights take place on Sundays between April and December, alternating between three stadiums outside the center, so ask which stadium to attend. The three most important fights are in April, mid-August and early December.

SHOPPING
Arequipa overflows with antique and artisan shops, especially on the streets around Monasterio Santa Catalina. High-quality alpaca, vicuña (threatened wild relative of alpacas) and leather goods, and other handmade items are what you'll see being sold most often.

Raices Peru (☎ 22 0951; Jerusalén 309A; ☺ 9am-7:30pm Mon-Fri, 9am-7pm Sat) This storefront sells all types of folk art – including textiles, woodcraft, ceramics, jewelry, alpaca goods and toys – made in indigenous communities from the Amazon to the Andes to the coast.

Casona Santa Catalina (☎ 28 1334; www.santacata lina-sa.com.pe; Santa Catalina 210; ☺ most shops 10am-6pm) Inside this polished tourist complex, you'll find a few shops of major export brands, such as Sol Alpaca and Biondi Piscos.

Patio del Ekeko (☎ 21 5861; Mercaderes 141) This high-end tourist mall has plenty of expensive but good alpaca- and vicuña-wool items, jewelry, ceramics and other arty souvenirs.

GETTING THERE & AWAY
Air
Arequipa's **airport** (code AQP; ☎ 44 3464) is about 8km northwest of the city center.

LAN (☎ 20 1224; Santa Catalina 118C) has daily flights to Lima and Cuzco. **Aero Condor Perú** (☎ 22 6660; Portal de San Agustín 119) has surprisingly cheap flights to Tacna near the Chilean border, but they're often booked up far in advance.

Servicios Aéreos AQP (☎ /fax 28 1800, 965 0206; www.saaqp.com.pe) flies nine-passenger Piper Cheyenne III planes anywhere you want to go, including sightseeing spots in the canyon country.

Bus

Although night buses to destinations are convenient, they are often not safe. Fatal accidents, hijackings, robberies and assaults have all occurred on these overnight routes. If you can afford to, consider flying instead. Alternatively, take day buses and/or plan to break up your journey along the way.

INTERNATIONAL

From the Terrapuerto bus terminal, **Ormeño** (☎ 42 4113) has two buses a week to Santiago, Chile (US$89, 2½ days), and three a week to Buenos Aires, Argentina (US$119, three days).

LONG-DISTANCE

Most bus companies have departures from Terminal Terrestre or the smaller Terrapuerto bus terminal, both of which are together on Av Andrés Avelino Cáceres, less than 3km south of the city center (take a taxi for US$1). Check in advance which terminal your bus leaves from and keep a close watch on your belongings while you're waiting there. There's a US$0.30 departure tax from either terminal. Both terminals have shops, restaurants and left-luggage facilities. More chaotic Terminal Terrestre also has a global ATM and a tourist information office.

For Lima (US$12 to US$40, 16 to 18 hours), **Cruz del Sur** (☎ 42 7375), **Ormeño** (☎ 42 4113) and several other companies operate daily buses, mostly leaving in the afternoon. Many Lima-bound buses stop en route at other south coast destinations, including Camaná ($4.50, 3½ hours), Nazca (US$7 to US$36, 10 to 12 hours) and Ica (US$9 to US$38, 13 to 15 hours); Pisco is about 6km west of the Panamericana, and few buses go direct (see p137). Many of the same companies also have overnight buses to Cuzco (US$7.50 to US$21, nine to 11 hours), either on a direct, mostly paved road or the asphalted highways via Juliaca.

If you're heading toward Lake Titicaca, direct buses to Juliaca (US$3.60, five hours) and Puno (US$4.50, six hours) leave every half hour throughout the day from Terminal Terrestre. Some continue to Desaguadero (US$7.50, seven to eight hours) on the Bolivian border. Direct services to La Paz, Bolivia, are supposedly offered, but these usually involve a change of buses or at least a stop for a couple of cold predawn hours while you wait for the border posts to open.

Transportes del Carpio (☎ 42 7049) has hourly daytime departures for Mollendo (US$1.50 to US$2.50, 1½ to two hours). Cruz del Sur has the most comfortable buses to Tacna (US$6.50, six to seven hours) via Moquegua (US$4.50, four hours). These southern destinations are also served by Ormeño, **Flores** (☎ 23 8741) and several smaller bus companies. For Ilo (US$5.50, five hours), Flores has 10 departures per day from either Terminal Terrestre or its own **Flores terminal** (☎ 23 4021, 24 4988), diagonally across the roundabout.

REGIONAL SERVICES

Many buses useful for sightseeing in the canyon country also leave from Terminal Terrestre and Terrapuerto. Travel times and costs can vary depending on road conditions. During the wet season (between December and April), expect significant delays.

Heading for the Cañón del Colca, there are only a few daily buses for Chivay (US$2.40, three hours); they continue to Cabanaconde (US$4.50, six hours) at the end of the canyon's main road. In order of recommendation, bus companies include **Andalucia** (☎ 44 5089, 53 1166), **Reyna** (☎ 43 0612) and **Transportes Colca** (☎ 42 6357). Try to catch the earliest daylight departure, usually around 5am.

For buses to Corire (US$3, three hours) to visit the Toro Muerto petroglyphs, Transportes del Carpio has hourly daytime services. Transportes del Carpio also goes hourly to the Valle de Majes (US$3, three hours) for river running, as do other small bus companies. **Transportes Trebol** (☎ 82 9319) usually has a service departing around 4am daily for Corire that continues to Andagua (US$8, 10 to 12 hours) to visit El Valle de los Volcanes. The bus leaves Andagua for the return trip to Arequipa at around 4pm.

For the Cañón del Cotahuasi (US$7.50 to US$10, 12 hours), Reyna has a 4pm departure and **Transportes Alex** (☎ 42 4605) has a 4:30pm departure.

Train

The train station is over 1km south of the Plaza de Armas. Services between Arequipa and Juliaca and Puno on Lake Titicaca have been suspended, although **PeruRail** (☎ 21 3530; www.perurail.com) will run trains as a private charter for large tourist groups. The Arequipa–Juliaca part of the route is bleak, but the views of the altiplano (Andean plateau) are appealing and you'll see vicuñas, alpacas and llamas along the way, plus flamingos if you're lucky.

GETTING AROUND
To/From the Airport

There are no airport buses, although mini-buses marked 'Río Seco' or 'Zamacola' go along Av Puente Grau and Ejército, passing within 700m of the airport – ask the driver exactly where to get off. A taxi from downtown costs about US$4.20. From the airport, *colectivo* (shared) taxis charge around US$2 per person to drop you off at your hotel.

Bicycle

Andes Bike (☎ 20 5078; Villalba 414) sells bicycles, spare parts and travel gear.

Bus

Combis and minibuses go south along Bolívar to Terminal Terrestre (US$0.60, 20 minutes), next door to the Terrapuerto bus terminal, but it's a slow trip via the market area.

Taxi

You can often hire a taxi with a driver for less than renting a car from a travel agency. Local taxi companies include **Presidencial Express** (☎ 20 3333) and **Ideal Taxi** (☎ 28 8888). A short ride around town costs around $0.70. A trip from the Plaza de Armas out to the bus terminals costs about US$1.

CANYON COUNTRY

A tour of the Cañón del Colca is the most popular excursion from Arequipa, but climbing the city's guardian volcano El Misti, rafting in the Majes canyon and visiting the petroglyphs at Toro Muerto, exploring El Valle de los Volcanes, and trekking down in the world's deepest canyon at Cotahuasi are more adventurous. Most of these places can be visited by a combination of public bus and hiking. Alternatively, friends can split the cost of hiring a taxi or 4WD vehicle and driver; a two-day trip will set you back over US$100.

RESERVA NACIONAL SALINAS Y AGUADA BLANCA

The paved road from Arequipa climbs northwest past El Misti and Chachani to this **national reserve** (☎ 054-25 7461; www.inrena

.gob.pe/areasprotegidas/rnsalinas/main.html; admission free; ⏰ 24hr), which covers 367,000 hectares at an average elevation of 4300m. Here, vicuñas are often sighted. Later in the trip, domesticated alpacas and llamas are frequently seen, so it is possible to see three of the four members of the South American camelid family in one day. Seeing the fourth member, the guanaco, is very hard, as they have almost disappeared from this area.

Past the reserve, the increasingly bumpy road continues through bleak altiplano and over the highest point of 4800m, from where the snowcaps of Nevado Ampato (6310m) are seen. Flamingos may also be seen around here between January and April. From there, you'll drop spectacularly into the Cañón del Colca as the road switchbacks down to the dust-choked village of Chivay.

CAÑÓN DEL COLCA

The 100km-long Cañón del Colca is set among high volcanoes (6613m-high Coropuna and 6310m-high Ampato are the tallest) and ranges from 1000m to more than 3000m in depth. For years there was raging controversy over whether or not this was the world's deepest canyon at 3191m, but recently it ranked a close second to neighboring Cañón del Cotahuasi, which is just over 150m deeper. Amazingly, both canyons are more than twice as deep as the Grand Canyon in the USA (see The Deepest Canyon, p51).

Despite its depth, the Cañón del Colca is geologically young. The Río Colca has cut into beds of mainly volcanic rocks, which were deposited less than 100 million years ago along the line of a major fault in the earth's crust. The climate is cool and dry on the plateau and slopes high above the Río Colca. However, the deep valley and generally sunny weather produce frequent updrafts, especially along the canyon's southern edge between Maca and Cabanaconde, and soaring condors can often be seen at close range. Viscachas (burrowing rodents closely related to chinchillas) are also common around the canyon rim, darting furtively among the rocks. Cacti dot many slopes and, if they're in flower, you may be lucky enough to see tiny nectar-eating birds braving the spines to feed. In the depths of the canyon it can be almost tropical, with palm trees, ferns and even orchids in some isolated areas.

The local people (especially the women) are known for their highly decorative traditional clothing. The women's dresses and jackets are intricately embroidered, and their hats are distinctive. In the Chivay area at the east end of the canyon, the white hats are usually woven from straw and are embellished with lace, sequins and medallions. At the west end of the canyon, the hats are of cotton and are painstakingly embroidered. The women don't particularly enjoy being photographed, so always ask permission. Those who pose for photographs expect a tip.

For more information on outdoor outfitters in Arequipa and activity gear rental, see p170. For guided tours of the canyon leaving from Arequipa, see p173.

Chivay

☎ 054 / pop 4600 / elev 3630m

At the head of the Cañón de Colca, the capital of the province of Caylloma is a small, dusty transportation hub.

INFORMATION

Limited tourist information can be gleaned from semiprofessional travel agencies cropping up around the main plaza. The police station is next to the *municipalidad* (town hall) on the plaza. There are no official money-changing facilities in the canyon, except for a few shops that exchange US dollars, euros and traveler's checks at unfavorable rates, so bring plenty of Peruvian cash. Slow, expensive internet access is available from a few cyber-cafés near the plaza.

SIGHTS & ACTIVITIES

At the Casa Andina hotel, a tiny **astronomical observatory** (☎ 53 1020; Huayna Cápac s/n; adult/student US$6/3) has nightly sky shows in Spanish and English, though the weather doesn't always cooperate, especially during the wet season between December and April.

Chivay's famous **hot springs** (admission US$3; ☉ 4:30am-8pm) are 3.5km to the northeast of the village by road. There are large, clean pools, showers, changing rooms, a snack shop and a tiny ethnographic museum. The mineral-laden water is said to have curative properties, but it's also handy when the hot-water supply in Chivay packs up. There are frequent *colectivos* (US$0.30) from the market area to the springs, or you can walk or cycle.

> **WARNING!**
>
> Quasi-official ticket vendors board all buses at Chivay to try and force all gringos to buy a *boleto turístico* (tourist ticket, US$7) that supposedly covers entrance fees to all of the canyon's points of interest. However, if you're just passing through Chivay en route to Cabanaconde and don't intend to visit Cruz del Cóndor, you don't have to buy it – all the proceeds benefit Chivay anyway, not less affluent villages in the canyon. If you politely but persistently refuse to pay, you'll be allowed through – eventually.

Several short hikes can easily be made around Chivay. For example, from where the road forks to the hot springs, stay to the left and walk beside the fertile fields to Corporaque, which has an arched colonial-era plaza. Head downhill and out of Corporaque past some small ruins and look for the orange bridge across the river. Notice the hanging cliff tombs as you cross the river over to Yanque, from where passing buses or *colectivos* return to Chivay. It's an all-day walk; alternatively, rent mountain bikes in Chivay.

It's also possible to walk about 27km further up the northern side of the canyon from Corporaque, past **Ichupampa** and **Lari**, to the rarely visited town of **Madrigal**, which is an interesting spot from which to trek into the deepest parts of the canyon. Occasional *combis* also run to these villages from the streets around the main market area in Chivay.

SLEEPING

Though it's a tiny town, Chivay has plenty of budget guesthouses to choose from.

Hostal Estrella de David (☎ 53 1233; Siglo XX 209; s/d/tr US$3/6/9) A simple, clean guesthouse with bathrooms, this *hospedaje* (small, family-owned inn) is a few blocks from the plaza in the direction of the bus terminal.

Hostal Municipal (☎ 53 1093; Plaza de Armas; s/d US$3/6) Though unexciting, this institutional place is fine for an exhausted traveler.

Hospedaje El Rey (☎ 80 8864; Puente Inca 110; s/d/tr US$4.50/7/9) Close to the plaza, this rustic place has decent rooms with private bathrooms, or cheaper bare-bones habitations for less, all arranged around rickety staircases.

Hospedaje Rumi Wasi (☎ 53 1146; Sucre 714; s/d/tr US$6/9/12) Half a dozen blocks from the main plaza, this guesthouse has a tiny garden where pet alpacas nibble on greenery. The meticulously clean rooms have enticing views of the surrounding countryside. Mountain bikes (US$1.50/10 per hour/day) and Spanish-, English- and French-speaking trekking guides are available for hire. Breakfast costs US$2.

Hostal Anita (☎ 53 1114; Plaza de Armas 606; s/d incl breakfast US$9/15) With a pretty interior courtyard, this friendly hostel smack on the main plaza has hot showers and affable owners. It's tricky to find, so ask at shops nearby.

Hostal La Pascana (☎ 53 1190, 53 1001; hrlapas cana@hotmail.com; Siglo XX 106; s/d/tr incl breakfast US$17.50/25/28) Just a stone's throw from the main plaza, La Pascana is a very good option with carpeted, well-decorated rooms and firm mattresses. It's several notches above the other more modest guesthouses near the plaza.

Wasi Kolping Hostel (☎ 53 1076; www.hoteleskolping .net/colcawasi; Siglo XX s/n; s/d/tr incl breakfast US$26/35/45) An off-the-beaten path midrange choice, this country inn is set in spacious grounds on the outskirts of town, a minute's walk from the bus terminal. The somewhat bedraggled, but still charming bungalows are also accessible to travelers with disabilities. There are nine double rooms, but just one single and two triples.

Casa Andina (☎ 53 1020, 53 1022; www.casa-andina .com; Huayna Cápac s/n; s/d incl breakfast US$60/70) This newly renovated tourist complex recreates a rustic idyll with quaint stone-and-thatch cottages, neatly sculptured bushes and garden views of snow-capped peaks. It has a good restaurant with live music some evenings. Foreign-currency exchange may be available.

EATING

Q'oka (Plaza de Armas 601; drinks US$1-2.50; ☯ closed Sun) Try this spot for decent coffee and snacks with terrace views of the plaza.

Lobo's (☎ 53 1081; Plaza de Armas; meals from US$2; ☯ 9am-10pm) This place offers a touristy menu (including big breakfasts), a backpacker bar and limited tourist information.

Casa Blanca (☎ 48 8616; Plaza de Armas; menús US$4; ☯ 11am-9:30pm) A warm subterranean restaurant with a fireplace, friendly Casa Blanca has a pick-and-choose menú that includes unusual local specialties. Portions are huge.

DRINKING

The nightlife in this tiny village revolves around the tourists. Peñas are everywhere, with shows of traditional dance and music starting around 8pm nightly. For dancing, there's **Latigo's** (cnr Puente Inca & Bolognesi; ☯ closed Sun) and a couple of other nightclubs within drunken stumbling distance. And yes, it's official: **M´elroys** (Plaza de Armas; ☯ closed Sun) proves that Irish pubs really are everywhere.

GETTING THERE & AROUND

The bus terminal is a 15-minute walk from the plaza. Buses to Arequipa (US$2.40, three hours) or to Cabanaconde (US$1, 2½ hours), stopping at towns along the southern side of the canyon and Cruz del Cóndor, leave four times daily.

Combis and *colectivo* taxis run to the surrounding villages from street corners in the market area, just north of the main plaza. Mountain bikes in varying condition can be readily hired from travel agencies on the plaza or at **BiciSport** (Zaramilla 112; ☯ 9am-6pm) behind the market for about US$1.50 per hour, or US$7 per day.

Traveling onward to Cuzco from Chivay may be possible, but it's overly complicated and not recommended. Although some travelers have managed to catch *combis* to Puente Callalli and flag down a bus there, it's much safer and probably just as fast to return to Arequipa instead.

Chivay to Cabanaconde

The road following the south bank of the upper Cañón del Colca leads past several villages that still use the Inca terracing that surrounds them. Those on the south side of the canyon are most easily accessible by buses traveling between Chivay and Cabanaconde. Occasional *combis* and *colectivo* taxis also leave from the market area in Chivay for most of the villages in the canyon, so ask around.

YANQUE
☎ 054

About 7km from Chivay, the peaceful rural village of Yanque has an attractive 18th-century church on the main plaza. Also on the plaza is the excellent **Museo Yanque** (admission US$0.90; ☯ 7am-6:30pm Tue-Sun), a university-run cultural museum with displays on traditional canyon life. In the central courtyard is a herbal garden of ancient medical remedies, some predating Inca times. Brief guided tours are given in Spanish, after which you can borrow foreign-language booklets that explain the main displays. Next door is a small local art gallery and shop.

From the plaza, a 30-minute walk down to the river brings you to some local hot springs (US$0.30). There are a few simple, family-run guesthouses scattered around town, most charging from around US$3 per person per night. Travelers have recommended **Sumaq Huayta Wasi** (☎ 83 2174; Cusco 303), just two blocks from the main plaza. Out on the main road, you'll find the delightful **Tradicíon Colca Albergue** (☎ 42 4926, 20 5336; www.tradicioncolca.com; Av Colca 119; s/d incl breakfast US$25/30), a European-run country inn with 24-hour hot water; a small swimming pool, sauna and Jacuzzi; and a restaurant, café and bar with a billiards table. Rates include an afternoon guided hike and mountain-bike ride.

CORPORAQUE TO MADRIGAL

Across the river from Yanque, in the village of Corporaque, is the excellent **La Casa de Mamay-acchi** (www.lacasademamayacchi.com; s/d incl breakfast from US$30/35). Hidden away downhill from the main plaza, this inn is built with traditional materials and boasts awesome canyon views. The cozy rooms have no TVs, but there's a games library, fireplace and bar make it sociable. Although it's often booked by tour groups, it also welcomes independent travelers, especially romantic couples. Make advance reservations through the **Arequipa office** (☎ 054-24 1206; Jerusalén 606).

Further up the northern side of the canyon is the upmarket **Colca Lodge** (☎ 054 53 1191; www .colca-lodge com; s/d/tr/q incl breakfast US$82/92/105/125, ste US$150-190), a large and attractive stone-and-thatch hotel tucked into the bend of the river amid Inca terracing. Activities including horseback riding, fishing, rafting and mountain biking can be arranged here. The stone-lined pools of the hotel's private hot springs are open from April to January. For advance reservations, visit the **Arequipa office** (☎ 054-20 2587, 054-20 3604; Jerusalén 212).

YANQUE TO PINCHOLLO

Further along the main road on the south side of the canyon, the spreading landscape is remarkable for its Inca and pre-Inca terracing, which goes on for many kilometers and is some of the most extensive in Peru. Some tours also stop at a small carved boulder that is supposed to represent a pre-Columbian map of the terracing.

The next big village along the main road is **Pinchollo**, about 30km from Chivay. From here, a trail climbs toward **Hualca Hualca** (a snowcapped volcano of 6025m) to an active geothermal area set amid wild and interesting scenery. Though it's not very clearly marked, there's a four-hour trail up to a bubbling geyser that used to erupt dramatically before a recent earthquake contained it. Ask around for directions, or just head left uphill in the direction of the mountain, then follow the water channel to its end. In Pinchollo, there is the very basic **El Refugio** (dm US$2) near the plaza, and the owner is also a local guide. A sleeping bag and flashlight are recommended.

CRUZ DEL CÓNDOR

You can continue on foot from Pinchollo to **Cruz del Cóndor** (admission with boleto turístico) in about two hours or flag down any passing bus headed toward Cabanaconde. This famed viewpoint, also known locally as Chaglla, is for many the highlight of their trip to the Cañón del Colca. A large family of Andean condors nests by the rocky outcrop and, with lots of luck, they can occasionally be seen gliding effortlessly on thermal air currents rising from the canyon, swooping low over onlookers' heads. It's a mesmerizing scene, heightened by the spectacular 1200m drop to the river below and the sight of **Mismi** reaching over 3000m above the canyon floor on the other side of the ravine.

Recently it has become more difficult to see the condors, mostly due to air pollution, including from travelers' campfires. Early morning (8am to 10am) or late afternoon (4pm to 6pm) are still the best times to see the birds, though they can appear at various hours during the day. The condors are less likely to appear on rainy days so it's best to visit during the dry season. You can walk from the viewpoint to Cabanaconde, 18km past Pinchollo and almost 50km from Chivay.

Cabanaconde

☎ 054 / pop 1300 / elev 3290m

The quiet rural town of Cabanaconde makes an ideal base for some spectacular hikes into the canyon. It's a very small place, with just a few simple spots to stay and eat. Bring everything you'll need to stay a couple of days, including plenty of Peruvian currency in small bills and any trekking equipment (eg sleeping bags).

ACTIVITIES

The most popular short trek is one that involves a steep two-hour hike down to **Sangalle** (also popularly known as 'the oasis') at the bottom of the canyon, where several sets of basic bungalows and campgrounds have sprung up, all costing from about US$3 per person. There are two natural pools for swimming, the larger of which is claimed by Oasis Bungalows, which charges US$3 (free if you are staying in its bungalows) to swim. Paradaíso Bungalows doesn't charge for the smaller swimming pool, and there is a local dispute over whether travelers should be charged to use the pools at all. Do not light campfires as almost half of the trees in the area have been destroyed in this manner, and take all trash out of the canyon with you (those garbage cans you see lying about are not emptied properly). The return trek to Cabanaconde is a stiff climb and thirsty work; allow about three to four hours.

An adventurous five- to seven-day trek goes down to the canyon bottom, passes through the village of Tapay, then goes up the other side of the canyon by the village of Choco and over a 5500m pass, before descending through the town of Chacas and El Valle de los Volcanes. Another pass brings you to Andagua, where there are buses back to Arequipa (US$8, 10 hours) at around 4pm.

The charming village of **Tapay** is a destination in itself and is also a base camp for other shorter treks, including to **Bomboya**. Readers have recommended camping or staying overnight at Hostal Isidro, whose owner is a guide and has a shop, satellite phone and rental mules. Accommodations are also available in Tapay and closer to Cabanaconde in San Juan de Chuccho, where travelers have recommended Roy's campground, bungalows and simple restaurant.

Local guides, guesthouse owners and other travelers can suggest a wealth of other day hikes and longer treks to *miradors*, Inca ruins, waterfalls and geysers. You can buy topographic and trekking maps and rent gear from **Colca Trek** (☎ 054-20 6217, 054-960 0170; www.colcatrek .com.pe; colcatrek@gmail.com; Jerusalén 401-B) back in Arequipa.

TOURS & GUIDES

Although most treks are DIY, hiring a local guide typically costs US$5 to US$10 per day, depending on their experience. Horse or mule rentals can also be easily arranged for about US$8 per day.

SLEEPING & EATING

Accommodation options are extremely limited in Cabanaconde. Most people eat where they're sleeping, although there are a couple of cheap local restaurants near the main plaza, too.

Hostal Valle del Fuego (☎ 83 0032, 83 0035, 83 2158; hvalledelfuego@hotmail.com; s/d with shared bathroom US$3/6) This budget hostel is an established travelers' scene, with DVDs, a full bar, solar-powered showers and owners who are knowledgeable about trekking. Ask about free passes to the Sangalle pools. Rooms are very basic and most share bathrooms. There's also a newer private annex that costs more. You can contact the hostel in advance through Pablo Tours (☎ 054-20 3737), located at 400 Jerusalén in Arequipa.

Hospedaje Villa Pastor (hospedaje_villa_pastor@ hotmail.com; Plaza de Armas; s/d US$3/6) This small, upstart guesthouse is the Hostal Valle del Fuego's only competition in the budget category, offering lukewarm showers and a simple restaurant and bar. Travelers give the friendly staff good reviews, although the place can look deserted at times.

La Posada del Conde (☎ 44 0197; San Pedro s/n; s/d incl breakfast US$8/15) This small modern hotel mostly has double rooms, but they are well-cared for with clean bathrooms. The rates often include a welcome *mate* (herbal tea) or pisco sour (grape brandy cocktail) in the downstairs restaurant.

Hotel Kuntur Wassi (☎ 21 8166, 83 0034; www .kunturwassi.com; Cruz Blanca s/n; s/d/tr/ste incl breakfast $40/50/60/60) This charming upmarket hotel is built into the hillside above town, with stone bathrooms, trapezoidal windows overlooking the gardens and a nouveau-rustic feel. Suites boast enormous bathtubs. There's also a bar, restaurant, library, laundry and foreign-currency exchange. In low season prices may drop significantly.

GETTING THERE & AWAY

Buses for Chivay (US$1, 2½ hours) and Arequipa (US$4.50, six hours) via Cruz del Cóndor leave Cabanaconde from the main plaza several times per day. Departure times change frequently though, so check locally. All buses will stop upon request at towns along the main road on the southern side of the canyon.

TORO MUERTO PETROGLYPHS

This is a magnificent and quite unusual archaeological site in the high desert. It consists of thousands of black volcanic boulders carved with stylized animals, people and birds, which are spread over several square kilometers of desert. Archaeologists are uncertain of the cultural origins of this site, but it is thought that it was made by the Wari culture about 1200 years ago.

To reach the site by public transport, take a bus to Corire from Arequipa (US$3, three hours). If you don't want to sleep in Corire, take an early bus (they start as early as 4am) and get off at a small church 2km before the town of Corire, where you'll see a sign for Toro Muerto. From there, a dirt track goes up a valley to the petroglyphs. Otherwise continue to Corire itself, from where you can walk to the petroglyphs in about 1½ hours or catch a taxi (round-trip US$7.50). In Corire there is the basic **Hostal Willy** (☎ 054-47 2046; s/d with shared bathroom US$3/6, s/d US$6/9), which can provide information on reaching the site. Bring plenty of water, sunblock and insect repellent (as there are plenty of mosquitoes en route).

Buses return from Corire to Arequipa once an hour, usually leaving at 30 minutes past the hour. The Toro Muerto petroglyphs can also be visited more conveniently on expensive full-day 4WD tours from Arequipa.

EL VALLE DE LOS VOLCANES

El Valle de los Volcanes is a broad valley, west of the Cañón del Colca and at the foot of Nevado Coropuna (6613m), famed for its unusual geological features. The valley floor is carpeted with lava flows from which rise many small (up to 200m high) cinder cones, some 80 in total, aligned along a major fissure, with each cone formed from a single eruption. Given the lack of erosion of some cones and minimal vegetation on the associated lava flows, the volcanic activity occurred no more than a few thousand years ago, and some was likely very recent – historical accounts suggest as recently as the 17th century.

The lava flows have had a major influence on drainage in the valley. They have controlled the course of the Río Challahuire, constraining it against the east side of the valley and forming the dam behind which Laguna de Chachas is impounded. The outlet of Laguna de Chachas then runs beneath lava flows for nearly 20km before emerging at Laguna Mamacocha. Despite being relatively young, Laguna de Chachas is rapidly being reclaimed by the deltas of the Río Challahuire and other streams.

The 65km-long valley surrounds the village of **Andagua**, near the snowy summit of Coropuna. It is a weird and remote area that is seldom visited by travelers. There are some *chullpas* (funery towers) at **Soporo**, a two-hour hike or half-hour drive from Andagua. En route to Soporo are the ruins of a pre-Columbian city named **Antaymarca**. Northeast of Andagua, at a place called **Izanquillay**, the Río Andahua runs through a narrow lava canyon, forming a spectacular 40m-high waterfall.

There are several cheap and basic hostels and restaurants in Andagua. To get to the valley from Arequipa, take a bus to Andagua (US$8, 10 to 12 hours). Return buses leave Andagua around 4pm and arrive in Arequipa at around 4am, as bus companies always underestimate the time it takes to get anywhere remote.

CAÑÓN DEL COTAHUASI

While the Cañón del Colca has stolen the limelight for many years, it is actually this remote canyon, 200km northwest of Arequipa as the condor flies, that is the deepest known canyon in the world. It is around twice the depth of the Grand Canyon, with stretches dropping down below 3300m. While the depths of the ravine are only accessible to experienced river runners (p172), the rest of the fertile valley is also rich in striking scenery and trekking opportunities. The canyon also shelters several traditional rural settlements that currently see only a handful of adventurous travelers.

Sights & Activities

The main access town is appropriately named **Cotahuasi** (pop 3200) and is at 2620m above sea level on the southeast side of the canyon. Northeast of Cotahuasi and further up the canyon are the villages of **Tomepampa** (10km away; elevation 2500m) and **Alca** (20km away; elevation 2660m), which also have basic accommodations. En route you'll pass a couple of **thermal baths** (admission US$0.30).

Trails lead into the canyon, and **waterfalls** and **hot springs** can be visited. You can allegedly hike from Cotahuasi to the coast along the canyon in about two weeks, but more popular short treks include the waterfall of **Sipia** and the Inca ruins near **Pampamarca**, north of Cotahuasi.

Trekking trips of several days' duration can be arranged in Arequipa (p170); some can be combined with the Toro Muerto petroglyphs, and, if you ask, they may return via a collection of dinosaur footprints on the west edge of the canyon.

Sleeping & Eating

Unless stated otherwise, accommodation is in shared rooms of up to four beds.

Hostal Villa (☎ 054-58 1018; Independencia 118, Cotahuasi; r with shared bathroom per person US$3) Hostal Villa has a flowery stone courtyard and basic rooms sharing one bathroom, which may have hot water.

Alojamiento Chávez (☎ 054-58 1028; Cabildo 125, Cotahuasi; r with shared bathroom per person US$3) Señor Chávez offers lodging in a colonial house with a muddy central patio. You'll have to request hot water.

Hostal Hatunhuasi (☎ 054-58 1054, in Lima 01-531 0803; catyborda@hotmail.com; Centanario 309, Cotahuasi; r with shared bathroom per person US$3) This friendly guesthouse has plenty of rooms with shared bathrooms. There is some warm water available during the day. The owners are skilled in independent trip planning and are good sources of hard-to-get information for travelers.

Hostal Fani Luz (☎ 054-58 1002; Independencia 117, Cotahuasi; r with shared bathroom per person US$3, s/d US$6/8) Opposite Hostal Villa, this friendly spot has almost a dozen rooms (some with an ancient black-and-white TV) and shared hot-water bathrooms. Private bathrooms are cold water only.

Hostal Alcalá (☎ 054-28 0455; Plaza de Armas, Alca; dm US$4, r with shared/private bathroom US$6/8) In Alca, this guesthouse has a good mix of clean rooms and prices – including some of the most comfortable digs in the whole valley. There is 24-hour hot water here.

Hospedaje Wuasi Punko (☎ 054-26 6941, 054-26 8210; r with shared bathroom per person US$5) Conveniently near the hot springs at Luicha on the road to Alca, this rustic building has shared bathrooms with hot showers.

In Pampamarca, there is only the basic **Casa Albergue** (dm US$3).

Getting There & Away

The 420km bus journey from Arequipa, half of which is on unpaved roads, takes 12 hours if the going is good (US$7.50 to US$10). Over three-quarters of the way there, the road summits a 4500m pass between the huge glacier-capped mountains of Coropuna (6613m) and Solimana (6323m) before dropping down to Cotahuasi. Buses return to Arequipa at around 4:30pm and 5pm.

There are hourly *combis* from Cotahuasi plaza up to Alca (US$0.90, one hour) via Tomepampa (US$0.60, 30 minutes). For Pampamarca, there are two daily buses (US$1.50, two hours) departing in the early morning and again in the midafternoon.

LAGUNA DE SALINAS

This lake (4300m above sea level), east of Arequipa below Pichu Pichu and El Misti, is a salt lake that becomes a white salt flat during the dry months of May to December. Its size and the amount of water in it vary from year to year depending on the weather. During the rainy season it is a good place to see all three flamingo species, as well as myriad other Andean water birds.

Buses to Ubinas (US$4, 3½ hours) pass by the lake, but catching a bus from the lake back to Arequipa is difficult because the bus begins at the village of Ubinas and is very full by the time it passes the lake. You can hike around the lake, which can take about two days, then return on the packed daily afternoon bus at around 3pm (expect to stand) or try to catch a lift with workers from the nearby mine. One-day minibus tours from Arequipa, which may include a stop at a hot springs, cost about US$40 per person; mountain biking tours are also available (p172). Finally, some mountain-climbing expeditions to Ubinas (p171) stop off at the lake en route to base camp.

Lake Titicaca

At the crossroads of the mighty Andes and Peru's windswept altiplano (Andean plateau) grasslands, fertile Lake Titicaca was a cradle for Peru's ancient civilizations.

Settled life began here in 200 BC with the Pukara culture, which erected huge pyramids and monuments. A millennium later, the influential Tiahuanaco culture spread into Bolivia. Warlike tribes such as the Collas and Aymaras arose shortly thereafter, only to be violently shoved aside by the Inca empire. Hot on the heels of the Inca warriors were Spanish conquistadors, who came lusting for mineral riches to be wrested from the bowels of the earth.

Today the department of Puno, focused on magnificent Lake Titicaca, is a stronghold of rural Peruvian life. You can amble around peaceful lakeside communities where Aymara and Quechua are still first languages, or dive into celebrations of traditional dance and music during the wildly colorful *folklórico* festivals for which the region is world-famous.

Meanwhile, Lake Titicaca is the world's highest navigable lake with passenger boat services, and South America's largest lake – over 170km in length and 60km in breadth. According to legend, this is where the first Inca Manco Capac, son of the sun god Inti, emerged.

At this altitude, temperatures average less than 15°C year-round. But luminescent sunlight suffuses the highland altiplano and the lake's deep waters. The earthy tones of the scenery are reflected in the crumbling colonial churches and ancient funerary towers scattered around the lakeshore. As the air is unusually clear, horizons seem limitless.

HIGHLIGHTS

- Gawking at the windswept ancient funerary towers at **Sillustani** (p202) and **Cutimbo** (p202)
- Overnighting with islanders on **Isla Taquile** (p204) or Bolivia's **Isla del Sol** (p218)
- Catching one of the lake district's myriad *folklórico* **dance and music celebrations** (p196), especially in Puno
- Taking a tour with a genial captain aboard the 19th-century steamship **Yavari** (p195)
- Navigating local buses to visit rural **altiplano towns** (p191 and p215) en route to Cuzco or along Lake Titicaca's south shore

Towns en route to Cuzco

Sillustani ★
Puno ★   ★ Isla Taquile
★Cutimbo   Isla del Sol ★

Towns of Lake Titicaca's south shore

- BIGGEST CITY: JULIACA, POPULATION 198,600
- AVERAGE TEMPERATURE: JANUARY 8°C TO 14°C, JULY 4°C TO 10°C

JULIACA

☎ 051 / pop 198,600 / elev 3826m

The large, brash workaday town of Juliaca has the department's only commercial airport and a railway junction with connections to Puno and Cuzco. That said, it deservedly sees far fewer tourists than its more picturesque lakeside neighbor Puno. Most people will end up transiting through here at some point – it's almost unavoidable. There is little to see in Juliaca itself, but it's a handy hub for excursions to nearby traditional villages. Picking your way through the fleets of *mototaxis* (three-wheeled motorcycle rickshaw taxis) and colorful piles of Andean woolen goods in the Sunday market will help pass the time.

Information

For emergencies, visit the **police station** (☎ 32 2091; cnr San Martín & San Román; ☽ 24hr). *Casas de cambio* (foreign-exchange bureaus) sprawl around the intersection of Bolívar and M Nuñez, where you'll find cheap internet cafés. **Interbank** (M Nuñez 231) has a 24-hour global ATM. **BCP** (M Nuñez 136) has an ATM that accepts Visa, Plus and Amex cards. **Clínica Americana**

Adventista (☎ 32 1639; Loreto 315; ☽ 24hr) offers emergency medical services. The **post office** (Sandía at Butrón; ☽ 8:15am-7pm Mon-Sat) is a stiff walk northwest of Plaza Bolognesi.

Dangers & Annoyances

If you arrive from the coast, especially by air, take it easy for a few days to help avoid problems with altitude sickness (see p534).

Sleeping

With Puno so close by, there's usually no need to overnight here. Most of the following places will give discounts if you ask for their best price. In addition, there are many barebones *hostales* (guesthouses) around Plaza Bolognesi, near the train station.

Hostal San Antonio (☎ 33 1803; San Martín 347; s/d with shared bathroom US$5/7.50, s/d US$7.50/12) San Antonio has a large array of basic but clean rooms; the better options in the new wing have hot showers and national TV. There's also an attached sauna (entry US$3) that's open daily.

Hostal Sakura (☎ 32 2072; San Román 133; s/d US$7.50/10.50, with cable TV US$10.50/12) Just northwest of the plaza, this guesthouse has positive

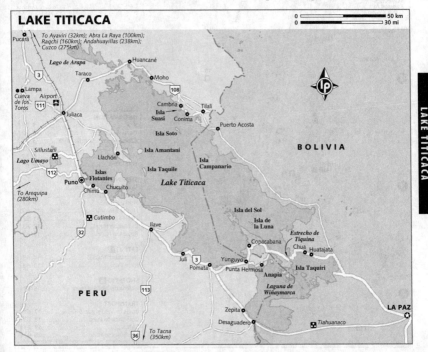

LAKE TITICACA

0 _____ 50 km
0 _____ 30 mi

To Ayaviri (32km); Abra La Raya (100km);
Raqchi (160km); Andahuaylillas (238km);
Cuzco (275km);

Pucará

Lago de Arapa

Huancané

Taraco

Moho

108

Lampa
Cueva de los Toros   111   Airport   Juliaca

Cambria   Tilali
Isla
Suasi   Conima

Isla Soto

Puerto Acosta

BOLIVIA

Sillustani
Lago Umayo   112   Llachón   Isla Amantaní

Islas   Isla Taquile   Isla
Flotantes   Campanario
Puno   Chucuito   Lake Titicaca
Chimú

To Arequipa
(280km)

Cutimbo   Ilave

Isla del Sol
Isla de
la Luna   Estrecho de
Tiquina
Copacabana   Chua   Huatajata

32

Juli   3   Yunguyo   Isla Taquiri
Pomata   Punta Hermosa   Anapia
Anapia
Laguna de
Wiñaymarca

PERU   113

Zepita   La Paz

Desaguadero   Tiahuanaco

36   To Tacna
(350km)

LAKE TITICACA

vibrations, and most rooms have private hot showers.

Hotel San Martín (☎ 32 5317; M Nuñez 233; s/d US$10.50/19.50) This is a fairly modern option with plain homey rooms, good showers and cable TV. Although the atmosphere isn't very friendly, the location is conveniently close to regional bus stops.

La Maison Hotel (☎ 32 1444; www.lamaisonhotel .com; 7 de Junio 535; s/d/tr/q US$18/28/38/44, ste US$34, all incl breakfast) Next to a video pub and disco, sociable La Maison has notably comfortable if classless rooms with cable TV and plastic chairs. The downstairs restaurant opens early for breakfast.

Hostal Don Carlos (☎ 32 3600; www.hotelesdon carlos.com; 9 de Diciembre 124; s/d/tr/ste incl breakfast US$30/40/45/50) Though the building isn't aging as gracefully as it could, Don Carlos is still the best hotel right on Plaza Bolognesi. As well as a restaurant, the hotel has clean and pleasant rooms with a surprising number of amenities, including heating, cable TV and minibar.

Royal Inn Hotel (☎ 32 1561, 32 8626; www.royalinnho teles.com; San Román 158; s/d/tr US$45/50/60, ste US$60–65) An excellent choice for the price, the towering Royal Inn boasts newly revamped modern rooms with hot showers, heating and cable TV, plus one of Juliaca's best restaurants.

Don Carlos Suites Hotel (☎ 32 1571, 32 7260; www .hotelesdoncarlos.com; Manuel Prado 335; s/d/ste incl breakfast US$50/60/80) Easily the best hotel in town, the three-star Don Carlos Suites has spacious, new-and-improved rooms that are several

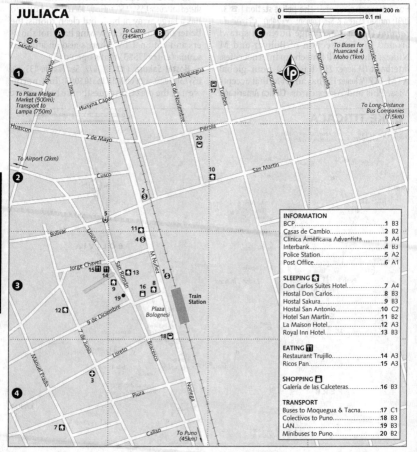

JULIACA

0 ———— 200 m
0 ———— 0.1 mi

To Cuzco (345km)

To Buses for Huancané & Moho (1km)

To Plaza Melgar Market (500m); Transport to Lampa (750m)

To Long-Distance Bus Companies (1.5km)

To Airport (2km)

Train Station

Plaza Bolognesi

To Puno (45km)

INFORMATION	
BCP.....................................**1** B3	
Casas de Cambio.....................**2** B2	
Clínica Américana Adventista........**3** A4	
Interbank..............................**4** B3	
Police Station.........................**5** A2	
Post Office.............................**6** A1	

SLEEPING	
Don Carlos Suites Hotel..............**7** A4	
Hostal Don Carlos....................**8** B3	
Hostal Sakura........................**9** B3	
Hostal San Antonio..................**10** C2	
Hotel San Martín.....................**11** B2	
La Maison Hotel......................**12** A3	
Royal Inn Hotel......................**13** B3	

EATING	
Restaurant Trujillo...................**14** A3	
Ricos Pan.............................**15** A3	

SHOPPING	
Galería de las Calceteras............**16** B3	

TRANSPORT	
Buses to Moquegua & Tacna.........**17** C1	
Colectivos to Puno...................**18** B3	
LAN...................................**19** B3	
Minibuses to Puno...................**20** B2	

blocks away from the action. The old wing is less plush, but all rooms boast cable TV and a minibar.

Eating & Drinking

Ricos Pan (cnr Unión & Jorge Chavez; items US$0.50-4.50; ☺ 8:30am-12:30pm & 2:30-6:30pm) is the best place for coffee and yummy baked goods. **Restaurant Trujillo** (San Román 163; mains US$3-6; ☺ breakfast, lunch & dinner) is good for more substantial meals and boasts a decent drinks list. The restaurant at the **Royal Inn Hotel** (☎ 32 1561; San Román 158; mains US$3-9) is the best in town.

There is a paucity of *peñas* (bars or clubs with live folkloric music), though discos come and go in the town center.

Shopping

If you're hot for some haggling, Juliaca has some of the cheapest prices for alpaca goods you'll find. Sunday is the best market day, while Monday hosts a large, raw-materials market. The markets are held west of the center in Plaza Melgar. You'll find a daily indoor handicrafts market called Galería de las Calceteras on Plaza Bolognesi.

Getting There & Away

AIR

The **airport** (☎ 32 8974) is 2km west of town. **LAN** (☎ 32 2228; San Román 125) allegedly has daily flights to/from Lima, Arequipa and Cuzco. However, if flights aren't full they may not operate, so be prepared for cancellations.

BUS & TAXI

Rumor has it that a Terminal Terrestre is under construction. For now, long-distance bus companies are located on *cuadra* 12 of San Martín, 2km east of town. Buses from Juliaca travel to the same destinations as from Puno (p201). Regular buses go to Arequipa and Cuzco with **Cruz del Sur** (☎ 32 2011), **Ormeño** (☎ 54 5057), **Cromotex** (☎ 33 2733) and several other companies. At the time of writing, Ormeño had the only direct bus to Lima, which is a Royal Class service (US$39, 18 hours).

More centrally located, **San Martín** (☎ 32 7501) and other companies along Tumbes between Moquegua and Piérola have *económico* night buses to Tacna (US$9, 11 hours) via Moquegua. They tend to leave around 6pm.

Combis (minibuses) to Huancané (US$0.60, one hour) leave every 15 minutes from Ballón

and Sucre, about four blocks east of Apurímac and 1½ blocks north of Lambayeque.

To get to Puno, *colectivo* (shared) taxis (US$0.60, 50 minutes) leave when they are full from the southeast corner of Plaza Bolognesi. More frequent *combis* (US$0.50, one hour) depart from around the intersection of Piérola and 8 de Noviembre, northeast of the plaza.

TRAIN

Juliaca's **train station** (☎ 32 1036; Plaza Bolognesi 353; ☺ 7am-noon & 1-5pm Mon-Fri, 7-11am Sat & Sun) was once the busiest railway crossroad in Peru, serving Puno, Cuzco and Arequipa. However, improved roads have led to a suspension of services to Arequipa. Trains still run from Puno to Cuzco but can be erratic, especially out of high season. They pass through Juliaca an hour or so after leaving Puno. See p201 for schedules, fares and more details on this route. Watch your belongings with an eagle eye while in the ill-lit Juliaca station.

Getting Around

A bus with an 'Aeropuerto' placard cruises around town and down 2 de Mayo before heading to the airport (US$0.30). Taxis cost around US$1.50. At the airport you'll usually find *colectivos* heading directly to Puno, charging around US$1.50 per passenger and taking less than an hour for the trip.

AROUND JULIACA
Lampa

☎ 051 / pop 5000

This charming little town, 36km northwest of Juliaca, is known as *La Ciudad Rosada* (the Pink City) for its dusty, pink-colored buildings. The beautifully constructed church of **Iglesia de la Inmaculada** holds a few secrets worth seeing: leading local citizen Don Enrique Torres Belón had a huge domed tomb constructed here, topped by a copy of Michelangelo's famous statue *La Pietà*. The structure below it is lined with hundreds of skeletons of Spaniards apparently dredged up from the catacombs below and arranged in ghoulishly decorative, skull-and-crossbones patterns. The caretaker will show you around the church and take you down into the catacombs for a tip. If no one's at the church, ask around at the mural-covered Municipalidad on the plaza.

Staff at the shop opposite the tiny **Museo Kampac** (Ugarte 462; admission by donation; ☺ hrs vary)

BORDER CROSSING: BOLIVIA VIA THE NORTH SHORE

This little-traveled route into Bolivia is recommended only for hardy off-the-beaten-track travelers with little concern for time or comfort. Speaking at least a little Spanish is essential, as is lots of luck.

First get an exit stamp from the Peruvian *oficina de migraciónes* in Puno (see opposite) and ask them to predate the stamp by three or four days. Then catch a regular *combi* from Juliaca to the small town of Huancané (see p191). If you need them, there are basic *hostales* (guesthouses) near where the buses stop and around Huancané's Plaza de Armas.

Several buses and trucks leaving daily from Juliaca and Huancané travel the unpaved road to the friendly little village of Moho (US$2, two hours), though these get crowded so you may have to stand. Nicknamed *el jardin de altiplano* (the garden of the altiplano), the lovely town of Moho is a restful place to break your journey. There are a couple of cheap, basic but adequate *hospedajes* (small, family-owned inn) with rooms for around US$3 on the cobbled streets around the main plaza. On the plaza, a fancier tourist hotel offers doubles for around US$10. The town's electricity is limited, so bring spare batteries for your flashlight.

Buses and trucks leave Moho for Tilali most mornings, but you can also walk in about five hours to Conima, which has the colonial church of San Miguel Arcangel, then follow the lakeshore for another two hours to Tilali near the Bolivian border. There are no hotels or restaurants in Tilali, but local families may rent rooms – ask around. It's also possible to stay near Conima on Isla Suasi (see p214).

Another option from Juliaca is to take a direct night bus that goes to Tilali via Huancané, Moho and Conima. Buses usually depart Juliaca on Tuesday, Friday and Sunday from the 10th block of Lambayeque, at the corner with the Colegio Encinas.

However you get there, from Tilali it's about four hours to the nearest Bolivian town of Puerto Acosta. There is a big border market on Wednesday and Saturday mornings, when it becomes easier to find bus and truck transport from Tilali to the market and onward to Puerto Acosta, but you might get stuck otherwise. There are very few private vehicles along this route, so don't count on hitchhiking.

The police on the Bolivian border can be unhelpful, so make sure your documents are in order. Ask them where the Bolivian immigration post currently is to get your passport stamped, and keep in mind that there may simply not be one before La Paz. Transportation out of Puerto Acosta does not leave regularly, so take the first vehicle you can, be it truck or bus, heading toward La Paz.

The nearest Bolivian consulate is in Puno (opposite). See p214 for details of entering Bolivia via simpler, more popular routes along Lake Titicaca's south shore.

will give you a quick, informative Spanish-language guided tour of the museum's small collection and, at their discretion, may show you a unique vase inscribed with the sacred cosmology of the Incas.

About 4km west of town over a bridge hides **Cueva de los Toros**, a bull-shaped cave with prehistoric carvings of llamas and other animals. The cave is in some rocks on the right side of the road, and en route you'll see several *chullpas* (funerary towers), not unlike the ones at Sillustani (p202) and Cutimbo (p202).

Most visitors come on day trips, but you could overnight at any of the few cheap and friendly *hospedajes* (small, family-owned inns) scattered around the center. *Combis*

headed for Lampa leave Juliaca when full from Jirón Huáscar, a couple of blocks west of the market area (US$0.40, 45 minutes). Their arrival point is a short walk from Lampa's main plaza.

Pucará
☎ 051 / pop 2500 / elev 3860m

More than 60km northwest of Juliaca, the sleepy village of Pucará is famous for its celebrations of **La Virgen del Carmen** on July 16, and its earthy colored **ceramics** – not least the ceramic *toritos* (bulls) often seen perched on the roofs of Andean houses for good luck. Asking around on weekdays may lead you to several local workshops. The **Museo Lítico Pucará** (admission US$1.50; ⏱ 8:30am-5pm) displays

a surprisingly good little selection of anthropomorphic monoliths from the town's pre-
Inca site, which was connected to the ancient
Tiahuanaco culture. The ruins themselves sit
above the town, a short walk up the same road
that the museum sits on, which leads away
from the main plaza. If you get stuck, there
are a few simple places to overnight either
near the plaza or out on the highway by the
lonesome bus stop.

Ayaviri
☎ 051 / pop 2100 / elev 3928m

Almost 100km northwest of Juliaca is Ayaviri, the first sizable settlement on the road
to Cuzco. It's a bustling, chilly market town
with a colonial **church**, and a few kilometers
away are the hot springs of **Pojpojquella** (admission
US$1.50), where you can bathe. There are several
simple hotels to stay overnight in town, but
little else to do here.

Abra la Raya

From Ayaviri, the route climbs for almost
another 100km through windswept altiplano
to this Andean **mountain pass** (4319m), the
highest point on the trip to Cuzco. Buses
often stop here to allow passengers to take
advantage of the cluster of handicraft sellers and the photogenic view of snowcapped
mountains. The pass also marks the departmental line between Puno and Cuzco, and
points of interest north of here are described
starting on p278.

PUNO
☎ 051 / pop 102,800 / elev 3830m

The small port of Puno is by far the most
convenient departure point to make forays
to Lake Titicaca's various islands or to surrounding archaeological sites. The capital
of its department, the town was founded on
November 4, 1668, near the site of the now-
defunct colonial silver mine of Laykakota. Few
colonial buildings remain, but the streets are
merrily claustrophobic and the markets filled
with local women garbed in many-layered
dresses and bowler hats.

Orientation

Puno is handily compact. If you've got energy
to spare, you can walk into the center from the
port or the bus terminals, or hop into a *mototaxi* instead. Everything in the town center
is within easy walking distance.

Information

EMERGENCY

Police (☎ 36 6271; Deustua 530; ☾ 24hr)
Policía de Turismo (☎ 35 3988; Deustua 558; ☾ 24hr)
May provide some assistance in cases of emergency.

IMMIGRATION

Bolivian consulate (☎ 35 1251; 3rd fl, Arequipa 136;
☾ 8:30am-2pm Mon-Fri)
Oficina de migraciónes (immigration office; ☎ 35
7103; Ayacucho 240; ☾ 8am-2pm Mon-Fri) Gives tourist-
card extensions (see Visas on p513), though it's cheaper to
go to Bolivia and return.

INTERNET ACCESS

Internet cafés are found near the main plaza
and along Calle Lima.
Choza@net (2nd fl, Lima 339; ☾ 8am-11pm) Speedy
computers, printers, photo CD burning and cheap telephone
calls are available here.

LAUNDRY

Lavaclin (Valcárcel 132; ☾ 8am-noon & 2-7pm Mon-
Sat; per kg US$1.40)

MEDICAL SERVICES

Botica Fasa (☎ 36 6862; Arequipa 314; ☾ 24hr)
A well-stocked pharmacy.
Hospital Nacional Manuel Nuñez Butrón (☎ 36
9286, 36 9696, 35 1021, 35 2931; Av El Sol 1022;
☾ 7:30am-2:30pm) OK option, but better medical
services are available in Juliaca (see p189).

MONEY

Bolivianos can be exchanged in Puno or at the
border near Yunguyo; rates vary so ask travelers coming from Bolivia which is currently the
best choice. You'll find an ATM inside Terminal Terrestre that accepts most bank cards and
dispenses US dollars and nuevos soles.
BCP (Lima at Grau) Visa/Amex/MasterCard ATM and gives
Visa cash advances.
Interbank (Lima 444) Global ATM and changes traveler's
checks.

POST & TELEPHONE

Serpost (Moquegua 267; ☾ 8am-8pm Mon-Sat) Northeast of the Plaza de Armas.
Telefónica-Perú (cnr Moquegua & Federico More) Office
stays open late, but phone calls from internet cafés near
the Plaza de Armas are typically cheaper.

TOURIST INFORMATION

The website www.titicacaalmundo.com has
good general information on the area.

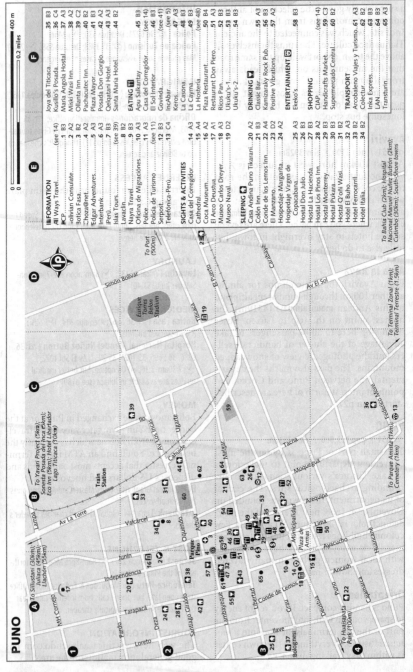

PUNO

INFORMATION
All Ways Travel	(see 14)
BCP	1 B3
Bolivian Consulate	2 A2
Botica Fasa	3 B2
Choza@net	4 A2
Edgar Adventures	5 A3
Interbank	6 A3
Perú	7 B3
Islas Tours	(see 39)
Lavacín	8 B2
Nayra Travel	9 B3
Oficina de Migraciónes	10 A3
Police	11 A3
Policía de Turismo	(see 11)
Serpost	12 B3
Telefónica-Perú	13 C4

SIGHTS & ACTIVITIES
Casa del Corregidor	14 A3
Cathedral	15 A4
Coca Museum	16 A2
El Arco Deustua	17 A1
Museo Carlos Dreyer	18 A3
Museo Naval	19 D2

SLEEPING
Casa Andina Puno Tikarani	20 A2
Colón Inn	21 B3
Conde de los Lemos Inn	22 A4
El Manzano	23 D2
Hospedaje Margarita	24 A2
Hospedaje Virgen de Copacabana	25 A3
Hostal Don Julio	26 B3
Hostal La Hacienda	27 B3
Hostal Los Pinos Inn	28 A3
Hostal Monterrey	29 B3
Hostal Q'oñi Wasi	30 B3
Hotel El Buho	31 B2
Hotel Ferrocarril	32 A3
Hotel Italia	34 B2
Joya del Titicaca	35 B3
Kusillo's Posada	36 C4
Maria Angola Hostal	37 A3
Miski Wasi Inn	38 A2
Ollanta Inn	39 C2
Pachacutec Inn	40 B2
Plaza Mayor	41 B3
Posada Don Giorgio	42 A2
Qelqatani Hotel	43 A3
Santa Maria Hotel	44 B2

EATING
Apu Salkantay	45 B3
Casa del Corregidor	(see 14)
El Sol Interior	46 A3
Govinda	(see 41)
IncAbar	(see 5)
Keros	47 A3
La Casona	48 B3
La Cayma	49 B3
La Hostería	(see 48)
Plaza Restaurant	50 B4
Restaurant Don Piero	51 A3
Ricos Pan	52 B3
Ukuku's-1	53 B3
Ukuku's-2	54 B3

DRINKING
Classic Bar	55 A3
Kamizaraky Rock Pub	56 B3
Positive Vibrations	57 A2

ENTERTAINMENT
Ekeko's	58 B3

SHOPPING
CIAP	(see 14)
Handicrafts Market	59 C3
Supermercado Central	60 B2

TRANSPORT
Arcobaleno Viajes y Turismo	61 A3
Colectur	62 B2
Inka Express	63 B3
LAN	64 B3
Transturin	65 A3

iPerú (☎ 36 5088; iperupuno@promperu.gob.pe; Plaza de Armas, cnr Lima & Deustua; ⏱ 8:30am-7:30pm) Puno's helpful, if ruthlessly efficient, tourist office. Also runs Indecopi, the tourist protection agency, which registers complaints against travel agencies and hotels.

TRAVEL AGENCIES

All Ways Travel (☎ 35 3979; www.titicacaperu.com; Deustua 576) This agency run by multilingual staff has a decently responsible attitude toward the islanders.

Edgar Adventures (☎ 35 3444; www.edgaradventures .com; Lima 328) An agency run by knowledgeable folks.

Islas Tours (☎ 952 1093; islastours@hotmail.com; Ollanta Inn, Ilo E-1) A family-run outfit offering typical island and south-shore tours.

Nayra Travel (☎ 36 4774, 975 1818; www.nayratravel .com; Office 105, Lima 419) An agency offering personalized service, especially for off-the-beaten-track destinations.

Dangers & Annoyances

Puno's high altitude gives it extreme weather conditions. Nights here get especially cold, particularly during the winter months of June to August, when temperatures can drop well below freezing. Despite the cold, the sun is very strong at this altitude and sunburn is a common problem. The elevation also means that travelers arriving directly from the coast run a real risk of getting *soroche* (altitude sickness; see p534). Plan on spending some time in Arequipa (2350m) or Cuzco (3326m) first to acclimatize, or take it very easy after arrival in Puno.

Attacks on travelers have been reported on the outskirts of Puno. Exercise caution there, even during the day.

Sights & Activities

On the western flank of the Plaza de Armas is Puno's baroque **cathedral** (admission free; ⏱ 7:30-11am & 3-6pm), which was completed in 1757. The interior is more spartan than you'd expect after seeing the well-sculpted façade, though there is a silver-plated altar that, following a 1964 visit by Pope Paul VI, has a Vatican flag to its right.

Just off the plaza is the 17th-century **Casa del Corregidor** (☎ 35 1921; www.casadelcorregidor.com .pe; Deustua 576; admission free; ⏱ 10am-10pm Tue-Fri, 10am-2:30pm & 5-10pm Sat 21 Jan-20 Dec, also 10am-2:30pm & 5-10pm Sun May-Oct), one of Puno's oldest houses, which has a cultural center and café-bar

---

THE YAVARI PROJECT

The much-loved **Yavari** (☎ 36 9329; www.yavari.org; suggested donation US$6; ⏱ 8am-5:30pm) is the oldest steamship on Lake Titicaca. In 1862 the *Yavari* and its sister ship, the *Yapura,* were built in Birmingham, England, of iron parts – a total of 2766 for the two vessels. These were shipped around Cape Horn to Arica, from where they were moved by train to Tacna, before being hauled by mule over the Andes to Puno – an incredible undertaking that took six years to complete.

The ships were assembled in Puno and the *Yavari* was launched on Christmas Day 1870. The *Yapura* was later renamed the *BAP Puno* and became a Peruvian Navy medical ship; it can still be seen in Puno. Both had coal-powered steam engines, but due to a shortage of coal, the engines were powered by dried llama dung! In 1914 the *Yavari* was further modified with a unique Bolinder four-cylinder, hot-bulb, semidiesel engine.

After long years of service, the ship was decommissioned by the Peruvian Navy and the hull was left to rust on the lakeshore. In 1982, Englishwoman Meriel Larken visited the forgotten boat and decided it was a piece of history that could and should be saved. She formed the Yavari Project to buy and restore the vessel, and was fortunate in gaining the royal support of Britain's Prince Philip as well as finding the perfect captain in the enthusiastic Carlos Saavedra, formerly of the Peruvian Navy.

Now open as a museum, the *Yavari* is moored by the Sonesta Posada Hotel del Inca (catch almost any minivan heading northbound along Av el Sol, US$0.15). The captain happily gives guided tours of the ship and, with prior notice, enthusiasts may be able to see the engine fired up. In 1999, to mark the restoration of the engine, the *Yavari* left port under her own power for the first time in nearly half a century, and in the foreseeable future the vessel should be ready for passage across Lake Titicaca.

The Yavari Project is always looking for support in the way of money and volunteers. To send donations and receive information, contact the **Yavari Project** (☎ /fax 44-208-874-0583; info@yavari .org; 61 Mexfield Rd, London, SW15 2RG, UK) or call direct to the captain in Puno.

(see p199). The word *corregidor* refers to the Spanish colonial position of governor, judge and tax collector. This historical monument also served as a chaplaincy, and its porch is made of the same type of stone as the town's cathedral.

Around the corner is the small but exquisitely curated **Museo Carlos Dreyer** (www.museo dreyer.com; Conde de Lemos 281; foreigner US$5, Peruvian adult/student US$1.40/0.60; 10am-10pm). It houses a collection of precious archaeological artifacts and colonial art that was bequeathed to the city upon the owner's death. Upstairs there's a full-scale model of a *chullpa* as seen at archaeological sites around Puno, such as Sillustani and Cutimbo.

Toward the port, the **Museo Naval** (Titicaca at Av Fl Sol; 8am-5pm Mon-Fri, 9am-1pm Sat & Sun) has a

fascinating if tiny exhibit on navigating the lake, from rudimentary reed boats up to 19th-century steamers. The Spanish-speaking staff will show you around for a tip.

Puno's tiny **Coca Museum** (36 5087; www .cocamuseo.com; Deza 301; admission by donation; 9am-1pm & 3-8pm) is also worth a peek. Although the exhibits created by an Aymara family are less extensive than at the more-famous coca museum in La Paz, Bolivia, the displays here are still stimulating, as is the gift shop.

A 10-minute walk west of the Plaza de Armas brings you to **Huajsapata Park** atop a little hill crowned by a larger-than-life white statue of the first Inca Manco Capac looking out over the legendary site of his birth. The view is excellent but do not walk here alone as several robberies have been reported. The

---

FIESTAS & FOLKLORE AROUND LAKE TITICACA

Puno is often said to be the folklore capital of Peru, boasting as many as 300 traditional dances and celebrating numerous fiestas throughout the year. Although they often occur during celebrations of Catholic feast days, many dances have their roots in pre-colonial celebrations usually tied in with the agricultural calendar. The dazzlingly ornate and imaginative costumes worn on these occasions are often worth more than an entire household's everyday clothes, and range from strikingly grotesque masks and animal costumes to glittering sequined uniforms.

Accompanying musicians play a host of traditional instruments, from Spanish-influenced brass and string to percussion and wind instruments that have changed little since Inca times. The ancient instruments include *tinyas* (wooden hand drums) and *wankaras* (larger drums formerly used in battle), and of course there has to be a chorus of *zampoñas* (panpipes), which range from tiny, high-pitched instruments to huge bass panpipes almost as tall as the musician. Keep an eye out for *flautas* (flutes), from simple bamboo pennywhistles, called *quenas*, to large blocks that look as though they've been hollowed out of a tree trunk. The most esoteric is the *piruru*, which is traditionally carved from the wing bone of an Andean condor.

Seeing street fiestas can be planned, or can simply be a matter of luck. Some celebrations are held in one town and not in another or, at other times, the whole region lets loose. Ask at the tourist office in Puno about any fiestas in the surrounding area while you're in town. The following festivals mentioned are particularly important in the Lake Titicaca region, but many country-wide celebrations are used as an excuse for a party, too.

La Virgen de la Candelaria is one of the most spectacular and is spread out for several days around the actual date (February 2), depending upon which day of the week Candlemas falls. If it falls on a Sunday to Tuesday, things get under way the previous Saturday; if it falls on a Wednesday to Friday, things get going the following Saturday. Puno Week (the first week of November), centered on Puno Day (November 5), is also celebrated in style and marks the legendary birth of Manco Capac, the first Inca.

No list of regional holidays and fiestas could ever be exhaustive. Most are celebrated for several days before and after the actual day, including Epiphany (January 6); the Feast of St John the Baptist (March 8); Alacitas (May 2), with a miniature handicrafts fair in Puno; Las Cruces (May 3–4), with celebrations on Isla Taquile and in Huancané; the Feast of St James (July 25), celebrated mostly on Isla Taquile; and Our Lady of Mercy (September 24). All of these festivals feature traditional music and dancing, as well as merry mayhem of all sorts.

If you plan to visit during any of these festivals, either make reservations in advance or show up a few days early, and expect to pay premium rates for lodgings.

same applies to the walk to **El Arco Deusta** (Independencia cuadra 2), an arch built to commemorate war heroes, which has good views.

Although the frothy green waters of the lake make going for a swim unappealing, the **Bahía Club** (admission US$1.50) has a pool 2km outside town towards Chimú.

Tours & Guides

It pays to shop around for agencies in Puno. Several of the cheaper tour agencies have reputations for ripping off the islanders of Amantaní and Taquile so ask how your money will be distributed. Also beware of street touts hanging around the popular gringo hotels and on the train from Cuzco. Never part with your money until you are in a hotel or travel agency or you may never see the guide again.

Even with the better agencies, the island-hopping tours are often disappointing, even exploitative. We strongly recommend that you take time to do it yourself instead. Ask around (eg at your guesthouse) to hire a local guide, preferably someone with family ties to the islands, then simply go down to the docks early in the morning and get on the next boat headed to the island you want to visit with your guide.

No tour operator can ever be 100% recommended, but see p195 for well-established travel agencies.

In the foreseeable future, the historic steamship *Yavari* (see p195) will offer pleasure cruises on Lake Titicaca. For waterborne tours to Bolivia, see p200. For sightseeing bus tours to Cuzco, see p201.

Sleeping

The prices given here are for the high season (June to August) and during fiestas. Prices drop to as little as half during other months, and bargaining almost always reaps rewards. If you're the kind of person who runs colder than most, pay extra for a room with heating.

BUDGET

Some barest-bones hostels in Puno have only cold showers, which can be painful at this altitude. If you want to economize yet avoid freezing off any appendages, use the public hot showers dotted around town. Most of the following budget-traveler haunts drop their prices especially low outside of high season and major festivals.

Hospedaje Virgen de Copacabana (☎ 36 3766; Ilave 228; dm US$4.50) This friendly, if darkish and ramshackle, HI-affiliated hostel has clean, homely rooms with shared bathrooms, tucked off a side street along a narrow passageway. You may have trouble finding the often absent staff, though.

El Manzano (☎ 36 4697; www.gratisweb.com/peru _lodgemanzano/hospedaje.htm; El Puerto 449; s/d/tr with shared bathroom US$5/10/12, s/d US$8/14, all incl breakfast) Highly recommended by Lonely Planet readers, this clean, family-run guesthouse is located near the port and has a flowery courtyard. All of the simple accommodations come with woolen blankets and generous breakfasts. The small on-site café offers room service too – bonus!

Santa María Hotel (☎ 36 8608; Ugarte 171; s/d with shared bathroom US$5/8, s/d/tr incl breakfast US$10/13/18) A personable choice, the Santa María has smart if spartan rooms and 24-hour hot water. Rooms without bathrooms are uncarpeted and much more basic.

Hostal Monterrey (☎ 35 1691; Lima 441; s/d/tr with shared bathroom US$7/11/15, s/d/tr from US$10/20/30) The Monterrey is right in the thick of things on the main pedestrianized boulevard, Calle Lima. The hot showers may have erratic hours, and rooms without bathrooms are basic compared to those with, which are very comfortable and boast cable TV. Expect ambient noise from neighboring nightclubs.

Hostal Q'oñi Wasi (☎ 36 5784; qoniwasi@mundomail .net; Av La Torre 119; s/d with shared bathroom US$7.50/12/18, s/d/tr US$10.50/21/24) The small, quirky Q'oñi Wasi has snug, if rundown, older rooms, electric showers, common kitchen and staff who are used to the shoestring backpacker crowd. Maybe not the best value in town, but a decent crash pad nonetheless. French spoken.

Kusillo's Posada (☎ 36 4579; kusillos@latinmail.com; Federico More 162; s/d incl breakfast US$9/15) Run by the indefatigable Jenny Juño and her wonderful family, this heartwarming homestay has cozy rooms with electric showers. It's not far from the bus stations, just a short walk southeast of the Plaza de Armas.

Hostal Los Pinos Inn (☎ 36 7398; hostalpinos@hotmail .com; Tarapacá 182; s/d US$10/15) A recommended budget guesthouse, Los Pinos has large, spotless rooms with wool blankets, lukewarm water and cable TV, but they tend to get chilly at night. Ask for one facing away from the noisy street to ensure a quiet night's sleep.

Also recommended:

Hotel El Buho (☎ 36 6122; Lambayeque 142; s/d/tr US$9/13.50/16.50) Decent rooms away from the plaza have hot water, phones and national TV. There's a restaurant, café and bar.

Hospedaje Margarita (☎ 35 2820; Tarapacá 130; s/d incl breakfast US$10/15) Long-established choice has cozy rooms with national TV. Limited hot showers.

Pachacutec Inn (☎ 36 4827; Arbulu 235; s/d incl breakfast US$11/15.50) Well-cared-for rooms with hot showers, but the hosts are not always accommodating.

There are dozens more cheap guesthouses on streets east of the Plaza de Armas, as well as a secure, if very basic, *hospedaje* at Terminal Terrestre for those arriving by bus at odd hours.

MIDRANGE

Hostal Don Julio (☎ 36 3358; hostaldonjulio@hotmail.com; Tacna 336; s/d/tr incl breakfast US$15/20/25) Don Julio has a relaxed atmosphere and is set back from the road. Spacious, if blandly modern, rooms have cable TV and heating on request.

Joya del Titicaca (☎ 35 1823; joyadeltiticaca_hotel@ hotmail.com; Arequipa 522; s/d/tr with shared bathroom US$15/20/30, s/d/tr US$36/46/60) Recommended by readers, the Joya del Titicaca has fairly good quality rooms with alpaca furnishings and cable TV. French, Italian and some English are spoken.

Ollanta Inn (☎ 36 6743; ollanta_inn@latinmail.com; Ilo E-1; s/d incl breakfast US$20/30) Handy to the central market, this family-run small hotel inhabits a narrow, multistory tower. It has warm, cozy and extremely tidy rooms with flowery décor, 24-hour hot water and cable TV.

Miski Wasi Inn (☎ 36 5861; miskiwasiinn@hotmail .com; Santiago Giraldo 177; s/d US$20/30) Another well-kept small hotel, Miski Wasi is located at the quieter end of Calle Lima, a few blocks away from the Plaza de Armas. The light-filled rooms have hot showers, cable TV and heating. Service is extremely professional.

Posada Don Giorgio (☎ 36 3648; dongiorgio@titica calake.com; Tarapacá 238; s/d/tr incl breakfast US$25/35/45) An excellent choice with a mellow interior courtyard and exceptionally comfy rooms, Don Giorgio is still small enough to provide personal service. Rooms have phones, cable TV and deep armchairs. Beware of street noise, however.

Hostal Pukara (☎ 36 8448; pukara@terra.com.pe; Libertad 328; s/d incl breakfast US$25/40) This quirky, rapidly aging hotel may be noisy and service

may be lackadaisical, but it leaves no corner undecorated, with an eye-catching four-story-high relief in the entrance, plus murals, unusual tiling and other touches throughout the hallways. Rooms are heated, have hot showers, cable TV and phone, and there's a glass-covered rooftop café.

Hotel Ferrocarril (☎ 35 1752; www.hotelferrocar ril.com; Av La Torre 185; s/d/tr incl breakfast US$33/44/55) Though it has seen grander days, this large railway hotel retains old-fashioned, attentive service and has comfortable rooms with cable TV, phone, hot showers and heating. Buffet meals are served in the restaurant, and boxed lunches are available for day-trippers and those taking the train to Cuzco.

Hotel Italia (☎ 36 7706; www.hotelitaliaperu.com; Valcárcel 122; s/d/tr incl breakfast buffet US$33/44/55) Rooms have cable TV, hot showers and heating but vary in quality at this large, well-established midrange hostelry. The quiet environs are a respite from the chaotic street outside, and the restaurant, which serves international and vegetarian dishes, is often suffused with sunshine.

Conde de los Lemos Inn (☎ 36 9898; www.condelem osinn.com; Puno 675-681; s/d/tr US$35/45/60) Highly recommended by travelers for its personable staff and high standards, this small hotel with airy, light-filled rooms (with bathtubs) is a short walk west of the Plaza de Armas, away from central Puno's hurly-burly.

Maria Angola Hostal (☎ 36 4596; Bolognesi 190; s/d/tr US$36/53/65) Situated away from the hustle of the center, the funky Maria Angola has a fixation with intricately carved wood paneling and doors. It offers big reductions in low season.

Hostal La Hacienda (☎ 35 6109; www.lahacienda puno.com; Deustua 297; s/d incl breakfast US$43/55) This excellent little colonial-style hotel has an intimate patio covered in trailing plants, and warm-colored rooms that boast cable TV, heating and phone. The upper stories have lake views.

Qelqatani Hotel (☎ 36 6172; www.qelqatani.com; Tarapacá 355; s/d/tr/ste incl breakfast buffet US$43/56/72/85) Qelqatani is a large, modern hotel with helpful staff and spacious, though worn, rooms with heaters and cable TV. Bathrooms are first-class and have a tub and shower.

Plaza Mayor (☎ 36 6089; www.plazamayorhostal.com; Deustua 342; s/d/tr/ste incl breakfast buffet US$43/56/72/85) The Plaza Mayor is a high-class, newly renovated hotel right by the Plaza de Armas. It has a glamorous entrance and very comfy carpeted rooms with heaters, telephones and bathtubs. Service can be almost ridiculously attentive.

Colón Inn (☎ 35 1432; www.titicaca-peru.com/colon1e .htm; Tacna 290; s/d/tr US$45/55/70) This colonial-style property was formerly a Best Western chain hotel. It has classy, if overly flowery, rooms with all mod cons (including heating), as well as a tiny indoor patio dripping with plants, and a restaurant offering room service.

TOP END
Casa Andina Puno Tikarani (☎ 36 7803; www.casa -andina.com; Independencia 185; d from US$63) A short walk from the plaza, this Peruvian chain hotel is in sparkling nick, with good, firm beds, quality furnishings and heating. Walls are decked out in bold, primary colors, and stone, tiling and modern furnishings are harmoniously combined. There are also lofty public areas for lounging, a restaurant and wi-fi internet access. Casa Andina has two other hotels in Puno; see the website for details.

Eco Inn (☎ 36 5525; www.ecoinnpuno.com; Chulluni 195, Huaje; s/d incl breakfast buffet US$65/70; 🖵) Never mind the stark exterior: the small, friendly Eco Inn has over 60 exceptionally bright and airy rooms, with large windows, individually controlled heaters, telephones and cable TV. There's a glass-walled restaurant looking onto an attached enclosure with pet alpacas. It's on the quieter outskirts of town.

Sonesta Posada del Inca (☎ 36 4111; www.son esta.com/peru_puno; Sequicentenario 610, Huaje; s/d/tr US$105/115/140) This relaxing Posada chain hotel is about 5km from Puno on the shores of Lake Titicaca. Half of the tastefully decorated 62 rooms have lake views, and all have cable TV, telephone and heating. The reputable restaurant and bar Inkafé offers lake-view dining. Extensive lawns run down to where the steamship *Yavari* is moored (see p195). Rates drop 25% between December and July.

Hotel Libertador Lago Titicaca (☎ 36 7780, in Lima 01-442 0166; www.libertador.com.pe; Isla Esteves; r US$140-190, ste US$190-260; 🖵) This local landmark dominates its own private island in the western part of Lake Titicaca. The island is connected to Puno by a 5km road over a causeway. Taxis charge about US$3 for the trip, or frequent *combis* leave from Av El Sol at the northeastern edge of Puno (US$0.30). Half of the 111 luxurious rooms and all

of the dozen suites have fabulous views out over the lake, plus there are beautiful gardens on the island's slopes and a collection of pet llamas. There is also a good restaurant, bar and gift shop.

Eating
Tourist haunts huddle together on the glitzy pedestrian street Calle Lima. Note that many don't advertise their set meals (*el menú*), which are cheaper than ordering à la carte. During the evening, many restaurants welcome visitors with a flaming cauldron in the doorway to warm your hands.

Ricos Pan (Moquegua 326; items US$0.45-3; 🕑 8am-9:30pm Mon-Sat) Puno's best bakery is a quiet find for lovers of Peruvian comfort food, especially melt-in-your-mouth cakes. There are several branches scattered around town, but this one is most popular with locals.

Casa del Corregidor (Deustua 576; items US$1-3; 🕑 10am-10pm Tue-Fri, 10am-2:30pm & 5-10pm Sat 21 Jan-20 Dec, also 10am-2:30pm & 5-10pm Sun May-Oct) This café, in a 17th-century colonial house (see p195), is a great place to hobnob with local expats and artists over a cappuccino and pastry. There's a decent book exchange and newspapers to browse.

Govinda (Deustua 312; 3-course menús US$1.50-2; 🕑 noon-8pm) True to form, the Hare Krishna-run Govinda serves up its hippie vegetarian *menús* without burning a hole in your pocket. The environs are cramped and dank, though.

El Sol Interior (Libertad 352; mains US$1.80-4.75; 🕑 11:30am-9:30pm) This holistic, health-minded vegetarian restaurant has amazing Peruvian fake-meat dishes, with a cornucopia of sides such as quinoa and locally grown vegetables, plus Amazonian-style jungle juices and potions.

Restaurant Don Piero (Lima 364; mains US$3-5; 🕑 lunch & dinner) Don Piero doesn't match the other restaurants on Calle Lima for glitz, but has excellent local food and an elegant simplicity; the number of locals dining is testament to its quality. There's live music after 7pm on some evenings.

La Casona (Lima 517; mains US$3.60-7.50; 🕑 9am-10pm) Calling itself a 'restaurant-museum,' La Casona retains an old-fashioned 1920s air with a collection of antique irons on the walls. Impeccably mannered waiters serve regional Peruvian fare, especially lovingly prepared fish dishes.

LAKE TITICACA

La Hostería (Lima 501; mains US$3.60-7.50, 3-course menús US$4.50; ☺ closed lunch Sun) Within its almost tropically thatched walls, La Hostería dishes up great apple pie, chocolate cake and coffee. The space around its low, semicircular bar is heated, a plus in Puno.

Keros (Lambayeque 131; mains US$3.60-7.50; 3-course menús US$4.50; ☺ closed lunch Sun) Though it may look deserted, low-key Keros has a full bar and serves variations on typical local dishes, such as excellent trout with wine and almond sauce. It's motto is 'Eat like an Inca, pay like a peasant.'

IncAbar (Lima 348; mains US$4.50-7; ☺ closed lunch Sat) This stylishly low-slung restaurant does creative international food with a local twist, such as alpaca with whisky or curried chicken with papaya.

Plaza Restaurant (Puno 425; mains US$4.50-9; ☺ lunch & dinner) This large, formally staffed restaurant on the plaza has a surreptitiously jazzy feel with subtle leopard-print cloths and mirrored walls. It reputedly serves great fish dishes.

Ukuku's (2nd fl, Pasaje Grau 172; mains US$5-7.50; ☺ 10am-10pm) Crowds of travelers and locals thaw out in this toasty restaurant that dishes up good local and Andean food (don't miss the alpaca steak with baked apples), as well as pizzas, pastas, Asian-style vegetarian fare and espresso drinks – all of which are top-notch. There's a second, less-popular branch at Libertad 216.

La Cayma (Arequipa 410; meals US$5.50-9; ☺ lunch & dinner) Hidden well away from Calle Lima, this courtyard restaurant doubles as a local art gallery. Here you can dine on nouveau Andean fusion fare while gazing at impressive photographs of ancient ruins. The atmosphere is as warm as a ski hut, and there's a good drinks list.

Apu Salkantay (Lima 425; mains US$5.50-9; ☺ lunch & dinner) This rustic, popular place serves up bland touristy dishes (such as *flambre salkantay*, which includes alpaca, trout and sweet potato), but has live *música folklórica* every night.

Puno's crowded Supermercado Central is a great place to stock up, but watch out for pickpockets.

Drinking & Entertainment

Central Puno's nightlife is geared toward tourists, with plenty of lively bars scattered around the bright lights on Calle Lima, where touts hand out free drink coupons. Elsewhere

a few traditional *peñas* advertise nightly performances of *música folklórica*.

Kamizaraky Rock Pub (Pasaje Grau 158; ☺ 5pm-late) With our vote for southern Peru's best watering hole, this place feels like your best friend's living room. It has a classic rock soundtrack, unbelievably cool bartenders and liquor-infused coffee drinks essential for staying warm during Puno's bone-chilling nights.

Ekeko's (2nd fl, Lima 355; ☺ 5pm-late) Travelers and locals alike tend to gravitate to this tiny, ultraviolet dance floor splashed with psychedelic murals and moving to a thumping mixture of modern beats and old favorites, from salsa to techno trance, that can be heard several blocks away. Movies are shown at around 5pm daily.

Classic Bar (Tarapacá 338; ☺ 5pm-late) Off the beaten path, this side-alley bar opens up into a hangar-sized, yet convivial, space with a familiar soundtrack of travelers' favorite tunes and a long drinks list. It's a cool, unhurried place to chat with local rockers.

Positive Vibrations (Lambayeque 127; ☺ 8pm-late) This 'rock 'n' reggae' travelers' haunt is just off Lima. The enthusiastic young staff all dream of being DJs someday, and friendly service lives up to the promise of the bar's name.

Shopping

Puno is a good town to get quality woolen and alpaca sweaters at a fair price. Stop by **CIAP** (Deustua 576; ☺ 9am-7pm), a local nonprofit cooperative inside the Casa del Corregidor, just off the Plaza de Armas. More typical tourist goods are sold at the open-air **handicrafts market** (cnr Cahuide & Deustua) and **Artesanias La Cholilla** (Lima), the indoor shopping complex on Calle Lima just north of Deustua.

Getting There & Away

AIR

The nearest airport is in Juliaca, about 45km away. See above for more information on flights. Several travel agents in Puno will sell tickets and provide a shuttle service direct to the airport for about US$3 per person, though these services can be painfully slow. **LAN** (☎ 36 7227; Tacna 299) is currently the only airline with an office in Puno.

BOAT

Boats from the Puno dock leave for various islands on the lake (see p203). Tickets bought directly from the boats at the dock are invariably cheaper than those bought from agencies in town.

There are no passenger ferries across the lake from Puno to Bolivia, but tour-bus services connect with expensive hydrofoil and catamaran services on the Bolivian side of the border. **Transturin** (☎ 35 2771; www.transturin.com; Ayacucho 148) offers catamaran trips to Bolivia (US$120 to US$180). Groups leave Puno by bus between 6am and 6:30am and go to Copacabana, Bolivia, from where a catamaran sails to the Isla del Sol for a quick but interesting visit before continuing to the Bolivian port of Chua and on to La Paz by bus, arriving around 5:30pm. This service includes hotel transfers, lunch and a guide. Transturin also offers longer trips including an overnight stay and buffet breakfast on board a catamaran with comfortable private cabins (US$185 to US$235). Last-minute discount tickets may be available (US$70/90 for day/overnight tours). These trips can also be done in reverse from La Paz, where there's another **Transturin office** (☎ 591-2-242 2222; info@transturin.com; Alfredo Ascarrunz 2518, Sopocachi).

Arcobaleno Viajes y Turismo (☎ 35 1052, 35 1884; Lambayeque 355) is the Puno agent for **Crillon Tours** (www.titicaca.com), which has thrice-weekly tours to Bolivia via Isla del Sol and the Bolivian port of Huatajata, departing Puno at 7:30am on Tuesday, Thursday and Saturday and arriving in La Paz around 6:30pm. Full-day tours cost US$175, while the two-day tour (US$250) overnights in a hotel in Copacabana, Bolivia.

BUS

About 2km southeast of the Plaza de Armas, **Terminal Terrestre** (☎ 36 4733; Primero de Mayo 703) houses Puno's long-distance bus companies. There is a departure tax of US$0.30 for all passengers.

The roads to Arequipa and Cuzco are now paved, and fast and efficient services run to Lima (US$11 to US$45, 18 to 21 hours), Arequipa (US$3.60 to US$7.50, five to six hours) and Cuzco (US$4.50 to US$10.50, six to seven hours), almost all going via Juliaca (US$0.60, one hour). To get to Tacna (US$7.50, 10 hours) via Moquegua, **San Martín** (☎ 36 3631) has a few daily and overnight *económico* buses that stop at Desaguadero on the Bolivian border. Warning: this is a rough trip that's only for hardy shoestring travelers. It's far more

comfortable to go to Arequipa, then change to another bus bound for Tacna.

Inka Express (☎ 36 5654; www.inkaexpress.com; Tacna 314B) and other companies run luxury tour buses sporting panoramic windows to Cuzco, with departures every morning. The splurge-worthy US$25 fare includes beverages and an English-speaking tour guide, who talks about sites that are briefly visited en route, including Pucará (p192), Abra la Raya (p193), Raqchi (p279) and Andahuaylillas (p279).

Minibuses to Juliaca (US$0.50, one hour), towns along Lake Titicaca's south shore (see p215) and also the Bolivian border (see p214) leave from **Terminal Zonal** (Simón Bolívar), a few blocks northwest of Terminal Terrestre.

TRAIN

Following the suspension of services to Arequipa, Puno's **train station** (☎ 36 9179, 35 1041; www.perurail.com; Av La Torre 224; ◷ 7am-noon & 1-5pm Mon-Fri, 7-11am Sat & Sun) only has trains to Cuzco via Juliaca.

Fares to Cuzco have skyrocketed in recent years – they are now US$119 for first-class 'Andean Explorer' tickets, which include a glass-walled observation car and complimentary lunch, or US$17 for non-reservable seats in the more basic 'Backpacker' carriage where drinks and snacks are sold.

The train is scheduled to leave at 8am daily, supposedly arriving at 5:30pm in Cuzco, though it's often hours late. Departures are also subject to whether there are enough passengers, so the line suffers routine cancellations. Extra trains occasionally run for group bookings made by travel agents. It is therefore essential to check schedules in person at the station.

The journey to Cuzco has great views along the shores of Lake Titicaca and of the Andes, but note that even in the best class, seats are not very comfortable and the ride is known for being a bit of a bone-shaker. Most travelers now take the faster (and almost as scenic) bus services to Cuzco.

Getting Around

A short taxi ride anywhere in town costs about US$1. One taxi company to call is **Movil** (☎ 36 8000). *Mototaxis* are a fun way to get around and are cheaper than ordinary taxis, but make sure that the negotiated fare is per ride, not per person.

AROUND PUNO
Sillustani
Sitting on rolling hills on the Lake Umayo peninsula, the funerary towers of **Sillustani** (admission US$2; ☺ sunrise-sunset) stand out for miles against the desolate altiplano landscape.

The ancient Colla people who once dominated the Lake Titicaca area were a warlike, Aymara-speaking tribe who later became the southeastern arm of the Incas. The Colla, along with the rival Lupaca tribe, buried their nobility in funerary towers called *chullpas* that can be seen scattered widely around the hilltops of the region.

The most impressive of these towers are at Sillustani, where the tallest reaches a height of 12m. The cylindrical structures once housed the remains of complete family groups, along with plenty of food and belongings for their journey into the next world. The towers' only opening was a small hole facing east, just large enough for a person to crawl through, which would be sealed immediately after a burial. Nowadays, nothing remains of the burials. The *chullpas*, however, are well-preserved and worth seeing, both for their architecture and their awe-inspiring location. The afternoon light is the best for photography, though the site can get crowded at this time.

The outside walls of the towers are made from massive coursed blocks reminiscent of Inca stonework, but considered even more complicated (perhaps partly because conservationists are still struggling to rebuild some of them). Carved but unplaced blocks and a ramp used to raise them are among the points of interest at the site, and you can also see the site of the makeshift quarry. A few of the blocks are decorated, including the well-known carving of a lizard on one of the *chullpas* closest to the car park. There is a small on-site museum and gift shop, too. Dress warmly and bring sunblock.

Sillustani is partially encircled by the sparkling Lago Umayo (3890m), which is home to a wide variety of plants and Andean waterbirds, plus a small island with vicuñas (threatened wild relatives of llamas). Birders should particularly watch for the giant Andean coot, white-tufted and silvery grebes, puna ibis, Andean goose, black-crowned night-heron, speckled and puna teals, yellow-billed pintail, Andean lapwing, and Andean gull (though it's strange to see a 'sea' gull so far from the ocean!) and, if you're very lucky, one of the

three species of flamingo found in the Andean highlands.

Travel agencies run tours to Sillustani that leave Puno at around 2:30pm daily and cost at least US$7.50, including the site entrance fee. The round-trip takes about 3½ hours and allows you about 1½ hours at the ruins plus a stop at a specially built 'traditional' homestead nearby.

If you'd prefer more time at the site, hire a private taxi for US$15 with waiting time. Or to save money, catch any bus to Juliaca and ask to be let off where the road splits. From there, occasional *combis* run to the village of Atuncolla (US$0.60, 10 minutes), a 4km walk from the ruins. During high season, *combis* will occasionally continue to the ruins, but don't bank on this.

Cutimbo
Just over 20km from Puno, this dramatic windswept **site** (admission US$2; ☺ sunrise-sunset) has an extraordinary position atop a table-topped volcanic hill surrounded by a fertile plain. Its modest number of well-preserved *chullpas*, built by the Colla, Lupaca and Inca cultures, come in both square and cylindrical shapes. You can still see the ramps used to build them. Look closely and you'll find several monkeys, pumas and snakes carved into the structures.

This remote place receives few visitors, which makes it as enticing as it is potentially dangerous for independent travelers, especially women. Go in a group and keep an eye out for local nogoodniks who wait to prey on tourists, especially by hiding behind rocks at the top of the 2km trail leading steeply uphill from the road.

Combis en route to Laraqueri leave the cemetery by Parque Amista, 1km from the center of Puno (US$0.60, 30 minutes). You can't miss the signposted site, which is on the left-hand side of the road – just ask the driver where to get off. A taxi to both Sillustani and Cutimbo will cost approximately US$24 with waiting time.

Llachón
☎ 051 / pop 1300 / elev 3820m
Almost 75km northeast of Puno, this pretty little village community is found on the peninsula of Capachica, which offers some fantastic views and short hikes to surrounding pre-Inca sites. It's an area that thankfully sees very few tourists. With advance notice, families

welcome visitors into their homes, provide basic accommodations and cook meals for around US$4 per person per night. Nayra Travel (see p195) can help make arrangements and explain how to get here via local buses from Puno (US$4.50, 2½ hours).

LAKE TITICACA ISLANDS

The only way to really see Lake Titicaca is to spend a few days visiting its fairy-tale islands. That said, negative impacts from tourism are already being deeply felt in many communities. When enterprising individuals from Puno first began bringing tourists to visit these remote islands, the islanders fought the invasion. It wasn't the tourists they objected to but the Puno entrepreneurs. Often justified antipathy toward tour groups and independent travelers remains. Unfortunately, there are also rare instances of thieving and begging.

If you do decide to visit the islands, do your best to be respectful and responsible. Carry out your trash, bring gifts of fresh fruits and vegetables for your host family and ensure that your tour guide or travel agency has ties to local communities and ideally shares profits. See p197 for more advice on choosing tours and guides.

If you prefer to go independently, you could also hop across the Bolivian border to the quiet town of Copacabana (p217), from where boats depart for the restful Islas del Sol and de la Luna (p218). Allow at least two days, and preferably three, for this side trip from Puno.

Whichever islands you decide to visit, remember to bring sunblock for the slow boat journey, because the intensity of the high-altitude sun bouncing off the lake can cause severe sunburn, as well as plenty of insect repellant.

Islas Flotantes

Just 5km east of Puno's harbor, the unique **floating islands** (admission US$1) of the Uros people (and often referred to as the Uros islands) are Lake Titicaca's top tourist attraction. Though their popularity has led to shocking and dismaying over-commercialization, there is still nothing quite like them to be found anywhere else in the world.

Intermarriage with the Aymara-speaking indigenous people has seen the demise of the pure-blooded Uros, who nowadays all speak Aymara. Always a small tribe, they began their unusual floating existence centuries ago in an effort to isolate themselves from the aggressive Collas and the Incas. Today, several hundred people still live on the islands and eke out a living from fishing and tourism.

The biggest of the islands contains several buildings, including an overabundance of souvenir shops. The buildings' walls are still made of *totora* (see Islands Built by Hand, below), but some of the roofs are now tin. The inhabitants of some islands have built small huts ('museums') with stuffed birds inside or observation platforms so that you can survey the surroundings from the rickety perch. Small donations are requested.

Some islands may also have elaborately designed versions of traditional tightly bundled reed boats on hand. When they are made well, these unmistakable canoe-shaped boats can carry a whole family for several months before beginning to rot. You can usually persuade one of the Uros to give you a joyride, but be prepared to pay and give a tip for taking photographs.

It's worth noting that more authentic reed islands do still exist; these are located further from Puno through a maze of small channels and can only be visited with a private boat. The islanders there continue to live in a relatively traditional fashion, and prefer not to be photographed.

There used to be a problem with begging on the Uros islands and, while this has abated, you are asked not to give candy to kids.

Getting to the Islas Flotantes is easy; just go down to the dock in Puno and within minutes you'll be asked to take a trip to the islands. You can go with the next tour

---

ISLANDS BUILT BY HAND

Peru's famous floating islands are built using the buoyant *totora* reeds that grow abundantly in the shallows of Lake Titicaca. The lives of the Uros are interwoven with these reeds, which are partially edible and are also used to make their homes and boats and the crafts they churn out for tourists. The islands are constructed from many layers of the *totora*, which are constantly replenished from the top as they rot from the bottom, so the ground is always soft and springy. Be careful not to put your foot through any rotten sections!

TAQUILE'S TRADITIONS

The island of Taquile has a particularly fascinating tradition of handicrafts, and the islanders' creations are made according to a system of deeply ingrained social customs. The menfolk wear tightly woven woolen hats that resemble floppy nightcaps, which they take great pride in knitting themselves. It's a common sight to see them wandering about the island with knitting needles in hand. These hats are closely bound up with social symbolism: men wear red hats if they are married and red-and-white hats if they are single, and different colors can denote a man's current or past social position.

The women weave thick colorful waistbands for their husbands, which when worn with their knitted caps, roughly spun white shirts and thick, calf-length black pants, give them an altogether raffish air. The women also look eye-catching in their multilayered skirts and delicately embroidered blouses. These fine garments are among the best-made traditional clothes in Peru, and can be bought in the cooperative store on the island's main plaza.

group (US$3) or hire a private boat (US$20 to US$25). Tour boats leave regularly from 7am until late afternoon according to passenger demand, but it's best to leave as early as possible to avoid being surrounded by tour groups. Pay only at the dock's official ticket booth, or the captain directly when hiring a private boat.

The standard tour, visiting the main island and one or two others, takes around two hours. Boats leave when they have 15 to 20 passengers. Many agencies in Puno will sell tickets and provide a guide from about US$6 per person, which often includes transport to the dock, but it's hardly worth the extra hassle. Trips to other islands on the lake sometimes stop at the Islas Flotantes on the way out.

Isla Taquile

Inhabited for thousands of years, **Taquile Island** (admission US$1.50), 35km east of Puno, is a tiny 7-sq-km island with a population of around 2000 people. The Quechua-speaking islanders are distinct from most of the surrounding Aymara-speaking island communities and maintain a strong sense of group identity. They rarely marry non-Taquile people, and their lives are somewhat untrammeled by the modernities of the mainland.

ORIENTATION & INFORMATION

A steep stairway of over 500 steps leads from the dock to the center of the island. The climb takes a breathless 20 minutes or more if you're not acclimatized.

A limited electricity supply was introduced to the island in the 1990s, but is still not widely available so remember to bring a flashlight.

Take in the lay of the land while it's still light as travelers have been known to get so lost in the dark that they end up roughing it for the night.

Make sure you already have lots of small bills in local currency, because change is limited and there's nowhere to exchange dollars. You may also want to bring extra money to buy some of the exquisite crafts sold in the cooperative store.

SIGHTS & ACTIVITIES

Taquile often feels like its own little world, completely detached from the rest of the earth. Its scenery is beautiful with deep, red-colored soil that, in the strong highland sunlight, contrasts with the intense blue of the lake and the glistening backdrop of Bolivia's snowy Cordillera Real on the far side of the lake. Several hills boast Inca terracing on their sides and small ruins on top. Visitors are free to wander around, exploring the ruins and enjoying the tranquility, but you can't do this on a day trip without skipping lunch or missing the returning boat, so stay overnight if you can. The island is a wonderful place to catch a sunset and gaze at the moon, which looks twice as bright in the crystalline air, rising over the breathtaking peaks of the Cordillera Real.

FESTIVALS & EVENTS

The **Fiesta de San Diego** (Feast of St James; 25 July) is a big feast day on Taquile. Dancing, music and general carousing go on for several days until the start of August, when islanders make traditional offerings to Pachamama

(Continued on page 213)

Ocean view from Parque del Amor,
Miraflores (p102), Lima

La Catedral de Lima (p93), Plaza de Armas,
Lima

Palacio Arzobispal (Archbishop's Palace; p92), Plaza de Armas, Lima

CHRIS BEALL

Burial ground, near Nazca (p142)

Monasterio de la Recoleta (p167), Arequipa

MARK DAFFEY

JEFFREY BECOM

Church façade, Yanque (p183)

Reed boat, Lake Titicaca (p203)

JANE SWEENEY

ERIC L WHEATER

Aymara woman with *totora* reeds, Lake Titicaca
(p203)

Archway on Isla Taquile (p204)

MARK DAFFEY

JUDY

Handicrafts for sale (p250), Cuzco

Templo y Convento de la Merced (p234), Cuzco

RICHARD I'ANSON

WOODS WHEAT

Plaza de Armas (p230), Cuzco

Backstreets, Cuzco (p221)

KRZYSZTOF DYDYNSKI

LEANNE WALKER

La Catedral (p230), Plaza de Armas, Cuzco

Food vendor, Cuzco (p221)

RICHARD I'ANSON

Hikers at Warmiwañusca (Dead Woman's Pass; p276), Inca Trail

MARK

WOODS WHEATCROFT

Ruins, Machu Picchu (p269)

Ruins, Machu Picchu (p269)

WOODS WHEATCROFT

JEFFREY BECOM

Mountain road between Aguas Calientes and Machu Picchu (p274)

JOHN BORTHWICK

Inca stairway, Machu Picchu (p269)

The final descent into Machu Picchu on the Inca Trail (p278)

WOODS WHEATCROFT

Machu Picchu train (p264), Ollantaytambo

MARK DAFFEY

MARK

Inca ruins (p262), Ollantaytambo

Inca ruins, Saqsaywamán (p254)

ERIC L WH

(Continued from page 204)

(Mother Earth). **Easter** and **New Year's Day** are also festive and rowdy. Many islanders go to Puno for La Virgen de Candelaria and Puno Week (see p196), when the island becomes somewhat deserted.

SLEEPING & EATING

Staying overnight on Taquile is worthwhile because tours tend to inundate the island with day-trippers between noon and 2pm, when it can be difficult to appreciate the place in its normal serene state.

At the dock, local porters are on hand to help carry your luggage for around US$3. Independent travelers will be met by a group of inhabitants next to the arch at the top of the stairs up from the dock. These islanders can arrange accommodation in familial guesthouses that sleep up to 10 people. There is a standard charge of about US$3 per person per night. Beds are basic but clean, and facilities are minimal. You will be given some blankets, but if possible bring a sleeping bag, too, as it gets very cold at night. Bathing here means doing what the locals do: washing in cold water from a bucket. Toilets are usually basic outhouses. Campers are charged about half of the cost of a bed in someone's house.

Simple restaurants in the center sell fresh trout, potatoes, rice and fried eggs. The San Santiago, on the main plaza, is a cooperatively owned restaurant, the profits from which benefit the community. Recently, more islanders have been opening their own small eateries, too. However, most close by late afternoon, so you should consider asking your host family about arranging dinner in advance. You can buy bottled drinks, and boiled tea is usually safe to drink, though it's worth bringing purifying tablets or a filter as backup.

GETTING THERE & AWAY

Passenger boats for the excruciatingly slow 35km trip to Taquile leave Puno's dock every day between 7:30am and 8:30am (US$6, three hours). Boats sometimes include a brief stop at the floating islands en route. Get to the dock early and pay the captain directly. The return trip leaves the island in the early afternoon, arriving in Puno around nightfall.

Travel agencies in Puno (p195) offer this trip for about US$9 with a guide, or US$15 with an overnight stay including accommodation and meals, though the islanders benefit much more directly from travelers who go independently. During high season, full-day tours (US$36) in fast boats are occasionally offered by upmarket hotels and the travel agencies. The companies drop you off on one side of the island and pick you up on the other side, giving you time to trek across Taquile.

Isla Amantaní

Less-frequently visited, **Amantaní Island** (admission US$1.50) is a few kilometers north of the smaller Taquile. Almost all trips to Amantaní (pop 4000) involve an overnight stay with basket-weaving islanders. Basic food and accommodations are available. The villagers sometimes organize rousing traditional dances, letting travelers dress in their traditional partying gear to dance the night away. Of course, you'll look quite comical in your hiking boots!

The island is very quiet, boasts great views and has no roads or vehicles. Several hills are topped with ruins, among the highest and best-known of which are **Pachamama** and **Pachatata** (Mother and Father Earth), which date to the Tiahuanaco culture. This was a largely Bolivian culture that appeared around Lake Titicaca and expanded rapidly between 500 BC and AD 1000. There are eight village communities on the island, each housing a cluster of adobe dwellings. As with Taquile, the islanders speak Quechua, but their culture is more heavily influenced by the Aymaras.

SLEEPING & EATING

Upon arrival, island families can find you accommodation according to a rotating system. A bed and full board costs around US$3 per person per night. Or you can stay in more comfort at the family-run **Kantuta Lodge** (☎ 81 2664, 963 6172, ask for Segundino Cari's family; www.punored.com/titicaca/amantani/img/english.html; r per person incl meals US$20). The accommodations are *hospedaje*-style, and the basic but cheery rooms have private bathrooms, striped woven bedcovers and sunset views over the lake. There's live local music some evenings in the lodge's simple **restaurant** (meals US$5).

GETTING THERE & AWAY

Boats to Amantaní leave the Puno dock between 7:30am and 8:30am most mornings (US$7.50, 3½ hours). Though many people at the dock will tell you they are from Amantaní, there was only one regular boat service genuinely run by islanders at the time of writing. Do your best to ensure that you catch the islanders' boat (thereby helping the islanders) and be sure to only pay the captain directly.

Boat connections make it easiest to travel from Puno to the Islas Flotantes then to Amantaní and on to Taquile, rather than in reverse as boats often stop at the floating islands on the way out, but not on the return trip. A daily boat from Amantaní sometimes runs to Taquile for about US$2 one way, but you can't rely on it. Another option is to take a one-day guided tour, but let your travel agency know you'll be staying on Amantaní overnight and ask them to make arrangements for your onward travel the following day.

Travel agencies in Puno (see p195) charge at least US$15 for a two-day tour to Amantaní, with a quick visit to Taquile and the floating islands. Three-day, two-night tours are also available, with the first night at Amantaní and the second at Taquile. But if you take a tour, remember that the islanders see less money that way.

Isla Suasi

This idyllic 5-acre **island** (www.islasuasi.com) is reached via the mainland village of Cambria on the north shore of Lake Titicaca. In the late 1990s, a small hotel – the only building on the island – was built here using local resources. The **hotel** (r incl meals from US$150) runs on solar power and provides modern services such as bathrooms, hot showers and heating in a rustic, stone-and-thatch structure that blends harmoniously with its surroundings. The flowering terraces almost all have lake views. There are rowboats, a sauna and a garden of native plants, herbs and vegetables. The island also hosts a few flocks of camelids.

You must book in advance to stay here, which is most easily done through the **Puno office** (☎ 051-36 5968, 962 2709; Deustua 576). Programs of two days/one night or three days/two nights are usually offered, with either land or lake transport or a combination of the two.

Isla Suasi can be used as a base to visit other islands or north-shore towns such as Moho (p192).

BORDER CROSSING: BOLIVIA VIA THE SOUTH SHORE

For many travelers, Puno and Lake Titicaca are stepping stones to Bolivia, which borders the lake to the south and east. It's a fascinating side trip that's worth your time.

There's a Bolivian consulate in Puno (p193). Visa regulations change frequently, but citizens of the USA and most European countries can stay 90 days without a visa, while citizens of Canada, Ireland, Australia and New Zealand can stay 30 days without a visa. A few other nationalities, including South Africans, require a visa in advance (usually issued for a 30-day stay).

Remember that Bolivian time is one hour ahead of Peruvian time. 'Exit taxes' are sometimes asked for at the border but these are not legal and the money only lines the official's pockets. There have also been unconfirmed reports of a scam in which police search travelers' luggage for 'fake dollars' that are then confiscated, so hide your cash before reaching the border. You are not required to visit the Peruvian police station before leaving the country, so if anyone asks you to go there with them, politely but firmly refuse.

There are two overland routes from Puno along the lake's south shore to Bolivia – via Yunguyo or Desaguadero. (The rarely used third route from Juliaca via the north shore is described on p192.) The Yunguyo route is safer, easier and more attractive, and many travelers break the trip in the chill-out Bolivian lakeshore town of Copacabana, from where the Islas del Sol and de la Luna can be visited. The unsavory Desaguadero route is nevertheless faster, slightly cheaper and more direct than Yunguyo and can be combined with a visit to the Bolivian ruins at Tiahuanaco. However, it's also less safe and rarely used by independent travelers.

Via Yunguyo

The most convenient option to get from Puno to Copacabana or La Paz is with a cross-border bus company. **Colectur** (☎ 051-35 2302; Tacna 221, Puno) has departures at 7:30am to Yunguyo, and will stop at a *casa de cambio* (foreign-exchange bureau), show you where to go for exit and entrance formalities, and then drive you to Copacabana (US$3.60, three hours), where you are met by another bus for the trip to La Paz (US$7.50, eight hours). Officials will board the bus in Copacabana and make you pay an 'entry fee' (US$0.15) even if you're just passing through town.

Anapia

Well off the beaten track, this pristine island is in Laguna de Wiñaymarca near the Bolivian border. It sees very few tourists, so it can be visited as an alternative to the popular islands of Amantaní and Taquile. Families will take in travelers and prepare their meals for around US$4 per night. The tiny island of **Yupinsque** nearby hosts a vicuña reserve. Travel agencies in Puno (see p195) can organize trips here or you can catch a boat from Punta Hermosa near Yunguyo (US$2, two hours). Boats usually run between noon and 3pm on Sunday, when the islanders return after visiting Yunguyo's market.

SOUTH-SHORE TOWNS

The road to Bolivia via Lake Titicaca's southern shore passes through several bucolic villages, notable for their myriad colonial churches, busy market days and stunning views. Traveling this route is an easy way to get a relatively untouristed peek at the region's traditional culture. If you start early enough,

you can visit all of the following south-shore towns in a day and either be back in Puno by nightfall or continue onward to Bolivia.

For public transport to any south-shore town, go to Puno's Terminal Zonal on Simón Bolívar, a few blocks northwest of Terminal Terrestre. Cheaper, slower minibuses and faster *combis* leave from there for Chimú (US$0.30, 15 minutes), Chucuito (US$0.60, 40 minutes), Juli (US$1, 1½ hours), Pomata (US$1.20, 1¾ hours) and the Bolivian border at Yunguyo or Desaguadero (US$1.40, 2½ hours). Direct transport to the towns closer to Puno are more frequent, but if you're patient you should be able to leave for the town of your choice within about an hour.

Chimú

The road east of Puno closely follows the margins of the lake. After about 8km, it reaches the village of Chimú, whose inhabitants have close ties with the Uros and are famous for their *totora* industry. You might spy bundles of reeds piled up to dry as you pass by, and

---

You can save a little money by going independently. Frequent buses leave from Puno's Terminal Zonal for Yunguyo (US$1.40, 2½ hours), which has a couple of basic hotels. You will find moneychangers in Yunguyo's plaza and by the border, about 2km away in Kasani (*combis* US$0.30) – count your money carefully. Then walk about 200m under a stone archway into Bolivia, where the Bolivian border post is open from 9am to 7pm daily, and formalities are fairly straightforward. From the border, it's another 10km to Copacabana (*combis* US$0.50). Transportation is more frequent on Sunday, which is market day in Yunguyo; on weekdays you may have to wait up to an hour.

Copacabana has much better hotels and restaurants than Yunguyo, and most people continue straight through the border. If you leave Puno early enough, you can reach La Paz in a day. See p218 for transportation between Copacabana and La Paz.

Via Desaguadero

Buses (US$2) and minibuses (US$1.40) leave Puno's Terminal Terrestre and Terminal Zonal, respectively, for Desaguadero (2½ hours). Basic hotels there include **Hostal Panamericano** (☎ 051-85 1021; Panamericana 151; s/d/tr with shared bathroom US$3/6/9), near the border, which has simple little rooms and cold showers.

Border-post hours are usually 8am to 8pm, though you can cross back and forth outside these hours if you stay within the border area. Remember that Bolivia is an hour ahead of Peru, so you can't enter Bolivia after 7pm Peru time. Moneychangers at the border and *casas de cambio* in Yunguyo usually have exchange rates roughly comparable to La Paz or Puno.

There are many daytime buses from Desaguadero to La Paz (US$1.80, three hours), but these peter out in the afternoon. If you leave Puno at dawn, you can cross into Bolivia early enough for a quick stop at the archaeological site of Tiahuanaco (admission US$10; ☉ 9am-5pm) before continuing on to La Paz (the bus passes the turnoff to the ruins, from where connecting combis run to the site).

The best direct bus from Puno to La Paz is with Ormeño's Royal Class service (US$15, six hours), but there are plenty of cheaper options.

there are usually a few reed boats in various stages of construction.

Chucuito

☎ 051 / pop 1600

In the village of Chucuito, about 20km southeast of Puno, the principal attraction is the outlandish **Templo de la Fertilidad** (Inca Uyu; admission free; ⊗ 8am-6pm), the dusty grounds of which are scattered with large, stone phalluses, some up to 1.2m in length. Local guides tell various entertaining stories about the carvings, including tales of maidens sitting atop the stony joysticks to increase their fertility. Whether you buy into their theories or believe another suggestion that the temple may in fact be a fake is up to you. Further uphill from the main road is the main plaza, which has two attractive colonial churches, Santo Domingo and Nuestra la Señora de la Asunción, though you'll have to track down the elusive caretakers to get a glimpse inside. A five-minute walk south of the plaza, you'll come to a breathtaking **mirador** (observation point), where stone arches frame a picture-perfect view of Lake Titicaca.

Albergue Las Cabañas (☎ 35 2176, 36 8494; www .chucuito.com; Tarapacá 153; dm/s/d from US$7.50/15/30) is a large, rambling, HI-affiliated hostel not far from the main plaza; it has a spacious, overgrown garden and a superb view of the lake. Rooms are in rustic stone cabins and familial bungalows come complete with wood-burning fires. Prices are extremely flexible and only estimations are given here. Camping is also allowed.

The unmissable, New Age **Taypikala Hotel** (☎ 36 9689; www.taypikala.com; Km18 Panamericana Sur; s/d/tw/ste US$51/67/87/95) is buried under a confusion of model condors and jagged artificial rocks by the road. Its main entrance is at the back near the temple, but the rooms have lake and garden views and are decorated with copies of local rock art. It also has all the modern amenities expected of accommodations in this price range, including an upscale restaurant with a touristy menu that includes some regional Peruvian dishes (US$4.50 to US$15).

The only restaurants in town are near the plaza and at the Taypikala Hotel.

Juli

☎ 051 / pop 7200

Past Chucuito, the road curves southeast away from the lake and through the commercial center of **Ilave**. About 80km from Puno, Juli is called Peru's *pequeña Roma* (little Rome) on account of its four colonial churches dating from the 16th and 17th century, which are slowly being restored. Nominal admission fees are charged and opening hours vary wildly. Your best bet is to turn up in Juli on market days on Wednesday and Sunday (especially the latter). Dating from 1570, the adobe baroque church of **San Juan de Letrán** contains richly framed, colonial Cuzqueña paintings that depict the lives of saints. The 1557 church of **Nuestra Señora de la Asunción** has a pulpit covered in gold leaf and there are excellent vistas of Lake Titicaca from its expansive courtyard. Its belfry was struck by lightning several years ago. The church of **Santa Cruz** has lost half of its roof and remains closed for the foreseeable future, while the 1560 stone church of **San Pedro**, on the main plaza, is in the best condition, with carved ceilings and a marble baptismal font.

A couple of basic guesthouses can be found near the plaza.

Pomata

☎ 051 / 1900

Beyond Juli, the road continues southeast to Pomata, 105km from Puno. As you arrive, you'll see a Dominican **church** dramatically located on top of a small hill. It was founded in 1700 and is known for its windows made of translucent alabaster and its intricately carved baroque sandstone façade. Look for the puma carvings – the town's name means 'place of the puma' in Aymara. The only local accommodation is **Hostal Rosario** (Plaza de Armas; s/d with shared bathroom US$3/6), which has limited hot water.

Walk downhill from the plaza to the main road and flag down any passing transport to continue heading south. Just out of Pomata, the road forks. The main road continues southeast through Zepita to the border town of Desaguadero (p215), which has a frenzied market and another crumbling colonial church. A side road, leading to the other border crossing at Yunguyo (p214), hugs the shore of Lake Titicaca.

If you're going to Bolivia via Yunguyo, consider stopping off at the **Mirador Natural de Asiru Patjata**, a few kilometers from Yunguyo. Here, a 5000m-long rock formation resembles a *culebra* (snake), whose head is a viewpoint looking over to Isla del Sol. The area around here is known for its isolated villages and shamans.

BOLIVIA

If you find yourself irresistibly drawn to the idea of staying longer in Bolivia, Lonely Planet's *Bolivia* guidebook has more comprehensive information.

Copacabana

☎ 02 / pop 54,500 / elev 3800m

Just across the border from Yunguyo, Copacabana is a restful Bolivian town on Lake Titicaca's south shore. Though its famous name may lead you to imagine more glamorous South American beach resorts, this is a modest, even at times sleepy, place.

In the 16th century the town was presented with an image of the Virgin of Candelaria (now Bolivia's patron saint), sparking a slew of miracles. The town became a pilgrimage destination, and today it's known for its Moorish cathedral, fervent fiestas and lake views.

Copa makes for a rejuvenating stopover between Puno and La Paz, as well as a handy base for visiting the famous Islas del Sol and de la Luna. Be prepared for heavy rains, especially during December and January, and chilly nights year-round.

ORIENTATION & INFORMATION

Travel agencies surround Plaza Sucre, where many buses arrive and depart. Not far away, **Alf@Net** (6 de Agosto at 16 de Julio; per hr US$1.75; ☼ 9am-10pm) offers slow internet access. Other internet cafés are found on 6 de Agosto heading downhill toward the lake or uphill from Plaza Sucre toward Plaza 2 de Febrero. Copacabana has no ATMs, but banks and *casas de cambio* along 6 de Agosto heading uphill from Plaza Sucre will change cash (US dollars or nuevos soles) or traveler's checks for a commission. Banks may also give Visa cash advances, but don't count on it.

SIGHTS & ACTIVITIES

The sparkling Moorish-style **cathedral** (Plaza 2 de Febrero), built between 1605 and 1820, dominates the town. Holy water used by the devout to bless their *movilidades* (anything that moves, ie vehicles) is sold at the cathedral from 8am to noon and 2pm to 6pm daily. The famous wooden statue of La Virgen de Copacabana is housed around the side of the

cathedral in the **Capilla de Velas** (admission by donation; ☼ 9am-noon & 2:30-6pm), where hundreds of candles illuminate an arched sepulchre and wax graffiti cakes the walls.

The hill north of town is **Cerro Calvario** (3966m), the summit of which can be reached in under an hour and is well worth the climb, especially at sunset. Many pilgrims also make this climb, stopping at the stations of the cross as they ascend. Far less impressive are the town's minor **Inca sites** lying a few kilometers outside town.

Head down to the waterfront to rent bicycles, motorcycles, boats and kayaks.

FESTIVALS & EVENTS

The blessing of miniature objects, for example cars and houses, happens during **Alasitas** (Festival of Ekeko; January 24) as a prayer that the real thing will be obtained in the coming year. Miniatures are sold in stalls around Copa's main plaza and at the top of Cerro Calvario.

The fiesta of **La Virgen de Candelaria** is celebrated on the first two days of February. Dancers from Peru and Bolivia perform traditional Aymara dances amid much music, drinking and feasting. On **Good Friday** during Semana Santa (Holy Week), the town fills with pilgrims, who join a solemn procession at dusk.

The biggest fiesta of the year, which is held for a week around Bolivia's **Independence Day** (August 6), features parades, brass bands, fireworks and not much sobriety.

SLEEPING

There are plentiful places to snooze in Copa. During festivals, however, everything fills up and prices can jump threefold. The cheapest *alojamientos* (guesthouses), which cost around US$2 per person for rooms with shared bathrooms, are scattered west of the Plaza 2 de Febrero, especially around the market area.

Residencial Brisas del Titicaca (☎ 862 2178; www .hostellingbolivia.org; 6 de Agosto s/n; r per person US$3.50) The reception is more hostile than hostel, but this HI-affiliated place is perennially popular, especially with groups, and it overlooks the lakeshore. Two- or three-bed rooms are basic but shipshape. Money exchange is available.

Hotel Ambassador (☎ 862 2216; Jáuregui at Bolívar; r per person US$4) This ex-HI affiliate offers rooms with TV and private bathrooms with piped-in shower music. It's by noisy Plaza

Sucre, but the atmosphere remains relatively peaceful, even though the hallways echo. The hotel's rooftop garden restaurant is open for breakfast.

Hotel La Cúpula (☎ 862 2029; www.hotelcupula.com; Michel Pérez 1-3; s/d/tr with shared bathroom US$6-12/14-17/20, s/d/tr US$14/20-24/28, ste $14-40) This romantic retreat hides away on a shady, hammock-equipped hillside overlooking the lake. None of the 17 rooms are alike, but all are inviting. A Tower of Babel's worth of languages is spoken, and the staff are also full of helpful travel tips. There's a restaurant, TV/video room, shared kitchen and laundry facilities. Reservations are essential.

Hotel Rosario del Lago (☎ 862 2141; www.hotelrosa rio.com/lago; cnr Av Costanero & Rigoberto Paredes; s/d/tr/ste incl buffet breakfast from US$33/44/58/90; ☐) The lake-side branch of La Paz' excellently managed Hotel Rosario, this cream-colored colonial hotel sprawls just uphill from the beach, a short walk southwest of Plaza Sucre. Though some of the lovely rooms are smallish, many have French doors looking out onto the lake and all have satellite TV and hot showers. Ask for an upper-floor room for the best views and quietest night's sleep.

EATING & DRINKING
The local specialty is *trucha* (trout) farmed on Lake Titicaca. Competitive stalls along the beachfront have set menus (US$2) featuring trout cooked in a variety of styles. Many more restaurants and bars line 6 de Agosto from the beach all the way uphill past Plaza Sucre.

Mankha Uta (set meals US$1.50-3; ☉ 9am 10pm) When it's cold outside, never fear because the fire will be burning bright inside this cozy restaurant, which has board games, magazines and a long list of drinks. Unbelievably filling set meals come with hot bread, soup and salad, a meat or vegetarian main dish, and dessert. Boxed lunches are available.

Sudna Wasi (Jáuregui 127; mains US$2-3; ☉ 8am-8pm) A convivial backpacker café with a court-yard set back from the hectic market streets. The home-cooked menu includes hearty breakfasts, a dozen different salads and a few Bolivian specialties.

Cafe Bistrot (Baptista s/n; mains US$3-5; ☉ lunch & dinner) European cool kids hang out here while chain-smoking, drinking espresso and forking into anything from Thai seafood curries to creative vegetarian fare. The service is slow, but nobody seems to mind.

La Orilla (6 de Agosto s/n; mains US$3-6; ☉ lunch & dinner) With a full bar and huge portions of Tex-Mex fajitas, pesto pasta, coconut curry and more, this eclectic grill restaurant is definitely worth seeking out, though opening hours are, ahem, 'flexible.'

Hostal La Cúpula (Michel Pérez 1-3; mains US$4-8; ☉ breakfast & dinner daily, lunch Wed-Mon) It's worth hiking uphill as much for the views as the tasty, internationally inspired vegetarian fare at this inviting hotel eatery.

GETTING THERE & AWAY
Several bus and minibus companies offer frequent daily departures for La Paz (US$2 to US$4, three to five hours), which include a crossing over the 800m-wide Estrecho de Tiquina. This memorable crossing involves transferring to a passenger boat while your overloaded bus gets shipped across on a rick-ety barge – loads of fun! Note that buses often depart Copacabana from Plaza Sucre, but ar-rive at Plaza 2 de Febrero. You can usually buy same-day tickets from company offices found near both of Copacabana's main plazas.

For boat trips to Isla del Sol, see opposite.

Islas del Sol y de la Luna
The most famous island on Lake Titicaca is Isla del Sol (Island of the Sun), the legendary birthplace of Manco Capac and his sister-wife Mama Huaca (or Mama Ocllo), and suppos-edly the sun itself. Both Isla del Sol and Isla de la Luna (Island of the Moon) have Inca ruins, which can be reached by delightful walking trails across the islands that pass traditional villages. Sunshine and altitude can take their toll, so bring extra water, food and sunscreen. Though you may be able to visit the main sites on Isla del Sol in one long day, it's more rejuvenating to stay overnight.

SIGHTS & ACTIVITIES
Isla del Sol has some fine sandy **beaches**. The largest villages are Yumani to the south and Ch'allapampa at the north end. The island's **Inca ruins** include fortress-like **Pilkokayna** at the southern end and the **Chincana** labyrinth com-plex in the north. The latter is the site of the sacred Titi Khar'ka (Rock of the Puma) that features in the Inca creation legend and in fact gave the lake its name. At Ch'allapampa there's also an interesting **museum** with gold artifacts from nearby underwater excavations. In the middle of the island near Ch'alla, the

Museo Templo del Sol (admission US$0.65) features a collection of all things Aymara, but opening hours are erratic.

Far less touristed, quiet Isla de la Luna boasts the partially rebuilt **ruins** of the convent that in ancient times housed virgins of the sun. Many tour boats do not stop here, so if you want to visit, ask before buying tickets.

SLEEPING & EATING

Isla del Sol is the best of the two islands for accommodations options, though you can camp on both islands.

Local infrastructure on Isla del Sol is very basic but improving, and no doubt there will be more options by the time you read this. You'll need a flashlight and sleeping bag at night. Food is more expensive than on the mainland and self-catering shops are scarce.

There are at least a half-dozen *alojamientos* on the hilltop in Yumani. All charge around US$3 per person, offer rooms with shared cold showers (though a few are installing private bathrooms with hot water), offer meals for under US$2 and have spectacular views. There are a few simple restaurants at the top of the Inca Stairway and on the town's hilltop.

A peaceful refuge in Yumani, **Casa de Don Ricardo B&B** (☎ 719 34427; birdyzehnder@hotmail .com; s/d incl breakfast US$12/20) is perched halfway up the hill from the jetty. Argentine activist Ricardo runs this place with his Aymara neighbors, cooks fantastic meals on request and knows everything about the islands. It's worth a stay for the spectacular views alone. Rooms have private hot showers.

At the north end of the island, you'll find basic lodging and meals in houses around Ch'allapampa's main plaza.

GETTING THERE & AROUND

For a full-day tour (US$4), boats depart Copacabana around 8:15am and arrive at Ch'allapampa at about 10am. A Spanish-speaking guide shows groups around the museum and accompanies them to Chincana. From there it's a moderately strenuous three-hour walk along the ridgeline to Yumani, where the Escalera de Inca (Inca Stairway) goes down to the jetty at Fuente del Inca. Tour boats leave around 4pm for the return trip. Most stop to visit the Pilkokayna ruins on the way back, finishing at Copacabana at around 6pm.

The half-day tours (US$2) only allow you under an hour on Isla del Sol, which is not enough time to do much more than climb the Inca Stairway and snap a few postcard photos. Morning boats leave at 8:15am and return around 11am; the afternoon boats leave at 1:30pm, returning around 6pm. Most tour-boat tickets theoretically let you return on a later day so you can stay on the island to explore, but hooking up with your original company isn't always easy. Purchasing two one-way tickets instead allows you more flexibility.

If you have the time and energy, it's an adventure to walk from Copacabana to Yampupata, then float across to Isla del Sol by rowboat or motorboat. The initial 17km hike takes three to four hours – if you don't get lost. Always ask locals for directions before setting out. Returning to Copacabana, some sort of *movilidad* (US$0.50) usually leaves Yampupata early in the morning or after lunch most days.

The only way to get to Isla de la Luna is on a tour.

Cuzco & the Sacred Valley

As the heart of the once mighty Inca empire, the magnetic city of Cuzco heads the list of many a traveler's itinerary. Each year it draws hundreds of thousands of tourists to its cobbled streets, lured by the city's unique combination of colonial and religious splendors built on the hefty stone foundations of the Incas. And lying within easy hopping distance of the city is the country's biggest drawcard of all, the 'lost' city of the Incas, Machu Picchu, a lofty Inca citadel perched high on an isolated mountaintop.

The department of Cuzco boasts a long list of flamboyant fiestas and carnivals in which the nation's proud pagan past collides colorfully with solemn Catholic rituals and modern Latin American mayhem. And in no other place in Peru can you descend from the breathtaking altitudes of Andean peaks down through cloud forests painted with rare orchids to the lush lowlands of the Amazon jungle so quickly – and you can do it while trekking on foot, mountain biking, river running (white-water rafting) or simply hopping on local buses and trucks, which bravely drive into remote corners of the far-reaching department.

Yet you don't have to go to the ends of the Amazon or the Andes to discover some of South America's most fascinating archaeological sites, not least of which are those to be found in the Inca's ancestral homeland in the Sacred Valley of the Río Urubamba, where quaint colonial towns, hectic artisan markets and head-spinning trekking routes also await. Just remember not to overexert yourself during your first few days if you've flown in from low altitudes.

HIGHLIGHTS

- Being awed by **Machu Picchu** (p269), Peru's most venerable mountaintop Inca citadel

- Witnessing the colorful **Inti Raymi** (p239) outside Cuzco, **La Virgen del Carmen** (p283) in Paucartambo or **Q'oyoriti** (p284) at Ausangate

- Trawling through the **artisan workshops** (p250) of Cuzco's eclectic San Blas *barrio*

- Exploring idyllic towns and ancient ruins scattered around the **Sacred Valley** (p255)

- **Rafting** (p235) the Ríos Apurímac and Tampobata or **mountain biking** (p236) down into the Amazon jungle

- Taking an awe-inspiring **alternative trekking route** (p277) to Machu Picchu

  ★ Machu Picchu ★ Paucartambo
  Sacred Valley ★
  Río Apurímac ★ ★ Cuzco
  ★ Ausangate
  Río Tambopata ★

■ BIGGEST CITY: CUZCO, POPULATION 322,000 ■ AVERAGE TEMPERATURE: JANUARY 7°C TO 20°C, JULY -1°C TO 21°C

CUZCO

☎ 084 / pop 322,000 / elev 3326m

The high-flying Andean city of Cuzco (also Cusco, or Qosq'o in the Quechua language) is the uneasy bearer of many grand titles. It was once the foremost city of the Inca empire, and is now the undisputed archaeological capital of the Americas, as well as the continent's oldest continuously inhabited city. Few travelers to Peru will skip visiting this premier South American destination, which is also the gateway to Machu Picchu.

Although Cuzco was long ruled by an *inca* (king) or a Spanish conquistador, there's no question of who rules the roost in the 21st century: city life is almost totally at the whim of international tourists. These days nearly every building surrounding the historic Plaza de Armas seems to be a tourist hotel, restaurant, shop, travel agency or busy internet café.

While Cuzco has rapidly developed infrastructure to at least partly cope with the influx of tourism over the last few decades, its historical past retains a powerful grip on the present. Massive Inca-built walls line steep, narrow cobblestone streets and form the foundations of modern buildings. The plazas are thronged with Quechua-speaking descendants of the Incas, and ancient treasures are carefully guarded inside colonial mansions and churches.

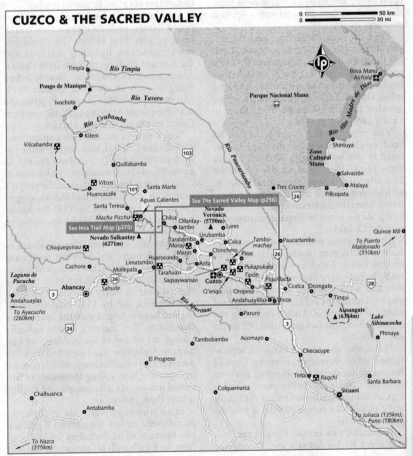

CUZCO & THE SACRED VALLEY

HISTORY

Legend tells that in the 12th century, the first *inca*, Manco Capac, was charged by Inti, the ancestral sun god, to find the navel of the earth (*qosq'o* in the Quechua language) – the spot where he could plunge a golden rod into the ground until it disappeared. When at last Manco discovered such a spot, he founded the city that was to become the thriving capital of the Americas' greatest empire.

The Inca empire's main expansion likely occurred in the hundred years prior to the arrival of the conquistadors in 1533. When the Spanish reached Cuzco, they began keeping chronicles, including Inca history as related by the Incas themselves. The most famous of these accounts was *The Royal Commentaries of the Incas,* written by Garcilaso de la Vega, the son of an Inca princess and a Spanish military captain.

The ninth *inca*, Pachacutec, gave the empire its first bloody taste of conquest. Until his time, the Incas had dominated only a modest area close to Cuzco, though they frequently skirmished with other highland tribes. One such tribe was the Chanka, whose growing thirst for expansion led them to Cuzco's doorstep in 1438.

Viracocha Inca fled in the belief that his small empire was lost, but his third son refused to give up the fight. With the help of some of the older generals, he rallied the Inca army and, in a desperate final battle, in which legend claims that the very boulders transformed themselves into warriors to fight alongside the Incas, he famously managed to rout the Chanka.

The victorious younger son changed his name to Pachacutec, proclaimed himself *inca* and, buoyed by his victory over the Chanka, embarked upon the first wave of Inca expansion that was eventually to create the Inca empire. During the next 25 years, he bagged much of the central Andes, including the region between the two great lakes of Titicaca and Junín.

Pachacutec also proved himself a sophisticated urban developer, devising Cuzco's famous puma shape and diverting rivers to cross the city. He also built some fine buildings, including the famous Qorikancha temple and a palace on a corner of what is now the Plaza de Armas.

Pachacutec's successor, Túpac Yupanqui, was every bit his father's son. During the 1460s he helped his father subdue a great area to the north, including the northern Peruvian and southern Ecuadorian Andes of today, as well as the northern Peruvian coast. And as the 10th *inca*, his empire continued to expand dramatically, extending from Quito in Ecuador to south of Santiago in Chile by his death.

Huayna Capac, the 11th *inca*, was the last to rule over a united empire, an empire so big that it seemed to have little left to conquer. Nevertheless, Huayna Capac doggedly marched to the northernmost limits of his empire, along the present-day Ecuador–Colombia border, and fought a long series of campaigns during which he sired his son Atahualpa, who was possibly born of a *quiteña* (inhabitant of Quito, Ecuador) mother.

Then something totally unexpected happened: Europeans discovered the New World, bringing with them various Old World diseases. Epidemics, including smallpox and the common cold, swept down from Central America and the Caribbean. Shortly before dying of such an epidemic around 1525, Huayna Capac divided his empire, giving the northern part to Atahualpa and the southern Cuzco area to another son, Huascar.

Both sons were suited to ruling an empire – so well suited, in fact, that neither wished to share power, and an Inca civil war ensued. As a pure-blooded native *cuzqueño* (inhabitant of Cuzco), it was Huascar who had the people's support, but Atahualpa had the backing of the northern army and in 1532 his battle-hardened troops won a key battle, capturing Huascar outside Cuzco.

Meanwhile, Francisco Pizarro landed in northern Ecuador and marched southward in the wake of Atahualpa's conquests. Atahualpa himself had been too busy fighting the civil war to worry about a small band of foreigners, but by 1532 a fateful meeting had been arranged with the Spaniard in Cajamarca. This meeting was to radically change the course of South American history, as Atahualpa was ambushed by a few dozen armed conquistadors, who succeeded in capturing him, killing thousands of unarmed indigenous tribespeople and routing tens of thousands more.

In an attempt to regain his freedom, the *inca* offered a ransom of a roomful of gold and two rooms of silver, including gold stripped from the temple walls of Qorikancha. But after holding Atahualpa prisoner for a number of months, Pizarro murdered him anyway, and soon marched on Cuzco. Mounted on horseback, protected by armor and swinging steel swords, the Spanish cavalry was virtually unstoppable at the time.

Pizarro entered Cuzco on November 8, 1533, by which time he had appointed Manco, a half-brother of Huascar and Atahualpa, as the new puppet *inca*. But after a few years of keeping to heel, the docile puppet rebelled. In 1536, Manco Inca set out to drive the Spaniards from his empire, laying siege to Cuzco with an army estimated at well over a hundred thousand people. Indeed, it was only a desperate last-ditch breakout and violent battle at Saqsaywamán that saved the Spanish from complete annihilation.

Manco Inca was forced to retreat to Ollantaytambo and then into the jungle at Vilcabamba. After Cuzco was safely recaptured, looted and settled, the seafaring Spaniards turned their attentions to the newly founded colonial capital, Lima. Cuzco's importance quickly waned, becoming just another quiet colonial backwater. All the gold and silver was gone, and many Inca buildings were pulled down to accommodate churches and colonial houses. For more on Inca culture and history, see p67.

Few events of historical significance have rocked Cuzco since the Spanish conquest, except for earthquakes in 1650 and 1950, and an infamous Inca uprising led by Túpac Amaru II in 1780. His was the only indigenous revolt that ever came close to succeeding, but eventually he too was defeated by the Spaniards. Not coincidentally, just over two centuries later in 1984, a Peruvian Marxist guerrilla group named itself after the Inca warrior.

Battles for Peruvian independence in the 1820s achieved what the Inca armies never had. Yet as it was the descendants of the conquistadors who wrested power from Spain, life continued much as before. It was the 'rediscovery' of Machu Picchu in 1911 that affected Cuzco far more than any event since the arrival of the Spanish, changing the city from a provincial backwater into Peru's foremost tourist hub.

ORIENTATION

The center of the city is the Plaza de Armas, while traffic-choked Av El Sol nearby is the main business thoroughfare. Walking just a few blocks north or east of the plaza will lead you onto steep, twisting cobblestone streets little changed for centuries, while the areas south and west of the Plaza de Armas are mostly flat land.

CUZCO & THE SACRED VALLEY IN...

Two Days

Start your day with rich pastries and coffee in the *barrio* (neighborhood) of **San Blas** (p246), then savor the treasures of the city's many museums, especially the **Museo de Arte Precolombino** (p232) and **Museo Inka** (p232). After lunch, gawk at the most imposing relics left by the Incas and Spanish conquistadors, respectively, at **Qorikancha** (p233) and **La Catedral** (p230). Wake up early the next morning and board a train to **Machu Picchu** (p269).

Four Days

Follow the first day of the two-day itinerary, then early on the second day catch a bus from Cuzco into the **Sacred Valley** (p255). Be caught up in the frenetic markets of **Pisac** (p256) and **Chinchero** (p264), hike around the ancient terraces of **Moray** (p261) and the salt pans of **Salinas** (p261), and soak up the ancient ambience in **Ollantaytambo** (p262), from where cheaper trains go to Machu Picchu. Overnight in **Aguas Calientes** (p265) just to beat the crowds by taking the first morning bus up the mountain to **Machu Picchu** (p269) the next day.

One Week

Spend the first two days acclimatizing in Cuzco, exploring the impressive fortress of **Saqsaywamán** (p254) and nearby archaeological sites in the **Sacred Valley** (p255). On the third day, start trekking the **Inca Trail** (p274) or a less touristed **alternative route** (p277) to reach towering **Machu Picchu** (p269).

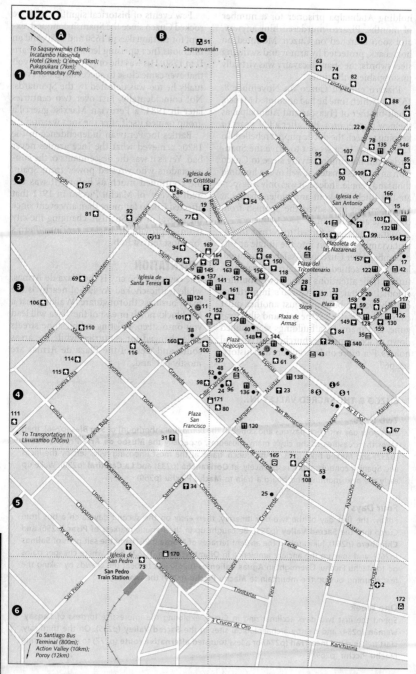

CUZCO

To Saqsaywamán (1km);
Incatambo Hacienda
Hotel (2km); Q'enqo (3km);
Pukapukara (7km);
Tambomachay (7km)

Saqsaywamán

Iglesia de
San Cristóbal

Iglesia de
San Antonio

Iglesia de
Santa Teresa

Plaza del
Tricentenario

Plazoleta de
las Nazarenas

Plaza de
Armas

Plaza
Regocijo

Plaza
San
Francisco

To Transportation in
Llmatambo (700m)

Iglesia de
San Pedro

San Pedro
Train Station

To Santiago Bus
Terminal (800m);
Action Valley (10km);
Poroy (12km)

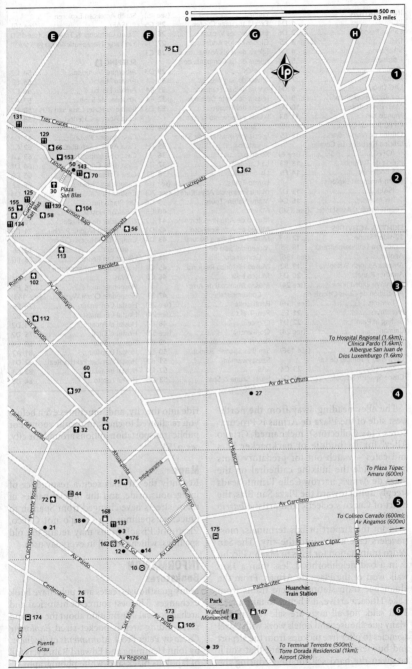

INFORMATION			
BCP	**1** D4	Enigma	(see 48)
Clínica Paredes	**2** D6	Excel Language Center	**25** C5
DHL	**3** F5	Expediciones Vilca	**26** B3
InkaFarma	**4** D4	Globos de los Andes	**27** G4
Interbank	**5** D4	Iglesia de Jesús María	**28** C3
iPerú	**6** D4	Iglesia de La Compañía de	
Jerusalén	**7** C4	Jesús	**29** D3
LAC Dolar	**8** D4	Iglesia de San Blas	**30** E2
Los Andes Bookshop	**9** C4	Iglesia de San Francisco	**31** B4
Main Post Office	**10** F6	Iglesia de Santo Domingo	**32** E4
Mundo Net	**11** B3	Iglesia del Triunfo	**33** D3
OFEC Branch Office	(see 45)	Iglesia y Convento de Santa	
Oficina de Migraciónes	**12** F5	Clara	**34** B5
Oficina Ejecutiva del Comité		Iglesia y Monasterio de Santa	
(OFEC)	(see 6)	Catalina	**35** D3
Policía de Turismo	**13** B3	Kcosñipata	**36** C4
SBS Bookshop	**14** F5	La Catedral	**37** D3
South American Explorers		Llama Path	**38** B3
(SAE)	**15** D2	Loreto Tours	(see 16)
Telser Internet	**16** C4	Manu Ecological Adventures	(see 26)
Tourist Medical Assistance	(see 136)	Manu Nature Tours	**39** G6
		Mayuc	**40** C3
SIGHTS & ACTIVITIES		Museo de Arte Precolombino	**41** D2
12-sided Stone	**17** D3	Museo de Arte Religioso	**42** D3
Academia Latinoamericana	**18** E5	Museo de Historia Natural	**43** D4
Agotur	(see 136)	Museo del Sitio de	
Amauta Spanish School	**19** B2	Qorikancha	**44** E5
Another Planet	**20** D3	Museo Histórico Regional	**45** C4
Apumayo Expeditions	(see 24)	Museo Inka	**46** C3
Asociación de Guías Oficials de		Museo Municpal de Arte	
Turismo	(see 136)	Contemporaneo	**47** B3
Aventours	**21** E5	Pantiacolla	(see 26)
Birding in Peru	**22** D1	Peru Treks	(see 24)
Caiman	(see 24)	Q'ente	**48** C4
Colegio de Licenciados en		Qorikancha	(see 32)
Turismo	(see 136)	Reserv Cusco Ltda	**49** C3
Convento y Templo de La		San Blas Spanish School	**50** E2
Merced	**23** C4	Saqsaywamán	**51** B1
Cusco Spanish School	**24** C4	SAS	**52** C4
		Siluet Sauna & Spa	**53** D5

South American Explorers			
(SAE)	(see 15)		
Tatoo Outdoors & Travel	(see 151)		
Yin Yang Therapeutic Massage	(see 9)		
SLEEPING 🏠			
Albergue Municipal	**54** C2		
Amaru Hostal	**55** E2		
Amaru Hostal II	**56** F2		
Andenes de Saphi	**57** A2		
Boutique Hotel Casa San Blas	**58** E2		
Casa Andina Catedral	**59** D3		
Casa Andina Koricancha	**60** E4		
Casa Andina Plaza	**61** C4		
Casa Andina San Blas	**62** G2		
Casa de Campo Hostal	**63** D1		
Casa de la Gringa	**64** D1		
Casa Grande	**65** D3		
Casona los Pleiades	**66** E2		
Cristina Hostal	**67** D4		
Del Prado Inn	**68** C3		
El Balçón Hostal	**69** A3		
El Mirador de la Ñusta	**70** E2		
Gran Hostal Machu Picchu	**71** C5		
Gringo Bill's Hostal (Cuzco			
office)	**72** E5		
Hogar San Pedro	**73** B6		
Hospedaje Familiar Kuntur			
Wasi	**74** D1		
Hospedaje Inka	**75** F1		
Hospedaje Q'oñi Wasi	(see 143)		
Hostal Centenario	**76** F6		
Hostal Corihuasi	**77** B2		
Hostal el Arcano	**78** D2		
Hostal el Grial	**79** D2		
Hostal el Solar	**80** C4		
Hostal Familiar	**81** A2		
Hostal Familiar Pakcha Real	**82** D1		
Hostal Incawasi	**83** C3		
Hostal Loreto	**84** D3		

The alley heading away from the northwest side of the Plaza de Armas is Procuradores (Tax Collectors), nicknamed 'Gringo Alley' for its huddle of backpacker bars and cafés – watch out for predatory touts here. Beside the hulking cathedral on the Plaza de Armas, narrow Calle Triunfo leads steeply uphill toward the Plaza San Blas, the heart of Cuzco's eclectic and artistic *barrio* (neighborhood).

From the airport or bus terminals, most travelers take a taxi into the city. The San Pedro train station for trips to Machu Picchu is in a bad neighborhood, less than a 1km walk west of the Plaza de Armas. From the Huanchac train station, where trains from Lake Titicaca arrive, it's better to take a taxi. That said, not all taxis are safe (see p229). Many guesthouses and hotels work with travel agencies to offer free pickups from the airport and bus terminals, but be aware that you'll be given the hard sell for tours during the ride into the city, and sometimes even before you're allowed to check into your room. For public transportation options around the city, see p254.

Maps
Recently the city has seen a resurgence of indigenous pride, and the official names of many streets have changed from Spanish to Quechua spellings (eg Qosq'o not Cuzco, Pisaq not Pisac). Maps may retain the old spellings, which are still in everyday use.

INFORMATION
Bookstores
Many guesthouses, cafés and pubs have book exchanges. The best source of historical and archaeological information about the city and surrounding area is pocket-sized *Exploring Cuzco* by Peter Frost. *Monuments of the Incas*, by John Hemming and Edward Ranney, is full of fabulous black-and-white photographs.

CUZCO & THE SACRED VALLEY

Recommended bookstores:

Jerusalén (☎ 23 5428; Helaldeos 143; ⏱9am-9pm Mon-Sat) Book exchange in several languages, plus new titles and music CDs for sale.

Los Andes Bookshop (☎ 23 4231; Portal Comercio 125; ⏱9:30am-1:30pm & 4:15-9pm Mon-Sat) Conveniently on the Plaza de Armas.

SBS Bookshop (☎ 24 8106; Av El Sol 781A; ⏱9am-9pm Mon-Sat) Small, but specializes in foreign-language books, especially in English.

South American Explorers (SAE; ☎ 24 5484; www.saexplorers.org; No 4, Choquechaca 188; ⏱9:30am-5pm Mon-Fri, 9:30am-1pm Sat) Foreign-language guidebooks and maps are sold at the SAE clubhouse, which also has a members-only book exchange.

Cultural Centers

South American Explorers (SAE; ☎ 24 5484; www.saexplorers.org; No 4, Choquechaca 188; ⏱9:30am-5pm Mon-Fri, 9:30am-1pm Sat) SAE's Cuzco clubhouse has a huge stock of travel information, along with wi-fi access, filtered water, recycling bins, a book exchange and helpful staff, plus good-quality maps, books and brochures for sale. Weekly events and limited volunteer information are available to nonmembers. For more information about the club, see p93.

Embassies & Consulates

Most foreign embassies and consulates are located in Lima (p503). Honorary consul representatives in Cuzco:

Belgium (☎ 22 1098, 22 4322)
France (☎ 23 3610)
Germany (☎ 23 5459, 24 2970)
Italy (☎ 22 4398)
Spain (☎ 65 0106)
UK (☎ 22 6671, 23 9974)
USA (☎ 962 1369)

Emergency

Policía de Turismo (Tourist Police; ☎ 24 9654; Saphi 510; ⏱24hr) Some English is spoken by the police, although travelers have written to complain of corruption scams in which the victims of crimes are actually considered suspects until proven innocent. If you have something stolen, you'll usually need an official police report for insurance claims.

Immigration

Oficina de migraciónes (immigration office; ☎ 22 2741; Av El Sol 612; ⏰ 8am-1pm & 2-4:30pm Mon-Fri) Extend your Peruvian visa (see p513) here.

Internet Access

Internet cafés are found on almost every street corner.

Mundo Net (☎ 26 0285; Santa Teresa 172; per hr US$0.60; ⏰ 7am-10pm Mon-Sat) Not far from the Plaza de Armas, this oasis of calm has private telephone booths and an espresso bar.

Telser Internet (☎ 24 2424; Medio 117; ⏰ 7am-11pm) Fast computers, printing and telephone booths.

Internet Resources

About Cusco (www.aboutcusco.com) General background and travel information.

CuscoPeru.com (www.cuscoperu.com) Touristy overview, but with live webcam images.

Cusco Views (www.cuscoviews.com) Hundreds of visual images, including panoramic photographs, virtual postcards, screen savers and e-books.

Diario del Cusco (www.diariodelcusco.com in Spanish) Online edition of the local newspaper.

Municipalidad del Cusco (www.municusco.gob.pe in Spanish) The city's official website.

Laundry

Lavanderías (laundries) clustered just off the Plaza de Armas on Suecia, Procuradores and Plateros will wash, dry and fold your clothes for around US$1.50 per kilogram. During the busiest months, however, don't bet your last pair of hiking socks on their promise of 'in by 10am, ready by 6pm.'

Left Luggage

If you're going trekking for a few days or even just on an overnight excursion, many guesthouses and hotels will store your bags for free. Always get a receipt, and lock your bags. The bags should have identifying tags showing your name and the drop-off and expected pickup dates. For soft-sided bags, we recommend placing them inside a larger plastic bag and sealing them shut with tape. Then sign your name across the seal, so you can tell if your bag has been opened while you're away. It's best to keep all valuables (eg passport, credit cards, money) on your person. Trekkers are required to carry their passport with them on the Inca Trail.

Medical Services

Cuzco's medical facilities are limited; head back to Lima for serious procedures.

Clínica Panamericana (☎ 27 0000, 65 1888; www .cuscohealth.com; Urb Larape Grapple C-17 San Jerónimo; ⏰ 24hr) Medical care specifically for tourists, including visits with a doctor, nurse and ambulance at your hotel.

Clínica Pardo (☎ 24 0387; Av de la Cultura 710; ⏰ 24hr) Consultation US$10.50.

Clínica Paredes (☎ 22 5265; Lechugal 405; ⏰ 24hr) Consultation US$30.

Hospital Regional (☎ 23 9792, emergencies 22 3691; Av de la Cultura s/n; ⏰ 24hr) Cheaper than private clinics, but not as consistently good. Consultation is US$7.50. Yellow-fever vaccinations available 9am to 1pm Saturday.

InkaFarma (☎ 24 2967; Av El Sol 214; ⏰ 24hr) A well-stocked pharmacy.

Tourist Medical Assistance (TMA; ☎ 26 0101; Heladeros 157; ⏰ 24hr) Offers emergency medical services, health information and legal assistance.

Money

Many banks on Av El Sol and shops around the Plaza de Armas have foreign-card-friendly ATMs, as do the airport and the main bus terminal. *Casas de cambio* (foreign-exchange bureaus) give varying exchange rates and are scattered around the main plazas and along Av El Sol. Moneychangers can be found outside banks, but their rates aren't much better than *casas de cambio* and rip-offs are common.

BCP (Av El Sol 189) Has a Visa ATM, gives cash advances on Visa, and changes US dollars and traveler's checks.

Interbank (Av El Sol 380) 24-hour global ATM machines accept American Express, Cirrus, MasterCard, Plus, Visa etc.

LAC Dolar (☎ 25 7969; Av El Sol 150; ⏰ 9am-8pm Mon-Sat) Reliable *casa de cambio* that has fair rates and changes traveler's checks into nuevos soles for no commission.

Post

DHL (☎ 24 4167; Av El Sol 627A; ⏰ 8am-7pm Mon-Fri, 9am-noon Sat) International express mail and package courier services.

Main post office (☎ 22 4212; Av El Sol 800; ⏰ 8am-8pm Mon-Sat) General delivery (poste restante) mail is held here at the main post office; bring proof of identity.

Telephone

Local, long-distance and international calls can be made from any public pay phone using a phonecard (see p511). Many cybercafés offer cheaper and more convenient 'net-to-phone' services from private indoor *cabinas* (cabins, or booths).

Tourist Information

Travel agencies are all too willing to help out with travel arrangements – for a hefty commission, of course.

iPerú (www.peru.info); airport (☎ 23 7364; Aeropuerto Alejandro Velasco Astete, Main Hall; ☼ 6am-4pm); city center (☎ 23 4498; Office 102, Galerías Turísticas, Av El Sol 103; ☼ 8:30am-7:30pm) Apart from providing tourist information, iPerú runs Indecopi (☎ 25 2974), the tourist protection agency, from its efficient, helpful and knowledgeable city-center office.

South American Explorers (SAE; ☎ 24 5484; www .saexplorers.org; No 4, Choquechaca 188; ☼ 9:30am-5pm Mon-Fri, 9:30am-1pm Sat) Loads of unbiased advice and information booklets for sale, including on alternatives to the Inca Trail and Amazon jungle adventures.

DANGERS & ANNOYANCES

While most travelers will experience few problems in Cuzco, it's a fact that more tourists are robbed here than in any other Peruvian city. Take special care going to and from the train stations and central market, as these are prime areas for pickpockets and bag slashers.

Ruthless robberies in taxis have been on the rise. When taking cabs, use only official taxis – look for the company's lit telephone number on top of the taxi. Lock your doors from the inside, and never allow the driver to admit a second passenger.

Avoid walking by yourself late at night or very early in the morning. Revelers returning late from bars or setting off for the Inca Trail before sunrise are particularly vulnerable to 'choke and grab' attacks. For tips on avoiding theft and other common scams, see p501.

Don't buy drugs. Dealers and police often work together, and Procuradores is one of several areas in which you can make a drug deal and get busted all within a couple of minutes. Women especially should try not to let go of their glass or accept drinks from strangers; spiking drinks with drugs has been frequently reported.

Take care not to overexert yourself during your first few days if you've flown in from lower elevations, such as Lima. You may find yourself quickly becoming winded while traipsing up and down Cuzco's narrow streets. A few luxury hotels offer in-room oxygen supplements, which may ease some of the headaches and insomnia that are common ailments at high elevations. For more advice on altitude sickness, see p534.

SIGHTS

Tourists can't easily buy individual entrance tickets to many of Cuzco's sights. Instead, you are forced to buy a *boleto turístico* (tourism ticket; below). Only a few museums, churches

---

BOLETO TURÍSTICO

Cuzco's official *boleto turístico* (tourism ticket) is exasperating. It represents good value only if you visit nearly all of the 16 participating sights; that said, you can't visit any of them without it. The biggest drawback to the *boleto turístico* is that each sight can only be visited once.

The ticket, which should be valid for 10 days, costs US$21 for adults, US$10.50 for students under 26 with ISIC cards, and is free for children under 10. In Cuzco, it's valid for the Santa Catalina religious-art museum, the archaeological museum at Qorikancha (but not Qorikancha itself), the Museo Histórico Regional, Museo de Arte Popular, Museo Municipal de Arte Contemporaneo, Pachacutec Monument and an evening performance of Andean dances and live music at the Centro Qosqo de Arte Nativo. It also covers the outlying sites of Saqsaywamán, Q'enqo, Pukapukara, Tambomachay, Pisac, Ollantaytambo, Chinchero, Tipón and Piquillacta. If you are in a hurry and only plan to visit archaeological sites near Cuzco or around the Sacred Valley, it's possible to buy partial *boletos* costing US$12, but they are valid only for one day and receive no student discount.

You can buy *boletos turísticos* from the **Oficina Ejecutiva del Comité** (OFEC; ☎ 22 7037; Av El Sol 103; ☼ 8am-5:30pm Mon-Fri, 8:30am-12:30pm Sat), in the back of the *municipalidad* (town hall), or at the **OFEC branch office** (☎ 22 6919; Calle Garcilaso s/n; ☼ 8am-5pm Mon-Sat, 8am-2pm Sun) around the corner from the Museo Histórico Regional. Tickets may also be purchased from a travel agent or at some of the sites themselves. Students will need to show their ID card along with the *boleto turístico* when entering any site.

and colonial buildings in and around the city can be visited for free or for a modest admission charge. Almost all have local guides who persistently offer their services. Some speak a varying amount of English or other foreign languages. For more extensive tours at major sites, such as Qorikancha or the cathedral, you should always agree to a fair price in advance. Otherwise, a respectable minimum tip for a short tour is US$1 per person in a small group, a little more for individuals.

Opening hours are erratic and can change for any reason – from Catholic feast days to the caretaker slipping off for a beer with his mates. A good time to visit Cuzco's well-preserved colonial churches is in the early morning from 6am to 8am, when they are open for Mass. Officially, they are closed to tourists at these times, but if you go in quietly and respectfully as one of the congregation, you can see the church as it should be seen – as a place of worship, not just a tourist attraction. Flash photography is normally not allowed inside churches or museums.

Plaza de Armas

In Inca times, the plaza, called Huacaypata or Aucaypata, was the heart of the Inca capital. Today it's the nerve center of the modern city. Two flags usually fly here – the red-and-white Peruvian flag and the rainbow-colored flag of Tahuantinsuyo, representing the four quarters of the Inca empire. Foreigners often mistake the latter for an international gay-pride banner, to which it bears a remarkable resemblance!

Colonial arcades surround the plaza, which in ancient times was twice as large as it is today, also encompassing the area now called the Plaza Regocijo. On the plaza's northeastern side is the imposing cathedral, fronted by a large flight of stairs and flanked by the churches of Jesús María and El Triunfo. On the southeastern side is the strikingly ornate church of La Compañía de Jesús. The quiet pedestrian alleyway of Loreto, which has Inca walls, is a historic means of access to the plaza.

LA CATEDRAL

Started in 1559 and taking almost a hundred years to build, the **cathedral** (Plaza de Armas; adult/student US$4.75/2.30, religious-circuit ticket US$10/5.35; ☉ 10am-6pm Mon-Sat, 2-6pm Sun) squats on the site of Viracocha Inca's palace and was built using

blocks pilfered from the nearby Inca site of Saqsaywamán. The cathedral is joined with **Iglesia del Triunfo** (1536) to its right and **Iglesia de Jesús María** (1733) to the cathedral's left. El Triunfo, Cuzco's oldest church, also houses a vault containing the remains of the famous Inca historian, Garcilaso de la Vega, born in Cuzco in 1539. His remains were only recently returned to Cuzco by the king and queen of Spain.

The cathedral is one of the city's greatest repositories of colonial art, especially for works from the *escuela cuzqueña* (Cuzco school) of painting, noted for its decorative combinations of 17th-century European devotional painting styles with the motifs and customs of indigenous Andean artists. One of the most striking examples is *The Last Supper* by Quechua artist Marcos Zapata, which is found in the northeast corner of the cathedral. This famed painting depicts one of the most solemn occasions in the Christian faith, but graces it with a small feast of Andean ceremonial food; look for the plump and juicy-looking roast *cuy* (guinea pig) stealing the show with its feet held plaintively in the air.

Also look for the **oldest surviving painting** in Cuzco, showing the entire city during the great earthquake of 1650. The inhabitants can be seen parading around the plaza with a crucifix, praying for the earthquake to stop, which miraculously it did. This precious crucifix, called **El Señor de los Temblores**, or 'the Lord of the Earthquakes,' can still be seen in the alcove to the right of the door leading into El Triunfo, blackened by the countless votive candles that have been lit beneath it.

The **sacristy** of the cathedral is covered with paintings of Cuzco's bishops, starting with Vicente de Valverde, the friar who accompanied Pizarro during the conquest. The crucifixion at the back of the sacristy is attributed to the Flemish painter Anthony van Dyck, though some guides claim it to be the work of 17th-century Spaniard Alonso Cano. The original wooden **altar** is at the very back of the cathedral, behind the present silver altar, and opposite both is the magnificently carved **choir**, dating from the 17th century. There are also many glitzy silver and gold **side chapels** with elaborate platforms and altars that contrast with the austerity of the cathedral's stonework. The last side chapel to the left of the altar has a painting of Pope John Paul II during his visit to Saqsaywamán in 1985.

The huge main doors of the cathedral are open to genuine worshippers between 6am and 10am. Religious festivals are a superb time to see the cathedral. During the feast of Corpus Christi (p239), for example, it is filled with pedestals supporting larger-than-life statues of saints, surrounded by thousands of candles and bands of musicians honoring them with mournful Andean tunes.

IGLESIA DE LA COMPAÑÍA DE JESÚS

This **church** (Plaza de Armas; adult/student US$3/1.50; 9-11:30am & 1-5:30pm) is often lit up at night and can be seen from the train as you come in from Machu Picchu after dark. Its foundations are built upon the palace of Huayna Capac, the last *inca* to rule an undivided, unconquered empire.

The church was built by the Jesuits in 1571, and was reconstructed after the 1650 earthquake. The Jesuits planned to make it the most magnificent of Cuzco's churches. However, the archbishop of Cuzco complained that its splendor should not rival that of the cathedral, and the squabble grew to a point where Pope

Paul III was called upon to arbitrate. His decision was in favor of the cathedral, but by the time word had reached Cuzco, La Compañía de Jesús was just about finished, complete with an incredible baroque façade that makes it one of Cuzco's most ornate churches.

Two large canvases near the main door show early marriages in Cuzco, and are worth taking note of for their wealth of period detail. Local student guides are available to show you around the church, as well as the catacombs underneath the main altar, and the grand view from the choir on the second floor, reached via rickety steps. Tips are gratefully accepted.

MUSEO DE HISTORIA NATURAL

This university-run **museum** (Plaza de Armas; admission US$0.60; 9:30am-1pm & 3-6:30pm Mon-Fri) houses a motley collection of stuffed local animals and birds and a few other dusty items, including over 150 snakes from Parque Nacional Manu and various Amazon biodiversity projects. The entrance is hidden off the Plaza de Armas, to the right of the church of La Compañía de Jesús. But if you can't find it, don't worry: you're not missing much.

DETOUR: INCA WALLS

If you walk southeast away from the Plaza de Armas along the narrow alley of **Loreto**, there are Inca walls on both sides. The wall on the right-hand side belongs to Amaruqancha (Courtyard of the Serpents). Its name may be derived from the pair of snakes carved on the lintel of the doorway near the end of the enclosure. Amaruqancha was the site of the palace of the 11th *inca*, Huayna Capac. The church of La Compañía de Jesús was built here after the conquest, and there is now a touristy market behind the church. On the other side of Loreto is one of the best and oldest Inca walls in Cuzco. The wall belonged to the Acllahuasi (House of the Chosen Women). Following the conquest, the building became part of the closed convent of Santa Catalina and so went from housing the Inca virgins of the sun to pious Catholic nuns.

Heading northeast away from the Plaza de Armas uphill along Calle Triunfo, you soon come to the street of **Hatunrumiyoc**, named after the well-known **12-sided stone**. The stone is on the right, about halfway along the second city block, and can usually be recognized by the knot of small children standing next to it who beg for tips after loudly pointing it out to tourists. This excellently fitted stone belongs to a wall of the palace of the 6th *inca*, Inca Roca. It is technically brilliant but is by no means an unusual example of polygonal masonry. In Machu Picchu there are stones with more than 30 angles (though these are corner stones and are therefore counted in three dimensions), and a block with 44 angles in one plane has been found at Torontoy, a minor ruin roughly halfway between Machu Picchu and Ollantaytambo.

There is a great difference between the wall of Hatunrumiyoc and that of the Acllahuasi. The first is made of polygonal stone blocks in no regular pattern, while the other is made from carefully shaped rectangular blocks that are coursed, or layered, in the manner of modern-day bricks. In general, the polygonal masonry was thought to be stronger and was therefore used for retaining walls in terraces. The coursed masonry, which was considered more aesthetically appealing, was used for the walls of Inca temples and palaces.

IGLESIA Y MONASTERIO DE SANTA CATALINA

This tranquil **convent** (Arequipa s/n; entry only with boleto turístico; 🕙 9am-5:30pm Sat-Thu, 8am-4pm Fri) has a musty museum of religious art, with many colonial paintings of the *escuela cuzqueña*, plus a dramatically friezed baroque side chapel, with the convent's main altar of carved cedar.

San Blas

Everything in the artistic San Blas *barrio* is a stiff uphill walk from the Plaza de Armas, but your trip through the narrow cobblestone streets will be rewarded with panoramic views – the more you climb, the better they are. Whenever you feel winded, stop to browse and perhaps buy treasures from artisan shops along the way (see p250).

MUSEO DE ARTE PRECOLOMBINO

Inside a Spanish colonial mansion with an Inca ceremonial courtyard, this dramatically curated **pre-Columbian art museum** (MAP; ☎ 23 3210; http://map.perucultural.org.pe; Plazoleta Nazarenas 231; adult/student US$6/3; 🕙 9am-10pm) showcases a stunningly varied, if selectively small, collection of archaeological artifacts previously buried in the vast storerooms of Lima's Museo Rafael Larco Herrera (p100). Dating from between 1250 BC and AD 1532, the artifacts show off the artistic and cultural achievements of many of Peru's ancient cultures, with exhibits labeled in Spanish, English and French. Highlights include the Nazca and Mochicha galleries for multicolored ceramics, as well as *queros* (ceremonial Inca wooden drinking vessels) and dazzling displays of jewelry made with intricate gold- and silverwork.

MUSEO INKA

This charmingly modest **museum** (☎ 23 7380; Tucumán at Ataúd; admission US$3; 🕙 8am-5pm Mon-Fri, 9am-5pm Sat), a steep block northeast of the Plaza de Armas, rests on Inca foundations; it's also known as the Admiral's House, after the first owner, Admiral Francisco Aldrete Maldonado. It was badly damaged in the 1650 earthquake and rebuilt by Pedro Peralta de los Ríos, the count of Laguna, whose crest is above the porch. Further damage from the 1950 earthquake has now been fully repaired, restoring the building to its position among Cuzco's finest colonial houses.

But it's what's inside that counts. Look for the massive stairway guarded by sculptures of mythical creatures, as well as a corner window column that from the inside looks like a statue of a bearded man but from the outside appears to be a naked woman. The façade is plateresque, an elaborately ornamented 16th-century Spanish style suggestive of silver plating. The ceilings are ornate, and the views from the windows are good.

Even more importantly, this is also the best museum in town for those interested in the Incas. The restored interior is jam-packed with a fine collection of metal- and goldwork, jewelry, pottery, textiles, mummies and more. The museum has 450 *queros*, which is the largest such collection in the world, although some are in storage.

Downstairs in the sunny courtyard, highland Andean weavers demonstrate their craft and sell traditional textiles directly to the public – a bonus for socially conscious shoppers.

MUSEO DE ARTE RELIGIOSO

Originally the palace of Inca Roca, the foundations of this **museum** (Hatunrumiyoc; adult/student US$3/1.50, religious-circuit ticket US$10/5.35; 🕙 8am-6pm Mon-Sat, 10am-6pm Sun) were converted into a grand colonial residence and later became the archbishop's palace. The beautiful mansion is now home to a musty religious-art collection, notable for the accuracy of its period detail and especially its insight into the interaction of indigenous peoples with the Spanish conquistadors. There are some impressive ceilings, as well as the curious Sala de Arzobispos (Room of Archbishops), filled with jovially grinning life-sized models. The colonial-style tilework of the interior is not original, having been replaced during the 1940s.

IGLESIA DE SAN BLAS

This simple adobe **church** (Plaza San Blas; admission US$1.80, religious-circuit ticket US$10/5.35; 🕙 10am-6pm Mon-Sat, 2-6pm Sun) is comparatively small, but you can't help but be awed by the baroque, gold-leafed principal altar. The exquisitely carved pulpit has been called the finest example of colonial wood-carving in the Americas. Legend claims that its creator was an indigenous man who miraculously recovered from a deadly disease and subsequently dedicated his life to carving this pulpit for the church. Supposedly, his skull is nestled in the topmost part of the carving. In reality, no one is certain of the identity of either the skull or the woodcarver.

Avenida El Sol

Running south from the Plaza de Armas, Av El Sol is choked with honking taxis, pollution-spewing buses and more pedestrian traffic than you'd thought possible in the Andes. It's better to approach the following sights from the backstreets just further east.

QORIKANCHA

If you visit only one site in Cuzco, make it these **Inca ruins** (Plazoleta Santo Domingo; adult/student US$3.60/1; ⊙ 8am-5pm Mon-Sat, 2-5pm Sun), which form the base of the colonial church and convent of Santo Domingo. Once the richest temple in the Inca empire, all that remains of Qorikancha today is the masterful stonework.

In Inca times, Qorikancha (Quechua for 'Golden Courtyard') was literally covered with gold. The temple walls were lined with some 700 solid-gold sheets, each weighing about 2kg. There were life-sized gold and silver replicas of corn that were ceremonially 'planted' in agricultural rituals. Also reported were solid-gold treasures such as altars, llamas and babies, as well as a replica of the sun, which was lost. But within months of the arrival of the first conquistadors, this incredible wealth had all been looted and melted down.

Various other religious rites took place in the temple. It is said that the mummified bodies of several previous *incas* were kept here, brought out into the sunlight each day and offered food and drink, which was then ritually burnt. Qorikancha was also an observatory from which high priests monitored celestial activities. Most of this is left to the imagination of the modern visitor, but the remaining stonework ranks with the finest Inca architecture in Peru. A curved, perfectly fitted 6m-high wall can be seen from both inside and outside the site. This wall has withstood all of the violent earthquakes that have leveled most of Cuzco's colonial buildings.

Once inside the site, the visitor enters a courtyard. The octagonal font in the middle was originally covered with 55kg of solid gold. Inca chambers lie to either side of the courtyard. The largest, to the right, were said to be temples to the moon and stars, and were covered with sheets of solid silver. The walls are perfectly tapered upward and, with their niches and doorways, are excellent examples of Inca trapezoidal architecture. The fitting of the individual blocks is so precise that, in some places, you can't tell where one block

ends and the next begins as you glide your finger over them.

Opposite these chambers, on the other side of the courtyard, are smaller temples dedicated to thunder and the rainbow. Three holes have been carved through the walls of this section to the street outside, which scholars think were drains, either for sacrificial *chicha* (fermented corn beer), for blood or, more mundanely, for rainwater. Alternatively, they may have been speaking tubes connecting the inner temple with the outside. Another feature of this side of the complex is the floor in front of the chambers; it dates from Inca times and is carefully cobbled with pebbles.

The temple was built in the mid-15th century during the reign of the 10th *inca*, Túpac Yupanqui. After the conquest, Francisco Pizarro gave it to his brother Juan Pizarro, but Juan was not able to enjoy it for long, because he died in the battle at Saqsaywamán in 1536. In his will, he bequeathed Qorikancha to the Dominicans, in whose possession it has remained ever since. Today's site is a bizarre combination of Inca and colonial architecture, topped with a roof of glass and metal.

IGLESIA DE SANTO DOMINGO

The church of Santo Domingo is most famous as the site of Qorikancha. The church has twice been destroyed by earthquakes, first in 1650 and again in 1950, as well as being damaged in the 1986 earthquake. Photographs in the entrance show the extent of the 1950 damage; compare the state of the colonial building with that of the Inca walls, which sustained minimal damage in these earthquakes. Also in the entrance is a doorway carved in the Arabic style – a reminder of the centuries of Moorish domination in Spain. The remains of the Inca temple are inside the cloister. Colonial paintings around the outside of the courtyard depict the life of St Dominic. The paintings contain several representations of dogs holding torches in their jaws. These are God's guard dogs (*dominicanus* in Latin), hence the name of this religious order.

MUSEO DEL SITIO DE QORIKANCHA

Next to the church of Santo Domingo, this small underground **archaeological museum** (entry only with boleto turístico; ⊙ 9am-5:30pm Mon-Sat, 8am-1pm Sun) is entered off Av El Sol. There are sundry archaeological displays interpreting Inca and pre-Inca cultures.

Plaza Regocijo

This park just west of the Plaza de Armas is a locus of tourist traffic. None of the sights around here are unmissable, but if you've got time on your hands, they're of minor interest.

TEMPLO Y CONVENTO DE LA MERCED

Cuzco's third most-important colonial church, **La Merced** (☎ 23 1821; Mantas 121; admission US$1; ☯ 8am-noon & 2-5pm Mon-Sat) was destroyed in the 1650 earthquake, but was quickly rebuilt. To the left of the church, at the back of a small courtyard, is the entrance to the monastery and museum. Paintings based on the life of San Pedro Nolasco, who founded the Order of La Merced in Barcelona in 1218, hang on the walls of the beautiful colonial cloister. The church on the far side of the cloister contains the tombs of two of the most famous conquistadors, Diego de Almagro and Gonzalo Pizarro. Also on the far side of the cloister is a small religious museum that houses vestments rumored to have belonged to conquistador and friar Vicente de Valverde. The museum's most famous possession is a priceless solid gold monstrance, 1.3m high and covered with precious stones, including no fewer than 1500 diamonds and 1600 pearls. Ask to see it if the display room is locked.

MUSEO HISTÓRICO REGIONAL

This **museum** (Calle Garcilaso at Heladeros; entry only with boleto turístico; ☯ 8am-5pm Mon-Sat) is housed in the colonial Casa Garcilaso de la Vega, the house of the Inca-Spanish historian who now lies buried in the cathedral. The chronologically arranged collection begins with arrowheads from the Preceramic Period and continues with a few pots of the Chavín, Vicus, Mochica, Chimu, Chancay and Inca cultures. There is also a Nazca mummy, a few Inca weavings and some small gold ornaments excavated from Qorikancha and the Plaza de Armas. Also on display are a few dozen paintings from the *escuela cuzqueña*, as well as rooms full of colonial furniture.

MUSEO MUNICIPAL DE ARTE CONTEMPORANEO

There's a small collection of contemporary Andean art on display at this **museum** (Plaza Regocijo; entry only with boleto turístico; ☯ 9am-5pm Mon-Sat) in the municipality building.

IGLESIA DE SAN FRANCISCO

This monastery and **church** (Plaza San Francisco; admission US$1.50; ☯ hrs vary), dating from the 16th and 17th centuries, is more austere than many of Cuzco's other churches, but it does have a large collection of colonial religious paintings and a well-carved cedar choir. One of the paintings measures 9m by 12m (supposedly the largest painting in South America) and shows the family tree of St Francis of Assisi, the founder of the order. His life is celebrated in the paintings hung around the colonial cloister. Also of macabre interest are the two crypts, which are not totally underground. Inside are plenty of human bones, some of which have been carefully arranged in designs meant to remind visitors of the transitory nature of life.

IGLESIA Y CONVENTO DE SANTA CLARA

This 16th-century **church** (Santa Clara s/n; admission free; ☯ hrs vary), part of a strict convent, is difficult to visit but it's worth making the effort to go for morning services, because this is one of the more bizarre churches in Cuzco. Mirrors cover almost the entire interior; apparently, the colonial clergy used them to entice curious indigenous peoples into the church for worship. The nuns provide the choir during Mass, sitting at the very back of the church and separated from both the priest and the rest of the congregation by an ominous grille of heavy metal bars stretching from floor to ceiling.

ACTIVITIES

Scores of outdoor outfitters in Cuzco offer trekking, rafting and mountain-biking adventures, as well as mountaineering, horseback riding and paragliding. Price wars can lead to bad feeling among locals, with underpaid guides and overcrowded vehicles. The cheaper tours are liable to be the most crowded, multilingual affairs. Due to tax exemptions for new agencies, cheaper outfits also regularly change names and offices, so ask other foreign tourists for the most recent recommendations.

Once you've asked travelers about their experiences, approach the agency forearmed with questions. Is there an English-speaking guide? How big will the group be? What kind of transport is used? How long will everything take? Can I check out the equipment? Can I meet the guide in advance? Will you explain a special diet to the cook? If you're unsure about anything, get any and all guarantees in writing, as some agencies will literally say anything to get your business. Also be aware they may be selling you a trip run by someone else, just to secure a commission.

No company can ever be 100% recommended, but those listed in the following sections are reputable outfits that have received mostly positive feedback from readers.

Trekking

The Inca Trail is on most hikers' minds, but there is a dizzying array of alternate routes to Machu Picchu (see Inca Trails Less Traveled, p277), as well as other rewarding Andean treks in the mountains around Cuzco. Many agencies will organize trips to more remote Inca ruins, such as Vilcabamba (p281), which the Spanish conquistadors called Espíritu Pampa, or Choquequirau (p285). The latter can be combined with other routes, including a further five-day hike to Machu Picchu, or you can take a longer, more spectacular seven- to nine-day trek from Huancacalle, which reaches altitudes up to 5000m. Another popular trek is the five- to seven-day circuit around southern Peru's highest peak, Ausangate (6384m), which travels over two breathtaking passes above 5000m (see p283 for details).

The best time to go trekking in the Andes or the Amazon is during the colder dry season, which lasts roughly from May until September. Make reservations for treks during high seasons several months in advance, up to a year for the Inca Trail. In the wettest months of January to March, trails have a tendency to turn into muddy slogs, and views disappear under a blanket of clouds. Note that the Inca Trail is completely closed during the month of February for its annual cleanup.

For trekkers going it alone or on a private guided tour, topographic trekking maps are sold by the **South American Explorers** (SAE; ☎ 24 5484; www.saexplorers.org; No 4, Choquechaca 188; ✆ 9:30am-5pm Mon-Fri, 9:30am-1pm Sat). Tents, sleeping bags, backpacks and stoves can all be rented in Cuzco, usually for around US$2 per item per day. Check all equipment carefully before you agree to rent it, as some is pretty shoddy and rarely is it ultralightweight. To buy new, **Tatoo Outdoors & Travel** (☎ 26 3099; Plazoleta Nazarenas 211; ✆ 10am-9pm Mon-Sat, 1-9pm Sun) has a good-quality selection of packs, tents, sleeping bags and other gear.

Prices for large-group guided treks offered by tour operators are *not* fixed. Shop around and ask lots of questions. Some agencies ask that you carry 'a small day pack,' which ends up being your regular backpack, so clarify this. Find out how many people sleep in tents, how many porters each group has, what the arrangements are for special diets and whether trekkers will be collected from their hotel if the tour leaves very early (early starters walking along Cuzco's deserted streets can be caught off guard by muggers). Make your wishes clear and get them in writing. Be aware that the cheapest agencies change names regularly in order to retain tax benefits afforded to new companies, so ask around for up-to-date recommendations from other shoestring backpackers if you're on a very tight budget.

Travelers often recommend the following agencies:

Andean Treks (☎ in USA 617-924 1974, 800 683 8148; www.andeantreks.com) Run by Tom Hendrickson, a local mountaineering pioneer who has lived in Cuzco for 20 years, this agency has some of the best guides and equipment for climbing the local peaks. It also organizes trekking and jungle trips.

Aventours (☎ 22 4050; www.aventours.com; Av Pardo 545) This agency is expensive, but it has top-of-the-line guides, equipment, food and services. Its llama treks and private Inca Trail entrance camp at Km 82 are unique.

Enigma (☎ 22 2155; www.enigmaperu.com; Office 103, Calle Garcilaso 210) Specializes in tailor-made treks for small groups, and in alternative tourism.

Llama Path (☎ 24 0822; www.llamapath.com; San Juan de Dios 250) Friendly, small trekking company that has received good reports from some travelers.

Peru Treks (☎ 50 5863; www.perutreks.com; 2nd fl, Calle Garcilaso 265) Locally owned, ecoconscious company with experienced guides; it also invests in the ethical treatment of porters. Highly recommended.

Q'ente (☎ 24 7836; www.qente.com; Calle Garcilaso 210) Offers many alternatives to the classic Inca Trail.

SAS (☎ 25 5205; www.sastravelperu.com; Portal de Panes 167) A mammoth operator that takes huge groups along the Inca Trail; however, it has many detractors.

River Running

Rafting down the Río Urubamba is the most popular trip. It's not very wild and offers some spectacular scenery, as well as a chance to visit some of the best Inca ruins near Cuzco. Trips typically last half a day (three hours of rafting plus a couple of hours for transportation at either end) and start at US$25. Full-day tours, combining a raft trip with a lunch and a visit to the Pisac or Ollantaytambo ruins, are also offered for a little more. Two-day trips offer two half-days of rafting on different sections of the river, and ruin visits and overnight stays in the Urubamba valley are possible at extra cost.

Three sections of the Río Urubamba are frequently run. The Huambutiyo-to-Pisac section is the easiest and includes three or four hours of fun rafting, as well as a chance to explore the Pisac ruins or market. This section can be run year-round, although during the dry season it is far from wild. The run from Ollantaytambo to Chilca is also very popular – it combines the ruins of Ollantaytambo with some exciting rapids and reaches class III level of difficulty. The most exciting nearby section is the short but action-packed Cañón Huaran, with class III rapids, however, this is not a frequently offered trip. Further downstream, the river becomes unraftable as it approaches Machu Picchu. Beyond Machu Picchu the Urubamba offers more possibilities, but access is limited.

Other rivers that can be run are further from Cuzco. For these, you definitely need to book with a top-quality outfit using highly experienced rafting guides who know first aid as well as rafting, because you will be days away from help in the event of illness or accident. Several travelers have died on these rivers in recent years, often due to carelessness or error on the part of their rafting guides, who aren't always vetted by tour operators.

The Río Apurímac offers three- to 10-day trips through deep gorges and protected rainforest, but can only be run from May to November. The rapids are exhilarating (classes IV and V), and the river goes through remote and wild scenery with deep gorges. Rafters camp on sandy beaches (where sand flies can be a nuisance), and sightings of condors and even pumas have been recorded. The end of the run enters the Zona Reservada del Apurímac, a huge protected area of rainforest with no tourist services. Three- or four-day trips are most often offered, but this stretch of river has limited camping places, and those that exist are becoming increasingly trashed. Make sure your outfitter removes everything and leaves behind a clean campsite.

An even wilder expedition is the 10- to 12-day trip along the demanding Río Tambopata, which can only be run from June to October. You'll start in the Andes mountains north of

Lake Titicaca and end at Reserva Nacional Tambopata in the Amazon jungle. It takes two days just to drive to the put-in point from Cuzco! The first days on the river are full of technically demanding rapids (classes III and IV) in wild Andean scenery, and the trip finishes with a couple of gentle floating days in the rainforest. Tapirs, capybara, caiman, giant otters and jaguars have all been seen by keen-eyed boaters.

Rafting agencies that have received some good reports from travelers:

Amazonas Explorer (☎ 25 2846, 976 5448, 976 5447; www.amazonas-explorer.com; Collasuyo 910, Urb Marivelle) This professional international operator with top-quality equipment and guides offers rafting trips on the Ríos Apurímac and Tambopata. Private trips on even more remote rivers, such as Río Cotahuasi near Arequipa (p172), can also be arranged.

Apumayo (☎ 24 6018; www.apumayo.com; Interior 3, Calle Garcilaso 265) Another professional outfitter, which takes advance international bookings for Río Tambopata trips; it's also equipped to take travelers with disabilities.

Loreto Tours (☎ 22 8264; www.loretotours.com; Medio 111) Runs cheaper one-day trips along the Río Urubamba, as well as multinight kayaking adventures on the Río Apurímac and Laguna de Huacarpay.

Mayuc (☎ 24 2824; www.mayuc.com; Portal Confiturías 211) This knowledgeable, long-running company organizes rafting day and overnight trips on the Ríos Urubamba and Apurímac, including transportation, food and camping, as well as nine-day trips (five days of rafting) on the Río Tambopata. It has recently had serious safety problems, however.

Mountain Biking

Mountain-biking tours are another growing industry in the Cuzco area. The rental bikes available are not always up to scratch, so serious mountain bikers may prefer to bring their own from home. However, the selection is always improving. The cheapest bikes can be rented for about US$10 per day, but they aren't really up to the rigors of unpaved roads on the wilder rides. Better bikes are available for US$15 to US$20 per day, but you should check them carefully as well. Make sure you get a helmet, puncture-repair kit, pump and tool kit.

If you're an experienced rider, there are awesome mountain-biking possibilities around the Sacred Valley, especially from Moray to Calca and Lares. Longer trips are possible, but a professionally qualified guide and a support vehicle are necessary. From

Ollantaytambo, you can go by bus to the Abra de Malaga (Malaga Pass; 4600m) and then downhill to the Amazon jungle in a couple of days. If heading to Manu, you can break up the long bus journey by biking from Tres Cruces to La Unión – a beautiful, breathtaking downhill ride – or you could go all the way down by bike. The outfitters of Manu trips can arrange bicycle rental and guides. The descent to the Río Apurímac makes a great burn, as would the journey to Río Tambopata, which boasts a descent of 3500m in five hours. Beat that if you can. A few bikers attempt the 500km-plus trip all the way to Puerto Maldonado, which gets hot and sweaty near the end but is a great challenge.

Be aware that not all mountain-biking guides are experienced, and serious accidents have befallen clients. Ask to meet your guides beforehand, and then question them carefully about their qualifications. The following agencies have received mostly positive reviews from travelers, although none can ever be 100% recommended:

Amazonas Explorer (☎ 25 2846, 976 5448, 976 5447; www.amazonas-explorer.com; Collasuyo 910, Urb Marivelle) Mainly organizes river running, but also offers excellent two- to 10-day mountain-biking adventures.

Loreto Tours (☎ 22 8264; www.loretotours.com; Medio 111) Particularly recommended for its mountain-biking tours, it runs half-day trips to the ruins around Cuzco, full-day and overnight trips in the Sacred Valley, and four-day rides down into the Amazon jungle. Rentals available.

Peru Discovery (☎ 24 7007; www.perudiscovery.com; Mariscal Gamarra 1 Etapa 19F) This outfit runs recommended mountain-bike tours around the Sacred Valley and downhill into the Manu area.

Reserv Cusco Ltda (☎ 26 1548; www.reserv-cusco -peru.com; Plateros 326) Offers cheap Sacred Valley mountain-biking trips and Inka Jungle Trail tours, which start with mountain biking from the Abra de Malaga, then trekking to Aguas Calientes to reach Machu Picchu.

Horseback Riding

Most agencies can arrange a morning or afternoon's riding from US$10, or you can walk to Saqsaywamán, where many of the ranches are, and negotiate your own terms. However, choose carefully as many horses are in a sorry state.

Other horseback-riding options require more legwork. Select agencies will offer multi-day trips to the area around Limatambo, and there are some first-rate ranches with Peruvian *paso* horses in Urubamba (see p259).

Bird-watching

Serious birders should definitely get hold of *Birds of the High Andes,* by Jon Fjeldså and Niels Krabbe. One of the best birding trips is from Ollantaytambo to Quillabamba, over the Abra de Malaga. This provides a fine cross section of habitats from 4600m down below 1000m, but you need to rent a truck or jeep to do it. Englishman Barry Walker, owner of the Cross Keys, is a self-confessed 'birding bum' and the best resident ornithologist to give serious birders plenty of enthusiastic advice. He has also written a field guide, *The Birds of Machu Picchu,* and runs a tour agency, **Birding in Peru** (www.birding-in-peru.com; Atocsaycuchi s/n), for bird-watching trips all around Peru, as well as into Bolivia and Chile.

Kayaking

Kayaking is increasingly popular in the Cuzco area. Some of the river-running trips described earlier can be accompanied by experienced kayakers, many of whom bring their own kayaks from home. A few outfitters also rent kayaks (see opposite).

Mountaineering & Skiing

Andean Treks (☎ in USA 617-924 1974, 800 683 8148; www.andeantreks.com) is your best source for information and guides for scaling any of the high peaks in the Cuzco area.

There are no commercial skiing areas, but adventurous and expert mountain skiers have been known to carry their skis to an Andean summit and ski back down – quite an adventure!

Other Activities

For outdoor activities around Urubamba in the Sacred Valley, see p259.

Action Valley (☎ 24 0835; www.actionvalley.com; 9am-5pm Sun-Fri Apr-Nov) is an adventure park with a climbing wall (US$10), 120m-high free rappel (US$10), 60m-long flying fox cable ride (US$10), giant tower swing (US$20), 122m bungee jump (US$59) and a bungee slingshot (US$59) at the ready. The park is 11km outside Cuzco on the road to Poroy (taxi US$3 each way). It's closed in the wet season.

Globos de los Andes (☎ 23 2352; www.globosperu .com; Suite 36, Av de la Cultura 220) Runs hot-air ballooning trips over the Sacred Valley, which can be combined with 4WD tours. It costs US$300 per person for an extended trip, or US$60 for a short ride with a moored balloon, which requires a minimum of 15 people to take a trip per day.

For those interested in local shamans, or who are curious to try the healing properties of the notorious San Pedro and Ayahuasca plants, contact Lesley Myburgh at **Another Planet** (☎ 22 9379; www.anotherplanetperu.net; Triunfo 120). Never buy these plants in the street or try to prepare them yourself, as they can be highly toxic in the wrong hands.

For some pampering or a post-trekking splurge, enterprising individuals and a blossoming number of spas offer massage services, including **Yin Yang Therapeutic Massage** (☎ 25 8201; 2nd fl, Portal Comercio 121; ☺ 8am-10pm) and the newly renovated **Siluet Sauna & Spa** (☎ 23 1504; Quera 253; ☺ 10am-10pm).

COURSES

Cuzco is one of the best places in the country to study Spanish. Most language schools will arrange family homestays, cultural activities and volunteer opportunities for additional fees, though not all such programs are legitimate – be skeptical and ask lots of questions.

Academia Latinoamericana de Español (☎ 24 3364; www.latinoschools.com; Plaza Limacpampa 565) Charges US$265 per week for mini group (maximum four students) classes, plus a US$40 registration fee. Tuition fees include a family homestay, three meals per day, laundry service, airport pickup, luggage storage, mail service, wi-fi access and weekly social activities.

Amauta Spanish School (☎ 26 2345; www.amauta spanish.com; Suecia 480) This popular Spanish school offers 20 hours of classes per week for US$98 in a small group or US$184 individually, plus a US$33 enrollment fee. Spanish classes for kids, teens, families, seniors or medical professionals can also be arranged (minimum four people). For something exotic, it will also run programs in the Sacred Valley and the Amazon jungle near Manu (minimum six people).

Cusco Spanish School (☎ 22 6928; www.cuscospanish school.com; 2nd fl, Calle Garcilaso 265) Costs from US$255 per week for individual classes, or from US$205 in a small group; prices include 20 hours of Spanish-language instruction per week, three meals per day, a city tour and salsa-dancing lessons. The intensive program doubles the amount of class time (from US$575 per week). The school can also arrange classes in Peruvian cookery, the Quechua language, Andean musical instruments and ceramics.

Fairplay (www.fairplay-peru.org) A unique nonprofit NGO, Fairplay trains Peruvian single mothers and local families to provide Spanish lessons and homestays, and it also organizes volunteer opportunities for travelers. Instead of paying tuition fees to a for-profit company, travelers pay their teachers and host families directly, thereby helping the community more. Tuition fees range from US$5 to US$7.50 for an hour-long language class, and up to US$800 for a four-week Spanish course.

Excel Language Center (☎ 23 5298; www.excelin spanish.com; Cruz Verde 336) Highly recommended for its professionalism, Excel charges US$7 an hour for private lessons, US$5 in a group of two or US$4 in a group of three to four. All-inclusive program rates are US$250 per week, including 20 hours of classes and family homestay with meals. Tuition fees include extracurricular cultural activities and weekly social events. Inquire about college credit.

San Blas Spanish School (☎ 24 7898; www.spanish schoolperu.com; Tandapata 688) Has group lessons with a maximum of four students from US$4/80 per hour/week. Private lessons cost from US$6/120 per hour/week.

TOURS & GUIDES

There are hundreds of registered travel agencies in Cuzco, but none can ever be 100% recommended, so ask other travelers for recent recommendations. Be aware that many travel agencies are actually selling you a trip run by someone else, just to secure a commission. Many are clustered around the Plaza de Armas, Procuradores and Plateros. For outdoor outfitters offering activity-based tours, see p234.

Some key questions to ask before handing over your money to any travel agency or tour operator: Is there an English-speaking guide? Where will we stop for lunch and is it expensive? How big will the group be? What kind of transport is used? How long will everything take? Try to get all of the important details in writing.

Most of the standard tours offered in Cuzco are a complete waste of your time and money. They're very rushed, overcrowded and usually visit sites that you can get to on your own either by walking or via taxi and public transportation. Average options include a half-day tour of the city and/or nearby ruins, a half-day trip to the Sunday markets at Pisac or Chinchero and a full-day tour of the Sacred Valley (ie Pisac, Ollantaytambo and Chinchero).

Agents also offer expensive Machu Picchu tours that include train tickets, the bus from Aguas Calientes to/from the ruins, admission tickets to the archaeological site, an English-speaking guide and lunch. Since you only get to spend a few hours at the ruins before it's time to return to the train station, it's more enjoyable (not to mention much cheaper) to DIY.

Cuzco is still an excellent place to organize trips to the Amazon jungle, especially to Puerto Maldonado and Parque Nacional Manu. None are cheap, though. Try the following:

Caiman (☎ 25 4041, 25 4042; www.manucaiman.com; Office 207, Calle Garcilaso 210)

Expediciones Vilca (☎ 24 4751; www.cbc.org.pe /manuvilca; Plateros 359)

InkaNatura Travel (☎ 25 5255; www.inkanatura.com; Ricardo Palma J1, Urb Santa Monica) Has lodges in the Puerto Maldonado and Manu areas.

Kcosñipata(☎ 23 1625; www.cuscoselva.com; Portal Comercio 195) Shorter trips to areas nearby Cuzco; recommended for its work with indigenous peoples.

Manu Ecological Adventures (☎ 26 1640; www .manuadventures.com; Plateros 356)

Manu Expeditions (☎ 22 6671, 23 9974; www .manuexpeditions.com; Humberto Vidal Unda G5, Urb Magisterial)

Manu Nature Tours (☎ 25 2721; www.manuperu .com; Pardo 1046)

Pantiacolla (☎ 23 8323; www.pantiacolla.com; Plateros 360 & Saphi 554)

For trips closer to Cuzco, licensed private guides registered with Inrena (Instituto Nacional de Recursos Naturales; the government agency administering national parks, reserves, historical sanctuaries and other protected areas) can be contacted through many tour agencies or via the following two organizations:

Asociación de Guías Oficiales de Turismo (Agotur; ☎ 24 9758; www.agoturcusco.org.pe; Office 34F, Heladeros 157)

Colegio de Licenciados en Turismo (Colitur; ☎ 24 2065; www.colitur.org; Office 34F, Heladeros 157)

FESTIVALS & EVENTS

Cuzco and the surrounding highlands celebrate many lively fiestas and holidays. In addition to national holidays (p505), the following are the most crowded times, when you should book all accommodations well in advance:

El Señor de los Temblores (the Lord of the Earthquakes) This procession on the Monday before Easter dates from the earthquake of 1650 (p230).

Crucifix Vigil On May 2 to 3, a Crucifix Vigil is held on all hillsides with crosses atop them.

Q'oyoriti Less well-known than the spectacular Inti Raymi are the more traditional Andean rites of this festival, which

is held at the foot of Ausangate in May or June (see Apu Ausangate, p284).

Corpus Christi Held on the 9th Thursday after Easter, Corpus Christi usually occurs in early June and features fantastic religious processions and celebrations in the cathedral.

Inti Raymi Cuzco's most important festival, the 'Festival of the Sun,' is held on June 24. It attracts tourists from all over Peru and the world, and the whole city celebrates in the streets. The festival culminates in a reenactment of the Inca winter-solstice festival at Saqsaywamán. Despite its commercialization, it's still worth seeing the street dances and parades, as well as the pageantry at Saqsaywamán.

Santuranticuy artisan crafts fair A crafts fair held in the Plaza de Armas on December 24 (Christmas Eve).

SLEEPING

Cuzco has hundreds of hotels of all types, and just about the only thing they have in common is that they charge some of the highest room rates in Peru – while in the rest of Peru, midrange rooms cost up to US$75, in Cuzco they cost up to US$100. Unless otherwise stated, all prices quoted here are for high season. It gets the most crowded between June and August, especially during the 10 days before Inti Raymi on June 24 and during Fiestas Patrias (National Independence Days) on July 28 and 29. During the rest of the year, it is always worth bargaining for better rates.

Remember that rates quoted here are never to be taken as gospel. Prices are market driven and vary dramatically according to the season and demand. Budget travelers are at a distinct advantage outside of peak season, when room prices automatically drop and even midrange accommodations can be reduced to high-end budget rates with a little polite haggling. Beware that the very cheapest hotels are not always in safe areas, so either take official taxis after dark or walk back in a group.

Though the Plaza de Armas is the most central area, you won't find any bargains there. As Cuzco is such a compact city, it's just as convenient to stay in another neighborhood nearby. The hilly San Blas neighborhood has a cornucopia of fetching accommodations, while places to stay along Av El Sol tend to be bland, expensive and set up for tour groups. Spreading northwest of the Plaza de Armas, especially on the side streets heading uphill and around the Plaza Regocijo, are some unusually good finds, though you'll usually want to avoid the central market area by San Pedro train station.

Many of Cuzco's guesthouses and hotels are located in charming colonial buildings with interior courtyards, which can echo resoundingly with noise from other guests or the street outside. Those places that offer breakfast sometimes start serving as early as 5am to accommodate Inca Trail trekkers and Machu Picchu day-trippers. Watch out for early check-out times, which are often between 8:30am and 10am. The good news is that if you arrive on an early-morning flight or bus, you shouldn't have to wait long until a room is ready for you. With advance notice, most places will send a travel agent to pick you up for free at the airport, train station or bus terminal.

Casas de Hospedaje (Family House Association; ☎ 24 2710; www.cusco.net/familyhouse) provides local lodging in small, family-run hostels, with prices ranging from US$5 to US$12 per person, depending on the season and the facilities. Check the website for heartwarming descriptions of each *cuzqueño* home, including its location and all available amenities.

Unless otherwise noted, all of the following midrange places offer rooms with cable TV and 24-hour hot-water showers.

Cuzco's swanky, top-end hotels are usually booked solid during high season. Making reservations through a travel agency or via the hotel's website may result in better rates than making reservations yourself by phone or by walking in off the street. Unless otherwise stated, the top hotels all feature rooms with heating and telephone. Prices quoted here may not include taxes.

For more-general information and advice about finding accommodations, see p496.

Plaza de Armas
BUDGET
There are almost no good-value budget choices right on the plaza itself, though you'll find plenty of places within strolling distance. Side streets northwest of the plaza (especially Tigre, Tecsecocha and Suecia, off the end of Procuradores, and Kiskapata, accessed via steep, pedestrian-only Resbalosa) are bursting with cheap crash pads.

Hostal Residencial Rojas (☎ 22 81814; Tigre 129; s/d with shared bathroom US$6/9, s/d US$9/12) What may be Cuzco's tiniest guesthouse is run by an earnestly hospitable family who make sure the doors are securely shut at night. It's in an incredibly central, if noisy, location.

Hostal Mira Sol (☎ 23 5824; mirasolhostal@hotmail.com; Suecia 504; s/d/tr with shared bathroom $7.50/15/22.50) Downhill from the Colegio Salesiano, this home-style Italian-run guesthouse offers basic, tidy rooms (those below ground level are quiet, but also dark) and a huge upstairs lounge with a stereo, cable TV and shared kitchen. The views on the walk up are breathtaking, literally speaking.

Albergue Municipal (☎ /fax 25 2506; albergue@municusco.gob.pe; Kiskapata 240; dm US$9, d with shared bathroom US$18) Cuzco's official youth hostel is less institutional than the norm. It's tucked away off a steep, pedestrian-only street that affords great city views. Spotless dorm rooms have four to eight bunk beds, while basic twins are laughably overpriced. There's hot water and laundry facilities.

Also recommended:

Casa Grande (☎ 26 4156; Santa Catalina Ancha 353; s/d/tr with shared bathroom US$6/9/12, s/d US$9/12) More than a little ragged round the edges, but popular, especially with Israeli backpackers. Hot water? Hrmph.

Hospedaje Q'oñi Wasi (☎ 25 7576; Tigre 124; s/d with shared bathroom US$7.50/10.50) A ramshackle colonial house hidden uphill behind the plaza. The staff sure aren't smiley, but the price is right.

Hostal Suecia I (☎ 23 3282; hsuecia1@hotmail.com; Suecia 332; s/d US$7.50/10.50, with bathroom US$12/15) This pint-sized guesthouse has nondescript rooms arranged around a sociable indoor courtyard.

Hostal Suecia II (☎ 23 9757; Tecsecocha 465; s/d with shared bathroom US$7.50/12, s/d US$9/15) This safe colonial-style guesthouse is often full. It has stuffy rooms (very few singles) with hot-water showers. There's a glassed-in courtyard, too.

Hostal Incawasi (☎ 22 3992; Portal de Panes 147, s/d/tr with shared bathroom US$10/16/21, s/d/tr US$15/23/30) A great, if incredibly noisy, location smack on the Plaza de Armas, but ghoulishly dark rooms and limited hot water. It's the prime position you're paying for.

Hostal Saphi (☎ 26 1623; hostalsaphi@yahoo.es; Saphi 107; s/d/tr US$15/25/35) Over two dozen plain, carpeted rooms but with hot-water showers and cable TV.

MIDRANGE
Hostal Loreto (☎ 22 6352; www.hloreto.com; Loreto 115; s/d/tr incl breakfast US$25/40/50) Hidden off the Plaza de Armas, this amiable place has four basic, carpeted rooms with Inca walls, which make them rather dark and musty – but then again how often do you get to sleep next to an Inca wall? There's limited hot water, a curious mix of old and new furnishings and a helter-skelter-like staircase in the center.

Hostal Corihuasi (☎ 23 2233; www.corihuasi.com; Suecia 561; s/d/tr incl breakfast US$35/45/55) A brisk walk uphill from the main plaza, this cozy guesthouse inhabits a mazelike colonial building with postcard views of the Andes mountains. Amply sized rooms are outfitted in a warm rustic style with alpaca-wool blankets, handwoven rugs and solid wooden furnishings. Room 1 is the most in demand for its wraparound windows that are ideal for soaking up panoramic sunsets.

Del Prado Inn (☎ 22 4442; www.delpradoinn.com; Suecia 310; s/d/tr/ste US$75/110/145/150) Del Prado is a very welcome addition, located almost on the Plaza de Armas. The all-professional staff give highly personalized service, and there are just over a dozen snug rooms reached by elevator. Rooms come with lots of extras, including wooden floors, central heating, bathtubs and wi-fi access. Some rooms have tiny balconies with corner views of the plaza, though these can be noisy, especially on weekends. Best of all, the dining room has original Inca walls.

TOP END
None of the top-shelf hotels on the plaza can be recommended, though there are some respectable, if unexciting, options just a short taxi ride away.

Hotel Ruinas (☎ 26 0644; www.hotelruinas.com; Ruinas 472; s/d/ste US$95/125/155) This glass-enclosed colonial-style courtyard hotel was only built in 1997 and has smart, spacious rooms. Though it's a shade on the characterless side, it's favored by Peruvian business travelers and pan-American tour groups. Carpeted rooms have minibars and music players, while suites have fireplaces. One drawback is the noisy street outside, though.

San Blas
Guesthouses of all kinds abound around the Plaza San Blas. You'll have to huff and puff to get up here, but once you've arrived the atmosphere is fantastic.

BUDGET
Hospedaje Familiar Kuntur Wasi (☎ 22 7570; Tandapata 352A; s/d with shared bathroom US$6/12, s/d US$15/25) Kuntur Wasi has an exceptionally hospitable environment, with limited views over downtown Cuzco, reliably warm showers and kitchen privileges. What really makes it a star is the *dueña* (owner), whose concern for travelers' well-being is genuine.

Hospedaje Inka (☎ 23 1995; americopacheco@hotmail .com; Suytuccato 848; s/d incl breakfast US$7.50/15) This scruffy but charming converted hillside farmhouse high above the Plaza San Blas affords some great views. There's erratic hot water, private bathrooms and a large farm kitchen available for cooking your own meals. Taxis can't climb the final uphill stretch, so be prepared for a stiff walk.

Casa de la Gringa (☎ 24 1168; www.anotherplanet peru.net/hostel.htm; Pasnapacana 148; dm US$9, d with shared/private bathroom US$26/30) This laid-back hostel is a spiritual, New Age retreat overrun by a garden of healing plants. In the main house, the funky rooms are wildly colorful. There's a mixed-sex dormitory for backpackers, a shared kitchen, and a TV-and-games lounge. Out back in the cottage annex are disappointingly basic digs with shared bathrooms.

Amaru Hostal (☎ 22 5933; www.cusco.net/amaru; Cuesta San Blas 541; s/d/tr with shared bathroom US$12/16/24, s/d US$17/25/36, all incl breakfast) In a characterful old building, this delightful guesthouse perches uphill from the Plaza de Armas. For the price and the location, it can't be beat. Flowerpots sit outside relatively peaceful rooms, which have windows to let the sunshine in and perhaps even rocking chairs. Those in the outer courtyard are noisier, while those at the back are newer. All have hot water and cable TV. Amaru Hostal II has only a handful of rooms, but they lack atmosphere and many amenities, though the views are sweeping.

Also recommended:

Moon Hospedaje Familiar (Canchipata s/n; s/d with shared bathroom US$5/7.50, s/d US$9/12) It's like the waaaay most chilled-out crash pad in Cuzco, mon!

Hostal Familiar Pakcha Real (☎ 23 7484; www .hostalpakchareal.com; Tandapata 300; s/d with shared bathroom US$6/9, s/d US$9/12) Basic guesthouse with a TV lounge and open fireplace for relaxing.

Hostal el Arcano (☎ /fax 23 2703; Carmen Alto 288; s/d with shared bathroom US$6/10.50, s/d US$9/12) El Arcano is an intimate, friendly little place, though rooms are nothing to write home about.

El Mirador de la Ñusta (☎ 24 8039; elmiradorde lanusta@hotmail.com; Tandapata 682; s/d US$10/15) Conveniently right on the Plaza San Blas, though there are better-value guesthouses with larger rooms found further west on Tandapata.

MIDRANGE
Hostal Marani (☎ 24 9462; www.hostalmarani.com; Carmen Alto 194; s/d/tr/q incl breakfast US$25/36/46/60) This airy guesthouse has a light-filled courtyard

surrounded by humble rooms that vary in size and shape, but a few upstairs have vaulted ceilings, skylights and city views. It's a tranquil oasis from the hustle and bustle of the artistic scene happening just outside. Although proceeds from this Dutch-run guesthouse don't directly benefit the HoPe Foundation (p513), you can learn more about its social commitment from the owner or in the on-site library.

Hostal Pensión Alemana (☎ 22 6861; www.cuzco -stay.de; Tandapata 260; s/d/tr incl breakfast US$33/45/57) With well-kept rooms locked up tight against chilly Andean nights and a flower garden in the inner courtyard, this rustic Swiss-German lodge wouldn't look out of place in the Alps. For the price, it's an exceedingly comfortable place to stay near the Plaza San Blas. Taxis can make it uphill almost all the way to the front door, a boon for the older European travelers who favor staying here.

Orquidea Real Hostal (☎ 22 1662, in Lima 01-444 3031; www.orquidea.net; Alabado 520; s/d/tr/q incl breakfast US$33/44/55/66, ste incl breakfast $55) Owned by a package-tour company, this efficiently run small guesthouse has rustic rooms with working fireplaces, exposed wooden beams and skyline views over the city. All rooms have cable TV, phones and safes; matrimonial doubles also have king-sized beds. The inn's only suite, which has panoramic windows and a small sitting area, is well-priced.

Casa de Campo Hostal (☎ 24 3069; www.hotel casadecampo.com; Tandapata 296B; s/d/tr/q incl breakfast US$35/55/65/70) After climbing steeply to reach this rambling hillside inn, a favorite with members of the South America Explorers club, you may have to persevere for many more flights of stone steps before reaching your room. But the reward is huge: condor's-eye views over the city. Not all rooms are created equal, however. Take a taxi back here at night.

Hostal Rumi Punku (☎ 22 1102; www.rumipunku.com; Choquechaca 339; s/d/tr/q incl breakfast US$37/40/55/68) Recognizable by the monumental Inca stonework around the entrance, family-run Rumi Punku (Stone Door) is in a stylish, older colonial house with a rooftop terrace and gardens. Rooms have been steadily rising in quality and cost in recent years, but are worth the asking price. They sport central heating, wooden floors with throw rugs and thermal blankets on the beds. A Finnish sauna and whirlpool tub are coming soon.

Hotel Arqueólogo (☎ 23 2569; www.hotelarqueologo .com; Pumacurco 408; s/d/ste incl breakfast US$64/72/97; 💻) Its name an echo of the Inca stonework in the narrow street running beside it, this antique French-owned guesthouse keeps adding on amenities. Tastefully done rooms overlook a vast interior courtyard. You can relax in the garden deck chairs, or sip a complimentary pisco sour (grape brandy cocktail) in the fireplace lounge. The hostelry not only supports local artisans, whose weavings are on sale here, but also helps fund public libraries. French, English and German are spoken.

Boutique Hotel Casa San Blas (☎ 25 1563; www .casasanblas.com; Tocuyeros 566; s/d US$65/87, ste US$88-110; 🆒 💻) Unusually haute for the San Blas neighborhood, this polished three-star inn inside an 18th-century colonial house makes for a soothing retreat. Arranged around a courtyard, straightforward rooms are not as luxurious as the rates would suggest, but they're spacious, and furnished with traditional textiles, extralong beds and in-room safes, while upper-story suites have kitchenettes and balconies with city views. The staff provide personalized attention and a bouquet of little luxuries for guests.

Los Apus Hotel & Mirador (☎ 26 4243; www.losa pushotel.com; Atocsaycuchi 515; s/d US$89/109; 🆒) Los Apus is a neat, classy little hotel under Swiss management, with an airy courtyard and quality rooms with wooden furnishings. It's so eye-catching that Peruvian feature films have been shot here. Although the place is overpriced, central heating and IDD telephones are welcome luxuries. And when it comes to security, this hotel has no equal, with a high-tech alarm system and an emergency water supply. The rooftop terrace is ideal for meeting other travelers. Expect plenty of ambient noise inside your room, however. A wheelchair-accessible room for travelers with disabilities is available.

Also recommended:

Inkafe Hostal (☎ 22 7610; www.inkafe.com.pe; Choquechaca 261; s/d/tr US$18/27/36) Cozy rooms and caring staff, just around the corner from the 12-sided stone.

Casona los Pleiades (☎ 50 6420; www.casonapleia des.com; Tandapata 116; s/d incl breakfast US$20/30) A sun-drenched B&B with tidy rooms overlooking the city, plus a TV and video lounge.

Hostal el Grial (☎ 22 3012; www.cusco-peru.pl; Atocsaycuchi 594; s/d/tr US$20/30/40) In a rickety old wooden-floored building attached to a Spanish school, all rooms have orthopedic mattresses and some have views.

Koyllur Tourist Hostal (☎ 24 1122; www.koyllur hostal-peru.com; Carmen Bajo 186; s/d/tr with shared bathroom US$20/30/36, s/d/tr US$25/35/52, all incl breakfast; 🖵) On a busy side street east of the Plaza San Blas, this tourist-class hotel has comfy, if bland rooms. It's a prime location, though.

TOP END

Novotel Cuzco (☎ 58 1030; www.novotel.com; San Agustin 239; d incl breakfast US$165-205; 🖵) With 99 rooms, the elegant French-owned Novotel is small enough to devote personal attention to guests, but still big enough to offer every imaginable service, especially those catering to business travelers. Think of it as the best of the old and new: the hotel separates its tariffs according to whether accommodations are in the spit-and-polish contemporary wing or the more expensive, but more characterful colonial courtyard, where each room is different.

Hotel Monasterio (☎ 24 1777; www.monasterio .orient-express.com; Palacio 136; r US$470, ste US$560-1240; 🍴 🖵) Draped in graceful 16th-century cloisters, the Monasterio is indisputably Cuzco's top hotel, with majestic public areas and over 100 exquisitely designed rooms and suites surrounding its genteel courtyards. Although it has been wholly renovated over the years, the accommodations still show their Jesuit roots, with irregular floor plans and varying room sizes. If high-altitude acclimatization headaches worry you, take comfort in the fact that oxygen supplements ($30) are available in most rooms. This indubitably five-star hotel boasts two high-class restaurants, along with absolutely everything else expected of an establishment of this sterling caliber.

Avenida El Sol

BUDGET

Hostal San Juan Masías (☎ 43 1563; www.sanjuanmasias .com; Ahuacpinta 600; d/tr with shared bathroom US$12/18, d/tr/q US$15/22.50/30) An excellent alternative guesthouse run by Dominican nuns on the grounds of the busy Colegio Martín de Porres, this place is clean, safe and friendly and overlooks frequent games lessons on the courtyard. Breezy, simple and spic-and-span rooms with hot water are arranged off of a long, sunny hallway brightened by fresh flowers.

MIDRANGE

La Posada del Abuelo (☎ 80 7285, 22 2646; www.la posadadelabuelocusco.com; Av Pardo 869; s/d/tr incl breakfast US$25/30/35) In an offbeat location south of the city center, this charming hotel comes recommended by readers for its cozy, carpeted rooms and gracious staff. The interior hallways are splashed with artwork.

Hostal Pascana (☎ 22 5771; www.hostalpascana.com; Ahuacpinta 539; s/d incl breakfast US$33/42) Tucked away on a side street behind Qorikancha, Pascana is a small, well-run inn that's a real gem. It's filled with sunlight, and the well-kept rooms come with heaters upon request. Rooms 201 and 202 have windows facing the Inca walls of Qorikancha. If you're severely jet-lagged, take heart – there's 24-hour room service.

Torre Dorada Residencial (☎ 24 1698; www.torredo rada.com; Los Cipreses N-5, Residencial Huancaro; s/d/tw incl breakfast US$52/50/60) Torre Dorada is a modern, family-run hotel in a quiet residential district close to the bus terminal. It's recommended for the high quality of the service, including free pickup from and drop off to the airport and train stations. Fluent English is spoken.

Also recommended:

Cristina Hostal (☎ 22 7251; www.hcristina.com; Av El Sol 341; s/d/tr incl breakfast US$45/55/65) Cristina has curvy little rooms. It's one of the best values right on the hectic avenue, but that's not saying much.

Hostal Centenario (☎ 22 4235; www.hostal centenario.com; Centenario 689; d/tr/ste US$55/70/80) Small, serene but snooty place off the beaten path. Modern rooms have heating.

TOP END

Hotel Libertador Palacio del Inka (☎ 23 1961; www .libertador.com.pe; Plazoleta Santo Domingo 259; d US$200-250, ste US$235-365; 🍴 🖵) Even if you were yearning to stay at Hotel Monasterio, Cuzco's second-best hotel won't disappoint. Set in a huge, opulently furnished colonial mansion with a fine interior courtyard, the Libertador boasts Inca foundations, while other parts of the building date back to the 16th century, when Francisco Pizarro was an occupant. Refined guest rooms boast all the comforts you would expect, and even some you wouldn't, such as free wi-fi access. A business center, artisan gift shop and the respected Inti Raymi restaurant make this top-tier Peruvian chain hotel almost a small city unto itself.

Plaza Regocijo

BUDGET

Loki Backpackers Hostel (☎ 24 3705; www.lokihostel .com; Cuesta Santa Ana 601; dm US$5.50-8.50, s/d US$10.50/21; 🖵) This is where the party's at! Expats have rescued this 450-year-old national monument from near ruin, then transformed it into a jovial place to put down your rucksack for a few days. There are basically furnished private rooms and mixed or single-sex dormitories. Amenities include a shared kitchen, hot showers and free internet access.

Qorichaska Hostal (☎ 22 8974; www.qorichaskaperu .com; Nueva Alta 458; s/d with shared bathroom US$8/16/24, s/d/tr US$12/20/30, all incl breakfast) Hidden behind several gates, Qorichaska feels a bit like a secret society. It's basic but friendly and safe. There are hot-water showers and guests have access to a shared kitchen and internet hookup for laptops.

Gran Hostal Machu Picchu (☎ 23 1111; Quera 282; s/d/tr US$10/20/30) Set around two pretty courtyards with intricate old wooden balconies, this antique-looking *hostal* (guesthouse) has hot water most of the time. Don't let the grandiose name fool you, as it's not that much to look at. Still, discounts are often readily available.

Also recommended:

Hostal el Solar (☎ 38 0254; Plaza San Francisco 162; s/d US$9/15) Run-down exterior, but with colorful rooms and low, arched ceilings. Friendly and family owned.

MIDRANGE

Los Aticos (☎ 23 1710; www.losaticos.com; Quera 253; s/d/apt US$25/35/45; 💻) Hidden in an alley, this sleepy place stays under the radar. With just a handful of simple home-style rooms and suites, it's ideal for families, language-school students or other extended stays. Rates include free internet access and drinking water, a self-service laundry room and a full guest kitchen, where Peruvian cooking classes are taught. Its modern sister hotel, Los Aticos II, is less safely located.

Hogar San Pedro (☎ 23 1118; Cascaparo 116; s/d/tr US$35/45/55) You'll be greeted with smiling faces at this delightful guesthouse next to the sta-

tion for trains to Machu Picchu. The hostel is run by missionaries to help fund a home for girls. The building has several courtyard gardens, surprisingly comfortable rooms for the price and a convenient wake-up call from church bells.

El Balcón Hostal (☎ 23 6738; balcon1@terra.com.pe; Tambo de Montero 222; s/d/tr incl breakfast US$35/55/65; 💻) El Balcón is in an attractively renovated building dating from 1630 with just 16 guest rooms with balconies. It has a beautiful little garden filled with curiosities and some great views over Cuzco. There's also a sauna on the premises.

Hotel Garcilaso I (☎ 23 3031; www.hotelesgarcilaso .com; Calle Garcilaso 233; s/d/tr US$40/55/69) Though some rooms are a little drab, staying here will give you the thrill of staying in part of Garcilaso de la Vega's own mansion, which extends into the next-door Museo Histórico Regional. There's a second, more modernized location just up the street at No 285.

Hotel los Marqueses (☎ 26 4249; www.hotelmar queses.com; Calle Garcilaso 256; s/d/tr incl breakfast from US$40/60/80) An air of mystery and romance perfumes this fabulously refurbished colonial villa, built in the 16th century by Spanish conquistadors. Traditional *cuzqueño* paintings, courtyard fountains and balconies with views of the cathedral on the Plaza de Armas will all seduce you. The wood-floored rooms are large and airy; some have split-level sleeping areas and skylights. Most guests here are on package tours.

Hotel Royal Inka (☎ 22 2284; www.royalinkahotel .com; s/d/tr US$50/70/85; 💻) Hotel Royal Inka I (Plaza Regocijo 299); Hotel Royal Inka II (Santa Teresa 335) Built atop a 300-year-old national monument, the Royal Inka I faces the plaza. Reliably well-cared-for lodgings are popular with package tourists, but anyone can appreciate the bustling atmos-

---

THE AUTHOR'S CHOICE

Niños Hotel (☎ 23 1424; www.ninoshotel.com; Meloc 442; s/d with shared bathroom US$14/28, d US$34) This Dutch-run hotel comes with a wonderful story to tell. It's run by a nonprofit foundation that helps underprivileged children in Cuzco by providing food, medical aid and after-school activities. But even if it didn't, we'd still love this near-perfect small hotel, which inhabits a fetching colonial-era house with a sunny courtyard surrounded by a balcony. Although the simplest rooms are not much bigger than the bed contained within, all have thick wool blankets and portable heaters. Even the shared bathrooms are sparkling clean and have 24-hour hot water. The café downstairs offers a book exchange and a crackling fire on chilly Andean nights, and the front-desk staff speak several languages. The hotel's second property is even quieter, but also has a more out-of-the-way location. Inquire in advance about extended-stay apartment rentals.

phere and convenient location. Unfortunately, not all of the rooms have windows. While the more upscale Royal Inka II nearby has a gorgeous atrium dominated by a mural of Cuzco's history, it has not been as recently renovated as the Royal Inka I.

Also recommended:

Perezosos Bed & Breakfast (☎ 25 5341; Nueva Alta 424; s/d incl breakfast from US$15/30) An arty family home. It also has a popular curry restaurant (p248) downstairs.

Teatro Inca B&B (☎ 24 7372, in Lima 01-976 0523; www.teatroinka.com; Teatro 391; s/d/tr incl breakfast from US$30/40/50; 🖳) Outside is a tumbledown colonial façade, while inside is a jungle-plant-laden patio and oversized, if unfashionably decorated rooms.

TOP END

Casa Andina (www.casa-andina.com; r from US$87; 🞬 🖳) Catedral (☎ 23 3661; Santa Catalina Angosta 149); Plaza (☎ 23 1733; Portal Espinar 142); Private Collection (☎ 23 2610; Plazoleta de Limacpampa Chico 473); Korikancha (☎ 25 2633; San Agustín); San Blas (☎ 25 2400, 26 3694; Chihuampata 278) Among the most central of Cuzco's top-end hotels, the Casa Andina has five properties in Cuzco. Its Plaza hotel lies unobtrusively between the Plaza de Armas and Plaza Regocijo. The Catedral branch is even closer to the action and boasts some original Inca walls. The Qorikancha hotel inhabits a charming colonial courtyard house, while the San Blas branch has city views. But top billing goes to the so-called Private Collection hotel, which inhabits a graceful 16th-century colonial mansion. All of these Peruvian chain hotels have modern, well-equipped rooms and tourist restaurants with good-value buffet meals.

Other Neighborhoods

Hostal Familiar (☎ 23 9353; hostalfamiliar@hotmail.com; Saphi 661; s/d with shared bathroom US$7.50/15, s/d incl breakfast US$12/18) Well off the beaten path, this slightly ramshackle family-owned guesthouse boasts a well-kept colonial courtyard filled with flowering plants and clean, if spartan rooms. It's often full, but when it's not, prices are flexible. Some English is spoken.

Albergue San Juan de Dios Luxemburgo (☎ /fax 24 0135; www.sanjuandedioscusco.com; Av Manzanares 264, Urb Manuel Prado; s/d incl breakfast US$15/30; 🖳) A truly heartwarming place, this spotless guesthouse with modern décor is part of a nonprofit enterprise that supports a hospital clinic and also provides job opportunities for young people with disabilities. All of the quiet, carpeted

rooms have large windows; most have twin beds, though there's one matrimonial double. The wonderful staff can help with everything from making international phone calls to laundry services. Discounts may be available for online reservations. Take a taxi from the city center (US$1).

Andenes de Saphi (☎ 22 7561; www.andenesdesaphi .com; Saphi 848; s/d/tr incl breakfast US$41.50/48.50/55.50) Strangely standing at the far end of Saphi, where the city starts to become more rural, this dependably modern hotel has effected a rustic, wooden construction and fantastic colorful murals in every room.

Incatambo Hacienda Hotel (☎ 22 1918; incatambo hotel@terra.com.pe; Km 2 Carretera Cuzco-Saqsaywamán; s/d/tr US$65/70/80, ste US$85-115) This is a good place to stay in the countryside yet be within minutes of Cuzco and a short walk from the site of Saqsaywamán. Part of the colonial hacienda was once Francisco Pizarro's home, this place now houses faded but comfortable enough rooms. Fields and woodlands surround the hotel and horse rides can be arranged for guests.

EATING

Cosmopolitan Cuzco is packed with a variety of restaurants catering to every taste and budget. Book ahead for tables at the top restaurants during high season.

A multitude of touristy restaurants litter the Plaza de Armas, most of which have only a disappointing pastiche of Peruvian and international dishes; these restaurants are visited by bands who wander in and out during the evening. A marginally better hunting ground is the first *cuadra* (block) of Plateros, just off the plaza. A new breed of trendy eclectic eatery is taking over the San Blas area uphill from the center, where foreign tourists, expats, and Peruvian artists and musicians all mix.

If you don't treasure childhood memories of pet guinea pigs and you want to try something distinctively Andean, roast *cuy* is a delicacy. Other typical dishes include *anticucho de corazon* (shish kebab made from beef hearts), *adobo* (spicy pork stew), *chicharrones* (pork or chicken cracklings), *lechón* (suckling pig), *tamales* (corn dough stuffed with meat, beans or chilies) and various *locros* (meat and vegetable stews). The meal is often washed down with the infamous *chicha*, a fermented, mildly alcoholic corn beer, sometimes mixed with fruits.

A few restaurants around town serve up limited menus of tasty, authentic Andean specialties – there are no opt-out vegetarian clauses for the suddenly faint of heart. Called *quintas*, these spots are usually open only for lunch or afternoon snacks so expect to be out by early evening. There are also several hole-in-the-wall places along Pampa del Castillo that serve *chicharrones* hot from the grill, which is often placed in the door. Get them *para llevar* (to go) at lunchtime, when they're fresh.

Plaza de Armas

Some of the foreigners' bars around the plaza serve yummy victuals, including filling English breakfasts at Cross Keys (p248) and sloppy burgers at Norton's Rat (p248).

I Due Mondi (☎ 24 7677; Santa Catalina Ancha 366; snacks from US$0.50) If it's ice cream you want, you'll find over a dozen seductive flavors (including coca and *chicha*!) to choose from at this chic Italian-style café. Takeout is also available.

Coco Loco (☎ 24 3707; Espaderos 135; snacks US$1-3; ☿ till 4am Mon-Sat) This hectic fast-food joint serves international- and Peruvian-style snacks into the wee hours. It's just the place to satisfy your postclubbing cravings.

El Encuentro (☎ 24 7977; Santa Catalina Ancha 384; menús $1.20-3; ☿ 9am-3pm & 6-9pm Mon-Sat) This busy, happy vegetarian kitchen offers all-day breakfasts, a lunchtime salad bar and dinners featuring fake meats. It comes recommended by many readers.

Trotamundos (☎ 23 2387; 2nd fl, Portal Comercio 177; snacks US$1.50-4.50; ☿ 9am-11pm; 🖳) This coffeehouse has a dead-on view of the cathedral and sells a bit of everything, with especially good coffees and baked goods. It's also a popular late-night bar-cum-café.

Kin Taro (☎ 22 6181; Heladeros 149; mains US$2-4.50; ☿ 11am-10pm Mon-Sat) As authentic a Japanese menu as you'll find anywhere outside of Lima, with sake to swill and trout sushi among the more unusual fusion dishes.

Victor Victoria (☎ 25 2854; Tigre 130; mains US$2.50-6; ☿ lunch & dinner) Around the corner from the plaza is this no-frills budget restaurant, which slips a few French, Israeli and vegetarian dishes into its primarily Peruvian menu. Backpackers can't recommend it enough, especially for its filling portions.

Lemon Bee (Plateros 348B; mains US$3-7.50; ☿ 11:30am-10:30pm) Extending back from busy Plateros, this lime-green-colored eatery and lounge with globe lamps may not have the swiftest service, but each small plate is exquisitely done, from salads with glazed fruit and Andean cheeses to *lomo* (beef) in gourmet wine sauce. The cocktail list is lusciously long.

Chez Maggy (☎ 23 4861; Procuradores 344, 365, 374; mains US$3.50-5.50; ☿ 9am-10:30pm) The original travelers' haunt is still the best; Chez Maggy has virtually taken over Gringo Alley with three déjà vu–inducing branches, all serving up wood-fired pizzas and pastas.

Sumaq Misky (☎ 22 3353; www.sumaqmisky.com; 2nd fl, Plateros 334; mains US$4.50-12; ☿ 9am-10:30pm) Hidden up an alley of souvenir stalls, this friendly family-owned restaurant and bar targets adventurous travelers with special foodie nights such as alpaca Fridays and *cuy* Sundays, when you can order your guinea pig roasted tandoori style (we're not kidding, folks). '*Alpurguesas*' (alpaca hamburgers), *ensaladas* (salads) and all-you-can-eat specials are everyday affairs.

Blueberry Lounge (☎ 24 9458; Portal de Carnes 236; mains US$5-10; ☿ 8:30am-midnight) Global fusion rules the roost here, with a menu that throws together everything from South Asian curries to teriyaki alpaca steaks. The atmosphere after dark is more hip than at the touristy, run-of-the-mill plaza restaurants. There's an older branch called Greens (☎ 24 3379) at Tandapata 700, near Plaza San Blas; it's open 8:30am to 11pm.

Pomodoro (☎ 22 1397; Loreto 125; mains US$5-15; ☿ lunch & dinner) Hidden behind Inca walls off the Plaza de Armas, this romantic Italian restaurant concocts almost everything from scratch, including its pasta dough. Pizzas are cooked in a terra-cotta wood-fired oven that warms the subdued, artistically designed space. The best deals are at lunchtime.

Small grocery shops that stock trekking and camping food supplies include **Gato's Market** (Portal Belén 115; ☿ 7am-10pm) and the original **Market** (Mantas 119; ☿ 8am-11pm).

San Blas

El Buen Pastor (☎ 24 0586; Cuesta San Blas 579; items US$0.30-1.50; ☿ 7am-8pm Mon-Sat) You can't get much better than El Buen Pastor for a morning bakery. The warm glow isn't just from sipping a rich cappuccino with your pastries – it's also from the knowledge that all profits benefit charity.

Muse (☎ 974 4669; Tandapata 684; items US$0.75-4.20; ☺ 8am-late) A long-established bohemian hangout, this café has tables spilling out onto and around Plaza San Blas. It's always a popular spot for taking in the sun or curling up with a book on the cushioned window seats. The farm-fresh menu features bold salads and tons of other vegetarian options.

Kaschiwache Coffee Zone (Carmen Alto 260; items US$1-2.50; ☺ 11am-late) This hole-in-the-wall joint will irresistibly draw you in from the street with the carnivorous aromas of hot grilled sandwiches and savory kebabs – the *diablito* (little devil) is a feast. Some vegetarian items also available.

Cicciolina (☎ 23 9510; Calle Triunfo 393; bakery snacks & meals US$1.50-5.50, restaurant mains US$4.50-11.50; ☺ bakery 8am-6pm, restaurant 6pm-late) Inhabiting a lofty colonial courtyard mansion, this eclectic bakery and restaurant has just about everything to tickle your palate. Head downstairs to the bakery for generous breakfasts, sandwiches made from sliced bread that's hot out of the oven, and afternoon tea. Upstairs is a svelte tapas bar and Spanish restaurant with a balcony and a stellar wine list for tasting, including some European vintages.

Café Cultural Ritual (☎ 68 2223; Choquechaca 140; mains US$2-7.50, 3-course menús US$2.50-4.50; ☺ 8:30am-11pm) This is a bright, cute little option near the South American Explorers. A mostly vegetarian menu boasts Andean specialties such as quinoa pancakes, fried yucca and fresh trout cooked in all sorts of delicious ways, including stuffed with mushrooms and orange slices. There is a more carnivorous branch on the Plaza San Blas.

Moni (☎ 23 1029; San Agustín 311; dishes US$2.25-4.25; ☺ closed Sun) Moni is run by a Peruvian-English couple and is highly recommended for its à la carte vegetarian fare, including a mean veg curry and adapted organic Peruvian dishes. There's a laid-back coffee-bar ambience and sweet-tooth desserts.

Granja Heidi (☎ 23 8383; 2nd fl, Cuesta San Blas 525; meals US$3-6.50; ☺ 8:30am-9:30pm Mon-Sat) Follow the pictures of cows upstairs to this light Alpine café with terrific fresh produce, yogurts, cakes and other snacks on offer. The hot breakfasts are gigantic, and can satisfy any carnivorous cravings you may have.

Jack's Cafe (☎ 80 6960; Choquechaca 509; mains US$3.50-7.50; ☺ 9am-10:30pm) Before struggling uphill to the Plaza San Blas, refuel here on a hearty menu of modern international fusion fare and nouveau comfort food, such as gourmet grilled-cheese sandwiches. The ginger-lemon tea alone will cure all ills.

Sweet Temptation (Herrajes 138A; mains US$3.50-5.50; ☺ 11am-9pm) This cozy bakery and café is the perfect spot for a light meal or sweet snack, with fresh salads, quiche, fruit juices and generous slices of cake and pie on the sinfully delicious menu.

Al Grano (☎ 22 8032; Santa Catalina Ancha 398; mains US$3.50-5.50; ☺ 10am-9pm Mon-Sat) Al Grano has a nonspicy menu of hot plates from nine Asian countries, including Thailand, India, Vietnam and Indonesia, plus big breakfasts and coffee. Downstairs there's a pool table, cards and games, and a book exchange.

Inkafe Café (☎ 25 8073; Choquechaca 131A; mains US$4.50-10; ☺ 7am-11pm) With an art gallery on the walls and magazines scattered on the front table, this intimate café does a stellar job not only with breakfast, but also with regional Peruvian dinners and desserts, real Italian espresso and a short but sassy wine list.

Pachapapa (☎ 24 1318; Plaza San Blas 120; mains US$4.50-13.50; ☺ 11:30am-10pm) With rustic wooden tables and a crackling fire pit just off the Plaza San Blas, this airy outdoor restaurant has a menu full of classic Peruvian dishes with African, European and Asian accents, from *cuzqueño* lamb soup to roast trout with wild fennel, plus oven-fired pizzas and fruit-flavored pisco cocktails. There's live Andean harp music on most evenings.

Inka Panaka (Tandapata 140; mains US$6-9; ☺ breakfast, lunch & dinner) Along an alleyway west of the plaza, this ambitious and artistic restaurant has just a half-dozen candlelit tables at which you can fork into *novoandina* (Peruvian nouvelle cuisine) fare, including delicious breakfasts, steaks and desserts. There's a chill-out soundtrack and artisan crafts for sale.

MAP Café (☎ 23 3210; Plazoleta Nazarenas; dinner mains US$7.50-15; ☺ 11am-10pm) Inside the gorgeous Museo de Arte Precolombino, this is the city's most sophisticated restaurant and lounge. Outdoor tables with starched white tablecloths sit royally upon a glass-enclosed patio, while attentive waiters pour ruby red glasses of fantastic South European and New World wines. The menu ranges from Italianesque salads to Andean steak and guinea-pig confit. The crowd of movers and shakers is always dressed to the nines. There's live music almost every night. Make reservations for dinner.

Avenida El Sol

Inka's Hut (Av El Sol 751; menús US$1.50-2.50, mains US$2-5; ☻ lunch) Though all-business Av El Sol is almost a wasteland when it comes to restaurants, this humble locals' joint with a few outdoor and indoor tables is a real gem. Skip the à la carte menu and instead go for the special *menú* (set meal) of the day, which features true Peruvian fare, including some of the most lip-smackingly good ceviche (raw seafood marinated in lime juice) in the Andean highlands.

Plaza Regocijo

Though you need to keep your wits about you, the central market next to the San Pedro train station has many vendors for excellent fresh juices.

Café Dos X 3 (Marquez 771; snacks US$1.50) This retro café spins jazz tunes and has black-and-white tiling straight out of a 1950s movie. Don't you dare leave without tasting its out-of-this-world passion-fruit cheesecake.

Cusco Curry House (☎ 25 5341; Nueva Alta 424; mains US$4.50-7.50; ☻ 7am-10pm) A favorite with British expats, this family-run kitchen dishes up a rainbow of Indian curries and desserts, along with enough artery-choking pub grub to chase those homesick daydreams away.

El Truco (☎ 23 5295; Plaza Regocijo 261; lunch menús US$6, mains US$7.50-10.50, buffet US$9) This restaurant combines a mix of lofty architecture with murals, an original ceiling and a nightly dinner show starting at 8pm (admission US$2). Make reservations in the high season, because it's popular with tour groups.

Don Antonio (☎ 24 1364; Santa Teresa 356; lunch buffet US$12, dinner buffet US$16) Don Antonio is another top-notch dinner-and-show restaurant in a huge barn of a venue off the Plaza Regocijo. It is more elegant than El Truco, but it also is often booked out by large tour groups.

DRINKING

Most clubs open early, but crank up a few notches after 11pm. Savvy travelers will soon realize just how intense the competition is between Cuzco's nocturnal establishments, and will discover that they can count on enough free drinks to forget those aching feet fresh from the Inca Trail. The free drinks in question are almost exclusively *cuba libre* (rum and Coke), cheap wine or the ubiquitous pisco sour.

Plaza de Armas

In popular backpacker bars, especially right on the Plaza de Armas, both sexes should beware of drinks being spiked – don't let go of your glass, and think twice about using free-drink coupons.

Cross Keys, Norton's Rat, Paddy Flaherty's and Rosie O'Grady's are all good places to track down those all-important soccer (football) matches, with satellite TVs more or less permanently tuned into sports.

Ukuku's Pub (☎ 24 2951; Plateros 316; ☻ 8pm-late) The most consistently popular nightspot in town, Ukuku's plays a winning combination of crowd pleasers – Latin pop, reggae, alternative, salsa, ska, soul, jazz et al – and hosts live local bands nightly starting at 10:30pm. Usually full to bursting after midnight, it's good, sweaty dance-a-thon fun, with as many Peruvians as foreign tourists. Happy hour is from 8pm to 10:30pm.

Cross Keys (Portal Confiturías 233; ☻ 11am-late) Cross Keys is the most established watering hole in town, housed in a rickety old building on the plaza and smothered in the trappings of a typical British pub. There's cable TV, a dartboard and the most challenging pool table in town – its banana-like trajectory is as yet unparalleled. Happy hours are from 6:30pm to 7:30pm and 9:30pm to 10pm.

Norton's Rat (Loreto 115; ☻ 9am-late) Run by a motorcycle enthusiast, this down-to-earth bar overlooking the Plaza de Armas has the best damn burgers in town. They've also got TVs, darts and billiards to help you work up a thirst. Happy hour is from 7pm to 9pm nightly.

Paddy Flaherty's (Triunfo 124; ☻ 11am-late) This cramped little Irish pub is filled with high stools, games, TVs and a laughably big foam leprechaun. It's usually packed to the gills with homesick European travelers. Happy hours are from 7pm to 8pm and 10pm to 10:30pm.

Extreme (Portal de Carnes 298; ☻ 8pm-late) Though it may change names, it usually has the most up-to-the-minute electronic music collection, with techno, trance and hip-hop mixed in with mainstream. There are chill-out sofas upstairs but this isn't the place for chat. There's plenty of cheap booze during happy hour from 9pm to midnight.

Mama Africa (2nd fl, Portal Harinas 191; ☻ 7pm-late) Mama Africa is the classic backpackers' hangout, usually packed with people sprawled

IS THAT A TOAD IN YOUR BEER?

Ever wondered what *cuzqueños* (inhabitants of Cuzco) do to relax instead of whiling away the hours over a game of darts or pool in the local bar? Well, next time you're in a *picantería* (local restaurant) or *quinta* (house serving typical Andean food) look out for a strange metal *sapo* (frog or toad) mounted on a large box and surrounded by various other holes and slots. Men will often spend the whole afternoon drinking *chicha* (fermented corn beer) and beer while competing at this old test of skill in which players toss metal disks as close to the toad as possible. Top points are scored for landing it smack in the mouth. Legend has it that the game originated with Inca royals, who used to toss gold coins into Lake Titicaca in the hopes of attracting a *sapo*, believed to possess magical healing powers and to have the ability to grant wishes.

across cushions or swaying to rock and reggae rhythms. Unfortunately it also has a bad reputation as a haven for pickpockets, scam artists and other evildoers. It has a happy hour from 8:30pm to 11pm.

Big Blue Martini (☎ 24 8839; Tecsecocha 148; ☺ 7pm-late) This post-modern 'sofa bar' not only serves James Bond's signature cocktail, but boasts an eclectic range of sounds to tickle your eardrums, from hot fusion tribal beats to cool bossa nova.

Mystique (Suecia 320; ☺ 5pm-midnight) Built on Inca foundations and with a hulking back wall made up of enormous Inca blocks, Mystique is a relaxed, cavernous bar with chatty staff. Happy hours are from 7pm to 8:30pm and 10pm to 11:30pm.

Rosie O'Grady's (Santa Catalina Ancha 360; ☺ 11am-late) Rosie's is another spot for a Guinness that's got more room to breathe than its smaller compatriot Paddy's – in fact, it's usually bereft of any customers at all. Happy hours are from 1pm to 2pm and 8:30pm to 9:30pm.

El Muki (Santa Catalina 110-114; ☺ 9pm-late Thu-Sun) Just off the plaza, El Muki is a dark, intimate club with plenty of barely lit alcoves and a couples-only rule at the door (though they rarely count when a group goes in).

San Blas

Many of the *barrio*'s eclectic restaurants double as cafés and bars, too.

Mandela's (3rd fl, Palacio 121; ☺ 6pm-late) A bar with a true South African twist, Mandela's has a tempting menu of snacks and a funky atmosphere that will make you want to hang out here for hours, as well as plenty of live music and special events. Happy hours runs from 9pm to 11pm.

Km 0 (☎ 25 4240; Tandapata 100; ☺ 8:30am-late) With the slogan *Arte y Tapas*, this Spanish-

themed bar located off the Plaza San Blas is a convivial place for expats to gather. It often has live Latin and jazz music after 8:30pm. Show up early to taste the special US$3 dinner *menú*.

Le Nomadé (☎ 43 8369; Choquechaca at Hatunrumiyoc) This Francophile café has live bands some nights, but its real draws are the lounge chairs with hookah pipes for smoking and an open-air balcony overlooking a busy pedestrian intersection.

7 Angelitos (Siete Angelitos 638; ☺ 6pm-late Mon-Sat) This tiny hillside haunt is the city's unofficial hipster lounge. Their motto is Coffee, Music, Cocktails. And how can you argue with that? The live entertainment runs the cool-factor gamut from local rock bands to DJs spinning retro funk. Happy hour is from 7pm to 8pm.

Fallen Angel (☎ 25 8184; Plazoleta Nazarenas 221; ☺ 6pm-late) This is an ultrafunky restaurant and lounge that's falling all over itself in the rush to cram in as much kitsch as possible, with glitterballs, fake fur and even bathtub-cum-aquarium tables complete with live goldfish. Devilishly unangelic cocktails are expensive, but creative. The same folks also own jungle-themed Macondo (☎ 22 9415) at Cuesta San Blas 571; it's also open 6pm till late.

Plaza Regocijo

Kamikase (☎ 23 3865; Plaza Regocijo 274; ☺ 8pm-late) Kamikase is an older, more intimate bar that doesn't offer free drinks, but it has a disarmingly large variety of music that can switch from seductive salsa to live *música folklórica* in an instant. Try the bar's dangerously named *el camino a la ruina* (the path to ruin) cocktail. Happy hour runs from 8pm to 10pm, and there's also often a live show beginning at 10:45pm.

ENTERTAINMENT

Live Music

Several restaurants have evening *folklórica* music and dance shows, especially around the Plaza Regocijo (see p248). For live acoustic music in San Blas, head for Muse (p247) after 9:30pm.

Centro Qosqo de Arte Nativo (☎ 22 7901; Av El Sol 604; admission US$4.50, free with boleto turístico) Locals attend this center, one of the best places for nightly shows starting at around 7pm.

Teatro Municipal (☎ 22 7321; Mesón de la Estrella 149) This theater has a range of music and dance shows, plays and other performances, mostly on weekends.

Cinema

Sunset (☎ 80 7434; Tecsecocha 2) and **Film Lounge** (☎ 962 5898; 2nd fl, Procuradores 389) are small video bars showing three different recently released movies daily for a nominal admission charge (US$1 or less). Several bars and nightclubs also show movies during the afternoon; check in person for current show times and listings.

SHOPPING

Tourists inevitably equal rich targets for the innumerable street sellers of Cuzco. Though it can be wearisome, the only thing you can do is smile, say a firm '*No, gracias,*' and be careful not to show the slightest spark of curiosity in their wares, which would inevitably result in at least five minutes of hard sell.

The area surrounding Plaza San Blas is Cuzco's artisan quarter, packed with the workshops and showrooms of local craftspeople. There are also many shops along Hatunrumiyoc and Cuesta San Blas heading downhill to the Plaza de Armas. Some of the better ones offer the chance to watch artisans at work and to take a look into the interiors of colonial buildings while hunting down that perfect souvenir. Prices and quality vary greatly, so shop around and expect to bargain, except in the most expensive stores, where prices are often fixed.

Art & Crafts

Museo de Arte Precolombino (MAP; ☎ 23 3210; http://map.perucultural.org.pe; Plazoleta Nazarenas 231; ☼ 9am-10pm) For high-quality reproductions of ancient ceramics, textiles and jewelry, stop by the shop at this museum.

Centro de Textiles Tradicionales del Cusco (☎ 22 8117; www.textilescusco.org; Av El Sol 603A; ☼ 8am-8pm Mon-Fri, 8am-6pm Sat) For insight into Andean textiles, head to this nonprofit organization, founded in 1996, which promotes the survival of traditional weaving. You may be able to catch a shop-floor demonstration that illustrates the different weaving techniques in all of their finger-twisting complexity.

Agua y Tierra (☎ 22 6951; Calle Garcilaso 210; ☼ 9am-8pm) This beautiful high-ceilinged gallery specializes in authentic art and crafts, including pottery, textiles, paintings and more, all handmade by indigenous tribespeople living in the Amazon jungle.

Jatum Maqui (☎ 25 1744; Tecsecocha 432; ☼ 10:30am-9:30pm) A stone's throw from Gringo Alley, this youthful artists' workshop sells ceramics with quirky contemporary designs. They'll even box 'em up in international-post-ready packaging for a small additional charge.

High-quality artisan workshops around town:

Camero Workshop (☎ 995 7705; Palacio 122) For silver jewelry and ornaments, check out this family-owned shop.

Taller Olave (☎ 23 1835; Plaza San Blas 651) To the left of the church, there's a treasure trove of reproductions of colonial sculptures and precolonial ceramics here.

Taller Mendivil (☎ 23 3247; Plaza San Blas) Nationally famous for its giraffe-necked religious figures.

Taller Mérida (☎ 22 1714; Carmen Alto 133) For striking earthenware statues.

Clothing

Werner & Ana (☎ 23 0176; Plaza San Francisco 295A) This sleek Dutch-Peruvian designer showroom sells innovative high-end alpaca-wool clothing for both sexes, including uniquely gorgeous sweaters, scarves and hats. You may pay more here than at any of Cuzco's markets, but the quality is exceptional.

Andean Expressions (Choquechaca 210) Hailing from the mountain town of Huaraz in northern Peru, the owner of this unusual T-shirt shop is also the graphic designer – no Inka Kola logos here.

Artesania Alpasuri (☎ 80 5529; Cuesta San Blas 521) This humble family-owned shop sells handmade alpaca goods of all types, from sweaters to hats and mittens. If you're a knitting fan, you can even buy skeins of yarn dyed in natural colors.

Markets

For mass-produced woolen goods, textiles, pottery, jewelry and other crafty souvenirs, head for the vast **Centro Artesenal Cuzco** (cnr El Sol & Tullumayo; ☺ 9am-10pm), where you can literally shop till you drop. Other standard souvenir markets line Av El Sol heading north toward the Plaza de Armas.

Near the San Pedro train station, the Mercado Central isn't the place for crafts, but can be a good spot to pick up fruit or that vital spare pair of socks. Go in a group and don't take any valuables, as the thieves here are extremely professional and persistent.

GETTING THERE & AWAY

Cuzco is a major South American travel hub, with thousands of travelers passing through every week.

Air

Nearly all departures and arrivals from Cuzco's **Aeropuerto Internacional Alejandro Velasco Astete** (code CUZ; ☎ 22 2611), a few kilometers south of the city center, are in the morning, because climatic conditions in the afternoon typically make landings and takeoffs more difficult. Several airlines offer regular daily flights to and from Lima. These may get canceled or lumped together with other flights during quiet periods. Your best bet is to reserve the earliest flight available, as later ones are the most likely to be delayed or canceled. A few domestic carriers also have regularly scheduled flights to Puerto Maldonado, Juliaca and Arequipa.

Flights tend to be overbooked, especially in high season, so confirm your flight when you arrive in Cuzco, then reconfirm 72 hours in advance and again 24 hours before departure. If you buy your ticket from a reputable travel agent, the staff will reconfirm for you.

Check in at least two hours before your flight. Beware that check-in procedures are often chaotic, and even people with confirmed seats and boarding passes occasionally have been denied boarding because of overbooking errors. During the rainy season, flights can be postponed for 24 hours due to bad weather. Bring all valuables and essentials with you on the plane, and securely lock any checked baggage.

When flying from Cuzco to Lima, try to check in as early as possible so you can get a seat on the right-hand side of the plane for the best views of Salkantay's 6271m peak. Some pilots like to fly quite close to the mountain, and the views are sometimes stupendous.

(Sit on the left from Lima to Cuzco.) Very occasionally a different route is taken over Machu Picchu.

At the time of research, airlines serving Cuzco included the following:

Aero Condor Perú (☎ 25 2774; www.aerocondor .com.pe) Daily flights to Lima and thrice weekly to Puerto Maldonado.

LAN (☎ 25 5555; www.lan.com; Av El Sol 627B) Major domestic airline has regular direct flights to Lima, Arequipa, Juliaca and Puerto Maldonado.

Star Perú (☎ 23 4060; www.starperu.com; Office 1, Av El Sol 679) Two daily flights to Lima.

TACA (☎ 24 9921; www.taca.com; Av El Sol 602B) Daily flights to Lima (except on Wednesdays).

Bus & Taxi

The journey times given here are only approximate and apply only if road conditions are good. Long delays are likely during the rainy season, especially from January to April.

INTERNATIONAL

All international services depart from Cuzco's main long-distance bus terminal.

For Bolivia, several companies offer through buses to Copacabana (US$15, 13 hours) and La Paz (US$18 to US$20, 18 hours). Many will swear blind that their service is direct, though the buses usually stop in Puno for several hours in the middle of the night until the border opens. **Transportes Zela** (☎ 24 9977) and **Imexso** (☎ 22 9216) have daily buses departing around 9pm or 10pm. **Ormeño** (☎ 22 7501) has the only direct service to La Paz, leaving at around 10pm (US$33, 14 hours), but it goes via the border post at Desaguadero and does not pass through Copacabana.

For Tacna, by the Chilean border, Cruz del Sur has a bus departing every afternoon around 3pm (US$22.50, 15 hours).

LONG-DISTANCE

Terminal Terrestre, the town's main long-distance bus terminal (departure tax US$0.30), is 2km southeast of the Plaza de Armas, several blocks off Av El Sol. This is where you'll find all of the major luxury bus companies, including **Cruz del Sur** (☎ 22 1909) and **Ormeño** (☎ 22 7501), as well as scores of smaller *económico* (economic) bus operators, too. Buses to most major cities leave from this terminal, though buses for more unusual destinations (eg the Amazon jungle) still leave from elsewhere, so check carefully in advance.

Regular buses depart frequently for Puno (US$4.50 to US$10.50, six to seven hours) via Juliaca. But why not treat yourself? **Inka Express** (☎ 24 7887; www.inkaexpress.com; Pardo 865) runs luxury tourist-class buses with panoramic windows to Puno, with departures every morning. The splurge-worthy US$25 fare includes beverages and an English-speaking tour guide, who talks about the various sites that are briefly visited en route, including Andahuayillas, Raqchi, Abra la Raya and Pucará.

There are now two options to get to Lima. Most direct buses now ply the quicker route via Abancay and Nazca to Lima (US$18 to US$33, 17 to 23 hours), but this can be a rough ride and is prone to crippling delays during the rainy season. Companies include the most luxurious Cruz del Sur and the cheapest **Expreso Molino** (☎ 23 6144). The alternative is to go via Arequipa, a longer but more comfortable and reliable route for reaching Lima (US$19.50 to US$47.50, 25 to 27 hours). Ormeño's Royal Class has a daily departure at 9am.

Many buses also run just to Arequipa (US$7.50 to US$21, nine to 11 hours), but these services are mostly overnight. Buses to Abancay (US$4.50, five hours) and Andahuaylas (US$8, 10 hours) usually leave in the early morning and early evening. You can change at Andahuaylas to a bus bound for Ayacucho in Peru's central highlands via rough roads that get very cold at night. Wear all of your warm clothes and if you have a sleeping bag, bring it onboard the bus.

Buses to Quillabamba (US$4.50, seven to eight hours) via Santa María leave a few times per day from the Santiago bus terminal in western Cuzco (take a taxi from the city center, US$0.60). For this trip, most locals recommend the bus company **Turismo Ampay** (☎ 24 5734), which has three departures daily and conveniently staffs a ticket counter at Cuzco's main long-distance terminal. Daytime buses to Quillabamba are safer and have spectacular scenery while climbing the 4600m Abra de Malaga and then dropping down into the jungle.

For other Amazon jungle destinations, you have to fly, risk a hazardous journey by truck or find an expedition. There are daily trucks to Puerto Maldonado during the dry season along a wild and difficult road, and the trip from Cuzco takes anything from two days to over a week in the wet season (for more details, see p283). These trucks leave from near Plaza Túpac Amaru, east of Tacna along Garcilaso (US$10, two to seven days). You could also get a bus to Urcos and wait for a truck there. **Transportes Huayna Ausangate** (☎ 965 0922; Av Tomasa Tito Condemayta) has buses that go as far as Ocongate and Tinqui (US$4.20, seven hours) and leave around 10am daily except Sunday.

Getting to Manu is just as problematic. **Expreso Virgen del Carmen** (☎ 22 6895; Diagonal Angamos 1952) has buses to Paucartambo (US$3, five hours) leaving from behind the Coliseo Cerrado daily. Continuing from Paucartambo to Manu, there are only passing trucks or expedition buses, though buses for Pillcopata leave from Av Angamos in Cuzco on Monday, Wednesday and Friday mornings (US$4.50, 10 hours). For onward travel from Pillcopata to Shintuya, take a truck (US$2.50, eight hours).

REGIONAL SERVICES

Minibuses to Pisac (US$0.60, one hour) and Urubamba (US$0.90, two hours) leave frequently from Av Tullumayo, south of Av Garcilaso, from approximately 5:30am until 8pm. Roughly during those same hours, there are speed-demon *colectivo* (shared) taxis that leave when full bound for Urubamba (US$1.50, 1½ hours) via Chinchero (US$1, 45 minutes), as well as minibuses to the same destinations; you'll find them along the 300 block of Grau, near the Puente Grau (Grau Bridge). To get to Ollantaytambo, it's easiest to change at Urubamba, or you can try and catch an infrequent direct bus from Puente Grau (US$1, 2½ hours). Slower highway buses to Quillabamba (left) stop in Ollantaytambo, too, but you'll have to pay the full fare (US$4.50, 2½ hours).

Minibuses to Urcos (US$1) leave from Manco Capac, east of Tacna, and from Av de la Cultura opposite the regional hospital. Take these to visit Tipón, Piquillacta, Rumicolca and Andahuaylillas en route to Puno or to wait for passing trucks to Puerto Maldonado.

Trucks, *combis* (minibuses) and faster *colectivo* taxis for Limatambo (US$1.50 to US$2, 1½ to two hours), only a few of which continue onward to Abancay, leave from various places on Arcopata, a couple of blocks west of Meloc.

Car & Motorcycle

Given all the headaches and potential hazards of driving yourself around (see p526), consider hiring a taxi for the day – it's cheaper than renting a car anyway.

Motorcycle rentals are offered by a few outdoor outfitters and travel agencies in Cuzco. You can go for short runs around town or, when seasonal road conditions allow, into the surrounding areas, but not much further. Even for experienced riders who purchase full-coverage insurance, the risks and dangers are considerable.

Train

Cuzco has two train stations. Estación Huanchac, near the end of Av El Sol, serves Juliaca and Puno on Lake Titicaca. Estación San Pedro, next to the Mercado Central, serves Ollantaytambo in the Sacred Valley and Machu Picchu. The two stations are unconnected, so it's impossible to travel directly from Puno to Machu Picchu. Make reservations and buy tickets as far ahead of time as possible. Click to www.perurail.com for updated schedules, fares and reservations.

Estación Huanchac (Estación Wanchaq; ☎ 23 8722; ☟ 8:30am-4:30pm Mon-Fri, 8:30am-noon Sat & Sun) has trains for Puno that usually leave at 8am on Mondays, Wednesdays and Saturdays and take about 9½ hours (though they are often late). Fares have skyrocketed in recent years – they are now US$119 for first-class 'Andean Explorer' seats, which include a glass-walled observation car and a complimentary lunch,

or just US$17 for nonreservable seats in the more basic 'Backpacker' carriage, where drinks and snacks are sold separately. The journey has great views of the Andes and along the shores of Lake Titicaca, but even in the best class, seats are not very comfortable, and the ride is known for being a bone shaker.

At the time of research, tickets for the Machu Picchu train to Aguas Calientes were only sold from the Huanchac station (bring your passport to buy tickets), but soon they may also be available at the station that the Machu Picchu trains actually leave from, **Estación San Pedro** (☎ 22 1992). The station is a prime target for thieves, and though security around the station has been tightened it's best to remain vigilant.

From Cuzco, there are at least three tourist trains to Machu Picchu a day, with more during the high season. It is no longer possible for foreigners to use the *tren local* (the cheaper local train). The *trenes de turismo* (tourist trains) leave Cuzco between 6am and 7am and stop at Poroy (6:40am to 7:40am), Ollantaytambo (8am to 9am) and Aguas Calientes (9:40am to 11am), aka Machu Picchu Pueblo. Services return between 3:30pm and 5pm, arriving back in Cuzco between 7:20pm and 9:25pm. You can cut the return journey short by up to 45 minutes by getting off at Poroy and catching a taxi (around US$5) back to Cuzco.

At press time, one-way/round-trip tickets cost US$46/73 on backpacker trains, or US$66/113 in the first-class Vistadome train,

---

RIDING THE RAILS TO THE 'LOST' CITY OF THE INCAS

The railway journey to Machu Picchu begins with a steep climb out of Cuzco. Too steep for normal railroad curves, this is accomplished in four back-and-forth switchbacks. It takes at least 30 minutes before the train starts leaving Cuzco proper, and late-risers who miss it can often make a dash for the station at Poroy (US$5 in a taxi) to catch up.

The tracks then drop gently through agricultural countryside to Ollantaytambo. As the train draws out of that station, you may be able to catch a glimpse of the Ollantaytambo ruins as well as Nevado Verónica (5750m) to your right. The train descends down the narrow gorge, affording superb views of the white water of the lower Río Urubamba. Km 82 is where hikers begin the Inca Trail and the stop at Km 104 is for the shorter two-day Inca Trail.

The last station on the line is Aguas Calientes, aka Machu Picchu Pueblo. It is an 8km bus trip from the town up to Machu Picchu itself. The tracks beyond Aguas Calientes used to continue into the jungle at Quillabamba, but catastrophic damage during the 1998 El Niño closed the line.

On the return trip to Cuzco, the view of the city is enhanced by the beautifully floodlit church and cathedral on the Plaza de Armas, but unfortunately, the slow-moving trains on the switchbacks have become the target for angry locals throwing water and even rocks; don't stick any expensive cameras out of the windows, which you should shut here.

which is the earliest and fastest service and includes snacks and drinks. These prices have skyrocketed in recent years, though, and it's likely they will rise again every year or so. Despite local pressure to break PeruRail's monopoly on the line, more competitive prices are not likely in the near future.

Anyone interested in visiting the Sacred Valley should note that they can travel for less on Vistadome trains to Machu Picchu from Ollantaytambo, which is also where the cheapest backpacker train service leaves from. For more details, see p264.

GETTING AROUND
To/From the Airport

The airport is a few kilometers south of the city center. Frequent *colectivos* run along Av El Sol to just outside the airport (US$0.30). A taxi from the city center to just outside the airport costs US$2.70, or US$3.60 to the airport terminal itself (drivers have to pay a surcharge to enter the precinct). With advance reservations, many hotels and guesthouses offer free pickup services.

Bus

Local rides on public transportation cost only around US$0.30, though it's much easier to walk or just take a taxi than to figure out where any given minibus or minivan is headed.

Taxi

Always negotiate the fare in advance, as there are no meters. Trips within the city center should cost around US$1. Official taxis, identified by a lit company telephone number on the roof, are more expensive than taxis flagged down on the street, but they are safer and more reliable. Unofficial 'pirate' taxis, which only have a taxi sticker in the window, have been complicit in muggings, violent assaults and kidnappings of tourists. Before getting into any taxi, do as savvy locals do and take conspicuous note of the registration number. One recommended company is **Aló Taxi** (☎ 22 2222; www.alocusco.com), whose drivers are all licensed and should carry photo ID.

Tram

The **Tranvia** (☎ 22 4377) is a free-rolling tourist tram that conducts a two-hour hop-on, hop-off city tour; the fare for adults is US$2. It leaves at 10am and 1pm daily from Portal Comercio on the Plaza de Armas.

AROUND CUZCO

The four ruins closest to Cuzco are Saqsaywamán, Q'enqo, Pukapukara and Tambomachay. They can all be visited in a day, or far less if you're whisked through on a guided tour. If you only have time to visit one site, Saqsaywamán is less than a 2km trek uphill from the Plaza de Armas in central Cuzco.

Entry to each site is only with the *boleto turístico* (p229). They're officially open daily from 7am to 6pm, though there's little to stop you visiting outside these times – apart from the risk of violent muggings and sexual assaults. Attacks against tourists have occurred even during daylight hours. Go with as large a group as possible, and give yourself enough time to get back before nightfall.

The cheapest way to visit the sites is to take a bus bound for Pisac and ask the driver to get off at Tambomachay, the furthest site from Cuzco and, at 3700m, the highest. It's an 8km walk back to Cuzco, visiting all four ruins along the way. Alternatively, a taxi will charge roughly US$20 to US$25 to all four sites, giving you enough time to explore.

Locals in their traditional finery with their most photogenic llamas wait near each site, hoping to be photographed for a tip of a couple of nuevos soles. Local guides also hang around while offering their services, sometimes quite persistently; agree on a price before beginning any tour.

SAQSAYWAMÁN

This immense ruin of both religious and military significance is the most impressive in the immediate area around Cuzco. The long Quechua name means 'Satisfied Falcon,' though tourists will inevitably remember it by the mnemonic 'sexy woman.' Saqsaywamán feels huge, but what today's visitor sees is only about 20% of the original structure. Soon after the conquest, the Spaniards tore down many walls and used the blocks to build their own houses in Cuzco, leaving the largest and most impressive rocks, especially those forming the main battlements.

In 1536 the fort was the site of one of the most bitter battles of the Spanish conquest. Over two years after Pizarro's entry into Cuzco, the rebellious Manco Inca recaptured the lightly guarded Saqsaywamán and used it as a base to lay siege to the conquistadors in Cuzco. Manco was on the brink of defeating the Spaniards when a desperate last-ditch attack by 50 Spanish cavalry led by Juan Pizarro, Francisco's brother, succeeded in retaking Saqsaywamán and putting an end to the rebellion. Manco Inca survived and retreated to the fortress of Ollantaytambo, but most of his forces were killed. Thousands of dead littered the site after the Incas' defeat, attracting swarms of carrion-eating Andean condors. The tragedy was memorialized by the inclusion of eight condors in Cuzco's coat of arms.

The site is composed of three different areas, the most striking being the magnificent three-tiered zigzag fortifications. One stone incredibly weighs over 300 tons. It was the ninth *inca*, Pachacutec, who envisioned Cuzco in the shape of a puma, with Saqsaywamán as the head, and these 22 zigzagged walls as the teeth of the puma. The walls also formed an extremely effective defensive mechanism that forced attackers to expose their flanks when attacking

Opposite is the hill called **Rodadero**, with retaining walls, polished rocks and a finely carved series of stone benches known as the Inca's Throne. Three towers once stood above these walls. Only the foundations remain, but the 22m diameter of the largest, Muyuc Marca, gives an indication of how big they must have been. With its perfectly fitted stone conduits, this tower was probably used as a huge water tank for the garrison. Other buildings within the ramparts provided food and shelter for an estimated 5000 warriors. Most of these structures were torn down by the Spaniards and later inhabitants of Cuzco.

Between the zigzag ramparts and the hill lies a large, flat parade ground that is used for the colorful tourist spectacle of **Inti Raymi**, held every June 24 (p239).

To reach the site from central Cuzco, climb the steep street of Resbalosa to where it ends beneath Iglesia de San Cristóbal. Turn right and continue around a hairpin bend in the road. On your left look for a stone staircase, which is actually an old Inca road. From there, the climb to the top is a stiff one and often deserted – don't go alone. Guards will quickly demand to see your *boleto turístico* here. From the Plaza de Armas, the entire walk takes 20 to 40 minutes, so make sure you're acclimatized before attempting it. Arriving at dawn will let you have the site almost to yourself, though

a few opportunistic robberies have been reported, both early and late in the day.

Q'ENQO

The name of this small but fascinating ruin means 'Zigzag.' It's a large limestone rock riddled with niches, steps and extraordinary symbolic carvings, including the zigzagging channels that probably gave the site its name. These channels were likely used for the ritual sacrifice of *chicha* or, perhaps, blood. Scrambling up to the top you'll find a flat surface used for ceremonies and, if you look carefully, some laboriously etched representations of a puma, condor and a llama. Back below you can explore a mysterious subterranean cave with altars hewn into the rock.

Q'enqo is about 4km before Cuzco, on the left of the road as you descend from Tambomachay. Off the beaten path, the ruins of **Salapunco** (Temple of the Moon) are about 1.5km from Q'enqo; head back uphill, turn right and head out into the fields. Ask locals for directions as you go. Don't go alone as, due to its remote location, this is one of the most likely spots for being mugged or attacked.

PUKAPUKARA

Just across the main road from Tambomachay is this commanding structure looking down on the Cuzco valley. In some lights the rock looks pink, and the name literally means 'Red Fort,' though it is more likely to have been a hunting lodge, guard post and stopping point for travelers. It is composed of several lower residential chambers, storerooms and an upper esplanade with panoramic views.

TAMBOMACHAY

In a sheltered spot about 300m from the main road, this site consists of a beautifully wrought ceremonial stone bath channeling crystal-line spring water through fountains that still function today. It is thus popularly known as El Baño del Inca (the Bath of the Inca), and theories connect the site to an Inca water cult. Pukapukara can be seen from the small signaling post opposite.

THE SACRED VALLEY

The beautiful Río Urubamba valley, popularly known as El Valle Sagrado (the Sacred Valley), is about 15km north of Cuzco as the condor

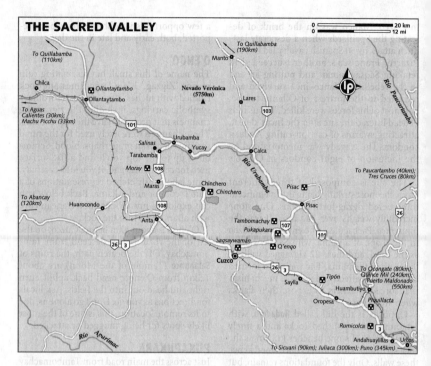

THE SACRED VALLEY

flies. The star attractions are the lofty Inca citadels of Pisac and Ollantaytambo, which preside over its undulating twists and turns, but the valley is also packed with other Inca sites, as well as hectic markets and fetching Andean villages. It's also famous for some high adrenaline activities, from rafting to trekking to drifting off in a hot-air balloon. Most activities can be organized in Cuzco (p234) or at some hotels in Urubamba.

A multitude of travel agencies in Cuzco offer whirlwind tours of the Sacred Valley, stopping at markets and the most significant archaeological sites, but even if you only have a day or two to spare, it's immeasurably rewarding to explore this peaceful, often overlooked corner of the Andes at your own leisure. Visiting the archaeological sites of Pisac, Ollantaytambo and Chinchero requires a *boleto turístico* (p229), which usually can be bought directly from the guards at the sites.

PISAC

☎ 084 / pop 2000 / elev 2715m

Lying 33km northeast of Cuzco by paved road, Pisac is the most convenient starting point for a visit to the Sacred Valley. There are two distinct parts to Pisac (also spelled Pisaq): the colonial village lying beside the river and the Inca fortress perched dramatically on a mountain spur above.

Information

There's a pay phone on the main plaza. A small, slow **cybercafé** (Bolognesi s/n; per hr US$0.60; ☯ 9am-10pm Mon-Sat, noon-10pm Sun) and a mini supermarket that doubles as a BCP agent for exchanging US dollars are further south on Bolognesi.

Sights & Activities

In Pisac, Bolognesi has several craft workshops and you can visit any of the clay-oven bakeries on Mariscal Castilla for the hot-out-of-the-oven flatbread rolls typical of the area. Keep an eye out for the elaborate *castillos de cuyes* (miniature castles inhabited by guinea pigs).

PISAC RUINS

This hilltop **Inca citadel** (admission only with boleto turístico; ☯ 7am-6pm) lies high above the village on a triangular plateau with a plunging gorge on either side. Though it's a truly awesome site, you'll see relatively few tourists here, except mid-morning on Sundays, Tuesdays and Thursdays, when it becomes flooded with tour groups.

To get here, either walk up the steep 4km footpath from the plaza or hire a taxi (there are usually some waiting on the east side of the market area) to drive you up the 10km paved road (one-way US$4.50). You can sometimes catch a truck carrying workers up from Pisac around 7am, and occasional minibuses run to within a kilometer of the ruins. On market day, *combis* may also make the trip from the eastern edge of the village (US$0.60).

The footpath to the site starts from above the west side of the church. Allow 90 minutes to two hours for this stiff but spectacular climb. There are many crisscrossing trails, but if you keep heading upward toward the terracing, you won't get lost. To the west, or the left of the hill as you climb up on the footpath, is the Río Kitamayo gorge; to the east, or right, is the Río Chongo valley.

Pisac is famous for its agricultural **terracing**, which sweeps around the south and east flanks of the mountain in huge and graceful curves, almost entirely unbroken by steps, which require greater maintenance and promote erosion. Instead, the terracing is joined by diagonal flights of stairs made of flagstones set into the terrace walls. Above the terraces are cliff-hugging footpaths, watched over by caracara falcons and well defended by massive stone doorways, steep stairs and a short tunnel carved out of the rock. Vendors meet you at the top with welcome drinks, and after carrying the bottles this far, they certainly deserve to make a few nuevos soles.

This dominating site guards not only the Urubamba valley below, but also a pass leading into the jungle to the northeast. Topping the terraces is the site's **ceremonial center**, with an Intihuatana (Hitching Post of the Sun), several working water channels and some painstakingly neat masonry in the well-preserved **temples**. A path leads up the hillside to a series of ceremonial baths and around to the military area. Looking across the Kitamayo gorge from the back of the site, you'll also see hundreds of holes honeycombing the cliff wall. These are **Inca tombs** that were plundered by *huaqueros* (grave robbers), and are now completely off-limits to tourists.

The site is large and warrants several hours of your time.

MARKET

For most of the week, colonial Pisac is a quiet, rural Andean village. It comes alive on Sunday, however, when the famous weekly market takes over. This bustling spectacle attracts traditionally dressed locals from miles around and, despite also drawing tourists from the world over, still retains traditional aspects.

Around 10am the tour buses deposit their hordes into an already chaotic scene, thronged with buyers and overrun with artisans. The selling and bartering of everyday produce, including dozens of potato varieties, goes on alongside the masses of souvenir stalls. Nonetheless, the market is a professional affair and, even after hard bargaining, both the prices and the selection are comparable to Cuzco.

The main square becomes packed with locals early on and becomes even more crowded after the morning Mass (given in Quechua) when the congregation leaves the church in a colorful procession, with men in traditional highland dress blowing horns and sometimes led by the mayor holding his silver staff of office. Things start winding down well before lunchtime, and by evening the village has returned to its usual somnolent state.

There's a smaller craft market on Thursday and one smaller still on Tuesday, and a few stallholders also sell souvenirs daily during the high season.

Festivals & Events

Pisac celebrates **La Virgen del Carmen** in mid-July, from around the 15th to the 18th.

Sleeping

Pisac has only limited accommodations, so get there very early on market days during high season. Cheap guesthouses are scattered on and around the main plaza.

Hospedaje Beho (☎ 20 3001; hospedajebeho@yahoo .es; Intihuatana 113; s/d with shared bathroom US$4.50/9, s/d US$9/18) On the path to the ruins and easily hidden by market stalls, this family-run handicrafts shop offers no-frills lodging with warm showers. If you reach the entrance to the footpath to the ruins, you've gone too far; turn around and look back downhill for a yellow sign.

CUZCO & THE SACRED VALLEY

Hospedaje Familiar Samana Wasi (☎ 20 3018; Plaza Constitución 511; s/d US$10.50/15) Facing the main plaza, this place has plain but clean rooms and hot water. There's a cheap restaurant serving trout dishes downstairs.

Hotel Pisaq (☎ 20 3062; www.hotelpisaq.com; Plaza Constitución; s/d with shared bathroom US$13/26, s/d incl breakfast US$20/35) Recognizable by its funky geometric designs, this plaza hotel has a pretty courtyard and rustic rooms with hand-painted native-inspired murals. Massages and entry to the natural-rock sauna cost extra. German, English and French are spoken.

Paz y Luz Bed & Breakfast (☎ 20 3204; www.maxart .com/window/gateway.html; s/d incl breakfast US$20/35) A 1km walk east along a dirt road beside the river, this spiritual spot is surrounded by

green fields and run by a North American who also organizes mystical tours. Ask about apartment rentals for extended stays.

Royal Inka Hotel Pisac (☎ 20 3064, 20 3065; www .royalinkahotel.com; campsites per person US$3, s/d/tr/q incl breakfast US$54/78/93/108; ⬛) About 1.5km from the plaza up the road to the ruins, this large converted hacienda is operated by Cuzco's Royal Inka group. Though many of the rooms lack character, some on the upper floors have panoramic views. The hotel also has an impressive list of amenities: restaurant, bar, sauna, massage, indoor swimming pool and tennis and basketball courts; it also offers horseback rides and sightseeing tours. There's a public campground (tent hire US$10 to US$15) with good facilities, too.

Eating

Hotel Pisaq (☎ 20 3062; www.hotelpisaq.com; Plaza Constitución; mains US$4-10) The café at this hotel serves home-style Peruvian meals, and also fires up a wood-burning pizza oven on market days and Saturday evenings.

Restaurante Valle Sagrado (☎ 20 3009; Amazonas 116; mains US$2.40-3.60; ☯ lunch & dinner) Few tourists know about this family-run restaurant, just a few blocks west of where all the buses stop. It's nothing fancy, but the house specialty is delicious trout cooked in a rainbow variety of styles. The staff's smiles are heartwarmingly sincere.

Mullu (☎ 20 3033; Plaza Constitución; mains US$2.50-5.50; ☯ closed Mon) Hanging above an art gallery, this alt-cultural café has a prime position with balcony seats overlooking the plaza, and a deliciously long list of juices and smoothies (US$1.25 to US$3), sandwiches and *novoandina* fusion fare. Bohemians will want to hang out for hours on the sofas and floor cushions.

Ulrike's Café (☎ 20 3195; Plaza Constitución; 3-course menús US$3.60; ☯ 9am-9pm) This sunny café serves up a great vegetarian *menú*, plus homemade pastas and melt-in-the-mouth cheesecake and brownies. There's a book exchange, DVDs and special events like yoga classes. English, French and German are spoken.

Getting There & Away

Buses to Urubamba (US$0.60, one hour) and to Av Tullumayo in Cuzco (US$0.60, one hour) leave frequently from the downtown bridge between 6am and 8pm; the latter may be standing-room only, while the former go

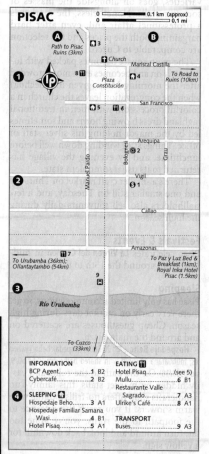

PISAC

0 — 0.1 km (approx)
0 — 0.1 mi

Path to Pisac Ruins (3km)

Church

Mariscal Castilla

Plaza Constitución

To Road to Ruins (10km)

San Francisco

Arequipa

Manuel Pardo

Bolognesi

Grau

Vigil

Callao

Amazonas

To Urubamba (36km);
Ollantaytambo (54km)

To Paz y Luz Bed & Breakfast (1km); Royal Inka Hotel Pisac (1.5km)

Río Urubamba

To Cuzco (33km)

INFORMATION		
BCP Agent	1	B2
Cybercafé	2	B2
SLEEPING		
Hospedaje Beho	3	A1
Hospedaje Familiar Samana Wasi	4	B1
Hotel Pisaq	5	A1

EATING		
Hotel Pisaq	(see 5)	
Mullu	6	B1
Restaurante Valle Sagrado	7	A3
Ulrike's Café	8	A1
TRANSPORT		
Buses	9	A3

via Calca (US$0.30, 30 minutes). Many travel agencies in Cuzco also operate tour buses to Pisac, especially on market days.

CALCA

☎ 084 / pop 8500 / elev 2928m

Less than 20km beyond Pisac, Calca is a key market town in the Sacred Valley, though it has few facilities for tourists. There are some small Inca sites and hot springs in the vicinity, which are best explored by mountain bike.

The clean, flowery **Hospedaje Familiar Villa María** (☎ 20 2110; Mariano de Los Santos 388; 4-bed dm with shared/private bathroom US$3/4.50, s/d/tr US$6/12/18) is the best choice in town, with amiable service, hot-water bathrooms and a small orchard. It's a few blocks west of where most buses stop. Good food is served at **Quinta Jacaranda** (☎ 20 2026; mains US$4.50-10; ☉ closes 6pm), 1km west of town along the main highway.

Buses from Cuzco (US$0.75, 1½ hours) that go via Pisac (US$0.30, 30 minutes) en route to Urubamba (US$0.30, 30 minutes) usually stop at Calca. Minivans also frequently shuttle between Calca and those towns.

YUCAY

☎ 084 / pop 3000 / elev 3000m

The pretty little village of Yucay is approximately 4km before Urubamba. There's nothing to speak of in the town itself, but there are three excellent hotels around a grassy plaza that make it an inviting place to stay overnight or break for lunch.

Hostal Y'llary (☎ 20 1112; fax 22 6607; Plaza Manco II No 107; campsites per person US$6, s/d incl continental breakfast US$25/30), which means 'Dawn' in Quechua, is run by a charming old gent and has pleasant rooms with private hot showers. There's also a large garden and camping area with a separate hot shower and bathroom.

La Casona de Yucay Hotel (☎ 20 1116; www.lacasona deyucay.com; Plaza Manco II No 104; s/d/tr/ste incl breakfast from US$60/80/100/140) is a colonial house built in 1810, in which the liberator Simón Bolívar stayed in 1825. Indeed, if you book ahead you may even be allowed to stay in his antique-filled room. Almost 40 spacious guest rooms surround a traditional stone courtyard with hand-carved arches, and there is a restaurant and bar. The staff are gracious.

The entrance to **Sonesta Posada del Inca** (☎ 20 1107, in USA & Canada ☎ 800 766 3782; www.sonesta.com /peru_yucay1/; Plaza Manco II No 123; s/d/ste US$115/125/155; ▣) is through an 18th-century building of a Spanish colonial hacienda, formerly a monastery built upon the summer palace of *inca* Huayna Capac. Most of the 84 rooms are in modern buildings, but a few in the original part are more creaky and characterful; one is supposedly haunted. Also on the sprawling grounds are flower-filled gardens, a chapel and a little museum, as well as a global ATM that may or may not be working, a public pay phone and a money-exchange desk for US dollars and euros. The hotel can arrange local activities, or you can simply unwind in the Kallpa Wasi Spa, which offers massages (from US$45) and has a steam room, sauna and Jacuzzi. The hotel's open-air restaurant Inkafé, open from 5:30am until 10:30pm daily, puts on a generous lunch buffet (US$10).

Get to Calca on any bus heading between Pisac and Urubamba.

URUBAMBA

☎ 084 / pop 8000 / elev 2870m

At the junction of the valley road leading from Pisac with the Chinchero road back to Cuzco, Urubamba is an unappealing but necessary transit hub. Although it has little of historical interest, it's surrounded by beautiful countryside and makes a convenient base from which to explore the extraordinary Salinas and terracing of Moray, and to perhaps participate in some of the valley's top-flight outdoor activities.

Orientation & Information

Urubamba is quite spread out, so expect to do a lot of walking or to pay for *mototaxi* (three-wheeled motorcycle rickshaw taxi) rides. There's a global ATM at the *grifo* (gas station) on the main highway, about 1km east of the main bus terminal. **Banco de la Nación** (Mariscal Castilla s/n) changes US dollars. You can get online at a few cybercafés nearby the plaza, which is where you'll find the post office.

Activities

Many outdoor activities that are organized from Cuzco (see p234) take place at Urubamba, including horseback riding, mountain biking, paragliding and hot-air balloon trips.

Perol Chicho (☎ 21 3386, 962 4475; www.perolchico .com), run by Dutch-Peruvian Eduard van Brunschot Vega, has an excellent ranch outside Urubamba with Peruvian *paso* horses. Eduard organizes horseback-riding tours that last up to two weeks; a one-day trip to Moray and Salinas costs roughly US$110. Advance bookings are required.

Adventure Club Viento Sur (☎ 20 1620; www .aventurasvientosur.com; Sol y Luna Lodge) organizes a variety of activities, from horse-riding tours on Peruvian *paso* horses (half-day/full-day/two-day tour US$60/100/275) to paragliding (in high season only, tandem flight per person US$125), mountain biking (half-day/full-day tours US$55/90) and guided hikes. Make reservations in advance.

Sleeping

Although it lacks the charm of Ollantaytambo, Urubamba has a surprising number of tourist accommodations. There are only a few places to stay in the city center; most of the hotels, guesthouses and campgrounds are lined up along the highway, west of town and the bus terminal, on the way to Ollantaytambo.

BUDGET

Hotel Urubamba (☎ 20 1062; Bolognesi 605; s/d with shared bathroom US$3/6, s/d US$6/9) Hotel Urubamba, a couple of blocks from the central plaza, is a basic but friendly choice in the town center. The shared showers on the 2nd floor may have hot water upon request.

Señor de Torrechero (☎ 20 1033; Mariscal Castilla 114; s/d/tr US$6/9/12) This old standby guesthouse offers fair-value, if unexciting, rooms right on a busy thoroughfare. It's just uphill from the *grifo*, near some yummy bakeries.

Camping

Los Cedros (☎ 20 1416; campsites per person US$5) This pastoral campground is about 4km above the town on winding country roads.

MIDRANGE

Quinta los Geranios (☎ 20 1093; Cabo Conchatupa; s/d/tr US$15/30/45) Los Geranios has spotless new rooms with bathrooms, and a garden running down to the river. It's also a popular open-air restaurant (mains US$4.50 to US$10), open from noon to 6pm.

Las Chullpas (☎ 968 5713, 969 5030; www.geocities .com/laschullpas; Pumahuanca Valley; r per person from US$20) Hidden 3km above town, these woodland cottages with fireplaces and private bathrooms make for the perfect getaway. The site is nestled beneath a mountain and thick eucalyptus trees. There's a sweat lodge, garden hammocks and an open kitchen where vegetarian

food is available. Spanish lessons and treks to the Lares Valley and Choquequirau can be arranged here. A *mototaxi* from town should cost around US$1.

Hostal el Maizal (☎ 20 1194; maizal@speedy.com .pe; r from US$45) West of the bus terminal just past Km 73, El Maizal is a quiet place with a large grassy garden. German and English are spoken, and rates may include continental breakfast.

Quinta Patawasi (☎ 20 1386; quinta-patawasi@telser .com.pe; r from US$45) On a small street right behind Hostal el Maizal, Quinta is a characterful spot recommended for extremely cheerful, attentive service. English is spoken.

San Agustín Hotel Urubamba (☎ 20 1444; www.hotelessanagustin.com.pe; s/d/tr/ste incl breakfast US$60/70/80/90; ☑) Part of the Cuzco based chain, this San Agustín hotel is a spacious option about a kilometer east of town at Km 69 along the highway. Rooms all have TV and minibar, and there's also a swimming pool, massage room, sauna, Jacuzzi, and a restaurant and bar at which to sip a pisco sour.

TOP END

Willka T'ika Garden Guesthouse (☎ 20 1508, in USA 503-252 1492, in USA & Canada 888 737 8070; www.magical journey.org) Just past Km 75, about 3km west of town, this alternative guesthouse staffed by Quechua-speaking locals has offbeat rooms set in riotously colorful gardens. Yoga classes, massage and meditation rooms, healing and shamanism workshops, and vegetarian meals are offered. Call or email for rates; it is essential to make advance reservations here, and it sometimes closes on weekends. Willka T'ika is run by tour operator Magical Journey.

San Agustín Hotel Monasterio de la Recoleta (☎ 22 1666; www.hotelessanagustin.com.pe; Jirón Recoleta s/n; s/d/tr/ste incl breakfast US$70/80/90/90) This 15th-century building is a hauntingly beautiful mission on the outskirts of town. It has a chapel, cloistered courtyards and nearly three dozen colonial-style rooms and suites that were recently renovated.

K'uychi Rumi (☎ 20 1169, 969 0952; www.urubamba .com; d/q US$90/140) Between Km 74 and Km 75 on the main highway, over 2km west of town, you'll find a half-dozen two-story rustic private cottages built of colorful clay. Each comes with its own kitchenette, fireplace, terrace balcony and two bedrooms; a buffet breakfast costs US$5. The name means 'Rainbow Stone' in Quechua.

Sol y Luna Lodge (☎ 20 1620; www.hotelsolyluna.com; s/d/tr/q incl breakfast US$120/140/185/220, ste d US$220; ⊠) Just over 1km west of town along a side street running north of the highway, this swish red-walled complex has secluded guest bungalows made of wood, stone and clay and color-fully accented with local artisans' handiwork. There's also a restaurant with dinner shows, and spacious gardens with tennis courts and a horse stable, plus a spa offering facials, scrubs, wraps, and Thai and Swedish massage.

Eating & Drinking

Many hotels have buffet-style restaurants (you'll pay at least US$12 for lunch) that are filled by tour groups.

Muse, Too (☎ 960 6966; Comercio 347; mains US$3-6; ⏱ 10am-late) Far removed from the touristy restaurants along the highway, this laid-back alternative café and bar just off the main plaza dishes up generously sized portions of in-ternational comfort food. DVD movies are shown and there's occasionally live music or a poker game going on in the evenings.

Tres Keros Restaurant Grill & Bar (☎ 20 1701; Av Señor de Torrechayoc; mains US$4.50-10; ⏱ lunch & dinner) This stylish chef-owned restaurant dishes up flavorful *novoandina* fusion fare to pique any gourmet's interest. There's also a fully-stocked bar with satellite TV.

Shopping

Seminario Ceramicas (☎ 20 1002; www.ceramicasemin ario.com; Berriozabal 111) The prolific and well-known local potter Pablo Seminario creates original work with a preconquest influence that is different from anything you'll see in Cuzco. He speaks English and is happy to explain his art to visitors. The workshop is in western Urubamba, just off the main highway.

Getting There & Away

Urubamba serves as the valley's principal transportation hub. Every 15 minutes buses leave the terminal on the main highway for Cuzco (US$0.90, two hours) via Calca (US$0.30, 30 minutes) and Pisac (US$0.60, one hour) or via Chinchero (US$0.50, 50 minutes). *Colectivo* minibuses and taxis to Ollantaytambo (US$0.30, 30 minutes) also leave from the bus terminal. It's located about 1km west of the main intersection at the *grifo*, where faster *colectivo* taxis to Cuzco (US$1.50, 1½ hours) leave when full. You can buy tickets

for the morning bus to Quillabamba (US$4.50, five to six hours) via Ollantaytambo from a small shop just east of the *grifo*.

SALINAS

About 6km further down the valley from Uru-bamba is the village of Tarabamba. Cross the Río Urubamba by footbridge in Tarabamba, turn right and follow a footpath along the south bank to a small cemetery, where you turn left and climb roughly southward up a valley to the **salt pans** (admission US$1.50; ⏱ 9am-4:30pm) of Salinas. It's about a 3km uphill hike. A rough dirt road that can be navigated by taxi enters Salinas from above, giving spec-tacular views. Tour groups visit via this route most days.

Thousands of salt pans have been used for salt extraction since Inca times. A hot spring at the top of the valley discharges a small stream of heavily salt-laden water, which is diverted into salt pans and evaporated to produce a salt used for cattle licks. The local salt-extracting cooperative charges for entry to this incredible site, but there's rarely any-one to collect the money if you enter from the path climbing up from the river.

MORAY

Over 10km east of Urubamba, the impres-sively deep amphitheater-like terracing of Moray (admission US$1.50; ⏱ 9am-4:30pm) is a fasci-nating spectacle. Different levels of concentric terraces are carved into a huge earthen bowl, each layer of which apparently has its own microclimate, according to how deep into the bowl it is. For this reason, some theorize that the Incas used them as a kind of laboratory to determine the optimal conditions for grow-ing crops of each species. There are two large bowls and one small, the first of which has once again been planted with various crops as a kind of living museum.

Though refreshingly off the beaten path, this site is not all that challenging to reach. First, catch one of the frequent buses or *com-bis* from Urubamba's bus terminal bound for Chinchero (US$0.30, 30 minutes to the Moray turnoff). From Cuzco, take any bus (U$0.60, 1½ hours) or *colectivo* taxi (US$1, 70 minutes) heading to Urubamba via Chinchero (be aware that those via Pisac take a different highway). Ask the driver to drop you at the turnoff for the road to Maras. Taxis usually wait at this turnoff to drive tourists to Moray (round-trip around US$9, including waiting time), which can be combined with a visit to Salinas (US$12). Alternatively, take a taxi trip direct from Urubamba (round-trip US$12, or US$16 including Salinas). The road to the ruins is extremely rough.

You could also tackle the 3km walk to the village of Maras yourself. From there, follow the trail another 7km to Moray, asking locals for directions. From Moray, it is supposedly possible to continue walking to Salinas about 6km away and then onward down to the Río Urubamba, which can fill a long but satisfying day. Ask the guard in Moray to point out the faint and not well-used trail, as it can be very hard to find. Most locals recommend backtracking to Maras first.

OLLANTAYTAMBO

☎ 084 / pop 2000 / elev 2800m

Dominated by a massive Inca fortress above, the quaint village of Ollantaytambo is the best surviving example of Inca city planning, with narrow cobblestone streets that have been continuously inhabited since the 13th century. Originally this rural village was divided into blocks called *canchas*, and each *cuncha* had just one entrance, which led into a courtyard. Today hulking tour buses roar along the streets as they race to meet trains arriving from and departing for Aguas Calientes, aka Machu Picchu Pueblo.

Information

Slow and expensive internet access is available at a few cybercafés near the main plazas. At the corner of the road leading down to the train station, the **public toilet** (admission US$0.15) is a model of cleanliness that the whole country should seek to emulate; its motto is *Ciudad Inka Viviente, Te Quiero Limpia* (Living in the Incas' City, I Want it to Be Clean for You).

Sights & Activities

OLLANTAYTAMBO RUINS

The spectacular, huge, steep terraces that guard Ollantaytambo's **Inca ruins** (entry only with boleto turístico; ☺ 7am-6pm) mark one of the few places where the Spanish conquistadors lost a major battle. It was to this fortress that the rebellious Manco Inca retreated after his defeat at Saqsaywamán. Then in 1536, Hernando Pizarro (Francisco Pizarro's younger half-brother) led a force of 70 cavalrymen here,

supported by large numbers of indigenous and Spanish foot soldiers, in an attempt to capture Manco Inca.

Pizarro's men were showered with arrows, spears and boulders from atop the steep terracing and were unable to climb to the fortress. They were further hampered when Manco Inca, in a brilliant move, flooded the plain below the fortress through previously prepared channels. The Spaniards' horses were bogged down in the water and Pizarro ordered a hasty retreat – which almost became a rout when the conquistadors were followed down the valley by thousands of Manco Inca's victorious soldiers.

However, the Incas' victory was short lived. The Spanish forces soon returned with a quadrupled cavalry force and Manco fled to his jungle stronghold in Vilcabamba.

Though Ollantaytambo was a highly effective fortress, it was as much a temple as a fort. A finely worked **ceremonial center** is at the top of the terracing. Some extremely well-built walls were under construction at the time of the conquest and have never been completed. The stone was quarried from the mountainside 6km away, high above the opposite bank of the Río Urubamba. Transporting the huge stone blocks to the site was a stupendous feat that must have involved the sweat and blood of thousands of indigenous workers. Their crafty technique to move the massive blocks across the river was to leave the blocks by its side then divert the entire river channel around them!

A good walk from Ollantaytambo is the 6km trail to the **Inca quarry** on the opposite side of the river. The trail starts from the Inca bridge by the entrance to the village and takes a few hours to reach the site, passing several abandoned blocks known as 'the tired stones.' Looking back towards Ollantaytambo, you can see the enigmatic optical illusion of a pyramid in the fields and walls in front of the fortress, which a few scholars believe marks the legendary place where the original Incas first emerged from the earth.

MUSEO CATCCO

Local community history and ethnography are the main focus of the lovingly tended **Museo CATCCO** (☎ 20 4024; www.ollanta.org; Patacalle s/n; suggested donation US$1.50; ☺ 10am-1pm & 2-4pm Tue-Sun). Its historical and cultural displays hold a wealth of fascinating information, from

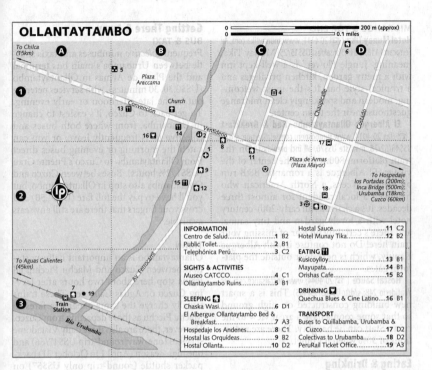

OLLANTAYTAMBO

0   200 m (approx)
0   0.1 miles

To Chilca
(15km)

Plaza
Araccama

Church

Convención

Ventiderio

Chaupicalle

Costado

Plaza de Armas
(Plaza Mayor)

To Hospedaje
los Portadas (200m);
Inca Bridge (500m);
Urubamba (18km);
Cuzco (60km)

To Aguas Calientes
(45km)

Av Ferrocarril

Train
Station

Río Urubamba

INFORMATION		Hostal Sauce.....................11 C2
Centro de Salud...................1 B2		Hotel Munay Tika.................12 B2
Public Toilet........................2 B1		
Telephónica Perú.................3 C2		**EATING**
		Kusicoylloy........................13 B1
SIGHTS & ACTIVITIES		Mayupata..........................14 B1
Museo CATCCO....................4 C1		Orishas Cafe.......................15 B2
Ollantaytambo Ruins.............5 B1		
		DRINKING
SLEEPING		Quechua Blues & Cine Latino....16 B1
Chaska Wasi.........................6 D1		
El Albergue Ollantaytambo Bed &		**TRANSPORT**
Breakfast..........................7 A3		Buses to Quillabamba, Urubamba &
Hospedaje los Andenes...........8 C1		Cuzco.............................17 D2
Hostal las Orquídeas..............9 B2		Colectivos to Urubamba..........18 D2
Hostal Ollanta....................10 D2		PeruRail Ticket Office............19 A3

archaeology and agriculture to the town's many traditional Andean festivals. Downstairs are artisan workshops where you can interact with indigenous weavers and potters. Ask at the front desk about locally guided hikes, horseback rides, mountain biking, and rafting and birding trips.

Festivals & Events

Ollantaytambo is a great place to be when the locals are having a fiesta, many of which are tied to the Catholic church but intricately overlaid with indigenous Andean traditions.

Feast of Epiphany Held on January 6, this feast is celebrated with music, dancing and colorful processions.

Feast of Pentecost Held in late May or early June, it commemorates the local miracle of El Señor de Choquechilca.

Sleeping
BUDGET

Hospedaje los Portadas (☎ 20 4008; Principal s/n; s/d with shared bathroom US$3/6, s/d US$6/12) Located just east of the Plaza de Armas, this family guesthouse has a sunny courtyard. Although all of the tourist and local buses pass by outside, it

still manages to achieve tranquillity. Camping on the grassy lawn may be allowed for a small fee.

Chaska Wasi (☎ 20 4045; katycusco@yahoo.es; Medio s/n; dm US$4, s/d with shared bathroom US$6/12) North of the plaza, the friendly folks here live up to their simple motto of Bed, Food and Drinks. Cheerful basic rooms have electric showers. There are bicycles for rent and a DVD library. It's just 3½ blocks north of the plaza where all the buses stop.

Hostal las Orquídeas (☎ 20 4032; lasorquideas3@hotmail.com; Av Ferrocarrill s/n; s/d incl breakfast US$20/24) Las Orquídeas has a small, grassy courtyard with deck chairs, and less than a dozen basic rooms, some with shared bathrooms. The local family who runs it has a gaggle of smiling kids.

Also recommended:

Hostal Ollanta (☎ 20 4116; Plaza de Armas; s/d with shared bathroom US$7.50/15) Situated behind a village shop, this cavernous place has clean rooms and hot water.

Hospedaje los Andenes (☎ 20 4095; Ventiderio s/n; s/d with shared bathroom US$7.50/15) This reluctantly recommended spot has a convenient location and hot water; it's connected to a hole-in-the-wall café outside.

MIDRANGE & TOP END

Hotel Munay Tika (☎ 20 4111; www.munaytika.com; Av Ferrocarril 118; s/d incl breakfast US$15/25) Munay Tika, meaning 'Jungle Flower,' is a well-kept inn with a pretty garden, kitchen privileges and a tropical-style bar. It's the most welcoming, modern and sparklingly clean midrange guesthouse near the town center.

El Albergue Ollantaytambo Bed & Breakfast (☎ /fax 20 4014; www.rumbosperu.com/elalbergue; s/d/tr US$48/62/78, mini ste US$70, all incl breakfast) On the train platform, 800m from the center of the village, El Albergue is a romantic B&B run by Wendy Weeks, a North American who has been a local resident for almost three decades. It's a characterful early-20th-century hotel with a lovely garden and tiny sauna, and there's certainly no fear of missing your train here! Do not confuse it with Albergue Kapuly, which is next door outside the platform gates.

Hostal Sauce (☎ 20 4044; www.hostalsauce.com.pe; Ventiderio 248; s/d/tr US$69/79/105) This is a smart new building constructed on high ground so that some rooms have a great view to the ruins. Staff can be haughty. There are reductions of 30% when it's quiet.

Eating & Drinking

Restaurants are found around both of the village's main plazas.

Orishas Cafe (Av Ferrocarril s/n; items US$1.50-4.50; ☯ 9am-9pm) Opposite Munay Tika, this riverside spot offers breakfasts, set meals and à la carte snacks, all accompanied by the melodious sound of the river waters rushing by.

Kusicoylloy (☎ 20 4114; Plaza Araccama; mains US$4.50-9; ☯ 9am-10pm) This stylish underground café right next to the Inca ruins has golden décor, a tempting wine list and eclectic victuals, from Amazon-grown coffee to Swiss fondue. It's all done to high culinary standards, and the staff are quite knowledgeable about the town and surrounding area.

Mayupata (☎ 20 4000; Convención; mains US$6-9; ☯ lunch & dinner) This riverside restaurant serving classic Peruvian fare has a breezy garden and a roaring fireplace for those cold Andean nights.

Quechua Blues Bar & Cine Latino (☯ noon-late) Hidden on a side street, this is Ollantaytambo's best – and truthfully, only – watering hole, serving up colorful jungle cocktails. It usually shows movies during the afternoons and has live music some evenings.

Getting There & Away

BUS & TAXI

Frequent *colectivo* minibuses and taxis shuttle between Urubamba's main bus terminal and the Plaza de Armas in Ollantaytambo (US$0.30, 30 minutes), with services petering out in the late afternoon or early evening. To get back to Cuzco, it's easiest to change in Urubamba, from where both buses and *colectivo* taxis frequently leave, or you can catch the morning or evening buses direct from Ollantaytambo to Cuzco's Puente Grau (US$1, 2½ hours). Buses between Cuzco and Quillabamba also stop in Ollantaytambo, but you'll have to pay the full fare (US$4.50) and cross your fingers that there are still any seats available.

TRAIN

Ollantaytambo is an important halfway station between Cuzco and Machu Picchu; all trains stop here about two hours after leaving Cuzco or Aguas Calientes. These trains usually charge the same expensive fares to Machu Picchu as those departing from Cuzco. However, there are also three daily Vistadome services (one-way/round-trip US$47/66) and one high-season (April 1 to October 31) backpacker shuttle (round-trip only US$57) on the Sacred Valley line that leave from Ollantaytambo itself. The PeruRail ticket office just outside Ollantaytambo's train station is open only sporadically. It always helps to show up at least the day beforehand to buy tickets. For seats during high season, make reservations as far in advance as possible. Click to www.perurail.com for updated schedules, fares and reservations.

CHINCHERO

☎ 084 / pop 2000 / elev 3762m

Known to the Incas as the birthplace of the rainbow, this typical Andean village is at an elevation almost 400m higher than Cuzco, so take it easy if you aren't yet acclimatized. The town combines Inca ruins with a colonial church, some wonderful mountain views and a colorful Sunday market. Entry to the Inca ruins, church and museum requires a *boleto turístico*, while the market is free for everyone.

Sights & Activities

Steep steps run up to the main village square, which features a massive ancient **Inca wall** with trapezoidal niches. The colonial church situated just above the square is built on Inca foundations and the interior is decked out in elaborate floral and religious designs. It's open for tour groups on Tuesday and Thursday, and is open for worship on Sunday. Chinchero also has a small **museum** focused on local archaeology, which is located opposite the church.

The most extensive Inca ruins here consist of terracing; if you start walking away from the village through the terraces on the right-hand side of the valley, you'll also find various rocks carved into seats and staircases. On the opposite side of the valley, a clear trail climbs upward before heading north and down to the Río Urubamba valley about four hours away. At the river, the trail turns left and continues to a bridge at **Wayllabamba**, where you can cross. From here, the Sacred Valley road will take you to Calca (turn right, about 13km) or Urubamba (turn left, about 9km). You can flag down any passing bus until mid-afternoon.

The Sunday **markets** at Chinchero are marginally less touristy than those in Pisac. One in front of the old church sells crafts with prices similar to Pisac and Cuzco, but it's also good to see local people still dressed in traditional garb, a habit that isn't just for the tourists. A local produce market is also held at the bottom of the village. Both markets are held to a smaller extent on Tuesday and especially Thursday.

Sleeping & Eating

There's no need to stay overnight here, but there are a few simple guesthouses near the main plaza and along the highway. **Hospedaje Mi Piuray** (☎ 30 6029; Garcilaso 187; s/d with shared bathroom US$3/4.50, s/d US$7/10.50) is a welcoming family hostelry set around an open courtyard. Though some rooms have bathrooms, the hot showers are communal. There's a good café overlooking the main plaza by the entrance to the ruins.

Getting There & Away

Only some of the buses traveling between Urubamba (US$0.50, 50 minutes) and Cuzco (US$0.75, 70 minutes) go via Chinchero instead of via Pisac. Faster *colectivo* taxis between Cuzco (US$1, 45 minutes) and Urubamba (US$1, 45 minutes) also stop in Chinchero.

MACHU PICCHU & THE INCA TRAIL

AGUAS CALIENTES
☎ 084 / pop 2000 / elev 2410m

Also known as Machu Picchu Pueblo, this town lies in the deep valley below the ancient Inca ruins and enclosed by towering walls of stone and cloud forest. Sounds beautiful, doesn't it? Trust us, it's not: unplanned tourist development and perpetual construction makes this one of the ugliest, most exploitative towns you'll run across anywhere in Peru. However, all travelers to and from Machu Picchu must pass through here. There's only one good reason to stay overnight, though: to avoid being engulfed by the hordes of day-trippers arriving from Cuzco by train each morning. Only those who sleep here get to catch the first morning bus up the mountain to Machu Picchu and stay at the ruins until late afternoon, when the tour crowds magically vanish.

Orientation

The footpath from the tourists' train station to the Machu Picchu bus stop is short and stepped, and passes through a scrum of handicraft sellers. Wheelchairs should be directed across the small bridge and through the center of town.

Information

There's a helpful branch of **iPerú** (☎ 21 1104; Edificio del Instituto Nacional de Cultura, Pachacutec cuadra 1; ⏱ 9am-1pm & 2-8pm) in the same building as the **Machu Picchu ticket office** (⏱ 5am-10pm), where independent travelers must buy their entrance tickets before heading up to the ruins, unless a travel agency or tour operator has already done this for you. **BCP** (Av Imperio de los Incas s/n) has a Visa ATM, and small amounts of US dollars and traveler's checks can usually be exchanged at highly unfavorable rates in tourist shops, but don't rely on these options – you should bring plenty of Peruvian cash with you instead. Pay phones that accept phonecards, and cybercafés offering slow internet access are scattered around the town. For emergencies, there's a small **centro de salud** (medical center; ☎ 21 1161; ⏱ 8am-8pm, emergencies 24hr) by the train station and the **police** (☎ 21 1178; Av Imperio de los Incas s/n) are further west alongside the tracks. For local, long-distance and international phone calls, there's a branch office of **Telefónica-Peru** (Av Imperio de los Incas s/n) on the opposite side of the train tracks. There's a small **post office** (Pachacutec s/n).

Sights & Activities

By Puente Ruinas at the base of the footpath to the Machu Picchu ruins, **Museo de Sitio Manuel Chávez Ballón** (admission US$6, free with Machu Picchu entrance ticket; ☺ 9:30am-4pm Wed-Mon) has superb multimedia displays on archaeological excavations of Machu Picchu, and on the ancient Inca building methods, cosmology and culture. Stop here on the day before you visit the ruins or immediately afterward to truly understand the grandeur of Machu Picchu. A small botanical garden, where you can wander among exotic jungle plants, is usually in bloom outside.

Just staggered in from the Inca Trail? Weary trekkers soak away their aches and pains in the town's **hot springs** (admission US$3; ☺ 5am-8:30pm), 10 minutes' walk up Av Pachacutec from the train tracks. Granted, these tiny, natural thermal springs, from which

Aguas Calientes derives its name, are not very exciting. But they're certainly useful for when the hot water runs out at your guesthouse. Swimsuits and towels can both be rented cheaply outside the entrance to the thermal springs.

And for those who still have energy left for trekking, there are some good walks in the vicinity, including one up the steep **Putucusi** mountain directly opposite Machu Picchu; follow the railway tracks about 250m west of the station and you'll see a steeply ascending pathway. Parts of the walk are up ladder rungs, which get slippery in the wet season, but the view across to Machu Picchu is worth the trek.

Sleeping

As in Cuzco, prices in Aguas Calientes are higher than in the rest of the country. Prices given here are for high season between late May and early September. You can expect to pay up to 50% less (after some hard bargaining, that is) during the rest of the year. Early check-out times between 8:30am and 10am are the norm.

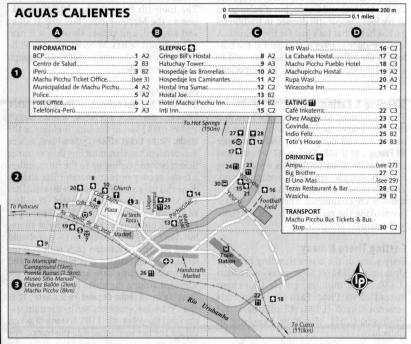

AGUAS CALIENTES

0 — 200 m
0 — 0.1 miles

INFORMATION
BCP	1 A2
Centro de Salud	2 B3
iPerú	3 B2
Machu Picchu Ticket Office	(see 3)
Municipalidad de Machu Picchu	4 A2
Police	5 A2
Post Office	6 C2
Telefónica-Perú	7 A3

SLEEPING
Gringo Bill's Hostal	8 A2
Hatuchay Tower	9 A3
Hospedaje las Bromelias	10 A2
Hospedaje los Caminantes	11 A2
Hostal Ima Sumac	12 C2
Hostal Joe	13 B2
Hotel Machu Picchu Inn	14 B2
Inti Inn	15 C2
Inti Wasi	16 C2
La Cabaña Hostal	17 C2
Machu Picchu Pueblo Hotel	18 C3
Machupicchu Hostal	19 A2
Rupa Wasi	20 A2
Wiracocha Inn	21 C2

EATING
Café Inkaterra	22 C3
Chez Maggy	23 C2
Govinda	24 C2
Indio Feliz	25 B2
Toto's House	26 B3

DRINKING
Ampu	(see 27)
Big Brother	27 C2
El Uno Mas	(see 29)
Tezas Restaurant & Bar	28 C2
Wasicha	29 B2

TRANSPORT
Machu Picchu Bus Tickets & Bus Stop	30 C2

To Hot Springs (150m)

To Putucusi

Church
Colla Suyo
Colla Raymi
Plaza
Av Imperio de los Incas
Av Sinchi Roca
Market

Lloque Yupanqui
Pachacutec
Mayta Capac
Yawar Huaca
Wiracocha
Football Field

To Municipal Campground (1km);
Puente Ruinas (1.5km);
Museo Sitio Manuel Chávez Ballón (2km);
Machu Picchu (8km)

Handicrafts Market

Train Station

Río Urubamba

To Cuzco (110km)

BUDGET

True bargains are as rare as Inca gold in this ridiculously overpriced town.

Inti Wasi (☎ 21 1036, 80 2024; jddggk@latinmail.com; dm US$4.50, s/d/tr with shared bathroom US$5/10/15) This woodsy family-owned guesthouse is hidden up an overgrown walking path on the locals' side of the river. It offers basic bunk beds and rooms with shared hot-water bathrooms, as well as campsites and tent rentals for a nominal fee. Breakfasts and boxed picnic lunches are also available for an extra charge.

Hostal Joe (☎ 21 1190; Mayta Cápac 103; s/d with shared bathroom US$4.50/9, s/d US$10/15) Uphill from the plaza, friendly Joe's has bare, cell-like rooms and limited hot water, with communal showers that are a mite exposed for those chilly Andean nights.

Hospedaje los Caminantes (☎ 21 1007; Av Imperio de los Incas 140; s/d/tr US$7.50/15/22.50) Well, it ain't much to look at, but this ramshackle multi-story guesthouse overlooking the noisiest part of town along the west end of the train tracks just couldn't be cheaper. It's for penny-pinchers, or anyone else who finds themselves stuck without a room.

Hospedaje las Bromelias (☎ 21 1145; Colla Raymi; s/d US$7.50/12) On the plaza, this standby guesthouse has plain rooms with hot-water bathrooms. The whole package is only slightly above average, but the value is pretty fair for Aguas Calientes.

Hostal Ima Sumac (☎ 23 9648, 975 2300; www.machupicchulodging.com; Av Imperio de los Incas s/n; s/d/tr US$10/15/20; ▣) Ima Sumac is an eccentric favorite with bathrooms and reliable hot water, friendly atmosphere and plenty of hippie-dippy touches. Ambient noise from the neighboring bars and discos can be overwhelming in some rooms, so inspect a couple of different ones first.

Camping

Municipal campground (campsites per person US$3) This small, often eerily deserted campground has basic facilities. It's a 1km walk downhill from the center of town on the road to Machu Picchu, by the bridge over the Río Urubamba.

MIDRANGE

Machupicchu Hostal (☎ 21 1034, in Cuzco 084-24 4598; presidente@terra.com.pe; s/d/tr US$26/30/45) One of the tidy midrange inns right next to the train tracks, this place has a small flower-festooned interior courtyard. The noise from

other guests echoes endlessly, and you will certainly hear every train that goes by, but it's still a decent value.

Rupa Wasi (☎ 21 1101; http://perucuzco.com/rupa wasi; Huanacaure 110; d/ste incl breakfast US$30/50) Built haphazardly into the hillside, this 'ecolodge' still looks and feels like a work in progress. Although some rooms are in terrible repair, anyone with Rastafarian, hippie or alt-cultural leanings will feel right at home. Things don't often run like clockwork, yet the hospitality is genuine. Bargain hard. Waterfall hikes can be arranged.

Wiracocha Inn (☎ 21 1088; wiracocha-inn@peru.com; Wiracocha s/n; s/d US$30/40) On a side street crowded with midrange hotels, this newer option has well-kept and polished rooms, amiable service and a sheltered patio area near the river. In some rooms you'll be lulled to sleep by the Andean mountain waters rushing by.

La Cabaña Hostal (☎ 21 1048; Pachacutec M-20; s/d/tr incl breakfast US$40/55/75; ▣) Further uphill than most of the hotels is this popular spot, which has warm, woody rooms and a rustic feel, plus 24-hour hot water and free internet access.

Inti Inn (☎ 21 1137; www.grupointi.com; Pachacutec cuadra 4; s/d incl breakfast from US$55/80) This upscale modern hotel is built in a more rustic style that's designed to blend in with the town's natural surroundings. Most of the 30 guest rooms are doubles and have timber-beamed ceilings, colorful modish furnishings, phones, TVs and heating, with oxygen tanks available for a surcharge. There's also a cafeteria, bar-and-grill restaurant, massage services and free pickups from the train station.

Gringo Bill's Hostal (☎ 21 1046; www.gringobills .com; Colla Raymi 104; s/d US$60/80, ste US$70-90) It's one of the original places for tourists to stay in Machu Picchu town. Service is iffy at best, but the white-walled, flower-bedecked inn still has an enchanting look. What you'll get is a mostly comfortable room with plain furnishings and perhaps a balcony. The plumbing is notoriously unreliable, so insist upon looking at your room before checking in. Always reconfirm your reservation in advance at the office in Cuzco (☎ 084-211 046), located at Av El Sol 520, especially during the high season.

TOP END

Hotel Machu Picchu Inn (☎ 21 1011; reservas@ keyholdingperu.com; Pachacutec 109; s/d/tr US$105/105/135) This airy hotel is positioned right amid the budget accommodations and gringo restaurants on Pachacutec, but has 75 very smart and comfortable rooms. Swedish massage is available for an extra fee.

Hatuchay Tower (☎ 21 1201; www.hatuchaytower .com; Carretera Puente Ruinas 4; r US$196-206, ste US$218) What Hatuchay lacks in soul, it makes up for in comfort. Situated opposite the riverside down from the train tracks, it has welcoming public areas for lounging and five floors of smart rooms, many with dual-voltage outlets and balconies overlooking the river.

Machu Picchu Pueblo Hotel (☎ 21 1122; www.inka terra.com; Km 110 Machu Picchu; d US$375-430; ✪ ▯) For nature-lovers who crave creature comforts, this trendy ecohotel is a 100m walk southeast of the train station. Set amid tropical gardens featuring a bamboo-and-eucalyptus sauna, the hotel's hand-hewn cottages are done up in nouveau Andean style and are connected by stone pathways. True, there are many things not to love here, including management that is far from flawless. That said, you'll have a more peaceful stay here than at the Machu Picchu Sanctuary Lodge, located right outside the ruins.

Eating

Tourist restaurants cluster along the railway tracks and on Pachacutec on the way to the hot springs.

Govinda (Pachacutec s/n; 3-course menús US$3; ✪ noon-8pm) This trusty vegetarian haunt has stone floors and good-value fare made by the Hare Krishna.

Café Inkaterra (☎ 21 1122; Machu Picchu Pueblo Hotel, Km 110 Machu Picchu; snacks US$3-8, buffet from US$15; ✪ 11am-9pm) A high-class spot for a filling Peruvian fusion spread, this restaurant is hidden behind the train station. With flickering votive candles and a chilled-out soundtrack to match the tantalizing *novoandina* menu, the atmosphere here is truly an escape from the masses.

Chez Maggy (Pachacutec 156; mains US$4.50-9; ✪ 10am-10pm) Chez Maggy has stained-glass walls, sociable long tables, board games and an international menu that includes tasty nachos and wood-fired pizzas.

Toto's House (☎ 21 1020; Av Imperio de los Incas s/n; mains US$6-13.50, lunch buffet US$12; ✪ lunch daily, dinner Mon-Sat) This upmarket eatery is popular with tour groups for its traditional buffets set up in a large, glass-roofed building overlooking the river.

Indio Feliz (☎ 21 1090; Lloque Yupanqui 4; meals from US$10; ✪ noon-4pm & 6-10pm) Indio Feliz is owned by a friendly French-Peruvian couple, and the French cook whips up some fantastic meals made from farm-fresh ingredients, as well as good espresso drinks. The restaurant itself is very cozy, with walls plastered with the business cards of satisfied customers.

Drinking

Backpacker bars that have extra-long happy hours, serve pizzas and show movies are all crowded together at the top of Pachacutec before reaching the hot springs. **Tezao Restaurant & Bar** (Pachacutec s/n) boasts an open-air 2nd-floor terrace, while **Big Brother** (Pachacutec s/n) and **Ampu** (Pachacutec s/n) just across the street also stay open late. Nearer the plaza, **Wasicha** (☎ 21 1282; Lloque Yupanqui MZ 12-L-2) has dancing till the wee hours, while the bar **El Uno Mas** (Lloque Yupanqui s/n) next door is a locals' hangout.

Getting There & Away

BUS

At the time of research there was only one way for diehard travelers to avoid taking the train to Aguas Calientes. But check with locals to see if the following route is still feasible before setting off! First, board a bus from Cuzco bound for Quillabamba (see p252) and get off at Santa María, where there's a simple lodge, run by Lorenzo Cahuana (lorenzocahuana@hotmail.com), where you can stay overnight and hire local guides to trek to Aguas Calientes via Santa Teresa. Otherwise, you can usually catch a minibus leaving Santa María in the wee hours of the morning for Santa Teresa (US$1.50, two hours), where there's an adrenaline-fueled cable-car river crossing. It's about a two-hour walk from there to the hydroelectric plant, then another two hours along the defunct train tracks to Aguas Calientes. It's not an easy journey, but it's a memorable one, and it'll save you loads of money, too. You can also do this route as a guided multisport tour; see p277 for more information.

TRAIN

Except for a nearby hydroelectric plant, Aguas Calientes is the end of the line from Cuzco. Tourist trains arrive at the new station close to the Machu Picchu Pueblo Hotel. You can buy tickets in front of the station, but during high season make reservations as far in advance as possible. Trains from Cuzco (p253) arrive in Aguas Calientes after about four hours, while cheaper services from Ollantaytambo (p264) take around 1½ hours.

The Vistadome services (one-way/round-trip US$66/113) leave at 3:30pm and 5pm daily, and are usually full with returning day-trippers. They are scheduled to arrive in Cuzco at 7:20pm and 9:25pm, respectively. The other Cuzco-bound backpacker train (US$46/73) leaves at 3:55pm, arriving in Cuzco at 8:20pm. If you want to speed things along a little, catch a taxi back to Cuzco's city center from Poroy station (around US$5).

The Sacred Valley line to Ollantaytambo runs three Vistadome services (one-way/round-trip US$47/66) that return from Aguas Calientes at 8:35am, 1:20pm and 4:45pm, arriving in Ollantaytambo at 10:05am, 2:40pm and 6:15pm, respectively. There's also a high-season (April 1 to October 30) backpacker train (round-trip only US$57) leaving Aguas Calientes at 4:20pm and arriving in Ollantaytambo around 6pm.

Check www.perurail.com for updated schedules, fares and reservations.

Getting Around

To get to the ruins, you can either walk or take a bus. See p274 for more details.

MACHU PICCHU

For many visitors to Peru and even South America, a visit to the lost Inca city of Machu Picchu is the sweet cherry on the top of their trip. With its spectacular location, it's the best-known archaeological site on the continent. This awe-inspiring ancient city was never revealed to the conquering Spaniards and was virtually forgotten until the early part of the 20th century. In the high season from late May until early September, the maximum limit of 2500 people arrive daily. Despite this great tourist influx, the site manages to retain its air of grandeur and mystery, and is a must for all visitors to Peru.

History

Machu Picchu is not mentioned in any of the chronicles of the Spanish conquistadors. Apart from a few indigenous Quechuas, nobody knew of Machu Picchu's existence until American historian Hiram Bingham stumbled upon it in 1911 while being guided around by locals. You can read Bingham's own account of his 'discovery' in the classic book *Inca Land: Explorations in the Highlands of Peru*, first published in 1922 and now available as a free download from Project Gutenberg (www.gutenberg.org).

Bingham's search was for the lost city of Vilcabamba, the last stronghold of the Incas, and he thought he had found it at Machu Picchu. We now know that the remote ruins at Espíritu Pampa, much deeper in the jungle, are actually the remains of Vilcabamba. The Machu Picchu site was initially overgrown with thick vegetation, forcing Bingham's team to be content with roughly mapping the site. Bingham returned in 1912 and 1915 to carry out the difficult task of clearing the thick forest, when he also discovered some of the ruins on the so-called Inca Trail. Peruvian archaeologist Luis E Valcárcel undertook further studies in 1934, as did a Peruvian-American expedition under Paul Fejos in 1940–41.

Despite scores of more recent studies, knowledge of Machu Picchu remains sketchy. Even today archaeologists are forced to rely heavily on speculation and educated guesswork as to its function. Over 50 burial sites and 100 skeletal remains have been discovered over the course of excavations. Initially the remains were thought to be 80% female, leading to an early theory that it was a city of 'chosen women,' but this lost support when it emerged that the male/female ratio was actually 50/50. Some believe the citadel was founded in the waning years of the last Incas as an attempt to preserve Inca culture or rekindle their predominance, while others think it may have already become an uninhabited, forgotten city at the time of the conquest. A more recent theory suggests that the site was a royal retreat or country palace abandoned at the time of the Spanish invasion.

What is obvious from the exceptionally high quality of the stonework and the abundance of ornamental work is that Machu Picchu must once have been vitally important as a ceremonial center. Indeed, to some extent, it still is: Alejandro Toledo, the country's first indigenous Andean president, impressively staged his inauguration here in 2001.

Information

The ruins are typically open from dawn till dusk, but they are most heavily visited between 10am and 2pm. Many tours combine visits of Machu Picchu with the Sunday

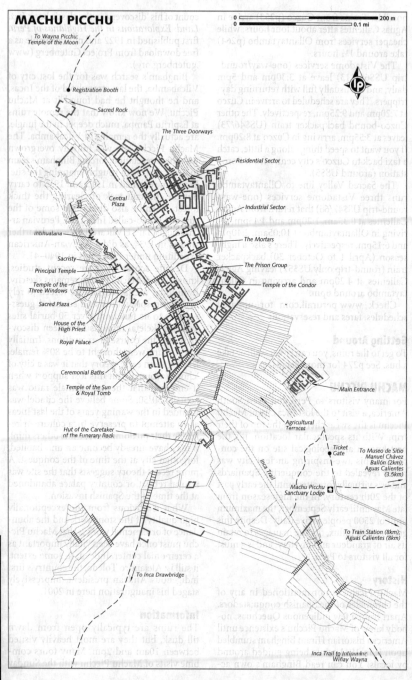

MACHU PICCHU

To Wayna Picchu;
Temple of the Moon

Registration Booth

Sacred Rock

The Three Doorways

Residential Sector

Central
Plaza

Industrial Sector

The Mortars

Intihuatana

The Prison Group

Sacristy

Principal Temple

Temple of the
Three Windows

Temple of the Condor

Sacred Plaza

House of the
High Priest

Royal Palace

Ceremonial Baths

Temple of the Sun
& Royal Tomb

Main Entrance

Hut of the Caretaker
of the Funerary Rock

Agricultural
Terraces

Ticket
Gate

To Museo de Sitio
Manuel Chávez
Ballón (2km);
Aguas Calientes
(3.5km)

Machu Picchu
Sanctuary Lodge

Inca Trail

To Train Station (8km);
Aguas Calientes (8km)

To Inca Drawbridge

Inca Trail to Intipunku;
Wiñay Wayna

0   200 m
0   0.1 mi

markets at either Pisac or Chinchero, so Sunday is fairly quiet. June to August are the busiest months. Plan your visit early or late in the day, which is possible if you stay overnight in Aguas Calientes, and you'll avoid the worst of the crowds, plus you'll get the chance to view the mesmerizing changes in light as the sun comes up over or goes down behind the mountains. A visit early in the morning midweek during the rainy season guarantees you more room to breathe, especially during February, when the Inca Trail is closed.

Entrance tickets for the **Machu Picchu historical sanctuary** (www.inc-cusco.gob.pe; one-day ticket adult/student under 26 with ISIC card US$23.50/12) are expensive and must be bought in advance at the **Machu Picchu ticket office** (Edificio del Instituto Nacional de Cultura, Pachacutec cuadra 1; ☾ 5am-10pm) in Aguas Calientes or from a travel agency or tour operator in Cuzco. You are not allowed to bring large packs, food or walking sticks into the ruins. All bags have to be checked at the luggage-storage office just before the main entrance gate. Although this service is free, it's not entirely secure, so bring as little as possible.

There is no official visitors center. Most people come on an organized tour or guided trek, so local guides aren't as readily available for hire here as at other tourist sites around Cuzco. That said, the information and map provided in this book should be enough for a self-guided tour. For really in-depth explorations, take along a copy of *Exploring Cuzco* by Peter Frost. If you do decide to hire a guide, make sure to agree upon a price in advance and clarify whether it's per person or covers the whole group.

Dangers & Annoyances

Inside the ruins, do not walk on any of the walls – this loosens the stonework and prompts an cacophony of whistle-blowing from the guards. Trying to spend the night here is also illegal, and guards do a thorough check of the site before it closes.

Sights & Activities

Don't miss the new Museo de Sitio Manuel Chávez Ballón (see p266) by Puente Ruinas at the base of the footpath to Machu Picchu. Buses headed back from the ruins to Aguas

LOSING MACHU PICCHU

As Peru's showpiece site, everyone wants a piece of Machu Picchu. Even as thousands of visitors marvel at the seemingly untouchable beauty of Machu Picchu, the popularity of this age-old site has placed it under the shadow of significant environmental and political threats.

Japanese scientists from the University of Kyoto caused a scare in early 2001 when they announced that the steep slopes on the western side of Machu Picchu were slipping downwards at the rate of 1cm per month, prefacing a possible catastrophic landslide in the not-too-distant future. While the scientists conceded that their results were exaggerated by excessive rainfall and construction work at the time, the area has seen many landslides in the past, and the fear is that constant busloads of tourists are further unsettling the subsoil of the sacred mountain.

While a long mooted plan to build a cable car to the summit has been put firmly on the back burner following condemnation from the national and international community, the threat of private interests encroaching on the site has also long simmered in the background, periodically rearing its ugly head with worrying new plans. One unbelievable accident even saw a TV crew filming a beer commercial smash a crane into the site's showpiece, the Intihuatana (Hitching Post of the Sun), breaking a large chip off the old granite block!

Unesco has also warned that the site cannot support more than 500 visitors per day without sustaining damage – a number dwarfed by current visitor numbers, especially during peak season. But their exhortations have not always found an echo in Lima. Back-and-forth negotiations between the Peruvian government and Unesco have resulted in several revisions of long-term plans for the site, as well as international monitoring of the situation.

For locals, the number-one issue is the private monopoly on the railway line between Cuzco and Aguas Calientes. Periodic local protests have shut down the trains for days at a time, after which things usually return to normal. However, the Peruvian government's response has been to point out that anyone can apply for the necessary permits to operate other trains along the Machu Picchu line, but no one has done so yet.

Calientes will stop upon request at the bridge, from where you can head back to town later, usually less than a half hour's walk.

INSIDE THE RUINS

Unless you arrive via the Inca Trail, you'll officially enter the ruins through a ticket gate on the south side of Machu Picchu. About 100m of footpath brings you to the mazelike main entrance of Machu Picchu proper, where the ruins lie stretched out before you, roughly divided into two areas separated by a series of plazas.

To get a visual fix of the whole site and snap the classic postcard photograph, climb the zigzagging staircase on the left immediately after entering the complex, which leads to a hut. Known as the **Hut of the Caretaker of the Funerary Rock**, it is one of a few buildings that has been restored with a thatched roof, making it a good shelter in the case of rain. The Inca Trail enters the city just below this hut. The carved rock behind the hut may have been used to mummify the nobility, hence the hut's name.

If you continue straight into the ruins instead of climbing to the hut, you pass through extensive terracing to a beautiful series of 16 connected **ceremonial baths** that cascade across the ruins, accompanied by a flight of stairs.

Just above and to the left of the baths is Machu Picchu's only round building, the **Temple of the Sun**, a curved and tapering tower that contains some of Machu Picchu's finest stonework. It appears to have been used for astronomical purposes. Inside are an altar and a curiously drilled trapezoidal window that looks onto the site. The Temple of the Sun is cordoned off to visitors, but you can see into it from above, which is how you'll be approaching it if you take the stairs leading down and to the left from the caretaker's hut.

Below the temple is an almost hidden, natural rock cave that has been carefully carved, with a steplike altar and sacred niches, by the Inca stonemasons. It is known as the **Royal Tomb**, though no mummies were actually ever found here.

Climbing the stairs above the ceremonial baths, you reach a flat area of jumbled rocks, once used as a quarry. Turn right at the top of the stairs and walk across the quarry on a short path leading to the four-sided **Sacred Plaza**. The far side contains a small viewing platform (with a curved wall) that offers a

view of the snowy Cordillera Vilcabamba in the far distance and the Río Urubamba below.

Important buildings flank the remaining three sides of the Sacred Plaza. The **Temple of the Three Windows** commands an impressive view of the plaza below through the huge trapezoidal windows that give the building its name. With this temple behind you, the **Principal Temple** is to your right. Its name derives from the massive solidity and perfection of its construction. The damage to the rear right corner of the temple is the result of the ground settling below this corner rather than any inherent weakness in the masonry itself. Opposite the Principal Temple is what is known as the **House of the High Priest**.

Behind and connected to the Principal Temple lies a famous small building called the **Sacristy**. It has many well-carved niches, perhaps used for the storage of ceremonial objects, as well as a carved stone bench. The Sacristy is especially known for the two rocks flanking its entrance; each is said to contain 32 angles, but it's easy to come up with a different number whenever you count them.

A staircase behind the Sacristy climbs a small hill to the major shrine in Machu Picchu, the **Intihuatana**. This Quechua word loosely translates as the 'Hitching Post of the Sun' and refers to the carved rock pillar, often mistakenly called a sundial, which stands at the top of the Intihuatana hill. The Inca astronomers were able to predict the solstices using the angles of this pillar. Thus, they were able to claim control over the return of the lengthening summer days. Exactly how the pillar was used for these astronomical purposes remains unclear, but its elegant simplicity and high craftwork make it a highlight of the complex. It is recorded that there were several of these Intihuatanas in various important Inca sites, but the Spaniards smashed most in an attempt to wipe out the pagan blasphemy of sun worship.

At the back of the Intihuatana is another staircase. It descends to the **Central Plaza**, which separates the ceremonial sector of Machu Picchu from the more mundane residential and industrial sectors, which were not as well-constructed. At the lower end of this latter area is the **Prison Group**, a labyrinthine complex of cells, niches and passageways, positioned both under and above the ground. The centerpiece of the group is the **Temple of the**

Condor, which contains a carving of the head of a condor, with the natural rocks behind it resembling the Andean bird's outstretched wings. Behind the condor is a well-like hole and, at the bottom of this, the door to a tiny underground cell that can only be entered by bending double.

WAYNA PICCHU
The most famous of several short walks around Machu Picchu is the climb up the steep mountain of Wayna (also spelled Huayna) Picchu at the back of the ruins. Wayna Picchu is normally translated as 'Young Peak,' but the word *picchu*, with the correct glottal pronunciation, refers to the wad in the cheek of a coca-leaf chewer.

At first glance, it would appear that Wayna Picchu is a difficult climb but, although the ascent is steep, it's not technically difficult. Beyond the central plaza between two open-fronted buildings is a registration booth, where you have to sign in. Note that it's only open from around 7am until 1pm, and you must return by 4pm. The 45-minute to 1½-hour scramble up a steep footpath takes you through a short section of Inca tunnel. For all the huffing and puffing it takes to get there, the fabulous views from the top are definitely worth the effort, even for trekkers just stumbling in off the Inca Trail. Take care in wet weather as the steps get dangerously slippery.

Another walk begins part way up Wayna Picchu, where a marked path plunges down to your left, continuing down the rear of Wayna Picchu to the small **Temple of the Moon**. The trail is easy to follow, but involves steep sections, a ladder and an overhanging cave, where you have to bend over to get by. The descent takes about an hour, and the ascent back to the main Wayna Picchu trail longer. The spectacular trail drops and climbs steeply as it hugs the sides of Wayna Picchu before plunging into the cloud forest. Suddenly, you reach a cleared area where the small, very well-made ruins are found. Unfortunately, they are marred by graffiti. From the Temple of the Moon, another cleared path leads up behind the ruin and steeply onward up the back side of Wayna Picchu.

INCA DRAWBRIDGE
On the other side of the ruins, a scenic but level walk from the Hut of the Caretaker of the Funerary Rock takes you right past the top of the terraces and out along a narrow, cliff-clinging trail to the Inca drawbridge. In under a half hour's walk, the trail gives you a good look at cloud-forest vegetation and an entirely different view of Machu Picchu. You'll have to be content with photographing the bridge from behind a barrier a few hundred meters above it, however, as someone crossed the bridge some years ago and tragically fell to their death.

INTIPUNKU
The Inca Trail ends after its final descent from the notch in the horizon called Intipunku (Sun Gate). Looking at the hill behind you as you enter the ruins, you can see both the trail and Intipunku. This hill, called Machu Picchu, or 'old peak,' gives the site its name. It takes about an hour to reach Intipunku, and if you can spare at least a half-day for the round trip, it may be possible to continue as far as Wiñay Wayna (p278). Expect to pay US$3 or more as an unofficial reduced-charge admission fee to the Inca Trail, and be sure to return before 3pm, which is when the checkpoint typically closes.

Sleeping & Eating
Most people either arrive on day trips from Cuzco or stay overnight nearby in Aguas Calientes.

Machu Picchu Sanctuary Lodge (☎ 21 1038, 21 1039; www.monasterio.orient-express.com; patio/standard/mountain-view r US$715-885, r with panoramic view US$1005, ste US$1165) The Sanctuary Lodge is the only place to stay at Machu Picchu itself. Rates have skyrocketed recently and are criminally overpriced for what you get, though it's still often full, so book as far ahead as possible, especially during the high season. Only two of the rooms have views of the ruins, but all of the rooms and suites are equipped with every modern convenience, and there's a common terrace with a partial view of the site. One of the hotel's polished restaurants serves a good but expensive lunch buffet from 11:30am until 3pm.

There's a pricey snack bar serving light meals on a patio below the entrance to the ruins. If you bring your own boxed lunch and drinks, you'll have to leave them in a checked pack at the luggage-storage room outside the main entrance to the ruins.

Getting There & Away

There are only two options to get to Machu Picchu: trek it or catch the train to Aguas Calientes (p253, p262, p268).

From Aguas Calientes, buses for Machu Picchu leave from a ticket office along the main road for the tightly winding 8km trip up the mountain (round-trip US$12, 25 minutes). Departures are hourly, roughly between 5:30am and the early afternoon, plus extra buses to handle the crowds when trains arrive. Buses return from the ruins when full, with the last departure usually around 5:30pm.

Otherwise, it's a 20-minute walk from Aguas Calientes to Puente Ruinas, where the road to the ruins crosses the Río Urubamba, nearby the museum. A breathtakingly steep, but well-marked trail climbs another 2km up to Machu Picchu, taking about an hour to hike (less coming down!).

THE INCA TRAIL

The most famous hike in South America, the four-day Inca Trail, is walked by many thousands of backpackers every year. Although the total distance is only 33km, the ancient trail laid by the Incas from the Sacred Valley to Machu Picchu winds its way up and down and around the mountains, snaking over three high Andean passes en route, that have collectively led to the route being dubbed 'the Inca Trial.' The views of snowy mountain peaks, rural hamlets where llamas graze and cloud forests flush with orchids can be stupendous, and walking from one cliff-hugging pre-Columbian ruin to the next is a mystical and unforgettable experience. Except for the sad fact, of course, that you'll never have a moment's peace to really soak it all up. What savvy tourism officials and tour operators call *the* Inca Trail is just one of dozens of footpaths that the Incas built to reach Machu Picchu, and some of these overland routes are still being dug out of the jungle by archaeologists. You may have a more rewarding experience by taking one of the many alternative trekking routes (see Inca Trails Less Traveled, p277). See also p62 for more on the Inca Trail.

Regulations & Fees

The Peruvian government keeps introducing more reforms to the Inca Trail in an attempt to reduce the number of trekkers and prevent further damage to the trail caused by overcrowding. The most recent regulations state that all Inca Trail hikers must now go with a licensed guide, and no more than 200 hikers are allowed to start the trail per day. All trekkers are required to carry their passport (a copy will not do) and ISIC card with them at all times to show at appropriate checkpoints along the trail.

Registered tour agencies also have to pay huge annual fees and taxes, which often increase annually, and so tour prices have consequently shot up. At the time of writing, trail fees had reached US$60 per person (or US$30 for students under 26 with a valid ISIC card), which doesn't include the one-day entrance fee to Machu Picchu. Tickets must be bought at the Instituto Nacional del Cultura (INC) office in Cuzco at least 72 hours before the trek, but tour operators will normally handle this for you.

When to Go

Groups leave year-round, except for February, when the annual cleanup of the trail takes place. However, in the wettest months from December to April, trails can be slippery and campsites muddy, and views are often obscured behind a thick bank of rolling clouds. In contrast, the coldest and driest months (June to August) are the most popular time to trek, as well as the most crowded. Temperatures can drop below freezing year-round, and it occasionally rains even during the dry season (late May to early September).

What to Bring

Sleeping bags and other trekking gear can be hired at travel agencies in Cuzco. The trail gets extremely cold at night so make sure the sleeping bag you rent is warm enough (down is preferable) and bring plenty of layers of clothing. Also remember sturdy shoes,

---

WARNING!

Due to the Inca Trail's overwhelming popularity, book at least six weeks in advance for trips outside of high season and up to a full year beforehand for departures between late May and early September. Just don't turn up in Cuzco and expect to start trekking within a few days – it's not likely to happen, even during the rainy months! And remember that the trail is completely closed during the month of February.

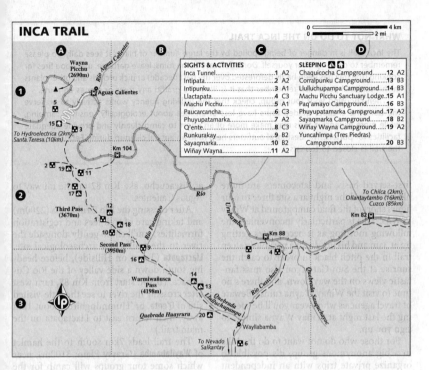

INCA TRAIL

SIGHTS & ACTIVITIES		SLEEPING	
Inca Tunnel.....................1	A2	Chaquicocha Campground......12	A2
Intipata........................2	A2	Corralpunku Campground......13	B3
Intipunku.....................3	A1	Llulluchupampa Campground...14	B3
Llactapata....................4	C3	Machu Picchu Sanctuary Lodge.15	A1
Machu Picchu................5	A1	Paq'amayo Campground.........16	B3
Paucarcancha...............6	C3	Phuyupatamarca Campground..17	A2
Phuyupatamarka............7	A2	Sayaqmarka Campground.......18	B2
Q'ente.........................8	C3	Wiñay Wayna Campground....19	A2
Runkurakay..................9	B2	Yuncachimpa (Tres Piedras)	
Sayaqmarka................10	B2	Campground...............20	B3
Wiñay Wayna...............11	A2		

rain gear, insect repellent, sunblock, a flashlight (with fresh batteries), basic first-aid supplies and water-purification tablets. Optional trekking maps are sold by **South American Explorers** (SAE; ☎ 084-24 5484; www.saexplorers .org; No 4, Choquechaca 188; ◷ 9:30am-5pm Mon-Fri, 9:30am-1pm Sat) in Cuzco. Metal-tipped walking sticks are no longer allowed on the trail or inside the ruins, though if you would like some added support, locals sell cheap bamboo canes with an embroidered cloth handle for about US$1 at various places near the start of the Inca Trail, including in Ollantaytambo, where many trekking groups have breakfast.

Apart from bottled drinks sold by locals over the first stretch of the trail, there is almost nowhere to buy food en route. You'll be served three square meals a day but stocking up on snacks is not a bad idea as the digestive system slows with altitude. Also take a small stash of cash for tipping the guide, cook and especially the porters, who work the hardest of all. It's also a good idea to take money to spend on your last day in Aguas Calientes and also for any emergencies, especially dur-

ing the rainy season when it's not unknown for landslides along the railway to delay the return to Cuzco.

Tours & Guides

For the classic four-day Inca Trail, you should expect to pay over US$300 for a tour run by a reliable company (students under 26 with a valid ISIC card may get small discounts of 10% to 15%). That tour price includes a tent, food, porters, a cook, one-day admission to the ruins and the train fare back to Cuzco. Some agencies ask that you carry 'a small day pack,' which ends up being your regular backpack, so clarify this. Find out how many people sleep in tents, how many porters each group has, what the arrangements for special diets are and, above all, make your wishes clear and get them in writing. For more details about tours and some reputable trekking agencies to choose from, see p235.

There are many benefits to booking ahead and reconfirming in advance. First, this prevents you from missing out on the Inca Trail due to bottlenecks in high season. Second, campsites are allotted according to a first-come,

---

WHAT NOT TO DO ON THE INCA TRAIL

The Inca Trail is in danger of being spoiled by the large number of hikers it sees daily, so please remember to clean up after yourself. Don't defecate in the ruins, leave garbage, use wood fires for cooking (the trail has been badly deforested over the past decade) or pick orchids and other plants in this national park. Also remember that it is illegal to graffiti any trees or stones en route.

When choosing your tour group, check that the trekking agency works actively to preserve the trail. The cheaper guided tours have less of an idea about ecologically sensitive camping, while more expensive trips may make more of an effort to camp cleanly and provide adequate facilities for porters. The best local outfitters help fund an annual cleanup during February, when the trail is closed to tourists.

---

first-served basis, and latecomers are more likely to spend the night at a site three to four hours short of the final campground at Wiñay Wayna. This is particularly inconvenient the following morning as it necessitates getting up at 3am and hiking down a perilously steep trail in the pitch black in order to catch the sunrise at the Sun Gate (you also miss fantastic views on the way down, and there's no time to visit the Wiñay Wayna ruins). Beware of travel agencies who swear you'll be spending the last night at Wiñay Wayna simply to sign you up.

For those who do not want to do the hike in a big anonymous group, it's possible to organize private trips with an independent licensed guide registered with the governing body Inrena. This option allows hikers some degree of flexibility, but can be expensive (up to US$1000 per person). That said, for groups of six or more it may in fact be cheaper than the standard group treks. Prices vary considerably depending on which company you choose to organize your private trek through, so shop around.

Danger & Annoyances

Occasional theft and violent attacks on tourists happen on the trail, and you are advised to take all gear into your tents at night. There are very few staffed park stations along the Inca Trail. Although the rangers have radios, these don't always work. Medical facilities are almost nonexistent. If you have an accident on the trail, it could be days before evacuation can be arranged (and the standard procedure is to carry people out, not to send in a helicopter).

The Hike

Most trekking agencies run tour buses to the start of the trail near the village of Chilca

at Piscacucho, aka Km 82 on the railway to Aguas Calientes.

After crossing the Río Urubamba (2200m) and taking care of trail fees and registration formalities, you'll climb gently alongside the river to the trail's first archaeological site, **Llactapata** (Town on Hillside), before heading south down a side valley of the Río Cusichaca. (If you start from Km 88, turn west after crossing the river to see the little-visited site of **Q'ente**, or 'Hummingbird,' about 1km away, then return east to Llactapata on the main trail.)

The trail leads 7km south to the hamlet of **Wayllabamba** (Grassy Plain; 3100m), near which some tour groups will camp for the first night. You can buy bottled drinks and high-calorie snacks here, and take a breather to look over your shoulder for views of the snowcapped **Nevado Verónica** (5750m).

Wayllabamba is situated near the fork of the Llullucha and Cusichaca Rivers. The trail crosses the Río Llullucha on a log bridge, then climbs steeply up along the river. This area is known as **Tres Piedras** (Three White Stones), though these boulders are no longer visible. From here it is a long, very steep 3km climb through humid *Polylepis* woodlands. At some points, the trail and streambed become one, but stone stairs keep hikers above the water.

The trail eventually emerges on the high, bare mountainside of **Llulluchupampa**, where water is available and the flats are dotted with campsites that get very cold at night. This is as far as you can reasonably expect to get on your first day, though many groups will actually spend their second night here.

From Llulluchupampa, a good path up the left-hand side of the valley climbs for a two- to three-hour ascent to the pass of **Warmiwañusca**, also colorfully known as 'Dead Woman's Pass.' At 4198m above sea level, this is the highest

INCA TRAILS LESS TRAVELED

Let's face it: the Inca Trail is being loved to death. Overcrowded campsites, ethical issues with porter welfare, the limited availability of trail permits and the rising cost of taking a mandatory guided trek has made lesser-known routes to Machu Picchu look ever more appealing. After all, there were many trails used by the Incas, not just one!

The following alternative routes are not always a method of avoiding the sky-high trekking prices, as many treks link up with the principal trail, in which case the regulations regarding licensed guides and some or even all of the trail fees still apply. Ultimately, prices and availability for these alternative treks depend upon demand, so make sure you shop around (see p235 for some recommended trekking agencies).

For more detailed information, purchase an *Alternative Inca Trails Information Packet* from the **South American Explorers** (SAE; ☎ 084-24 5484; www.saexplorers.org; No 4, Choquechaca 188; ☯ 9:30am-5pm Mon-Fri, 9:30am-1pm Sat) in Cuzco.

The Shorter Inca Trail

A shorter version of the Inca Trail leaves from Km 104, and gives a good idea of what hiking the Inca Trail is like. You'll be let off the train shortly before Aguas Calientes where the signed trail crosses the river on a footbridge before climbing very steeply for three or four hours to Wiñay Wayna. The average price for the all-inclusive two-day trek is US$200 to US$250.

The Valley Inca Trail

A longer but less strenuous version of the Inca Trail follows the Río Urubamba from Km 82 to Km 104, where it picks up the trail of the short hike mentioned earlier. Along the way it passes less often visited archaeological sites and lush jungle favored for bird-watching. The all-inclusive four-day trek usually costs about the same as the classic Inca Trail.

The Lares Valley Trek

This route wanders around the Sacred Valley, trekking between rural Andean villages and past hot springs, lesser-known Inca archaeological sites, lush lagoons and river gorges. You'll finish by taking the train from Ollantaytambo to Aguas Calientes. Although this is more of a cultural trek than a technical trip, the highest mountain pass (4450m) is certainly nothing to sneeze at. An all-inclusive four-day trek costs US$200 to US$300.

The Salkantay Trek

An even longer, more spectacular approach to Machu Picchu, starts from the village of Mollepata, off the Cuzco–Abancay road. Climbing over 4800m-high passes near the magnificent glacier-clad peak of Salkantay (6271m), this week-long trek joins the classic Inca Trail after three or four days at Wayllabamba, where there is an official checkpoint. An all-inclusive seven-day trek costs over $500.

The Inka Jungle Trail

Fans of DIY trekking rejoice: at the time of research, there was still one alternative to taking an expensive guided tour to Machu Picchu. The four-day Inka Jungle Trail is a heart-stopping adventure that starts off with a bus ride over the Abra la Raya (4319m), followed by mountain biking downhill to the small jungle village of Santa María, where there's a trekking lodge run by the genial Lorenzo Cahuana (lorenzocahuana@hotmail.com). From Santa María, you'll walk through the Amazon jungle to Santa Teresa, camping overnight by some hot springs, then take a crazy cable car across the Río Urubamba and follow defunct train tracks into Aguas Calientes. If you don't want to book a multisport guided tour from Cuzco (the all-inclusive four-day trip costs around US$150 to US$250), you can save money by going independently, if you don't mind skipping the mountain biking. To do this, take a Quillabamba-bound bus from Cuzco as far as Santa María (US$4.50, six to seven hours), then hire a local guide at Lorenzo's lodge. For more information, see p268. Note that this route is open even during February, when the Inca Trail is closed for its annual cleanup.

point of the trek, and leaves many a seasoned hiker gasping. From Warmiwañusca, you can see the Río Pacamayo (Sunrise River) far below, as well as the ruin of Runkurakay halfway up the next hill, above the river.

The trail continues down a long and knee-jarringly steep descent to the river, where there are large campsites with toilets at **Paq'aymayo**. At an altitude of about 3500m, the trail crosses the river over a small footbridge and climbs toward **Runkurakay** (Basket-Shaped Building), a round ruin with superb views. It's about an hour's walk away.

Above Runkurakay, the trail climbs to a false summit before continuing past two small lakes to the top of the second pass at 3950m, which has views of the snow-laden Cordillera Vilcabamba. The clear trail descends past an uninvitingly green lake to the ruin of **Sayaq-marka** (Dominant Town), a tightly constructed complex perched on a small mountain spur, and offering incredible views. The trail continues downward and crosses an upper tributary of the Río Aobamba (Wavy Plain). There are campsites here, though the ground gets too boggy for camping in the wet season.

The trail then leads on across an Inca causeway and up a gentle climb through some beautiful cloud forest to the third pass at almost 3700m. Along the way, you'll pass through an Inca tunnel carved from the rock. There are also grand views of the Río Urubamba valley from the pass.

Soon you'll reach the beautiful and well-restored ruin of **Phuyupatamarka** (Town Above the Clouds), about 3600m above sea level. The site contains a beautiful series of ceremonial baths with water running through them. A ridge here offers campsites where some groups spend their final night, with the advantage of watching the sun set over a truly spectacular view, but with the disadvantage of having to leave at 3am in the race to reach the Sun Gate in time for sunrise.

From Phuyupatamarka, the trail makes a dizzying dive into the cloud forest below, following an incredibly well-engineered flight of many hundreds of Inca steps (which can be nerve-racking in the early hours – take extra batteries for your flashlight). After two or three hours, the trail eventually zigzags its way down to a red-roofed white building that provides last-night youth-hostel facilities for those who want to pay a bit extra. More popularly, it also offers hot showers, meals and bottled drinks. The hostel is usually quite full, but there are some campsites nearby.

A 500m trail behind the hostel leads to the exquisite little Inca site of **Wiñay Wayna** (also spelled Huiñay Huayna), which is variously translated as 'Forever Young,' 'To Plant the Earth Young' and 'Growing Young,' (as opposed to 'growing old'). Peter Frost writes that the Quechua name refers to an orchid that blooms here year-round. A rough trail leads from this site to another newly uncovered, terraced ruin called **Intipata**.

From the Wiñay Wayna guard post, the trail winds around through the cliff-hanging cloud forest for about two hours to reach **Intipunku** (Sun Gate) – the penultimate site on the trail, where those who are very lucky can catch their first glimpse of majestic Machu Picchu and wait for the sun to rise over the encompassing mountaintops.

The final triumphant descent takes almost an hour. Backpacks are not allowed into the ruins and park guards will pounce on you to check in your pack and have your trail permit stamped. Though it is rather a brusque return to rules and regulations, trekkers generally arrive long before the morning trainloads of tourists, and can enjoy the exhausted exhilaration of reaching their goal without having to push past enormous groups of tourists fresh off the first train from Cuzco.

CUZCO TO PUNO

The rickety railway and the paved road to Lake Titicaca shadow each other as they both head southeast from Cuzco. En route you can investigate ancient ruins and pastoral Andean towns that are great detours for intrepid travelers who want to leave the beat-up Gringo Trail far behind. Most of the places described can be reached on day trips from Cuzco; for points of interest closer to Puno, see p191. Inka Express runs luxury bus tours (p252) between Cuzco and Puno that visit some, but not all, of these places. Local and long-distance highway buses run more frequently along this route and are less expensive.

TIPÓN

A demonstration of the Incas' mastery over their environment, this extensive **Inca site** (entry only with boleto turístico; ☉ 7am-6pm) consists of some excellent terracing at the head of a small valley and boasts an ingenious irrigation system. Take any Urcos-bound bus from Manco Capac or Av de la Cultura in Cuzco and ask to be let off at the Tipón turnoff (US$0.75, 45 minutes), about 30km from Cuzco and just before Oropesa. A steep dirt road from the turnoff (an excellent spot for eating at cheap *cuyerías* – guinea-pig roasteries – to build up your strength) climbs the 4km to the ruins. A taxi from Cuzco to Tipón and Piquillacta costs US$20 or more with waiting time.

PIQUILLACTA & RUMICOLCA

Literally translated as 'the Place of the Flea,' **Piquillacta** (entry only with boleto turístico; ☉ 7am-6pm) is the only major pre-Inca ruin in the area. It was built around AD 1100 by the Wari culture. It's a large ceremonial center of crumbling two-story buildings, all with entrances that are strategically located on the upper floor. It is surrounded by a defensive wall. The stonework here is much cruder than that of the Incas, and the floors and walls were paved with slabs of white gypsum, which you can still see traces of. The site can be reached on any Urcos-bound bus from Manco Capac or Av de la Cultura in Cuzco. It's under 40km east of Cuzco, just past a lake on the left-hand side of the road. On the opposite side of the road about 1km further east is the huge Inca gate of **Rumicolca**, built on Wari foundations. The cruder Wari stonework contrasts with the Inca blocks. The area's swampy lakes are also interesting, and you can see indigenous people making roof tiles from the mud that surrounds the lakes. The **Centro Recreacional Huacarpay** (☎ 084-74 6652; dm US$3) has youth-hostel accommodations and a games pitch by Laguna de Nukré, not far below Piquillacta.

Urcos-bound buses from Cuzco pass by both sites (US$1, one hour).

ANDAHUAYLILLAS

☎ 084 / pop 2500 / elev 3123m

Don't confuse this place with Andahuaylas, west of Cuzco. Andahuaylillas is over 45km southeast of Cuzco, about 7km before the road splits at Urcos. This pretty Andean village is most famous for its lavishly decorated **Jesuit church** (admission US$1.20; ☉ 8am-noon & 2-5pm Mon-Sat, 8:30-10am & 3-5pm Sun), which is almost oppressive in its baroque embellishments. The church dates from the 17th century and houses many carvings and paintings, including a canvas of the Immaculate Conception by Esteban Murillo. There are reportedly many gold and silver treasures locked in the church, and the villagers are all involved in taking turns guarding it 24 hours a day. Is the rumor true or not? All we can tell you is that they take their job *very* seriously.

Hospedaje El Sol (☎ in Cuzco 084-22 7264; Garcilaso 514; r per person from US$10) has inviting accommodations in a colonial house, and **Hostal el Casona** (Cuzco 410; s/d US$15/25) is a spa hotel set around a cool, tree-filled courtyard. Back on the main plaza to the side of the church is a cooperative yarn, weaving and traditional textiles **workshop** where you can buy highland handicrafts.

To reach Andahuaylillas (US$1.50, 1½ hours), take any Urcos-bound bus from Manco Capac or Av de la Cultura in Cuzco.

URCOS TO SICUANI

The road splits at **Urcos**, less than 60km southeast of Cuzco, where one road heads northeast to Puerto Maldonado in the jungle (p283), while another continues southeast toward Lake Titicaca.

About 65km southeast of Urcos is the village of **Tinta**, which has a fine colonial church and a basic place to stay. About 25km further is **Sicuani**, a market town of 40,000 people, which can be used as a base for visiting the pretty highland **Lago Sibinacocha**. To get to the lake, ask locals about the early Wednesday *combi* to Santa Barbara (two hours), then catch any available ongoing transport. You won't be able to make it back in one day so plan on spending the night. One economical place to stay in Sicuani is **Hostal Samariy** (☎ 084-35 2518; Centenario 138; s/d US$6/9), which has limited hot water.

A few kilometers before Sicuani is the little village of **San Pedro** and the ruins of **Raqchi** (admission US$1.50; ☉ 7am-5pm), which look like a huge aqueduct from the road. These are the remains of the Temple of Viracocha, which was once one of the holiest shrines in the Inca empire. Twenty-two columns made of stone blocks helped support the largest-known Inca roof; most were destroyed by the Spanish, but their foundations are clearly seen. The remains of many houses and storage buildings are also visible and reconstruction is an ongoing process. Outside the site are several artisan workshops. In early June, Raqchi is the site of a colorful **fiesta** with much traditional music and dancing.

The trip from Cuzco to Raqchi (US$1.75, 2½ hours) or Sicuani (US$2, three hours) can be done in any bus bound for Puno. The train (p253) between Cuzco and Puno also passes by the site but far less frequently and reliably. There are also *combis* to Raqchi from Sicuani (US$0.30, 30 minutes).

CUZCO TO THE JUNGLE

There are three overland routes from Cuzco to the jungle, all by roads that frequently get bogged down in the wettest months. One road goes northwest from Ollantaytambo over the Abra de Malaga to Quillabamba and Ivochote; another through Paucartambo, Tres Cruces and Shintuya to reach the area around Parque Nacional Manu; and the third heads east from Urcos through Ocongate and Quince Mil all the way to Puerto Maldonado. Most travelers fly into the Amazon jungle, so think twice before deciding to travel overland. All of these roads are muddy, slow and dangerous, especially during the wettest months (January through April); fatal accidents commonly occur even during the dry (or more accurately, drier) season from June to September. An invaluable resource for independent travelers is the *Peruvian Jungle Information Packet*, sold by the **South American Explorers** (SAE; ☎ 084-24 5484; www.saexplorers.org; No 4, Choquechaca 188; 🕑 9:30am-5pm Mon-Fri, 9:30am-1pm Sat) in Cuzco.

CUZCO TO IVOCHOTE
Quillabamba
☎ 084 / pop 16,300 / elev 1000m

Lying on the Río Urubamba at the end of a heart-pounding route over the pass of Abra de Malaga, Quillabamba is one of Peru's most important tea- and coffee-producing regions. The narrow road from Ollantaytambo, with its stomach-testing twists and turns, quickly passes through several ecological zones, from subglacial plunging down to subtropical. Quillabamba is a hot and humid town of the high jungle, known as the City of Eternal Summer. It's quite listless and not particularly interesting, but it can be used as a base for trips deeper into the jungle.

INFORMATION
BCP (Libertad 549) has a Visa ATM and changes US dollars. There's slow but cheap internet access at a few places around the Plaza de Armas. Limited information is available for tourists at the *municipalidad* (town hall). For phone calls, **Telefónica-Perú** (Libertad cuadra 4) is also on the plaza, next to the post office and on the same block as the police station. There's also a hospital.

TOURS & GUIDES
Travel agencies around town are only open during the drier months from June to November. Ask around to find the office of Kiteni Tours, which offers excursions to the Pongo de Manique (p282) and Vilcabamba, as well as a one-day tour of local waterfalls.

SLEEPING
There is a handful of cheap, cold-water hostels around the Plaza de Armas.

Hostal Pinoda (☎ 28 1447; Libertad 530; s/d US$1.50/9; 🕑 Jun-Nov) This guesthouse has poky rooms with cold-water bathrooms above the owner's grocery store. Some English is spoken.

Hostal Alto Urubamba (☎ 28 1131; altourub@ec-red .com; 2 de Mayo 333; s/d/tr with shared bathroom US$6/8/10.50, s/d/tr US$12/16.50/19.50) This long-running place is clean, economical and overrun with nosy local men. Dozens of comfortable-enough rooms with fans encircle a sunny but echoingly noisy courtyard.

Hostal Quillabamba (☎ 28 1369; fax 28 1015; Grau 590; s US$13.50, d US$18-24; 🏊) This is a large, semi-professionally run place reluctantly recommended for clean rooms with hot showers and TV, a terrace restaurant and a rooftop garden. It's near the sketchy market area.

Hostal Don Carlos (☎ 28 1150; doncarlos@viabcp.com; Libertad 556; s/d/tr US$14/20/24, ste US$21) This elegant small hotel is by far the best place in town to stay, with a pretty courtyard garden and rooms with TVs and 24-hour hot showers.

EATING & DRINKING
Pizzeria Alamos (Bolognesi 342; snacks US$0.50-2, pizzas from US$3.50; 🕑 11am-9:30pm) No other place in town is quite so kind to foreign tourists. Staffed by enthusiastic youth, this restaurant fires up pizzas that are big enough to feed an army of Inca warriors, and the open-air courtyard bar is a local hangout after dark.

Heladería la Esquina (cnr Espinar & Libertad; mains US$1.50-3; 🕑 closed Sun) This retro café serves up delicious juices, cakes, ice cream and fast-food snacks. Service is grouchy, though, and if you order chicken, you may have to listen to them slaughtering the poor bird out back.

along a cliff-hanging dirt road with exhilarating views of the mountains and the Amazon Basin beyond.

Paucartambo is famous for its riotously colorful celebration of **Virgen del Carmen**, a festival held annually around July 15 to 17, with hypnotic street dancing, wonderful processions and all manner of weird costumes. The highly symbolic dances are inspired by everything from fever-ridden malaria sufferers to the homosexual practices of the Spanish conquistadors. The Inca ruins of **Macha Cruz** and **Pijchu** are also within walking distance of the village – ask locals for directions.

Few tourists make it here, simply because it's so difficult to reach; you either have to camp, find a room in one of a few extremely basic hotels or hope a local will give you some floor space. Many tourist agencies in Cuzco run buses specifically for the fiesta and can help arrange accommodations with local families.

Expreso Virgen del Carmen (☎ in Cuzco 084-27 7755, 084-22 6895; Diagonal Angamos 1952, Cuzco) has three daily bus services from Cuzco (US$3, five hours).

Tres Cruces

About 45km beyond Paucartambo is the extraordinary jungle view at Tres Cruces, off the Paucartambo–Shintuya road. The sight of the mountains dropping away into the Amazon Basin is gorgeous in itself, but is made all the more magical by the sunrise phenomenon that occurs from May to July (other months are cloudy), especially around the time of the winter solstice on June 21. The sunrise here gets optically distorted, causing double images, halos and an incredible multicolored light show. At this time of year, many travel agencies and outdoor adventure outfitters run sunrise-watching trips from Cuzco.

You can also take a truck en route to Pillcopata and ask to be let off at the turnoff to Tres Cruces (a further 13km walk). There are buses from Av Angamos in Cuzco to Pillcopata that usually leave on Monday, Wednesday and Friday mornings (US$4.50, 10 hours). During Paucartambo's Fiesta de la Virgen del Carmen, minibuses run back and forth between Paucartambo and Tres Cruces all night long. Alternatively, ask around in Paucartambo to hire a truck for about US$50 round-trip. Make sure you leave in the middle of the night to catch the dawn.

For details of the onward trip to Shintuya and the Manu area, see p466.

CUZCO TO PUERTO MALDONADO

According to Peruvian road engineers, this is Peru's worst road between two major towns. It's almost 500km long and takes at least 2½ days to travel in the dry season, and much longer in the wet. Most tourists travel from Cuzco to Puerto Maldonado by air, but the difficult, adventurous trip by road is a chance to see the impressive scenery of the Andes' eastern slopes. But don't take it lightly: the journey requires hardiness, self-sufficiency and loads of good luck. Fatal accidents are not uncommon.

Trucks leave daily from near the Plaza Túpac Amaru in Cuzco. Fares to Puerto Maldonado start around US$10; the cheapest places are in the back, and more expensive ones are in the cab with the driver. The least comfortable but fastest trucks are *cisternas* (gasoline trucks), with a narrow ledge on top upon which to crouch. The trucks stop about three times daily to let the driver eat, and once more so he can sleep (never for long though). If you want to split up the journey, the best places to stop are Ocongate and Quince Mil, which have basic accommodations.

The route heads toward Puno until Urcos (see p278), where the dirt road to Puerto Maldonado begins. (You could take a bus to Urcos from Manco Capac or Av de la Cultura in Cuzco and wait there for a truck; the bus costs about US$1.50.) About 125km and seven or eight hours from Cuzco, you come to the highland town of **Ocongate**, which has a couple of basic hotels around the plaza.

From here, trucks go to the village of **Tinqui**, an hour's drive beyond Ocongate, which is the starting point for the spectacular seven-day trek encircling **Ausangate** (6384m), the highest mountain in southern Peru. The route begins in the rolling brown *puna* (grasslands of the Andean plateau, known as the altiplano) and crosses four high passes (two over 5000m) en route. It features stunningly varied scenery, including fluted icy peaks, tumbling glaciers and turquoise lakes, and green marshy valleys. There are warm **mineral springs** near Tinqui, at the start and finish of the walk. Along the way you'll stumble across huge herds of alpacas and tiny hamlets unchanged in centuries.

APU AUSANGATE

The mountains (apus) are sacred deities for the Andean people and are possessed of kamaq (vital force). Ausangate, the region's highest mountain, is the most important apu in the area and the subject of many legends. It is considered the pakarina (mythical place of sacred origin) of llamas and alpacas, and controls the health and fertility of these animals. Its heights are also where condemned souls are doomed to wander, as absolution for their sins.

Today, the mountain spirits are celebrated through fiestas. Like many extant festivals they have their origins in a mixture of Quechua legend and Catholic imagery. Ausangate is the site of the traditional festival of **Q'oyoriti**, held in late May or early June between the Christian feasts of the Ascension and Corpus Christi. It takes place at an altitude of 4750m, where glaciers flow down into the Sinakara valley, on the site where an image of Christ is supposed to have appeared in 1783. Thousands of locals converge on the mountain's icy slopes to celebrate the 'star of the snow' with a night trek to the top of a glacier – during which any bad spirits encountered may need to be subdued – to return with glacial ice to be used as holy water for the subsequent year.

Despite its overtly Christian aspects, the festival remains primarily a celebration and appease-ment of the apu. In this respect it dates from at least Inca times, when offerings were regularly made to Ausangate. In modern times, the fiesta usually lasts for three days and involves much colorful dancing, traditional Andean highland music and chicha (fermented corn beer) drinking bouts. Tinqui is the gathering point. Travel agencies and outdoor outfitters in Cuzco can arrange guided trips to Ausangate.

There is a basic hotel back in Tinqui, and the locals rent pack mules (about US$15 per day with an *arriero*, or mule driver) to do the trek. Apart from trucks, **Transportes Huayna Ausangate** (☎ 084-965 0922; Tomasa Tito Condemayta, Cuzco) has a bus to Tinqui leaving Cuzco near the Coliseo Cerrado at 10am daily except Sunday (US$4.20, seven hours).

After Tinqui, the road drops steadily to **Quince Mil**, 240km from Cuzco, less than 1000m above sea level, and the halfway point of the journey. The area is a gold-mining center, and the hotel here is often full. After another 100km, the road into the jungle reaches the flatlands, where it levels out for the last 140km into Puerto Maldonado.

CUZCO TO THE CENTRAL HIGHLANDS

Traveling by bus from Cuzco to Lima via Abancay and Nazca takes you along a remote route closed from the late 1980s until the late 1990s by guerilla activity and banditry; however, it now is safer (of course, you should check recent news reports before heading out this way) and largely paved. Going west from Abancay to Andahuaylas and Ayacucho is a tough ride on a rough road rarely used except by the most hard-core travelers.

LIMATAMBO
pop 1000

This speck of a village, set in mountainous countryside 80km west of Cuzco by road, is at the upper end of the valley of a headwater tributary of the Río Apurímac. It is named after the Inca site of Rimactambo, also popu-larly known as **Tarawasi** (adult/student US$1.50/0.60), which is situated beside the road, about 2km west of Limatambo. The site's painstakingly constructed stonework suggests that it was used as a ceremonial center, as well as a resting place for the Inca *chasquis* (Inca runners used to deliver messages over long distances). The exceptional polygonal retaining wall, note-worthy for its 28 human-sized niches, is in itself worth the trip from Cuzco; look for a half-dozen flower shapes and a nine-sided heart amid the patchwork of perfectly inter-locking stones.

You can reach Limatambo from Cuzco via *colectivo* taxis (US$1.80, 1½ hours) or minibuses (US$1.50, two hours) that all leave from Arcopata, two long blocks west of Meloc in central Cuzco, or on buses bound for Aban-cay from Cuzco's Terminal Terrestre. If you leave early in the morning, you can visit the ruins and return to Cuzco on an afternoon bus (passing between 2pm and 3:30pm), al-though there's also the basic **Hostal Rivero** (dm US$3) in a farmhouse just off the highway west of town.

SAIHUITE

The Inca site of **Saihuite** (adult/student US$3/1), 45km east of Abancay, has a sizable, intricately carved boulder called the Stone of Saihuite, which is similar to the famous sculpted rock at Q'enqo, near Cuzco, though it's smaller and more elaborate. The carvings of animals are particularly intricate. To get to Saihuite, catch any bus bound for Abancay from Cuzco (US$2.40, 3½ to four hours) and ask to be let off at the turnoff to the ruins, from where it is a 1km walk downhill.

CHOQUEQUIRAU

The recently rediscovered ridgetop Inca site of **Choquequirau** (admission US$3) is a remote ruin lying in a cloud forest above a river canyon. The site is currently only reached on foot (a great attraction for some people), so get to it quickly before tourist authorities make the site more accessible to the masses. It has an incredible location at the junction of three valleys, and though much of the ruins are still covered by cloud forest, they display clear religious and agricultural elements. The most common trekking route begins from Cachora, a village off the road to Abancay – the turnoff is shortly after the ruins of Saihuite. Buses and *colectivo* taxis sometimes run direct from Abancay to Cachora, or it's a matter of hitchhiking the final stretch. Most tour agencies follow the route from Cachora. Independent travelers will find simple guesthouses, a campground and local guides and mules for hire in Cachora.

ABANCAY

☎ 083 / pop 101,600 / elev 2378m

This sleepy rural town is the capital of the department of Apurímac, one of the least-explored regions in the Peruvian Andes. Despite its status as a capital, the place has a forlorn, forgotten air. Travelers may opt to use it as a rest stop on the long, tiring bus journey between Cuzco and Ayacucho.

Information

BCP (Arequipa 218-222) changes US dollars and has a Visa ATM. Several cheap but slow cybercafés are clustered on Arenas.

Sights & Activities

During the dry season (late May to September), hikers and climbers may want to take advantage of the best weather to head for

NOTE

Due to severe rainfall and mudslides that made all routes nearly impassable, plus nationwide political strikes (always more extreme in the highlands), our author could not access Abancay, Andahuaylas and around. Our research in this area consisted of personal contacts by phone and internet, and input from local citizens and fellow travelers.

the sometimes snowcapped peak of **Ampay** (5228m), about 10km north-northwest of town. The mountain is also the center of the 3635-hectare **Santuario Nacional Ampay**, where camping and birding are good.

Festivals & Events

Abancay has a particularly colorful **Carnaval** held in the week before Lent, which is a chance to see festival celebrations uncluttered by the trappings of tourism. It includes a nationally acclaimed folk-dancing competition. Book ahead or arrive before the festivities start. **Abancay Day** happens on November 3, the anniversary of the town's founding.

Sleeping & Eating

Hostal Gran Hotel (☎ 32 1144; Arenas 196; s/d with shared bathroom US$3/5, s/d US$4.50/6) This large, noisy hostel is adequate but old; only a few rooms have hot water.

Hostal Victoria (☎ 32 1301; Arequipa 305; s/d with shared bathroom US$5/7.50, s/d US$7.50/10.50) This is an excellent, very clean little hostel not far from the BCP. Rooms that come with cable TV cost a bit extra.

Hostal Imperial (☎ 32 1578; Díaz Bárcenas 517; s/d with shared bathroom US$7.50/10.50, s/d incl breakfast US$13.50/21) The Imperial has an unprepossessing entrance, but opens up to a light courtyard; it has decent rooms with 24-hour hot water and cable TV.

Hoturs Hotel de Turistas (☎ 32 1017; fax 32 1628; Díaz Bárcenas 500; s/d/tr 2nd fl US$25/40/50, 3rd fl US$30/45/55, ste US$75) Located opposite the Hostal Imperial, the best hotel in town is housed in an old-fashioned country mansion. The 3rd-floor rooms have cable TV, minibar and phone. This hotel also has Abancay's best restaurant.

There are plenty of cheap cafés and local restaurants on Arenas. Conveniently just a block away from the BCP, **Cafe Mundial** (Arequipa s/n; items US$1.50-3; 11am-8pm) mixes up killer juices, fruit salads, homemade cakes and ice cream, and portions are huge. Elsewhere, **Restaurant La Delicia** (32 1702; Elias 217; 2-course menús US$2; closed Sat) is a tiny health-food joint serving dirt-cheap vegetarian food. If you get stuck here overnight, **Punto A** (Arequipa) is a bar that expats recommend.

Getting There & Away

Most bus companies leave from Arenas near Nuñez. Several companies go to Lima (from US$12, 18 to 20 hours) via the Nazca road; you need to book a day in advance to ensure a seat. All of the bus companies leaving for Cuzco (US$4.50, five hours) or Andahuaylas (US$4, five hours) have four departures daily, usually around 6am, 1pm and 8pm. Journeys may take much longer during the wet season. Transfer in Andahuaylas for onward buses to Ayacucho.

ANDAHUAYLAS

083 / pop 30,000 / elev 2980m
Andahuaylas, 135km west of Abancay on the way to Ayacucho, is the second most important town in the department of Apurímac, and a convenient halfway stop on the rough but scenic route between Cuzco and Ayacucho.

Information

BCP (Ramon Castilla s/n) has a Visa ATM and changes US dollars. The best internet connection is at **Telefónica-Perú** (JF Ramos 317).

Sights & Activities

Andahuaylas' main attraction, the beautiful **Laguna de Pacucha**, is 17km from town and accessible by bus or taxi. There are meals, fishing and rowboat rental available there. *Combis* to the lake run along Chanka at the north end of town (US$1.20, 30 minutes). A one-hour hike from the lake brings you to the imposing hilltop site of **Sondor**, built by the Chanka culture, traditional enemies of the Incas. The site is accessible by taxi from town (round-trip US$15), and has panoramic mountain views.

Both Andahuaylas and Pacucha have Sunday **markets** that are worth perusing.

The colonial **cathedral** on the Plaza de Armas is worth a look, though it's more sober than its counterparts elsewhere in Peru. There's also a **municipal pool** (Lázaro Carrillo; adult/child US$0.60/0.30; 9am-4pm Tue-Sun).

Festivals & Events

The annual **Fiesta de Yahuar** (Blood Feast) is on July 28, when traditional dances and music are performed. In the village of Pacucha, the festival includes lashing a condor to the back of a bull and allowing the two to fight in a representation of the highland people's struggle against the Spanish conquistadors.

Sleeping

Hostal los Libertadores Wari (72 1106; JF Ramos 424; s/d with shared bathroom US$4.50/6, s/d US$6/9) This bare-bones hostel is clean and safe and has hot water, but it closes its doors by 11pm.

Hostal Delicias (72 1104; JF Ramos 525; s/d US$7.50/10.50) Delicias is a light, well-kept place run by welcoming folks; rooms have hot showers.

Encanto de Apurimac Hotel (72 3527; JF Ramos 401; s/d/tr US$7.50/10.50/13.50) This hotel, which has its door on JA Trelles, has modern, shiny rooms with hot water.

Hotel Turístico Andahuaylas (72 1229; www .hoteturisticoandahuaylas.com; Lázaro Carrillo 620; s/d/tw/tr US$12/15/18/21) This place has boxy rooms with cable TV, and has the advantage of being next door to the swimming pool. There's also a sauna in the hostel, open weekends only (US$3). English and French are spoken.

El Encanto de Oro Hotel (72 3066; elencanto rohotel@hotmail.com; Av Casafranca 424; s/d/tr US$13.50/18/24) El Encanto has good rooms with private hot showers (some rooms even have two bathrooms), cable TV and telephone.

Imperio Chanka (72 3065; Vallejo 384; s/d US$15/20) This new hostel is by the Expreso Molino bus station and has very good, clean rooms and cable TV, though it lacks character.

Sol de Oro (72 1152; JA Trelles 164; s/d/tr US$15/22.50/30) This is the best hotel in town, boasting extremely smart modern rooms with hot water, cable TV and attentive service.

Eating & Drinking

The plaza is one of the few spots in town for nightlife.

El Dorado (72 1152; Sol de Oro, JA Trelles; mains US$1.50-5; breakfast, lunch & dinner) Located at the Sol de Oro hotel, this restaurant is surprisingly elegant considering the low prices.

Chifa El Dragón (72 1956; cnr JF Ramos & JA Trelles; 3-course menús from US$2; 11:30am-8:30pm) El Dragón is a smart restaurant serving Chinese meals with a touch of *criollo* (spicy Peruvian fare with Spanish and African influences).

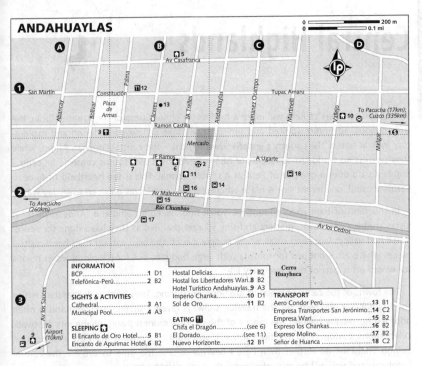

ANDAHUAYLAS

INFORMATION			Hostal Delicias................7 B2	Cerro
BCP....................................1 D1			Hostal los Libertadores Wari.8 B2	Huayhuca
Telefónica-Perú.......................2 B2			Hotel Turístico Andahuaylas.9 A3	
			Imperio Chanka...............10 D1	**TRANSPORT**
SIGHTS & ACTIVITIES			Sol de Oro.......................11 B2	Aero Condor Perú.............................13 B1
Cathedral................................3 A1				Empresa Transportes San Jerónimo...14 C2
Municipal Pool.........................4 A3			**EATING**	Empresa Wari..................................15 B2
			Chifa el Dragón.............(see 6)	Expreso los Chankas......................16 B2
SLEEPING			El Dorado....................(see 11)	Expreso Molino................................17 B2
El Encanto de Oro Hotel......5 B1			Nuevo Horizonte..............12 B1	Señor de Huanca 18 C2
Encanto de Apurimac Hotel.6 B2				

Nuevo Horizonte (☎ 80 1870; Constitución 572; 2-course menús US$1.50; ⊗ closed Sat) Nuevo Horizonte, just off the plaza, is a simple place with cheap, tasty vegetarian fare.

Getting There & Away

AIR

Aero Condor Perú (☎ 72 2877; Cáceres 326) has flights to Lima three times weekly. The flight sometimes goes via Ayacucho, but not on a regularly scheduled basis. Minibuses run from the airline office to the regional airport, a 20-minute drive south of town (US$1.80). A taxi to the airport will cost about US$3.

BUS

Heading east, **Señor de Huanca** (☎ 72 1218; Martinelli 170) has four daily buses to Abancay (US$4, five hours). **Empresa Transportes San Jeronimo** (☎ 72 1400; Andahuaylas 116) has an evening bus to Cuzco (US$8, 10 hours) via Abancay.

Expreso los Chankas (☎ 72 2441; Av Malecon Grau 232) runs a twice-daily service west to Ayacucho (US$6, 10 hours), as well as running buses to Abancay and Cuzco. The road to Ayacucho goes over very high *puna*, may be snow covered, and is very cold at night. Make sure to wear warm clothes and bring a sleeping bag on board if you have one.

Empresa Wari (☎ 72 1936; Av Malecon Grau s/n) and **Expreso Molino** (☎ 72 1248; Av los Sauces s/n) each have three daily buses to Lima (from US$15, 22 to 24 hours) that go through Nazca. Both also have a daily service to Ayacucho.

ABANCAY TO NAZCA

The road down to Nazca and the coast passes through **Chalhuanca**, roughly 120km from Abancay, then about 190km further on it reaches **Puquio**, which has the basic **Hostal los Andes** (☎ 45 2103; s/d US$5/10) and simple restaurants. For the last 50km before Puquio, the road traverses an incredibly wild-looking area of desolate, lake-studded countryside that is worth staying awake for. About 65km beyond Puquio and 90km before Nazca, the road passes through the **Reserva Nacional Pampas Galeras** (p146), a sanctuary for vicuñas (threatened wild relatives of llamas).

Several bus companies travel between Abancay and Lima (from US$12, 18 to 20 hours) via Nazca; book a day in advance.

Central Highlands

While most travelers to Peru will make a beeline for either Cuzco or the Amazon Basin, the truly curious, adventure spirited and time rich will take a slow, meandering and exploratory look at one of the country's lesser-known regions – the central Peruvian Andes. While they possess no world-famous sights or ruins or even high-tech tourist centers, the central highlands do offer a glimpse of Peru at it's most normal. This is the heartland of Andean Peru – its soul, one might say. A place where the Inca spirit lives on in an everyday way.

In this land of bare rocky mountains you'll find sweeping altiplano (Andean plateau) vistas studded with lakes, glaciers and tiny villages that live as they have done for aeons. You'll find valleys large and small where people live off the land and off their handicrafts – places where art is not just for tourists with large budgets, but for people of lesser means for whom art is part of their everyday life.

The towns of the central highlands are unprepossessing. They neither deliberately entice tourists nor live off them. Yet the traveler is always given a smiling welcome and is often afforded hospitality beyond the means of the region's modest-living inhabitants. Festivals, celebrations, customs and traditions thrive. If you want to slip away from the well-trodden Gringo Trail look no further than Peru's heartland; take the time to explore the central highlands and you will be rewarded more than you might expect.

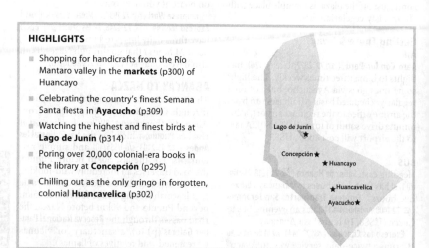

HIGHLIGHTS

- Shopping for handicrafts from the Río Mantaro valley in the **markets** (p300) of Huancayo
- Celebrating the country's finest Semana Santa fiesta in **Ayacucho** (p309)
- Watching the highest and finest birds at **Lago de Junín** (p314)
- Poring over 20,000 colonial-era books in the library at **Concepción** (p295)
- Chilling out as the only gringo in forgotten, colonial **Huancavelica** (p302)

Lago de Junín ★

Concepción ★   ★ Huancayo

★ Huancavelica

Ayacucho ★

■ BIGGEST CITY: HUANCAYO, POPULATION 387,700

■ AVERAGE TEMPERATURE: JANUARY 12°C TO 24°C, JULY 8°C TO 24°C

CENTRAL HIGHLANDS

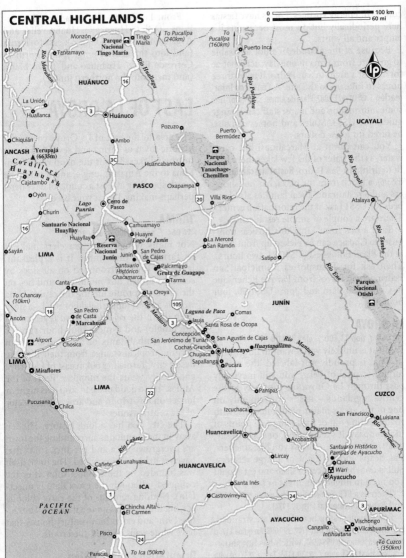

LIMA TO LA OROYA

SAN PEDRO DE CASTA & MARCAHUASI

San Pedro de Casta (population 500, elevation 3200m) is a good place to start your central Andes adventure. This mountainside locale is a small village about 40km from Chosica (80km from Lima). People come here in order to visit the little-known archaeological site of Marcahuasi, a 4-sq-km plateau at 4100m; it's 3km from San Pedro on foot. Marcahuasi is famed for its weirdly eroded rocks shaped into animals such as camels, turtles and seals. These have a mystical significance for some people, who claim they are signs of a pre-Inca culture or energy vortices. Locals have fiestas here periodically but on most occasions it's empty and all yours.

Because of the altitude, it's not advisable to go there from Lima in one day; acclimatize for at least a night in San Pedro. It takes three hours to hike up to the site. A **Centro de Información** (☎ 01-571 2087; Plaza de Armas, San Pedro) has some information and maps; staff can arrange guides for US$3. Mules and horses can also be hired for a few dollars.

You can camp at Marcahuasi but carry water, as the water of the few lakes there isn't fit to drink. In San Pedro, **Hostal Marcahuasi** (s/d US$3/6), a block from the plaza, has hot showers and a restaurant. Local families also have beds for US$1 (ask at the information center). There are a couple of simple restaurants.

Take a bus from Lima to Chosica; minibuses to Chosica can be picked up from Arica at the Plaza Bolognesi (US$0.75, two hours). Then ask for Transportes Municipal San Pedro, which leaves from Parque Echenique in Chosica at 9am and 3pm (US$1.50, four hours).

LA OROYA

☎ 064 / pop 33,600 / elev 3731m

While it is unlikely you'll want to linger long in what is proudly self-labeled 'the metal-lurgical capital of Peru,' you will inevitably pass through La Oroya on your way to the central highlands – it sits conveniently on one of the area's major road junctions, with roads leading out of the town to all points of the compass. It's a cold and, one has to say, unattractive place – unless you like smelters, slag heaps and the sight of a large refinery. Still, it does have places to sleep and eat should you need to linger for a night or so.

There is a **BCP** (formerly Banco de Crédito; ☎ 39 1191) and **Banco Continental** (☎ 39 1174).

Few travelers stop here. If you are stranded, try the basic **Hostal Inti** (☎ 39 1098; Arequipa 117; d with shared bathroom US$4.50), which has hot showers, or **Hostal Chavín** (☎ 39 1185; Tarma 281; s/d with shared bathroom US$3/6), with hot showers and a restaurant. About 2km or 3km from the center toward Lima, near the prison on the edge of town, the **Hostal San Juan** (☎ 39 2566; fax 39 1539; RH Rubio 114; s with shared bathroom US$7, s/d US$10/16) is clean and has hot showers. **Hostal San Martín** (☎ 39 1278, 39 1963; RH Rubio 134; s/d US$13/20) is the best option. Rooms have hot showers, cable TV and heaters.

From La Oroya, roads lead in all directions: south to Huancayo, Huancavelica and Ayacucho (and on to Cuzco); east to Tarma (and into the central jungle); and north to Cerro de Pasco, Huánuco and Tingo María (and then into the northern jungle).

EAST OF LA OROYA

The area to the east of La Oroya covers the historic town of Tarma and several pleasant nearby villages. This is the main route from Lima to the Amazon jungle, and it would be worth spending at least a couple of days here, perhaps making Tarma your base.

TARMA

☎ 064 / pop 51,800 / elev 3050m

Not many independent travelers make it to Tarma and then linger. It is a pleasant, laid-back town surrounded on all sides by scrubby, brown dirt mountains and lies on the important route linking the capital Lima with its nearest jungle neighborhood – a steep drop down the *ceja de la selva* (eyebrow of the jungle) and a mere four-hour run for *limeños* (inhabitants of Lima) seeking an exciting tropical change from their bustling desert city. Tarma lies 60km east of La Oroya and locally wears the moniker 'Pearl of the Andes.' It is a good place to stop overnight or longer on any trip in and around this sector of the central Andes.

The city also has a long history. Hidden away in the mountains surrounding the town are overgrown Inca and pre-Inca ruins that have yet to be fully excavated. The town itself was founded by the Spanish soon after the conquest (although the exact date is uncertain). Nothing remains of the early colonial era, but the town has quite a number of attractive 19th- and early-20th-century houses that have white walls and red-tiled roofs.

Orientation & Information

While the center of Tarma is fairly compact, most buses and taxis to/from Lima arrive about 800m to the west of the Plaza de Armas. Taxis from Huancayo arrive and depart from a rather inconvenient location on the southwest side of town, while Amazon transport leaves from the east side of town.

Casas de cambio (foreign-exchange bureaus) are at the western end of Lima.

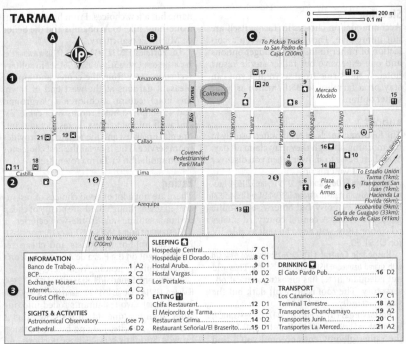

TARMA

0 —————— 200 m
0 —————— 0.1 mi

Banco de Trabajo (Lima) Has an ATM near the *casas de cambio*.

BCP (☎ 32 2149; Lima at Paucartambo) You can change money here; also has an ATM.

Internet (Paucartambo 567)

Tourist office (☎ 32 1010 ext 20; fax 32 3483; 2 de Mayo 775; ☼ 8am-1pm & 3-6pm Mon-Fri) On the Plaza de Armas and has brochures and information about local tours, in Spanish.

Sights

Tarma is high in the mountains and the clear nights of June, July and August provide some ideal opportunities for stargazing, though the surrounding mountains do limit the amount of observable heavens. To make it easier to observe the stars, there is a small **astronomical observatory** (☎ 32 2625; Huánuco 614; admission US$1; ☼ 8-10pm Fri) run by the owners of Hospedaje Central. The owners are usually away in Lima, but public use is permitted.

The town's **cathedral** is modern (1965), and it contains the remains of Peruvian president Manuel A Odría (1897–1974). He was born in Tarma and organized the construction of the cathedral during his presidency. The old clock in the cathedral tower dates from 1862.

Nearby excursions include visits to the religious shrine of El Señor de Muruhuay in Acobamba (9km from Tarma; see p293) and the Gruta de Guagapo (33km away; see p293).

Festivals & Events

The big annual attraction is undoubtedly Easter.

Semana Santa (Holy Week) Many processions are held, including several by candlelight after dark. They culminate on the morning of Easter Sunday with a marvelous procession to the cathedral along an 11-block route entirely carpeted with flower petals. This attracts thousands of Peruvian visitors and the hotels are usually full, with prices increasing by up to 50%.

Tarma Tourism Week Another fiesta, held near the end of July. It involves dress-up parades, music, dancing and much raucous merriment.

El Señor de los Milagros (Lord of the Miracles) This annual fiesta takes place in late October; the main feast days are the 18th, 28th and 29th. This is another good opportunity to see processions over beautiful, flower-petal carpets.

Sleeping

Accommodation choices in Tarma itself are not impressive. They range between a collection of rather uninspiring budget options and one expensive but rather sterile resort hotel. A short ride from town and you can stay on a farmhouse B&B, which is a far better option.

BUDGET

The following hotels have hot water, usually in the morning, though they may claim all day. Your best bet is to shower when you discover that the hot water is on.

Hospedaje El Dorado (☎ 32 1914; fax 32 1634; Huánuco 488; s/d with shared bathroom US$3/4.50, s/d US$4.50/8) Rooms can be noisy, but otherwise are quite good and clean. A central courtyard invites relaxation. Box-watchers can rent a cable TV for US$1.50.

Hospedaje Central (☎ 32 2625; Huánuco 614; s/d with shared bathroom US$4.50/6, s/d US$7/9) This old but adequate hotel has an astronomical observatory. The rooms are a bit dark but the staff is friendly.

Hostal Vargas (☎ 32 1460; fax 32 1721; 2 de Mayo 627; s/d with shared bathroom US$4.50/6, s/d US$8/11) Ignore the rather gloomy entrance and you'll find a clean hotel with spacious rooms and hard beds if you're fed up with sagging mattresses. The staff is upfront with the hot-water hours: 5am to 10am only. TV rental is US$1.50.

Hostal Aruba (☎ 32 2057; Moquegua 452; s/d US$10/14.50) A very secure hotel located by the ever-busy *mercado modelo* (market); ring the bell for admittance. The rooms are clean, showers are hot and local cable TV is provided.

MIDRANGE & TOP END

Hacienda La Florida (☎ 34 1041, 01-344 1358; www .haciendalaflorida.com; s/d US$25/50) Six kilometers from Tarma on the road to Acobamba, this 250-year-old working hacienda is now a B&B owned by a welcoming Peruvian-German couple, Pepe and Inge. The solid-walled and individually named rooms boast attractive wooden parquet floors and private bathrooms, and there are a couple of rooms for backpackers plus secure space for campers (US$5). A filling breakfast as well as homemade lunches and dinners can be had for US$6 per person. Visitors can partake in farm life or in two-day workshops (minimum of six) in relaxation techniques, cooking classes and reiki, to

name but a few choices. From here it's about a one-hour hike to Acobamba and the Señor de Muruhuay sanctuary.

Los Portales (☎ 32 1411; fax 32 1410; www.hoteles losportales.com; Castilla 512; s/d US$52/76) Set in solitary seclusion away from the center and amidst pleasant gardens at the west end of town, this hotel features a children's playground and 45 standard hotel rooms with cable TV and wi-fi internet access. Rates include continental breakfast and the restaurant provides room service. This is by far the best choice for accommodation in Tarma town itself.

Eating

There are not a lot of good choices of restaurant in town, though there are plenty of cheap and unassuming hole-in-the-wall eateries.

Restaurant Grima (☎ 32 1892; Lima 270; meals US$1-2; ☼ 7am-7pm) For breakfasts and cheap set lunches right on the Plaza de Armas you won't go far wrong by heading right here.

Restaurant Señorial/El Braserito (☎ 32 3334; Huánuco 138/140; menús US$1.20, mains US$2-5; ☼ 8am-3pm & 6-11pm) Two restaurants rolled into one (they open just one side if it's slow), this is the locals' favorite, judging by the nonstop crowds. Sprightly service, huge portions and bright, cheerful surroundings with mirrored walls and neon signs lure diners in. They aren't disappointed by the menu of Peruvian standards, plus traditional dishes such as *cuy* (guinea pig).

El Mejorcito de Tarma (☎ 32 3500; Arequipa 501; mains US$2-5; ☼ lunch & dinner) From Chiclayo, the owner of this restaurant decided upon arrival in Tarma some years ago that the restaurant food in town wasn't good enough. The positive result is the Mejorcito (the 'littlest and bestest'). The modest menu runs the gamut of Peruvian favorites, with grilled trout being a less obvious but excellent choice.

Chifa Restaurant (cnr Amazonas & 2 de Mayo; mains US$2-5; ☼ lunch & dinner) While the blue neon lights might not provoke an appetite, the mainly chicken-based Peruvian dishes will fill you, as will the very tasty and enormously portioned special fried rice.

Drinking

El Gato Pardo Pub (Callao 227) For a town with little to choose from in the nightlife stakes, this dark and noisy pub is also a club with recorded and live Latin music and draws a mainly local crowd.

Getting There & Around

The forlorn, minuscule but official Terminal Terrestre has just one bus daily leaving for Lima at 10pm (US$3, six hours).

Bus companies usually have their own terminals here:

Los Canarios (☎ 32 3357; Amazonas 694) Has small buses to Huancayo (US$2.50, three hours) leaving almost hourly from 5am to 6pm.

Transportes Chanchamayo (☎ 32 1882; Callao 1002) Has 9am, 2pm and 11pm departures to Lima (US$4.50). Buses coming through from Lima go to La Merced.

Transportes Junín (☎ 32 1234, 32 3494; Amazonas 669) Has five daily buses to Lima including bus-camas at 11:30am and also 11:45pm (US$4.50 to US$7.30). It also has 5:30am and 1pm departures for Cerro de Pasco.

Transportes La Merced (☎ 32 2937; Vienrich 420) Has buses to Lima at 8:45am, 11:30am, 1:30pm, 10:30pm, 11pm and 11:30pm (US$4.50). The evening services offer bus-cama (bed bus) options for US$8 (upstairs) or US$9 (downstairs).

Transportes San Juan (☎ 32 3139) In front of the Estadio Unión Tarma at the northeastern end of town (a three-wheeled motorcycle rickshaw – mototaxi – ride here costs US$0.20). Has big buses to Huancayo ($2.50, 3½ hours) via Concepción and Jauja, as well as frequent buses to La Merced (US$1.50, two hours).

By the gas station opposite the Terminal Terrestre, colectivo (shared) taxis take up to four passengers to Lima (US$8.50 each) or local destinations such as Junín (US$4) or La Oroya (US$4). If you want to go to Cerro de Pasco or Huánuco, you can take colectivos from here too, though you will have to change cars up to three times to get there. Fast colectivo taxis to Huancayo (US$5) leave from Jauja, about 600m south of the Terminal Terrestre.

Almost opposite Transportes San Juan, colectivos to La Merced charge US$3. This is a spectacular trip, dropping about 2.5km vertically to the jungle edge in the space of just over an hour. For destinations beyond La Merced, change at the convenient Transportes San Juan La Merced bus terminal. Ask around the stadium area for other destinations. During the day frequent, inexpensive minibuses for Jauja (US$1.90) leave from the roundabout next to the Terminal Terrestre as soon as they are full. A bus stop next to Transportes San Juan has minibuses going to Acobamba and Palcamayo. Pickup trucks and cars for San Pedro de Cajas leave from the northern end of Moquegua. The tourist office can advise on getting to other villages.

ACOBAMBA
☎ 064

The village of Acobamba, about 9km from Tarma, is famous for the religious sanctuary of **El Señor de Muruhuay**, which is visible on a small hill about 1.5km away.

The sanctuary is built around a rock etching of Christ crucified. Historians claim that it was carved with a sword by a royalist officer who was one of the few survivors after losing the Battle of Junín (a major battle of independence fought on August 6, 1824). Despite this, legends relating to the image's miraculous appearance persist. The first building erected around the image was a roughly thatched hut, which was replaced in 1835 by a small chapel. The present sanctuary, inaugurated in 1972, is a modern building with an electronically controlled bell tower and is decorated with huge weavings from San Pedro de Cajas.

The colorful feast of El Señor de Muruhuay, held throughout May, has been celebrated annually since 1835. Apart from the religious services and processions, there are ample opportunities to sample local produce and to see people dressed in traditional clothes. There are dances, fireworks and even a few gringos. Stalls sell chicha (corn beer) and cuy, but be wary unless your stomach is used to local food. Visitors usually stay in nearby Tarma.

PALCAMAYO
☎ 064

This attractive village, 28km from Tarma, is serviced by several colectivo taxis a day. From Palcamayo you can visit the **Gruta de Guagapo**, a huge limestone cave in the hills about 4km away. The cave has been the subject of various international expeditions and is one of Peru's largest and best-known caves, officially protected as a National Speleological Area. Several other, lesser-known caves in the area would also be of interest to speleologists.

A descent into the Gruta de Guagapo requires caving equipment and experience. The cave contains waterfalls, squeezes and underwater sections (scuba equipment required), and although it is possible to enter the cave for a short distance, you soon need technical gear. A local guide, Señor Modesto Castro, has explored the cave on numerous occasions and can provide you with ropes and lanterns to enter the first sections. He lives in one of the two houses below the mouth of the cave and has a collection of photographs and newspaper clippings describing the exploration of the cave. He doesn't do much caving himself any more but his son, Ramiro, can be of assistance.

SOUTHEAST OF LA OROYA

This section of Peru's central highlands is dominated by the Río Mantaro valley, which runs between the towns of Jauja and Huancayo. Split by the Río Mantaro throughout its length, the valley is a large and fertile agricultural plain and home to a number of colorful villages.

Festivals are a way of life in the valley. Valley residents say that there is a festival occurring each day of the year, so don't be surprised if you stumble upon some colorful happenings. The valley is also one of the few places in the central Andes where cycling is popular. Southwards from Huancayo the road leads through narrow valleys to Huancavelica and further south through a rough but scenic route to Ayacucho.

JAUJA

☎ 064 / pop 21,200 / elev 3250m

Coming from Lima, the first place you pass along this route is Jauja, a friendly and historic town about 80km southeast of La Oroya, 60km south of Tarma and 40km north of Huancayo. It's a busy commercial town and while it superficially offers little to entice tourists, it is pleasant enough and makes for an alternative base.

Orientation & Information

Jauja is a long, spread-out town that is easily navigable on foot. Transportation arrives 500m north of town.

You can change money at **BCP** (☎ 36 2011; Junín 785), which also sports an ATM. Internet *cabinas* dot most of the central blocks. For good general information (in Spanish only), click to www.jaujamiperu.com.

Sights & Activities

Before the Incas, this area was the home of an important Huanca indigenous community, and **Huanca ruins** can be seen on a hill about 3km southeast of town. A brisk walk or *mototaxi* will get you there. Jauja was Pizarro's first

capital in Peru, though this honor was short lived. Some finely carved wooden altars in the main church are all that remain of the early colonial days.

About 4km from Jauja is **Laguna de Paca**, a small lakeside resort offering restaurants, rowboats and fishing. A boat ride in a covered rowboat around the lake will cost about US$1 per passenger (five-person minimum). There are ducks and gulls, and you can stop at the **Isla del Amor** – a tiny artificial island not much bigger than the boat you're on.

There is a colorful **market** in the town center every Wednesday morning.

Tours & Guides

For adventure hiking get in touch with **Tampu Tours** (☎ 36 2314; www.tampu.info, in Spanish; Bolívar 1114), which runs challenging four-day trekking tours in the area.

Sleeping

Many visitors stay in Huancayo and travel to Jauja on one of the frequent minibuses or *colectivo* taxis.

Cabezon's (☎ 36 2206; Ayacucho 1025; s with shared shower US$4.50, d US$11.50) Has hot water and rooms with TV.

Hotel Santa Rosa (☎ 36 2225; Ayacucho 792; s/d US$5/10) On the corner of the Plaza de Armas, has a restaurant, hot water and rooms with showers.

Hotel Ganso de Oro (☎ 36 2165; Ricardo Palma 249; s/d with shared shower US$5/6) Try also this simple option, two blocks from the train station on the north side of town. The fairly tiny rooms all have sinks and toilets and 24-hour hot water is promised, but the showers are shared.

Hostal Manco Cápac (☎ 36 1620; Manco Cápac 575; s/d incl breakfast US$10/15) If you choose to stay in Jauja, a good choice is this relaxing house with a garden, three blocks north of the Plaza de Armas. Rates include a hearty continental breakfast and real coffee.

Hostal Maria Nieves (☎ 36 2543; Gálvez 491; s/d incl breakfast US$11.50/14.50) This is a good option, with TVs in the rooms.

Eating

Out by Laguna de Paca, a string of lakeshore restaurants attempts to entice diners with loud music and menu boards. The lakeside tables are pleasant enough to sit at, but hardly quiet as each restaurant tries to outdo its neighbor with piped Andean music. Of the bunch there is not much to choose between them in either quality or price, though Las Brisas near the beginning of the strip is generally considered to be one of the better ones and does offer a fairly solid plate of *pachamanca* (meat, potatoes and vegetables cooked in an earthen 'oven' of hot rocks).

Jauja has several cheap, basic restaurants near the Plaza de Armas.

Hotel Ganso de Oro (☎ 36 2166; Ricardo Palma 247; mains US$2.50-5; ☾ lunch & dinner) Has a good restaurant. Trout and (during the rainy season) frog are local specialties.

El Paraíso (☎ 36 2400; Ayacucho 917; mains US$2.50-5; ☾ lunch & dinner) Just north of the Plaza, this place is pretty reputable with dishes such as the traditional dish *papa a la huancaína* (boiled potato topped with a creamy cheese sauce) or *picante de cuy* (roast guinea pig in a spicy sauce) usually on offer. It's close to the center.

D'Chechis (☎ 36 2638; Bolívar 1166; mains US$2.50-5; ☾ lunch & dinner) Another well-regarded dining choice that serves up a variety of local dishes.

Getting There & Away
Jauja has the regional airport, but there are currently no scheduled flights.

Buses, minibuses and taxis all congregate at the south side of town at the junction of Ricardo Palma and Junín about 500m from the Plaza de Armas. During the day, frequent, inexpensive minibuses leave from here for Huancayo (US$1.60), Tarma (US$1.90) and La Oroya (US$1.25) as soon as they are full. *Colectivo* taxis normally take five passengers and that means two in the front seat. Pay the extra fare if you don't want a passenger in your lap.

Getting Around
Mototaxis run anywhere in town for around US$0.90. Take a *mototaxi* to get to Laguna de Paca (US$1.90).

Jauja is one of the few towns in the central highlands that sell bicycles. You can pick up a fairly reliable mountain bike from one of the shops on Junín if you plan to stay for a while.

CONCEPCIÓN
☎ 064/elevation 3283m
South of Jauja, the road branches to follow both the west and east sides of the Río

Mantaro valley to Huancayo. Local bus drivers refer to these as *derecha* (right, or west) and *izquierda* (left, or east).

Concepción, a village halfway between Jauja and Huancayo on the *izquierda* side, is the entry point for the famous convent of **Santa Rosa de Ocopa** (admission US$1.50; ☾ 9am-noon & 3-6pm Wed-Mon). Admission is by 45-minute guided tour every hour. There is a 50% student discount. Set in a pleasant garden, this beautiful building was built by the Franciscans in the early 18th century as a center for missionaries heading into the jungle. During the years of missionary work, the friars built up an impressive collection that is displayed in the convent's museum. Exhibits include stuffed jungle wildlife, indigenous artifacts, photographs of early missionary work, old maps, a fantastic library of some 20,000 volumes (many are centuries old), a large collection of colonial religious art (mainly of the style of *escuela cuzqueña*, whereby colonial artists combined Spanish and Andean artistic styles) and many other objects.

Frequent *colectivos* to the convent leave from Concepción for Ocopa, about 5km away. Concepción is easily visited by taking a Huancayo–Jauja *izquierda* bus.

HUANCAYO
☎ 064 / pop 387,700 / elev 3244m
Arriving in Huancayo you get the impression of arriving in some Wild West frontier town. Tumbledown outer suburbs, dusty, chaotic streets, people wandering seemingly at random and all around the mountains rise and surround. Yet the altiplano (Andean plateau) on which Huancayo is built gives the whole scene an air of welcome space often missing in the Andes. Huancayo is an arresting town. Once you've dusted your spurs and settled in, the real town reveals itself. It's modern yet traditional. There's good accommodation and top-class wine-and-dineries in which to wash off the dust of the mountains and taste hearty local fare, all to the accompaniment of crisp Peruvian wines or local boutique beer.

Above all Huancayo is a center of activity for this whole section of the central highlands, and on a local level the Río Mantaro valley. There are culture and fiestas to be savored, crafts to be learned, musical instruments to be dabbled with (maybe even mastered one day) and for the adventurous there's Andes trekking, extreme mountain biking and jungle tramping. Polyglots can add another linguistic arrow to their bow by learning Spanish at well-organized language courses. Huancayo challenges at first, then bids you to hang around a while. Most travelers eventually do.

Orientation & Information

Huancayo is a sizable town and you'll end up doing a lot of walking. Buses arrive at either the north or the south side of the Plaza de la Constitución.

BCP, Interbank, Banco Continental, Banco Wiese and other banks and *casas de cambio* are on Real. Most banks open on Saturday morning and have ATMs. Many places offering internet access are found along Giráldez and other central streets.

Clínica Ortega (☎ 23 2921; Carrín 1124; ☒ 24hr) English is spoken.

Dr Luis Mendoza (☎ 23 9133; Real 968) For a dentist, try here.

Incas del Perú (☎ 22 3303; fax 22 2395; www.incas delperu.org; Giráldez 652) A recommended source for information on just about anything in the area.

Lavandería Chic (☎ 23 1107; Breña 154; ☒ 8am-10pm Mon-Sat, 10am-6pm Sun) Offers both self-service (US$3 per load, wash and dry, soap included) and drop-off laundry.

Locutorio Telefónica (Puno 200) Combines internet access with cheap phone calls.

Main post office (Centro Cívico)

Policía de Turismo (☎ 23 4714; Ferrocarril 580) Can help with tourist information as well as with emergencies.

Tourist office (☎ 20 0550, 20 0551; Casa del Artesano, Real 481; ☒ 10am-1:30pm & 4-7:30pm Mon-Fri) Located upstairs in the indoor crafts market and has information about sightseeing in the Río Mantaro valley and how to get around on public transport.

Sights

Museo Salesiano (☎ 24 7763; Jirón Arequipa 105; admission US$0.60) can be entered from the Salesian school, and has Amazon fauna, pottery and archaeology exhibits. Hours vary.

Head northeast on Av Giráldez for a great view of the city. About 2km from the town center is **Cerro de la Libertad**, a popular recreational and dining locale where, apart from the city view, there are artwork stalls and a playground. About 2km further (there is a sign and an obvious path), you will come to the eroded geological formations known as **Torre Torre**. Some of the formations look like towers – hence the name (*torre* means 'tower').

In the city itself, the church of **La Merced**, on the first block of Real, is the most interesting; this is where the Peruvian Constitution was approved in 1839. In the suburb of San Antonio, the **Parque de la Identidad Huanca** is a fanciful park full of stone statues and miniature buildings representing the area's culture.

Activities

The ever-active Lucho Hurtado of **Incas del Perú** (☎ 22 3303; www.incasdelperu.org; Giráldez 652), in the same building as the restaurant La Cabaña, organizes most activities. He is a local who speaks English and knows the surrounding area well. Mountain bikers can participate in easy one-day tours, relaxing two-day biking and camping tours or, for the really adventurous and fit, 12-day Andean cycling marathons that cover over 100km of rigorous mountain biking. You can also participate in an Andean mountain-trekking expedition to the lake and glacier of Huaytapallana for up to three days; the three-day trek costs US$105 per person.

Incas del Perú arranges Spanish and even Quechua lessons, which include meals and accommodations with a local family (if you wish) starting at US$110 a week for the budget course through to US$260 per week for the busy interactive course. Lessons can be modified to fit your interests. You can also learn to cook local dishes, find out how to make jewelry, engage in gourd carving, try your feet at dancing, dabble with natural dyes, play the panpipes, create back-strap or pedal-loom weavings or make a stab at other local crafts.

Tours are arranged by Lucho, who guides treks down the eastern slopes of the Andes and into high jungle on foot, horseback or public transport. It isn't luxurious, but it's a good chance to experience something of the 'real' rural Peru. Lucho's father has a ranch in the middle of nowhere, where you can stay and meet all kinds of local people. If you are unable to get a group together, you may be able to join up with another group. The trips last anywhere from four to eight days and cost about US$35 per person per day including simple food. Accommodations are rustic and trips may involve some camping.

Festivals & Events

There are hundreds of fiestas in Huancayo and surrounding villages – supposedly almost every day somewhere in the Río Mantaro valley. Ask at the tourist office.

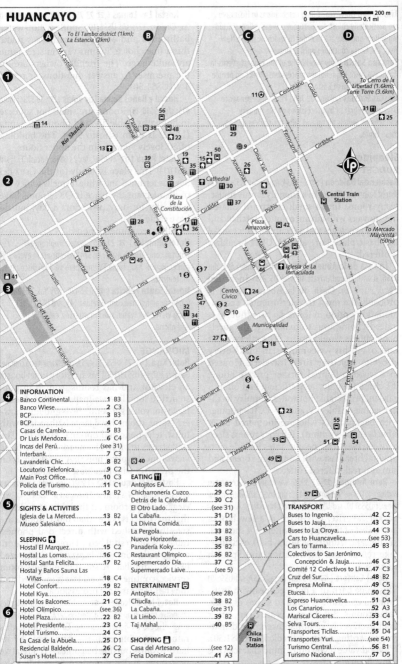

HUANCAYO

0 ——— 200 m
0 ——— 0.1 mi

To El Tambo district (1km);
La Estancia (2km)

To Cerro de la
Libertad (1.6km);
Torre Torre (3.6km)

To Mercado
Mayorista
(50m)

Río Shulcas

Plaza
de la
Constitución

Plaza
Amazonas

Iglesia de la
Inmaculada

Centro
Cívico

Municipalidad

Sunday Craft Market

Chilca
Train
Station

Central Train
Station

INFORMATION
Banco Continental	1	B3
Banco Wiese	2	C3
BCP	3	B3
BCP	4	C4
Casas de Cambio	5	B3
Dr Luis Mendoza	6	C4
Incas del Perú	(see 31)	
Interbank	7	C3
Lavandería Chic	8	B2
Locutorio Telefonica	9	C2
Main Post Office	10	C3
Policía de Turismo	11	C1
Tourist Office	12	B2

SIGHTS & ACTIVITIES
Iglesia de La Merced	13	B2
Museo Salesiano	14	A1

SLEEPING
Hostal El Marquez	15	C2
Hostal Las Lomas	16	C2
Hostal Santa Felicita	17	B2
Hostal y Baños Sauna Las Viñas	18	C4
Hotel Confort	19	B2
Hotel Kiya	20	B2
Hotel los Balcones	21	C2
Hotel Olímpico	(see 36)	
Hotel Plaza	22	B2
Hotel Presidente	23	C4
Hotel Turismo	24	C3
La Casa de la Abuela	25	D1
Residencial Baldeón	26	C3
Susan's Hotel	27	C3

EATING
Antojitos EA	28	B2
Chicharronería Cuzco	29	C2
Detrás de la Catedral	30	C2
El Otro Lado	(see 31)	
La Cabaña	31	D1
La Divina Comida	32	B3
La Pergola	33	B2
Nuevo Horizonte	34	B3
Panadería Koky	35	B2
Restaurant Olímpico	36	B2
Supermercado Día	37	C2
Supermercado Laive	(see 5)	

ENTERTAINMENT
Antojitos	(see 28)	
Chuclla	38	B2
La Cabaña	(see 31)	
La Limbo	39	B2
Taj Mahal	40	B5

SHOPPING
Casa del Artesano	(see 12)	
Feria Dominical	41	A3

TRANSPORT
Buses to Ingenio	42	C2
Buses to Jauja	43	C3
Buses to La Oroya	44	C3
Cars to Huancavelica	(see 53)	
Cars to Tarma	45	B3
Colectivos to San Jerónimo, Concepción & Jauja	46	C3
Comité 12 Colectivos to Lima	47	C3
Cruz del Sur	48	B2
Empresa Molina	49	C5
Etucsa	50	C2
Expreso Huancavelica	51	D4
Los Canarios	52	A3
Mariscal Cáceres	53	C4
Selva Tours	54	D4
Transportes Ticllas	55	D4
Transportes Yuri	(see 54)	
Turismo Central	56	B1
Turismo Nacional	57	D5

Año Nuevo (New Year's Day) Celebrations in Huancayo are particularly colorful – partygoers wear yellow (including yellow underwear!) in order to welcome in the New Year. The fiesta continues until 6 January.

Semana Santa (Holy Week) One of the biggest events in Huancayo, with big religious processions attracting people from all over Peru at Easter.

Fiestas Patrias (28 and 29 July) Peru's Independence Days are celebrated by processions by the military and schools. Hotels fill up and raise their prices during these times.

Sleeping

BUDGET

Residencial Baldeón (☎ 23 1634; Amazonas 543; s/d with shared bathroom US$3/6) In a friendly family house, teeny rooms line a small courtyard. Shared hot showers with advance notice, kitchen and laundry privileges make this basic place fair value. A US$1 breakfast is offered.

La Casa de la Abuela (☎ 22 3303; Giráldez 691; dm US$6, d with shared/private shower US$8/9) Incas del Perú runs La Casa de la Abeula, which is probably the most traveler-oriented accommodation option in town. *La casa* (house) is indeed a home away from home, as the guestbook entries would testify. The effervescent Lucho and his welcoming staff make every effort to welcome tired travelers. Housed in a wooden-floored former private home, it's clean, friendly, very efficient and offers a garden, predictable hot water, laundry facilities, games, cable TV and DVD. It's popular with backpackers who are mothered by *la Abuela* (Lucho's mom). Ten cozy rooms sleep between two to six people; rates include continental breakfast with homemade bread and jam and real, filtered coffee.

Peru Andino (☎ 22 3956; www.geocities.com/peru andino_1; Pasaje San Antonio 113; dm US$3, s/d with shared shower US$5/10, s/d US$6/12, all incl breakfast) A backpacker favorite, this place is a few blocks northwest of the map and offers hot showers, kitchen and laundry facilities, book exchange, bike rental, tour information and Spanish lessons.

Hotel Confort (☎ 23 3601; Ancash 237; s/d US$6/9) This huge barn of a hotel echoes with institutional corridors leading to scores of stark, faded rooms. But the rooms are clean, larger than average, have hot showers, good mattresses, writing desks and cable TV (US$1.50). It's good value if you don't mind characterless convenience.

Hostal Las Lomas (☎ 23 7587; laslomashyo@yahoo .es; Giráldez 327; s/d US$8/10) Spotless hot-water bathrooms and excellent mattresses make this a fine choice. Rooms vary in size; some are quite large. The friendly owners are on the premises to answer questions or rent a TV (US$1.50).

Hostal y Baños Sauna Las Viñas (☎ 36 5236; Piura 415; s/d US$10/13) Rooms are small but squeeze in hot baths, cable TV and phone. Its sauna (US$2) is open 6am to 9pm. The building offers lovely views from the upper floors.

Hotel Plaza (☎ 21 4507; fax 23 6858; Ancash 171; s/d US$11/14) This place is handy for the Cruz del Sur bus terminal and while it smells somewhat of disinfectant the place is OK. Rooms have hot water for only two hours a day, but do have cable TV.

Other recommendations:

Hotel Olímpico (☎ 21 4555; hotelolimpicohyo@ hotmail.com; Ancash 408; r US$24) Eclectic art in every corner. Rooms have cable TV and there's a 30% discount for tourists.

Hostal Santa Felicita (☎ 23 5476, ☎ /fax 23 5285; irmaleguia@hotmail.com; Giráldez 145; s/d US$11/15) Plaza views, hot water, solid mattresses, cable TV and phone.

MIDRANGE

Hotel Kiya (☎ 21 4955, 21 4957; hotelkiya@terra.com.pe; Giráldez 107; s/d US$13/20) This six-story hotel boasts an elevator and has rooms painted in pink stencil to look like wallpaper. If this doesn't faze you, you'll get comfy beds and hot showers (some rooms have large bathrooms with tubs), telephone and optional cable TV. The staff strives to please. Some rooms have plaza views (but also plaza noise). A restaurant is on the premises with breakfast available.

Hostal El Marquez (☎ 21 9026; www.elmarquezhuan cayo.com; Puno 294; s/d/ste incl breakfast US$22/27/40) An elegant sitting room off the lobby says clearly that this hotel is better than most. Rooms are sweetly furnished with direct-dial phones, cable TV and restful beds. Three suites feature a large bathroom with Jacuzzi tub, king-sized bed and minibar. A small café offers room service, continental breakfast is included and the staff is pleasingly professional.

Hotel los Balcones (☎ 21 1041; www.losbalcones huancayo.com; Puno 282; s/d/ste US$22/27/40; 🖵) Sitting cheek-by-jowl next to El Marquez, this rather imposing edifice – noticeable by its hard-to-miss outside balconies – is a relative newcomer and is a modern new-style hotel that is both airy and spacious. The rooms are simply and perhaps a bit gaudily decorated, but have the obligatory cable TV and phone. There is a busy in-house restaurant too.

Susan's Hotel (☎ 20 2251; susans_hotel@yahoo.com; Real 851; s/d incl breakfast US$21/27) Multinational flags over the entrance welcome visitors to this spotless and cheerful hotel. Rooms have good-sized bathrooms, cable TV, writing desks, quality mattresses and dazzlingly bright bedspreads. Reception staff are, however, a bit stuffy, but if you can ignore this, it is a good choice. There is a restaurant, the Marisquería, and breakfast is included.

Hotel Turismo (☎ /fax 23 1072; www.hoteles-del -centro.com; Ancash 729; s/d US$34/48; 🖳) This pleasant-looking old building with wooden balconies and public areas has a certain faded grandeur. Rooms vary in size and quality but all have bathrooms. The hotel has a restaurant and bar and is part of the same organization as the Hotel Presidente.

Hotel Presidente (☎ /fax 23 5419, 23 1736; www .hoteles-del-centro.com; Real 1138; s/d incl breakfast US$34/48; 🖳) This good modern hotel includes breakfast in the price, has nicely carpeted rooms and larger-than-average bathrooms.

Eating
BUDGET
Panadería Koky (☎ 23 4707; Puno 298; snacks from US$1; 🕑 7am-9pm) This modern bakery–coffee shop serves tasty sandwiches, pastries, empanadas, real espresso and other coffees.

Nuevo Horizonte (Ica 578; meals US$1-1.50; 🕑 7:30am-10pm Sun-Fri) Inside an atmospheric older house with attractive ceilings, this place has an excellent vegetarian menu using soy to recreate Peruvian plates such as *lomo saltado* (strips of beef stir-fried with onions, tomatoes, potatoes and chili), as well as straightforward veggie meals. Vegetarian products are for sale.

Antojitos (☎ 23 7950; Puno 599; meals US$1.50-8; 🕑 5pm-late Mon-Sat) This restaurant-cum-bar, housed in an antique-filled, wood-beamed, two-story building with the obligatory Lennon and Santana posters, brings in friendly crowds of upscale locals bent on having roaring conversations over the sounds of anything from *cumbia* (popular dance music from Colombia) to Pink Floyd. The well-prepared bar food is burgers, pizzas and grills.

La Pergola (☎ 21 9344; Puno 444; set lunch US$2; 🕑 lunch & dinner) Upstairs with a plaza view and courtly atmosphere, La Pergola offers a varied menu ranging from sandwiches and snacks to full-blown meals. The *menú* (set meal) is usually a very good option (US$1.40) though the chicken fried rice is exceptionally filling and goes down well with a bottle of beer.

Chicharronería Cuzco (Cuzco 173; meals US$2) This hole-in-the-wall is run by Doña Juana Curo Ychpas, who makes excellent traditional plates of *chicharrones* (fried pork ribs) – for dedicated carnivores only – for about US$2.

La Divina Comida (Arequipa 712; mains US$2) Capitalizing no doubt on Dante's comedy classic, there is nonetheless nothing infernal about the simple meatless fare at this busy hole-in-a-wall. Hearty fried rice and tortillas with spinach feature on a small but refreshing menu in an otherwise meat-dominated culinary scene.

Restaurant Olímpico (☎ 23 4181, Giráldez 199; breakfasts, set lunch US$2; mains US$4-8) Here for over six decades, this is Huancayo's oldest (though modernized) restaurant. It features a large open kitchen where you can see the traditional Peruvian dishes prepared, and a popular Sunday buffet lunch (US$5).

Detrás de la Catedral (☎ 21 2969, Ancash 335; mains US$2.70-5; 🕑 11am-11pm) A relative newbie for Huancayo, this well-run and attractively presented place exudes a woody, warm feeling and has garnered a good following of regular patrons with a surprisingly broad menu selection – helped by its user-friendly picture menu decoder. Dine in colder weather next to a charcoal brazier, admire Picasso-like surrealist paintings on the wall and enjoy either a filling burger (veggie and carnie options both supported), or a couple of specials like *asado catedral* (barbecued meats done in the style of Detrás de la Catedral) or *chuleta* (pork in a white-wine sauce). The desserts bear exotic names such as the chocolate-drenched *pionono helado*.

PAPA A LA HUANCAÍNA

Visitors to Huancayo should try the local specialty, *papa a la huancaína*, which consists of a boiled potato topped with a creamy white sauce of fresh cheese, oil, hot pepper, lemon and egg yolk. The whole concoction is served with an olive and sliced boiled egg, and is eaten as a cold potato salad. Despite the hot pepper, its flavor is pleasantly mild.

THE AUTHOR'S CHOICE

La Cabaña (☎ 22 3303; Giráldez 652; mains around US$4.50; ⏰ 5-11pm) This popular haunt has become a bit of an establishment eatery for locals and travelers alike, and there is nothing quite like it in town for its relaxed ambience, good food – oh, and let's not forget its pisco sours (grape brandy cocktails): they have a stronger kick than usual, yet are oh-so-smooth. When you're suitably mellow order a scrumptious pizza or graze on trout, juicy grills, *al dente* pastas, or nibble on a variety of less filling appetizers. The house drink is sangria, available in three sizes; and if you want to party, then Thursday to Saturday a local *folklórica* band will perform for you. Next door and part of the same establishment, El Otro Lado (☎ 22 3303) is open for lunch from April to October. *Cuy* (guinea pig) is available upon request. *¡Salud!*

Self-Catering

Self-caterers can try **Supermercado Dia** (Giráldez) or **Supermercado Laive** (Real at Lima).

MIDRANGE

La Estancia (☎ 22 3279; M Castilla 2815; meals US$7) Northwest of town, Real becomes Av Mariscal Castilla in the El Tambo district. La Estancia does a great lunchtime *pachamanca* containing *cuy*, pork, lamb, potatoes, beans and tamales among other possible ingredients, wrapped in leaves and cooked in an underground earth oven (basically, a hole in the ground). Go early and watch them disinter it. Cheaper plates also available.

Entertainment

The entertainment scene is fairly patchy with clubs opening and closing regularly.

La Limbo (Cuzco 374) Offers live local rock bands.

Taj Mahal (Huancavelica 1052) This club with video karaoke and dancing caters to a somewhat more mature crowd.

Antojitos (☎ 23 7950; Puno 599; ⏰ 5pm-late Mon-Sat) Local bands perform at this bar-restaurant most nights from 9pm.

La Cabaña (☎ 22 3303; Giráldez 652; ⏰ 5-11pm) This popular eatery has live *folklórica* music and dancing on weekends.

Chucclla (Ayacucho) and a couple of other places on the same block are also worth checking out.

Shopping

Huancayo has two main markets.

The colorful daily produce market spills out from Mercado Mayorista (which is covered) east along the railway tracks. In the meat section you can buy Andean delicacies such as fresh and dried frogs, guinea pigs, rabbits and chickens. Although it's a daily market,

the most important day is Sunday, coinciding with Huancayo's weekly craft market.

Feria Dominical (Huancavelica), the Sunday craft market, occupies numerous blocks along Huancavelica to the northwest of Piura. Noncraft items range from cassette tapes to frilly underwear. Weavings, sweaters, textiles, embroidered items, ceramics and wood carvings are also sold here, as well as *mates burilados* (carved gourds) and many other items from various villages in the Río Mantaro valley – handy if you don't have the time to make the trek out to the villages yourself. The gourds are made in the nearby villages of Cochas Grande and Cochas Chico. This is definitely a place to keep an eye on your valuables.

More handy, **Casa del Artesano** (south corner, Plaza de la Constitución) has a wide range of art souvenirs for sale in a somewhat more secure environment.

Getting There & Away

BUS

As in many Peruvian towns, bus terminals are in diverse locations, but none are particularly far from the center. Bus services change depending on season and demand, as do the location of their offices – particularly for the smaller companies. In this section we do not list all companies, as some are less than reliable. Companies listed here are either the better options or the only options.

Bus links focus naturally on Lima. One-way ticket prices range from US$6 to US14. For US$14 you get a bed seat on a *bus cama*; for US$6 you get an ordinary seat. There are other levels of comfort in between the two. The best company for comfort would be **Cruz del Sur** (☎ 23 5650; Ayacucho 251), followed by **Etucsa** (☎ 23 6524; Puno 220), which has somewhat more frequent departures. Next is **Mariscal Cáceres** (☎ 21 6633; Real 1241). Check each company's buses, or at least brochures, before deciding. If you are in a hurry, **Comité 12** (☎ 23 3281; Loreto 421) has *colectivo* taxis to Lima (US$14, five hours).

For Ayacucho (US$7.50, 10 to 12 hours) the recommended service is **Empresa Molina** (☎ 22 4501; Angaraes 334), with morning and night departures on a mostly rough, unsealed road.

Huancavelica (US$3, five hours) is served most frequently by **Transportes Ticllas** (☎ 20 1555; Ferrocarril 1590) with six daily buses. **Expreso Lobato** (☎ 75 2964; M Muñoz 489) has comfortable overnight buses via Huancayo to Huancavelica. Others include the nearby Turismo Nacional, Expreso Huancavelica and Transportes Yuri, with late-night buses only.

Transportes San Juan (☎ 21 4558; Ferrocarril 131) has minibuses almost every hour to Tarma (US$2.50, 3½ hours) and can drop you off at Concepción or Jauja. It also has services to La Merced (US$4.50, five hours), with stops at Jauja and Tarma. **Los Canarios** (Puno 739) serves Tarma (US$2.50, three hours).

For Satipo (US$4.50, eight to nine hours) the best service is **Selva Tours** (☎ 21 8427; Ferrocarril 1587) with four daily buses.

Turismo Central (☎ 22 3128, Ayacucho 274) has buses north to Cerro de Pasco (US$3.50, five hours), Huánuco (US$6, seven hours), Tingo María (US$8, 10 hours) and Pucallpa (US$14, 22 hours).

Inexpensive minibuses for Jauja (US$1.60) leave from a depot on Calixto.

TAXI
Colectivo taxis for Huancavelica (US$8, 2½ to three hours) leave when full (four-passenger minimum) from the Terminal Terrestre.

TRAIN
Huancayo has two train stations in different parts of town linked by an unused section of track. A special tourist train, the **Ferrocarril Central Andino** (☎ 22 2395), runs up from Lima between mid-April and October for US$55 round-trip. It leaves Lima at 7am Friday and arrives in Huancayo 12 hours later. It returns from Huancayo at the rather inconvenient time of 6pm Sunday, arriving back in Lima at 6am Monday. For this return night leg bring along warm clothes and perhaps a blanket and a neck pillow.

It's a fabulous run, passing through La Galera (4829m), the world's second-highest station (the Tibetans are the record holders),

on a single-gauge track and is popular with train enthusiasts the world over. The best way to book it is to visit the Incas del Perú website www.incasdelperu.com, where there is an online booking form.

The **Chilca train station** (☎ 21 7724; www.fhh.com .pe) for Huancavelica is at the southern end of town. It's a fair hike so take a taxi. From here, *expreso* services depart for Huancavelica at 6:30am Monday to Sunday (five hours) and *ordinario* services depart at 12:30pm Monday to Saturday (five to six hours). Tickets are about US$2.50/3/4 in 2nd/1st/buffet class. The buffet class is reasonably comfortable with padded seats and has guaranteed seating; 1st class has reserved padded seats with perhaps a tad less padding while 2nd class offers wooden bench-type seats and no seat reservations. The ticket office is open from noon to 6pm on the day before travel and at 6am on the day of travel.

On Sunday and Monday, there's a faster *autovagón* (electric train) that leaves at 6pm (US$4.50, around four hours).

Getting Around
Local buses to nearby villages leave from the street intersections shown on the map. Just show up and wait until a bus is ready to leave. Ask other passengers for more details. The tourist office is a good source of local bus information.

RÍO MANTARO VALLEY
Two main road systems link Huancayo with the villages of the Río Mantaro valley, and are known simply as the left and right of the river. *Izquierda* (left) is the east and *derecha* (right) is the west side of the river, as you head into Huancayo from the north. It is best to confine your sightseeing on any given day to one side or the other because there are few bridges linking the sides.

Perhaps the most interesting excursion is on the east side of the valley, where you can visit the twin villages of **Cochas Grande** and **Cochas Chico**, about 11km from Huancayo. These villages are the major production centers for the incised gourds that have made the area famous. Oddly enough, the gourds are grown mainly on the coast and are from the Chiclayo and Ica areas. Once they are transported into the highlands, they are dried and scorched, then decorated using woodworking tools.

MARKET DAYS AROUND HUANCAYO

Each little village and town in the Río Mantaro valley has its own *feria*, or market day. If you enjoy these, you'll find one on every day of the week.

Monday – San Agustín de Cajas, Huayucachi
Tuesday – Hualhuas, Pucara
Wednesday – San Jerónimo, Jauja
Thursday – El Tambo, Sapallanga
Friday – Cochas
Saturday – Matahuasi, Chupaca, Marco
Sunday – Huancayo, Jauja, Mito, Comas

Other villages known for their handicrafts include **San Agustín de Cajas**, **Hualhuas** and **San Jerónimo de Tunán**. Cajas is known for the manufacture of wicker furniture. Hualhuas is a center for the manufacture of wool products – ponchos, weavings and other items. San Jerónimo is known for its filigree silverwork and also has a 17th-century church with fine wooden altars. While the villages can be visited from Huancayo, most buying and selling is done in Huancayo, and the villages have few facilities. The key is the ability to speak Spanish and make friends with the locals.

IZCUCHACA
☎ 067

Izcuchaca, the main village between Huancayo and Huancavelica, has a basic hotel, a pottery center, hot springs and archaeological ruins, which are accessible only on foot. There is also a **historic bridge** that, as legend has it, was built by the Incas and was defended by Huascar against the advance of Atahualpa's troops during the civil war that was raging in the Inca empire when the Spaniards arrived.

There's not much reason to linger here other than to make a train connection to Huancavelica if coming from Ayacucho. However, because the arrival of the buses and the departure of the train do not match, this will require an overnight stay; there's a small hotel near the train station. You *might* be lucky to find a spare place in a Huancavelica-bound *colectivo* taxi, but don't bank on it. A bus pickup is a more reliable option.

HUANCAVELICA
☎ 067 / pop 42,500 / elev 3690m

Given that it can be a challenge to get to Huancavelica, travelers justifiably expect to find something worthwhile. What they will find is a small, cozy town nestled among craggy peaks, more reminiscent of Switzerland than the Andes. Its location means that the town can experience some bone-chilling winds, and the weather can be unpredictable in the wet season. Huancavelica is 147km south of Huancayo and is the capital of its own department. It's a relaxed kind of town that grows on you and, like other towns in the country, activity centers on its main square, where there are reasonable hotels and a few quality eating options.

This historic city was a strategic Inca center, and shortly after the conquest the Spanish discovered its mineral wealth. By 1564 the Spaniards were sending indigenous Peruvian slaves to Huancavelica to work in the mercury and silver mines. The present town was founded in 1571 under the name of Villa Rica de Oropesa and retains a very pleasant colonial atmosphere and many interesting churches. Not many travelers make it here, but it is worth the effort – particularly during the sunny days of the dry season between May and October.

Information
More than a dozen central places provide internet access.

@Internet (Segura 166) On the Plaza de Armas.
BCP (☎ 75 2831; V Toledo 384) Has a Visa ATM and changes money.
Dirección de Turismo (☎ 75 2938; dreceturhvc@yahoo.es; 2nd fl, V Garma 444; ☼ 8am-1pm & 2-5pm Mon-Fri) Provides good directions (in Spanish) for local hikes.
Lavandería Sam (Toledo 346) A reasonably modern place to get your gear washed and freshened up.
Main post office (Pasaje Ferrua 105) Near Iglesia de Santa Ana.
Multired (M Muñoz) A stand-alone ATM next to the Municipalidad, but it doesn't work with all cards.

Sights & Activities
INSTITUTO NACIONAL DE CULTURA
The **INC** (☎ 75 2544; Raymondi 205; admission free; ☼ 10am-1pm & 3-6pm Tue-Sun), in a colonial building on Plaza San Juan de Dios, has information and displays about the area; don't hesitate to ask the helpful director if you have any questions. A small **museum** features the usual Inca artifacts plus a display of local costumes. You even have the option of taking a class in *folklórica* dancing or music.

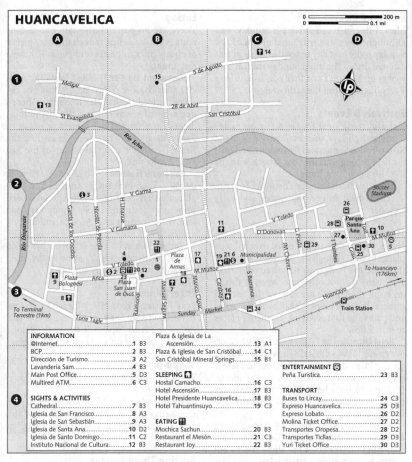

HUANCAVELICA

0   200 m
0   0.1 mi

INFORMATION		Plaza & Iglesia de La	
@Internet...................................1	B3	Ascensión............................13	A1
BCP...2	B3	Plaza & Iglesia de San Cristóbal......14	C1
Dirección de Turismo.................3	A2	San Cristóbal Mineral Springs.........15	B1
Lavanderia Sam.........................4	B3		
Main Post Office.......................5	D3	SLEEPING	
Multired ATM............................6	C3	Hostal Camacho.....................16	C3
		Hotel Ascensión.....................17	B3
SIGHTS & ACTIVITIES		Hotel Presidente Huancavelica...18	B3
Cathedral..................................7	B3	Hotel Tahuantinsuyo...............19	C3
Iglesia de San Francisco.............8	A3		
Iglesia de San Sebastián.............9	A3	EATING	
Iglesia de Santa Ana.................10	D2	Mochica Sachun......................20	B3
Iglesia de Santo Domingo...........11	C2	Restaurant el Mesón...............21	C3
Instituto Nacional de Cultura......12	B3	Restaurant Joy........................22	B3

ENTERTAINMENT	
Peña Turistica...........................23	B3

TRANSPORT	
Buses to Lircay.........................24	C3
Expreso Huancavelica...............25	D3
Expreso Lobato........................26	D2
Molina Ticket Office.................27	D2
Transportes Oropesa................28	D2
Transportes Ticllas...................29	D3
Yuri Ticket Office.....................30	D3

CHURCHES

Huancavelica churches are noted for their silver-plated altars, unlike the altars in the rest of Peru's colonial churches, which are usually gold-plated. There are several churches of note here, although they are generally closed to tourism. However, you can go as a member of the congregation when they are open for services, usually early in the morning on weekdays, with longer morning hours on Sunday.

The oldest church in Huancavelica is **Santa Ana**, founded in the 16th century. The **cathedral**, built in 1673, has been restored and contains what some say is the best colonial altar in Peru. Other 17th-century churches include **San Francisco**, renowned for its 11 intricately worked altars; **Santo Domingo**, with famous statues of Santo Domingo and La Virgen del Rosario, which were made in Italy; **San Sebastián**, which has been well restored; **San Cristóbal** and **La Ascensión**.

SAN CRISTÓBAL MINERAL SPRINGS

These **mineral springs** (pool/private shower US$0.30/0.50; 5:30am-4pm Sat-Thu, to noon Fri) are fed into two large, slightly murky swimming pools. The water is lukewarm and supposedly has curative properties. You can rent a towel, soap and a bathing suit if you've forgotten yours (though the selection is limited and unlovely). You can reach the springs via a steep flight of stairs – enjoy the view of the city as you climb.

MARKETS

Market day in Huancavelica is Sunday, and although there are smaller daily markets, Sunday is the best day to see the locals in traditional dress. The main Sunday market area snakes up Barranca and then continues along Torre Tagle behind the cathedral.

Festivals & Events

Colorful traditional fiestas occur on major Peruvian holidays, such as Carnaval, Semana Santa, Todos Santos and Christmas, and others held throughout the year. Check with the INC for upcoming festivals.

Huancavelica's Semana Turística (Tourism Week) is held in late September and early October.

Sleeping

Huancavelica does in fact boast over a dozen places to stay, though the greater majority of them are the budget to superbudget variety and many do not offer hot water. If this is an issue then there are always the natural mineral baths in town to soak away the aches and pains and to freshen up. The better places to stay follow.

Hotel Ascensión (☎ 75 3103; Manco Cápac 481; s/d with shared shower US$3/4, s/d US$4.25/5) In a good location on the Plaza de Armas, this hotel has larger rooms than its posher neighbor the Presidente. It claims 24-hour hot water but you're better taking your shower when you see that the water is hot.

Hostal Camacho (☎ /fax 75 3298; Carabaya 481; s/d with shared shower US$2.50/4.30, s/d US$4/7) This clean, well-run budget choice has small rooms but pretty decent mattresses with piles of blankets for those chilly Andean nights. Showers are hot in the mornings only.

Hotel Tahuantinsuyo (☎ 75 2968; Carabaya 399; s/d with shared shower US$3/4.25, s/d US$3.60/8) Abutting busy Calle Muñoz, this is another reasonable budget option. The rooms are pretty basic and the ones with bathrooms have hot water in the morning only.

Hotel Presidente Huancavelica (☎ /fax 75 2760; s/d US$23/29) In a quite presentable old building on the Plaza de Armas, Hotel Presidente Huancavelica is the only nonbudget hotel in town, and a bit pricey for what you actually get. The rooms are very plain, though they do have guaranteed hot showers, a laundry service, telephone and cable TV – not forgetting a handy restaurant.

Eating

There are no particularly standout restaurants in Huancavelica, though there are plenty of cheap chicken places and *chifas* (Chinese restaurants).

Restaurant Joy (☎ 75 2826; V Toledo 216; menús US$2, mains US$2.50-6; ☺ 9am-2pm & 5-10pm) For excellent grilled trout cast a line here. There's not a lot of room but it pulls in the local diners for a limited but honest selection of Peruvian dishes. The owner must like the Beatles – there's a signed poster of the Fab Four on the wall.

Restaurant El Mesón (☎ 45 3570; Muñoz 153; mains US$2.50-5; ☺ 9am-2pm & 5-10pm) Another busy little place that has a changing daily specials board sometimes featuring *criollo* (spicy Peruvian fare with Spanish and African influences) dishes.

Mochica Sachun (V Toledo 303) Another solid choice. It offers much the same as the other two and prices are pretty similar.

Entertainment

Peña Turística (☎ 45 3623; V Toledo 319; ☺ 6pm-midnight Thu, Fri, Sat) For a spot of music and culture as you drink Esparta, listening to folkloric groups such as Rammi, Llantuy and Taipuy.

Shopping

There are small daily markets, but Sunday is market day.

Handicrafts are sold almost every day on the north side of the Plaza de Armas and also by the Municipalidad. Colorful wool leggings are especially popular.

Getting There & Away

Huancavelica can be a bit hard to get to directly, but can be approached from Huancayo (the easiest option), Pisco and (indirectly) from Ayacucho. The most interesting way to get to Huancavelica is by train from Huancayo, which is marginally faster than the buses and follows in the main the river valley, taking a rather circuitous but necessarily less challenging route. Buses are of the local variety – filled with locals and their goods and produce – and take their time. Not all take the scenic alpine route.

If you are in a hurry, from Huancayo it's a good idea to take a *colectivo* taxi, which takes between 2½ and three hours, and runs through some spectacular scenery. From Huancayo there is a fast new road as far as Izcuchaca, at which point the road skews right and upward along an unsealed section for 78km. It first heads up following the mountains' contours, then ducks into a narrow valley with tiled-roof villages and a running river. It then opens out into lush alpine meadowland with thatched-roof settlements and freely wandering herds of llamas. It then spirals downwards into the narrow valley where Huancavelica lies. It's a highly recommended trip.

BUS

All major buses depart from the Terminal Terrestre, inconveniently located about 2km to the west of the town center. A taxi here costs US$1. Bus tickets are sold in downtown offices and though there are ticket booths at the terminal, none were in operation at the time of research.

Companies serving Huancayo (US$3, five hours) include **Transportes Ticllas** (☎ 75 1562; Prado 56) with six daily departures. Other companies go less often or at night, or may go via Huancayo en route to Lima.

For Lima (about US$9, 12 to 15 hours) some companies go via Huancayo while others go via Pisco. Via Huancayo is usually a little faster but it depends on road conditions. The Pisco route goes over a 4850m pass and is freezing at night; bring warm clothes. **Transportes Oropesa** (☎ 75 3181; O'Donovan 599) departs for Pisco at 6pm (US$8, nine hours), Lima at 6pm (US$8, 12 hours) and also has an overnight bus to Ica (US$8.50, 11 hours). **Expreso Lobato** (☎ 75 2964; M Muñoz 489) has comfortable overnight buses via Huancayo. Also try **Expreso Huancavelica** (☎ 50 3171; M Muñoz 516).

For Ayacucho things are a little trickier (see The Missing Link, p312). The 'easiest' option is to take a 4:30am(!) minibus to Rumichaca (US$3, six hours) and wait for an Ayacucho-bound bus coming from the coast – usually from Lima. The trouble is that most day buses from Lima don't get to Rumichaca until about 2pm so you might want to try your hitchhiking skills rather than waiting for 3½ hours in what is by all accounts a pretty bleak place. Ensure, however, that there are at least two of you, and remember that hitchhiking always contains an element of risk. The other more adventurous option is to minibus it to Lircay, find another onward minibus passage to Julcamarca and finally seek yet another minibus from Julcamarca to Ayacucho. Allow a full day to execute this option.

You can get to Lircay by minibus from Huancavelica (US$2, 3½ hours).

TAXI

Colectivo taxis for Huancayo (US$8, 2½ to three hours) leave when full (four-passenger minimum) from the Terminal Terrestre.

TRAIN

Trains leave from **Huancavelica station** (☎ 75 2898) for Huancayo at 6:30am daily and 12:30pm Monday to Saturday. A faster *auto-vagón* leaves at 5:30pm Friday. Buy tickets in advance if possible. See p301 for more details on this route.

LIRCAY
☎ 067

The small, colonial town of Lircay is almost 80km southeast of Huancavelica. Its main claim to fame is as the center for the department's traditional clothing, which can be seen at Huancavelica's Sunday market. The predominant color is black, but the men wear rainbow-colored pom-poms (supposedly love tokens from women), and the women wear multicolored shawls over their otherwise somber clothing. Stay at **Hostal Rosario** (Jirón Puno; s/d with shared bathroom US$3/4.50). Beds are OK and showers are sometimes hot. You can get to Lircay by minibus from Huancavelica (US$2, 3½ hours).

AYACUCHO
☎ 066 / pop 143,100 / elev 2750m

Arguably Peru's most enticing Andean city after Cuzco, Ayacucho is well worth a visit. It has retained its colonial atmosphere more than most Peruvian cities, and colonial buildings and churches dominate the town's skyline. The city overflows during the Semana Santa celebrations, which are easily the most colorful yet most devout in Peru. As yet Ayacucho does not have a large traveler presence and this is due largely to its fairly tenuous links with other Andean towns to the north and south. But it is nonetheless a popular destination for Peruvians who, apart from Semana Santa, come for the town's bracing mountain air, its numerous archaeological attractions and its excursions in the surrounding mountains.

As mentioned at the beginning of this chapter, the central Andes is one of Peru's least-visited areas. Ayacucho is no exception to this. Its first road link with the Peruvian coast was not finished until 1924 and in 1960 there were only two buses and a few dozen vehicles in the city. The paving of the road to Lima, completed in 1999, has turned Ayacucho to face the 21st century, but without forgetting its storied past.

History

The first signs of human habitation in Peru were discovered in the Pikimachay caves, near Ayacucho. (There is nothing of interest to be seen there.)

Five hundred years before the rise of the Inca empire, the Wari empire dominated the Peruvian highlands. The Wari's ruined capital, 22km northeast of Ayacucho, can be reached along a paved road. Ayacucho played a major part in the battles for Peruvian independence, and a huge nearby monument marks the site of the important Battle of Ayacucho, fought in 1824. And it was here, in a rural university campus, that Professor Abimael Guzmán nurtured the Sendero Luminoso (Shining Path) Maoist revolutionary movement in the 1970s, which became an armed guerrilla organization bent on overthrowing the government.

Today, Ayacucho is a safe place to visit. The populace doesn't discuss the dark days of the 1980s much, and welcomes travelers with enthusiasm and good cheer.

Orientation

The Plaza de Armas is also known as Plaza Mayor de Huamanga. The street names of the four sides of the plaza, clockwise from the east (with the cathedral), are Portal Municipal, Portal Independencia, Portal Constitución and Portal Unión.

Information

EMERGENCY
Police (☎ 31 2332; 28 de Julio 325; 🕒 24hr)
Policía de Turismo (☎ 31-2179; 2 de Mayo 100; 🕒 7:30am-8pm)

INTERNET ACCESS
There are many options.
Hueco Internet (☎ 31 5528; Portal Constitución 9) Among the better ones, it has newer machines, a spacious environment and excellent – and quiet – phone booths where you can make cheap calls overseas.

INTERNET RESOURCES
www.ayacucho.com Good general reference site for tourist information.

LAUNDRY
Lavandería Arco Iris (Bellido 322) Provides both wash-and-dry and dry-cleaning services.

MEDICAL SERVICES
Clínica de La Esperanza (☎ 31 7436; Independencia 355; 🕒 8am-8pm) English spoken.
Clínica Dental García Tresierra (☎ 964 1763; Cuzco 200)
Hospital Central (☎ 31 2180/1; Independencia 335; 🕒 24hr) Provides basic services.
Inka Farma (☎ 31 8240, 83 6273; 28 de Julio 250; 🕒 7am-10:30pm) Pharmacy.

MONEY
BCP (☎ 31 4102; Portal Unión 28) Visa ATM.
Interbank (☎ 31 2480; 9 de Diciembre 183)
Moneychangers (Portal Constitución) On the southwest corner of the Plaza de Armas.

POST
Post office (☎ 31 2224; Asamblea 293; 🕒 8am-8pm Mon-Sat) It's 150m from the Plaza de Armas.

A NOT-SO-SHINING PATH

The Sendero Luminoso's (Shining Path) activities in the 1980s focused on deadly political, economic and social upheaval. In remote towns and villages, mayors were murdered, community leaders assassinated, uncooperative villagers massacred, police stations and power plants bombed, and government- and church-sponsored aid projects destroyed. The government responded by sending in the armed forces, who were often equally brutal, and in the ensuing civil war between 40,000 and 60,000 people died or disappeared, most of them in the central Andes. Ayacucho was almost completely off-limits to travelers during most of the 1980s. Things finally changed when the Sendero Luminoso's founder, Guzmán, was captured and imprisoned for life in 1992, followed quickly by his top lieutenants, leading to a halt in activities that lasted for some 12 years. In recent years the fragmented group has been only sporadically active, with its political idealism giving way to pragmatism – drug trafficking has been its most notable activity in recent times.

AYACUCHO

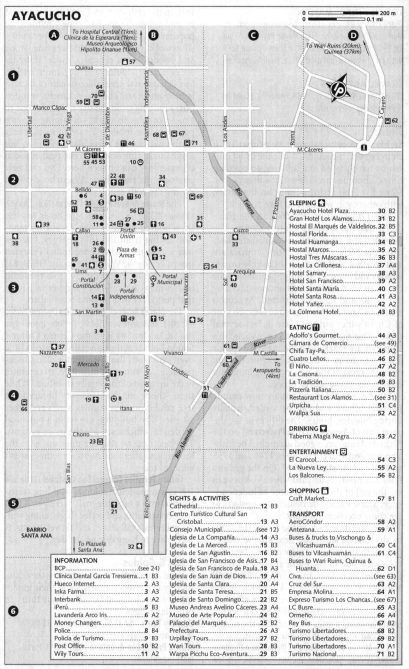

0   200 m
0   0.1 mi

To Hospital Central (1km);
Clínica de la Esperanza (1km);
Museo Arqueológico
Hipólito Unanue (1km)

To Wari Ruins (20km);
Quinea (37km)

SLEEPING
Ayacucho Hotel Plaza...............30 B2
Gran Hotel Los Alamos............31 B2
Hostal El Marqués de Valdelirios...32 B5
Hostal Florida..........................33 C3
Hostal Huamanga....................34 B2
Hostal Marcos.........................35 A2
Hostal Tres Máscaras...............36 B3
Hotel La Crillonesa..................37 A4
Hotel Samary..........................38 A3
Hotel San Francisco.................39 A2
Hotel Santa María....................40 C3
Hotel Santa Rosa.....................41 A3
Hotel Yañez.............................42 A2
La Colmena Hotel....................43 B3

EATING
Adolfo's Gourmet.....................44 A3
Cámara de Comercio.............(see 49)
Chifa Tay-Pa...........................45 A2
Cuatro Leños...........................46 B2
El Niño...................................47 A3
La Casona...............................48 A3
La Tradición............................49 B3
Pizzería Italiana.......................50 B2
Restaurant Los Alamos.........(see 31)
Urpicha..................................51 C4
Wallpa Sua.............................52 A2

DRINKING
Taberna Magía Negra...............53 A2

ENTERTAINMENT
El Carocol...............................54 C3
La Nueva Ley...........................55 A2
Los Balcones...........................56 B2

SHOPPING
Craft Market...........................57 B1

TRANSPORT
AeroCóndor............................58 A2
Antezana................................59 A1
Buses & trucks to Vischongo &
  Vilcashuamán......................60 C4
Buses to Vilcashuamán.............61 C4
Buses to Wari Ruins, Quinua &
  Huanta................................62 D1
Civa....................................(see 63)
Cruz del Sur............................63 A2
Empresa Molina.......................64 A1
Expreso Turismo Los Chancas...(see 67)
LC Busre.................................65 A3
Ormeño...................................66 A4
Rey Bus..................................67 B2
Turismo Libertadores...............68 B2
Turismo Libertadores...............69 B2
Turismo Libertadores...............70 A1
Turismo Nacional....................71 B2

SIGHTS & ACTIVITIES
Cathedral...............................12 B3
Centro Turístico Cultural San
  Cristobal............................13 A3
Consejo Municipal................(see 12)
Iglesia de La Compañía............14 A3
Iglesia de La Merced...............15 B3
Iglesia de San Agustín.............16 B2
Iglesia de San Francisco de Asis..17 B4
Iglesia de San Francisco de Paula..18 A3
Iglesia de San Juan de Dios......19 A4
Iglesia de Santa Clara..............20 A4
Iglesia de Santa Teresa............21 B5
Iglesia de Santo Domingo........22 B2
Museo Andreas Avelino Cáceres..23 A4
Museo de Arte Popular............24 B2
Palacio del Marqués................25 B2
Prefectura..............................26 A3
Urpillay Tours.........................27 B3
Wari Tours.............................28 B3
Warpa Picchu Eco-Aventura.....29 B3

INFORMATION
BCP.....................................(see 24)
Clínica Dental García Tressierra....1 B3
Hueco Internet.........................2 A3
Inka Farma..............................3 A3
Interbank................................4 A2
iPerú.....................................5 B3
Lavandería Arco Iris.................6 A2
Money Changers......................7 A3
Police...................................8 B4
Policía de Turismo...................9 B3
Post Office............................10 B2
Wily Tours............................11 A2

BARRIO
SANTA ANA

To Plazuela
Santa Ana

TOURIST INFORMATION

iPerú (☎ 31 8305; iperuayacucho@promperu.gob.pe; Municipalidad Huamanga, Plaza Mayor, Portal Municipal 48; ☺ 8:30am-7:30pm Mon-Sat, 8:30am-2:30pm Sun) Not a lot of material, but good advice. English is spoken.

TRAVEL AGENCIES

Wily Tours (☎ 31 4075; 9 de Diciembre 107) Good for flights and bus reservations.

Sights

Sights in Ayacucho consist primarily of churches and museums. While the listed museums have posted and adhered-to opening times, churches are a law unto themselves. Some list their visiting times on the doors; with others you will have to take potluck.

The 17th-century **cathedral**, on the Plaza de Armas, has a religious-art museum. The cathedral and a dozen other colonial churches from the 16th, 17th and 18th centuries are well worth a visit for their incredibly ornate facades and interiors, mainly Spanish baroque but often with Andean influences evinced by the plants and animals depicted. Ayacucho claims to have 33 churches (one for each year of Christ's life) but there are in fact several more. The most important of Ayacucho's churches are marked on the map. Except for during Semana Santa (when churches are open for most of the day), opening hours are erratic; ask at the tourist office.

Most of the old mansions are now mainly political offices and can be visited, usually during business hours. The offices of the department of Ayacucho (the **Prefectura**) on the Plaza de Armas are a good example. The mansion was constructed between 1740 and 1755 and sold to the state in 1937. On the ground floor is a pretty courtyard where visitors can see the cell of the local heroine of independence, María Parado de Bellido. Go upstairs to see some excellent tilework.

Also worth a look is the Salon de Actas in the **Consejo Municipal**, next to the cathedral, with its excellent view of the plaza. On the north side of the plaza are several more fine colonial houses, including the **Palacio del Marqués**, at Portal Unión 37, which is the oldest and dates from 1550. There are various others scattered around the town center, many housing professional offices; the tourist office can suggest which ones to visit.

The **Museo de Arte Popular** (Portal Unión 28; admission free; ☺ 9am-6:30pm Mon-Thu, 9am-7:30pm Fri, 9am-1pm

Sat) is in the 18th-century Casa Chacón, owned by and adjoining the Banco de Crédito. The popular art covers the *ayacucheño* spectrum – silverwork, rug and tapestry weaving, stone and woodcarvings, ceramics (model churches are especially popular) and the famous **retablos** (an ornamental screenlike structure located behind an altar). These are colorful wooden boxes ranging from the size of a matchbox to a meter or more in height, containing intricate papier-mâché models; Peruvian rural scenes or the nativity are particularly popular, but some interesting ones with political or social commentary can be seen here. Old and new photographs show how Ayacucho changed during the 20th century.

The **Museo Andres Avelino Cáceres** (28 de Julio 512; admission US$0.60; ☺ 9am-1pm & 2-5pm Mon-Fri, 9am-noon Sat) is housed in the Casona Vivanco, a mansion dating from the 16th century. Cáceres was a local man who commanded Peruvian troops during the War of the Pacific (1879–83) against Chile. Accordingly, the museum houses maps and military paraphernalia from that period, as well as some colonial art.

The **Museo Arqueológico Hipolito Unanue** (Museo INC; ☎ 31 2056; admission US$0.60; ☺ 9am-1pm & 3-5pm Mon-Sat, 9am-1pm Sun) is in the Centro Cultural Simón Bolívar at the university, located a little over 1km from the town center along Independencia – you can't miss it. Wari ceramics make up most of the small exhibition. While there, check out the university library for a free exhibition of mummies, skulls and other niceties. The buildings are set in a botanical garden in which cacti are the main exhibits. The best time to visit the museum is in the morning, as afternoon hours sometimes aren't adhered to.

Centro Turístico Cultural San Cristobal (28 de Julio 178) is a remodeled colonial building transformed into a hip little mall. Here you'll find bars, restaurants and coffee shops, along with art galleries, craft stores and flower stands. A nice place to hang during the day.

Tours & Guides

Several agencies arrange local tours; they cater mainly to Peruvian tourists and their guides mainly speak Spanish. Ask about tours in other languages.
Urpillay Tours (☎ 31 5074; Portal Unión 33-D)
Wari Tours (☎ 31 3115; Lima 148)
Warpa Picchu Eco-Aventura (☎ 31 5191; Portal Independencia 66)

Festivals & Events

Ayacucho's **Semana Santa** celebration, held the week before Easter, has long been considered Peru's finest religious festival and it attracts visitors – though relatively few foreigners – from all over the country. Rooms in the better hotels are booked well in advance, and even the cheapest places fill completely. The tourist office has lists of local families who provide accommodations for the overflow.

Each year, iPerú prints a free brochure describing the Semana Santa events with street maps showing the main processions. Visitors are advised to use this detailed information. The celebrations begin on the Friday before Palm Sunday and continue for 10 days until Easter Sunday. The Friday before Palm Sunday is marked by a procession in honor of La Virgen de los Dolores, or 'Our Lady of Sorrows,' during which it is customary to inflict 'sorrows' on bystanders by firing pebbles out of slingshots. Gringos have been recent targets, so be warned.

Each succeeding day is marked with solemn yet colorful processions and religious rites, which reach a fever pitch of Catholic faith and tradition. They culminate on the Saturday before Easter Sunday with a huge all-night party leading up to dawn fireworks to celebrate the resurrection of Christ.

In addition to the religious services, Ayacucho's Semana Santa celebrations include numerous secular activities – art shows, folkdancing competitions and demonstrations, local music concerts, street events, sporting events (especially equestrian ones), agricultural fairs and also the preparation of traditional meals.

The tourist office here is a good source of information about the large number of minor fiestas held throughout the department (there seems to be one almost every week).

Sleeping

The revival of tourism in the late 1990s has resulted in a hotel boom, with over 50 hotels and *hospedajes* (small, family-owned inns) listed by the tourist office. The majority are small affairs with generally limited facilities and comforts. There is a handful of more comfortable options with decent-sized rooms, predictable shower times and occasional creature comforts. Even these better places are not expensive and are really worth considering unless all you want is a bed to crash for the

night. During Semana Santa prices rise markedly – from 25% to even 75%.

BUDGET

Hostal Huamanga (☎ 31 3527, 31 1871; Bellido 535; s/d with shared shower US$3/6, s/d US$6/12) The rooms here are basic, but generally OK. There seems to be abundant hot water all day and it also offers a café and a garden.

La Colmena Hotel (☎ 31 2146, 31-1318; Cuzco 140; s with shared bathroom US$5, s/d US$8/10) This popular hotel is often full by early afternoon, partly because it's one of the longest-standing places in town, and partly because it's steps from the plaza. It's a great building, but has rather been resting on its laurels – the shared bathrooms are run-down and rates are lower than in recent years. Still, it has a locally popular restaurant, a courtyard with balconies and a great location, so check it out.

Hotel Samary (☎ 31 2442, 31 3562; Callao 329; s/d with shared bathroom US$6.50/8.50, s/d US$8/10) A simple but clean hotel with great rooftop views and hot water in the early morning and evening.

Gran Hotel Los Alamos (☎ /fax 31 2782; Cuzco 215; s/d US$6/11.50) This hotel is over one of the town's most favored restaurants. The smallish and essentially functional rooms overlook the restaurant action (not very noisy) and supposedly have hot showers all day, but, as with most budget hotels, ask.

Hostal Tres Máscaras (☎ 31 2931, 31 4107; Tres Máscaras 194; s/d with shared bathroom US$4.50/7.50, s/d US$8/12.50) The pleasing walled garden and friendly staff make this an enjoyable place to stay. Hot water is on in the morning and later on request. For an extra US$1.50 you can have a room with a TV. Breakfast is available for US$2.

Hotel La Crillonesa (☎ 31 2350; www.hotelcrillonesa .cib.net; Nazareno 165; s/d with shared shower US$5/8, s/d US$9/15) A small but popular and helpful hotel, it offers a rooftop terrace with photogenic church-tower views, a café, TV room with cable, tour information and 24-hour hot water. Its rather small rooms have comfy beds; those with shower may have cable TV.

Hostal Florida (☎ 31 2565; fax 31 6029; Cuzco 310; s/d US$10/16) This traveler-friendly *hostal* (guesthouse) has a relaxing courtyard garden and clean rooms with bathrooms and TV, hot water in the morning and later on request. There is also a small cafeteria.

Hotel Yañez (☎ /fax 31 4918; www.hotelyanez .com; M Cáceres 1210; s/d incl breakfast US$11/17) Spacious rooms, comfortable mattresses, large mirrors, maroon bedspreads, kitsch wall art, cable TV and hot showers are the hallmarks of this well-run hotel. The large rooms tend to echo and are noisy – not helped by the casino parlor downstairs – but the hotel is clean and the roof has pleasant views. A cafeteria serves breakfasts, included in the rates.

Hostal El Marqués de Valdelirios (☎ 31 8944; fax 31 4014; Bolognesi 720; s/d US$13/18) This lovely, un-signposted colonial building is about 700m from the center. While it is in a quiet loca-tion, the walk back at night involves passing through some dark neighborhoods. There is a restaurant, bar and a grassy garden where food can be served. Rooms vary in size and in amenities (views, balconies, telephone) but all have beautiful furniture, cable TV and hot showers.

Hotel San Francisco (☎ 31 2353, ☎/fax 31 4501; Callao 290; s/d incl breakfast US$14/18) This rather rambling, oldish hotel is pretty convenient for the center of town. It's not flash, but it is presentable. It has a restaurant and bar and will serve meals on its inside patio. Outside double rooms are better as the single inside rooms can be very pokey. Check before you commit.

Hostal Marcos (☎ 31 6867; 9 de Diciembre 143; s/d incl breakfast US$13/21) Twelve spotless rooms in a little place somewhat sequestered away at the end of an alley, which is clearly signposted off 9 de Diciembre. This place is often full so call ahead if you can. Rooms offer 24-hour hot water and cable TV, and a light breakfast is included.

MIDRANGE
Hotel Santa María (☎/fax 31 4988; santamaria hotel2@hotmail.com; Arequipa 320; s/d US$18/27) Of the places opened during the hotel rush of the late '90s, this new one seems to have got it right. It looks impressive from the outside, while the interior is nonetheless a little sterile and could perhaps do with some greenery. That said, the rooms are very comfortable, quite spacious and tastefully decorated. There's a bar and café-restaurant too. A good second choice.

Hotel Santa Rosa (☎ 31 4614; ☎/fax 31 2083; Lima 166; www.hotel-santarosa.com; s/d incl breakfast US$18/33) Less than a block from the Plaza de Armas, this capacious hotel with its twin courtyards is perhaps the best overall choice in its cat-egory. The rooms are spacious, airy and well furnished. They come with a fridge (a

rare luxury in Peru), a TV and DVD player and a phone. The bathrooms are large and the shower space enormous, with oodles of hot water. There's a decent and well-priced on-site restaurant for meals (US$1.20 for the lunch *menú*), which also serves the included breakfast.

Ayacucho Hotel Plaza (☎ 31 2202, 31 4467, 31 4461; fax 31 2314; 9 de Diciembre 184; s/d US$46/62) Once con-sidered the best in town, it's an impressive-looking colonial building and the interior does admittedly exude a certain kind of co-lonial charm. However, for what you pay the rooms are oh-so-plain and in reality no more than adequate. The better ones do have balconies (request one) and some have plaza views.

Eating
Restaurants within two blocks of the Plaza de Armas tend to be better deals. They are slightly more expensive than places a little further out but it's a fair trade-off for the ambience, convenience and pleasure of dining in the company of fellow travelers and other Peruvian visitors. Regional specialties include *puca picante*, a potato and beef stew in a spicy red peanut and pepper sauce, served over rice; *patachi*, a wheat soup with various beans, dehydrated potatoes and lamb or beef; and *mondongo*, a corn soup cooked with pork or beef, red peppers and fresh mint. *Chicharrones* and *cuy* are also popular; vegetarians may be challenged to find meatless fare.

Chifa Tay-Pa (☎ 31 5134; M Cáceres 1131; mains average US$2; ⏰ 5-11pm) Good-value Chinese food with some vegetarian options.

Wallpa Sua (☎ 31 2006; G de la Vega 240; mains US$2-5; ⏰ 6-11pm Mon-Sat) This is an upscale, locally popular and ever-busy chicken restaurant, with a quarter chicken and fries starting at US$2, and various other meat plates available. *Wallpa sua* is Quechua for 'chicken thief' – makes you wonder where it gets its poultry supplies from.

La Casona (☎ 31 2733; Bellido 463; mains US$2-6; ⏰ 7am-10:30pm) This popular restaurant has been recommended by several travelers for its big portions. It focuses on Peruvian food and occasionally has regional specialties. This place also may have musicians, especially on weekend nights.

Adolfo's Gourmet (☎ 31 3110; Portal Constitución 4; mains US$2-6; ⏰ lunch & dinner) If you can score one of the seven outside balcony tables, you'll dine with one of the best views in Ayacucho: the Plaza de Armas and all its activity. Upstairs on the 2nd floor Adolfo's does pizzas, pastas and a sprinkling of Peruvian dishes. Good sangria and excellent pizza make for a satisfying feed.

Restaurant Los Alamos (☎ 31 2782; Cuzco 215; mains average US$3; ☺ 7am-10pm) In an attractive patio within the hotel of the same name, though operated as a separate entity, this restaurant has good service and a long menu of Peruvian selections and a few vegetarian plates; it may have musicians in the evening.

El Niño (☎ 31 4537, 31 9030; 9 de Diciembre 205; mains US$3-6; ☺ 11am-2pm & 5-11pm) In a colonial mansion with a sheltered patio containing tables overlooking a garden, El Niño specializes in grills yet dishes up a variety of Peruvian food. The individual *parrillada* (grilled meats) is worth trying, though in practice it is enough for two modest eaters. Service is efficient and friendly

Urpicha (☎ 313905; Londres 272; mains average US$4; ☺ 11am-8pm) This is a homey place, with tables in a flower-filled patio, familial attention, and an authentic menu of traditional dishes including *cuy* and the ones listed in the Eating introduction. It has a bit of a local cult following and not many outsiders make it down here. However, the neighborhood isn't great, so take a taxi after dark.

Pizzería Italiana (☎ 31 7574; Bellido 490; pizzas US$4-8; ☺ 4:30pm-11:30pm) The wood-burning oven makes this a very cozy place on cold nights; musicians may wander in and the pizza is excellent.

Cuatro Leños (☎ 970 6197; M Cáceres 1038; mains US$5-10) Chronic carnivores can take pleasure in sinking their teeth into a variety of ample *parrilladas* including *anticucho de corazón* (beef-heart kebabs) or a filling *parilla mixta especial* with pork and chicken. There's also karaoke performances in the evenings.

The 400 block of San Martín has several decent inexpensive places, including the following:

Cámara de Comercio (☎ 31-4191; San Martín 432; mains US$2-4; ☺ 9am-10pm) Serves Peruvian food.

La Tradición (☎ 31-2595; San Martín 406; menús US$1.50; ☺ 8am-3pm Mon-Sat) Locals flock here for good, cheap set lunches.

Drinking
Taberna Magía Negra (9 de Diciembre 293) A bar-gallery with good local art, beer and pizza.

Entertainment
Outside of Semana Santa this is a quiet town, but there is a university so you'll find a few bars to dance or hang out in, mostly favored by students. There are a few *peñas* (bars or clubs featuring live folkloric music) on weekends (as usual, they start late, go until the wee hours and feature Peruvian music). It's best to ask locally about these.

Los Balcones (2nd fl, Asamblea 187) This popular venue has occasional live Andean bands (US$1 cover) and a variety of recorded Andean, Latin, reggae and Western rock music to dance to. Its balconies offer a less-loud environment for conversation.

La Nueva Ley (Cáceres 1147) does disco and salsa dancing, while **El Carocol** (Arequipa 285) is a disco catering to a mainly local crowd.

Shopping
Ayacucho is famous as a handicraft center, and a visit to the Museo de Arte Popular will give you an idea of local products. The tourist office can recommend local artisans who will welcome you to their workshops. The Santa Ana *barrio* (neighborhood) is particularly well known for its crafts. The area around the Plazuela Santa Ana has various workshops, including that of **Alfonso Sulca Chavez** (☎ 32 990; Plazuela de Santa Ana 83), whose family has been weaving here for three generations. Sulca's weavings cost considerably less when bought directly from the artist rather than from shops in Lima.

A **craft market** (Independencia & Quinua) is open during the day.

Getting There & Around
AIR
The airport is 4km from the town center. Taxis charge under US$2.

Flight times and airlines can change without warning, so check airline websites for the latest schedules.

Aero Condor (☎ 31 2418, ☎ /fax 31 3060; 9 de Diciembre 123) has a 6am flight from Lima on Tuesday, Thursday, Friday and Sunday, via Andahuaylas, from where it departs for Ayacucho at 7:35am, returning to Lima at 8:45am. The Andahuaylas leg may be cancelled if there are not enough passengers.

LC Busre (Lima 178) has a daily 6:15am flight from Lima, returning at 7:35am.

The departure tax for domestic flights is $3.57.

BUS

Buses arrive at and depart from a bewildering array of individual company terminals scattered throughout the town, but all relatively close to one another. There was supposed to be a new Terminal Terrestre constructed next to the airport; at the time of research, it had not yet materialized.

Most transport connections are with Lima via the relatively fast and spectacular Hwy 24 that traverses the Andes via Rumichaca to Pisco. Night departures outnumber day departures, but day trips are naturally more interesting for the wild scenery en route. Choose your bus and company carefully. Ticket prices to/from Lima range from US$6 for a regular seat to US$15 for a reclining armchair that you can sleep in. The trip takes on average around nine hours. Take warm clothing if traveling by night and especially if taking a cheaper ticket option.

For Lima, **Empresa Molina** (☎ 31 2984; 9 de Diciembre 459) is probably the best overall option. There are two daily departures and no less than seven night departures with the 'special' *cama* service being the best one to take for comfort. Next up, **Civa** (☎ 31 9948; M Cáceres 1242) also offers a *cama* service at 9:30pm. **Cruz del Sur** (☎ 31 2813; M Cáceres 1264) and **Ormeño** (☎ 31 2495; Libertad 257) offer executive-style services with comfortable seats, but not fully reclinable. Other cheaper options include **Turismo Libertadores** (☎ 31 3614; Tres Mascaras 493, Pje Cáceres,

Manco Capác), **Antezana** (☎ 31 3048; Manco Capác 273) and **Rey Bus** (☎ 31 9413; Pje Cáceres 166).

Traveling north or south to other Andean towns presents some challenges as many roads are unsealed and subject to washouts in the rainy season. Destinations in this category include Huancayo to the north and Abancay, Andahuaylas and Cuzco to the south and southeast. Be prepared for delays. For Cuzco (US$14, 22 hours) and Andahuaylas (US$6, 10 hours), seek out **Expreso Turismo Los Chancas** (☎ 31 2391; Pje Cáceres 150), which has four departures daily. It's a long and rough trip, and the journey can be broken at Andahuaylas.

Huancavelica to the northwest is notoriously hard to get to from Ayacucho (see The Missing Link, below).

For Pucallpa, Satipo, Tingo María and Huánuco go to **Turismo Nacional** (☎ 31 5405; M Cáceres 884).

For Huancayo (US$7, 10 to 12 hours), Empresa Molina is the preferred choice with one daily and five night departures. Take note: this is a tough 250km trip and is not for the faint of heart. Around 200 of those kilometers take you along a rough, narrow, potholed and unpaved road between Huanta and Mariscal Cáceres through the wild Río Mantaro valley. The road runs at times high along unguarded cliff faces with nothing but space between your bus window and the foaming river below. Sit on the right side of the bus if you don't like vertiginous drops.

THE MISSING LINK

On the map Huancavelica looks tantalizingly close to Ayacucho. A shortish haul northwest across the Andes and you're there, right? Simple. The town is a convenient way station for travelers on a south–north loop through the central highlands. There's even a handy train out of Huancavelica heading north to Huancayo (see p301) – the next logical stop. That's where plans almost meet a dead end.

The bad news is that there is no direct bus route from Ayacucho to Huancavelica; the good news is that it *can* be done. The first option is complex and requires an early start. Take a local minibus at 4am from Ayacucho to Julcamarca, where you can take a short break while looking for an onward minibus to Lircay. You can stay the night here if you wish. From Lircay seek out yet another local minibus to Huancavelica. Total traveling time: 10 hours.

Option two: take an early-morning Lima-bound bus as far as Rumichaca (2½ to three hours). Disembark here and hopefully catch a connecting minibus to Huancavelica. This is supposed to arrive from Huancavelica at 10:30am, but delays (especially in the wet season) may occur. The Huancavelica-bound minibus doesn't 'connect' as such with the Lima buses; you just need to be at Rumichaca by 10:30am. Total traveling time: nine to 10 hours.

The coward's way out (and this author's final choice) is to bus it to Huancayo and backtrack by train to Huancavelica. At least it gets you there – assuming there are no washouts or landslides, or worse, on the way to Huancayo.

Buses to Julcamarca, Cangallo and Vischongo (US$2.50, four hours) leave from the Puente Nuevo area, which is the bridge on Castilla over the Río Alameda. Departures are normally in the morning. Buses leave for Vilcashuamán (five hours) at 5am, 6am, 7am, 8am and 9am.

Pickup trucks and buses go to many local villages, including Quinua (US$0.80, one hour), and to the Wari ruins, departing from the Paradero Magdalena at the traffic circle at the east end of M Cáceres.

WARI RUINS & QUINUA

An attractive 37km road climbs about 550m to Quinua, 3300m above sea level. After about 20km, you will pass the extensive **Wari ruins** (admission incl small museum US$0.60; ⏰ 8am-5:30pm) sprawling for several kilometers along the roadside. The five main sectors of the ruins are marked by road signs; the upper sites are in rather bizarre forests of *Opuntia* cacti. If you visit, don't leave the site too late to look for onward or return transport – vehicles can get hopelessly full in the afternoon. Note that you have to pay the full fare to Quinua (US$0.80) and remind the driver to drop you off at the ruins.

The ruins have not been well restored and the most interesting visits are with a guide from Ayacucho. Agencies charge about US$8 per person for a one-day tour combined with Quinua (you need to speak Spanish).

Wari is built on a hill, and as the road from Ayacucho climbs through it, there are reasonable views. The road climbs beyond Wari until it reaches the pretty village of **Quinua**; buses usually stop at the plaza. Steps from the left-hand side of the plaza, as you arrive from Ayacucho, lead up to the village church on an old-fashioned cobblestone plaza. A small **museum** (admission US$1; ⏰ 10am-4:30pm) nearby displays various relics from the major independence battle fought in this area. It's of little interest, however, unless you are particularly fascinated by the battle fought here. Beside the museum you can see the room where the Spanish royalist troops signed their surrender, leading to the end of colonialism in Peru.

To reach the battlefield, turn left behind the church and head out of the village along Jirón Sucre, which, after a walk of about 10 minutes, rejoins the main road. As you walk, notice the red-tiled roofs elaborately decorated with ceramic model churches. Quinua is famous as a handicraft center and these model churches are especially typical of the area. Local stores sell these and other crafts.

The **white obelisk**, which is intermittently visible for several kilometers as you approach Quinua, now lies a few minutes' walk in front of you (bus drivers may drive here if there is enough demand). The impressive monument is 40m high and features carvings commemorating the Battle of Ayacucho, fought here on December 9, 1824. The walk and views from Quinua are pleasant. The whole area is protected as the 300-hectare **Santuario Histórico Pampas de Ayacucho**.

There are no accommodations in Quinua, but simple local meals are available. There is a small market on Sunday.

VISCHONGO & VILCASHUAMÁN

Vilcashuamán (sacred falcon) was considered the geographical center of the Inca empire. Here the Inca road between Cuzco and the coast crossed the road running the length of the Andes. Little remains of the city's earlier magnificence; Vilcashuamán has fallen prey to looters, and many of its blocks have been used to build more modern buildings. The once-magnificent Temple of the Sun now has a church on top of it! The only structure still in a reasonable state of repair is a five-tiered pyramid called an *usnu*, topped by a huge double throne carved from stone and used by the Incas.

To get there, take a vehicle from Ayacucho to Vischongo (about 110km by rough but scenic road). From here, it's about 45 minutes by car, or almost two hours uphill on foot, to Vilcashuamán, where there are basic accommodations such as Hostal El Pirámide and Hostal Fortaleza (both single/double US$2/4).

From Vischongo, you can also walk about an hour to an **Intihuatana ruin** (admission US$0.80), where there are reportedly **thermal baths**. If coming from Ayacucho, the turnoff to the ruin is about 2km before the village, and then another 2km on a trail. You can also walk to a *Puya raimondii* **forest** (see Giants of the Mountains, p54), which is about an hour away by foot.

If you don't want to spend the night, you can do a day tour with an agency from Ayacucho for about US$20 per person. Independent travelers will find buses returning to Ayacucho in the afternoon; ask for times.

NORTH OF LA OROYA

North of La Oroya the highway passes through some of the more visually stark and tropically lush scenery in Peru in relatively short succession. Climbing high on to the altiplano, you pass through Junín, perched on the southern edge of the eponymous lake, before lurching upwards to Peru's highest town, the breath-sapping mining town of Cerro de Pasco. Your breathing seems to be revitalized by the minute as the road now plunges downwards in a series of twists and turns towards thriving Huánuco before plunging to the *ceja de la selva* in lush, tropical and warm Tingo María.

JUNÍN & AROUND
☎ 064 / elev 4125m

An important independence battle was fought at the nearby pampa (large, flat area) of Junín, just south of Junín, 55km due north of La Oroya. This is now preserved as the 2500-hectare **Santuario Histórico Chacamarca**, where there is a monument 2km off the main road.

At the south end of Junín village is a modern **villa artesanal** (craft market). Stay at the cold-water **Hostal San Cristobal** (☎ 34 4215; Manuel Prado 255; s/d US$2.80/4) and eat at restaurants around the Plaza de Libertad.

About 10km beyond the village is the interesting **Lago de Junín**, which, at about 30km long and 14km wide, is Peru's largest lake after Titicaca. Over 4000m above sea level, it is the highest lake of its size in the Americas. Lago de Junín is known for its birdlife, and some authorities claim that one million birds live on the lake or its shores at any one time. It is a little-visited area and a potential destination for anyone interested in seeing a variety of the water- and shorebirds of the high Andes. The lake and its immediate surroundings are part of the 53,000-hectare **Reserva Nacional Junín**. Visit by taking a *colectivo* 5km north to the hamlet of **Huayre**, from where a 1.5km path leads to the lake. Otherwise it can be quite hard to actually visit or even see the lake as it is mostly surrounded by swampy marshlands and no main highway gets within eyeshot of the lake itself.

A further 5km from Huayre brings you to the village of **Carhuamayo**, where there are basic restaurants and the cold-water **Residencial Patricia** (Tarapacá 862; s/d US$2/4).

The wide, high plain in this area is bleak, windswept and very cold, so be prepared with warm, windproof clothing. There are several villages along the road and buses stop quite often. Between these settlements, herds of llama, alpaca and sheep are seen.

CERRO DE PASCO
☎ 063 / pop 79,800 / elev 4333m

Few travelers stop at, or would want to stop at, this rather bleak and *soroche* (altitude sickness) rich altiplano mining town. Cerro de Pasco is the highest city of its size in the world, the capital of the department of Pasco and overall is an uninspiring place with no real reason for anyone to linger, or sight to offer. That said, it is lively enough, the inhabitants are friendly and unassuming and if you are traveling by *colectivo* taxi around the altiplano it is the best place to pick up a connecting ride. The high, oxygen-poor altitude makes the town bitterly cold at night and *soroche* sufferers will really feel its dizzying effects.

Change your money at **BCP** (☎ 72 2123; Daniel Carrión 12). Emergency health care is available at **Clínica Gonzales** (☎ 72 1515; Daniel Carrión 99).

The friendly **Hotel El Viajero** (☎ 72 2172; s/d with shared bathroom US$3.50/5), on the Plaza de Armas, has clean rooms and hot water in the mornings. Nearby, the basic **Hotel Santa Rosa** (☎ 72 2120) is similar.

Hostal Arenales (☎ 72 3088; Arenales 162; s/d US$4/6) is near the bus terminal. Clean rooms have hot showers and TV. **Villa Minera** (☎ 72 3073; Angamos at Parque Universitario; s/d US$7.50/10), in the suburbs, has rooms with hot-water showers, heating and cable TV. Similar facilities are offered at **Hostal Rubi** (☎ 72 1011; Antonio Martínez 306; s/d US$6/13).

The congested bus terminal five blocks south of the Plaza de Armas has buses to Huánuco (US$2, three hours), Huancayo (US$3.50, five hours), Lima (US$5, eight hours), La Oroya (US$2, 2½ hours) and Tarma. There are also minibuses to Tarma (US$2, three hours). Faster *colectivos* from the plaza or bus terminal charge US$4.50 to either Huánuco or Tarma; however, the Tarma trip actually involves three changes of taxi.

SOUTHWEST OF CERRO DE PASCO

A poor and infrequently used road goes southwest of Cerro de Pasco to Lima. West of Lago de Junín, the road goes close to the village of Huayllay and nearby the 6815-hectare **Santuario Nacional Huayllay**, known for its strange geological formations. Several hours further southwest is the small town of **Canta**, which has a basic hotel and restaurant and is a few kilometers away from the pre-Columbian ruins of **Cantamarca**, which can be visited on foot.

HUÁNUCO
☎ 062 / pop 151,200 / elev 1894m

After the oxygen deprivation of the altiplano, coming down to the busy little town of Huánuco is a pleasant relief. It makes for a convenient and decidedly more tempting stopover on the Lima–Pucallpa jungle route. Huánuco is the capital of its department, and is the site of one of Peru's oldest Andean archaeological sites, the Temple of Kotosh (aka the Temple of the Crossed Hands). The town has a museum and a pleasant, shady Plaza de Armas. Although Huánuco was founded in 1541, little is left of its colonial buildings. The town's inhabitants boast that the perfect elevation and location gives Huánuco the best climate in Peru.

Orientation
Huánuco looks a little congested and confusing at first sight, but is easy enough to get around once you have your bearings. Most transport options arrive and depart from within 200m of the main square, and hotels and restaurants are all reachable on foot.

Information
You're spoiled for choice with internet access, with at least one almost identical set of *cabinas* on every block.

Banco Continental (☎ 51 3348; 2 de Mayo 1137) Has a pair of ATMs.

BCP (☎ 51 2213; 2 de Mayo 1005) With a Visa ATM.

Locutorio Público (28 de Julio 810) Make cheap overseas phone calls here.

Tourist office (☎ 51 2980; 28 de Julio 940; 8am-1:30pm & 4-6pm Mon-Fri) Has a few brochures.

Sights
The archaeological site of the **Temple of Kotosh** (adult/student incl guided tour US$0.90/0.50; 9am-3pm) is also known as the Temple of the Crossed Hands because of the life-sized mud molding of a pair of crossed hands, which is the site's

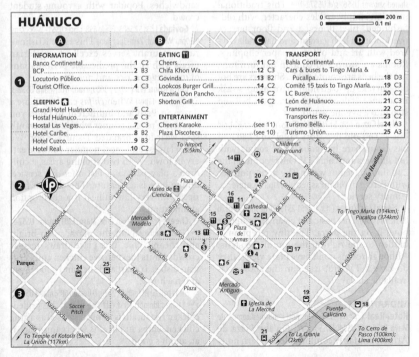

HUÁNUCO

| | | 0 ——— 200 m |
| | | 0 ——— 0.1 mi |

INFORMATION		
Banco Continental	1	C2
BCP	2	B3
Locutorio Público	3	C3
Tourist Office	4	C3

SLEEPING		
Grand Hotel Huánuco	5	C2
Hostal Huánuco	6	C3
Hostal Las Vegas	7	C3
Hotel Caribe	8	B2
Hotel Cuzco	9	B3
Hotel Real	10	C2

EATING		
Cheers	11	C2
Chifa Khon Wa	12	C3
Govinda	13	B2
Lookcos Burger Grill	14	C2
Pizzería Don Pancho	15	C2
Shorton Grill	16	C2

ENTERTAINMENT		
Cheers Karaoke	(see 11)	
Plaza Discoteca	(see 10)	

TRANSPORT		
Bahía Continental	17	C3
Cars & buses to Tingo María & Pucallpa	18	D3
Comité 15 taxis to Tingo María	19	C3
LC Busre	20	C2
León de Huánuco	21	C3
Transmar	22	C2
Transportes Rey	23	C2
Turismo Bella	24	A3
Turismo Unión	25	A3

highlight. The molding dates to about 2000 BC and is now at Lima's Museo Nacional de Antropología, Arqueología y Historía del Perú; a replica remains. Little is known about Kotosh, one of the most ancient of Andean cultures. The temple site is not in great shape, but is easily visited by taxi (US$4.50, including a 30-minute wait and return) or the bus to La Unión. The site is about 5km west of town off the road to La Unión.

About 25km south of Huánuco the road goes through the village of **Ambo**, noted for its *aguardiente* distilleries. This locally popular liquor is made from sugarcane, which can be seen growing nearby. Sometimes the bus stops and passengers can buy a couple of liters.

Sleeping

BUDGET

Hotel Caribe (☎ 51 9708; fax 51-3753; Huánuco 546; s/d with shared shower US$2.20/3.75, s/d US$3.75/4.50) Showers are hot, cable TV is included in the price and there's a karaoke café downstairs. This is among the best run of several basic, budget hotels near the market.

Hostal Huánuco (☎ 51 2050; Huánuco 777; s with shared shower US$6, s/d US$7.50/9) This traditional mansion simply exudes character, with old-fashioned, tiled floors, a 2nd-floor terrace overlooking a lush garden, and hall walls covered with art and old newspaper clippings. Rooms are worn and contain old furniture, but the beds are comfortable. Showers are hot but can take up to an hour to warm up, so ask in advance. If door is locked, ring the bell and step into a bygone world.

Hotel Cuzco (☎ 51 7653; fax 51-3578; Huánuco 614; s/d US$6/9) This old five-story hotel isn't bad and has clean, bare but good-sized rooms with hot showers and cable TV. Only rooms on the 2nd floor have hot water. The hotel, popular with Peruvian businesspeople, has a cafeteria, laundry service.

Hostal Las Vegas (☎ /fax 51 2315; 28 de Julio 934; s/d US$7.50/10.50) This basic but clean and popular hotel is on the plaza. The tiny reception is hidden to the right at the top of the stairs. Although rooms don't have plaza views, they do have a TV. Hot water in the showers is available all day.

MIDRANGE

Hotel Real (☎ 51 1777; real_hotel@hotmail.com; 2 de Mayo 1125; s/d US$40/37.50; 🖳) On the Plaza de Armas, this fairly comfortable, modern hotel has unattractive scuffed, bare hallways leading to large rooms with good beds, cable TV and phone. It has a sauna, restaurant and a handy 24-hour café.

Grand Hotel Huánuco (☎ 51 4222; www.grand hotelhuanuco.com; D Beraún 775; s/d US$37.50/51.50; 🖳) Also on the Plaza de Armas, this is the grande dame of Huánuco hotels. Its public areas are airy and pleasant, and the hotel has character. High-ceilinged rooms have solid parquet floors as well as a phone and a fuzzy, mainly Spanish-language cable-TV service. A sauna, Jacuzzi, pretty good restaurant and bar are on the premises.

Eating

The 24-hour café at the Hotel Real is an excellent choice for midnight munchies or predawn breakfasts, and for more formal dining the stately dining room at the Grand Hotel Huánuco offers quality food in a relaxed and unhurried environment.

Lookcos Burger Grill (☎ 51 2460; Abtao 1021; meals US$1-2; ⏰ 6pm-midnight) This is a squeaky-clean, white restaurant (with black-and-white photos on the wall) that serves burgers and sandwiches. Popular with a young student crowd.

Govinda (☎ 52 5683; Prado 658; plates US$1-2; ⏰ 7am-9:30pm Mon-Sat, 7am-3pm Sun) This Hare Krishna–run restaurant serves excellent vegetarian meals with all the predictable permutations of tofu, veggies, rice and noodles.

Chifa Khon Wa (☎ 51 3609; Prado 816; mains US$2-3; ⏰ 10:30am-11pm) When *chifas* can be a dime a dozen in Peru and indifferent to boot, you know you're on a winner when a restaurant's staff wear logo-branded T-shirts. Khon Wa is the largest and most popular Chinese eatery in town. With two cooking areas, a children's play park and fast attentive service, dining here is a pleasure. The chicken fried rice (with very hot chilies) is a good option at lunchtime.

Cheers (☎ 51 4666; 2 de Mayo 1201; mains US$2-3; ⏰ 11am-midnight) On the plaza, neon-bright and cheaply chic, this place draws regular crowds for its inexpensive chicken and Peruvian dishes. It's fast and slick and good if you are in a hurry.

Shorton Grill (☎ 51 2829; D Beraún 685; mains US$2-3; ⏰ 11am-midnight) Just off the plaza, this grilled-chicken restaurant is thinly disguised as a grill; chicken, chips and beer is where this place is at, and it's good.

Pizzeria Don Pancho (☎ 51 6906; Prado 645; meals US$3; ⏱ 6-11pm Mon-Sat) This place does good, though rather small pizzas – not such a bad thing given the tendency in Peru to make portions overlarge. Don Pancho also serves up a small line of pasta dishes. The dining area is a bit squashy, but you overlook this shortcoming after you sip on a refreshing jug of house sangria.

Entertainment

Cheers Karaoke (☎ 51 4666; 2 de Mayo 1201) If you're cool with karaoke, stop by this restaurant on a Friday or Saturday night to catch a could-be Peruvian singing star.

Plaza Discoteca (☎ 51 1777; Hotel Real, 2 de Mayo 1125; ⏱ 8pm-4am) A small door at the side of the Real Hotel leads down into a largish dance club with fairly standard Latin and top-40 recorded music. Locals and the occasional gringo troop in at weekends.

La Granja, also known as La Nueva Granja, is on the outskirts of town and advertises local bands. Taxi drivers know it.

Getting There & Away

AIR

Flight services were fairly stable at the time of research. **LC Busre** (☎ 51 8113; 2 de Mayo 1357) flies to and from Lima daily. The domestic departure tax is $3.57. The airport is 5km from town. Take a cab (US$3.50) to get there.

BUS & TAXI

Buses go to Lima (US$6 to US$10, eight hours), Pucallpa (US$8, 12 hours), La Merced (US$5.50, six hours), Huancayo (US$5, six hours) and La Unión (US$3, five hours), with companies all over town. Among the best:

Bahía Continental (☎ 51 9999; Valdizán 718) Regular bus to Lima at 10am, plus *bus camas* at 10pm and 10:15pm (regular/*bus cama* US$9/11).

León de Huánuco (☎ 51 1489, 51 2996; Robles 821) To Lima at 10am, 8:30pm and 9:30pm; La Merced at 8pm; Pucallpa at 7:30pm.

Transmar (28 de Julio 1067) Pucallpa at 6am.

Transportes Rey (☎ 51 3623; 28 de Julio 1215) Lima 9am and 10:15pm; Huancayo 8:30pm.

Turismo Bella (San Martión 571) Tantamayo at 6:30am and 7:30am.

Turismo Unión (☎ 52 6308; Tarapaca 449) La Unión at 7:15am.

Other companies near Turismo Unión and Turismo Bella also go west toward villages

on the eastern side of the Cordillera Blanca: rough roads, poor buses.

For Tingo María (US$2, 3½ hours), take a Pucallpa-bound bus or a *colectivo* taxi (US$3.50) with **Comite 15** (☎ 51 8346) at General Prado near the river. There are more *colectivo* taxis for Tingo María on the other side of the river such as Trans Milagros, or wait here for a passing bus.

For Cerro de Pasco, minibuses (US$2, three hours) or *colectivo* taxis (US$4.50) leave from a bus stop about 3km southwest of town. *Mototaxis* charge US$0.30.

LA UNIÓN

This remote village is between Huánuco and Huaraz via rough roads. A three-hour walk (one way) from La Unión are the extensive and impressive Inca ruins of **Huánuco Viejo** (admission US$1.50; ⏱ 7am-5pm). Take the path from behind the market heading toward a cross on a hill. Vehicles can also be found to take you almost to the site, which is worth a visit.

La Unión lacks banks, has a few public but no listed phones, several simple eateries and two or three basic hotels like **Hostal Picaflor** (2 de Mayo 840; s/d with shared shower US$5.50/9).

Buses leaves the plaza early in the day for Lima via Chiquián. There are also buses to Huancayo (US$3, five hours).

TINGO MARÍA

☎ 062 / pop 54,000 / elev 649m

The inclusion of Tingo María in this Andes chapter is an odd one, for Tingo María (Tingo for short) is as different as it can be from any of the cities and towns previously described. This languid, humid and warm university and market town lies in the *ceja de la selva*, and while it has its back to the mountains its feet are firmly planted in the lush vegetation of the Amazonas region. It is verdant, tropical, humid and – most importantly – warm, a real bonus if you have just come down from the bone-chilling heights of the upper Andes. Tingo is known locally by the moniker *La Ciudad de la Bella Durmiente* (the City of the Sleeping Beauty) in honor of a mountain in the Tingo María National Park that bears the shape of a sleeping woman wearing an Inca crown.

Tingo María is as much a popular way station as it is a destination in its own right. *Limeños* come here in droves to escape their *garúa* (coastal fog, mist or drizzle) and desert city status, while travelers pause here on their way to the Amazon. Many go to the great river itself – or more accurately, its feeder the Río Ucayali – and end up coming back to Tingo to linger longer and relax in its unhurried embrace.

This thriving town has had bad press in the past – and still does to some extent. To the north in the Huallaga valley coca is grown and is jealously guarded by *narcotraficantes* (drug traffickers) who, if steered clear of, leave all and sundry alone. To the east a lonely jungle road spears across the *selva* to the port of Pucallpa, but it is a road with its own possible dangers (see p478).

Surrounded by mountains, waterfalls and caves, Tingo begs for the traveler's attention.

Pause for just one day and you may end up here a week.

Orientation & Information

Tingo María is an airy, spacious town that can easily be navigated on foot. Arrivals tend to happen at the southwest corner of town.

There are internet places on most blocks.

Banco Continental (☎ 56 2141; A Raymondi 543) US cash can be changed here. It has a US dollar and nuevo sol ATM machine.

BCP (☎ 56 2111; A Raymondi 249) Also changes US cash here. It has a Visa ATM and may change traveler's checks.

Clínica Santa Lucila (☎ 56 1020; Ucayali 637) A private, better option than the hospital.

Hospital (☎ 56 2017/8/9; Ucayali 114) A block east of Alameda Perú.

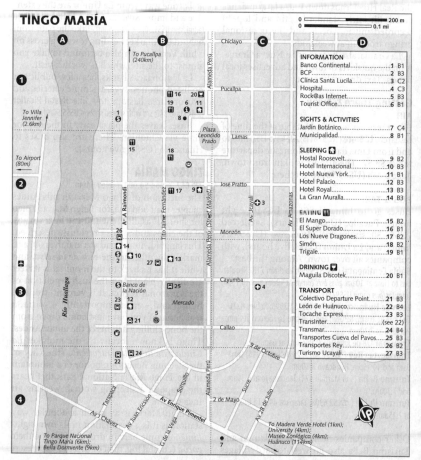

TINGO MARÍA

0 _____ 200 m
0 _____ 0.1 mi

INFORMATION	
Banco Continental..............1	B1
BCP..............2	B3
Clínica Santa Lucila..............3	C2
Hospital..............4	C3
Rock@as Internet..............5	B3
Tourist Office..............6	B1

SIGHTS & ACTIVITIES	
Jardín Botánico..............7	C4
Municipalidad..............8	B1

SLEEPING 🛏	
Hostal Roosevelt..............9	B2
Hotel Internacional..............10	B3
Hotel Nueva York..............11	B1
Hotel Palacio..............12	B3
Hotel Royal..............13	B3
La Gran Muralla..............14	B3

EATING 🍴	
El Mango..............15	B2
El Super Dorado..............16	B1
Los Nueve Dragones..............17	B2
Simón..............18	B2
Trigale..............19	B1

DRINKING 🍸	
Maguila Discotek..............20	B1

TRANSPORT	
Colectivo Departure Point..............21	B3
León de Huánuco..............22	B4
Tocache Express..............23	B3
TransInter..............(see 22)	
Transmar..............24	B4
Transportes Cueva del Pavos..............25	B3
Transportes Rey..............26	B2
Turismo Ucayali..............27	B3

To Pucallpa (240km)

To Villa Jennifer (2.6km)

To Airport (80km)

Río Huallaga

Chiclayo

Pucallpa

Plaza Leoncido Prado

Lamas

José Pratto

Monzón

Cayumba

Mercado

Callao

Banco de la Nación

9 de Octubre

2 de Mayo

To Madera Verde Hotel (1km); University (4km); Museo Zonológico (4km); Huánuco (114km)

To Parque Nacional Tingo María (6km); Bella Dormiente (9km)

Av J Chávez

Av Juan Ericsson

Av Enrique Pimentel

Tarapacá

Surquillo

Crla de la Vega

Alameda Perú

Sucre

Av 28 de Julio

Alameda Perú

Tito Jaime Fernández

A Raimondi

Av Jcvayli

Av Amazonas

Main post office (Plaza Leoncido Prado)

Rock@as Internet (Tito Jaime 101) Open till late.

Tourist office (☎ 56 2351; Alameda Perú 525) On Plaza Leoncido Prado, but has little to offer other than paintings and photos.

Sights & Activities

For a tour guide, ask at the tourist office, or try **Segundo Cordova** (☎ 56 2030, 969 5383). He knows the waterfalls, lakes and caves of the area well.

UNIVERSIDAD NACIONAL AGRARIA DE LA SELVA (UNAS)

The university runs a **jardín botánico** (botanical garden; ☎ university 56 2341; admission free; ☟ 8am-2pm Mon-Fri, 8am-11am Sat), which, though rather run-down and overgrown, has labels on some of the plants with useful information. The garden is at the south end of Alameda Perú and you may need to yell for the gatekeeper.

The university itself, 4km south of town, has a small **museo zoológico** (zoological museum) with a collection of living and mounted animals from around the region.

PARQUE NACIONAL TINGO MARÍA

This 18,000-hectare park lies on the south side of town around the mouth of the Río Monzón, a tributary of the Río Huallaga. Within the park is the **Bella Dormiente** (Sleeping Beauty), a hill overlooking the town. From some angles, the hill looks like a reclining woman.

Also in the park is **La Cueva de las Lechuzas** (the Cave of the Owls), which, despite its name, is known for the colony of oilbirds that

lives inside. In addition, there are stalactites and stalagmites, bats, parrots and other birds around the cave entrance, but the oilbirds are the main attraction.

The caves are about 6km away from Tingo María, and taxis can take you there. There is a US$1.50 national-park fee, and guides are able to show you around. Locals say the best time to visit the park is in the morning, when sunlight shines into the mouth of the cave, though dusk, when the oilbirds emerge, may also be good. Don't be tempted to use your flashlight to see the birds as it disturbs their sleeping and breeding patterns. Instead, use it to see where you are going only so that your shoes don't get covered in bat and bird droppings.

Sleeping

The hotel scene has seen a marked improvement in recent times, with a much-needed injection of a few decent hotels in the midrange bracket. Budget hotels are, on the whole, of a low standard with little to recommend them except their price. Showers are cold unless stated otherwise.

BUDGET

Hotel Palacio (☎ 56 2319, 56 2055; Av A Raymondi 158; s/d with shared shower US$4.50/7.50, s/d US$7.50/12) It looks well run and clean, with rooms surrounding a plant-filled courtyard with caged parrots. Although the rooms are a bit spartan, they have fans and TV. A café is on the premises.

Hostal Roosevelt (☎ 50 5448; watts300866@hotmail.com; José Pratto 399; s/d US$6/8) The most recent

---

LA RUTA DE COCA

Growing the coca plant itself is not illegal. It's leaves are used for chewing, making infusions of *mate de coca* (coca-leaf tea) and for other medicinal purposes. In itself it is a fine plant.

However it is the mashing of coca leaves into *pasta básica* (basic paste) that gets people into trouble. This is the stuff that has hitherto been surreptitiously been ghosted out of the region to processing centers – notably in Colombia – where the refined drug cocaine is produced. Coca grows in profusion in the hidden corners of the long Huallaga valley than runs from Tingo María to Tarapoto in the north. Close to Tingo, Monzon and its valley is a particularly troublesome area where police rarely tread. This is primary army territory.

But the battle against cocaine is a tough one. Farmers who make a pittance out of growing fruit or coffee can earn a viable living out of coca. It is a perverse logic played out equally in Afghanistan with its poppies, or further north in the tropical valleys of Colombia where coca again is the crop of choice. *Narcotraficantes* (drug traffickers) have now upped the ante by establishing hidden processing centers within the Huallaga region instead of exporting the *pasta básica*. Pure cocaine now flows out of the region via various routes and methods and while the police and army try hard to stem the flow, it is ultimately a losing battle.

addition to the accommodations scene, this neat little hostelry is a midrange option with budget prices. A cool black-and-white tiled floor leads you to series of smallish, but very clean rooms. If you don't mind the kitsch colors (purple and yellow) or the wall-length mirror next to the bed (!) you won't go wrong for the price. Cable TV and piped radio are also provided.

Hotel Nueva York (☎ /fax 56 2406; www.hotelnueva york.net; Alameda Perú 553; s/d from US$7/9) Spacious rooms have fans and showers hooked up to rooftop tanks so water gets a bit warmer in the afternoon. For an extra US$3 you can have cable TV. Breakfast is an additional US$1.50. The rooms are set back from the road and quiet.

Hotel Royal (☎ 56 2166; fax 56 2167; Tito Jaime 214; s/d US$8/11) All rooms have showers; an extra US$3 buys you hot water and cable TV. This well-kept property with clean blue walls, small courtyard and plenty of plants is a good budget choice.

MIDRANGE

Hotel Internacional (☎ /fax 56 3035; hinternacional _TM2@hotmail.com; s/d US$9/14) Close to the bus stations and handy for pretty much every amenity, this newcomer to the accommodations scene is unquestionably a pleasant choice and beckons the jaded *viajero* (traveler) with its cool, tiled interior and well-designed rooms. These have 24-hour hot water, cable TV and phone.

La Gran Muralla (☎ /fax 56 2934; Raymondi 277, lagranmuralla_hotel@hotmail.com; s/d US$12/20; 🖳) One of the newer midrange offerings to spring up, this breezy riverside complex is a fine choice if you want to be next to the action. It has a light, bright feel to it, exemplified by its welcoming lobby. Its modern, pleasantly furnished rooms are of a decent size and have cable TV, fans and phones. From the 2nd-floor terrace you can gaze over the river to the airport and the jungle beyond.

Madera Verde Hotel (☎ /fax 56 1800, 56 2047; s/d incl breakfast US$50/60; 🖳) Just over 1km south of town. Walk-in rates can be discounted, and continental breakfast is included. The rooms are good sized, have bathrooms and hot water, TV and minibar. Quadruple bungalows are also available. The hotel is set in pleasant gardens with a playground and simple but adequate restaurant and bar.

Eating

Eating out is improving all the time in Tingo. There's a proliferation of the usual hole-in-the-wall options that are OK for a quick feed, but for a more relaxed dine time, check out the following select eateries.

Simón (☺ Tito Jaime Fernández 416; mains US$2-3; ☺ 7am-3pm & 6-10pm) On Tito Jaime, between José Prado and Lamas, this sweaty restaurant has few cooling fans and little breeze. The food is good and varied – including a few *criollo* dishes. Locals say it's the best value in town. You can get most Peruvian dishes here; try the *bistec à la Simón* – large and juicy. Order a big beer, and you'll get a 1L bottle.

El Mango (☎ 56 1671, 56 3454; Lamas 232; ☺ 8am-3pm Mon-Sat & 7-11pm daily; sandwiches & breakfasts US$1-2, mains US$2.50-5.50) A surprising garden restaurant; good food including pizzas, friendly service and a place to linger. Look for the mango-colored façade.

THE AUTHOR'S CHOICE

Villa Jennifer (☎ 960 3509; www.villajennifer.net; Km 3.4 Castillo Grande; s/d US$14/22; 🖳) North of the airport, this relaxing tropical hacienda and lodge is run by a Danish-Peruvian couple. They have done wonders out of a lush expanse of tropical bushland bounded by rivers on two sides. Apart from the rustically stylish accommodations that range from simple rooms with shared bathrooms to airy mini-homes that can sleep up to 10 people, there so much more. You can play table tennis, darts, badminton or table soccer – there is even a mini soccer pitch. Catch a movie on DVD if you become jungle-blasé, or go see the animals that include crocodiles, tortoises, a sloth and a couple of monkeys. Oh, and you can watch exotic birds too. Then there's the swimming: two pools to choose from, or let the cool current of the river nurse your bush-weary body. Tired already? Take a novel (they are scattered around) and hang in a shaded hammock until dinnertime (upon request). The food is excellent and the local fruit – including *anonas* (custard apples), guavas, *pomarosas* (Malay apples) and mangoes – is to die for. Stay here too long and you may never want to leave.

Trigale (☎ 56 1638; Tito Jaime Fernández 540; mains US$2.50-4.50; ☻ 6-11pm) Tingo María's best pizza and pasta restaurant will deliver if you are too lazy to forsake the fan and the TV in your hotel room.

El Super Dorado (☎ 56 3394; Tito Jaime Fernández 594; mains US$2.50-4.50; ☻ lunch & dinner) It's big 'n' brash and locals love it for its no-nonsense chicken *parilladas* that they wash down with lashings of cold beer – the best recipe on a hot sticky evening.

Los Nueve Dragones (☎ 40 6451; Tito Jaime Fernández 394; mains US$3-5; ☻ lunch & dinner) Where most eateries forego the niceties of décor in favor of taste and portion size, the 'Nine Dragons' *chifa* has put some effort into making its restaurant a pleasant, bright and cheery eating environment. The food here is predictable, with a range of Peruvian-Chinese fusion plates.

Drinking

Maguila Discotek (Plaza Leoncido Prado) On Tingo María's main plaza, Maguila Discotek is a typically dark and seedy outback-town disco, rife with noise, beer and macho men looking for an easy night with a friendly *chica* (girl). Sample with caution.

Getting There & Away

AIR

The airport is 1.5km from town, though at the time of research there were no scheduled services. At the airport you may be able to find light aircraft flying to nearby towns.

BUS & TAXI

Schedules change frequently, but the focus is essentially on moving passengers to and from Lima and destinations in between such as Huánuco. Buses also serve local villages and Pucallpa. The road between Tingo and Pucallpa can be risky; see p478.

Buses to Lima (US$7 to US$12, 12 hours) are operated by **Transportes León de Huánuco** (☎ 56 2030), **Transmar** (☎ 56 3076), **Transportes Rey** (☎ 56 2565; Raymondi 297) and TransInter. Buses usually leave at 7am or 7pm. Some operators go to Pucallpa (US$5, nine hours). Faster service to Pucallpa is with Turismo Ucayali, which has *colectivo* taxis (US$14, six hours).

Tocache Express (☎ 56 3324) has cars to Tocache (US$8.50, four hours) from where trucks continue another five hours on to Juanjui.

Transportes Cueva del Pavos is a signed stop with *mototaxis* to the Cave of the Owls in Parque Nacional Tingo María.

NORTH COAST

North Coast

Southern Peru can keep its Machu Picchu. The unruly northern coast is flush with enough ancient chronicles to fill a library of memoirs, and boasts beaches and surf that are the envy of Peru. Here, the coastal desert spreads out from Lima all the way to Ecuador as the Pan-American Hwy heroically divides restless sand dunes and burly cliffs from the Pacific Ocean's belligerent waves.

This heaving coastline is scattered with more antediluvian ruins that you can poke a pre-Inca civilization at. The few travelers who manage to slip the familiar clutches of the Gringo Trail and venture this far north scratch their collective heads at the 5000 year-old remnants of the Americas' oldest civilization. They drool at the gold-laden million-dollar treasures buried in long-forgotten pyramids and tombs, and listen to tall tales of modern-day treasure hunters clashing wits with archaeologists in a race to uncover the untold wealth of the region.

Occasional oases of bottle green farmland lie scattered along the coastline, and animated colonial towns will doff their collective *campesino* (peasant) hats to all who make the effort to visit. Meanwhile, the graceful surf that continually pounds the coast has had surfers board-waxing lyrical for years, while the enduring sunny months and frisky seaside resorts beckon modern-day sun worshippers to the coast's sandy shores.

HIGHLIGHTS

- Day-tripping from Trujillo to visit the ruins of **Chan Chan** (p336) and the beautifully preserved friezes of **Huacas del Sol y de la Luna** (p339)

- Indulging in sun, surf and sand at **Máncora** (p362), Peru's premier beachside hot spot

- Drooling over a vast wealth of once buried treasure around **Chiclayo** (p349)

- Dragging your board up the coast in search of that elusive perfect swell at **Huanchaco** (p340), **Puerto Chicama** (p343), **Pacasmayo** (p343) and around **Máncora** (p362)

- Seeking out **shamans** (p360) for the perfect cure – or curse – in the mountain wilds of Huancabamba

- BIGGEST CITY: TRUJILLO, POPULATION 768,300

- AVERAGE TEMPERATURE: JANUARY 18°C TO 28°C, JULY 16°C TO 25°C

NORTH COAST

LIMA TO BARRANCA

The Carretera Panamericana (Pan-American Hwy) winds its way north out of chaotic Lima through nonstop desert all the way to Ecuador. At Km 105, a marked dirt road heads 4km east to **Reserva Nacional Lomas de Lachay** (admission US$1.50; ☼ dawn-dusk), a 5070-hectare natural reserve where moisture from coastal mists creates the unique microenvironment of a dwarf forest, which conceals a plethora of small animals and birds. The park has campsites and picnicking areas, pit toilets and trails, but there are no buses – you will have to hire a vehicle or hike from the Panamericana to get here.

Further north, the village of **Huaura**, opposite **Huacho**, is where José de San Martín proclaimed Peru's independence. Ask for someone to show you the building where it occurred. There is an inconsequential **museum** (admission US$0.90; ☼ 9am-5pm) and a Spanish-speaking guide who'll show you the balcony from where the desire for self-rule was decreed.

BARRANCA

☎ 01 / pop 44,000

Barranca, located 195km north of Lima, has a relaxed, fountain-spouting plaza and a cacophony of traffic plowing through on the Carretera Panamericana, which dissects the town. Neighboring Pativilca, located 10km further north, is where the road branches off to Huaraz and the Cordillera Blanca. This spectacular route climbs inland through cactus-laden cliff faces, and you can watch the cathedrals of sheer rock slowly turn into a carpet of greenery as the road climbs up to Huaraz.

Sights
PARAMONGA

The adobe temple of **Paramonga** (admission US$0.90) is situated 4km beyond the turnoff for the Huaraz road and was built by the Chimu culture, which was the ruling power on the north coast before it was conquered by the Incas (see p336). The fine details of the massive temple have long been eroded, yet the multi-tiered construction is nonetheless impressive and affords fantastic panoramas of the lush valley. Local buses from Barranca will drop you off at a spot 3km from the entrance (US$0.50, 25 minutes), or a taxi here will cost US$3.

CARAL

About 25km inland from Barranca lie the monumental ruins of **Caral** (adult/student US$3/0.90; ☼ 9am-5pm), which confounded Peruvian archaeologists when they proved to be part of the oldest civilization in all of South America. Before Caral's discovery, the city of Chavín de Huántar near Huaraz, built around 900 BC, held that particular title. This earlier civilization arose in the Supe valley between an incredible 4500 and 5000 years ago, making it one of the earliest city-states in the world, alongside Mesopotamia, Egypt, India and China. This ancient culture was a conglomeration of 18 city-states and controlled the three valleys of Supe, Pativilca and Fortaleza, with the main seat of government at Caral. At the site, six stone-built pyramids (most of which have been excavated) were found alongside amphitheaters, ceremonial rooms, altars, adobe complexes and several circular plazas. Most of the pyramids have stairways leading to their peaks, where offerings were once made; the stairs can be climbed for great views.

Considering how few people visit Caral, and how even fewer know about it, the site is well set out for visitors. There are plaques in both Spanish and English illustrating points of interest. **Projecto Especial Arqueológico Caral** (www.caralperu.gob.pe) is in charge here, and its **Lima office** (Map pp94-5; ☎ 01-431 2235; Jirón Belén 1040, Central Lima) has tons of information and also does informative full-day tours on the last Sunday of each month for US$24 per person. **Lima Tours** (Map pp94-5; ☎ 01-424 5110; www.limatours.com.pe; Jirón Belen 1040, Central Lima; ☼ 8:30am-5:30pm Mon-Fri, 9am-1pm Sat) in Lima arranges expensive private tours to Caral on request. *Colectivo* (shared transport) taxis depart from Barranca to the nearby hamlet of Caral fairly regularly for US$1.50 (two hours), or alternatively a taxi will cost US$25 for the return journey (including waiting time). The road out here is rough and may be impassable during the December to March wet season. Spanish-speaking local guides are also available at the site for US$6 per group.

Sleeping & Eating

Most hotels are along Barranca's main street.

Hostal Birch (Pedro Reyes Barbosa 159; s/d US$4.50/7.50) This is the cheapest place to stay, with slightly run-down but reasonably clean rooms and a friendly family running the show – look for colorful jungle murals lining the entryway. It's one block east of the plaza.

Hostal Residencial Continental (☎ 235-2458; A Ugarte 190; s/d US$6/13.50) A step up from Hostal Birch, this spot has great little rooms that are clean, secure and brightened by loud bedspreads.

Hotel Chavín (☎ 235 2358, 235 2253; www.hotelchavin .com.pe; Gálvez 222; s/d US$19.50/24; ☒) The best place in town, Hotel Chavín has comfortable rooms that are perfectly preserved in their resplendent '70s style. There's a decent restaurant called El Liberador below it.

Sech (A Ugarte 190; snacks US$0.90-1.80; ☼ 8am-10pm) For a tasty bite, visit this busy modern café with warm yellow walls and a varied menu.

Getting There & Away

To get to Lima, flag down one of the many buses heading in that direction. Most buses from Lima going up the coast can drop you in Barranca. For Huaraz, catch a minibus (US$0.30) to the petrol station at the Huaraz turnoff. From there, infrequent buses stop to pick up passengers (US$4 to US$6, five hours) or you can catch a much faster *colectivo* taxi (US$7.50, 3½ hours).

CASMA

☎ 043 / pop 21,400

A small and unflustered Peruvian coastal town, Casma has little to do except watch the whirring of passing buses. The big draw here is the archaeological site of Sechín, about 5km away. Casma's once important colonial port (11km from town) was sacked by various pirates during the 17th century, and the town today is merely a friendly blip on the historical radar.

From here, the Panamericana branches off for Huaraz via the Callán Pass (4225m). This route is tough on your backside but offers excellent panoramic views of the Cordillera Blanca. Most points of interest in town lie along the Panamericana, between the Plaza de Armas in the west and the petrol station in the east.

Information

There's no tourist office, but **Sechín Tours** (☎ 41 1421; www.sechintours.com; Nepeña 16) has a small office in the Hostal Monte Carlo that dishes out tourist information and travelers' assistance, and also arranges local tours. There's a branch of **BCP** (☎ 71 1314, 71 1471; Bolívar 111) here and several internet cafés line the plaza.

Sights

Sechín (adult/student US$1.50/0.80; ♥ 8am-5pm), 5km southeast of Casma, is one of Peru's granddaddy archaeological sites, dating from about 1600 BC. It is among the more important and well-preserved ruins along this coast, though it has suffered some damage from grave robbers and natural disasters.

The warlike people who built this temple remain shrouded in mystery. The site consists of three outside walls of the main temple, which are completely covered in gruesome 4m-high bas-relief carvings of warriors and captives being vividly eviscerated in a grisly fashion. Ouch. Inside the main temple are earlier mud structures that are still being excavated; you can't go in, but there is a model in the small on-site **museum**. If you visit the museum first, you may be able to pick up a Spanish-speaking guide (ie one of the caretakers) for around US$4.50.

To get here, a *mototaxi* (three-wheeled motorcycle rickshaw taxi) from Casma costs around US$1.50. You can also visit on a tour organized by Sechín Tours in Casma, or by using pedal power if you rent one of the company's bicycles. The route is well signposted.

Other early sites in the Sechín area have not been excavated due to a lack of funds. From the museum, you can see the large, flat-topped hill of **Sechín Alto** in the distance. The nearby fortress of **Chanquillo** consists of several towers surrounded by concentric walls, but it is best appreciated from the air. Aerial photographs are on display at the museum.

The entry ticket to Sechín also allows you to visit the Mochica ruins of **Pañamarca**, 10km inland from the Panamericana on the road to Nepeña. These ruins are badly weathered, but you can see some of the covered murals if you ask the guard.

Tours & Guides

The friendly folk at **Sechín Tours** (☎ 41 1421; www.sechintours.com; Hostal Monte Carlo, Nepeña 16) arrange full-day trips to Sechín and Tortugas, including entrance fees, lunch and a Spanish-speaking guide, for US$15 per person (minimum two people). You can rent mountain bikes here to explore the ruins under your own steam (US$3 for three hours, US$6 per day). They also rent sandboards (US$1.50 per day) for plummeting down the nearby **Manchan** dunes, a US$3 *mototaxi* ride away.

Sleeping & Eating

Hostal Gregori (☎ 9631 4291; L Ormeño 579; s/d with shared bathroom US$4.50/7.50, s/d US$9/10.50) Probably the best and most popular budget pick. This funky white hotel has random potted plants in specially designed crevices, architecturally rakish wall angles and very comfortable, fresh rooms. Hot water and TVs are available on request and the whole place has radiantly airy feng shui.

Hostal Selene (☎ 71 1065; L Ormeño 595; s/d US$6/10.50) This budget affair is a little frayed but friendly and clean enough for a night's kip. There's hot water, cable TV and a risqué collection of business cards at the front desk.

Las Dunas (☎ 41 1226; L Ormeño 505; s/d US$7.50/10.50) Housed in a newish building, Las Dunas has immaculate rooms with a bounty of space, cable TV and hot water.

Hostal Monte Carlo (☎ 41 1421; Nepeña 16; s/d US$10.50/15) The big rooms here couldn't be any cleaner if your mother had scrubbed them herself. All come with TV. Sechín tours operates out of the reception, and there's a neat little café serving cheap snacks (US$0.50 to US$1.20) and breakfasts (US$1.10 to US$1.50). It's just east of the plaza.

Hotel El Farol (☎ 41 1064, in Lima 01-424 0517; Túpac Amaru 450; s/d US$21/30; ⬛) One of the fanciest places to bed down in Casma, El Farlo curves around a fetching garden, complete with a dainty gazebo and a bamboo-lined restaurant and bar. The walled-in compound supplies an oasis of calm from the street clamor and has great rooms. There are useful maps and photographs in the lobby if you plan to explore surrounding ruins.

Hotel Los Poncianos (☎ 41 1599, ☎ /fax 41 2123; Panamericana Norte Km 376; s/d US$21/30; ⬛) Just a block off the main highway and six blocks from the Plaza de Armas, this place is in a hushed spot and has both an Olympic-sized pool and a children's pool in its grounds. The restaurant will feed you, hot showers will bathe you, cable TV will entertain you and a ceiling fan will keep you cool.

There are no fancy restaurants in town, but for a coffee and early breakfast snacks try the bakery **Sol Caribeño** (L Ormeño 544; snacks US$0.30-0.90; ♥ 7am-6pm). **La Careta** (Peru 895; meals around US$3.60; ♥ 7-11pm) is a popular meatery serving sizzling grills nightly – though be warned that the only 'greens' you'll come across here are the indoor potted plants. **Chifa Tío Sam** (☎ 71 1447; Huarmey 138; mains around US$3.30; ⏰ 7am-9pm) is also a good place to grab a bite.

Getting There & Away

Colectivo taxis to Chimbote (US$1.50, 45 minutes) leave frequently from the Plaza de Armas.

Several bus companies, including Cruz del Norte, Movil and Turismo Paraiso, have a communal **booking office** (☎ 41-2116; L Ormeño 145) in front of the petrol station at the eastern end of town. Most buses stop here to pick up extra passengers. There are frequent buses to Lima (US$5.50 to US$11, six hours), to Trujillo (US$4.50, three hours) and buses to Huaraz (check which route they take; Yungay Express and Transportation Huandoy have buses that take the scenic route via the Callán Pass) at 6:30am, 10:30am and 10:30pm (US$5.50 to US$7, five to six hours). Nearby **Tepsa** (☎ 41 2658; L Ormeño 546) has comfortable buses to Lima (US$9 to US$15), a direct 8pm bus all the way to Tumbes (US$21, 11 hours) and a 10pm bus to Cajamarca (US$18, seven hours).

TORTUGAS

This small beach resort hugs a diminutive, calm bay about 22km northwest of Casma, off the Panamericana at Km 392. There's a decent, pebbly beach with clean water, and pleasant swimming in the bay. It's a popular weekending spot, and a visit can be combined with an all-day Sechín tour from Casma. Stay at the **Hotel Farol Beach Inn** (☎ 968 2540; Tortugas; s/d US$12/18), which has big rooms with hot water and top vistas from its airy communal areas. *Colectivo* taxis to Tortugas (US$0.90, 20 minutes) leave frequently from the Plaza de Armas in Casma.

CHIMBOTE

☎ 043 / pop 320,600

Chimbote is Peru's largest fishing port – and with fish-processing factories lining the roads in and out of Chimbote you'll probably smell that fact before you see it. The odor of fermenting fish may take a while to get used to, but the quiet, open (and odorless) plaza in the town's heart makes for a refreshing change. The fishing industry has declined from its 1960s glory days due to overfishing, but you'll still see flotillas of brightly colored

boats moored offshore every evening. This roguish port town is not a tourist destination, and there's little to do, but you may have to stay overnight if you're catching an early morning bus to Huaraz via the hair-raising Cañón del Pato route.

Information

Internet cabins are found on E Aguirre to the south of J Pardo.

Banco Continental (F Bolognesi)
Banco Wiese (F Bolognesi)
BCP (F Bolognesi)
Interbank (F Bolognesi)
Oficina de migraciónes (immigration office; ☎ 32 2481; 2nd fl, Centro Civico Comercial de Chimbote) Does visa extensions.
Police (☎ 32 4485; cnr E Palacios & L Prado)
Post office (☎ 32 2943; cnr Tumbes & L Prado; ⏰ 9am-7pm Mon-Fri, 9am-1pm Sat)

Sleeping

There are lots of hotels in Chimbote, though little in the top-end range.

BUDGET

Hostal Chimbote (☎ 34 4721; J Pardo 205; s/d US$6/7.50) The cell-like rooms here have windows onto the corridor, but it's an acceptable cheapie that boasts cold-water showers and TV. There are cheaper rooms without showers or the aforementioned TV.

Cesar's Hostal (☎ 32 4946; L Espinar 286; s/d US$7.50/ 10.50) Still glossy from a Teletubbies-inspired blue-on-yellow paint job, these spartan abodes are clean and come with cable TV thrown is – a bargain at this price. It's more hushed than most hotels in Chimbote and has cold water.

Hostal Karol Inn (☎ 32 2727; M Ruiz 277; s/d US$7.50/12) Using mothballs as air freshener may not be the best marketing ploy, but there's space enough in the rooms to swing a few cats and a rowdy local bar right downstairs.

Hostal Residencial el Parque (☎ 34 1552, 34 5572; E Palacios 309; s/d US$9/15) With spartan, windowless rooms, this friendly, secure venture is right on the Plaza de Armas and continues to be a popular spot for passing *extranjeros* (foreigners). Hot showers and cable TV come as standard.

Tany (☎ 32 3441; E Palacios 553; s/d incl breakfast US$12/21) Though it's a little spendier than most budget options, Tany has massive and immaculately kept rooms with polished floorboards, a quiet location and a free breakfast, giving it a decent bang-for-buck ratio.

MIDRANGE

Hotel Vertiz (☎ 32 4856; F Bolognesi 305; s/d US$18/30) A quiet, sparkling new setup that has orderly rooms with fridge and TV. It's guarded by a foyer with lots of wooden finishings and more than its fair share of mirrors and glittery bits.

Hotel San Felipe (☎ 32 3401; J Pardo 514; s/d incl breakfast US$19.50/28.50) The clean rooms here are reached by elevator and have strong hot showers and cable TV. Be sure to take your continental breakfast on the 5th-floor terrace with plaza views. A glitzy downstairs casino will help you live out your Las Vegas card-shark fantasies.

Hostal D'Carlo (☎ 34 4044, ☎ /fax 32-1047; Villavicencio 376; s/d incl breakfast US$25.50/33) Cheerfully painted walls, nice bedspreads, fans and cable TV welcome you here. Rooms are spacious but the bathrooms (with hot water) can be Lilliputian. There's room service from the hotel café between 7am to 10pm, and some rooms overlook the plaza.

Hostal Chifa Canton (☎ 34 4388; F Bolognesi 498; s/d incl breakfast US$28.50/33) The town's best hotel, Hostal Chifa Canton has large, attractive rooms with modern amenities. Some rooms look onto the sea. It has a good *chifa* (Chinese restaurant) and a pool hall on the premises.

Real Hotel Gran Chimú (☎ 32 3721, 32-8104; Gálvez 109; s/d US$29.50/39; 🕸) This charming and dignified old building is roomy and aloof, lazing by the sea and espousing a laissez-faire life philosophy that's a welcome reprieve from Chimbote's showy bustle. Upstairs, 76 rooms and three suites supply either fans or air-con, cable TV and phone, and some come with a view over the fishing-trawler-filled bay. It has a decent restaurant and bar.

Eating

Vegetariano (cnr J Pardo & E Palacios; meals around US$1.50; 🕙 8am-10pm) A ramshackle veggie oasis, this veritable hole-in-the-wall has tasty vegetarian options and filling breakfasts.

Restaurant Paola's (☎ 34-5428; Bolognesi 401; sandwiches US$2.40-4.50; 🕙 1-10pm) Try this place for sandwiches, snacks and ice creams.

Restaurant Venecia (☎ 32 5490; Bolognesi 386; mains around US$5.50; 🕙 6am-1am) This is a popular place for chunks of grilled meaty goodies, seafood and breakfasts.

The restaurants at **Hostal Chifa Canton** (☎ 34 4388; F Bolognesi 498; 🕙 8am-10pm) and **Real Hotel Gran Chimú** (☎ 32 3721, 32-8104; Gálvez 109; 🕙 8am-10pm) are both good.

Getting There & Away

For Casma (US$1.50, 45 minutes), whale-sized old American *colectivo* taxis leave when full from in front of the market.

All long-distance buses leave from the Terminal Terrestre, about 5km east of town (a US$1.20 taxi ride). **America Express** (☎ 35 3468) has buses leaving for Trujillo every 15 minutes from 6am to 9pm (US$2.10, two hours). Dozens of companies run overnight buses to

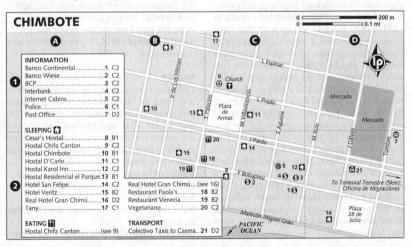

CHIMBOTE

0 ———— 200 m
0 ———— 0.1 mi

L Espinar
L Prado
L Prado
Church
Plaza de Armas
J Pardo
F Bolognesi
Malecón Miguel Grau
PACIFIC OCEAN
Mercado
Mercado
To Terminal Terrestre (5km); Oficina de Migraciónes
Plaza 28 de Julio

NORTH COAST

Lima, leaving between 10pm and midnight; costs range from US$9 to US$24 (six hours). Reputable companies include **Oltursa** (☎ 35 3586), **Linea** (☎ 35 4041), **Civa** (☎ 35 1808) and **Cruz Del Sur** (☎ 35 5665). Linea has extra Lima-bound buses at 10am and 12:30pm, as well as Chiclayo buses at 9am and 3:40pm (US$6, four hours).

Buses to Huaraz and the Cordillera Blanca run either via the dazzling yet rough route through the Cañón del Pato (p402), via an equally rough road that climbs through the mountains from Casma, or via the longer, comfortably paved route through Pativilca. Travel times on these routes range from seven to nine hours. **Transportation Huandoy** (☎ 35 3086) has an 11:30am bus to Caraz (US$7.50, eight hours) through the *cañón* (canyon) and 6am, 10am and 1pm buses to Huaraz (US$6) through Casma. **Yungay Express** (☎ 35 1304, 35 2850) has an 8:30am Caraz bus (US$7, eight hours) through the Cañón del Pato and a 9pm bus to Huaraz (US$7) via Casma. Ritzy **Movil Tours** (☎ 35 3616) has a 10pm bus to Huaraz (US$7.50) via Pativilca that also goes onto Caraz. It pays to book Huaraz buses a day in advance.

TRUJILLO
☎ 044 / pop 768,300

Stand in the right spot and the glamorously colonial streets of old Trujillo look like they've barely changed in hundreds of years. Well, OK, there are more honking taxis now – but the city still manages to put on a dashing show with its flamboyant buildings and profusion of churches. Pizarro founded Trujillo in 1534, and he thought so highly of this patch of desert he named it after his birthplace in Spain's Estremadura. Spoiled by the fruits of the fertile Moche Valley, Trujillo never had to worry about money – wealth came easily. With life's essentials taken care of, thoughts turned to politics and life's grander schemes; the city has a reputation for being a hotbed of revolt. The town was besieged during the Inca rebellion of 1536, and in 1820 was the first Peruvian city to declare independence from Spain. The tradition continued into the 20th century as bohemians flocked, poets put pen to paper (including Peru's best poet, César Vallejo), and rebels raised their fists defiantly in the air. It was here the Alianza Popular Revolution Americana (APRA) workers' party was formed.

The behemoth Chimu capital of Chan Chan is nearby, though little remains of what was once the largest adobe city in the world. Other Chimu sites bake in the surrounding desert, among them the immense and suitably impressive Moche Huacas del Sol y de la Luna (Temples of the Sun and Moon), which date back 1500 years. When you get yourself ancient-cultured out, the village of Huanchaco beckons with a sandy beach, respectable surf and a more contemporary interpretation of sun worship.

Information

EMERGENCY
Policía de Turismo (Tourist Police, Poltur; ☎ 29 1705, 20 4025; Independencia 630)

IMMIGRATION
Oficina de migraciónes (☎ 28 2217; Larco cuadra 12) Does visa extensions.

INTERNET ACCESS
InterWeb (Pizarro 721; per hr US$0.50; ☯ 8:30am-11pm) One of many internet places, this spot offers a decent connection.

LAUNDRY
Most midrange hotels supply laundry services at reasonable rates.
Lavanderías Unidas (☎ 20 0505; Pizarro 683; per kg US$2.40; ☯ 8am-9pm)

MEDICAL SERVICES
Clínica Americano-Peruano (☎ 23 1261; Mansiche 702) The best general medical care in town, with English-speaking doctors. It charges according to your means, so let the clinic know if you don't have medical insurance.
Hospital Regional (☎ 23 1581, Napoles 795) For more rudimentary care.

MONEY
Changing money in Trujillo is a distinct pleasure; some of the banks are housed in well-preserved colonial buildings. All have ATMs that accept Visa and MasterCard. If lines are long, visit the *casas de cambio* (foreign-exchange bureaus) near Gamarra and Bolívar, which give good rates for cash.
Banco Continental (Pizarro 620) Housed in the handsome Casa de la Emancipación. Good rates for cash.
Banco Wiese (Pizarro 314)
BCP (Gamarra 562) Has the lowest commission for changing traveler's checks.
Interbank (Gamarra at Pizarro) Reasonably fast service.

POST
Post office (Independencia 286; 9am-7pm Mon-Fri, 9am-1pm Sat)

TOURIST INFORMATION
Local tour companies can also provide you with some basic information on the area. **iPerú** (29 4561; Pizarro 412, Municipalidad de Trujillo, mezzanine level; 8am-7pm Mon-Sat, 8am-2pm Sun) Provides tourist information and a list of certified guides and travel agencies.

Dangers & Annoyances
Single women tend to receive a lot of attention from males in Trujillo bars – to exasperating, even harassing, levels. If untoward advances are made, firmly state that you aren't interested. Inventing a boyfriend or husband sometimes helps get the message across. See p514 for more advice for women travelers.

Sights
Trujillo's colonial mansions and churches, most of which are near the Plaza de Armas, are worth seeing, though they don't keep very regular opening hours. Hiring a good local guide is recommended if you are seriously interested in history. The churches often are open for early morning and evening masses, but visitors at those times should respect worshippers and not wander around.

The creamy pastel shades and beautiful wrought-iron grillwork fronting almost every colonial building are unique Trujillo touches. Several buildings have changing **art shows** (admission free) at various times and are best visited then.

PLAZA DE ARMAS
Trujillo's spacious and fetching main square hosts an impressive statue dedicated to work, the arts and liberty. The plaza is fronted by the **cathedral**, begun in 1647, destroyed in 1759, and rebuilt soon afterward. The cathedral has a famous basilica and a museum of religious and colonial art.

One elegant colonial mansion now houses the **Hotel Libertador** (Independencia 485). Another, **Casa de Urquiaga** (Pizarro 446; admission free; 9am-3pm Mon-Fri, 10am-1:30pm Sat & Sun), belongs to the Banco Central de la Reserva del Perú.

At 8am on Sunday there is a **flag-raising ceremony** on the Plaza de Armas, complete with a parade. On some Sundays there are also *caballos de paso* (pacing horses) and performances of the *marinera* (a typical coastal Peruvian dance involving much romantic waving of handkerchiefs).

EAST OF PLAZA DE ARMAS
The **Iglesia de la Merced**, built in the 17th century, has a striking organ and cupola. Uniquely, an altar here is painted on the wall, an economical shortcut when funds ran out for a more traditional gold or carved-wood alternative.

Now the Banco Continental building, the **Casa de la Emancipación** (Pizarro 620; 9am-6pm Mon-Fri) is where Trujillo's independence from colonial rule was formally declared on December 29, 1820. Nearby, the canary yellow 19th-century mansion **Palacio Iturregui** (Pizarro 688; 9am-7pm Mon-Sat) is unmistakable and impossible to ignore unless you're color-blind. Built in neoclassical style, it has beautiful window gratings, slender interior columns and gold moldings on the ceilings. General Iturregui lived here after he famously proclaimed independence.

Colonial-art pundits will not want to miss the Carmelite museum in the **Iglesia del Carmen** (cnr Colón & Bolívar; museum admission US$0.90; 9am-1pm Mon-Sat).

The **Museo de Arqueología** (24 9322; Junín 682; adult/student US$1.50/0.80; 9am-3pm Mon, 9am-1pm & 3-7pm Tue-Fri, 9am-4pm Sat & Sun) displays a rundown of Peruvian history from 12,000 BC to the present day. There's also a small but interesting collection of artifacts from the Huaca de la Luna. The museum is housed in La Casa Risco, a restored 17th-century mansion.

Casona Orbegoso (Orbegoso 553; 9am-6pm), named after a former president of Peru, is a beautiful 18th-century manor with a collection of well-worn art and period furnishings. On the opposite side of Bolívar, **Iglesia de San Agustín** has a finely gilded high altar and dates from 1558. Further southwest is **Iglesia de Belén** and north of here is another mansion, **Casa de Mayorazgo de Facala** (Pizarro 314; 9am-6pm Mon-Fri), which houses Banco Weise.

NORTH & WEST OF PLAZA DE ARMAS
Northeast of the cathedral is **Casa Ganoza Chopitea** (Independencia 630), also known as Casa de los Léones, which is considered to be the best mansion of the colonial period in Trujillo. The tourist police are housed here. Good contemporary Peruvian art is sometimes shown here, as are some rather arcane pieces that

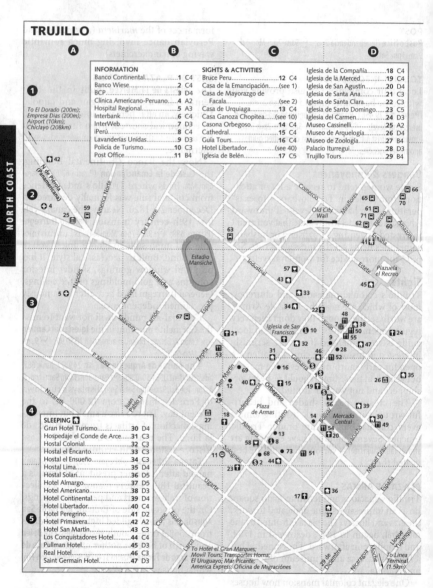

TRUJILLO

INFORMATION
Banco Continental.............................1 C4
Banco Wiese......................................2 C4
BCP..3 D4
Clínica Americano-Peruano............4 A2
Hospital Regional.............................5 A3
Interbank..6 C4
InterWeb...7 D3
iPerú..8 C4
Lavanderías Unidas..........................9 D3
Policía de Turismo..........................10 C3
Post Office.......................................11 B4

SIGHTS & ACTIVITIES
Bruce Peru..12 C4
Casa de la Emancipación...........(see 1)
Casa de Mayorazgo de
  Facala....................................(see 2)
Casa de Urquiaga.............................13 C4
Casa Ganoza Chopitea............(see 10)
Casona Orbegoso.............................14 C4
Cathedral..15 C4
Guía Tours..16 C4
Hotel Libertador.......................(see 40)
Iglesia de Belén...............................17 C5

Iglesia de la Compañía.................18 C4
Iglesia de la Merced......................19 C4
Iglesia de San Agustín..................20 D4
Iglesia de Santa Ana.....................21 C3
Iglesia de Santa Clara...................22 C3
Iglesia de Santo Domingo...........23 C3
Iglesia del Carmen........................24 D3
Museo Cassinelli.............................25 A2
Museo de Arqueología..................26 D4
Museo de Zoología........................27 C3
Palacio Iturregui............................28 D3
Trujillo Tours..................................29 B4

SLEEPING
Gran Hotel Turismo.........................30 D4
Hospedaje el Conde de Arce.........31 C3
Hostal Colonial.................................32 C3
Hostal el Encanto.............................33 C3
Hostal el Ensueño............................34 C3
Hostal Lima......................................35 D4
Hostal Solari.....................................36 D5
Hotel Almargo.................................37 D5
Hotel Americano..............................38 D4
Hotel Continental............................39 D4
Hotel Libertador..............................40 C4
Hotel Peregrino................................41 D2
Hotel Primavera..............................42 A2
Hotel San Martín.............................43 C3
Los Conquistadores Hotel.............44 C4
Pullman Hotel..................................45 D3
Real Hotel...46 C3
Saint Germain Hotel.......................47 D3

To El Dorado (200m);
Empresa Dias (200m);
Airport (10km);
Chiclayo (208km)

To Hotel el Gran Marques;
Movil Tours; Transportes Horna;
El Uruguayo; Mar Picante;
America Express; Oficina de Migraciones

To Hotel el Gran Marques;
To Linea
Terminal
(1.5km)

---

you may never have a chance to see elsewhere. Hours vary. Further north of the mansion is **Iglesia de Santa Clara**.

The **Museo Cassinelli** (N de Piérola 601; admission US$2.10; 9:30am-1pm & 3-6pm Mon-Sat) is a private archaeological collection housed in the basement of a gas station. The museum is fascinating, with hundreds of pieces that certainly

don't belong under a gritty petrol dispensary. Have a look at the bird-shaped whistling pots, which produce clear notes when air is blown into them (ask the curator to show you). Superficially the pots are very similar, but when they are blown each produces a completely different note that corresponds to the calls of the male and female birds.

EATING 🍴
Asturias	48 D3
Chifa Ah Chau	49 D4
Diet Light	50 D3
El Mochica	51 C4
El Sol Restaurante Vegetariano	52 D3
El Valentino	53 B3
Jugería San Augustine	54 D4
Restaurant de Marco	(see 48)
Restaurant Romano	(see 48)
Supermercado Merpisa	55 D3

DRINKING 🍷
Mecano Bar	56 D4
Restaurante Turístico Canana	57 C3
Ributo Bar	58 C4

TRANSPORT
Buses to El Esperanza	59 A2
Cial	60 D2
Civa	61 D2
Combis to Chan Chan, Huanchaco & Huaca Esmeralda	62 D2
Combis to Chan Chan, Huanchaco & Huaca Esmeralda	63 C2
Combis to Las Huacas del Sol y de la Luna	64 E4
Cruz del Sur	65 D2
Flores	66 D2
Ittsa	67 B3
LAN	68 C4
Linea Booking Office	69 C4
Oltursa	70 D2
Ormeño	71 D2
Provincial Bus Terminal Interurbano	72 F5
Star Peru	73 C4

Museo de Zoología (San Martín 368; admission US$0.60; 🕑 7am-7pm Mon-Fri, 8am-1pm Sat), just west of the Plaza de Armas, is mainly a taxidermic collection of Peruvian animals (many so artificially stuffed they look like nightmarish caricatures of their former selves).

There are three other interesting churches near the Plaza de Armas; **Iglesia de la Compañia** (Independencia), **Iglesia de Santa Ana** (cnr Mansiche & Zepita) and **Iglesia de Santo Domingo** (Larco).

Activities
The aid organization **Bruce Peru** (☎ 23 2664; www.volunteertrujillo.com; San Martín 444) helps kids that are unable to attend school. Volunteer opportunities are best arranged beforehand, though short-term, walk-in volunteers are sometimes needed.

Tours & Guides
There are dozens of tour agencies. Some agencies, though, have been criticized for supplying guides who speak English but don't know much about the area, or vice-versa. Friendly and recommended **Trujillo Tours** (☎ 23 3091; Almagro 301) has three- to four-hour tours to Chan Chan and Huanchaco (US$18), and to Huacas del Sol y de la Luna (US$15), as well as city tours (US$14). Entrance fees are included and some English, French and German is spoken. The long-established **Guía Tours** (☎ 24 5170; Independencia 580) organizes similar trips for US$12 to US$22 per person (two-person minimum). Its guides speak some English.

If you prefer your own guide, it's best to go with a certified official guide who knows the area well. Ask at **iPerú** (☎ 29 4561; Pizarro 412, Municipalidad de Trujillo, mezzanine level; 🕑 8am-7pm Mon-Sat, 8am-2pm Sun) for a list of certified guides and contact details.

Festivals & Events
Fiesta de la Marinera Held in the last week in January, this is the national *marinera* contest.
El Festival Internacional de la Primavera (International Spring Festival) Trujillo's major festival is celebrated with parades, national dancing competitions (including, of course, the *marinera*), *caballos de paso* displays, sports, international beauty contests and other cultural activities. It all happens in the last week in September, and better hotels are booked out well in advance.

Sleeping
Decent budget places are a thin on the ground in Trujillo, but pay a little extra and you'll be soaking up colonial ambience. Some travelers prefer to stay in the nearby beach town of Huanchaco.

BUDGET
Hostal Lima (☎ 23 2499; Ayacucho 718; s/d US$3.30/5.50) If you've been on a tour of Alcatraz and thought, 'I could live here,' this is your chance.

The prison-bare, cell-like rooms in this se-cure building are sometimes used by super-shoestringing gringos.

Hotel Americano (☎ 24 1361; Pizarro 764; s/d US$6/9) The absolutely humongous foyer in this rambling, renowned old institution looks like Grand Central Station. Echo, echo, echo. The rooms haven't changed in nearly a century either; they're well-used, creaky and reasonably clean. They do drip with a certain charisma, however, and many have beautifully carved balconies looking down onto the street below.

Hospedaje el Conde de Arce (☎ 29 1607; Independencia 577; s/d US$6/12) With a tiny patio, this is a simple, small, safe and friendly budget lodging right in the center. The rooms are a little weathered, but it's not a bad deal by Trujillo standards.

Hotel Primavera (☎ /fax 23 1915; N de Piérola 872; s/d US$7.50/12; 🖳) You can't miss the pseudo-modern, semicircular blue flourishes lining the side of this '70s relic. It's only slightly shabby, fairly clean and convenient to several northbound bus stations. The invigorating concrete pool may help you overlook the general mustiness.

Hostal el Ensueño (☎ 20 7744; Junín 336; s/d US$9/15) After navigating the narrow and dark hallways here, you will find clean rooms with giant bathrooms. The owners also run Hostal El Encanto (Junín 319), located across the street with cheaper but danker rooms.

Hotel San Martín (☎ /fax 25 2311; San Martín 745; s/d US$12/16.50) Although characterless, this massive hotel (furnished with faux-wood floor tiles for insta-charm) is fair value for rooms with cable TV and phone. It has a restaurant and bar.

Hostal Almagro (☎ 22 3845; Almagro 748; s/d US$13.50/18) No pretensions of a colonial past here, just modern, well-maintained, sparse rooms with TVs and glistening bathrooms. There's a café downstairs.

Hostal Colonial (☎ 25 8261; hostcolonialtruji@hot mail.com; Independencia 618; s/d US$13.50/19.50) Easily a winner in the budget category, this tastefully renovated, rose-colored colonial mansion has a great location just a block from the Plaza de Armas. Chatty and helpful staff, a tour desk, a pleasant courtyard and a garden synergically come together to keep attracting travelers. Cozy rooms have hot showers, and some have balconies and great views of Iglesia de San Francisco opposite.

Gran Hotel Turismo (☎ 24 4181; Gamarra 747; s/d US$14.50/21.50; 🔀) Live out your swinging Austin Powers fantasies at this hotel, which has its original hip décor, hallways the length of football fields and spotless, cozy rooms. Everything here is decked out in the 'latest' '60s trends. Groovy.

MIDRANGE

Most of these hotels can be noisy if you get the streetside rooms. All hotels here have hot showers and many offer discounts to walk-in guests.

Hotel Continental (☎ 31 0046; www.hotelconti nentaltrujillo.com; Gamarra 663; s/d US$18/27) High on professionalism, low on inspirational décor, this place has shipshape rooms, some of which look onto a concrete garden light well. There's a restaurant downstairs.

Hostal Solari (☎ 24 3909; www.hostalsolari.com.pe; Almagro 715; s/d incl breakfast US$21/33) A contemporary spot, this place has massive, sensibly decorated 'executive' rooms, which feature polished floorboards, a separate sitting area, excellent mattresses, cable TV, minifridge and phone. A café provides room service, and the helpful front-desk staff will arrange tours, confirm airline tickets and try to do whatever you need.

Hotel Peregrino (☎ 20 3990; www.peregrinohotel .com; Independencia 978; s/d incl breakfast US$24/30; 🖳) No backyard? Plant an indoor garden! The green atrium downstairs is lovely, and the rest of the hotel is clean, pleasant and quiet. Carpeted, comfortably furnished rooms have minibar, cable TV, phone and writing desk. Suites have Jacuzzis and a sitting area. Midnight munchies can be quelled by room service and the front desk strives to please.

Pullman Hotel (formerly Hotel la Alameda del Peregrino; ☎ 47 1645, 47 0517; www.pullmanhotel.com; Pizarro 879; s/d US$24/30; 🖳) The swanky lobby here faces a pedestrian street near the Plazuela el Recreo and therefore doesn't suffer from street noise. Neat and spotless, the parquet-floored rooms boast a minibar, cable TV and phone with internet connection. The fake antique chairs look a little out of place.

Real Hotel (☎ /fax 25 7416; crealh@viabcp.com; Pizarro 651; s/d incl breakfast US$24/36; 🔀) In the middle of Trujillo's busy shopping district, Real Hotel is crisp, bright and splashy. It has good, airy rooms with all the conveniences, but it sits over a casino and disco so it can get noisy at night.

Saint Germain Hotel (☎ 25 0574; www.perunorte .com/saintgermain; Junín 585; s/d US$24/42) The boutiquey Saint Germain has great rooms to get comfortable in and the usual slew of modern conveniences, as well as immaculate bathrooms. The rooms facing inward are silent and have windows onto a bright light well. There's a bar and café here.

Los Conquistadores Hotel (☎ 24 4505; www.loscon quistadoreshotel.com; Almagro 586; s/d US$48/60, ste from US$103, all incl breakfast; ⌘ 💻) Courteous doormen will eagerly greet you at the entrance of this contemporary venture, a few steps away from the Plaza de Armas. The relaxing rooms here are carpeted, and come with cable TV, phone, minibar and 24-hour room service. Suites have Jacuzzis. The swanky downstairs restaurant and bar is a good place to unwind over a pisco sour. Rates include airport transfers, wall-to-wall wi-fi, a travel service and the use of exercise rooms.

TOP END

Hotel el Gran Marques (☎ 24 9161, 24 9366; Diaz de Cienfuegos 145; s/d US$59/70, ste from US$106; ⌘ 💻) A couple of kilometers southwest of the city center, this hotel offers a sauna, gym, restaurant and bar. Unfortunately, it has to be content playing second fiddle in the top-end stakes to Hotel Libertador.

Hotel Libertador (☎ 23 2741; www.libertador.com.pe; Independencia 485; d US$88, ste US$135-180, both incl breakfast; 💻) The classy dame of the city's hotels, the Libertador is in a beautiful building that's the Audrey Hepburn of Trujillo – it wears its age with refined grace. It earns its four stars with a sauna, good restaurant, amiable bar, 24-hour coffee shop and comfortable rooms with the all the conveniences you might expect. Try to avoid the streetside rooms unless you want to watch the goings-on, as they are apt to be noisy.

Eating

The 700 block of Pizarro is where the cool cats hang out, and they're kept well-fed by a row of trendy yet reasonably priced cafés and restaurants. Some of the best eateries in Trujillo are found a short taxi ride outside of the town center.

Jugería San Augustíne (Bolivar 526; juice US$0.50; ⌚ 8am-10pm) You can spot this place by the near-constant lines snaking around the corner in summer as locals queue for the drool-inducing juices.

Diet Light (Pizarro 724; snacks US$0.80-2.50; ⌚ 9:30am-10pm) This perennially busy place serves not-very-diet, but yummy nonetheless, ice creams (US$1.50) and whopping servings of mixed fruit (US$0.80) – with ice cream.

El Sol Restaurante Vegetariano (Pizarro 660; meals US$0.90-2.40; ⌚ 8am-10pm) A limited menu attests to experience; the cooks have been here a long time and know what you want. A few nonvegetarian items occasionally sneak onto the menu.

Asturias (Pizarro 741; breakfast & sandwiches US$1.50-3, mains US$3.60-7; ⌚ 7:30am-midnight) Tidy and cozy, this café serves up a little bit of everything. There's a long menu of Peruvian and international plates and the smartly dressed elderly waiters will make sure you're well looked after.

Restaurant Romano (☎ 25 2251; Pizarro 747; mains US$1.80-4.50; ⌚ 7am-midnight) This place has been around since 1951, so you know these guys have been doing something right. Whipping up a decent espresso, as well as breakfast, snacks and meals all day, the Romano is one of the most popular eateries in town. Expect meaty and meatless sandwiches, desserts, and a mainly Peruvian menu.

Restaurant de Marco (☎ 23 4251; Pizarro 725; breakfast US$2.10-3, mains US$10-13; ⌚ 7:30am-11pm) This small bistro specializes in Italian food – if you read Italian, so much the better for deciphering the extensive menu. It has enjoyable desserts and ice cream, as well as good coffees.

Mar Picante (☎ 22 1544; America Sur 2199; meals US $2.10-4.50; ⌚ 11am-10pm). This large, bamboo-lined seafood palace specializes in some of Trujillo's best and freshest ceviche (raw seafood marinated in lime juice) and is packed daily with hundreds of savvy locals. Try the heaped *ceviche mixto*, which has various kinds of fish and crustaceans (US$2.70). The restaurant is a US$0.80 taxi ride south of town.

El Mochica (☎ 29 3441; Bolívar 462; mains US$3-9; ⌚ noon-10pm) Industrially hygienic and scattered with bits of art to take the edge off, this place has a variety of midpriced steaks and seafood, as well as cheaper local dishes. They have a snug *salón de té* (tea room) next door.

El Valentino (☎ 24 6643, 29 5339; Orbegoso 224; mains US$4.50-9; ⌚ 5pm-1am) This popular place is currently the best Italian restaurant in town. Pasta and meat dishes are on the menu.

El Uruguayo (☎ 28 3369; America Sur 2219; meals US$4.50-7.50; ⌚ 6:30pm-1am) Vegetarians might want to take a wide berth around this place. Located a US$0.80 taxi ride south of town, little El Uruguayo serves up delicious BBQ meat to a nightly crowd of salivating in-the-know patrons. A massive sizzling plate of mixed meats (Argentinean steak, chicken, chorizo, beef heart plus a few surprises), salad and fries – enough for two to three people – will set you back US$10. Dig in.

Chifa Ah Chau (☎ 24 3351; Gamarra 769; mains around US$5; ☒ 6pm-10pm). This is a funky, faded but fun place with individual private curtained booths and genuine Chinese food. Portions are elephantine – order to share.

Supermercado Merpisa (Pizarro 700; ☒ 9:15am-1:15pm & 4:30-9pm) Good for self-catering.

Drinking & Entertainment

Trujillo's local newspaper *La Industria* is the best source for information about local entertainment, cultural exhibitions and other events.

Mecano Bar (☎ 20 1652; www.mecanobarperu.com; Gamarra 574; admission US$6; ☒ 9pm-late) This is the current top spot to see and be seen in Trujillo. Sway your hips to salsa, reggae and techno alongside a mix of well-to-do Peruvians and expats. It's very busy on weekends.

Restaurante Turístico Canana (☎ 23 2503, 23 1482; San Martín 791; admission US$3; ☒ 5pm-late) Although this place is open every night and serves good Peruvian coastal food (mains US$4.50 to US$11), late Thursday to Saturday is the time to go. Local musicians and dancers perform, starting at around 11pm, and the audience joins in – or watches, if they are chowing down *chicharrones* (pork cracklings).

Ributo Bar (☎ 29 4546; cnr Pizarro & Almagro; ☒ 9pm-late) This pleasant bar on the corner of the plaza is great for a quiet tipple and a chat with your friends. It attracts a younger, livelier crowd on weekends, when there is live music or hot DJs.

Getting There & Away

AIR

The **airport** (code TRU; ☎ 46 4013) is 10km northwest of town. There's the usual US$3.57 departure tax.

LAN (☎ 22 1469; Pizarro 340) has a daily 5pm flight from Trujillo to Lima for US$110, returning at 6:35pm. The newcomer **Star Perú** (☎ 41 0009; Almagro 545) has two daily flights to Lima (US$96), one at 8:10am via Chiclayo (US$49), and one direct flight at 7:10pm.

BUS

Buses often leave Trujillo full, so booking a little earlier is advised. Several companies that go to southern destinations have terminals on the Panamericana Sur, the southern extension of Moche; check where your bus actually leaves from when buying a ticket.

Linea (booking office ☎ 24 5181; cnr San Martin & Orbegoso; ☒ 8am-8pm Mon-Fri; bus terminal ☎ 24 3271; Panamericana Sur 2857) has services to most destinations of interest to travelers and is one of the more comfortable bus lines. The company's booking office is conveniently located in the historical center, although all buses leave from the terminal on Panamericana Sur, a US$0.80 taxi ride away. Linea goes to Lima (US$9 to US$21, eight hours) 10 times daily, with most departures going overnight; to Piura (US$9, six hours) at 11pm; to Otuzco (US$1.50, two hours) five times a day, to Cajamarca (US$4.50 to US$10.50, six hours) at 10:30am, 1:30pm, 10pm and 10:30pm; to Chiclayo (US$3.60, three hours) hourly from 6am to 6pm, stopping at Pacasmayo (US$1.80, 1¾ hours) and Guadalupe (US$2.40, two hours); to Chimbote (US$1.80, two hours) eight times a day; and to Huaraz (US$12, nine hours) at 9pm.

There's an enclave of bus companies around España and Amazonas offering Lima-bound night buses (eight hours). **Cruz del Sur** (☎ 26 1801; Amazonas 237), one of the biggest and priciest bus companies in Peru, goes to Lima five times a day for US$10.50 to US$31.50. **Ormeño** (☎ 25 9782; Ejército 233) has three night buses to Lima for between US$10.50 and US$21, leaving between 9pm and 10pm, as well as two night buses to Tumbes (US$15 to US$21, 10 hours), near the Ecuador border. **Cial** (☎ 20 1760; Amazonas 395), **Flores** (☎ 20 8250; Ejército 350), **Oltursa** (☎ 26 3055; Ejército 342) and **Civa** (☎ 25 1402; Ejército 285) all have at least one night bus to Lima leaving between 9:30pm and 10:30pm, with prices averaging between US$16.50 and US$21.

For Chimbote, **America Express** (☎ 26 1906; La Marina 315) is a US$0.90 taxi ride south of town and has buses every 15 minutes between 5am and 9pm (US$2.10, two hours).

If you're heading north, **El Dorado** (☎ 29 1778; N de Piérola 1070) has rudimentary buses to Piura and Sullana (US$6 to US$7, six hours) at 12:45pm and 10:20pm, as well as buses to Tumbes (US$7.50 to US$9, 10 hours) at 7pm, 8pm and 8:30pm. **Empresa Días** (☎ 20

1237; N de Piérola 1079), opposite El Dorado, has an 11:30am bus to Cajamarca (US$4.50, six hours). **Ittsa** (☎ 25 1415; Mansiche 145) has buses for Piura (US$3.30 to US$9, six hours) leaving at 1:30pm, 11:30pm and 11:45pm, as well as Lima buses (US$16.50 to US$21) at 1pm, 10pm and 10:30pm. **Transportes Horna** (☎ 25 7605; America Sur 1368) has an 8:30am and 10:30am bus to Huamachuco (US$4.50, seven hours) and several morning buses to Cajamarca (US$4.50, six hours).

Movil Tours (☎ 28 6538; Panamericana Sur 3959) specializes in very comfortable long-haul tourist services. It has a 10pm service to Lima (US$19.50, eight hours), a 9pm overnight bus to Huaraz (US$13.50, eight hours), a 4pm bus to Chachapoyas (US$15, 13 hours) and a 2:30pm bus to Tarapoto (US$22.50, 18 hours). If you want to travel to Huaraz by day, you'll need to go to Chimbote and catch a bus from there. For more frequent buses to Cajamarca and the northern highlands, head to Chiclayo.

White-yellow-and-orange B *combis* to Huaca Esmeralda, Chan Chan and Huanchaco pass the corners of España and Ejército, and España and Industrial every few minutes. Buses for La Esperanza go northwest along the Panamericana and can drop you off at La Huaca Arco Iris. *Combis* leave every half hour from Suarez for the Huacas del Sol y de la Luna. Fares range from US$0.30 to US$0.50 on these routes. Note that these buses are worked by professional thieves; keep valuables hidden and watch your bags carefully.

A taxi to most of these sites will cost US$3 to US$4.50.

El Complejo Arqueológico la Huaca el Brujo, about 60km northwest of Trujillo, is harder to reach. Start at the Provincial Bus Terminal Interurbano off Atahualpa, and head to Chocope (US$0.60, 1½ hours). Ask there for *combis* going toward the site (US$0.50).

Getting Around

The **airport** (☎ 46 4013), 10km northwest of Trujillo, is reached cheaply on the Huanchaco *combi* (minibus), though you'll have to walk the last kilometer. It will cost US$0.60 and take around 30 minutes. A taxi from the city center costs US$3 to US$4.50.

A short taxi ride around town costs about US$0.50. For sightseeing, taxis charge about US$7.50 to US$9 per hour, depending on distance.

AROUND TRUJILLO

The Moche and Chimu cultures left the greatest marks on the Trujillo area, but they were by no means the only cultures in the region. In a March 1973 *National Geographic* article, Drs ME Moseley and CJ Mackey claimed knowledge of over 2000 sites in the Río Moche valley, and many more have been discovered since then.

Five major archaeological sites can be easily reached from Trujillo by local bus or taxi. Two of these are principally Moche, dating from about 200 BC to AD 850. The other three, from the Chimu culture, date from

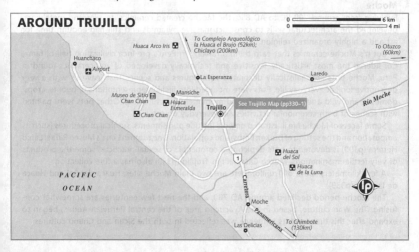

AROUND TRUJILLO

0   6 km
0   4 mi

Huaca Arco Iris

To Complejo Arqueológico la Huaca el Brujo (52km); Chiclayo (200km)

To Otuzco (60km)

Huanchaco

Airport

La Esperanza

Laredo

Museo de Sitio Chan Chan

Mansiche

Huaca Esmeralda

Trujillo

See Trujillo Map (pp330–1)

Río Moche

Chan Chan

Huaca del Sol

Huaca de la Luna

PACIFIC OCEAN

Carretera

Moche

Panamericana

Las Delicias

To Chimbote (130km)

about AD 850 to 1500. The recently excavated Moche ruin of La Huaca el Brujo (60km from Trujillo) can also be visited, but it's not as convenient.

Joining a tour to the archaeological sites isn't a bad idea, even for budget travelers. The ruins will be more interesting and meaningful with a good guide. Alternatively, you could hire an on-site guide.

The entrance ticket for Chan Chan is also valid for the Chimu sites of La Huaca Esmeralda and La Huaca Arco Iris, as well as the Chan Chan museum, but it must be used within two days. All sites are open from 9am to 4:30pm and tickets are sold at every site, except La Huaca Esmeralda.

Chan Chan

Built around AD 1300 and covering 28 sq km, **Chan Chan** (adult/student US$3.30/1.70; ☯ 9am-4:30pm) is the largest pre-Columbian city in the Americas, and the largest adobe city in the world. At the height of the Chimu empire, it housed an estimated 60,000 inhabitants and contained a vast wealth of gold, silver and ceramics. The wealth remained more or less undisturbed after the city was conquered by the Incas, but once the Spaniards hit the stage

PRE-COLUMBIAN PEOPLES OF THE NORTH COAST

Northern Peru has played host to a series of civilizations stretching back as far as 5000 years ago. Listed below are the major cultures that waxed and waned in Peru's coastal desert areas over the millennia.

Huaca Prieta

One of first peoples on the desert scene, the Huaca Prieta lived at the site of the same name (p340) from around 3500 BC to 2300 BC. These hunters and gatherers grew cotton and varieties of beans and peppers, and subsisted mainly on seafood. They were a Stone Age people who didn't use jewelry, but had developed netting and weaving. At their most artistic, they decorated dried gourds with simple carvings. Homes were single-room shacks half buried in the ground, and most of what is known about these people has been deduced from their middens.

Chavín

Based around Huaraz in Peru's central Andes, the Chavín also had a significant cultural and artistic influence on coastal Peru, particularly between the years 800 BC and 400 BC. For more information on the Chavín culture, see p415.

Moche

Evolving from around 200 BC to AD 850, the Moche created ceramics, textiles and metalwork, developed the architectural skills to construct massive pyramids and still had enough time for art and a highly organized religion.

But it's Moche ceramics that earn them a ranking in Peru's pre-Inca civilization hall of fame. Considered the most artistically sensitive and technically developed of any ceramics found in Peru, Moche pots are realistically decorated with figures and scenes that leave us with a very descriptive look at everyday life. Pots were modeled into lifelike representations of people, crops, domestic and wild animals, marine life and monumental architecture. Other pots were painted with scenes of both ceremonial activities and everyday objects.

Some facets of Moche life illustrated on pots include punishments, surgical procedures (such as amputation and the setting of broken limbs) and copulation. One room in Lima's Museo Rafael Larco Herrera (p100) is devoted to pots depicting a cornucopia of sexual practices, some the products of very fertile imaginations. Museo Cassinelli in Trujillo (p330) also has a fine collection.

A few kilometers south of Trujillo, there are two main Moche sites: Huaca del Sol and Huaca de la Luna (p339).

The Moche period declined around AD 700, and the next few centuries are somewhat confusing. The Wari culture, based in the Ayacucho area of the central Peruvian Andes, began to expand after this time, and its influence was reflected in both the Sicán and Chimu cultures.

the looting began. Within a few decades little but gold dust remained. Remnants of what was found can be seen in museums. Although Chan Chan must have been a dazzling sight at one time, devastating El Niño floods and heavy rainfall have severely eroded the mud walls of the city. Today the most impressive aspect of the site is its sheer size; you'll need an active imagination to fill in the details.

The Chimu capital consisted of nine major subcities, also called royal compounds. Each contained a royal burial mound filled with vast quantities of funerary offerings, including dozens of sacrificed young women and chambers full of ceramics, weavings and jewelry. The Tschudi complex, named after a Swiss naturalist, is the only section of Chan Chan that's partially restored. It is possible that other areas will open in the future, but until they are properly policed and signed, you run the risk of being mugged if you visit them.

At the Tschudi complex you'll find an entrance area with tickets, snacks, souvenirs, bathrooms, a small unsigned **site museum** (admission free with Chan Chan ticket) and guides (US$6). The complex is well marked by fish-shaped pointers, so you can see everything without a guide if you prefer. Your entry ticket for Chan

NORTH COAST

Sicán

The Sicán were probably descendants of the Moche and flourished in the same region from about AD 750 to 1375. Avid agriculturalists, the Sicán were also infatuated with metallurgy and all that glitters. The Sicán are known to many archaeologists for their lost-wax (mold-cast) gold ornaments and the manufacture of arsenical copper, which is the closest material to bronze found in prehistoric New World archaeology. These great smiths produced alloys of gold, silver and arsenic copper in vast quantities, using little more than hearths fired by *algarrobo* (carob tree) wood and pipe-blown air to achieve the incredible 1000°C temperatures needed for such work.

Artifacts found at Sicán archaeological sites suggested that this culture loved to shop, or at least trade. They were actively engaged in long-distance trade with peoples along the length and breadth of the continent, acquiring shells and snails from Ecuador, emeralds and diamonds from Colombia, bluestone from Chile, and gold from the Peruvian highlands.

With a structured and religiously controlled social organization, the Sicán engaged in bizarre and elaborate funerary practices, examples of which can be seen at the Museo Nacional Sicán in Ferreñafe (p352).

Unfortunately, as was the case with many pre-Inca societies, the weather was the ultimate undoing of the Sicán. Originally building their main city at Batán Grande (p352), northeast of Trujillo, they were forced to move to Túcume (p352) when El Niño rains devastated that area in the 13th century.

Chimu

The Chimu were contemporaries of the Sicán and lasted from about AD 850 to 1470. They were responsible for the huge capital at Chan Chan (opposite), just north of Trujillo. The artwork of the Chimu was less exciting than that of the Moche, tending more to functional mass production than artistic achievement. Gone, for the most part, was the technique of painting pots. Instead, they were fired by a simpler method than that used by the Moche, producing the typical blackware seen in many Chimu pottery collections. While the quality of the ceramics declined, skills in metallurgy developed, with gold and various alloys being worked.

The Chimu are best remembered as an urban society. Their huge capital contained about 10,000 dwellings of varying quality and importance. Buildings were decorated with friezes, the designs molded into mud walls, and important areas were layered with precious metals. There were storage bins for food and other products from across the empire, which stretched along the coast from Chancay to the Gulf of Guayaquil (southern Ecuador). There were huge walk-in wells, canals, workshops and temples. The royal dead were buried in mounds with a wealth of offerings.

The Chimu were conquered by the Incas in 1471 and heavy rainfall has severely damaged the adobe moldings of this once vast metropolis.

Chan is also valid for the Chimu sites of La Huaca Esmeralda and La Huaca Arco Iris.

Combis to Chan Chan leave Trujillo every few minutes, passing the corners of España and Ejército, and España and Industrial.

TSCHUDI COMPLEX

Inside a 4m-thick defensive wall lies the massive restored **Ceremonial Courtyard**, whose interior walls are mostly decorated with recreated geometric designs. The ground-level designs closest to the door, representing three or four sea otters, are the only originals left and are slightly rougher looking than the modern work. A ramp at the far side of the high-walled plaza enters the second level (early wheelchair access?). Though all the Chan Chan walls have crumbled with time, parts of Tschudi's walls once stood over 10m high.

Head out of the Ceremonial Courtyard and walk along the **outside wall**, one of the most highly decorated and best restored of Tschudi's walls. The adobe friezes show waves of fish rippling along the entire length of the wall above a line of seabirds. Despite their time-worn appearance, the few rougher-looking originals retain a fluidity and character somehow lacking in the contemporary version.

At the end of this wall, the marked path goes through the labyrinthine **Audience Rooms**. Their function is unclear, but their importance is evident in both the quantity and quality of the decorations – the rooms have the most interesting friezes in Tschudi. Living so close to the ocean, the Chimu based much of their diet on seafood, and the importance of the sea reached venerable proportions. Fish, waves, seabirds and sea mammals are represented throughout the city, and in the Audience Rooms you'll find all of them in the one place. For the Chimu, both the moon and the sea were of religious importance (unlike the Incas, who worshipped the sun and venerated the earth).

Further on, the **Second Ceremonial Courtyard** also has a ramp to the second level. From behind this plaza, you can see a huge rectangular depression that was once a **walk-in well** supplying the daily water needs of the royal compound.

To the left is an area of several dozen small, crumbling cells that has been called the **Military Sector**. Perhaps soldiers lived here, or the cells may have been used for storage. Next is the **Mausoleum**, where a king was buried along

with human sacrifices and ceremonial objects. To the left of the main tomb, a pyramid containing the bodies of dozens of young women was found.

The final area is the **Assembly Room**. This large rectangular room has 24 seats set into niches in the walls, and its amazing acoustic properties are such that speakers sitting in any one of the niches can be clearly heard all over the room.

MUSEO DE SITIO CHAN CHAN

The site museum contains exhibits explaining Chan Chan and the Chimu culture. It is on the main road, about 500m before the Chan Chan turnoff. The museum has a few signs in Spanish but none in English so a guide is useful. A sound-and-light show plays in Spanish every 30 minutes. The aerial photos and maps showing the huge extension of Chan Chan are fascinating, as tourists can only visit a tiny portion of the site.

Huaca Esmeralda

Halfway between Trujillo and Chan Chan, this Chimu **temple** (admission free with Chan Chan ticket) is to the south of the main road, four blocks behind the Mansiche Church. Thieves reportedly prey on unwary tourists wandering around, so go with a large group or a guide, and keep your eyes open.

Huaca Esmeralda was buried by sand and was accidentally discovered by a local landowner in 1923. He attempted to uncover the ruins, but El Niño of 1925 began the process of erosion, which was exacerbated by the floods and rains of 1983. Although little restoration work has been done on the adobe friezes, it is still possible to make out the characteristic Chimu designs of fish, seabirds, waves and fishing nets.

White-yellow-and-orange B *combis* to Huaca Esmeralda leave Trujillo every few minutes; they pass the corners of España and Ejército, and España and Industrial.

Huaca Arco Iris

Also known locally as Huaca del Dragón, **Huaca Arco Iris** (Rainbow Temple; admission free with Chan Chan ticket) is in the suburb of La Esperanza, about 4km northwest of Trujillo.

Huaca Arco Iris is one of the best preserved of the Chimu temples simply because it was covered by sand until the 1960s. Its location was known to a handful of archaeologists and *huaqueros* (grave robbers), but excavation did not begin until 1963. Unfortunately, the 1983 El Niño caused damage to the friezes.

The *huaca* used to be painted, but these days only faint traces of yellow hues remain. It consists of a defensive wall over 2m thick enclosing an area of about 3000 sq meters, which houses the temple itself. The building covers about 800 sq meters in two levels, with a combined height of about 7.5m. The walls are slightly pyramidal and covered with repeated rainbow designs, most of which have been restored. Ramps lead the visitor to the very top of the temple, from where a series of large bins, found to contain the bones of infants – possibly human sacrifices – can be seen. This may have been a fertility temple since in many ancient cultures the rainbow represents rain, considered to be the bringer of life.

There is a tiny on-site **museum**, and local guides are available to show you around.

Buses for La Esperanza go northwest along the Panamericana and can drop you off at La Huaca Arco Iris.

Huacas del Sol y de la Luna

The **Temples of the Sun and the Moon** (adult/student US$3.30/1.70; 9am-4pm) are over 700 years older than Chan Chan and are attributed to the Moche period. They are on the south bank of the Río Moche, about 10km southeast of Trujillo by a rough road. The entrance price includes a guide.

The Huaca del Sol is the largest single pre-Columbian structure in Peru, although about a third of it has been washed away. The structure was built with an estimated 140 million adobe bricks, many of them marked with symbols representing the workers who made them.

At one time the pyramid consisted of several different levels connected by steep flights of stairs, huge ramps and walls sloping at 77 degrees. Around 1500 years have wrought their inevitable damage, and today the pyramid looks like a giant pile of crude bricks partially covered with sand. The few graves within the structure suggest it may have been a huge ceremonial site. Certainly, its size alone makes the pyramid an awesome sight, and the views from the top are excellent.

But size isn't everything. The smaller but more interesting Huaca de la Luna is about 500m away across the open desert. This structure is riddled with rooms that contain ceramics, precious metals and some of the beautiful polychrome friezes for which the Moche were famous. The *huaca* was built over six centuries to AD 600, with six succeeding generations expanding on it and completely covering the previous structure. Archaeologists are currently onion skinning selected parts of the *huaca*, and have discovered that there are friezes of stylized figures on every level, some of which have been perfectly preserved by the later levels built around them. It's well worth a visit; you'll see newly excavated friezes every year. Reproductions of some of the murals are displayed in the Museo de Arqueología in Trujillo (p329).

As you leave, check out the souvenir stands, some of which sell pots made using the original molds found at the site. Also look around for one of the unique Peruvian hairless dogs that hang out here; their body temperature is higher than the normal dog, and they have traditionally been used as body warmers for people with arthritis.

Combis leave for the Huacas del Sol y de la Luna every half hour from Suarez in Trujillo. It's also possible to take a taxi.

EL NIÑO

The weather phenomenon known as El Niño (the Baby) has played a ferocious role in the history of coastal Peru. El Niño is a major fluctuation in the surface temperature of the eastern Pacific Ocean that occurs roughly every two to seven years. The phenomenon was called El Niño since it appears on the South American coast around Christmastime.

Lasting for up to two years, El Niño wreaks havoc with heavy, unremitting rains and floods along Peru's coast. It played a significant role in the collapse of both the Sicán and Moche civilizations.

El Niño still manages to mess things up today; as recently as 1998, months of rain deluged northern Peru, washing away much of the infrastructure of that region (including roads, bridges and entire towns) and destroying nearly all of the coast's crops.

NORTH COAST

Complejo Arqueológico la Huaca el Brujo

This **archaeological complex** (admission negotiable; ☿ 9am-5pm) consists of the Huaca Prieta site, the recently excavated Moche site of Huaca Cao Viejo with its brilliant mural reliefs, and Huaca el Brujo, which has yet to be excavated. The complex is 60km from Trujillo on the coast and is hard to find without a guide. It's technically not open to the public as there is little to see of the excavations so far, but tour agencies in Trujillo can arrange a visit to the area on request.

To get to the complex, take a bus from the Provincial Bus Terminal Interurbano in Trujillo to Chocope (US$0.60, 1½ hours), then jump on a *combi* going toward the site (US$0.50).

HUACA CAO VIEJO

The main section of Huaca Cao Viejo is a 27m truncated pyramid with some of the best friezes in the area. They show multicolored reliefs with stylized life-sized warriors, prisoners, priests and human sacrifices. There are also many burial sites from the Lambayeque culture, which followed the Moche. Many other ruins, few of which have been properly studied, are in the area.

HUACA PRIETA

Huaca Prieta, on the other hand, has been one of the most intensively studied early Peruvian sites. However, for nonarchaeologists, it's generally more interesting to read about than to tour. Although it's simply a prehistoric pile of refuse, it does afford extensive vistas over the coastal area and can be visited along with the other *huacas* in the archaeological complex.

HUANCHACO

☎ 044 / pop 18,000

This once tranquil fishing hamlet, 12km outside of Trujillo, woke up one morning to find itself a brightly highlighted paragraph on Peru's Gringo Trail. Managing to retain much of its villagey appeal, Huanchaco has cottoned onto its own popularity and today is happy to dish up a long menu of sleeping and dining options to tourists. Come summertime, legions of local and foreign tourists descend on its lapping shores, and this fast-growing resort town makes a great alternative base for exploring the ruins surrounding Trujillo.

Orientation & Information

Victor Larco is the main drag running the length of the bay and there's a small pier in the middle of Huanchaco, often filled with hobbyist fishermen. There's a US$0.20 entry charged to the pier on the weekends. House numbering can be a bit confusing as the local council changed all the house numbers in 2003, and many places still use the old ones.

See www.huanchaco.com for lots of useful tourist information. There's a Banco Continental ATM next to the *municipalidad* (town hall) accepting Visa cards. Next door is **Internet K.M.E.K** (La Riviera 269A; per hr US$0.30; ☿ 8am-11pm), which moonlights as a Western Union office and can change US dollars. There's a small **post office** (Manco Capac 220; ☿ 9am-7pm Mon-Fri, 9am-1pm Sat) a block back from the pier.

Dangers & Annoyances

Be careful walking the streets late at night as robberies are not uncommon.

Sights & Activities

Things change slowly here. So slowly that local fishermen are still using the very same narrow reed boats depicted on 2000-year-old Moche pottery. The fishermen paddle and surf these neatly crafted boats like seafaring cowboys, with their legs dangling on either side – which explains the nickname given to these elegantly curving steeds, *caballitos de tortora* (little horses). The inhabitants of Huanchaco are among the few remaining people on the coast who remember how to construct and use the boats, each one only lasting a few months before becoming waterlogged. You'll see rows of these iconic craft extending their long fingers to the sun as they dry along the beach of Huanchaco. At the northern end you can see the reeds that are gown to manufacture the boats. To try surfing the 2000-year-old way, ask the fishermen on the beach to show you how to use their *caballitos*. Just US$1.50 will get you paddled out and surfed back in Huanchaco style. If that whets your appetite, you can ask one of the locals to take you out fishing with them for a few hours; the price is highly negotiable.

The curving, grey-sand beach here is fine for swimming from the December to April summer, but expect serious teeth chatter during the rest of the year. The good surf here, perfect for beginners, draws its fair share of followers and you'll see armies of bleached-blond surfer types ambling the streets with boards in hand. You can rent surfing gear (US$6 to US$9 per day for a wetsuit and surfboard) from several places along the main drag, including **Wave** (☎ 58 7005; Victor Larco 525). For surfing lessons, visit **Un Lugar** (☎ 957 7170; www.otracosa.info; cnr Bolognesi & Atahualpa), two blocks back from the main beach road. This place is run by the superfriendly and highly skilled Juan-Carlo and provides private two-hour lessons for US$12. It also rents boards and suits, organizes surfing safaris to Puerto Chicama and, best of all, runs a volunteer program helping local street children. Travelers are welcome to volunteer.

Otra Cosa (☎ 46 1346; www.otracosa.info; Victor Larco 921; ⏰ 9am-8pm Wed-Sun), a Middle Eastern restaurant, also organizes several volunteer projects in the area; see its website for more information.

The church above town, **Santuario de la Virgen del Socorro** (⏰ dawn-dusk), is worth a visit. Built between 1535 and 1540, it is said to be the second-oldest church in Peru. There are sweeping views from the restored belfry.

Festivals & Events

Carnaval Held in February/March, Carnaval is a big event in Huanchaco.

Festival del Mar Held every other year (even years) during the first week in May, this festival re-enacts the legendary arrival of Takaynamo, founder of Chan Chan. Expect surfing and dance competitions, cultural conferences, food, music and much merrymaking.

Sleeping

BUDGET

You can find Naylamp, Huanchaco's Garden and Las Brisas Hostal in the northern part of Huanchaco, while at the southern end of town there are a few guesthouses in the small streets running perpendicular to the beach.

Naylamp (☎ 46 1022; www.geocities.com/hostal naylamp; Victor Larco 1420; campsite/dm US$2.40/3.60, s US$7.50-9, d US$10.50-13.50) Top of the pops in the budget stakes, Naylamp has one building on the waterfront and a second, larger building on a hill overlooking the bay a few blocks back. Great budget rooms share a spacious sea-view patio, and the lush camping area has perfect sunset views and hammocks for everyone! Kitchen and laundry facilities, hot showers and a café are all thrown in.

Hospedaje los Ficus de Huanchaco (☎ 46 1719; www.huanchaco.net/losficus; Los Ficus 516; r with shared bath-room per person US$4.50) This spotless family house provides guests with hot showers, breakfast on request and kitchen privileges. Many rooms have tons of space and are neat and bright, though they all differ so check out a few before you decide.

La Casa Suiza (☎ 46 1825; www.casasuiza.com; Los Pinos 451/310; r per person US$4.50; 🖳) This tired backpacker favorite is very late for a date with the paintbrush, with the once colorful rooms slowly falling into patchy disrepair. Still, it's a very popular place with the surfing set and its rooftop hangout is often rowdy till the wee hours.

Hostal Solange (☎ 46 1410; hsolange@yahoo.ed; Los Ficus 484; d US$9) Often full, this quiet, simple place is run by a slightly deaf older lady – so practice enunciating your Spanish loudly.

Huanchaco's Garden (☎ 46 1194; huanchacosgarden@ yahoo.es; Av Circumvallatioń 440; d US$12; 🖳) Back from the beach, the clinically clean rooms here are in low white adobe buildings surrounding the promised shady garden. There are a couple of small swimming pools and lots of grass in the walled-in compound, and the friendly family that runs the place will try their best to make your stay enjoyable.

Las Brisas Hostal (☎ 46 1186; Raymondi 146; d US$12) A white multistory monolith that seems to have gotten lost on it's way to the Greek isles, this *hostal* (guesthouse) has decent rooms, many with views of the sea. There's a cheap restaurant on site.

MIDRANGE

All these hotels have hot showers and TVs. You can get discounts of up to 50% outside of festival and holiday times.

Huanchaco Hostal (☎ 46 1688; Plaza de Armas; s/d US$18/25.50; 🖳) This neat red building looks cute enough to have housed the three little pigs in a past life. On the town's small Plaza de Armas, this little place has spartan white rooms and a handsome backyard concealing a secluded pool and garden. There's plenty of arty touches to make it feel homely.

Hostal Caballito de Totora (☎ 46 1154; totora@terra .com.pe; La Rivera 219; s/d/ste US$18/27/51; 🖳) Although there are lots of different rooms at Caballito de Tortora, it's the suites that take the cake, each with perfect sea views and private patios. There's also lots of greenery and the white walls with blue flourishes give it a truly Mediterranean feel. The regular rooms can be a little stuffy.

Hostal Bracamonte (☎ 46 1162; www.hostalbraca monte.com; Los Olivos 503; s/d US$21/31.50, bungalows from US$54; ☐ ☒) Popular, friendly, welcoming and secure behind high walls and a locked gate, the Bracamonte has nice gardens, a games room, video room, barbecue, restaurant, bar, and toddlers' playground. The rooms include cable TVs, fans and phone. This is the oldest of Huanchaco's good hotels, and it remains among the best choices.

Huankarute Restaurant & Hospedaje (☎ 46 1705; www.hostalhuankarute.com; La Rivera 233; s US$21, d US$24-33; ☒) A small place with bright rooms that have fan and cable TV. The top-floor doubles afford great vistas as well as a real treat – bathtubs! The kidney-shaped pool has an 'aqua bar' attached, and the restaurant features seafood and lunch specials starting at US$2.10.

Las Palmeras (☎ 46 1199; www.laspalmerasdehuan chaco.com; Victor Larco 1150; s/d US$22.50/36; ☒ ☐ ☒) Probably the nicest place to stay in town, this well-trimmed, mellow-yellow resort hotel has spotless rooms (some with sea views), a secluded green lawn, a lovely pool, spots of shade and a restaurant to boot. It's in an enclosed compound right near the beach and is a great place for travelers with kiddies.

Hostal el Malecon (☎ 46 1275; www.hostalelmalecon .com; La Rivera 225; s/d US$24/30) This 'highly qualified lodging company' features a café, a terrace with views of surfers and a pub that plays videos on demand. English and German are spoken.

Eating

Not surprisingly, Huanchaco has oodles of seafood restaurants, especially near the *caballitos de tortora* stacked at the north end of the beach.

Otra Cosa (☎ 46 1346; www.otracosa.info; Victor Larco 921; dishes US$1.20-2.40; ☼ 9am-8pm Wed-Sun) Decorated with Middle Eastern flair, this cozy, hammock-filled beachside pad serves up yummy vegetarian victuals like falafel and hummus.

Grill A Bordo (☎ 937 4026; Los Pinos 491; dishes US$2.40-6; ☼ 6-11pm Mon-Sat, 11am-11pm Sun) The ships-ahoy theme, complete with waiters dressed as sailors, may be unnecessary as this *parrillada* (grill house) serves only one fish dish – but there are plenty of scrumptiously grilled meats on offer. A few blocks back from the beach, it's a cozy little place that also houses a small ceramics gallery.

El Caribe (Victor Larco at Atahualpa; dishes US$3-4.50; ☼ 10am-7pm) Recommended for its seafood, particularly the reasonably priced ceviche.

Club Colonial (☎ 461 015; Grau 272; meals US$4.50-7.50; ☼ noon-11pm) On the plaza, this Belgian-run place is in a striking, candlelit colonial mansion and serves up finely prepared Peruvian and French dishes. It also doubles as a gallery for quality local artists and is the best place in town for a romantic rendezvous.

Mamma Mía (☎ 997 3635; Victor Larco at Independencia; pasta US$5.50, pizza US$9; ☼ 6-11pm) Come here for delicious concoct-your-own pizzas prepared with the freshest ingredients. The pastas are also great, but for a real treat you should check to see if the Peruvian owner, Fernando, is making any of his famous secret-recipe crab lasagna. Yum.

Restaurant Big Ben (☎ 46 1378; Victor Larco 836; mains US$6-12; ☼ 11am-11pm) At the far north end of Huanchaco, Big Ben specializes in lunchtime ceviches and has a reputation for its other top-notch seafood.

Restaurante Mococho (☎ 46 1350; Bolognesi 535 at Independencia; 3-course meals about US$18; ☼ 1-3pm) This tiny place sits secluded in a walled garden where patrons wait to see what amazing seafood concoctions the skilled Don Victor will serve up that day. It's not cheap, but ceviche and seafood does not get any better than this, as regular patron ex-President Fujimoro will attest.

Getting There & Away

Combis to Huanchaco frequently leave from Trujillo (US$0.50). To return, just wait on the beachfront road for the bus as it travels from the north end. A taxi from Trujillo is US$3 to US$4.50.

OTUZCO

☎ 044 / pop 10,300 / elev 2627m

The small town of Otuzco is only two hours away from Trujillo, making it the only place in Peru where you can go coast-to-Andean peaks in such a short amount of time. The cobblestone streets, cool weather and relaxed pace of life make this a great day trip or stopover on the mountain route to Cajamarca. The modern church here houses the Virgen de la Puerta, the object of a popular Peruvian pilgrimage.

The trip itself is worthwhile, as you'll be greeted by excellent scenery while your fillings jitter on the rough journey through coastal subtropical crops and into the highland agricultural regions.

There are some modest places to stay, the best being the cheap **Hostal Los Portales** (Santa Rosa 680; s/d US$3/6). A few inexpensive restaurants serve Peruvian food, but none are outstanding.

Linea has buses to between Otuzco and Trujillo ($1.50, two hours). *Colectivos* to Huamachuco leave regularly from the southern part of town (US$2.20, four hours).

PUERTO CHICAMA

☎ 044

The small fishing outpost of Puerto Chicama might not look like much, but it's the offshore action that draws a dedicated following. Puerto Chicama, also called Malabrigo, lays claim to one of the longest left-hand point breaks in the world. Originally a busy port for the sugar and cotton grown on nearby haciendas, Puerto Chicama now draws adrenaline-seeking surfers who try their luck catching that rare, long ride.

The lengthy break is caused by a shallow, flat beach and on a good day waves can reach up to 2m and travel for an incredible 2km. Good waves can be found year-round, but the marathon breaks only come about when the conditions are just so, usually between March and June. There is some gear available for hire at El Hombre, though it's best to bring your own just in case. The water is very cold for much of the year, except for December through March.

El Hombre (☎ 57 6077; s/d from US$5/8) is the original surfers' hostel and is run by local legend 'El Hombre,' a surfer guru who's been at it for over 40 years. Facing the ocean, the hostel has comfy beds, good simple meals, kitchen privileges and a communal TV often seen flickering with surf videos. Next door, the French-owned **El Inti** (☎ 57 6138; s/d US$10/12) has a sea-view restaurant where Peru doffs its hat to French influences. There are a few garden bungalows here, a BBQ and a pool table. A few doors down, **Hostal los Delfines** (☎ 57 6103; losdelfineschicama@hotmail.com; s/d/ste US$18/25/40; 🖳) is the top-end choice, with more ocean views, a heart-shaped pool and Jacuzzis in the suites.

Some surf shops in Huanchaco, including Un Lugar (p341), arrange surfing safaris to Puerto Chicama. Buses leave frequently from Trujillo's Provincial Bus Terminal Interurbano to the town of Paiján, 40km further north on the Panamericana (US$1.40, 1½ hours). From here you can catch *colectivos* for the 16km to Puerto Chicama (US$0.40, 20 minutes).

PACASMAYO

☎ 044 / pop 14,400

This lively, mostly forgotten beach town is crammed with colonial buildings in various states of disrepair and blessed with a pretty stretch of beach. Check out the pier here; it's one of the largest in Peru. Dedicated surfers often drop in, particularly from May to August when there is a decent offshore break. It's also a great place to spend some time away from the more popular resort towns and get swept up in the aging nostalgia of the whole place.

The **Balin Surf Shop** (Junin 84) rents boards and does repairs. There's a **BCP** (Ayacucho 20)

THE NORTH COAST'S TOP FIVE SURF BREAKS

Dedicated surfers will find plenty of action on Peru's North Coast, from the longest break in the world at Puerto Chicama to consistently good surf at Máncora. Most spots have reliable swell from April to October. For the inside scoop on surfing throughout Peru, see p64.

Los Organos (p362) – a rocky break with well-formed tubular waves reaching up to 2m; it's for experienced surfers only

Cabo Blanco (p362) – a perfect pipeline ranging between 1m and 3m in height and breaking on rocks; again, it's for experienced surfers only

Puerto Chicama (above) – on a good day, this is the longest break in the world (up to 2km!); it has good year-round surfing for all skill levels

Máncora (p362) – a popular and easily accessible with consistently decent surf up to 2m high; it's appropriate for all skill levels

Huanchaco (p340) – long and well-formed waves with a pipeline; it's suitable for all skill levels

bank on the small plaza near the beach with a Visa ATM. Internet access is available all over town.

A few kilometers north, just before the village of Guadalupe, a track leads toward the ocean and the little-visited ruins of **Pacatnamú**, a large site that was inhabited by the Gallinazo, Moche and Chimu cultures.

There are several cheap, basic but clean hotels in town and some swisher converted colonial mansions along the beach. **Hotel San Francisco** (☎ 52 2021; L Prado 21; s/d with shared bathroom US$4.50/5.50, s/d US$6/9) is on the main commercial strip and has clean, bare-bones rooms. **Hostal Duke** (☎ 52 2017; Ayacucho 44; s/d US$7.50/10.50) is a laid-back *hostal* in a rambling colonial edifice and has a huge variety of rooms – have a good look around before you choose one. It's covered in surfing paraphernalia, and the Peruvian owner surfs, shows surf videos and rents boards. **Hotel Pakatnamú** (☎ 52 1051; fax 52 3255; Malecón Grau 103; s/d/ste US$18/27/36; ⚄) is in a freshly painted colonial building along the waterfront. The plush rooms here come with TV, fridge and even a mounted car stereo with 'surround sound.' A few doors down, **La Estación Pacasmayo Hotel** (☎ 52 1515; Malecón Grau 103; s/d US$20/30; ⚄) is a similarly majestic colonial building with a lovely terrace restaurant, though the rooms here are a little bare. For good seafood, visit **Se Salio el Mar** (Ayacucho 145; meals US$1.80-3.60; ⏰ 11am-10pm), several blocks back from the beach.

In Guadalupe village, try **Hotel el Bosque** (☎ 56 6490; s/d US$15/21).

Frequent buses to and from Trujillo (two hours), Chiclayo (two hours) and Cajamarca (four hours) pass through the northern end of town.

CHICLAYO
☎ 074 / pop 592,100

Spanish missionaries founded a small rural community on this site in the 16th century. Either by chance, or through help from 'above,' Chiclayo has prospered ever since. In one of the first sharp moves in Peruvian real estate, the missionaries chose a spot that sits at the hub of vital trade routes between the coast, the highlands and the deep jungle. Chiclayo's role as the commercial heart of the district has allowed it to overtake other once vital organs of the region, such as the nearby city of Lambayeque. This bustling metropolis shows few signs of slowing down.

La Ciudad de la Amistad (the City of Friendship) holds a friendly, outstretched hand to the wayward venturer. While it's shaking hands hello, it will probably slip in a bold mix of unique regional dishes to tickle your taste buds. Known for its *brujos* (witch doctors), the fascinating market here is a Wal-Mart of shamanistic herbs, elixirs and other sagely curiosities. While the town itself is pretty light on tourist attractions, the dozens of tombs with Moche and Chimu archeological booty surrounding the area should not be missed.

Information

EMERGENCY
Policía de Turismo (☎ 23 6700; Saenz Peña 830) Useful for reporting problems.

IMMIGRATION
Oficina de migraciónes (☎ 20 6838; La Plata 070) Near Paseo de Las Museos; does visa extensions.

INTERNET ACCESS
Internet abounds.
Ciber C@fe (MM Izaga 716; per hr US$0.30; ⏰ 8am-11pm) Has a cozier feeling than most.

LAUNDRY
Lavandería (☎ 23 3159; 7 de Enero 639; per kg US$1.20)

MEDICAL SERVICES
Clínica del Pacífico (☎ 23 6378; JL Ortiz 420) The best medical assistance in town.

MONEY
There are several banks on *cuadra* (block) 6 of J Balta. Moneychangers outside the banks change cash quickly at good rates.
Banco Continental (☎ 23 9110; J Balta 643)
Banco Weise (☎ 22 4724; J Balta 609)
BCP (☎ 23 7291; J Balta 630) Has a 24-hour Visa and MasterCard ATM.
Interbank (☎ 23 8361; cnr Colón & E Aguirre)

POST
Post office (E Aguirre 140; ⏰ 9am-7pm Mon-Fri, 9am-1pm Sat) West of Plaza Aguirre.

TOURIST INFORMATION
Centro de Información Turístico (☎ 23 3132; Saenz Peña 838) Has lots of information.
Information booth (Plaza de Armas) We've yet to see this open.

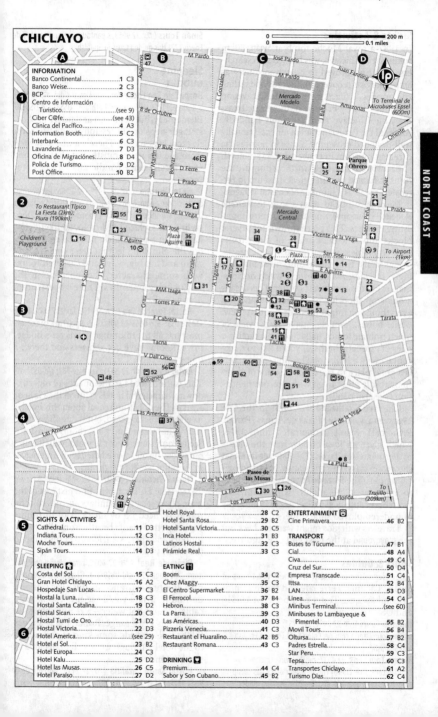

CHICLAYO

NORTH COAST

Sights & Activities

In 1987 a royal Moche tomb at **Sipán**, 30km southeast of Chiclayo, was located by researchers. This find proved to be extraordinary as archaeologists recovered hundreds of dazzling and priceless artifacts from the site. Excavation continues. Partly because of these rare treasures, the Chiclayo area has single-handedly cornered the Peruvian market for exceptionally well-designed museums; a case in point is the excellent museum, 11km north of Chiclayo. Other sites worth visiting are the ruins at **Túcume**, another great museum in **Ferreñafe**, as well as a number of coastal villages.

Make sure not to miss a visit to **Mercado Modelo** (◔ 9am-5pm), one of Peru's most interesting markets. This place sprawls for several blocks and is a thick maze of fresh fruits and vegetables, woven goods, handicrafts, live animals, fish, meats and, most interestingly, the *mercado de brujos* (witch doctors' market) in the southwest corner. This area is a one-stop shop for medicine men and has everything you might need for a potent brew: whale bones, amulets, snake skins, vials of indeterminate tonics, hallucinogenic cacti and piles of aromatic herbs. If you'd like to make contact with a *brujo* for a healing session, this is a good place to start, but be wary of sham shamans. It's best to go with a recommendation (see also p360).

Chiclayo's **cathedral** was built in the late 19th century, and the Plaza de Armas (Parque Principal) wasn't inaugurated until 1916, which gives an idea of how new the city is by Peruvian standards. The **Paseo de las Musas** showcases classical-style statues of mythological figures. The **Plaza de Armas** is a great place to amble as it fills nightly with sauntering couples, evangelical preachers and an army of underemployed shoe shiners.

Travelers with kids might want to check out the **playground** at the west end of E Aguirre.

Tours & Guides

Agencies offer frequent inexpensive tours of Sipán, Túcume, Ferreñafe and the museums in Lambayeque. Tours cost between US$10 and US$20.

Indiana Tours (☎ 22 2991, 22-5751; indianatours@terra.com.pe; Colón 556) Tours in English and Spanish.

Moche Tours (☎ 22 4637; mochetours_chiclayo@ hotmail.com; 7 de Enero) This new tour office has cheap daily tours with Spanish- and English-speaking guides.

Sipán Tours (☎ 22 9053, sipantours@terra.com.pe; 7 de Enero 772) Has guided tours in Spanish.

Sleeping

BUDGET

Hospedaje San Lucas (formerly Hostal Lido; ☎ 49 9269; E Aguirre 412; s with shared bathroom US$3, s/d US$6/9) Elementary, but kept trim and tidy, this shoe-stringer steps up successfully to its Welcome Backpackers motto. There's a nice city view from the top floor, mostly hot showers, and some locally made handicrafts for sale at reception.

Hotel Europa (☎ 23 7919, 22 2066; hoteleuropa chiclayo@terra.com; E Aguirre 466; s with shared bathroom US$4.50, s/d US$6/9) With grandiose Art Deco styling, this place kind of looks like it may have been a psychiatric hospital in a previous life. But don't let that deter you. It's kept clean and has big, worn and carpeted rooms with some character, though little in the way of fancy amenities. There's a restaurant here as well.

Hostal Tumi de Oro (☎ 22 7108; fax 23 7767; L Prado 1145; s US$6-9, d US$9-13.50) This spartan place almost has all the midrange goods for a budget price. Rooms have hot showers and there's a lobby with cable TV.

Hotel Royal (☎ 23 3421; San José 787; s/d US$7/10) This is the choice for aficionados of old, run-down, characterful hotels right on the Plaza de Armas. The only thing royal about this hotel is its elegant visiting card, but it does have large rooms, hot water, and a TV room downstairs. Some rooms overlook the plaza, which is fun but noisy. If you enjoyed the Hotel Americano in Trujillo, you'll fit right in.

Hostal Victoria (☎ 22 5642; MM Izaga 933; s/d US$7.50/13.50) This is a great find just east of the main plaza. It's quiet, sanitary and has colorful rooms spruced up by nice bits of furniture. Lots of potted plants breathe some life to the indoors and there's a friendly family vibe to the whole place.

Pirámide Real (☎ 22 4036; piramidereal@hotmail .com; MM Izaga 726; s/d US$9/15) Blink and you'll miss the tiny entrance to this place. If you do find it, inside you'll see tidy rooms with cable TV and hot water – a reasonably good deal at this price range. Romanesque statues fill the halls and add some kind of personality to the hotel – though we're still undecided as to what kind.

Hostal Santa Catalina (☎ 27 2119; Vincente de la Vega 1127; s/d US$10.50/13.50) Its 10 rooms with electric hot showers and cable TV are clean and quiet.

Hostal Sican (☎ 23 7618; MM Izaga 356; s/d US$10.50/15) An appealing pick with lots of polished wood and wrought iron creating an illusion of grandeur. The rooms are small, comfortable and cool. All have more wood paneling, as well as some tasteful bits of art and a TV. This great choice also has a laundry service.

Hotel Paraíso (☎ 22 8161, 22 2070; www.hoteles paraiso.com; P Ruiz 1064; s/d US$12/15; 💻) Brighter and cheerier than its immediate neighbors, the value equation falls in Hotel Paraíso's favor. Spotless and modern tiled rooms boast decent furniture, a hot shower and cable TV. Breakfast is available in its café. It's the cheapest of several hotels on this block, but holds its head up in comparisons with any of them.

Hotel Kalu (☎ 22 9293, 22 8767; hotelkalu@hotmail .com; P Ruiz 1038; s/d US$14.50/22) Almost boutique-like, these quarters are dressed with stylish '80s pizzazz. With dazzling colors, a wall-mounted aquarium and an attentive door-man, it's a spiffy-looking hotel all round. Carpeted rooms have fan, cable TV and hot showers, and some have a minifridge.

Hotel Santa Victoria (☎ /fax 22 5074; La Florida 586; s/d incl breakfast US$15/21) Overlooking the leafy Paseo de las Musas, the laid-back Hotel Santa Victoria is a longish walk from the center but is top value. Rooms have fan, cable TV and phone; a restaurant with room service is also available.

Hotel el Sol (☎ 23 2120; www.hotelsoltresestrelias .com; E Aguirre 119; s/d US$15/21; 🛈) This fastidiously maintained and professionally run deal has tip-top rooms with all the mod-cons – a steal at this price. The varied rooms have TV, fans and phones, though we wouldn't want to be responsible for cleaning the spotless white leather couches downstairs. It's run by the same owners as Hotel Vicus in Piura.

Hostal la Luna (☎ 20 5945; Torres Paz 688; s/d US$15/21) The airy rooms here are OK, with some bamboo furniture and lots of hush on tap. The downstairs frontage is easily spotted from the street; look for the glass wall completely covered by indoor plants.

Hotel Santa Rosa (☎ 22 4411; fax 23 6242; L Gonzales 927; s/d incl breakfast US$18/24) This quiet, clean and pleasant hotel has comfortable rooms with fan, cable TV and phones. The size of the bathrooms varies from unit to unit, so look around. There's a good restaurant.

Hotel America (☎ 22 9305, 27 0664; www.hotel americachiclayo.com; L Gonzales 943; s/d US$18/21; 💻) Part underground beatnik club, part '70s ca-sino, the America is dark and moody, with lots of velvet, plush carpeting and kitsch gold trimmings (gold deer statues anyone?). The good-sized rooms are nicely appointed and have fans, cable TV and minifridges.

MIDRANGE

Latinos Hostal (☎ 23 5437; MM Igaza 600; s/d US$24/36) An excellent choice, this new-looking hotel is thoroughly maintained with perfect little rooms; some of the corner rooms have giant curving floor-to-ceiling windows for great street views and plenty of light. The staff are very helpful.

Inca Hotel (☎ 23 5931, 23 7803; www.incahotel.com; L Gonzales 622; s/d incl breakfast US$35/46; 🛒) Finally, air-con! The carpeted rooms have sound-proofed windows – some of which have city panoramas – and there's 'Inca'-style art throughout the hotel. Other features include direct-dial phones, hairdryer, minifridge and cable TV. There's also a room with a Jacuzzi if you're willing pay US$55. Ask about discounts if the going is slow.

Hotel las Musas (☎ 23 9884-86; nazih@viabpc.com; Faiques 101; s/d incl breakfast US$40/60; 🛒 💻) Over-looking the peaceful Paseo de las Musas, this hotel has modern, spacious rooms with cable TV, phone and minifridge. There's a cascad-ing 'waterfall' backed by a mossy green wall in the foyer, and the bathrooms all have bathtubs as well as showers – a rarity in Peru. Some rooms have good views of the Paseo de las Musas. A restaurant is open 7am to 11pm, and room service is available 24 hours. There is a karaoke-disco, small casino and tourist information, and tours are available.

Costa Del Sol (☎ 22 7272; www.costadelsolperu .com; Balta 399; s/d/ste US$60/70/96; 🛒 📺 💻) Part of a northern Peru chain, this establishment has all the creature comforts, including pool, gym, sauna, Jacuzzi and impeccable service. The tastefully and simply designed rooms have cable TV, minibar, safe, and direct-dial phone.

TOP END

Gran Hotel Chiclayo (☎ 23 4911; www.granhotelchiclayo .com.pe; F Villarreal 115; s/d US$69/84; 🛒 💻 📺) The top end of Chiclayo living, it's all superswanky here, with everything you'd expect, includ-ing room service, laundry, travel agency, car rental, cappuccino bar, karaoke and casino. Serious-looking businessmen flock here in droves.

Eating

Las Américas (☎ 20 9381; E Aguirre 824; sandwiches US$1.20, mains US$1.80-5.50; ☒ 7:30am-11:30pm) This bright, popular place off the southeast corner of the plaza is a perennial favorite. With '60s-style red-and-white booths, Las Américas has a varied menu of soups, meats and fish dishes – try the fish in a savory onion and spicy tomato sauce. This place can be a little hygienically challenged.

Boom (☎ 27 0549; San José 677; meals US$1.40-4.20; ☒ 7am-late) This buzzing, neon-lit young thing whips out local dishes, sandwiches, pizzas and cakes faster than you can blink and is filled every night with hungry diners. The upstairs seating is a little quieter. The portions here are elephantine.

La Parra (☎ 22 7471, 22 5198; MM Izaga 752; mains US$1.80-4.50; ☒ 11:30am-midnight) There are two restaurants side by side here; one is a *chifa* and the other is a grill, but they share an entrance and a kitchen. Go figure. Both menus are available in each dining room.

Restaurant Romana (☎ 22 3598; J Balta 512; breakfasts US$2.30, mains US$3-6; ☒ 7am-late) This locally popular place serves a bunch of different dishes, all of them local favorites. If you're feeling brave, try the *chirimpico* for breakfast; it's stewed goat tripe and organs and is guaranteed to either cure a hangover or give you one. Otherwise, you can have pastas, steaks, seafood, chicken or pork *chicharrones* with yucca.

Chez Maggy (☎ 20 9253; J Balta 413; pizzas US$2.70-3.30; ☒ 6-11pm) It's not how Papa Giuseppe used to make it, but the wood-fired pizzas at this restaurant are fairly good. It's run by the same owners as the Chez Maggy in Cuzco's gringo ghetto.

El Ferrocol (Las Americas 168; meals US$3-7.50; ☒ 11am-7pm) This hole-in-the-wall, a little out of the center, is well worth the trip, as chef Lucho prepares some of the best ceviche in all of Chiclayo. Treat yourself.

Hebron (☎ 22 2709; J Balta 605; mains about US$4; ☒ 24hr) This flashy, contemporary and bright two-story restaurant is a luxury *pollería* (restaurant specializing in roast chicken) on steroids. Lots of windows, impeccable service and a giant children's playground that would put McDonalds to shame keep this restaurant marked on the calendars of most Chiclayans.

Pizzería Venecia (☎ 23 3384; Balta 413; half pizza US$4; ☒ 6:30pm-late) This rip-roaring pizzeria attracts a young crowd that listens to rock and Latin favorites while they chug beer with their food.

Restaurant el Huaralino (☎ 27 0330; Libertad 155; mains US$5-10; ☒ noon-11pm Mon-Sat, noon-5pm Sun) One of Chiclayo's most upscale restaurants, this place serves good Chiclayan specialties, Creole dishes and international cuisine. Bonus brownie points for some of the cleanest bathrooms in Peru.

Restaurant Típico la Fiesta (☎ 20 1970; Salaverry 1820; mains US$5-12; ☒ 9:30am-11pm) Another quality top-end choice, La Fiesta is in the Residencial 3 de Octubre suburb, about 2km west of central Chiclayo. It's expensive by Peruvian standards, but the food is a delicious variety of local meats and seafood.

El Centro Supermarket (cnr L Gonzales & E Aguirre; ☒ 8am-10pm) For self-catering.

Drinking

Premium (☎ 22 6689; J Balta 100; ☒ 9pm-late) Turns into a popular place for a tipple and a dance after hours, with loud international music, a mixed crowd, free entry and a boisterous vibe.

Sabor y Son Cubano (☎ 27 2555; San Jose 155; ☒ 9pm-late Fri-Sun) This spot gives the over-35 crowd somewhere to shake their rumps on the weekends, with jazz, classic salsa and Cuban music setting the pace.

Entertainment

Cine Primavera (☎ 20 7471; L Gonzales 1235) This place has five screens, often showing some Hollywood flicks.

Getting There & Away

AIR

The **airport** (code CIX; ☎ 23 3192) is 1.5km east of town; a taxi ride there is a US$0.60 and departure tax is US$3.57. **LAN** (☎ 27 4875; MM Izaga 770) flies from Lima to Chiclayo (US$110) daily at 6:30am and 7:50pm, returning to Lima at 10:40am and 8:55pm. LAN also flies to Piura (US$64) at 8:30am, returning at 9:30am. **Star Perú** (☎ 27 1173; Bolognesi 316) has two flights from Lima leaving at 7am and 5pm and returning to Lima from Chiclayo at 9am and 6:30pm (US$85). It also flies to Trujillo at 6:30pm, returning at 8:10am (US$48) the next day.

BUS

Cruz del Sur, Movil Tours and Linea usually have the most comfortable buses.

Cial (☎ 20 5587; Bolognesi 15) Has a 9pm Lima bus (US$18 to US$24, 10 hours) and a 6pm bus to Tarapoto (US$12, 12 hours).

Civa (☎ 22 3434; Bolognesi 714) Lima buses at 8pm and 8:30pm (US$15 to US$24, 10 hours), Jaén buses at 10am and 9:30pm (US$4.50, six hours), a Tarapoto bus at 6pm (US$12, 12 hours) and a Chachapoyas bus at 5:30pm (US$6, 10 to 11 hours).

Cruz del Sur (☎ 22 5508; Bolognesi 888) Has six departures to Lima (US$13 to US$30, 10 hours) between 7pm and 10pm.

Empresa Transcade (☎ 23 2552; J Balta 110) Has buses to Jaén (US$4.50) at 8:30am and 8:30pm.

Ittsa (☎ 23 3612; Bolognesi 155) *Bus-cama* (bed bus) to Lima (US$16.50 to US$24, 10 hours) at 8pm.

Linea (☎ 23 3497; Bolognesi 638) Has a comfortable Lima service (US$13.50 to US$24, 10 hours) at 8pm and 8:30pm, and regular hourly services to Trujillo (US$3.60, two hours) and Piura (US$3.60, three hours). Also has buses to Chimbote at 9:15am and 3:15pm (US$6, four hours), buses to Cajamarca at 10:45am, 10pm and 10:45pm (US$4.50 to US$9, six hours) and buses to Jaén at 1:15pm and 11pm (US$5.50 to US$7).

Movil Tours (☎ 27 1940; Bolognesi 199) Has a Lima bus (US$22.50, 10 hours) at 8:30pm, a Tarapoto bus (US$21, 12 hours) at 6:30pm and a Chachapoyas bus (US$12, 10 to 11 hours) at 8pm.

Oltursa (☎ 23 7789; Vincente de la Vega 101) Three *bus-cama* services to Lima (US$21 to US$24, 10 hours) between 8pm and 9pm.

Padres Estrella (☎ 20 4879; J Balta 178) Has Tarapoto buses (US$12, 12 to 14 hours) at 5am, 7am and 4pm, with the 4pm bus going onto Yurimaguas (US$21, 20 to 24 hours).

Tepsa (☎ 23 6981; Bolognesi 504) *Bus-cama* services to Lima (US$18, 10 hours) at 7:30pm, 8:15pm and 9:15pm.

Transportes Chiclayo (☎ 23 7984; JL Ortiz) Has buses to Piura (US$3.60, three hours) every hour from 6am to 9:30pm, with the last bus going on to Tumbes (US$6, eight hours).

Turismo Dias (☎ 23 3538; J Cuglievan 190) Has a cheaper bus to Lima (US$12 to US$15, 10 hours) at 7pm as well as departures to Cajamarca (US$6, six hours) at 6:45am, 5pm and 10:30pm.

Behind Tepsa there is a minibus terminal where a dozen small companies have at least six buses throughout the day to Cajamarca (US$4.50 to US$6), a night bus to Tumbes at 8:30pm (US$6), buses at 7:30pm, noon and 8:30pm to Chachapoyas (US$7.50), 9:30am and 3:30pm buses to Tarapoto (US$10.50),

a 3:30pm bus to Yurimaguas (US$16.50) and frequent services to Jaén (US$4.50). These times tend to change with the setting of each moon, so check the schedule ahead of time.

The minibus terminal at the corner of San José and Lora y Lora has regular buses to Lambayeque (US$0.50, 20 minutes) and Pimentel (US$0.50, 25 minutes).

Buses for Ferreñafe (US$0.50), Sipán (US$0.80), Monsefú (US$0.40), Zaña (US$0.80) and Chongoyape (US$1.50) leave frequently from **Terminal de Microbuses Epsel** (Nicolás de Píerola at Oriente).

Buses to Túcume (US$0.50) leave from Angamos near M Pardo – it's hard to find this bus stop, so ask.

AROUND CHICLAYO
Pimentel & Santa Rosa
☎ 074

Two coastal municipalities, Pimentel and Santa Rosa, can be conveniently visited from Chiclayo on day trips.

Pimentel, 14km from Chiclayo, has a long, sandy beach with a huge, decaying jetty curving out well into the sea. There are some gracefully aging colonial buildings around the Plaza Diego Ferre, and at the south end of the beach you can sometimes see fishermen building *caballitos*. This place gets very crowded on summer weekends (January to March), as Chiclayans flock to the dozens of low-rise summer apartments lining the oceanfront. The surf here is also good. Stay at

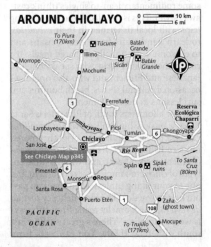

AROUND CHICLAYO

To Piura (170km)
Túcume
Batán Grande
Illimo
Morrope
Sicán
Batán Grande
Mochumí
Ferreñafe
Reserva Ecológica Chaparri
Río Lambayeque
Lambayeque
Picsi
Tumán
Chongoyape
Chiclayo
Río Reque
San José
See Chiclayo Map p345
Sipán
Sipán ruins
To Santa Cruz (80km)
Pimentel
Monsefú
Reque
Santa Rosa
Puerto Etén
Zaña (ghost town)
108
PACIFIC OCEAN
To Trujillo (171km)
Mocupe

0 .... 10 km
0 .... 6 mi

HUAQUEROS

The word *huaquero* is heard frequently on the north coast of Peru and literally means 'robber of *huacas*.' *Huacas* are pyramids, temples, shrines and burial sites of special significance.

Since the Spanish conquest, *huaqueros* have worked the ancient graves of Peru, selling valuables to anybody prepared to pay. To a certain extent, one can sympathize with a poor *campesino* (peasant) hoping to strike it rich, but the *huaquero* is one of the archaeologist's greatest enemies. The *huaqueros'* efforts have been so thorough that archaeologists rarely find an unplundered grave.

Hostal Garuda (☎ 45 2964; Quiñones 109; s/d US$9/21). In a well-preserved colonial house, this *hostal* has excellent rooms sporting some refined aesthetics and enormous bathrooms. It's a block back from the coast.

At Playa las Rocas, a 20-minute walk south, sprawls **Katuwira Lodge** (☎ 970 0484, 976 9188; www.katuwira.com; campsite/r with shared bathroom per person US$5/10, both incl full board), a funky, hippyish beachside hangout made of bamboo and sporting vibes and art in equal measures. Katuwira has distinctive pyramid bungalows sleeping five to seven people, complete with beautifully finished bamboo lounges downstairs, and bedrooms with awesome sea views upstairs. There are a few smaller double rooms and some rudimentary lean-to singles (think castaway style). This is the place to arrange fishing trips with local fishermen in their *caballitos*, to learn handicrafts from local artisans and to eat some sensationally prepared meals. It's run by the helpful Mario, who speaks English, Japanese and French, and who also organizes occasional cultural shows, beach bonfires and surf lessons in nearby Pimentel.

A few kilometers south of Pimentel is Santa Rosa, a busy fishing village where *caballitos* can also be seen among the brightly colored modern fishing fleet. Its famed for its *chicha* (fermented corn beer), and with 28 different types of *chicha* to sample, you're bound to find one to your liking (unless, of course, you pass out before you do). The local delicacy *tortilla de reya* (Spanish omelet made from stingray) is worth sampling. There's great surfing just south of here at **El Faro**. You can walk from Pimentel to Santa Rosa in less than an hour or take a *colectivo* taxi (US$0.30).

Colectivos from Santa Rosa head south to the small port of **Puerto Etén**, once an important commercial center. Legend has it that Jesus himself appeared here in 1649; the small Capilla del Milagro (Chapel of the Miracle) now stands in that spot. Check out the 19th-century train engine in the (disused) train station.

You can return to Chiclayo via the village of **Monsefú**, 15km south of Chiclayo. Monsefú is known for its flowers and handicrafts, and has an artisanal market selling hats, bags and baskets made of straw and rattan, as well as ponchos and cotton goods. A craft festival called **Fexticum** is held in the last week of July. The simple and rustic Restaurant Tradiciones is recommended for good local fare.

Transportation to Pimentel leaves regularly from Chiclayo's minibus terminal (US$0.50, 25 minutes); during summer (January to March), they continue from Pimentel along the so-called *circuito de playas* (beach circuit) through Santa Rosa, Puerto Etén and Monsefú before returning to Chiclayo.

Sipán

The story of Sipán reads like an Indiana Jones movie script: buried treasure, *huaqueros*, police, archaeologists and at least one killing. The archaeological **site** (☎ 80 0048; adult/student US$2.30/0.90; 9am-5pm), also known as Huaca Rayada, was discovered by *huaqueros* (see left) from the nearby hamlet of Sipán. When local archaeologist Dr Walter Alva saw a huge influx of intricate objects on the black market in early 1987, he realized that an incredible burial site was being ransacked in the Chiclayo area. Careful questioning led Dr Alva to the Sipán mounds. To the untrained eye the mounds look like earthen hills, but in AD 300 these were huge truncated pyramids constructed from millions of adobe bricks.

At least one major tomb had already been pillaged by looters, but fast protective action by local archaeologists and police stopped further plundering. Luckily several other, even better, tombs that the grave robbers had missed were unearthed, including an exceptional royal Moche burial which became known as the Lord of Sipán. One *huaquero* was shot and killed by police in the early, tense days of the struggle over the graves. The Sipán locals were not too happy at losing what they considered their treasure trove. To solve this problem, the locals were invited to train to become excavators, researchers and guards at the site, which now provides steady employment to many of them.

The full story has been detailed by Dr Alva in the October 1988 and June 1990 issues of *National Geographic,* and the May 1994 issue of *Natural History.*

Some of the tombs have been restored with replicas to show what they looked like just before being closed up over 1500 years ago. The actual artifacts went on a world tour, and most returned to Lambayeque's Museo Tumbas Reales de Sipán, where they are now displayed. Opposite the entrance is a small on-site **museum**, which is worth a visit. Spanish-speaking guides can be hired (US$4.50).

Daily guided tours are available from tour agencies (p346) in Chiclayo for around US$15. Alternatively, buses for Sipán (US$0.80) leave frequently from Chiclayo's Terminal de Microbuses Epsel.

Lambayeque
☎ 074 / pop 44,400

About 11km north of Chiclayo, Lambayeque was once the main town in the area but now plays second fiddle to Chiclayo. The town's museums are its best feature. La Casa de Logia, a block south of the main plaza, has a 67m-long, 400-year-old balcony, said to be the longest balcony in Peru.

SIGHTS
The two museums in Lambayeque are both within a 15-minute walk of the plaza.

Museo Tumbas Reales de Sipán
Opened in November 2002, the **Museum of the Royal Tombs of Sipán** (☎ 28 3977, 28 3988; www .tumbasreales.org; admission US$2.30; ⏰ 9am-6pm Tue-Sun, last admission 5pm) is the pride of northern Peru, as well it should be. With its burgundy pyramid construction rising gently out of the earth, it's a world-class facility specifically designed to showcase the marvelous finds from Sipán. Photography is not permitted and all bags must be checked.

Visitors are guided through the museum from the top down, and are shown some of the numerous discoveries from the tomb in the same order that the archaeologists found them. The first hall contains detailed ceramics representing gods, people, plants,

llamas and other animals. Descending to the 2nd floor there are delicate objects like impossibly fine turquoise-and-gold ear ornaments showing ducks, deer and the Lord of Sipán himself. The painstaking and advanced techniques necessary to create this jewelry place them among the most beautiful and important objects of the pre-Columbian Americas. Finally, the ground floor features exact reproductions of how the tombs were found. Numerous dazzling objects are displayed, the most remarkable of which are the gold pectoral plates representing sea creatures such as octopuses and crabs. Even the sandals of the Lord of Sipán were made of precious metals since he was carried everywhere and never had to walk. Interestingly, since nobility were seen as part animal god, they used the *nariguera* (a distinctive nose shield) to conceal their very human teeth – and the fact that they were no different from everyone else.

The lighting and layout is exceptional, but the signage is all in Spanish. Guides are available for US$6; some speak English.

Bruning Museum
This **museum** (☎ 28 2110, 28 3440; adult/student US$2.30/0.90; ⏰ 9am-5pm) houses a good collection of archaeological artifacts from the Chimu, Moche, Chavín and Vicus cultures. Budding archaeologists will enjoy the exhibits showing the development of ceramics from different cultures, and the exhibits explaining how ceramics and metalwork were made. There are models of several important sites. English-speaking guides charge US$4.50.

EATING
El Cantaro (☎ 28 2196, 2 de Mayo 180; mains US$2.40-4.50; ⏰ 10am-6pm) Continue past La Casa de Logia to this popular local restaurant with typical food and good service. Try the famous *arroz con pato* (spiced rice with roast duck).

El Rincón del Pato (☎ 28 2751; Leguia 270; meals US$1.80-5.50; ⏰ 11am-3pm) This place also gets the thumbs-up from people who are authorized to give such thumb ratings for good ceviches, grills and local specialties.

GETTING THERE & AWAY
The minibus terminal at the corner of San José and Lora y Lora in Chiclayo has regular buses to Lambayeque (US$0.50, 20 minutes), which will drop you off a block from Bruning Museum.

Ferreñafe

☎ 074 / pop 34,900

This old town, 18km northeast of Chiclayo, is worth visiting for the excellent **Museo Nacional Sicán** (☎ 28 6469; http://sican.perucultural.org .pe; adult/student US$2.30/0.90; ☯ 9am-5pm Tue-Sun). Sicán culture thrived in the Lambayeque area between AD 750 and 1375 (see p336), around the same time as the Chimu. The main Sicán site at Batán Grande lies in remote country to the north and is hard to visit unless you're on a tour. This splendid museum displays replicas of the 12m-deep tombs found there, among the largest tombs found in South America. Enigmatic burials were discovered within – the Lord of Sicán was buried upside down, in a fetal position with his head separated from his body. Beside him were the bodies of two women and two adolescents, as well a sophisticated security system to ward off grave robbers: the red-colored *sinabrio* dust, which is toxic if inhaled. Another important tomb contained a nobleman sitting in a cross-legged position, and wearing a mask and headdress of gold and feathers, surrounded by smaller tombs and niches containing the bodies of one man and 22 young women. The museum is worth the ride out and it's never crowded. Guided tours from Chiclayo to Ferreñafe and Túcume cost around US$15 to US$20 per person, or buses for Ferreñafe (US$0.50) leave frequently from Chiclayo's Terminal de Microbuses Epsel.

Túcume

☎ 074 / pop 7200

This vast and little-known **site** (☎ 80 0052; adult/student US$2.30/0.90; ☯ 8am-4:30pm Tue-Sun) lies around 30km to the north of Lambayeque on the Panamericana. This vast area – with over 200 hectares of crumbling walls, plazas and no fewer than 26 pyramids – was the final capital of the Sicán culture (see p336), who moved their city from nearby Batán Grande around AD 1050 after that area was devastated by the effects of El Niño. The pyramids you see today are a composite of structures made by several civilizations; the lower levels belonged to the Sicán while the next two levels, along with the distinctive surrounding walls, were added by the Chimu. While little excavation has been done and no spectacular tombs have been found, it's the sheer size of the site that makes it a memorable visit.

The site can be surveyed from a stunning *mirador* (lookout) atop Cerro Purgatorio (Purgatory Hill). The hill was originally called Cerro la Raya (Stingray Hill), but the name was changed after the Spaniards tried to convert local pagans to Christianity by dressing as demons atop the hill and throwing non-believers to their deaths. There is a small but attractive on-site **museum** with some interesting tidbits. Guides are available for US$4.50.

Buses from Chiclayo (US$0.50) and Lambayeque (ask at the Bruning Museum) go here. Guided tours cost around US$15 to US$20 per person (p346).

Reserva Ecológica Chaparrí

This 34,000-hectare private **reserve** (☎ 43 3194; www.chaparri.org; admission US$3), located 75km east of Chiclayo, was established in 2000 by the community of Santa Catalina and the famous Peruvian wildlife photographer Heinz Plenge. This is one of the few places in the world where you can spot the rare spectacled bear in its natural habitat. This area is an ornithologist's dream, with over 140 species of birds, including rare white-winged guans, Andean condors, king vultures and several species of eagle. A large number of threatened species are also found here, including pumas, collared anteaters, and the Andean weasels. Nearly a third of these vertebrates are not found anywhere else in the world.

You can visit the reserve on your own by catching a bus from Chiclayo's Terminal de Microbuses Epsel to Chongoyape (US$1.50), from where you can hire a local guide and car for about US$30 to tour the reserve. Alternatively, Moche Tours (p346) in Chiclayo arranges day tours, including transportation and guide, for US$27 per person (minimum four people).

Batán Grande & Chota

About halfway from Chiclayo to Chongoyape a minor road on your left leads to the Sicán ruins of **Batán Grande**. This is a major archaeological site where about 50 pyramids have been identified and several burials have been excavated. With the urging of Dr Walter Alva, among others, the site has recently become the **Santuario Histórico Bosque de Pomac**, but there is no tourist infrastructure. The reserve protects a forest of *algarrobo* (carob trees). As there is almost no public transportation to Batán

Grande, you will have to find a taxi or tour to take you.

A rough but scenic road climbs east from Chongoyape into the Andes until it reaches **Chota** (at an altitude of around 2400m), a 170km journey that takes about eight hours. Two or three buses a day from Chiclayo travel there, from where a daily bus makes the rough journey via Bambamarca and Hualgayoc to Cajamarca (five hours).

Zaña
☎ 074

The old site of this town is a ghost town about 50km southeast of Chiclayo. Founded in 1563, Zaña was once an opulent city that controlled the shipping lanes between Panama and Lima from the nearby Cherrepe port. It was even slated to become the nation's capital at one stage, but the excessive wealth and rich churches and monasteries soon attracted the eye of robbers and pirates. During the 17th century it was sacked by pirates, including the famous Edward Davis, and survived several slave uprisings, only to be destroyed by the great flood of 1720. Today, great walls and the arches of four churches poke eerily out of the desert sands. Nearby, the present-day village of Zaña houses about 1000 people and is famous for its *brujos*. Stay at the **Centro Vacacional Santa Ana** (☎ 43 1052; Victór RH de La Torre 102; s/d US$5.50/6.50). Buses go to the new town from Chiclayo's Terminal de Microbuses Epsel (US$0.80).

PIURA
☎ 073 / pop 328,600

After several hours of crossing the vast emptiness of the Sechura Desert, Piura materializes like a mirage on the horizon, enveloped in quivering waves of heat. It's hard to ignore the sense of physical isolation forced on you by this unforgiving environment; the self-sufficiency imposed upon early settlers may explain why they identify as Piuran rather than Peruvian. Being so far inland, the scorching summer months will have you honing your radar for air-conditioning as you seek out chilled venues in which to soothe your sweltering skin. But the lovely narrow, cobbled streets and charismatic colonial houses of central Piura make up for the fact that there's little else for tourists to do here. Its role as a hub for the spokes of the northern towns means that you'll probably end up spending

some time here sighing in the relief of the occasional afternoon breeze.

Francisco Pizarro settled the first city in this district in 1532 as he whirred past on his way to trounce the Incas. It was originally located in Sullana, which was not the smartest move given that the oppressive heat and disease-ridden river there meant that settlers had a rather unpleasant time of it all. Fed up, they moved the city around a few times before resettling in Paita on the coast. The run of bad luck continued as Paita was sacked by English pirates in 1577. The very miffed settlers finally moved their city for the last time to its current spot.

Intense irrigation of the desert has made Piura a major agricultural center that feeds the masses, while rich coastal oil fields near Talara run overtime fueling the machinery of development. The department was hard hit by the El Niño floods of 1983, which destroyed almost 90% of the rice, cotton and plantain crops, and also caused serious damage to roads, bridges, buildings and oil wells in the area.

Information
Casas de cambio are at the Ica and Arequipa intersection.

Akasa (Tacna 630; per hr US$0.50; ⏰ 8am-11pm) Finding somewhere to get online is no problem in Piura, but try this place for some air-con comfort.

Banco Continental (☎ 33 1702; Tacna 598)

Banco Wiese (☎ 32 8200; cnr Huancavelica & Libertad)

BCP (☎ 33 6822; Grau 133)

Centro de Promoción Turistico (☎ 31 0772; www .munipiura.gob.pe; Ayacucho 377; ⏰ 8am-7pm Mon-Fri, 9am-7pm Sat, 9am-noon Sun) Has tourist information.

Clínica San Miguel (☎ 30 9300, 33 5913; Los Cocos 111; ⏰ 24hr) The best medical attention in Piura.

Delta Reps (☎ 32 1784; Libertad 640) A recommended full-service travel agency.

Lavas (☎ 30 4741; Callao 602; per kg US$1.20) For some reason, laundry services are fiendishly difficult to come by; thankfully, Lavas will wash your *ropas* (clothes) for only US$1.20 per kilo.

Oficina de migraciónes (☎ 33 5536; cnr Sullana & Circunvalación) Does visa extensions.

Post office (☎ 30 9595; cnr Ayacucho & Libertad; ⏰ 9am-7pm Mon-Fri, 9am-1pm Sat) Also on the plaza.

Sights
Jirón Lima, a block southeast of the Plaza de Armas, has preserved its colonial character more than most areas in Piura.

NORTH COAST

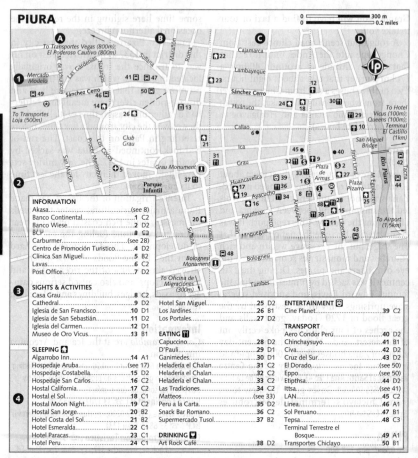

PIURA

INFORMATION
Akasa..(see 8)	
Banco Continental.................................**1** C2	
Banco Wiese..**2** D2	
BCP..**3** C2	
Carburmer.......................................(see 28)	
Centro de Promoción Turístico............**4** D2	
Clínica San Miguel...............................**5** B2	
Lavas..**6** C2	
Post Office..**7** D2	

SIGHTS & ACTIVITIES
Casa Grau...**8** C2	
Cathedral..**9** D2	
Iglesia de San Francisco.....................**10** D1	
Iglesia de San Sebastián.....................**11** D2	
Iglesia del Carmen..............................**12** D1	
Museo de Oro Vicus.............................**13** B1	

SLEEPING
Algarrobo Inn.....................................**14** A1	
Hospedaje Aruba............................(see 17)	
Hospedaje Costabella..........................**15** D2	
Hospedaje San Carlos..........................**16** C2	
Hostal California.................................**17** C2	
Hostal el Sol......................................**18** C1	
Hostal Moon Night.............................**19** C2	
Hostal San Jorge................................**20** B2	
Hotel Costa del Sol.............................**21** B2	
Hotel Esmeralda.................................**22** C1	
Hotel Paracas....................................**23** C1	
Hotel Peru...**24** C1	

Hotel San Miguel................................**25** D2		**ENTERTAINMENT**	
Los Jardines......................................**26** B1		Cine Planet...**39** C2	
Los Portales......................................**27** D2			
		TRANSPORT	
EATING		Aero Condor Perú...............................**40** D2	
Capuccino..**28** D2		Chinchaysuyo.....................................**41** B1	
D'Pauli..**29** D1		Civa...**42** D2	
Ganimedes...**30** D1		Cruz del Sur.......................................**43** D2	
Heladería el Chalan..............................**31** C2		El Dorado.......................................(see 50)	
Heladería el Chalan..............................**32** C2		Eppo...(see 50)	
Heladería el Chalan..............................**33** C2		Etipthsa..**44** D2	
Las Tradiciones..................................**34** C2		Ittsa...(see 41)	
Matteos.......................................(see 33)		LAN..**45** C2	
Peru a la Carta...................................**35** D2		Linea...**46** A1	
Snack Bar Romano..............................**36** C2		Sol Peruano..**47** B1	
Supermercado Tusol.............................**37** B2		Tepsa...**48** C3	
		Terminal Terrestre el	
DRINKING		Bosque..**49** B1	
Art Rock Café.....................................**38** D2		Transportes Chiclayo...........................**50** B1	

MUSEUMS

The small **Museo de Oro Vicus** (Museo Municipal; ☎ 30 9267; Huánuco 893; admission US$0.90; 🕘 9am-5pm Tue-Sun) has an underground museum with gold from nearby Vicus culture sites. Some excellent pieces are displayed, including a gold belt decorated with a life-sized gold cat head that puts today's belt buckles to shame.

Casa Grau (☎ 32 6541; Tacna 662; entry by donation; 🕘 8am-noon & 3-6pm Mon-Fri, 8am-noon Sat & Sun) is the house where Admiral Miguel Grau was born on July 27, 1834. The house was restored by the Peruvian navy and is now a naval museum. Admiral Grau was a hero of the War of the Pacific against Chile (1879–80), and the captain of the British-built warship *Huáscar*, a model of which can be seen in the museum.

CHURCHES

The **cathedral** on the Plaza de Armas was originally constructed in 1588, when Piura was finally built in its current location. The impressive gold-covered side altar of the Virgin of Fatima, built in the early 17th century, was once the main altar in the church. Famed local artist Ignacio Merino painted the canvas of San Martín de Porres in the mid-19th century.

Other churches worth seeing are the **Iglesia de San Francisco** (Jirón Lima), where Piura's independence was declared on January 4, 1821, and the colonial churches of **San Sebastián** (cnr Moquegua & Tacna) and **El Carmen** (Sánchez Cerro), which has a religious art museum and the chair used by the pope in 1985.

Sleeping

BUDGET

Hospedaje Aruba (☎ 30 3067; Junin 851; s/d with shared bathroom US$4.50/6) All white and bright, the small, spartan rooms here all share bathrooms. This *hospedaje* (small family-owned inn) has a few random decorations that give it a slight edge over your run-of-the-mill cheapie.

Hostal Moon Night (☎ 33 6174; Junín 899; s/d with shared bathroom US$4.50/6, s/d US$9/10.50) Five floors of bare, but supertidy, faux-wood-lined abodes with hot water and cable TV. Grab a top-floor room for some silence and city views.

Hostal California (☎ 32 8789; Junín 835; s/d with shared bathroom US$4.50/7.50) Popular with shoe-string travelers, this clean hotel has small, slightly stuffy rooms with fans and cold showers. Walls are thin, however, so pray for unamorous neighbors.

Hospedaje San Carlos (☎ 20 1059; Ayacucho 627; s/d US$7.50/10.50) Winning the budget stakes by a nose, this brand-spanking-new little *hospedaje* has immaculate and trim rooms, each with TV. The back rooms are best for light sleepers. The smiles here are broader and more genuine than anywhere else in town.

Los Jardines (☎ 32 6590; Los Cocos 436; s/d US$9/13.50) Located in a smart, quiet residential area around Club Grau, the rooms here are enormous and all have TV. The friendly family who runs the joint offers laundry facilities and shares its small communal garden area.

Hostal San Jorge (☎ 32 7514; fax 32 2928; Loreto 960; s/d US$10.50/15) This is a cookie-cutter standard-issue hotel with hot showers. Rooms have table fans and, for US$1.50 extra, cable TV.

Hospedaje Costabella (☎ 30 7807; Libertad 1082; s/d US$10.50/15) These supertidy little digs right near the Iglesia San Sebastian are in a bright yellow building and are popular with Peace Corps volunteers. The staff are friendly, and all rooms have TV.

Hotel Peru (☎ 33 3421, fax 33 1530; Arequipa 476; s/d US$12/17.50, d with air-con US$24.50; ⚹) This place has the goods: a pleasant bamboo lounging area, an elegant restaurant (with lots of gold fixtures, unfortunately) and neat, spacious rooms with hot water and TV. Worth its weight in nuevos soles.

Hotel Paracas (☎ /fax 33 5412; Loreto 339; s/d US$13.50/18) The small, dark lounge with slowly turning fan at this central hotel is reminiscent of a smoky Humphrey Bogart classic. The passable rooms have hot water, cable TV and fan, and there's a communal laundry.

Hotel San Miguel (☎ 30 5122; Apurímac 1007; s/d US$12/21) Modern, sterile and overlooking a quiet park, this place dishes out standard but spotless rooms. There's a café and the staff are helpful.

Algarrobo Inn (☎ 30 7450; www.ahorapiura.com.pe /hosteles; Los Cocos 389; s/d US$13.50/15, d with air-con US$24, all incl breakfast; ⚹) The walled-in compound here has both grass and shade in spades, both at a premium in Piura. Rooms are just OK, but there's a decent restaurant and – this may well be the deal clincher – you get free use of the Club Grau pool next door!

Hotel Vicus (☎ 34 3201; Guardia Civil B-3; s/d US$14.50/21; ☕) The well-appointed rooms here are spaced out around a drive-in, motel-styled layout and have everything you might crave, except air-con. They're neat and spotless nonetheless, with lots of splashy color; there's also room service.

MIDRANGE

Hostal El Sol (☎ 32 4461, 32 6307; mailservitucoral@terra.com.pe; Sánchez Cerro 455; s/d US$18/30; ☕) An elegant lobby leads to rooms that are good-sized and reasonable value, with a ceiling fan and cable TV. A restaurant is available for breakfast and a US$1.50 *menú* (set meal).

Hotel Esmeralda (☎ 33 1205, 33 1782; www.hotelesmeralda.com.pe; Loreto 235; s/d US$21/29.50, s/d with air-con US$37/48, all incl breakfast; ⚹ 💻) This place is a shining white-and-bright cocktail of glass, gold and tiles. The carpeted rooms look like they were decorated by your grandmother, but are comfy and have cable TV, phone and minifridge. There is an elevator, restaurant and room service, and staff are efficient and helpful.

Hotel Costa del Sol (☎ /fax 30 2864; www.costadelsolperu.com; Loreto 649; s/d US$62/72; ⚹ 💻 ☕) This attractive old-fashioned hotel has a well-stocked bar, elegant restaurant with room service, Jacuzzi, small gym and a casino (naturally). Well-kept and comfortably furnished rooms offer cable TV, a direct-dial phone and minibar. Ask about airport transfers.

TOP END

Los Portales (☎ 32 3072, 32 1161; losportales@cpi.udep.edu.pe; Libertad 875; s/d/ste incl breakfast US$70/90/110; ⚹ 💻 ☕) Live out dreams of conquistador grandeur in this beautiful and fully refurbished colonial building on the Plaza de Armas. Handsome public areas with iron grillwork and black-and-white checkered floor lead to a poolside restaurant and bar, indoor restaurant, games room with pool table and slot machines, and a smart bar. The comfortable rooms are decorated with an old-fashioned touch, yet have large cable TV, direct-dial phone, minibar and great beds. A welcome cocktail is included in the rates.

Eating

To tuck into some regional delicacies, a lunch-time trip to the nearby town of Catacaos is a must.

D'Pauli (Jirón Lima 451; cakes around US$0.90; ☑ 9am-1pm & 4-10pm) Leave room for dessert after your meal and visit here – it's a great cake shop.

Heladería el Chalan (snacks US$1.50-4.50; ☑ 7:30am-10pm); Grau (Grau 173 & 453); Tacna (Tacna 520) This fast-food joint has multiple outlets whipping up burgers and sandwiches, but our money's on the excellent selection of juices and the dozens of flavors of cool, cool ice cream.

Ganimedes (☎ 32 9176; Jirón Lima 440; menús US$1.50, mains US$2-3; ☑ 7am-10pm Mon-Sat, 11am-9pm Sun) A magnet for patchouli-oil-wafting dreadlocked types, this hippie hangout sticks diligently to its vegetarian pledge. No goat-head soups here, but plenty of refreshing fruit juices, yummy yogurts, wholegrain biscuits, and lots and lots of salads.

Snack Bar Romano (☎ 32 3399; Ayacucho 580; menús US$1.70, mains US$2.10-6; ☑ 7am-11pm, closed Sun) With an excellent *menú*, this local favorite has been around as long as its middle-aged waiters. It gets the double thumbs-up for ceviches and local specialties.

Las Tradiciones (☎ 32 2683; Ayacucho 579; menús US$1.80; ☑ 10am-10pm) With wicker chairs spread throughout a gently crumbling colonial building, this is another decent place to sample cheap local fare.

Matteos (☎ 30 8924; Tacna 532; meals US$2.40-3.60; ☑ 7am-10pm) On the Plaza de Armas, Matteos serves as an antidote to the hills of *parrillada* found all over Peru. The all-veggie menu has lots of I-can't-believe-it's-not-meat versions of local dishes, salads, and heaped plates of fruit and yogurt.

Capuccino (☎ 30 1111; Libertad 1048; sandwiches US$2.40-3.60; ☑ 10am-2pm & 5-11pm) It would be hard to beat the great desserts and massive sandwiches these guys bang together, all served in a bright and showy, artsy space. The Capuccino club sandwich (US$3.60), with grilled chicken, ham, egg, cheese and fries, is as delicious as it is enormous. Also

try their ice-cream-headache-inducing frozen fruit juices (US$1.20).

Peru a la Carta (☎ 31 3596; Tacna 786; meals US$3-5.50; ☑ 8:30am-10pm) A slightly more upmarket eatery serving local faves in a cavernous old building that's fitted out with lots of wood and a few bits of art. With excellent food and very attentive service, it's popular with Peace Corps volunteers.

Carburmer (☎ 30 9475; Libertad 1014; mains US$3.60-9; ☑ 6-11pm; ☒) This cozy and romantic place is the best Italian restaurant in town. Dripping with moodily lit ambience (check out the wacky pulley system that opens the door), this is the ideal place for that special night out. It has an excellently executed menu where Italian dishes vie for your attention with Peruvian specialties.

Supermercado Tusol (Plaza Grau; ☑ 8:30am-10:30pm) For self-catering.

Drinking

Art Rock Café (☎ 976 5098; Apurímac 343; ☑ 6pm-late Thu-Sun) This is a modish wood-covered drinking hideaway with a drink selection as long as your arm, plus lots of cocktails, pool and foosball tables, live music, Swiss bar snacks and an über-friendly vibe. It's the sort of place that, after your fourth Crystal, is guaranteed to make you feel like you've been coming here for years.

Queens (cnr Guardia Civil & Cayeta; admission US$4.50; ☑ 9pm-late Thu-Sun) If you really need to shake your rump, head down to Queens, which is not in New York, but just east of town. On rowdy weekend nights the place is filled with gringos and well-heeled Peruvians shakin' their money-maker to an eclectic international music mix.

Entertainment

Cine Planet (☎ 30 3714; Huancavelica 537; admission US$2-2.60) In a brand-spanking-new shopping complex, this cinema shows Hollywood flicks in blissful air-conditioned comfort.

Getting There & Away

AIR

The **airport** (code PIU; ☎ 34 4505) is on the south-eastern bank of the Río Piura, 2km from the city center. Schedules change often. The usual US$3.57 airport tax is charged.

LAN (☎ 30 2145; Grau 140) flies from Lima to Piura (US$111) at 6:30am and 6pm daily, returning to Lima at 9:30am and 8pm. LAN also has a 9:30am flight to Chiclayo (US$64), returning at 8:30am. **Aero Condor Perú** (☎ 31 3668; Libertad 777) flies from Lima (US$100) at 5:30pm, returning at 8:30pm.

BUS
International

The standard route to Ecuador goes along the Panamericana via Tumbes to Machala. Alternatively, **Transportes Loja** (☎ 30 9407; Sánchez Cerro 228) goes via La Tina to Macará (US$3.60, four hours) and Loja (US$8.50, eight hours) at 9:30am, 1pm, 9:30pm and 10pm. These buses stop for border formalities, then continue; see p369 for warnings about the Ecuador–Peru border.

Domestic

Services to Lima take 12 to 16 hours. Several companies have offices on the 1100 block of Sánchez Cerro, though for Cajamarca and across the northern Andes, it's best to go to Chiclayo and get a connection there.

Chinchaysuyo (☎ 30 4651; Sánchez Cerro 1156) Has been known to run direct buses to Huaraz (US$16.50, 12 to 14 hours) at 10:30pm.

Civa (☎ 34 5451; Tacna 101) Has a 5pm and a 6pm bus to Lima (US$15 to US$21), frequent buses to Chulucanas (US$0.90, 45 minutes), and a bus to Huancabamba (US$6, eight to 10 hours) at 8:30am.

Cruz del Sur (☎ 33 7094; Bolognesi at Lima) Three Lima buses (US$27 to US$37.50) between 6:30pm and 7:30pm.

El Dorado (☎ 32 5875, 33 6952; Sánchez Cerro 1119) Buses for Tumbes (US$4.50, five hours) every two hours, and six buses a day to Máncora (US$4.50, 2½ hours).

El Poderoso Cautivo (☎ 30 9888; Sullana Norte 7) Buses for Ayabaca (US$4.50, six hours) at 8:30am and 3pm.

Eppo (☎ 30 4543; Sánchez Cerro 1141) Has buses to Sullana (US$0.60, 45 minutes) and Talara (US$2.40, two hours) every 30 minutes. Also fast services to Máncora (US$3.60, 3½ hours) hourly.

Etiptsha (☎ 34 5174; Tacna 277) Buses to Huancabamba (US$6, eight to 10 hours) leaving at 7:30am and 5:30pm.

Ittsa (☎ 33 3982; Sánchez Cerro 1142) Has a bus to Trujillo (US$3.30 to US$9, six hours) and Chimbote (US$7.50, seven hours) at 11pm, and a *bus-cama* to Lima at 6:30pm (US$30).

Linea (☎ 32 7821; Sánchez Cerro 1215) Hourly buses to Chiclayo (US$3.60, three hours), an 11pm bus to Trujillo (US$9, six hours) and a 6am and 6:30pm bus to Cajamarca (US$11 to US$14.50, 10 hours).

Sol Peruano (☎ 41 8143; Sánchez Cerro 1112) Goes direct to Tarapoto at 1pm (US$15, 18 hours).

Tepsa (☎ 30 6345, Loreto 1198) Lima buses (US$25.50) at 5pm and 7:30pm.

Transportes Chiclayo (☎ 30 8455; Sánchez Cerro 1121) Hourly buses to Chiclayo (US$3.60, three hours) and a bus to Tumbes (US$4.50, five hours) at 10:15am.

Transportes Vegas (☎ 30 8729; Panamericana C1, Lot 10) Has buses leaving for Ayabaca (US$4.50, six hours) at 8:30am and 3pm.

East of the San Miguel pedestrian bridge, Terminal el Castillo has buses for departmental towns east of Piura. Buses and *combis* for Catacaos (US$0.30, 15 minutes), Sullana (US$0.60, 45 minutes) and Paita (US$0.80, one hour) leave from **Terminal Terrestre el Bosque** (Sánchez Cerro, cuadra 12).

TAXI

If you are heading to Tumbes, you can catch a much faster *colectivo* taxi (US$6, 3½ hours).

CATACAOS
☎ 073 / pop 57,500

Catacaos, a small, dust-blanketed town 12km southwest of Piura, is the self-proclaimed capital of *artesanía* (handicrafts) in the region. And justifiably so: its **arts market** (☼ 10am-4pm) is the best in northern Peru. Sprawling for several blocks near the Plaza de Armas, here you will find excellent weavings, gold and silver filigree jewelry, wood carvings, ceramics, leather goods and more. The weekends are the best and busiest times to visit.

Not satisfied with the *artesanía* crown, Catacaos is also shooting for the culinary medal, with dozens of *picanterías* (local restaurants) open for lunch daily. You can get local specialties like *chicha, seco de chabelo* (a thick plantain and beef stew), *seco de cabrito* (kid goat), *tamales verdes* (green corn dumplings), *copus* (dried goat heads cured in vinegar and then stewed) and loads of other dishes, not all of them that adventurous. We've had reports of certain restaurants severely overcharging foreigners, so look at a few places and check prices before you tuck in.

Catacaos is famous for its elaborate **Semana Santa** (Holy Week) processions and celebrations. Reach it by *colectivo* from the Terminal Terrestre el Bosque in Piura (US$0.30, 15 minutes).

PAITA
☎ 073 / pop 57,400

The main port of the department of Piura is the historic town of Paita, 50km due west of Piura by paved road. This dusty, crumbling colonial port town looks like it sprouted organically from the desert that surrounds it and has a roguish, Wild West feel to it – understandable when you look at its history.

In 1527 Pizarro became the first European to land here, and Paita has been attracting seafaring conquistadors ever since. It became a Spanish colonial port and was frequently sacked by pirates and swashbuckling buccaneers such as Sir Francis Drake. Raids continued, and in the 18th century Protestant adventurer George Anson attempted to decapitate the wooden statue of Our Lady of Mercy. The statue, complete with slashed neck, can still be seen in the church of La Merced. The only flotilla you're likely to see nowadays is a scrappy Technicolor shipping fleet bobbing offshore.

Information

There are several banks here and a basic hospital.

Sights & Activities

Manuela Sáenz, the influential Ecuadorian mistress of Simón Bolívar, arrived here upon Bolívar's death in 1850. Her **house** still stands (and people live there), and a plaque commemorates its history. Across the street is **La Figura**, a wooden figurehead from a pirate ship.

To the north and south of the port are good beaches popular with summer holidaymakers. About 13km north (by road) is the good beach of **Colán**, home to the oldest colonial church in Peru. This white-sand beach is a trendy summer destination for the Peruvian jet set, but is practically deserted for rest of the year. The curving bay has a shallow beach that's excellent for swimming.

The beach of **Yasila**, some 12km to the south, is also popular.

Sleeping & Eating

PAITA

Despite the town's historic interest and beaches, Paita has only a few hotels, and most visitors stay in Piura.

Hostal El Mundo (☎ 61 1401; Bolívar 402; s/d US$6/9) Offers basic rooms with showers and little else.

Hostal Miramar (☎ 21 1083; Jorge Chávez 418; d US$12) Our pick of the bunch is this place, housed in a funky, weathered colonial building standing at bright orange alert on the

waterfront. There are bright pastel colors throughout and the massive rooms have tall ceilings and large windows.

Hostal Las Brisas (☎ 21 2175; fax 61 2175; Ayurora 201 at A Ugarte; s/d from US$12/18) This place has small, carpeted rooms with phones, cable TV, hot-water bathrooms and a hospital-white restaurant.

Hotel El Farlo (☎ 32 0322; Junin 320; s/d US$15/21) This hotel has bigger rooms near the waterfront, though they're slightly tattered and vary from downright stuffy to bright and airy.

Tiny fresh-seafood stands line the waterway near the main pier. The best place to eat is **Club Liberal** (☎ 61 1173; Jorge Chávez 162; meals US$2.70-5.50; ☼ 7am-10pm), which has creaky wooden floors and lots of rickety charm in its 2nd-floor pier location; the breezy, sweeping vistas are excellent.

COLÁN

Hospedaje Frente del Mar (☎ 966 6914; d US$6) Run by the ever helpful Alfredo, this *hospedaje* has a good seaside restaurant and rents out a couple of 'rustic' rooms at the back.

Bahia del Sol (☎ 997 6488; bahiadelsol_colan@hotmail .com; r per person US$25 per person) On the south part of the beach, this spot has clean, austere, modern rooms sleeping up to four people.

Playa Colán Lodge (☎ 32 6778; www.playacolanlodge .com.pe; 2-/4-/5-person cabin US$55/65/75; ☲) Further south, this has to be the best place to stay. Built from a combination of natural materials it has an upmarket Robinson Crusoe feel and hosts cute, pastel-colored bungalows along the beach. There are lots of hammocks, shady palm trees, a tennis court, and restaurant and bar. In the low season ask for a US$20 discount.

Getting There & Away

There are buses every 10 minutes to Paita from the Terminal Terrestre el Bosque in Piura (US$0.80, one hour). *Colectivos* leave from the main terminal in Paita, near the market, to Colán (US$0.60, 20 minutes) and Sullana (US$1.20, 1¼ hours).

SULLANA

☎ 073 / pop 161,500 / elev 90m

Abandoned as a location for modern-day Piura, Sullana today is a hot and dusty little city with several parks and more shops than you can poke a S/20 bill at. It's also a transportation hub for destinations north of Piura. There's little to see here except the hustle and bustle of a commercial Peruvian market town, however.

Be wary of personal safety outside of central areas and take *mototaxis* to and from the outskirts of town.

Decent budget hotels include the **Hostal Lion's Palace** (☎ 50 2587; Grau 1030; s/d US$6/9), with large, dark and cool rooms with bathrooms, and the slightly more spiffy **Hostal El Churre** (☎ 50 7006; Tarapacá 501; s/d US$10.50/15), which has contemporary rooms that get a bit of noise due to its corner location. The best is **Hostal La Siesta** (☎ /fax 50 2264; Av La Panamericana 404; s/d from US$30/39; 🈂 🛢), on the outskirts of town, with hot water (but do you really need it?), cable TV and a restaurant.

Restaurant Park Plaza (☎ 50 9904; Plaza de Armas; menús US$1.20; 🕑 8am-10pm) is owned by a fanatical fan of Hollywood (the walls are covered with pictures of stars) and has a good Peruvian menu.

Buses to Piura leave from the **Terminal Terrestre** (José de Lama 481) every few minutes (US$0.60, 45 minutes). There are also buses to Máncora (US$3, 2½ hours).

CHULUCANAS

☎ 073 / pop 70,400 / elev 95m

This village is about 55km east of Piura, just before the Sechura Desert starts rising into the Andean slopes. It's known Peru-wide for its distinctive **ceramics** – rounded, glazed, earth-colored pots that depict humans. Chulucanas ceramics have officially been declared a part of Peru's cultural heritage and are becoming famous outside of Peru.

The best place to buy ceramics around here is in **La Encantada**, a quiet rural outpost just outside of Chulucanas whose inhabitants work almost exclusively in *artesanía*. La Encantada was home to the late Max Inga, a local legend who studied ceramic artifacts from the ancient Tallan and Vicus cultures and sparked a resurgence in the art form. The friendly artisans are often happy to demonstrate the production process, from the 'harvesting' of the clay to the application of mango-leaf smoke to get that distinctive black-and-white design. The village is reached from Chulucanas by a 10-minute *mototaxi* ride (around US$1.50).

There are a few basic hotels in Chulucanas, including **Hostal Chulucanas Soler** (☎ 37 8576; Ica 209; s/d US$6/10.50), two blocks from the plaza.

Civa has frequent buses to and from Piura (US$0.90, 45 minutes).

HUANCABAMBA

☎ 073 / pop 8700 / elev 1957m

For the daring adventurer, Huancabamba, deep in the eastern mountains, is well worth the rough 10-hour journey from Piura. This region is famed in Peru for the powerful *brujos* and *curanderos* (healers) that live and work at the nearby lakes of Huaringas. Peruvians from all over the country flock to partake in these ancient healing techniques (see Shopping for Shamans, p360). Many locals (but few gringos) visit the area, so finding information and guides is not difficult.

The mystical town of Huancabamba is surrounded by mountains shrouded in mist and lies at the head of the long, narrow Río Huancabamba. The banks of the Huancabamba are unstable and constantly eroding and the town is subject to frequent subsidence and slippage. It has earned itself the nickname *La Ciudad que Camina* (the Town that Walks). Spooky.

There's a small **tourist information office** (☎ 47 3321; 🕑 8am-6pm) at the bus station that has an elementary map of the area and a list of accredited *brujos* and *curanderos*. You can also change US dollars at the bus station. There's a basic **hospital** (☎ 47 3024).

Hotels are all rudimentary and most share cold-water bathrooms. **Hostal El Dorado** (☎ 47 3016; Medina 116; s/d with shared bathroom US$3/4.50) is on the Plaza de Armas, and has one of the best restaurants in town and a helpful owner. **Hospedaje Tres Estrellas** (☎ 47 3077; San Martin 115; s/d with shared bathroom US$3/9) is another bare-bones budget deal in an old building on the plaza; it also has ludicrously friendly staff. **Hostal Danubio** (☎ 47 3200; Grau 206; s/d with shared bathroom US$4.50/7.50, s/d US$9/12), on the corner of the plaza, has the most solid rooms in town, all with TVs.

Restaurants to try include the busy **Casa Blanca** (Union 304; menús US$1.10, meals US$1.20-1.80; 🕑 7am-11pm), which serves Peruvian food and has a cheap *menú*. The local beverage is *rompope*, a concoction of sugarcane alcohol with raw egg, honey, lemon and spices – a pauper's pisco sour.

At the Huancabamba bus terminal, **Etipthsa** (☎ 47 3000), **Civa** (☎ 47 3488) and **Turismo Express** (☎ 47 3320) each have a morning service between 8am and 9am to Piura (US$6, eight to

SHOPPING FOR SHAMANS

When people from the 'West' think of witchcraft, visions of pointed hats, broomsticks and bubbling brews are rarely far away. In Peru, consulting *brujos* (witch doctors) and *curanderos* (healers) is widely accepted and has a long tradition predating Spanish colonization.

Peruvians from all walks of life visit *brujos* and *curanderos* and often pay sizable amounts of money for their services. These shamans are used to cure an endless list of ailments, from headaches to cancer to chronic bad luck, and are particularly popular in matters of love – whether it's love lost, love found, love desired or love scorned.

The **Huaringas** lake area near Huancabamba, almost 4000m above sea level, is said to have potent curative powers and attracts a steady stream of visitors from all corners of the continent. The most famous lake in the area is **Laguna Shimbe**, though the nearby **Laguna Negra** is the one most frequently used by the *curanderos*.

Ceremonies can last all night and entail hallucinogenic plants (such as the San Pedro cactus), singing, chanting, dancing, and a dip in the lakes' painfully freezing waters. Some ceremonies involve more powerful substances like *ayahuasca* (Quechua for 'vine of the soul'), a potent and vile mix of jungle vines used to induce strong hallucinations. Vomiting is a common side effect. The *curanderos* will also use *ícaros*, which are mystical songs and chants used to direct and influence the spiritual experience. Serious *curanderos* will spend many years studying the art, striving for the hard-earned title of *maestro curandero*.

If you are interested in visiting a *curandero* while in Huancabamba, be warned that this tradition is taken very seriously, and gawkers or skeptics will get a hostile reception. *Curanderos* with the best reputation are found closer to the lake district. The information booth at the bus station has a list of registered *curanderos*. In Salala, closer to the lakes, you will be approached by *curanderos* or their 'agents', but be wary of scam artists – try get a reference before you arrive. Know also that there are some *brujos* who are said to work *en el lado oscuro* (on the dark side). Expect to pay around US$60 for a visit.

These days, busy Peruvian professionals can get online and consult savvy, business-minded shamans via instant messenger. Not quite the same thing as midnight chants and icy dunks in the remote lakes of the Andes.

ten hours). Two afternoon buses also depart for Piura at 4:30pm and 5pm. To visit the lakes, catch the 5am *combi* from this terminal to the town of Salala (US$3, two hours), from where you can arrange treks to the lakes (US$6 return).

AYABACA
☎ 073 / pop 5400 / elev 2715m

For the final three hours of the journey between Piura and Ayabaca the bumpy road starts to climb through cultivated fields and dense clouds and doesn't stop until it reaches the pretty town of Ayabaca. This aged colonial highland hamlet is surrounded by green valleys and foggy peaks – there's something to be said for waking up to a blanket of clouds filling up the valley below you like a fluffy meringue pie.

Information
You can change US dollars at the **Banco de la Nación** (Grau 448). Limited tourist information is

available at the **municipalidad** (☎ 47 1003; Cáceres 578), on the Plaza de Armas.

Sights & Activities
The overgrown Inca site of **Aypate** (admission free) contains walls, flights of stairs, terraces (some still in use), ceremonial baths and a central plaza. This territory here is stunning and you will see hazy mountains full of orchids, bromeliads, birds, white-tailed deer and other species. It's 2½ hours by truck, then three hours on foot. There are other, unexplored Inca and pre-Inca sites in the area, as well as mysterious caves, lakes and mountains, some of which are said to be bewitched. Ornithologists report excellent **bird-watching** habitats.

Visit the area in the May to November dry season when the trails are passable. **Raul Bardales** (☎ 47 1043; Piura 331) guides tourists to Aypate (US$60). **Segundo Celso Acuña Calle** (☎ 47 1209; Cáceres 257) is very knowledgeable on the area, and will talk your ear off if you go with him on one of his five-day treks (US$50 per day, guiding only), which take in Inca ruins and trails, pre-Inca sites and lagoons.

Festivals & Events

Held from October 12 to 15, the gaudy religious festival of **El Señor Cautivo**, rarely seen by tourists, packs every hotel in town. Pilgrims pour in from all over the country for this, some who have walked continuously for months and crawl their last few miles on hands and knees. It's an unforgettable sight.

Sleeping & Eating

Hostal Alex (☎ 47 1101; Bolívar 112; s/d US$3/9) One of the cheapest choices in town.

Hospedaje Plaza (☎ 47 1085; Caceres 423; s/d US$4.50/6) This *hospedaje* has hot water, cozy rooms with TVs and plaza views.

Hostal Oro Verde (☎ 41 0028; Slavery 381; s/d with shared bathroom US$3/6, s/d US$7.50/10.50) Just off the plaza, this place has the usual budget bare-bones rooms as well as much nicer, newer rooms with TV, bathroom and steaming hot water.

Hotel Samanaga Municipal (☎ /fax 47 1049; s/d US$7.50/12) On the Plaza de Armas, Hotel Samanaga Municipal is the pick of the bunch, with friendly staff, a decent restaurant and rooms with TV and hot showers.

For meals, there are *pollerías* aplenty, but the 'best' restaurant is **Flor de Milan** (☎ 47 1093; Tacna 111; meals US$0.90-2.40; ☺ 7am-10pm), with fancy checkered tablecloths and a small menu serving local dishes.

Getting There & Away

Transportes Vegas (☎ 47 1231) and **El Poderoso Cautivo** (☎ 47 1247) on the plaza both have buses

to Piura (US$4.50, six hours) at 8:30am and 3pm. From Ayabaca there is access to the Ecuadorian village of Amaluza (five hours by various *combis*).

TALARA

☎ 073 / pop 100,400

Once a small fishing village, Talara today is the site of Peru's largest oil refinery, producing 60,000 barrels of petroleum a day. Although there are some good beaches near Talara, the town has little to interest the tourist.

Negritos, 11km south of Talara by road, is on Punta Pariñas and is the most westerly point of the South American continent.

Some 20 hotels house oil workers, but water supply is an ongoing problem. **Hostal Grau** (☎ 38 2841; Grau A77; s/d US$6/9) is clean and friendly and has hot water for part of the day. **Gran Hotel Pacifico** (☎ 38 5449; www.ghotelpacificotalara.com.pe; s/d US$29/43; 🅿 🛗) is the best place in town and has a bar, café and restaurant.

Buses leave for Piura (US$2.40, two hours) and Tumbes (US$2.20, two hours) at least every hour.

CABO BLANCO

☎ 073

The Panamericana runs parallel to the ocean north of Talara, with frequent glimpses of the coast. This area is one of Peru's main oil fields, and oil pumps are often seen scarring both the land and the sea with offshore oil rigs.

About 40km north of Talara is the sleepy town of Cabo Blanco, one of the world's most famous fishing spots. Set on a gently curving bay strewn with rocks, the town has a flotilla of fishing vessels floating offshore where the

---

BORDER CROSSING: ECUADOR VIA LA TINA

The border post of La Tina lacks hotels, but the Ecuadorian town of Macará (3km from the border) has adequate facilities. La Tina is reached by *colectivo* (shared) taxis (US$4.50, two hours) leaving Sullana throughout the day. **Transportes Loja** (☎ 073-30 9407; Sánchez Cerro 228, Piura) buses from Piura conveniently go straight through here and on to Loja (US$8.50, eight hours).

The border is the international bridge over the Río Calvas and is open 24 hours. Formalities are relaxed as long as your documents are all in order. There are no banks, though you'll find moneychangers at the border or in Macará. The Peruvian immigration office is on the left, before the international office.

Travelers entering Ecuador will find taxis (including *colectivos*) to take them to Macará, where the Ecuadorian immigration building is found on the 2nd floor of the *municipalidad* (town hall), on the plaza. Most nationalities are simply given a tourist card, which must be surrendered when leaving. There is a Peruvian consulate in Macará. See Lonely Planet's *Ecuador & the Galápagos Islands* for further information on Ecuador.

confluence of warm Humbolt currents and El Niño waters creates a unique microcosm filled with marine life. Ernest Hemingway was supposedly inspired to write his famous tale *The Old Man and the Sea* after fishing here in the early 1950s. The largest fish ever landed on a rod here was a 710kg black marlin, caught in 1953 by Alfred Glassell Jr. The angling is still good, though 20kg tuna are a more likely catch than black marlin, which have declined and are now rarely over 100kg. Fishing competitions are held here and 300kg specimens are still occasionally caught. From November to January, magnificent 3m-high pipeline waves attract hard-core surfers to Cabo Blanco.

La Cristina is a 32ft deep-sea fishing boat, with high-quality Penn tackle, which can be rented through Hostal Merlin and other hotels in the area for US$350 per six-hour day, including drinks and lunch. January, February and September are considered the best fishing months.

Hostal Merlin (☎ 25 6188, in Lima 01-442 8318; www .geocities.com/hotelmerlin; s/d incl breakfast US$21/31) has 12 massive rooms with handsome stone-flagged floors, private cold showers and balconies with ocean views. This cavernous hotel doesn't get many visitors.

Cabo Blanco is several kilometers down a winding road from the Panamericana town of Las Olas. Catch a ride in one of the regular pickup trucks that ply the route (US$0.50, 20 minutes).

MÁNCORA
☎ 073 / pop 9300

Peru's worst-kept secret, Máncora is *the* place to see and be seen along the Peruvian coast – in the summer months foreigners flock here to rub sunburned shoulders with the frothy cream of the Peruvian jet set. It's not hard to see why – Peru's best sandy beach stretches for several kilometers in the sunniest region of the country, while dozens of plush resorts and their budget-conscious brethren offer up rooms within meters of the lapping waves. On shore, a plethora of restaurants provides fresh seafood straight off the boat as fuel for the long, lazy days. The consistently good surf draws a sun-bleached, board-toting bunch, and raucous nightlife keeps visitors busy after the sun dips into the sea in a ball of fiery flames. However, even though it has seen recent explosive growth, Máncora has

somehow managed to cling to its fishing community roots.

Located about halfway between Talara and Tumbes, Máncora has the Panamericana passing right through its middle, within 100m of the surf. During the December to March summer period, the scene can get rowdy and accommodation prices tend to double. But year-round sun means that this is one of the few resort towns on the coast that doesn't turn into a ghost town at less popular times.

Orientation
The Panamericana, called Calle Piura at the south end of town and Calle Grau at the north, is the main drag, with businesses lining both sides. From the bridge at the south end, the Antigua (Old) Panamericana is a dirt road following the coast and sprinkled with remote, upscale hotels. The Antigua rejoins the Panamericana about 12km further south near Los Organos.

Addresses are not used much here – just look for signs in the center.

Information
There is no information office, but the website www.vivamancora.com has tons of useful information. Two ATMs (no bank) accept Visa and MasterCard.

Banco de la Nación (☎ 25 8193; Piura 625; ☒ 8:30am-2:30pm Mon-Fri) Change US dollars here.
Internet Marlon (☎ 25 2437; Piura 320; per hr US$0.60; ☒ 9am-midnight) Attached to Marlon; has the newest computers and the most reliable service.
Marlon (☎ 25 2437; Piura 520) The best general store; it sells phonecards and has several telephone booths.

Activities
There are remote, deserted beaches around Máncora; ask your hotel to arrange a taxi or give you directions by bus and foot, but be prepared to walk several kilometers.

SURFING & KITESURFING
Surf here is best from November to February, although good waves are found year-round and always draw dedicated surfers. Los Organos is a popular surfing spot. You can rent surfboards from several places at the southern end of the beach in Máncora (US$6 per day). **Soledad** (☎ 929 1356; Piura 316) sells boards, surf clothing and organizes surf lessons for US$13.50 per hour (including board rental). The friendly Pilar, at **Laguna Camp** (☎ 9401 5628;

www.vivamancora.com/lagunacamp), also does surf lessons for US$15 for 90 minutes of instruction. For something a little more extreme, you can get lessons in kitesurfing (US$40 per hour); ask about it at **Del Wawa** (☎ 25 8427; www.delwawa.com).

MUD BATHS
About 11km east of town, up the wooded Fernandez valley, a natural **hot spring** (admission US$0.60) has bubbling water and powder-fine mud – perfect for a face pack. The slightly sulfurous water and mud is said to have curative properties. The hot spring can be reached by *mototaxi* (US$9 including waiting time).

TREKKING
To see some of the interior of this desert coast, hire a pickup (around US$20, including waiting time) to take you up the Fernandez valley, past the mud baths, and on until the road ends (about 1½ hours). Continue for two hours on foot through mixed woodlands with unique birdlife to reach Los Pilares, which has pools ideal for swimming. You can also visit these areas as part of a tour.

OTHER ACTIVITIES
Máncora Rent (Hospedaje Las Terrazas; ☎ 25 8351; Piura 496) rents off-road motorbikes (US$4.50 per hour, US$30 for 24 hours) as well as small quad-bikes for teens (US$20 per hour) and jet skis (US$30 per 30 minutes). For transportation with a mind of its own, **horses** are available for hire along the beach for US$6 per hour.

Tours & Guides
Ursula Behr from **Iguana's** (☎ 9853 5099; urs _behr@hotmail.com; Piura 245) organizes full-day trips to the Los Pilares dry forest, which include wading through sparkling waterfalls, swimming, horseback riding and a soak in the mud baths, for US$30 per person. She's also a professional rafting guide (earned her stripes in Cuzco) and has set up a two-day class III river-running trip through the tropical forest at Rica Playa (US$100 per person). Sea kayaking trips, ideal for bird-spotting, cost US$30 per person for the day.

Sleeping
Rates for accommodations in Máncora are seasonal, with the January to mid-March high season commanding rates up to 50% higher

than the rest of the year, especially at weekends. During the three major holiday periods (Christmas to New Year, Semana Santa and Fiestas Patrias) accommodations can cost triple the low-season rate, can require multinight stays, is very crowded and is generally best avoided. High-season rates are given here. Many pricier hotels accept payment in US dollars.

BUDGET
Budget rooms are spendier here than other parts of the coast, but there are cheap beds in *hospedajes* in the center of town and the southern part of the beach. Most places offer triples and quad rooms for slightly less per person.

HI La Posada (☎ 25 8328; Panamericana Km 1164; campsite per person US$1.50, dm/s/d US$4.50/7.50/35) Our personal pick of the litter, La Posada is a hushed compound close to the beach and perennially popular with backpackers. Safe, with a pleasant garden, hammocks and basic kitchen facilities, this HI-affiliated *hostal* has recently added a restaurant and improved, more comfortable rooms. Owner-manager Luisa goes out of her way to make guests feel comfortable. It's by the bridge at the south end of town.

Hospedaje Crillón (☎ 25 8017; Paita 168; r per person with shared/private bathroom US$4.50/7.50) One quiet block back from the beach, this place has cubbylike cells with four walls, four beds and no room for anything else – though surfers manage to get their boards in here. It is surprisingly busy.

Hostal Sol y Mar (☎ 25 8106, 25 8088; www.viva mancora.com/solymar; Piura 220; r per person from US$4.50, d US$12; 🏊) With 67 rooms, this motel is close to good waves, and attracts a bizarre mix of Peruvian families, surfers and the party-till-you-drop crowd. The huge speakers out front can tell you what to expect – loud music and dancing till the wee hours. Table tennis, foosball and a bar-restaurant complete the picture, but the quality of the rooms varies widely and it's only marginally more secure than sleeping on the beach.

Laguna Camp (☎ 9401 5628; www.vivamancora.com /lagunacamp; r per person US$6) This laid-back pad is a hidden gem, sandwiched between the town's lagoon and the ocean. Indonesian-style bamboo bungalows sit around a pleasant sandy garden right near the water, and lots of swinging, shady hammocks will provide days of entertainment. There's a small communal kitchen and the whole vibe is chilled and friendly. The cheery owner Pilar is also a surf instructor.

Hospedaje Don Carlos (☎ 25 8007; Piura 641; s/d US$6/10.50) Of the many cheap places in the center of Máncora, this is among the best run, with helpful owners. Barely passable concrete rooms sleep two to six, and have cold water showers and fans.

El Pirata (☎ 25 8459; www.vivamancora.com/elpirata; Panamericana Km 1164; s/d with shared bathroom US$7.50/9, s/d US$10.50/18) A mishmash of austere split-bamboo rooms, some with more gaps in the walls than bamboo. Other, slightly more solid rooms have attached bathrooms. There's a kitchen, a few hammocks to laze in and little else. It's very relaxed and the owners have a laissez-faire attitude to the whole endeavor.

Hostal Sausalito (☎ 25 8058, in Lima 01-479 0779; jcvigoe@terra.com.pe; Piura cuadra 4; s/d US$9/15) If the intense colors of the walls here don't keep you up at night, the traffic noise might. The tiny rooms are acceptably clean and well kept, and have TVs and ceiling fans. Be careful with your valuables here.

Casa Palmera (☎ 9825 8793; r per person US$15) Behind Las Olas, the new rooms here are in a bright lemon-colored building and face a small patch of vibrant grass. The abodes are immaculate and quiet, but lack any view. It's one row of houses back from the beach.

Del Wawa (☎ 25 8427; www.delwawa.com; s/d US$15/30) This surfer's mecca has a great setup right on the beach; the warm-colored adobe rooms all face the ocean. There's lots of hammock space, a chill space with great views of the best breaks on the beach, and surfboard rental. Del Wawa also organizes kitesurfing lessons for US$40 per hour.

Hostal las Olas (☎ 85 8109; lasolasmancora@yahoo.com; r per person incl breakfast US$20) Rooms here are minimalist white and some come with ocean views, though they're all the same price. The small, cozy restaurant looks onto the beach's best breaks and is a surf-spotter's dream. You can rent boards here for US$6 per day.

MIDRANGE

South of Máncora, along Antigua Panamericana, are multiple tranquil resorts spread out over several kilometers of beaches, including Las Pocitas and Vichaito beach. All have restaurants and can be reached by *mototaxi* (US$1.50 to US$3). The places further south are the quietest and are more likely to have individual bungalow accommodation. The

following places are listed in the order you will reach them when traveling from Máncora.

Punta Ballenas Inn (☎ 25 8136; www.puntaballenas.com; Panamericana Km 1164; d US$50; ☒) At the south end of town where the Antigua Panamericana branches off, this hotel is far enough away from town to be silent but still close enough to allow frequent visits. White brick all round and designed with a raunchy mood in mind, this laid-back place has a great restaurant, a tiny pool, a colorful bar, foosball tables and lots of art gracing the walls. The rooms are comfortable but possibly overpriced.

Casa de Playa (☎ 25 8005; www.vivamancora.com/casadeplaya; s/d US$35/55; ☒) About a kilometer further along the old Panamericana, this large place offers up modern, slick dwellings colored in warm orange and yellow tones and constructed with lots of gently curving lines. All the large rooms have hot water, arty bits and a balcony with a hammock and fine sea views. The restaurant here is good and a lovely two-story lounge hangs out over the sea.

Sunset (☎ 25 8111; www.hotelsunset.com.pe; d/f US$50/100; ☒) Another smooth and showy resort, the ultrahip, boutique-styled Sunset wouldn't be out of place on the cover of *Condé Nast Traveler*. It has beautifully furnished interiors and great aqua-themed rock sculptures, and good-sized rooms supply solid mattresses, hot showers, balconies and views of the seascape. The pool is tiny and ocean access is rocky, though a short walk brings you to a sandy beach. The hotel's Italian restaurant is excellent.

Las Pocitas (☎ 25 8432; www.laspocitasmancora.com; d US$60-70; ☒) Las Pocitas' rooms have white-stone walls timbered with bamboo, and are cool, inviting and bespeckled with shell decorations (in case you'd forgotten you were at the beach). Patios with a hammock and sea views are standard and a children's playground, table tennis, foosball, *sapo* (a game in which brass disks are tossed into a table with holes in it) and a grassy lawn are featured.

Balcones de Máncora (☎ 997 5755; balcones_de_mancora@yahoo.es; 8-person bungalows US$120) If you have money to burn, let this be your pyre: this place easily wins the 'most beautiful bungalows' plaudit. Set on a cliff overlooking the beach, these three deluxe bamboo-and-thatch dwellings have giant overhanging roofs, a full kitchen (complete with microwave), two bedrooms, a living space and lots of glass frontage for an unimpeded panorama of the coast. Inside, they're elegantly decorated and have all the creature comforts needed for extended stays. The upstairs double bedroom is completely open to the ocean and has its own bathroom. At the time of writing, plans were afoot to build smaller, and cheaper, double bungalows.

Los Corales (☎ 25 8309, 969 9170; www.vivamanorca .com/loscorales; s/d incl breakfast US$35/50; 🛄) The alluring little rooms here are filled with seashell decorations and painted in forcibly cheery colors. All have balconies, cable TVs and hammocks, though only some have sea views. There is a tiny pool and a small children's playground, and the beachfront is rocky.

Las Arenas (☎ 25 8240, in Lima 01-9643 0659; www .lasarenasdemancora.com; d US$65-75; 🅿️ 🛄) A 5km *mototaxi* ride from Máncora brings you to this spruced-up resort with a slick, angular pool. Enshrined in fastidiously trimmed lawn, the Mediterranean-like white-and-blue bungalows are scattered along the beachfront and come with air-con and DVD players (with a free movie library). The staff are very professional and there's a kiddy playground to keep the little tykes entertained. Sea kayaks, bicycles and horse rides are available.

Playa Palmera (☎ in Lima 01-9362 1182; www.playa palmeras.com; r per person US$25) Located 7km from Máncora, this small and restful little enterprise has just a few perfectly aligned bungalows facing a quiet stretch of beach. Sitting on a manicured lawn and shaded by strategically shaped palms, the neat rooms here have nice arty touches and you have free use of sea kayaks and a boogie board. You can also arrange horseback riding from here for US$6 per hour.

Vichayito (☎ 825 6942, in Lima 01-9947 6558; www .vichayito.com; s/d US$50/60, 6-person bungalows US$100; 🛄) About 8km south of Máncora, this is an attractively constructed hotel with lovely cane, bamboo and wood bungalows, all finished in soothing white tones and sporting soaring roofs. Isolated and quiet, the minimalist styling here makes it a great place to unwind. Travelers with cars can reach the hotel by turning off the Panamericana at Km 1155 (2km north of the village of Los Organos), and following the old Panamericana for 3km to the hotel.

Eating

Seafood rules the culinary roost in Máncora, while other ingredients tend to be pricier due to transportation costs. There is all manner of ceviches, *majariscos* (a mix of seafood nib-

bles), *chicharrones, sudados* (seafood soup or stew) and just plain *pescado* (fish) on offer. It's good and it's always fresh. Most midrange hotels have their own restaurants, but in town there are loads of other eating choices.

Jugería Mi Janett (Piura 250; juices US$0.30-0.90; 🕙 7am-2:30pm & 5:30-10pm) The best juice place in town – come here for massive jugs of your favorite tropical fruit juice.

La Bajadita (☎ 25 8385; Piura 424; dishes US$0.90-3; 🕙 10am-10pm Tue-Sun) This is the place to sink your sweet tooth into some great cakes, including tiramisu, pecan pie, brownies and the ever popular apple pie. They also do small meals and all-day breakfasts here.

El Faro Lounge (☎ 9745 2928; Piura 233; meals US$1.80-6; 🕙 6-11pm) Packed to the rafters nightly with salivating gringos, this budget eatery is a Pandora's box of gastronomical specimens, with everything from grilled meats to fish to *wantans* (wontons) to sandwiches on the varied menu.

Punto Pollo (☎ 9662 6647; Piura 609; quarter chicken US$2.10; 🕙 6pm-midnight) Arguably the best *pollería* in town – and who are we to argue?

Green Eggs & Ham (☎ 25 8004; Piura 112; breakfast US$3; 🕙 7:30am-1pm) This tiny beachfront shack near Sol y Mar has, without doubt, the best create-your-own breakfast around. Stock up on carbs for a hard day's surfing (or lazing) with big plates of waffles, French toast or eggs – just make sure you order a side of the scrumptious spicy home-fried potatoes.

Hnos Lama (☎ 25 8215; Grau 503; meals US$3-4.50; 🕙 8am-8pm) The best of three Lama restaurants, all owned by different family members, this one is owned by Orlando and has a reputation for some of the best ceviche (what else?) in town. It's opposite the Eppo terminal.

Las Gemelitas (☎ 51 6115; Micaela Bastidas 154; mains US$3-6; 🕙 11am-9pm) Three blocks off the Panamericana, behind the Cruz del Sur office, this cane-walled restaurant does great seafood and nothing else. Ceviches and *chicharrones* are the specialty, and the portions are ginormous.

Regina's (☎ 49 6802; Piura 668; mains US$3.60-6; 🕙 7:30am-10pm) The ceviches are also good at this simple but friendly place, which also serves a few meat dishes.

El Espada (☎ 258 338; Piura cuadra 5; mains US$4.50-9; 🕙 11am-8pm) This place, with two locations close to one another, is among the most tourist-oriented seafood eateries in the center. Similar places are nearby.

Chan Chan (☎ 25 8146; Piura 384; meals US$5.50-7.50; ☺ 6:30-11pm Wed-Mon) Run by Italian chef Udo, this Italian eatery has a cozy atmosphere and lots of bright, white, curving adobe walls smartly decorated with tasteful art. The food here is great, the pizzas look like the real, thin-crust deal, and the service is very attentive – it's well worth the splurge. Get here early for a breezy patio seat. To find it, look out for the palm-frond-concealed frontage.

Sunset (☎ 25 8111; mains US$5.50-11.50; ☺ 8am-11pm) With a short menu of excellent Italian food, this is the most gourmet restaurant in town when the Italian chef is on, disappointing when he isn't. It's in the hotel of the same name.

Getting There & Away

Many bus offices are in the center, though most southbound trips originate in Tumbes. *Combis* leave for Tumbes (US$1.80, two hours) regularly; they drive along the main drag until full. *Bus-camas* from Máncora go direct to Lima (14 hours); other services can drop you in intermediate cities on the way to Lima (16 hours). Regular minibuses run between Máncora and Punta Sal (30 minutes).

Cial (☎ 25 8558; Piura 654) Has Lima-bound buses at 3pm (US$15), 7pm (US$30 to US$36) and 8pm (US$21 to US$24).

Civa (☎ 01-9805 5131; Piura 688) Has an economical 3:30pm service to Lima (US$15), as well as a nicer bus at 5:30pm (US$27).

Cruz del Sur (☎ 25 8232; Grau 208) Has a *bus-cama* service to Lima at 4:30pm (US$39 to US$48).

El Dorado (☎ 25 8582; Grau 111) Six buses a day to Piura (US$4.50, 2½ hours) with fast transfers to Chiclayo (US$8.50, six hours) and Trujillo (US$9, nine hours).

Eppo (☎ 25 8027; Grau 470) Fast and regular hourly buses to Talara (US$1.50, 1½ hours), Sullana (US$3, 2½ hours) and Piura (US$3.60, 3½ hours) between 4am and 7pm.

Oltursa (☎ 25 8267; Piura 509) Lima bus (US$36 to US$48) at 5:30pm.

Ormeño (☎ 25 8334; Piura 611) Lima buses (US$27 to US$36) at 2:30pm and 7:30pm. Also has buses direct to Quito (US$35, 16 hours) at 6am on Wednesdays and Fridays.

Tepsa (☎ 25 8043; Grau 113) Lima bus (US$28.50) at 4pm.

PUNTA SAL
☎ 072

The long, curvy bay at Punta Sal, 25km north of Máncora, has fine sand and is dotted with rocky bits – but it's still great for a dip in the ocean. The sea here is calm, and the lack of surfer types means that this tranquil oasis of resorts is particularly popular with families.

One of the few budget options on this beach, **Las Terrazas** (☎ 54 0001; lasterrazaspuntasal@yahoo.com; r per person US$7.50) has solid rooms inside the main house, as well as some poky small bamboo rooms at the back, all for the same price – choose wisely! The terrace restaurant here has awesome sunset views.

Hua Punta Sal (☎ 54 0023/43; www.huapuntasal.com; r per person US$10) is a friendly, family-run hotel with a comely yellow-brick-and-thatch approach to design. Rooms with and without sea views are available, and a restaurant sits on the beach. The hotel rents canoes and boats.

A wooden sundeck nearly hangs out over the sea at **Sunset Punta Sal** (☎ 54 0004; www.sunsetpuntasal.com; r per person incl breakfast/full board US$15/25) and is indeed a great place to admire the setting sun. The bright white adobe is reminiscent of a Greek isle and fishing paraphernalia adorns the walls. The rooms themselves are plain but come with some fine wooden touches, balconies and sea views. The staff can arrange inexpensive fishing trips.

The 23 ocean-view rooms at **Hotel Caballito de Mar** (☎ 54 0048, in Lima 01-446 3122; www.hotelcaballitodemar.com; r per person incl breakfast/full board US$20/35; ☒) have private patios, and there's a restaurant, bar, Jacuzzi, TV room and games room. The gorgeous pool here practically dips its toe into the sea, and activities such as fishing, boating, horseback riding, waterskiing and surfing can be arranged.

Hotel Bucanero (☎ 54 0118; www.elbucaneropuntasal.com; d incl breakfast US$30; ☒) has 14 rooms by the beach, each with cold shower, fan and patio or balcony. The hotel has a games room, TV room, restaurant, two bars, a grassy garden and a lookout with an ocean seascape. Rates include a welcome drink.

Off the Panamericana at Km 1192, the seaside **Punta Sal Club Hotel** (☎ 54 0088, in Lima 01-442 5992; www.puntasal.com.pe; r per person incl full board US$63-83; ☒ ☒ ☒) has the full-service deal. Perfect for families, it has minigolf, laundry facilities, banana-boat rides, waterskiing, tennis, volleyball, table tennis, billiards and a wooden-decked pool – and what resort would be complete without with a near-life-sized replica of a conquistador galleon? It also offers deep-sea fishing trips for US$600 per day in a boat that will take up to six anglers.

Regular minibuses run between Máncora and Punta Sal (30 minutes).

ZORRITOS

☎ 072

About 35km south of Tumbes, Zorritos is the biggest fishing village along this section of coast. While the thin beach here isn't as nice as beaches further south, it's home to interesting coastal **birdlife**. Look out for frigate birds, pelicans, egrets and other migratory birds.

A few kilometers south of central Zorritos is **Hostel Casa Grillo** (☎ 9764 2836; www.casagrillo.com .pe; Panamericana Km 1236; r per person with shared/private bathroom US$4.50/6). The rooms are quite basic, but HI members receive a US$1.50 discount. It has a restaurant with vegetarian specials (sandwiches US$0.90 to US$1.80, mains US$2.40 to US$7.50) and information about tours to nearby national reserves. Horseback riding and hiking to nearby mud baths can also be arranged. The hostel runs popular five-day *hostal*-and-camping tours that take in beaches, trekking, lagoons and mud baths and cost only US$175 per person – including everything! Longer trips are also available.

At Km 1235 is **Tres Puntas Ecological Tourist Center** (☎ 9764 2836; campsite US$3, r with shared bathroom per person US$7.50). Constructed (mainly by volunteers) from natural materials such as bamboo and cane, everything here, including water, is recycled. Breezy, rustic cabins with balconies and hammocks sit on the beach, and campsites have electricity and a shade roof. All rooms share interesting outdoor communal bathrooms covered in mosaic tiles and seashells. Dog-lovers should ask the owner to show you his 14 Peruvian hairless dogs – he breeds them. HI members get a US$1.50 discount

Right in Zorritos, **Puerta del Sol** (☎ 54 4294; hosppuertadelsol@hotmail.com; s/d US$9/18) is a skinny little *hospedaje* that is just too lovely for words. It has a miniature garden dissected by a winding, yellow-brick path and patches of vibrant lawn. The only accessory missing is a garden gnome. The rooms are simple and neat, and beach access is available, but there are no views.

Midrange choices include the beachfront **Hotel Los Cocos** (☎ 9867 1259; www.hotelloscocos.com; Panamericana Km 1242; r per person US$20, r per person incl full board US$30; 🏊), with big rooms filled with bamboo furniture, a few arty bits, and balconies with hammocks and sea vistas. The pool has rock features and a separate children's section. There's also a small kids' play area, a trampoline and a beach-volleyball court here.

Bungalows Costa Azul (☎ 54 4268; www.vivaman cora.com/costaazul; r per person US$22, r per person incl full board US$35) is a huge sprawling complex of various-sized spartan bungalows, all with TV. Some sleep up to six people and sit right on the beach.

Combis to Zorritos leave regularly from Tumbes (US$0.60, about one hour). Coming from the south, just catch any bus heading toward Tumbes.

TUMBES

☎ 072 / pop 128,500

Only 30km from the Ecuadorian border, Tumbes is in a uniquely green part of coastal Peru, where dry deserts magically turn into mangroves and an expanse of ecological reserves stretches in all directions. It's also the springboard for trips to the excellent and popular beaches of Máncora, two hours further south.

An Ecuadorian village until Peru's victory in the 1940–41 border war, Tumbes remains a garrison town with a strong military presence. It's hot and (depending on season) dusty or mosquito-bugged, and most travelers don't stay long. The nearby national reserves are distinctive and a boon for nature buffs.

Tumbes was an Inca town when it was first sighted by Pizarro in 1528. Pizarro invited an Inca noble to dine aboard his ship and sent ashore two of his men, who reported the existence of an obviously well-organized and fabulously rich civilization. Based on those accounts Pizarro returned a few years later to begin his conquest of Peru.

Present-day Tumbes is about 5km northeast of the old Inca city, which is marked on maps as San Pedro de los Incas. The Panamericana passes through the site, but there is little to see.

Information

Apart from offering tours to local sights, Tumbes tour companies can also provide some tourist information.

Banco Continental (☎ 52 3914; Bolívar 129)

BCP (☎ 52 5060; Bolívar 261) Changes traveler's checks and has an ATM.

Clinica Feijoo (☎ 52 5341; Mariscal Castilla 305) One of the better medical clinics in Tumbes.

Ecuadorian Consul (☎ 52 5949; 3rd fl, Bolívar 129; ☽ 9am-1pm & 4-6pm Mon-Fri) On the Plaza de Armas.

Ministerio de Turismo (☎ 52 3699, 52 4940; 2nd fl, Bolognesi 194) Provides useful tourist information.

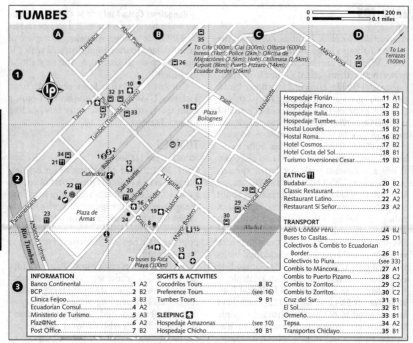

TUMBES

Hospedaje Florián...	**11** A1
Hospedaje Franco...	**12** B2
Hospedaje Italia...	**13** B3
Hospedaje Tumbes...	**14** B3
Hostal Lourdes...	**15** B2
Hostal Roma...	**16** B2
Hotel Cosmos...	**17** B2
Hotel Costa del Sol...	**18** B1
Turismo Inversiones Cesar...	**19** B2

EATING 🍴
Budabar...	**20** B2
Classic Restaurant...	**21** A2
Restaurant Latino...	**22** A2
Restaurant Sí Señor...	**23** A2

TRANSPORT
Aéro Cóndor Perú...	**24** B2
Buses to Casitas...	**25** D1
Colectivos & Combis to Ecuadorian Border...	**26** B1
Colectivos to Piura...	(see 33)
Combis to Máncora...	**27** A1
Combis to Puerto Pizarro...	**28** C2
Combis to Zorritos...	**29** C2
Combis to Zorritos...	**30** C2
Cruz del Sur...	**31** B1
El Sol...	**32** B1
Ormeño...	**33** B1
Tepsa...	**34** A2
Transportes Chiclayo...	**35** B1

INFORMATION
Banco Continental...	**1** A2
BCP...	**2** B2
Clínica Feijoo...	**3** B3
Ecuadorian Consul...	**4** A2
Ministerio de Turismo...	**5** A3
Plaz@Net...	**6** A2
Post Office...	**7** B2

SIGHTS & ACTIVITIES
Cocodrilos Tours...	**8** B2
Preference Tours...	(see 16)
Tumbes Tours...	**9** B1

SLEEPING 🛏
Hospedaje Amazonas...	(see 10)
Hospedaje Chicho...	**10** B1

Oficina de migraciónes (☎ 52 3422; Tumbes 1751) Along the Panamericana 2km north of town. Does visa extensions.
Plaz@Net (Bolivar 161; per hr US$0.30; ☯ 8am-11pm) Internet access.
Police (☎ 52 5250; Tumbes 1742) Located north of town.
Post office (☎ 52 3866; San Martín 208; ☯ 9am-7pm Mon-Fri, 9am-1pm Sat) On the block south of Plaza Bolognesi.

Sights

There are several **old houses** dating from the early 19th century on Grau, east of the Plaza de Armas. These rickety abodes are made of split-bamboo and wood and it seems like they are only defying gravity by sheer will. The plaza has several outdoor restaurants and is a nice place to relax. The **pedestrian streets** north of the plaza (especially Bolívar) have several large, modern monuments and are favorite hangouts for young and old alike.

About 5km south of town, off the Panamericana, is an overgrown archaeological site that was the home of the Tumpis people and, later, the site of the Inca fort visited by Pizarro. The story is told in the tiny site museum,

Museo de Cabeza de Baca (adult/student US$0.60/0.30; ☯ 9am-2pm Mon-Sat), which also displays some 1500-year-old ceramics vessels.

Tours & Guides

The following companies run various local tours, including trips to the reserves:
Cocodrilos Tours (☎ 52 4133; cocodrilostours@terram ail.com.pe; Huáscar 309) Does tours to the reserves as well as to local beaches, mud baths and Puerto Pizarro.
Preference Tours (☎ 52 4757; turismomundial@terra .com.pe; Grau 427) Runs some of the most economical tours in town if you have a group of three or more.
Tumbes Tours (☎ 52 6086; www.tumbestours.com; Tumbes 341)

Sleeping

Almost all of Tumbes' hotels are in the budget range and most hotels have only cold water, but that's no problem in the heat. Be sure your room has a working fan if you're here in the sweltering summer (December to March). During the wet season and the twice-yearly rice harvests, mosquitoes can be a big problem, and there are frequent water and electricity outages.

BUDGET

Hospedaje Tumbes (☎ 52 2203; Grau 614; s/d US$6/9) Dark but welcoming, the good-sized rooms here have fans. TV costs US$1.80 extra. The walls are decorated with oh-so-hip '80s posters and a few plants help spruce the place up.

Hospedaje Franco (☎ 52 5295; San Martín 107; s/d US$6/9) Clean enough and quieter than most, this place made some tile vendor very wealthy – they cover nearly every surface. TV costs US$1.50 extra.

Hospedaje Italia (☎ 52 3396; Garu 733; d US$7.50) The Italia is a good deal for double rooms, each of which has plenty of natural light and space, tiled floors and TVs as standard.

Hospedaje Florián (☎ 52 2464; Piura 414; s/d US$7.50/9) Has warm showers and fans, plus cable TV for US$1.30 extra. It's a little hygienically challenged.

Hospedaje Amazonas (☎ 52 5266; Tumbes 317; s/d US$7.50/10.50) Aged but well maintained, the huge rooms here have fans, and a communal TV lounge offers some entertainment.

Hospedaje Chicho (☎ 52 2282, ☎ /fax 52 3696; Tumbes 327; s/d US$7.50/10.50) Very clean rooms in a central location, helpful and friendly staff, hot showers, cable TV, fan, minifridge and phone all add up to solid budget fare. Mosquito nets are also provided on request.

Turismo Inversiones Cesar (☎ 52 2883; Huáscar 311; s/d US$12/15) Warm colors throughout and well-worn, creaky polished floorboards give this place a pleasant lived-in feeling. Throw in a gregarious owner, some interesting design choices and clean rooms with TV, and you should definitely give this place a second look.

Hostal Lourdes (☎ 52 2966; Mayor Bodero 118; s/d US$12/18) Clean, safe and friendly, the Lourdes includes a top-floor restaurant among its amenities. Austere rooms have fans, phones, TV and hot showers.

Hotel Cosmos (☎ 52 4366; Piura 900; s/d US$12/19.50) Recently graduated from mere *hostal* (guesthouse) status, Hotel Cosmos has solid rooms with TVs and space in spades. Potted plants in the hallway brighten things up a bit. There are poker machines and a snack bar downstairs if you get the urge to munch, gamble or both.

Hostal Roma (☎ 52 4137, 52 2494, 52 5879; hotel romatumbes@hotmail.com; Bolognesi 425; s/d US$13.50/19.50) A modern hotel with top Plaza de Armas real estate, the Roma is a little more upscale than the rabble and affords guests clean, comfortable rooms with hot shower, fan, phone and cable TV.

MIDRANGE

Hotel Chilimasa (☎ 52 4555; Andrés Araujo, Manzana 2A; s/d US$24/36; ⌘) About 2km north of town en route to the airport, this hotel supplies comfortable rooms and a restaurant, but it's the pool that will probably get your attention.

Hotel Costa del Sol (☎ 52 3991; www.costadelsol peru.com; San Martín 275; s/d/ste incl breakfast US$60/70/95; ⌘⌘) This is by far the best hotel in town, with a decent restaurant, a pleasant bar and a garden, plus a Jacuzzi, adult and children's

---

WARNING: BORDER-CROSSING BLUES

Shady practices at the border crossing between Ecuador and Peru at Aguas Verdes have earned it the dubious title of 'the worst border crossing in South America.' Whether it deserves to wear that crown is hard to prove empirically, but it pays to be wary.

Try not to change dollars into soles here as 'fixed' calculators are common and many bills offered to foreigners are fake (see p508). If you must change money, find out the exchange rate before you arrive and change just enough to get you to the nearest bank in Tumbes. Try to get S/10 notes as these are the least likely to be forgeries. Don't listen to helpful advice like 'you can't change dollars in Tumbes,' 'the banks are closed,' 'there's a strike,' or 'Tumbes is flooded.'

Taxi drivers will use similarly persuasive methods to convince you that *combis* (minibuses) and *colectivo* (shared) taxis aren't running. Overcharging here can be audacious. *Combis* run from the border to Tumbes all day and charge US$0.50, and a *colectivo* costs around US$0.90 per person or US$4.50 for the whole taxi. Establish a price before you get into the vehicle, and make sure it covers the fare all the way to Tumbes, not just to the immigration post 3km away.

Many people will offer their services as porters or guides. Most are annoyingly insistent, so unless you really need help, they're more of a hassle than they're worth.

Remember that there are no entry fees into either country. If the border guards say otherwise, always be polite but insistent in your refusal to pay.

swimming pools, a small casino and a gym. The comfortable rooms have cable TV, direct-dial phone, fan, minifridge, and bathroom, hot shower and hair drier. A cold cocktail is included – and is most welcome.

Eating

There are several bars and restaurants on the Plaza de Armas, many with shaded tables and chairs outside – a real boon in hot weather. It's a pleasant place to sit and watch the world go by as you drink a cold beer and wait for your bus.

Restaurant Sí Señor (☎ 52 1937; Bolívar 115; menús US$1.50, meals US$3-3.90; ☺ 7:30am-2am) With pleasant streetside tables outside and quixotic, slow-turning fans inside, Sí Señor serves traditional Peruvian fare and is a cheaper version of the nearby Restaurant Latino.

Las Terrazas (☎ 52 1575; Andres Araujo 549; meals US$3-5.50; ☺ 9am-8pm) A little bit out of the town center, this popular place is well worth the US$0.30 mototaxi ride. Packed with hungry diners daily, it serves up heaped plates of seafood, and will ceviche or cook anything from fish to lobster to octopus. It's all prepared in the northern coastal style and they have live folk music on the weekends. It's on a classy 3rd-floor terrace, and has flowing tablecloths, lots of decorations and a festive mood.

Classic Restaurant (☎ 52 4301; Tumbes 185; mains US$3.30-4.80; ☺ 8am-5pm; ☒) Small, quiet and dignified, Classic Restaurant is a wonderful place to escape torrid Tumbes and relax with a long lunch, as many of the town's better-connected locals do. The food is good and mainly coastal, but secretly we love this place for its air-con.

BORDER CROSSING: ECUADOR VIA TUMBES

Colectivo (shared) taxis (US$0.90 per person, 25 minutes) and combis (minibuses; US$0.50, 40 minutes) for Aguas Verdes on the Peru–Ecuador border leave from the corner of Abad Puell and Tumbes. It's US$4.50 for the whole taxi. Unless you have a real love for loitering at dirty border towns, it's far better to take a **Cifa** (☎ 072-52 7120; Tumbes 572) bus straight through to Machala (US$2, two hours) or Guayaquil (US$5, five hours) in Ecuador.

The Peruvian **immigration office** (El Complejo; ☎ 072-56 1178; ☺ 24hr) is in the middle of the desert at Aguas Verdes, about 3km from the border. Travelers leaving Peru obtain exit stamps here – if you're catching public transportation make sure you stop to complete these border formalities. If you're entering Peru and require a visa, ensure you obtain it before reaching the border; otherwise, you'll have to go back to the Peruvian consulate in Machala to get one. Although a ticket out of Peru is officially required to enter the country, gringo travelers are rarely asked for one unless they look thoroughly disreputable. A bus office in Aguas Verdes sells (nonrefundable) tickets out of Peru, and the immigration official can tell you where it is.

From the immigration office, mototaxis can take you to the border town of Aguas Verdes (US$0.30).

Aguas Verdes is basically a long, dusty street full of vendors that continues into the near-identical Ecuadorian border town of Huaquillas via the international bridge across the Río Zarumilla. If you are forced to stay the night at the border, there are a few basic hotels in Aguas Verdes, but they're all noisy and pretty sketchy. You're better off catching a US$0.60 mototaxi to the quiet Peruvian town of Zarumilla, 5km away. Here, **Hostal Prisalex** (☎ 072-56 5601; www.prisalex.mbperu .com; Del Ejercito 112; s/d US$6/9) offers immaculate, large and recently painted rooms for bargain prices in their quiet, blue hostal (guesthouse).

The Ecuadorian immigration office, about 4km to the north of the bridge, is also open 24 hours. Taxis from the bridge charge about US$1. Few tourists need a visa for Ecuador, but everyone needs a T3 embarkation card, available free at the immigration office. You must surrender your T3 when you leave Ecuador, so don't lose it. Exit tickets out of Ecuador and sufficient funds (US$20 per day) are legally required, but rarely asked for. Stays of up to 90 days are allowed, but often only 30 days are given. Tourists are allowed only 180 days per year in Ecuador – if you have stayed more and try to return you'll be refused entry.

There are a few basic hotels in Huaquillas, but most people make the two-hour bus trip to the city of Machala, where there are much better facilities. See Lonely Planet's Ecuador & the Galápagos Islands for more information.

Budabar (☎ 50 4216; Grau 309; meals US$3.60-5.50; 😋 8am-2am) Occupying a huge cavernous space and with streetside tables, this place has a full bar and serves typical Peruvian fare, including the usual chicken, fish and beef suspects.

Restaurant Latino (☎ 52 3198; Bolívar 163; mains US$3.90-6; 🕐 7am-11pm) This popular place serves from a long menu of Peruvian food, especially seafood. You can eat inside, or outside on the shaded pavement.

Getting There & Away
AIR
The **airport** (code TBP; ☎ 52 5102) is 8km north of town; the usual US$3.57 airport departure tax is charged. **Aero Condor Perú** (☎ 52 4835; Grau 454) has a daily flight from Lima to Tumbes (US$102) leaving at 5:30pm and returning to Lima at 7:30pm.

BUS
You can usually find a bus to Lima within 24 hours of your arrival in Tumbes, but they're sometimes (especially major holidays) sold out a few days in advance. You can take a bus south to another major city and try again from there.

Buses to Lima take 16 to 18 hours. Some companies offer a limited-stop special service, with air-con, bathrooms and video; some have deluxe, nonstop *bus-cama* services. Slower services stop at Piura (five hours), Chiclayo (seven to eight hours) and Trujillo (nine to 10 hours). If you are heading to Piura, you can catch a much faster *colectivo* taxi (US$6, 3½ hours).

If you're going to Ecuador, it's easiest to go with Cifa, an Ecuadorian company that stops at the border for you to complete passport formalities.

Cial (☎ 52 6350; Tumbes 572) Services to Lima at 1:15pm (US$15), 5pm (*bus-cama* US$27 to US$36) and 5:45pm (US$15).

Cifa (☎ 52 7120; Tumbes 572) Heads to Machala (US$2, two hours) and Guayaquil (US$5, five hours), both in Ecuador, about every two hours.

Civa (☎ 52 5120; Tumbes 518) Lima services at 1:30pm (US$15), 4pm (*bus-cama* US$25.50 to US$36) and 6:15pm (US$15).

Cruz del Sur (☎ 52 6200; Tumbes 319) To Lima (*bus-cama* US$39 to US$48) at 3pm.

El Sol (☎ 50 9252; Piura 403) Economy buses to Chiclayo (US$4.50) at 8:30am and 9:30am. Also a service to Lima (US$15) via Chiclayo (US$4.50) and Trujillo (US$7) at 8:20pm.

Oltursa (☎ 52 6524; Tumbes 946) *Bus-cama* service to Lima (US$36 to US$45) at 4pm.

Ormeño (☎ 52 2288, 52 2228; Tumbes 314) Two classes of bus to Lima (US$22.50 to US$33) via Chiclayo (US$9 to US$13.50) and Trujillo (US$13.50 to US$19.50), the cheaper one leaving at 1pm and the pricier one at 5:30pm.

Tepsa (☎ 52 2428; Tumbes 199) To Lima (US$28.50) at 2:30pm.

Transportes Chiclayo (☎ 52 5260; Tumbes 464) Daily bus to Chiclayo (US$6) at 2:30pm via Piura (US$4.50).

If you're heading for Puerto Pizarro (US$0.30, 15 minutes), Zorritos (US$0.60, about one hour) or Máncora (US$1.80, two hours), there are *combi* stops in Tumbes near the market area. Ask locals, as the stops aren't marked. Buses to Casitas leave at 1pm (US$3, five hours), while the Rica Playa bus leaves at midday (US$0.90, two hours).

Getting Around
A taxi to the airport is about US$4.50, depending on your bargaining abilities. There are no *combis* to the airport.

AROUND TUMBES
Puerto Pizarro
☎ 072
About 14km north of Tumbes, the character of the oceanfront changes from the coastal desert, which stretches over 2000km north from central Chile to northern Peru, to the mangrove swamps that dominate much of the Ecuadorian and Colombian coastlines. There's an explosion of **birdlife** here, with up to 200 different migrating species visiting these areas. Boats can be hired to tour the mangroves; one tour goes to a **crocodile sanctuary** where you can see Peru's only crocodiles being nursed back from near extinction. The nearby **Isla de Aves** can be visited (but not landed on) to see the many nesting seabirds, especially between 5pm to 6pm, when huge flocks of birds return to roost for the night. **Isla del Amor** has lunch restaurants and attractive swimming beaches. Boat line the waterfront of Puerto Pizarro and cost US$12 per hour per boat; you can do a tour of the mangroves and the above-mentioned sites for US$24. Tour companies in Tumbes also provide guided tours to the area.

Most visitors stay in Tumbes and visit Puerto Pizarro on a day trip; however, accommodation is available at **Bayside Hotel** (☎ 54 3045; s/d US$12/15; 🏊) on the waterfront. The

Bayside has a faded Palm Springs attitude and its yellow concrete bungalows are large and weathered, but supply plenty of character. It's a good place to chill, with a pleasant thatch-roofed restaurant and seaside hammocks to watch the world float by. The hotel also rents kayaks for US$1.50 per hour and jet skis for US$18 per hour – though you won't see much wildlife zooming around on one of those.

There are regular *combis* between Puerto Pizarro and Tumbes (US$0.30, 15 minutes).

Reserva de Biosfera del Noroeste

The Northwestern Biosphere Reserve consists of four protected areas that cover 2344 sq km in the department of Tumbes and northern Piura. A lack of government funding means that there is little infrastructure or tourist facilities – much of what exists was funded by organizations such as the Fundación Peruana para la Conservación de la Naturaleza (FPCN; also called ProNaturaleza), with assistance from international bodies such as the WWF.

Information about all four areas is available from the Tumbes office of **Inrena** (☎ 972-52 6489; www.inrena.gob.pe; Tarapacá 427, Ministerio de Agricultura; ☷ 9am-5:30pm), the government department in charge of administering this region. The biologist in charge is Oscar Garcia Tello, and this office has lots of pamphlets and information on the area, some maps, and may be able to give you a lift to one of the reservations if it has people heading there that day. It's here you will need to get permission papers to visit any of the protected areas on your own; these are free and take minutes to organize.

Tour companies in Tumbes can arrange tours, as can Hostel Casa Grillo (p367) in Zorritos. There are few roads into these areas and visiting during the wet months of December to April can prove very difficult.

PARQUE NACIONAL CERROS DE AMOTAPE

The tropical, dry-forest ecosystem of Cerros de Amotape is protected by this 913-sq-km national park, which is home to flora and fauna including jaguars, condors and anteaters, though parrots, deer and peccaries are more commonly sighted. Large-scale logging, illegal hunting and overgrazing are some of the threats facing this habitat, of which there is very little left anywhere in Peru. **Guides** are essential for spotting wildlife and can be arranged in the town of **Rica Playa**, a small, friendly village located just within the park.

Although there are no hotels here, you can camp and local families will sell you meals.

During the dry season, a bus leaves for Rica Playa from the Tumbes market (US$0.90, two hours) at midday. Most of the route, bar the last 18km, is paved.

Another way to visit the park is to go to the village of **Casitas** near Caña Veral; buses leave from the Tumbes market at 1pm (US$3, five hours).

Agencies in Tumbes also organize tours for US$10 to US$30 per person, depending on the number of people.

ZONA RESERVADA DE TUMBES

This reserve is probably the best place to spot a wide range of wild animals. The forest is similar to the tropical dry forest of Cerros de Amotape, but because it lies more on the easterly side of the hills, it is wetter and has slightly different flora and fauna, including crocodiles, howler monkeys and nutria. You can also see various orchids and a wide variety of birds. There is no public transportation here, so you'll need to either have your own wheels or come on a tour, which can cost anywhere between US$10 to US$30 per person.

COTO DE CAZA EL ANGOLO

This 650-sq-km extension at the southwest border of Cerros de Amotape is the most remote section of the tropical dry forest. It's a hunting preserve.

SANTUARIO NACIONAL LOS MANGLARES DE TUMBES

This national sanctuary was established in 1988 and lies on the coast, separated from the other three dry-forest areas. Only about 30 sq km in size, it plays an essential role in conserving Peru's only region of mangroves.

You can travel here by going to Puerto Pizarro and taking a dirt road northeast to the tiny community of **El Bendito**. From here, ask around for someone to guide you by canoe. Guided tours are available from Puerto Pizarro as well, though the mangroves here are not technically within the protection of the sanctuary. Another way to visit is to go to **Zarumilla**, 5km before the Ecuador border, and seek out **Oriol Cedillo Ruiz** (☎ 50 7816; Independencia 690). He can arrange two- to three-hour kayak tours (US$12 per kayak). Access depends on the tides. Agencies in Tumbes also arrange tours for US$15 to US$30 per person.

Huaraz & the Cordilleras

The mountainous region of the Cordillera Blanca is where superlatives crash and burn in a brave attempt to capture the beauty of the place. A South American mecca for worshippers of outdoor adventure, this is one of the preeminent hiking, trekking and backpacking spots on the continent. Every which way you throw your gaze, perennially glaciered white peaks razor their way through expansive mantles of lime-green valleys. In the recesses of these prodigious giants huddle scores of pristine jade lakes, ice caves and torrid springs. This is the highest mountain range in the world outside of the Himalayas, and its 22 ostentatious summits of over 6000m will not let you forget it for a second.

Huaraz is a fast-beating heart linking the trekking trails and roads that serve as the mountains' arteries. It's here that plans of daring ice climbs, mountain-biking exploits and rock-climbing safaris are hatched over ice-cold beers in fireplace-warmed bars. Meanwhile in the eastern valley, the enigmatic 3000-year-old ruins of Chavín de Huántar await daily rediscovery, while further north picture-perfect villages, steeped in pre-Inca traditions, dispense affectionate smiles like they're going out of style.

HIGHLIGHTS

■ Traipsing for weeks around the magnificent peaks of the **Cordillera Blanca** (p387) and **Cordillera Huayhuash** (p391)

■ Tunneling through the mysterious millennia-old ruins of **Chavín de Huántar** (p414)

■ Plummeting down precipitous mountain-bike trails and clambering up vertical rock-climbing cliffs around **Huaraz** (p377)

■ Winding your way through the 1000m sheer rock walls of the staggering **Cañón del Pato** (p402)

■ Experiencing days of butt-smacking bus rides to the remote and serene traditional mountain villages of **Chacas** (p418) and **Pomabamba** (p419)

Cañon del Pato ★ ★ Pomabamba

★ Chacas

★ Cordillera Blanca

Huaraz ★   ★ Chavín de Huántar

Cordillera Huayhuash ★

■ BIGGEST CITY: HUARAZ, POPULATION 88,300

■ AVERAGE TEMPERATURE: JANUARY 10°C TO 16°C, JULY 12°C TO 17°C

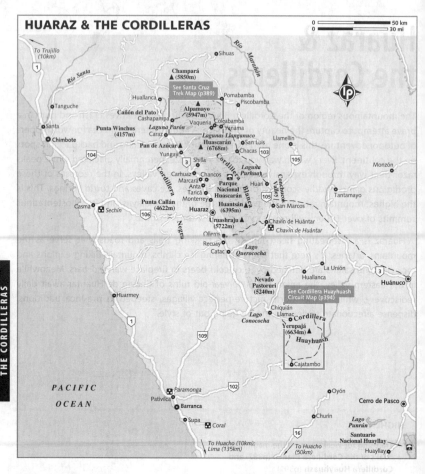

HUARAZ & THE CORDILLERAS

| 0 | 50 km |
| 0 | 30 mi |

HUARAZ

☎ 043 / pop 88,300 / elev 3091m

Huaraz is the restless capital of this Andean adventure kingdom and its rooftops command exhaustive panoramas of the city's dominion: one of the most impressive mountain ranges in the world. Nearly wiped out by the earthquake of 1970, Huaraz isn't going to win any Andean-village beauty contests anytime soon, but it does have personality – and personality goes a long way.

This is first and foremost a trekking metropolis. During the high season the streets buzz with hundreds of backpackers and adventurers freshly returned from arduous hikes, or planning their next expedition as they huddle in one of the town's many fine watering holes. Dozens of outfits help plan trips, rent equipment and organize a list of adventure sports as long as your arm. An endless lineup of quality restaurants and hopping bars keep the belly full and the place lively till long after the tents have been put away to dry. Mountain adventures in the off-season can be equally rewarding, but the vibe is more subdued and some places go into hibernation over the rainy season.

INFORMATION
Emergency

Casa de Guías (☎ 42 1811; Plaza Ginebra 28G; ⏱ 7-11am, 5-11pm) Can arrange mountain rescue;

register here before heading out on a climb. All trekkers and climbers should carry rescue insurance, best purchased before leaving home. A helicopter rescue will cost several thousand dollars. (Also see p400.)

Local Police (☎ 42 1221, 42 1331; José Sucre near San Martín)

National Police (☎ 42 6343; 28 de Julio 701)

Policía de Turismo (☎ 42 1341; Plaza de Armas; ☼ 8am-1pm Mon-Sat & 5-8pm Mon-Fri) On an alley on the west side of the Plaza de Armas, above iPerú. Some officers speak limited English.

Internet Access
There are literally dozens of places on Plaza Ginebra and the corresponding block of Luzuriaga.

Laundry
Both of these are good for washing down gear and dry cleaning:

B&B/Pressmatic (☎ 42 1719; José de la Mar 674; per kg US$0.90)

Lavandería Dennys (☎ 42 9232; José de la Mar 561; per kg US$0.90)

Medical Services
Clínica San Pablo (☎ 42 8811; Huaylas 172; ☼ 24hr) North of town, this is the best medical care in Huaraz. Some doctors speak English.

Farmacia Recuay (☎ 42 1391; Luzuriaga 497) Will restock expedition medical kits.

Hospital Regional (☎ 42 4146; Luzuriaga cuadra 13) At the south end of town. For rudimentary medical care.

Money
Banco Wiese (☎ 42 1500; José Sucre 760)

BCP (☎ 42 1692; Luzuriaga 691) Has an ATM and is the only bank that doesn't charge a commission for changing traveler's checks.

Interbanc (☎ 42 1502; José Sucre 687)

Oh NaNa Casa de Cambio (northeast cnr Plaza de Armas) Changes US dollars and euros at good rates.

Post
Post Office (☎ 42 1031; Luzuriaga 702)

Tourist Information
The travel agencies mentioned on p386 and popular meeting points for tourists in Huaraz can be good sources of local and trekking information.

iPerú (☎ 42 8812; Oficina 1, Pasaje Atusparia, Plaza de Armas; ☼ 8am-6:30pm Mon-Sat, 8:30am-2pm Sun) Has general tourist information but nothing in the way of trekking info.

Parque Nacional Huascarán Office (☎ 42 2086; Sal y Rosas 555) Staff have limited information about visiting the park.

DANGERS & ANNOYANCES
Time to acclimatize is important. Huaraz' altitude will make you feel breathless and may give you a headache during your first few days, so don't overexert yourself. The surrounding mountains will cause altitude sickness if you venture into them without spending a few days acclimatizing in Huaraz first. See p534 for more advice on altitude sickness.

Unfortunately, during late 2002 and early 2003, there was a series of armed robberies of tourists going by foot on day trips to sites around Huaraz. Ask locally what the current situation is, and while no robberies have been reported since that time, consider hiring somebody to go with you.

SIGHTS
The **Museo Regional de Ancash** (☎ 42 1551; Plaza de Armas; adult/student incl guided tour US$1.70/1.10; ☼ 8am-6:30pm) houses the largest collection of ancient stone sculptures in South America. Small but interesting, it has a few mummies, some trepanned skulls and a garden of stone monoliths from the Recuay culture (400 BC to AD 600) and the Wari culture (AD 600 to 1000).

At the trout hatchery **Piscigranja de Truchas** (admission US$0.30; ☼ 9am-1pm & 3-5pm), you can see the stages of the trout-hatching process from eggs to adults. By the entrance, the **Recreo de los Jardínes** serves trout for lunch. It's a half-hour walk from the center; walk east on Raimondi to Confraternidad Este, then turn left and cross the bridge over the Río Quilcay. The hatchery is just beyond.

Jirón José Olaya, also east of town, is on the right-hand side of Raimondi a block beyond Confraternidad. It's the only street that remained intact through the earthquakes and shows what old Huaraz looked like; go on Sunday when a street market sells regional foods.

Mirador de Retaquenua is about a 45-minute walk southeast of the center and has great views of the city and its mountainous backdrop. Ask locally for directions.

Monumento Nacional Wilcahuaín (adult/student US$1.40/0.60; ☼ 8am-5pm), the small Wari ruin about 8km north of Huaraz, is remarkably well preserved. Dating from about AD 600 to 900, it's an imitation of the temple at Chavín

HUARAZ

HUARAZ & THE CORDILLERAS

INFORMATION
B&B/Pressmatic.....................1 C4
Banco Wiese...........................2 C5
BCP..3 C5
Casa de Guías........................4 C4
Farmacia Recuay....................5 C4
Interbanc................................6 C4
iPerú..7 C5
Lavandería Dennys................8 C4
Local Police............................9 B5
National Police.....................10 C6
Oh NaNa Casa de Cambio...11 C5
Parque Nacional Huascarán
  Office.................................12 B6
Policía de Turismo...........(see 7)
Post Office............................13 C5

SIGHTS & ACTIVITIES
Andean Kingdom..................14 C4
Bruce Peru.............................15 C6
Galaxia Expeditions.............16 B5
Huaraz Chavín Tours............17 C4
Huascaran..............................18 E6
Montañero.............................19 C4
Monttrek................................20 C5
Mountain Bike Adventures.21 C4
MountClimb...........................22 B4
Museo Regional de Ancash..23 C5
Pablo Tours............................24 C4
Sechín Tours..........................25 C4
Sierra Verde Spanish
  School............................(see 21)

SLEEPING
Albergue Churup....................26 E5
Alojamiento Soledad............27 E5
B&B My House........................28 B5
Caroline Lodging..................29 A6
Edward's Inn.........................30 A4
Familia Meza Lodging......(see 21)
Grand Hotel Huaraz..............31 D5
Hostal Raimondi.....................32 C3

Hostal Schatzi.......................33 D4
Hostal Tany............................34 C4
Hostal Gyula Inn...................35 C5
Hotel Brit's.............................36 B4
Hotel Colomba......................37 C1
Hotel Del Valle......................38 C4
Hotel El Tumi.........................39 B6
Hotel Los Portales................40 D3
Jo's Place...............................41 D1
La Casa de Zarela.................42 E6
Monte Blanco Hotel.............43 C4
Olaza's Guest House.............44 E6
Oscar's Hostal.................(see 43)
Piramide Hotel......................45 C5
San Sebastian........................46 F4
Way Inn..................................47 D6

EATING
Bistro de los Andes...............48 D4
Café Andino....................(see 21)
California Cafe.......................49 B6
Chifa Jim Hua.......................50 C5
Crêperie Patrick....................51 C4
El Fogón.................................52 B6
El Rinconcito Minero............53 C4
Encuentro...............................54 C4
La Brasa Roja.........................55 C4
Mercado Ortiz.......................56 C3
Monte Rosa/Inca Pub...........57 C4
Pachamama...........................58 B5
Piccolo....................................59 C4
Pizza Bruno............................60 B6
Sabor Salud Pizzería.............61 C5
Siam de los Andes................62 D4

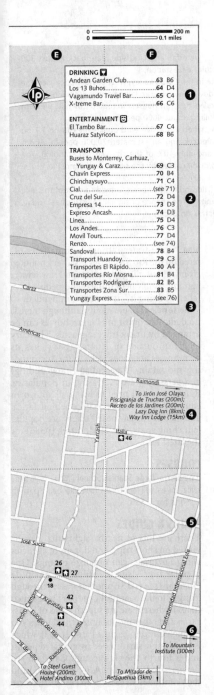

done in the Tiahuanaco style. Wilcahuaín means 'grandson's house' in Quechua. The three-story temple has seven rooms on each floor, each originally filled with bundles of mummies. The bodies were kept dry using a sophisticated system of ventilation ducts. The rooms are now lit, and entertaining kids in the area will take you inside the ruin and show you around for a tip.

Taxis cost a few dollars, or ask for a *combi* (minibus; around US$0.30) at the bus stops by the Río Quilcay in town. The two-hour walk up can be a rewarding glimpse into Andean country life, passing farms and friendly *pueblos* (villages). Ask locally if it is safe before you set off.

Instead of returning to Huaraz, you could walk down to the hot springs at Monterrey (see p398) along a footpath (one hour).

ACTIVITIES
Trekking & Mountaineering
Whether you're arranging a mountain expedition or going for a day hike, Huaraz is the place to start – it is the epicenter for planning and organizing local Andean adventures. Numerous outfits can prearrange entire trips so that all you need to do is show up at the right place at the right time. Many experienced backpackers go camping, hiking and climbing in the mountains without any local help, and you can too if you have the experience. Just remember, though, that carrying a backpack full of gear over a 4800m pass requires much more effort than hiking at low altitudes. See p385 for more details.

Rock Climbing
Rock climbing is taking off in a big way in the Cordillera Blanca. Avid climbers will find some great bolted sport climbs, particularly at Chancos (p399), Monterrey and Recuay. For some big-wall action that will keep you chalked up for days, head to the famous Torre de Parón, known locally as the Sphinx. Most trekking tour agencies (see p386) offer climbing trips, both for beginners and advanced, as part of their repertoire. Many also rent gear, and with a bit of legwork and some information-gathering you could easily arrange your own do-it-yourself climbing expedition. Galaxia Expeditions (p386), Andean Kingdom (p386) and the Andean Garden Club (p383) all have indoor climbing or bouldering walls.

HUARAZ &
THE CORDILLERAS

TREMORS & LANDSLIDES

Records of *aluviónes*, a deadly mix of avalanche, waterfall and landslide, date back almost 300 years, but three recent ones have caused particular devastation.

The first occurred in 1941, when an avalanche in the Cojup valley, west of Huaraz, caused the Laguna Palcacocha to break its banks and flow down onto Huaraz, killing about 5000 inhabitants and flattening the city. Then, in 1962, a huge avalanche from Huascarán roared down its western slopes and destroyed the town of Ranrahirca, killing about 4000 people.

The worst disaster occurred on May 31, 1970, when a massive earthquake, measuring 7.7 on the Richter scale, devastated much of central Peru, killing an estimated 70,000 people. About half of the 30,000 inhabitants of Huaraz died, and only 10% of the city was left standing. The town of Yungay was completely buried by the *aluvión* caused by the quake, and almost its entire population of 18,000 was buried with the city.

Since these disasters, a government agency (Hidrandina) has been formed to control the lake levels by building dams and tunnels, thus minimizing the chance of similar catastrophes. Today, warning systems are in place, although false alarms do occur.

Mountain Biking

Mountain Bike Adventures (☎ 42 4259; www.chakina niperu.com; 2nd fl, Lúcar y Torre 530; ☯ 9am-1pm & 4-8pm Mon-Sat) has been in business for over a decade and receives repeated visits by mountain bikers for its decent selection of bikes, knowledgeable, friendly service and good safety record. The owner is a lifelong resident of Huaraz who speaks English and has spent time mountain biking in the USA – he knows the region's single-track possibilities better than anyone. The company offers bike rentals for independent types or guided tours, ranging from an easy five-hour cruise to 12-day circuits of the Cordillera Blanca. Rates start at US$20 per day for equipment rentals and US$30 for one-day tours. Some experienced technical riders have noted that the organized tours are more suited for beginner/intermediate riders.

Volunteering

For the latest on volunteering opportunities, check out the community notice boards at popular gringo cafés and hangouts around Huaraz. **Bruce Peru** (☎ 42 7487; www.volunteerhuaraz .com; Damaso Antuez 782) is an aid organization that works with children who can't afford to go to school. It's best to arrange volunteer activities in advance, but it sometimes takes short-term, walk-in volunteers.

Other Activities

Skiers will not find ski lifts in the Cordillera Blanca, but there is limited mountain **skiing** for diehards who want to climb with skis. Ask locally for current conditions. **River run**ning (white-water rafting) is sometimes offered on the Río Santa, but it's a very polluted river (mine-tailings upstream and raw sewage certainly don't help things) and people have fallen ill doing it – it's not recommended.

Horse riding is a possibility; although there is no dedicated outfit in Huaraz, horses can be arranged by many travel agencies. The Lazy Dog Inn outside of Huaraz (p381) has its own horses and does treks to the surrounding mountains. **Parapenting** (hang gliding) and **parasailing** are increasing in popularity, though you will need to bring all your own equipment. Aparac, a precipice behind Taricá, and Pan de Azúcar near Yungay are popular launching spots. Ask at Monttrek (p386) for the latest info.

COURSES

The **Sierra Verde Spanish School** (☎ 42 7954; sierra verde_sp@hotmail.com; Lúcar y Torre 530) has Spanish lessons for US$6.

TOURS & GUIDES

There are lots of nearby sights that can be visited on short trips, and dozens of agencies along Luzuriaga can organize outings. One popular tour visits the ruins at Chavín de Huántar (see p415); another passes through Yungay to the beautiful Lagunas Llanganuco (p401), where there are superb vistas of Huascarán and other mountains; a third takes you through Caraz to Laguna Parón (p402), which is ravishingly surrounded by glaciated peaks; and a fourth travels through Caraz to see the massive *Puya raimondii* plant (p403) and then continues on to Nevado Pastoruri, where you can view ice caves, glaciers and mineral springs.

Any of these trips cost between US$8 and US$12 each; prices may vary depending on the number of people going, but typically include transport (usually in minibuses) and a guide (who may or may not speak English). Admission fees are extra. Trips take a full day; you should bring a packed lunch, warm clothes, drinking water and sunblock. Tours depart daily during the high season, but at other times departures depend on passenger demand.

Out of the throng of agencies in Huaraz, **Pablo Tours** (☎ 42 1145; pablotours@terra.com.pe; Luzuriaga 501), **Huaraz Chavín Tours** (☎ 42 1578; hct@chavintours.com.pe; Luzuriaga 502), and **Sechín Tours** (☎ 42 1419; www.sechintours.com; Morales 602), which also has a satellite office in Casma, have fairly solid reputations.

For details on trekking tours, see p386.

FESTIVALS & EVENTS

Semana Santa (Holy Week) is very busy, with Peruvian tourists flooding to town. On the Tuesday before Easter there's a day of intense water fights – stay inside your hotel if you don't want to get soaked. **Ash Wednesday** is much more interesting and colorful, with funeral processions for *ño carnavalón* (king of carnival) converging on the Plaza de Armas. Here, his 'will' is read, giving the opportunity for many jabs at local politicians, police and other dignitaries, before the procession continues to the river where the coffin is thrown in. Participants dress in colorful costumes with papier-mâché heads, some of which are recognizable celebrities.

Huaraz pays homage to its patron, **El Señor de la Soledad**, beginning May 3. This weeklong festival involves fireworks, music, dancing, elaborately costumed processions and lots of drinking.

Semana de Andinismo is held annually in June. It attracts mountaineers from several countries, and competitions and exhibitions are held.

SLEEPING

The prices given here are average high (dry) season rates. Hotel prices can double during holiday periods and rooms become very scarce. Perhaps because Huaraz is seen as a trekking, climbing and backpacking center, budget hotels predominate.

Budget

Especially during the high season, locals meet buses from Lima and offer inexpensive accommodations in their houses. Hostels also employ individuals to meet buses, but beware of scams or overpricing – don't pay anybody until you've seen the room.

Caroline Lodging (☎ 42 6398; carolinelodging@yahoo .com; Urb Avitentel Mz-D, Lt 1; dm/d US$3/12) Recently renovated, this delightful homestay continues to get rave reviews from budget travelers. The incredibly friendly family will bend over backwards to make your stay enjoyable. There are bright, neat rooms with attached bathrooms, hot water and a top-floor kitchen with a large chill-out space, continental breakfasts, a TV lounge and Huaraz' signature mountain views. Call – you can be picked up. Once you find out where it is (beyond the west end of 28 de Julio, down a flight of stairs) you won't have any problem finding it again.

Hospedaje Ezama (☎ 42 3490; ezama_623@yahoo .es; M Melgar 623; dm/s/d US$3/4.50/9) Going north of town on Centenario and then right on M Melgar brings you to this quiet, friendly, seven-room place that has spacious rooms and good hard beds. Hot water and tourist information are available.

Familia Meza Lodging (☎ 42 6763; Lúcar y Torre 538; s/d US$4.50/9) In the same building as Café Andino and Mountain Bike Adventures, this charming family guesthouse has cheery rooms and is decorated throughout with homely, frilly touches. What's more, the owners are friendly and helpful enough to cure the worst bout of homesickness. Hot showers are shared and there's a top-floor communal area with a small kitchen.

Jo's Place (☎ 42 5505; www.huaraz.com/josplace; Villazon 278; dm/s/d US$4.50/6/10.50) Bright splashes of color and a rambling grassy area mark this informal and slightly chaotic place. Popular with trekkers and climbers (camping is allowed and there's plenty of room to dry out your gear), it has four floors linked by spindly staircases that lead to a warren of basic rooms, only some with bathrooms. Owner Jo provides UK newspapers, makes bacon and eggs for breakfast and has free coffee on tap.

Way Inn (☎ 42 8714; www.thewayinn.com; Buenaventura Mendoza 821; dm US$5.50, d US$12-15) Run by the friendly UK team of Alex and Bruni, the Way Inn has decent rooms, with several lounging areas and a roof-top terrace thrown in for good measure. The big draw here is its connection to the isolated Way Inn Lodge (opposite), a peaceful lodge nestled in the mountains of the Cordillera Blanca.

Oscar's Hostal (☎ 42 2720; José de La Mar 624; s/d US$6/9) Centrally located, Oscar's offers passable rooms with TV – though noise from the outside can be an issue.

Hostal Gyula Inn (☎ 42 1567; www.hostalgy.on.to; Plaza Ginebra 632; s/d US$6/9) Set around a quiet plaza right in the middle of town, Gyula has good rooms with comfortable mattresses, 24-hour hot showers and some climbing and trekking gear rental.

Hostal Tany (☎ 42 7680; Lúcar y Torre 648; s/d US$6/9; 🖳) The big and bright rooms here have massive windows to help you appreciate the awesome mountain vistas around. There's an internet café downstairs.

Alojamiento Soledad (☎ 42 1196; www.cordillera -adventure.com; Amadeo Figueroa 1267; s/d US$6/12; 🖳) A cozy family house with eight rooms – six with bathrooms and hot showers. Its rooftop terrace has the prerequisite sweeping views and a barbecue for sunset cook outs. Helpful owners speak English and German, have a book exchange, free internet, a cable-TV room, kitchen and laundry facilities.

Albergue Churup (☎ 42 2584; www.churup.com; Amadeo Figueroa 1257; dm US$6-7; s/d incl breakfast US$16/25) Fresh from another round of renovations, this immensely popular family-run hostel continues to win the top budget-choice accolade. Immaculate and comfortable rooms share cushy, colorful lounging areas on every floor. The building is topped by a massive, fireplace-warmed lounge space with magnificent 180-degree views of the Cordillera. If that isn't enough, the affable Quirós family has built a sauna, café and bar, communal kitchen and pretty garden, and has a book exchange, laundry facilities and a travel office that rents trekking gear and arranges Spanish lessons. Reservations are advised.

Hostal Raimondi (☎ 42 1082; Raimondi 820; s/d US$7.50/10.50) Greeted by an immense antique foyer reminiscent of an echoing train station, inside you'll find dark, austere rooms painted in dizzying, bright patterns. All come with comfy beds and writing desks, and hot showers are provided in the morning. It's convenient for buses and has a small café for early breakfasts.

La Casa de Zarela (☎ 42 1694; www.lacasadezarela .com; J Arguedas 1263; s/d US$7.50/15) Zarela's helpfulness is legendary. Double and triple rooms

here have hot showers and there are kitchen facilities as well as lots of neat little patio areas in which to relax with a book. The scenic black-and-white photos of the environs are worth perusing.

Monte Blanco Hotel (☎ 42 6384; José de la Mar 620; s/d incl breakfast US$9/18) Recently repainted blindingly pink, the digs here are spartan, clean and shiny. Big cushioned couches await slumping in the hallways – this is a solid back-up choice.

Edward's Inn (☎ 42 2692; www.edwardsinn.com; Bolognesi 121; r per person US$10.50) Rooms in this popular place all have hot water, but are otherwise elementary. There is a nice grassy bit and the owner, Edward, speaks excellent English and is a knowledgeable guide.

Hotel Del Valle (☎ 42 7399; Larroa y Loredo 700, s/d US$10.50/16.50) Not a bad deal for this price range. It has nice communal sitting areas and the orderly rooms are rather presentable.

Olaza's Guest House (☎ 42 2529; info@andeanexplorer .com; J Arguedas 1242; s/d US$10.50/16.50) This small, spick-and-span guesthouse has excellent hot showers in every room, a book exchange, laundry facilities and wonderful views from the rooftop terrace. Breakfast is served up here, and the owners can arrange mountain-biking trips and have an excellent gift shop. Bus station pickup is free with reserved rooms.

Hotel Brit's (☎ 42 6720; www.huarazinfo.net/brits; M Cáceres 391-399; s/d US$12/15) A six-storey monolith with good rooms for the price; each is clean, carpeted and comes with cable TV. It's a secure place and some of the top-floor rooms have good views.

Midrange

B&B My House (☎ 42 3375; bmark@ddm.com.pe; 27 de Novembre 773; s/d incl breakfast US$13.50/21) A small, bright patio and six rooms decorated like a home away from home welcome you to this hospitable B&B. Rooms have a writing desk and hot shower and there's a cheery communal yard. English and French are spoken.

Hostal Schatzi (☎ /fax 42 3074; www.schatzihostal .com; Bolívar 419; s/d US$15/21) Plenty of leafage in the pleasant courtyard here manages to keep the cement at bay. Charismatic little rooms surround this garden and inside have exposed wood-beam ceilings and great top-floor views. This is a reliable bet.

Hotel El Tumi (☎ 42 1784, 42 1852; www.hoteleltumi .8m.com; San Martín 1121; s/d US$16.50/30; 🖳) If serious businessmen lodged in chalets, this large and comfortable establishment is where they would flock. The rooms are handsomely finished with dark wood, come with cable TV and many have great mountain views. It all has a cozy mountain-retreat feel. Downstairs there's a lounge, posh restaurant with room service and wi-fi for laptopping mountain-road warriors.

Grand Hotel Huaraz (☎ 42 2227, grandhotel@terra .com.pe; Larrea y Loredo 721; s/d US$19.50/30; ☐) Spiffy and new, the Grand Hotel Huaraz is a little short on personality, but the solid rooms have everything you'll need for a comfortable stay.

Hotel Sierra Nevada (☎ 44 9613; Monterrey Km 3.5; s/d US$21/36) Laid out in a large V shape, this hotel sits perched on a hilltop 3.5km north of town and has sensational views of the valley below. The rooms are just comfortable enough, and you can take your breakfast in the dainty garden gazebo while the pet alpaca roams the grounds aimlessly.

Hotel Los Portales (☎ 42 8184; Raimondi 903; s/d incl breakfast US$21/36) A little swisher than most choices in Huaraz, the quiet, carpeted rooms here are clean and without fault. A games room (pool and table tennis) adds some attraction and there is a restaurant and sauna to boot. At night, the whole place is dimly lit with romantic mood lighting.

Steel Guest House (☎ 42 9709; www.steelguest.com; Pje A Maguina 1467; s/d US$22/38; ☐) Exceptionally welcoming, this guesthouse, a short walk south of town, decks out its fetching rooms with oodles of flair. Loads of facilities round out the offerings, including outdoor hammocks, billiards, a restaurant, kitchen, TV room, sauna and roof terrace. Gets our double thumbs up for excellent all-round value.

Piramide Hotel (☎ 42 8250, 42 5801; filiberto@terra .com.pe; Plaza Ginebra U-22; s/d/ste incl breakfast US$25/30/60) This is a modern hotel with phones and TVs, and some rooms have a balcony looking out into the plaza or toward the mountains. There's a restaurant with room service and rates include an American breakfast.

Hotel La Joya (☎ 42 5527; www.hotellajoya.com; San Martín 1187; s/d US$36/57; ☐) With true, glittering '80s panache, this towering, mirror-lined monolith offers hotel-standard rooms, with TV and writing desk. There's a very cheesy but comfortable lounge downstairs with endless muzac on tap. The top-floor rooms come with views and for some reason a disturbing statue of a mountaineer guards the elevator.

Hotel Colomba (☎ 42 7106, 42 1501; www.huaraz hotel.com; Francisco de Zela 278; s/d US$37.50/45) One of the best picks in town, the bungalows here are speckled around a dense and compulsively trimmed hedge forest. Each bungalow has a relaxing veranda, TV and telephone and

---

MOUNTAIN RETREATS

If trudging around the mountains for days at a time doesn't appeal to you, a good alternative is to make a home right among them. These mountain lodges let you explore deep in the stunning hills by day, and still come back to a comfortable bed every night.

Way Inn Lodge (☎ 42 8714; www.thewayinn.com/lodge.htm; camping US$3, dm US$6-9, d US$21, bungalows US$30-42, all incl breakfast) Located several hours into the picturesque Cordillera Blanca, this lodge is operated by the friendly folk from Huaraz' Way Inn (see p379). Rooms range from bunks in one of their Flintstone-esque 'cave' rooms to deluxe, well-appointed bungalows with fireplaces. A sauna and hot tub round off the long list of facilities rather nicely. There's tons of information here about one-day and multiday treks and trails you can do right from the front door, and hiking equipment is available for rent. All rates include breakfast, and other meals are available. Contact the Way Inn for directions or visit its website.

Lazy Dog Inn (☎ 978 9330; www.thelazydoginn.com; d US$40-60, cabins US$75-90, all incl breakfast) Run by maple-leaf-waving rugged Canadians Diana and Wayne, this deluxe ecolodge is at the mouth of the Quebrada Llaca, 8km east of Huaraz. It's made entirely of adobe and built by hand, and you can stay in either comfortable double rooms in the main lodge or in fancier private cabins, which have fireplaces and bathtubs. All rates include breakfast, and other meals are prepared. Lots of trekking opportunities are available here, there are some rock-climbing walls nearby and you can rent horses for US$7 per hour. Call ahead or visit its website for directions.

See also The Italian Connection (p400) for a list of modest and remote refuges deep in the Cordillera, all run by an Italian aid organization.

the sprawling gardens conceal a kids' playground, huge bird enclosures and a dainty restaurant.

San Sebastian (☎ 42 6960; www.huaraz.org/sansebastian; Italia 1124; s/d incl breakfast US$45/53) A fetching white-walled and red-roofed building with balconies and arches overlooking a grassy garden and an inner courtyard with a soothing fountain – this four-story hotel is a neocolonial architectural find. All rooms have a writing desk, good beds, hot shower and TV on request. A few rooms have balconies.

Top End

Hotel Andino (☎ 42 1662; www.hotelandino.com; Pedro Cochachín 357; s/d US$87/105, with balcony US$98/121; ☐) This Swiss-run hotel, up on a hill overlooking the town, is an outstanding place to stay and has one of the best, and most romantic, restaurants in Huaraz. The beautifully furnished rooms have all the necessary mod-cons and all have top views. It's very popular with international trekking and climbing groups; reservations are a good idea during the high season.

EATING

Restaurant hours are flexible in Huaraz, with shorter opening times during low-season slow spells and later hours at busy times.

Chifa Jim Hua (☎ 42 4468; 2nd fl, Luzuriaga 645; dishes US$1.50-6; ☺ 8am-10pm) This cozy Chinese restaurant gets good reviews as one of the better places in town to get your wonton on.

Café Andino (☎ 42 1203; www.cafeandino.com; 3rd fl, Lúcar y Torre 530; breakfast US$1.80-5.40; ☺ 8am-8pm Tue-Sun) This modern top-floor café has both space and light in spades, comfy lounges, art, photos, books and groovy tunes – it's the ultimate all-day hangout and meeting spot. You can get breakfast anytime (Belgian waffles – yum!) and this place is serious about its coffee – it roasts its own. Ask Chris, the US owner, about information on trekking in the area and check out the message board for local info.

Pachamama (☎ 42 1834; San Martín 687; snacks & mains US$1.80-7) This warm and delightful restaurant-bar features a glass roof, plant-filled interior garden, fireplace, pool table, table tennis, art on the walls and giant chessboard on the floor. It's a hip, fun and popular locale that may have live music and dancing at weekends (not *folklórica*!). The menu is Peruvian and international with a Swiss twist.

California Cafe (☎ 42 8354; www.huaylas.com/californiacafe; 28 de Julio 562; breakfast US$1.90-5.40; ☺ 7:30am-7pm; ☐) Run by Tim, from California no less, this hip pad does breakfasts at any time, light lunches and salads, and is a funky, chilled space to while away many hours. You can spend the day listening to the sublime word-music collection or reading one of the hundreds of books available for exchange. Wi-fi is a god-send to laptop junkies, and rich espressos and dozens of herbal teas will keep you sipping till closing time. Tim is active in the development of eco-tourism in the Cordillera Huayhuash and is a goldmine of information on that area. He organizes ultimate-Frisbee games every Friday.

Sabor Salud Pizzería (☎ 42 3443; 2nd fl, Luzuriaga 672; pizzas from US$2.10; ☺ 7:30am-10pm) If all Italians were vegetarian, this is where they would eat. Flavor and health are the bywords for this little place, which also serves up spinach lasagna and other pastas, soy burgers, yogurt, fruit salads, vegetable salads, omelets, garlic bread, muesli – it's almost enough to entice hardened carnivores. Almost.

El Fogón (☎ 42 1267; 2nd fl, Luzuriaga 928; mains US$2.40-4.50; ☺ noon-11pm) A bright, modern and slightly upscale twist on the traditional Peruvian grill house, this place will grill anything that moves – including the usual chicken, trout and rabbit, and it does great *anticuchos* (kebabs). Everything is very tasty and the place gets packed nightly with Peruvians in on the secret. Vegetarians will go hungry here.

Encuentro (☎ 42 7971; Luzuriaga, 6ta Cuadra; mains US$2.70-5.40; ☺ 9am-11pm) One of the most popular eateries in town, Encuentro has a niche market in well-prepared Peruvian fare, including everyone's favorite Andean delicacy, *cuy* (guinea pig). It's all served in a great space that has indoor and outdoor seating on a quiet plaza away from the street hubbub.

Pizza Bruno (☎ 42 5689; Luzuriaga 834; pizza US$3-6.30; ☺ 5-11pm) Serves pizza and has good steaks, salads, seafood and top-notch espresso. The French owner also rents out a 4WD vehicle for US$70 per day (plus US$0.30 per kilometer) with driver included.

La Brasa Roja (☎ 42 7738; Luzuriaga 919; mains US$3-6.60; ☺ noon-midnight Mon-Sat) This scrumptious *pollería* (restaurant specializing in rotisserie chicken) is the ultimate budget refueling stop. The 'Red-Hot Coals' also serves up sandwiches, pastas and beef – but stick with the chicken, it's what it does best.

Piccolo (☎ 42 7306; Morales 632; mains US$3.30-7.50; ☻ 7am-midnight) Very popular with gringos attracted to the outdoor pavement seating, friendly service and reasonable prices, the Piccolo is a café and pizzeria that moonlights as a restaurant. It has a good Italian and international menu, but make sure you see its Peruvian menu.

Monte Rosa/Inca Pub (☎ 42 1447; José de la Mar 661; pizzas US$3.90-5.40, mains US$6-12; ☻ 11am-11pm) This excellent, snug Swiss-run restaurant has an Alpine vibe; it does an international menu that includes fondue and raclette as well as pizzas and Peruvian plates. Service is good. The owner sells and rents climbing equipment and Victorinox Swiss army knives.

Crêperie Patrick (☎ 42 3364; Luzuriaga 422; mains around US$5; ☻ 8am-10pm) This French- influenced place is recommended for crepes, ice cream and continental dinners (trout, fondue, pasta). It has a rooftop patio that's open in the mornings for enjoying breakfast under the sun.

El Rinconcito Minero (☎ 42 2875; Morales 757; mains around US$5; ☻ 7am-11pm) This place comes highly recommended by readers. It's open all day and has a popular outdoor patio.

Bistro de los Andes (☎ 42 6249; www.huaraz.com/bistro; Morales 823; mains around US$5.50; ☻ 7am-10pm Tue-Sun, 6-10pm Mon, high season only) This restaurant with a European air is owned by a multilingual Frenchman. It serves an international and Peruvian menu ranging from pancakes to pastas. Good coffees, delectable desserts, fabulous fish dishes – there's something here for everyone at any time of day. It has a book exchange, the ambience is as elegant as you'll find anywhere in Huaraz and the service is always obliging.

Siam de los Andes (☎ 42 8006; Gamarra 560; mains US$7.50-11.70; ☻ 6-10pm) More expensive than many Huaraz restaurants, the authentic Thai fare is prepared by a Thai chef and well worth the few extra soles. Vegetarians will find plenty of dishes to choose from and a fireplace cranks up on cold evenings, creating a nice ambience.

Mercado Ortiz (Luzuriaga at Raimondi; ☻ 8am-10pm) This supermarket is a good place to pick up goodies for trekking or self-catering.

DRINKING

Huaraz is the best place in this part of the Andes to take a load off and get pleasantly inebriated.

Los 13 Buhos (2nd fl, José de la Mar 812; ☻ 5pm-late) Located upstairs from Makondos, the 13 Owls is a chilled-out bar that is currently the most popular place in town to kick back and chat in the early evening while listening to excellent, funky sounds. Warm lighting flickers over graffiti-covered walls and climbing paraphernalia clings to the rafters, while couches help you ease into the evening's frivolities over a cold Crystal.

Vagamundo Travel Bar (Morales 753; ☻ 10am-late) Opens late morning and has erratic hours. Come in for a beer, snack and a game of foosball. Enjoy rock and blues while perusing the many maps on the walls, or sit outside on the patio.

Andean Garden Club (Luzuriaga 1032; ☻ 11am-6pm, high season only) Owned by the same people as the X-treme Bar, this laid-back option has an outdoor garden setting and sells beer and snacks, and has a climbing wall for the perennially active. Just don't drink and climb.

X-treme Bar (☎ 42 3150; upstairs, cnr Uribe & Luzuriaga; ☻ dusk-late) This classic watering hole hasn't changed in years. Bizarre art, drunken graffiti, strong cocktails and good rock and blues keep things rambunctious into the night as it fills to the brim with a steady stream of bodies.

ENTERTAINMENT

There are plenty of discos and *peñas* (bars or clubs featuring folkloric music) around, though names and levels of popularity change with the seasons.

El Tambo Bar (☎ 42 3417; José de la Mar 776; ☻ 9pm-4am) If you're hankerin' to shake your groove-thang, this is the most popular disco in town. Fashionable with both *extranjeros* (foreigners) and Peruvians, the music swings from techno-*cumbia* to Top 20, to salsa to reggae and most things in between – all in a space of 20 minutes. Occasional live bands also play. Although there's no cover charge, you may want to consult your accountant before buying a round of drinks – the prices are astronomical.

Huaraz Satyricon (☎ 955 7343; Luzuriaga 1036; admission US$1.20) This place may just be the world's most perfect little cinema. A small and intimate space that has snug couches, fresh popcorn, snacks, espresso and shows quality international and repertoire flicks (all with English subtitles) on a private projection screen. Look out for flyers around town advertising the changing schedule.

SHOPPING

Inexpensive thick woolen sweaters, scarves, hats, socks, gloves, ponchos and blankets are available if you need to rug up for the mountains; many of these are sold at stalls on the pedestrian alleys off Luzuriaga. Quality climbing gear and clothes are sold by several outfits around town (p387). Tooled leather goods are popular souvenirs.

High-quality, attractive T-shirts with appropriately mountainous designs are made by **Andean Expressions** (☎ 42 2951) and sold in several outlets in town.

GETTING THERE & AWAY
Air

The Huaraz **airport** (☎ 44 3095) at Anta, 23km north of town, takes only chartered flights

Bus

Combis for Caraz (US$1.40, 1½ hours) leave every few minutes during the day from near the petrol station on 13 de Diciembre. These will drop you in any of the towns along the way. Minibuses south along El Callejón de Huaylas to Recuay, Catac and other villages leave from the Transportes Zona Sur terminal on A Gridilla at 27 de Novembre.

A plethora of companies have departures for Lima (seven to eight hours), so shop around for the price/class/time you prefer. Most depart mid-morning or late evening. Some buses begin in Caraz and stop in Huaraz to pick up passengers.

Three bus routes reach Chimbote on the north coast. Most buses take the paved road to Pativilca (the same route as Lima-bound buses, eight hours) and then head north on the Panamericana. A second, bumpier route follows El Callejón de Huaylas and passes through the narrow, thrilling Cañón del Pato (eight to nine hours, see p402) before descending to the coast at Chimbote. A third route crosses the 4225m-high Punta Callán (seven hours) and provides spectacular views of the Cordillera Blanca before plummeting down to Casma. This road is in rough shape.

For services across the Andes to the towns east of Huaraz, there are many small companies with brave, beat-up buses. Buses to Chavín are timed to meet the limited opening hours of the Cahuish tunnel, which was under construction at the time of writing, and are likely to change once building is complete.

Of the following long-haul companies, Movil Tours and Linea are recommended:

Chavín Express (☎ 42 4652; M Cáceres 338) Has 4am, 9:30am, 3pm and 8:30pm services to Chavín (US$3, two hours), going on to San Marcos (US$3, 2½ hours) and Huari (US$3.60, four hours). Also has a bus to Llamellin at 9:30am (US$4.50, six hours).

Chinchaysuyo (☎ 42 6417; Morales 650B) Has a 9pm bus to Trujillo (US$9, nine to 10 hours) via Pativilca.

Cial (☎ 42 9253; Morales 650) Good midpriced night buses to Lima (US$12 to US$13.50).

Cruz del Sur (☎ 42 8726; Bolívar 491) Has 11am and 10pm luxury nonstop services to Lima for US$12.

Empresa 14 (☎ 42 1282; Bolívar 407) Leaves at 8:45pm to Trujillo (US$9) via Pativilca, and at 10pm to Lima (US$7.50).

Expreso Ancash (☎ 42 5371; Raimondi 835) Has cheap services to Lima at 1:45pm and 8:45pm (US$6).

Linea (☎ 42 6666; Bolívar 450) Has excellent buses at 9:30pm to Trujillo ($12, nine hours) via Pativilca and Chimbote.

Los Andes (☎ 42 7362; Raimondi 744) Has a 6am bus to Pomabamba (US$7, eight hours) via Piscobamba, Yanama, Colcabamba and Vaqueria.

Movil Tours (☎ 42 2555; Bolívar 542) Buses to Lima at 9am and 1pm and several night buses between 10pm and 11pm (US$7.50 to US$16.50). Has 9pm and 9:30pm buses to Chimbote via Pativilca (US$7.50 to US$12) and on to Trujillo (US$13.50).

Renzo (☎ 42 9673; Raimondi 835) Has a rambling 6am and 7pm service to Pomabamba (US$7, eight hours) stopping at Piscobamba, Yanama, Colcabamba and Vaqueria. Another service leaves at 6:15am and 2:30pm for San Luis (US$5.50, five hours) via Chacas (US$4.50, four hours).

Sandoval (☎ 42 8069; M Cáceres 338) Has buses to Huari (US$3.60) via Chavín (US$3) at 4am, 10am, 3pm and 8:30pm. Also has a bus to Huánuco at 8pm (US$6, eight hours).

Transport Huandoy (☎ 42 7507; Fitzcarrald 261) There's a bus at 11am to Chimbote via Cañón del Pato (US$6, eight hours), as well as 8am, 10am and 1pm Chimbote buses (US$6, seven hours) via Casma.

Transportes El Rápido (☎ 42 2887; Bolognesi 261) Buses leave at 5:30am and 2pm to Chiquián via Recuay (US$3, 2½ hours); 6am, 1pm and 3pm to Huallanca (US$4.50, four hours); and 1pm to La Unión (US$6, five hours).

Transportes Río Mosna (☎ 42 6632; 27 de Novembre) Has buses at 10am and 3pm to Chavín (US$3, two hours) and Huari (US$3.60, four hours).

Transportes Rodríguez (☎ 42 1353; 27 de Novembre 622) Night buses to Lima at 10:30pm (US$7.50).

Yungay Express (☎ 42 4377; Raimondi 744) There's a morning bus at 7am to Chimbote via Cañón del Pato (US$7, eight hours), and a night bus via Pativilca (US$7, seven hours).

HUARAZ & THE CORDILLERAS

GETTING AROUND

A taxi ride around Huaraz costs about US$0.60. A taxi ride to Caraz is at least US$12. Look for taxis at the bridge on Fitzcarrald or along Luzuriaga.

TREKKING IN THE CORDILLERAS

Huaraz lies sandwiched in a valley carved out by the Río Santa, flanked to the west by the brown Cordillera Negra and to the east by the frosted Cordillera Blanca. More commonly known as El Callejón de Huaylas, a paved road runs the valley's length linking a string of settlements while furnishing visitors with perfect views of lofty elevations.

The Cordillera Negra, though an attractive range in its own right, is snowless and often eclipsed by the stunning, snow-covered crown of the Cordillera Blanca.

The Cordillera Blanca, about 20km wide and 180km long, is an elaborate collection of toothed summits, razor-sharp ridges, pea-colored lakes and green valleys draped with crawling glaciers. In this fairly small area there are more than 50 peaks of 5700m or higher. North America, in contrast, has only three mountains in excess of 5700m, and Europe has none. Huascarán, at 6768m, is Peru's highest mountain and the highest pinnacle in the tropics anywhere in the world.

South of the Cordillera Blanca is the smaller, more remote, but no less spectacular Cordillera Huayhuash. It contains Peru's second-highest mountain, the 6634m Yerupajá, and is a more rugged and less frequently visited range.

Where once pre-Columbian and Inca cultures used the high valleys as passageways to eastern settlements, backpackers and mountaineers now explore and marvel at the spectacle of Mother Nature blowing her own trumpet.

The main trekking areas of the Cordilleras include sections of the Cordillera Blanca, which is mostly encompassed by Parque Nacional Huascarán, and the Cordillera Huayhuash, to the south of Huaraz. There's something here for scramblers of all skill and fitness levels: from short, easy hikes of a day or two, to multiweek adventures requiring technical mountain-climbing skills. Foreign-

ers flock here yearly, and favorite hikes like the Santa Cruz trek can see a lot of hiking-boot traffic in the high season. While the more remote 10-day Cordillera Huayhuash Circuit doesn't see half as many visitors as the Santa Cruz trek, savvy travelers are rapidly discovering its rugged beauty and appreciating the friendly highland culture. Dozens of shorter routes crisscross the Cordillera Blanca and can provide an appetizing taste of the province's vistas, or can be combined with longer treks to keep you walking in the hills for months on end.

See p60 for advice and information about responsible trekking in Peru.

Information

To get the low-down on trekking and the latest condition, your first port of call should be **Casa de Guías** (☎ 42 1811; Plaza Ginebra 28G, Huaraz; ☽ 7-11am & 5-11pm), which has information on weather, trail conditions, guides and mule hire. Some IGN and Alpenvereinskarte topographic maps are sold here.

Trekking and equipment-rental agencies are also good sources of local knowledge, and can also advise on day hikes. For more impartial advice, be sure to visit popular Huaraz haunts such as California Cafe (p382) and Café Andino (p382), whose foreign owners keep abreast of local developments, sell hiking maps and guides, and freely dole out advice alongside tasty treats. While you're there, be sure to check out their notice boards and talk to other travelers and mountaineers – recently returned climbers will have the best advice on what to expect.

When to Go

People hike year-round, but the dry season of mid-May to mid-September is the most popular time to visit, with good weather and the clearest views. It's still advisable to check out the latest weather forecasts, however, as random heavy snowfalls, winds and electrical storms are not uncommon during this period. December to April is the wettest time, when it is often overcast and wet in the afternoons and trails become boggy. With the appropriate gear and some preparation hiking is still possible, and some trekkers find hiking then more rewarding since many of the most popular trails are empty. For serious mountaineering, climbers pretty much stick to the dry season.

Trail Guidebooks & Maps

Lonely Planet's *Trekking in the Central Andes* covers the best hikes in the Cordillera Blanca and the Cordillera Huayhuash. A great resource for the Huayhuash region is the detailed *Climbs and Treks of the Cordillera Huayhuash of Peru* (2005) by Jeremy Frimer, though it's only available locally in Huaraz.

Felipe Díaz' 1:286,000 *Cordilleras Blanca & Huayhuash* is a popular and excellent map for an overview of the land, with towns, major trails and town plans – though it may not be detailed enough for remote treks. The Alpenvereinskarte (German Alpine Club) produces the most detailed and accurate maps of the region; look for the regularly updated 1:100,000 *Cordillera Blanca Nord* (sheet 0/3a) and *Cordillera Blanca Sur* (sheet 0/3b) maps. For the Cordillera Huayhuash, get the Alpine Mapping Guild's 1:50,000 *Cordillera Huayhuash* topographic map. These maps are available in Caraz, Huaraz and at South American Explorers' clubhouses.

IGN produces six 1:100,000 scale maps covering the Cordilleras, although they're somewhat dated and often use atypical place names.

Tours & Guides

Mountaineers and trekkers should check out Casa de Guías (see p374) for a list of certified guides – it's the headquarters of the **Mountain Guide Association of Peru** (agmp@terra.com.pe).

Agencies in Huaraz arrange full trekking and climbing expeditions that include guides, equipment, food, cooks, porters and transport. Depending on the number of people and length of your trip, expect to pay around US$30 to US$50 per person per day. Try not to base your selection of agency solely on price, as is often the case you get what you pay for. The list below is by no means exhaustive; things change, good places go bad, and bad places get good. Be sure to ask around for references – other traveler's experiences are an invaluable resource.

Andean Kingdom (☎ 42 5555; www.andeankingdom .com; Luzuriaga 522) One of the cheapest and more popular agencies in town. Be sure to double-check the equipment here and confirm exactly what's included in your trip before you set off.

Galaxia Expeditions (☎ 42 5691; M Cáceres 428) Peruvian-run agency with a fine reputation and good gear. Also does local tours, climbing trips and has an indoor climbing wall.

Huascaran (☎ 42 2523; Pedro Campos 711) Gets repeatedly good reviews from satisfied travelers. Also does tours.

Montañero (☎ 42 6386; Parque Ginebra) This good agency arranges treks and climbs, and rents or sells gear.

Monttrek (☎ 42 1124; www.monttrek.com; 2nd fl, Luzuriaga 646) A reputable agency that has lots of local information and arranges rock-climbing, mountain-biking and parapenting trips.

As always, check your equipment before you leave – finding out your tent has holes in it in the middle of a thunderstorm is not our idea of fun.

If you wish to put together a support team for your own expedition, trekking agencies can also arrange individual guides, cooks or pack animals. Casa de Guías (see p374) is a good place to start your search for qualified mountain guides, *arrieros* (mule drivers) and cooks. Pony Expeditions (p403) in Caraz, on the way to the trailheads, can also help set things up or point you in the right direction.

If your Spanish is up to it and you're not in a great hurry, you can hire *arrieros* and mules in trailhead villages, particularly Cashapampa, Colcabamba and Vaqueria, among others. Horses, donkeys and mules are used as pack animals, and while llamas are occasionally provided, they cannot carry as much weight. Try to get a reference for a good *arriero* and establish your trekking goals (ie pace, routes) before you depart. Check the state of the pack animals before you hire them – some *arrieros* overwork their beasts of burden or use sick or injured animals.

Prices are generally set by the Dirección de Turismo and the guides' union. Expect to pay

---

STOP PRESS

Just before this book went to print, Inrena (Instituto Nacional Recursos Naturales; the government agency administering national parks, reserves, historical sanctuaries and other protected areas) announced new regulations governing Parque Nacional Huascarán. Under these new regulations, the use of local guides will be mandatory for everywhere except designated recreation zones, and climbers attempting difficult routes will need a local climbing guide to accompany them.

around US$5 per day for a horse, donkey or mule and US$10 per day for an *arriero*. Official rates for guides are US$30 to US$50 per day for a trekking guide, US$50 to US$75 for a climbing guide and US$100 to US$120 for a technical climbing guide.

Qualified guides and *arrieros* are issued with photo identification by the tourism authority – ask for credentials. Even experienced mountaineers would do well to add a local guide, who knows exactly what has been happening in the mountains, to their group. Prices do not include food and you may have to provide your *arriero* with a tent and pay for their return journey. Confirm what's included before you set off.

Equipment & Rentals

If you lack the experience or equipment required to mountain it, fear not, as dozens of savoir-faire businesses offer guides, gear rental and organize entire adventures for you, right down to the *burros* (donkeys). If you go on a tour, trekking agencies (see opposite) will supply everything from tents to ice axes. Some of them also rent out gear independently. **Skyline Adventures** (☎ 964 9480; www.sladventureschool.com), based outside of Huaraz, comes highly recommended and has some of the best-quality rental equipment in town. It also provides guides for treks and mountain climbs and leads two- and three-day mountaineering courses.

Another reliable rental agency is **Mount-Climb** (☎ 42 6060; M Cáceres 421, Huaraz), which has top-end climbing gear. **Monte Rosa/Inca Pub** (☎ 42 1447; José de la Mar 661, Huaraz) sells and buys good-quality climbing gear and skis and is an official Swiss Army knife outlet.

It often freezes at night, so make sure you have an adequately warm sleeping bag, wet-weather gear (needed year-round), and a brimmed hat and sunglasses. It's best to bring strong sunblock and good insect repellant from home as they're difficult to find in Huaraz.

CORDILLERA BLANCA

One of the most breathtaking parts of the continent, the Cordillera Blanca encompasses some of South America's highest mountains. Andean leviathans include the majestic Nevado Alpamayo (5947m), once termed 'the most beautiful mountain in the world' by the German Alpine Club. Others include Nevado Huascarán (at 6768m, Peru's highest),

Nevado Pucajirca (6039m), Nevado Quitaraju (6036m) and Nevado Santa Cruz (6241m). Peruvian mountaineer César Morales Arnao first suggested protecting the flora, fauna and archaeological sites of the Cordillera in the early 1960s, but it didn't become a reality until 1975, when Parque Nacional Huascarán was established. This 3400-sq-km park encompasses practically the entire area of the Cordillera Blanca above 4000m.

Visitors to the park should bring their passports to register at the park office in Huaraz (p375) and pay the park fee. This is US$1.50 per person for a day visit, or US$20 for a one-month pass. You can also register and pay your fee at one of the control stations, though their locations and operating hours vary – it's best to pay in Huaraz before you set off.

Money from fees is used to help maintain trails, pay park rangers and offset the effects of the legions of visitors to the area. It makes sense that as foreign visitors are among those frequenting the area and causing the greatest change, they should contribute to the financing of the national park with their user fees. Although it's sometimes possible to dodge paying the park fee, remember that the cheapest option isn't always the correct one.

Santa Cruz Trek

Heading up the spectacular Quebrada Santa Cruz, this trek ascends the valley and crosses the Punta Union pass (4760m) before tumbling into Quebrada Huaripampa on the other side. Head-turning sights along the way include picturesque emerald lakes, sensational views of many of the Cordillera's peaks, beds of brightly colored alpine wildflowers and stands of red *quenua* trees. As it's one of the most popular routes in Peru for international trekkers, it is clearly signposted for much of its length.

The building of a major tourist road to the Llanganuco lakes and beyond means that the trek is now shorter and can be completed in three days by acclimatized parties. Side trips

FAST FACTS

Duration: 4 days
Distance: 50km
Difficulty: easy–moderate
Start: Cashapampa
Finish: Vaqueria

to Laguna Quitacocha, Alpamayo Base Camp, Quebrada Paria and Quebrada Ranincuray are possible and four days allows more scope for viewing alpine flora and exploring side valleys. The trek can be extended beyond Vaqueria (as for the original route), following the road out and picking up the walking trail over the Portachuelo de Llanganuco pass to Quebrada Llanganuco and its jade-green lakes.

Colectivo (shared-transport) taxis frequently head out from Caraz to the main trailhead at Cashapampa (US$1.80, 1½ hours).

The trek can be done in reverse – daily *colectivos* from Huaraz to Vaqueria provide access to the trailhead.

DAY 1: CASHAPAMPA TO LLAMACORRAL
5 hours / 11km / 700m ascent

From the bus stop in Cashapampa (2900m), walk up the dirt road (northeast) to the signpost signifying the start of the trek. Pass through the gate and follow the path (north) past a small bridge on the right (do not cross this) and continue climbing steadily, through stands of tall eucalypt trees, into Quebrada Santa Cruz. Stick to the southeast side of the river and hike steeply up the rocky trail for 2½ hours. The well-defined trail turns east and continues along the valley floor past stone walls and a jumble of moss-covered boulders, with the Río Santa Cruz rushing past on the left.

The walking becomes easier from here, and after a further 2½ hours, the extensive meadow area (or *pampa*) of Llamacorral (3600m) is reached. This is the first night's impressive campsite. Water for cooking and drinking is available from the Río Santa Cruz, but be sure to boil it before drinking.

DAY 2: LLAMACORRAL TO TAULLIPAMPA
7 hours / 13km / 650m ascent

Just beyond Llamacorral, the valley floor widens. Many small waterfalls can be seen cascading down the rocky walls along this stretch, and a series of lakes and interconnecting marshy areas appears up ahead. The first, smaller lake is Laguna Ichiccocha (also referred to as Laguna Chica), closely followed by the much larger Laguna Jatuncocha (or Laguna Grande). The main trail continues to skirt the lakes on their right shore, rising slightly and passing through many bushy clusters of purple and blue lupins. To reach this point takes four hours, and an alterna-

tive grassy camp site is among the trees. The trail crosses a log bridge over the Río Santa Cruz to the left bank and then divides, with the right fork, heading east, continuing the Santa Cruz trek, and climbs gently for one hour before leveling out and traversing soft, marshy swamp ground.

Quebrada Arteson is a side valley that connects with Quebrada Santa Cruz from the south. Continue along the main trail east, climbing steadily until the second night's campsite is reached at Taullipampa (4250m). This gorgeous **meadow** rests at the foot of majestic Nevado Taulliraju (5830m). The glacial icefall on the flanks of Taulliraju is very active and large chunks regularly break off, especially under the influence of the afternoon sun. To the south, Nevado Artesonraju (6025m) and Nevado Parón (5600m) dominate the skyline.

Side Trip: Laguna Quitacocha
5–6 hours / 14km / 800m ascent/descent

A small bridge heads left (north) off the Santa Cruz trail just as Laguna Jatuncocha is reached. Follow this track along the northern shore of the lake for 30 minutes until it turns sharply left (north) again and ascends steeply to Laguna Quitacocha and a spectacular **valley** below Nevado Quitaraju (6036m).

Side Trip: Alpamayo Base Camp (South Side)
7–8 hours / 12km / 700m ascent/descent

This steep hike takes you to the climber's base camp underneath the southern aspect of the magnificent Nevado Alpamayo (5947m), at the head of the valley known as Quebrada Arhueycocha. Where the trail crosses a log bridge over the Río Santa Cruz, the left, signposted fork heads north up to Alpamayo Base Camp. The track is steep and zigzags upward in a series of tight switchbacks into Quebrada Arhueycocha. Just before the climb to Laguna Arhueycocha on the right (northwest), the trail divides. The left fork climbs very steeply through moraine on the west (opposite) side of the valley toward Nevado Quitaraju. Take the right fork (moving northeast) and follow it up steep switchbacks to a camping area in the trees well below the moraine that forms Laguna Arhueycocha. Camp here or, if you're still full of energy, hike the two hours back to the Quishuar junction and continue along the Quebrada Santa Cruz.

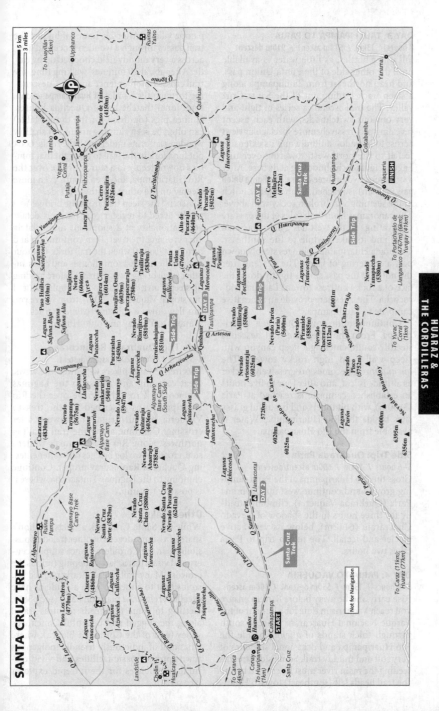

SANTA CRUZ TREK

HUARAZ & THE CORDILLERAS

DAY 3: TAULLIPAMPA TO PARIA
8 hours / 13km / 510m ascent / 910m descent

Fill water bottles, as little water is available until the other side of the Punta Union pass, and head northeast from Taullipampa along a steep track leading out of the Santa Cruz valley. The trail ascends a series of tight and very obvious switchbacks, with each ascent revealing progressively more spectacular **views** across to Nevado Taulliraju and its extensive icefall to the northwest, towering over tiny Laguna Taullicocha huddling at its base. After a strenuous two to three hours, the **Punta Union pass** (4760m) is reached, at an angular notch in the seemingly unbroken rocky wall above. The panoramas from both sides of the pass are captivating. To the west lies Quebrada Santa Cruz and its lakes, while to the southeast, Quebrada Huaripampa plunges steeply down past a scattering of lakes. The descent after the notch at the pass spirals tightly down the face of a rocky buttress toward Lagunas Morococha. The lakes here provide an alternative campsite to Taullipampa.

Continue south down Quebrada Huaripampa. From the lakes, the trail descends steadily south, entering a deep canyon with steep walls and high rocky towers. The *quenua* forest becomes progressively thicker as altitude is lost, and after four to five hours an established campsite is reached at Paria (3850m), with pit toilets and beautiful grassy sites beside the Río Huaripampa. Water is available from the Río Huaripampa.

Side Trip: Quebrada Paria
5–6 hours / 10km / 600m ascent/descent

Cross the Río Huaripampa at the Paria camping ground and continue west up Quebrada Paria (Quebrada Vaqueria), climbing steadily for three hours in the shadow of Nevado Chacraraju (6112m), below its very active glacier and icefall. The return trip to Paria takes two hours.

DAY 4: PARIA TO VAQUERIA
3–4 hours / 13km / 550m descent / 400m ascent

Rise early and be away before 8am to ensure you reach Vaqueria in time for a bus out of the Parque Nacional Huascarán. Proceed south through thick stands of *quenua* beside the Río Huaripampa and occasional stretches of very soft and muddy trail. Some side streams feeding the main river must be crossed before the trail heads left (southeast) toward Huari-

pampa village. After 2½ hours of hiking, the trail passes through a wooden fence and gate, across a very muddy field chopped up by cattle. After about 20 minutes' walking time, the trail crosses another fence and gate, descending through the hamlet of **Huaripampa** and its traditional thatched-roof Quechua houses. Guinea pigs (destined for the dinner table) can often be seen running around in shallow wooden platforms underneath the roofs. Look out for a fork in the trail to the right that tumbles down steeply to a sturdy bridge over the Río Huaripampa, and then climbs even more steeply up the other (southwest) side.

Ascend the steep trail from the bridge. You will be asked to register your passport details and nationality at a shopfront immediately after crossing the river, then continue up and turn right (south) when the trail forks. Contour around the hill past some houses and cross another small bridge over a stream before heading up steeply on a dirt road to the shopfronts and bus stop at Vaqueria (3700m), from where you can flag down a *colectivo, camión* (truck) or minibus to Yungay and onto Huaraz.

Side Trip: Quebrada Ranincuray
4–5 hours / 11km / 800m ascent/descent

This trek rewards hikers with awesome views, great camping and access to the Lagunas Tintacocha. Cross the bridge over the Río Huaripampa as described for the trek to Vaqueria, but turn right (northwest) after crossing. Continue along the trail heading northwest along Río Huaripampa's western side, crossing two log bridges soon after entering Quebrada Ranincuray proper. Continue climbing to the Lagunas Tintacocha, where it is possible to camp.

Other Treks

While the Santa Cruz trek attracts the lion's share of visitors, dozens of other trekking possibilities in the Cordillera Blanca supply scenery and vistas just as jaw-dropping (minus the crowds). Many trails aren't clearly marked yet, so it's best to either go with a guide or have excellent reference maps on hand (see p386). Getting to some trailheads requires travel along the rugged and beautiful Conchucos valley (east of the Cordillera Blanca), where a handful of ludicrously friendly indigenous towns provide basic facilities and vivid cultural experiences for the intrepid explorer (see p414).

ALPAMAYO BASE CAMP

This is one of the more dazzling and demanding treks of the Cordillera. The seven-day, 90km route involves very long ascents to high passes, incredible alpine scenery (including the regal north side of Nevado Alpamayo) and traditional Quechua communities with no road access. Starting in Cashapampa (same as the Santa Cruz trek) and ending in Pomabamba, it is only recommended for experienced and acclimatized hikers who are familiar with navigation. The route is relatively straightforward, but not signposted. You can treat yourself to well-earned dips in hot mineral spring baths at both ends of this trek.

LAGUNA 69

This is a beautiful, short overnight trek through backdrops dripping with marvelous views. The campsite on the way to the *laguna* is a true highlight, where you can wake up to a crystal morning vision of Chopicalqui (6354m), Huascarán Sur (6768m) and Norte (6655m). In the morning you scramble up to Laguna 69, which sits right at the base of Chacraraju (6112m), and then hike down past the famous Llanganuco lakes. That's a lot of impressive lakes crammed into just two days. The trails to Laguna 69 commence near the Yurac Corral (3800m), on the northern tip of a big bend in the Llanganuco road.

CONCHUCOS VALLEY TREKS

If you're short on time but still want to cross the Cordillera and soak in some icy-peak time, the relatively easy two- to three-day **Olleros to Chavín de Huántar** trek comes to the rescue. You can start the 40km trek in either town, though most people start in Olleros, where you can arrange llamas as pack animals. There are pretty villages along the way, interlaced with pre-Inca roads and great views of the Uruashraju (5722m), Rurec (5700m) and Cashan (5716m) mountains as you head up to the 4700m Punta Yanashallash high pass. The valley on the Conchucos side is absolutely gorgeous. Best of all, in Chavín you can soak your weary bones in hot springs and get up early the next day to visit the ruins without the usual throng of tourists. Dedicated riders have mountain-biked this route. To get to Olleros, catch a south-heading *combi* from Huaraz, get off at the Bedoya bridge and hike the 30 minutes up to Olleros. A taxi there costs US$9 to US$12.

If this trek whets your appetite for ambling, you can continue on to Huari by bus (see p416) or by walking along the road, and commence the equally impressive **Huari to Chacas** trek. Be sure to make time to camp near the Laguna Purhuay – this picturesque spot deserves an overnight visit. The easy two- to three-day route passes several other lakes, reaches its zenith at a 4550m pass and finishes up through misty high-altitude tropical forests of the Parhua valley (3500m) to Chacas.

After a rest in the fetching town of Chacas, you can continue on to do the one- to two-day **Chacas to Yanama** trek. This is the shortest of the three hikes and has the lowest pass of the lot, at a 'mere' 4050m. From Chacas you hike through the municipalities of Sapcha and Potaca, and can either finish the trek at Yanama or continue to the Keshu valley, where there are several good places to camp. Colcabamba, a few hours further on from Yanama, is the end of the Santa Cruz trek and endurance hikers can tag this trek onto the end of their herculean circuit before returning to Huaraz.

INCA TRAIL

This three- to four-day hike along an Inca trail, between Huari and the city of Huánuco, is just starting to be developed. Hikers cross well-preserved parts of the old Inca trail and end up in Huánuco Viejo, which was one of the most important military sites of the Incas in northern Peru. This route is being organized in conjunction with the Inka Naani project. It aims to encourage tourism that respects the cultural heritage of the region and ties together several independent grassroots tourism initiatives. If you are interested, contact the **Mountain Institute** (☎ 42 3446; mtorres@mountain .org; Ricardo Palma 100) in Huaraz.

CORDILLERA HUAYHUASH

Often playing second fiddle to its limelight-stealing cousin the Cordillera Blanca, Huayhuash hosts an equally impressive medley of glaciers, summits and lakes – all packed into a hardy area only 30km across. Increasing numbers of travelers are discovering this rugged and remote territory, where trails skirt around the outer edges of this stirring, peaked range. Several strenuous high-altitude passes of over 4500m throw down a gauntlet to the hardiest of trekkers. The feeling of utter wilderness, particularly along the unspoiled eastern edge, is the big draw, and you are more likely to spot the graceful Andean condor here than dozens of *burro*-toting trekking groups.

In the waning moments of 2001, Peru's Ministry of Agriculture declared the Cordillera Huayhuash a 'reserved zone', giving a transitory measure of protection to nearly 700 sq km of almost-pristine land. Since then, the Ministry has backed away from official support as a unique, private and community-managed conservation effort has taken root. The six communities whose traditional territory lies at the heart of the Huayhuash range are becoming formally recognized as 'Private Conservation Areas.' Several districts along the circuit now charge user fees of US$3 to US$4, with costs for the entire circuit approaching US$16. Part of the fees goes to improved security for hikers, and part goes to continued conservation work – support this grassroots preservation attempt by paying your fees, carrying enough small change, and by always asking for an official receipt.

Cordillera Huayhuash Circuit

Circling a tight cluster of high peaks, including Yerupajá (6634m), the world's second-highest tropical mountain, this stunning trek crosses multiple high-altitude passes with spine-tingling views. The dramatic lakes along the eastern flanks provide great campsites (and are good for trout fishing) and give hikers a wide choice of routes to make this trek as difficult as they choose to make it. Described here is the classic Huayhuash Circuit trek, but there are many side trips and alternate routes along the way that can add a day or two to your trekking time.

Most trekkers take extra rest days along the way, partly because the length and altitude make the entire circuit very demanding, and partly to allow for the sensational sights to sink in. Others prefer a shorter version, and can hike for as few as five days along the remote eastern side of the Huayhuash. Trekkers should be prepared for aggressively territorial dogs along the way; bending down to pick up a rock usually keeps them off – though refrain from throwing it.

For information on getting to Chiquián, and transport to Llamac for the trailhead, see p414. In Llamac there is a soccer field where camping is permitted. There are three *hospedajes* (small, family-owned inns) here,

FAST FACTS

Duration: 10 days
Distance: 115km
Difficulty: demanding
Start/finish: Chiquián
Nearest towns: Chiquián, Llamac and Cajatambo

including the plain, four-room, cold-water Hotel Santa Rosam and the slightly better Hospedaje Huayhuash. Both have rooms for around US$1.50 to US$2 per person and provide meals.

DAY 1: LLAMAC TO LAGUNA YAHUACOCHA
5½–8 hours / 1000m ascent / 250m descent
Llamac is the last town for several days as the trail leaves 'civilization' and climbs to the first of many top Cordillera panoramas before dropping to a lake. The early part of the trail takes you past a small pre-Inca platform with excellent mountainscapes up and down the valley. The trail also passes many 4m-high *cholla* cacti as it climbs south up a hill to a ridge where there are two large, cube-shaped water tanks used for irrigation, two hours from Llamac.

Take the more scenic left fork from here and climb southeast toward the low, flat 4300m Pampa Llamac pass. At times the trail braids, but continuing southeast will bring you to the pass a little over an hour from the water tanks.

The **Pampa Llamac pass** is marked by some stone cairns visible from below. When the cairns are reached, the trail bursts out on a fabulous **view** of glaciated peaks: Rondoy (5870m), the double-fanged Jirishanca (6094m), Yerupajá Chico, Yerupajá (6634m) and others. This is what you have come to see!

The trail takes you past a canal trail, corrals and the canal irrigation control buildings, and eventually after two hours to your first glimpse of Laguna Yahuacocha (4050m). Here there's a rustic house where bottled drinks are sold. Nearby, the west end of the lake is a popular camping area. To the south, the waterfalls of Quebrada Huacrish are visible, with a trail zigzagging up the right side toward Punta Yaucha. Hike around the north side of the lake for another 30 minutes to find more camp ites at the lake's east end.

Alternative Route: Chiquián to Matacancha
6–8 hours / 750m ascent

An alternative start, from Chiquián to Matacancha via Mahuay, bypasses the beautiful Punta Rondoy pass and has become increasingly popular since the road to Llamac opened to traffic. To follow this route, catch the 9am minibus from Chiquián to Quero (US$1.50, 2½ hours), which is at the intersection of several small rivers and has hot springs that can be reached by a one-hour walk. Follow Quebrada Mahuay east to Mahuay, where camp may be made. On the second day, follow Quebrada Pariash east, continuing cross-country along poor trails past Cerro Azulcocha to Quebrada Asiac and follow this southeast to Matacancha. A guide is recommended, unless you are confident with maps and using poorly defined trails and can speak passable Spanish.

DAY 2: LAGUNA YAHUACOCHA TO MATACANCHA
4½–7 hours / 700m ascent / 550m descent

The trail heads east from the lake's northeast corner, passing well to the left of a few stone huts, beyond which the trail divides – you need to stay on the lower right trail.

To your right (southeast) is a huge moraine hiding Laguna Solteracocha. Half an hour beyond the east end of Yahuacocha, turn left and follow the best of several braided donkey tracks. Soon the surprisingly blue waters of Solteracocha come into view behind you and the trail crosses a flourishing meadow set with highland grasses, a few low bushes and ground-hugging flowers.

The trail switchbacks toward a spiky ridge and you climb through a scree slope along a clear mule trail until a **pass** is reached, two or three hours from Yahuacocha. The vistas of Rondoy and Yerupajá looming over blue Solteracocha are suitably impressive and make the climb worthwhile. Continue walking north-northeast for about five minutes on a clear trail to the **Punta Rondoy pass** (4750m), and views of Ninashanca (5607m) will appear behind Rondoy.

From here, don't take the obvious trail going north, zigzag down northeast into the bowl below, to the valley bottom at **Quebrada Rondoy** after 45 minutes. There is good camping all along the river. Keep heading north for at least an hour, staying above a mining road

and passing the spread-out farming settlements of Rondoy and Matacancha (4150m). After a further 45 minutes, the trail joins the road near the stone marker for Km 39 (the distance to Huallanca). Follow the road for about 1km until it makes a hairpin bend. At this point, keep heading north or northeast instead of following the road, and good camping is found almost immediately, near some corrals.

Note that the trek can be started from nearby Matacancha.

DAY 3: MATACANCHA TO LAGUNA MITACOCHA
5½–7½ hours / 550m ascent / 450m descent

Today, another high pass, with frequent condor sightings, leads to the first of a string of beautiful lakes on the east side of the Cordillera Huayhuash. From the campsite, head northeast, climbing up animal and donkey trails zigzagging upward and eastward toward the base of some large cliffs. Keep an eye out for condors. The unnamed **pass** (4685m) is often very windy and is reached two to three hours after leaving camp.

The trail heads steeply east, switchbacking into the swampy Quebrada Caliente valley, staying well above the right (southeastern) bank to avoid the swamps. The trail passes a **metal cross** erected in 2000 by Canoandes in honor of a Polish explorer who died here. The trail flattens and contours around to the southeast, then slopes gently toward the confluence of the Quebrada Caliente with

---

WARNING

Over the past few years there have been two serious events in the Huayhuash involving robbery and death. Two foreign trekkers were murdered near Cajatambo in August 2002, and in 2004 there was a series of robberies at the Huayhuash camp, and on the pass to Laguna Viconga, that resulted in one death. In both of these isolated cases the motive appears to have been robbery. In recent years, community-based conservation work has improved the situation somewhat, with mandatory registration points and armed security guards accompanying trekkers for sections of the circuit. Inquire locally regarding safety in the area before you head off.

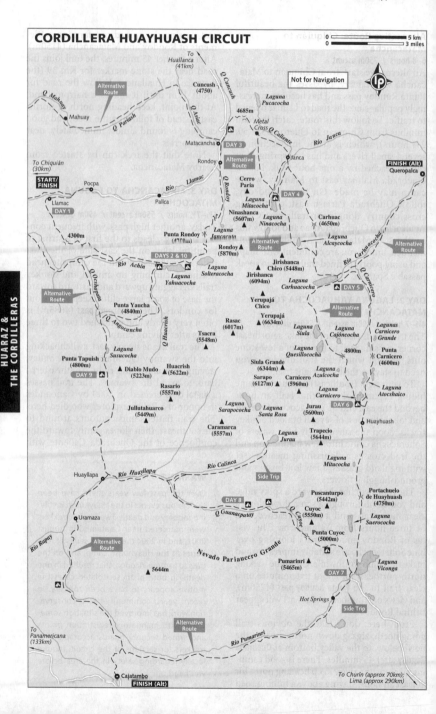

CORDILLERA HUAYHUASH CIRCUIT

0 |————————| 5 km
0 |————————| 3 miles

Not for Navigation

the Río Janca. The tiny community of **Janca** (4200m) is about two to three hours from the pass and while you can camp near here, there are more exciting views if you turn south-southwest and follow the right bank of the Río Janca, climbing gently, to Laguna Mitacocha (4230m) over an hour away.

DAY 4: LAGUNA MITACOCHA TO LAGUNA CARHUACOCHA
4–5 hours / 20m ascent / 510m descent
In this leg, high-country hiking leads to the most scenic lake on the eastern side of the circuit; many trekkers spend a rest day (or even two) exploring the Carhuacocha area. Head north from Mitacocha and swing around to the northeast as the valley widens out. After 45 minutes, jump over a tiny stream and climb east past a single house, aiming for a grassy saddle. The trail is faint, mainly cattle paths, but after zigzagging up to the saddle for 20 minutes you'll find a clearer trail heading off to the southeast. Just beyond the top, jump back over the stream you had crossed below. After 15 minutes, the trail follows the right side of a flat, grassy meadow and is unusually marked by a series of stones stuck upright into the ground like daggers. Next, climb up the right of a small, steep valley and emerge into another grassy field.

To the right, the mountains of Siula Grande (6344m) and Yerupajá loom into view. Continue heading southeast to the **Carhuac pass** (4650m), reached after about 1½ hours, for excellent mountain panoramas. Twenty-five minutes of southbound descent brings you to a narrowing of the valley where the trail crosses to the left side and continues high above a sheep-filled boggy meadow. After about 20 minutes cross back over to the right side and continue south for 20 more minutes. Here, you'll reach a clifftop that spectacularly overlooks Laguna Carhuacocha (4138m) below you and glaciated mountains behind.

Head east, high above the north shore of Carhuacocha, past a farmhouse where beer and soft drinks are sold. Drop down to the east end of the lake to camp; the best sites are near the stream at the southeast corner.

DAY 5: LAGUNA CARHUACOCHA TO LAGUNA CARNICERO
4–5½ hours / 500m ascent / 200m descent
Cross the Río Carhuacocha at its mouth at the southeast corner of the lake via stepping

stones, climb up to the farmhouse visible above and head northeast along the right-hand side of the Río Carhuacocha valley.

After about 40 minutes the trail goes above a house and crosses the Quebrada Carnicero. Shortly beyond the stream turn hard right and climb up parallel to the stream for about 50m until you find a clear, steep trail zigzagging up, climbing east and then southeast away from the Río Carhuacocha valley.

After about 45 minutes of climbing, the trail tops out on the left side of the Quebrada Carnicero and flattens out. About 20 minutes more brings you to a short section of paved **Inca trail**, about 1.5m wide and 50m long, the remnants of an Inca road heading south from the archaeological site of Huánuco Viejo near La Unión. The trail crosses over to the right side of the Quebrada Carnicero after half an hour, and immediately after the crossing is a short, angled section of paved Inca trail again, attesting to the ancient use of this route.

Keep heading due south, past a series of small lakes to the trail's left and to the low pass of **Punta Carnicero** (4600m), marked by small piles of rocks decorated by twigs of lycopodium and other plants.

A clear trail continues south from the pass, climbing briefly up above the first Laguna Atocshaico to your left before continuing its descent southwest on a very clear trail.

After a few minutes Laguna Carnicero (4430m), locally called Juraucocha, appears to the right. As soon as the lake is sighted, look for a minor trail angling off to the right toward the southeast side of the lake. For camping, it's better to continue southwest around the lake until you reach a small stream at the south end, crossed by stepping stones.

DAY 6: LAGUNA CARNICERO TO BEYOND LAGUNA VICONGA
5–6½ hours / 500m ascent / 400m descent
You're now following an Inca trail – short remnants of paving and arrow-straight paths are a dead giveaway.

Head along a faint trail on the right side (west) of the valley, and join a more defined trail after about 20 minutes. Once this trail joins the faint one, it continues quite clearly heading south-southwest, and is fairly flat. After 20 minutes, the community of Huayhuash is reached, and south of here the main river is crossed as you climb up to the ridge above the east bank to find the trail again.

Now, the trail climbs gently but steadily, with views of Trapecio (5644m) to the west. The trail passes the lower **Laguna Mitucocha** (to the right of the trail) about an hour beyond Huayhuash, and upper Laguna Mitucocha (4485m) 10 minutes later. After the lakes, the trail veers around to the south-southeast and the pass is visible straight ahead.

En route to the next pass, the trail climbs through talus slopes with dozens of **viscachas** stealthily scampering around. The top of **Portachuelo de Huayhuash** (4750m) is reached along well-marked tracks in about 1¼ hours from Laguna Mitucocha.

Just over an hour past the pass, the **Laguna Viconga** (4407m) comes into your line of sight. At the southwest end of the lake, the trail climbs steeply for a few minutes, finally topping out at a small **pass** (4475m), where several glaciated mountain crowns come into view, including the double-peaked Cuyoc (5550m) to the northwest.

You can either head northwest to camp below Punta Cuyoc and continue the main circuit, or you can head southwest along the Río Pumarinri valley toward **Cajatambo**, leaving the circuit early. Many trekkers prefer the challenge of the 5000m Punta Cuyoc pass.

For the high pass, continue on the main trail as it drops, winding around with a small dam visible to your left and a building with solar panels housing the dam controller. Head down to this building, crossing an irrigation canal via a footbridge on the way.

From the dam controller's house, head north on a rough trail heading up the right side of the valley. After half an hour, you'll reach a water wheel and some concrete and metal construction housing controls of the irrigation canal. You can camp anywhere above there. The camp, although close to a lofty 4500m, is well protected and makes a good place to acclimatize before tomorrow's high ascent.

DAY 7: BEYOND LAGUNA VICONGA TO QUEBRADA GUANACPATAY
4–6 hours / 525m ascent / 650m descent
From the camping areas, a narrow trail climbs north-northwest up the middle of the valley. At the head of the valley the trail heads around the left-hand side of talus slopes and well to the left of a waterfall. Soon, the trail flattens out and becomes indistinct for about 300m. Look for a pile of rocks on the horizon to the

west, and after crossing the flat area, zigzag up toward the rock pile.

Ahead are the double peaks of Cuyoc and the long ridge of Puscanturpo (5442m). To your left is an icy and rocky summit locally called Pumarinri (5465m), which in Quechua means 'puma's ear,' due to a supposed resemblance. It is variously marked on maps as Jirishanca Chico or Cuyocraju.

About 1½ hours above the camp, the trail crests a small ridge and you get face-on **views** of Cuyoc. A clear trail falls steeply and then climbs to the pass and a more scenic trail goes higher to the left of the large rock hill, avoiding the steep drop and climb.

The higher trail continues climbing northwest to a point a little above the actual pass. Look out for the hardy *Stangea henricii*, a grayish-green, flat, rosette-shaped plant of overlapping tongue-like leaves that only grows above 4700m. Finally, about 2½ hours after leaving camp, the highest point on the trek is reached, marked by a single pile of stones. If you brought champagne, this would be a good time to pop the cork.

From the top, head down to the left on a steep, slippery trail passing under a strangely eroded rock – a giant mushroom or penis, depending on your sense of humor. The trail continues to the northwest and after 45 minutes the Quebrada Cuyoc, which the trail has been paralleling, becomes a waterfall. Below the fall, the trail becomes somewhat boggy as it drops diagonally across the valley; beyond this are dry camping areas. It tends to be exposed and windy here.

The trail continues westward along the right side of the valley, staying above the valley bottom as it negotiates the falling terrain. After 40 minutes you come across an apparently **deserted farm** (4350m) with two thatched buildings and a series of stone corrals. These act as a good windbreak and camp is often made here, with good Cordillera views looking back up the valley.

DAY 8: QUEBRADA GUANACPATAY TOWARD PUNTA TAPUISH
8–11 hours / 1200m ascent / 800m descent
Good morning! There are several possible choices today: continue the direct circuit by hiking past the village of Huayllapa; exit the circuit through Huayllapa and the town of Uramaza to Cajatambo; or make a side trip up the Río Calinca valley to Lagunas Jurau,

Santa Rosa and Sarapococha, where there are some of the best mountain panoramas of the entire trek.

To continue with the traditional circuit, leave camp heading west along the north bank of the Quebrada Guanacpatay. After 30 minutes the trail becomes faint, the valley becomes narrower and you'll cross over the river to the left (south) side. Ten minutes later, you'll see some **quenua trees** on the north side of the river – make some time to hug them, these are the first trees that you will have seen for some days. A few minutes later, the glacier-clad pyramid of Jullutahuarco (5449m) comes into view on the right-hand side.

Continue northwest on the left bank of the Quebrada Guanacpatay for one hour to the steep sides of the Río Huayllapa. The trail will tumble precipitously and foot travelers can carefully negotiate this very steep descent, which parallels a stupendous 100m-high **waterfall** to the right, and arrive at the Río Huayllapa trail after a hard 30 minutes.

At the Río Huayllapa, turn left and head west on the south bank of the river, crossing the river on a footbridge after 20 or 30 minutes. The village of Huayllapa comes into sight half an hour later. A **stone wall** with a gap for the trail to pass through marks the village's entrance. About 100m beyond the gap, the trail to Punta Tapuish goes off to the right. For Cajatambo, go straight ahead on the trail into Huayllapa (10 to 15 minutes, reached by a steep descent), and on through Uramaza.

The trail to Punta Tapuish goes north from shortly before Huayllapa and climbs steeply. After crossing and re-crossing a stream, the trail smoothes out to a flat area (4350m) between two forks and provides good camping.

However, if you have the energy for a long day, continue climbing north up the left side of the right fork for about 1km. The trail then bears northwest, away from the stream, and climbs, steeply at first and then more gently, to a flat area at the base of Punta Tapuish near a small lake (4700m) about two hours beyond the earlier suggested camp. There is good high-altitude camping here.

DAY 9: PUNTA TAPUISH TO LAGUNA YAHUACOCHA
6–8 hours / 500m ascent / 1200m descent

From the high camp before the Punta Tapu-ish, continue up the left side of the valley heading north-northeast for about an hour to reach the pass (4800m). As you crest the top, a brilliant white range is visible to the northwest – this is the southern part of the Cordillera Blanca. The trail continues north, dropping gently to **Laguna Susucocha** (4750m) about 15 minutes beyond the pass.

The trail follows the left bank of the river until shortly before the **junction** (4400m) with Quebrada Angocancha. About an hour below the Punta Tapuish pass, wade across the Quebrada Ocshapata shortly before the junction and then climb east up the Quebrada Ango-cancha valley toward the Punta Yaucha pass. The trail skirts boggy meadows and climbs into rock and scree before reaching **Punta Yaucha** (4840m), about two to three hours above the river junction.

The pass gives a wonderful view of the range's major peaks, including Yerupajá, to the east and many of the minor glaciated high points to the southeast. Look out for fossils on the ground – they are the imprints of ammonites and other creatures that once dwelled under the sea – and imagine the Andes relegated to the ocean's bottom.

The trail descends steeply from the pass, heading east toward the Quebrada Huacrish valley, which is reached in under an hour. As you drop down, keep your eyes upward for condors floating effortlessly on outstretched 'fingered' wings. When the river is reached (4400m), turn left (north) and follow the left (west) side of the valley. This area is also known for herds of semiwild bulls. Avoid wearing red today.

For almost an hour, the trail drops slowly, mainly northwest, before reaching a steep, switchbacking section paralleling the waterfalls of the lower Quebrada Huacrish. From the top of the falls is an excellent view of the beautiful Laguna Yahuacocha, backed by the Cordillera Huayhuash – haul out the camera yet again. Stay on the west side of the falls all the way to the bottom before heading to the lake and camp.

DAY 10: LAGUNA YAHUACOCHA TO LLAMAC
4–6 hours / 700m ascent / 600 descent

This last day essentially backtracks the route on Day 1. By now, trekkers are well acclimatized and can trek to Llamac in the morning, from where midday transport to Chiquián, and on to Huaraz, can be arranged.

NORTH OF HUARAZ

As the Río Santa slices its way north through the El Callejón de Huaylas, a road shadows its every curve past several subdued towns to Caraz, and on to the menacingly impressive Cañón del Pato. The Andean panorama of the Cordillera Blanca looms over the length of the valley like a wall of white-topped sentries, with the granddaddy of them all, Huascarán, barely 14km away from the road as the condor flies. Many hiking trailheads are accessible from towns along this route and two unsealed roads valiantly cross the Cordillera, one via Carhuaz and another via Yungay.

MONTERREY

🗺 043 / pop 1100 / elev 2800m

Huddled around a scattered spine of tourist facilities, this tiny *pueblo*, 6km north of Huaraz, earns a spot on the map for its natural hot springs (admission US$0.90; ⏲ 6am-6pm). It also makes for a low-key sleeping alternative to Huaraz. The baths are run by the Real Hotel Baños Termales Monterrey next door, which fronts a popular rock-climbing wall. Buses terminate right in front.

The hot springs are divided into two sections; the lower pools are more crowded while the upper pools are nicer and have private rooms (20 minutes for US$0.90 per person). Before you wrinkle your nose at the brown color of the water, know that it's due to high iron content rather than questionable hygiene practices. It's best to visit in the morning as the baths are cleaned overnight. The pools get crowded on weekends and holidays.

Sleeping & Eating

All the hotels are within a five-minute walk of the springs. Some of the restaurants are a little further afield, but still within walking distance.

Hostal El Nogal (☎ 42 5929; s/d US$10.50/19.50) The slightly dank rooms at Hostal El Nogal find redemption in its attractive, wood-lined building and flourishing rear garden.

Real Hotel Baños Termales Monterrey (☎ 42 7690; s/d US$21/28, 2-/4-person bungalows US$36/54; 🛇) Crowning the hill like a thermal-bath overlord, you can hear the history of this grand old structure through its creaky wooden floors. Old-world charm oozes from every crack in the wall. It is set in a motley garden,

there's a simple restaurant with outdoor dining (overlooking the pool) and reasonably priced meals. Rather spartan rooms have hot showers and a TV that shows local channels. The four bungalows sleep either two or four. Rates include access to the springs.

El Patio de Monterrey (☎ 42 4965; elpatio@terra .com.pe; s/d US$51/56) The fanciest venture around, this has colonial-style architecture around a toothsome hacienda, complemented by the colonial-style furniture. Most of the ship-shape rooms are spacious, and have bathtubs, phones and local TV. Some rooms (US$85) sleep up to four and a few have a fireplace. Most rooms look out onto a bountiful garden that's strewn with wagon wheels and fountains; some have a balcony. Meals are available in the fireplace-heated restaurant-bar.

Apart from the hotel restaurants, there are several eateries worth mentioning.

El Regimontano (meals US$0.90-1.80; ⏲ 8am-7pm) Opposite the baths, this place is guarded by mannequins dressed in traditional mountain garb and opens into a secret garden. Local specialties – including *cuy, chicharrones* (pork cracklings) and trout – are the norm, and the large benches, protected from the elements by thatch roofs, are popular with groups.

Recreo Mochica (☎ 42 9074; Km 2.5; mains US$2.50-5; ⏲ 8am-8pm) This is a small but locally popular place.

Recreo Buongiorno (☎ 42 7145; Km 2.5; meals US$3-6; ⏲ 11am-8pm) You can't miss the rock model of the Cordillera Blanca outside this joint. Local and national food is served and there are yummy pastries. Outside is a nice garden with a play set for children that attracts families.

El Ollon de Barro (☎ 42 3364; Km 7; meals US$3-9; ⏲ 10am-7pm) This is surrounded by a near-impenetrable wall of hedge guarding a large, enticing garden with a fronton court, children's swings and trees. Typical plates such as *rocoto relleno* (spicy hot pepper stuffed with rice and pepper) and *ají de gallina* (chicken in chili sauce) are on offer, as well as the usual country grills.

El Cortijo (☎ 42 3813; mains US$6-10.50; ⏲ 10am-7pm) An excellent grillery that chars ostrich alongside *cuy* and other meats, as well as serving 'ordinary' food. Outdoor tables are arranged around a fountain (complete with little boy peeing) in a grassy flower-filled garden, with swings for children.

Restaurant Cordillera Blanca (near El Cortijo; ⏲ 10am-7pm) Also good and slightly cheaper.

Getting There & Away

Local buses from Huaraz go north along Lu-zuriaga, west on 28 de Julio, north on 27 de Novembre, east on Raimondi and north on Fitzcarrald. Try to catch a bus early in the route, as they soon fill up. The fare for the 15-minute ride is US$0.30. A taxi ride be-tween Huaraz and Monterrey costs US$1.20 to US$1.50.

MONTERREY TO CARHUAZ

About 5km north of Monterrey, the road goes through the little village of **Taricá**, which earns its tourist stripes with locally made pottery. Stop at the friendly **Hostal Sterling** (☎ 49 1277, 49 0299; s/d US$6/11.50), which has funky, concrete-block rooms with electric showers, a small restaurant and a bar that looks like it's barely been touched since the 1950s – the dust is piled high. Behind the hotel is an elevation called Aparac, which is used for hang-gliding.

About 18km north of Monterrey is mi-nuscule Anta airport, and 2km beyond is the hamlet of **Marcará**. From here, minibuses and trucks leave regularly for the hot springs and natural saunas of **Chancos**, 4km to the east, where the waters supposedly harbor curative properties. The rustic Chancos hot springs are popular with weekending locals and tend to be crowded then. There are some great 'steam baths' here in natural vapor caves (US$1.50 for 15 minutes), where you can purchase herbs to aromate and medicate your sauna experience. The smaller caves tend to be hotter so check out a few. The pools, on the other hand, are rather tepid; private pools cost US$0.60 and the public pool US$0.30 for as long as you like. There's a popular, pre-bolted **climbing wall** just before the hot pools.

Buses occasionally continue another 4km to **Vicos**, beyond which the Quebrada Honda trail (for hikers only) continues across the Cordillera Blanca and passes the **Laguna Lejíacocha**.

Marcará serves as the base for a very active Italian nonprofit organization that's been helping disenfranchised local youth for decades (see p400). The **Cooperative Artesanal Don Baso** (☎ 74 3061; Los Pinos 3A) has a large work-shop here where you can see adolescents busy creating superior-quality carvings, ceramics, sculptures, furniture and other crafts.

The **Hostal Los Jazmines** (main plaza; r per person US$5) is predictably austere and has shared bathrooms.

CARHUAZ

☎ 043 / pop 5100 / elev 2638m

Carhuaz, 35km north of Huaraz, lays claim to one of the prettiest Plazas de Armas in the valley, with a combination of rose gardens and towering palm that make lingering here a pleasure. The Sunday market is a kaleido-scopic treat as *campesinos* (rural inhabitant) descend from surrounding villages to sell a medley of fresh fruits, herbs and handicrafts. A road passes over the Cordillera Blanca from Carhuaz, via the beautiful Quebrada Ulta and Punta Olímpica pass, to Chacas and San Luis.

Carhuaz' annual **La Virgen de La Merced fiesta** is celebrated from September 14 to 24 with processions, fireworks, dancing, bullfights and plenty of drinking; it's one of the area's best and wildest festivals. The small, municipal **tourist office** (☎ 39 4249; Plaza de Armas) claims to have some information.

Sleeping & Eating

A number of rudimentary, family-run *hos-tales* have simple, clean rooms with hot-water bathrooms. **Hostal Río Santa** (☎ 39 4128; 28 de Julio; s/d US$4.50/6), **Hostal Las Bromelias** (☎ 39 4033; Brazil 208, s/d US$4.50/6) and **Hostal Las Torrecitas** (☎ 39 4213; Amazonas 412; s/d US$6/9) all provide little to differentiate between them. One of the oldest running ventures, **Hotel La Merced** (☎ 39 4241; Ucayali 724; s/d US$6/9), has lots of windows for Cordillera adulation, and plenty of religious posters for internal speculation. Rooms are clean and have hot showers. The haughtiest place to stay in town is **Hostal El Abuelo** (☎ 39 4456; hostalelabuelo@terra.com.pe; 9 de Diciembre 257; s/d incl breakfast US$30/40; 🖳), which has immaculately neat rooms with good mattresses and hot showers in a large, older-styled house. There's a lovely restaurant on the premises.

On the plaza, **La Punta Olímpica** (☎ 39 4022; meals around US$1.50; 🕙 8am-10pm) slaps together cheap local dishes and *menús* (set meals) for an appreciative local crowd. **Café Heladería El Abuelo** (☎ /fax 39 4149; meals US$1.20-4.50; 🕙 8am-9pm), also on the plaza, is owned by local cartographer Felipe Díaz (you probably have his map, everyone does). It serves breakfast, snacks and ice cream made from local fruits, and provides local information.

El Mirador (☎ 49 4244; meals US$3-5), about 2km south of Carhuaz on the south of a hill, is a lunchtime restaurant with typical food. It delivers on its promise of great views.

THE ITALIAN CONNECTION

Established by the pioneering Father Ugo de Censi, a priest of the Salesian order, the Italian nonprofit organization Don Basco has a long and active history in South America, particularly the eastern Cordillera Blanca.

Since 1976, enterprising and well-meaning Italians have been working overtime to help indigenous youth of the region. They've established the School and Workshop of Carpentry and Woodcarving, where orphans and street children can accumulate free hands-on experience and training in carpentry and woodcarving. The Italians have also been busy founding schools and artisan cooperatives in the area, and organizing re-forestation and agricultural programs. In Chacas, the best hospital in the eastern Cordillera was built and staffed by this organization, and many churches have had extensive renovations paid for through its funding efforts. Oh, and we can't forget the too-large-to-ignore statue of Christ blessing your journey as you approach Chavín – these guys also had a hand in that.

Three **refuges** (☎ 44 3061; www.rifugi-omg.org) have also been constructed by this organization, all deep within the belly of the Cordillera. Each refuge is heated and has a radio, basic medical supplies, 60 beds, and charges US$30 per night for bed, breakfast and dinner. Profits go to local aid projects. Refuges include **Refugio Perú** (4765m), a two-hour walk from Llanganuco and a base for climbing Pisco; **Refugio Ishinca** (4350m), a three-hour walk from Collón village in the Ishinca valley; and **Refugio Huascarán** (4670m), a four-hour walk from Musho. Trekkers, mountaineers and sightseers are all welcomed.

The founder of this Andean mission, Father Ugo de Censi, continues to be actively involved at the sprightly old age of 82. He is the parish priest in Chacas.

Getting There & Away

The Plaza de Armas is where you can pick up passing minibuses to Huaraz (US$0.80, 50 minutes), Yungay (US$0.30, 30 minutes) and Caraz (US$1.10, 45 minutes). Morning and afternoon buses from Huaraz to Chacas and San Luis also pass by the plaza. Buses between Caraz and Lima, and Huaraz and Chimbote, pass by here also.

YUNGAY

☎ 043 / pop 11,300 / elev 2458m

Light on overnighting visitors, serene little Yungay has relatively few tourist services. It has the best access for the popular Lagunas Llanganuco, via a dirt road that continues over the Cordillera to Yanama and beyond. Surrounded on all sides by lush hills wafting brisk mountain air, it's difficult to believe the heartrending history of this little junction in the road.

The original village of Yungay is now a rubble-strewn zone about 2km south of the new town and marks the site of the single worst natural disaster in the Andes. The earthquake of May 31, 1970 loosened 15 million cu meters of granite and ice from the west wall of Huascarán Norte. The resulting *aluvión* reached a speed of 300km/h as it dropped over three vertical kilometers on its way to Yungay,

14km away. The town and almost all of its 18,000 inhabitants were buried (see p378).

Information

Policía de Montaña (USAM; ☎ 39 3327, 39 3333, 39 3291; usam@pnp.gob.pe) has two helicopters, trained search-and-rescue dogs, and police officers who have taken mountaineering courses. They often work with experts from the Mountain Guide Association at the Casa de Guías (p374) in Huaraz. It's located behind Hostal Gledel.

Sights & Activities

The site of old Yungay (Yungay Viejo), **Campo Santo** (admission US$0.60; ⊙ 8am-6pm) is marked by a towering white statue of Christ standing on a knoll and overlooking the path of the *aluvión*. Flower-filled gardens top the hill, with occasional gravestones and monuments commemorating the thousands of people who lie buried beneath the 8m to 12m of soil. At the old Plaza de Armas, you can just see the very top of the cathedral tower and a few palm-tree tips (one of them remarkably still alive). A replica of the cathedral's facade has been built in honor of the dead.

If you're interested in DIY mountain-biking adventures, visit **Cycle World** (☎ 30 3109; Arias Graciani; ⊙ 9am-6pm). It rents mountain bikes for US$10 per day, including a helmet, puncture repair kit and simple map. You can do several trails in the area, but the most popular one involves catching a *colectivo* to Portachuelo (US$3) and cycling back downhill over three to four hours. A park entry fee of US$1.50 applies.

Sleeping & Eating

Hostal Gledel (☎ 39 3048; Calle 13; s/d US$3/4.50) There are 13 impossibly cute and spartan rooms rented out by the gregarious and generous Señora Gamboa. Expect at least one hug and a sample of her cooking during your stay. Showers are shared and you can get breakfast here. This is both the cheapest and best place to stay in town – it's deservedly popular.

  Hostal Yungay (☎ 39 3053; Santo Domingo 1; s/d US$4.50/6) Also decent, this place has 25 simple rooms that have electric showers.

  Hostal Sol de Oro (☎ 39 3116; Santo Domingo 7; s/d US$4.50/9) Another good pick – it has bright, clean rooms with solid mattresses and hot showers.

  There are several cheap and rustic places to eat in Yungay's market, next to the plaza. In garden surrounds, **Restaurant Turístico Alpamayo** (☎ 39 3090; meals US$2.10-3.60; 🕑 7am-7pm), off the main highway at the north end of town, is the best restaurant.

Getting There & Away

Minibuses run from the Plaza de Armas to Caraz (US$0.40, 15 minutes) and Huaraz (US$1.10, 1¼ hours). Buses from Caraz to Lima and from Huaraz to Chimbote pick up passengers at the Plaza de Armas.

  Departures on beat-up buses from Huaraz to Pomabamba via Lagunas Llanganuco pass by daily.

LAGUNAS LLANGANUCO

A dirt road climbs the Llanganuco valley to its two stunning Llanganuco lakes, also called Laguna Chinancocha and Laguna Orcon-cocha, 28km east of Yungay. Nestled in a glacial valley just 1000m below the snow line, these pristine lagoons practically glow in their bright turquoise and emerald hues. There's a 1½-hour trail hugging Chinancocha and passing rare *polylepis* trees. You can rent boats at this lake – it's a popular day-tripping spot. There are killer views of the mountain giants of Huascarán (6768m), Chopicalqui (6354m), Chacraraju (6112m), Huandoy (6395m) and others, particularly if you drive a few kilo-

meters beyond the lakes. The road continues over the pass beyond the lakes to Yanama on the other side of the Cordillera Blanca; there are several early-morning vehicles from Huaraz going to Yanama and beyond.

  To reach the Lagunas Llanganuco, you can take a tour from Huaraz or use buses or taxis from Yungay. During the June to August high season, frequent minibuses leave from Yungay's Plaza de Armas (US$5), allowing about two hours in the lake area. A national-park admission fee of US$1.50 is charged. During the rest of the year, minibuses do the trip if there's enough demand. *Colectivo* taxis are available for US$3 per person each way. Go in the early morning for the clearest views.

CARAZ

☎ 043 / pop 11,000 / elev 2270m

With an extra helping of superb panoramas of the surrounding mountains and a more kick-back attitude than its rambunctious brother Huaraz, Caraz makes for an excellent alternate base of operations. Trekking and hiking trails meander in all directions – some of the short, day-trip variety, some much longer sojourns. One of the few places in the valley spared total destruction by earthquake or *aluvión*, a gentle whiff of colonial air still hangs about the town, and its lazy Plaza de Armas wouldn't be out of place in a much smaller *pueblo*.

  Caraz is both the end point of the time-honored Llanganuco-to-Santa-Cruz trek (which can also be done in reverse starting here) and the point of departure for rug-ged treks into the remote northern parts of the Cordillera Blanca. The north side of Al-pamayo (5947m), enthusiastically labeled the most beautiful mountain in the world for its knife-edged, perfectly pyramidal northern silhouette, is easily accessible from here.

Information

The **Municipalidad** (☎ 39 1029; San Martín 1121; 🕑 8am-1pm & 2-5pm Mon-Fri), on the Plaza de Armas, has limited tourist information.

  For internet access, try the new **Dan Clau** (José Sucre 1122), on the Plaza de Armas, with relatively fast access for the standard US$0.30. **BCP** (☎ 39 1010; Daniel Villar 217) changes cash and traveler's checks but lacks an ATM. Pony Expeditions can change US cash and euros and arrange Visa advances. The **post office** (San Martín 909; 🕑 8am-8pm Mon-Fri) is north of the cathedral.

Sights & Activities

The partially excavated Chavín ruins of **Tumshukaiko** are about 2km on a dirt road north of Caraz. There is no sign or fee. The extensive walls (now in poor condition) and buried underground chambers indicate this was once an important Chavín site. A *mototaxi* to get here costs US$0.60, while a taxi is US$1.20.

The pastel-blue **Laguna Parón** (4200m), 32km east of Caraz, is surrounded by spectacular snow-covered peaks, of which Piramide (5885m), at the end of the lake, looks particularly brilliant. The challenging rock-climbing wall of Torre de Parón, known as the Sphinx, is also found here. The road to the lake goes through a canyon with 1000m-high granite walls – this drive is as spectacular as the better-known Llanganuco trip. Fit and acclimatized hikers can trek to the lake in one long day, but it's easier to catch local transport to Pueblo Parón and hike the remaining four hours.

If you continue north from Caraz along El Callejón de Huaylas, you will wind your way through the outstanding **Cañón del Pato**. It's here that the Cordillera Blanca and the Cordillera Negra come to within kissing distance for a battle of bedrock wills, separated in parts by only 15m, and plummeting to vertigo-inducing depths of up to 1000m. The road snakes along a path hewn out of sheer rock, over a precipitous gorge and passes through 35 tunnels, hand-cut through solid

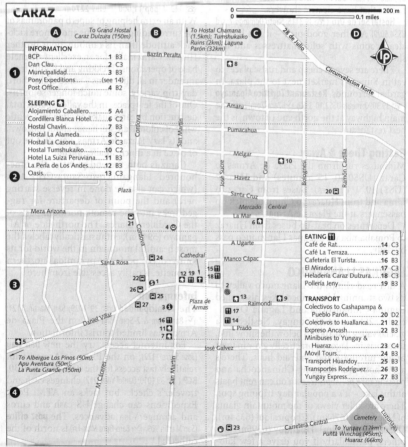

CARAZ

0 — 200 m
0 — 0.1 miles

To Grand Hostal
Caraz Dulzura (150m)

To Hostal Chamana
(1.5km); Tumshukaiko
Ruins (2km); Laguna
Parón (32km)

INFORMATION
BCP.................................1 B3
Dan Clau..........................2 C3
Municipalidad....................3 B3
Pony Expeditions..............(see 14)
Post Office........................4 B2

SLEEPING
Alojamiento Caballero..........5 A4
Cordillera Blanca Hotel........6 C2
Hostal Chavín.....................7 B3
Hostal La Alameda..............8 C1
Hostal La Casona................9 C3
Hostal Tumshukaiko...........10 C2
Hotel La Suiza Peruviana.....11 B3
La Perla de Los Andes.........12 B3
Oasis..............................13 C3

EATING
Café de Rat......................14 C3
Café La Terraza.................15 C3
Cafeteria El Turista............16 B3
El Mirador........................17 C3
Heladería Caraz Dulzura......18 C3
Pollería Jeny....................19 B3

TRANSPORT
Colectivos to Cashapampa &
  Pueblo Parón..................20 D2
Colectivos to Huallanca......21 B2
Expreso Ancash.................22 B3
Minibuses to Yungay &
  Huaraz..........................23 C4
Movil Tours......................24 B3
Transport Huandoy.............25 B3
Transportes Rodríguez........26 B3
Yungay Express.................27 B3

Bazán Peralta
28 de Julio
Circunvalación Norte
Amaru
Pumacahua
Melgar
Havez
Santa Cruz
Mercado Central
La Mar
A Ugarte
Manco Cápac
Raimondi
L Prado
José Galvez
Plaza
Meza Arizona
Santa Rosa
Cathedral
Plaza de Armas
Daniel Villar
Cordova
San Martín
José Sucre
Grau
Bolognesi
Ramón Castilla

To Albergue Los Pinos (50m);
Apu Aventura (50m);
La Punta Grande (150m)

Carretera Central
Cemetery
To Yungay (12km);
Punta Winchus (45km);
Huaraz (66km)

HUARAZ & THE CORDILLERAS

stone. Gargantuan, crude walls tower above the road on all sides, and as the valley's hydro-electric plant comes into sight you realize that it's dramatic enough to house the secret lair of a James Bond arch-villain. Sit so you're looking out of the right-hand side of the bus (as you face the driver) for the best views along the way.

Punta Winchus, a remote 4157m pass in the Cordillera Negra 45km west of Caraz and reached by tour vehicles, is the center of a huge stand of 5000 rare *Puya raimondii* plants. This is the biggest known stand of these 10m-tall members of the pineapple family, which take 100 years to mature and in full bloom flaunt up to 20,000 flowers each! On a clear day you have an astounding 145km panorama from the Cordillera Blanca all the way to the Pacific Ocean.

For detailed trekking information you can visit one of the two main trekking outfits in Caraz. Alberto Cafferata at **Pony Expeditions** (☎ /fax 39 1642; www.ponyexpeditions.com; José Sucre 1266; ☯ 8am-10pm) speaks English, French and Spanish and provides equipment rental (including bicycles), transport, guides, *arrieros* and various excursions. Books, maps, fuel and other items are for sale at the shop. You can also visit Luis at **Apu Aventura** (☎ 9683 2740; www.apuaventura.com), based at Albergue Los Pinos (right). Luis is an experienced guide who can also help arrange treks, horse riding, climbing and equipment rental.

Sleeping

Caraz is yet to see the tourist development of Huaraz, and offers straightforward facilities and budget sleeping options. Prices remain quite stable throughout the year.

Hostal La Casona (☎ 39 1334; Raimondi 319; s/d with shared bathroom US$3/4.50; s/d US$4.50/6) Although many of the large rooms here are dark and windowless, the attractive patio still makes this place a budget fave.

Alojamiento Caballero (☎ 39 1637; Daniel Villar 485; s/d US$3/9) It's a small, simple, clean, friendly, family-run place with views and shared hot showers.

Hotel La Suiza Peruviana (☎ 58 8217; San Martín 1133; s/d US$6/7.50) You wouldn't think that exposed concrete could look inviting, yet somehow this place manages to exude a certain bucolic appeal. This large, rambling brick building has modest rooms that are kept reasonably clean by the friendly owners.

Cordillera Blanca Hotel (☎ 39 1625; Grau 903; s/d US$6/9) This multistory hotel opposite the market is decidedly lacking in anything that might resemble character, but the immaculate pink rooms and gleaming bathrooms are without fault and good value for money. The restaurant downstairs, Chifa El Dragon Rojo, has a Chinese twist on the traditional *pollería*.

Oasis (☎ 39 1785; Raimondi 425; s/d US$6/12; ☐) Some people will call this place a rat hole, but we prefer the term inner-urban rodentia habitat. It's as basic as it gets, but it has a restaurant and internet access on site to tempt passersby.

Albergue Los Pinos (☎ 39 1130; Parque San Martín 103; campsites per person US$3; s/d with shared bathroom US$6/12, s/d US$12/21; ☐) This popular, International Youth Hostel–affiliated place offers outstanding rooms in a massive, multicolored mansion that is thoughtfully decorated inside and out. There are several great garden courtyards and a funky restaurant that serves breakfast and snacks. The owner, Luis, organizes trekking and tours of the area.

Hostal Chavín (☎ 39 1171; hostalchavin@latinmail.com; San Martín 1135; s/d US$7.50/10.50) The friendly owner knows the area and provides information, tours and local transportation. Rooms are simple, but all have TV and hot showers. Breakfast is available and some interesting handicrafts collect dust in a wall cabinet.

Grand Hostal Caraz Dulzura (☎ 39 1523; www.huaraz.com/carazdulzura; Saenz Peña 212; s/d US$7.50/13.50) About 10 blocks north of town along San Martín, this is a clinically clean and modern rural retreat that provides good bang for your buck. Rooms are bright and have hot showers and comfortable beds. There's a patio backed by a rocky hill and covered in lots of greenery, a TV room, book exchange and restaurant for doing breakfast (US$1.80) and dinner (mains US$3 to US$4.50).

Hostal La Alameda (☎ 39 1177; Bazán Peralta 262; s with shared bathroom US$10-20, s/d US$12/18) There are lots of places to sit and relax around the flourishing garden here, and while the cheaper rooms are a little cell-like, the better rooms are relatively good value. The old ladies running this show are ridiculously friendly. Hot showers and breakfasts are an added bonus.

La Perla de Los Andes (☎ /fax 39 2007; Plaza de Armas 179; s/d US$10.50/16.50) A swish place that wears its multiple layers of polished wood with pride, La Perla has a great location right on Caraz' quiet plaza. Although rooms are a mite small, they all have cable TV, solid mattresses and hot showers, and some have balconies with an ideal plaza view. A restaurant serves breakfast and the staff are helpful.

Hostal Tumshukaiko (☎ 39 2212; Melgar 114; s/d US$10.50/21) Five blocks north of town is this hotel with fine, modern 2nd-floor rooms decorated in a rustic theme and featuring excellent mattresses and hot showers. Downstairs is a cactus garden and a Spanish-influenced restaurant that serves bonza buffet breakfasts (US$2.50). There's a small discount in the off season.

Hostal Chamana (☎ 969 1645; Nueva Victoria 185; s/d US$20/30) It's less than 2km from the center on the road to Cashapampa (ask locals for directions and take a taxi at night). The Chamana has six pleasant cabins, all with hot showers, set in a bucolic garden. Recently, however, there's been a change of management and the bungalows are starting to dabble with the 'abandoned' look – call ahead to make sure that it's still open.

Eating

Heladería Caraz Dulzura (Daniel Villar, Plaza de Armas; ice cream US$0.60-1.20; ✆ 8am-9:30pm) This popular ice-cream place gets packed on hot days. It also serves some local meals, but the ice cream is what it's really all about.

Pollería Jeny (☎ 39 1101; Plaza de Armas; meals US$1.20-2.70; ✆ 7am-10:30pm) Good set lunches and the best chicken in town attract the indigent; slightly pricier à la carte items include steak and trout. Breakfast, snacks and sandwiches are also available.

DO-IT-YOURSELF ANDEAN EXPLORATION

An alternate and well-off-the-beaten-track route to the eastern side of the Cordillera Blanca involves heading north from Caraz to Huallanca, and then catching a series of *colectivos* through small, traditional Andean towns all the way to Sihuas, and eventually on to Pomabamba. Modest accommodations and restaurants can be found along the way, and buses connect most towns at least once a day. This path is rarely traversed by gringos and promises a true Andean adventure as well as magnificent views of the rarely seen northern Cordillera. Plenty of time and patience are required. Godspeed!

El Mirador (☎ 39 1806; José Sucre 1202; meals US$1.20-3; ✆ 9am-10pm) A very good grill house, this place has *menús* (set meals), grilled chicken and steaks – all served with plaza views from its balcony.

Cafeteria El Turista (☎ 30 1518; San Martín 1127; breakfast US$1.40-2.10; ✆ 7am-noon & 5-8pm) A great place to grab an early breakfast, this tiny little café is a one-woman show run by the exuberant Maria. It's filled with a warren of crafts and knickknacks – all for sale.

La Punta Grande (☎ 39 2101; Daniel Villar 595; meals US$1.50-3.30; ✆ 7am-7pm) A short walk from the town center, this stadium-sized place is not for romantics – but it is the place for a typical highland lunch. It has a menu and serves dishes like *cuy*. There's a plant-filled garden to eat in, which houses a pond, gazebo and a kids' playground. If you don't feel like *cuy*, try a bowl of soup, *lomo saltado* (grilled strips of beef mixed with French fries) or tamales.

Café de Rat (☎ /fax 39 1642; José Sucre 1266, above Pony Expeditions; meals US$1.80-4.50, large pizzas US$6.50-8.50; ✆ 7am-11pm Mon-Sat) Don't mind the name, the menu has been cleared of rodents. But this atmospheric wood-beamed restaurant and café does serve sandwiches, pastas, coffees and drinks throughout the day, as well as a massive buffet breakfast (US$3.60). It also has a book exchange, darts, a bar and music; it's a top spot to hang out. There's a fireplace and you can gaze onto the plaza from its upstairs balcony.

Café La Terraza (☎ 30 1226; José Sucre 1107; dishes US$1.80-4.50; ✆ 7am-11pm) Does some of the best coffee in town and has lots of breakfast options (pancakes!), pizzas and pastas – all in a cavernous but cheerful art-covered space.

Getting There & Around

Caraz is often the final destination for buses heading from the coast to El Callejón de Huaylas. Most coastal buses go via Huaraz.

BUS
Long Distance
Transportes Rodríguez (☎ 39 1184; Cordova 141) has a Lima bus at 8pm (US$7.50, 10 hours), while **Expreso Ancash** (☎ 39 1126; Cordova 139) has one at 7:30pm (US$6). **Movil Tours** (☎ 39 1922; cnr Cordova & Santa Rosa) has comfortable Lima buses at 8am and 8:30pm (US$7.50 to US$9), as well as a *semi-cama* (semi-sleeper) Trujillo bus via Pativilca at 7:30pm (US$13.50, 12 hours).

(Continued on page 413)

Main gate, Kuélap (p440)

TOM COCKREM

Mummy in the Bruning Museum (p351), Lambayeque

COREY WISE

Street singers, Chachapoyas (p435)

TOM COCKREM

406

Shoe repairman, Huancavelica (p302)

Local woman, Huancayo (p295)

Railway worker on the Huancayo–
Huancavelica train (p301)

Powdered pigments, Huancavelica (p302)
JEFFREY BECOM

Two women, Lircay (p305)
JEFFREY BECOM

Church on Plaza San Juan de Dios, Huancavelica (p302)
COREY WISE

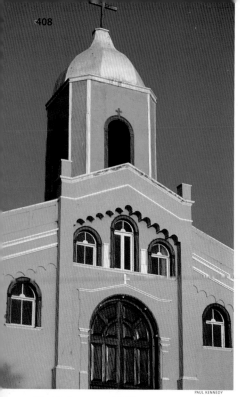

Church, Pacasmayo (p343)

PAUL KENNEDY

Mototaxi (three-wheeled motorcycle rickshaw taxi), Pacasmayo (p343)

PAUL KENNEDY

Reed boats, Huanchaco (p340)

TOM COCKR

Fresco detail, Chan Chan (p336)

TOM COCKREM

Fishing boat, Pacasmayo (p343)

PAUL KENNEDY

CINE RAMON CASTILLA

PAUL KENNEDY

Abandoned cinema, near Piura (p353)

Colonial architecture on the Plaza de Armas (p329), Trujillo

JANE SWEENEY

PAUL KENNEDY

Campsite, Laguna Yahuacocha (p392), Cordillera Huayhuash

Hot-drink seller, Huaraz (p374)

AARON MCCOY

PAUL KE

Trekkers near Punta Cuyoc (p396), Cordillera Huayhuash

PAUL KENNEDY

A local man and daughter, Laguna
Mitacocha (p395), Cordillera Huayhuash

ALFREDO MAIQUEZ

Laguna Jatuncocha (p388), Cordillera Blanca

Laguna Comercocha, Ausangate trek (p283)

GRANT DIXON

ALISON WRIGHT

Yagua man, near Iquitos (p490)

JOHN BORT

Floating market, Amazon Basin (p450)

Tree frog (p51), Amazon Basin

JASON EDWARDS

Local children, near Tarapoto (p444)

AARON

(Continued from page 404)

Yungay Express (☎ 39 1693; Daniel Villar 316) has three buses a day to Chimbote via the Cañón del Pato leaving at 8:30am, noon and 3pm (US$6, seven hours). **Transport Huandoy** (☎ 39 1236; Daniel Villar 224) also has a 12:30pm Chimbote bus through the Cañón (US$6).

Caraz Area
Minibuses to Yungay and Huaraz leave from the station on the Carretera Central. From the corner of Ramón Castilla at Santa Cruz are 4am, 7am, 11am and 1pm buses to Pueblo Parón (US$0.90, 45 minutes) for the famous Laguna Parón, which is about 9km further on foot or by truck.

TAXI
Colectivo taxis for Cashapampa (US$1.80, 1½ hours) for the northern end of the Llanganuco-to-Santa-Cruz trek leave when full from the corner of Ramón Castilla at Santa Cruz. *Colectivos* to Huallanca, for the Cañón del Pato and onwards, leave from the corner of Cordova and La Mar when full (US$1.50, 1½ hours).

Taxis (US$0.60 to US$0.90) and *mototaxis* (US$0.30) trundle around town.

SOUTH OF HUARAZ

Covering the southern extent of the Cordillera Blanca and the majestic Cordillera Huayhuash, this part of the Andes refuses to be outdone in the 'breathtaking mountain scenery' stakes. Several peaks here also pass the 6000m mark, huddling to form a near-continuous, saw-toothed ridge of precipitous summits. **Yerupajá** (6634m), Peru's second-highest mountain, is the icing on the Cordillera cake and is followed in height by its second lieutenant **Siulá Grande** (6356m), where climber Joe Simpson fell down a crevice to his near death and lived to tell the tale in the book and movie *Touching the Void*.

The rugged and rewarding 10-day Cordillera Huayhuash Circuit (p392), accessed through the town of Chiquián, is the glittering star attraction. This fairly strenuous hike is less accessible and receives fewer visitors than its Cordillera Blanca counterpart, but rewards those who make the effort with stunning and remote azure lakes, snow-covered peaks and green carpeted valleys.

The Puente Bedoya bridge, about 18km south of Huaraz, marks the beginning of a 2km dirt road to the community of **Olleros**, the starting point for the three-day trek across the Cordillera Blanca to Chavín de Huántar (see p391). **Recuay**, a town 25km from Huaraz, is one of the few municipalities to have survived the 1970 earthquake largely unscathed. **Catac**, 10km south of Recuay, is an even smaller hamlet and the starting point for trips to see the remarkable *Puya raimondii* plant.

CHIQUIÁN
☎ 043 / pop 5000 / elev 3400m
A subdued hill-town, Chiquián was traditionally the base of operations for folk trekking the Cordillera Huayhuash Circuit. Now, however, it can be bypassed using the new road that extends to a trailhead at Llamac. There are great views of the Huayhuash as you drive into the village.

Trekking services can be arranged through a couple of small agencies in town. Look for Yoder, the owner of Restaurante Yarupaja, who is a good source of info on the Huayhuash area and can help you cobble together a trek. Daily rates are roughly the same as in Huaraz.

The annual festival in Chiquián is **Santa Rosa de Lima**, held in late August and celebrated with dances, parades, music and bullfights. There is also a **Semana Turística** in early July. **Club Esperanza** (☎ 44 7161; Comercio 310) sells good-quality alpaca products hand-knitted by local artisans.

Sleeping & Eating
Hotel Los Nogales (☎ 44 7121; hotel_nogales _chiquian@yahoo.com; Comercio 1301; s/d with shared bathroom US$3/6, s/d US$6/12) Clean and attractive, this place is about three blocks from the central plaza. Rooms surround a comely, colonial-style courtyard and meals are available on request. There is hot water.

Hostal Chavín (San Martín 1st block; d US$5) An adequate pick for shoestring travelers trying to squeeze value out of their soles.

Gran Hotel Huayhuash (☎ 44 7049, 44 7183; Figueredo Amadeo 216; s/d US$6/12) Some rooms at this more contemporary place have cable TV and afford good vistas; hot water is available and the hotel has the town's best restaurant. The hotel owner here is a good source of information.

Chifa Huaycayinita (☎ 58 8604; Saenz Peña; meals US$1.50-3; ☺ noon-4pm & 7-11pm) A decent hole-in-the-wall restaurant that serves Chinese and Peruvian fare.

Getting There & Away

If you're interested in heading straight to Chiquián and the Cordillera Huayhuash, you'll find direct buses from Lima. However, as you'll probably need a few days to acclimatize, note that Huaraz offers a wider selection of distractions. **Turismo Cavassa** (☎ 44 7036; Bolognesi 421) has buses to and from Lima, leaving at 9am daily from either city (US$6, nine hours).

El Rápido (☎ 42 2887) and **Virgen Del Carmen** (☎ 44 7003) have buses that leave from Chiquián's Plaza de Armas to Huaraz at 5am and 2pm (US$2.40 to US$3.60, 2½ hours).

If you're starting the Huayhuash Circuit, catch a 9am *combi* to Llamac or Pocpa (US$2, three hours). There is also a 9am *combi* to Quero (US$1.50, 2½ hours), from where you can hike to Mahuay and Matacancha for the trek's alternate start (see p393). It's possible to get from Chiquián to Huallanca, although service is erratic at best. Ask locally. Huallanca has a basic hotel, and transport continues on from here to La Unión and Huánuco.

CAJATAMBO

☎ 01 / pop 3000 / elev 3380m

This small market town on the far side of the Cordillera Huayhuash is reached by trekking, or by snaking up a hair-raising dirt road from Lima. The plaza, topped by the standard colonial church, is rather nice. Because it is at the north end of the department of Lima, it has Lima-style seven-digit phone numbers.

Hotel Miranda (Tacna 141; s/d US$4/8) is a pretty good ambassador for the several cold-water cheapies around town. **Tambomachay** (☎ 244 2046; Bolognesi 140; r per person US$3-4.50) supplies better service, hot water and arranges local bus tickets. The top of the price range in Huayhuash, though probably not really worth the money, is **International Inn** (☎ 244 2071; international.inn@hostal.net; Benavides cuadra 4; s/d US$40/50). The small rooms have comfortable beds, hot water and TV. Bargain hard for a discount. There's an expensive restaurant here as well. Cheap *pollerías* encircle the Plaza de Armas if you're in need of sustenance.

Empresa Andia (Plaza de Armas) has 6am buses to Lima (US$8, nine hours).

EAST OF THE CORDILLERA BLANCA

The Conchucos Valley, running parallel to El Callejón de Huaylas, lolls on the eastern side of the Cordillera, sprinkled liberally with remote and rarely visited gems. This captivating dale is steeped in history and blessed with isolated, postcard-perfect Andean villages so tranquil that they'd fall into comas if they were any sleepier. Interlaced with excellent yet rarely visited hiking trails, this untapped region begs for exploration. Tourist infrastructure is still in its infancy, with a handful of welcoming but modest hotels and erratic transport along rough, unsealed roads that can be impassable in the wet season. If you do make the effort to get here, the highland hospitality of Quechua *campesinos* and awe-inspiring scenery will more than make up for the butt-smacking, time-consuming bumps in the road.

Chavín de Huántar, at the south end of the valley, is the most accessible area of the lot and lays claim to some of the most important and mysterious pre-Inca ruins on the continent. From Huari, just north of Chavín, you can either catch rides on pseudo-regular buses north to Pomabamba, or hike your way north, skirting the eastern peaks of the Cordillera Blanca to Chacas and Yanama (see p391).

CHAVÍN DE HUÁNTAR

☎ 043 / pop 2900 / elev 3250m

The unhurried town of Chavín abuts the northern end of the ruins and is too often whizzed through by visitors on popular day trips from Huaraz. A shame really, as this attractive Andean township has excellent tourist infrastructure, a slew of nature-centered activities and some of the best value accommodations in the Cordillera. Public transport between here and Huaraz is fast, cheap and frequent. If you decide to overnight it here, you get to visit the impressive archaeological site in the early morning and have it all to yourself.

The main drag of Chavín town is 17 de Enero, which leaves the peaceful Plaza de Armas southbound, passing rows of restaurants, internet cafés and the entrance to the archaeological site. You can't change money in town, but there is a **Banco de la Nación** in

San Marcos, 8km away, that will change US dollars.

Sights

CHAVÍN DE HUÁNTAR RUINS

This archaeological **site** (adult/student US$3.30/1.70; ☺ 8am-5pm) is thought to be the only large structure left behind by the Chavín culture, one of the oldest civilizations on the continent. Quite possibly a major ceremonial center, it's a stupendous achievement of ancient construction that at first sight may leave you feeling a little underwhelmed. Take a good look around, however, as most of the interesting bits are underground and the area was covered by a huge landslide in 1945. To get the most from your visit, enter the chambers below ground (which are electrically lit) – it's worth hiring a guide to show you around.

The site is a series of older and newer temple arrangements built between 1200 BC and 800 BC. In the middle is a massive central square, slightly sunken below ground level, with an intricate and well-engineered system of channels for drainage. From the square, a broad staircase leads up to the single entrance of the largest and most important building – the Castillo. Built on three different levels of dry stone masonry, the walls here were at one time embellished with *tenons* (keystones of large projecting blocks carved to resemble stylized human heads). Only one of these remains in its original place; the others have been moved to museums.

These underground tunnels are an exceptional feat of engineering, comprising a maze of complex alleys, ducts and chambers. In the heart of this complex is an exquisitely carved rock known as the Lanzón de Chavín. Several beguiling construction quirks, such as the strange positioning of water channels and the use of shined, coal mirrors, lead Stanford archaeologists to believe that the complex was used as an instrument of shock-and-awe. To instill fear in nonbelievers, priests manipulated sights and sounds. They blew on echoing Strombus trumpets, amplified the sounds of water running through specially designed channels and reflected underground lights through ventilation shafts. The disoriented were probably given hallucinogens like San Pedro cactus shortly before entering the darkened maze. These tactics endowed the priests with awe-inspiring power, and thus one of the earliest stratified societies arose from what was once an egalitarian civilization.

Don't miss the small **museum** for some first-rate examples of the intricate and terrifyingly carved *tenons*. During the summer months you may see Stanford University archaeology students excavating the site – have a chat to them for some interesting insights.

The site is best visited in the morning before the crowds from Huaraz arrive.

CENTRO ARTESONAL CEO CHAVÍN

A few hundred meters along the road to Huari, **Centro Artesonal CEO Chavín** (J Tello Sur 350;

CHAVÍN CULTURE

Named after its type site at Chavín de Huántar, this is considered one of the oldest major cultures in Peru, strutting its stuff on the pre-Inca stage from 1000 BC to 300 BC. The Chavín wielded their influence with great success, particularly between the formative years of 800 BC and 400 BC. Its people didn't conquer by warfare; they influenced the artistic and cultural development of all of northern Peru by example – there's a lesson in that for all of us. Archaeologists formerly referred to this cultural expansion as the Chavín Horizon, though Early Horizon is now preferred.

The principal Chavín deity was feline (jaguar or puma). Lesser condor, snake and human deities were also worshipped. Representations of these deities are highly stylized and cover many Chavín sites. The mind boggles to think this beautifully carved and fine work was carried out 3000 years ago with relatively primitive tools.

Because the artistic work of Chavín is more stylized and cultist than the naturalistic art of later Moche and Nazca cultures, archaeologists lack an accurate picture of everyday life in Chavín times. However, excavations of ancient garbage dumps (the treasure of archaeologists' dreams) indicate that corn became a staple food, and agriculture improved with the introduction of squash, avocados, yucca and other crops. Better agriculture allowed more leisure time, which in turn set the stage for art and religion to flourish. Impressive to think that corn could lead to the Early Horizon and influence the art and religion of an entire continent.

(☽ dawn-dusk) sells locally made textiles, alpaca weavings and stone carvings – visit in the afternoon to see weavers weaving wildly.

Activities

There are relaxing sulfur **thermal baths** (admission US$0.60) a 30-minute walk south of town, which house four private baths and one larger pool. Keep your eyes peeled for a small, signed path that leads down to the river. **Horse riding** on Peruvian pacing horses can be arranged through the Cafeteria Renato (see right) for US$6 per hour (including a guide).

From Chavín you can hike for a few hours into a lofty valley, in the direction of Olleros, to a high pass with stirring views of Huantsan (6395m) – the highest mountain in the southern Cordillera Blanca. If you're interested in longer treks originating here, **Don Donato** (☎ 45 4136; J Tello Sur 275) of the Asociación de Servicios de Alta Montaña, offers a four-day trek that circles the back side of the Cordillera Blanca, passes by several alpine lakes and exits through the Carhuascancha valley.

Sleeping & Eating

Chavín has a surprisingly good selection of accommodations. Camping by the ruins is also possible with permission of the guard.

Hostal Inca (☎ 45 4092; Plaza de Armas; s/d US$7.50/15) The reputation of this secure, popular place is as solid as its hot showers, and it boasts very respectable rooms. There's a small garden and the family that runs it is superfriendly and helpful. Hostal Inca also houses the lab for the ongoing excavation project of the ruins.

La Casona (☎ 45 9004; Plaza de Armas 130; s/d US$7.50/15) In an old house, the well-kept rooms here are a little on the dark side, but the beautiful courtyard, dripping with plants, is an excellent place to hang out and soak in the ambience. The hot water here can be erratic, however. Some rooms have a TV or a plaza balcony and there's a restaurant.

Hotel Chavín (☎ 45 4055; Inca Roca 141; s/d US$9/15) This hotel is modern, has hot water and a TV in all rooms and a restaurant. Around the corner is the affiliated but cheaper and more basic Hostal Chavín. Between the two of them you'll find a room to suit; guests bargain for the best deal.

Gran Hotel Rickay (☎ 45 4068; 17 de Enero 600; s/d US$12/18) With slightly pricier digs, this grandiose colonial option has top rooms, is newly renovated and has a patio, restaurant (serving

pizzas and pastas) and modern rooms with hot showers and a TV.

Most of the town's eateries can be found along 17 de Enero and in hotels. Restaurants have a reputation for closing soon after sunset, so dig in early.

Chavín Turístico (☎ 45 4051; 17 de Enero 439; meals US$1.20-2.40; ☽ 11am-9pm) A good lunch option, this place has a chalkboard of traditional plates and rickety tables around a tiny courtyard. The food is tasty and popular with tour groups.

Cafeteria Renato (☎ 50 4279; Plaza de Armas; breakfast & snacks US$1.80-3; ☽ 7am-4pm) On the casual Plaza de Armas, this cozy place serves yummy local and international breakfasts alongside homemade yogurt, cheese and *manjar blanco* (homemade caramel spread). There's a lovely garden you can laze in while waiting for your bus and the owners organize horse trekking from here.

Buongiorno (☎ 45 4112; 17 de Enero 439; meals US$3-4.80; ☽ 10am-9pm) Probably the best restaurant in town, Buongiorno serves well-executed local dishes and a few gringo usuals in a cordial garden backdrop. The *lomo a la pimiento*, a Peruvian fave of grilled steak in wine, cream and cracked-pepper sauce (US$4.20), is excellent. Keep an eye out for the unnatural-looking stuffed deer guarding the entrance.

Getting There & Away

The scenic drive across the Cordillera Blanca via Catac passes the Laguna Querococha at 3980m. From here, there are views of the peaks of Pucaraju (5322m) and Yanamarey (5237m). The road is now paved most of the way to Chavín and may be completely finished by the time you read this. Along the way it passes through the Cahuish tunnel, at 4178m above sea level, which cuts through the 4480m Cahuish pass. As you exit the tunnel and descend toward Chavín, look out for the massive statue of Christ, built by Italian missionaries (see p400), blessing your journey.

Tour buses make day trips from Huaraz. See p384 for details of Chavín Express and other companies that have multiple daily departures to Chavín (US$3, two hours). Returning to Huaraz is straightforward with Chavín Express or Sandoval – ask about departure times at the Plaza de Armas.

Continuing north along the east side of the Cordillera Blanca involves asking around. Most of the buses originating in Huaraz continue on to Huari (US$1.20, two hours), from where you can catch onward transport on some of the infrequent buses that pass through from Lima. Frequent minibuses to San Marcos depart from the plaza (US$0.30, 20 minutes).

Hikers can walk to Chavín from Olleros in about three days; it's a popular but uncrowded hike (see p391).

NORTH OF CHAVÍN

The road north of Chavín goes through the villages of San Marcos (after 8km), Huari (40km, two hours), San Luis (100km, five hours), Pomabamba and eventually Sihuas. The further north you go, the more inconsistent transport becomes, and it may stop altogether during the wet season.

From Sihuas, it is possible to continue on to Huallanca (at the end of Cañón del Pato) via Tres Cruces and thus return to El Callejón de Huaylas (see Do-It-Yourself Andean Exploration, p404). This round trip is scenic, remote and rarely made by travelers.

There are two roads that offer picturesque crossings back to El Callejón de Huaylas. The road from Chacas to Carhuaz, via the Punta Olímpica pass (4890m), is spectacular. A road from Yanama to Yungay takes passengers over yet another breathtaking pass (4767m) and into the valley made famous by the Llanganuco lakes, with top views of the towering Huascarán, Chopicalqui and Huandoy (6356m).

Huari

☎ 043 / pop 4300 / elev 3150m

A small Quechua town barely clinging to the mountainside, Huari has nearly 360-degree mountain panoramas from its steep, cobbled streets. Market day here is Sunday, when *campesinos* from surrounding towns descend on Huari to hawk fruits and vegetables. The

annual town **fiesta**, Señora del Rosario, is held in early October and has a strange tradition of cat consumption (see below). The town has a small and modern Plaza de Armas, and a larger Plaza Vigil (known as El Parque) one block away. All buses leave from Plaza Vigil. You should be able to change US dollars into soles at the Banco de la Nación near the market.

For sweeping panoramas of the valley, keep walking uphill from the El Dorado hotel until you come to a *mirador* (lookout). A good day hike is to **Laguna Purhuay**, a beautiful lake about 5km away. An excellent two- or three-day backpacking trip continues past the lake to emerge at the village of Chacas. Another three- to four-day trek trails along the old Inca highway to Huánuco (see p391).

There are several cheap hotels in town, but **El Dorado** (☎ 45 3028; Simon Bolívar 353; r per person without/with bathroom US$3/4.50; 🖳) is the pick of the bunch with hot water, the cleanest rooms, smiling staff and internet on tap. **Hostal Paraíso** (☎ 45 3029; Simon Bolívar 263; s/d US$4.50/9) is up the hill from El Dorado and has more modest rooms and a courtyard with some greenery. For breakfast, try **Restaurant Turístico El Milagro** (San Martín 589; dishes US$0.60-1.20; 🕑 7am-8:30pm), which also does local food and ceviche (raw seafood marinated in lime juice). For a real treat, be sure to eat at **Chifa Dragón Andino** (☎ 45 4110; Magisterial 300; dishes US$1.20-3; 🕑 10am-11pm), which serves some of the best Chinese food in the Cordillera. It's behind the main market.

Buses for Huaraz and Lima leave most days from Plaza Vigil. Sandoval, Chavín Express and Rio Mosna all have 9am, 3pm and 8:30pm buses to Huaraz (US$3.60, four hours). Turismo Andino has daily buses to Lima at 9am (US$10.50, 12 hours) and two buses a week to Chacas via San Luis (8:30am on Saturday and Tuesday, US$3, four hours) as well as two weekly buses to Pomabamba (US$6, seven

---

HUARI CATS

The annual fiesta of Señora del Rosario in Huari is also know locally as the Fiesta de los Gatos. It's held in October, and the people of Huari have an odd tradition of cooking up *miche broaster* – roasted cat. Though no one's quite sure how this all began, it probably arose when an alternative source of protein was needed during a particularly tough growing season, and thus a tradition was formed. Locals get quite excited by this fried feline fetish. So much so that in 2005 there was no cat on the menu – too many felines were consumed at a previous fiesta to sustain the cat population. Check out the fountain in the Plaza de Armas, it has eight cat statues pawing and peeing into a central pool.

hours) at around 10pm. For Laguna Purhuay you can hire a taxi to take you for US$9 return, including waiting time.

San Luis

☎ 043 / elev 3130m

This simple municipality is little more than a crossroad blip on the tourist radar. It's reached by daily buses from Huaraz, via Yungay and Yanama, or by buses between Huari and Pomabamba (you get some super views coming from Huari). The best of several basic hotels here is **Hostal San Lucho** (☎ 83 3435; 28 de Julio 250; r per person without/with bathroom US$3.60/6), with passable rooms around a typical Andean courtyard open to the mountain air.

Regular *combis* leave for Chacas when full (US$0.90) and several buses depart for Huaraz ($5.40, five hours) throughout the day.

Chacas

☎ 043 / elev 3360m

This ornate mountain town sits atop a hill crest, surrounded by fertile hills and with guest appearances by the occasional snow-capped Cordillera peak. The charismatic main plaza is dominated by a brilliant church built by a religious Italian aid organization (see p400), many of whom use Chacas as their base for helping operations.

White-walled houses around the plaza look idyllic against the mountain backdrop, and many have intricate wooden balconies and brightly colored doors and window shutters just screaming to have their picture taken. Best of all, the town is whisper quiet as there's no traffic to speak of. Look out for the impossibly petite, smiling Andean ladies that sit meditatively spinning wool on every second corner. This is an excellent place to while away a few days. The whole town has only five phones, yet surprisingly there's internet access across from the church (US$0.30 per hour). The Chacas **fiesta** is held on August 15.

You can do great two- to three-day treks from here to Huari or Yanama, from where energetic hikers can continue on to do the Santa Cruz trek (see p387).

The friendly and very simple **Hostal Saragoza** (Bolognesi; 370; r per person without/with bathroom US$3/4.50) is on the Plaza de Armas – a couple of rooms have windows onto the plaza and the place manages to scrap together a certain bucolic appeal. **Hospedaje Alameda** (Lima 305; r per person without/with bathroom US$3/9) has some similarly

modest rooms as well as much nicer, newer abodes with attached bathrooms. Both places have hot water. Pilar Ames (the owner of El Cortijo restaurant in Monterrey; see p398) has the most comfortable digs in town at **Hostal Pilar** (☎ in Monterrey 42 3813; Ancash 110; d US$40), with decent modern facilities. This place is used as part of a local tour and is open only to those with prior reservations. There are a few hole-in-the-wall restaurants and *pollerías* around, all serving similar local dishes.

Copa and Transporte Renzo run buses to Huaraz (via Punto Olímpica and Carhuaz) at 7am and 2pm (US$4.50, four hours). *Combis* leave for San Luis from in front of the cathedral when full (US$0.90) and from San Luis you can catch passing buses to Pomabamba or Huari.

Yanama

☎ 043 / elev 3400m

A tiny, mountain-enveloped *pueblo*, where the most exciting thing to happen this decade is a connection to the electricity grid in 2005. The town is only about 1½ hours' walk from the end of the popular Santa Cruz trek (see p387) and makes a good stopover point, where trekkers and mountain bikers can refuel and recharge. The town **festival** of Santa Rosa is held here in August.

A daily morning bus links Yungay with Yanama, passing the famed Lagunas Llanganuco (p401) and traveling within 1km of the village of **Colcabamba**, the starting point for the Llanganuco-to-Santa-Cruz trekking circuit. Facilities are rudimentary in Yanama and showers can be as frosty as the mountain air. A couple of *hospedajes* supply austere rooms for around US$3 per person, but the best option in town is **Hospedaje El Pino** (☎ 83 3449; www.hospedajeelpino.com; r per person with shared bathroom US$3), behind the church with a huge pine tree outside. Exceptionally friendly, it's basic but has comfortable beds and the owners will heat up hot water on request for a 'bucket' shower. You'll also find the best restaurant in town here – misty views of the mountains come standard.

In Colcabamba you'll find several home-stays that offer beds with dinner for US$5 per person.

Colectivos leave for Yungay from the plaza around midday (US$3, three hours) or you can catch one of the buses originating in Pomabamba.

Pomabamba

☎ 043 / pop 4500 / elev 2950m

Known as the City of Cedars (check out the specimen on the plaza), Pomabamba is a great place to spend some time between trekking trips. Soak in lungfuls of the crisp mountain troposphere and the small-town ambience. Several cross-Cordillera treks begin and end at this township, and you'd be forgiven for failing to notice that this is supposed to be the 'largest' settlement north of Huari.

There's a small **museum** by the plaza and several sets of natural private **hot springs** (admission US$0.30) lie in wait for weary hikers on the outskirts of town. These may make up for the fact that there are no hot showers in town. It's sometimes possible to arrange trekking guides from here – ask at your hotel. There are several internet cafés near the plaza.

The next town along toward San Luis or Huari, **Piscobamba**, has decent views of the mountains, and that's 'bout it.

Pomabamba single-handedly dominates the Cordillera Blanca's SBC (simple, basic, clean) *hostal* market. **Hostal Pomabamba** (☎ 45 1276; Huamachuco 338; r per person without/with bathroom US$1.50/4.50), on the main plaza, is one of the more economical rudimentary alternatives. The genial **Alojamiento Estrada** (☎ 50 4615; Huaraz 209; r per person US$3), by the church, has a small courtyard and just trumps the competition in the charm stakes. **Albergue Turístico Vía** (☎ 44 1052; Primavera 323; r per person US$3-6) has typical shared-bathroom basics as well as nicer, newer rooms with bathrooms attached.

If you are a *pollería* connoisseur, as we have become on our travels in Peru, check out **Mikey's Pollería** (Huamachuco 330; meals US$1.20-2.40) on the plaza for some of the best darn grilled chicken south of the equator. **Davis David** (Huaraz 269; menús US$1.50) has local usuals and a respectable daytime *menú*.

All buses to Huaraz and Lima leave from near the Plaza de Armas. **Turismo Andino** (☎ 45 1290) has buses to Huaraz at 7am and 7pm (US$7, eight hours) via Yanama (US$3, four hours), a 6am bus to Lima (US$12, 18 hours) on Monday and Thursday via Huari (US$3, four hours), and occasional buses to Sihuas (US$3, three hours). **Transporte Renzo** (☎ 45 1088) has an early Huaraz bus at 5:30am on Monday, Wednesday and Saturday as well as regular daily buses at noon and 7pm (US$7). **El Solitario** (☎ 45 1133) has a 6:30am Lima bus (US$13.50) via Huari (US$3) on Sunday, Monday and Wednesday. There are also daily *combis* to Sihuas and Piscobamba from the town center.

Northern Highlands

Vast tracts of unexplored jungle and mist-shrouded mountain ranges guard the secrets of the northern highlands like a suspicious custodian. Here, Andean peaks and a blanket of luxuriant forests stretch from the coast all the way to the deepest, darkest jungles of the Amazon. Interspersed with the relics of Inca kings and the jungle-encrusted ruins of cloud-forest-dwelling warriors, these outposts of Peru remain barely connected by disheveled and circuitous roads.

The cobbled streets of Cajamarca testify to the beginning of the end of the once powerful Inca empire, and remnants of the work of these famed Andean masons still line the surrounding countryside. The delicate colonial structures lining Cajamarca's heart, meanwhile, attest to the final outcome of the 16th-century battle of swords and wills.

The hazy forests of Chachapoyas have only recently revealed their archaeological bounty – the rarely seen yet staggering stone fortress of Kuélap, which clings for dear life to a craggy limestone peak. Hundreds of misplaced archaeological remnants from this mysterious alliance of city-states can be visited on a trek or by horse while meandering through pristine forgotten countryside. At Tarapoto, where the paved road reaches its final conclusion, the jungle waits patiently, as it has for centuries, endowed with a cornucopia of wildlife and exquisite good looks.

HIGHLIGHTS

- Scrambling through **Kuélap** (p440), an immense citadel that rivals Machu Picchu in grandeur but lacks its crowds
- Hiking through cloud forests to boldly (re)discover long-forgotten cities, Indiana Jones-style, in the region of **Gran Vilaya** (p438) near Chachapoyas
- Following Inca footsteps to soak in **Los Baños del Inca** (p430), the steaming baths once used by kings
- Getting to within a hairbreadth of the fracas of the jungle at **Tarapoto** (p444) without leaving the comfort of the paved highway
- Surviving filling-jolting travels to reach the tranquil traditional villages of **Celendín** (p433) and **Leimebamba** (p442)

Gran Vilaya ★
Kuélap ★   Tarapoto ★
Celendín ★ ★Leimebamba
★ Los Baños del Inca

- BIGGEST CITY: CAJAMARCA, POPULATION 135,000
- AVERAGE TEMPERATURE: JANUARY 10°C TO 20°C, JULY 10°C TO 21°C

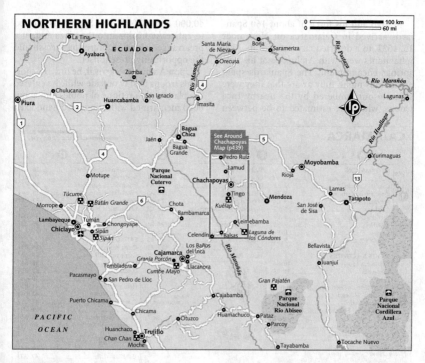

NORTHERN HIGHLANDS

CAJAMARCA

☎ 076 / pop 135,000 / elev 2650m

The most important town in the northern highlands, Cajamarca is a dainty colonial metropolis cradled in a languid valley and stone-walled by brawny mountains in every direction. Descending into the vale by road, Cajamarca's mushroom field of red-tile-roofed abodes surely confesses a secret desire to cling to its village roots. Fertile farming land carpets the entire valley, and Cajamarca's streets belong as much to the wide-brimmed-hat-wielding *campesinos* (peasants) bundled in brightly colored scarves as the young city slickers that frequent the boutique restaurants and bars. In the colonial center, the capacious Plaza de Armas is bordered by majestic churches. From here, once decadent baroque mansions spread out in concentric circles along the cobbled streets, many enclosing ethereal hotels and fine restaurants.

Things have changed slowly here. Only recently has the Yanacocha gold mine (see There's Gold in Them There Hills, p424) injected Cajamarca with an avalanche of cash and a steady stream of moneyed engineers.

Not many tourists pass through this way, but dozens of sights from the town's pivotal past, including the famous Baños del Inca, will keep those that make it here absorbed for days.

History

In about 1460, the Incas conquered the local Cajamarca populace, and Cajamarca evolved into a major city on the Inca Andean highway linking Cuzco and Quito.

After the death of the *inca* (king) Huayna Capac in 1525, the remaining Inca empire, which then stretched from southern Colombia to central Chile, was pragmatically divided between his sons, with Atahualpa ruling the north and Huascar the south. Obviously not everyone was in concord as civil war soon broke out, and in 1532 Atahualpa and his victorious troops marched southward toward Cuzco to take complete control of the empire. Parked at Cajamarca to rest for a few days, the Inca emperor was camped at the natural thermal springs, known today as Los Baños del Inca, when he heard the news that the Spanish were nearby.

Pizarro and his force of about 160 Spaniards arrived in Cajamarca on November 15, 1532, to a deserted city; most of its 2000 inhabitants were with Atahualpa at his hotsprings encampment. The Spaniards spent an anxious night, fully aware that they were severely outnumbered by the nearby Inca troops, who were estimated to be between 40,000 and 80,000. The Spaniards plotted to entice Atahualpa into the plaza and, at a prearranged signal, capture the *inca* should the opportunity present itself.

Upon Atahualpa's arrival, he ordered most of his troops to stay outside while he entered the plaza with a retinue of nobles and about 6000 men armed with slings and hand axes.

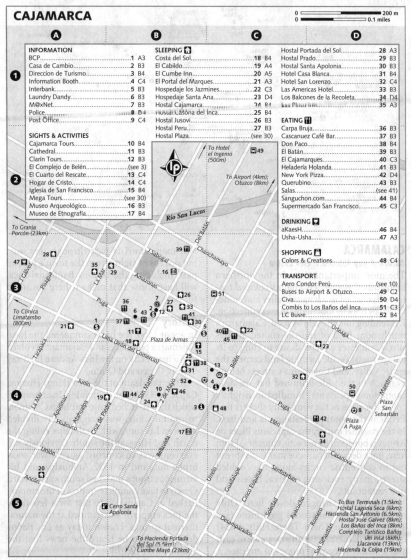

CAJAMARCA

0 ————— 200 m
0 ————— 0.1 miles

INFORMATION
BCP...**1** A3
Casa de Cambio..........................**2** B3
Dirección de Turismo.................**3** B4
Information Booth.......................**4** C4
Interbank...................................**5** B3
Laundry Dandy...........................**6** B3
M@xNet......................................**7** B3
Police...**8** B4
Post Office..................................**9** C4

SIGHTS & ACTIVITIES
Cajamarca Tours.......................**10** B4
Cathedral..................................**11** B3
Clarín Tours..............................**12** B3
El Complejo de Belén..............(see 3)
El Cuarto del Rescate...............**13** C4
Hogar de Cristo........................**14** C4
Iglesia de San Francisco...........**15** B4
Mega Tours.............................(see 30)
Museo Arqueológico................**16** B3
Museo de Etnografía................**17** B4

SLEEPING
Costa del Sol............................**18** B4
El Cabildo.................................**19** A4
El Cumbe Inn............................**20** A5
El Portal del Marques................**21** A3
Hospedaje los Jazmines............**22** C3
Hospedaje Santa Ana...............**23** D4
Hostal Cajamarca.....................**24** B4
Hostal Casona del Inca.............**25** B4
Hostal Jusovi............................**26** B3
Hostal Peru..............................**27** B3
Hostal Plaza...........................(see 30)

Hostal Portada del Sol..............**28** A3
Hostal Prado.............................**29** B3
Hostal Santa Apolonia..............**30** B3
Hotel Casa Blanca....................**31** B4
Hotel San Lorenzo....................**32** C4
Las Americas Hotel...................**33** B3
Los Balcones de la Recoleta......**34** D4
Los Pinos Inn...........................**35** A3

EATING
Carpa Bruja..............................**36** B3
Cascanuez Café Bar..................**37** B3
Don Paco..................................**38** B4
El Batán...................................**39** B3
El Cajamarques........................**40** C3
Heladería Holanda....................**41** B3
New York Pizza.........................**42** D4
Querubino.................................**43** B3
Salas.....................................(see 41)
Sanguchon.com.........................**44** B4
Supermercado San Francisco.....**45** C3

DRINKING
aKaesH.....................................**46** B4
Usha-Usha................................**47** A3

SHOPPING
Colors & Creations....................**48** C4

TRANSPORT
Aero Condor Perú...................(see 10)
Buses to Airport & Otuzco........**49** C2
Civa..**50** D4
Combis to Los Baños del Inca....**51** C3
LC Busre...................................**52** B4

To Hotel el Ingenio (500m)

To Airport (4km); Otuzco (8km)

To Granja Porcón (23km)

Río San Lucas

J Sabogal
Chanchamayo
Amazonas
Del Batán

To Clínica Limatambo (800m)

Puga
Puga
Puga
Pisagua
La Mar
J Galvez
Tarapacá

Lima (Jirón del Comercio)
Plaza de Armas
Junín
La Mar
Apurímac
Atahualpa
Cruz de Piedra
San Martín
2 de Mayo
Huánuco
Unión

Belén
Urteaga
Inca
Etén
Maestro

Plaza San Sebastián
Plaza A Puga
Casanova

Bellavista
Guadalupe
Cinco Esquinas
Soledad
Santisteban
Desamparados
Ayacucho
Romero
San Sebastián

Ancón
Unión

Cerro Santa Apolonia

To Hacienda Portada del Sol (5.5km); Cumbe Mayo (23km)

To Bus Terminals (1.5km); Hostal Laguna Seca (6km); Hacienda San Antonio (6.5km); Hostal Jose Galvez (8km); Los Baños del Inca (8km); Complejo Turístico Baños del Inca (8km); Llacanora (13km); Hacienda la Colpa (15km)

He was met by the Spanish friar Vicente de Valverde, who attempted to explain his position as a man of God and presented the *inca* with a Bible. Reputedly, Atahualpa angrily threw the book to the ground, and Valverde needed little more justification to sound the attack.

Cannons were fired, and the Spanish cavalry attacked Atahualpa and his troops. The indigenous people were terrified and bewildered by the fearsome onslaught of never-before-seen cannons and horses. Their small hand axes and slings were no match for the well-armored Spaniards, who swung razor-sharp swords from the advantageous height of horseback to slaughter 7000 indigenous people and capture Atahualpa. The small band of Spaniards were now literally conquistadors (conquerers).

Atahualpa soon became aware of the Spaniards' lust for gold, and offered to fill a large room in the town once with gold and twice with silver in return for his freedom. The Spanish agreed, and slowly the gold and silver began pouring into Cajamarca. Nearly a year later the ransom was complete – about 6000kg of gold and 12,000kg of silver had been melted down into gold and silver bullion. At today's prices, this ransom would be worth almost US$60 million, but the artistic value of the ornaments and implements that were melted down to create the bullion is impossible to estimate.

Atahualpa, suspecting he was not going to be released, sent desperate messages to his followers in Quito to come to Cajamarca and rescue him. The Spaniards, panic stricken by these messages, sentenced Atahualpa to death. On July 26, 1533, Atahualpa was led out to the center of the Cajamarca plaza to be burned at the stake. At the last hour, Atahualpa 'accepted' baptism, and as a reward his sentence was changed to a quicker death by strangulation.

Most of the great stone Inca buildings in Cajamarca were torn down and the stones used in the construction of Spanish homes and churches. The great plaza where Atahualpa was captured and later killed was in roughly the same location as today's Plaza de Armas, though in Atahualpa's time it was much larger. The Ransom Chamber, or El Cuarto del Rescate, where Atahualpa was imprisoned, is the only Inca building still standing.

Information

There are moneychangers near the Plaza de Armas; take the usual precautions. There's internet access practically on every block.

BCP (☎ 36 2742; Lima at Apurímac) Changes traveler's checks and has an ATM accepting Visa and MasterCard.

Casa de Cambio (Del Batán) Changes US dollars quickly.

Clínica Limatambo (☎ 36 4241; Puno 265) Has the best medical service; it's west of town.

Dirección de Turismo (☎ 36 2903; El Complejo de Belén; ☘ 7:30am-1pm & 2:30-6pm Mon-Fri) Tourist information and a list of reputable travel agencies.

Information booth (Lima at Belén) For tourist information, though opening hours are erratic.

Interbank (☎ 36 2460; 2 de Mayo 546) Changes traveler's checks and has an ATM accepting Visa and MasterCard.

Laundry Dandy (☎ 36 3454; Puga 545; per kg US$1.50)

M@xNet (☎ 36 5385; Del Batan 177; ☘ 8am-midnight) Internet access.

Police (☎ 36 2165; cnr Puga & Ayacucho) Toward the eastern part of town.

Post office (☎ 36 4065; Puga 668; ☘ 9am-7pm Mon-Fri, 9am-1pm Sat) Behind the Iglesia de San Francisco.

Sights

All the following sights are officially open 9am to 1pm and 3pm to 6pm daily – most of the time. They don't have addresses but are in the center of town. The US$1.40 ticket to El Cuarto del Rescate includes El Complejo de Belén and Museo de Etnografía if they are all visited on the same day.

EL COMPLEJO DE BELÉN

Construction of this sprawling colonial complex, church and hospital of Belén, made entirely from volcanic rock, occurred between 1627 and 1774. The hospital was run by nuns, and 31 tiny, cell-like bedrooms line the walls of the T-shaped building. In what used to be the women's hospital, there is a small archaeology museum. The façade here has a fascinating statue of a woman with four breasts – it was carved by local artisans and supposedly represent an affliction (supernumary nipples, that is) commonly found in one of the nearby towns. The kitchen and dispensary of the hospital now houses an unimpressive art museum.

The baroque church next door is one of Cajamarca's finest and has a prominent cupola and a well-carved pulpit. There are several interesting wood carvings, including an extremely tired-looking Christ sitting cross-legged on his throne, propping up his chin

NORTHERN HIGHLANDS

THERE'S GOLD IN THEM THERE HILLS

The hills outside of Cajamarca are laced with gold. Tons of it. But don't reach for your shovel and pan just yet, as this gold is not found in the kind of golden nuggets that set prospectors' eyes ablaze. It's 'invisible gold,' vast quantities of minuscule specks that require advanced and noxious mining techniques to be pried out of its earthly ore.

The American-run Yanacocha mine has quarried open pits in the countryside surrounding Cajamarca, becoming one of the most productive gold mines in the world. Over US$7 billion worth of the shiny stuff has been extracted so far. That, combined with plenty of new jobs and an influx of international engineers into Cajamarca, has meant a surge in wealth for the region – but locals are only now beginning to question the environmental and social costs they've had to pay.

According to a joint investigation by the *New York Times* and the PBS program *Frontline World* (a US news-magazine on public television), the history of the mine is clouded by charges of corruption.

In 2000, a large spill of toxic mercury raised doubts about Yanacocha's priorities: gold over safety seemed to be the predictable marching cry. The mine makes its profit by washing vast quantities of mountainside with cyanide solution, a hazardous technique that utilizes masses of water – the very stuff farmers' lives depend on. An internal environmental audit carried out by the company in 2004 verified villagers' observations that water supplies were being contaminated and fish stocks were disappearing.

In the autumn of 2004, disillusioned *campesinos* (peasants) rallied against the opening of a new mine in the area of Quilish, and clashed violently with the police employed to protect the mine's interests. After weeks of conflict, the company eventually gave in and has since re-evaluated its priorities. It currently pumps millions of dollars back into the community and is starting to pay more than lip service to the need for community consent. Several environmental concerns have been addressed and the company's safety record has indeed improved. What remains to be seen, however, is whether Yanacocha can keep its promises once the profits run dry; the millions of tons of acid-contaminated earth left behind will require treatment for decades to come.

with a double-jointed wrist and looking as though he could do with a pisco sour after a hard day's miracle working. Look out for the oversized cherubs supporting the elaborate centerpiece, which represents the weight of heaven. The outside walls of the church are lavishly decorated. The tourist office is housed in one of the interior complex rooms.

EL CUARTO DEL RESCATE

The Ransom Chamber is the only Inca building still standing in Cajamarca. Although it's called the Ransom Chamber, the room shown to visitors is actually where Atahualpa was imprisoned, not where the ransom was stored. The small room has three trapezoidal doorways and a few similarly shaped niches in the inner walls – signature Inca construction. Although well built, the chamber does not compare with the Inca buildings in the Cuzco area. In the entrance to the site are a couple of modern paintings depicting Atahualpa's capture and imprisonment. The stone of the building is weathered and has only recently been covered by a large protective dome.

MUSEO DE ETNOGRAFÍA

This small, sparsely filled museum, just a few meters from El Complejo de Belén, has limited exhibits of local costumes and clothing, domestic and agricultural implements, musical instruments, and crafts made from wood, bone, leather and stone, as well as other examples of Cajamarca culture. Large-scale photographs and modern art interpretations illustrate traditional lives of the district's farmers.

MUSEO ARQUEOLÓGICO

This small, university-run **museum** (Del Batán 289; admission free; 8am-2:30pm Mon-Fri) is worth visiting; just knock on the door to enter. Its varied ceramics collection includes a few examples of pots from the Cajamarca culture and an unusual collection of ceremonial spears, also from the same period. The Cajamarca culture, which existed here before the Inca empire conquered the region, is little studied and relatively unknown. The Museo Arqueológico also has black-and-white photographs of historic and prehistoric sites in the Cajamarca area; its director is knowledgeable, and is willing to talk to visitors about the museum's exhibits.

PLAZA DE ARMAS

The genial plaza has a well-kept topiary garden with hedges trimmed into the shape of llamas and other Andean animals. The fine central **fountain** dates from 1692 and commemorates the bicentenary of Columbus' landing in the Americas. Come evening, the town's inhabitants congregate in the plaza to stroll and mull over the important events of the day – a popular pastime in this area of northern Peru.

Two churches face the Plaza de Armas: the **cathedral** (admission free; ☺ hrs vary) and the **Iglesia de San Francisco** (admission US$0.90; ☺ 9am-noon & 4-6pm Mon-Fri). Both are often imaginatively illuminated in the evenings, especially on weekends. The cathedral is a squat building that was begun in the late 17th century and only recently finished. Like most of Cajamarca's churches, this cathedral has no belfry. This is because the Spanish Crown levied a tax on finished churches and so the belfries were not built, leaving the church unfinished and thereby avoiding the tax.

Iglesia de San Francisco's belfries were finished in the 20th century – too late for the Spanish Crown to collect its tax. Inside are elaborate stone carvings and decadent altars, and at the entrance is an interesting collection of dangling silver sacred hearts. Visit the church's small **Museo de Arte Religioso** to see 17th-century religious paintings done by indigenous artists, and the creepy **catacombs**, where many monks lie buried. The intricately sculpted **Capilla de la Dolorosa** (to the right of the church) is considered one of the finest chapels in the city.

CERRO SANTA APOLONIA

This garden-covered **hilltop** (admission US$0.30; ☺ 9am-1pm & 3-5pm) overlooks the city from the southwest and is a prominent Cajamarca landmark. It's easily reached by climbing the stairs at the end of 2 de Mayo. The pre-Hispanic carved rocks at the summit are mainly from the Inca period, but some are thought to originally date back to the Chavín period. One of the rocks, known as the Seat of the Inca, has a shape that suggests a throne, and the *inca* is said to have reviewed his troops from here.

Activities

Hogar de Cristo (☎ 36 5778; www.hogardecristoperu.org in Spanish; Belén 676; ☺ 8am-6pm) is a charity that is always looking for volunteers to help with its various programs for street children.

Tours & Guides

Tour companies provide information and inexpensive guided tours of the city and its surrounds. The companies claim to have English-speaking guides, but only a few really pass muster. Tours to Cumbe Mayo (US$5), Hacienda la Colpa and Baños del Inca (US$3.90), Granja Porocón (US$4.50) and Ventanillas de Otuzco (US$4) are the most popular. The companies will often pool tours. They can also help you arrange car hire for around US$80 per day. The following companies have received recommendations:

Cajamarca Tours (☎ 36 5674; 2 de Mayo 323)
Clarín Tours (☎ 36 6829; clarintours@hotmail.com; Del Batán 161)
Mega Tours (☎ 35 7793; jpilcon@yahoo.es; Puga 691)

Festivals & Events

Carnaval Held in the last few days before Lent, the Carnaval festivities here are reputed to be one of the most popular and rowdy events in the country (see p426).
Corpus Christi A popular feast day in Cajamarca; it's held on the ninth Thursday after Easter.
Fiestas Patrias Celebrations marking National Independence Days (28 and 29 July) may include a bullfight.
Tourist Festival Various cultural events include art shows, folk music and dancing competitions, beauty pageants and processions. It's held around the second week in August.

Sleeping

Hotel rates (and other prices) rise during festivals and special events, and are also usually slightly higher in the dry season (May to September). Prices given here are for October to April.

BUDGET

Most of the budget options in Cajamarca have hot-water showers, though often for only a few hours each day.

Hostal Plaza (☎ 36 2058; Puga 669; s/d with shared bathroom US$4.50/7.50, s/d US$7.50/10.50) Sleeping in this central cheapie, located right on the plaza, is like slipping on an old pair of comfy slippers. Sure, they're a little tattered around the edges, but the basic, creaky rooms, worn with age, fit like a glove. There's hot water in the

---

CARNAVAL CAJAMARCA

The Peru-wide pageantry of Carnaval is celebrated at the beginning of Lent, usually in February. Not all Carnavals are created equal, however. Ask any Peruvian where the wildest celebrations are at, and Cajamarca will invariably come out trumps.

Preparations begin months in advance; sometimes, no sooner have Carnaval celebrations wound down than planning for the following year begins. Cajamarcans take their celebrations seriously. The festival is nine days of dancing, eating, singing, partying, costumes, parades and general rowdy mayhem. It's also a particularly wet affair, and water fights here are worse (or better, depending on your point of view) than you'd encounter elsewhere. Local teenagers don't necessarily limit themselves to soaking one another with water – paint, oil and other unsightly liquids have all been reported.

Hotels fill up weeks beforehand, prices skyrocket and hundreds of people end up sleeping in the plaza. Considering it's one of the most rambunctious festivals in Peru, it certainly seems worth it.

---

mornings and evenings, and while the communal bathrooms can be on the smelly side of things, the eight rooms with bathrooms are great value. Try to snag a room with a balcony and plaza views.

Hostal Peru (☎ 36 4030; Puga 605; s/d US$6/9) This hotel on the plaza has private bathrooms with hot showers all day, but is a little more worn than most and is exposed to dinnertime noise from El Zarco restaurant below.

Hostal Prado (☎ 36 6093, La Mar 582; s/d with shared bathroom US$6/12, s/d US$12/21) This well-kept, clean property has a café and hot water all day. Rooms have TVs, and you'll have to fork out extra for cable. Some of the staff speak English.

Hostal Jusovi (☎ 36 2920; Amazonas 637; s/d US$9/15) Boasting what must be the smallest rooms in town, Hostal Jusovi's abodes are kept perfectly clean and manage to squeeze in private showers with morning hot water. Some rooms have cable TV, and the rooftop terrace with views of the cathedral spire is a welcome addition.

Hospedaje los Jazmines (☎ /fax 36 1812; assado@hotmail.com; Amazonas 775; s/d with shared bathroom US$9/13.50, s/d US$12/18) This six-room German-run *hospedaje* (small, family-owned inn) isn't much to look at, but its excellent café, comfortable beds, hot showers and practice of hiring disabled people keep attracting altruistic travelers.

Hospedaje Santa Ana (☎ 34 0427; J Sabogal 1130; s/d US$10.50/15) A great budget pick, this brightly colored shoebox of a place has neat modern rooms, complete with gently curving yellow walls and cable TV. At the entrance you'll be greeted by both a statue of the Virgin Mary

and smiling, helpful staff. This place is popular with visiting Peace Corps volunteers.

Hotel San Lorenzo (☎ 36 2909; Amazonas 1070; s/d US$10.50/16.50) Helpful, friendly owners provide dark but good-sized rooms (though the street-side ones can be noisy), cable TV, hot showers and a café.

Los Balcones de la Recoleta (☎ /fax 36 3302, 36 4446; Puga 1050; s/d US$10.50/21; 🖳) Polished wood glistens throughout this 19th-century building. The 12 rickety rooms ooze charisma and encircle a lovely plant-filled courtyard. It's a relaxing place, and with hot showers all day, cable TV, internet connections in each room and good beds, what more do you need? OK, throw in a small restaurant, crafts on most of the walls and friendly staff, and you're onto a real winner.

Hostal José Galvez (☎ 34 0396, s/d US$13.50/18) Near Los Baños del Inca, this clean hotel has a bar and is popular with large groups. The rooms all have hot thermal showers.

Hostal Santa Apolonia (☎ 36 7207, ☎ /fax 82 8574; Puga 649; s/d US$15/24) Secure and spotless, this place takes the cake in the plaza-side accommodations stakes. The comfortable, carpeted rooms have 24-hour hot showers, cable TV and minifridges, and some come with views of the plaza. There's also a comfortable sitting area inside, complete with the Virgin Mary enshrined in a curious freestanding cavelike obelisk.

MIDRANGE
All hotels in this range have 24-hour hot water and many throw in a free breakfast.

Hostal Casona del Inca (☎ 36 7524; www.casonadel incacajamarca_peru.com; 2 de Mayo 458-460; s/d US$18/27) You might begin questioning your sobriety when you notice that all the brightly painted walls of this plaza-side colonial seem to be on a slight angle. Don't worry – they are. The aged carnival fun-house appearance just adds to the charm, however. The rooms follow in the footsteps of this slightly wonky theme, and are clean and cozy. This place is justifiably popular with gringos.

El Cabildo (☎ 36 7025; cabildoh@latin.com; Junín 1062; s/d incl breakfast US$18/28.50) One of the town's best-value sleeping options, this huge historic mansion conceals an eclectic collection of well-maintained and graceful older rooms. Some of the rooms come with split levels, and all are filled with plenty of gleaming wood and tasteful decorations. At the mansion's heart, a gorgeous courtyard area is filled with greenery, a fountain and a cacophony of sculptures and statues.

Complejo Turístico Baños del Inca (☎ /fax 34 8385; bungalows/albergue US$18/36) Right behind Los Baños del Inca are eight spacious bungalows, each with sitting room, bedroom, minifridge and cable TV. Too bad they don't have a kitchenette. They have views of reservoirs of scalding 78°C water, steaming Dante-esquely – the water must be mixed with cold water before it flows into the spa complex.

El Cumbe Inn (☎ 36 8221; www.elcumbeinn.com; Atahualpa 345; s/d incl breakfast US$19.50/33) This good find, located in the quieter southern part of town, has nicely furnished, pristine and bright rooms, all with glistening bathrooms on hand. A small garden lies out the back and the stairway here is guarded by large, scary Carnaval masks.

Hostal Portada del Sol (☎ 36 3395; portasol@amet .com.pe; Pisagua 731; s/d incl breakfast US$21/30; 🖳) The bright colors in this cozy colonial are as warm as the staff. Inside you will find thoughtfully decorated spaces with polished floorboards and exposed wooden beams, as well as a skylight-protected courtyard to while away the time in. A good on-site restaurant offers room service. The owners also have a rammed-earth hacienda (☎ 36 3395; Pisagua 731), 5.5km away in the countryside on the unpaved road to Cumbe Mayo. The 15 rooms here are tranquil, private and many have countryside vistas. A tree house and playground make this a top getaway for families and groups.

Hotel Casa Blanca (☎ 36 2141; 2 de Mayo 446; s US$21, d US$30-37, all incl breakfast) This dignified old structure on the Plaza de Armas exudes plenty of character while also providing a few mod cons in the medley of rooms. Quarters range from poky to good sized, and come with cable TV, direct-dial telephone and mini-fridge. The hotel café provides room service, and the staff also arrange car rental and free airport transfers. Some of the larger rooms have bathtubs, while a family room with five beds costs US$58.

Los Pinos Inn (☎ 36 5992, 36 5991; pinoshostal@yahoo .com; La Mar 521; s/d incl breakfast US$21/32) This majestic and drafty colonial building, dripping in marble staircases and intricate tilework, and strewn about with antiques, looks like a museum yet manages to refrain from being ostentatious. Hallways with enormous gilded mirrors lead to 21 large and varied rooms, all with distressed floorboards and more antique flourishes, as well as solid beds. Continental breakfast (included in the price) is served in a pleasing courtyard café covered with a stained-glass roof. This hotel is often full, so call ahead.

Hostal Cajamarca (☎ 36 2532; fax 36 2813; 2 de Mayo 311; s/d US$26/33) Presentable, spacious hotel in a colonial house, with a courtyard and a recommended restaurant that occasionally hosts live music.

El Portal del Marques (☎ /fax 36 8464; www.portal delmarques.com; Lima 644; s/d/ste incl breakfast US$29/39/79; 🖳) Set around an immaculately groomed garden, this restored colonial mansion has standard carpeted rooms with TVs and minifridges. There's a fancy-looking restaurant on site that provides room service and, if bathing in Baños del Inca doesn't do it for you, you can splurge on the hotel's suite, which comes with a Jacuzzi. The mood lighting in the garden makes it a romantic evening hangout.

Las Americas Hotel (☎ 36 8863, ☎ /fax 82 3951; Amazonas 618; s/d incl breakfast US$34.50/43.50) Breaking away from the 'cozy colonial hotel' pack, this contemporary property is all business. It has a central atrium flowing with plenty of plants and a rooftop terrace giving plaza and church views. The 28 rooms are all carpeted and have direct-dial phones, minifridges, cable TVs and excellent mattresses; five of them have Jacuzzi tubs and three have balconies, so it pays to check around. A restaurant provides room service.

Hacienda San Antonio (☎ /fax 34 8237; csananton io@terra.com.pe; s/d incl breakfast US$35/45) An ideal rural getaway, this lovely and rustic-looking ranch has gracefully renovated rooms with some antique flourishes and hot showers.

One room even has a fireplace. The property also has a children's playground, and horseback riding is included in the price. An artificial stream and pond have fishing and canoeing, and walks can be taken to enjoy the fresh country air. To get to the hacienda, head 5km out on the road to Los Baños del Inca, then 1.5km left (just past the El Porongo gas station) to San Antonio (a US$3 taxi ride from Cajamarca).

Hotel el Ingenio (☎ /fax 36 7121; www.elingenio .com; Vía de Evitamiento 1611-1709; s/d/ste incl breakfast US$40/50/75) Built in the style of an attractive colonial hacienda, this modern and relaxing alternative has charisma in spades. Stone archways lead to plenty of garden areas to loll around in, and the warm-colored rooms are large, comfortable and classically decorated. Cable TV, direct-dial telephones, minifridges and tubs in the bathrooms are standard, while some rooms have patios or balconies. The six minisuites each have a Jacuzzi. The staff are very attentive. It's a 20-minute walk into town.

TOP END

Costa del Sol (☎ 36 2472; www.costadelsolperu.com; Cruz de Piedra 707; s/d US$68/83, ste US$115-140; 🖥 🖳) The only top-end choice right in town, Costa del Sol is part of a chain of Peruvian luxury hotels and has recently taken over the southwest corner of the Plaza de Armas. No colonial bent here, just uncluttered, slick rooms filled with all the mod cons and catering to the Peruvian jet set. A stylish restaurant and a top-floor pool, gym and sauna round off an extensive list of amenities.

Hostal Laguna Seca (☎ 59 4600; www.lagunaseca .com.pe; s/d US$89/110, ste US$135-160; 🔣 🖳) Situated 6km from Cajamarca near Los Baños del Inca, this Swiss-owned resort runs, not surprisingly, like clockwork. It features a huge heated swimming pool, Jacuzzi and Turkish bath, and the hot water in all rooms is fed by the natural thermal springs nearby. Rooms have large bathrooms with deep tubs for soaking, direct-dial phones, cable TVs, minifridges and radios. Horseback riding (US$8.50 per hour) and bicycle rental (US$2.40 per hour) are available, and massages and spa health treatments pamper to the hedonists among you. There's also a pleasant garden with children's playground and a decent restaurant. Call ahead for free transfers from Cajamarca's airport.

Eating

Heladería Holanda (☎ 34 0113; Puga 657; ice creams US$0.80; 🕙 9am-7pm) Don't miss the tiny entrance on the town's Plaza de Armas; it opens into a large, bright café selling what might be the best ice cream in northern Peru. The café has about 20 changing flavors, including some locally made fruit concoctions. Excellent espressos, creamy cappuccinos and homemade pies round out the menu and draw in the daytime punters.

Cascanuez Café Bar (☎ 36 6089; Puga 554; desserts US$1-2; 🕙 7am-11pm) This café sells snacks and meals, but people flock here for the good choice of fine desserts and respectable coffee.

New York Pizza (☎ 50 6215; Puga 1045; pizzas US$1.10-2.70; 🕙 4-11pm) OK, it's not real New York pizza, but then again nothing else is. They still make a great pie though, as the yummy smells wafting down the street will verify. They get double bonus points for their delivery service.

Carpa Bruja (☎ 34 2884; Puga 519; sandwiches US$1.50-4.20, meals US$4.50-7.50; 🕙 noon-11pm) Cajamarca's modern antidote to old-world colonial style, this slick, modern and bright affair serves up international dishes, gourmet sandwiches (on whole-wheat ciabatta!), lots of salads and several vegetarian choices. There's a happy hour in the evening, and for dessert you'll have to go a long way to beat their specialty cheesecake (US$1.80).

Sanguchon.com (Junín 1137; mains around US$2.10; 🕙 6pm-late) Popular hamburger and sandwich joint with an excellent bar that often remains rowdy till the wee hours.

Don Paco (☎ 36 2655; Puga 726; meals US$2.70-5.50; 🕙 8:30am-11pm) Tucked away near the plaza, Don Paco has a big following among both residents and expats. There's something for everyone here, including typical breakfasts and great renditions of Peruvian favorites, as well as a whole bunch of veggie options, all served by friendly staff.

Salas (☎ 36 2867; Puga 637; mains US$3.30-6; 🕙 7am-10pm) This barn of a restaurant on the Plaza de Armas has been a local favorite since 1947 – and some of the diners look like they have been patronizing the joint since the very beginning. Knowledgeable elderly staff in white suits will help you navigate the extensive menu, which lists local specialties such as goat, tamales (corn dough stuffed with meat, beans or chilies) and even *sesos* (cow brains). More-standard plates are also available.

El Batán (☎ 36 6025; anabufet@hotmail.com; Del Batán 369; menús US$4.50-6, mains US$3.90-6; 🕙 10am-11pm) One of the town's best places to eat, this gallery-restaurant-*peña*-cultural-center serves varied Peruvian and international dishes and has a decent wine list. The *menú* (set meal) is an excellent deal. On Friday and Saturday nights, El Batán has live shows of local music, anything from folk songs to traditional Andean music to Afro-Peruvian dance rhythms. There is a full bar and an upstairs art gallery.

Querubino (☎ 34 0900; Puga 589; mains US$3.90-6; 🕙 noon-midnight) Modern and stylish, warm and busy, this place has a ponderous menu of Peruvian and international dishes, and is renowned for its great pastas. It also has a solid wine selection.

El Cajamarques (☎ 36 2128; Amazonas 770; mains US$4.50-6; 🕙 8:30am-11pm) For high-end Peruvian cuisine, dip into this elegant restaurant. The colonial courtyard is filled with tropical birds that will happily sing along as Peruvian and international dishes are presented on spiffy white tablecloths. Rowdy parties are held here during Carnaval.

Supermercado San Francisco (☎ 36 2128; Amazonas 780; 🕙 7am-8pm) For self-catering.

Drinking

aKaesH (☎ 36 8108; 2 de Mayo 334; 🕙 9pm-late) Currently the most popular watering hole in town, aKaesH, roughly translated to 'here it is,' gets busy most nights with wall-to-wall gringos and well-to-do Peruvians. It has a well-stocked bar and flashy retro styling with changing nightly events, including Tuesday-night movies, as well as the occasional live band. Look out for flyers around town.

Usha-Usha (Puga 142; admission US$1.50; 🕙 9pm-late) For something a little more intimate, this place is a graffiti-covered hole-in-the-wall bar run by an eccentric local musician. It serves strong mixed drinks and hosts live jazz music most nights of the week. It's definitely worth searching out.

Shopping

There are lots of local handicrafts available near the market and along Belén.

Colors & Creations (☎ 34 3875; Belén 628; 🕙 9:30am-1:30pm & 2:30-7pm Mon-Sat, 10am-6pm Sun) A neat artisan-owned-and-run cooperative, this shop sells excellent-quality crafts, including some of the best replicas of Inca pottery in Peru, created by the internationally renowned local artist Don Lorenzo.

Getting There & Away

AIR

Schedules are subject to change, as well as occasional cancellations and delays, so reconfirm and arrive early at the **airport** (code CJA; ☎ 36 2523). The airport departure tax is $3.57.

Aero Condor Perú (☎ 36 2814, 36 5674; 2 de Mayo 323) has a morning flight from Lima to Cajamarca (US$109) at 5:45am, returning to Lima at 7:15am, daily from Monday to Saturday. On Sunday this flight leaves Lima at 3pm and returns at 5:30pm. **LC Busre** (☎ 36 1098; Lima 1024) also plies this route, with two daily flights leaving Lima (US$124) at 3:30pm and 3:45pm, and returning at 5:30pm and 5:45pm.

BUS

Cajamarca continues its ancient role as a crossroads, with buses heading to all four points of the compass. Most bus terminals are close to *cuadra* (block) 3 of Atahualpa, about 1.5km southeast of the center (not to be confused with the Atahualpa in the town center), on the road to Los Baños del Inca.

The major route is westbound to the Panamericana near Pacasmayo on the coast, then north to Chiclayo (six hours) or south to Trujillo (six hours) and Lima (14 hours).

The southbound road is the old route to Trujillo (at least 15 hours) via Cajabamba (4½ hours) and Huamachuco (7½ hours). For Huamachuco and on to Trujillo, change at Cajabamba. The trip to Trujillo takes two or three times longer on this rough dirt road than it does along the newer paved road via Pacasmayo, although the old route is only 60km longer. The scenery is prettier on the longer route, but most buses are less comfortable and less frequent beyond Cajabamba.

The rough northbound road to Chota (five hours) passes through wild and attractive countryside via Bambamarca, which has a busy market on Sunday morning. Buses run from Chota to Chiclayo along a knobby, rough road.

The staggeringly scenic eastbound road winds to Celendín (five hours), then bumps its way across the Andes, past Chachapoyas and down into the Amazon lowlands. The road between Celendín and Chachapoyas is beautiful but in bad condition and transport can be sporadic; if you're going to Chachapoyas, consider traveling via Chiclayo and Bagua Grande, unless you have plenty of time and patience.

Cial (☎ 36 8701; Independencia 288) Has buses to Lima at 7pm (US$18 to US$24).

Civa (☎ 36 1460; Ayacucho 753) Good buses to Lima (US$24) at 7pm.

Cruz del Sur (☎ 36 1737; Via de Evitamiento 750) Luxury *bus-cama* (bed bus) to Lima (US$26.50) at 7pm. This terminal is several kilometers further along the road to Los Baños del Inca.

El Cumbe (☎ 36 3088; Atahualpa 300) Cheap buses to Chiclayo (US$4.50 to US$5.50) at 7am, 11:30am, 3pm and 9pm.

Flores (☎ 34 1294; Atahualpa 248) Cheap bus to Lima (US$12 to US$21) at 5pm.

Linea (☎ 36 2056; Atahualpa 318) Good-quality buses go to Lima (US$27) at 7pm, Chiclayo (US$4.50 to US$9) at 11am, 10:45pm and 11pm, and Trujillo (US$4.50 to US$10.50) at 10:30am, 1:30pm, 10pm and 10:30pm.

Ormeño (☎ 36 9885; Independencia 304) Good buses to Lima (US$13.50) at 8pm.

Royal Palace's (☎ 34 3063; Atahualpa 337) Services to Celendín (US$3) at 9am, and cheap buses to Trujillo (US$4.50) at 11am and Lima (US$9) at 7:30pm.

Tepsa (☎ 36 3306; Atahualpa 300) Comfortable *semi-cama* (half bed) Lima service (US$24) at 6pm.

Transportes Atahualpa (☎ 36 3060; Atahualpa 299) Buses to Cajabamba (US$3) at noon, Celendín (US$3) at 7am and 1pm and Chota (US$4.50) via Bambamarca at 11am.

Transportes Horna (☎ 36 7671; Atahualpa 313) Buses to Lima (US$9) at 6pm, Trujillo (US$4.50) at 8am and 10pm and Cajabamba (US$3) at 2am and 5pm.

Transportes Rojas (☎ 34 0548; Atahualpa 405) Services to Cajabamba (US$3) at 2am, 9am, 11am, 2pm and 4pm.

Turismo Diaz (☎ 36 8289; Sucre 422) Lima buses (US$4.50 to US$9) at 5pm, 6pm and 7pm, Trujillo buses (US$4.50 to US$9) at 10am, 1pm and 10pm, and Chiclayo buses (US$4.50 to US$6) at 10:30am, 2pm and 10:30pm.

Turismo Nacional (☎ 34 0357; Atahualpa 309) Services to Celendín (US$3) at 7am and 1pm, and Chota (US$3) via Bambamarca at 11am.

There are also several minibuses to Cajamarca (US$4.50 to US$6), also leaving from *cuadra* 3 of Atahualpa.

Buses for Ventanillas de Otuzco (US$0.60, 20 minutes) leave from 500m north of the plaza. These pass the airport (US$0.20), though taking a taxi is much faster (US$1.50).

Combis (minibuses) for Los Baños del Inca (US$0.20, 25 minutes) leave frequently along

J Sabogal, near 2 de Mayo. Some of these buses also continue onto Hacienda la Colpa (US$0.30, 40 minutes).

AROUND CAJAMARCA

Places of interest around Cajamarca can be reached by public transport, on foot, by taxi or with a guided tour. Tour agencies pool their clients to form a group for any trip, although more expensive individual outings can be arranged.

Los Baños del Inca

Atahualpa was camped by these natural **hot springs** (⏱ 4:30am-8pm) when Pizarro arrived, hence the name. Now you can take a dip in the same pools that an Inca king used to bathe his war wounds – though they've probably been cleaned since then. Set around flourishing grounds with sculpted shrubbery, this attractive compound has hot water channeled into private cubicles (US$0.90 to US$1.50 per hour), some large enough for up to six people at a time. There is a public pool (US$0.60), which is cleaned on Monday and Friday, and sauna rooms and massages are available for US$3 each. This place gets hundreds of visitors daily, so it's best to come in the morning to avoid the rush. There's a **Complejo Recreativo** (admission US$0.60; ⏱ 8am-8pm) opposite the main bath complex that has swimming pools, a children's playground and 'waterslides of the Incas,' which are a big hit with kids. The *baños* (baths) are 6km from Cajamarca and have a few hotel possibilities (see p427). *Combis* for Los Baños del Inca (US$0.20, 25 minutes) leave from J Sabogal in Cajamarca.

Cumbe Mayo

About 20km southwest of Cajamarca, Cumbe Mayo (derived from the Quechua *kumpi mayo*, meaning 'well-made water channel') is an astounding feat of pre-Inca engineering. These perfectly smooth aqueducts were carved around 2000 years ago and zigzag at right angles for 9km, all for a purpose that is as yet unclear since Cajamarca has an abundant water supply. Other rock formations are carved to look like altars and thrones. Nearby caves contain **petroglyphs**, including some that resemble wooly mammoths. The countryside is high, windswept and slightly eerie. Superstitious stories are told about the area's eroded rock formations, which look like groups of shrouded mountain climbers.

The site can be reached on foot via a sign-posted road from Cerro Santa Apolonia in Cajamarca. The walk takes about four hours if you take the obvious shortcuts and ask every passerby for directions. Guided bus tours (around US$5) are offered by tour companies in Cajamarca; these can be a good idea as public transport to Cumbe Mayo is sporadic at the best of times.

Ventanillas de Otuzco & Combayo

These pre-Inca necropolises have scores of funerary niches built into the hillside, hence the name Ventanillas (Windows). Ventanillas de Otuzco is in alluring countryside, 8km northeast of Cajamarca, and is easily walkable from either Cajamarca or Los Baños del Inca (ask for directions). The larger and better-preserved Ventanillas de Combayo are 30km away and are best visited on a US$10 tour. Buses to Ventanillas de Otuzco leave frequently from north of the Plaza de Armas in Cajamarca (US$0.60, 20 minutes), or tours cost around US$4.

Llacanora & Hacienda la Colpa

The picturesque hamlet of Llacanora lies 13km from Cajamarca. Some inhabitants still play the traditional 3m-long bamboo trumpet called the clarín.

A few kilometers away is the Hacienda la Colpa, often visited on a tour combined with Llacanora or the Baños del Inca (about US$4 per person). The hacienda is a working cattle ranch, complete with a lake and gardens, that was made famous by ranch hands who would herd cows into their stalls by calling out to each animal by name. An impressive feat when the herd numbered in the hundreds, a little less so now that there are only half a dozen head of cattle. This is a locally famous tourist attraction that can be reached by combi from Cajamarca (US$0.30, 40 minutes).

Granja Porcón

Located about 23km by road from Cajamarca, this is a successful evangelical cooperative that began in 1975 and is still going strong. The community has its own Plaza de Armas, plus two pueblos (towns or villages), Tinte and Huaquin. Overlooked by 'God loves you' billboards in Spanish and Quechua, about 1200 residents work in fields, a dairy, trout hatchery, wood mill, looms, craft shops, simple restaurants, and a lodge (☎ 36 5631; granjaporcon@yahoo.com). There's even a small zoo here housing a condor, jaguars, speckled bears (the only type of bear found in South America), ostriches and monkeys. It's an interesting ongoing project and is visited by daily tours (US$4.50). A highlight is the herd of vicuñas (threatened, wild relatives of alpacas) running free among deer and alpaca herds.

CAJABAMBA

☎ 076 / pop 12,600 / elev 2655m

The old route from Cajamarca to Trujillo takes at least 15 hours along 360km of mostly dirt road via Cajabamba and Huamachuco. Although this route passes through more interesting scenery and towns than the road via Pacasmayo, the bus trip is very rough and few tourists come through.

The friendly town of Cajabamba sits on a natural ledge overlooking swaths of farms and plantations. With a 19th-century atmosphere, the town has more mules than cars in the streets, and the whitewashed houses and red-tiled roofs lend the place a colonial aesthetic. The feast of La Virgen del Rosario is celebrated around the first Sunday in October with bullfights, processions, dances and general bucolic carousing. There are several sights within an hour's walk of Cajabamba, including the caverns of Chivato and the fetching mountain lagoons of Ponte and Quengococha. Ask at Hostal La Casona (☎ 35 8285; Bolognesi 720) for information on visiting these sights.

Most of the town's simple hotels line the Plaza de Armas and can fill up fast before the feast of La Virgen del Rosario. They also suffer from periodic water shortages and dim lighting. Hostal Flores (☎ 55 1086; L Prado 137; s/d with shared shower US$3/9) has rooms with a balcony onto the plaza. Hostal Ramal (☎ 50 5539; Cárdenas 784; s/d with shared bathroom US$3/9) has basic rooms with cold-water bathrooms. Hostal La Casona (☎ 35 8285; Bolognesi 720; s/d US$6/9) gets the ribbon for the top place to stay in town, with DVD players in the rooms, a DVD library (US$0.30), hot showers and several rooms with balconies and plaza views.

La Casona Restaurant (☎ 35 8285; Bolognesi 720; meals US$1.20-3; ☧ 7am-10pm), below the hotel of the same name, is one of the better places to grab a bite in town. It serves the usual Peruvian victuals and has a menu in English. Chifa Chacato (Cardenas 735; meals US$1.50-3.60; ☧ noon-11pm) has good Chinese food prepared by a Lima-trained chef.

Transportes Rojas (☎ 55 1399; Bolognesi 700) has buses to Cajamarca (US$3, 4½ hours) at 3am, 5am, 8:30am and 2pm. **Transportes Horna** (☎ 55 1397; Prado 153) has daily Cajamarca buses (US$3, 4½ hours) at noon, 4:30pm and 7pm and buses to Huamachuco (US$1.80, three hours) at 4am and 3:30pm. **Los Andes** (☎ 80 5594; Grau 1170) also go to Huamachuco at 4am, 9am and 4pm (US$1.80).

HUAMACHUCO

☎ 044 / pop 22,100 / elev 3160m

This small colonial town is located between Cajabamba and Trujillo. It has an impressive Plaza de Armas, said to be Peru's largest, and a large contemporary church.

The massive ruins of the pre-Inca mountain fort of **Marcahuamachuco** (admission free) lie 10km away via a track passable only by 4WD or truck. This 2.5km-long site dates from around 400 BC and has tall defensive perimeter walls and interesting circular structures of varying sizes. Marcahuamachuco culture seems to have developed independently of surrounding civilizations of the time. A taxi can reach within 5km of the site in the dry season (US$2), but you'll have to hike along the dirt road the rest of the way. Bring all necessary food and drink with you.

There is transport east to the mining town of **Pataz** during the dry season, from where expeditions can be mounted to the little-explored ruins of various jungle cities. The largest of these are the vast Chachapoyas ruins of **Gran Pajatén**. The ruins are north of the recently formed Parque Nacional Río Abiseo, which has no infrastructure for travelers at this time and is very hard to get to. This is an undertaking for determined explorers, archaeologists, or Indiana Jones only.

A BRIEF HISTORY OF THE GUINEA PIG

Love it or loathe it, *cuy*, or guinea pig (or *Cavia porcellus* if you really must know), is an Andean favorite that's been part of the local culinary repertoire since pre-Inca times. And before you dredge up childhood memories of cuddly mascots in protest, know that these rascally rodents were gracing Andean dinner plates long before anyone in the West considered them worthy pet material.

Pinpointing the gastronomic history of the *cuy*, a native of the New World, is harder than trying to catch one with your bare hands. It's believed that *cuy* may have been domesticated as early as 7000 years ago in the mountains of southern Peru, where wild populations of *cuy* still roam today. Direct evidence from Chavín de Huántar shows that they were certainly cultivated across the Andes by 900 BC. Arrival of the Spanish in the 18th century led to the European debut of *cuy*, where they rode a wave of popularity as the must-have exotic pet of the season (Queen Elizabeth I supposedly kept one).

How they earned the name guinea pig is also in doubt. Guinea may be a corruption of the South American colony of Guiana, or it may refer to Guinea, the African country that *cuy* would have passed through on their voyage to Europe. Their squeals probably account for the latter half of their name.

Cuy are practical animals to raise and have adapted well over the centuries to survive in environments ranging from the high Andean plains to the barren coastal deserts. Many Andean households today raise *cuy* as part of their animal stock, and you'll often see them scampering around the kitchen in true free-range style. *Cuy* are the ideal livestock alternative: they're high in protein; feed on kitchen scraps; breed profusely; and require much less room and maintenance than traditional domesticated animals.

Cuy is seen as a true delicacy, so much so that in many indigenous interpretations of 'The Last Supper,' Jesus and his disciples are sitting down to a hearty final feast of roast *cuy*.

An integral part of Andean culture, even beyond the kitchen table, *cuy* are also used by *curanderos* (healers) in ceremonial healing rituals. *Cuy* can be passed over a patient's body and used to sense out a source of illness, and *cuy* meat is sometimes ingested in place of hallucinogenic plants during shamanistic ceremonies.

If your can overcome your sentimental inhibitions, sample this furry treat. The rich flavors are a cross between rabbit and quail, and correctly prepared *cuy* can be an exceptional 7000-year-old feast.

Basic and clean, **Hostal San José** (Bolívar 361; s/d US$3/5) has cold water and offers little else in the way of amenities. The better **Hostal Huamachuco** (☎ 44 1393; Castilla 354; s/d with shared bathroom US$4.50/7.50, s/d US$7.50/9) is on the plaza and has hot water and TV. **Hostal Colonial** (☎ 51 1101, 44 1334; Castilla 347; s/d US$7.50/13.50), in a pleasant colonial house (no surprises there), is similar and has a good restaurant downstairs.

Several minivans leave throughout the day bound for Cajabamba (US$1.80, three hours). Transportes Horna and Los Andes both have several early-morning and evening buses to Cajamarca (US$2.40 to US$3, seven hours) and Trujillo (US$4.50, seven hours). *Colectivo* (shared) buses to Otuzco leave when full from near the plaza (US$2.20, four hours).

CELENDÍN

☎ 076 / pop 14,800 / elev 2625m

The unpaved road from Cajamarca to Celendín passes through an undulating sea of green hills stretching to every horizon. Celendín itself is a delightfully sleepy little town that receives few travelers except for those taking the wild and scenic route to Chachapoyas.

There's a **Banco de la Nación** (2 de Mayo 530) here that can change US dollars. The annual **fiesta** (July 29 to August 3) coincides with Fiestas Patrias and features bullfighting with matadors from Mexico and Spain. The fiesta of **La Virgen del Carmen** is celebrated on July 16.

Hot springs (admission free) and mud baths will help soothe aching bones and can be found at Llanguat, reached by a 30-minute drive. You can also take a 7am *combi* from the Plaza de Armas (US$0.90, 45 minutes). It returns at around midday.

The nearby hamlet of **José Gàlvez** is a tranquil mountain town with rustic adobe houses, a nice Plaza de Armas, a small waterfall and, supposedly, the most beautiful women in all of Peru (you will have to decide that for yourself). *Colectivo* taxis for José Gàlvez leave every 20 minutes from near the hospital (US$0.30, 20 minutes).

Less-than-frequent transport connections mean that you may have to dust off the dirt from your rough journeys and unwind in Celendín for a night.

The cheapest digs in town, **Hotel José Gàlvez** (☎ 31 1503; 2 de Mayo 334; r per person US$2.40) has musty wooden rooms on the verge of collapse and cold-water showers. **Hostal Raymi**

Wasi (☎ 55 5374; José Gàlvez 420; s/d with shared bathroom US$3/4.50) is a small space with dark but acceptable rooms. Pay only a little more at **Hostal Loyers** (☎ 55 5210; José Gàlvez 440; s/d with shared bathroom US$3/5.50, s/d US$4.50/8.50) and you'll get colorful rooms, a fetching courtyard and hot(ish) electric showers. The new kid on the block, **Hostal Imperial** (☎ 55 5492; 2 de Mayo 568; s/d with shared bathroom US$3.90/8, s/d US$5.50/8.50) has the best rooms of this bunch, though the singles with shared bathrooms are poky.

Kept fastidiously clean and with a decent selection of rooms, **Hostal Amazonas** (☎ 55 5093; 2 de Mayo 316; r per person US$6) is rather unnecessarily filled with a few '80s kitsch tidbits. It has hot water in the morning. Finally, the best place to stay in town is **Hostal Celendín** (☎ 55 5041; Unión 305; s/d US$8/11.50; 🖳). Right on the Plaza de Armas, it has reliable hot water and worn but inviting rooms, many with balconies and grand plaza views. It also has a good restaurant and, for some reason, an odd stuffed-bird collection in the reception area. The town's disco is held here on Saturday nights (bring earplugs). The staff are extra helpful. Be sure to ask about discounts.

Snack Cafe (José Gàlvez 512; meals US$1.20-2.40; 🕙 6-10pm) makes a valiant attempt at pizza. The best restaurant in town is at **Hostal Celendín** (Plaza de Armas; meals US$1.80-3; 🕙 8am-11pm), which boasts a Lima-trained chef and serves pizzas and lots of local specialties, including the tasty *cuy tipico* – fried guinea pig with mashed sweet potato and spring-onion-and-lemon sauce (US$1.80). **La Reserva** (☎ 50 5817; José Gàlvez 420; meals US$1.80-3.30; 🕙 7pm-midnight) is another popular eating choice, with multilevel seating and a warm ambience.

The rough road from Cajamarca is far better than the one from Chachapoyas. Most bus companies are found around the Plaza de Armas.

Inca Atahualpa (☎ 31 9749; Pardo 438) has daily buses to Cajamarca (US$2.40, five hours) at 5:45am and at 12:15pm. **Royal Palace's** (☎ 55 5322; Union 504) and **Transportes Atahualpa** (☎ 55 5256; Pardo 362) both have departures at about 7am and 1pm to Cajamarca (US$2.40 to US$3, five hours). **Virgen del Carmen** (☎ 55 5238; Caceres 110), located behind the market, has buses to Chachapoyas (US$9, 12 to 14 hours) via Leimebamba (US$6, eight to nine hours) at 11am on Sundays and Thursdays only. Hiring a taxi for this route costs around US$90. If you hang out at the intersection called

---

BORDER CROSSING: ECUADOR VIA JAÉN

If your next port of call is Ecuador, remember that you don't have to spend days on winding roads to get back to the Peruvian coast. From Jaén, a good northbound road heads 107km to San Ignacio near the Ecuadorian border. Since the peace treaty was signed with Ecuador in late 1998, it has become possible to cross into Ecuador at this remote outpost.

Begin at the fast-growing agricultural center of **Jaén** (population 52,900), where there are a couple of banks and over a dozen hotels. Good ones include the budget **Hostal Jaén** (☎ 076-43 1333; San Martín 1528; s/d US$4.50/7.50), with friendly staff and cold showers, and the family-run **Hostal Diana Gris** (☎ 076-43 2127; 2nd fl, Urreta 1136; s/d US$7.50/9), which has hot showers, fans, cable TVs and a restaurant. Also try the recommended **Prim's Hotel** (☎ 076-43 2970; Palomino 1353; s/d US$13.50/25.50; 🖵), which has a *chifa* (Chinese restaurant), or the town's best option, **Hotel El Bosque** (☎ 076-43 492; M Muro 632; s/d US$23/31; 🍴 🖵), with bungalows set in gardens.

From Jaén, *colectivo* (shared) buses leave for **San Ignacio** (US$3.60, 2½ hours), where there's a simple hotel and places to eat. Change here for another *colectivo* for the rough road to **La Balsa** (US$3.60, 2½ hours) on the Río Blanco dividing Peru from Ecuador. There used to be a *balsa* (ferry) here (hence the name), but there's now a new international bridge linking the countries. Border formalities are straightforward if you have your papers in order, although the immigration officers don't get to see many gringos coming through.

Once in Ecuador, curious yet typical *rancheras* (trucks with rows of wooden seats) await to take you on the uncomfortable 10km drive to Zumba. From here, buses go to the famed 'valley of longevity' of Vilcabamba (US$4, three hours) where you'll be ready to relax in one of the comfortable hotels and read Lonely Planet's *Ecuador & the Galápagos Islands* book. If you leave Jaén at dawn, you should be able to make it to Vilcabamba in one day.

El Monumento, you may be able to flag down a ride with a passing truck or private vehicle as a paying passenger; bring enough food and snacks for the long journey.

CELENDÍN TO CHACHAPOYAS

This rough but beautiful route may be temporarily impassable during the wet season. It's worth finding transportation that will let you take in the scenery by daylight.

The road climbs over a 3085m pass before plummeting steeply to the Río Marañón at the shabby village of **Balsas** (975m), 55km from Celendín. There's a scruffy guesthouse here where you can rent what apparently passes for a room for US$1.80 per night. The road climbs again, through gorgeous cloud forests and countryside swathed in a lush quilt a million shades of green. It emerges 57km later at the 3678m high point of the drive, aptly named **Abra de Barro Negro** (Black Mud Pass), which suggests what road conditions you can expect during the rainy season. Ghostly low-level clouds and mists hug the dispersed communities in this part of the trip and creep eerily amongst the hills. The road then drops 32km to Leimebamba at the head of the Río Utcubamba valley and follows the river as it descends past Tingo and on to Chachapoyas.

The final 20km approach into Chachapoyas is freshly paved, and after at least 12 butt-smacking hours from Celendín it will feel like a smooth balm on your backside. Travelers should carry water and food, as the few restaurants en route are poor and unhygienic.

The normal route to Chachapoyas is from Chiclayo via Bagua Grande; it's a much easier, but considerably less spectacular, route.

CHICLAYO TO CHACHAPOYAS

This is the usual route for travelers to Chachapoyas. From the old Panamericana 100km north of Chiclayo, a paved road heads east over the Andes via the 2145m Porculla Pass, the lowest Peruvian pass going over the Andean continental divide. The route then tumbles to the Río Marañón valley. About 190km from the Panamericana turnoff, you reach the town of **Jaén**, the beginning of a newly opened route to Ecuador (see above). Continuing east, a short side road reaches the town of **Bagua Chica** in a low, enclosed valley (elevation about 500m), which Peruvians claim is the hottest town in the country. The bus usually goes through **Bagua Grande** on the main road, and follows the Río Utcubamba valley to the crossroads town of Pedro Ruiz, about 90 minutes from Bagua Grande. From here, a bumpy and rough southbound road branches to Chachapoyas, 54km and about 90 minutes away.

CHACHAPOYAS

☎ 041 / pop 20,700 / elev 2335 m

Also known as Chachas, Chachapoyas is a laid-back town insulated by a buffer of rough unpaved roads and high-altitude cloud forests. The town was an important junction on jungle–coast trade routes until a paved road was built in the 1940s through nearby Pedro Ruíz, bypassing Chachapoyas altogether. The unlikely capital of the department of Amazonas, this pleasant colonial settlement is now a busy market town and makes an excellent base for exploring the awesome ancient ruins left behind by the fierce civilization of the Chachapoyas ('People of the Clouds').

Vast zones of little-explored cloud forest surround the city of Chachapoyas, concealing some of Peru's most fascinating and least-known archaeological treasures. Although the ravages of weather and time, as well as more recent attentions of grave robbers and treasure seekers have caused damage to many of the ruins, some have survived remarkably well. Kuélap is by far the most famous of these archaeological sites, though dozens of other ruins lie besieged by jungle and make for tempestuous exploration.

Over a dozen tour agencies in Chachapoyas will vie for your custom and help you arrange trekking trips that include guides, horses, accommodations and all food. Some hikes will require at least sleeping bags; check what you will need ahead of time. The driest months (May to September) are the best time to go hiking and to organize a group to share costs. October to December isn't too wet, but January to April can be soggy.

The traditional evening pastime of strolling around the Plaza de Armas provides the town's main form of entertainment, relaxation and socializing.

History

The Chachapoyas culture was conquered but not fully subdued by the Incas a few decades before the Spaniards arrived (see p440). When the Europeans showed up, local chief Curaca

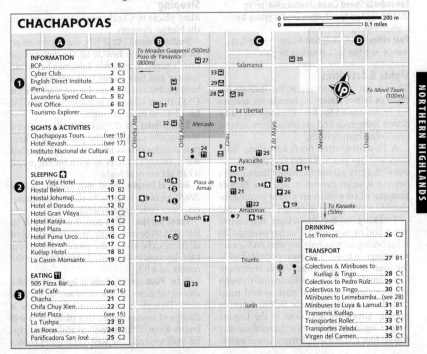

CHACHAPOYAS

0 ——— 200 m
0 ——— 0.1 miles

INFORMATION
BCP..1 B2
Cyber Club.......................................2 C3
English Direct Institute.................3 C3
iPerú...4 B2
Lavandería Speed Clean...............5 B2
Post Office......................................6 B2
Tourismo Explorer..........................7 C2

SIGHTS & ACTIVITIES
Chachapoyas Tours................(see 15)
Hotel Revash...........................(see 17)
Instituto Nacional de Cultura
    Museo..8 C2

SLEEPING
Casa Vieja Hotel............................9 B2
Hostal Belén..................................10 B2
Hostal Johumaji............................11 C2
Hotel el Dorado.............................12 B2
Hotel Gran Vilaya..........................13 C2
Hotel Karajia..................................14 C2
Hotel Plaza....................................15 C2
Hotel Puma Urco...........................16 C2
Hotel Revash.................................17 C2
Kuélap Hotel..................................18 B2
La Cason Monsante.......................19 C2

EATING
505 Pizza Bar.................................20 C2
Café Café................................(see 16)
Chacha..21 C2
Chifa Chuy Xien.............................22 C2
Hotel Plaza.............................(see 15)
La Tushpa.......................................23 B3
Las Rocas.......................................24 B2
Panificadora San José...................25 C2

DRINKING
Los Troncos....................................26 C2

TRANSPORT
Civa...27 B1
Colectivos & Minibuses to
    Kuélap & Tingo........................28 C1
Colectivos to Pedro Ruíz...............29 C1
Colectivos to Tingo.......................30 C1
Minibuses to Leimebamba....(see 28)
Minibuses to Luya & Lamud..........31 B1
Transervis Kuélap..........................32 B1
Transportes Roller..........................33 C1
Transportes Zelada........................34 B1
Virgen del Carmen.........................35 C1

To Mirador Guayamil (500m); Pozo de Yanayacu (800m)

Salamanca

La Libertad

Mercado

Ayacucho

Plaza de Armas

Amazonas

Church

Triunfo

Junín

To Movil Tours (100m)

To Karaoke (50m)

Chincha Alta
Ortiz Arrieta
Grau
2 de Mayo
Merced
Unión

NORTHERN HIGHLANDS

Huáman supposedly aided them in their conquest to defeat the Inca. Because of the relative lack of Inca influence, the people didn't learn to speak Quechua and today Spanish is spoken almost exclusively here. Local historians claim that San Juan de la Frontera de las Chachapoyas was the third town founded by the Spaniards in Peru (after Piura and Lima) and it was, at one time, the seventh-largest town in the country.

Information

There are at least five internet cafés on the Plaza de Armas, though they're often full in the evenings. Several stores on the plaza will change US dollars at reasonable rates.

BCP (Ortiz Arrieta; Plaza de Armas) Changes US dollars and traveler's checks and has a Visa and MasterCard ATM.

Cyber Club (Triunfo 769; per lb US$0.60; ☒ 8am-midnight) Try internetting here.

English Direct Institute (Trufino 761; ☒ 3-9pm) If you're desperate for new reading materials you can exchange books here, though the selection is poor.

iPerú (☎ 47 7292; Plaza de Armas, Ortiz Arrieta 588; ☒ 8am-7pm) You can pick up some rudimentary maps and pamphlets on the area here.

Lavandería Speed Clean (Ayacucho 964; per kg US$0.90; ☒ 7am-1pm, 2-10pm) Good at getting the smelliest trekking clothes clean.

Post office (☎ 47 7019; Ortiz Arrieta; ☒ 9am-7pm Mon-Fri, 9am-1pm Sat) Just south of the plaza.

Sights & Activities

There's not much to see at the **Instituto Nacional de Cultura Museo** (INC; Ayacucho 904; admission free; ☒ 9am-noon & 3-5pm Mon-Sat) except for half a dozen mummies and ceramics from several pre-Columbian periods.

A 10-minute stroll northwest along Salamanca brings you to **Mirador Guayamil**, a lookout with a city panorama. About three blocks beyond it is an overrated well, the **Pozo de Yanayacu**, where visitors are said to become enchanted so they will return to Chachapoyas.

Trekking to the numerous impressive sights and ruins around Chachapoyas (p438) is becoming increasingly popular and is easy to arrange in town. The most popular trek is the four- or five-day Gran Vilaya trek, from Choctámal to the Marañón canyon, through pristine cloud forest and past several ruins and the heavenly Valle de Belén. Another popular adventure heads out to the Laguna de los Cóndores (p442), an arduous three-day trip on foot and horseback from Leimebamba.

Treks to any of the other ruins in the district can be arranged and tailored to suit your needs – though there's so much to see here that several weeks would not be enough.

Tours & Guides

All the tour agencies are found near the Plaza de Armas. Ask around for other travelers' experiences before you choose an agency. Expect to pay US$35 to US$45 per person for multiday treks (a little more for groups of less than four) and around US$20 for day tours.

Chachapoyas Tours (☎ 47 8078; www.huelapperu .com; Hotel Plaza, Grau 534) These guys get rave reviews for their day tours of the area. The company also organizes multiday treks and has some English-speaking guides.

Tourismo Explorer (☎ 47 8060; cnr Amazonas & Grau) This company also has a great reputation and specializes in multiday treks. It has guides who speak excellent English.

Hotel Revash (☎ 47 7391; revash@terra.com; Grau 517) Though not officially registered as a tour company, these guys are great salesmen; walk in wanting a day tour to Kuélap and you may just walk out having booked an eight-day trek. They specialize in tours around Lamud and the Gran Vilaya.

Sleeping

Most places in Chachapoyas fall squarely in the budget category.

Hostal Johumaji (☎ 47 7279; olvacha@terra.com.pe; Ayacucho 711; s US$4.50, d US$7.50-12) The better of the town's supercheap hotels, Johumaji has small, spartan and tidy rooms that are well lit and have electric hot showers. Laundry service for US$1.10 per kilogram is available, as is a TV for US$1.50 extra per night.

Kuélap Hotel (☎ 47 7136; kuelaphotel@hotmail.com; Amazonas 1057; s/d US$6/9) The plain rooms here pass the cleanliness inspection and have hot water, though mattresses are a bit saggy and it can get noisy at night.

Hotel el Dorado (☎ 47 7047; Ayacucho 1062; s/d US$6/9) An older house with electric hot showers, clean rooms and helpful staff.

Hotel Karajía (☎ 31 2606; 2 de Mayo 546; s/d US$7.50/10.50) Secure, basic and clean is about all that can be said of this place – though the kaleidoscopic bedspreads do tend to cheer the rooms up a bit.

Hotel Plaza (formerly Hostal El Tejado; ☎ 47 7654; eltejado@viabcp.com; Grau 534; s/d incl breakfast US$10.50/13.50) Though it has recently undergone a change of management, this plaza hotel still boasts some of the friendliest and most helpful staff around. The well-kept, quiet rooms here are aesthetically decorated and good value. There's an upstairs terrace restaurant overlooking the plaza, and a popular travel agency. Enthusiastically recommended by Lonely Planet readers.

Hostal Belén (☎ 47 7830; www.hostalbelen.com.pe; Ortiz Arrieta 540; s/d US$10.50/15) Also on the plaza in a well-maintained building, Belén has very small but tidy rooms, each with one brightly painted wall to cheer up the relative darkness.

Hotel Revash (☎ 47 7391; fax 47 7356; revash@terra .com; Grau 517; s/d US$10.50/15; 🖳) The showers seem endlessly hot (as eagerly demonstrated by the staff) in this older, classic Chachapoyas hotel. The thickly forested courtyard and wooden floors add plenty of character, and there are laundry facilities and US dollars can be exchanged. The staff here can be overly pushy with their tours.

Hotel Puma Urco (☎ /fax 47 7871; Amazonas 833; s/d US$12/18) A basic, new and contemporary hotel with lots of wood throughout and a small café downstairs.

Hotel Gran Vilaya (☎ 47 7664; hotelvilaya@viabcp .com; Ayacucho 755; s/d US$15/21) This modern deal has the standard Peruvian hotel setup, with carpeting, faux-wood-lined walls and a casino next door. Rooms are spacious, showers are hot, but the ambience is rather unexciting. For some reason, the back garden doubles as a corn plantation.

La Cason Monsante (☎ 47 7702; www.lacasonamon sante.com; Amazonas 746; s/d US$18/24) This lovely colonial mansion is one of the town's top picks. Walk in to find a large, plant-filled stone courtyard and unwind in the inviting and supercomfy rooms decorated with photos of the region and paintings (in which Jesus and Mary make regular guest appearances). Rooms come with cable TV and there's a cafeteria on the premises.

Casa Vieja Hostal (☎ /fax 47 7353; www.casaviejaperu .com; Chincha Alta 569; s/d US$18/30; 🖳) Very comfortable quarters in a classy converted mansion make Casa Vieja Hostal a very special choice. Waking up to the sounds of birds chirping in the lovely courtyard, rather than roaring *mototaxis* (three-wheeled motorcycle rickshaw taxis), is a real pleasure. There's a colorful and comfortable lounge, and the bright rooms all have handcrafted decorations and big windows facing onto the verdant garden. The showers are hot and breakfast (in bed!) is available.

Eating

Moving east across the Andes, Chachapoyas is the first place where you begin finding Amazonian-style dishes, though with local variations. *Juanes* (steamed rice with fish or chicken, wrapped in a banana leaf) are made with yucca instead of rice. *Cecina*, a dish made from dehydrated pork in the lowlands, is often made with beef.

Café Café (Amazonas 829; desserts US$0.30-0.60; ☯ 7am-10pm) A popular, flashy and bright little place under Hotel Puma Urco doing simple sandwiches (US$0.80 to US$1.20), sweet cakes and hot beverages.

505 Pizza Bar (☎ 47 7328; 2 de Mayo 505; pizzas US$0.90; ☯ noon-late) The name says it all: cheap pizzas in a tiny, austere joint with a full bar and music to keep you lingering over a pisco sour long after the last slice is gone.

Panificadora San José (Ayacucho 816; breakfasts US$0.90-1.80; ☯ 6:30am-10pm) This bakery features a few tables where you can enjoy a tamal, *humita* (tamal filled with spiced beef, vegetables and potatoes) or sandwich with coffee for breakfast, and snacks and desserts all day. Be sure to try their rich hot chocolate (US$0.60).

Chacha (☎ 47 7107; Grau 545; menús US$1; mains US$2-4; ☯ 7am-10pm) This is an old standby on the plaza – it's a toss-up whether Chacha or Las Rocas is better.

Chifa Chuy Xien (☎ 47 8587; Amazonas 840; mains US$1.50-9; ☯ 12-4pm & 6-10pm) Behold, the town's best (only?) Chinese restaurant.

Hotel Plaza (☎ 47 7554; 2nd fl, Grau 534; menús US$1.80) It's ambience galore at this plaza-view restaurant, though unfortunately there are only a few tables by the window. Recommended for its set lunches; the service can be slow, though.

Las Rocas (☎ 47 8158; Ayacucho 932; mains US$1.80-3; ☯ 7:30am-9pm Mon-Sat, 6-9pm Sun) Nothing too fancy here, just huge, finger-lickin' portions of Peruvian usuals for a mere handful of soles.

La Tushpa (☎ 80 3634; Ortiz Arrieta 753; meals US$2.10-4.50; ☯ noon-10pm) The ideal place to satisfy a carnivorous hunger, this steak house does sensational grills and mouthwatering steak cooked just the way you like it – whatever way you like it. The place gets packed nightly with locals in the know.

Drinking

Los Troncos (☎ 47 7239; 2 de Mayo 561; ☯ 7pm-5am) The top spot to get your boogie on at the moment is this place, which fills up by 10pm on weekends and blasts international music to a gyrating crowd. The cover on weekends is US$0.30.

Entertainment

Karaoke (Merced 604; 🕥 7pm-late) Come here if you feel like belting out your own unique rendition of Céline Dion.

Getting There & Away

AIR

Although Chachapoyas has an airport, at the time of writing no carriers flew in or out of it. This may change, though probably not soon.

BUS & TAXI

The frequently traveled route to Chiclayo (10 to 11 hours) and on to Lima (20 to 23 hours) starts along the unpaved but vista-lined route to Pedro Ruíz, and then is paved throughout. **Transervis Kuélap** (🕾 47 8128; Ortiz Arrieta 412) has a daily bus to Chiclayo (US$9) at 7pm. **Civa** (🕾 47 8048; Salamanca 956) has a daily 6pm bus to Chiclayo (US$6), and buses bound for Lima at noon on Monday, Wednesday and Friday (US$21). **Transportes Zelada** (🕾 37 8066; Ortiz Arrieta 310) goes to Lima (US$19.50) at 11:30am, stopping at Chiclayo (US$7.50). It also has a direct bus to Chiclayo only at 8pm. The very comfortable **Movil Tours** (🕾 47 8545; La Libertad 464) has an express bus to Lima (US$27, 20 hours) at 1pm, as well as a 10pm bus to Trujillo (US$15, 13 hours) via Chiclayo (US$12).

Virgen del Carmen (Salamanca 650) departs for Celendín (US$9, 12 to 14 hours) on Tuesdays and Fridays at 6am, stopping at Leimebamba (US$3, four hours).

Transportes Roller (Grau 302) has two buses to Kuélap (US$3.60, 3½ hours), via Tingo, Choctámal and María, at 4pm. These return from Kuélap at 6am and 8am.

Colectivo taxis to Kuélap (US$4.50, three hours) depart throughout the day when full from Grau. This block also has frequent minibuses (US$1.80, 1½ hours) and *colectivo* taxis for Tingo (US$2.40, 1½ hours); the taxis may continue on to María (US$3.60, three hours). Minibuses to Leimebamba leave at noon and 4pm (US$3, three to four hours).

To continue further into the Amazon Basin, take a *colectivo* taxi to the crossroads at Pedro Ruíz (US$3.60, 1½ hours) and wait for an eastbound bus. Ask around for trucks and minibuses to other destinations.

If you start early and have plenty of time on your hands, you can see some of the attractions around Chachapoyas by public minibus. For Karajía, you can take a minibus to Luya (US$2.40, 50 minutes), from where regular minibuses go to the nearby village of Cruz Pata (US$1.80, 50 minutes).

A taxi for the day to Kuélap or to sites around Chachapoyas costs US$36; for Leimebamba it's US$45.

AROUND CHACHAPOYAS

Relics of Chachapoyas and Inca civilizations and daring, rugged scenery speckle the mountains surrounding Chachapoyas. There are scores of archaeological sites in this area, most of them unexcavated and many reclaimed by vivacious jungle. Below is a list of some of the main points of interest, though there are many others – and even more await discovery.

Gran Vilaya

The name Gran Vilaya refers to the bountiful valleys that spread out west of Chachapoyas, reaching toward the rushing Río Marañón. Abutting the humid Amazon, this region sits in a unique microcosm of perennially moist high-altitude tropics and cloud forests – an ecological anomaly that gave rise to the Chachapoyas culture's moniker, the People of the Clouds. The fertility of this lush area was never a big secret – the valley successfully supported huge populations from first the Chachapoyas and then the Inca cultures, and to date over 30 archaeological sites have been found dotting the mountains. Important sites like **Paxamarca**, **Pueblo Alto**, **Pueblo Nuevo** and **Pirquilla** lie connected by winding goat-tracks as they did hundreds of years ago, completely unexcavated, and can be visited on multiday hikes. Immaculately constructed Inca roads weave up and around the hills, past many ruined cities camouflaged by centuries of jungle.

The breathtaking, impossibly green and silt-filled **Valle de Belén** lies at the entrance of Gran Vilaya. The flat valley floor here is dissected by the mouth of the widely meandering Río Huaylla, coiled like a languid serpent. Filled with grazing cattle, horses and surrounded on all sides by mist-covered hills, the vistas here are mesmerizing.

Roads barely make a dint into this terrain, so the only way to really explore it is on foot or by horse. If your Spanish is up to it and you have the gear, it is possible to hike independently – but trails are not always marked and the overgrown ruins are difficult to find. Most travel agencies in Chachapoyas offer trekking tours of this region.

Karajía

This extraordinary funerary site hosts six sarcophagi perched high up a sheer cliff face. Each long-faced tomb is constructed from wood, clay and straw, and is uniquely shaped like a stylized forlorn individual. The characters stare intently over the valley below, where a Chachapoyas village once stood; you can see stone ruins scattered among the fields of today. Originally there were eight coupled sarcophagi, but the third and eighth (from

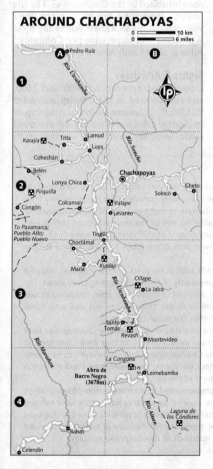

AROUND CHACHAPOYAS

the left) collapsed, opening up the adjoining coffins – which were found to contain mummies, and various crafts and artifacts related to the deceased. Look out for scattered bones below the coffins. Only important individuals were buried with such reverence: shamans, warriors and chieftains. The skulls above the tombs are thought to have been trophies of enemies or possibly human sacrifices. Locals charge a US$1 admission fee.

Karajía is a 45-minute walk from the tiny outpost of Cruz Pata. Minibuses from Chachapoyas travel to Luya (US$2.40, 50 minutes), from where there are minibuses to Cruz Pata (US$1.80, 50 minutes).

Levanto

A great day trip from Chachas is Levanto, a small village three- to four-hours' walk south along an Inca road, or 1½ hours by minibus (US$1.80), which leave from near the market in Chachapoyas in the early morning. You can stay here at the **Levanto Lodge** (r per person US$6), which is built in the style of a traditional round Chachapoyas house. Twenty minutes' walk outside of Levanto, at **Colla Cruz**, sits another reconstructed Inca building with round Chachapoyas walls, meticulous Inca stone foundations and a three-story thatch roof. Ask around for directions.

Revash

Near the town of Santo Tomás, Revash is the site of several brightly colored funerary buildings tucked into limestone cliff ledges. Looking a bit like attractive yet inaccessible summer cottages, these *chullpas* are made of small, mud-set stones that were plastered over and embellished with red and cream paints. This bright taste in décor is still clearly visible today. While much of the site was looted long ago, the skeletons of 11 adults and one child, along with a wealth of artifacts such as musical instruments and tools made from bones, were found inside by archaeologists. A number of pictographs decorate the walls of the cliff behind the tombs, and a funerary cave, originally containing over 200 funerary bundles, lies 1km from the main set of tombs.

The ruins are a steep 3½-hour walk from the turnoff for Santo Tomás, which can be reached by Leimebamba-bound *combis* from Chachapoyas, which leave at noon and 4pm.

NORTHERN HIGHLANDS

La Jalca (Jalca Grande)

This lovely little mountain town, also known as Jalca Grande, is a small, cobblestoned municipality that has managed to retain much of its historical roots, though modernization is slowly creeping its way in. Quechua is still spoken throughout much of the town, and traditional, Chachapoyas-influenced round-walled houses with thatch roofs hide around the corners. Look for **Choza Redonda**, a tall-roofed traditional Chachapoyas house that was supposedly continually inhabited until 1964. It is still in excellent condition and was used as a model for the re-creation of Chachapoyas houses in Kuélap and Levanto. At the ruins of **Ollape**, half an hour's walk west of La Jalca, you can see several house platforms and circular balconies decorated with complex designs. To get here, catch a Chachapoyas–Leimebamba bus and ask to be let off at the La Jalca turnoff, from where it's a one-hour walk up a dirt road.

Yalape

On the road between Chachapoyas and Levanto, these ruins of limestone residential buildings make an easy day trip from Chachas. With good views of Levanto below, Yalape has some decent defense walls with some frieze patterns, all impressed with lots of forest growth. Yalape is four hours' hike from Chachapoyas or half an hour's walk from Levanto. Occasional *combis* head to Levanto early in the morning from near the market in Chachapoyas; they can let you off at Yalape.

KUÉLAP

elev 3100m

Matched in grandeur only by the ruins of Machu Picchu, this fabulous ruined citadel city in the mountains southeast of Chachapoyas is the best preserved and most accessible of the district's extraordinary archaeological sites. This monumental stone-fortified city crowns a craggy limestone mountain and affords exceptional panoramas of a land once inhabited by the Chachapoyas. The site receives remarkably few visitors, but those who make it get to witness one of the most significant and impressive pre-Columbian ruins in all of South America.

Sights & Activities

Constructed between AD 900 and 1100, and rediscovered in 1843, **Kuélap** (adult/student US$3.30/1.70; ☉ 8am-noon & 1-5pm) is made up of millions of cubic feet of remarkably preserved stone. Some say more stone was used in its

---

THE CHACHAPOYAS

The Chachapoyas, or 'People of the Clouds,' controlled the vast swath of land around present-day Chachapoyas from AD 800 to the 1470s, when they were conquered by the Incas. Very little is known about this civilization, whose inhabitants were thought to be great warriors, powerful shamans and prolific builders who were responsible for one of the most advanced civilizations of Peru's tropical jungles. Today, among the many dozens of cliff tombs and hamlets of circular structures left behind, archaeologists match wits with grave robbers in a race for a deeper understanding of the Chachapoyas.

The Chachapoyas were heavily engaged in trade with other parts of Peru. However, isolated in their cloud-forest realm, they developed independently of these surrounding civilizations. The Chachapoyas cultivated a fierce warrior cult; the heads of enemies were often displayed as war trophies. The eventual expansion of the Inca empire in the 15th century was met with fierce resistance, and sporadic fighting continued well after the initial conquest.

Environmentalists long before Greenpeace got into rubber dinghies, the Chachapoyas built structures that were in perfect harmony with their surroundings and that took advantage of nature's aesthetic and practical contributions. The Chachapoyas religion is believed to have venerated some of the salient natural features of these territories; the serpent, the condor and the puma were worshipped as powerful representatives of the natural world.

The unique use of circular construction was complemented by intricate masonry friezes, which used zigzags and rhomboids. The buildings were covered by thatch roofs, which were tall and steep to facilitate the run-off of the area's frequent rains. Hundreds of ruins illustrate Chachapoyas architecture, but none stand out as much as the impressive fortified city of Kuélap, surrounded by a colossal 20m-high wall and encompassing hundreds of dwellings and temples.

construction than for the Great Pyramid of Egypt. Though the stonework is not as elaborate as that of the Incas, the 700m-long oval fortress is surrounded by an imposing, near-impenetrable wall that towers 6m to 12m high. Entrance into this stronghold is via three deep, lean gates – an ingenious security system that forced attacking parties into easily defeated single files.

Inside are three levels scattered with the remnants of over 400 circular dwellings. Some are decorated with zigzag and rhomboid friezes, and all were once topped by soaring thatch roofs. One dwelling has been reconstructed by Canadian archaeologist Morgan Davis. In its heyday, Kuélap housed up to 3500 people and, surrounded by wispy cloud, must have been a breathtaking sight. The most impressive and enigmatic structure, named **El Tintero** (Inkpot), is in the shape of a large inverted cone. Inside, an underground chamber houses the remains of animal sacrifices, leading archaeologists to believe that it was a religious building of some kind. Recent evidence suggests it may have also been a solar calendar. Another building is a lookout tower with excellent 360-degree vistas. The mountain summit on which the whole city sits is surrounded by abundant greenery, towering bromeliad-covered trees and exotic orchids.

Tours & Guides

The guardians at Kuélap are very friendly and helpful; one is almost always on hand to show visitors around and answer questions. Don José Gabriel Portocarrero Chávez has been there for years; he can guide you and is a good source of information on this and other ruins in the area. Other local guides congregate at the car park under the ruins – tip accordingly.

Sleeping & Eating

There are limited sleeping options at Kuélap itself, though nearby towns provide a good range of accommodations and can be used as a base for exploring the area.

Hospedaje El Bebedero (r per person US$4) sits just beneath the Kuélap ruins and has very basic rooms without electricity or running water; bringing your own sleeping bag is recommended. There is also free camping at the nearby INC Hostel, which has rooms that are permanently occupied by the Kuélap excavation team. The caretaker of the ruins is happy

to cook up a basic dinner for you if you ask, and you can buy drinks and some snacks near the ticket office. Alternatively, for truly local fare, go to the second house down the road from the Kuélap car park; it has an unsigned home **kitchen** (meals US$0.60-1.20; 8am-4pm). Try the free-range *cuy* (you can hear them scampering around the kitchen) or egg soup with *motte* (corn dumplings).

The next closest sleeping choices are in the hamlet of María, two hours' walk from Kuélap and connected to Chachapoyas by daily minibuses. Here you will find a cottage industry of half a dozen charming and near-identical **hospedajes** (r per person US$3) – they all even go to the same sign-maker. All offer clean, modest rooms with electric hot water and will cook up hearty meals for guests for under US$2. Try Hospedaje el Torreon or Hospedaje Lirio. One hour further down the road from María, and 3km above the village of Choctámal, the pleasant **Choctámal Lodge** (r per person US$7.50) sits perched on a hillcrest with stunning 360-degree panoramas of the valley and Kuélap. There are seven comfy rooms here, all with some arty decorations and electric hot water. There's also an outdoor hot tub. Basic meals are available.

In Tingo (elevation 1900m), at the far base of Kuélap, there's the bare-bones **Albergue Léon** (r with shared bathroom per person US$3), with tiny, bucolic rooms and electric hot water. On the outskirts, the inviting **Valle Kuélap Hotel Inn** (041-81 3025, in Chachapoyas 041-47 8258; vallekuelap@hotmail.com; s/d US$9/18) is a great deal for furnished and comfortable duplex bungalows, all with smart decorations. You can get hot showers here and the restaurant has agreeable river views. **Estancia Chillo** (041-83 0108; www.estanciachillo.com; r per person incl meals US$35), 5km south of Tingo, is one of the nicest places to stay in the area. The beautiful hacienda-style compound has rustic and well-designed rooms, complete with ranch props, wagon wheels and brightly colored pet parrots wandering the grounds. All the fixtures you see were handmade by the owner Oscar Arce Cáceres. You can organize guides from here (US$12 per day) as well as horses or donkeys (US$7.50 per day) to go out and explore nearby ruins.

Getting There & Around

A 9.8km trail climbs from the south end of Tingo to the ruins, situated about 1200m above the town. There are some signposts on the way and the trail is not difficult to follow, but it is an exhausting, often hot climb; allow five to six hours. Remember to bring water as there is none available along the trail. During the rainy season (October to April), especially the latter half, the trail can become very muddy and travel can be difficult. You can hike to Kuélap from Choctámal Lodge in about three hours, and from María in about two hours.

Colectivo taxis to Kuélap (US$4.50, three hours) depart from Chachapoyas throughout the day. **Transportes Roller** (Grau 302) has buses to Kuélap (US$3.60, 3½ hours), via Tingo, Choctámal and María, leaving Chachapoyas at 4pm and returning from Kuélap at 6am and 8am the next morning. Alternatively, at Kuélap you can ask about getting a ride back to Chachapoyas with returning private colectivos or combis. There are frequent combis (US$1.80, 1½ hours) and colectivo taxis (US$2.40, 1½ hours) between Tingo and Chachapoyas. Tour agencies arrange day trips from Chachapoyas.

LEIMEBAMBA

pop 1100 / elev 2050m

This convivial cobblestoned town lies at the head of the Río Utcubamba. It has a delightfully laid-back allure that can only be maintained by its relative isolation – the nearest big city is many hours away by rough dirt roads. Horses outnumber people here two to one (watch out for droppings), and the friendliness of the townsfolk is legendary in the region. Surrounded by a multitude of archaeological sites from the Chachapoyas era, this is a great place to base yourself while exploring the province.

Information

Two phone offices and a police station are on the plaza.

Sights & Activities

In Leimebamba there is small **tourist center & museum**, open erratically on the main plaza. A new **tomb**, three day's walk south from Leimebamba, was discovered in 1999.

LAGUNA DE LOS CÓNDORES

This part of Peru hit the spotlight in 1996 when a group of farmers found six chullpas (ancient Andean burial towers) on a ledge 100m above a cloud-forest lake. This burial site was a windfall for archaeologists, and its 219 mummies and over 2000 artifacts have given researchers a glimpse past the heavy curtain of history that conceals the details of the Chachapoyas civilization. So spectacular was the find that a Discovery Channel film was made about it, and a museum was built in Leimebamba to house the mummies and cultural treasures.

Some of the tombs, plastered and painted in white or red-and-yellow ochre, are decorated with signature Chachapoyas zigzag friezes. All lie huddled against the cliff on a natural ledge overlooking the stunning Laguna de los Cóndores. Don't get too excited about spotting any of the wide-winged Andean wonders though – this lake was renamed after the find to make it more 'tourist friendly.'

The only way to get to the Laguna is by a strenuous 10- to 12-hour hike on foot and horseback from Leimebamba. The return journey takes three days; horses and guides can be arranged either in Leimebamba or at travel agencies in Chachapoyas.

LA CONGONA

The most captivating of the many ancient ruins strewn around Leimebamba, La Congona is definitely worth the three-hour hike needed to get here. The flora-covered site contains several well-preserved circular houses that, oddly for Chachapoyas culture, sit on square bases. Inside, the houses are adorned with intricate niches, and outside there are wide circular terraces surrounding each house. This archaeological site is renowned for the intricate decoration on the buildings, and particularly for the numerous sophisticated masonry friezes. A tall tower can be climbed by a remarkable set of curving steps for wide-angle panoramas of the surrounding valley. Based on the location of this site, it's believed that it may have been a military bunker.

The site is reached in three hours from Leimebamba along a path beginning at the lower end of 16 de Julio. A guide is recommended, expect to pay around US$7.50 to US$9.

MUSEO LEIMEBAMBA

The mummies found at Laguna de los Cóndores are now being studied in the **Museo Leimebamba** (www.centromallyui.org.pe; adult/student US$3/1.50; 10:30am-4:30pm Tue-Sun), located 3km south of town. The museum is in a wonderfully constructed complex with multi-tiered roofs, all generously funded by the Austrian Archaeological Society. Most of the mummies are wrapped in bundles and can be seen in glass cases; some have been unwrapped for your gruesome viewing pleasure. Well-presented artifacts on display include ceramics, textiles, wood figures and photos of Laguna de los Cóndores.

Tours & Guides

Local guides (inquire at the museums) will arrange trips to the tombs and various other sites; some are easily visited on a day trip, while others require several days. Homer Ullilen, the son of the owner of the **Albergue Turístico de la Laguna de los Cóndores** (Amazonas 320), can guide you to sites near their land. Expect to pay around US$7.50 to US$9 per day for a guide (not including food), and US$6 to US$7.50 for horses.

Sleeping & Eating

One of the better cheapies in town, **Hotel Escobedo** (16 de Julio 514; s/d with shared bathroom US$3/9) has rickety wooden rooms. **Albergue Turístico de la Laguna de los Cóndores** (Amazonas 320; s/d with shared bathroom US$3/9, s/d US$7.50/9), located half a block from the plaza, is a family-run affair that has a verdant courtyard and lots of comfortable sitting areas draped in thick, colorful blankets. There are hot showers, cozy rooms, and tours of the area can be arranged from here. Further along the same street, **La Casona** (☎ 83 0106; Amazonas 221. s/d US$6/12) has polished floors in its neat rooms and new bathrooms with electric hot water. Some rooms have little balconies looking onto the quiet, cobblestoned street below. There's also a small restaurant at La Casona.

On the plaza, **Restaurant Tushpa** (16 de Julio 624; menús US$0.90; ♥ 7am-10pm) does one of the better *menús* in town and has outdoor courtyard seating. The pick of the eateries in town, however, is **Cely's Pizza** (La Verdad 530; pizzas US$1.80-4.50; ♥ 6:30am-10:30pm), which does pizza (as promised), as well as a bunch of Peruvian dishes.

Shopping

AMAL (San Agustine 429; ♥ 9am-6pm) Located on the plaza, AMAL is a women's artisan cooperative selling top-grade handicrafts and local weavings.

Getting There & Away

Minibuses for Chachapoyas leave frightfully early at 3am and 5am (US$3, three to four hours) from in front of one of the telephone offices on the plaza; there's a sign. Reserve a seat the night before. A taxi to Chachapoyas costs US$25. The two weekly buses to Chachapoyas (US$3, four hours) from Celendín pass through at about 7pm on Sundays and Thursdays. In the reverse direction they pass at about 9am on Tuesdays and Fridays heading toward Celendín (US$6, eight to nine hours). There are occasional trucks and private vehicles to Chachapoyas and Celendín.

PEDRO RUÍZ

☎ 041 / elev 1400m

This dusty transit town sits at the junction of the Chiclayo–Tarapoto road and the turnoff to Chachapoyas. When traveling from Chachapoyas, you can board east- or west-bound buses here. The pick of the sorry hotels in Pedro Ruiz is the **Casablanca Hotel** (☎ 83 0135; s/d US$9/13.50), by the road junction, but try to get a room away from the noisy highway. Hostal Amazonense is cheaper, simpler and, more often than not, closed.

Buses from the coast pick up passengers heading to Rioja or Moyobamba (US$6 to US$7.50, five hours) and Tarapoto (US$7.50 to US$9, seven hours). Several come through daily, but they may be crowded. The road is paved to Tarapoto.

Buses bound for Chiclayo pass by mostly in the late afternoon and cost US$7.50 to US$10.50 (eight hours). If coming from Tarapoto, you'll find plenty of *colectivo* taxis for Chachapoyas (US$3.60, 1½ hours) leaving from the junction.

The journey east from Pedro Ruíz is spectacular, climbing over two high passes, traveling by a beautiful lagoon, and dropping into fantastic high-jungle vegetation in between.

MOYOBAMBA

☎ 042 / pop 46,300 / elev 860m

Moyobamba, the capital of the department of San Martín, was founded in 1542, but earthquakes (most recently in 1990 and 1991) have contributed to the demise of any historic buildings. Nevertheless, Moyobamba is a pleasant enough town to spend a few days in, and local tourist authorities are slowly drumming up sites of interest to visit.

Information

Alt@ntin Internet (A de Alvarado 863; per hr $0.90) Email your folks here.

BCP (☎ 56 2572; A de Alvarado 903) Changes money and has an ATM.

Dirección Regional de Industria y Turismo (☎ 56 2043; www.turismosanmartin.com; San Martín 301) Has limited tourism information.

Sights & Activities

Hot springs (admission US$0.30; ☺ 6am-8pm) with temperatures of around 40°C are 4km south of town (taxi US$1.20). On weekends they get crowded with locals, who know the waters are curative; travelers rarely make it here. The Cascadas Paccha and Lahuarpía are impressive **waterfalls**, each 30 minutes away by car. The region is famed for its orchids; there's an orchid festival held in October. A giant orchid statue guards the town's entrance. You can see these and other exotic plants in a giant geodesic-domed hothouse at the **Jardín Botánico San Francisco** (admission US$0.30; ☺ 8am-5pm). It's 2km from town, a US$1.20 *mototaxi* ride away.

The **Instituto Nacional de Cultura** (INC; ☎ 56 2281; Benavides 352; admission US$0.30; ☺ 9am-noon & 2-5pm Mon-Fri) is a small museum and has some information as well.

Tours & Guides

Tingana Magic (☎ 56 1436; www.tinganaperu.com; Reyes Guerra 422; ☺ 10am-6pm) can arrange tours around the area to waterfalls, diamond caves and ecological reserves. There's no sign outside.

Sleeping & Eating

Hospedaje Santa Rosa (☎ 80 9890; P Canga 478; s/d US$3.60/7.50) A great shoestringer pick with a few rudimentary, newly painted rooms set around a brick patio. The occasional potted plant helps liven up the concrete-jungle feel.

Hostal Royal (☎ 56 2662; A de Alvarado 784; s/d US$6/9) With cubby-sized rooms and friendly service, this cheap option also has a basic restaurant downstairs.

Atlanta Hotel (☎ 56 2063; A de Alvaro 865; s/d US$9/15) With a Motel 6–inspired setup around a tiled courtyard, this place has good, clean rooms with hot water and smiles all round

Country Club Hostal (☎ 56 2110; www.moyabamba .net/countryclub; M de Aguila 667; s/d US$7.50/10.50; ⚑) Spartan tiled rooms have hot showers and sit around a green lawn lined with scraggly bushes. There's a tiny pool, though it was empty when we last visited.

Hostal Marcoantonio (☎ 56 2045; www.altomay operu.com; P Canga 488; s/d US$19.50/32) This is the place to come for a touch of comfort in Moyobamba. The spotless rooms have the necessary mod cons, such as TV and hot water, but lack flair or any distinguishing features. The downstairs restaurant has room service and staff arrange local tours.

Hotel Puerto Mirador (☎ /fax 56 2050; pmirador hotel@terra.com.pe; Jirón Sucre; s/d US$34.50/46, bungalows incl breakfast US$58; ⚑) Located 1km northeast of town, this fine hotel has oodles of luxuriant lawn, a great pool and lots of sitting areas made from natural materials. There are relaxing views over the Río Mayo and a restaurant provides room service.

Chifa Shanghai (☎ 962 7436; A de Avaro; meals US$1.80-3.60) Packed nightly with more diners than you can poke a *wantan* (wonton) at, this is the place to go for a taste of the Middle Kingdom.

La Olla de Barro (☎ 56 3450; P Canga at S Filomeno; mains US$2.10-6; ☺ 8am-11pm) This local institution is set up like a tiki lounge, complete with faux flames licking around a 'bubbling' pot, lots of bamboo and jungle knickknacks. This is the best place in town to sample local jungle dishes – don't miss it.

Getting There & Away

Colectivos to Rioja (US$0.90, 30 minutes) and Tarapoto (US$6, two hours) leave frequently from the corner of Benavides and S Filomeno, three blocks east of the Plaza de Armas.

The bus terminal is on Grau, about 1km from the center. Most buses between Tarapoto and Chiclayo stop here to pick up passengers.

TARAPOTO

☎ 042 / pop 128,500 / elev 356m

Tarapoto straddles the base of the Andean foothills and the edge of the vast jungles of eastern Peru. A sweltering rainforest metropolis, it dips its toe into the Amazon Basin while managing to cling to the rest of Peru by the umbilical cord of a long paved road back to civilization. From here you can take the plunge deeper into the Amazon, or just enjoy the easily accessible jungle lite, with plenty of places to stay and eat, and reliable connections to the coast. There's a bunch of natural sights to explore nearby, from waterfalls to lagoons, and river-running opportunities will entertain the adventure-seeking contingent.

The largest and busiest town in the department of San Martín, Tarapoto's recent growth can be accounted for by coca-growing enterprises in the middle and upper Río Huallaga valley to the south. Tourists don't usually encounter problems and the situation has been improving since the peace agreement with Sendero Luminoso (Shining Path) guerillas. The exception is the Saposoa region; the trip through there to Tingo María is not recommended. The route from Moyobamba through Tarapoto and on to Yurimaguas is safe, but be sure to check the latest conditions.

Information

Internet cafés hide around every corner.

Banco Continental (☎ 52 3228; R Hurtado 149)

BCP (☎ 52 2682; Maynas 130) Cashes traveler's checks and has an ATM.

Clínica San Martín (☎ 52 3680, 52 7860; San Martín 274; ☼ 24hr) The best medical care in town.

DirSetur (Ministerio de Cultura; ☎ 52 2567; Angel Delgado; ☼ 8am-1pm & 2-5pm Mon-Fri) Has a couple of brochures on the area and a list of hotels and travel agents. The office is a US$0.50 *mototaxi* ride west of town.

Interbank (☎ 89 5092; Grau 119)

Lavanderia Tintoreria (☎ 52 6263; Manco Cápac; per kg US$1.50; ☼ 8am-9pm) This is the place to restock your clean underwear pile.

Post office (☎ 50 3450; San Martín 482; ☼ 9am-7pm Mon-Fri, 9am-1pm Sat) Tarapoto's main post office.

Puerto Net (cnr R Hurtado & Bolognesi; per hr US$0.60; ☼ 8am-midnight) Has new computers with big screens.

Quiquiriqui Tours (☎ 52 4016; www.quiquiriquitours .com; Pimentel 309; ☼ 8am-7pm Mon-Fri, 8am-6pm Sat, 9am-noon Sun) A full-service travel and tour agency that can directly book flights, offer information on the area and arrange tours to most of the district's attractions.

Turismo Selva (☎ 52 7419; San Pablo de la Cruz 233; ☼ 8am-6pm Mon-Sat, 9am-noon Sun) Smiley staff here can book numerous local tours and flights.

Sights & Activities

There is not much to see or do in Tarapoto itself, apart from just hanging out in the town's Plaza de Armas (also called the Plaza Mayor) or visiting the tiny **Museo Regional** (Maynas 174; admission US$0.30; ☼ 8am-noon & 12:30-8pm Mon-Fri), but you can make several excursions to nearby sights. The land around Tarapoto is rugged, and waterfalls and lakes are abundant.

TARAPOTO

0 ———— 300 m
0 ———— 0.2 miles

INFORMATION	
Banco Continental	1 C2
BCP	2 C2
Clínica San Martín	3 C2
Interbank	4 C2
Lavanderia Tintoreria	5 D2
Post Office	6 B1
Puerto Net	7 D1
Quiquiriqui Tours	8 B3
Turismo Selva	9 D2

SIGHTS & ACTIVITIES	
Los Chancas Expeditions	10 D3
Museo Regional	11 C2

SLEEPING	
Alojamiento Arevalo	12 D2
Alojamiento Grau	13 C1
Alojamiento July	14 C1
El Paso Texas II	15 C2
Hospedaje Misti	16 C1
Hostal Luna Azul	(see 5)
Hostal Pasquelandia	17 C3
Hostal San Antonio	18 C2
Hotel Lily	19 B3
Hotel Monte Azul	20 C1
Hotel Nilas	21 D2
La Patarascha	22 D2
La Posada Inn	23 C2

EATING	
Banana's Burgers	24 C2
Café d' Mundo	25 C2
Chifa Tai Pai	26 D2
El Brassero	27 D2
El Rincón Sureño	28 B1
La Patarascha	(see 22)
Real Grill	29 C2
Supermercado la Inmaculada	30 C2

DRINKING	
La Alternativa	31 C1
Stonewasi Taberna	32 D2

TRANSPORT	
LAN	33 C2
Star Peru	34 C2

To DirSetur (2km); Hostal la Cumbre (2.8km)

To Bus Terminals (2.5km); Morales district (3km); Papillón (3km)

To Motos Ride (50m)

To Airport (3km); Lamas (20km); Chazuta

To La Collpa (50m)

To Takiwasi Centre (1.5km)

To El Mirador (150m)

Plaza de Armas

To Banda de Shilcayo district (500m); Hotel Río Shilcayo (2km); Puerto Palmeras (6km)

Mercado

NORTHERN HIGHLANDS

Lamas is an indigenous highland village with a sprinkling of colonial buildings and is a standard tour destination. The large indigenous population here has an annual **Feast of Santa Rosa de Lima** in the last week of August. Although minibuses (US$2.40, 45 minutes) and *colectivos* go to Lamas, it's easiest to visit with a guided tour (US$10 to US$16 per person, four to six hours), which usually includes a visit to Ahuashiyacu waterfalls. There is a small museum and some crafts on offer.

The town of **Chazuta** is growing as another popular destination. A two-hour drive away, it boasts the impressive **Tununtunumba** waterfalls, another small museum showcasing pre-Inca funerary urns, artisanal crafts and a port on the Río Huallaga with great fishing. Agencies in Tarapoto are starting to promote 'mystical tourism,' where trips include a visit to local *brujos* (witch doctors). Really the only way to get to Chazuta is on a day tour (US$27) or by private transport.

Several lakes lie tucked away in the surrounding mountains. **Laguna Azul** (also called Laguna de Sauce) is a popular local spot reached by crossing the Río Huallaga, 45km away, on a vehicle raft ferry and continuing by car for another 45 minutes. Day tours (US$21 to US$25.50 per person, minimum three people) and overnight excursions are available. There is good swimming, boating and fishing here, and accommodations, ranging from camping to upscale bungalows, are available. Several *combis* a day go to nearby Sauce (US$4.50, four hours) from a bus stop in the Banda de Shilcayo district, east of the town. Taxi drivers know it. Meanwhile, **Laguna Venecia** and the nearby **Cataratas de Ahuashiyacu** are about 45 minutes toward Yurimaguas. There's a small restaurant nearby and a locally favored swimming spot. Five-hour tours cost US$15 per person. Also popular is a similarly priced trip to the **Cataratas de Huacamaillo**, which involves two hours of hiking, and wading across the river several times. These places can be reached by public transport and then on foot, but go with a guide or get detailed information to avoid getting lost.

River running (white-water rafting) on the Río Mayo, 30km from Tarapoto, and on the lower Río Huallaga is offered from June to November. The shorter trips (half- and full-day trips, from US$21 per person) are mainly class II and III white water, while longer trips (up to six days, from July to October only)

ride out class III and class IV rapids. Rafting trips to the class III rapids of the upper Mayo, 100km from Tarapoto, are possible. Inflatable kayaks are available for rent for US$15/25 for a half/full day. Check with **Los Chancas Expeditions** (☎ 52 2616; www.geocities.com/amazonrainforest; Rioja 357), the local river-running specialists.

Brujos play a pivotal role in the *pueblos* of the jungle. A few kilometers north of Tarapoto, you'll find the **Takiwasi Center** (☎ 52 2818; www.takiwasi.com; Prologación Alerta 466). Started in the early 1990s by French physician Jacques Mabit, this rehabilitation and detox center combines traditional Amazonian medicines and plants, as used by *brujos* or *curanderos* (healers), with a combination of psychotherapy. This treatment is not for the fainthearted; intense 'vomit therapy' and *ayahuasca* (hallucinogenic brew made from jungle vines) are used as part of the healing process. Rehabilitation programs run for nine months and cost around US$500, though no one is turned away for lack of funds. Information and introductory sessions can be organized.

Festivals & Events
Patronato de Tarapoto A festival in mid-July that celebrates the town's indigenous heritage.
Aniversario de Tarapoto The anniversary of the town (August 20) is the city's biggest fiesta, with music, dancing and frivolities in the streets. *Uvachado*, made by steeping macerated grapes in cane liquor, keeps the party fueled. The fiesta lasts for an entire week around the anniversary.

Sleeping
BUDGET
Hostal Pasquelandia (☎ 52 2290; Pimentel 341; s/d shared bathroom US$2.40/3.60) It's a dirt-cheap, beat-up, wooden affair with cold water.

El Paso Texas II (☎ 52 3799; AA de Morey 115; s/d US$6/7.50) Don't ask us where Paso Texas I is. All we know is this place has basic digs with private bathrooms and a few cheesy paintings livening things up. The front rooms are noisy, while the rear rooms are a little dark.

Alojamiento Grau (☎ 52 3777; Grau 243; s/d US$6/9) Family run and friendly, this place has quiet, clean, elementary rooms, all with exposed brick walls and windows to the inside. A very solid budget option.

Hospedaje Misti (☎ 52 2439; L Prado 341; s/d US$6/9) The typically modest rooms here are redeemed by the skinny, leafy courtyard and a laid-back café. Tiny bathrooms with cold water leave little maneuvering room, but you get a TV and ceiling fan – good shoestring value. There are discounts for groups and monthly rentals.

Hostal San Antonio (☎ 52 5563, ☎ /fax 52 2226; Pimentel 126; s/d US$7.50/10.50) A great, laid-back, budget-focused deal right in town, with a quiet courtyard filled with greenery. Helpful staff and good, clean standard rooms with hot showers, fans and cable TVs round off the facilities nicely.

Alojamiento July (☎ 52 2087; AA de Morey 205; s/d US$7.50/10.50) Cheerfully painted rooms with electric shower, cable TV, minifridge and fan are OK for the price. Every wall here is covered with jungle murals, endless rows of beads and knickknacks clank in the hallways, and the whole place is run by a gregarious Imelda Marcos type. There's a nice 2nd-floor patio.

La Patarashca (☎ 52 3899, 52 7554; www.lapatarashca .com; Lamas 261; s/d incl breakfast US$10.50/18) Don't miss this little gem of a *hospedaje*. Tucked away between a couple of restaurants, all the rooms have cold-water showers and cable TVs, and nice bits of furniture and crafty lamps to make them feel homely and welcoming. There's a green lounging area under a giant thatch roof, hammocks, couches and some English-speaking staff. Look out for the bilingual talking parrots, which, while cute initially, can be a little annoying at 6am. Best of all, you can get room service at a discount from the identically named restaurant next door.

El Mirador (☎ 52 2177; San Pedro de la Cruz 517; s/d US$13.50/18) This spick-and-span hotel has 13 rooms, all with big fans and great mattresses. Some of the rooms have hot showers, and doors have linen curtains that can be left open for a cool breeze (but little privacy). Being a few blocks away from the center cuts down most of the *mototaxi* noise. You can take breakfast on the rooftop terrace with views of the city one way and treetops the other.

Alojamiento Arevalo (☎ 52 5265, 52 7467; Moyobamba 223; s/d US$9/13.50) The best thing about this quiet hotel is the large rooms – there's space enough to swing a couple of cats. Each has a cold shower, cable TV, fan and minifridge. A large public area with tables adjoins a lush courtyard.

Hostal Luna Azul (☎ 52 5787, lunaazulhotel@hotmail .com; Manco Cápac 262; s/d US$15/21, s/d with air-con US$18/24; 🌡 💻) So clinically clean you could eat off the floors, the Luna Azul is a modern hotel with comfortable, small rooms, some with air-con. Hot water, direct-dial phones,

grinning staff and cable TV put this close to the midrange class. It has a snack bar.

Hotel Monte Azul (☎ 52 2443, 52 3145; http://webs .amarillastelefonica.com/hotelmonteazul; C Morey 156; s/d US$13.50/24, s/d with air-con US$13.50/27; 🌡) Adorned with some nice flopping areas, it's cozy, orderly and bright, and at this price is pretty good bang for your buck. The staff are always switched on and friendly, and the rooms all have quality mattresses, direct-dial phones and minifridges.

Hostal la Cumbre (☎ 52 9987; Circunvalación 2040; s/d incl breakfast US$18/24) This friendly family-run affair, 3km (a US$0.50 *mototaxi* ride) northwest of town, gets good reviews from readers. It's in a modern building, and good-sized rooms come with TV and minifridges. There is a garden area to relax in and great views of the surrounding misty mountains. The best thing is the Amazonian breakfasts.

MIDRANGE

All hotels in this range have cable TV and hot water.

La Posada Inn (☎ 52 5557, 52 2234; laposadainn@ latinmail.com; San Martín 146; s/d incl breakfast US$21/30; 🌡) This quaint boutique hotel has beamed ceilings, traditional ironwork and a sweeping wooden staircase, as well as pretty rooms with today's necessities thrown in. The classy rooms are an eclectic mix: some have balconies, some have air-con and some have electric showers. Even though it's right in the town center, La Posada manages to remain quiet. Call for airport transfers.

Hotel Lily (☎ 52 3154; Pimentel 407; s/d incl breakfast US$33/45; 🌡 💻) Unpretentious but secure and restful, this business-oriented hotel features a sauna and a breakfast room by the pool. Rooms are spacious, with writing desks, minifridges, phones and vivid colors (think blue carpet and lime green blankets). Streetside rooms have balconies but can be noisy.

Hotel Nilas (☎ 52 7331/2; nilas-tpto@terra.com.pe; Moyobamba 173; s/d US$39/54; 🌡 💻 💻) A canary yellow hotel like this would not be out of place swaying over a Miami beach – and the palm-fringed 3rd-floor pool rounds off the illusion nicely. The good-sized rooms have the all the necessary mod cons, and you'll find a gym, restaurant and conference center tucked away among the maze of cheery floors.

Hotel Río Shilcayo (☎ 52 2225, ☎ /fax 52 4236; www.rioshilcayo.com; Pasaje La Flores 224; s/d/bungalows incl breakfast US$45/55/65; 🌡 💻) Almost 2km east of town, this hotel is quiet and cool, and has a sauna, good restaurant, bar, and rooms with good amenities – and a tropical bird enclosure thrown in for good measure. Rates include airport transfer.

TOP END

Puerto Palmeras (☎ 52 3978, 52 4100; www.puerto palmeras.com; Presidente FB Terry Km 614; s/d US$47/87, ste US$117-153; ✕ ☒ ☒) This resort, 6km east of town, has the whole kit and caboodle. Set on sprawling green grounds, the decked-out rooms are spread out in hacienda-style complexes constructed with white adobe walls and decorated with loads of attractive pieces of art. The resort grounds have a large fishing pond, a beautiful pool, artfully decorated restaurant and sitting areas, billiard tables, horses, a fleet of 4WDs for hire and more. It's a US$1.20 taxi ride from town, or you can call for a pickup.

Eating

Banana's Burgers (☎ 52 3260; AA de Morey 102; US$1-2; ☾ 24hr) A good burger joint, this place is always open, and there's a bar on the 2nd floor.

Chifa Tai Pai (☎ 52 4393; L Prado 250; meals US$2.40-6; ☾ 12-3pm & 6-11pm) Modern and shiny, this *chifa* (Chinese restaurant) serves up good Chinese fare to eager locals and families.

Real Grill (☎ 52 2183; Moyobamba 131; mains US$2.40-9; ☾ 8am-midnight) An institution right on the Plaza de Armas, this place has (noisy) outdoor tables and serves pastas, Chinese meals, local dishes, meat, seafood, burgers and so on. The food is middle of the road.

Café d' Mundo (☎ 50 3223; AA de Morey 157; meals US$3-7; ☾ 7pm-midnight) A funky establishment illuminated nightly by moody candlelight, this hip restaurant and bar has outdoor seating and snug indoor lounges. Good pizzas, pastas and other tidbits are on the small menu, and a full bar will help you pass the rest of the evening away comfortably. The continually roaring *mototaxis* tend to detract from the mood a little, however.

El Brassero (☎ 52 2700; Lamas 231; mains US$3-6.50; ☾ noon-late) Carnivores congregate at this great grill. Choose your cut; pork ribs are the specialty, funky acid-jazz tunes are a bonus. The owners love to chat – they only close when the coals die down and people leave.

La Patarashca (☎ 52 3899; Lamas 261; mains US$3-7.50; ☾ 8am-11pm) Regional Amazon cuisine is

featured here, as well as standard chicken, fish and meat dishes. The 2nd floor, with street views and tropical ambience, is popular on weekends. See and be seen.

La Collpa (☎ 52 2644; Circunvalación 164; mains US$4.20-7.50; ☾ 10am-11pm) For a meal where you can practically taste the jungle air, this stilt restaurant, with a bamboo balcony over a river and a patch of rainforest, is the place to go for an ecomeal. The menu tries to offer up everything imaginable, from ceviche (raw seafood marinated in lime juice) to typical jungle food to grills to Chinese food to pastas. It's best to come for lunch to appreciate the views, though candlelit dinners are also a treat.

El Rincón Sureño (☎ 52 2785; Leguia 458; meals US$4.50-7.50; ☾ noon-11pm) One of the best grills in town, this owish-looking establishment has intimate wood-lined rooms as well as a bustling outdoor seating area. The grilled meats here are delicious and El Rincón Sureño boasts what must be one of the largest wine collections in all of South America.

Supermercado la Inmaculada (☎ 52 7598; M de Compagnon 126; ☾ 8:30am-10pm) This supermarket has everything you might need for self-catering.

Drinking

Stonewasi Taberna (☎ 52 4681; Lamas 222; ☾ 6pm-late) This is the place to see and be seen in Tarapoto. The whole intersection of Lamas and La Cruz transforms each evening into a cruising scene, with several good people-watching restaurants and bars. Stonewasi is the pick of the bunch and lays out streetside tables where punters and *mototaxi* drivers throng nightly to the sound of international rock and house music. Check out the path leading to one of the entryways – it's made entirely of conch-shell fossils.

La Alternativa (☎ 52 7898; Grau 401; ☾ 9am-8pm) This 'alternative' hole-in-the-wall bar is more like a medieval pharmacy than a bar – shelves are stacked with dusty bottles containing *uvachado* and various homemade natural concoctions based on soaking roots, lianas etc in cane liquor. All the potent Amazonian tonics and brews are for the tasting – but not for the faint-hearted.

Entertainment

Papillón (☎ 52 2574; Peru 209; admission US$3; ☾ evening Fri & Sat) This nightclub has live salsa bands or DJ-fuelled dancing. Popular with young locals and travelers, it's in the Morales district, by the

Río Cumbaza about 3km west of the center. *Mototaxis* go out there for under US$1.

Getting There & Away

AIR

The **airport** (code TTP; ☎ 52 2278) is 3km southwest of the center. Airport departure tax is US$3.57.

Star Perú (☎ 52 8765; San Pablo de la Cruz 100) has daily flights from Lima to Tarapoto (US$98) at 1:30pm, returning at 3pm This airline was also planning to set up regular flights to Iquitos ($68) at the time of writing. **LAN** (☎ 52 9318; R Hurtado 184) also has a daily flight from Lima (US$111) at 8:10pm, returning to Lima at 10pm. None of the *avionettas* (small airline companies – often just one guy with a four-seater plane) that once plied chartered routes between the smaller airports of the region have offices in Tarapoto anymore – the declining drug trade has eliminated much of the demand for private chartered flights (who would have thought!). Things are continually changing, however, and you can try your luck at the airport or ask at one of the tour agencies in town to see if any scheduled flights are expected.

BUS & TAXI

Several companies head west on the paved road to Lima (24 to 28 hours) via Moyobamba (two hours), Chiclayo (14 to 16 hours) and Trujillo (18 to 20 hours), generally leaving between 8am and 4pm. All these companies can be found along the same block of Salaverry in the Morales district, a US$0.60 *mototaxi* ride from the town center. If you're heading to Chachapoyas, you'll need to change in Pedro Ruíz (seven hours).

Cial (☎ 52 7629; Salaverry) Has a noon express bus to Lima (US$33) and a 4:30pm Chiclayo bus (US$15).

Civa (☎ 52 2269; Salaverry) Has a comfortable 2pm bus to Lima (US$33) stopping at Chiclayo (US$15) and Trujillo (US$24). Also has a 6pm bus to Chiclayo.

Ejetur (☎ 52 6827; Salaverry) Has a bus to Lima (US$24) at 11:15am via Chiclayo (US$13.50) and Trujillo (US$16.50). Also has direct Trujillo buses at 7:30am, 8:30am and 1:30pm. A bus leaves for San Ignacio (US$12, 18 hours) at 7:30am for the alternative Ecuador border crossing (see p434).

Expreso Huamanga (☎ 52 7272; Salaverry) Slower buses to Chiclayo (US$12, 16 hours) via Jaén (US$9, nine hours) at 8:30am, Chiclayo direct at 11:30am (US$12), Lima at 2:30pm (US$24) and Yurimaguas at 8am (US$3.60, six to eight hours).

Movil Tours (☎ 52 9193; Salaverry) Top-end express buses to Lima (US$36, 24 hours) leave at 8am and 1pm, with a 3pm departure to Trujillo (US$22.50) and a 4pm bus to Chiclayo (US$19.50).

Paredes Estrella (☎ 52 1202; Salaverry) Has a cheaper 11am service to Lima (US$24) stopping at Chiclayo (US$12) and Trujillo (US$15), as well as a 2:30pm bus to Trujillo, a 3pm bus to Chiclayo and a 7am bus to Yurimaguas (US$3, six to eight hours).

Sol Peruano (☎ 52 3232; Salaverry) On the opposite side of the road from the other companies, Sol Peruano has a comfortable bus to Lima (US$27) at 1pm via Chiclayo (US$15) and Trujillo (US$18). There is also a 2:30pm bus to Piura (US$15, 18 hours).

Turismo Tarapoto (☎ 52 5240; Salaverry) A cheaper 3pm bus to Trujillo (US$13.50) via Chiclayo (US$15) as well as an 11am bus to Piura (US$15, 18 hours).

Minibuses, trucks and *colectivo* taxis for Yurimaguas (US$4.50 to US$7.50) leave when full from the *mercado* (market) in the eastern suburb of Banda de Shilcayo and take five to six hours in the dry season, more in the wet. The unpaved road is in terrible shape, though it's one of the most beautiful drives in the area. The 130km road climbs over the final foothills of the Andes and emerges on the Amazonian plains.

Colectivo taxis to Moyobamba (US$3.60) leave when full from Salaverry in the Morales district. Minibuses to Lamas (US$2.40, 45 minutes) can also be found along this road.

The southbound journey via Bellavista to Juanjuí (145km) and on to Tocache Nuevo and Tingo María (485km), though safer than it once was, is still dangerous and not recommended because of drug-running and problems with bandits. If you go, avoid traveling at night, and see if any flights are available. Bellavista, Juanjuí and Tocache Nuevo all have basic hotels. Tingo María is safe enough.

Getting Around

Mototaxis cruise the streets like circling sharks. A short ride in town is around US$0.30, to the bus stations US$0.60, and to the airport US$0.90. A great way to see the region is to rent your own motorbike and go off and explore. **Motos Ride** (☎ 53 1314; Alfonso Ugarte 424) rents 110cc scooters (US$1.80/US$18 per hour/day), and 125cc off-road bikes (US$3/US$30 per hour/day). Assuming you can handle the road conditions (eg nonexistent road rules), you can visit many of the sights mentioned earlier. Wear a helmet.

Amazon Basin

When you step out of an air-conditioned plane and a blast of hot, muggy tropical air hits your face, you will know immediately that you have arrived in the Peruvian Amazon Basin. This at least is what most travelers experience when they come to the Amazonas – as it is known in Spanish – for few roads and just a few rivers connect this vast tract of jungle territory with the rest of Peru.

The Amazonas comprises approximately 50% of the nation yet only 5% of Peruvians live here. It is nonetheless a fast-growing tourist destination. Judicious protection of the Peruvian jungle has meant that the biosphere of the eastern flank of the Andes preserves some of the most diverse fauna and flora reserves in the whole world. Unlike neighboring Brazil, where ecotourism is almost a dirty word, Peru has managed to look after its natural heritage for future generations.

Divided into three primary areas, the Peruvian Amazonas offers a mixture of river life, jungle trekking, birding and animal-spotting, coupled with a dash of raucous city living when the need arises. There are only three towns of any size: one, Pucallpa, is reachable by a paved road, another, Puerto Maldonado, by a rough dirt track and the third, Iquitos, is not even connected to the rest of Peru by road.

The Peruvian Amazonas is a vivid, bright, exotic and challenging frontier zone. It deserves your time and attention.

HIGHLIGHTS

- Visiting the Ashaninka people from **Puerto Bermúdez** (p473)
- Spotting Amazonian animals and birds at **Manu** (p465), **Pacaya-Samiria** (p482) and the **upper Río Tambopata** (p462)
- Swinging in a hammock on a riverboat heading to/from **Iquitos** (p493) along the Amazon
- Buying Shipibo ceramics and cloth near **Yarinacocha** (p478)

- BIGGEST CITY: IQUITOS, POPULATION 430,000
- AVERAGE TEMPERATURE: JANUARY 22°C TO 32°C, JULY 21°C TO 30°C

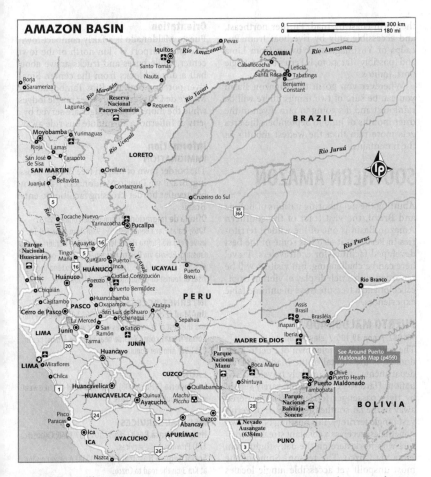

AMAZON BASIN

Geography & Climate

A number of jungle areas of Peru are accessible to the traveler. In the southeast, near the Bolivian border, there's Puerto Maldonado, a port at the junction of the Ríos Tambopata and Madre de Dios. Puerto Maldonado is most easily reached by air (particularly from Cuzco) or by an atrociously bad dirt road (an uncomfortable two- or three-day journey by truck). South of Puerto Maldonado are numerous lodges and campsites in the Reserva Nacional Tambopata and in the Parque Nacional Bahuaja-Sonene.

North of Cuzco, and fairly easily accessible from there, is Parque Nacional Manu, one of the best areas of protected rainforest in the Amazon.

In central Peru, east of Lima, is the area known as Chanchamayo, which consists of the two small towns of San Ramón and La Merced, both easily accessible by road from Lima, and several nearby villages including Puerto Bermúdez and Oxapampa. From La Merced a paved road continues to the boomtown of Satipo, a major coffee-growing area.

A very rough jungle road goes north from La Merced, and past Puerto Bermúdez, to the important river port of Pucallpa, the capital of the department of Ucayali. Most travelers going to Pucallpa, however, take the better roads from Lima via Huánuco and Tingo María, or fly.

Further north, in the department of Loreto, is the small port of Yurimaguas, reached from the north coast by road. Further northeast, and accessible only by riverboat from Pucallpa or Yurimaguas, or by air from Lima and (possibly) Tarapoto, is Peru's major jungle port, Iquitos.

Wherever you go in the Amazon Basin you can be sure of two things: there will be rainforest and it's going to rain. Even in the drier months of June to September, the area gets more rain than the wettest months in the mountains.

SOUTHERN AMAZON

Abutting the neighboring nations of Bolivia and Brazil, the vast tract of the southern Amazon Basin is one of the wildest territories in Peru, yet it also has some of the best developed facilities for ecotravelers. Travel here can be challenging, but visitors will be rewarded with a rich display of vibrant tropical color and a treasure trove of unforgettable experiences.

PUERTO MALDONADO

☎ 082 / pop 39,100 / elev 250m

The ramshackle jungle town of Puerto Maldonado is the capital of the Madre de Dios department – and an unlikely traveler destination. Hard to get to by land, rarely served by river passenger ferries and sequestered away in the far southeastern sector of Peru's vast jungle territory, this bustling boomtown nonetheless receives a constant stream of visitors who flock here on the daily flight from Lima via Cuzco. The reason? Some of the most unspoilt yet accessible jungle locales in the country, served by some excellent accommodation options for travelers who want just a touch of luxury. Puerto Maldonado gives the traveler the chance to see, feel and hear the Amazonian jungle like nowhere else in Peru.

The town itself has been important over the years for rubber, logging and even for gold and oil prospecting, and its role as a crossroads is about to take on even greater dimensions as the interoceanic highway linking the Atlantic Ocean with the Pacific Ocean via Brazil and Peru slowly takes shape. Few travelers stay long in Puerto Maldonado, though its languid, relaxing ambience certainly invites you to linger and there are enough distractions to keep you occupied for a day or two.

Orientation

Puerto Maldonado is a fairly compact town. The small airport is 7km north of the town center, while buses and trucks arrive about half a dozen blocks from the center. Small river ports on both the Ríos Tambopata and Madre de Dios serve the closer jungle lodges, while the more distant lodges are served by a jetty at Infierno, a 45-minute bus ride away.

Information

IMMIGRATION

The border town of Iñapari (see Border Crossing: Brazil via Puerto Maldonado, p456) now has regular border-crossing facilities to enter Brazil.

Oficina de migraciónes (immigration office; ☎ 57 1069; Ica at Plaza Bolognesi; 9am–1pm Mon–Fri) To leave Peru via Puerto Heath for Bolivia (see Border Crossing: Bolivia via Puerto Maldonado, p457), get your passport stamped here. Travelers can also extend their visas or tourist cards for the standard US$28 fee.

INTERNET ACCESS

UnAMad (2 de Mayo 287; per hr US$1.50) University run, and the best of several places downtown.

ZonaVirtual.com (Velarde near Plaza de Armas; per hr US$1.50) Another popular choice.

LAUNDRY

Lavandería (Velarde 898) Wash your mud-caked, sweat-soaked, repulsive jungle rags.

MEDICAL SERVICES

Hospital Santa Rosa (☎ 57 1019, 57 1046; Cajamarca 171) Provides basic services.

Social Seguro Hospital (☎ 57 1711) A newer option at Km 3 on the road to Cuzco.

MONEY

Brazilian reais and Bolivian bolivianos used to be hard to exchange here, though there is now a growing presence of Brazilian visitors since the opening of new bridge link at Iñapari, and Brazilian reais are becoming more acceptable.

Banco de la Nación (Plaza de Armas) Limited facilities but also has a Multired ATM that does not take all cards.

BCP (formerly Banco de Crédito; ☎ 57 1210; Plaza de Armas) Changes US cash or traveler's checks; has Visa ATM.

Casa de Cambio (Puno at G Prada) Has standard rates for US dollars.

POST

Post office (Velarde) Southwest of the Plaza de Armas.

PUERTO MALDONADO

0 ——————— 200 m
0 ——————— 0.1 miles

INFORMATION
Banco de la Nación.........................1 C2
BCP..2 C2
Casa de Cambio.............................3 B3
Inrena...4 C3
Lavandería.....................................5 B4
Ministerio de Industria y Turismo....6 A4
Post Office.....................................7 B3
UnAMad..8 C3
ZonaVirtual.com.............................9 C2

SLEEPING 🏠
Corto Maltes office........................10 D2
Estancio bello Horizonte Office....(see 28)
Hospedaje Principe.......................11 B3
Hospedaje Rey Port.......................12 C3
Hospedaje Royal Inn.....................13 B3
Hostal Cabaña Quinta....................14 B2

Hostal Cahuata.............................15 A4
Hostal El Solar..............................16 B3
Hostal Moderno............................17 C1
Inkaterra office.............................18 B2
Rainforest Expeditions office.........19 C3
Tambopata Jungle Lodge office.....20 C3
Wasai Lodge................................21 D2

To Social Seguro Hospital (3km);
Brombus (4km); ProNaturalezas
Butterfly Conservation Center
Japipi (6.5km); Airport (7km);
Cuzco (533km)

Río Madre de Dios

Municipalidad

Plaza de Armas

Río Tambopata

DRINKING 🍸
Anaconda Pub..............................31 C2
Coconut Pub.................................32 C2
Discoteca Witite............................33 C2

SHOPPING 🛍
Artesanía Shabuya.......................34 C2

Mercado
Modelo
To Oficina de
Migraciones (250m);
Obelisco (400m)

To Tambopata Language Centre (50m);
Hospital Santa Rosa (150m);
Hotel Don Carlos (250m)

EATING 🍴
Chifa Wa-Seng.............................22 C2
El Califa.......................................23 B2
El Tigre..24 A3
Frutos del Mar.............................25 B4
La Casa Nostra.............................26 C3
La Estrella....................................27 C3
Los Gustitos del Cura...................28 C2
Pizzería El Hornito/Chez Maggy....29 C2
Pollería Astoria............................30 B3

TRANSPORT
AeroCondor..................................35 C2
Agencia Moto...............................36 B3
Buses to Laberinto........................37 A4
Cars to Laberinto..........................38 A3
Colectivo taxi to Iñapari................39 A3
Empresa Transportes Imperial....(see 39)
LAN Peru.....................................40 C1
Madre de Dios Ferry Dock.............41 D2
River-Boat Hire.........................(see 41)
Trucks to Cuzco.........................(see 37)

TOURIST INFORMATION

Inrena (☎ 57 1604; Cuzco 135) The national park office gives information and collects entrance fees; currently US$8.50 if you stay on the north side of the Río Tambopata, but US$20 if you enter the south side.

Ministerio de Industria y Turismo (☎ 57 1413, 57 1164; Fitzcarrald 252; ⏲ 7am-3:30pm Mon-Fri) Has some tourist information; there is also an airport booth that provides limited information.

Sights & Activities

Although the strangely cosmic, blue **Obelisco** (Fitzcarrald & Madre de Dios; admission US$0.30, with use of elevator US$1; ⏲ 10am-4pm) was designed as a modern *mirador* (lookout tower), its 30m height unfortunately does not rise high enough above the city for viewers to glimpse the riv-

ers, though plenty of corrugated-metal roofs can be admired! The tower is often closed during rainstorms because water from the roof drains down the stairwells, making them impassable.

Just outside the airport gates you will find the **ProNaturalezas Butterfly Conservation Center Japipi** (☎ 01-264 2736; www.pronaturaleza.org; admission US$5), an impressive operation that was set up in 1996 with the initial aim of re-creating Peru's first commercial butterfly farm. It is has since morphed into the present nonprofit butterfly-conservation center and has a well-developed program for butterfly preservation, as well as gripping live exhibits of butterflies in their various forms of development.

The **Madre de Dios ferry** (per person US$0.15; ☽ dawn-dusk), at Puerto Capetania close to the Plaza de Armas, is a cheap way of seeing a little of this major Peruvian jungle river, which is about 500m wide at this point. The river traffic is colorfully ramshackle: *peki-pekis* (canoes powered by two-stroke motorcycle engines with outlandishly long propeller shafts) leave from the dock several times an hour, tracking at an almost impossible angle of 45 degrees to counter the strong flow of the river. Drivers heading for Brazil can ferry their vehicles across on wooden or metal catamarans to a rather desultory-looking ferry 'terminal' on the opposite side.

Courses

Tambopata Language Centre (☎/fax 57 3935; www .geocities.com/tambopata_language; Cajamarca 895; per week US$100-255) offers Spanish classes one-on-one or in small groups, and also family home-stays, cultural and jungle tours, and an English book exchange. Cajamarca is parallel to and southwest of Fitzcarrald.

Tours & Guides

Most visitors arrive with prearranged tours and stay at a jungle lodge – and in all fairness it really is the most convenient way to do it. You *can* arrange a tour when you arrive, either by going to the lodge offices where you might get a small discount on a tour that would cost more in Lima or Cuzco, or by looking for a guide. Beware of guides at the airport, who often take you to a 'recommended' hotel (and collect a commission) and then hound you throughout your stay. There are crooked operators out there – shop around, don't prepay for any tour and if paying an advance deposit, insist on a signed receipt. If you agree to a boat driver's price, make sure it includes the return trip.

There are about 30 guides with official licenses granted by the local Ministerio de Industria y Turismo. Unfortunately, many of the best ones work full time for one of the local jungle lodges. Still, having a licensed guide does give you some recourse in the unlikely event of a disastrous trip. In almost all cases boat rides are needed to get out of Puerto Maldonado, and boats use a lot of gas and are notoriously expensive to run. Guides charge from US$25 to US$60 per person per day depending on the destination and number of people, plus park fees.

The following are recommended:
Hernán Llavé (☎ 57 2243) Speaks some English. If he's not on a tour, you'll find him in the baggage reception area of the airport waiting for incoming flights.
Nadir Gnan (☎ 57 3833, 57 3860; nadirgnan@yahoo.es) Speaks English and Italian, and has firsthand expertise on mining activities.
Victor Yohamona Dumay (☎ 968 6279, 57 1742; victorguideperu@hotmail.com) A well-known guide who can be contacted through Hostal Cabaña Quinta (opposite).

Sleeping

The greater majority of hotels in Puerto Maldonado itself are of the budget variety – basic and strictly functional. The better midrange hotels are probably worth opting for if you want a decent start (or end) to your jungle adventure

BUDGET

Hostal Moderno (☎ 30 0043; Billinghurst 359; s/d/tr US$3.20/6.50/9) Despite the up-to-date name, this family-run place has been around for decades. Rooms are simple but clean and the owners invest in a new coat of paint every few years to keep this quiet budget choice presentable and popular. Meals are served on request.

Hostal Cahuata (☎ 57 2111; Fitzcarrald 517; s/d with shared bathroom US$3.20/6.50, s/d US$6.50/9.50) The marketside location won't give you much sleep during the day, but it quietens down at night. Rooms are small but neat, have fans and are good value for the price. Rooms with bathrooms even offer a TV.

Hostal El Solar (☎ 57 1634; G Prada 445; s/d with shared bathroom US$4.50/7.50, s/d US$7.50/10) The rooms are fairly basic but do have fans, and a TV is provided on request if you want to practice your Spanish.

Hospedaje Principe (☎ 57 2838; G Prada 355; s/d with shared bathroom US$4.50/7.50, s/d US$7.50/10.50) The rooms with bathroom also boast fans, which makes them more comfortable, though still quite basic. The owners offer discounts for groups and multinight stays, and a simple café and air-travel agency are on the premises.

Hospedaje Rey Port (☎ 57 1177; Velarde 457; s/d with shared shower US$6/9, s/d US$10/14) The rooms are clean and have fans, but aren't remarkable. The upper floors do have good views though, which is the hotel's best feature. Owners Dora and Boris reputedly provide excellent breakfasts and delicious sandwiches.

Iñapari Lodge (☎ 57 2575; fax 57 2155; r per person US$6) Five kilometers away from the center, near the airport, this rustic but pleasant and friendly *hostal* (guesthouse) has rooms with communal showers, plus a restaurant and bar. Inexpensive horseback, bicycle and other tours can be arranged.

Hospedaje Royal Inn (☎ 57 1048; 2 de Mayo 333; s/d US$7.50/10.50) Large, clean rooms with fans make this a good choice for travelers needing to spread out their gear. There are also cheaper rooms with shared bathrooms.

There's also Brombus (p456) for peaceful accommodations.

MIDRANGE

Hotel Don Carlos (☎ 57 1323, 57 1029; reservasmaldonado@hoteldoncarlos.com; León Velarde 1271; s/d incl breakfast US$30/35; ✿ ☑) The wood-paneled rooms here are reasonably sized and have hot showers, minifridge and TV. The location – about 1km southwest of the center – is quiet, and the Río Tambopata can be seen from the grounds. A little restaurant that opens on demand has an outdoor dining balcony and room service, and an airport transfer is included in the rates. The promotional lower rates are for walk-in guests or in the low season.

Hostal Cabaña Quinta (☎ 57 1045; fax 57 3336; perutoursytravel@hotmail.com; Cuzco 535; s/d standard US$16/25, superior US$31.50/41; ✿) This is the hotel of choice for folks wanting economical comfort in the town center. Standard rooms have cold showers, fans and TV; superior rooms boast air-con, minifridge and hot shower as well. A decent and moderately priced restaurant saves you walking into the town center, and the staff try to please. Room service is available.

Wasai Lodge (☎ 57 2290; www.wasai.com; Billinghurst at Arequipa; s/d US$36/48; ✿ ☑) This small lodge consists of comfortable wooden bungalows overlooking the Madre de Dios. A few rooms offer air-con for an extra US$10. However, minifridge, hot showers, cable TV and a river view are standard. The room lighting is pretty abysmal so bring a flashlight for good measure. There is, however, a good restaurant (mains US$5 to US$6), room service and bar. The lodge arranges one-day and overnight trips into the area.

Outside Puerto Maldonado are a dozen jungle lodges (see p458 and p462).

Eating

There are no fancy restaurants in Puerto Maldonado, just a selection of chicken shops, pizzerias and one or two down-to-earth but excellent-value places that serve up good Peruvian food. Regional specialties to look out for include *juanes* (rice steamed with fish or chicken in a banana leaf), *chilcano* (a broth of fish chunks flavored with the native cilantro herb) and *parrillada de la selva* (a barbecue of marinated meat, often game, in a Brazil-nut sauce). A *plátano* (plantain) is served boiled or fried as a side dish to many meals.

La Casa Nostra (☎ 57 2647; 2 de Mayo 287a; snacks & breakfast US$1-3; ✿ 7am-1pm & 5-11pm) This used to be the best café in town and served as a local hangout for guides; it has now moved to smaller premises and lost its hangout status. It still serves varied breakfasts, tamales, great juices, snacks, desserts and coffee.

Los Gustitos del Cur (☎ 57 3107; Velarde 474; meals US$2; ✿ 11am-10pm) For a sweet treat or the best ice cream in town, drop into this French-owned patisserie. Sandwiches, cakes and drinks are also dished up and if that wasn't enough there are local *objets d'arte* on sale too.

La Estrella (☎ 57 1058; Loreto 258; snacks US$2; ✿ 11am-10pm) This chicken restaurant looks like a US fast-food outlet and its clean, bright décor attracts locals happy to spend US$2 for a quarter-chicken, fries and chicken broth – the standard and most popular menu item. It's one of the best budget options in town.

Pollería Astoria (☎ 57 1422; Velarde 701; meals US$2) This is exactly the same yet precisely opposite to La Estrella. Same food, same price, same value, yet served in a neon-lit restaurant that has more of an Amazonian feel and an equally large local following. Your choice!

Frutos del Mar (☎ 57 2334; Moquegua 787; mains US$2-4) This reader-suggested *cevichería* (restaurant serving ceviche) is also a good choice. Praised for its excellent seafood and its cheap prices, the food is simple and unassuming, but is of a high quality.

El Califa (☎ 57 1119; Piura 266; mains US$2-5; ✿ 10am-4:30pm) This is a rustic place serving good regional specialties including heart of palm salad, *juanes*, fried *plátano* and game meat. It's sultry and a few blocks away from the center, but always attracts a following of daily diners who consider it the best lunch in town.

Pizzería El Hornito/Chez Maggy (☎ 57 2082; D Carrión 271; individual/family pizzas US$3.50/8.50; ✿ 6pm-late) This popular but dimly lit hangout on the Plaza de Armas serves pasta and wood-fired, ample-sized pizzas – the best in town. There's no lunches – the oven makes it too hot during the day!

AMAZON BASIN

El Tigre (☎ 57 2286; Tacna 456; mains average US$4; ☺ lunch only) Recommended for its ceviche (raw seafood marinated in lime juice), this place is popular in the morning and for lunch. Other local fish dishes are also offered.

Chifa Wa-Seng (Cuzco 244; mains US$4-6; ☺ noon-2pm Tue-Sun & 6-11pm daily) The Peruvian Amazon version of Chinese food is actually quite tasty, though somewhat different from the fare in Shanghai. Come with an open mind and mouth – portions are big.

Brombus (☎ 57 3230) Also consider this place, 4km out of Puerto Maldonado on the way to the airport. In a peaceful riverside setting that combines adobe walls and thatched roofs, Fernando Rosemberg and his wife serve local delicacies and international dishes. A few simple rooms are available for rent – call ahead.

Other good options include the satisfactory Hotel Cabaña Quinta (p455) restaurant, and the pricier, well-recommended Wasai Lodge (p455).

Drinking

A handful of nightclubs sputters into life late on weekend nights, usually with recorded and occasionally live music. Listen around for other possibilities.

Discoteca Witite (☎ 57 2419, 57 3861; Velarde 151) The best known.

Anaconda Pub (Loreto 228) On the Plaza de Armas.

Coconut Pub (Plaza de Armas; ☺ 9:30pm-late) At the southwest corner of the plaza.

La Choza del Candamo (☎ 57 2872; ☺ 7pm-late) Outside of town you might want to head to this relaxed *peña* (bar or club featuring live folkloric music) restaurant where you can sample various appetizers from all three regions of Peru – coast, mountain and jungle – and listen to the latest live musical offerings. You'll find it 4km along the airport road.

Shopping

Artesanía Shabuya (☎ 57 1854; Arequipa 279) For a good selection of honestly crafted artisanal wares, visit this place on the Plaza de Armas where local craftspeople have their wares on show and for sale.

Getting There & Away

Most travelers fly here from Lima or Cuzco. The long road or river trips are only for travelers prepared to put up with discomfort and delay. A new highway is slowly being established to link western Brazil with the Andes. When complete, road travel from Cuzco to Puerto Maldonado will be a viable option.

AIR

The airport is 7km out of town. Scheduled flights leave every day to and from Lima via Cuzco with **LAN Peru** (☎ 57 3677; Velarde 503) and **AeroCondor** (☎ 57 1733; Loreto 222). Schedules and airlines can change from one year to the next but numerous travel agents in the town center have the latest details. At the time of writing rates are US$112 one-way to/from Lima and US$84.50 one-way to/from Cuzco.

Light aircraft to anywhere can be chartered as long as you pay for five seats and the return trip. Ask at the airport.

BOAT

Hire boats at the Río Madre de Dios ferry dock for local excursions or to take you downriver to the Bolivian border. It's difficult to

---

BORDER CROSSING: BRAZIL VIA PUERTO MALDONADO

An unpaved but developing road goes from Puerto Maldonado to Iberia and on to Iñapari, on the Brazilian border. This is the future to-be-paved Interoceánica. Along the road are small settlements of people involved in the Brazil-nut industry, some cattle-ranching and logging. After 170km you reach **Iberia**, which has a couple of very basic hotels. The village of **Iñapari** is another 70km beyond Iberia.

Peruvian border formalities can be carried out in Iñapari. Stores around the main plaza will accept and change both Peruvian and Brazilian currency; if leaving Peru, it's best to get rid of your soles here. Small denominations of US cash are often negotiable. A block north of the plaza, **Hostal Milagritos** (☎ 57 4274; s/d US$8/16) has the best rooms. From Iñapari, you can cross to **Assis Brasil** in Brazil over the new road bridge. Assis has better hotels and rates start at around US$9 per person. US citizens need to get a Brazilian visa beforehand. From Brasiléia, it's a further 244km by paved road to the important Brazilian city of Rio Branco.

BORDER CROSSING: BOLIVIA VIA PUERTO MALDONADO

There are two ways of reaching Bolivia from the Puerto Maldonado area. One is to go to Brasiléia in Brazil (see opposite), and cross the Río Acre by ferry or bridge to **Cobija** in Bolivia, where there are hotels and an airstrip with erratically scheduled flights further into Bolivia. There is also a gravel road to the city of **Riberalta** (12 hours in the dry season).

Alternatively, hire a boat at Puerto Maldonado's Madre de Dios dock to take you to the Peru–Bolivia border at **Puerto Pardo** (Puerto Heath is on the Bolivian side, a few minutes away from Puerto Pardo by boat). The trip takes half a day and costs about US$100 – the boat will carry several people. With time and luck, you may also be able to find a cargo boat that's going there anyway and will take passengers more cheaply.

It's possible to continue down the river on the Bolivian side, but this can take days (even weeks) to arrange and isn't cheap. Travel in a group to share costs, and avoid the dry months of July to September (when the river is too low). From Puerto Heath, continue down the Río Madre de Dios as far as Riberalta (at the confluence of the Madre de Dios and Beni, far into northern Bolivia), where road and air connections can be made. Basic food and shelter (bring a hammock) can be found en route. When the water is high enough, a cargo and passenger boat plies from Puerto Maldonado to Riberalta and back about twice a month, but this trip is rarely done by foreigners.

The Peruvian and Bolivian border guards can stamp you out of and into their respective countries. Visas are not available, however, so get one ahead of time if you need it. Formalities are generally slow and relaxed.

---

find boats up the Madre de Dios (against the current) to Manu. Cuzco is a better place than Puerto Maldonado from which to reach Manu. Occasionally, people reach Puerto Maldonado by boat from Manu (with the current) or from the Bolivian border (against the current), but transportation is infrequent. Be prepared for waits of several days.

At the Tambopata dock, several kilometers south of town and reached by *motocarros* (three-wheeled motorcycle rickshaw), there are public boats up the Tambopata as far as the community of Baltimore. The *Tiburon* leaves twice a week (currently Monday and Thursday, but subject to change) and can drop you off at any of the lodges between Puerto Maldonado and Baltimore. The fare is US$5 or less, depending on how far you go. All passengers must stop at La Torre Puesto de Control (checkpoint) where passports and Inrena permits (US$8.50) are needed. (See p453, for more details on Inrena permits.)

When transporting visitors upriver, some Río Tambopata lodges avoid the first two hours of river travel by taking the bumpy dirt road to the indigenous community of Infierno, almost an hour away, and continuing by boat from there. Going to Infierno needs to be arranged ahead of time because there is nowhere to stay there and no boats await passengers.

BUS & TAXI

Trucks, minibuses and *colectivo* (shared) taxis leave Puerto Maldonado for Laberinto (US$2, 1½ hours), passing the turnoff to Baltimore at Km 37 on the road to Cuzco. They leave frequently during the morning and less often in the afternoon from the corner of Ica and E Rivero. *Colectivo* taxis to Iñapari (US$8, four hours), near the international borders with Brazil and Bolivia, leave from **Empresa Transportes Imperial** (☎ 57 4274; Ica cuadra 5) when they have four passengers. Some other companies on the same block also advertise this trip.

Although it's only about 500km, the road to Cuzco is so rough that the journey by truck can take 60 hours or more, depending on weather conditions (see p283). During the rainy season, the journey can take days longer. That said, plans are well underway to upgrade the road as it will necessarily become part of the Interoceánica link previously mentioned. Until then this option is for the severely travel-struck or highly budget-minded. It is an incredibly scenic drive and in the future will undoubtedly become a great and much easier journey. During the highland dry season, trucks to Cuzco leave from the Mercado Modelo on E Rivero, or from outside the public swimming pool, which is located two blocks south of the *mercado* (market) on the same street.

AMAZON BASIN

Getting Around

Motocarros take two or three passengers (and light luggage) to the airport for US$2. Short rides around town cost under US$1. There are also *mototaxi* Honda 90s that will take one passenger around town for about US$0.25.

You can rent motorcycles if you want to see some of the surrounding countryside; go in pairs in case of breakdowns or accident. There are several motorcycle-rental places, mainly on G Prada between Velarde and Puno. They charge US$1.20 per hour and have mainly small, 100cc bikes. Bargain for all-day discounts.

AROUND PUERTO MALDONADO
Laberinto

A bus trip to the nearby gold-rush town of Laberinto enables you to see the countryside around Puerto Maldonado. You can leave in the morning and return in the afternoon, but don't miss the last bus, as the one hotel in Laberinto is a real dive and usually full of drunk miners. Laberinto itself is a shanty-town. However, you can take trips up and down the Río Madre de Dios from here to nearby communities. You may see buyers blowtorching gold to melt and purify it. The miners come into Laberinto to sell their gold at the Banco de Minero. If the bank runs out of money, the miners may barter their gold in exchange for gas, food and other supplies. Trucks, minibuses and *colectivo* taxis for Laberinto leave from the corner of Ica and E Rivero in Puerto Maldonado (US$2, 1½ hours) frequently during the morning and less often in the afternoon.

Río Madre de Dios

This important river flows past Puerto Maldonado, eastbound, heading into Bolivia and Brazil, and the Amazon proper. In the wet season it is brown-colored, flows swiftly and looks very impressive, especially when it carries huge logs and other jungle flotsam and jetsam downstream. The main reason people come here is to stay for a few days in one of several jungle lodges, all of which are to be found between one and two hours upstream from Puerto Maldonado itself.

Additionally, travelers can partake in fishing and nature trips, and visit beaches, indigenous communities, salt licks and gold-panning areas along the Madre de Dios. Some excursions involve camping or staying in simple thatched shelters, so bring a sleeping pad and bag and/or hammock. Be prepared for muddy trails – two pairs of shoes are recommended, a dry pair for camp use and a pair that can get thoroughly wet and covered with mud. Long rubber boots (wellies or gumboots) are ideal. Insect repellent, sunblock and a means of purifying water are also essential.

SIGHTS & ACTIVITIES

The **ITA Aceer Tambopata en Inkaterra** (www.inkaterra .com/ita/aceer.htm) is an important research center that was built on the site of a 19th-century house formerly occupied by one of the first doctors to practice in this part of the Amazon. ITA retains parts of the original house while providing modern research facilities in the new construction. Although the modern accommodations are mainly for researchers, ITA can be visited by ecotourists who examine the small exhibit about local conservation issues, and attend lectures.

You can reach **Lago Sandoval** from some of the lodges here.

SLEEPING

Most lodge-style accommodations are based along the rivers. However, there is one superb getaway that is based away from the rivers and can be found in the jungle itself.

Estancia Bello Horizonte (☎ /fax 57 2748; www .estanciabellohorizonte.com; Loreto 258, Puerto Maldonado; per 3 days & 2 nights US$95, 4 days & 3 nights US$180; ☒) For a touch of Franco-Swiss style and comfort you won't go far wrong at this relaxing hideaway resort, which is built all in local wood and situated in a large open clearing on a ridge overlooking the rainforest. Located 20km from Puerto Maldonado on the east side of the Río Madre de Dios, the final approach to the Estancia is along a 6km private road through dense Amazon jungle. The wooden accommodation bungalows contain smallish but very comfortable rooms with bathrooms, and each room has a hammock and reclining chairs for lounging in. The main building contains a relaxing dining, reading, drinking and chill-out space where you can enjoy impressive views over the virgin rainforest. There's lots of open space, plus banana and papaya trees, a small soccer pitch and volleyball court. Kids will love it – especially the swimming pool and the signposted walks in the jungle.

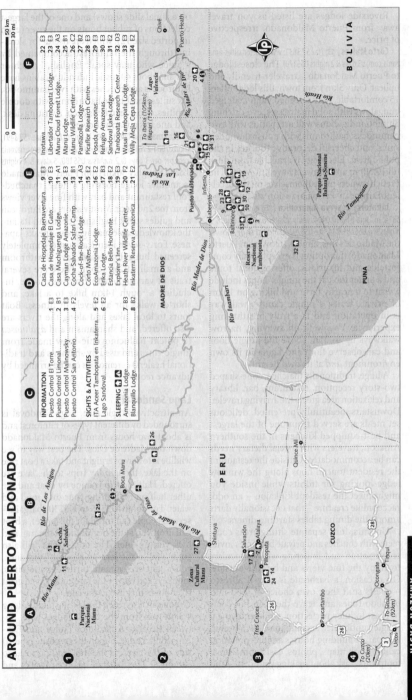

AROUND PUERTO MALDONADO

AMAZON BASIN

Riverside lodges are listed as you travel away from Puerto Maldonado, irrespective of price.

Corto Maltes (☎ /fax 57 3831; www.cortomaltes-amazonia.com; s 3 days & 2 nights US$170) The closest lodge to Puerto Maldonado is traveler-friendly and upbeat. Only 5km from town, this lodge offers 15 comfortable, fully screened, high-ceilinged bungalows with solid mattresses, eye-catching Shipibo indigenous wall art, patios with two hammocks, bathrooms with unusual wooden sinks, and cheerful decorative touches in the public areas. Electricity is available from dusk till 10:30pm and showers have hot water. The French owners pride themselves on the excellent European-Peruvian fusion cuisine.

Inkaterra Reserva Amazonica (☎ in Cuzco 084-24 5314, in Lima 01-610 0404; www.inkaterra.com; 3 days & 2 nights s/d US$183/314, cto US$292/100) Further down the Madre de Dios, almost 16km from Puerto Maldonado, this option is exceptionally comfortable and luxurious, offering local tours and a better look at the jungle. Tours include a visit to a nearby farm and hiking on 10km of private trails; a jungle canopy walkway is in operation and is a truly breathtaking experience. You walk on swaying, narrow walkways up to 35m above the jungle floor and can observe flora and fauna in its own environment *and* at its own height.

A huge, traditionally thatched, cone-shaped two-story reception, restaurant, bar, library and relaxation area greets the arriving traveler. Downstairs, beautifully presented, delicious set meals are served from one of the largest and best-equipped kitchens in the southern Amazon; travelers with special dietary needs can be accommodated. Outside the restaurant the resident toucan hops along the window ledge looking for tidbits while inside you might meet the resident kinkajou – an odd, raccoonlike creature – that occasionally darts among the dining tables startling diners.

Upstairs, four separate sitting areas complete with couches and private balconies invite conversation and lingering with binoculars to enjoy the fine views and birdlife outside. On occasion, a barbecue is served alfresco – guests stuff their own choice of food into bamboo tubes and leave them on hot coals to roast to juicy perfection, while enjoying a jungle sundowner accompanied by a guitar. A separate building houses an interpretation center (with maps, photos, casts of mammal footprints – ask about making your own – and

occasional slide shows) and one of the largest collections of rubber boots on the river (even imported size 12), which are useful for sloshing through the rainforest accompanied by a guide who may speak English, French or Italian. About 40 rustic individual cabins have bathrooms and porches with two hammocks. Six suites boast huge bathrooms with double vanities, two queen beds each, a writing desk, and one has a warm shower.

EcoAmazonia Lodge (☎ in Puerto Maldonado 57 3491, in Cuzco 084-23 6159, in Lima 01-242 2708; www.ecoamazonia .com.pe; per 3 days & 2 nights s US$180, 5 days & 4 nights US$290) Roughly 30km from Puerto Maldonado is another lodge boasting a huge, thatched-roof restaurant and bar, with fine river views from the 2nd floor. Most visitors are European and guides speak English, French and Italian; the knowledgeable manager also speaks Japanese. Forty-seven identical, rustic, completely screened bungalows each have a bathroom and a small sitting room. There are several trails of varying length from this lodge, including a tough 14km hike to a lake, and shorter walks for all levels of fitness. Boat tours to local lakes and along the rivers are also offered, and shamanism and *ayahuasca* (a potent hallucinogenic brew made from jungle vines and used by shamans and traditional healers) ceremonies can be arranged by advance request.

Lago Sandoval

An attractive jungle lake, Lago Sandoval is surrounded by different types of rainforest and is about two hours from Puerto Maldonado down the Madre de Dios. The best way to see wildlife is to stay overnight and take a boat ride on the lake, though day trips to the lake are offered. Half the trip is done by boat and the other half on foot. Bring your own food and water. For about US$25 to US$30 (bargain – several people can travel for this price), a boat will drop you at the beginning of the trail and pick you up later. The boat driver will also guide you to the lake on request. With luck, you might see caiman, turtles, exotic birds, monkeys and maybe the rare endangered giant river otters that live in the lake.

You can also reach the lake by hiking along a 3km trail from the jungle lodges here. Between Reserva Amazonica Lodge and Eco-Amazonia Lodge, but on the opposite (south) side of the river, is the trail leading to Lago Sandoval. The flat trail has boardwalks and gravel and is easily passable year-round. From the end of this trail, you can continue 2km on a narrower, less-maintained trail to an inexpensive lodge, or take a boat ride across the lake to the best lodge in this area.

The inexpensive lodge is the family-run **Willy Mejía Cepa Lodge** (r per person US$20). Willy's father, Don César Mejía Zaballos, homesteaded the lake 50 years ago and has been offering basic accommodations to budget travelers for 16 years. The lodge has room for 20 people; showers and bathrooms are shared and are separate from the sleeping areas. Mosquito nets and meals are included; bottled drinks are sold. For groups of 10 or more, rates are US$15 per person per day including transportation from Puerto Maldonado, simple family meals, a bed and excursions (in Spanish). Book in Puerto Maldonado at Velarde 487.

The best lodge is **Sandoval Lake Lodge** (per 3 days & 2 nights s/d US$295/430, extra nights per person US$70), which is on the other side of the lake to Willy Mejía. Getting there is half the fun. After hiking the 3km to the lake (bicycle rickshaws are available for luggage and for people with walking difficulties), you board canoes to negotiate narrow canals through a flooded palm-tree forest inhabited by hundreds of nesting red-bellied macaws. Emerging from the flooded forest, you are silently paddled across the beautiful lake to the lodge. With luck, you may spot the endangered giant river otter, several pairs of which live in the lake and can sometimes be seen during early-morning boating excursions. Various monkey species and a host of birds can also be spotted, as well as caiman, frogs and lizards. Hikes into the forest are offered, and guides are multilingual and knowledgeable.

The spacious lodge is built on a hilltop about 30m above the lake and is surrounded by primary forest. The hilltop was a former farm, and the lodge was built from salvaged driftwood, so the owners pride themselves on the fact that no primary forest was cut during construction. (This is also true of some other lodges, though not always mentioned.) The rooms (with heated and tiled showers and ceiling fans) are the best in the area, and the restaurant-bar area is huge, airy and conducive to relaxing and chatting. Rates include transport from Puerto Maldonado and all meals. Book with **InkaNatura** (www.inkanatura.com; Cuzco ☎ 084-25 1173; Ricardo Palma J1, Urb Santa Monica; Lima ☎ 01-440 2022; Manuel Bañón 461, San Isidro).

FRIAJES

Although the Puerto Maldonado region is hot and humid year-round, with temperatures averaging 27°C and often climbing above 32°C, there are occasional cold winds from the Andes. Known as *friajes*, these winds can make temperatures plunge to 9°C or even lower. It's worth having a light jacket or sweater in case this happens. The *friajes'* effect on the wildlife contributes to the high species diversity and endemism of the region.

Lago Valencia

Just off the Río Madre de Dios and near the Bolivian border, Lago Valencia is about 60km from Puerto Maldonado. At least two days are needed for a visit here, though three or four days are recommended. This lake reportedly offers the region's best **fishing**, as well as good **bird-watching** and **wildlife-watching** (bring your binoculars). There are trails into the jungle around the lake.

Río Heath

About two hours south of the Río Madre de Dios and along the Río Heath (the latter forming the border between Peru and Bolivia), the **Parque Nacional Bahuaja-Sonene** (admission US$8.50) has some of the best wildlife in Peru's Amazon region, though much of it is hard to see. Infrastructure in the park, one of the nation's largest, is limited, and wildlife-watching trips have only just started up here. The entrance fee into the park should be paid at Inrena (p453) in Puerto Maldonado, because the checkpoints along the way don't have tickets.

The simple, six-room **Heath River Wildlife Center** (5 days & 4 nights with first & last night at Sandoval Lake Lodge s/d US$800/1320) is owned by the Ese'eja indigenous people of Sonene, who provide guiding and cultural services. Trails into the new Parque Nacional Bahuaja-Sonene are available, and field biologists have assessed this area as one of the most biodiverse in southeastern Peru. Capybaras are a frequent highlight along the river. The center also arranges guided tours to a nearby *colpa* (clay lick), a popular attraction for macaws and parrots (binoculars are recommended). Contact **InkaNatura** (www.inkanatura.com) Cuzco ☎ 084-25 1173; Ricardo Palma J1, Urb Santa Monica); Lima (☎ 01-440 2022; Manuel Bañón 461, San Isidro).

AMAZON BASIN

LIFE IN THE JUNGLE

If you've not been to the jungle before, read on. The Peruvian jungle (*selva* in Spanish) is a damp, humid place, with dense overgrowth, lots of muddy paths (in the rainy season), a lot of wildlife – though you have to look hard to find it at times – and a veritable panoply of exotic flora. The jungle you will encounter close to the tourist lodges is not quite like what you see it in the movies: it has been tamed and packaged to protect delicate travelers like yourself – and the jungle itself. In short it can be a pretty pleasant experience.

It has its shortcomings though. Because it is so humid, your clothes, once they are damp, will take forever to dry out – and you *will* perspire a lot … Mosquitoes are crafty little insects. They don't buzz you annoyingly like they do in hotel rooms: they just surreptitiously find your unprotected skin and suck your blood without you knowing it.

Ants live on the jungle floor and if you step on a column, they will bite you – hard. Fire ants live in tree trunks and as long as you don't put your hand on them they won't set you alight with bites. Piranhas leave humans alone for the most part unless you decide to catch one and it gets nasty with you for pulling it out of its river home. Then you need to watch your fingertips.

On a practical side there is little electricity, so reading a book at night is a challenge. There's not much radio to be heard on your trannie, so sing yourself to sleep. Cell phones? Forget 'em! You are at one with nature and, equally importantly, with your fellow travelers. Relearn the ancient art of conversation; maybe forget about talking when you walk the jungle trails and let silence – or at least the sounds of the jungle – take over.

Life in the jungle is getting back to nature and, for many visitors, a chance to find their inner selves once more.

Río Tambopata

The Río Tambopata is a major tributary of the Río Madre de Dios, joining it at Puerto Maldonado. Boats go up the river, past several good lodges, and into the **Reserva Nacional Tambopata** (admission US$8.50, incl Tambopata Center US$20), an important protected area divided into the reserve itself and the **zona de amortiguamiento** (buffer zone). The park entrance fee needs to be paid for at the Inrena office (p453) in Puerto Maldonado, unless you are on a guided tour, in which case you will pay at the lodge office.

Travelers heading up the Río Tambopata must register their passport numbers at the Puesto Control (guard post) El Torre next to the Explorer's Inn and show their national-park entrance permits obtained in Puerto Maldonado. Visiting the reserve is quite easy if you book a guided stay at one of the lodges within it. One of the highlights of the reserve is the Colpa de Guacamayos (macaw clay lick), one of the largest natural clay licks in the country. It attracts hundreds of birds and continues to be a spectacular sight (see the January 1994 *National Geographic* for a photographic story).

Lodges are listed in the order in which you would arrive at them if traveling from Puerto Maldonado.

Posada Amazonas (per 3 days & 2 nights s/d US$205/410) is about two hours from Puerto Maldonado along Río Tambopata, followed by a 10-minute uphill walk. The *posada* is on the land of the Ese'eja native community of Infierno, and tribal members, as well as local *mestizos* (persons of mixed indigenous and Spanish descent), are among the guides. (Several other lodges use 'native' guides, but these are often *mestizos* rather than tribal members.) There are excellent chances of seeing macaws and parrots on a small salt lick nearby, and giant river otters are often found swimming in lakes close to the lodge. Guides at the lodge are mainly English-speaking Peruvian naturalists with varying interests. Your assigned guide stays with you throughout the duration of your stay. Visits are also made to the Centro Ñape ethnobotanical center where medicine is produced for members of the Ese'eja community. Visitors are shown round a medicinal plant trail where a staff member explains the uses of the various plants. A short hike from the lodge is a 30m-high observation platform giving superb views of the rainforest canopy. The lodge has 30 large double rooms with private showers and open (unglazed) windows overlooking the rainforest. Mosquito nets are provided. Rainforest Expeditions also operates the Refugio Amazonas (p464) and Tambopata

Research Center (p464). Book with **Rainforest Expeditions** (www.perunature.com; Cuzco ☎ /fax 084-23 2772; cusco@rainforest.com.pe; Portal de Carnes 236; Lima ☎ 01-421 8347; fax 01-421 8347; postmaster@rainforest .com.pe; Aramburu 166, Miraflores; Puerto Maldonado ☎ /fax 57 2575; pem@rainforest.com.pe; Avenida Aeropuerto Km 6, CPM La Joya.

Inotawa (☎ in Puerto Maldonado 57 2511, in Lima 01-467 4560; www.inotawaexpeditions.com; per person 3 days & 2 nights US$150, extra nights US$45) lies a few kilometers beyond Posada Amazonas and is a good budget option. Campers can bring their own tent and pitch it on the grounds for a small fee. Rates include transfers from Puerto Maldonado, meals, guided walks and boat rides. The lodge features a high roof with a transparent window at the ceiling apex, allowing more light than most other lodges. Electricity is available from 6pm to 10pm when guests can charge their video camera batteries. Most of the 10 rooms have shared bathrooms, but there are also a couple of rooms with their own bathrooms. A large, cool hammock room invites relaxation and the Swiss-Peruvian owners deliver excellent food with a European flair. German-, French- and English-speaking guides are available on advance request.

Explorer's Inn (www.peruviansafaris.com; 3 days & 2 nights incl meals & guided tours excl tours to the salt lick s/d US$195/360) Cuzco (☎ 084-23 5342, Plateros 365); Lima (☎ 01-447 8888, 447 4761; fax 01 241 8427; sails@peruviansafaris.com; Alcanfores 459, Miraflores); Puerto Maldonado (☎ 57 2078; Fitzcarrald Mz. H, Lote 15 Ur. Fonavi) is 58km from Puerto Maldonado (three to four hours of river travel) and features 15 rustic double and 15 triple rooms, all with bathroom and screened windows. It is a pleasant and folksy kind of place and predisposes the visitor to linger. The central lodge room has a restaurant, a bar, a foosball table, and a small museum. Outside there is a small soccer pitch and even an archery range, while you can browse through an assortment of herbs and plants in the medicinal garden. The lodge is located in the former 5500-hectare Zona Preservada Tambopata (itself now surrounded by the much larger Reserva Nacional Tambopata). More than 600 species of birds have been recorded in this preserved zone, which is a world record for bird species sighted in one area. There are similar records for other kinds of wildlife, including over 1200 butterflies. Despite these records (which are scientifically documented), the average tourist won't see much more here than anywhere else during the standard two-night visit, yet the area is more pristine than that surrounding the lodges on the Madre de Dios. The 38km of trails around the lodge can be explored independently or with naturalist guides. Some guides are local or from Lima. German, English and French are spoken.

Next up is the new **Cayman Lodge Amazonie** (☎ /fax 082-57 1970; www.cayman-lodge-amazonie .com; 28 de Julio 954, Puerto Maldonado; 2 days & 3 nights s/d US$210/240), some 70km from Puerto Maldonado. This is one of the few places that advertises its existence along the Tambopata with a prominent sign on the river bend. This lodge is a little different to the others. It has an open, relaxing environment with banana, *cocona* (peach tomato) and mango trees in a lush tropical garden that is lorded over by Felix the cat and two ducks. Activities include visits to the oxbow Lagunas Sachavacayoc and Condenado, and there is also a five- to seven-day shamanism program where you can learn about tropical medicine and even be treated for any ailment you may have. There is a large bar and restaurant area served by a large and very modern kitchen. The rooms are a little on the small side, but are more than comfortable and the windows are meshed to protect from insects. One of its more arresting features is the hammock house, from where you can watch the sun set over the Río Tambopata. Run by the effervescent French Anny and her English-speaking Peruvian partner Daniel, the Cayman promises a tropical jungle vacation with a dash of Gallic panache.

Picaflor Research Centre (www.picaflor.org), 74km from Puerto Maldonado, is a real find for budget travelers, and has received repeated recommendations from volunteers and researchers. Owners are Dr Laurel Hanna (a British biologist) and her boat-captain Peruvian husband, 'Pico' Maceda-Huinga. Visitors can volunteer, research or take guided tours. Volunteers work three hours daily and pay US$140 for 10 nights of food and accommodation (plus park fees and US$3 transportation from Puerto Maldonado). Researchers pay about US$20 a night and tourists pay US$190 for an all-inclusive three-day/two-night tour. The center is small (six rooms with solar lights) but replete with guidebooks and trails. The library has a power outlet for laptops. Check out the website for ongoing research projects and volunteer opportunities.

Further along is the **Libertador Tambopata Lodge** (☎ 082-57 1726, 082-968 0022; fax 082-57 1397; www.tambopatalodge.com; Gonzalez Prada 269, Puerto Maldonado; 3 days & 2 nights s/d US$287/465). Set mainly near secondary forest and some farms, this considerably more luxurious lodge is still within the Reserva Tambopata, and a short boat ride will get you out into primary forest. Tours to nearby lakes and to the salt lick are offered, and naturalist guides are available. There are 12km of well-marked trails, which you can wander at will without a guide. The lodge consists of a series of spacious individual bungalows, some of which have solar-generated hot water. Each enjoys a tiled patio with table and chairs and all look out onto a lush tropical garden. There is the mandatory restaurant and a cozy separate bar complex. You won't miss Willy the minuscule howler monkey who clambers among the woodwork chattering at guests, nor Veronica the rather indolent and otherwise disinterested parrot.

New in 2006, the latest addition to the jungle accommodation scene is the rather impressive **Refugio Amazonas** (4 days & 3 nights s/d US$330/590). This lodge is better for a longer stay as it is a fairly lengthy boat ride up the river to get here. It is built on a 2000-hectare private reserve in the buffer zone of the Tambopata National Reserve. While it feels just that little more isolated, the lodge is not lacking in creature comforts, with a large reception, dining and drinking area. Rooms are comfortable and similar in style and open architecture to those of its sister lodge, the Posada Amazonas. Activities include a Brazil-nut trail and camp and, for children, a dedicated rainforest trail. The increased remoteness usually means better opportunities for spotting wildlife. Book with **Rainforest Expeditions** (www.perunature.com; Cuzco ☎ /fax 084-23 2772; cusco@rainforest.com.pe; Portal de Carnes 236; Lima ☎ 01-421 8347; postmaster@rainforest .com.pe; fax 01-421 8347; Aramburu 166, Miraflores; Puerto Maldonado ☎ /fax 57 2575; pem@rainforest.com.pe; Avenida Aeropuerto Km 6, CPM La Joya).

A little further up the Tambopata, near the community of **Baltimore**, are several small *hospedajes* (small, family-owned inns); inquire in Puerto Maldonado about these or just show up and hope for the best (maybe bring some food). Baltimore is reached by a twice-weekly passenger boat from Puerto Maldonado, or by bus and foot. Take any vehicle from Puerto Maldonado heading to Laberinto, and ask to get off at Km 37. From there, a footpath goes

to Baltimore (about five hours). In Baltimore is the **Casa de Hospedaje Buenaventura** (r per person US$6-10) with seven two- and three-bed rooms, mosquito nets, two showers and an attractive octagonal communal room with river views and a few English novels to read. Food is extra. This seems the best option. Across the river, **Casa de Hospedaje El Gato** (r per person US$20), owned by the Ramirez family, has basic beds, showers at waterfalls in the river, and includes meals and walks in the forests.

Shortly past Baltimore is the small **Wasai Tambopata Lodge** (www.wasai.com; s/d per day US$70/140). This is the penultimate lodge on the river and, unlike the others, it does not feature programmed ecoactivities. So if you just want to relax, read a book, enjoy a beer or just amble around a series of well-signed trails yourself – totalling 20km in all – this is the place to do it. You can engage in a spot of fishing or canoe paddling if you can tear yourself away from hammock hanging for an hour or two. The lodge consists of four large bungalows and two smaller ones than can accommodate a maximum of 40 guests. There is a tall observation tower from where you get good views of the surrounding jungle. Contact **Wasai Lodge** (☎ 57 2290; fax 57 1355; www.wasai.com; Billinghurst at Arequipa, Puerto Maldonado).

Finally, and about seven hours' river travel from Puerto Maldonado, the **Tambopata Research Center** (6 days & 5 nights s/d US$835/1560) is known for a famous salt lick nearby that attracts four to 10 species of parrots and macaws on most mornings. Research here focuses on why macaws eat clay, on their migration patterns, their diet, nesting macaws and on techniques for building artificial nests. The lodge itself is fairly simple, with 18 double rooms sharing four showers and four toilets, but because of the distances involved, rates are higher than the other places. If you're interested in seeing more macaws than you ever thought possible, it's worth the expense, although the owners point out that occasionally, due to poor weather or other factors, the macaws aren't found at the lick. Still, about 75% of visitors get good looks at macaws, though you shouldn't expect to get the kinds of photos in the *National Geographic* article. Travel time to the lodge varies, depending on river levels and the size of your boat motor, and a stopover is usually made at Refugio Amazonas on the first and last nights. The last section of the ride is through remote country with excellent chances of seeing capybara and maybe more unusual animals. Have your passport ready at the Puesto Control Malinowsky. Book with **Rainforest Expeditions** (www.perunature .com; Cuzco ☎ /fax 084-23 2772; cusco@rainforest.com.pe; Portal de Carnes 236; Lima ☎ 01-421 8347; fax 01-421 8347; postmaster@rainforest.com.pe; Aramburu 166, Miraflores; Puerto Maldonado ☎ /fax 57 2575; pem@rainforest.com.pe; Avenida Aeropuerto Km 6, CPM La Joya).

MANU AREA

The Manu area encompasses the Parque Nacional Manu and much of the surrounding area. The park covers almost 20,000 sq km (about the size of Wales) and is one of the best places in South America to see a wide variety of tropical wildlife. The park is divided into three zones: the largest sector, to the west, is the *zona natural* comprising 80% of the total park area and is essentially closed to unauthorized visitors. Entry to this sector is restricted to a few indigenous groups, mainly the Machiguenga, some of whom continue to live here as they have for generations; some groups have had almost no contact with outsiders and do not seem to want any. Fortunately, this wish is respected. A handful of researchers with permits is also allowed in to study the wildlife. The second sector is the *zona experimental* where controlled research and tourism activities are permitted. There is only one official accommodation option here. This is the northeastern sector and comprises about 10% of the park area. The third sector, covering the lower southeastern area and comprising 10% of the park area, is the *zona cultural*, where most other visitor activity is concentrated. In addition, the areas around the park proper provide good wildlife-watching opportunities, especially near the Manu Wildlife Center (p468), which is outside the park.

Tours to the Manu Area

It's important to check exactly where the tours are going, because Manu is a catchall word that includes the national park and much of the surrounding area. Some tours, such as to the Manu Wildlife Center, don't actually enter Parque Nacional Manu at all (although the wildlife center is recommended for wildlife-watching, nevertheless). Some companies aren't allowed to enter the park, but

offer what they call 'Manu tours' either outside the park or acting as agents for other operators. Other companies work together and share resources such as lodges, guides and transportation services. Most will combine a Manu experience with a full Peru tour on request. Confusing? You bet!

The companies listed in this section were all recently authorized to operate within Manu by the national-park service and maintain some level of conservation and low-impact practices. The number of permits to operate tours into Parque Nacional Manu is limited, and allow only about 3000 visitors annually. It is essential that intending visitors book well in advance, and you should be flexible with onward travel plans as delays are common.

Tour costs depend on whether you camp or stay in a lodge, and whether you arrive/depart overland or by air. The more expensive companies offer more reliable and trained multilingual guides, better maintained equipment, a wider variety of food, suitable insurance and emergency procedures, and intangibles such as local experience. All companies provide transportation, food, purified drinking water, guides, permits and camping equipment or screens in lodge rooms. Personal items such as a sleeping bag (unless staying in a lodge), insect repellent, sunblock, flashlight with spare batteries, suitable clothing and bottled drinks are the client's responsibility. Binoculars are highly recommended.

Manu Expeditions (☎ 084-22 6671, 084-23 9974; www.manuexpeditions.com; Umberto Vidal Unda G-5, Cuzco) – owners of the only tented camp within the national park, and co-owners of the Manu Wildlife Center – comes highly recommended, with over two decades of Manu experience. Its guides are excellent, experienced and highly knowledgeable, but if you are lucky enough to go with the owner, British ornithologist and longtime Cuzco resident, Barry Walker, you will really be in excellent hands, particularly if birding is your main interest. (Barry was featured in Michael Palin's *Full Circle* travel series on the BBC.) The most popular trip leaves Cuzco every Sunday (except January, February and March when it's the first Sunday of the month only) and lasts nine days, including overland transportation to Manu with two nights of camping, three nights at Manu Wildlife Center, three nights at other lodges and a flight back to Cuzco. This costs US$1595. The overland section can include a

AMAZON BASIN

mountain-biking descent if arranged in advance. Shorter, longer and customized trips are offered.

Manu Nature Tours (☎ 084-25 2721; fax 084-25 4793; www.manuperu.com; Pardo 1046, Cuzco) operates the respected Manu Lodge, which is open year-round. The lodge has 12 double rooms (bathrooms are planned) plus a bar-cum-dining-room next to a lake that's is home to a breeding family of giant otters. A 20km network of trails and guided visits to lakes and observation towers are also provided. A five-day tour, flying in or out, is US$1403 per person, double occupancy, with fixed departures every Friday. The trip has a bilingual naturalist guide and all meals are provided. For an extra fee, mountain biking or river running (white-water rafting) can be incorporated into the road descent. Longer tours are also available. This company also has departures to its Manu Cloud Forest Lodge (right).

Pantiacolla Tours (☎ 084-23 8323; fax 084-25 2696; www.pantiacolla.com; Saphy 554, Cuzco) is often recommended by budget travelers for jungle trips. Pantiacolla Tours' owners were raised in the area and are knowledgeable; they offer a variety of tours, including the opportunity to study Spanish at their jungle lodge. Trips start at US$745 per person for five days, flying out, or US$785 per person for nine days, all overland, and include a mixture of camping and lodge accommodations. More expensive options are also available. Pantiacolla Tours also works with local indigenous groups in their Yine Project, which is outlined on their website.

InkaNatura (www.inkanatura.com; Cuzco ☎ 084-25 5255; fax 084-24 5973; Ricardo Palma J1; Lima ☎ 01-440 2022; fax 01-422 9225; Manuel Bañón 461, San Isidro; USA Tropical Nature Travel ☎ 1-877 888 1770, 1-352 376 3377; POB 5276, Gainesville FL32627-5276) is a highly respected international agency and is co-owner of Manu Wildlife Center. The operators can combine a visit here with visits to other parts of the southeastern Peruvian rainforest, including Puerto Maldonado and Pampas del Heath.

Manu Ecological Adventures (☎ 084-26 1640; fax 084-22 5562; www.manuadventures.com; Plateros 356, Cuzco) has camping trips using tents on the beaches of the national park; an eight-day trip costs US$610 per person. There are bilingual guides, and all gear and bus transportation is provided.

CUZCO TO MANU

This journey provides opportunities for some excellent **bird-watching** at the lodges en route.

If traveling overland, the first stage of the journey involves taking a bus or truck from Cuzco via Paucartambo (see p282) to Shintuya. Buses run by **Gallito de las Rocas** (☎ 084-27 7255; Manco Cápac, Cuzco) leave at 10am for Pilcopata (US$6, 12 hours in good weather) along the one-way road on Monday, Wednesday and Friday. Cheaper trucks leave the same days and possibly Sunday from the Coliseo Cerrado in Cuzco. In the dry season they take about 24 hours to reach Shintuya. Breakdowns, flat tires, extreme overcrowding and delays are common, and during the rainy season (and even during the dry) vehicles slide off the road. It's safer, more comfortable and more reliable to take the costlier tourist buses (which are basically heavy-duty trucks) offered by Cuzco tour operators. Many tour companies in Cuzco offer trips to Manu (see p239).

There are two lodges between Paucartambo and Pilcopata. **Cock-of-the-Rock Lodge** (3 days & 2 nights d US$900) is just a few minutes' walk from a *lek* (mating ground) for cocks-of-the-rock (brightly colored rainforest birds that live on rock cliffs and outcrops; they conduct elaborate communal mating 'dances'). This lodge offers exceptional cloud-forest birding at a pleasant 1600m elevation. The owners claim you can get photos of male cocks-of-the-rock displaying about 7m from your camera. The lodge has a restaurant and 10 rustic double cabins with hot showers. Normally, visitors overnight here en route to Manu, but the lodge can be used as a destination in itself for cloud-forest birding. Rates include meals and round-trip transportation from Cuzco, which can take six to 10 hours. Discounts are available for longer stays and larger groups. Contact **InkaNatura** (www.inkanatura.com; Cuzco ☎ 084-25 1173; Ricardo Palma J1, Urb Santa Monica; Lima ☎ 01-440 2022; Manuel Bañón 461, San Isidro).

Nearby, **Manu Cloud Forest Lodge** (☎ 084-25 2721; www.manuperu.com; Pardo 1046, Cuzco; 3 days & 2 nights per person on a shared basis US$466) is near the same stretch of road. The 16-to-20-bed lodge provides six rooms with hot showers, a restaurant, a sauna (US$10) and birding opportunities in the high cloud forest. Transportation is extra. Nearby is the **Manu Cloud Forest Tented Camp** (☎ 084-25 2721; www.manuperu.com; Pardo 1046,

Cuzco; d US$76). Five large tents on platforms sleep two people each (bedding, showers, toilets and meals provided).

The truck trip to these lodges is often broken at **Pilcopata**, which is the biggest village along the road and is currently the end of the public bus route. There are a couple of basic hotels and a few stores in town. A bed costs about US$5, or floor/hammock space is US$2.50. Pickup trucks leave early every morning for Atalaya and Shintuya (US$3, about five hours).

About 40km before Shintuya is the village of Atalaya (not to be confused with the village of the same name on the Río Ucayali, see p473) on the Río Alto Madre de Dios. Across the river is the very pleasant **Amazonia Lodge** (☎ /fax 084-23 1370; www.amazonialodge.com; Matará 334, Cuzco; r per person US$60), in an old hacienda in the foothills of the Andes. The lodge offers clean, comfortable beds and communal hot showers; simple but satisfactory meals are also included. There is no electricity, but that is more than compensated for by the low number of mosquitoes. There are trails into the forest, and the birding is excellent. Birders could profitably spend a few days here in relative comfort, or fully guided birding tours are offered. The lodge can make transportation arrangements on request, or the tour agencies in Cuzco can make reservations. From Atalaya, boats leave for **Erika Lodge** (r per person US$40); contact **Ernesto Yallico** (☎ 084-22 7765; Casilla 560, Cuzco). Within a private reserve on the banks of the Alto Madre de Dios, this lodge provides simple accommodations and meals, and camping is allowed.

The village of **Salvación**, about 10km closer to Shintuya, has a national park office and a couple of basic hotels. Ask here for boats continuing down the river but note that park entry is restricted to tour groups and there are very few other boats available.

Shintuya is the end of the road at this time and is the closest village to the park, but it has only a few places to stay. You may be able to camp at the mission station by talking to the priest.

The Ecuadorian-Dutch Moscoso family lives 30 minutes downriver from Shintuya and operates **Pantiacolla Lodge** (r per person US$55). There are 14 double rooms with shared bathrooms here. Rates include meals but not transportation or tours, though you can hike on the forest trails nearby. Various transportation

and guided-tour options are available starting at US$750 per person for five days. The lodge is on the fringe of the national park, and good wildlife sightings have been reported. Contact **Pantiacolla Tours** (☎ 084-23 8323; www.pantiacolla.com; Saphy 554, Cuzco).

Boats can travel from Pilcopata, Atalaya, Salvación or Shintuya toward Manu. People on tours often start river travel from Atalaya after a night in a lodge. The boat journey down the Alto Madre de Dios to the Río Manu takes almost a day, depending on how fast the boat is. At the junction is the village of **Boca Manu**, with simple stores and bars. This village is known for building the best riverboats in the area, and it is interesting to see them in various stages of construction. There is an inexpensive lodge here, but reservations are hard to make – just show up and hope for the best. A few minutes from the village is the Boca Manu airstrip, often the start or exit point for commercial trips into the park. **Trans Andes** (☎ 084-22 4638; Cuzco airport) and **Malu Servicios Aereos** (☎ 084-24 2104; Cuzco airport) fly small aircraft here most days for US$120. Most seats are taken up with tour groups, but empty seats are often available. A US$10 airport fee is charged.

PARQUE NACIONAL MANU

The great biodiversity of this national park is due to it starting in the eastern slopes of the Andes and plunging down into the lowlands, thus covering a wide range of cloud forest and rainforest habitats. The most progressive aspect of the park is the fact that so much of it is very carefully protected – a rarity anywhere in the world.

After Peru introduced protection laws in 1973, Unesco declared Manu a Biosphere Reserve in 1977 and a World Natural Heritage Site in 1987. One reason the park is so successful in preserving such a large tract of virgin jungle and its wildlife is that it is remote and relatively inaccessible to people, and therefore has not been exploited by rubber tappers, loggers, oil companies or hunters.

It is illegal to enter the park without a guide. Going with an organized group can be arranged in Cuzco (see p239) or with international tour operators. It's an expensive trip; budget travelers should arrange their trip in Cuzco and be very flexible with travel plans. Travelers often report returning from Manu three or four days late. Don't plan an international airline connection the day after a Manu trip!

Permits, which are necessary to enter the park, are arranged by tour agencies. Transportation, accommodations, food and guides are also part of tour packages. Most visits are for a week, although three-night stays at a lodge can be arranged.

The best time to go is during the dry season (June to November); Manu may be inaccessible or closed during the rainy months (January to April), except to visitors staying at the two lodges within the park boundaries (following).

Virgin jungle lies up the Río Manu northwest of Boca Manu. At the Puesto Control Limonal (guard post), about an hour from Boca Manu, you pay a park entrance fee of US$20 per person. Continuing beyond is only possible with a guide and permit. Near Limonal are a few trails.

Six hours upstream is **Cocha Salvador**, one of the park's largest and most beautiful lakes, where there are guided camping and hiking possibilities. With patience, wildlife is seen in most areas. This is not a wide-open habitat as is the African plains. The thick vegetation will obscure many animals, and a skilled guide is very useful in helping you to see them.

During a one-week trip, you can reasonably expect to see scores of different bird species, several monkey species and possibly a few other mammals. Jaguars, tapirs, giant anteaters, tamanduas, capybaras, peccaries and giant river otters are among the common large mammals of Manu. But they are elusive, and you can consider a trip very successful if you see two or three large mammals during a week's visit. Smaller mammals you might see include kinkajous, pacas, agoutis, squirrels, brocket deer, ocelots and armadillos. Other animals include river turtles and caiman (which are frequently seen), snakes (which are less often spotted) and a variety of other reptiles and amphibians. Colorful butterflies and less pleasing insects also abound.

There are two lodges within the park.

At Manu Lodge a row of 14 simple double rooms is screened and has comfortable beds; a separate building has cold showers and toilets. The lodge is on Cocha Juarez, a 2km-long oxbow lake, and is about 1km from the Río Manu; a breeding family of giant river otters is often encountered. For an extra fee, a climb up to a canopy platform or river running can be arranged. A 20km network of trails from the lodge around the lake and beyond provides ample opportunities for spotting monkeys and birds. Contact **Manu Nature Tours** (☎ 084-25 2721; www.manuperu.com; Pardo 1046, Cuzco).

Cocha Salvador Safari Camp lies beyond Manu Lodge. This camp has raised platforms supporting large walk-in screened tents containing cots and bedding. Modern showers, toilets and meals are available. Manu Expeditions occasionally uses the more rustic Casa Machiguenga Lodge, which was built in traditional style by the Machiguenga indigenous people in 1998. Contact **Manu Expeditions** (☎ 084-22 6671, 084-23 9974; www.manuexpeditions.com; Umberto Vidal Unda G-5, Cuzco).

More primitive camping, usually on the sandy beaches of the Río Manu or on the foreshore of a few of the lakes, is another possibility. Tour operators can provide all necessary equipment. During the rainy season (January to April) these beaches are flooded and the park is closed to camping. Campers should come prepared with plenty of insect repellent.

MANU WILDLIFE CENTER & AROUND

A two-hour boat ride southeast of Boca Manu on the Río Madre de Dios takes you to **Manu Wildlife Center** (5 days/4 nights s/d US$1250/2100). The center is a jungle lodge owned by **InkaNatura Travel** (☎ in Cuzco 084-25 5255; www.inkanatura.com; Ricardo Palma J1, Urb Santa Monica, Cuzco) and **Manu Expeditions** (☎ 084-22 6671, 084-23 9974; www.manu expeditions.com; Umberto Vidal Unda G-5, Cuzco), both of which take reservations. Although the lodge is not in Manu Biosphere Reserve, it is recommended for its exceptional wildlife-watching and birding opportunities. There are 22 screened double cabins with hot showers, a dining room and a bar–hammock room. The lodge is set in tropical gardens.

There are 48km of trails around the wildlife center, where 12 species of monkeys, as well as other wildlife, can be seen. Two canopy platforms are a short walk away, and one is always available for guests wishing to view the top of the rainforest and look for birds that frequent the canopy.

A 3km walk through the forest brings you to a natural salt lick, where there is a raised platform with mosquito nets for viewing the nightly activities of the tapirs. This hike is for visitors who can negotiate forest trails by flashlight. Visitors may wait for hours to see the animals. Nothing is guaranteed, but the chances are excellent if you have the patience. Note that there isn't much happening at the lick during the day.

A short boat ride along the Madre de Dios brings visitors to another well-known salt lick that attracts various species of parrots and macaws. Most mornings you can see flocks in the hundreds. The largest flocks are seen from late July to September. As the rainy season kicks in the numbers diminish, though there are usually some birds all year, except June when birds don't visit the salt lick at all. May and early July aren't reliable either, though ornithologists report the presence of the birds in other nearby areas during these months, and birders will usually see them.

The macaw lick is visited on a floating catamaran blind, with the blind providing a concealed enclosure from which 20 people can view the wildlife. The catamaran is stable enough to be able to use a tripod and scope or telephoto lens, and gets about halfway across the river. The boat drivers won't bring the blind too close to disturb the birds.

In addition to the trails and salt licks, there are a couple of nearby lakes where paddled catamarans provide transportation and giant otters may be seen (as well as various birds and other animals). If you wish to see the macaw and tapir lick, lakes and canopy, and hike the trails in search of wildlife, you should plan on a three-night stay at the Manu Wildlife Center, though shorter and longer stays are workable.

Near the Manu Wildlife Center, the rustic Blanquillo Lodge has rooms with shared bathrooms. Some companies in Cuzco combine this cheaper option with a tour including other lodges in the Manu area, but prices vary. Staying at just Blanquillo itself isn't offered.

If you continue down the Madre de Dios past gold-panning areas to Puerto Maldonado, you won't see much wildlife. This takes 14 hours to two days and may cost as little as US$10 if you can find a boat heading that way. But transportation to Puerto Maldonado is infrequent, and almost all visitors return to Cuzco.

CENTRAL AMAZON

For a quick Amazon fix on long weekends and holidays, *limeños* (inhabitants of Lima) tend to head for this relatively easily accessible Amazon

region. Reachable in just under eight hours by bus – less by car – the tropical Chanchamayo region is as different to the coastal desert strip or the Andes as you can get. The last hour's stretch in particular is remarkable for the rapid change in vegetation and climate as you slip down the harsh shoulder of the Andes ranges to the lush green of La Selva Central, as it is known in Spanish. Comprising the two main towns of San Ramón and La Merced, plus a scattering of remoter communities, the area is noted for coffee and fruit production and is the central portal to the vast Amazonas region that makes up 50% of the Peruvian landmass.

SAN RAMÓN & LA MERCED

☎ 064 / pop 40,000 / elev 800m

San Ramón is 295km east of Lima and La Merced is 11km further along. The two towns are quite likable in their own languid sort of way and if you're arriving from the heights of the Andes it is a relief to be able to breathe in unrarified air – albeit hot and humid. Both towns have a good selection of hotels and restaurants and, as testimony to their popularity as holiday destinations in their own right, accommodation bookings are recommended at busy periods. Room rates are also more expensive at these times.

Orientation

San Ramón is the quieter of the two towns, though it does own the regional airstrip. La Merced, while hardly large, is nonetheless a bustling kind of place with squadrons of buzzing *autotaxis* careening down the streets. La Merced is also the main transport center, with buses, minibuses and *colectivos* departing from here to all parts of the Selva Central.

While San Ramón is essentially one long main street, La Merced is compact and most traveler facilities are within a coconut's throw of the main plaza.

Information

Both towns have a BCP with an ATM, and plenty of public telephones. La Merced has internet places scattered around town.

Bayoz Internet (Plaza de Armas, La Merced) Internet access.

Cambios Beto (Plaza Central, La Merced) Seems to do most of the money-changing business in town.

Hospital (☎ 53 1002, 53 1408, La Merced) Small.

Internet Exchange (Progreso 353; per hr US$1.30) As good as any.

Police station (Julio Piérola at Passuni, La Merced)
Post office (2 de Mayo, La Merced)
Telecentro (Palca 12, La Merced) Make cheap calls here.

Sights & Activities

Both towns are more for strolling around and taking in the local color than for anything else. That said, there is a colorful **daily market** in La Merced. A **weekend market** at San Luis de Shuaro, 22km beyond La Merced, is also interesting – local indigenous peoples visit it. Ashaninka tribespeople occasionally come into La Merced to sell handicrafts.

Av 2 de Mayo is good for **views** of La Merced; the stairs at the northwest end afford a good view of the town, and from the balcony at the southwest end there's a photogenic river view.

An interesting **botanical garden** (Fjército 490) is on the grounds of El Refugio Hotel in San Ramón.

Sleeping

LA MERCED

Hospedaje Santa Rosa (☎ 53 1012; 2 de Mayo 447; s/d with shared shower US$3.20/5, s/d US$6.50/8) The cleanest of the cheapest hotels, the Santa Rosa boasts light rooms with cable TV, large windows but cold showers.

Hostal Residencial Primavera (☎ /fax 53 1433; Arequipa 175; r with cold/hot shower US$8/11) Singles cost the same as doubles at this bright, tidy but bland hostel. Rooms have a fan and cable TV.

Hospedaje Cristina (☎ 53 1276; Tarma 582; s/d US$8/10.50) Good-sized rooms feature cable TV and decent mattresses, but the décor is plain and the cold-shower bathrooms cramped.

Hospedaje Cosmos (☎ /fax 53 1051; hospedaje cosmos@hotmail.com; Julio Piérola at Passuni; s/d US$9/11.50) The lack of a sign makes finding this place a bit hard, but it does exist. It's a rather old-fashioned, institutionalized sort of joint and the rooms are somewhat spartan with cold showers, but certainly clean.

Hostal Rey (☎ /fax 53 1185; Junín 103; s/d US$14.50/20.50) Bright, inviting hallways decorated with flowers and pictures lead to attractive rooms with fan, cable TV and hot shower complete with towels and soap. A restaurant on the top floor serves decent breakfasts, lunches and dinners while offering good views of the town.

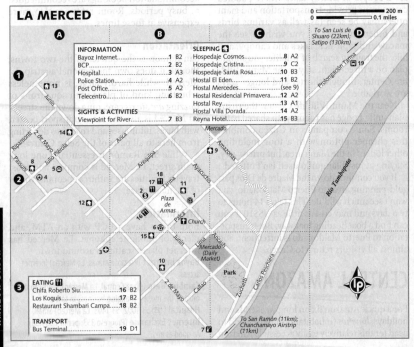

Reyna Hotel (☎ /fax 53 1780, 53 2196; www.hotel reyna.com; Palca 259; s/d US$16/22) You can't go wrong with this modern, brightly tiled hotel and its sparkling cafeteria. Rooms feature direct-dial phone, fan, cable TV, excellent beds and hot shower. A nice, comfy choice.

Other choices:

Hostal Villa Dorada (☎ 53 1221; Julio Piérola 265; s/d with shared bathroom US$3/6, s/d US$6/8) Large rooms but small, cold showers.

Hostal Mercedes (☎ /fax 53 1304; Tarma 576; s/d US$10/13) Rooms seem without charm but the hot showers and TVs make up for that.

Hostal El Eden (☎ 53 1183; fax 53 2340; eleden@hotmail.com; Ancash 347; s/d US$19/28) You pay for the plaza location, but the rooms are OK with TV, fan and cold shower.

SAN RAMÓN
Hotel Chanchamayo (☎ 33 8038; ferructzzy_7@hotmail.com; Progreso 291; s/d with shared shower US$3/6, s/d US$6/9) A good budget choice, this hotel has hot water and TV (US$3) in the rooms.

Hotel Conquistador (☎ /fax 33 1771; conquistador@viabcp.com; Progreso 298; s/d US$7.50/12) This modern hotel with motel-like rooms (complete with cable TV and hot shower) doubles its rates in high season. There is also an in-house restaurant.

Hotel El Parral (☎ 33 1128; ☎ /fax 33 1536; Uriarte 361; s/d US$12/19) This modern hotel has a locally popular restaurant serving jungle specialties, such as *paiche* (a large freshwater fish) and *tacahco* (pork and plantain). Rooms are simple but comfortable with hot shower, fan and cable TV.

El Refugio Hotel (☎ /fax 33 1082; www.hotelelrefugio.com.pe; Ejército 490; d high season US$43, s/d/tr US$10/16/22 Jan-Mar; 🖳 🖭) About a 10-minute walk from the town center, this hotel is the best in town and features grounds containing a small, well-designed botanical garden. The various exotic plants are labeled and tend to attract butterflies and birds. The rooms are comfortable bungalows with hot shower, fan and cable TV; rates include breakfast.

Eating
LA MERCED
Consider any one of many chicken restaurants on Ayacucho at Tarma, where a quarter-chicken with fries will set you back US$1.30. The *mercado* at Tarma and Amazonas has plenty of stalls selling juice and cake – for travel-hardened stomachs.

Restaurant Shambari Campa (☎ 53 2842; Tarma 389; menús US$3, mains US$3-5; 🕑 6:30am-12:30am) On the plaza, this famous hole-in-the-wall restaurant has been serving good local food for decades. The menu, including the set lunches, is very extensive and you can be literally lost for choice. Service is quick and attentive.

Chifa Roberto Siu (☎ 53 1207; Junín 310; mains US$3-4.50; 🕑 11am-2pm & 6-11pm) Also on the plaza, this is the best *chifa* (Chinese restaurant) in town for a fairly wide selection of Peruvian Chinese staples.

Los Koquis (☎ 53 1536; Tarma 376; mains US$3-6; 🕑 11am-11pm) Also on the plaza, this place advertises its jungle specialties to lure punters in. Its *pachamanca* chicken (marinated and cooked in an earthen 'oven' of hot rocks) and ceviche are also well regarded.

SAN RAMÓN
The hotel restaurants are worth a visit.

Chifa Felipe Siu (☎ 33 1078; Progreso 440; 🕑 11am-2pm & 6:30-11pm) This reliable place is recommended by locals – it's a bit of an establishment here.

Getting There & Away
AIR
Air service is provided by local companies with light aircraft. There are daily flights to Puerto Bermúdez. For other destinations, go to the airport early in the morning and ask around for a flight. Planes carry five to nine passengers and leave when full. Planes can be chartered to almost anywhere in the region. The Chanchamayo airstrip is a 30-minute walk from San Ramón. *Colectivos* and taxis will take you there.

BUS
The bus terminal is a 1km downhill walk east of the center of La Merced. Most buses arrive/leave from here. Schedules are haphazard – go down there as early as you can and ask around.

Direct buses go from Lima to Chanchamayo, though some travelers find it convenient to break the journey at Tarma. It is worth trying to travel the 70km stretch from Tarma to San Ramón in daylight for the views during the spectacular 2200m descent. Companies going to Lima (US$7, eight hours) include **Junín** (☎ 53 1256), which has two day buses and two night sleeping buses daily to Lima (upstairs/downstairs US$8/9.50) and is considered the most reliable service. Expreso Satipo, Transportes Lobato and others also go to Lima with several daily departures. **Empresa de Transportes San Juan** (☎ 53 1522) charges US$4.50 for the five-hour journey to Huancayo (with stops at Tarma and Jauja). Frequent buses (various companies) go to Tarma (US$2, 2½ hours).

Most transportation into the jungle is by large minibus. The minibuses leave for Pichanaqui (US$1.80, one hour) about every half-hour. Change at Pichanaqui for another minibus to Satipo. **Empresa Santa Rosa** (☎ 53 1084) has frequent minibuses to Oxapampa (US$3.50, three hours), with a few continuing to Pozuzo (US$5.50, six to seven hours). For Puerto Bermúdez (US$10, seven to 12 hours), Empresa Fisel and Transdife leave at 4am; these are trucks with seats in the cabin. The journey depends on weather and road conditions.

In San Ramón **Empresa de Transportes** (☎ 33 1410; cnr Progreso & Paucartambo) runs buses to Tarma and Cerro de Pasco.

TAXI
Colectivo taxis seating four passengers go to Tarma (US$4.50) and Pichanaqui (US$2.50). Ask at the bus terminal.

Getting Around
Minibuses link La Merced with San Ramón every few minutes (US$0.25; 15 minutes), leaving from outside the bus terminal. *Mototaxis* charge US$0.30 to drive you from the terminal up into La Merced center or anywhere round town.

PICHANAQUI
☎ 064 / pop 13,200 / elev 500m
Almost 70km east of La Merced on the newly paved road to Satipo, Pichanaqui is a fast-growing center for coffee production. Sitting on the Río Perené, the town attracts some local tourism during the April to August dry months when water levels drop and sandy beaches are revealed. **Playa El Pescador** is a favorite beach, with several restaurants serving mainly fish – El Bambú and El Parralito are locally recommended. Hotels are popping up almost overnight in this booming town; try **Hospedaje Brice's** (☎ 34 7745; 7 de Junio 375; d US$10-12), which has private showers and fans; the better rooms also have cable TV.

Frequent minibuses from Pichanaqui run to Satipo (US$1.25, 45 minutes) and La Merced (US$1.80, one hour).

SATIPO
☎ 064 / pop 15,700 / elev 630m
This jungle town is the center of a coffee- and fruit-producing region and lies about 130km by road southeast of La Merced. This road was paved in 2000 to provide an outlet for produce, and as a result Satipo is growing quickly. It is also linked by a poor road to the highlands of Huancayo. There is a BCP (ATM).

There are several other cheap and more basic hotels than the following.

Half a block from the plaza, **Hostal Palmero** (☎ 54 5020, 54 5543; eliana0301@yahoo.es; Manuel Prado 229; s/d US$8/12) has varied rooms at varied rates. The best ones have cold shower, fan and cable TV, while the cheapest have communal showers and no TV. A restaurant is attached.

Modern, clean and the best in town, **Hostal San José** (☎ 54 5105, 54 5990; eri369@hotmail.com; AB Leguía 684; s/d US$8/12) has cool tiled floors, hot water and cable TV.

On the Central Plaza, **Hotel Majestic** (☎ /fax 54 5762; Colonos Fundadores Principal 408; s/d US$10/15) is a simple but clean choice with private cold showers and cable TV.

The nearby airport has light aircraft for charter. Flights to Pucallpa and other jungle towns leave irregularly, when there are enough passengers.

AGUARDIENTE: PERUVIAN FIREWATER

While it is considered primarily a Colombian tipple, *aguardiente* is an equally popular drink in Peru. Distilled from sugarcane molasses, flavored with anise and given its characteristic sweet flavor with the addition of extra sugar, this South American firewater sure packs a punch. Unlike other aperitif spirits, *aguardiente* is not considered a gentle sipping tipple. Said one hardened *aguardiente* imbiber when pressed, 'It's not a sipping drink. You get a table and a bottle and sit there until it's gone.' At 60% proof when finally bottled, the drink is not to be taken lightly. Andean farm workers often carry a flask to ward off the chill mountain air. Travelers might pick up a bottle for sale by the roadside in the jungle areas of Peru where it is mostly made.

AMAZON BASIN

Minibuses leave many times a day for Pichanaqui, where you can change for La Merced. A few slower, larger buses leave every morning and evening for La Merced, some continuing on to Lima. **Selva Tours** (☎ 54 5631; Manuel Prado 455) has four daily buses to Huancayo (US$4.50, eight to nine hours) via the spectacular but difficult direct road through Comas.

EAST OF SATIPO

It's possible to continue east into the jungle. A fairly good unpaved road goes through **Mazamari**, 20km away, where there's the clean **Hospedaje Divina Montaña** (☎ 54 8042; d US$5). It offers hot showers, a sauna and a popular restaurant serving jungle and game dishes. Another 40km further and you'll come to **Puerto Ocopa**, reached by *colectivo* from Satipo in a couple of hours. Beyond Puerto Ocopa, a rough road continues to **Atalaya** at the intersection of the Ríos Urubamba, Tambo and Ucayali. The road may be impassable, in which case boats go down the Río Tambo to Atalaya, taking a full day.

In Atalaya, there are simple hotels and an airstrip with connections to Satipo. Boats can be found to Pucallpa every few days (US$14, one to three days). Atalaya is two or three days away by boat from Sepahua to the east, though there are few boats.

OXAPAMPA

☎ 063 / pop 7800 / elev 1800m

This is a ranching and coffee center, 75km north of La Merced. Look around at your fellow passengers on the bus north from La Merced – occasional blond heads and blue eyes attest to the several hundred German settlers who arrived in the mid-19th century. Their descendants inhabit Oxapampa and smaller, lower **Pozuzo** (three to four hours north of Oxapampa by daily minibus; longer in the wet season), and have preserved many Germanic customs. Buildings have a Tyrolean look to them, Austrian-German food is prepared and an old-fashioned form of German is still spoken by some families. Although the area has been long settled, it is remote and rarely visited. The people are friendly and interested in talking with tourists.

Oxapampa has a BCP and several simple and cheap hotels. The cold-water *hostales* **Rocío** (☎ 76 2163), **Santa Isolina** (☎ 76 2305/6), Arias and Liz have been recommended as clean

and charge about US$3 to US$6 per person. Pozuzo also has several hotels, of which El Tirol is the best at about US$10 per person including meals.

PUERTO BERMÚDEZ

☎ 063 / pop 1000 / elev 500m

Looking at the huddle of dugout canoes tied up to the mud bank of the little Río Pachitea flowing past sleepy Puerto Bermúdez, it is difficult to imagine that one can embark here on a river journey that would eventually lead down the Amazon to the Atlantic.

The area southeast of Puerto Bermúdez is the home of the Ashaninka tribespeople, the largest indigenous Amazon group in Peru. In the late 1980s and early '90s, Sendero Luminoso guerrillas attempted to indoctrinate the Ashaninka. When the guerrillas were unable to get the indigenous peoples' total support, they tried intimidation by massacring dozens. Thankfully, Sendero activity has been reduced since the capture of the guerrilla leaders. People interested in learning more about the Ashaninka can get information in Puerto Bermúdez. Contact Albergue Humboldt (below) if you want to visit the Ashaninka.

Located near the river, **Albergue Humboldt** (☎ 83 0020; www.alberguehumboldt.com; r US$4) is the best place to stay in the region. You can enjoy rustic rooms with shared cold showers and electricity from 8am to 11pm, or sleep in a hammock, or camp. Three meals, plus drinking water, tea and coffee, can be had for an extra US$5 per day. The friendly and hospitable Basque-born owner Jesus López de Dicastillo will arrange all manner of trekking, wildlife and cultural expeditions into Ashaninka territory for US$18 to US$30 per person per day, depending on group size and including food, boat and accommodation in simple shelters. Highly recommended for budget adventurers!

Hostal Tania (r per person US$3) is another basic hotel right by the river; it offers four walls and a river view that is pretty, especially at dawn and dusk.

The town's main street has a few simple eateries.

Trucks carrying passengers go to La Merced daily. Continuing north the road deteriorates, and erratic transportation to Ciudad Constitución, Zungaro, Puerto Inca and Pucallpa is often by truck. This trip is very rough and can take two days. Boats go north to Ciudad

Constitución and Puerto Inca, but do not have particular schedules. During the dry season, the river may be too low for passage, and the road is the better bet. During the wet months, the road can be barely passable, and boats are better. You can also fly from the airstrip near Puerto Bermúdez. The folks at Albergue Humboldt know what's going on.

PUCALLPA

☎ 061 / pop 324,900 / elev 154m

For the uninitiated it is quite a revelation to arrive at Pucallpa (pu-kal-pa), the capital of the department of Ucayali, after miles of lush jungle travel from the raw and rocky Andes. The sight of the sweeping Río Ucayali pushing its way through Amazonian hinterland is impressive. You feel as if you have reached the coast. In fact you can reach the coast – eventually – in Brazil via the Río Ucayali and its major partner the Río Amazonas.

Pucallpa is the Amazon region's only town to be linked to Lima by a paved road. For that reason it is an important river port for the distribution of goods along the broad Río Ucayali. It's a fast-growing place and a busy and lively river port. Bedeviled by dust and hovered over by flocks of ominous-looking vultures, the town nonetheless comes to life at night when people flock to meander around the Plaza de Armas.

Travelers come to Pucallpa in search of that riverboat north to Iquitos or beyond, to visit the local indigenous communities or to simply relax for a few days at a comfortable river lodge a short ride north of the town. While the town has a frontier feel to it with its mix of modernity and shantytown simplicity, it is nonetheless a friendly and engaging place and worth a day or two to pause and take stock.

Information

Internet cabinas abound on every block. Several banks change money and traveler's checks and have ATMs. Foreign-exchange houses are found along the 4th, 5th and 6th cuadras (blocks) of Raimondi. For jungle guides go to Yarinacocha.

Clínica Santa Rosa (☎ 57 1689; Inmaculada 529; ☼ 24hr) Quite good for stool, urine or blood tests.

Clínica Zar Nicolas (☎ 57 2854; Saenz Peña 166) Also good.

Lavandería Gasparin (☎ 59 1147; Portillo 526; ☼ 9am-1pm & 4-8pm Mon-Sat) Provides both self-service and drop-off laundry services.

Tourist booth (☎ 57 1303; 2 de Mayo 111) At the airport, a small booth that is more often than not unattended.

Utopi@.net (cnr Morey & Immaculada; ☼ 8am-11pm) As good as any internet cabina and is close to the eating options in 'pizza strip.'

Viajes Laser (☎ 57 1120; fax 57 3776; Raimondi 399) Western Union is here, at one of the better travel agencies in Pucallpa.

Sights

Many travelers visit nearby Yarinacocha, which, although it is more interesting than Pucallpa, is far from touristy yet has some good accommodation options.

About 4km from the center of Pucallpa, off the road to the airport, is **Parque Natural** (admission US$0.70; ☼ 9am-5pm). Here you'll find an Amazon zoo, a museum displaying Shipibo pottery and a few other objects, a small children's playground and a snack bar. Buses heading to the airport can drop you here, or a *motocarro* is about US$1.

Usko-Ayar (☎ 57 3088; Sánchez Cerro 465) is the gallery of the visionary local artist Pablo Cesar Amaringo Shuna, whose work and biography can be accessed at www.egallery.com. Other promising Amazonian artists study, work and display here – it's well worth a visit. Tell drivers it's near the Iglesia Fray Marcos.

Agustín Rivas (☎ 57 1834; 2nd fl, Tarapaca 861) is a famed local woodcarver whose work graces the lobbies of some of Pucallpa's best hotels and businesses. Ring the bell to enter his house-gallery.

Sleeping

BUDGET

Hostal Perú (☎ 57 5128; Raimondi 639; s/d with shared bathroom US$4.25/5.50, s/d from US$5.50/7.50 or US$9/11.50) A Shipibo pot collection brightens the faded entry stairs of this large, older property. Rooms are tiny but clean with small fan. More expensive rooms have been refurbished. Showers are cold and TVs are an extra US$1.50.

Hostería del Rey (☎ 57 5815; Portillo 753; s/d US$5/6) High ceilings indicate this hotel was built for the tropics – hot air rises. Cold showers and fans keep you cool, and a TV can be added for US$1.50.

Hospedaje Barbtur (☎ 57 2532; Raimondi 670; s/d with shared bathroom US$7.50/8, s/d US$10/11) Small, friendly, well maintained and family run, this hotel has cold showers and includes cable TV in its en suite rooms.

PUCALLPA

| | 0 | 300 m |
| | 0 | 0.2 mi |

INFORMATION
Clínica Santa Rosa	1	C3
Clínica Zar Nicolas	2	B2
Lavandería Gasparin	3	C5
Utopi@.net	4	C3
Viajes Laser	5	C4
Western Union	(see 5)	

SIGHTS & ACTIVITIES
| Agustín Rivas Gallery | 6 | C4 |

SLEEPING 🏠
Antonio's Hospedaje	7	B4
El Gran Dorado	8	C3
Hospedaje Amazonas	9	C5
Hospedaje Barbtur	10	C5
Hospedaje El Virrey	11	D4
Hospedaje Komby	12	B4
Hospedaje Sisley	13	C5
Hostal Arequipa	14	B4
Hostal Happy Day	15	C5
Hostal Perú	16	C5
Hostal Tariri	17	C5
Hostería del Rey	18	C5
Hotel America	19	D4
Hotel Mercedes	20	C4
Hotel Sol del Oriente	21	C4
Ruíz Hotel	22	C4

EATING 🍴
Cebichería El Escorpión	23	B4
C'est Si Bon	24	B4
Chez Maggy	25	C3
Chifa Mey Lin	26	C3
El Portal Chicken	27	B4
Fuente Soda Tropitop	28	C4
Parrilladas El Braserito	29	C4
Restaurant El Golf	30	D4
Restaurant Kitty	31	D4
Restaurant Pizzeria Sofia	32	C4
Supermercado Los Andes	33	C5

TRANSPORT
Copacabana	34	B4
LC Busre	35	C4
León de Huánuco (to Lima)	36	C4
Star Perú	37	C5
Trans Amazonica (to Lima)	38	C4
Transmar (to Lima)	39	C5
Transportes El Rey (to Lima)	40	C5
Transportes Palcazu (to Amazon Towns)	41	C5
Turismo Ucayali	42	C5

Hospedaje Sisley (☎ 57 5137; Portillo 658, upstairs; s/d US$8.50/12) Friendly older ladies run this decent budget hotel. Tidy, secure rooms include private cold shower, fan and TV.

Hospedaje Komby (☎ 57 1562; www.hospedaje kombi.com.pe; Ucayali 360; s/d US$10/12; 🏊) Rooms are clean but basic, though the small pool and restaurant make up for that.

Hostal Happy Day (☎ 57 2067; fax 57 3263; Huáscar 440; s US$10-17.50, d US$13-20, all incl breakfast; ❄) You can't miss this orange-and-ochre-colored building. Rooms are tiny but quiet.

El Gran Dorado (☎ /fax 57 4592; Independencia 204; s/d US$12.50/19) The electric blue tiled reception and hallways ooze hygiene. Rooms are small-ish but spotless and have a minifridge. Rates

AMAZON BASIN

include a continental breakfast daily except Sunday. Discounts are readily available for longer stays.

Also consider the following:

Hospedaje Amazonas (☎ 57 1080; Portillo 729; s/d US$4.50/6) Basic, dingy rooms have a cold shower and fan, and the price is right.

Hostal Tariri (☎ 57 5147; Raimondi 733; s US$4.50-6, d US$6-9) Rooms with cold shower vary substantially in size and quality.

MIDRANGE

All the following have rooms with bathroom, fan and cable TV.

Hospedaje El Virrey (☎ 57 5611; ☎/fax 59 0579; hotelvirrey@speedy.com.pe; Tarapaca 945; s US$14-27.50, d US$17-38; ⚇) Rooms are neat and well kept. The pricier rooms have warm shower and air-con and include an American breakfast in the hotel restaurant.

Hotel America (☎/fax 57 5989; hotelamerica@viabcp .com; Portillo 357; s US$14-30, d US$20-40, mini ste US$39-47, all incl breakfast; ⚇ ⚇) Rooms are modern but small and amenities vary; minifridges, telephones and hot showers are available. There is a small restaurant, and continental or American breakfast is included.

Hostal Arequipa (☎ 57 3171, 57 3112; www.hostal -arequipa.com; Progreso 573; s US$17-28, d US$20.50-34.50; ⚇) This is a popular and often full mid-range choice, and has attractive public areas, hot water, minifridges, restaurant and airline ticket sales and reconfirmation. The pricier rooms with air-con also include a continental breakfast.

Antonio's Hospedaje (☎ 57 3721, 57 4721; www .antonios-pucallpa.com; Progreso 545; s US$18-25, d US$22-31.50; ⚇) Rooms here are huge and have hot shower, comfortable mattresses and mini-fridge. A small garden with armchairs allows outdoor relaxation.

Hotel Mercedes (☎ 57 5120; ☎/fax 57 1191; ghotelmercedes@hotmail.com; Raimondi 610; s US$20-22, d US$26-29, ste US$61; ⚇ ⚇) This was Pucallpa's first good hotel and has a certain dated charm and character. Rooms, though faded, are well looked after and have comfortable beds and minifridge. The pool (US$3 for nonguests) is set in a lush garden and there is a good restaurant-bar on the premises. Some rooms can be noisy. The four suites have a full sitting room.

Ruíz Hotel (☎ 57 1280, 57 2771; hotelruiz@speedy .com.pe; San Martín 475; s/d incl breakfast US$29/36; ⚇) An odd-looking hotel with only three of its

six stories completed, it nonetheless takes guests. Rooms are spartan but bigger than average, and have phone, warm shower, cable TV and minifridge.

TOP END

Hotel Sol del Oriente (☎ 57 5154; ☎/fax 57 5510; hsoloriente@qnet.com.pe; San Martín 552; s/d/ste US$65/80/130, s/d with Jacuzzi US$75/90; ⚇ ⚇) This is about the best you'll get in Pucallpa proper. It's not that flash but it's comfortable. The rooms are of a decent size, have air-con, TV and a welcome minibar and good, always-hot showers. Within, the hotel boasts a pool and palm-shaded garden punctuated with life-sized carved wooden statues.

Eating

The town abounds with cheap and midrange restaurants, though few are noteworthy. The heat in the middle of the day means that restaurants tend to open by 7am for breakfast. Many are closed Sunday.

Restaurant Kitty (☎ 57 4764; Tarapaca 1062; menús US$1.50) The Kitty is clean and popular and brings in local lunch crowds. Join 'em!

Restaurant Pizzeria Sofia (☎ 57 2629; Sucre 415; menús US$1.90 ⏰ 7am-11pm) Slap-bang on the main square, this friendly little joint is a great spot for hearty breakfasts, while its lunchtime *menús* are good value. Pizzas are the specialty and they deliver too.

El Portal Chicken (☎ 57 1771; Independencia 510; mains about US$3; ⏰ 5pm-midnight) You can hardly miss this three-story restaurant with its open-air plaza views and the brightest neon lights in town. It is the best of several chicken restaurants in the area and it also serves a few other meaty dishes.

Chez Maggy (☎ 57 4958; Inmaculada 643; mains/large pizza US$3/7) Maggy has pizza from a wood-burning oven and tasty pastas. The interior is modern and not plasticized like some of its neighbors, and the pizzas really are good. The Maggy special topped with an egg is worth a try. The unusual, tropical-tasting sangria goes down well with all dishes.

Chifa Mey Lin (☎ 57 4687; Sucre 698; mains US$3; ⏰ closed Sun) There are a lot of *chifas* in town but this one gets the gong for being the best of the bunch.

Cebichería El Escorpión (☎ 57 4516; Independencia 430; meals US$3-6) This option has a prime plaza location, with (noisy) sidewalk tables, and serves good seafood for breakfast and lunch

The ceviche, despite Pucallpa's distance from the sea, is tender and fresh.

Restaurant El Golf (☎ 57 4632; Huáscar 545; mains US$3.50-7; 🕙 10am-5pm; ❄) Diagonally opposite the Mey Lin is this more upscale seafood restaurant with a variety of ceviches – try the local *doncella* rather than the endangered *paiche*.

Parrilladas El Braserito (San Martín 498; mains US$5-8; 🕙 11:30am-4pm daily & 6-11pm Mon-Sat) For good grills (steak, fish and venison) in an elegant atmosphere, this is a good choice.

C'est Si Bon (☎ 57 1893; Independencia 560) and **Fuente Soda Tropitop** (☎ 57-2860; Sucre 401; 🕙 7am-11pm), on opposite corners of the plaza, are bright spots serving ice creams, snacks, breakfasts and sandwiches for US$1 to US$3.

For long trips, stock up at **Supermercado Los Andes** (Portillo 545).

Shopping
The local Shipibo tribespeople wander the streets of town selling souvenirs. More of their work is seen near Yarinacocha. For details on their handicrafts, see p479.

Getting There & Away
AIR
Pucallpa's pleasant and decent-sized airport is 5km northwest of town. It currently only handles two flights daily to/from Lima. **LC Busre** (☎ 57 5309; Tarapaca) has direct flights to/from Lima (US$75) leaving midmorning, while **Star Perú** (☎ 59 0586; 7 de Julio 865) has an alternative direct flight for around the same price leaving early afternoon. Luggage on these flights is limited to 10kg. You'll have to pay around US$1.30 for each excess kilogram. Departure tax is US$3.57, payable at the booth in the concourse lounge before check-in.

Other towns and settlements (including Atalaya, Contamaná, Juanjuí, Puerto Breu, Purus, Sepahua, Tarapoto and Yurimaguas) are served by small local airlines using light aircraft. **Aero Andino** (☎ 59 2072; fax 57 2291) sometimes flies to Tarapoto, among other destinations; **North American** (☎ 57 2351; fax 57 3168, Aeropuerto) flies to Contamaná daily and sometimes to Tarapoto. Note that luggage on these flights is limited to 10kg per passenger.

BOAT
Pucallpa's port moves depending on water levels. During high water (January to April) boats dock at the town itself, abutting Parque

San Martín. As water levels drop, the port moves to about 3km northeast of the town center, reached by minibuses from the center (US$0.50).

Wherever the port is, riverboats sail the Río Ucayali from Pucallpa to Iquitos (US$18 to US$30 including basic meals, three to five days). Cabins with two or four bunks cost an extra US$1.50 per bunk per day, and come with better food service. Boats announce their departure dates and destinations on chalkboards on the boats themselves, but these can unreliable. Talk to the captain or the cargo loadmaster for greater dependability. They must present boat documents on the morning of their departure day at the **Capitanía** (☎ 57 2517; M Castilla 860). Many people work here, but only the official in charge of documents knows the real scoop and can give you accurate sailing information. Passages are daily when the river is high, but in the dry season low water levels result in slower, less frequent passages.

The quality of the boats varies greatly both in size and comfort. Choose a boat that looks good. The *Henry V* when it is in port is one of the better-equipped outfits and can take up to 250 passengers.

This is not a trip for everyone; see p523 for more details on traveling by boat. Come prepared – the market in Pucallpa sells hammocks, but the mosquito repellent may be of poor quality. Bottled drinks are sold on board, but it's worth bringing some large bottles of water or juice.

Jungle 'guides' approaching you on the Pucallpa waterfront are usually unreliable and sometimes dishonest. For jungle excursions, look for a reliable service in Yarinacocha. For a riverboat passage, ask at any likely looking boat, but don't pay until you and your luggage are aboard the boat of your choice. Then pay the captain and no one else.

The river journey can be broken at various villages, including Contamaná (15 to 20 hours) and Requena, and continued on the next vessel coming through. Or ask around for speedboats to Contamaná (US$23, about five hours). The return trip (US$29, six to seven hours) goes against the current. Boats leave daily about noon in each direction.

BUS
A direct bus to and from Lima (US$13) takes 20 hours in the dry season; the journey can

WARNING

The long and lonely section of road between Pucallpa and Tingo María is the only paved link between Peru's Amazonas region and the rest of the country. It can also be a risky road to travel on. Armed robberies have happened on many occasions and travelers have been caught up in the holdups. It used to be that robbers only targeted victims at night, and these included passengers in cars, trucks and buses. A series of daylight robberies (around 6pm to be precise) at the time of research has meant that the villains are getting bolder. Robbers take money and valuables and, assuming no one resists, they then allow onward passage. The police seem powerless to prevent these highway heists. Buses do make the trip daily to and from Tingo, but you take your own risk. Holidays and feast days seem to be the worst times. The safest option is to fly to Pucallpa from Lima.

be broken in Huánuco (US$8, nine hours) or Tingo María (US$5, nine hours).

León de Huánuco (☎ 57 2411, 57 9751; Tacna 655) serves Lima at noon and 5:30pm, as do **Transportes El Rey** (☎ 57 5545, 57 6793; Raimondi at 7 de Junio) at 11am and 11:30am; **Transmar** (☎ 57 4900, 59 2264; Raimondi 793) at 1pm and 4:30pm; and **Trans Amazonica** (☎ 57 1292; Tacna 628) at 5pm daily.

Turismo Ucayali (☎ 59 3002; 7 de Junio 799) has cars to Aguaytía (US$8) and Tingo María (US$14, six hours) leaving about every hour all day and night. At the same cross street, small companies have cars and minibuses to Aguaytía and Tingo María.

Transportes Palcazu (☎ 57 1273; Raimondi 730) has trucks and buses to Puerto Bermúdez and Puerto Zungaro.

Getting Around

Motocarros to the airport or Yarinacocha are about US$2; taxis are US$3.20. *Colectivos* to Yarinacocha (US$0.25) leave from 9 de Diciembre near the market, San Martín at Ucayali, and other places.

In Pucallpa, motorcycles can be rented from **Copacabana** (☎ 50 5304; Ucayali 265; per hr US$2.20, per day US$15-20).

YARINACOCHA

About 10km northeast of the center of Pucallpa, Yarinacocha is a lovely oxbow lake where you can go canoeing, observe wildlife, and visit indigenous communities and purchase their handicrafts. The lake, once part of the Río Ucayali, is now entirely landlocked, though a small canal links the two bodies of water during the rainy season. Boat services are provided here in a casual atmosphere. It's well worth spending a couple of days here.

A part of the lake has been set aside as a reserve. There is also a **botanical garden** (admis-

sion US$0.60; ☒ 8am-4pm), which is reached by a 45-minute boat ride followed by a 30-minute walk. Go early in the morning to watch birds on the walk there.

The lakeside village of **Puerto Callao** is a welcome relief from the chaos of downtown Pucallpa's streets. It's still a ramshackle kind of place with only a dirt road skirting the busy waterfront. Large and indifferent buzzards amble among the pedestrians and *peki-peki* boats come and go to their various destinations all day.

Here you'll find limited choice but generally good accommodations as well as some decent food. You can also hire **boats** here – in fact you'll be nabbed as soon as you turn up by boat touts seeking to lure you to their vessel. Choose your boat carefully and make sure it has new-looking life jackets. Wildlife to watch out for includes freshwater pink dolphins, sloths and meter-long green iguanas, as well as exotic birds such as the curiously long-toed wattled jacana (which walks on lily pads) and the metallic green Amazon kingfisher. If you like **fishing**, the dry season is said to be the best time.

Internet is available at three or four places, most near or on the main square up the hill.

Tours & Guides

Whatever your interests, you'll find plenty of *peki-peki* boat owners ready to oblige. Take your time in choosing a tour; there's no point in going with the first offer unless you are sure you like your boat driver. Guides are also available for walking trips into the surrounding forest including some overnight hikes.

A recommended guide is **Gilber Reategui Sangama** (☎ 061-962 7607, 061-985 5352; www.sacredherit age.com/normita), who owns the boat *La Normita* on Yarinacocha. He has expedition supplies (sleeping pads, mosquito nets, drinking water) and is both knowledgeable and environmentally aware. He speaks some English, is safe and reliable, and will cook most of your meals for you. He charges about US$35 per person per day, or US$7 per hour, with a minimum of two people, for an average of three to five days. Gilber works with Arcesio Morales and Roberto 'Jungle Man' Tamani, who don't speak English. He also recommends his uncle and nephew, Nemecio and Daniel Sangama, with their boat *El Rayito*.

Others who have been recommended for local day tours include the friendly **Miguel 'Pituco' Tans** (☎ 59 7494) and his boat *Pituco*; **Eduardo Vela** (☎ message 57 5383; 2 de Mayo, Nuevo Eden), with *The Best*; Gustavo Paredes with *Poseidon*; Mauricio (nicknamed 'Boa'); and Jorge Morales.

Note that other guides will claim that the above are unavailable or don't work there. Don't believe all you hear. A good boat driver will float slowly along, so that you can look for birdlife at the water's edge, or sloths *(perezosos)* in the trees. Sunset is a good time to be on the lake.

Trips to the **Shipibo villages** of either San Francisco (which is now reached by road) or, better, Santa Clara, which is reached by boat, are also popular. For short trips, boat drivers charge about US$5 an hour for the boat, which can carry several people. It's always worth bargaining over the price.

Sleeping & Eating
PUERTO CALLAO
There is really only one decent place to stay in the port and that is **La Maloka Ecolodge** (☎ 59 6072; lamaloka@soldeloriente.com; s/d US$25/37.50). It's worth forking out the extra cash for the comfort. Located at the right-hand (southern) end

of the waterfront, this lodge is built right out on the water, with the ample-sized but unadorned rooms sitting on stilts over the lake. There's a relaxing outdoor restaurant and bar area overlooking the lake and pink dolphins regularly flash their flippers for guests. The only downside is a small menagerie of sad-looking caged animals.

Several inexpensive restaurants and lively bars line the Puerto Callao waterfront. The better ones are toward the south side, where you'll find the aforementioned La Maloka Ecolodge as well as the Catahua, the Anaconda or the Puerto Rico, to name three of the more appealing choices.

NUEVA LUZ DE FATIMA
This village of about 50 families is a 20-minute boat ride from Puerto Callao. **Gilber Reategui Sangama** (☎ message 57 9018; junglesecrets@yahoo.com; r per person US$15) and his family offer rustic home hospitality, including all meals and very basic shared showers. Gilber's father is a shaman with over 50 years' experience who conducts ceremonies.

LAKESIDE
Both La Cabaña and La Perla arrange tours, and are within an hour's walk of the botanical garden.

La Cabaña (☎ 57 1689; per person incl meals US$35) A 10-minute *peki-peki* ride from Puerto Callao across the lake, this lodge has 15 simple bungalows with private bathroom and electricity.

La Perla (☎ 061-961 6004; www.eproima.net/laperla; per person incl meals & airport transfer US$30) A few minutes beyond La Cabaña is this family-run boarding house with double rooms sharing showers, and a family bungalow. Solar-powered electricity is available in the evening.

SHIPIBO TRIBESPEOPLE
The matriarchal Shipibo tribespeople live along the Río Ucayali and its tributaries in small loose villages of simple, thatched platform houses. Often visited are San Francisco, at the northwest end of Yarinacocha and accessible by dirt road from Pucallpa, and the boat-access-only village of Santa Clara. San Francisco even has simple lodgings (from US$3 per person).

Shipibo women craft delicate pots and textiles, decorated with highly distinctive, geometric designs. In Puerto Callao they run a fine craft store, Maroti Shobo, which collects work from about 40 villages. Each piece is handmade so though patterns are similar, each one is unique. They range from inexpensive small pots and animal figurines to huge urns valued at hundreds of dollars (and more, internationally). The friendly staff arrange international shipping if you buy a large piece. Prices are fixed but fair.

Pandisho Albergue (☎ 57 5041, 962 0030; incl meals dm US$3, s/d US$25/50) About 30 minutes from Puerto Callao in a different direction, this place has eight rooms with bathroom, and electricity from 6am to 10pm. Its bar is popular with locals on weekends when there's music, but it's quiet otherwise.

CONTAMANÁ TO REQUENA

Contamaná has a colorful waterfront market, a frontier-town atmosphere and, like most river towns, is settled mainly by *mestizo* colonists. It also boasts an airstrip, 24-hour electricity and some internet cafés.

Stay in 10-room **Hostal Augusts** (☎ 065-85 1008; s/d US$9/12) on the plaza. It's the best in town and rooms have a shower, fan and TV. **Hotel Venezia** (☎ 065-85 1031, 065-85 1047; s/d US$3/6, r with shower, TV & fan US$9) has friendly staff servicing 40 rooms with shared bathroom and nine with bathroom. There are several other cheaper and dingier options.

The next major port is **Orellana**, which has electricity from 6:30pm to 10:30pm and half a dozen basic hotels charging US$3/5 or less for singles/doubles with shared bathroom. Rooms with bathroom are under construction. Further on, the village of **Juancito** has some very basic rooms.

In the town of **Requena** (two to four days from Pucallpa), with 24-hour electricity, the nicest sleeps are tiny but cute **Hostal Jicely** (☎ 065-41 2216, 065-41 2493; M Manaos 292; s/d US$9/10), and friendly **Hotel Río Seco** (☎ 065-41 2242; s/d US$7/10) with rooms with TV and fan, and the Palo Alto restaurant next door. There's several other more basic places. Boats to Iquitos leave on most days, taking 12 to 15 hours.

NORTHERN AMAZON

Raw, vast and encapsulating the real spirit of the Amazon, the northern Amazon Basin is home to the eponymous river that wells up from the depths of the Peruvian jungle before making its long, languorous passage to the distant Atlantic Ocean. This is Peru at its Amazonian truest.

YURIMAGUAS

☎ 065 / pop 42,800 / elev 181m

Yurimaguas is a quiet, pleasant town little changed in the last decade – quite different from the bustling boomtown atmosphere of Pucallpa. There are signs of the rubber days, such as the expensive imported tiles decorating buildings at the end of Av Arica, but generally it is a sleepy port where you may wait a day or two for a riverboat to Iquitos. Locals call Yurimaguas 'the pearl of the Huallaga.' It is the major port on the Río Huallaga, and is also reached by road from Tarapoto or air from Lima.

Orientation & Information

Yurimaguas is a compact town and can be walked around in a short space of time. The central Plaza de Armas abuts the Río Huallaga, and minibuses to the town arrive on Tacna, 400m from the plaza.

The **Consejo Regional** (Plaza de Armas) can give information. **Manguaré Expediciones** (Lores 126) arranges tours, sells handicrafts and gives information. BCP and Banco Continental (with a Visa ATM) will change US cash and traveler's checks. Internet places come and go frequently but there are a few around the center of the town.

Sleeping

Few hotels have hot water, though most have bathrooms.

Quinta Lucy (☎ 35 1575; Jáuregui 305; s with shared shower US$3, s/d US$3.50/4.50) This cheap place is decently run, although it is basic and rooms look like jail cells.

Hostal César Gustavo (☎ 35 1585; Atahualpa 102; s/d US$4.50/7.50) The best of the basic places, this is clean and quiet but has no hot water. It has decent beds and portable fans, plus local TV stations.

Hostal de Paz (☎ /fax 35 2123; Jáuregui 431; s/d US$6/8.50) This hotel lacks a sign but it's good value. Some of the rooms have a ceiling fan and cable TV.

Leo's Palace (☎ 35 3008, ☎ /fax 35 2213; Lores 108; s/d US$6/9) The oldest of the better hotels and now a bit run-down, Leo's has a few simple but spacious rooms with fan and a balcony overlooking the Plaza de Armas. TV is available on request and there is a restaurant serving decent cheap lunches (US$1.50).

Hostal El Naranjo (☎ 35 2650, 35 1560; elnaranjo@hotmail.com; Arica 318; s US$14-21, d US$15-23; ❖ 🖥 🖵) This clean, quiet and recommended hotel has rooms with ceiling fan and cable TV. The higher tariff is for air-con. There's hot water and internet access (US$1), plus it has a good restaurant.

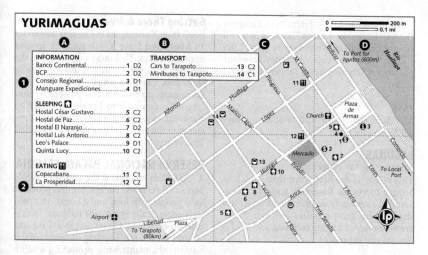

YURIMAGUAS

Hostal Luis Antonio (☎ 35 2065, ☎ /fax 35 2061; antonio@viabcp.com; Jáuregui 407; s US$15-21, d US$18-24; ✷ ✷) Prices here vary depending on whether you want cable TV and/or air-con. There is a decent restaurant and small pool, and all standard rooms have a fan; all are well maintained.

Porta Péricos (☎ 35 2009; San Miguel 720; s/d incl breakfast US$30/40; ✷) On the northern outskirts, overlooking the Río Paranapura, this hotel's breezy location negates the necessity for air-con, the staff claim. Rates include use of a games room (table tennis and foosball) but seem a tad high.

Eating

Many restaurants close between meals. The hotel restaurants are among the best, but they aren't anything special.

Copacabana (M Castilla at López) OK for standard food such as snacks, sandwiches and so on. Cheap and generally middle of the road.

La Prosperidad (☎ 35 2057; Progreso 107) Has tropical juices, burgers and chicken. It's popular as a local teenage hangout.

Shopping

Stores selling hammocks for river journeys are on the north side of the market.

Getting There & Around

AIR

No airline company currently serves Yurimaguas. The nearest mainline airport is at Tarapoto. A few local companies charter planes out of Yurimaguas, but choices are limited and the costs generally prohibitive.

BOAT

The main port 'La Boca' is 13 blocks north of the center. Cargo boats from Yurimaguas follow the Río Huallaga to the Río Marañón and on to Iquitos. The trip takes between three and five days with numerous stops for loading and unloading cargo. There are usually departures daily, except Sunday, at about 6pm. Passages cost US$15 to US$20 on deck (sling your own hammock and receive very basic food) or US$25 to US$30 for a bunk in double or quadruple cabins on the top deck, where the food is better and your gear is safer. Bottled water, soft drinks and snacks are sold onboard. Bring insect repellent and a hat. Boat information is available from the **Bodega Davila store** (☎ 35 2477) by the dock. The *Eduardo* boats (of which there are five) are considered the best. The journey can be broken at Lagunas (10 hours), just before the Río Huallaga meets the Marañón.

About every three or four weeks, the *MV Arca* cruise ship sails for Iquitos, taking five days.

BUS

For Tarapoto (US$3, six to eight hours), Paredes Estrella and Expreso Huamanga usually leave at 7am from their offices on the outskirts of town on the road to Tarapoto. Through tickets to Chiclayo and the Lima area are available.

Minibuses and pickup trucks to Tarapoto (US$4) leave town from Tacna when full several times daily from 4am to 6pm. Cars (US$7, five hours) leave when they have four passengers. The trip takes longer in the wet season.

TAXI

Mototaxis charge US$0.30 to take you anywhere around town.

LAGUNAS

☎ 065 / pop 300 / elev 148m

This village is the best point from which to begin a trip to the Reserva Nacional Pacaya-Samiria. Lagunas is small and remote, so you should bring most supplies with you. There are no money-changing facilities, and food is limited and expensive.

Tours & Guides

Spanish-speaking guides are locally available to visit Pacaya-Samiria. It is illegal to hunt within the reserve, but you may need to remind the guides of that (though fishing for the pot is OK). The going rate is a rather steep US$50 per person per day for guide, boat and accommodation in huts, tents and ranger stations. Food and park fees are extra. Often the guides will cook for you.

To avoid harassment and price-cutting, there is now an official guides association, **Estpel** (☎ 40 1007), which gives guides jobs in turn, so it is harder to get a particular guide. That said, the organization is currently headed by **Gamaniel Valles** (☎ 40 1005) who is himself a recommended guide with good knowledge of wildlife. Other recommended guides are Job Gongora and his nephews, and also Edinson and Kleber Saldaña, Juan Huaycama and Genaro Mendoza. However, you don't know whom you will get until you arrive.

Sleeping & Eating

Hotels are very basic, but choice is limited. The hostels provide cheap meals and are your best bet for food.

Hostal La Sombra (☎ 40 1063; r per person US$2) Has hot, stuffy little rooms with a shared shower.

Hostel (☎ 40 1009; r per person US$2) Above the Farmacia, this is a clean place that doesn't have showers (buckets of water are provided).

Hostal Miraflores (☎ 40 1001; Miraflores 249; s/d US$3/5) The best option, with clean rooms and a shared shower.

Getting There & Away

Boats from Yurimaguas to Lagunas take about 10 hours and leave Yurimaguas at around 6pm most days. This means an arrival in the wee hours, so make sure you ask the crew to wake you. The boat usually docks for about 20 minutes to load/unload passengers and cargo. To continue to Iquitos or return to Yurimaguas, ask which radio station is in contact with the boat captains to get an expected time of arrival.

RESERVA NACIONAL PACAYA-SAMIRIA

At 20,800 sq km, this is the largest of Peru's parks and reserves. Pacaya-Samiria provides local people with food and a home, and protects ecologically important habitats. In this case, an estimated 42,000 people live on and around the reserve. Juggling the needs of the human inhabitants while protecting wildlife is the responsibility of 20 to 30 rangers. Staff also teach inhabitants how to best harvest the natural renewable resources to benefit the local people and to maintain thriving populations of plants and animals. Despite this, three rangers were murdered by poachers in late 1998.

The reserve is the home of aquatic animals such as Amazon manatees, pink and grey river dolphins, two species of caiman, giant South American river turtles and many others. Monkeys and birds are abundant.

The best way to visit the reserve is to go by dugout canoe with a guide from Lagunas (see left) and spend several days camping and exploring. Alternately, comfortable ships visit from Iquitos (see p493). The nearest lodge is the Pacaya-Samiria Amazon Lodge (p492). The area close to Lagunas has suffered from depletion by hunting, so you need several days to get deep into the least-disturbed areas. Ranger stations charge US$20 to enter the reserve and you can then stay as long as you want. Official information is available at the reserve office in Iquitos.

The best time to go is during the dry season, when you are more likely to see animals along the riverbanks. Although rains ease off in late May, it takes a month or so for water levels to drop, making July and August the best months to visit (with excellent fishing). September to November isn't too bad, and December and January often have fairly low water. The heaviest rains begin in January, and the months of February to May are the worst times to go. February to June tend to be the hottest months.

Travelers should bring plenty of insect repellent and plastic bags (to cover luggage), and be prepared to camp out.

IQUITOS

☎ 065 / pop 430,000 / elev 130m

Linked to the outside world by air and by river, Iquitos is the world's largest city that cannot be reached by road. It has a unique personality: friendly, noisy, sassy and slightly manic. Travelers come here for an excursion into the rainforest or a river trip along the Amazon, but they often stay a few days to relish this remote jungle capital of the huge department of Loreto.

Iquitos was founded in the 1750s as a Jesuit mission, fending off attacks from indigenous tribes who didn't want to be converted. The tiny settlement survived and grew slowly until, by the 1870s, it had 1500 inhabitants. Then came the great rubber boom, and by the 1880s the population had increased 16-fold. For the next 30 years, Iquitos was at once the scene of ostentatious wealth and abject poverty. The rubber barons became fabulously rich, and the rubber tappers (mainly local tribespeople and poor *mestizos*) suffered virtual enslavement and sometimes death from disease or harsh treatment. Signs of the opulence of those days are seen in some of the mansions and tiled walls of Iquitos.

By WWI, the bottom fell out of the rubber boom as suddenly as it had begun. A British entrepreneur smuggled some rubber-tree seeds out of Brazil, and plantations were seeded in the Malay Peninsula. It was much cheaper and easier to collect the rubber from orderly rows of rubber trees in the plantations than from wild trees scattered in the Amazon Basin.

Iquitos suffered economic decline during the decades after WWI, supporting itself as best it could by a combination of logging, agriculture (Brazil nuts, tobacco, bananas and *barbasco* – a poisonous vine used by indigenous peoples to hunt fish and now exported for use in insecticides) and the export of wild animals to zoos. Then, in the 1960s, a second boom revitalized the area. This time the resource was oil, and its discovery made Iquitos a prosperous modern town. In recent years tourism has also played an important part in the economy of the area.

Orientation

Downtown Iquitos is 5km from its airport – most visitors arrive by air. If you choose to arrive by river, you'll end up at one of two ports, which are between 1km and 2km north of the city center.

Information

Because everything must be 'imported,' costs are higher than in other cities.

EMERGENCY

National police (☎ 23 3330; Morona 126)
Tourism police (☎ 24 2081, 23 1852; Lores 834)

IMMIGRATION

Brazil has a consul in Leticia, Colombia. If arriving/leaving from Brazil or Colombia, get your entry/exit stamp at the border.

Colombian Consulate (☎ 23 1461; Araujo 431;
🕒 9am-12:30pm & 2-4:30pm Mon-Fri)
Oficina de migraciónes (☎ 23 5371; M Cáceres, cuadra 18) Extend your tourist card or visa here.
Spanish Consulate (Putumayo 559)

INTERNET ACCESS

Many places charge under US$1 per hour:
Manugare Internet (Próspero 273) Fast machines.
Sured Internet (☎ 23 6119; Morona 213; 🕸)

LAUNDRY

Other laundries can be found in town.
Lavandería Imperial (☎ 23 1768; Putumayo 150;
🕒 8am-8pm Mon-Sat) Coin-operated.

MEDICAL SERVICES

Clínica Ana Stahl (☎ 25 2535; Av La Marina 285;
🕒 24 hr) Good private clinic.
Dr Rafael Urrunaga (☎ 23 5016; Fitzcarrald 201) Dentist.
Dr Victor Antonioli (☎ 23 2684; Fitzcarrald 156)
Speaks English.

MONEY

Several banks change traveler's checks, give advances on credit cards or provide an ATM. They have competitive rates. For changing US cash quickly, street money changers are on Lores at Próspero. Most are OK, but a few run scams where they cream off a 100-soles note and replace it with a 20-soles note. Exercise caution when changing money on the street. Changing Brazilian or Colombian currency is best done at the border. Transfer money at **Western Union** (☎ 23 5182; Napo 359).

IQUITOS

0 ————— 200 m
0 ————— 0.1 mi

INFORMATION
Banco Continental.....................1 C4
Banco Wiese & Western Union.2 C3
BCP..3 C3
Colombian Consulate................4 C3
Dr Rafael Urrunaga (Dentist).....5 D2
Dr Victor Antonioli....................6 D3
Gerald Mayeaux....................(see 11)
Inrena's Reserva Nacional
   Pacaya-Samiria Office...........7 C5
Interbank.................................8 C4
International Telephone Booths.9 C3
Laundry..................................10 C2
Lavandería Imperial................11 D3
Manugare Internet...................12 C3
Municipalidad......................(see 17)
National Police.......................13 C4
Post Office..............................14 C4
Spanish Consulate..................15 C3
Sured Internet.........................16 C4
Tourist Office..........................17 D3
Western Union........................18 C3

SIGHTS & ACTIVITIES
Amazon Tours & Cruises..........19 D1
Biblioteca Amazónica..........(see 22)
Casa de Fierro........................20 D3
Dawn on the Amazon..............21 D3
Museo Etnográfico.................22 D4

SLEEPING
Cumaceba Lodge (Office)........23 D3
Doral Inn................................24 D3
Heliconia Lodge (Office)..........25 C4
Hobo Hideout.........................26 C3
Hospedaje El Sitio...................27 C6
Hostal Alfert...........................28 C6
Hostal Amazonas....................29 C3
Hostal Ambassador.................30 D2
Hostal El Colibrí......................31 D3
Hostal La Pascana...................32 D3
Hostal Libertad.......................33 C4
Hostal Lima............................34 C4
Hostal Maflo...........................35 C4
Hotel El Dorado Plaza.............36 D3
Hotel Europa...........................37 C4
Hotel Sandalo.........................38 C5
Hotel Victoria Regia................39 C4
Loving Light Amazon Lodge
   (Office)...............................40 D3
Mad Mick's Bunkhouse............41 D3
Marañón Hotel........................42 D3

Muyuna Amazon Lodge
   (Office)...............................43 D3
Pacaya-Samiria Amazon Lodge
   (Office)...............................44 D2
Paseos Amazonicos (Offices)....45 D2
Real Hotel Iquitos...................46 D3

EATING
Antica.....................................47 D3
Ari's Burger............................48 D3
Chez Maggy............................49 D3
Chifa Cuan Chu.......................50 C3
Chifa Long Fung......................51 B4
Fitzcarraldo Restaurant-Bar.....52 D3
Gran Maloka...........................53 D4
Kikiriki...................................54 C3
Lidia's....................................55 A5
Nuevo Mesón..........................56 D3
Parrillada Al Carbón................57 C2
Restaurant Cebichería Paulina.58 B4
Supermercado Los Portales......59 C4
Yellow Rose of Texas...............60 D3

DRINKING
Arandú Bar.............................61 D3
Café-Teatro Amauta................62 D3
Noa Noa Disco-Pub.................63 D2

ENTERTAINMENT
Agricobank..............................64 D1
La Paranda..............................65 D2

SHOPPING
Mad Mick's Trading Post.......(see 41)

TRANSPORT
Aero Condor...........................66 D3
Boats to Belén........................67 C6
Expreso Loreto........................68 D2
JB Moto-Rental.......................69 C1
LAN..70 C3
Local buses to Laguna Quistacocha,
   Airport etc...........................71 B5
Star Perú................................72 C3

To Clínica Ana Stahl (1km);
Avenida La Marina (2km);
Pilpintuwasi (4km);
Butterfly Farm

Requena
Pedro Rosell
Tavara
Plaza

Nanay
Ocampo
Loreto
Yavari
Condamine
Fitzcarraldo

Universidad Nacional
de la Amazonía Peruana

Pevas

Napo
Putumayo
Nauta

Araujo

Plaza
de
Armas

Iglesia de
San Juan
Bautista

Lores

Morona
Huallaga
Tacna

Brasil

Ricardo Palma

M
Cáceres

Malecón Maldonado
Malecón Tarapacá

Río Amazonas

To Tourism
Police (150m)

Plaza 28
de Julio

San Martín

Ucayali

2 de Mayo
G Sáenz

Bolognesi

Abtao

Moore

Plaza
Grau

Aguirre
Arica
Araña

9 de Diciembre

Grau

9 de Diciembre

R Hurtado

Market
Belén
Abtao

To Mercado de Artesanía
San Juan (3.5km);
Airport (4km)

POST

Post office (☎ 23 4091; Arica 402; ⏲ 8am-6pm Mon-Fri, 8am-4:30pm Sat) Near the town center.

TOURIST INFORMATION

Apart from the places listed here, various commercial jungle guides and jungle lodges give tourist information, obviously biased toward selling their services, which is fine if you are looking for guides, tours or jungle lodges.

Gerald Mayeaux (☎ 24 1010; theyellowroseoftexasiq uitos@hotmail.com; Putumayo 180) Former tourist-office director now aids travelers and dispenses information from his Yellow Rose of Texas restaurant-bar. If you need a shower or a place to hang out before your late flight, and don't have a hotel, ask to use its facilities!

Inrena's Reserva Nacional Pacaya-Samiria Office (☎ 23 2980; 4th fl, R Palma 113; ⏲ 8am-4pm Mon-Fri)

iPerú airport (☎ 26 0251; Main Hall, Francisco Secada Vignetta Airport; ⏲ 8am-1pm & 4-8pm); city center (☎ 23 6144; Plaza de Armas, Calle Napo 232; ⏲ 8:30am-7:30pm)

Iquitos Times (www.iquitostimes.com) A free monthly newspaper in English, aimed at tourists, is delivered to all hotels and restaurants.

Dangers & Annoyances

Street touts and self-styled jungle guides tend to be aggressive, and many are both irritatingly insistent and dishonest. They are working for commissions. It is best to make your own decisions by contacting hotels, lodges and tour companies directly. Petty thieving is common by opportunist young children who roam the streets looking for easy prey. That said, violent crime is almost unknown in Iquitos.

Sights & Activities

CASA DE FIERRO

Every guidebook tells of the 'majestic' Casa de Fierro (Iron House) designed by Eiffel (of Tower fame). It was made in Paris in 1860 and imported piece by piece into Iquitos around 1890, during the opulent rubber-boom days, to beautify the city. Although three different iron houses were imported, only one, at the southeast corner of the Plaza de Armas, survives. It looks like a bunch of scrap-metal sheets bolted together and was once a store and the Iquitos Club. There is now a store on the ground floor. There are plans afoot to open an upstairs restaurant and bar. Stay tuned.

AZULEJOS

Other remnants of those rubber-boom days include *azulejos*, handmade tiles imported from Portugal to decorate the mansions of the rubber barons. Many buildings along Raimondi and Malecón Tarapaca are lavishly decorated with *azulejos*. Some of the best are various government buildings along or near the Malecón.

LIBRARY & MUSEUM

On the Malecón, at the corner with Morona, is an old building housing the **Biblioteca Amazónica** and the small **Museo Etnográfico**. Both are open on weekdays. The museum includes life-sized fiberglass casts of members of various Amazon tribes.

BELÉN

A walk down Raimondi (which turns into Próspero) and back along the Malecón is interesting, not only to see some of the tile-faced buildings, but also because you can visit the Belén **market** area at the southeast end of town. Belén itself is a floating shantytown with a certain charm to it. It consists of scores of huts built on rafts, which rise and fall with the river. During the low-water months, these rafts sit on the river mud and are dirty and unhealthy, but for most of the year they float on the river – a colorful and exotic sight. Seven thousand people live here, and canoes float from hut to hut selling and trading jungle produce. The best time to visit the shantytown is at 7am, when people from the jungle villages arrive to sell their produce. To get here, take a cab to 'Los Chinos,' walk to the port and rent a canoe to take you around.

The market, located within the city blocks in front of Belén, is the raucous, crowded affair common to most Peruvian towns. All kinds of strange and exotic products are sold here among the more mundane bags of rice, sugar, flour and cheap plastic and metal household goods. Look for the bark of the *chuchuhuasi* tree, which is soaked in rum for weeks and used as a tonic (it's served in many of the local bars). *Chuchuhuasi* and other Amazon plants are common ingredients in herbal pain-reducing and arthritis formulas manufactured in Europe and the USA. The market makes for exciting shopping and sightseeing, but do remember to watch your wallet.

AMAZON BASIN

DETOUR: PILPINTUWASI BUTTERFLY FARM

A visit to this fascinating little venture is highly recommended. **Pilpintuwasi Butterfly Farm** (☎ 23 2665; www.amazonanimalorphanage.org; Padra Cocha; admission US$5; ⏰ 10am-4pm) is ostensibly a conservatorium and breeding center for Amazonian butterflies. Butterflies aplenty there certainly are, including the striking blue morpho (*Morpho menelaus*) and the fearsome-looking owl butterfly (*Caligo eurilochus*) with a big owl-like eye on its wing. But it's the farm's exotic animals that ultimately steal the show: raised as orphans and protected within the property are the mischievous Antonio Piraña, a small white capuchin monkey; Florian and Zecke, two frisky black saki monkeys; and cheeky Igor, a red-faced howler. All four run amok when visitors arrive. An orphaned baby howler and capuchin monkey joined them in March 2006. Then there's Lolita, a docile tapir, and Pedro Bello, a majestic orphaned jaguar, which live in their own enclosures. You'll be sure to meet the capricious Rosa, a giant anteater who wanders around freely looking for ants. Beware of her fearsome claws! If you are lucky you might just spot the elusive lettuce-eating Amazon manatee that lurks in the pond by the reception area. To get there take a small boat from Bellavista-Nanay, a small port 2km north of Iquitos, to the village of Padre Cocha. Boats run all day. The farm is signposted and is a 15-minute walk through the village from the Padre Cocha boat dock.

AMAZON GOLF CLUB

Amazing as it may seem, you can play a round or two on the nine holes of the wacky and wonderful **Amazon Golf Club** (☎ 963 1333, 975 4976; Quistacocha; admission per day incl golf-club hire US$20; ⏰ 6am-6pm), the only one in the whole of the Amazon. Founded in 2004 by a bunch of nostalgic expats, the 2140m course was built on virgin bushland and is now proud to boast, apart from its nine greens, a wooden clubhouse. When fully completed the clubhouse will also include a bar and restaurant and the grounds will feature a swimming pool and a tennis court. Meantime see cofounder 'Mad' Mick Collis (see p489) for information on how to get a piece of the swinging action.

Sleeping

There's a broad range of accommodation choices in Iquitos, from basic budget to five-star comfort. Mosquitoes are rarely a serious problem in town, so mosquito netting is not provided.

The best hotels tend to be booked up on Friday and Saturday. The busiest season is from May to September, when prices may rise slightly.

BUDGET

All these hotels have bathrooms and fans unless otherwise indicated.

Mad Mick's Bunkhouse (☎ 975 4976; michaelcollis@hotmail.com; Putumayo 163; dm US$3) 'Mad' Michael Collis of the Trading Post has an eight-bed dormitory (four bunks) at the back of his shop.

The sizable room has a separate dining area. For the price you won't get any closer to the action – 50m from the Plaza de Armas.

Hostal Alfert (☎ 23 4105; G Saenz 1; s/d US$4.50/7.50) With a view of the river and the floating neighborhood of Belén, the gaudy green-painted Alfert tends to attracts shoestringers. It does have warm showers and has a kind of laid-back charm, though its rather remote location in a rather insalubrious neighborhood is a disadvantage.

Hobo Hideout (☎ 23 4099; hobohideout@yahoo.com; Putumayo 437; dm/s/d US$5/9/11) A cool travelers' vibe reaches out through the iron-grill gate, and kitchen privileges, laundry area, bar, cable TV room and 2-sq-meter plunge pool with waterfall draw international hobos. One (pricier) room towers above the rest on jungle-style stilts; others are small and dark. Expeditions can be arranged.

Hostal Libertad (☎ 23 5763; Arica 361; s/d US$7.50/11.50; d with air-con US$15; ❄) Rooms are fairly simple with electric shower, though some have cable TV. Only two rooms have air-con. The *hostal* is on a noisy street.

Hostal Lima (☎ 22 1409; fax 23 4111; Próspero 549; s/d US$8/11) A small courtyard opens onto small, clean rooms (the fans are window-mounted for lack of space) with small bathroom. Front rooms are noisier. TVs are available on request and upstairs rooms are better and breezier. It's one for the budget traveler.

Hospedaje El Sitio (☎ 23 4932; R Palma 545; s/d US$8/11) Clean, extralarge rooms with TV are the draw here and all 19 rooms have fans.

Hostal Maflo (☎ 24 1257; fax 23 1110; hostalmaflo@ mixmail.com; Morona 177; s/d incl continental breakfast US$7.50/12) Simple, plain rooms are set back from the street and feature hot water and cable TV – a good deal.

Hospedaje La Pascana (☎ 23 1418; www.pascana .com; Pevas 133; s/d/t US$11/12.50/16) With a small, verdant garden, this safe and friendly place is deservedly popular with travelers and often full. A book exchange and breakfast area add to the attraction.

Hostal El Colibrí (☎ 24 1737; hostalelcolibri@hotmail .com; Nauta 133; s/d US$11/16) Perhaps the best over-all budget choice is this newish establish-ment close to the river and the main square. Rooms are sparkling clean and airy and most have high ceilings. Fans give welcome air and there's the almost-obligatory TV. Flowers add a homely touch to what is in all respects a very fine place.

MIDRANGE
All of the hotels listed here have fairly generic rooms with air-con and private bathroom, normally with hot water. Walk-in rates for standard rooms are given; advance reserva-tions or holiday rates may be higher.

Hotel Sandalo (☎ 23 4761; fax 23 4264; sandalo@ iquitos.net; Próspero 616; s US$12.50-19, d US$19-25, all incl breakfast; 🐾) Offers modern, motel-style car-peted rooms with cable TV, minifridge and phone. Room rates are with fan or with air-con. Breakfast is included.

Hostal Ambassador (☎ /fax 23 3110; Pevas 260; s/d incl breakfast US$20/30; 🐾) Comfortable rooms, cable TV, continental breakfast and free air-port transfers are provided and a restaurant offers room service.

Marañón Hotel (☎ 24 2673; fax 23 1737; hotel .maranon@terra.com.pe; Nauta 285; s/d incl continental break-fast US$30/35; 🐾 📭) One of the newer Iquitos hotels, this place has light tiles everywhere and a restaurant with room service. The rooms have notably good-sized bathrooms by Iqui-tos standards, as well as the usual amenities. Good value.

Hostal Amazonas (☎ /fax 24 2431; amazonas@tvs .com.pe; Arica 108; s/d US$30/40; 🐾) Has a prime location on the Plaza de Armas and is popular with Peruvian businesspeople. A restaurant is on the premises; rooms are carpeted and have cable TV, minifridge and phone.

Hotel Europa (☎ 23 1123; fax 23 5483; hotel europasac@yahoo.es; Próspero 494; s/d incl breakfast US$20/30; 🐾) This modern block hotel rises five floors

above Próspero with good views from the top. A restaurant is available and the bright new rooms have cable TV and minifridge.

Doral Inn (☎ 24 3386, ☎ /fax 24 1970; doralinn hotel_iquitos@hotmail.com; Raimondi 220; s US$25-35, d US$35-45, all incl continental breakfast; 🐾) This new hotel has a 5th-floor restaurant with a view where you can enjoy your breakfast. Neat rooms have the usual amenities plus room service, and the hotel arranges tours to its Amazon Adventure Lodge.

Real Hotel Iquitos (☎ /fax 23 1011; s/d US$45/55; 🐾) On Malecón Tarapaca, this is the grand dame of Iquitos' hotels. Rooms are spacious but could do with a spruce-up, though the river view compensates for the deteriorated décor. Hot water is by request, which makes these rates a bit steep. Cheaper rooms without river view are almost half the quoted price.

TOP END
Note that these top-end hotels have only a few dozen rooms and are often full, so reserva-tions aren't a bad idea.

Hotel Victoria Regia (☎ /fax 23 1983; info@victoria regiahotel.com; Ricardo Palma 252; s/d incl breakfast US$50/60, ste US$70/90; 🐾 📭 🔲) A blast of icy, air-condi-tioned air welcomes guests to this comfortable hostelry. It has excellent beds and comfort-able rooms with all the usual amenities, plus hairdryers in the bathroom. There is a small and well-maintained indoor pool. A fine res-taurant and bar attract upscale guests and businesspeople.

Hotel El Dorado Plaza (☎ 22 2555; iquitos@eldorado plazahotel.com; Napo 258; r incl breakfast US$130; 🐾 📭) With a prime plaza location, this modern hotel is easily the town's best, with 64 well-equipped, spacious rooms (some with plaza views, others overlooking the pool). Jacuzzi, sauna, gym, restaurant, 24-hour room serv-ice, two bars and attentive staff make this a five-star hotel. Rates for rooms are often discounted when the hotel is not busy.

Eating
Kikiriki (☎ 23 2020; Napo 159; quarter chicken & chips US$2; 🕑 dinner only) How does a Peruvian cock crow? '*Kikiriki.*' This is the best place in town for grilled chicken.

Lidia's (Bolognesi 1181 at Abtao; mains from US$2; 🕑 6-9pm Mon-Sat) This is pretty much inside Lidia's living room. She and her family grill meats, fish, *cecina*, tamales and plantains on a bar-becue outside the house. No sign, but plenty of sizzle and full of locals. Come early for the best food selection – when the restaurant's done, it closes.

Parrillada Al Carbón (☎ 22 3292; Condamine 115; mains US$2-5; ◯ dinner only) This grill serves tasty cuts of meat, as well as chicken and fish. Look out for local dishes such as *tacacho* (mashed bananas with bacon), *calabresa* (spicy Brazilian sausage) and the *patacones* (fried bananas).

Ari's Burger (☎ 23 1470; Próspero 127; meals US$2-6; ◯ 7am-3am) On the corner of the Plaza de Armas, this clean, brightly lit joint is known locally as 'gringolandia.' Two walls are open to the street allowing great plaza- and people-watching. It's almost always open, serves American-style food as well as some local plates and ice creams, changes US dollars and is generally helpful and popular with tourists.

Chifa Cuan Chu (Huallaga 173; mains US$3) It's a good budget *chifa*. Try the house specialty: sweet-and-sour chicken prepared with fresh pineapple.

Restaurant Cebichería Paulina (☎ 23 1298; Tacna 591; menús US$3, mains US$3-6) A huge menu of ceviches and local food (including caiman) attracts a Peruvian lunch crowd. Lunchtime specials are posted on blackboard in the street.

Chez Maggy (☎ 24 1816; Raimondi 181; pastas US$3, large pizza US$7.50; ◯ 6-11:30pm) A wood-burning oven produces fresh pizzas, just like its sister restaurants in Cuzco and other cities.

Fitzcarraldo Restaurant-Bar (☎ 24 3434; Napo 100; mains US$3-7; ◯ noon-late) The Fitzcarraldo anchors a whole block of riverside restaurants and is the most upscale of them, with good food and service. Dine indoors (the air-con can be extra chilly) or on the streetside patio. It does good pizzas (delivery available) and various local and international dishes.

Antica (☎ 24 1672; Napo 159; mains US$3-7; ◯ lunch & dinner) New in 2006, the Antica would have to be the best Italian restaurant in town. Primarily a pizza place – there's an impressive wood pizza oven – pasta also takes a predominant spot on the menu with the lasagna being an excellent choice. The range of fine imported Italian wines is unparalleled for the Amazon. So is the relaxed environment, with its solid wooden benches and tables and upstairs street views from the balcony.

Nuevo Mesón (☎ 23 1857; Malecón Maldonado 153; mains US$3-8; ◯ lunch-late) Another choice on riverside row, this place serves local specialties

(including jungle animals); the local turtles are protected and should not be served, but deer and peccary are fair game.

Yellow Rose of Texas (☎ 24 1010; Putumayo 180; breakfast from US$1.50, mains US$5-7.50; ◯ 24 hr) Run by ex–tourism director Gerald Mayeaux, this restaurant and bar specializes in Texas barbecue, but has a varied menu of international and regional dishes. Eat on the sidewalk, inside, or in a tiny, lantern-lit courtyard in back. The bar has comfortable Adirondack chairs you can fall asleep in, board games, darts, sports TV, an excellent book exchange as well as beers fridged at 4°C and served up in insulated wooden holders.

Chifa Long Fung (☎ 23 3649; San Martín 464; mains about US$6) There are several inexpensive *chifas* and other restaurants near the Plaza 28 de Julio, of which the Long Fung is a little more expensive but worth it.

Gran Maloka (☎ 23 3126; Loreto 170; menús US$3.50, mains US$7-9; ◯ noon-10pm; ✖) Enjoy elegant and quiet dining in this atmospheric Amazonian restaurant inside a tiled mansion from rubber-boom days. The menu can be adventurous, but has plenty of well-prepared and less startling meat and fish dishes. Locals consider this to be the town's best restaurant.

Supermercado Los Portales (Próspero at Morona) For food supplies.

Drinking

There are several places to meet for a cold beer or other drinks and hear music, both recorded and live. Several places are found along the pedestrian blocks of the Malecón north of Napo. A good beer bar here is Arandú Bar, next to the Fitzcarraldo.

Café-Teatro Amauta (☎ 23 3109; Nauta 250) Hosts live Peruvian music on most nights and has a well-stocked bar with local drinks as well as a café.

Entertainment

Agricobank (Condamine at Pablo Rosell; admission US$1.75) For dancing, the most locally popular venue is this, a huge outdoor place where hundreds of locals gather for drinking, dancing and socializing.

Noa Noa Disco-Pub (☎ 23 2902; Pevas 292; admission US$6) More upscale; a very trendy disco with salsa rhythms predominating.

La Paranda (Pevas 174) Also popular for dancing, this place fills up with locals strutting their stuff on weekends.

Shopping

There are a few shops on the first block of Napo selling jungle crafts, some of high quality and pricey. A good place for crafts is Mercado de Artesanía San Juan on the road to the airport – bus and taxi drivers know it. Although items made from animal bones and skins are available, we discourage their purchase. It is illegal to import many of them into North America and Europe.

Mad Mick's Trading Post (☎ 975 4976; michaelcollis@hotmail.com; Putumayo 163; ☾ 8am-8pm) Stop by here for a jungle expedition – you can buy, rent or trade almost anything. Don't need it afterwards? Mick will buy anything back (if it's in good nick) for half-price.

Getting There & Away

AIR

Iquitos' small but busy airport currently receives flights from Lima. The airport is closed between 9am and 6pm because of flocks of vultures in the vicinity of the airport and the subsequent danger of bird strike. Until the problem is resolved, you can only leave and arrive at Iquitos outside of these times.

Three main airlines link Iquitos with the outside world. **LAN** (☎ 23 2421; Próspero 232) operates the best and most expensive flights. **Star Perú** (☎ 23 6208; Napo 256) and **Aero Condor** (☎ 23 1086; Próspero 215) also operate flights to Lima. At the time of writing, Star Perú was planning to set up regular flights to Tarapoto (US$68). All airlines operate jet aircraft, though the more modern airbuses of LAN warrant the more expensive airfare over the less comfortable aircraft of the other two companies.

Charter companies at the airport have five-passenger planes to almost anywhere in the Amazon. Rates are around US$300 an hour. Other small airlines may have offices at the airport.

The airport departure tax is US$3.57/10 for domestic/international flights.

The airport is about 7km from the center of Iquitos. A taxi ride will cost around US$4, a *mototaxi* around US$2.

BOAT

Iquitos is Peru's largest and best-organized river port. You can in theory travel all the way from Iquitos to the Atlantic Ocean, but most boats out of Iquitos today ply only Peruvian waters, and voyagers necessarily change boats at the Colombian–Brazilian border (see p494).

Cargo boats normally leave from Puerto Masusa, on Av La Marina about 2km or 3km north of the town center (maybe closer if the water is very high from May to July). Chalkboards tell you which boats are leaving when, for where, and whether they are accepting passengers. The *Henry* boats to Pucallpa leave from their own port nearer to town. Although there are agencies in town, it's usually best to go to the dock and look around; don't trust anyone except the captain for an estimate of departure time. Be wary: the chalkboards have a habit of changing dates overnight! Boats often leave hours or even a few days late.

Upriver passages to Pucallpa (four to seven days) or Yurimaguas (three to six days) cost US$20 to US$30 per person. The journey takes longer when the river is high. Boats leave about three times a week to Pucallpa, more often to Yurimaguas, and there are more frequent departures for the closer intermediate ports. Some boats have cabins and charge more for those.

Downriver boats to the Peruvian border with Brazil and Colombia leave about twice a week and take two days. Fares are US$15 to US$20 per person.

You can often sleep aboard the boat while waiting for departure; this enables you to get the best hammock space. Never leave gear unattended; ask to have your bags locked up when you sleep.

If you're in a hurry, **Expreso Loreto** (☎ 23 4086, 24 3661; Loreto at Raimondi) has fast motor launches to the border at 6am every two days. The fare is US$50 for the 12-hour trip, including lunch. Other companies nearby offer similar trips.

Amazon Tours & Cruises (p493) has weekly cruises on comfortable ships that go from Iquitos to Leticia, Colombia, leaving on Sunday. Most passengers are foreigners on a one-week, round-trip tour, but cheaper one-way passages are sold on a space-available basis.

Getting Around

The ubiquitous *motocarros* cost less than a taxi and are fun to ride, though they don't provide much protection in an accident. Most rides around Iquitos cost a standard US$0.70.

Taxis are relatively few and are pricier than in other Peruvian cities. Squadrons of busy *motocarros* more than make up for the lack of taxis. Always enter *motocarros* from the sidewalk side – passing traffic pays scant heed to embarking passengers – and keep your limbs inside the *motocarro* at all times. Scrapes and fender-bending can happen with alarming frequency.

Buses and trucks for several nearby destinations, including the airport, leave from the Plaza 28 de Julio. They are marked Nanay-Belén-Aeropuerto.

A paved road now extends through the jungle as far as Nauta on the Río Marañón, just beyond its confluence with the Río Ucayali. Riverboat passengers from Yurimaguas can now alight at Nauta and pick up a local bus to Iquitos, thus making the journey shorter by some six hours. Boats from Pucallpa do not stop at Nauta.

JB Moto-Rental (Yavari 702; per hr US$2.50) rents motorcycles.

AROUND IQUITOS
Nearby Villages & Lakes
About 16km from town, past the airport, **Santo Tomás** is famous for its pottery and mask making, and has a few bars overlooking Mapacocha, a lake formed by an arm of the Río Nanay. You can rent boats by asking around. A motorboat with driver is US$5 to US$10 an hour, or you can paddle your own canoe for less. **Santa Clara** is about 15km away, on the banks of the Río Nanay. Boats can also be rented here, and locals swim off the pure white beaches formed during low water levels (July to October). Both villages can be reached by *motocarros* (about US$4) and taxis.

Corrientillo is a lake near the Río Nanay. There are a few bars around the lake, which is locally popular for swimming on weekends and has good sunsets. It's about 15km from town; a *motocarro* will charge about US$3.

Laguna Quistacocha
This lake, 15km south of Iquitos, is served by minibuses several times an hour from Plaza 28 de Julio. A small **zoo** of local fauna has been improved under an Australian director who is sometimes available to show you around.

An adjoining **fish hatchery** has 2m-long *paiche*, a river fish that tastes excellent, but its popularity and loss of habitat has caused a severe decline in its numbers. An attempt to rectify the situation is being made with the breeding program here. A pedestrian walk circles the lake (in which people swim, though it looks murky) and paddleboats are for hire. It's fairly crowded with locals on the weekend but not midweek. Admission is US$1.

Exploring the Jungle
Excursions into the jungle are of three types: visits to jungle lodges for wildlife viewing; a cruise on a riverboat outfitted for tourism (an increasingly popular option) to observe the way of life along the river; and the more demanding camping and walking trips. Some cruises or lodges offer dedicated fishing trips. July to September are by far the best months for this.

Jungle guides will approach you at the airport, in restaurants and on the street in Iquitos. Their quality varies considerably, so get references for any guide, and proceed with caution. Some guides have criminal records – some for robbing tourists. All guides should have a permit or license; if they don't, check with the tourist office. Travelers have had mixed experiences with private guides, and none are especially recommended. The better jungle-lodge companies snap up the best guides and can arrange wilderness trips.

JUNGLE LODGES
A wide range of options at varying prices can be booked from abroad or in Lima, but if you show up in Iquitos without a reservation you can certainly book a lodge or tour and it'll cost you less. Bargaining is not out of the question if you are on a tight budget, even though operators show you fixed price lists. If the lodge has space and you have the cash, they'll nearly always give you a discount, sometimes a substantial one. If planning on booking after you arrive, avoid the major Peruvian holidays, when many places are filled with local holidaymakers. June to September (the dry months and the summer vacation for North American and European visitors) is also quite busy, though bargains can be found if you're flexible with time. It's worth shopping around.

The lodges are some distance from Iquitos, so river transport is included in the price. Most of the area within 50km of the city is not virgin jungle, and the chance of seeing big mammals is remote. Any tribespeople will be acculturated and performing for tourism. Nevertheless, much can be seen of the jungle way of life, and birds, insects and small mammals can be observed. The more remote lodges have more wildlife.

A typical two-day trip involves a river journey of two or three hours to a jungle lodge with reasonable comforts and meals, a jungle lunch, a guided visit to an indigenous village to buy crafts and perhaps see dances (though tourists often outnumber tribespeople), an evening meal at the lodge, maybe an after-dark canoe trip to look for caiman by searchlight, and a walk in the jungle to see jungle vegetation (and, if you are lucky, monkeys or other wildlife). A trip like this will set you back about US$60 to US$150, depending on the operator, the distance traveled and the comfort of the lodge. On longer trips you'll get further away from Iquitos and see more of the jungle, and the cost per night drops.

There are many good lodges in the Iquitos area that will give you a rewarding look at the rainforest. All prices quoted here are approximate; bargaining is often acceptable, and meals, tours and transportation from Iquitos should be included. Bottled drinks (including water) are extra; however, lodges will provide containers of purified water for you to fill your own bottle, as well as 24-hour hot water with instant coffee and tea bags. Meals normally include juice. The following places are arranged in order of distance from Iquitos.

Amazon Jungle Camp Amazon Tours & Cruises (☎ 22 2440, 23 1611; www.amazontours.net; Requena 336, Iquitos) This camp is near the mouth of the Río Momón, an Amazon tributary just north of Iquitos. It provides optional first/last nights near Iquitos for passengers on one of the many river cruises offered by this company. The lodge has about two dozen rooms with private toilet, and is lit by kerosene lanterns. Cold showers are provided in a separate building. Book with Amazon Tours & Cruises in Iquitos.

Cumaceba Lodge (☎ 22 1456; fax 23 2229; www.cumaceba.com; Putumayo 184, Iquitos; 2 days & 1 night US$114, 3 days & 2 nights US$150, 4 days & 3 nights US$200 per person) About 35km downriver from Iquitos, this lodge has 15 screened rooms with private shower and can arrange more adventurous trips where you would stay in simple, open-sided shelters. This is a popular, nearby, quick budget option.

Heliconia Lodge (☎ 23 1959; www.heliconialodge.com.pe; R Palma 242, Iquitos; 4 days & 3 nights s/d US$310/580) Approximately 80km downriver from Iquitos, this comfortable lodge is associated with Iquitos' Hotel Victoria Regia and provides 21 good-sized rooms with private, tiled hot showers. Covered walkways connect rooms to the lobby, restaurant, bar and hammock room. Electricity is available in the evenings, kerosene lanterns later at night. The usual boat and foot tours are offered to see both wildlife and indigenous villages. Discounts are available.

Loving Light Amazon Lodge (Iquitos ☎ 24 3180; Putumayo 128; USA ☎ 425-836 9431; www.junglelodge.com; 7016 248th Ave NE, Redmond, WA 98053; 5 days & 4 nights per person US$600, ayahuasca ceremonies US$35) About 120km from Iquitos on the Río Yanayacu, this lodge has a circular thatched dining room–reception lodge that is connected by walkways to seven bungalows with private shower and screens. Each sleeps up to four people, and book-sized solar panels in the thatched roofs are used for lighting. The usual jungle tours are available, and there are opportunities to listen to musicians in the evening, or take part in spiritual ceremonies conducted by a local

---

CANOPY WALKWAY

Until the 1970s, biologists working in the rainforest made their observations and collected specimens from the forest floor and along the rivers, unaware that many plant and animal species spent their entire lives in the canopy. When scientists ventured into the treetops, they discovered so many new species that the canopy became known as the new frontier of tropical biology. Until recently, it was difficult to visit the canopy unless you were a researcher, but it is now possible for travelers to get to the top of the rainforest.

This awesome hanging walkway stretches over 500m through the rainforest canopy, reaching 35m above the ground. It is about a 10-minute walk from ACTS Field Station. The canopy is reached by stairs and is accessible to any able-bodied visitor. The views are excellent, and birders spend hours up there.

Some warnings, though. Visiting the Canopy Walkway involves a lot of travel if you are not staying nearby, and it may terrify you if you are afraid of heights. It can get hot on top of the trees, so bring sun protection and a water bottle. Also, go with realistic expectations. Binoculars and an expert guide will enable you to see scores of tropical bird species, but you are not likely to spot many mammals in the canopy.

AMAZON BASIN

shaman. Walk-in discounts are also offered during off-season.

Amazon Yarapa River Lodge (☎ 993 1172; www .yarapariverlodge.com; La Marina 124, Iquitos; per person with shared/private bathroom 4 days & 3 nights US$800/860; 🖥) Approximately 130km upriver from Iquitos on the Río Yarapa, this lodge is simply stunning. It has a huge and well-designed tropical biology laboratory, regularly used by the US Cornell University for research and postgraduate classes. The lab is powered by an expansive solar-panel system, which also provides electric power throughout the lodge (bring your laptop). The lodge has satellite phone connections. The facilities are beautifully maintained, with an impressive entrance pier, elaborate woodcarvings in the restaurant-bar and even on the bed heads, and fully screened rooms linked by screened walkways. Eight huge bedrooms with oversized private bathroom are available (professors stay here when Cornell is in residence) and 16 comfortable rooms share a multitude of well-equipped, modern bathrooms. Of course, with its scientific agenda, the lodge offers topnotch guides for its jungle tours, which visit remote areas. The boats take about three to four hours from Iquitos but have a bathroom aboard. Recommended.

Muyuna Amazon Lodge (☎ office 24 2858, 993 4424; www.muyuna.com; ground fl, Putumayo 163, Iquitos; per person 3 days & 2 nights US$300, 6 days & 5 nights US$520) About 140km upriver from Iquitos on the Río Yanayacu, this intimate, 10-bungalow lodge surrounded by 10 well-conserved lakes in a remote area gives visitors a good look at the jungle, which tends to be less traveled and colonized upriver than downriver. The helpful owners live in Iquitos and have a very hands-on approach to maintaining their lodge, ensuring that recycling occurs, staff set an ecofriendly example to visitors, and guests are happy. Each stilted, thatched bungalow has a private cold shower, two or three comfortable beds, is large enough for a writing desk and is fully screened. There is also a balcony with hammock. During high water the river rises up to the bungalows, which are connected to the lodge–dining building with covered, raised walkways. Lighting is by kerosene lanterns. The bilingual guides are excellent and they guarantee observation of monkeys, sloths and dolphins, as well as rich avian fauna typical of the nearby Amazonian *varzea* (flooded forest), including the *piuri* –

the wattled curassow (*crax globulosa*) which is a critically endangered bird restricted to western Amazonia and which can only be seen in Peru at Muyuna. Unlike most other lodges, the owners do not pay commissions, so street touts and taxi drivers don't recommend them.

Pacaya-Samiria Amazon Lodge (☎ /fax 23 4128; www.pacayasamiria.com.pe; Raimondi 378, Iquitos; 3 days & 2 nights per person US$699, 4-person minimum US$420). About 190km upriver on the Marañón, this excellent lodge is past Requena and on the outskirts of the Pacaya-Samiria reserve. It's four hours from Iquitos and can arrange overnights within the reserve. Rooms feature private shower and a porch with river view, and the lodge has electricity in the evening.

Paseos Amazonicos (☎ /fax 23 1618; www.paseos amazonicos.com; Pevas 246, Iquitos; r per person US$100-140) This company runs three lodges. One of the oldest and best established is Amazonas Sinchicuy Lodge, on a small tributary of the Amazon 30km northeast of Iquitos. The 32 rooms have private cold shower, can sleep up to four, and are lantern-lit. Some rooms are wheelchair-accessible. This lodge can be visited on a day trip from Iquitos. The palmthatched Tambo Yanayacu Lodge is 60km northeast of Iquitos and has 10 rustic rooms with private bathroom. Here, the staff can supply tents for jungle expeditions. Stays at these two lodges can be combined into one trip. Finally, the Tambo Amazonico Lodge is about 160km upriver on the Río Yarapa. It is less a lodge and more of a camping place, with two open-air dormitories sleeping up to 20 people, with beds and mosquito nets. Camping trips can be arranged, including into the Pacaya-Samiria reserve.

Explorama Lodges (☎ 25 2530; fax 25 2533; www .explorama.com; Av La Marina 340, Iquitos) This well-established and recommended company owns and operates lodges and is an involved supporter of the Amazon Conservatory of Tropical Studies (ACTS), which has a lab at the famed Canopy Walkway. You could arrange a trip to visit one or more lodges (each of which is very different) combined with a visit to the walkway. Sample rates are given; contact Explorama for other options and combinations or visit the detailed website. Explorama serves all-you-can-eat lunch and dinner buffets, has fast boats (50km/h) and half-price rates for under-12s. Ask about group discounts. The well-trained, friendly and knowledgeable guides are locals who speak English (other languages on request). The following are the lodges operated by Explorama:

ACTS Field Station (s/d US$140/240) Near the Canopy Walkway, the 20 rooms here are in buildings similar to those at Explorama Lodge. Book ahead, because accommodations are often used by researchers and workshop groups. (Note that the old name Aceer is still used by some companies.)

Ceiba Tops (2 days & 1 night s/d US$225/400; ✂ 🖥 ♨) Forty kilometers northeast of Iquitos on the Amazon, this is Explorama's and the area's most modern lodge and resort. There are 75 luxurious rooms and suites, all attractively decorated and featuring comfortable beds and furniture, fan, screened windows, porches and spacious bathroom with hot shower. A satellite TV room is available. Landscaped grounds surround the pool complex, complete with hydromassage, waterslide and hammock house. The restaurant (with better meals than at Explorama's other places) adjoins a bar with live Amazon music daily. Short guided walks and boat rides are available for a taste of the jungle; there is some primary forest nearby. One highlight is the *Victoria regia*, or giant Amazon water lily, which has 2m-diameter leaves that a child could sleep on without sinking. This lodge is a recommended option for people who really *don't* want to rough it. It even hosts business incentive meetings.

Explorama Lodge (3 days & 2 nights s/d US$305/570) Eighty kilometers away on the Amazon, near its junction with the Río Napo, this was one of the first lodges constructed in the Iquitos area (1964) and remains attractively rustic. The lodge has several large, palm-thatched buildings with 75 rooms with shared cold-water bathroom; covered walkways join the buildings, and lighting is by kerosene lantern. Guides accompany visitors on several trails that go deeper into the forest.

ExplorNapo Lodge (5 days & 4 nights s/d US$840/1640) On the Río Napo, 157km from Iquitos, this simple lodge has 30 rooms with shared cold-shower facilities. The highlights are guided trail hikes in remote primary forest, bird-watching, ReNuPeRu ethnobotanical garden of useful plants (curated by a local shaman) and a visit to the nearby Canopy Walkway (half-hour walk). Because of the distance involved, on five-day/four-night packages, you spend the first and last night at the Explorama Lodge.

ExplorTambos Camp (5 days & 4 nights s/d US$1022/1684) This lodge is a two-hour walk from ExplorNapo. It's a self-declared 'primitive' camp and creature comforts get short shrift here. Guests (16 maximum) sleep on mattresses on open-sided sleeping platforms covered with a mosquito net; don't plan a passionate honeymoon here! Basic toilets and washing facilities are provided, and wildlife-watching opportunities here are better than at the lodges. A Canopy Walkway visit (see p491) is included.

CRUISES

Dawn on the Amazon Tours & Cruises (☎ 23 3730, 993 9190, 994 3267; www.dawnontheamazon.com; Maldonado 185, Iquitos) This small but cozy outfit offers the best deal for independent travelers. It sports two modernly equipped wooden craft for either day trips or longer river cruises up to two weeks, and you can travel with host Bill Grimes and his experienced crew along the Amazon, or along its quieter tributaries. Dawn on the Amazon has exclusive permission to go twice as far into Pacaya-Samiria National Reserve as any other tour company. The larger *Amazon III* uniquely features deep-cell solar batteries to quietly run the few fan-cooled cabins and electrical equipment, and offers an observation deck, kitchen, dining area, toilets, showers and a swimming and fishing platform at the stern. Trips can be customized to individual group desires and cost US$289 per day including a bilingual guide, all meals and transfers. A small launch is carried for side trips. Drinks are extra. The smaller yet still commodious *Amazon I* is best for groups of up to eight persons and costs US$144.50 per day for the full works, or US$59 per day for day trips including a light lunch.

Amazon Tours & Cruises (www.amazontours.net) Iquitos (☎ 22 2440, 23 1611; fax 23 1265; 336 Requena, Iquitos); USA (☎ 305-227 2266, 800-423 2791; info@amazontours.com; Suite 173, 275 Fontainebleau Blvd, Miami, FL 33172) Off Av La Marina in Iquitos, this company has been operating comfortable cruises for over two decades. The *MV Río Amazonas* is its largest ship (146ft) and has 20 air-conditioned cabins with private shower and two or three beds. Three of the cabins are larger suites (two junior and one senior). There is also a dorm cabin with communal showers. The 31-passenger *MV Arca* has 13 cabins with air-con that have upper/lower bunks, and three cabins with three- or four-bed configurations. All cabins have private showers. In addition, there is a dorm bunkroom. Both boats have air-conditioned restaurants. The newer but much smaller *MV Amazon Explorer* has only four large cabins and will take between two and 12 passengers on either scheduled or chartered trips. Its shallower draft makes it more suitable for accessing remote areas.

The first two boats are typical three- or four-decked Amazon riverboats with a lot of romantic charm, and they are comfortable but not luxurious (with the exception of the *MV Río Amazonas'* suites). All have dining areas and bars and plenty of deck space for watching the river go by. Each is accompanied by a full crew, including an experienced bilingual local naturalist guide. Small launches are carried for side trips. The *MV Amazon Explorer* is available for private charter.

The *MV Río Amazonas* leaves Iquitos at noon on Sundays. Passengers spend three days sailing downriver to Leticia/Tabatinga and a further three days returning to Iquitos. Stops are made at jungle towns, indigenous villages (for dancing and crafts sales), and almost a day is spent looking around the colorful Colombian port of Leticia and neighboring Tabatinga in Brazil. Short side trips are made to lagoons and up tributaries, and hikes in the jungle last from one to a few hours. This trip is on a well-traveled and long-settled part of the Amazon and gives a good look at the river and its inhabitants today. Wildlife enthusiasts will see dozens of bird species, pink dolphins, butterflies and other insects, but there's no guarantee you'll see other mammals. Rates start at US$1449 per person, double occupancy, for the six-day round trip, with suites at US$1675 and US$1865. If you're just going one-way, the rate is just over half price.

The *MV Arca* leaves about twice a month, on Sundays, for a five-day cruise of the Pacaya-Samiria reserve. All tours end at Yurimaguas and return from there to Iquitos. Side trips, bilingual guides, birding trips, fishing excursions etc are offered. This is currently the most comfortable way of seeing Pacaya-Samiria. Rates are US$695 per person, double occupancy for a standard cabin or US$995 for a suite. For exact departure dates, see the website.

The *MV Amazon Explorer* runs trips twice a month out of the small port of Requena, reached by a fast speedboat transfer from Iquitos. The three day–two night trip follows the Río Ucayali along the south side of the Pacaya-Samiria Reserve and deviates for a full-day exploration of the Río Pacaya within

BORDER CROSSING: THE PERU–COLOMBIA–BRAZIL BORDER ZONE

Even in the middle of the Amazon, border formalities must be adhered to, and officials will refuse passage if documents are not in order. With a valid passport and visa or tourist card, border crossing is not a problem.

When leaving Peru for Brazil or Colombia, you'll get an exit stamp at a Peruvian guard post just before the border (boats stop there long enough for this; ask the captain).

The ports at the three-way border are several kilometers apart and connected by public ferries. They are reached by air or boat, but not road. The biggest town, Leticia in Colombia, boasts by far the best hotels and restaurants, and a hospital. You can fly from **Leticia** to Bogotá on almost daily commercial flights. Otherwise, infrequent boats go to Puerto Asis on the Río Putumayo; the trip takes up to 12 days. From Puerto Asis, buses go further into Colombia.

The two small ports in Brazil are **Tabatinga** and **Benjamin Constant**; both have basic hotels. Tabatinga has an airport with flights to Manaus. Get your official Brazilian entry stamp from the Tabatinga police station if flying on to Manaus. Tabatinga is a continuation of Leticia, and you can walk or take a taxi between the two with no immigration hassles, unless you are planning on traveling further into Brazil or Colombia. Boats leave from Tabatinga downriver, usually stopping in Benjamin Constant for a night, then continuing on to Manaus, Brazil, a week away. It takes about an hour to reach Benjamin Constant by public ferry. US citizens need a visa to enter Brazil. Make sure you apply for your visa in good time – either at home in the USA or in Lima.

Peru is on the south side of the river, where currents create a constantly shifting bank. Most boats from Iquitos will drop you at the small village of Santa Rosa, with Peruvian immigration facilities. Motor canoes reach Leticia in about 15 minutes. If you are heading for Colombia or Brazil, Lonely Planet has guidebooks for both countries.

If you are arriving from Colombia or Brazil, you'll find boats in Tabatinga and Leticia for Iquitos. You should pay US$20 or less for the three-day trip on a cargo riverboat, or US$50 for a *mas rápido* (fast boat; 12 to 14 hours), which leave daily. The cruise ships leave Wednesday and arrive in Iquitos on Saturday morning.

With three borders and four ports to choose from, the best place to base yourself is in Leticia, Colombia. Remember that however disorganized things may appear, you can always get meals, money changed, beds and boats simply by asking around.

the reserve itself. The final day includes a bird-watching expedition along the Río Tapiche before heading back to port at Requena. Rates are US$1095 per person on a twin-share basis or US$1865 for a single passenger. There is a longer six day–five night trip for US$1395 or US$2495.

International Expeditions (☎ in the USA 205-428 1700, 800-633 4734; www.ietravel.com; 1 Environs Park, Helena, AL 35080, USA; 9 days & 8 nights US$2598) This well-organized company operates three boats – the 15-cabin *MV Amatista*, the 14-cabin *MV Turmalina* and the larger 23-cabin *MV Turquesa*. Its relaxing and pampered nine-day river cruises take in the Ríos Amazon and Ucayali, passing through Requena en route to the Pacaya-Samiria Reserve. These are elegant boats with three decks, air-conditioned double cabins with private showers, excellent dining and viewing facilities and experienced guides. Contact the company directly in the USA for details; you need advance reservations.

PEVAS

About 145km downriver from Iquitos, Pevas is Peru's oldest town on the Amazon. Founded by missionaries in 1735, Pevas now has about 3000 inhabitants but no cars, post office or banks (or attorneys!); the first telephone was installed in 1998. Most residents are *mestizos* or indigenous people from one of four tribes and are friendly and easygoing. Pevas is the

most interesting town between Iquitos and the border and is visited regularly (if briefly) by the cruise boats traveling to Leticia.

The rustic but attractive Casa de la Loma lodge on a hill in the outskirts of Pevas offers Amazon views and interesting activities. With its hilltop breezes and views, it is the best place to stay between Iquitos and Leticia. This is a place to spend a few days and get to know the town and the inhabitants, join in a fiesta or shop at the market. There are five screened rooms, which share three clean showers. There is no phone, and reservations are problematic. Room rates are low midrange, but not fixed. Be adventurous and show up.

There is also the basic Hospedaje Rodríguez, near the Pevas Plaza, which offers beds and food for a few dollars. Artists have been known to stay at fellow-artist Francisco Grippa's house. Grippa handmakes his canvases from local bark, similar to that formerly used by local tribespeople for cloth.

You can eat at both Casa de la Loma and Hospedaje Rodríguez, and there is also a couple of basic local places.

If you haven't arranged transportation with one of the agencies, just go down to the Iquitos docks and get on a boat to Leticia – stops are made at Pevas. (The same applies if you are coming from Leticia.) There's an element of risk – you might get stuck here for a while – but a boat *will* eventually turn up.

Directory

CONTENTS

ACCOMMODATIONS

There are many more places to stay than we're able to list in this book, so we've included those that we think are the best. Many new places will have opened since this book was published, however, so be bold and try them out – and then let us know how it goes!

Accommodations in Peru range from backpacker hostels to luxury lodges. In general, the scruffiest accommodations are found in often dodgy neighborhoods near bus terminals, while the cushiest places to stay are near the main plaza. At tourist-oriented hotels, the

---

PRACTICALITIES

■ Don't fry your gadgets on Peru's 220V, 60Hz AC electricity supply; bring along an adapter with a built-in surge protector

■ Use the metric system except for gas (petrol), which is measured in US gallons

■ Ask if your hotel TV has cable, or you will be stuck with Spanish-language soap operas

■ Buy or watch videos on the NTSC system (compatible with North America)

■ Keep up to date with Lima's centrist **El Comercio** (www.elcomercioperu.com.pe) – dry, but considered the best Spanish-language newspaper – and read opposing viewpoints in the mildly left-wing **La República** (www.larepublica.com.pe); for alternative travel journalism in Spanish and English, pick up the glossy monthly magazine **Rumbos** (www.rumbosdelperu.com)

---

staff usually speak a smattering of English, but in rural areas you'll need to have a grasp of the Spanish basics. *Habitación simple* is a single room, *habitación doble* is a double room with two twin beds and *habitación matrimonial* is a double room with one large bed.

You won't find many campgrounds, except while trekking. A few youth hostels exist, but are similar value to budget guesthouses. Homestays may be offered to people taking Spanish courses, but are otherwise a rare option, as are B&Bs. Places to stay are required to have rooms with private hot showers, telephones and other facilities such as a restaurant before they can officially be called hotels. This has caused many former hotels to change their titles to *hospedaje* or *hostal*. This system hasn't entirely caught on yet.

Typically smaller than a hotel, a *hostal* is like a guesthouse, offering private rooms with attached bathrooms, fairly reliable hot water and a continental breakfast of plain bread and tea or weak coffee included in the rates. Better *hostales* offer hot breakfasts and many of the same services as small hotels, while cheaper ones may have shared bathrooms. *Hospedajes* and *albergues* are similar to family-owned hostels and inns, respectively. Usually they have fewer and more basic rooms, and perhaps dormitories and a shared kitchen, but don't count on hot showers, private bathrooms or many other amenities. In popular travelers' destinations, there are a handful of backpacker hostels.

Many places to stay will store your luggage for free if you arrive early in the morning, if you have a late bus or flight to catch after check-out, or even just if you're going trekking for a few days. It's always a good idea to lock your bags and get a receipt, though.

Rates

Accommodation costs vary greatly in Peru, depending mainly on the season and the region. Consider the rates in this book, which are normally quoted for the high season unless stated otherwise, to only be guidelines.

Cuzco is the most expensive town for hotels, despite being stuffed full of them. During the high season (June to August) demand is very high; the busiest times are Inti Raymi, Semana Santa and Fiestas Patrias (see p504), when advance reservations are a must. Other cities that are pricier than average include Lima, Iquitos, Huaraz and Trujillo. At off-peak times incredibly good deals can be found, especially in less-visited towns. Walk-in guests should negotiate for the 'best price,' especially during the low season. Paying cash may get you an additional discount.

A surcharge of 7% or more typically applies to all credit-card transactions, not including the foreign-currency exchange fee that your own bank may add to the total amount.

When paying cash, either local currency, nuevos soles (S/), or US dollars (US$) are often accepted. It's easiest to pay in the same currency that the room rate was quoted in, which means US dollars at expensive hotels. Otherwise, it may work out more cheaply to pay in nuevos soles. But it all depends on the arbitrary exchange rate that the front desk staff uses to calculate the bill, and that rate will always be less favorable than the going rate offered by banks and *casas de cambio* (foreign-exchange bureaus).

BUDGET

Basic one- and two-star hotels, *hostales, hospedajes, albergues* and backpacker hostels are Peru's cheapest accommodations, but the differences among them are ambiguous. All may call themselves hotels. Rates range from about US$5 to US$25 for a double. Rooms vary remarkably in quality and facilities, even inside the same establishment.

Although these places are the cheapest, they are not necessarily the worst. There are some excellent bargains to be had in this price range if all you need is a decent bed and a shared bathroom. Private rooms with en suite facilities are sometimes available. Bathrooms may have hot showers, at least some of the time.

Always ask to see a room before accepting it. Avoid rooms overlooking noisy streets, lacking windows or appearing insecure (test the locks on all doors and windows). Looking around might yield a much more suitable room for about the same rate.

MIDRANGE

Mid-priced *hostales* and hotels range from US$25 to US$75 a double, though in Cuzco a midrange place can cost up to US$100. You

---

SHOWER SHOCK

The cheapest places to stay in Peru don't always have hot water, or it may be turned on only at certain hours of the day, or may be available upon request with an hour's notice, or even at an extra cost. Always ask about this before checking in. Early birds often use up all the hot water, so if you're a late riser be mentally prepared for a freezing wake-up call.

Beware of those showers that are heated electrically, with a single cold-water showerhead hooked up to an electric heating element that is switched on when you want a hot (more likely, tepid) shower. Don't touch anything metal or raise your hand near the heating unit while you're in the shower, or you may get a shock – never strong enough to throw you across the room, but hardly pleasant nonetheless. Tall travelers are more at risk. Wearing rubber sandals will protect you from the shock. Regulate the temperature by adjusting the water flow – more water means less heat, theoretically.

will often be worse off at the cheapest mid-range places than at the best budget choices, so it pays to choose carefully.

At this level, rooms usually have private showers (remote jungle lodges are often an exception) and hot water is the norm. Small portable heaters or fans may be provided for climate control. Rooms tend to have more amenities, such as cable TV and telephones. In-room phones usually connect with reception, however, and only receive incoming calls. To make outgoing calls, guests have to give the number to reception, hang up, then wait to get called back. See p510 for more information about making calls.

TOP END

Hotels in this category cost upwards of US$75 for a double, apart from in Cuzco, when a top-end place will cost upwards of US$100. Typically hotels will add a tax of 18% to the quoted room rates; however, they are legally allowed to refund this 18% to a non-Peruvian traveler if they can keep a photocopy of your passport. Expect a nonrefundable 'service charge' of 10% to be tacked onto your bill, too.

Many of these hotels conform to international standards, with international direct dialing (IDD) phones, handy dual-voltage outlets, central heating and air-conditioning, hairdryers in the bathroom, in-room safes, a bar and restaurants with 24-hour room service, as well as obliging staff. Luxury hotels are found only in major cities and tourist areas. They often boast a swimming pool, gym, sauna, spa, shopping gallery, business center and many more amenities, but not all of these may be in working order. Wi-fi internet access is rare (see p506).

Reservations

Cheap budget places may not accept phone or email reservations, or may not honor them if you arrive late in the day. Call when you arrive in town to see if they still have a room available, then head over right away. Better hotels will tell you what time you have to arrive by, and may request prepayment by means of a deposit into their bank account.

Making reservations online is convenient, but you pay for the privilege. Rates secured this way are guaranteed, but walk-in rates off the street can be much lower, as long as rooms are still available. The exception is at top-end hotels, where discounted rates may

> **BOOK ACCOMMODATION ONLINE**
>
> For more accommodation reviews and recommendations by Lonely Planet authors, check out the online booking service at www.lonelyplanet.com. You'll find the true, insider lowdown on the best places to stay. Reviews are thorough and independent. Best of all, you can book online.

only be available by making advance reservations online. Overall, the peace of mind is probably worth the extra cost of guaranteed reservations if you're arriving late at night or during peak travel times, or you need a pickup from the airport or bus station.

ACTIVITIES

Most travelers are interested in visiting archaeological sites, watching wildlife and trekking and/or mountaineering. But there are many other outdoor adventures awaiting you, as described starting on p60.

Peak season for most outdoor activities is during the colder dry season (June to August). Avoid trekking during the wet season (December to March). These hotter summer months are the best time of year for beach swimming and surfing along the Pacific Coast. For more information on climate, see opposite.

The fledgling status of many outdoor activities in Peru is both an advantage and a pitfall. While you may dream about having a surf break, mountain-bike trail or white-water rapids all to yourself, there are serious drawbacks. Equipment rental can be expensive and hard to find. Organized tour agencies may have little concern for safeguarding the natural environment. Local guides are largely unregulated, untrained and inexperienced, which can lead to injury or even death for themselves or their clients.

To assure your greater safety, avoid the cheapest, cut-rate travel agencies and shell out more for a well-trained guide or a trip organized by a reputable outdoor outfitter. For specialized activities, try to bring your own high-quality gear from home.

BUSINESS HOURS

Hours are variable and liable to change. Be patient, as services can be slow. Some places may have posted hours and not adhere to them. Forget about getting anything done on a Sunday, when nearly everything is closed. A few 24-hour supermarkets have opened in Lima and other major cities. Taxi drivers often know where the late-night stores are.

Many shops and offices close for a lunch break (usually from 1pm until around 4pm), but some banks and post offices stay open. Reviews in this book won't list opening hours unless they vary from the standard. Typically, opening hours are as follows:

Banks 9am-6pm Mon-Fri, some open 9am-1pm Sat

Bars and clubs 5:30pm-midnight, some till 2am

Restaurants 10am-10pm, some closed 3-6pm

Shops 9am-6pm Mon-Fri, some open 9am-6pm Sat

CHILDREN

Foreigners traveling with children in Peru are a welcome curiosity, and will excite some extra attention and generally friendly, well-intentioned interest. As this is a country where people frequently touch each other, your children may be patted on the head a lot.

Often someone will give up a seat on public transportation for a parent traveling with a child, or they'll offer to put the child on their lap. Children are normally charged full fare on buses only if they occupy a seat. On flights, children under 12 are typically charged 50% to 75% of the fare and get a seat, while infants are charged 10% if they don't need a seat.

At hotels, children shouldn't be charged as much as adults, but the rate is open to discussion. Cots are not normally available. While 'kids' meals' are not offered in restaurants, adult portions are normally so large that small children may not need a separate order. High chairs are rarely available.

Breastfeeding in public is not uncommon, but most women discreetly cover themselves. Poorly maintained public bathrooms may be a concern for parents. Always carry toilet paper and wet wipes. While a woman may take a young boy into the ladies' bathroom, it would be socially unacceptable for a man to take a girl of any age into the men's room. Diapers are difficult to find in smaller towns, so stock up at supermarkets or pharmacies in major cities and tourist centers.

For more advice about keeping your family happy, healthy and sane on the road, see Lonely Planet's *Travel with Children*.

CLIMATE CHARTS

Peru has three main climatic zones: the tropical Amazon jungle to the east; the arid coastal

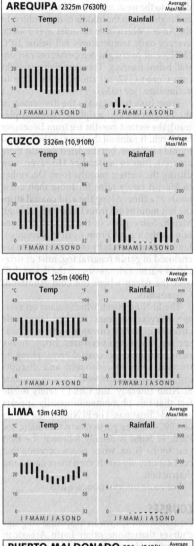

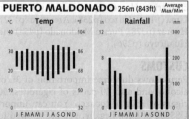

desert to the west; and the Andean mountains and highlands in the middle of the country. In the Andes, which have altitudes over 3500m, average daily temperatures fall below 10°C (50°F) and overnight temperatures can dip well below freezing. Travelers flying straight into Cuzco (3326m) should allow time to acclimatize (see p534).

From June to August is the dry season in the mountains and altiplano (Andean plateau); the wettest months are from December to March. It rains all the time in the hot and humid rainforest, but the driest months there are from June to September. However, even during the wettest months from December to May, it rarely rains for more than a few hours at a time. Along the arid coastal strip, the hot months are from December through March. Some parts of the coastal strip see rain rarely, if at all. From April to November, Lima and other areas by the Pacific Ocean are enclosed in *garúa* (coastal fog, mist or drizzle) as warmer air masses off the desert drift over the ocean where the cold Humboldt Current hits.

The El Niño effect, which occurs on average every seven years, is when large-scale changes in ocean currents and rising sea-surface water temperatures bring heavy rains and floods to coastal areas, plunging tropical areas into drought and disrupting weather patterns worldwide. The name El Niño (literally 'the Child') refers to the fact that this phenomenon usually appears around Christmas. The El Niño in the winter of 1997–98 was particularly traumatic for Peru. El Niño is usually followed the next year by La Niña, when ocean currents that cool abnormally create even more havoc and destruction.

For more information, see p18.

COURSES

Peru is less well-known for its Spanish-language courses than some other Latin American countries. However, there are schools in Lima (p106), Cuzco (p238), Arequipa (p172), Huaraz (p378), Puerto Maldonado (p454) and Huancayo (p296).

CUSTOMS

Peru allows duty-free importation of 3L of alcohol and also 20 packs of cigarettes, 50 cigars or 250g of tobacco. You can import US$300 of gifts. Legally, you are allowed to bring in such items as a laptop, camera, portable music player, kayak, climbing gear etc for personal use.

It is illegal to take pre-Columbian artifacts out of Peru, and it is illegal to bring them into most countries. Purchasing animal products made from endangered species or even just transporting them around Peru is also illegal. Coca leaves are legal in Peru, but not in most other countries – even in the form of tea bags, which are available in Peruvian shops. People subject to random drug testing should be aware that coca, even in the form of tea, may leave trace amounts in their urine.

Check with your own home government about customs restrictions and duties on any expensive or rare items you intend to bring back. Most countries allow their citizens to import a limited number of items duty-free, though these regulations are subject to change.

DANGERS & ANNOYANCES

Peru is often said to be one of the most dangerous countries in South America, but most travelers leave without ever feeling they've been in a sticky situation. Peru's widespread poverty means that street crimes (eg pickpocketing, bag-snatching and muggings) are common. Don't get too paranoid, though, since worrying can ruin your trip before it starts.

Remember that it's often safer to be a tourist than a resident, given Peru's tumultuous political climate. So, take the advice that locals give you with a grain of salt. However, warnings in heavily touristed areas such as Cuzco and the Sacred Valley may sometimes be accurate. Robberies and fatal attacks on trekkers have occurred even on popular hiking trails, especially around Huaraz and in the Cordilleras Blanca and Huayhuash. In other places, both residents and foreign embassies and consulates overestimate the everyday dangers, for example in Lima, where the situation has recently improved.

Kidnappings receive a lot of press, but these usually don't target foreigners. It's usually a matter of foreigners being in the wrong place at the wrong time. Political and economic turmoil have made public protests a familiar sight in Peru, so it's wise to stay aware of current events. Generally speaking, these protests have little effect on tourists other than blocking traffic. While waiting out a labor-related

---

GOVERNMENT TRAVEL ADVICE

The following government websites offer travel advisories and information on current hot spots.

Australian Department of Foreign Affairs (☎ 1300 139 281; www.smarttraveller.gov.au)

British Foreign Office (☎ 0845 850 2829; www.fco.gov.uk/countryadvice)

Canadian Department of Foreign Affairs (☎ 800 267 6788; www.dfait-maeci.gc.ca)

US State Department (☎ 888 407 4747; http://travel.state.gov)

---

strike, some travelers put their bus seats into full recline and take a nap.

The military and police (even sometimes the tourist police) have a reputation for being corrupt. While a foreigner may experience petty harassment (usually to procure payment of a bribe), most police officers are courteous to tourists, or otherwise leave them alone. The *policía de turismo* (tourist police, aka Poltur) are found in major cities and tourist areas. See p506 for more on legal matters.

Theft

Every year we hear from travelers who have been robbed. However, by taking basic precautions and exercising a reasonable amount of vigilance, you probably won't be. Often travelers are so involved in their new surroundings and experiences that they forget to stay alert – and that's when something is stolen.

Armed theft and 'choke and grab' attacks do not happen as frequently as sneak theft. Remember that crowded places are usually the haunts of pickpockets – bus terminals, train stations and bustling markets and fiestas are all common spots. Snatch theft can also occur if you place a bag on the ground for just a second, or while you're asleep on an overnight bus. Hotels aren't entirely trustworthy either: lock your valuables inside your luggage, or use safety deposit services where they are offered.

Thieves look for easy targets. Tourists carrying a wallet or passport in a hip pocket are asking for trouble. A small roll of bills loosely wadded under a handkerchief in your front pocket is as safe a way as any of carrying your daily spending money. The rest should be hidden. Always use at least a closable inside

pocket (or preferably a hidden body pouch or money belt) to protect your money and passport.

Thieves often work in pairs or groups. While your attention is being distracted by one, another is robbing you. The distraction can take the form of a bunch of kids fighting in front of you, an elderly person 'accidentally' bumping into you or asking you a question, someone dropping something in your path or spilling something on your clothes etc.

Razor-blade artists may slit open your luggage, whether it's a padlocked pack on your back or luggage on the rack of a bus, when you're not looking. Some travelers carry their day packs on their chests to avoid having them slashed in markets and other crowded public spaces. It is always a good idea to walk purposefully wherever you are going, even if you are lost.

Take out traveler's insurance (p506) before you leave. To make an insurance claim, you will need a police report of the theft. Airlines may reissue a lost ticket for a fee, if you have the original receipt. Stolen passports can be reissued at your embassy (p502), though you may be asked for an alternative form of identification first. After receiving your new passport, go to the nearest Peruvian immigration office (p513) to get a new tourist card.

Drugs, Kidnappings & Terrorism

Most of the kidnappings and violence associated with the illegal drug business in Peru are caused by domestic terrorists. The main terrorist group is the Sendero Luminoso (Shining Path), which has largely abandoned its Maoist origins for lucrative criminal activities. After its main leaders were captured in 1992, travel safety in Peru improved dramatically. Ten years later, the remaining Senderistas claimed responsibility for a car bombing near the US embassy in Lima. Sporadic attacks are still reported today, mostly in remote areas

---

WARNING!

All important documents (passport, credit cards, travel insurance policy, driving license etc) should be photocopied before you leave home. Leave one copy at home and keep another with you, separate from the originals.

WARNING!

Be wary when considering traveling on overnight buses, which are best avoided. Even on the well-traveled Pan-American Hwy route between Arequipa and Lima, overnight buses have been hijacked (recently by criminals posing as fellow passengers) and foreign tourists have been robbed and raped. Military checkpoints can appear anywhere, but road blockades by terrorist groups are common only in certain remote areas.

(eg the rural provinces of Ayacucho, Huancavelica, Huánuco, Junín, San Martín and Ucayali), and are not generally aimed at tourists.

In recent years, Peruvian farmers have increased their production of coca plants, from which cocaine is made. Peru is now the world's second-largest producer of cocaine. The Sendero Luminoso and other guerrilla groups have aligned with drug-trafficking cartels from Mexico and Colombia to protect coca-growing agricultural areas, which have expanded into Peru's central jungle. Backed by the USA, efforts by the Peruvian government to eradicate the crops have met with mass protests and riots. Travelers should especially avoid the upper Río Huallaga valley between Tingo María and Juanjui and the Río Apurímac valley near Ayacucho, where the majority of Peru's illegal drug-growing takes place (see also p319). Also exercise caution near the Colombian border, where incursions by armed guerrillas and kidnappings have occurred. For more information on drug-related legal matters, see p506.

In recent years there has been a rise in 'express' kidnappings. An armed attacker (or attackers) grabs someone out of a taxi or abducts them off the street, then forces them to go to the nearest bank and withdraw cash using their ATM cards. This usually happens in congested areas where traffic slows to a halt, particularly on roads leading to and from Lima's airport. Victims who do not resist their attackers generally don't suffer serious physical harm, although rapes have occurred.

Environmental Hazards

Some of the hazards you might encounter in Peru include altitude sickness, earthquakes, avalanches, animal and insect bites, sunburn, heat exhaustion and even hypothermia. You can take precautions for most of these, while the rest are, thankfully, rare. See p534 for more medical advice.

Landmines

A half century of armed conflict over the Cordillera del Condor region on Peru's northeastern border with Ecuador was finally resolved in 1998. However, unexploded ordinance (UXO) in the area has not been completely cleaned up. Only use official border crossings and don't stray from the beaten path when traveling in this region.

DISCOUNT CARDS

An official International Student Identity Card (ISIC), with a photograph, can get you a 50% discount at some museums and attractions and for organized tours. Senior discount cards are not recognized.

EMBASSIES & CONSULATES

Most foreign embassies are in Lima, with some consular services in major tourist centers. See p513 for *oficinas de migraciónes* (immigration offices), which issue entry cards, provide exit stamps and can extend the period of your stay in Peru.

It is important to realize what your embassy – the embassy of the country of which you are a citizen – can and can't do to help you if you get into trouble in Peru. Generally speaking, it won't be much help if the trouble you're in is even remotely your own fault. Your embassy will not be sympathetic if you end up in jail after committing a crime locally, even if such actions are legal in your own country.

In genuine emergencies, you might get some assistance, but only if other channels have been exhausted. If you need to get home urgently, a free ticket is exceedingly unlikely – the embassy would expect you to have travel insurance (p506). If all your money and documents are stolen, it should assist you with getting a new passport, but a loan for onward travel is out of the question.

Peruvian Embassies & Consulates

For countries not listed here, search the government website (www.rree.gob.pe) or click the 'Embassies & Consulates' link from PromPerú's home page (www.peru.info).

Australia ACT (☎ 02-6273 8752; www.embaperu.org
.au; 40 Brisbane Ave, Barton, ACT 2600); Sydney (☎ 02-
9262 6464; c-sydney4@conper.com.au; 3rd fl, 30 Clarence
St, Sydney, NSW 2000)
Bolivia La Paz (☎ 02-244 0631; www.conperlapaz.org;
Oficina 402, Edificio Hilda, Av 6 de Agosto 2455, Sopocachi,
La Paz)
Brazil Brasília (☎ 61-242 9435; www.embperu.org.br;
SES, Av das Nações lote 43, 70428-900 Brasília DF); Río de
Janeiro (☎ 21-2551 4496; conperio@terra.com.br; 2nd
fl, Av Rui Barbosa 314, Flamengo, CEP 22250-020, Río de
Janeiro); São Paulo (☎ 11-3063 5952; Calle Venezuela 36,
CEP 01439-000, Jarsim América, São Paulo)
Canada Ottawa (☎ 613-238 2721; www.embassyofperu
.ca; Suite 201, 130 Albert St, Ottawa, ON K1P 5G4);
Montréal (☎ 514-844 5123; www.consuladoperumon-
treal.com; Suite 970, 550 Sherbrooke Oeste, Montréal, QC,
H3A 1B9); Toronto (☎ 416-963 9696; www.conperu
toronto.com; Suite 301, 10 Saint Mary St, Toronto, ON, M4Y
1P9); Vancouver (☎ 604-662 8880; www.consuladoperu
.ca; 260-505 Burrard St, Vancouver, BC, V7X 1M3)
Chile Santiago (☎ 02-235 4600; conpersantiago@adsl.tie
.cl; Oficina 309, Calle Padre Mariano 10, Providencia,
Santiago 16277); Arica (☎ 058-23 1020;
conperarica@terra.cl; Av 18 de Septiembre 1554, Arica 17)
Colombia Bogotá (☎ 1-257 8763; cgperu@007mundo
.com; Oficina 417, No 14-26 Calle 90, Bogotá); Leticia
(☎ 8-592 7204; coplet@telecom.com.co; No 5-32 Calle
11, Leticia)
Ecuador Quito (☎ 02-225 2582; www.embajadadelperu
.org.ec; Av República de El Salvador 495e, Irlanda, Planta
Baja, Quito); Guayaquil (☎ 04-228 0114; conperu@gye
.satnet.net; Oficina 02, 14th fl, Edificio Centrum, Av
Francisco de Orellana Kennedy Norte, Guayaquil)
France Paris (☎ 01 42 70 65 25 10;
conperparis@wanadoo.fr; 25 rue de l'Arcade, 75008 Paris)
Germany Berlin (☎ 030 2 29 14 55; www.conperberlin
.embaperu.de; Mohrenstrasse 42, 10117 Berlin)
Ireland Dublin (☎ 01-288 9733; revillep@eircom.net;
67 Rocwood, off Leopardstown Rd, Blackrock Co, Dublin)
Honorary consul with only limited services.
Israel Tel Aviv (☎ 09-9957 8836; emperu@012.net.il; Entrada A, 2nd fl, 60 Medinat Hayehudim St, Herzliya 46766)
Italy Rome (☎ 06-8069 1510, 06-8069 1534; www
.ambasciataperu.it; Via Francesco Siacci 2B, 00197 Roma)
Netherlands Amsterdam (☎ 020-622 85 80; fax 020-
422 85 81; Kantoorgebouw Riverstate, Amsteldijk 166-7E,
1079 LH Amsterdam)
New Zealand Wellington (☎ 04-499 8087; www.embassy
ofperu.org.nz; Level 8, Cigna House, 40 Mercer St, PO Box
2566, Wellington)
Spain Madrid (☎ 91-56 29 012; www.consuladoperu
madrid.org; Calle Cristobal Bordiú 49, 28003 Madrid)
UK London (☎ 020 7235 1917; www.peruembassy
-uk.com; 52 Sloane St, London SW1X 9SP)

USA Washington, DC (☎ 202-833 9860; www.peruvian
embassy.us; 1700 Massachusetts Ave NW, Washington, DC
20036); Chicago (☎ 312-782 1599; www.consuladoperu
.com; Suite 1830, 180 N Michigan Ave, Chicago, IL 60601);
Los Angeles (☎ 213-252 5910; www.consuladoperu.com;
Suite 800, 3450 Wilshire Blvd, Los Angeles, CA 90010);
Miami (☎ 305-374 1305; www.consuladoperu.com;
Suite M-135, 444 Brickell Ave, Miami, FL 33131); New York
(☎ 646-735 3828; www.consuladoperu.com; 241 E 49th
St, New York, NY 10017)

Embassies & Consulates in Peru

For after-hours and emergency contact numbers of the embassies and consulates, check
the websites listed below. Other consulates are
listed under select cities in this book, notably
Cuzco (p227).

Australia Lima (Map p101; ☎ 01-222 8281; www.australia
.org.pe; Suite 1301, Torre Real 3, Av Victor A Belaúnde 147,
San Isidro; ☻ 9am-1pm & 2-5pm Mon-Fri)
Belgium Lima (Map p102; ☎ 01-241 7566; Av Angamos
Oeste 380, Miraflores; ☻ 8:30am-4pm Mon-Fri)
Bolivia Lima (Map p101; ☎ 01-422 8231; fax 01-222
4594; Los Castaños 235, San Isidro; ☻ 8:30am-4:30pm)
Puno (Map p194; ☎ /fax 051-35 1251; 3rd fl, Jirón
Arequipa 136, Puno; ☻ 8am-3pm Mon-Fri)
Brazil Lima (Map p102; ☎ 01-421 5660; www.embajada
brasil.org.pe; Av José Pardo 850, Miraflores; ☻ 9:30am-
noon Mon-Fri)
Canada Lima (Map p102; ☎ 01-444 4015; www.dfait
-maeci.gc.ca/latin-america/peru; Libertad 130, Miraflores;
☻ 8am-12:30pm & 1:15-5pm Mon-Tue & Thu-Fri, 8am-
1pm Wed)
Chile Lima (Map p101; ☎ 01-611 2211; www.embachile
.peru.com.pe; Av Javier Prado Oeste 790, San Isidro;
☻ 9am-12:30pm Mon-Fri)
Colombia Lima (Map p101; ☎ 01-441 0954; www.emba
jadacolombia.org.pe; Av Jorge Basadre 1580, San Isidro;
☻ 8:30am-12:30pm Mon-Fri) Iquitos (Map p484; ☎ 065-
23 1461; cniquitosperu@terra.com.pe; Calvo de Araujo 431,
Iquitos; ☻ 9am-12:30pm & 2-4:30pm Mon-Fri)
Ecuador Lima (Map p101; ☎ 01-212 4171; www.mecuador
peru.org.pe; Jirón Las Palmeras 356, San Isidro; ☻ 9am-
1pm Mon-Fri) Tumbes (Map p368; ☎ 072-52 5949; 3rd fl,
Jirón Bolívar 129, Plaza de Armas, Tumbes; ☻ 9am-1pm &
4-6pm Mon-Fri)
France Lima (Map p101; ☎ 01-215 8400; www.amba
france-pe.org; Av Arequipa 3415, San Isidro; ☻ 8:30am-
12:30pm)
Germany Lima (Map p101; ☎ 01-212 5016; www
.embajada-alemana.org.pe; Av Arequipa 4210, Miraflores;
☻ 8:30-11:30am Mon-Fri)
Ireland Lima (☎ 01-273 2903; irishconsulperu@yahoo
.ca; Miguel Alegré Rodriguez 182, Miraflores) Honorary
consul with only limited services.

Israel Lima (Map pp94-5; ☎ 01-433 4431; www.mfa
.gov.il; 6th fl, Natalio Sánchez 125, Santa Beatriz;
🕑 10am-1pm Mon-Thu, 10am-noon Fri)

Italy Lima (Map pp88-9; ☎ 01-463 2727; www.ital
embperu.org.pe; Av Gregorio Escobedo 298, Jesus María;
🕑 9am-1pm Mon-Fri)

Netherlands Lima (☎ 01-415-0660; www.nlgovlim
.com; 4th fl, Av Principal 190, Santa Catalina; 🕑 9am-
noon Mon-Fri)

Spain Lima (Map p101; ☎ 01-513 7930; www.mae.es
/consulados/lima; Calle Los Pinos, San Isidro; 🕑 8:30am-
1pm Mon-Fri)

Switzerland Lima (Map pp88-9; ☎ 01-264 0305; www
.eda.admin.ch/lima_emb/s/home.html; Av
Salaverry 3240, San Isidro; 🕑 8am-1pm & 2-5pm
Mon-Fri)

UK Lima (Map p102; ☎ 01-617 3000; www.british
embassy.gov.uk; 23rd fl, Torre Parque Mar, Av José Larco
1301, Miraflores; 🕑 8am-1pm Mon-Fri)

USA Lima (Map pp88-9; ☎ 01-434 3000; http://lima
.usembassy.gov; Av La Encalada cuadra 17, Surco;
🕑 7:30am-5:30pm Mon-Thu, 7:30am-12:30pm Fri)

FESTIVALS & EVENTS

Many Peruvian festivals echo the Roman
Catholic liturgical calendar and are celebrated
with great pageantry, especially in indigenous
highland villages, where Catholic feast days
are often linked with a traditional agricultural
festival, such as harvesttime. These days provide an excuse for a fiesta, and include much
drinking, dancing, rituals and processions.
Other holidays are of historical or political
interest, such as Fiestas Patrias (National Independence Days). Local fiestas and festivals
are held somewhere almost every week. Many
are described under individual towns earlier
in this book. See opposite for public holidays
that are observed nationally.

January
Año Nuevo (New Year's Day) This holiday, held on January 1, is particularly important in Huancayo (p298), where
a fiesta continues until Epiphany (January 6).

Fiesta de la Marinera (last week in January) National
dance festival in Trujillo (p331).

February
La Virgen de la Candelaria (Candlemas) Held on February 2, this highland fiesta is particularly colorful around
Puno (p196), where folkloric music and dance celebrations
last for two weeks.

Carnaval Held on the last few days before Lent (February/
March), this holiday is often 'celebrated' with weeks
of water fights, so be warned. It's popular in the highlands,

with the fiesta in Cajamarca (p426) being one of
the biggest. It's also busy in the beach towns.

March & April
Fiesta de la Vendimia (Wine Festival) Sample local
wine in Ica (p140). Held in the second week of March.

Semana Santa (Holy Week) The week before Easter
Sunday is celebrated with spectacular religious processions
almost daily, with Ayacucho (p309) being recognized as
having the best in Peru. Arequipa (p173), Huancayo (p298)
and Huaraz (p379) are also good for Easter processions.

May
Festival of the Crosses This festival is held on May 3
in Lima, Apurímac, Ayacucho, Junín, Ica and Cuzco.

Q'oyoriti At the foot of Ausangate, outside of Cuzco, in
May/June (p284).

June
Corpus Christi Processions in Cuzco (p239) are especially
dramatic. Held on the ninth Thursday after Easter.

Inti Raymi (Festival of the Sun, also the Feast of St John
the Baptist and Peasant's Day) The greatest of the Inca
festivals celebrates the winter solstice on June 24. It's certainly the spectacle of the year in Cuzco (p239), attracting
thousands of Peruvian and foreign visitors. It's also a big
holiday in many of the jungle towns.

San Pedro y San Pablo (Feasts of Sts Peter & Paul)
More fiestas on June 29, especially around Lima and in
the highlands.

July
La Virgen del Carmen Held on July 16, this holiday is
mainly celebrated in the southern sierra, with Paucartambo
(p283) and Pisac near Cuzco, and Pucará near Lake Titicaca
being especially important.

Fiestas Patrias (National Independence Days) Celebrated
nationwide on July 28 & 29, with festivities in the southern
sierra beginning with the Feast of St James on July 25.

August
Feast of Santa Rosa de Lima This involves major
processions on August 30 and is held in Lima, Arequipa
and Junín to honor the patron saint of Lima and of the
Americas.

September
El Festival Internacional de la Primavera (International Spring Festival) Supreme displays of horsemanship,
dancing and cultural celebrations in Trujillo during the last
week of September (p331).

October
La Virgen del Rosario Held on October 4 in Lima,
Ancash, Apurímac, Arequipa and Cuzco.

El Señor de los Milagros (Lord of the Miracles) Major religious processions (celebrants wear purple) in Lima on October 18, around which time the bullfight season starts.

November

Todos Santos (All Saints Day) Held on November 1, this is a religious precursor to the following day.

Día de los Muertos (All Souls Day) Celebrated on November 2 with gifts of food, drink and flowers taken to family graves; especially colorful in the sierra. Some of the 'gift' food and drink is consumed, and the atmosphere is festive rather than somber.

Puno Week Starting November 5, this weeklong festival involves several days of spectacular costumes and street dancing to celebrate the legendary emergence of the first Inca, Manco Capac; see p196.

December

Fiesta de la Purísima Concepción (Feast of the Immaculate Conception) This national holiday, held on December 8, is celebrated with religious processions in honor of the Virgin Mary.

Christmas Day Held on December 25, Christmas is less secular and more religious, especially in the Andean highlands.

La Virgen del Carmen de Chincha Frenzied dancing and all-night music in the *peñas* (bars or clubs featuring live folkloric music) of El Carmen on December 27 (p130).

FOOD

Reviews listed under Eating sections in this book are arranged by price, from cheapest to most expensive. Budget eateries generally serve dishes costing US$5 or less, while mains at midrange restaurants typically cost from US$5 to US$10. Top-end restaurants cost over US$10 for a main. Note that prices in Lima, Arequipa and Cuzco tend to be higher than in the rest of Peru. See p77 for more on Peruvian cuisine.

GAY & LESBIAN TRAVELERS

Peru is a strongly conservative, Catholic country. Gay rights in a political or legal context don't even exist as an issue for most Peruvians. (FYI: the rainbow flag seen around Cuzco is *not* a gay pride flag – it's the flag of the Inca empire.) When the issue does arise in public, hostility is most often the official response.

Sexuality is often heavily stereotyped in Latin countries, with the man playing a dominant macho role and the woman tagging along with that. This attitude spills over into homosexuality: straight-identifying macho men are not considered to be gay, even if they have sex with men (as long as they're on top), while an effeminate man, even if he is straight, may be called a *maricón* (which roughly translates as 'faggot').

Kissing on the mouth is rarely seen in public, either by heterosexual or homosexual couples. That said, Peruvians can be physically demonstrative with their friends, so kissing on the cheek in greeting or an *abrazo* (back-slapping hug exchanged between men) are innocuous, everyday behaviors. When in doubt, do as the locals do.

Few men in Peru are exclusively homosexual. This means that HIV/AIDS is often transmitted heterosexually, and is a growing problem in Peru, especially among women (see p531). Lesbians are a largely ignored segment of the population; most Peruvians realize they exist, but don't think much about them. Lima is by far the most accepting of gay people, while Cuzco, Arequipa and Trujillo are also more tolerant than the norm.

There are several organizations that provide resources for gay and lesbian travelers:

Deambiente.com (www.deambiente.com, www.intro spektivo.com) Spanish-language online magazine about politics and pop culture, plus nightlife listings.

Gayperu.com (www.gayperu.com) A modern, Spanish-language online guide to gay culture that lists bars to bathhouses; also runs a multilingual travel agency.

Global Gayz (www.globalgayz.com) Excellent, country-specific information about Peru's gay scene and politics, with links to international resources.

Movimiento Homosexual-Lesbiana (MHOL; Map pp88-9; ☎ 01-332 2945; www.mhol.org.pe; Mariscal Miller 822, Jesús María) Peru's best-known gay political organization.

Purpleroofs.com (www.purpleroofs.com) Massive GLBT portal with links to a few tour operators and gay-friendly accommodations in Peru.

Rainbow Peruvian Tours (Map p102; ☎ 01-610 6000, 01-215 6000; www.perurainbow.com; Jirón Rio de Janeiro 216, Miraflores, Lima) Gay-owned tour agency based in Lima, with a multilingual website.

HOLIDAYS

On major holidays, banks, offices and other services are closed, hotel rates can triple and transportation tends to be very crowded, so book ahead. If an official public holiday falls on a weekend, offices close on the following Monday. If an official holiday falls midweek, it may or may not be moved to the nearest Monday to create a long weekend. Major holidays may be celebrated for days around the official date.

Fiestas Patrias (National Independence Days) is the biggest national holiday, when the entire nation seems to be on the move. Major national, regional and religious holidays include the following:

New Year's Day January 1
Good Friday March/April
Labor Day May 1
Inti Raymi June 24
Feast of Sts Peter & Paul June 29
National Independence Days July 28–29
Feast of Santa Rosa de Lima August 30
Battle of Angamos Day October 8
All Saints Day November 1
Feast of the Immaculate Conception December 8
Christmas December 25

See also p504.

INSURANCE

Having a travel-insurance policy to cover theft, loss, accidents and illness is highly recommended. Many policies include a card with toll-free or collect-call hotlines for 24-hour assistance, and it's good practice to carry that with you. Not all policies compensate travelers for misrouted or lost luggage. Some policies specifically exclude 'dangerous activities,' which can include scuba diving, motorcycling, and even trekking. Also check if the policy coverage includes worst-case scenarios, such as evacuations and flights home. A variety of travel-insurance policies are available. Those handled by STA Travel and other budget travel organizations are usually good value.

Always read the fine print carefully. You may prefer a policy that pays doctors or hospitals directly rather than you having to pay on the spot and make a claim later. If your bags are lost or stolen, the insurance company may demand a receipt as proof that you bought the goods in the first place. You must usually report any loss or theft to local police within 24 hours. Make sure you keep all documentation to make any claim.

INTERNET ACCESS

Accessing the internet is a snap in Peru. Even tiny towns have an internet café, and larger cities have hundreds of them. A few of the most comfortable and convenient internet cafés are listed under destinations earlier in this book, but you will find many more.

Rates for high-speed connections at internet cafés average less than US$0.60 per hour,

and it's only in remote places that you will pay more for slower connection speeds. Most internet cafés are open from the early morning till late and also offer cheap phone calls (see p510). Almost all provide headphones. Hotel business centers are overpriced, charging up to US$6 per hour. A few top-end hotels are starting to offer wi-fi internet access in communal areas.

Before plugging in your laptop, ensure that your power source adheres to Peru's 220V, 60Hz AC electricity supply. A portable converter with a built-in surge protector is a must. Your PC-card modem may not work, but you won't know until you try. The easiest option is to buy a 'global' modem before you leave home. Dial-up internet access is generally a hassle because few ISPs have local access numbers in Peru, forcing you to make an international call. Only top-end hotel rooms have international direct-dial (IDD) phones. Peruvian telephone sockets use a North American RJ-11 jack.

A few internet cafés allow you to hook up your laptop to a cable connection at the same rates charged for using one of their terminals. Consider bringing along a portable USB flash drive. This keychain-sized device lets you seamlessly transfer files between your laptop and any other computer equipped with a high-speed USB port. A flash drive can also be used to store photo files uploaded from your digital camera memory cards.

See p20 for useful Peruvian websites.

LAUNDRY

Self-service laundry machines are available in only a few major cities. This means that you will have to pay someone to wash your clothes, or wash them yourself in the sink, a practice that's forbidden at many places to stay. The best hotels offer on-site laundry services and dry cleaning, but these can be expensive. In most towns, there are *lavanderías* (laundries) where you leave your clothes overnight or drop them off in the morning, then pick them up later the same day. Some *lavanderías* charge by the number of items and others by weight. Budget travelers advise bringing along a known weight (eg filled plastic water bottle) to test if the laundry's scales are accurate. Rates average US$2 per kilogram.

LEGAL MATTERS

Your own embassy is of limited help if you get into trouble with the law in Peru, where you

IS IT LEGAL?

Drinking alcohol	Yes – if you're 18 years old.
Drugs	No – except with a prescription.
Prostitution	Yes – though profiteering from such activities (eg pimping) is not.
Sex	Yes – age of consent is 14; homosexuality is not illegal.
Smoking in public	Yes – except on public transportation.

are presumed guilty until proven innocent. If you are the victim, the *policía de turismo* (tourist police, aka Poltur) can help, and usually have someone on hand who speaks at least a little English. There are Poltur stations in over a dozen cities, including Lima (p87).

Be aware that some police officers (even tourist police) are corrupt, but that bribery is illegal. Since most travelers won't have to deal with traffic police, the most likely place you'll be expected to pay officials a little extra is (sometimes) at land borders. This too is illegal, and if you have the time and fortitude to stick to your guns, you'll eventually be allowed in without paying a fee.

Definitely avoid having any conversation with someone who offers you drugs. In fact, talking to any stranger on the street can hold risks. There have been reports of travelers being stopped soon after by plainclothes police officers and accused of talking to a drug dealer. Should you be stopped by a plainclothes police officer, don't hand over any documents or money. Never get into a vehicle with someone claiming to a police officer, but insist on going to a bona fide police station on foot. Peru has draconian penalties for possessing even a small amount of drugs; minimum sentences are several years in jail.

If you are imprisoned for any reason, make sure that someone else knows about it as soon as possible. Being detained in prison for extended periods of time before a trial begins is not uncommon. Peruvians bring food and clothing to family members who are in prison, where conditions are extremely harsh.

If you think that you were ripped off by a hotel or tour operator, register your complaint with the **National Institute for the Defense of Competition and the Protection of Intellectual Property** (Indecopi; ☎ 01-224 7800) in Lima.

MAPS

The maps in this book will take you almost everywhere you want to go. The best road map of Peru is the 1:2,000,000 *Mapa Vial* published by Lima 2000 and available in better bookstores. The 1:1,500,000 *Peru South and Lima* country map, published by International Travel Maps, covers the country in good detail south of a line drawn east to west through Tingo Maria, and has a good street map of Lima, San Isidro, Miraflores and Barranco on the reverse side.

For topographical maps, go to the **Instituto Geográfico Nacional** (IGN; Map pp88-9; ☎ 01-475 9960; ventaign@ignperu.gob.pe; Aramburu 1198, Surquillo; ☷ 9am-4pm Mon-Fri). In January, the IGN closes around lunchtime. Its maps are for sale or for reference on the premises. Its good road map of Peru (1:2,000,000) is US$7, and a four-sheet 1:1,000,000 topographical map of Peru costs US$30. Departmental maps at various scales are US$6.50. High-scale topographic maps for trekking are available, though sheets of border areas might be hard to get. Geological and demographical maps are also sold.

The **Servicio Aerofotográfico Nacional** (Map pp88-9; ☎ 01-252 3401; ☷ 8am-2pm Mon-Fri), at Las Palmeras Air Force base in Surco, sells aerial photographs. Don't wear shorts when you go there, take a passport and expect a two-week waiting period for prints. Some aerial photos are also available from the IGN. The best way to find the base is to take a taxi.

Topographic, city and road maps are also at the South American Explorers' clubhouses in Lima (p93) and Cuzco (p227).

Up-to-date topo maps are often available from outdoor outfitters in major trekking centers such as Cuzco, Huaraz and Arequipa. If you are bringing along a GPS unit, ensure that your power source adheres to Peru's 220V, 60Hz AC standard and always carry a compass.

MONEY

Peru uses the nuevo sol (S/), which has traded at S/3.30 to S/3.50 per US dollar (US$) for several years, although you should keep an eye on current events. Prices in this book are quoted in US dollars unless otherwise stated. For more exchange rates, see the Quick Reference page inside the front cover.

Carrying cash, an ATM or traveler's check card and also a credit card that can be used for

FUNNY MONEY *Rafael Wlodarski*

Counterfeiting of both US and local-currency bills has become a serious problem. Merchants are extremely careful about accepting large-denomination notes; you should be, too. Everyone has their own technique for spotting a fake – some can feel the difference in paper quality, while others will sniff out counterfeit ink. You should look for a combination of signs; new forgeries simulate some security features, but never all of them. Politely refuse to accept *any* worn, torn or damaged bills, even small-denomination notes.

Things to watch out for:

■ Check the watermark – most fake bills have these, but real bills will have a section where the mark is made by discernibly thinner paper.

■ The writing along the top of the bill should be embossed – run your finger to see that it is raised from the paper and test the back for an impression.

■ The line underneath this writing is made up of tiny words – if it's a solid line, then it's a fake.

■ The value of the bill written on the side should appear metallic and be slightly green, blue, and pink at different angles – fake bills are only pink and have no hologram.

■ The metal strip running through the note has the word 'Peru' repeatedly written along its length in tiny letters when **held up** to the light – fake bills also have this, but the letters are messier and difficult to read.

■ The tiny pieces of colored thread and holographic dots scattered on the bill should be embedded in the paper, not glued on.

cash advances in case of emergency is advisable. When receiving local currency, always ask for small bills *(billetes pequeñas)*, as S/100 bills are hard to change in small towns or for small purchases. The best places to exchange money are normally *casas de cambio* (foreign-exchange bureaus), which are fast, have longer hours and often give slightly better rates than banks.

See also p19 for information on costs and money.

ATMs

Cajeros automáticos (ATMs) are found in nearly every city and town in Peru, as well as at major airports and bus terminals. ATMs are linked to the international Plus (Visa), Cirrus (Maestro/MasterCard) systems, American Express and other networks. They will accept your bank or credit card as long as you have a four-digit PIN. Before you leave home, notify your bank that you'll be using your ATM card abroad. Even better, leave your bank card at home and buy a traveler's check card instead.

ATMs are a convenient way of obtaining cash, but rates are usually lower than at *casas de cambio*. Both US dollars and nuevos soles are readily available from Peruvian ATMs. Your home bank may charge an additional fee

for each foreign ATM transaction. Surcharges for cash advances from credit cards vary, but are generally expensive, so check with your credit-card provider before you leave home.

ATMs are normally open 24 hours. For safety reasons, use ATMs inside banks with security guards, preferably during daylight hours.

Cash

The nuevo sol ('new sun') comes in bills of S/10, S/20, S/50, S/100 and (rarely) S/200. It is divided into 100 céntimos, with copper-colored coins of S/0.05, S/0.10 and S/0.20, and silver-colored S/0.50 and S/1 coins. In addition, there are bimetallic S/2 and S/5 coins with a copper-colored center inside a silver-colored ring.

US dollars are accepted by most tourist-oriented businesses, though you'll need nuevos soles to pay for local transportation, most meals etc. Paying in nuevos soles can be a time-consuming hassle at some midrange hotels and many top-end establishments. For specific advice on paying for accommodations, see p497.

Changing Money

Carrying cash entitles you to get the top exchange rates quickly. The best currency for exchange is the US dollar, although the euro is increasingly accepted. Other hard currencies can be exchanged, but usually with difficulty and only in major cities and tourist centers. All foreign currencies must be in flawless condition.

Cambistas (money-changers) hang out on street corners near banks and *casas de cambio* and give competitive rates (there's only a little flexibility for bargaining), but are not always honest. Officially, they should wear a vest and badge identifying them as legal. They're useful after regular business hours or at borders where there aren't any other options.

Credit Cards

Many top-end hotels and shops accept *tarjetas de credito* (credit cards) but usually charge you a 7% (or greater) fee for using them. The amount you'll eventually pay is not based on the point-of-sale exchange rate, but the rate your bank chooses to use when the transaction posts to your account, sometimes weeks later. Your bank may also tack on a surcharge and additional fees for each foreign-currency transaction.

The most widely accepted cards in Peru are Visa and MasterCard, although American Express and a few others are valid in some establishments, as well as for cash advances at ATMs. Before you leave home, notify your bank that you'll be using your credit card abroad.

Taxes, Tipping & Refunds

At Peruvian airports, international (p517) and domestic (p521) departure taxes are payable in US dollars or nuevos soles (cash only). Expensive hotels will add an 18% sales tax and 10% service charge, neither of which is normally included in quoted rates; non-Peruvians may be eligible for a refund of the sales tax only (see p498). A few restaurants charge combined taxes of more than 18%, plus a service charge *(servicio* or *propina)* of 10%. At restaurants that don't do this, you may tip 10% for good service. Taxi drivers do not expect tips, but porters and tour guides do. There is no system of sales-tax refunds for shoppers.

Traveler's Checks

If you carry some of your money as *cheques de viajero* (traveler's checks), these can be refunded if lost or stolen. However, exchange

rates for traveler's checks are quite a bit lower than for US cash. With the commissions sometimes charged, you can lose over 10% of the checks' value when you exchange them, and they may be impossible to change in small towns. Almost all businesses and some *casas de cambio* refuse to deal with them, so you will need to queue at a bank. American Express checks are the most widely accepted, followed by Visa and Thomas Cook.

Reloadable traveler's check cards work just like ATM cards, but are not linked to your home bank account. These cards enjoy some of the same protections as traveler's checks, and can be replaced more easily than a bank ATM card. During your trip, you can add more funds to a traveler's check card either online or by making an international collect call, or you can authorize someone else at home to do this for you, which eliminates the need for emergency wire transfers. **American Express** (www.americanexpress.com) offers traveler's check cards, as do many **Visa providers** (www.cashpassportcard.com).

PHOTOGRAPHY & VIDEO

Some locals think the camera's 'evil eye' can bring bad luck or steal a person's soul – always ask permission before pointing and shooting. In well-touristed locations, locals dressed in their finest traditional clothes stand beside their most photogenic llamas and expect a small payment for any photos you may take. Negotiate the price first. At markets, you may be able to photograph a vendor and/or their wares after making a purchase.

Print and slide film and replacement camera batteries are available in major cities and tourist centers, while digital memory cards and sticks are hard to find. Many internet cafés offer cheap CD-burning services that let you download and save files from your digital camera's memory. If your camera uses rechargeable batteries, be sure that your charger adheres to Peru's 220V 60Hz AC electricity standard before plugging it in.

It's best to carry film and digital memory cards with you onto airplanes. It's not advisable to put them into checked luggage because the scanners used for those bags are much stronger and likely to damage your film and erase digital memory cards. If you place all your film into a clear plastic bag, you may be able to get it hand-checked at security checkpoints (though this is often refused since 9/11).

POST

The privatized postal system is run by **Serpost** (www.serpost.com.pe). Its service is fairly efficient and reliable, but surprisingly expensive. Airmail postcards *(postales)* and letters *(cartas)* cost about US$4 to most foreign destinations and arrive in around two weeks from Lima, longer from the provinces.

Lista de correos (general delivery or poste restante) can be sent to any major post office. Bring your passport when picking up mail and ask the post-office clerk to check alphabetically under the initial letter of each of your first, last and middle names, as well as under 'M' (for Mr, Ms et al). Ask your correspondents to make sure that your name is clearly printed and to capitalize and underline your last name to avoid confusion. For example:

María HERNANDEZ
Lista de Correos
Correo Central
Miraflores, Lima 18
Peru

For express mail and packages, international couriers such as **Federal Express** (www.fedex.com.pe) are more reliable than post offices, but may only have drop-off centers in Lima or other major cities. They are also more expensive than Serpost.

SHOPPING

Arts and crafts are inevitably sold wherever tourists gather. Popular souvenirs include alpaca wool sweaters and scarves, woven textiles, ceramics, masks, gold and silver jewelry and the backpackers' fave, Inka Kola T-shirts. Avoid buying tourist-oriented products made by cutting up antique textiles, which is de-

---

PERUVIAN ADDRESSES

A post-office box is known as an *apartado postal* (abbreviated 'Apartado,' 'Apto' or 'AP') or a *casilla postal* ('Casilla' or 'CP'). Some addresses have *s/n* (short for *sin numero*, or 'without a number') or *cuadra* ('block,' eg Block 4) after the street name.

Only addresses in Lima and neighboring Callao require postal codes. Those used most often by travelers are Lima 1 (central Lima), Lima 4 (Barranco), Lima 18 (Miraflores) and Lima 27 (San Isidro). Note that the word 'Lima' is essential to these postal codes.

---

structive to indigenous peoples' cultural heritage. Expensive foreign-language books are stocked at better bookstores, especially in Lima (p87) and Cuzco (p226).

Bargaining is the norm at street stalls, markets and souvenir shops, where it's cash only. Prices are fixed in upscale stores, which may add a surcharge for credit-card transactions.

SOLO TRAVELERS

Traveling alone can be one of the most rewarding experiences in life. You're more likely to meet locals and other travelers without the protective shell of a partner. That said, it can get lonely at times, and it's certainly handy to have a companion to watch your bags while you answer nature's call. Overall, the freedom to do exactly what you want, whenever you want, usually outweighs any problems that a solo traveler may have. With Peru's abundance of organized tours and activities, you can easily hook up with other travelers if you're feeling homesick.

Unfortunately, traveling alone as a woman entails more risks than traveling as a man. But many foreign women travel by themselves safely every day in Peru. For more-specific advice for women travelers, see p514.

TELEPHONE

Public pay phones operated by **Telefónica-Perú** (www.telefonica.com.pe) are available on the street even in small towns. Most pay phones work with phonecards, many with coins. Often internet cafés have private phone booths with 'net-to-phone' capabilities, where an unlimited-time local call costs about US$0.06 and international calls can be as cheap as US$0.07 per minute to the USA or US$0.15 to Europe.

When calling Peru from abroad, dial the international access code for the country you're in, then Peru's country code (51), then the area code *without the 0* and finally, the local number. When making international calls from Peru, dial the international access code (00), then the country code of where you're calling to, then the area code and finally, the local phone number.

In Peru, any telephone number beginning with a 9 is a cell-phone number. Numbers beginning with 0800 are often toll-free only when dialed from private phones, not from public pay phones. See the inside front cover of this book for more useful dialing codes, including to contact an operator or directory assistance. To make a credit card or collect call using AT&T, dial ☎ 0800 50288. There's an online telephone directory at www.paginas amarillas.com.pe.

Cell Phones

It's possible to use a tri-band GSM world phone in Peru (GSM 1900). Other systems in use are CDMA and TDMA. This is a fast-changing field, so check the current situation before you travel: just do a Web search and browse the myriad products on the market. In Lima and other larger cities, you can buy cell phones that use SIM cards for about US$65, then pop in a SIM card that costs from US$6.50. Claro is a popular pay-as-you-go plan. Cell-phone rentals may be available in major cities and tourist centers. Expect

PERU'S AREA CODES

Each government region (called a department) has its own area code, listed immediately after each city or town entry in this book. If you are dialing within a department, don't dial the area code. To dial another department, dial the area code first.

There are 24 departmental (area) codes within the country:

Lima	☎ 01
Amazonas	☎ 041
Ancash	☎ 043
Apurímac	☎ 083
Arequipa	☎ 054
Ayacucho	☎ 066
Cajamarca	☎ 076
Cuzco	☎ 084
Huancavelica	☎ 067
Huánuco	☎ 062
Ica	☎ 056
Junín	☎ 064
La Libertad	☎ 044
Lambayeque	☎ 074
Loreto	☎ 065
Madre de Dios	☎ 082
Moquegua	☎ 053
Pasco	☎ 063
Piura	☎ 073
Puno	☎ 051
San Martín	☎ 042
Tacna	☎ 052
Tumbes	☎ 072
Ucayali	☎ 061

cell-phone reception to fade the further you get into the mountains or jungle.

Phonecards

Called *tarjetas telefónicas*, these cards are widely available and are made by many companies in many price ranges. Some are designed specifically for international calls. Some have an electronic chip that keeps track of your balance when the card is inserted into an appropriate phone. Other cards use a code system whereby you dial your own personal code to obtain balances and access; these can be used from almost any phone. The most common are Telefónica-Perú's 147 cards; you dial 147, then enter your personal code (which is on the back of the card), listen to a message telling you how much money you have left on the card, dial the number, and listen to a message telling you how much time you have left for this call. The drawback is it's in Spanish. The 147 card is best used for long-distance calls. For local calls, the Holá Peru card is cheaper, and works the same way except that you begin by dialing 0800. There are numerous other cards – ask around for which ones offer the best deal.

TIME

Peru is five hours behind Greenwich Mean Time (GMT). It's the same as Eastern Standard Time (EST) in North America. At noon in Lima, it's 9am in Los Angeles, 11am in Mexico City, noon in New York, 5pm in London, 4am (following day) in Sydney.

Daylight Saving Time (DST) isn't used in Peru, so add an hour to all of these times between the first Sunday in April and the last Sunday in October.

Punctuality is not one of the things that Latin America is famous for, so be prepared to wait a lot. Buses rarely depart or arrive on time. Savvy travelers should allow some flexibility in their itineraries. Bring your own travel alarm clock – tours and long-distance buses often depart before 6am.

TOILETS

Peruvian plumbing leaves something to be desired. There's always a chance that flushing a toilet will cause it to overflow, so you should avoid putting anything other than human waste into the toilet. Even a small amount of toilet paper can muck up the entire system – that's why a small, plastic bin is routinely provided for disposing of the paper. This may not seem sanitary, but it's definitely better than the alternative of clogged toilets and flooded floors. A well-run hotel or restaurant, even a cheap one, will empty the bin and clean the toilet every day. In rural areas, don't expect much more than a rickety wooden outhouse built around a hole in ground,

Public toilets are rare outside of transportation terminals, restaurants and museums. Those in terminals usually have an attendant who will charge you about S/0.50 to enter and then give you a miserly few sheets of toilet paper. Public restrooms frequently run out of toilet paper, so always carry an extra roll with you.

TOURIST INFORMATION
The government's official tourist agency, **PromPerú** (www.peru.info), doesn't have any international offices, but its website – in Spanish, English, French, German, Italian and Portuguese – is an easy way to obtain information before you depart. In the USA and Canada, you can call its toll-free **hotline** (☎ 866 661 7378). Some Peruvian embassies in foreign countries (see p502) supply tourist information as well.

PromPerú runs tourist information offices, called iPerú, in the following cities:

Lima airport (☎ 01-574 8000; Main Hall, Jorge Chávez International Airport; ☽ 24hr); Miraflores (☎ 01-445 9400; Module 14, Plaza Gourmet, LarcoMar Center; ☽ noon-8pm); San Isidro (☎ 01-421 1627; Jorge Basadre 610; ☽ 8:30am-6pm Mon-Fri)
Arequipa airport (☎ 054-44 4564; 1st fl, Main Hall, Rodríguez Ballón Airport; ☽ 6:30am-8:45pm); city center (☎ 054-22 1228; Casona Santa Catalina, Santa Catalina 210; ☽ 9am-7pm)
Ayacucho (☎ 066-31 8305; Municipalidad Huamanga, Plaza Mayor, Portal Municipal 48; ☽ 8:30am-7:30pm Mon-Sat, 8:30am-2:30pm Sun)
Chachapoyas (☎ 041-47 7292; Plaza de Armas, Jirón Ortiz Arrieta 588; ☽ 8am-7pm)
Cuzco airport (☎ 084-23 7364; Main Hall, Velasco Astete Airport; ☽ 6am-4pm); city center (☎ 084-23 4498; Office 102, Galerías Turísticas, Av Sol 103; ☽ 8:30am-7:30pm); Machu Picchu (☎ 084-21 1104; Oficina 4, Edificio del Instituto Nacional de Cultura, Av Pachacútec cuadra 1; ☽ 9am-1pm & 2-8pm)
Huaraz (☎ 043-42 8812; Oficina 1, Pasaje Atusparia, Plaza de Armas; ☽ 8am-6:30pm Mon-Sat, 8:30am-2pm Sun)
Iquitos airport (☎ 065-26 0251; Main Hall, Francisco Secada Vignetta Airport; ☽ 8am-1pm & 4-8pm); city

center (☎ 065-23 6144; Plaza de Armas, Napo 232; ☽ 8:30am-7:30pm)
Puno (☎ 051-36 5088; Plaza de Armas, Deustua at Lima; ☽ 8:30am-7:30pm)
Trujillo (☎ 044-29 4561; mezzanine level, Municipalidad de Trujillo, Plaza Mayor, Jirón Pizarro 412; ☽ 8am-7pm Mon-Sat, 8am-2pm Sun)

There is a 24-hour **iPerú hotline** (☎ 01-574 8000), which can provide general information and nonemergency assistance. Municipal tourist offices are listed under the relevant cities earlier in this book.

TRAVELERS WITH DISABILITIES
Peru's official tourism organization, **PromPerú** (www.peru.info), has a link to Accessible Tourism from the 'Special Interest' section of its website, where reports on wheelchair-accessible hotels, restaurants and attractions in Lima, Cuzco, Aguas Calientes, Iquitos and Trujillo are available.

Peru offers few conveniences for travelers with disabilities. Features such as signs in Braille or phones for the hearing-impaired are virtually nonexistent, while wheelchair ramps and lifts are few and far between, and the pavement is often badly potholed and cracked. Most hotels do not have wheelchair-accessible rooms, at least not rooms specially designated as such. Bathrooms are often barely large enough for an able-bodied person to walk into, so few are accessible to wheelchairs. Toilets in rural areas may be of the squat variety.

Nevertheless, there are Peruvians with disabilities who get around, mainly through the help of others. It is not particularly unusual to see mobility-impaired people being carried bodily to a seat on a bus, for example. If you need assistance, be polite and good-natured. Speaking Spanish will help immeasurably. If possible, bring along an able-bodied traveling companion.

Organizations that provide information for travelers with disabilities:
Access-Able Travel Source (www.access-able.com) Partial listings of accessible transportation and tours, accommodations, attractions and restaurants.
Apumayo Expediciones (Map pp224-5; ☎ /fax 084-24 6018; www.apumayo.com; Interior 3, Calle Garcilaso 265, Cuzco) An adventure-tour company that takes disabled travelers to Machu Picchu and other historical sites in the Sacred Valley, on river-running trips and into the Amazon jungle.

Conadis (Map pp94-5; ☎ 01-332 0808; www
.conadisperu.gob.pe; Av Arequipa 375, Santa Beatriz)
Governmental agency for Spanish-language information
and advocacy for people with disabilities.
Emerging Horizons (www.emerginghorizons.com)
Travel magazine for the mobility impaired, with handy
advice columns and news articles.
Mobility International USA (MIUSA; ☎ /TTY 541-343
1284; www.miusa.org; PO Box 10767, Eugene, OR 97440,
USA) International development and exchange programs
for people with disabilities.
Society for Accessible Travel & Hospitality (SATH;
☎ 212-447 7284; www.sath.org; Suite 610, 347 5th Ave,
New York, NY 10016, USA) A good resource for general
travel information.

VISAS

With a few exceptions (notably some Asian,
African and communist countries), visas
are not required for travelers entering Peru.
Tourists are permitted a 30- to 90-day stay,
which is stamped into their passports and
onto a tourist card, called a Tarjeta Andina
de Migración (Andean Immigration Card),
that you must return upon leaving the country. The actual length of stay is determined
by the immigration officer at the point of
entry. Be careful not to lose your tourist card,
or you will have to queue up an *oficina de
migraciónes* (immigration office), also simply
known as *migraciónes*, for a replacement
card. It's a good idea to carry your passport
and tourist card on your person at all times,
especially when traveling in remote areas
(it's required by law on the Inca Trail). For
security, make a photocopy of both documents and keep them in a separate place
from the originals.

Thirty-day extensions cost about US$28
and can be obtained at immigration offices in
major cities, with Lima (p87) being the most
painless place to do this. There are also immigration offices in Arequipa, Cuzco, Iquitos
Puerto Maldonado, Puno and Trujillo, as well
as near the Chilean and Ecuadorian borders.
Although extensions are a bureaucratic hassle,
you can keep extending your stay up to 180
days total. When your time is up, you can
leave the country overland and return a day
later to begin the process again.

Anyone who plans to work, attend school
or reside in Peru for any length of time must
obtain a visa in advance. Do this through
the Peruvian embassy or consulate in your
home country.

VOLUNTEERING

General advice for finding volunteer work
is to ask at language schools; they usually
know of several programs suitable for their
students. South American Explorers (SAE)
has an online volunteer database and also
folders with reports left by foreign volunteers at the SAE clubhouses in Lima (p93) and
Cuzco (p227).

Both nonprofit and for-profit organizations can arrange volunteer opportunities, if
you contact them in advance. These include
the following:
Action Without Borders (www.idealist.org) Free online
database of social work–oriented jobs, internships and
volunteer opportunities.
ADRA Perú (Map p102; ☎ 01-712 7700; www.adra.org
.pe; Av Angamos Oeste 770, Miraflores) A development
and relief agency with countrywide projects in health,
education and agriculture.
Cross-Cultural Solutions (☎ in USA 800 380 4777,
in UK 01273 666392; www.crossculturalsolutions.org) Educational and social-service projects in Lima and Ayacucho;
program fees include professional in-country support.
Earthwatch Institute (☎ in USA 800 776 0188; www
.earthwatch.org) Pay to help scientists on archaeological,
ecological and other real-life expeditions in the Amazon
Basin and the Andes.
Global Crossroad (☎ in USA & Canada 800 413 2008,
in UK 0800 310 1821; www.globalcrossroad.com) Volunteer, internship and job programs in the Andes. Summer
cultural immersion programs for 18- to 29-year-olds
include language instruction, homestays, volunteer work
and sightseeing.
Global Volunteers (☎ 800 487 1074; www.global
volunteers.org; 375 E Little Canada Rd, St Paul, MN 55117,
USA) Offers short-term volunteer opportunities helping
orphans in Lima.
HoPe Foundation (☎ 084-24 9885, in the Netherlands
0413-47 3666; www.stichtinghope.org; Casilla 59, Correo
Central, Cuzco) Provides educational and health-care
support in the Andes.
Kiya Survivors/Peru Positive Action (☎ 1273
721902; www.kiyasurvivors.org; 1 Sussex Rd, Hove BN3
2WD, UK) Organizes two- to six-month volunteer placements for assistant teachers and therapists to work with
special-needs children in Cuzco, Urubamba in the Sacred
Valley, and Máncora on the north coast.
ProWorld Service Corps (☎ in USA 877-733 7378,
in UK 0870 750 7202; www.proworldsc.org) Operating as
ProPeru, this highly recommended organization offers two-
to 26-week cultural, service and academic experiences,
including in the Sacred Valley and the Amazon. It has links
with affiliated NGOs throughout Peru and can organize
placements for individuals or groups.

Teaching & Projects Abroad (☎ 01903 708300; www.teaching-abroad.co.uk; Aldsworth Pde, Goring, Sussex BN12 4TX, UK) For summer, gap-year and career breaks, this UK-based organization has opportunities for community care and English teaching in the Sacred Valley and conservation in the Amazon jungle.

Volunteers for Peace (VFP; ☎ 802 259 2759; www .vfp.org; 1034 Tiffany Rd, Belmont, VT 05730, USA) Places volunteers in short-term workcamp programs, usually in Lima or Ayacucho. Program fees are more than reasonable, from $500 for three weeks (excluding airfare), and may be partially paid directly to local communities.

Working Abroad (www.workingabroad.com) Online network of grassroots volunteer opportunities (eg social development, environmental restoration, indigenous rights, traditional art and music) with trip reports from the field.

WOMEN TRAVELERS

Most female travelers to Peru don't encounter any serious problems, though you should come mentally prepared for being the center of attention. Machismo is alive and well in Latin America. Women with light-colored skin and hair often attract more attention, partly because gringas are considered more liberated and sexually available than Peruvian women.

It's not uncommon for fast-talking charmers to attach themselves to gringas and be surprisingly oblivious to a lack of interest from their quarry. Staring, whistling, hissing and catcalls in the streets are run-of-the-mill. Many men make a pastime of dropping *piropos* (cheeky, flirtatious or even vulgar 'compliments') at passing women, which can feel threatening at first. However, some men don't mean to be insulting; they're behaving as they've been taught to do, and normally don't follow up idle chatter with more aggressive behavior, unless they feel that you've insulted their manhood.

Ignoring all provocation and staring ahead is generally the best response. In the case of persistent harassment, try out some potentially ardor-smothering phrases such as *soy casada* (I'm married) or a sharper *déjame en paz* (leave me alone). If you appeal directly to locals, you'll find most Peruvians to be protective of lone women, expressing surprise and concern if you tell them you're traveling without your family or husband.

Use common sense when meeting men in public places, making it very clear if only friendship is intended. This goes double for

tour and outdoor-activity guides. If a stranger approaches you on the street and asks a question, go ahead and answer it, if you feel comfortable. But *don't* stop walking, which allows potential attackers to quickly surround you. Traveling in a group will somewhat reduce the risks.

Always avoid pirate taxis flagged down on the street; take only official taxis with a lit company phone number on their roof, stopping to take conspicuous note of the registration number before getting into the car. Some taxi drivers are known to be complicit in 'express kidnappings.' Do not take night buses, which are more likely to be hijacked, and on which a few foreign women have been robbed and raped. For more information on personal safety, see p500.

When hiring a private tour or activity guide, go through a reliable agency and ask around about the guide first. Take along at least one other traveler (preferably a man) on the trip, though this does not guarantee your safety. Always let someone know where you are going, with whom and when you're expected back.

Take care when visiting any remote areas, especially while trekking in the Andes or the Amazon jungle. Most of all, stay on guard at all archaeological ruins (even well-touristed sites around Cuzco and the Sacred Valley), as these are where assaults and rapes occur most often, even during broad daylight. If possible, take a self-defense course prior to your trip.

Travelers who are sexually assaulted can report it to the nearest police station or to the tourist police. However, Peruvian attitudes toward sexual assaults favor the attackers, not the survivors. Rape is often seen as a disgrace, and it is difficult to prosecute. Until recently, a rapist could avoid punishment by marrying the woman he attacked, something survivors were often pressured into doing by their own families. Because the police tend to be unhelpful, we recommend calling your own embassy or consulate (p503) first to ask for advice, including on where to seek medical treatment, which should be an immediate priority.

Tampons are difficult to find in smaller towns, so stock up in major cities, or investigate purchasing **The Keeper** (www.thekeeper.com), which could change your traveling life. Birth-control pills and other contraceptives (even condoms) are scarce outside of metropolitan areas and not always reliable, so bring your own supply from home. Rates of HIV infection are on the rise, especially among young women (see p531). Abortions are illegal, except to save the life of the mother.

These organizations provide useful information for female travelers:

Centro de La Mujer Peruana Flora Tristán (Map pp94-5; ☎ 01-433 2765; www.flora.org.pe; Parque Hernán Velarde 14, Lima; ☻ 1-5pm Mon-Fri) Feminist social and political advocacy group for women's and human rights in Peru, with a Spanish-language website and a library in Lima.

Instituto Peruano de Paternidad Responsable (Inppares; ☎ 01-583 9012; www.inppares.org.pe) Planned Parenthood–affiliated organization that runs a dozen sexual and reproductive health clinics for both women and men around the country, including in Lima.

WORK

Short-term business travelers can normally enter Peru on a tourist visa (p513). Not all top-end hotels have fully equipped business centers and international direct dialing (IDD) telephones in guest rooms, so ask about these when making reservations. Better hotels will provide dual-voltage outlets and electricity converters upon request, while luxury hotels have concierge staff to arrange everything from taxis to translators. Smaller hotels and guesthouses often have capable front desk staff

who can assist business travelers. See p506 for more information on internet access.

Officially, you will need a work visa to be employed in Peru. However, you might be able to get a part-time job teaching English in language schools, usually in Lima, without a work visa. This is illegal, however, and such jobs are increasingly difficult to get without a proper work visa. Occasionally, schools advertise for teachers in the newspapers, but more often, jobs are found by word of mouth. Schools expect you to be a native English speaker, and the pay is low. If you have teaching credentials, so much the better. Average pay is US$200 per week.

American and British schools in Lima sometimes hire teachers of math, biology and other subjects, but usually only if you apply in advance. They pay much better than the language schools, and might possibly be able to help you get a work visa if you want to stay. In Lima, the South American Explorers clubhouse (p93) and international cultural centers (p87) may have contacts with schools that are looking for teachers.

Most other jobs are obtained by word of mouth (eg bartenders, hostel staff, jungle guides), but the possibilities are limited. For internships and short-term job opportunities through volunteer organizations, see p513.

CLIMATE CHANGE & TRAVEL

Climate change is a serious threat to the ecosystems that humans rely upon, and air travel is the fastest-growing contributor to the problem. Lonely Planet regards travel, overall, as a global benefit, but believes we all have a responsibility to limit our personal impact on global warming.

Flying & Climate Change

Pretty much every form of motor transport generates CO_2 (the main cause of human-induced climate change) but planes are far and away the worst offenders, not just because of the sheer distances they allow us to travel, but because they release greenhouse gases high into the atmosphere. The statistics are frightening: two people taking a return flight between Europe and the US will contribute as much to climate change as an average household's gas and electricity consumption over a whole year.

Carbon Offset Schemes

Climatecare.org and other websites use 'carbon calculators' that allow travellers to offset the greenhouse gases they are responsible for with contributions to energy-saving projects and other climate-friendly initiatives in the developing world – including projects in India, Honduras, Kazakhstan and Uganda.

Lonely Planet, together with Rough Guides and other concerned partners in the travel industry, supports the carbon offset scheme run by climatecare.org. Lonely Planet offsets all of its staff and author travel.

For more information check out our website: www.lonelyplanet.com.

Transportation

CONTENTS

(side tab) TRANSPORTATION

GETTING THERE & AWAY

ENTERING THE COUNTRY

Arriving in Peru is typically a straightforward process, as long as your passport is valid for at least six months beyond your departure date. When arriving by air, US citizens must show a return ticket or open-jaw onward ticket – don't show up with just a one-way ticket to South America. Immigration officials at airports are efficient, while those at overland border crossings may take their time scrutinizing your passport before they stamp it. For information on Peruvian visas, see p513.

When arriving by air or overland, immigration officials may only stamp 30 days into your passport; if this happens, explain how many more days you need, supported by an exit ticket for onward or return travel. Bribery is illegal in Peru, but some officials may try to procure extra payment at borders.

AIR

Peru has flights linked up with North America, the UK and continental Europe, Australia and New Zealand, Asia and Africa, as well as the rest of Latin America. Many South American capitals have direct flights to Lima. Note that if you're headed to Cuzco, but are flying to Peru from another continent, your flight will most likely land in Lima during the late afternoon or evening, meaning you'll have to wait until morning to catch the next flight to Cuzco.

Airports & Airlines

In suburban Callao, Lima's **Aeropuerto Internacional Jorge Chávez** (code LIM; ☎ 01-517 3100; www.lap .com.pe) is a major hub, serviced by many flights from North, Central and South America, and a few direct flights from Europe. Travelers from other continents normally change planes in the USA or in a South American city. Check the airport website or call ☎ 01-511 6055 for updated departure and arrival schedules for domestic and international flights. See p121 for details of airport services and p123 for transportation options to/from the airport. At the time of research, international flights to and from the Peruvian regional airports in Cuzco and Iquitos were suspended.

AIRLINES FLYING TO/FROM PERU

The phone numbers and addresses listed below are for the airlines' Lima offices; add ☎ 01 if calling from outside the capital. If planning to visit an office, call before you go or check a phone directory under 'Lineas Aéreas', as they change addresses frequently. **Aerolineas Argentinas** (code ARG; Map p102; ☎ 444 0810; www.aerolineas.com.ar; Av José Pardo 805, Miraflores; hub Buenos Aires, Argentina)

THINGS CHANGE

The information in this chapter is particularly vulnerable to change. Check directly with the airline or a travel agent to make sure you understand how a fare (and the ticket you may buy) works, and shop carefully. Be aware of the security requirements for international travel. The details given in this chapter should be regarded as pointers and are not a substitute for your own careful, up-to-date research.

Aeroméxico (code AMX; ☎ 705 1111; www.aeromexico
.com; Aliaga 699 at Av José Pardo, San Isidro; hub Mexico
City, Mexico)
Aeropostal (code LAV; ☎ 444 1199; www.aeropostal
.com; Offices 501-02, Martir Olaya 129, Miraflores; hub
Caracas, Venezuela)
Air Canada (code ACA; Map p102; ☎ 241 1457;
www.aircanada.com; Office 101, Edificio Mar Azul,
Italia 389, Miraflores; hub Toronto, Canada)
Air France (code AFR; Map p102; ☎ 444 9285;
www.airfrance.com; Av José Pardo 601, Miraflores;
hub Paris, France)
Air Madrid (code DRI; Map p102; ☎ 214 1040;
www.airmadrid.com; Av José Pardo 269, Miraflores;
hub Madrid, Spain)
Alitalia (code AZA; ☎ 447 3899; www.alitalia.it;
Olaya 129, Miraflores; hub Rome, Italy)
American Airlines (code AAL; Map p101; ☎ 442 8595;
www.aa.com; Moreyra 380, San Isidro; hub Dallas-Forth
Worth, USA)
Avianca (code AVA; Map p102; ☎ 446 9902; www
.avianca.com; Av José Pardo 140, Miraflores; hub Bogotá,
Colombia)
British Airways (code BAW; Map p101; ☎ 411 7801;
www.britishairways.com; Office 902, Torre Central, Av
Camino Real 390, San Isidro; hub London, UK)
Continental Airlines (code COA; Map p101; ☎ 221
4340; www.continental.com; Camino Real, Belaúnde 147,
San Isidro; hub Houston, USA)
Copa Airlines (code CMP; Map p101; ☎ 610 0808;
www.copaair.com; Office 105, Torre Chocavento, Centro
Empresarial, San Isidro; hub Panama City, Panama)
Delta Airlines (code DAL; Map p101; ☎ 440 4328;
www.delta.com; Camino Real, Belaúnde 147, San Isidro;
hub Atlanta, USA)
Iberia (code IBE; Map p101; ☎ 411 7800; www.iberia
.com; Camino Real 390, San Isidro; hub Madrid, Spain)
KLM Royal Dutch Airlines (code KLM; Map p101;
☎ 421 9500; www.klm.com; Calderón 185, San Isidro;
hub Amsterdam, Netherlands)
LACSA (code LRC; Map p102; ☎ 511 8222; www.taca
.com; Av Espinar 331, Miraflores; hub San José, Costa Rica)
LAN (code LPE; Map p102; ☎ 213 8300; www.lan.com;
Av José Pardo 513, Miraflores; hub Lima, Peru)
Lloyd Aereo Boliviano (LAB; code LLB; Map p102;
☎ 241 5510; www.labairlines.com; Av José Pardo 231,
Miraflores; hub Bogota, Colombia)
TACA (code TAI; Map p102; ☎ 511 8222; www.taca.com;
Av Espinar 331; hubs San Salvador, El Salvador & Lima)
Varig (code VRG; Map p101; ☎ 422 1449; www.varig
.com; Camino Real 456, San Isidro; hub São Paulo, Brazil)

Tickets

From almost everywhere else in the world,
South America is a relatively costly destina-

INTERNATIONAL DEPARTURE TAX

Lima's departure tax for international flights
is US$28.10. Pay the tax in cash (dollars or
nuevos soles) before proceeding to departure gates.

tion. The high season for air travel to and
within Peru is late May to early September, as
well as around major holidays (p505). Lower
fares may sometimes be offered outside peak
periods.

Contacting a travel agent that specializes
in Latin American destinations and shopping
around the competing fares offered by online
booking agents often turns up the cheapest
tickets for Peru. Students with international
student ID cards (ISIC is one widely recognized card) and anyone aged under the age of
26 can often get discounts with budget travel
agencies and some airlines.

Tickets bought in Peru are subject to 18%
tax. It is essential to reconfirm all flights 72
hours in advance or you may get bumped off
the flight. If you are going to be in the boonies,
have a travel agent do this for you.

COURIER FLIGHTS

If you are flexible with dates and can manage
with only carry-on luggage, you can fly to
Lima as a courier. This is most practical from
major US gateways. Try:
AirCourier.org (in USA ☎ 800 461 8856; www.air
courier.org)
Air Courier International (in UK ☎ 0800 089 5888;
www.aircourieruk.com)
International Association of Air Travel Couriers
(IAATC; in USA ☎ 515 292 2458; www.courier.org)

INTERCONTINENTAL FLIGHTS

Some of the best deals for travelers visiting
many countries on different continents are
Round-the-World (RTW) tickets. Itineraries
from the USA, Europe or Australasia typically
require at least five stopovers, possibly including unusual destinations such as Tahiti or
South American cities. Fares vary widely, but
check **Air Treks** (www.airtreks.com) and **Air Brokers**
(www.airbrokers.com). These types of tickets have
restrictions, so read the fine print carefully.

Africa

Travel is normally via the USA or connecting
through another South American country

such as Colombia or Bolivia. **Rennies Travel** (www.renniestravel.com) and **STA Travel** (☎ 0861-781 781; www.statravel.co.za) have offices throughout South Africa and representatives in other African countries. Check the websites for locations.

Asia

Flights from Asia mostly connect via the USA.

Recommended travel agencies:

No 1 Travel (☎ 03-3205 6073; www.no1-travel.com) Discount flights from Japan, with offices in Tokyo, Osaka, Kobe, Nagoya and Fukuoka.

STA Travel (www.statravel.com) Student, youth and budget travel specialist; branches in Japan, China, Hong Kong, Taiwan, Malaysia, Singapore and Thailand.

STIC Travels (www.stictravel.com) Has offices in dozens of cities across India, and offers discounts to students.

Australia & New Zealand

Flights are usually via the USA or a South American gateway, such as Santiago (Chile).

In Australia there are many branches of **STA Travel** (☎ 1300 733 035; www.statravel.com.au) and **Flight Centre** (☎ 133 133; www.flightcentre.com.au). Try www.travel.com.au for online bookings.

Both **STA Travel** (☎ 0508-782-872; www.statravel .co.nz) and **Flight Centre** (☎ 0800 243 544; www .flightcentre.co.nz) have offices throughout New Zealand. Online, try www.travel.co.nz.

Canada

Canadians must typically take a connecting flight to a gateway US city (see opposite). **Travel CUTS** (☎ 866-246 9762; www.travelcuts.com) is Canada's national student travel agency.

Continental Europe

There are direct flights mainly from Amsterdam and Madrid, but travelers may find it cheaper if they take flights with connections in the USA, the Caribbean or Colombia.

Some recommended travel agencies:

FRANCE
Anyway.com (☎ 08 92 30 23 01; www.anyway.fr)
Expedia (www.expedia.fr)
Lastminute.com (☎ 08 99 78 50 00; www.lastminute.fr)
Nouvelles Frontières (☎ 08 25 00 07 47; www.nouvelles -frontieres.fr, in French)
OTU Voyages (☎ 01 55 82 32 32; www.otu.fr, in French) For student and youth travelers.
Voyageurs du Monde (☎ 08 92 68 83 63; www.vdm .com, in French)

GERMANY
Expedia (www.expedia.de)
Just Travel (☎ 089-747 333 0; www.justtravel.de)
Lastminute.de (☎ 01805-284 366; www.last minute.de)
STA Travel (☎ 069-743 032 92; www.statravel.de)

ITALY
CTS (☎ 06-44 1111; www.cts.it, in Italian) Specializes in student and youth travel.

NETHERLANDS
Airfair (☎ 026-750 1950; www.airfair.nl, in Dutch)

SPAIN
Barcelo Viajes (☎ 902-116 226; www.barceloviajes.com, in Spanish)

Latin America

Lima is connected to many South American cities. However, flights from Latin American countries are subject to high taxes, and good deals aren't often available. For Latin American airlines flying into Lima, see p516.

Recommended travel agencies:

ASATEJ Viajes (www.asatej.com, in Spanish) In Argentina, Mexico and Uruguay.
IVI Venezuela (☎ 0212-993 6082; www.ividiomas.com) In Venezuela.
Student Travel Bureau (STB; ☎ 11-3038 1555; www.stb.com.br) In Brazil.

UK & Ireland

Most flights from the UK or Ireland connect through gateway cities in continental Europe, the USA or Canada. A few fly via other Latin American countries.

Discount air travel is big business in London. Advertisements for travel agencies appear in the weekend newspapers, *Time Out London* (www.timeout.com/london), the *Evening Standard* (www.thisislondon.com) and *TNT* (www.tnt magazine.com).

An excellent place to start looking is **Journey Latin America** (☎ 020-8747 3108; www.journey latinamerica.co.uk). In Ireland try **Holidays Online** (☎ 01-6797399; www.holidaysonline.ie).

Other recommended travel agencies:

ebookers.com (☎ 0800 082 3000; www.ebookers.com)
Flight Centre UK (☎ 0800 587 0058; www.flight centre.co.uk)
North-South Travel (☎ 01245-608 291; www.north southtravel.co.uk) Donates part of its profits to projects in the developing world.
Quest Travel (☎ 0870-442 3542; www.questtravel.com)

STA Travel (☎ 0870-163 0026; www.statravel.co.uk)
Student, youth and budget travel specialist.
Trailfinders (☎ 0845-058 5858; www.trailfinders.co.uk)
Travel Bag (☎ 0800 082 5000; www.travelbag.co.uk)

USA

There are direct (nonstop) flights to Lima from Atlanta, Dallas-Fort Worth, Houston, Los Angeles, Miami and New York.

The largest student, youth and budget travel agency in the USA is **STA Travel** (☎ 800 781 4040; www.statravel.com). Latin American specialist **Exito Travel** (☎ 800 655 4053; www.exitotravel.com) offers competitive fares for everyone, as well as personalized service for complicated tickets, such as multi-city and extended stays.

Other discount travel agents found in the USA are known as consolidators (although you won't see a sign on the door saying 'Consolidator'). San Francisco is the ticket consolidator capital of America, although some pretty good deals can also be found in Los Angeles, New York and other major cities. You should check for ads in the travel sections of Sunday newspapers and some alternative weeklies.

For online bookings:
CheapTickets (www.cheaptickets.com)
Expedia (www.expedia.com)
Lowestfare.com (www.lowestfare.com)
Orbitz (www.orbitz.com)
Travelocity (www.travelocity.com)

LAND & RIVER

Because no roads cross the Darien Gap, it is not possible to travel to South America by land from the north (unless you spend a week hiking through drug-dealer-infested jungle), so bringing your own vehicle from North America is a costly undertaking.

Overland travel from neighboring Bolivia, Brazil, Chile, Colombia and Ecuador tends not to be as safe or straightforward as you might like. See p513 for important information on visas, immigration offices and other border-crossing formalities.

Getting to Peru by boat is possible from points on the Amazon River in Brazil and from Leticia, Colombia. **Ormeño** (☎ 01-472 1710; www.grupo-ormeno.com) is the main bus company offering cross-border travel, mostly from Lima to Chile, Ecuador and Colombia. The only rail service that crosses the Peruvian border is the train between Arica, Chile, and Tacna on Peru's south coast.

Whatever form of transport you choose, keep in mind that while it may be a bit cheaper to buy tickets to the border, cross over and then buy onward tickets on the other side, it's usually much easier, faster and safer to buy a cross-border through ticket. When traveling by bus, check carefully with the company about what is included in the price of the ticket, and whether the service is direct or involves a transfer (and possibly a long wait) at the border.

The following sections outline the principal points of entry to and exit from Peru.

Bolivia

Peru is normally reached overland from Bolivia via Lake Titicaca (p192); the border crossing at Yunguyo is much safer and a lot less chaotic than at Desaguadero. There are many transportation options for both of these routes, most of which involve changing buses at the Peru–Bolivia border before reaching Puno. Travel agents sell tickets for all-inclusive hydrofoil and catamaran tours between Puno and La Paz, Bolivia. It's also possible, but difficult, to reach Bolivia overland along the north shore of Lake Titicaca (p214) or by river and road from Puerto Maldonado (p457).

Brazil

You can travel overland between Peru and Brazil via Iñapari (p456). Traveling from Iquitos, it's more straightforward to voyage along the Amazon to Tabatinga in Brazil via Leticia, Colombia. For more information on boat trips, see Border Crossing: The Peru–Colombia–Brazil Border Zone, p494.

Chile

Traveling on the Pan-American Hwy, the major crossing point is between Arica, Chile, and Tacna on Peru's south coast (p160). Long-distance buses to Tacna depart from Lima, Arequipa and Puno. *Colectivo* (shared) taxis are the fastest and most reliable to travel between Tacna and Arica. It's also possible to make the crossing, albeit much more slowly, by train; border formalities are done at the respective stations. Flights to Tacna from Arequipa are cheap, but book up quickly. Alternatively, Ormeño runs through buses from Lima all the way to Santiago, Chile. From Arequipa, Ormeño goes to Santiago, Chile, and Buenos Aires, Argentina.

Colombia

It is easiest to travel between Peru and Colombia via Ecuador. Ormeño has through buses between Lima and Bogotá, Colombia via Ecuador. This long-haul trip is better done in stages, though.

It is more straightforward to voyage along the Amazon by boat between Iquitos and Leticia, Colombia, from where there are flights to Bogotá. For more details on border formalities there, as well as traveling from Leticia to Iquitos, see Border Crossing: The Peru–Colombia–Brazil Border Zone, p494.

Ecuador

The usual way to get to/from Ecuador is along the Pan-American Hwy via Tumbes (p370). Another route is via La Tina to Loja in Ecuador (p361). A third route is via Jaén (p434). **Cifa** (☎ 072-527120) runs buses between Tumbes in Peru and Machala or Guayaquil in Ecuador. **Transportes Loja** (☎ 073-30 9407) runs buses between Piura in Peru and Machala or Loja in Ecuador. Ormeño has weekly through buses between Lima and Quito, Ecuador.

TOURS

Scores of overseas companies offer tours of Peru for travelers who prefer not to travel on their own, or who have a limited amount of time and want to maximize their Peruvian experience, perhaps combining it with other South American countries. Usually, groups travel with knowledgeable guides, but you will pay a great deal extra for this privilege – it's worth it for highly specialized outdoor activities (eg river running, mountaineering, bird-watching). Otherwise, it's just as convenient and much cheaper to travel to Peru independently, then take organized day trips and overnight tours along the way (see p527).

From Australia & New Zealand

Peregrine Adventures (☎ 1300 85 44 44; www.peregrine.net.au; 380 Lonsdale St, Melbourne, VIC 3000) Hotel-based and trekking trips in Peru.

Tucan Travel (☎ 1300 769 249; www.tucantravel.com; 217 Alison Rd, Randwick, NSW 2031) Long-running tour operator specializing in Latin America provides a wide variety of tour options in Peru.

From Canada & the USA

With easy flight connections, the USA has more companies offering tours of Peru than the rest of the world. You can find tour operators' advertisements in outdoor and travel magazines, such as *Outside* and *National Geographic Adventure*.

Adventure Center (☎ 510-654 879, 800 227 8747; www.adventurecenter.com; Suite 200, 1311 63rd St, Emeryville, CA 94608) A clearinghouse for tour operators offering various trips.

Adventure Life (☎ 800 344 6118; www.adventure-life.com; Suite 1, 1655 S 3rd St W, Missoula, MT 5980) Andean trekking, Amazon exploring and multi-sport itineraries, plus combo trips with the Galapagos Islands. Uses bilingual guides, family-run hotels and local transportation.

Explorations (☎ 239-992 9660, 800 446 9660; www.explorationsinc.com; 27655 Kent Rd, Bonita Springs, FL 34135) Amazon trips include biologist-escorted cruises, lodge-based expeditions and fishing trips in the Pacaya-Samiria National Reserve.

GAP Adventures (☎ 800 708 7761; www.gap.ca; 19 Charlotte St, Toronto, ON M5V 2H5) The premier Canadian agency with branch offices in Vancouver; Boston, USA; and London, UK. Budget-priced tours include hotel-based, trekking, Amazon, festival and multicountry trips.

International Expeditions (☎ 205-428 1700, 800 633 4734; www.ietravel.com; One Environs Park, Helena, AL 35080) Offers Amazon tours, staying in jungle lodges or on river boats, with an emphasis on natural history, bird-watching or photography.

Mountain Travel Sobek (☎ 510-594 6000, 888-687 6235; www.mtsobek.com; 1266 66th St, Emeryville, CA 94608) Luxury trekking tours along the Inca Trail or in the Cordillera Blanca, and occasional rafting trips on the Río Tambopata.

Southwind Adventures (☎ 303 972 0701, 800-377 9463; www.southwindadventures.com; PO Box 621057, Littleton, CO 80162) Peruvian-American tour operator with trekking, cycling, rafting and boat-cruise itineraries in the Andes, Amazon and Galapagos Islands.

Tropical Nature Travel (☎ 352-376 3377, 877-888 1770; www.tropicalnaturetravel.com; PO Box 5276, Gainesville, FL 32627) Alliance of nature conservation groups offers multiday stays in Amazon wildlife lodges and trekking, river rafting and archaeological and cultural tours of Peru's highlights.

Wilderness Travel (☎ 510-558 2488, 800-368 2794; www.wildernesstravel.com; 1102 Ninth St, Berkeley, CA 94710) Offers luxury treks, ranging from four nights on the Inca Trail to two weeks in the remote Cordillera Huayhuash, with hotel stays and optional extensions to the Amazon, north coast and Arequipa's canyon country.

Wildland Adventures (☎ 206-365 0686, 800 345 4453; www.wildland.com; 3516 NE 155th St, Seattle, WA 98155) Prides itself on environmentally sound, culturally sensitive treks around Machu Picchu, the Sacred Valley and the Cordillera Blanca, as well as Amazon tours.

From the UK & Continental Europe

Amazonas Explorer (☎ 01437 891-743; www.ama
zonas-explorer.com) Rafting, mountain biking, trekking
and multi-activity trips in the Amazon and the Andes, plus
custom itineraries.

Andean Trails (☎ 0131-467 7086; www.andeantrails
.co.uk; The Clockhouse, Bonnington Mill Business Centre,
72 Newhaven Rd, Edinburgh, Scotland EH6 5QG) Mountain-biking, climbing, trekking and rafting tours in some
unusual spots.

clubaventure (☎ 08 26 88 20 80; www.clubaventure
.fr; 18 rue Séguier, 75006 Paris, France) A French-owned
company that organizes treks and tours in Peru.

Exodus (☎ 0870-240 5550; www.exodus.co.uk; Grange
Mills, Weir Rd, London SW12 0NE, UK) Award-winning
responsible-travel operator offers long-distance overland
trips and shorter cultural and trekking adventures.

Guerba Adventure & Discovery Holidays
(☎ 01373-826 611; www.guerba.co.uk; Wessex House,
40 Station Rd, Westbury, Wiltshire BA13 3JN, UK) Trekking, activity and family-focused tours of the Andes and
the Amazon.

Hauser Exkursionen (☎ 89-235 0060; www.hauser
-exkursionen.de, in German; Spiegelstras/se 9, D-81241
Munich, Germany) Hauser is among the best German
companies offering Andean treks.

Journey Latin America (☎ 020 8747 8315; www
.journeylatinamerica.co.uk; 12 & 13 Heathfield Terrace,
Chiswick, London W4 4JE, UK) Cultural, hotel-based trips
and treks in the Cordilleras Blanca and Huayhuash and to
Machu Picchu, plus tailor-made itineraries.

GETTING AROUND

AIR

Domestic-flight schedules and prices change
frequently. New airlines open every year, as
those with poor safety records close (check
out www.airsafe.com). Most cities are served
by modern jets, while some smaller towns are
served by propeller aircraft. A useful website
is www.traficoperu.com, which has schedules
and fares between major cities.

Airlines in Peru

Many domestic airlines have sprung up recently, but not all have proven to be long
lived. At press time, the following had the
most extensive services:

Aero Condor Perú (code ARD; ☎ 01- 614 6014; www
.aerocondor.com.pe) Flies to Cuzco, Iquitos and Lima,
as well as smaller destinations, including Andahuaylas,
Arequipa, Ayacucho, Cajamarca, Chiclayo, Piura, Puerto
Maldonado, Tacna and Trujillo.

> **DOMESTIC DEPARTURE TAX**
>
> The departure tax for domestic flights is
> US$6.05 from Lima, $4.28 from Cuzco. Pay
> the tax in cash (dollars or nuevos soles)
> before proceeding to departure gates.
> Elsewhere there's a US$3.57 domestic de-
> parture tax, payable after you get your
> boarding pass.

LAN (code LPE; ☎ 01-213 8200; www.lan.com) Peru's
major domestic carrier flies to the most-touristed destinations (Arequipa, Cuzco, Iquitos, Lima, Puerto Maldonado
and Trujillo), as well as to Arica, Chiclayo, Juliaca, Piura,
Tacna and Tarapoto.

LC Busre (code LCB; ☎ 01-619 1300; www.lcbusre.com
.pe) Mostly charter flights on small turbo-prop aircraft,
but some passenger services between Lima and Ayacucho,
Cajamarca, Huánuco and Pucallpa.

Star Perú (code SRU; ☎ 01-705 9000; www.starperu
.com) Flies most often to Cuzco, but also to Chiclayo,
Iquitos, Pucallpa, Tarapoto and Trujillo.

TACA (code TAI; ☎ 01-511 8222, 01-800 18222; www
.taca.com) International carrier offers limited services
between Lima and Cuzco only.

Most domestic airlines have offices in Lima
(p121). Branch offices for these and other
smaller carriers are listed under destinations
earlier in this book. More remote towns require connecting flights, and smaller towns
are not served every day. Many of the airports
for these places are often no more than a
grass strip in the jungle. They can be reached
on some of the small airlines or by chartered
light aircraft.

Be at the airport at least 60 minutes before
your flight departs (at least 90 minutes early
in Cuzco, and two hours in Lima). This is a
precaution as your flight may be overbooked,
baggage handling and check-in procedures
tend to be chaotic, and it's not unknown for
flights to leave *before* their official departure
time because predicted bad weather might
cancel the flight later. Also be aware that
flights are frequently late.

Tickets

Two one-way tickets typically cost the same
as a round-trip ticket. Most travelers travel
in one direction overland and save time returning by air. The peak season for air travel
within Peru is late May to early September, as
well as around major holidays. Buy tickets for

TRANSPORTATION

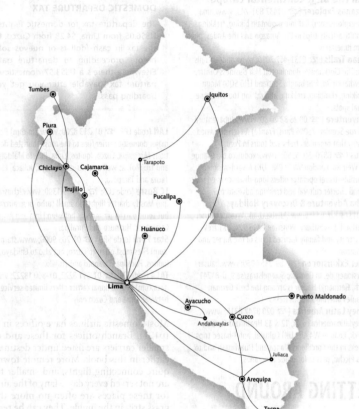

smaller destinations (ie anywhere other than Lima and Cuzco) as far in advance as possible, as these infrequent flights book up quickly.

Buying tickets and reconfirming flights is best done at airline offices; in remote areas, find a responsible travel agent to do this for you. You can sometimes buy tickets at the airport on a space-available basis, but don't count on it. It's almost impossible to buy tickets for just before major holidays (p505), notably Semana Santa (the week leading up to Easter) and Fiestas Patrias (the last week in July). Overbooking is the norm, not underbooking.

Ensure all flight reservations are *confirmed and reconfirmed* 72 and 24 hours in advance; airlines are notorious for bumping passengers

off flights. Flights are changed or canceled with surprising frequency, so it's even worth calling the airport or the airline just before leaving for the airport. Members of South American Explorers (SAE; see p93) can have the club reconfirm for them, though many hotels and guesthouses will do this free of charge if you ask. Confirmation is especially essential during the peak travel season, particularly during the busy months of June, July and August.

If you're planning to travel around the country only by air, all of the air passes currently available offer no substantial savings compared with buying individual one-way tickets. These passes inconveniently lock you into a pre-planned itinerary, with additional fees charged for making any changes. You'll enjoy more flexibility with flight schedules and a greater choice of airlines by *not* buying an air pass.

BICYCLE

The major drawback to cycling in Peru is motorists. On narrow, two-lane highways, drivers can be a serious hazard to cyclists. Cycling is more enjoyable and safer, though very challenging, off paved roads. Mountain bikes are recommended, as road bikes won't stand up to the rough conditions. See p65 for more about mountain biking and cycling in Peru.

Reasonably priced rentals (mostly mountain bikes) are available in popular tourist destinations, including Cuzco (p236), Arequipa (p172), Huaraz (p378) and Huancayo (p296). These bikes are rented to travelers for local excursions, not to make trips all over the country. For long-distance touring, bring your own bike from home. See p520 for organized tours.

Airline policies on carrying bicycles vary, so shop around. Some airlines will fly your bike as checked baggage if it's boxed. However, boxing the bike gives baggage handlers little clue to the contents, and the box may be roughly handled. If it's OK with the airline, try wrapping it in heavy-duty plastic, so baggage handlers can see the contents. Domestic airlines may charge up to US$60 extra per flight, and that's if they even allow a checked bike.

BOAT

There are no passenger services along the Peruvian coast. In the Andean highlands, there are boat services on Lake Titicaca. Small motorized vessels take passengers from the port in Puno to visit various islands on the lake (p203), while hydrofoils and catamarans zip over to Bolivia (p200).

In Peru's Amazon basin, boat travel is of major importance. Larger vessels ply the wider rivers. Dugout canoes powered by an outboard engine act as water taxis on smaller rivers. Some of the latter are powered by a strange arrangement that looks like a two-stroke motorcycle engine attached to a tiny propeller by a 3m-long propeller shaft. Called *peki-pekis,* these canoes are a slow and rather noisy method of transportation. In some places, modern aluminum launches are used.

The classic way to travel down the Amazon is while swinging in your hammock aboard a banana boat piloted by a grizzled old captain who knows the waters better than the back of his hand. You can travel from Pucallpa or Yurimaguas to Iquitos and on into Brazil this way (see p489). The lower deck of these boats is for cargo, and the upper deck (or decks) for passengers and crew.

At ports, there are chalkboards with ships' names, destinations and departure times displayed; the departure times are usually optimistic. The captain has to clear documents with the *capitanía* (harbor master's office) on the day of departure, so asking the person in charge of this at the *capitanía* can yield information. But asking the captain is best. Nobody else really knows. Departure time often depends on a full cargo, and *mañana* (tomorrow) may go on for several days if the hold isn't full. Usually, you can sleep on the boat while waiting if you want to save on hotel bills. Never leave your luggage unattended.

Bring your own hammock, or rent a cabin for the journey. If using a hammock, hang it away from the noisy engine room and not directly under a light, as these are often lit late at night, precluding sleep and attracting insects. Cabins are often hot, airless boxes, but are lockable (for your luggage) and not too hot at night. Sanitary facilities are basic but adequate, and there's usually a pump shower on board.

Basic food is usually included in the price of the passage, and may be marginally better on some bigger and better ships, or if you are in cabin class. Finicky eaters or people with dietary restrictions should bring their own food. Bottled soft drinks are usually available and priced very reasonably.

BUS

Buses are the normal form of transport for most Peruvians and many travelers. Fares are relatively cheap. Services are frequent on the major long-distance routes, but buses are of varying quality. Less-traveled and remote rural routes are often served by older, more uncomfortable vehicles, many with inadequate leg-room for taller travelers. Try to avoid seats at the back of the bus, because the ride is bumpier.

The scores of competing Peruvian bus companies have their own offices, and no one

TRANSPORTATION

company covers the entire country. In some towns, the companies have their offices in one main bus terminal. In many cities, bus companies are clustered around a few city blocks, while elsewhere, the terminals may be scattered all over town. Slowly, Peruvian cities are moving toward having just one long-distance bus terminal. For a rundown of major companies with offices in Lima, see p121.

Buses rarely arrive or depart on time, so the average trip times quoted in this book or by the operators themselves are almost certainly best-case scenarios. Buses can be much delayed during the rainy season, particularly in the highlands and the jungle. Especially from January through to April, quoted journey times can double or buses can even be delayed indefinitely because of landslides and bad road conditions.

Local and long-distance buses alike can be a risk to your personal safety, as fatal accidents are not unusual in Peru. Avoid overnight buses, on which muggings and assaults are more likely to occur. For important information on bus hijackings and road blockades, see p502.

Classes

The bigger companies often have luxury buses (called Imperial, Royal, Business, Executive or something similar), for which they charge up to 10 times more than *económico* buses. The former are express services with toilets, snacks, videos and air-conditioning. Some companies offer *bus-camas* (bed buses) on which the seat reclines halfway or almost fully – you can sleep quite well on them. But for trips under six hours, you may have no choice but to take an *económico* bus, which is usually pretty beat-up.

Better long-distance buses stop for bathroom breaks and meals (except on luxury buses, which serve paltry snacks and don't stop). Many companies have their own special rest areas, sometimes in the middle of nowhere, so you'll have no choice but to eat there. The food is fairly inexpensive, but not particularly appetizing, so many travelers bring their own food. Almost every bus terminal has a few convenience shops where you can stock up. Be aware that *económico* services don't stop for meals, although snack vendors will board the bus, and men and women alike

ROAD DISTANCES (KM)

	Arequipa	Ayacucho	Cajamarca	Chachapoyas	Chiclayo	Cuzco	Huancayo	Huaraz	Lima	Puno	Tacna	Trujillo	Tumbes
Arequipa	---												
Ayacucho	1135	---											
Cajamarca	1865	1439	---										
Chachapoyas	2132	1808	336	---									
Chiclayo	1677	1353	260	455	---								
Cuzco	518	582	1958	2337	1872	---							
Huancayo	705	318	1154	1523	1068	900	---						
Huaraz	1326	678	631	1000	545	1521	717	---					
Lima	907	1009	856	1225	770	1102	298	419	---				
Puno	584	323	2188	2557	2102	389	1289	1751	1332	---			
Tacna	963	368	2149	2518	2063	768	1477	1712	1293	419	---		
Trujillo	1468	1570	295	664	209	1663	859	336	561	1893	1854	---	
Tumbes	759	2329	810	805	550	2422	1618	1095	1320	2652	2613	759	---

MEMORABLE BUS MOMENTS *Rafael Wlodarski*

Love it or hate it, chances are you'll be spending time on the buses that brave the winding, potholed routes of the Andes and curving coastal highways of the deserts. We feel like we've spent half our lives on them – here's a hit list of memorable moments:

- Seatside shopping as armies of mobile vendors hawk fruits, vegetables and mysterious yet tasty snacks-on-a-stick. Look out for *choclo con queso* (grilled corn with cheese).

- Peruvian panpipe pop tunes (say that fast three times) that initially provide a rich, auditory tapestry to your trip, but manage to loose their luster somewhere around the 14th replaying.

- Snake oil vendors who zealously spout pseudo-scientific evidence for the magical medicinal properties of their ointment/powder/pill – everything from listlessness to cancer cured for only US$0.30!

- The unfortunate realization that Jean-Claude van Damme has made more movies than all of the world's martial-art-less actors combined.

- When the bus leaves on time, the air-conditioning works and is not set to arctic, the radio and TV are silent and the seat-back actually reclines – you realize you have stumbled upon the long lost bus-trip nirvana.

have to answer nature's call in the open at the side of the road – ladies, you may want to wear a skirt or tie a jacket around your waist.

Costs & Reservations

Schedules and fares change frequently and vary from company to company; therefore, the prices quoted in this book are only approximations. You can check schedules online (but not make reservations, at least not yet) for the major players, including **Cruz del Sur** (www.cruzdelsur.com.pe), **Ormeño** (www.grupo-ormeno .com) and **Transportes Línea** (www.transporteslinea .com.pe, in Spanish).

There is no bus-pass system. Students with international student cards may be able to get a small discount. During off-peak travel periods, some companies offer discounted fares. Conversely, fares can double around major holidays (see p505), especially for Christmas, Semana Santa (the week leading up to Easter) or Fiestas Patrias at the end of July, when tickets sell out several days ahead of time.

At other times, reservations for short journeys aren't usually necessary. Just go to the terminal and buy a ticket for the next bus to your destination. For long-distance or overnight journeys, or if you're headed someplace remote with only limited services, buy your ticket at least the day before. Most travel agencies will make reservations for you, but shockingly overcharge you for the ticket. Except in Lima, it's cheaper to take a taxi to the bus terminal and buy the tickets yourself.

Luggage

When waiting in bus terminals, watch your luggage very carefully. Some terminals have left-luggage facilities. If not, the bus company may agree to keep your bags behind the desk, especially if you have an onward ticket later that same day.

During the journey, your luggage will travel in the luggage compartment unless it is small enough to carry on board. This is reasonably safe. You are given a baggage tag in exchange for your bag, which should be securely closed or locked. Watch to be sure that your bag actually gets onto – and stays on – the bus.

Your hand luggage is a different matter. If you're asleep with a camera around your neck, you might wake up with a neatly razored strap and no camera. Hide all your valuables! Some travelers prefer to bring their rucksack on the bus with them, because there are occasional reports of theft from luggage compartments. This only works if your pack is small enough to shove between your legs or keep on your lap. Never place any bags into the overhead luggage racks, which are unsecured.

For more advice about theft, see p501.

CAR & MOTORCYCLE

It's a long way from Lima to most destinations, so it's better to take a bus or flight to wherever you want to go and rent a car once you get there. Given all the headaches and potential hazards of driving yourself around, consider hiring a taxi instead (p527).

At roadside checkpoints, where the police or military conduct meticulous document checks, you'll occasionally see Peruvian drivers slipping an officer some money to smooth things along The idea here is *not* to offer an (illegal) bribe, but simply a 'gift' or 'on-the-spot fine' so that you can get on your way. If you are driving and are involved in an accident that results in injury, know that drivers are routinely imprisoned for several days or even weeks until innocence has been established. For more advice on legal matters, see p506.

Driver's License

A driver's license from your own home country is sufficient for renting a car. An International Driving Permit (IDP) is only required if you'll be driving around Peru for more than 30 days.

Rental

Major car-rental companies have offices in Lima (p123), and a few other large cities. Renting a motorcycle is an option mainly in jungle towns, where you can go for short runs around town or the surrounding areas, but not much further.

Economy car rental starts at US$25 a day. But that doesn't include sales taxes of 19%, additional airport fees, 'super' collision-damage waiver, personal accident insurance and so on, which together can total at least $55 per day, not including excess mileage (around US$0.10 per kilometer). Vehicles such as 4WD jeeps are more expensive to rent.

Make sure you completely understand the rental agreement before you sign. A credit card is required, and renters normally need to be aged over 25.

Road Rules & Hazards

Bear in mind that the condition of rental cars is often poor, roads are potholed (even the paved Pan-American Hwy) and drivers are aggressive and commonly ignore speed limits, road signs and even traffic signals.

Drive on the righthand side of the road. Be aware that road signs are often small and unclear. Driving at night is not recommended because of poor road conditions, speeding buses and slow-moving, poorly lit trucks.

Theft is all too common, so you should not leave your vehicle parked in the street. When stopping overnight, park the car in a guarded lot (the better hotels have them).

Gasoline or petrol stations (called *grifos*) are few and far between. At the time of research, the average cost of *gasolina* in Peru was US$3.90 per US gallon.

HITCHHIKING

Hitchhiking is never entirely safe in any country in the world and is not recommended. Travelers who decide to hitch should understand that they are taking a serious risk. People who do choose to hitch will be safer if they travel in pairs and let someone know where they are planning to go. In Peru it's not very practical, as there are few private cars, buses are so cheap and trucks are often used as paid public transportation in remote areas.

LOCAL TRANSPORTATION

In most towns and cities, it's easy to walk everywhere or take a taxi. Using local buses, *micros* and *combis* can be tricky, but is less expensive than taxis.

Bus

Local buses are slow and crowded, but startlingly cheap. Ask locally for help, as there aren't any obvious bus lines in most towns.

A faster, more hair-raising alternative is to take *micros* or *combis,* sometimes called *colectivos* (though that term usually refers to taxis). Typically, *micros* and *combis* are, respectively, minibuses or minivans stuffed full of passengers. They can be identified by stickers along the outside panels and destination placards in the front windows. You can flag one down or get off anywhere on the route. A conductor usually leans out of the vehicle, shouting out destinations. Once inside, you must quickly squeeze into any available seat, or be prepared to stand up or crouch down. The conductor will come around and collect the fare, or you can pay when getting off. Know that safety is not a high priority for *combi* drivers. The only place for a passenger to safely buckle up is the front seat, but in the event of a head-on collision (not an unusual occurrence), that's the last place you'd want to be.

Taxi

Taxis seem to be everywhere. Private cars that have a small taxi sticker in the windshield aren't regulated. Safer, regulated taxis usually have a lit company number on the roof and are called for by telephone. These are more expensive than taxis flagged down on the street, but are more reliable. Solo women travelers should stick to regulated taxis, especially at night (see p514). See also p501 for more safety advice about kidnappings.

Always ask the fare in advance, as there are no meters. It's acceptable to haggle over a fare; try to find out what the going rate is before taking a cab, especially for long trips. The standard fare for short runs in most cities is around US$1. Tipping is not the norm.

TAXI

Hiring a private taxi for long-distance trips costs less than renting a car and takes care of many of the problems outlined earlier (see p525). Not all taxi drivers will agree to drive long distances, but if one does, you should carefully check the driver's credentials and vehicle before hiring.

Colectivo (shared) taxis for longer trips wait on busy corners and at major roundabouts, often by a signposted taxi stand.

TOURS

Major tourist towns have dozens of travel agencies offering group tours of the surrounding area. Whether you want to visit archaeological ruins, watch wildlife or be whisked around the city's sights in a private air-con minibus, there's a tour guide waiting for you.

In fact, the local tourism industry makes it *too* easy to join a tour, especially since doing it yourself can be more rewarding. Keep in mind that group tours rarely give you enough time to enjoy the places you want to visit. The major exception is trekking the Inca Trail (p274), for which you're legally required to sign up for a group tour in advance.

Lima, Cuzco, Arequipa, Puno, Trujillo, Huaraz, Puerto Maldonado and Iquitos have the most travel agencies offering organized tours; for details, see the Tours sections listed under these and many other destinations earlier in this book. For all-inclusive package tours from abroad, see p520.

For more specialized, individual or small-group tours, you can hire a good Spanish-speaking guide for about US$25 a day plus expenses; tours in English or other languages are more expensive. Some students or unregistered guides are cheaper, but the usual caveat applies – some are good, others aren't. A few local guides are listed in this book, but it's always good to ask other travelers for more up-to-date recommendations.

TRAIN

The privatized rail system, **PeruRail** (☎ 084-23 8722; www.perurail.com), has daily services between Cuzco and Aguas Calientes, aka Machu Picchu Pueblo, and services between Cuzco and Puno on the shores of Lake Titicaca three times a week; see p253 for details of both services. Passenger services between Puno and Arequipa have been suspended indefinitely, but will run as a charter for groups.

Train buffs won't want to miss the lovely **Ferrocarril Central Andino** (FCCA; ☎ 01-361 2828; www.ferroviasperu.com.pe), which reaches a head-spinning altitude of 4829m. It usually runs between Lima (p123) and Huancayo weekly from mid-April through October, but click to www.incasdelperu.org/statusofthetrain .htm for updates. In Huancayo, cheaper trains to Huancavelica leave daily from a different station. See p301 for details of both services. Another charmingly historic railway makes inexpensive daily runs between Tacna on Peru's south coast and Arica, Chile (see p160).

TRANSPORTATION

Health

CONTENTS

Prevention is the key to staying healthy while abroad. Travelers who receive the recommended vaccines and follow commonsense precautions usually come down with nothing more than a little diarrhea.

Medically speaking, Peru is part of tropical South America, which includes most of the continent except for the southernmost portion. The diseases found in this area are comparable to those found in tropical areas in Africa and Asia. Particularly important are mosquito-borne infections, including malaria, yellow fever, and dengue fever, although these are not a significant concern in the temperate regions of the country.

BEFORE YOU GO

Since most vaccines don't provide immunity until at least two weeks after they're given, visit a doctor four to eight weeks before departure. Don't forget to take your vaccination certificate with you (aka the yellow booklet); it's mandatory for countries that require proof of yellow-fever vaccination on entry.

Bring medications in their original, clearly labeled containers. A signed and dated letter from your physician describing your medical conditions and medications, including generic names, is also a good idea. If carrying syringes or needles, be sure to have a physician's letter documenting their medical necessity.

MEDICAL CHECKLIST

- antibiotics
- antidiarrheal drugs (eg loperamide)
- acetaminophen (Tylenol) or aspirin
- anti-inflammatory drugs (eg ibuprofen)
- antihistamines (for hay fever and allergic reactions)
- antibacterial ointment (eg Bactroban; for cuts and abrasions)
- steroid cream or cortisone (for poison ivy and other allergic rashes)
- bandages, gauze, gauze rolls
- adhesive or paper tape
- scissors, safety pins, tweezers
- thermometer
- pocket-knife
- insect repellent containing DEET (for the skin)
- insect spray containing permethrin (for clothing, tents and bed nets)
- sunblock
- oral rehydration salts
- iodine tablets (for water purification)
- syringes and sterile needles
- acetazolamide (Diamox; for altitude sickness)

If your health insurance doesn't cover you for medical expenses abroad, get extra travel insurance – check p506 for more information. Find out in advance if your travel insurance will make payments directly to providers or reimburse you later for overseas health expenditures. (Many doctors in Peru, though, expect payment in cash.)

ONLINE RESOURCES

There is a wealth of travel health advice on the internet. For further information, the website of **Lonely Planet** (www.lonelyplanet.com) is a good place to start. The **World Health Organization** (www.who.int/ith/) publishes a superb book called

IMMUNIZATIONS

The only required vaccine for Peru is yellow fever, and that's only if you're arriving from a yellow-fever-infected country in Africa or the Americas. A number of vaccines are recommended.

vaccine	recommended for	dosage	side effects
chickenpox	travelers who have never had chickenpox	two doses, one month apart	fever, mild case of chickenpox
hepatitis A	all travelers	one dose before trip; booster six to 12 months later	soreness at injection site, headaches, body aches
hepatitis B	travelers who will have long-term contact with the local population	three doses over six months	soreness at injection site, long-term fever
measles	travelers born after 1956 who've never had measles and who've had only one measles vaccination	one dose	fever, rash, joint pains, allergic reactions
rabies	travelers who will have contact with animals or won't have access to medical assistance	three doses over a four-week period	soreness at injection site, headaches, body aches
tetanus/ diphtheria	all travelers who haven't had a booster in 10 years	one dose every 10 years	soreness at injection site
typhoid	all travelers	four capsules by mouth, one taken every other day	abdominal pain, nausea, rash
yellow fever	travelers to jungle areas at altitudes below 2300m	one dose every 10 years	headaches, body aches, severe reactions are rare

International Travel and Health, which is revised annually and is available online at no cost. Another website of general interest is **MD Travel Health** (www.mdtravelhealth.com), which provides complete travel health recommendations and is updated daily.

It's usually a good idea to consult your government's travel health website before departure, if one is available:
Australia (www.dfat.gov.au/travel/)
Canada (www.travelhealth.gc.ca)
UK (www.doh.gov.uk/traveladvice/)
USA (www.cdc.gov/travel/)

FURTHER READING

For further information, see *Healthy Travel Central & South America,* also from Lonely Planet. If you're traveling with children, Lonely Planet's *Travel with Children* may be useful. The *ABC of Healthy Travel,* by E Walker et al, is another valuable resource.

IN TRANSIT

DEEP VEIN THROMBOSIS (DVT)

Blood clots may form in the legs during plane flights, chiefly because of prolonged

immobility. The longer the flight, the greater the risk. Though most blood clots are reabsorbed uneventfully, some may break off and travel through the blood vessels to the lungs, where they could cause life-threatening complications.

The chief symptom of DVT is swelling or pain of the foot, ankle or calf, usually – but not always – on just one side. When a blood clot travels to the lungs, it may cause chest pain and difficulty breathing. Travelers with any of these symptoms should immediately seek medical attention.

To prevent the development of DVT on long aeroplane flights, you should walk about the cabin, flex the leg muscles while sitting, drink plenty of fluids and avoid alcohol and tobacco.

JET LAG

The onset of jet lag is common when crossing more than five time zones, resulting in insomnia, fatigue, malaise or nausea. To minimize jet lag, try drinking plenty of (nonalcoholic) fluids and eating light meals. Upon arrival, get exposure to natural sunlight and readjust your schedule (for meals, sleep etc) as soon as possible.

IN PERU

AVAILABILITY OF HEALTH CARE

There are several high-quality medical clinics in Lima open 24 hours for medical emergencies (for details see p90). They also function as hospitals and offer subspecialty consultations. For a guide to clinics in Lima, check out the website for the **US embassy** (http://lima .usembassy.gov/acs_peru.html). There are also many English-speaking physicians and dentists in private practice in Lima, which are listed on the same website. Good medical care may be more difficult to find in other cities and impossible to locate in rural areas.

Many doctors expect payment in cash, regardless of whether you have travel insurance. If you develop a life threatening medical problem, you'll probably want to be evacuated to a country with state-of-the-art medical care. Since this may cost tens of thousands of dollars, be sure you have insurance to cover this before you depart. You can find a list of medical evacuation and travel insurance companies on the website of the **US State Department** (http://travel.state.gov/travel /tips/brochures/brochures_1215.html).

The pharmacies in Peru are known as *farmacias* or *boticas*, and are identified by a green or red cross in the window. They're generally reliable and offer most of the medications available in other countries. InkaFarma and Superfarma are two well-known pharmacy chains.

INFECTIOUS DISEASES

Of the diseases listed below, malaria, yellow fever and dengue fever are spread by mosquitoes. For information about protecting yourself from mosquito bites, see p535.

Cholera

An intestinal infection, cholera is acquired through ingestion of contaminated food or water. The main symptom is profuse, watery diarrhea, which may be so severe that it causes life-threatening dehydration. The key treatment is drinking oral rehydration solution. Antibiotics are also given, usually tetracycline or doxycycline, though quinolone antibiotics such as ciprofloxacin and levofloxacin are also effective.

Cholera occurs regularly in Peru, but it's rare among travelers. Cholera vaccine is no longer required to enter Peru, and is in fact no longer available in some countries, including the USA, because the old vaccine was relatively ineffective and caused side effects. There are new vaccines that are safer and more effective, but they're not available in many countries and are only recommended for those at particularly high risk.

Dengue Fever

This is a viral infection found throughout South America. Dengue is transmitted by aedes mosquitoes, which usually bite during the daytime and are often found close to human habitations. They breed primarily in artificial water containers, such as cans, cisterns, metal drums, plastic containers and discarded tires. As a result, dengue is especially common in densely populated, urban environments, including Lima and Cuzco.

Dengue usually causes flulike symptoms, including fever, muscle aches, joint pains, headaches, nausea and vomiting, often followed by a rash. The body aches may be quite uncomfortable, but most cases resolve uneventfully in a few days. Severe cases usually occur in children aged under 15 who are experiencing their second dengue infection.

There is no treatment for dengue fever except to take analgesics such as acetaminophen/paracetamol (Tylenol) and drink plenty of fluids. Severe cases may require hospitalization for intravenous fluids and supportive care.

Hepatitis A

A viral infection of the liver, hepatitis A is usually acquired by ingestion of contaminated water, food or ice, though it may also be acquired by direct contact with infected persons. Hepatitis A is the second most common travel-related infection (after travelers' diarrhea). The illness occurs throughout the world, but the incidence is higher in developing nations. Symptoms may include fever, malaise, jaundice, nausea, vomiting and abdominal pain. Most cases resolve without complications, though hepatitis A occasionally causes severe liver damage. There is no treatment; to aid recovery, avoid alcohol and eat simple, nonfatty foods.

The vaccine for hepatitis A is extremely safe and highly effective. If you get a booster six to 12 months later, it lasts for at least 10 years. You really should get it before you go to

Peru or any other developing nation. Because the safety of hepatitis A vaccine has not been established for pregnant women or children aged under two; they should instead be given a gamma globulin injection.

Hepatitis B

Like hepatitis A, hepatitis B is a liver infection that occurs worldwide but is more common in developing nations. Unlike hepatitis A, the disease is usually acquired by sexual contact or by exposure to infected blood, generally through blood transfusions or contaminated needles. The vaccine is recommended only for long-term travelers (on the road more than six months) who expect to live in rural areas or have close physical contact with the local population. Additionally, the vaccine is recommended for anyone who anticipates sexual contact with the local inhabitants or a possible need for medical, dental or other treatments while abroad, including transfusions or vaccinations.

Hepatitis B vaccine is safe and highly effective. However, a total of three injections is necessary to establish full immunity. Several countries added hepatitis B vaccine to the list of routine childhood immunizations in the 1980s, so many young adults are already protected.

HIV/AIDS

The Human Immunodeficiency Virus (HIV) may develop into Acquired Immune Deficiency Syndrome (AIDS; SIDA in Spanish). HIV/AIDS has been reported in all South American countries. Exposure to blood or blood products and bodily fluids may put an individual at risk. Be sure to use condoms for all sexual encounters. Fear of HIV infection should never preclude treatment of serious medical conditions as the risk of infection remains very small.

Malaria

Cases of malaria occur in every South American country except Chile, Uruguay and the Falkland Islands. It's transmitted by mosquito bites, usually between dusk and dawn. The main symptom is high spiking fevers, which may be accompanied by chills, sweats, headache, body aches, weakness, vomiting or diarrhea. Severe cases may affect the central nervous system and lead to seizures, confusion, coma and death.

Taking malaria pills is strongly recommended for all areas in Peru except Lima and its vicinity, the coastal areas south of Lima, and the highland areas (including around Cuzco, Machu Picchu, Lake Titicaca and Arequipa). The number of cases of malaria has risen sharply in recent years. Most cases in Peru occur in Loreto in the country's northeast, where malaria transmission has reached epidemic levels.

There is a choice of three malaria pills, all of which work about equally well. Mefloquine (Lariam) is taken once weekly in a dosage of 250mg, starting one to two weeks before arrival in an area where malaria is endemic, and continuing through the trip and for four weeks after returning. The problem is that some people develop neuropsychiatric side effects, which may range from mild to severe. Atovaquone/proguanil (Malarone) is a newly approved combination pill taken once daily with food starting two days before arrival, and continuing through the trip and for seven days after departure. Side effects are typically mild. Doxycycline is a third alternative, but may cause an exaggerated sunburn reaction.

In general, Malarone seems to cause fewer side effects than mefloquine and is becoming more popular. The chief disadvantage is that it has to be taken daily. For longer trips, it's probably worth trying mefloquine; for shorter trips, Malarone will be the drug of choice for most people. None of the pills is 100% effective.

If you may not have access to medical care while traveling, you should bring along additional pills for emergency self-treatment, which you should take if you can't reach a doctor and you develop symptoms that suggest malaria, such as high spiking fevers. One option is to take four tablets of Malarone once daily for three days. However, Malarone should not be used for treatment if you're already taking it for prevention. If taking Malarone, take 650mg of quinine three times daily and 100mg doxycycline twice daily for one week. If you start self-medication, see a doctor at the earliest possible opportunity. If you develop a fever after returning home, see a physician, as malaria symptoms may not occur for months.

Ensure that you take precautions to minimize your chances of being bitten by mosquitoes (p535).

Rabies

A viral infection of the brain and spinal cord, rabies is almost always fatal unless treated promptly. The rabies virus is carried in the saliva of infected animals and is typically transmitted through an animal bite, though contamination of any break in the skin with infected saliva may result in rabies. Rabies occurs in all South American countries. In Peru, most cases are related to bites from dogs or vampire bats.

The rabies vaccine is safe, but a full series requires three injections and is quite expensive. Those at high risk for rabies, such as animal handlers and spelunkers (cave explorers), should certainly get the vaccine. In addition, those at lower risk for animal bites should also consider asking for the vaccine if they might be traveling to remote areas and might not have access to appropriate medical care if needed. The treatment for a possibly rabid bite consists of rabies vaccine with rabies immune globulin. It's effective, but must be given promptly.

All animal bites and scratches must immediately be thoroughly cleansed with large amounts of soap and water, and local health authorities should be contacted to determine whether or not further treatment is necessary (see p534 for more details).

Tetanus

This potentially fatal disease is found in undeveloped tropical areas. It is difficult to treat, but it is preventable with immunization. Tetanus occurs when a wound becomes infected by a germ that lives in the feces of animals or people, so clean all cuts, punctures or animal bites. Tetanus is also known as lockjaw, and the first symptom may be discomfort in swallowing, or stiffening of the jaw and neck; this is followed by painful convulsions of the jaw and whole body.

Typhoid Fever

This fever is caused by ingestion of food or water contaminated by a species of salmonella known as *Salmonella typhi*. Fever occurs in virtually all cases. Other symptoms may include headache, malaise, muscle aches, dizziness, loss of appetite, nausea and abdominal pain. Either diarrhea or constipation may occur. Possible complications include intestinal perforation or bleeding, confusion, delirium or, rarely, coma.

Unless you expect to take all your meals in major hotels and restaurants, getting typhoid vaccine is a good idea. It's usually given orally, but is also available as an injection. Neither vaccine is approved for use in children under two.

The drug of choice for typhoid fever is usually a quinolone antibiotic such as ciprofloxacin (Cipro) or levofloxacin (Levaquin), which many travelers carry for treatment of travelers' diarrhea. However, if you self-treat for typhoid fever, you may also need to self-treat for malaria, since the symptoms of the two diseases may be indistinguishable.

Yellow Fever

A life-threatening viral infection, yellow fever is transmitted by mosquitoes in forested areas. The illness begins with flulike symptoms, which may include fever, chills, headache, muscle aches, backache, loss of appetite, nausea and vomiting. These symptoms usually subside in a few days, but one person in six enters a second, toxic phase characterized by recurrent fever, vomiting, listlessness, jaundice, kidney failure and hemorrhage, leading to death in up to half of the cases. There is no treatment except for supportive care.

Yellow-fever vaccine is strongly recommended for all those who visit any jungle areas of Peru at altitudes less than 2300m (7546ft). Most cases occur in the departments in the central jungle. Proof of vaccination is required from all travelers arriving in Peru from an area where yellow fever is endemic in Africa or the Americas.

Yellow-fever vaccine is given only in approved yellow-fever vaccination centers, which provide validated vaccination certificates. The vaccine should be given at least 10 days before any potential exposure to yellow fever and remains effective for about 10 years. Reactions to the vaccine are generally mild, though some people may experience severe side effects. While you may not be required to have proof of a yellow-fever vaccination to enter Peru, after visiting a region where yellow fever occurs, you'll need to have the vaccination to get to most other countries – even your home country. So you're better off getting your jab before you leave home.

Other Infections

Bartonellosis (Oroya fever) is carried by sand flies in the arid river valleys on the western slopes of the Andes in Peru, Colombia and Ecuador between altitudes of 800m and 3000m. The chief symptoms are fever and severe bone pains. Complications may include marked anemia, enlargement of the liver and spleen, and sometimes death. The drug of choice is chloramphenicol, though doxycycline is also effective.

Chagas' disease is a parasitic infection that is transmitted by triatomine insects (reduviid bugs), which inhabit crevices in the walls and roofs of substandard housing in South and Central America. In Peru, most cases occur in the southern part of the country. The triatomine insect drops its feces on human skin as it bites, usually at night. A person becomes infected when he or she unknowingly rubs the feces into the bite wound or any other open sore. Chagas' disease is extremely rare in travelers. However, if you sleep in a poorly constructed house, especially one made of mud, adobe, or thatch, you should be sure to protect yourself with a bed net and a good insecticide (see p535).

Leishmaniasis occurs in the mountains and jungles of all South American countries. The infection is transmitted by sand flies, which are about a third of the size of mosquitoes. In Peru, more cases have been seen recently in children aged under 15, due to the increasing use of child labor for brush clearing and preparation of farmlands on mountain slopes of the Andes. Most adult cases occur in men who have migrated into jungle areas for farming, working or hunting. Leishmaniasis may be limited to the skin, causing slowly growing ulcers over exposed parts of the body, or less commonly may disseminate to the bone marrow, liver and spleen. There is no vaccine. To protect yourself from sand flies, follow the same precautions as for mosquito bites (p535), except that netting must be made of finer mesh (at least 18 holes to the linear inch).

Leptospirosis is acquired by exposure to water contaminated by the urine of infected animals. Outbreaks often occur at times of flooding, when sewage overflow may contaminate water sources. The initial symptoms, which resemble a mild flu, usually subside uneventfully in a few days, with or without treatment, but a minority of cases are complicated by jaundice or meningitis. There is no vaccine. You can minimize your risk by staying out of bodies of fresh water that

may be contaminated by animal urine. If you're visiting an area where an outbreak is in progress, as occurred in Peru after flooding in 1998, you can take 200mg of doxycycline once weekly as a preventative measure. If you actually develop leptospirosis, the treatment is 100mg of doxycycline twice daily.

Gnathostomiasis is an intestinal parasite acquired by eating raw or undercooked freshwater fish, including ceviche. Note, though, that ceviche eaten on the coast will be almost certainly made from seafood.

Plague is usually transmitted to humans by the bite of rodent fleas, typically when rodents die. Symptoms include fever, chills, muscle aches and malaise, associated with the development of an acutely swollen, exquisitely painful lymph node, known as a bubo, most often in the groin. Cases of the plague are reported from Peru nearly every year, chiefly from the departments of Cajamarca, La Libertad, Piura and Lambayeque in the northern part of the country. Most travelers are at extremely low risk for this disease. However, if you might have contact with rodents or their fleas, especially in the above areas, you should bring along a bottle of doxycycline, to be taken prophylactically during periods of exposure. Those less than eight years old or allergic to doxycycline should take trimethoprim-sulfamethoxazole instead. In addition, you should avoid areas containing rodent burrows or nests, never handle sick or dead animals, and follow the guidelines for protecting yourself from mosquito bites (p535).

Taeniasis and the more serious **cysticercosis** are both caused by pork tapeworm (*Taenia solium*). Humans become hosts to the nasty parasite by eating infected or undercooked pork. Although pork tapeworm is rare, it does turn up in Peru, so be careful when eating pork.

TRAVELERS' DIARRHEA

You get diarrhea from taking contaminated food or water. See p534 and p536 for ideas for reducing the risk of getting diarrhea. If you develop diarrhea, be sure to drink plenty of fluids, preferably an oral rehydration solution containing lots of salt and sugar. A few loose stools don't require treatment but if you start having more than four or five stools a day, you should start taking an antibiotic (usually a quinolone drug) and an antidiarrheal agent (such as loperamide). If diarrhea is bloody, persists for more than 72 hours or is accompanied by fever, shaking chills or severe abdominal pain you should seek medical attention.

ENVIRONMENTAL HAZARDS
Altitude Sickness
Those who ascend rapidly to altitudes greater than 2500m (8100ft) may develop altitude sickness. In Peru, this includes Cuzco (3326m), Machu Picchu (about 2500m), and Lake Titicaca (3820m). Being physically fit offers no protection. Those who have experienced altitude sickness in the past are prone to future episodes. The risk increases with faster ascents, higher altitudes and greater exertion. Symptoms may include headaches, nausea, vomiting, dizziness, malaise, insomnia and loss of appetite. Severe cases may be complicated by fluid in the lungs (high-altitude pulmonary edema) or swelling of the brain (high-altitude cerebral edema). If symptoms are more than mild or persist for more than 24 hours (far less at high altitudes), descend immediately by at least 500m and see a doctor.

To help prevent altitude sickness, the best measure is to spend two nights or more at each rise of 1000m. Alternatively, take 125mg or 250mg of acetazolamide (Diamox) twice or three times daily starting 24 hours before ascent and continuing for 48 hours after arrival at altitude. Possible side effects include increased urinary volume, numbness, tingling, nausea, drowsiness, myopia and temporary impotence. Acetazolamide should not be given to pregnant women or anyone with a history of sulfa allergy. For those who cannot tolerate acetazolamide, the next best option is 4mg of dexamethasone taken four times daily. Unlike acetazolamide, dexamethasone must be tapered gradually upon arrival at altitude, since there is a risk that altitude sickness will occur as the dosage is reduced. Dexamethasone is a steroid, so it should not be given to diabetics or anyone for whom taking steroids is not advised. A natural alternative is gingko, which some people find quite helpful.

When traveling to high altitudes, it's also important to avoid overexertion, eat light meals and abstain from alcohol. Altitude sickness should be taken seriously; it can be life threatening when severe.

Animal Bites
Do not attempt to pet, handle or feed any animal, with the exception of domestic animals known to be free of any infectious disease. Most animal injuries are directly related to a person's attempt to touch or feed the animal.

Any bite or scratch by a mammal, including bats, should be promptly and thoroughly cleansed with large amounts of soap and water, followed by application of an antiseptic such as iodine or alcohol. The local health authorities should be contacted immediately for possible postexposure rabies treatment, whether or not you've been immunized against rabies. It may also be advisable to start an antibiotic, since wounds caused by animal bites and scratches frequently become infected. One of the newer quinolones, such as levofloxacin (Levaquin), which many travelers carry in case of diarrhea, would be an appropriate choice.

Snakes and leeches are a hazard in some areas of South America. In the event of a venomous snake bite, place the victim at rest, keep the bitten area immobilized and move the victim immediately to the nearest medical facility. Avoid tourniquets, which are no longer recommended.

Earthquakes & Avalanches
Peru is in an earthquake zone, and small tremors are frequent. Every few years, a large earthquake results in loss of life and property damage. Should you be caught in an earthquake, the best advice is to take shelter under a solid object, such as a desk or door frame. Do not stand near windows or heavy objects, and do not run out of the building. If you are outside, attempt to stay clear of falling wires, bricks, telephone poles and other hazards. Avoid crowds in the aftermath.

There's not much you can do when caught in an avalanche. Be aware that the main danger times are after heavy rains, when high ground may subside.

Food
Salads and fruit should be washed with purified water or peeled when possible. Ice cream is usually safe if it is a reputable brand name, but beware of street vendors and of ice cream that has melted and been refrozen. Thoroughly cooked food is safest, but not if it has been left to cool or if it has been reheated. Shellfish such as mussels, oysters and clams should be avoided, as should undercooked meat, particularly in the form of minced or

ground beef. Steaming does not make bad shellfish safe for eating. Having said that, it is difficult to resist Peruvian seafood dishes such as ceviche, which is marinated but not cooked. This is rarely a problem, as long as it is served fresh in a reputable restaurant.

If a place looks clean and well run, and if the vendor also looks clean and healthy, then the food is probably safe. In general, places that are packed with travelers or locals will be fine, while empty restaurants are questionable.

Hypothermia

Too much cold is just as dangerous as too much heat, as it may cause hypothermia. If you are trekking at high altitudes, particularly in wet and windy conditions, or simply taking a long bus trip over mountains, mostly at night, be prepared.

It is surprisingly easy to progress from very cold to dangerously cold due to a combination of wind, wet clothing, fatigue and hunger, even if the air temperature is above freezing. It is best to dress in layers; silk, wool and some of the new artificial fibers are all good insulating materials. A hat is important, as a lot of heat is lost through the head. A strong, waterproof outer layer is essential, because keeping dry is vital. Carry basic supplies, including food containing simple sugars to generate heat quickly, and lots of fluid to drink. A space blanket – an extremely thin, lightweight emergency blanket made of a reflective material that keeps heat in – is something all travelers in cold environments should carry.

Symptoms of hypothermia are exhaustion, numb skin (particularly toes and fingers), shivering, slurred speech, irrational or violent behavior, lethargy, stumbling, dizzy spells, muscle cramps and violent bursts of energy. Irrationality may take the form of sufferers claiming they are warm and trying to take off their clothes.

To treat mild hypothermia, first get the person out of the wind and/or rain, remove their clothing if it's wet and replace it with dry, warm clothing. Give them hot liquids – no alcohol – and some high-calorie, easily digestible food. Do not rub victims, as rough handling may cause cardiac arrest.

Mosquito Bites

To prevent mosquito bites, wear long sleeves, long pants, hats and shoes (rather than san-

dals). Bring along a good insect repellent, preferably one containing DEET, which should be applied to exposed skin and clothing, but not to eyes, mouth, cuts, wounds or irritated skin. Products containing lower concentrations of DEET are as effective, but for shorter periods of time. In general, adults and children aged over 12 should use preparations containing 25% to 35% DEET, which usually lasts about six hours. Children aged between two and 12 should use preparations containing no more than 10% DEET, applied sparingly, which will usually last about three hours. Neurologic toxicity has been reported from DEET, especially in children, but appears to be extremely uncommon and generally related to overuse. Compounds containing DEET should not be used on children under the age of two.

Insect repellents containing certain botanical products, including oil of eucalyptus and soybean oil, are effective but last only 1½ to two hours. DEET-containing repellents are preferable for areas where there is a high risk of malaria or yellow fever. Products based on citronella are not effective.

For additional protection, you can apply permethrin to clothing, shoes, tents, and mosquito nets. Permethrin treatments are safe and remain effective for at least two weeks, even when items are laundered. Permethrin should not be applied directly to skin.

Don't sleep with the window open unless there is a screen. If sleeping outdoors or in an accommodation where mosquitoes can enter, use a mosquito net, preferably treated with permethrin, with edges tucked in under the mattress. The mesh size should be less than 1.5mm. If the sleeping area is not otherwise protected, use a mosquito coil, which will fill the room with insecticide through the night. Repellent-impregnated wristbands are not effective.

Sunburn & Heat Exhaustion

To protect yourself from excessive sun exposure, you should stay out of the midday sun, wear sunglasses and a wide-brimmed sun hat, and apply sunblock with SPF 15 or higher and UVA and UVB protection, before exposure to the sun. Sunblock should be reapplied after swimming or vigorous activity. Be aware that the sun is more intense at higher altitudes, even though you may feel cooler.

Dehydration or salt deficiency can cause heat exhaustion. You should drink plenty of fluids and avoid excessive alcohol or strenuous activity when you first arrive in a hot climate. Long, continuous periods of exposure to high temperatures can leave you vulnerable to heatstroke, when body temperature rises to dangerous levels.

Water

Tap water in Peru is not safe to drink. Vigorous boiling of water for one minute is the most effective means of water purification. At altitudes greater than 2000m (6500ft), boil for three minutes.

Another option is to disinfect water with iodine or water purification pills. You can add 2% tincture of iodine to one quart or liter of water (five drops to clear water, 10 drops to cloudy water) and let stand for 30 minutes. If the water is cold, longer times may be required. Otherwise you can buy iodine pills, available at most pharmacies in your home country. The instructions for use should be carefully followed. The taste of iodinated water may be improved by adding vitamin C (ascorbic acid). Iodinated water should not be consumed for more than a few weeks. Pregnant women, those with a history of thyroid disease, and those allergic to iodine should not drink iodinated water.

A number of water filters are on the market. Those with smaller pores (reverse osmosis filters) provide the broadest protection, but they are relatively large and are readily plugged by debris. Those with somewhat larger pores (microstrainer filters) are ineffective against viruses, although they remove other organisms. Manufacturers' instructions must be carefully followed.

TRAVELING WITH CHILDREN

It's safer not to take children aged under three to high altitudes. Also, children under nine months should not be brought to jungle areas at lower altitudes because yellow-fever vaccine is not safe for this age group.

TRADITIONAL MEDICINE

Some common traditional remedies include the following:

problem	treatment
altitude sickness	ginko
jet lag	melatonin
mosquito-bite prevention	oil of eucalyptus/ soybean oil
motion sickness	ginger

When traveling with young children, be particularly careful about what you allow them to eat and drink, because diarrhea can be especially dangerous to them and because the vaccines for the prevention of hepatitis A and typhoid fever are not approved for use in children aged under two.

The two main malaria medications, Lariam and Malarone, may be given to children, but insect repellents must be applied in lower concentrations (see p535).

WOMEN'S HEALTH

Although travel to Lima is reasonably safe if you're pregnant, there are risks in visiting many other parts of the country. First, it may be difficult to find quality obstetric care, if needed, especially away from the main tourist areas. Second, it isn't advisable for pregnant women to spend time at high altitudes where the air is thin, which precludes travel to many of the most popular destinations, including Cuzco, Machu Picchu and Lake Titicaca. (If you are still determined to visit these places regardless, then ascend more slowly than normally recommended; see p534 for details.) Lastly, yellow-fever vaccine, strongly recommended for travel to jungle areas at altitudes less than 2300m, should not be given during pregnancy because the vaccine contains a live virus that may infect the fetus.

Language

CONTENTS

Spanish is the main language the traveler will need in Peru. Even though English is understood in the best hotels, airline offices and tourist agencies, it's of little use elsewhere. In the highlands, most indigenous people are bilingual, with Spanish as a second tongue. Quechua is the main indigenous language in most areas, except around Lake Titicaca, where Aymara is spoken. Outside Peru's very remote areas, where indigenous languages may be the only tongue, it's unlikely that travelers will encounter indigenous people with no Spanish at all.

SPANISH

If you don't speak Spanish, don't despair. It's easy enough to pick up the basics and for those who want to learn the language in greater depth, courses are available in Lima (see p106) and Cuzco (p238). Alternatively, you can study books, records and tapes while you're still at home and planning your trip. These study aids are often available free at public libraries – or you might consider taking an evening or college course. With the basics under your belt, you'll be able to talk with people from all parts of Latin America (except Brazil, where Portuguese is the predominant language).

For words and phrases that will come in handy when eating out, see p81.

For a more comprehensive guide to the Spanish of Peru, pick up a copy of Lonely Planet's *Latin American Spanish Phrasebook*. If you're planning on heading into more remote areas Lonely Planet's *Quechua Phrasebook* would also be a very handy addition to the backpack. Another useful resource is the compact and comprehensive University of Chicago *Spanish-English, English-Spanish Dictionary*.

PRONUNCIATION

Spanish spelling is phonetically consistent, meaning that there's a clear and consistent relationship between what you see in writing and how it's pronounced. In addition, most Spanish sounds have English equivalents, so English speakers should not have much trouble being understood if the rules listed below are adhered to.

Peruvian Spanish is considered one of the language's 'cleanest' dialects – enunciation is relatively clear, pronunciation is very similar to Castilian Spanish (the official language of Spain), and slang is a lot less common than in other parts of Latin America.

Vowels

a	as in 'father'
e	as in 'met'
i	as in 'marine'
o	as in 'or' (without the 'r' sound)
u	as in 'rule'; **u** is not pronounced after **q** and in the letter combinations **gue** and **gui**, unless it's marked with a diaeresis (eg *argüir*), in which case it's pronounced as English 'w'
y	at the end of a word or when it stands alone, it's pronounced as the Spanish **i** (eg *ley*); between vowels within a word it's as the 'y' in 'yonder'

Consonants

As a rule, Spanish consonants resemble their English counterparts. The exceptions are listed below.

While the consonants **ch**, **ll** and **ñ** are generally considered distinct letters, **ch** and **ll** are now often listed alphabetically under **c** and **l** respectively. The letter **ñ** is still treated as a separate letter and comes after **n** in dictionaries.

c	as in 'celery' before **e** and **i**; otherwise as English 'k'
ch	as in 'church'
d	as in 'dog,' but between vowels and after **l** or **n**, the sound is closer to the 'th' in 'this'
g	as the 'ch' in the Scottish *loch* before **e** and **i** ('kh' in our guides to pronunciation); elsewhere, as in 'go'
h	invariably silent. If your name begins with this letter, listen carefully if you're waiting for public officials to call you.
j	as the 'ch' in the Scottish *loch* ('kh' in our guides to pronunciation)
ll	as the 'y' in 'yellow'
ñ	as the 'ni' in 'onion'
r	a short **r** except at the beginning of a word, and after **l**, **n** or **s**, when it's often rolled
rr	very strongly rolled
v	like a soft English 'b'
x	as in 'taxi' except for a very few words, when it's pronounced as **j**
z	as the 's' in 'sun'

Word Stress

In general, words ending in vowels or the letters **n** or **s** have stress on the next-to-last syllable, while those with other endings have stress on the last syllable. Thus *vaca* (cow) and *caballos* (horses) both carry stress on the next-to-last syllable, while *ciudad* (city) and *infeliz* (unhappy) are both stressed on the last syllable.

Written accents will almost always appear in words that don't follow the rules above, eg *sótano* (basement), *América* and *porción* (portion). When counting syllables, be sure to remember that diphthongs (vowel combinations, such as the **ue** in *puede*) constitute only one. When a word with a written accent appears in capital letters, the accent is often not written, but is still pronounced.

GENDER & PLURALS

Spanish nouns are either masculine or feminine, and there are rules to help determine gender (with the obligatory exceptions).

Feminine nouns generally end with -**a** or with the groups -**ción**, -**sión** or -**dad**. Other endings typically signify a masculine noun. Endings for adjectives also change to agree with the gender of the noun they modify (masculine/feminine -**o**/-**a**). Where both masculine and feminine forms are included in this language guide, they are separated by a slash, with the masculine form first, eg *perdido/a*.

If a noun or adjective ends in a vowel, the plural is formed by adding **s** to the end. If it ends in a consonant, the plural is formed by adding **es** to the end.

ACCOMMODATIONS

I'm looking for ...

Estoy buscando ...	e·*stoy* boos·*kan*·do ...

Where is ...?

¿Dónde hay ...?	*don*·de ai ...

a hotel

un hotel	oon o·*tel*

a boarding house

una pensión/residencial/	oo·na pen·*syon*/re·see·den·*syal*/
un hospedaje	oon os·pe·*da*·khe

a youth hostel

un albergue juvenil	oon al·*ber*·ge khoo·ve·*neel*

I'd like a ... room.

Quisiera una habitación ...	kee·*sye*·ra oo·na a·bee·ta·*syon* ...

single

simple	*seem*·ple

double/twin (with two beds)

doble (con dos camas)	*do*·ble (kon dos *ka*·mas)

double (with one bed)

matrimonial (con una	ma·tree·mo·*nyal* (kon *oo*·na
cama)	*ka*·ma)

How much is it per ...?

¿Cuánto cuesta por ...?	*kwan*·to *kwes*·ta por ...

night

noche	*no*·che

person

persona	per·*so*·na

week

semana	se·*ma*·na

Does it include breakfast?

¿Incluye el desayuno?	een·*kloo*·ye el de·sa·*yoo*·no

May I see the room?

¿Puedo ver la	*pwe*·do ver la
habitación?	a·bee·ta·*syon*

I don't like it.

No me gusta.	no me *goos*·ta

MAKING A RESERVATION

To ...	A ...
From ...	De ...
Date	Fecha
I'd like to book ...	Quisiera reservar ... (see the list under Accommodations for bed/room options)
in the name of ...	en nombre de ...
for the nights of ...	para las noches del ...
credit card ...	tarjeta de crédito ...
number	número
expiry date	fecha de vencimiento
Please confirm ...	Puede confirmar ...
availability	la disponibilidad
price	el precio

It's fine. I'll take it.
  OK. La alquilo.   o·kay la al·kee·lo
I'm leaving now.
  Me voy ahora.   me voy a·o·ra

full board	pensión completa	pen·syon kom·ple·ta
private/shared bathroom	baño privado/compartido	ba·nyo pree·va·do/kom·par·tee·do
too expensive	demasiado caro	de·ma·sya·do ka·ro
cheaper	más económico	mas e·ko·no·mee·ko
discount	descuento	des·kwen·to

CONVERSATION & ESSENTIALS

In their public behavior, South Americans are very conscious of civilities, sometimes to the point of ceremoniousness. Never approach a stranger for information without extending a greeting, and use only the polite form of address, especially with the police and public officials. Young people may be less likely to expect this, but it's best to stick to the polite form unless you're quite sure you won't offend by using the informal mode. The polite form is used in all cases in this guide; where options are given, the form is indicated by the abbreviations 'pol' and 'inf.'

Hello.	Hola.	o·la
Good morning.	Buenos días.	bwe·nos dee·as
Good afternoon.	Buenas tardes.	bwe·nas tar·des
Good evening/night.	Buenas noches.	bwe·nas no·ches
Goodbye.	Adiós.	a·dyos

SIGNS

Entrada	Entrance
Salida	Exit
Información	Information
Abierto	Open
Cerrado	Closed
Prohibido	Prohibited
Comisaria	Police Station
Servicios/Baños	Toilets
Hombres/Varones	Men
Mujeres/Damas	Women

See you soon.	Hasta luego.	as·ta lwe·go
Yes.	Sí.	see
No.	No.	no
Please.	Por favor.	por fa·vor
Thank you.	Gracias.	gra·syas
Many thanks.	Muchas gracias.	moo·chas gra·syas
You're welcome.	De nada.	de na·da
Pardon me.	Perdón.	per·don
Excuse me.	Permiso.	per·mee·so
(used when asking permission)		
Forgive me.	Disculpe.	dees·kool·pe
(used when apologizing)		

How are things?
  ¿Qué tal?   ke tal
What's your name?
  ¿Cómo se llama?   ko·mo se ya·ma (pol)
  ¿Cómo te llamas?   ko·mo te ya·mas (inf)
My name is ...
  Me llamo ...   me ya·mo ...
It's a pleasure to meet you.
  Mucho gusto.   moo·cho goos·to
The pleasure is mine.
  El gusto es mío.   el goos·to es mee·o
Where are you from?
  ¿De dónde es/eres?   de don·de es/e·res (pol/inf)
I'm from ...
  Soy de ...   soy de ...
Where are you staying?
  ¿Dónde está alojado?   don·de es·ta a·lo·kha·do (pol)
  ¿Dónde estás alojado?   don·de es·tas a·lo·kha·do (inf)
May I take a photo?
  ¿Puedo sacar una foto?   pwe·do sa·kar oo·na fo·to

DIRECTIONS
How do I get to ...?
  ¿Cómo puedo llegar a ...?   ko·mo pwe·do lye·gar a ...
Is it far?
  ¿Está lejos?   es·ta le·khos
Go straight ahead.
  Siga/Vaya derecho.   see·ga/va·ya de·re·cho

LANGUAGE

EMERGENCIES

Help!
¡Socorro! so·ko·ro

It's an emergency.
Es una emergencia. es oo·na e·mer·khen·sya

Fire!
¡Incendio! een·sen·dyo

Could you help me, please?
¿Me puede ayudar, me pwe·de a·yoo·dar
por favor? por fa·vor

Where are the toilets?
¿Dónde están los baños? don·de es·tan los ba·nyos

I'm lost.
Estoy perdido/a. es·toy per·dee·do/a

I've been robbed.
Me robaron. me ro·ba·ron

Go away!
¡Déjeme! de·khe·me

Get lost!
¡Váyase! va·ya·se

Call ...!
¡Llame a ...! ya·me a
  the police
  la policía la po·lee·see·a
  a doctor
  un médico oon me·dee·ko
  an ambulance
  una ambulancia oo·na am·boo·lan·sya

Turn left.
Voltée a la izquierda. vol·te·e a la ees·kyer·da

Turn right.
Voltée a la derecha. vol·te·e a la de·re·cha

I'm lost.
Estoy perdido/a. es·toy per·dee·do/a

Can you show me (on the map)?
¿Me lo podría indicar me lo po·dree·a een·dee·kar
(en el mapa)? (en el ma·pa)

north	norte	nor·te
south	sur	soor
east	este/oriente	es·te/o·ryen·te
west	oeste/occidente	o·es·te/ok·see·den·te
here	aquí	a·kee
there	allí	a·yee
avenue	avenida	a·ve·nee·da
block	cuadra	kwa·dra
street	calle/paseo	ka·lye/pa·se·o

HEALTH

I'm sick.
Estoy enfermo/a. es·toy en·fer·mo/a

I need a doctor.
Necesito un médico. ne·se·see·to oon me·dee·ko

Where's the hospital?
¿Dónde está el hospital? don·de es·ta el os·pee·tal

I'm pregnant.
Estoy embarazada. es·toy em·ba·ra·sa·da

I've been vaccinated.
Estoy vacunado/a. es·toy va·koo·na·do/a

I'm allergic	Soy alérgico/a	soy a·ler·khee·ko/a
to ...	a ...	a ...
antibiotics	los antibióticos	los an·tee·byo·tee·kos
penicillin	la penicilina	la pe·nee·see·lee·na
peanuts	los manies	los ma·nee·es

I'm ...	Soy ...	soy ...
asthmatic	asmático/a	as·ma·tee·ko/a
diabetic	diabético/a	dya·be·tee·ko/a
epileptic	epiléptico/a	e·pee·lep·tee·ko/a

I have ...	Tengo ...	ten·go ...
altitude sickness	soroche	so·ro·che
diarrhea	diarrea	dya·re·a
nausea	náusea	now·se·a
a headache	un dolor de cabeza	oon do·lor de ka·be·sa
a cough	tos	tos

LANGUAGE DIFFICULTIES

Do you speak (English)?
¿Habla/Hablas (inglés)? a·bla/a·blas (een·gles) (pol/inf)

Does anyone here speak English?
¿Hay alguien que hable ai al·gyen ke a·ble
inglés? een·gles

I (don't) understand.
Yo (no) entiendo. yo (no) en·tyen·do

How do you say ...?
¿Cómo se dice ...? ko·mo se dee·se ...

What does ...mean?
¿Qué quiere decir ...? ke kye·re de·seer ...

Could you please ...?	¿Puede ..., por favor?	pwe·de ... por fa·vor
repeat that	repetirlo	re·pe·teer·lo
speak more slowly	hablar más despacio	a·blar mas des·pa·syo
write it down	escribirlo	es·kree·beer·lo

NUMBERS

1	uno	oo·no
2	dos	dos
3	tres	tres
4	cuatro	kwa·tro

5	cinco	seen·ko
6	seis	says
7	siete	sye·te
8	ocho	o·cho
9	nueve	nwe·ve
10	diez	dyes
11	once	on·se
12	doce	do·se
13	trece	tre·se
14	catorce	ka·tor·se
15	quince	keen·se
16	dieciséis	dye·see·says
17	diecisiete	dye·see·sye·te
18	dieciocho	dye·see·o·cho
19	diecinueve	dye·see·nwe·ve
20	veinte	vayn·te
21	veintiuno	vayn·tee·oo·no
30	treinta	trayn·ta
31	treinta y uno	trayn·ta ee oo·no
40	cuarenta	kwa·ren·ta
50	cincuenta	seen·kwen·ta
60	sesenta	se·sen·ta
70	setenta	se·ten·ta
80	ochenta	o·chen·ta
90	noventa	no·ven·ta
100	cien	syen
101	ciento uno	syen·to oo·no
200	doscientos	do·syen·tos
1000	mil	meel
5000	cinco mil	seen·ko meel
10,000	diez mil	dyes meel
50,000	cincuenta mil	seen·kwen·ta meel
100,000	cien mil	syen meel
1,000,000	un millón	oon mee·yon

SHOPPING & SERVICES

I'd like to buy ...
Quisiera comprar ... kee·sye·ra kom·prar ...
I'm just looking.
Sólo estoy mirando. so·lo es·toy mee·ran·do
May I look at it?
¿Puedo mirar(lo/la)? pwe·do mee·rar·(lo/la)
How much is it?
¿Cuánto cuesta? kwan·to kwes·ta
That's too expensive for me.
Es demasiado caro es de·ma·sya·do ka·ro
para mí. pa·ra mee
Could you lower the price?
¿Podría bajar un poco po·dree·a ba·khar oon po·ko
el precio? el pre·syo
I don't like it.
No me gusta. no me goos·ta
I'll take it.
Lo llevo. lo ye·vo

Do you	¿Aceptan ...?	a·sep·tan ...
accept ...?		
American	dólares	do·la·res
dollars	americanos	a·me·ree·ka·nos
credit cards	tarjetas de	tar·khe·tas de
	crédito	kre·dee·to
traveler's	cheques de	che·kes de
checks	viajero	vya·khe·ro
small bills	billetes pequeñas	bee·lye·tes
		pe·ken·yas
less	menos	me·nos
more	más	mas
large	grande	gran·de
small	pequeño/a	pe·ke·nyo/a
I'm looking	Estoy buscando ...	es·toy boos·kan·do
for (the) ...		
ATM	el cajero	el ka·khe·ro
	automático	ow·to·ma·tee·ko
bank	el banco	el ban·ko
bookstore	la librería	la lee·bre·ree·a
embassy	la embajada	la em·ba·kha·da
foreign exchange	la casa de	la ka·sa de
bureau	cambio	kam·byo
general store	la tienda	la tyen·da
laundry	la lavandería	la la·van·de·ree·a
market	el mercado	el mer·ka·do
pharmacy/	la farmacia/	la far·ma·sya/
chemist	la botica	la bo·tee·ka
post office	el correo	el ko·re·o
tourist office	la oficina de	la o·fee·see·na de
	turismo	too·rees·mo

What time does it open/close?
¿A qué hora abre/cierra?
a ke o·ra a·bre/sye·ra
I want to change some money/traveler's checks.
Quiero cambiar dinero/cheques de viajero.
kye·ro kam·byar dee·ne·ro/che·kes de vya·khe·ro
What is the exchange rate?
¿Cuál es el tipo de cambio?
kwal es el tee·po de kam·byo
I want to call ...
Quiero llamar a ...
kye·ro lya·mar a ...

airmail	correo aéreo	ko·re·o a·e·re·o
black market	mercado (negro/	mer·ka·do ne·gro/
	paralelo)	pa·ra·le·lo
letter	carta	kar·ta
phonecard	tarjeta telefónica	tar·khe·ta te·le·fo·
		nee·ka
postcards	postales	pos·ta·les
poste restante	lista de correos	lee·sta de ko·re·os

| registered (mail) | certificado | ser·tee·fee·ka·do |
| stamps | estampillas | es·tam·pee·lyas |

TIME & DATES

What time is it?	¿Qué hora es?	ke o·ra es
It's one o'clock.	Es la una.	es la oo·na
It's two o'clock.	Son las dos.	son las dos
midnight	medianoche	me·dya·no·che
noon	mediodía	me·dyo·dee·a
half past two	dos y media	dos ee me·dya
now	ahora	a·o·ra
today	hoy	oy
tonight	esta noche	es·ta no·che
tomorrow	mañana	ma·nya·na
yesterday	ayer	a·yer
Monday	lunes	loo·nes
Tuesday	martes	mar·tes
Wednesday	miércoles	myer·ko·les
Thursday	jueves	khwe·ves
Friday	viernes	vyer·nes
Saturday	sábado	sa·ba·do
Sunday	domingo	do·meen·go
January	enero	e·ne·ro
February	febrero	fe·bre·ro
March	marzo	mar·so
April	abril	a·breel
May	mayo	ma·yo
June	junio	khoo·nyo
July	julio	khoo·lyo
August	agosto	a·gos·to
September	septiembre	sep·tyem·bre
October	octubre	ok·too·bre
November	noviembre	no·vyem·bre
December	diciembre	dee·syem·bre

TRANSPORTATION
Public Transportation

What time does	¿A qué hora ...	a ke o·ra ...
... leave/arrive?	sale/llega?	sa·le/ye·ga
the bus	el autobus	el ow·to·boos
the plane	el avión	el a·vyon
the ship	el barco/buque	el bar·ko/boo·ke
the train	el tren	el tren
airport	el aeropuerto	el a·e·ro·pwer·to
train station	la estación de	la es·ta·syon de
	ferrocarril	fe·ro·ka·reel
bus station	la estación de	la es·ta·syon de
	autobuses	ow·to·boo·ses
bus stop	la parada de	la pa·ra·da de
	autobuses	ow·to·boo·ses

luggage check	guardería/	gwar·de·ree·a/
room	equipaje	e·kee·pa·khe
ticket office	la boletería	la bo·le·te·ree·a

I'd like a ticket to ...

| Quiero un boleto a ... | kye·ro oon bo·le·to a ... |

What's the fare to ...?

| ¿Cuánto cuesta hasta ...? | kwan·to kwes·ta a·sta ... |

student's	de estudiante	de es·too·dyan·te
1st class	primera clase	pree·me·ra kla·se
2nd class	segunda clase	se·goon·da kla·se
single/one-way	ida	ee·da
return/round	ida y vuelta	ee·da ee vwel·ta
trip		
taxi	taxi	tak·see

Private Transportation

I'd like to	Quisiera	kee·sye·ra
hire a/an ...	alquilar ...	al·kee·lar ...
bicycle	una bicicleta	oo·na bee·see·
		kle·ta
4WD	un todo terreno	oon to·do te·re·no
car	un auto	oon ow·to
motorbike	una moto	oo·na mo·to
pickup (truck)	camioneta	ka·myo·ne·ta
truck	camión	ka·myon
hitchhike	hacer dedo	a·ser de·do
diesel	diesel	dee·sel
gas (petrol)	gasolina	ga·so·lee·na

Where's a gas station?

| ¿Dónde hay una | don·de ai oo·na |
| gasolinera/un grifo? | ga·so·lee·ne·ra/oon gree·fo |

Please fill it up.

| Lleno, por favor. | ye·no por fa·vor |

I'd like (20) liters.

| Quiero (veinte) litros. | kye·ro (vayn·te) lee·tros |

Is this the road to (...)?

| ¿Se va a (...) por | se va a (...) por |
| esta carretera? | es·ta ka·re·te·ra |

(How long) Can I park here?

| ¿(Por cuánto tiempo) | (por kwan·to tyem·po) |
| Puedo aparcar aquí? | pwe·do a·par·kar a·kee |

Where do I pay?

| ¿Dónde se paga? | don·de se pa·ga |

I need a mechanic.

| Necesito un | ne·se·see·to oon |
| mecánico. | me·ka·nee·ko |

The car has broken down (in ...).

| El carro se ha averiado | el ka·ro se a a·ve·rya·do |
| (en ...). | (en ...) |

The motorbike won't start.
No arranca la moto.   no a·*ran*·ka la *mo*·to
I have a flat tire.
Tengo un pinchazo.   *ten*·go oon peen·*cha*·so
I've run out of gas.
Me quedé sin gasolina.   me ke·*de* seen ga·so·*lee*·na
I've had an accident.
Tuve un accidente.   *too*·ve oon ak·see·*den*·te

AYMARA & QUECHUA

The following list of words and phrases is obviously minimal, but it should be useful in areas where these languages are spoken. Pronounce them as you would a Spanish word. An apostrophe represents a glottal stop, which is the 'nonsound' that occurs in the middle of 'uh-oh.' In the following words and phrases, Aymara is the first entry, Quechua the second.

Hello.
Kamisaraki.   Napaykullayki.
Please.
Mirá.   Allichu.
Thank you.
Yuspagara.   Yusulipayki.
Yes.
Jisa.   Ari.

No.
Janiwa.   Mana.
How do you say ...?
Cun sañasauca'ha ...?   Imainata nincha chaita ...?
It is called ...
Ucan sutipa'h ...   Chaipa'g sutin'ha ...
Please repeat.
Uastata sita.   Ua'manta niway.
How much?
K'gauka?   Maik'ata'g?

father	auqui	tayta
food	manka	mikiuy
mother	taica	mama
river	jawira	mayu
snowy peak	kollu	riti-orko
water	uma	yacu

1	maya	u'
2	paya	iskai
3	quimsa	quinsa
4	pusi	tahua
5	pesca	phiska
6	zo'hta	so'gta
7	pakalko	khanchis
8	quimsakalko	pusa'g
9	yatunca	iskon
10	tunca	chunca

Also available from Lonely Planet:
Latin American Spanish Phrasebook

Latin American Spanish
phrasebooks
with 2000-word two-way dictionary

LANGUAGE

Glossary

See p81 for useful words and phrases about cooking and cuisine. See p537 for more useful words and phrases.

abrazo – backslapping hug exchanged between men
altiplano – literally, a high plateau or plain; specifically, it refers to the vast, desolate Andean flatlands of southern Peru, Bolivia, northern Chile and northern Argentina
aluvión – fast-moving flood of ice, water, rocks, mud and debris caused by the bursting of a dam or an earthquake in a mountainous region
ambulantes – street vendors; also called *vendedores ambulantes*
apartado postal – post-office box
apu – mountain deity
arenero – dune buggy
arequipeño – inhabitant of Arequipa
arriero – animal driver, usually of *burros* or *mulas*
avenida – avenue
ayahuasca – potent hallucinogenic brew made from jungle vines and used by shamans and traditional healers

barrio – neighborhood
blanca/blanco – white
bodega – winery, wine shop, wine cellar or tasting bar
boleto turístico – tourism ticket
bruja/brujo – shaman, witch doctor, or medicine woman or man
burro – donkey
bus-cama – long-distance, double-decker buses with seats reclining almost into beds; toilets, videos and snacks are provided on board

caballito – high-ended, cigar-shaped boat; found near Huanchaco
caballo – horse
cajón – percussion instrument consisting of a box upon which the musician sits and which is drummed with the palms of the hands; typically played by Afro-Peruvians
calle – street
camión – truck, lorry; may be used for transport in remote areas
campesino – peasant, farmer or rural inhabitant
cañón – canyon
capitanía – office of the port or harbor master
carretera – highway
casa – home, house
casa de cambio – foreign-exchange bureau
cerro – hill, mountain

chaccu – traditional capture, shearing and release of *vicuña* herds
charango – small, 10-stringed lute with a box traditionally made of an armadillo shell, though today most are wooden
chasqui – runner used for delivering messages during Inca times
chullpa – ancient Andean burial tower, notably found around Lake Titicaca
cocha – lake, from the indigenous Quechua language; often appended to many lake names, eg Conococha
colectivo – shared transportation; usually taxis, but sometimes minibuses, minivans or even boats
colpa – clay lick, usually found in the Amazonian rainforest and used by mammals and birds to obtain minerals
combi – minivan or minibus (usually with tiny seats, cramming in as many passengers as possible)
cordillera – mountain chain
criolla/criollo – Creole or native of Peru; also applies to coastal Peruvians, music and dance; *criollo* food refers to spicy Peruvian fare with Spanish and African influences
cuadra – city block
culebra – snake
curandera/curandero – traditional healer
cuzqueño – inhabitant of Cuzco (also spelled Cusco or Qosq'o)

derecha – right

escuela cuzqueña – Cuzco school; colonial artists who combined Spanish and Andean artistic styles
extranjera/extranjero – foreigner

feria – street market with vendor booths
flauta – flute
friaje – extremely cold wind that blows from the Andes into the Amazon rainforest

garúa – coastal fog, mist or drizzle
grifo – gasoline/petrol station
gringa/gringo – generally refers to all foreigners who are not from South or Central America and Mexico
guanaco – large, wild camelid that ranges throughout South America, now an endangered species in Peru
guano – seabird excrement, used as fertilizer

hospedaje – small, family-owned inn
hostal – guesthouse with fewer amenities and smaller than a hotel
huaca – sacred pyramid, temple or burial site

huaquero – grave robber

huayno – traditional Andean music using instrumentation with roots in pre-Columbian times

iglesia – church

IGN – Instituto Geográfico Nacional (National Geographic Institute); government agency that produces and sells topographic and other maps

impuestos – taxes, taxation

indígena – indigenous person (male or female)

Inrena – Instituto Nacional de Recursos Naturales (National Institute for Natural Resources); government agency that administers national parks, reserves, historical sanctuaries and other protected areas

Inti – ancient Peruvian sun god; husband of the earth goddess Pachamama

isla – island, isle

izquierda – left

jirón – road (abbreviated Jr)

limeño – inhabitant of Lima

listas de correos – general delivery, poste restante

marinera – a typical coastal Peruvian dance involving much romantic waving of handkerchiefs

mestizo – person of mixed indigenous and Spanish descent

micro – a small bus used as public transport

mirador – watchtower, observatory, viewpoint

mototaxi – three-wheeled motorcycle rickshaw taxi; also called *motocarro* or *taximoto*

mula – mule

museo – museum

negra/negro – black

nevado – glaciated or snow-covered mountain peak

niña/niño – girl/boy

nuevo sol – the national currency of Peru

oficina de migraciónes – immigration office

Pachamama – ancient Peruvian earth goddess; wife of the sun god Inti

pampa – large, flat area, usually of grasslands

Panamericana – Pan-American Highway (aka Interamericana); main route joining Latin American countries

para llevar – to go, take away

parque – park

peki-peki – wooden dugout canoe powered by a small outboard motor; the name derives from the explosive coughing sound made by the engine

peña – bar or club featuring live folkloric music

piropo – cheeky, flirtatious or even vulgar 'compliment'; often used by men trying to pick up women

piruru – flute carved from the wing bone of a condor

piso – floor, story; eg *segundo piso* (2nd floor)

playa – beach

pongo – narrow, steep-walled, rocky, jungle river canyon that can be a dangerous maelstrom during high water

pueblo – town, village

puna – high Andean grasslands of the *altiplano*

puya – spiky-leafed plant of the bromeliad family

quebrada – literally, a break; often refers to a steep ravine or gulch

quena – Andean pennywhistle, typically carved from bone or bamboo; also called *kena*

quero – ceremonial Inca wooden drinking vessel

río – river

sapo – game in which brass disks are tossed into a box or onto a table with holes in it; holes are scored according to difficulty, with the highest score for tossing a disk into the mouth of the *sapo* (toad) mounted in the center

selva – jungle, tropical rainforest

servicio – service charge; sometimes called a *propina*

SIDA – AIDS (Aquired Immune Deficiency Disease) in Spanish

sillar – off-white volcanic rock, often used for buildings around Arequipa

soroche – altitude sickness

SSHH – Servicios Higiénicos (public toilets)

tambo – resting place for *chasquis,* where messages would be relayed to waiting runners during Inca times

tarjeta de credito – credit card

tarjeta telefónica – phonecard

taximoto – see *mototaxi*

tinya – small Andean hand drum played with a stick

totora – reed of the papyrus family; used to build the 'floating islands' and traditional boats of Lake Titicaca

ventana – window

vicuña – threatened, wild relative of alpacas; smallest living members of the camelid family

wankara – large, round Andean bass drum

zampoña – larger traditional Andean panpipes

Behind the Scenes

THIS BOOK

This 6th edition of *Peru* was written and re-searched by Sara Benson (coordinating author), Paul Hellander and Rafael Wlodarski. Carolina A Miranda, Hugh Thomson and Dr David Goldberg MD also contributed. The 5th edition was written by Rob Rachowiecki and Charlotte Beech. The first four editions were also written by Rob Rachowiecki. This guidebook was commissioned in Lonely Planet's Oakland office, and produced by the following:

Commissioning Editors Kathleen Munnelly, David Zingarelli

Coordinating Editor Laura Stansfeld

Coordinating Cartographer Anthony Phelan

Coordinating Layout Designer Indra Kilfoyle

Managing Editor Imogen Bannister

Managing Cartographer Alison Lyall

Assisting Editors Carolyn Bain, Carolyn Boicos, Jackey Coyle, Kate Daly, Shawn Low, Susan Paterson, Tom Smallman

Assisting Cartographers Barbara Benson, David Connolly, Chris Crook, Julie Dodkins, Sally Gerden, Anneka Imkamp

Cover Designer Rebecca Dandens

Cover Artwork Cara Smith

Project Managers Nancy Ianni, Kate McLeod

Language Content Coordinator Quentin Frayne

Thanks to Jessa Boanas-Dewes, David Burnett, Sally Darmody, Jennye Garibaldi, Liz Heynes, Tasmin Mc-Naughtan, Carlos Solarte, Jessica Van-Dam, Celia Wood

THANKS
SARA BENSON

Many insider tips, jokes and late-night pints of beer from other travelers kept me going on the road. Big thanks to Rainer, Thomas, Gerd and Peru Treks guides Juvenal and Karin, who got me to Machu Picchu; Sara and Ellis, for sharing experiences and a dinner table in Nazca; David and Tara, for living to tell about that awful bus trip via Desaguadero; and especially David Youngblood and Trey Brown, whom fate kept putting in my path – lucky me! Local experts Mónica Moreno, Vlado Soto and Jorge Echeandia generously gave of their time, resources and knowledge, as did countless Peruvians on the streets who proved many times over that the kindness of strangers yet exists. *Muchas gracias* to my intrepid co-authors Paul and Rafael, who gladly researched everywhere from the Amazon to the Andes, and in the rainy season! Thanks to Carolyn Boicos, Kathleen Munnelly, Brice Gosnell, David Zingarelli, Alison Lyall and many more Lonely Planet staff in Oakland and Melbourne who worked on this edition of *Peru*.

PAUL HELLANDER

Firstly *muchas gracias* to Leo Rovayo and Mónica Moreno of Lima for a home away from home and their assistance in ferreting out extra facts as well as ferrying me to and from the airport; Kurt Holle of Rainforest Expeditions, Miraflores, for showing me the jungle the comfy way; and my guide Gerson from Puerto Maldonado for his diligence in

---

THE LONELY PLANET STORY

The story begins with a classic travel adventure: Tony and Maureen Wheeler's 1972 journey across Europe and Asia to Australia. There was no useful information about the overland trail then, so Tony and Maureen published the first Lonely Planet guidebook to meet a growing need.

From a kitchen table, Lonely Planet has grown to become the largest independent travel publisher in the world, with offices in Melbourne (Australia), Oakland (USA) and London (UK). Today Lonely Planet guidebooks cover the globe. There is an ever-growing list of books and information in a variety of media. Some things haven't changed. The main aim is still to make it possible for adventurous travellers to get out there – to explore and better understand the world.

At Lonely Planet we believe travellers can make a positive contribution to the countries they visit – if they respect their host communities and spend their money wisely. Every year 5% of company profit is donated to charities around the world.

keeping me safe from jungle critters. Hats off to the professional team at Inkaterra for their guided tour of the Río Madre de Dios. ¡Hola! to the indefatigable Lucho Hurtado of Huancayo for his enthusiasm, insight and insider knowledge of life in the Central Andes – not to mention his dancing. *Gracias* to Pepe and Inge of the Hacienda Florida in Tarma for *mate de coca* and magical potions to cure laryngitis. Then there is Bill Grimes from Iquitos who took me around in a wooden boat and showed me the Amazon. Let's not forget the ebullient Gerald Mayeaux, also of Iquitos, for his depth of local knowledge. I am indebted to Guillermo Piña of Miraflores for another home away from home. Thanks also to my colleagues Rafael and Sara, and also the editorial and cartographic folk at Lonely Planet who put it all together.

RAFAEL WLODARSKI

Thanks go out to the all the helpful folk who smoothed my speedy path through Peru, particularly the staff at the offices of iPerú and DirSetur far and wide, as well as armies of Peace Corps volunteers. A big bucket of thanks goes out to the people that went beyond the call of duty to help make this book possible: Segundo in Trujillo; Tim, Alex and Christopher in Huaraz; Drew in Chavín; Kim in Chiquián; Lorane in Cajamarca; Jeff in Cajabamba; Mario from Katuwira; and Adam from the Bay Area. Thanks to Kathleen Munnelly and Sara Benson for keeping it all together, and very special thanks are reserved, as always, for Suzanna.

OUR READERS

Many thanks to the travelers who used the last edition and wrote to us with helpful hints, useful advice and interesting anecdotes:

A Geneviève Abbott, Kyoko Abe, Geert Ackermans, Mark Addinall, Philip Adey, Tanja Adler, Vanessa Adnitt, Alicia Adornato, Ola Agledahl, Shlomi Agmon, Tamila Ahmadov, Ilze Aizsilniece, Diane Ako, Christian Albers, Bob Aldrich, Christina Alefounder, Mary Allen, Marcia Alpert, Eliot Alport, Jorge Altamirano, Andres Alvarez-Calderon, Julie Andersen, Klaus Andersen, Kathy Anderson, Tyler Anderson, Lilian Andrade, Frida Andrae, Linn Andreassen, Val Annison, Wolfgang Anton, Robin Appleberry, Jaime Arashiro, Hannah Arem, Lauren Armistead, Linda Armstrong, Vladimir Arnaoudov, Chris Arnberg, Jennifer Arterburn, David Ashworth, Richard Aspin, Yuval Avnery **B** Daan Baas, Eve Bach, Jill Baisinger, Steve Baker, Hannah Ballard, Ignacio Ballen, Susan Balzer, Matt Bannister, Ana Bao, Benoit Barbier, Eileen Barnett, Simon Barnett, Jo Barrett, Ken Barry, Sonia Bartolini, Roger Barton, Chris Bass, Christine Bass, Steve Batten, Irmgard Bauer, Corynne Bean, Ian Bean, George Beatty, Jane Beatty, Colin

Beekman, Oliver Beginn, Tony Bellette, Mirian Bellido, Sara Benson, Timothy Bergen, Eva Berger, Jessica Berger, Caryl Bergeron, Dominique Bergevin, Paul Bernet, Karyn Bertschi, Nienke Besselink, Don Bevington, Neil Bianco, Christian Biendl, Mary Birch, Clint & Carly Blackbourn, Caroline Blaikie, Ben Blair, Sarah Blake, Philippe Blank, Michael Blumenthal, Pippa Bobbett, Eric Bobek, Sean Bohan, Paul Böhlen, Fred Bosanquet, Brenda Bosch, Inge Bouwman, Alexandra Bradstock, Claudia Brambóck, Monika Brandner, Caroline Brandtner, Lea Brant, Richard Breakspear, Linda Brennan, Neil Broome, Louise Brown, Sam Brown, Stephen Brown, Astrid Brucker, Ian Bryant, Meg Buchanan, Sandra Buchanan, Sandra Buehler, Gerry Buitendag, Vanessa Burgess, Eric Burke, Mark Burley, Bryan Bushley, Sarah Butcher, Anita Buurman **C** Nuno Cacchinadinha, Jocelyn Cai, Rosana Calmet, Paul Cammaert, Claudia Canales, Brad Cannon, Annika Card, Geneviève Cardinal, Danielle Carpenter, Georgina Carrasco Sanllehi, Greg Carter, Miguel Carvalho, Roberto Castro, Sonia Castro, Maryanne Caughlin, Dan Cauley, Aymar Ccopacatty, Garett Chau, Doreena Chen, Wah Cheung, Rodrigo Chia, Calvin Chiang, Eric Christensen, Jorgen Christensen, Peter Churchill, Steve Ciuffini, Mike Cleary, Mike Climber, Courtney Cohn, Rachel Cole, John Coleman, Gabriele Colla, Adrian & Shamsiah Collett, Sharon Collins, Bay Corbishley, Sarah Corkill, Liesbet Cornelissens, Eric Coronado, Becky Corran, Neal Corson, Patrick Corveleijn, Martine Costa, Christian Cotting, Matthew Courtney, Curt Crandall, Robert Cromwell, Robert & Elizabeth Cromwell, Alan & Martha Currie, Robyn Cutright **D** Rafael D´Andrea, Roel Daenen, Armando D'agostino, Annika Dalén, Karie Daniel, Anne-Marie Dargan,

Sandip Dasgupta, Sera Davidson, Venetia Davie, Keith Davies, Anna Davis, Catherine Dawes, Fernando De Castilla, Theo De Geringel, Nathalie De Kock, Angelo De Mey, Katrien De Pauw, Alberto De Pedro, Elmer De Ronde, Marieke De Waard, Eric De Wilde, Doortje De Zoete, Klara Debeljak, Kerin G Deeley, Dorys Delgado, Kyile Dempsey, Jean Denaro, Felicitas Dennemann, Lisa Dervin, Aaron Deupree, Karen Diboll, Louise Dillon, Tiberiu Dima, Wafik Dimyan, Danny Dion, Guylaine Dion, Karena Doan, Mimi Dobryniewski, Markus Doebele, Evelyn Döning, Frauke Dorschky, Kelly Douglas, Monique Doussard, Joris Drabbe, Yaron Dror, Chris & Sally Drysdale, Shelley Ducker, Austin Duggar, Dominic Durand **E** Sue Earthrowl, Ben Eastwood, Robert Ehlert, Michael Eiche, Dan Eisenberg, Marc Eisinger, Daniela El Kady, Patrick Elliott, Tony Elson, Shirley Elward, Paul Elwick, Rob Elze, Matthieu En Marlous, Johan Engdahl, Alastair England, Tom Erichsen, Ralph Ermoian, Mira Essink, Gorka Etxeandia, Polly Everett **F** Marie-Andrée Fallu, Ofir Feldman, Carolyn Felgate, Eyal Felstaine, Patrick Fennessy, Laurence Fenton, Jeff & Katie Ferrand, Sunita Ferrao, Bruno Ferrari, Sylvain Ferrari, Jordi Ferrer, Roger Feytongs, Robert Fiehn, Ben Field, Zoe Fisher, Diane & Gary Flannery, Collin Flower, Andrea Forbriger, Judy Forney, Ken Forsberg, Marina Forti, Jason Fortner, Charless & Marjorie Fowlkes, Claudia Frattin, Kieron Freeman, Mark Freshney, Sabrina Frey, Sue Fricke, Katja Froebe, Amanda Fulmer, Wayne Fung, Marc Furnival, Alessandro Fuso, Anke Fydrich, Sophie Fyfe **G** Manuel Gadea, Meytav Gal, Susanne Galla, Ainsley Gallagher, Giancarlo Gallegos Peralta, Rhona Gardner, Katrena Garske, Amando Gaspar, Eva Gengenbach, Peggy Gibbons, Patricia Gil, Alex Gill, Richard Gillingham, Michel Givon, Lynle Go, Charles & Miriam Goevaers, Pierre Goguen, Uri Goldberg, Bettina Goldner, Peter Goltermann, Maria Blanca Gomez De Isidro, Raul Gonzales, Francisco Gonzalez, Wendy Goosen, Rayann Gordon, Ruth Gordon, Gena Gorrell, Nico Graaff, Przemek Grabowski, Coronel Grace, Vera-Maria Graubner, April Graves, Mark Gray, Narelle & Gez Green, Oliver Greenall, Iris Greenberg, Rina Gregsersen, Mari Griffin, Rupert Griffiths, Aaron Grimeau, Roeland Grommen, Illrike Grunwald, Albert Guardia, Mari Sol Pérez Guevara, Matt & Jess Gunning, Suchi Gururaj **H** Jonathan Haas, Marie-Hélène Hachey, Hans-Peter Hafner, Jochen Hager, Alan Hairabedian, Nicole Halbeisen, Delphine Halgand, Terry Halpin, Laurits Hamm, Roger Hansen, Florian Hanslik, Linda Harleman, George Hart, Helen Hatzimaggo, David Hawgood, Brad Hawke, Anne Hay, Andrew Hazlett, Kari-Anne Heald, Anna Healy, Siobhan Healy, Steve Heath, Erika Hedengård, Christian Heilbronn, Sandro Heinze, Daniel Hellendoorn, Aaron Heller, Jean-Paul Hemelaer, Roger Hennekens, Juergen Henning, Pauline Hensley, Gerald Henzinger, Keith Herndon, Gerald Hinxman, Caspar Hirschi, Tom Hiskey, Tamara Hoecherl, Shane Hoefer, Rene Hoevenaars, Daniel Hofer, Martin Hollinger, Witold Holubowicz, Roy Hoogmoed, Valerie Hooper, Ayse Hortacsu, Mildred Howard, Richard Howitt, Sue Hoylen, Lorenzo Huaraca, Frank Hubers, Stefan Hueppi, Keith & Isabel Huffman-Sanchez, Rebecca Hunter, Monika Hupperich, Chris Hutchins, Ortwin Hutten **I** Reynaldo Imana-Wendt, Jerome & Judith Brin Ingber, Shamin Islam **J** Celina Jaccachoury, Rob Jacobs, Marco Jacobsen, Gabriela Jahn, Jacqueline Jahnke, Mark Jansens, Anke Janssen, Bernd Jaunich, Alejandro Jauregui, Kristen Joy Jauregui, Joachim Jayet, Lorna Jennings, Barbara Jesser, Charlie Johnston, Bryn Jones, Jordan Jones, Rocet-Arwel Jones, Rosemary Jones, Sarah Jones, Rachel Jordana, Brigitta Jüni **K** Sonja Kahl, Bernd Kaltenhaeuser, Nadia Kamal, Yoav Kamar, Helena Kashevsky, Andrea Kasner, Gisela Kassoy, Caroline Keating, Jennifer Kefer, Lester Kelem, Barbara Kelly, Karen Kelly, Paul Kennedy, Stewart Kennedy, Venkatesh Kini, Jennifer Klein, Robert Knoops, Harold Kollmeier, Marieke Kolstee, Alexander Komm, George Kouseras, Kyle Kramer, Thorsten Krause, Sabrina Kreder, Natasha Krochina, Ulrich Krueth, Sandra Krupe, Marie Kuge, Moritz Kulawik, Melanie Kwa **L** Pat & Mike Laas, Hector Labbé, Martin Lang, Max Lansman, Christy Lanzl, Nestor Lara-Baeza, Dan Lauritsen, Anna Law, Rachel Lawrence, Andy Leach, Landon Leach, Kay Ledgerwood, Susan Lee, Gerard Robert Leitner, Pieter Lekkerkerk, John Lembi, Julia Lenz, Jason Leppi, Taal Levi, Avi Levy, Gary Levy, Drew Lewis, N H Lewis, Mark Leyland, Achim Lieth, Jelle Lieuwens, Francesco Liistro, Claas Linnewedel, Andreas Eg Lomborg, Ann-Christine Lomosse, Anabel Lopez, Lucinda Yunisa Lopez Huamani, Ainsley Lorych, Petra Lüttker, Dlaine Lucyk, Robert Lukacs, Shawn Lum, Andrew Lund, Martin Lundgren, Ulla Lütze, Jonathan Lyle, Jason Lynn **M** Alistair Mackworth Gee, Vivienne Maeyer, Toby Mailman, Sarah Mainprize, Carolyn Mak, Karine Mallet, Marie Marcoux, Kristi Margeson, Taimi Margus, Diane Marshall, Jason Martyn, Roy Masters, Manrique Mata-Montero, Chantal Matthee, Andrea Matthews, Robin May, Paul Mayers, Michelangelo Mazzeo, Nicolás Mazzoli, Margaret Mcaspurn, Rick Mccharles, Ian Mccombe, Dono Mcguinness, Niall Mchenry, Brad Mckay, Nina Mckenna, Mike Mckinley, Margaret Mclean, Brendan Mcnallen, Nelson Benito Medina, Martina Melcher, Jean-Pierre Mélon, Steve Merwin, Karin Messore, Filip Mestdagh, George Meyer, Paola Miglio Rossi, Willemijn Milders, Gina Mildner, Ed Millburn, Jared Miller, Laura Miller, Tara Miller, Danna Millett, Amorina Milone, Carolyn Miranda, Melanie Mireaux, Olivia Mirodone, Barry Mitcheson, Mollie Moll, Christian Mollard, Jarl Molvær, Carl Montgomery, Gareth Morgan, Sean Morris, Peter Morrison, Irene Moser, Fernando Luiz Motta Dos Santos, Todd Mulder, Ally Muller, José Muñoz-Figueroa, Ezra Murad **N** Matt Nagle, Paola Nesmith, Simon Nettleton, Maillekeul Newman, May Ng, Olivier Nguyen, Thomas Nguyen, Janet Nicol, Roland & Lisa Niederberger, Victor Junior Ñiquen Millones, Esther Nissyn, Ann Noon, Rowyna Noordermeer, Max Norbas, Yuri Novikov, Kathy Nussbaum **O** Rainer Oberguggenberger, Sheila O'Connor, Christoffer Odensten, Layla Oesper, Ea Helth Øgendahl, Fred Oliff, Cheryl Olson, Alice & Justin O'Neill, Helen Orchid-Beer, Jack Orman, Rachael Orr, Margaret Ortmans, Alla & Yevgen Osadchiy, Scott Oskins, Angela Ott, Martin Ottinger, Jolanda Oudeman, Jocelyn Ouellet **P** Luca Pajetta, Paul Pallada, George Palmer, Simone Panato, Aristea Parissi, Jim Parker, Nick Parr, Caroline Parrott, Deepesh Patel, Geoff Pavey, Margo Pearce, Jill Peary, Murray Peecock, Christine Penn, Anna Penna, Alison Perkins, Anna Perkins, Ed & Lilith Perkins, Ingrid Permann, Gina Perry, Clara Peters, Jan Peters, Jim Peters, Monica Petith, Andi Pfaff, Hoang Phan, Jayne Phan, Deborah Phillip, Bill Phillips, Eli Pickard, Rebecca Pilon, Enrica Piovesan, Bertha Pizarro De Garmendia, Thomas Polfeldt, Ellis Polin, Cristina Polo, Doreen Pon,

Nadja Poschung, Natalie Potter, Ilda Pozhegu, Carolyn Preece, Babette Prick, Maria Prieto, Klara Prinz, Mat Prout, Mariska & Erik-Jan Pullens, Catherine Pyun **R** Emma Raffle, Kesha Ram, Dave Ramont, Stuart Rankin, Meredith Rasch, Giorgio Raschio, Frederieke Rasenberg, Stuart Reed, Connie Regnersen, Michael Rehm, Max Reimpell, Heidi Reister, Dan Renfrow, Marieke Rensen, Ralf Resch, Keith D Rhoades, Andy Rice, Roberta Rice, Jana Richter, Niall Riddell, Ralph Riedel, Jodie Riedmann, Jenny Rienzo, Mario Righi, Brandon Rigoli, Rob Rijnswou Van, David Ritchay, Elizabeth Ritchie, David Rivel, Gareth Roberts, Jude Robinson, Katia Robinson, Caroline Rodgers, Andreas Rogall, Claudia Rogoff, Stefanie Rogoll, Susan Roh, Jeffrey Rosenbaum, Adam Ross, Miriam Ross, Claude Roulin, Arno & Karin Runge, Cameron Russo, Mary Ryan, Hélène Rybol **S** Elle Sabala, Marc Sacks, Wolfgang Salz, Stritof Samo, Karrie Sampson, Miguel Sancho, Anna Sandhammar, Kristin Sanne, Valter Maria Santoro, Thomas Sarosy, Hugo Savard, Margaret Scaramellini, Anja Schaefer, Mark Schaffer, Susan & Erik Scheel, Raf Schepers, Mary Jo Schiavoni, Tanja Schicker, Jason Schiffner, Ingrid Schlepers, Arwed Schmitt, Gwen Schmitt, Gabriel Schnaider, Rene Schnyder, Michael Schoute, Jan & Sacha Schreuder, Maximin Schubert, Liz Schuler, Jeff Schwagle, David Schwartz, Stefan Schwarz, Jochen Schweizer, Tracy Scott, Evan Sedgwick-Jell, Thomas Seebeck, Sybille Seliner, Peter Selley, Denis Seynhaeve, Jeremy Shafer, Andrew Shanahan, Helen & Wolfe Sharp, Martha Shepard, Darren Shepherd, Simon Shepherd, Lisa Sherk, Linda M Shipley, Kate Shower, Tom Shower, Shuchin Shukla, Steve Silver, Debbie Simpson, Jane Skalisky, Liesbeth Sluis, Martin Smetacek, Christopher Smith, Deborah Smith, Kate Smith, Mike Smith, Tim Smith, Karen Solberg, Ivar Sønstabø, Marc Souto, Flora Spannagel, Lorelle Speechley, Ivan & Joan Speidel, Jac Spijkers, Valerie Spink, Gary Spinks, Bronwyn Spiteri, Sam St. Clair-Ford, Menno Staarink, Marcel Stal, Daphne Stanley, Sarah Stannard, Harry Staymann, Assen Stefanov, Susanne Steiger-Escobar, Ole Steinert, Charlotte Stenermark, Anthony Stern, Ann Stewart, Cheryl Stewart, Franz Sticher, Alexandre Stoecklin, Helen Stone, David Stonehill, Patrick Sullivan, Judy & Ariana Svenson, David Swinehart **T** Lastina Tagle, Emanuela Tasinato, Dan Taylor, Ed Taylor, Mike Taylor, Worth Thomas, Skye Thompson, Tom & Anita Thompson, Laura Timm, Joanne Timms, Egle Tiskeviciute, Diane Tolentino, Paolo Tolusso, Richard Tooth, Samantha Tosh, Stefani Tovar, Paul Travers, Ondrej Trojan, Ana Trueno, Philippe Tulula, Nick Twynham U Christian Uribe **V** Irene Van Berlo, Leander Van De Visse, Ron Van Den Brink, Naomi Van Den Brom, Femke Van Den Einden, Judith Van Den Hengel, Hedwig Van Den Heuvel, Nienke Van Den Heuvel, Marc Van Der Holst, Pieter Van Der Luit, Hetty Van Der Stoep, Simone Van Der Veldt, Tim Van Der Wel, Peter Van Haren, Maarten Van Hoof, Anouk Van Limpt, Thomas Van Meerbeeck, Griet Van Mele, Wilma Van Riel, Han Van Roosmalen, Gerco Van Vulpen, Gerhard Van Wyngaardt, Matthew Vancleave, Karla Vaness, Carl Vannetelbosch, Hans Vanquathem, Rick Vecchio, Dineke Veerman, Jan Veldheer, Freek Vermeulen, Rebecca Verner, Fabim Verniere, Roberto Viajero, Nathalie Vial, Victoria Vine, Bianca Vitting, Kim Voermans, Christoph Von Uthmann, Roy Voortman, Nander Vrees **W** Richard C Walker, Keith Walkerdine, Julia Walter, Adrian Ward, Rachel Ward, Nic Warmenhoven, Jan Watts, Mareen Weber, Nancy Webster, Juerg Weingaertner, Sarah Wels, Christian Juergen Welz, Anika Wendle, Dana Weniger, Joel Werlen, Scott Whineray, James Whiston, Michael & Clara White Bravo, Torsten Wiberg, Darren Widenmaier, Rolien Wiersinga, Jaap Wijdeveld, Marie-Jose Wijntjes, Lisa Wildi, Kathleen & Terry Williams, Jennie Williamson, Chris Wilson, Randy Wilson, Maik David Winteler, Rebecca Wiseman, James Wood, Natalie Wood, Dave & Hannah Wright **Y** Tomoko Yasue, Christie Young **Z** Tyler Zajacz, Jacobo Zanella, Carlos Zanoni, Karla Zegarra, Austin Zeiderman, Paola Zimmermann, Phil Zirngast, Gerd Zoller

Index

000 Map pages
000 Photograph pages

INDEX

| 12am | 1am | 2am | 3am | 4am | 5am | 6am | 7am | 8am | 9am | 10am | 11am | 12pm |

ARCTIC OCEAN

Queen Elizabeth Is (Can)

Ellesmere Is (Can)

BAFFIN BAY

9am Greenland (Denmark)

11am

GREENLAND SEA

NORWEGIAN SEA

CHUKCHI SEA

Banks Is (Can)

Victoria Is (Can)

Baffin Is (Can)

Iceland

NORTH SEA

BEAUFORT SEA

Russia

Alaska (US)

3am

BERING SEA

GULF OF ALASKA

2am

4am

5am

Canada

6am

HUDSON BAY

LABRADOR SEA

8am

United Kingdom

Ireland

NORTH ATLANTIC OCEAN

8.30am

NORTH PACIFIC OCEAN

United States

Bermuda (UK)

Azores (Port)

Portugal Spain

Morocco

Canary Is (Sp)

Mauritania

Mali

1am Midway Is (US)

Hawaii (US)

Mexico

GULF OF MEXICO

The Bahamas

Cuba

Haiti

CARIBBEAN SEA

Eastern Caribbean Islands

Cape Verde

12pm

Senegal Burkina Guinea Faso

Liberia Ghana

GULF OF GUINEA

Guatemala

Nicaragua

Panama

Venezuela Guyana

Colombia Suriname

EQUATOR

Kiribati

Galapagos Is (Ecuador)

Ecuador

Ascension (UK)

Samoa

2.30am

Tahiti French Polynesia (Fr)

Peru

7am

8am

Brazil 9am

Tonga

12am

Cook Is (NZ)

2am

Pitcairn Is 3.30am (UK)

Easter Is (Chile)

Bolivia

Paraguay

SOUTH ATLANTIC OCEAN

1am

SOUTH PACIFIC OCEAN

Chile

Uruguay

Argentina

Tristan da Cunha (UK)

Gough Is (UK)

New Zealand

12.45am Chatham Is (NZ)

Falkland Is (UK)

South Georgia & South Sandwich Is (UK)

Bouvet I (Norway)

| 12am | 1am | 2am | 3am | 4am | 5am | 6am | 7am | 8am | 9am | 10am | 11am | 12pm |

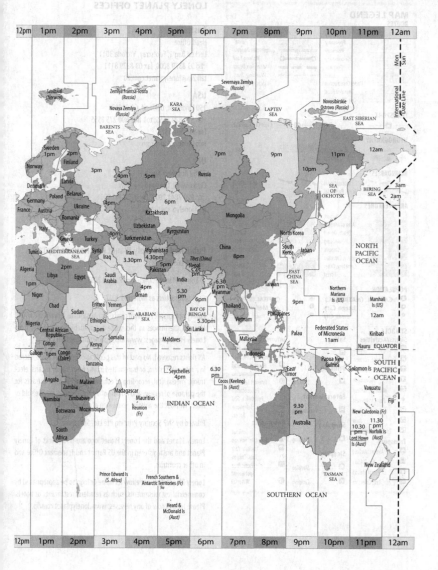

MAP LEGEND

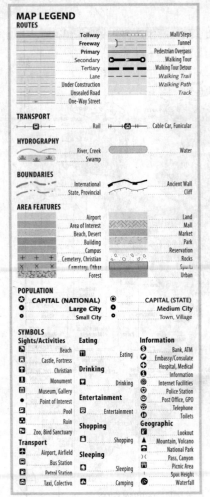

ROUTES

Tollway	Mall/Steps
Freeway	Tunnel
Primary	Pedestrian Overpass
Secondary	Walking Tour
Tertiary	Walking Tour Detour
Lane	Walking Trail
Under Construction	Walking Path
Unsealed Road	Track
One-Way Street	

TRANSPORT

Rail — Cable Car, Funicular

HYDROGRAPHY

River, Creek — Water
Swamp

BOUNDARIES

International — Ancient Wall
State, Provincial — Cliff

AREA FEATURES

Airport	Land
Area of Interest	Mall
Beach, Desert	Market
Building	Park
Campus	Reservation
Cemetery, Christian	Rocks
Cemetery, Other	Sports
Forest	Urban

POPULATION

◎ CAPITAL (NATIONAL)	◉ CAPITAL (STATE)
● Large City	● Medium City
● Small City	● Town, Village

SYMBOLS

Sights/Activities
- Beach
- Castle, Fortress
- Christian
- Monument
- Museum, Gallery
- Point of Interest
- Pool
- Ruin
- Zoo, Bird Sanctuary

Transport
- Airport, Airfield
- Bus Station
- Petrol Station
- Taxi, Colectivo

Eating
- Eating

Drinking
- Drinking

Entertainment
- Entertainment

Shopping
- Shopping

Sleeping
- Sleeping
- Camping

Information
- Bank, ATM
- Embassy/Consulate
- Hospital, Medical
- Information
- Internet Facilities
- Police Station
- Post Office, GPO
- Telephone
- Toilets

Geographic
- Lookout
- Mountain, Volcano
- National Park
- Pass, Canyon
- Picnic Area
- Spot Height
- Waterfall

LONELY PLANET OFFICES

Australia
Head Office
Locked Bag 1, Footscray, Victoria 3011
☎ 03 8379 8000, fax 03 8379 8111
talk2us@lonelyplanet.com.au

USA
150 Linden St, Oakland, CA 94607
☎ 510 893 8555, toll free 800 275 8555
fax 510 893 8572
info@lonelyplanet.com

UK
72-82 Rosebery Ave,
Clerkenwell, London EC1R 4RW
☎ 020 7841 9000, fax 020 7841 9001
go@lonelyplanet.co.uk

Published by Lonely Planet Publications Pty Ltd
ABN 36 005 607 983